More Than Just a Textbook

*Log on to **ca.gr4math.com** to…*

Access your book from home

- **Online Student Edition**
- **Student Workbooks**

See mathematical concepts come to life

- **Personal Tutor**
- **Concepts in Motion**

Practice what you've learned

- **Chapter Readiness**
- **Extra Examples**
- **Self-Check Quizzes**
- **Vocabulary Review**
- **Chapter Tests**
- **Standards Practice**

Try these other activities

- **Cross-Curricular Features**
- **Game Time**

Macmillan McGraw-Hill

California Mathematics

Concepts, Skills, and Problem Solving

4

Authors

Altieri • Balka • Day • Gonsalves • Grace • Krulik
Malloy • Molix-Bailey • Moseley • Mowry • Myren
Price • Reynosa • Santa Cruz • Silbey • Vielhaber

Macmillan
McGraw-Hill

About the Cover

California Focus About one-fourth of California's total land area is desert. The Mojave Desert has the highest and lowest points in the United States—not counting Alaska and Hawaii. The highest point is Mount Whitney, which is 14,495 feet above sea level, and the lowest is Bad Water in Death Valley, which is 282 feet below sea level. These two points are less than 100 miles apart.

Mathematics Focus This year you will learn about fractions. The rabbit on the cover is biking to Halftown. It is $\frac{3}{4}$ mile to Halftown and $\frac{1}{2}$ mile to Thirdsville. Which is farther away? Use the front wheel of the bike to help you decide.

Mc Graw Hill **Macmillan McGraw-Hill**

The McGraw-Hill Companies

Send all inquiries to:
Macmillan/McGraw-Hill
8787 Orion Place
Columbus, OH 43240-4027

ISBN-13: 978-0-02-105711-5
ISBN-10: 0-02-105711-7

Printed in the United States of America.

3 4 5 6 7 8 9 10 058/055 16 15 14 13 12 11 10 09 08

Contents in Brief

Authors

Mary Behr Altieri
Putnam/Northern Westchester BOCES
Yorktown Heights, New York

Don S. Balka
Professor Emeritus
Saint Mary's College
Notre Dame, Indiana

Roger Day, Ph.D.
Mathematics Department Chair
Pontiac Township High School
Pontiac, Illinois

Philip D. Gonsalves
Mathematics Coordinator
Alameda County Office of Education and California State University East Bay
Hayward, California

Ellen C. Grace
Consultant
Albuquerque, New Mexico

Stephen Krulik
Professor Emeritus
Mathematics Education
Temple University
Cherry Hill, New Jersey

Carol E. Malloy
Assistant Professor of Mathematics Education
University of North Carolina at Chapel Hill
Chapel Hill, North Carolina

Rhonda J. Molix-Bailey
Mathematics Consultant
Mathematics by Design
Desoto, Texas

Lois Gordon Moseley
Staff Developer
NUMBERS: Mathematics Professional Development
Houston, Texas

Brian Mowry
Independent Math Educational Consultant/Part-Time Pre-K Instructional Specialist
Austin Independent School District
Austin, Texas

Math Online Meet the Authors at ca.gr4math.com

Christina L. Myren
Consultant Teacher
Conejo Valley Unified School District
Thousand Oaks, California

Jack Price
Professor Emeritus
California State Polytechnic University
Pomona, California

Mary Esther Reynosa
Instructional Specialist for Elementary Mathematics
Northside Independent School District
San Antonio, Texas

Rafaela M. Santa Cruz
SDSU/CGU Doctoral Program in Education
San Diego State University
San Diego, California

Robyn Silbey
Math Content Coach
Montgomery County Public Schools
Gaithersburg, Maryland

Kathleen Vielhaber
Mathematics Consultant
St. Louis, Missouri

Contributing Authors

Viken Hovsepian
Professor of Mathematics
Rio Hondo College
Whittier, California

Donna J. Long
Mathematics Consultant
Indianapolis, Indiana

FOLDABLES™ **Dinah Zike**
Educational Consultant
Dinah-Might Activities, Inc.
San Antonio, Texas

California Mathematics Advisory Board

Macmillan/McGraw-Hill wishes to thank the following professionals for their invaluable feedback during the development of the program. They reviewed a variety of instructional materials at different stages of development.

Cheryl L. Avalos
Mathematics Consultant
Hacienda Heights, California

William M. Bokesch
Rancho Bernardo High School
San Diego, California

Patty Brown
Teacher
John Muir Elementary
Fresno, California

David J. Chamberlain
Secondary Mathematics Resource Teacher
Capistrano Unified School District
San Juan Capistrano, California

Eppie Chung
K-6 Teacher
Modesto City Schools
Modesto, California

Lisa Marie Cirrincione
Middle School Teacher
Lincoln Middle School
Oceanside, California

Carol Cronk
Mathematics Program Specialist
San Bernardino City Unified School District
San Bernardino, California

Ilene Foster
Teacher Specialist–Mathematics
Pomona Unified School District
Pomona, California

Grant A. Fraser, Ph. D.
Professor of Mathematics
California State University, Los Angeles
Los Angeles, California

Suzanne Bocskai Freire
Teacher
Kingswood Elementary
Citrus Heights, California

Beth Holguin
Teacher
Graystone Elementary
San Jose, California

Donna M. Kopenski, Ed. D.
Mathematics Coordinator K-5
City Heights Educational Collaborative
San Diego, California

Kelly Mack
6th Grade Teacher
Captain Jason Dahl Elementary
San Jose, California

Juvenal Martinez
Dual Immersion/ESL Instructor
Aeolian Elementary
Whittier, California

John McGuire
Associate Principal
Pacific Union School
Arcata, California

Dr. Donald R. Price
Teacher, Adjunct Professor
Rowland Unified School District
Rowland Heights, California

Kasey St. James
Mathematics Teacher
Sunny Hills High School
Fullerton, California

Arthur K. Wayman, Ph. D.
Professor of Mathematics Emeritus
California State University, Long Beach
Long Beach, California

Beverly Wells
First Grade Teacher
Mineral King Elementary School
Visalia, California

Frances Basich Whitney
Project Director, Mathematics K-12
Santa Cruz County Office of Education
Capitola, California

Consultants

Macmillan/McGraw-Hill wishes to thank the following professionals for their feedback. They were instrumental in providing valuable input toward the development of this program in these specific areas.

Mathematical Content

Viken Hovsepian
Professor of Mathematics
Rio Hondo College
Whittier, California

Grant A. Fraser, Ph.D.
Professor of Mathematics
California State University, Los Angeles
Los Angeles, California

Arthur K. Wayman, Ph.D.
Professor of Mathematics Emeritus
California State University, Long Beach
Long Beach, California

Assessment

Jane D. Gawronski
Director of Assessment and Outreach
San Diego State University
San Diego, California

Cognitive Guided Instruction

Susan B. Empson
Associate Professor of Mathematics and Science Education
University of Texas at Austin
Austin, Texas

English Learners

Cheryl Avalos
Mathematics Consultant
Los Angeles County Office of Education, Retired
Hacienda Heights, California

Kathryn Heinze
Graduate School of Education
Hamline University
St. Paul, Minnesota

Family Involvement

Paul Giganti, Jr.
Mathematics Education Consultant
Albany, California

Literature

David M. Schwartz
Children's Author, Speaker, Storyteller
Oakland, California

Vertical Alignment

Berchie Holliday
National Educational Consultant
Silver Spring, Maryland

Deborah A. Hutchens, Ed.D.
Principal
Norfolk Highlands Elementary
Chesapeake, Virginia

California Reviewers

Each California Reviewer reviewed at least two chapters of the Student Edition, giving feedback and suggestions for improving the effectiveness of the mathematics instruction.

Sherry G. Anderson
Teacher/G.A.T.E. Coordinator
Will Rogers Elementary
Lynwood, California

Ysaaca Axelrod
Kindergarten Teacher
El Monte Elementary
Concord, California

Cathy Bullock
Teacher
Capri Elementary
Encinitas, California

Michelle Callender
Teacher
Morgan/Kincaid Preparatory School of Integrated Studies
Victorville, California

M. Olivia Campos
4th Grade Teacher
Morrison Elementary
Norwalk, California

Malaura Page Easton, M.S.
Kindergarten Teacher
La Pluma School
La Mirada, California

Priscilla S. Edwards
5th Grade Classroom Teacher
David Reese Elementary
Sacramento, California

Lisa B. Friedberg
4th Grade Teacher
Alderwood Basics Plus School
Irvine, California

Wendy Smith Hernandez
Kindergarten Teacher
Herndon-Barstow Elementary
Fresno, California

Beth Holguin
Teacher
Graystone School
San Jose, California

Kristi Iverson
First Grade Teacher
Village Oaks Elementary
Stockton, California

Sheri Leiken
Teacher
Weathersfield Elementary
Thousand Oaks, California

Sarab H. Lopes
Teacher
Anza Elementary
El Cajon, California

Karen E. Lund
5th Grade Teacher
Meadow Park Elementary
Irvine, California

Efrain Melendez
Teacher
Livermore Valley USD
Livermore, California

Jean A. Nelson
Teacher
Fremont Elementary School
Alhambra, California

Tara Pahia
Elementary Teacher
Bear Gulch Elementary
Rancho Cucamonga, California

Dr. Donald R. Price
Teacher, Adjunct Professor
Rowland United School District
Rowland Heights, California

Kitty Ritz, M.A.
Teacher
Monte Vista Elementary
Rohnert Park, California

Corinne E. Schwartz
First Grade Teacher
Lincrest Elementary School
Yuba City, California

Deborah Shapiro
5th Grade Teacher
Nancy Cory
Lancaster, California

Maureen Smith
Curriculum Specialist
Fremont Unified School Dist. (retired 6/2006)
Fremont, California

Joseph M. Snodgrass
3rd Grade Teacher
Park Elementary School
Alhambra, California

Marie W. Stevens
Elementary Mathematics Coordinator
LAUSD
Los Angeles, California

Jane Traut
Classroom Teacher
Lang Ranch Elementary School
Thousand Oaks, California

Rachel C. Trowbridge
Teacher
Evergreen Elementary
San Jose, California

Cynthia H. Vandemoortel
Educator
Alderwood Basics Plus School
Irvine, California

Norine Yale
Teacher
Justin Elementary
Simi Valley, California

Dr. Darlene York
Education Consultant
Associate Professor
Antioch University
Seattle, Washington

Contents

Start Smart

Chapter 1 Place Value and Number Sense

CHAPTER 2 Addition and Subtraction

California Standards Practice
- 61, 67, 81, 87, 88, 89

H.O.T. Problems
Higher Order Thinking
57, 61, 66, 72, 80

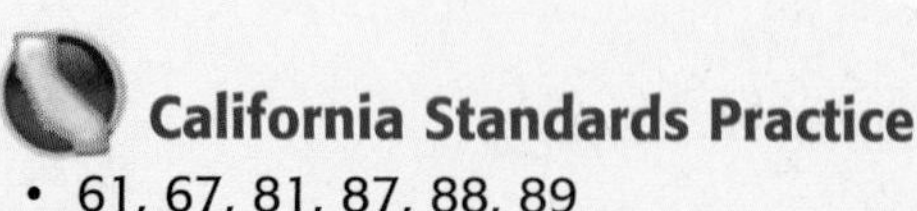

57, 61, 63, 66, 67, 69, 72, 75, 80, 87

Chapter 3 Algebra: Use Addition and Subtraction

CHAPTER 4 Statistics: Data and Graphs

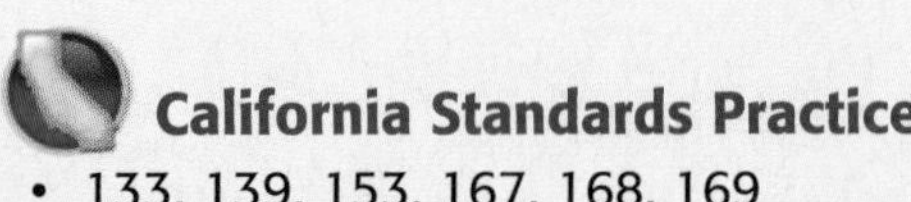

California Standards Practice

- 133, 139, 153, 167, 168, 169

H.O.T. Problems
Higher Order Thinking
129, 133, 138, 142, 152, 159

WRITING IN MATH 129, 133, 135, 138, 139, 142, 145, 149, 152, 155, 159, 167

CHAPTER 5 Multiplication and Division Facts

California Standards Practice

- 181, 185, 191, 197, 207, 211, 219, 220, 221

H.O.T. Problems
Higher Order Thinking
177, 181, 185, 190, 197, 202, 207, 210

WRITING IN MATH 174, 177, 181, 185, 187, 190, 191, 197, 199, 202, 207, 210, 219

CHAPTER 6 Algebra: Use Multiplication and Division

California Standards Practice

Multiply by One-Digit Numbers

Multiply by Two-Digit Numbers

California Standards Practice

H.O.T. Problems
Higher Order Thinking

CHAPTER 9 Divide by One-Digit Numbers

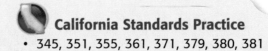

CHAPTER 10 Geometry

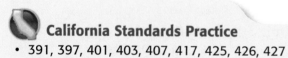

CHAPTER 11 Geometry and Measurement

CHAPTER 12 Algebra and Graphing

California Standards Practice

- 475, 479, 493, 501, 502, 503

H.O.T. Problems
Higher Order Thinking
471, 475, 478, 486, 492

WRITING IN MATH 471, 475, 478, 479, 483, 486, 489, 492, 495, 501

CHAPTER 13 Fractions

CHAPTER 14 Decimals

California Standards Practice

- 563, 569, 575, 580, 587, 588, 589

H.O.T. Problems
Higher Order Thinking
559, 563, 568, 575, 580

556, 559, 563, 565, 568, 569, 571, 575, 580, 587

CHAPTER 15 Decimals: Addition and Subtraction

California Standards Practice

- 596, 601, 609, 619, 625, 626, 627

H.O.T. Problems
Higher Order Thinking
596, 601, 608, 619

WRITING IN MATH 596, 601, 603, 605, 608, 609, 613, 615, 619, 625

Chapter 16 Probability

California Standards Practice

- 634, 639, 647, 655, 661, 662, 663

H.O.T. Problems
Higher Order Thinking
634, 639, 646, 655

WRITING IN MATH 634, 639, 641, 643, 646, 647, 651, 655, 661

California Standards Review

Looking Ahead to the Grade 5 Standards

H.O.T. Problems
Higher Order Thinking
669, 673, 677, 681

WRITING IN MATH 669, 673, 677, 681

California Standards for Mathematics Grade 4

🔑 denotes Key standards

Standard	Text of Standard	Primary Citations	Supporting Citations
Number Sense			
1.0	**Students understand the place value of whole numbers and decimals to two decimal places and how whole numbers and decimals relate to simple fractions. Students use the concepts of negative numbers:**	17–25, 28–31, 32–43, 62–63, 268–270, 469–471, 507–520, 522–533, 538–541, 555–563, 566–568, 572–580	36–40, 58–61, 64–66, 70–75, 268–271, 302–305, 348–350, 472–478, 480–481, 507–509, 516–518, 520, 528–531, 534–539, 555–563, 566–568, 572–575, 578–580, 636–639, 644–646, 652–655, 666–677
1.1	Read and write whole numbers in the millions.	17–25, 28–31, 32–34	50–51, CA4, CA6
🔑 1.2	Order and compare whole numbers and decimals to two decimal places.	28–30, 32–34, 42–43, 566–568, 578–580	36, 582, 585, 587, CA4, CA6
🔑 1.3	Round whole numbers through the millions to the nearest ten, hundred, thousand, ten thousand, or hundred thousand.	36–39, 268–270,	51, 58–61, 64–66, 70–72, 302–305, 348–350, CA4, CA6
🔑 1.4	Decide when a rounded solution is called for and explain why such a solution may be appropriate.	62–63	58–61, 67, 75, 87
1.5	Explain different interpretations of fractions, for example, parts of a whole, parts of a set, and division of whole numbers by whole numbers; explain equivalents of fractions (see Standard 4.0).	507–513, 516–520, 522–524, 532–533, 538–541	528–537, 555–563, 572–575, 636–639, 644–646, 652–677, CA5
1.6	Write tenths and hundredths in decimal and fraction notations and know the fraction and decimal equivalents for halves and fourths (e.g., $\frac{1}{2} = 0.5$ or $.50$; $\frac{7}{4} = 1\frac{3}{4} = 1.75$).	555–563, 572–575	566–568, 576–580, CA5, CA6
1.7	Write the fraction represented by a drawing of parts of a figure; represent a given fraction by using drawings; and relate a fraction to a simple decimal on a number line.	507–515, 572–575	507–509, 516–518, 536–539, CA6
🔑 1.8	Use concepts of negative numbers (e.g., on a number line, in counting, in temperature, in "owing").	469–471	473, 475–479, 480–481, CA3, CA6
🔑 1.9	Identify on a number line the relative position of positive fractions, positive mixed numbers, and positive decimals to two decimal places.	528–531, 539–541, 566, 578–580	517, 572, 574, 575, CA5
2.0	**Students extend their use and understanding of whole numbers to the addition and subtraction of simple decimals:**	59–61, 148–149, 593–596, 598–601, 604–608, 610–611, 614–619	58–61, 64–66, 598–601, 606–608, 616–619
2.1	Estimate and compute the sum or difference of whole numbers and positive decimals to two places.	148–149, 598–601, 604–608, 610–611, 614–619	58–61, 64–66, CA7, CA8, CA9
2.2	Round two-place decimals to one decimal or the nearest whole number and judge the reasonableness of the rounded answer.	593–596	598–601, 606–608, 616–619, CA7, CA8, CA9

Standard	Text of Standard	Primary Citations	Supporting Citations
3.0	**Students solve problems involving addition, subtraction, multiplication, and division of whole numbers and understand the relationships among the operations:**	58–61, 64–66, 68–72, 76–81, 299–301, 308, 312, 314–319, 322–324, 339–345, 348–350, 352–355, 358–364, 368–371, 442–443	67, 74–75, 85–89, 140–145, 268–270, 308–309, 313, 325, 326, 329, 330, 331, 337–345, 348–350, 352–355, 358–364, 368–371
3.1	Demonstrate an understanding of, and the ability to use, standard algorithms for the addition and subtraction of multidigit numbers.	58–61, 64–66, 68–72, 76–81, 602–603	67, 85–89, CA10, CA11, CA12
3.2	Demonstrate an understanding of, and the ability to use, standard algorithms for multiplying a multidigit number by a two-digit number and for dividing a multidigit number by a one-digit number; use relationships between them to simplify computations and to check results.	299–301, 310–312, 314–317, 322–324, 339–345, 348–350, 352–355, 358–364, 368–371	268–270, 302–305, 308–309, 337–338, CA10, CA12
3.3	Solve problems involving multiplication of multidigit numbers by two-digit numbers.	299–305, 308–312, 314–319, 322–324	313, 325, 326, 329–331, CA10, CA12
3.4	Solve problems involving division of multidigit numbers by one-digit numbers.	337–338, 366–367	339–345, 348–350, 352–355, 358–364, 368–371, CA11, CA12
4.0	**Students know how to factor small whole numbers:**	204–211	208–211, 448–449, 518, 524
4.1	Understand that many whole numbers break down in different ways (e.g., $12 = 4 \times 3 = 2 \times 6 = 2 \times 2 \times 3$).	204–207	208–211, 448–449, 518–520, 522, CA13, CA14, CA15
4.2	Know that numbers such as 2, 3, 5, 7, and 11 do not have any factors except 1 and themselves and that such numbers are called prime numbers.	208–211	522–524, CA13, CA14, CA15
Algebra and Functions			
1.0	**Students use and interpret variables, mathematical symbols, and properties to write and simplify expressions and sentences:**	93–100, 102–106, 114–115, 225–227, 230–240, 242–244, 486	55–57, 93–95, 104–106,121 225–227, 230–233, 239, 242–251, 454–457, 488–495
1.1	Use letters, boxes, or other symbols to stand for any number in simple expressions or equations (e.g., demonstrate an understanding and the use of the concept of a variable).	93–100, 102–103, 114–115, 225–227, 234–238	55–57, 104–106, 230–233, 242–244, 248–251, CA16
1.2	Interpret and evaluate mathematical expressions that now use parentheses.	230–233	55–57, 93–95, 225–227, CA16, CA17, CA18
1.3	Use parentheses to indicate which operation to perform first when writing expressions containing more than two terms and different operations.	230–233	94–95, 121, 225–227, 239, CA16, CA18
1.4	Use and interpret formulas (e.g., area = length $\times$ width or $A = \ell w$) to answer questions about quantities and their relationships.	438–440	444–446, 448–449, 454–457, CA17, CA18

Standard	Text of Standard	Primary Citations	Supporting Citations
1.5	Understand that an equation such as $y = 3x + 5$ is a prescription for determining a second number when a first number is given.	104–106, 242–244, 484–486	488–493, 494–495, CA17, CA18
2.0	Students know how to manipulate equations:	110–112, 248–251	120, 256, 275
2.1	Know and understand that equals added to equals are equal.	110–112	120, CA19, CA20, CA21
2.2	Know and understand that equals multiplied by equals are equal.	248–251	256, 257, CA19, CA20, CA21
Measurement and Geometry			
1.0	**Students understand perimeter and area:**	438–440, 444–446, 448–449, 454–457	446–457
1.1	Measure the area of rectangular shapes by using appropriate units, such as square centimeter (cm^2), square meter (m^2), square kilometer (km^2), square inch (in^2), square yard (yd^2), or square mile (mi^2).	444–446	447–449, 454–457, CA23–CA24
1.2	Recognize that rectangles that have the same area can have different perimeters.	448–449	446, 456, CA22
1.3	Understand that rectangles that have the same perimeter can have different areas.	448–449	446, 456, CA22, CA24
1.4	Understand and use formulas to solve problems involving perimeters and areas of rectangles and squares. Use those formulas to find the areas of more complex figures by dividing the figures into basic shapes.	438–440, 444–446, 454–457	442–443, 447, 450–452, CA24
2.0	**Students use two-dimensional coordinate grids to represent points and graph lines and simple figures:**	476–478, 480–481, 488–493	479, 498, 499, 501, 502, 503
2.1	Draw the points corresponding to linear relationships on graph paper (e.g., draw 10 points on the graph of the equation $y = 3x$ and connect them by using a straight line).	488–493	499, 501, 502, 503, CA2, CA25, CA27
2.2	Understand that the length of a horizontal line segment equals the difference of the x-coordinates.	476–478	479, 498, 502, CA26, CA27
2.3	Understand that the length of a vertical line segment equals the difference of the y-coordinates.	476–478	479, 498, 501, 503, CA26, CA27
3.0	**Students demonstrate an understanding of plane and solid geometric objects and use this knowledge to show relationships and solve problems:**	385–387, 395–400, 404–412, 414–417, 431–437	391, 399–400, 404–412, 417, 421, 423–427, 434–437, 441, 450–451, 455–457, 459, 464, 465
3.1	Identify lines that are parallel and perpendicular.	395–397	399–400, 410–412, 421, 426, CA28
3.2	Identify the radius and diameter of a circle.	414–417	424, 427, 437, CA29
3.3	Identify congruent figures.	431–433	434–437, 441, 459, 465, CA30
3.4	Identify figures that have bilateral and rotational symmetry.	434–437	441, 450–451, 459, 464, CA30

Standard	Text of Standard	Primary Citations	Supporting Citations
3.5	Know the definitions of a right angle, an acute angle, and an obtuse angle. Understand that 90°, 180°, 270°, and 360° are associated, respectively, with $\frac{1}{4}$, $\frac{1}{2}$, $\frac{3}{4}$, and full turns.	398–400	404–407, 417, 423, 425, CA30
3.6	Visualize, describe, and make models of geometric solids (e.g., prisms, pyramids) in terms of the number and shape of faces, edges, and vertices; interpret two-dimensional representations of three-dimensional objects; and draw patterns (of faces) for a solid that, when cut and folded, will make a model of the solid.	385–387, 408–409	391, CA29
3.7	Know the definitions of different triangles (e.g., equilateral, isosceles, scalene) and identify their attributes.	404–407	408–409, 417, 423, 425, 427, CA30
3.8	Know the definition of different quadrilaterals (e.g., rhombus, square, rectangle, parallelogram, trapezoid).	410–412	417, 423, 425, CA30
Statistics, Data Analysis, and Probability			
1.0	**Students organize, represent, and interpret numerical and categorical data and clearly communicate their findings:**	127–138, 140–142, 144–147, 150–153, 156–159	127–133, 136–139, 140–142, 144–145, 154–159, 161, 163, 165–169, 612–613, 678–681
1.1	Formulate survey questions; systematically collect and represent data on a number line; and coordinate graphs, tables, and charts.	127–129, 144–145, 154–159	136–138, 612–613, CA31, CA33
1.2	Identify the mode(s) for sets of categorical data and the mode(s), median, and any apparent outliers for numerical data sets.	130–133, 136–138	139, 161, 167–169, CA3, CA32, CA33
1.3	Interpret one- and two-variable data graphs to answer questions about a situation.	136–138, 140–142, 146–147, 150–153, 156–159	139, 161, 163, 165–167, CA32, CA33
2.0	**Students make predictions for simple probability situations:**	631–634, 640–646, 652–655	636–639, 642–643
2.1	Represent all possible outcomes for a simple probability situation in an organized way (e.g., tables, grids, tree diagrams).	631–634, 640–646, 652–655	636–639, CA34, CA35, CA36
2.2	Express outcomes of experimental probability situations verbally and numerically (e.g., 3 out of 4; $\frac{3}{4}$).	631–634, 636–639, 644–646, 648–649, 652–655	642–643, CA34, CA35, CA36
Mathematical Reasoning			
1.0	**Students make decisions about how to approach problems:**	*Used throughout the text.* For example: 26–27, 198–199, 452–453	
1.1	Analyze problems by identifying relationships, distinguishing relevant from irrelevant information, sequencing and prioritizing information, and observing patterns.	26–27, 40–41, 74–75, 102–103, 198–199, 240–241, 276–277, 320–321, 356–357, 392–393, 452–453, 482–483, 494–495, 570–571, 602–603, 640–641, 650–651	148–149, CA37, CA38
1.2	Determine when and how to break a problem into simpler parts.	442–443	CA37, CA38

Standard	Text of Standard	Primary Citations	Supporting Citations
2.0	**Students use strategies, skills, and concepts in finding solutions:**	*Used throughout the text.* For example: 64–66, 278–281, 606–608	
2.1	Use estimation to verify the reasonableness of calculated results.	272–274, 278–281, 284–287, 322–324, 352–355, 606–608, 616–619	64–66, 70–72, 311, 358–364, 369–371, CA40
2.2	Apply strategies and results from simpler problems to more complex problems.	526–527	546, CA40
2.3	Use a variety of methods, such as words, numbers, symbols, charts, graphs, tables, diagrams, and models, to explain mathematical reasoning.	20–21, 68–69, 96–97, 108–109, 134–135, 144–145, 148–149, 154–155, 175–177, 182–185, 204–207, 234–235, 306–309, 337–338, 402–403, 488–489, 514–517, 555–556, 564–565, 604–605, 614–615, 642–643	17–19, 22–25, 28–30, 32–34, 36–40, 98–113, 150–153, 156–159, 194–197, 302–305, 385–391, 404–407, 431–437, 469–478, 484–486, 507–513, 522–524, 572–575, 578–580, 593–596, 616–619, 652–655, 670–677, CA39
2.4	Express the solution clearly and logically by using the appropriate mathematical notation and terms and clear language; support solutions with evidence in both verbal and symbolic work.		134–135, CA40
2.5	Indicate the relative advantages of exact and approximate solutions to problems and give answers to a specified degree of accuracy.	62–63	67, 87, 267, CA40
2.6	Make precise calculations and check the validity of the results from the context of the problem.		74–75, 134–135, 148–149, 228–229, 276–277, 284–287, 320–321, 346–347, 494–495, 514–515, 526–527, 602–603, 650–651, CA39
3.0	**Students move beyond a particular problem by generalizing to other situations:**	*Used throughout the text.* For example: 173–174, 188–190, 266–267	
3.1	Evaluate the reasonableness of the solution in the context of the original situation.	266–267	276–277, CA41, CA42, CA43
3.2	Note the method of deriving the solution and demonstrate a conceptual understanding of the derivation by solving similar problems.	188–190	26–27, 74–75, 78–79, 102–103, 108, 175–177, 240–241, 284–287, 388–393, 482–483, 526–527, 532–539, 640–641, CA41, CA42, CA43
3.3	Develop generalizations of the results obtained and apply them in other circumstances.	173–174, 186–187	40–41, 62–63, 102–103, 175–177, 182–185, 263–267, 278–281, 284–287, 306–307, 388–393, 402–403, 442–443, 532–539, 604–605, 612–613, 640–641, 650–651, CA42, CA43

CHAPTER 1

Let's Get Started

Use the Scavenger Hunt below to learn where things are located in each chapter.

1. What is the title of Chapter 1?
2. What is the Main Idea of Lesson 1-1?
3. How do you know which words are vocabulary words?
4. What are the vocabulary words for Lesson 1-1?
5. What is the key concept shown in Lesson 1-6?
6. How many Examples are presented in Lesson 1-4?
7. What is the Web address where you could find extra examples?
8. On page 29, there is a Remember tip box. How does the Remember tip help you?
9. How many exercises are there in Lesson 1-5?
10. Suppose you need more practice on a concept. Where can you go for Extra Practice?
11. Suppose you're doing your homework on page 38 and you get stuck on Exercise 16. Where could you find help?
12. What is the web address that would allow you to take a self-check quiz to be sure you understand the lesson?
13. On what pages will you find the Chapter 1 Study Guide and Review?
14. Suppose you can't figure out how to do Exercise 36 in the Study Guide and Review on page 48. Where could you find help?

MATH SYMBOLS

Start Smart

Let's Review!

The California Sea Lion

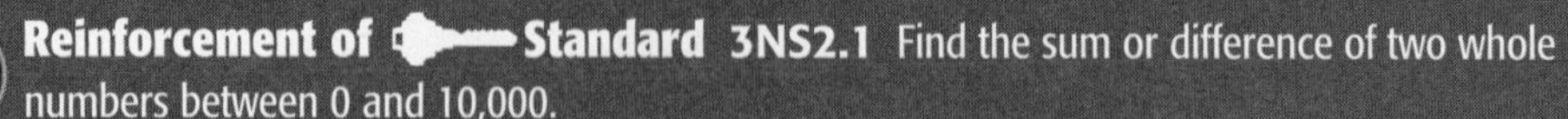

Reinforcement of Standard 3NS2.1 Find the sum or difference of two whole numbers between 0 and 10,000.

START SMART 1

Problem Solving

Climbing to the TOP!

Mountain climbing is a popular sport in California. The table shows the heights of the four tallest mountain peaks in the state.

What is the difference in height between Mount Whitney and North Palisade?

Mountain Peaks

Mountain	Height (ft)
Mount Whitney	14,494
Mount Williamson	14,370
North Palisade	14,242
White Mountain	14,246

Source: destination360.com

You can use the four-step problem-solving plan to solve math problems. The four steps are Understand, Plan, Solve, Check.

Understand

- **Read the problem carefully.**
- **What facts do you know?**
- **What do you need to find?**

The table lists the heights of the mountain peaks. You need to find the difference in height between Mount Whitney and North Palisade.

Plan

- **How do the facts relate to each other?**
- **Plan a strategy to solve the problem.**

To find the difference, subtract the height of North Palisade from the height of Mount Whitney.

Solve

- **Use your plan to solve the problem.**

14,494 feet	Mount Whitney
− 14,242 feet	North Palisade
252 feet	

So, Mount Whitney is 252 feet taller than North Palisade.

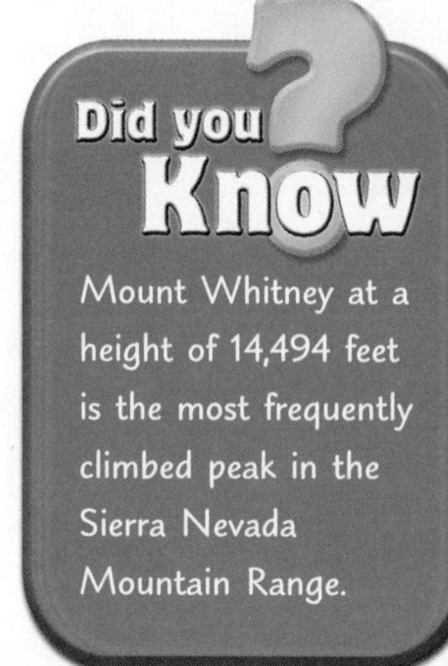

Did you Know
Mount Whitney at a height of 14,494 feet is the most frequently climbed peak in the Sierra Nevada Mountain Range.

Check

- **Look back at the problem.**
- **Does your answer make sense?**
- **If not, solve the problem another way.**

Mount Whitney is almost 14,500 feet tall. North Palisade is about 14,200 feet tall. So, an answer close to 300 makes sense.

1. List the four steps of the *four-step plan.*

2. WRITING IN MATH The table shows the elevation of cities in California. Write a real-world problem using the table. Ask a classmate to solve the problem using the *four-step plan.*

City Elevations

City	Elevation (ft)
Los Angeles	5,074
San Diego	823
San Francisco	934
San Jose	2,125

Source: U.S. Department of Interior

Reinforcement of Key Standard 3NS2.1 Find the sum or difference of two whole numbers between 0 and 10,000.

START 2 SMART

Number Sense

Math has a Seal of Approval

The California sea lion is a kind of seal. These animals can be found living off the west coast of North America.

Addition and Subtraction

For Exercises 1–3, use the table. It shows the average weight of California sea lions.

1. How much do two male sea lions weigh in all?
2. Find the total weight of two female sea lions.
3. Find the difference between the weight of two male sea lions and two female sea lions.

California Sea Lions

Type	Weight (lb)
Female	200
Male	600

Source: seaworld.org

CHECK What You Know Multiplication and Division

4. An adult male sea lion is about 8 feet long. What is the total length of five sea lions if lined up end-to-end?

5. Most California sea lion pups weigh between 13 and 20 pounds. What is the most that three sea lion pups could weigh?

6. An adult female sea lion ate 9 pounds of fish in one day. If she ate the same amount of food each day for the next six days, how many pounds would she eat that week?

Did you Know

When a sea lion dives, its nostrils automatically close up. This allows them to remain under water for 40 minutes at a time.

7. A male sea lion swam 80 miles in 5 hours. How many miles did the male sea lion swim per hour?

8. A group of 8 female sea lions ate 96 pounds of fish in one day. If each sea lion ate an equal amount of food, how many pounds did each female sea lion eat?

9. A sea lion pup swam 65 feet in 5 seconds. How many feet did the pup swim per second?

10. **WRITING IN MATH** Use the table to write a real-world problem about the weights of the predators of California sea lions.

California Sea Lion Predators

Predator	Weight (lb)
Bull shark	500
Great white shark	4,000
Killer whale	10,000

Source: Animal University

Reinforcement of Standard 3AF2.2 Extend and recognize a linear pattern by its rules.

START 3 SMART

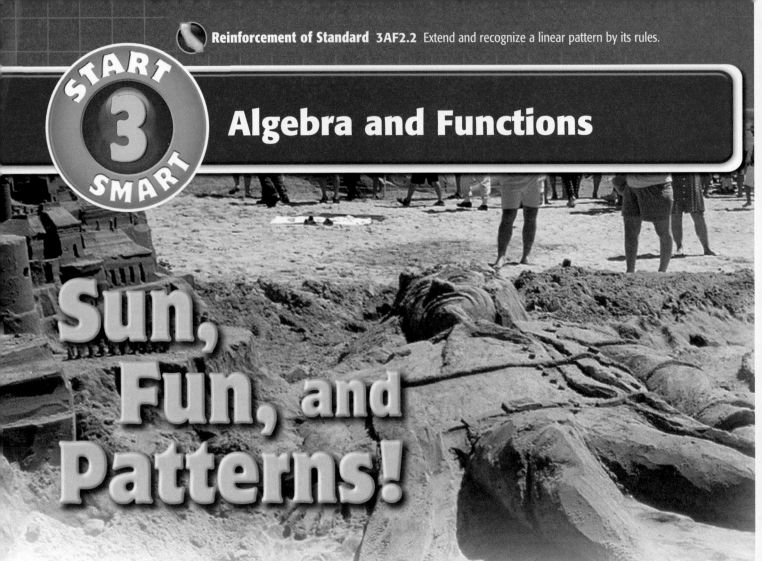

Algebra and Functions

Sun, Fun, and Patterns!

The U.S. Open Sandcastle Competition is the largest sandcastle competition in the United States. The competition is held each year in Imperial Beach, California.

Patterns

A pattern is a set of numbers or figures that follow a rule. Finding a pattern is a useful problem-solving strategy.

For Exercises 1 and 2, use the table. It shows the cost of sand buckets.

Cost of Sand Buckets

Number of Sand Buckets	Cost ($)
1	1.50
2	3.00
3	4.50

1. How much would 4 sand buckets cost?

2. Find the total cost of 8 sand buckets.

3. One bag of sea shells costs 45¢. Two bags cost 90¢. Three bags cost $1.35. How much will 5 bags cost?

Number Sentences

A sandcastle team has 6 members. In the competition, they built 48 small sandcastles. If each team member built the same number of sandcastles, how many sandcastles did they each build?

Number of sandcastles		Number of people		Number of castles built by each member
48	÷	6	=	■

You know that 48 ÷ 6 = 8. So, each member built 8 sandcastles.

Choose the number sentence that can be used to solve the problem. Then solve the problem.

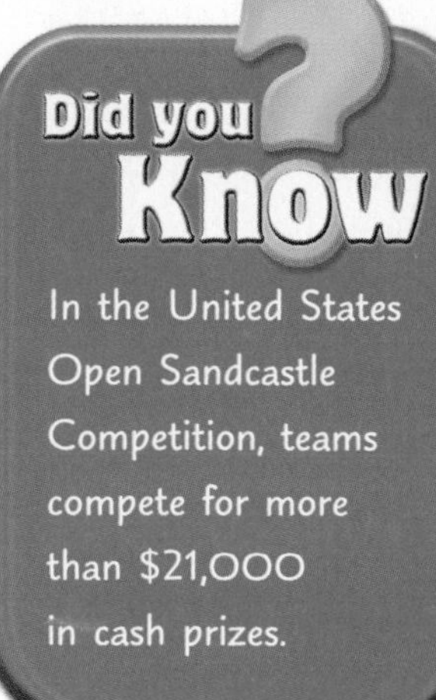

Did you Know
In the United States Open Sandcastle Competition, teams compete for more than $21,000 in cash prizes.

4. Tomas had 9 people on his sandcastle team. If each member built 5 castles, how many castles were built in all?

5. Holly had 14 tickets to the music concert. She gave some of the tickets away. If she had 5 tickets left, how many tickets did she give away?

6. Eric built 5 sandcastles. After 3 hours, he built a total of 14 castles. How many more sandcastles did Eric build?

7. Mrs. Thorne spent $45 on souvenir T-shirts. If she bought a total of 5 T-shirts, how much does each T-shirt cost?

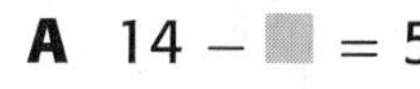

A 14 − ■ = 5

B 9 × 5 = ■

C 5 + ■ = 14

D 45 ÷ 5 = ■

8. **WRITING IN ▸MATH** Write a real-world multiplication problem. Represent the problem situation by using a number sentence. Then have a classmate solve it.

Reinforcement of Standard 3MG1.1 Choose the appropriate tools and units (metric and U.S.) and estimate and measure the length, liquid volume, and weight/mass of given objects.

Measurement

Math is Grape!

Grapes are one of the most popular fruits in the United States. The state of California produces 97% of grapes grown in the United States.

Weight

Weight tells how heavy an object is. An ounce (oz) and a pound (lb) are the customary units of weight.
16 ounces (oz) = 1 pound (lb)

1. Find the total weight of grapes shown.

2. What is the best estimate for the weight of 6 grapes, 1 ounce or 1 pound? Explain your answer.

Compare. Replace each ● with >, <, or =.

3. 10 oz ● 1 lb **4.** 32 oz ● 2 lb

Mass

Mass is the amount of matter an object has. The metric units of mass are the gram (g) and kilogram (kg).
1,000 grams (g) = 1 kilogram (kg)

5. What is the total mass of the grapes shown?

6. What is the best estimate for the mass of 8 bags of grapes, 10 grams or 4 kilograms? Explain your answer.

Did you Know?

One of California's nicknames is the Grape State. There are more than 300,000 tons of grapes grown in California every year!

Compare. Replace each ● with >, < , or = .

7. 100 g ● 1 kg
8. 3,000 g ● 3 kg
9. 1,500 g ● 1 kg

10. Order the weights from least to greatest:

300 g, 3 kg, 100 kg, 100 g

11. **WRITING IN ►MATH** Find two objects in the classroom that weigh more than one ounce. Find two objects that weigh less than one ounce. Explain each choice.

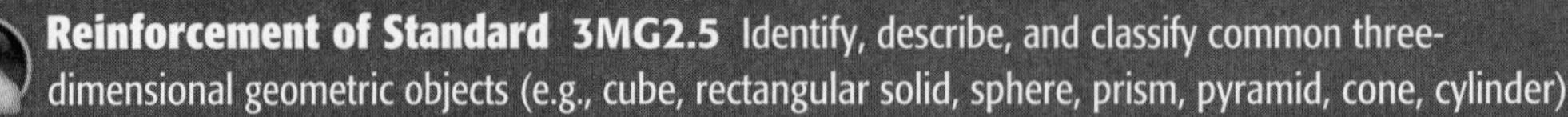

Reinforcement of Standard 3MG2.5 Identify, describe, and classify common three-dimensional geometric objects (e.g., cube, rectangular solid, sphere, prism, pyramid, cone, cylinder).

START SMART 5

Geometry

Artistic Shapes!

The Museum of Contemporary Art (MOCA) is located in Los Angeles. It has one of the finest collections of modern artwork.

CHECK What You Know Solid Figures

Solid figures are commonly found in architecture. Here are some characteristics of solid figures.

- Solid figures have length, width, and height.
- A flat side of a solid figure is called a **face**.
- An **edge** is the line segment where two faces meet.
- The point where three or more edges meet is a **vertex**.

(rectangular) prism

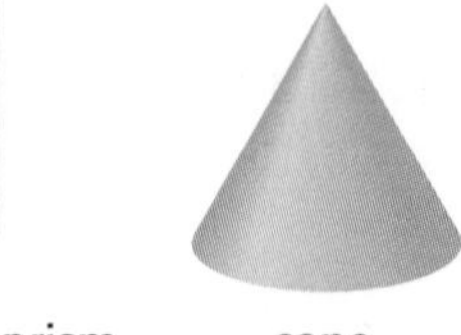
cone

cube

sphere

cylinder

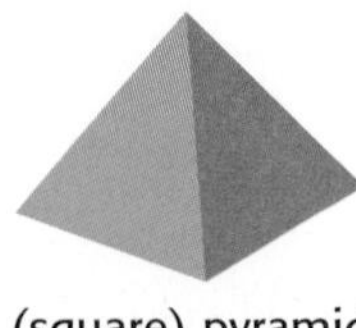
(square) pyramid

1. Which two solid figures have 6 faces?
2. Which solid figure has 5 vertices?
3. What solid figure does a basketball represent?

CHECK What You Know Plane Figures

A plane figure has length and width. Plane shapes are all around us. Just take a look at the traffic signs below.

stop sign

yield sign

speed limit

railroad sign

4. Which sign is an example of an octagon?
5. Which sign(s) contain right angles?
6. Explain the difference between an isosceles triangle and an equilateral triangle. Is a yield sign an equilateral or isosceles triangle?
7. Look for solid and plane figures in your classroom. Draw and label each figure.

8. WRITING IN MATH Describe a real-world solid figure. Then exchange papers with a classmate to see if he or she can guess the figure.

Did you Know
The Museum of Contemporary Art in Los Angeles holds about 5,000 pieces of modern art.

Reinforcement of **Standard** 3SDAP1.3 Summarize and display the results of probability experiments in a clear and organized way (e.g., use a bar graph or line plot).

START 6 SMART

Statistics, Data Analysis, and Probability

Hello Sports Fans!

Football is a popular sport. There are five professional teams in California, including two arena football teams.

CHECK What You Know **Pictographs**

A pictograph shows data by using pictures. The pictograph at the right shows the number of football games a football team played each month during a recent regular season.

1. What does each  represent?

2. How many games did the team play in November? December?

3. During which month was less than four games played?

Bar Graphs

A bar graph compares data by using bars of different lengths. The graph below shows the number of California's professional sports teams divided by sport.

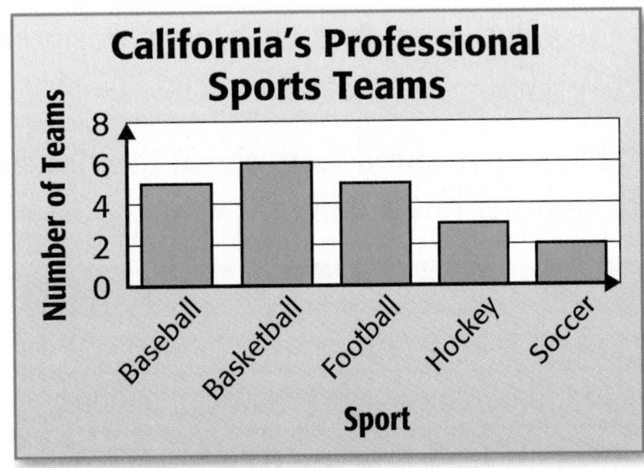

Arena football was invented during an indoor soccer game when its rules were written on an envelope.

4. Which sport has the fewest teams? the greatest?
5. Which two sports have five teams each? How do you know?
6. Which sport has two times as many teams as hockey teams? Explain.
7. What is the difference between the greatest and the least number of teams?
8. What is the total number of teams?
9. Follow these steps to take a survey. Then make a bar graph to show the results.
   - Ask each student to name his or her favorite sport.
   - Make a tally chart to show how many students like each sport.
   - Mark a bar graph from the tally chart.
10. **WRITING IN ▸MATH** Write a sentence that describes what your graph shows.

CHAPTER 1

Place Value and Number Sense

BIG Idea What is place value?

Place value is the value given to a digit by its position in a number.

Example The table shows some facts about the honeybee. Notice that each number has a different value.

Honeybee Facts
• Travels 15 miles per hour
• Makes 154 trips to make one tablespoon of honey
• Wing stroke of 11,400 times per minute

Source: honey.com

What will I learn in this chapter?

- Read and write whole numbers to millions.
- Compare and order whole numbers.
- Round whole numbers.
- Use the *four-step plan* to solve problems.

Key Vocabulary

place value
standard form
expanded form
is greater than (>)
is less than (<)

Student Study Tools
at ca.gr4math.com

FOLDABLES™
Study Organizer

Make this Foldable to help organize information about place value and number sense. Begin with one sheet of notebook paper.

1. **Fold** a sheet of paper. Leave a two-inch tab at the top.

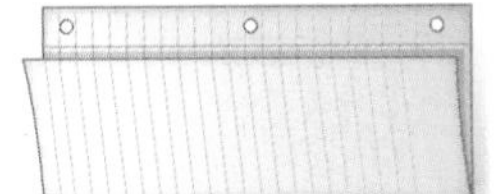

2. **Fold** the right side and the left side to make three equal sections.

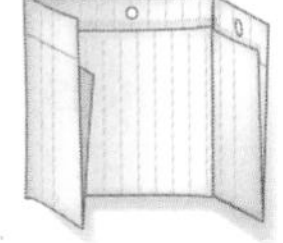

3. **Unfold** the sides. Then cut along the creases as shown.

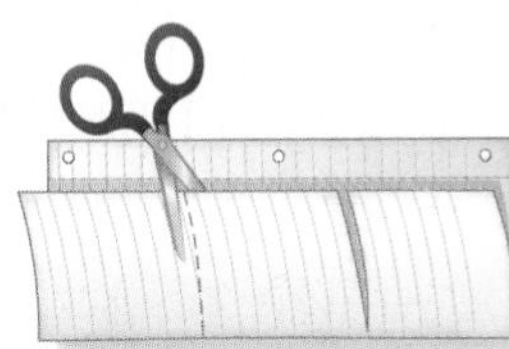

4. **Label** as shown. Take notes as you move through the chapter.

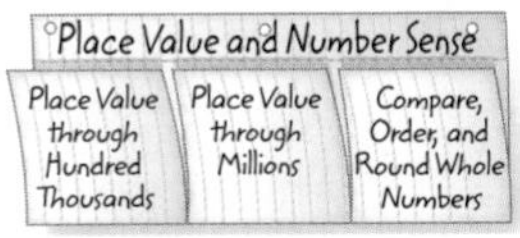

Place Value and Number Sense
Place Value through Hundred Thousands
Place Value through Millions
Compare, Order, and Round Whole Numbers

ARE YOU READY for Chapter 1?

You have two ways to check prerequisite skills for this chapter.

Option 2

Math Online Take the Chapter Readiness Quiz at ca.gr4math.com.

Option 1

Complete the Quick Check below.

QUICK Check

Write each number in word form and expanded form. **(Prior grade)**

1.

Ones		
hundreds	tens	ones
	6	4

2.

Ones		
hundreds	tens	ones
9	9	5

3. 79 **4.** 30 **5.** 90 **6.** 165

7. 347 **8.** 692 **9.** 1,840 **10.** 4,505

11. Write 300 + 20 + 1 in standard form and word form.

Compare. Use >, <, or =. **(Prior grade)**

12. 40 ● 4 **13.** 59 ● 59 **14.** 888 ● 898 **15.** 682 ● 700

16. Nora earned $425. She wants to buy a video game system that costs $375. Does she have enough money? Explain.

Round to the nearest ten. **(Prior grade)**

17. 26 **18.** 4 **19.** 18 **20.** 75

21. 152 **22.** 175 **23.** 347 **24.** 508

25. **Measurement** Carlsbad is 25 miles from San Diego. Would it be reasonable to say that Carlsbad is about 30 miles from San Diego? Explain.

Place Value Through Hundred Thousands

GET READY to Learn

The average lead pencil can draw a line that is almost 184,800 feet (about 35 miles) long. Do you know the value of each digit in 184,800?

MAIN IDEA

I will read and write whole numbers to hundred thousands.

Standard 4NS1.1 Read and write whole numbers in the millions.

New Vocabulary

digit
place value
period
standard form
word form
expanded form

A **digit** is any of the symbols used to write numbers 0, 1, 2, 3, 4, 5, 6, 7, 8, 9. A **place-value** chart shows the value of the digits in a number. Each group of three digits is called a **period**. Each period is separated by a comma.

Period			Period		
Thousands			Ones		
hundreds	tens	ones	hundreds	tens	ones
1	8	4,	8	0	0

EXAMPLE Identify Value of Digits

1 Write the value of the underlined digit in 18<u>4</u>,800.

Step 1 Write the number in a place-value chart.

Thousands			Ones		
hundreds	tens	ones	hundreds	tens	ones
1	8	(4),	8	0	0

Step 2 Identify the column where the 4 is located. Circle it.

Step 3 Replace all the digits that are to the right of the 4 with zeros.

The underlined digit has a value of 4,000. This is because the 4 is in the thousands place.

Standard form is the usual way to write a number using digits. **Word form** is the way you read or say a number. **Expanded form** shows the value of each digit.

Remember

When reading whole numbers in word form, the word *and* is not used.

EXAMPLES Read and Write Numbers

2 **Write 628,371 in word form and expanded form.**

Thousands			Ones		
hundreds	tens	ones	hundreds	tens	ones
6	2	8	3	7	1

Word form: six hundred twenty-eight thousand, three hundred seventy-one

Expanded form: 600,000 + 20,000 + 8,000 + 300 + 70 + 1

3 **Write *one hundred five thousand, twenty-six* in standard form and in expanded form.**

Standard form: 105,026

Expanded form: 100,000 + 5,000 + 20 + 6

Online **Personal Tutor at** ca.gr4math.com

CHECK What You Know

Write the value of the underlined digit. See Example 1 (p. 17)

1. 32,086 **2.** 78,387 **3.** 109,378 **4.** 590,320

Write each number in word form and in expanded form. See Examples 2 and 3 (p. 18)

5. 5,789 **6.** 18,046 **7.** 49,909 **8.** 270,006

9. Write *one hundred thousand, two hundred fifty-six* in standard form and expanded form. See Examples 2 and 3 (p. 18)

10. China has 555,200 fast food restaurants. Write 555,200 in word form.

11. Talk About It Do 800,600 and 860,000 represent the same values? Explain.

 Math Online **Extra Examples at** ca.gr4math.com

Practice and Problem Solving

EXTRA PRACTICE
See page R2.

Write the value of the underlined digit. See Example 1 (p. 17)

12. 59,833 **13.** 72,134 **14.** 93,743 **15.** 174,305

16. 593,802 **17.** 826,193 **18.** 830,259 **19.** 926,794

Write each number in word form and in expanded form. See Examples 2 and 3 (p. 18)

20. 5,050 **21.** 3,791 **22.** 57,402 **23.** 89,074

24. 243,895 **25.** 485,830 **26.** 649,320 **27.** 784,132

Write each number in standard form and in expanded form. See Examples 2 and 3 (p. 18)

28. twenty-five thousand, four hundred eight

29. forty thousand, eight hundred eleven

30. seven hundred sixty-one thousand, three hundred fifty-six

Write each number in word form and standard form.

31. 7,000 + 600 + 30 + 5 **32.** 20,000 + 900 + 70 + 6 **33.** 60,000 + 80 + 4

Real-World PROBLEM SOLVING

Science The photo shows an African elephant.

34. African elephants can weigh up to 14,432 pounds. What is the value of the underlined digit?

35. Write 14,432 in expanded form.

36. A zookeeper weighed a newborn African elephant. He was 232 pounds. After one year, the elephant had gained 1,000 pounds. Write the elephant's new weight in standard form and word form.

H.O.T. Problems

37. OPEN ENDED Write a five-digit number that has a 9 in the hundreds place and a 6 in the hundred thousands place.

38. WRITING IN MATH Explain how the value of the 4 in 694,213 will change if you move it to the tens place.

Math Activity for 1-2

How Big is One Million?

You can use models to help understand the value of 1,000,000.

MAIN IDEA

I will explore the concept of a million.

Standard 4NS1.1 Read and write whole numbers in the millions.

Standard 4MR2.3 Use a variety of methods, such as words, numbers, symbols, charts, graphs, tables, diagrams, **and models, to explain mathematical reasoning.**

You Will Need

thousand cube sheet
scissors
tape

ACTIVITY **Model 1,000,000.**

Step 1 **Model 1,000.**

Cut out a thousand cube model. Fold the edges where the sides meet and form a cube. This shows 1,000.

Step 2 **Model 10,000.**

Work with your classmates. Use 10 of the cubes to show 10,000.

Step 3 **Model 100,000.**

Make more cubes to build a model of 100,000.

Step 4 **Create 1,000,000.**

Suppose you were to build a model of 1,000,000. How many more 100,000 models would you need? (*Hint:* There are ten 100,000s in 1,000,000.)

Animation
ca.gr4math.com

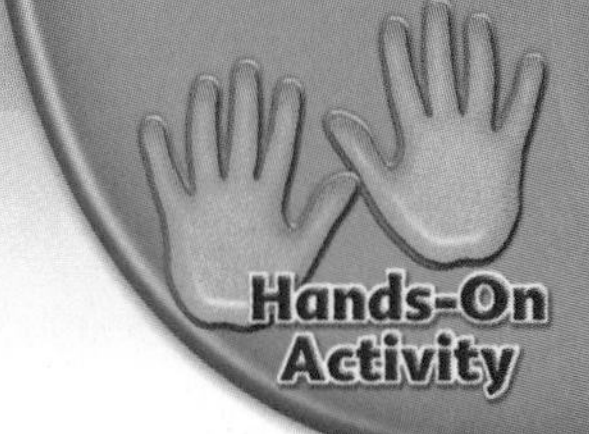

Think About It

1. How did you build a model of 10,000?
2. Describe what your model of 1,000,000 looks like.
3. How are the models you built and drew like the models for ones, tens, and hundreds?
4. What number patterns did you see as you built and drew these models?

CHECK What You Know

Write the number shown by each model.

5.

6.

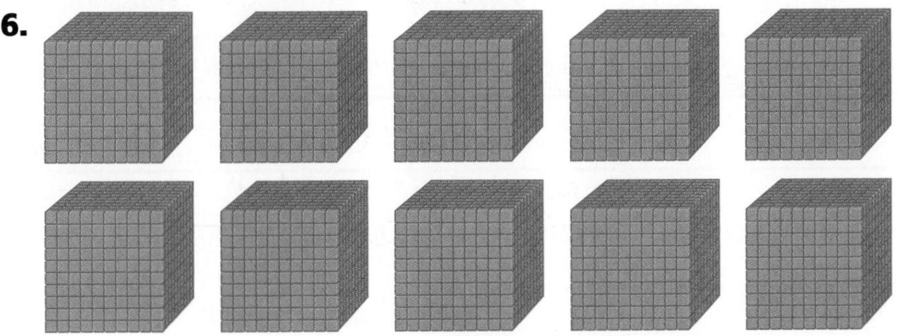

7. The model at the right shows 1,000. How many tens are in 1,000?
8. How many thousands are in 1,000,000?
9. Explain how to determine how long it would take to count to one million.
10. **WRITING IN ▶MATH** How many hundreds are there in 1,000,000? Explain your answer.

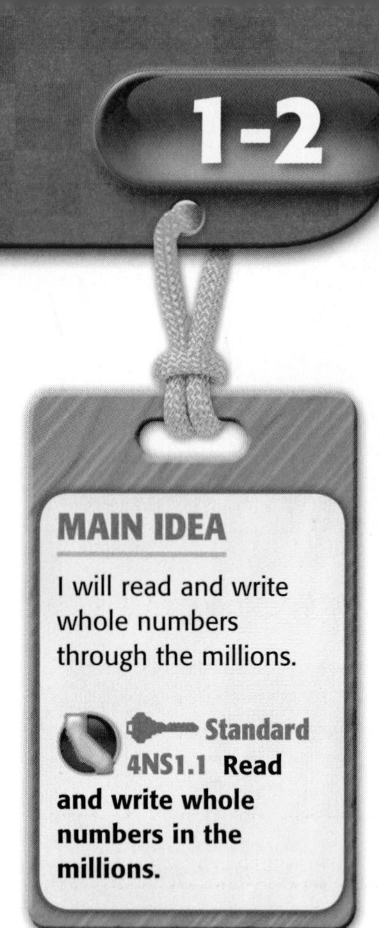

1-2
MAIN IDEA
I will read and write whole numbers through the millions.
Standard 4NS1.1 Read and write whole numbers in the millions.

Place Value Through Millions

GET READY to Learn

Baseball is one of America's favorite sports. The graph shows how many fans attended games for three teams during recent years. The attendance numbers are in the millions.

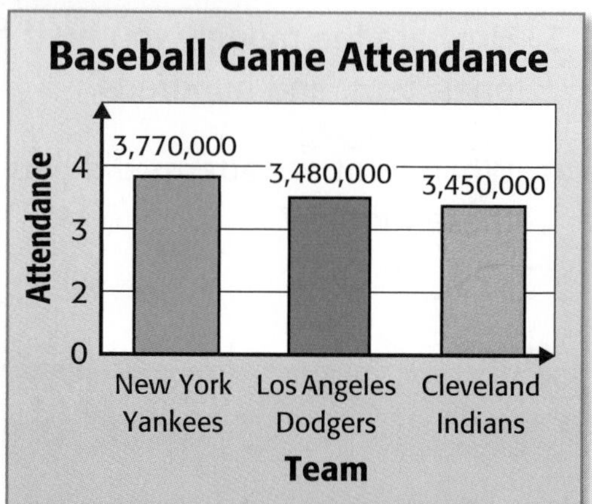

A place-value chart can be used to read and write numbers in the millions. The place-value chart below shows the value of each digit in 3,480,000, the attendance at the Los Angeles Dodgers baseball games.

Period			Period			Period		
Millions			**Thousands**			**Ones**		
		ones	hundreds	tens	ones	hundreds	tens	ones
		3	4	8	0	0	0	0

Real-World EXAMPLE Read and Write Numbers

1 SCIENCE The human eye blinks an average of 5,500,000 times a year. Write 5,500,000 in three ways.

Standard form: 5,500,000

Word form: five million, five hundred thousand

Expanded form: 5,000,000 + 500,000

Real-World EXAMPLE

2 **CARS United States citizens own *one hundred thirty-five million, seven hundred thousand* cars. Write this number in standard form and in expanded form.**

One hundred thirty-five million, seven hundred thousand is written in the place-value chart below.

Millions			Thousands			Ones		
hundreds	tens	ones	hundreds	tens	ones	hundreds	tens	ones
1	3	5,	7	0	0,	0	0	0

Standard form: 135,700,000

Expanded form: 100,000,000 + 30,000,000 + 5,000,000 + 700,000

Online **Personal Tutor at** ca.gr4math.com

CHECK What You Know

Write the value of the underlined digit. See Examples 1 and 2 (pp. 22–23)

1. 469,9$\underline{9}$9 **2.** $\underline{1}$,040,710 **3.** 35,0$\underline{9}$8,098 **4.** $\underline{8}$3,023,215

Write each number in word form and in expanded form. See Example 1 (p. 22)

5. 2,007 **6.** 43,980 **7.** 302,806 **8.** 38,000,875

Write each number in standard form and in expanded form. See Example 2 (p. 23)

9. nine hundred thousand, five hundred fifty-two

10. two hundred forty-six million, nine hundred thousand, eighteen

11. On Sunday, 2,617,000 newspapers were sold. Write the number of newspapers sold in word form and expanded form.

12. Talk About It Explain how to find the value of the underlined digit in the number 26,0$\underline{5}$7,928.

Practice and Problem Solving

Write the value of the underlined digit. See Examples 1 and 2 (pp. 22–23)

13. 132,<u>6</u>85 **14.** <u>3</u>09,573 **15.** 30<u>9</u>,841 **16.** 7,824,0<u>1</u>5

17. 40,2<u>4</u>5,854 **18.** <u>6</u>8,210,397 **19.** 73,581,<u>2</u>09 **20.** 9<u>7</u>,530,284

Write each number in word form and in expanded form. See Example 1 (p. 22)

21. 29,205 **22.** 82,009 **23.** 901,452 **24.** 200,013

25. 30,842,085 **26.** 63,930,053 **27.** 319,999,990 **28.** 800,493,301

Write each number in standard form and in expanded form. See Example 2 (p. 23)

29. two hundred thirty-eight thousand, three hundred seventy

30. four million, ninety-four thousand, two hundred fifteen

31. eighty three million, twenty-three thousand, seven

32. three hundred four million, eight hundred thousand, four hundred

Write each number in word form and in standard form.

33. 200,000 + 60,000 + 3,000 + 200 + 70 + 3

34. 1,000,000 + 900,000 + 50,000 + 6,000 + 200 + 20 + 5

35. As of 2004, the population of Los Angeles was 3,694,820. Write Los Angeles' population in word form.

36. **Measurement** The land area for California is 400,000 + 3,000 + 900 + 70 square kilometers. Write the area in word form.

Real-World PROBLEM SOLVING

Planets The Sun and Earth are shown.

37. The distance from Earth to the Sun is 92,955,793 miles. Write this number in word form and expanded form.

38. The amount of time that U.S. astronauts have spent in space is about 13,507,804 minutes. Is this number read as *thirteen million, fifty-seven thousand, eight hundred four*? Explain.

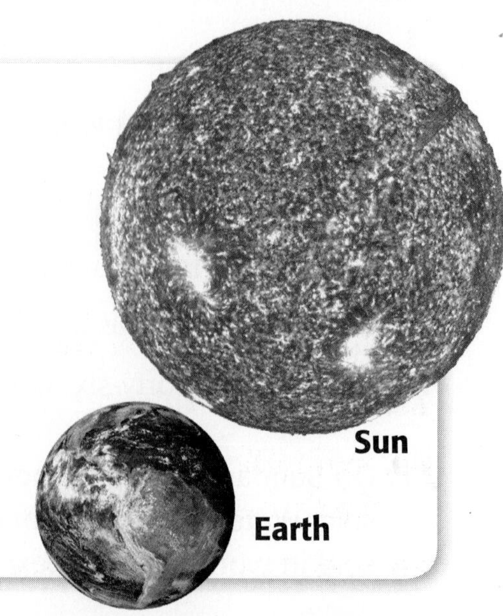

H.O.T. Problems

39. OPEN ENDED Write an eight-digit number that has a 7 in the ten millions place and a number in the thousands place with a value of 2,000.

40. CHALLENGE Write the number with the smallest value using the digits 1 through 9. Use each digit only once.

41. NUMBER SENSE Is the following statement *true* or *false*? Explain your answer.

1,000 thousands = 1,000,000

42. WRITING IN ▸MATH Explain how you know what number is missing in 3,947 = 3,000 + ■ + 40 + 7.

Standards Practice

43 Which number below is the word form of 57,302? **(Lesson 1-1)**

A five thousand, three hundred two

B fifty-seven thousand, three hundred twenty

C fifty-seven thousand, three hundred two

D five hundred thousand, three hundred two

44 Yosemite National Park hosts three million, three hundred seventy thousand visitors each year. What is this number in standard form? **(Lesson 1-2)**

F 3,307,000

G 3,370,000

H 30,307,000

J 30,370,000

Spiral Review

Write the value of the underlined digit. (Lesson 1-1)

45. 10,<u>4</u>98 **46.** 12,00<u>4</u> **47.** <u>3</u>0,182

Write each number in standard form and in expanded form. (Lesson 1-1)

48. three thousand five

49. four million, six hundred thirty-seven thousand, five hundred four

50. seventeen million, twenty thousand, four hundred fifty-eight

1-3 Problem-Solving Skill

MAIN IDEA I will solve problems using a four-step plan.

Standard 4MR1.1 Analyze problems by identifying relationships, distinguishing relevant from irrelevant information, sequencing and prioritizing information, and observing patterns. **Standard 4NS3.0 Students solve problems involving addition,** subtraction, multiplication, and division **of whole numbers** and understand the relationships among the operations.

There are six girls in Dina's scout troop. They are planning a trip to the local amusement park. Admission for children is $12. What is the total cost of admission for everyone to go?

Understand

What facts do you know?

- There are six scouts who want to go.
- The price of admission is $12 for each girl.

What do you need to find?

- The total cost of admission for all the girls.

Plan

To find the total cost, you can use addition. There are 6 girls, and it will cost $12 each. So, add 12 six times.

Solve

$\$12 + \$12 + \$12 + \$12 + \$12 + \$12 = \$72$

or $6 \times \$12 = \$72$

So, the troop needs $72 to go to the amusement park.

Check

Look back at the problem. One way to check the answer is to use a drawing.

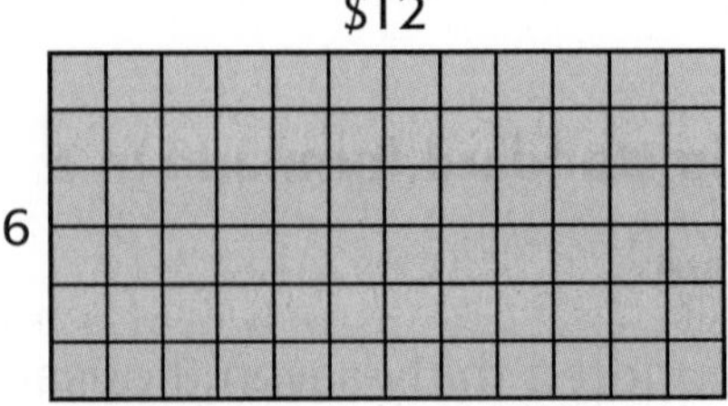

There are 6×12 or 72 squares, so the answer is correct.

ANALYZE the Skill

Refer to the problem on the previous page.

1. Explain why addition was used to solve the problem.

2. In the problem, the price for an adult admission was not included. Suppose the price of an adult ticket is $8 more than a child's ticket. Find the total cost of three adult tickets. Explain.

3. Refer to Exercise 2. Draw a model to check. Explain how the model shows that your answer is correct.

4. If three adults were to go on the trip with the scouts, how much would admission cost for everyone to go? Explain how you found your answer.

PRACTICE the Skill

EXTRA PRACTICE
See page R2.

Solve. Use the *four-step plan*.

5. A class is playing a game. Each correct answer is worth 5 points. Team 1 has 55 total points. Team 2 has answered 12 questions correctly. Who has answered more questions correctly?

6. Rosa is downloading music. It takes about 3 minutes to download one song. If she downloads an album with 10 songs, about how long will it take her to download the album?

7. Casey's mom is the baseball coach for his team. She spent $50 on 10 baseballs. How much would 1 baseball cost?

8. William can make 4 bracelets in an hour. With Daisy's help, they can make twice as many in an hour. If they work for 2 hours, how many bracelets can they make?

9. The opening phrase of the Gettysburg Address is shown. A score is 20 years. How many years would be in four score and seven years?

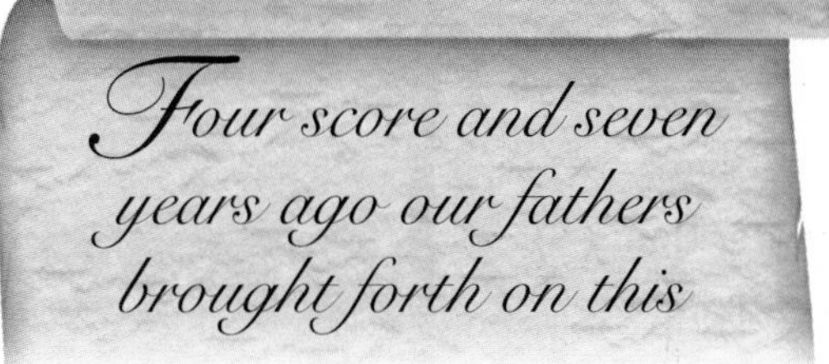
Four score and seven
years ago our fathers
brought forth on this

10. Scott spends 1 hour a day in math class. How many hours does he spend in math class in four weeks in which there are no days off except weekends?

11. Karl Freidrich Benz invented the first gasoline-powered automobile in 1885. Estimate how many years ago this automobile was invented.

12. **WRITING IN MATH** Select one problem from Exercises 5–11. Explain how you used the *four-step plan* to solve the problem.

1-4 Compare Whole Numbers

GET READY to Learn

A first year police officer earns $41,793 in one year. A first year firefighter earns $41,294 in one year. Which occupation pays more for the first year?

MAIN IDEA

I will compare whole numbers.

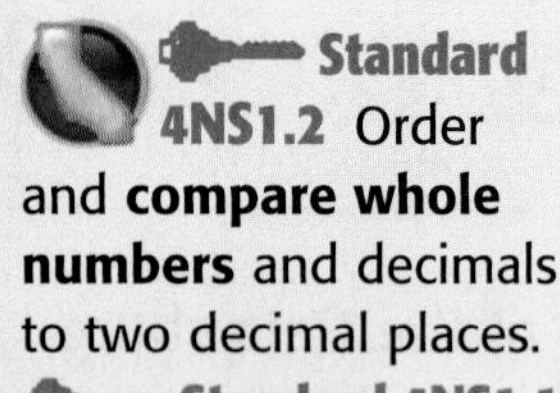

Standard 4NS1.2 Order and **compare whole numbers** and decimals to two decimal places.

Standard 4NS1.1 Read and write numbers in the millions.

New Vocabulary

number line
is greater than (>)
is less than (<)
is equal to (=)

You can use a number line to compare numbers. A **number line** is a line with numbers on it in order at regular intervals. The symbols below are used to show relationships of numbers.

is greater than	**is less than**	**is equal to**
>	<	=

Real-World EXAMPLE Use a Number Line

1 JOBS Which occupation pays more for the first year: police officer or firefighter?

On a number line, numbers to the right are greater than numbers to the left.

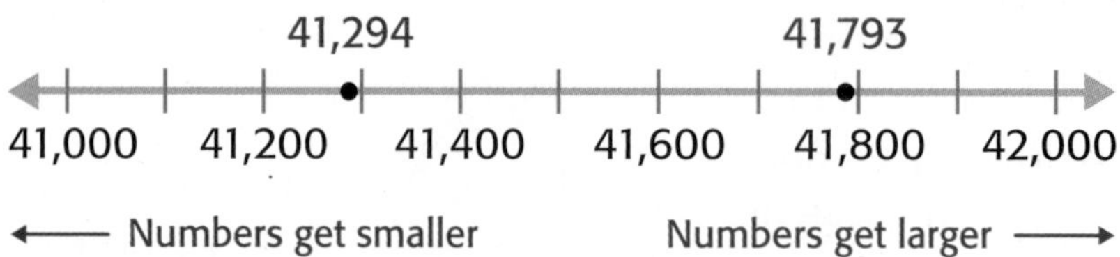

41,793 is to the right of 41,294.

So, 41,793 is greater than 41,294.

Therefore, 41,793 > 41,294.

So, police officers earn more money than firefighters.

To compare numbers, you can also use place value.

Real-World EXAMPLE Use Place Value

2 **DATA The table shows the two most popular names in the United States. Which name is more popular?**

Last Name	Number of People
Miller	1,253,913
Jones	1,836,509

Source: *Top 10 of Everything*

Remember

Before comparing numbers, always line up the ones place.

Step 1 Line up the numbers so that the digits in the ones place align.
1,253,913
1,836,509

Step 2 Begin at the greatest place. Compare the digits.
1,253,913
1,836,509
Since 1 = 1, go to the next place.

Step 3 Compare the digits in the next place on the right.
1,**2**53,913
1,**8**36,509
$8 > 2$

So, 1,836,509 is greater. Therefore, the more popular last name is Jones.

Personal Tutor at ca.gr4math.com

CHECK What You Know

Compare. Use $>$, $<$, or $=$. See Examples 1 and 2 (pp. 28–29)

1. 1,798 ● 1,789

2. 7,440 ● 7,436

3. 25,409 ● 26,409

4. 50,402 ● 50,406

5. 655,543 ● 556,543

6. 10,027,301 ● 10,207,301

7. Jun collects stamps and baseball cards. He has 1,834 stamps and 1,286 baseball cards. Does he have more stamps or more baseball cards?

8. **Talk About It** Explain why any five-digit number is less than any six-digit number.

Practice and Problem Solving

EXTRA PRACTICE
See page R3.

Compare. Use >, <, or =. See Examples 1 and 2 (pp. 28–29)

9. 3,030 ● 3,030
10. 5,980 ● 5,090
11. 6,789 ● 6,798
12. 9,623 ● 9,623
13. 23,001 ● 23,010
14. 18,041 ● 18,040
15. 76,101 ● 77,000
16. 12,683 ● 12,638
17. 304,999 ● 305,049
18. 701,010 ● 701,010
19. 2,999,214 ● 2,999,214

Copy and complete to make the number sentence true.

20. 658,431 < ■00,000
21. 1,342,646 > 1,■89,035

22. Delaney received 1,127 emails in a year. Patricia received 1,132 emails. Who received more emails?

23. Hassan read 2,365 pages during the school year. Anjelita read 2,382 pages during the school year. Who read more pages during the school year?

Real-World PROBLEM SOLVING

Technology The table shows the top four online languages.

24. Which language is used most on the Internet?

25. Which language is used less on the Internet, Japanese or Spanish?

Top Online Languages

Language	Internet Users
Chinese	105,736,236
English	286,642,757
Japanese	66,763,838
Spanish	55,887,063

Source: Nielsen/Net Ratings/International

H.O.T. Problems

26. OPEN ENDED Write a seven-digit number that is greater than 8,458,942.

27. WHICH ONE DOESN'T BELONG? Which number does not belong? Explain.

10,000 | 10 hundreds | ten thousand | 100 hundreds

NUMBER SENSE Compare. Use >, <, or =.

28. 3 thousands ● 3,200
29. 1,000,000 ● 1,000 thousands

30. **WRITING IN MATH** Explain how to compare numbers using place value.

Math Online Self-Check Quiz at ca.gr4math.com

Chapter 1 Mid-Chapter Check

Lessons 1-1 through 1-4

Write each number in word form and in expanded form. (Lesson 1-1)

1. 2,384

2. 917,022

Write each number in standard form and in expanded form. (Lesson 1-1)

3. nineteen thousand, two hundred six

4. two hundred seventy-two

5. There are 3 schools. Each school has 297 students. How many students are in all three schools? Write in standard form and word form. (Lesson 1-1)

6. **STANDARDS PRACTICE** Which sentence below is correct? (Lesson 1-1)

A 38,521 < 37,125

B 65,349 > 65,400

C 90,502 > 90,205

D 12,754 < 12,574

Write the value of the underlined digit. (Lesson 1-2)

7. 1,$\underline{6}$87

8. 3$\underline{2}$0,579

9. Erika is writing the greatest number possible using the digits shown.

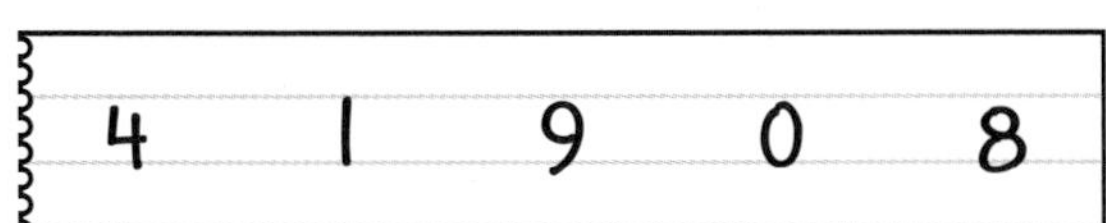

Write the number in expanded form. (Lesson 1-2)

10. What is 20,000,000 + 8,000,000 + 300,000 + 6,000 + 30 + 7 in standard form and in word form? (Lesson 1-2)

Compare. Use >, <, and =. (Lesson 1-4)

11. 2,481 ● 2,814

12. 200 + 70 + 8 ● 700 + 80 + 2

Algebra **Find the value of *x*.** (Lesson 1-4)

13. $5,000 + x + 9 = 5,709$

14. $40,000 + 6,000 + x = 46,009$

15. Rolando traveled 2,643 miles by air. Ramiro traveled 2,643 miles by car. Who traveled farther? Explain. (Lesson 1-4)

16. **STANDARDS PRACTICE** Which of these is 7,402,644? (Lesson 1-4)

F seven million, forty-two thousand, six hundred four

G seven thousand, four hundred two

H seven million, four hundred two thousand, six hundred forty-four

J seven million, two hundred four thousand, six hundred four

17. On Monday Dylan used a pedometer to record 15,725 steps. On Tuesday he took 15,806 steps. On which day did he take more steps? (Lesson 1-4)

18. **WRITING IN MATH** Explain how to find the number missing in the following expanded form sentence.
8,000,000 + 5,000 + 90 + 3 = 8,■05,093

1-5 Order Whole Numbers

MAIN IDEA

I will order whole numbers through the millions.

Standard 4NS1.2 Order and compare **whole numbers** and decimals to two decimal places.

Standard 4NS1.1 Read and write numbers in the millions.

GET READY to Learn

Having a dog is very popular. The table shows the number of Yorkshire Terriers, Beagles, and German Shepherds in the United States. Which dog is most popular? least popular?

Dog Breeds in the U.S.

Dog	Number
Yorkshire Terrier	47,238
Beagle	42,592
German Shepherd	45,868

Source: American Kennel Club

To order numbers, you can use a number line or place value.

Real-World EXAMPLE Use a Number Line

1 DOGS Order the dog breeds in the table above from most popular to least popular.

Graph each number on a number line.

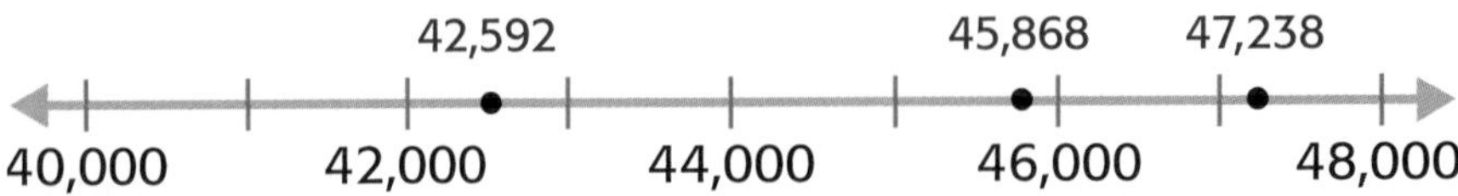

47,238 is farthest to the right.

45,868 is between 42,592 and 47,238.

42,592 is the farthest to the left.

The order is Yorkshire Terrier, German Shepherd, Beagle.

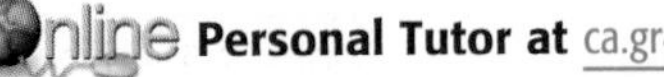

Personal Tutor at ca.gr4math.com

Real-World EXAMPLE Use Place Value

2 OIL The table shows the number of barrels of oil used each day in different countries. Use place value to order the data from greatest to least.

Oil Usage	
Country	**Barrels per Day**
Brazil	2,199,000
Canada	2,200,000
India	2,130,000
United States	19,650,000

Source: *CIA World Fact Book* (2005)

Remember

When ordering numbers, you can use number lines or place value.

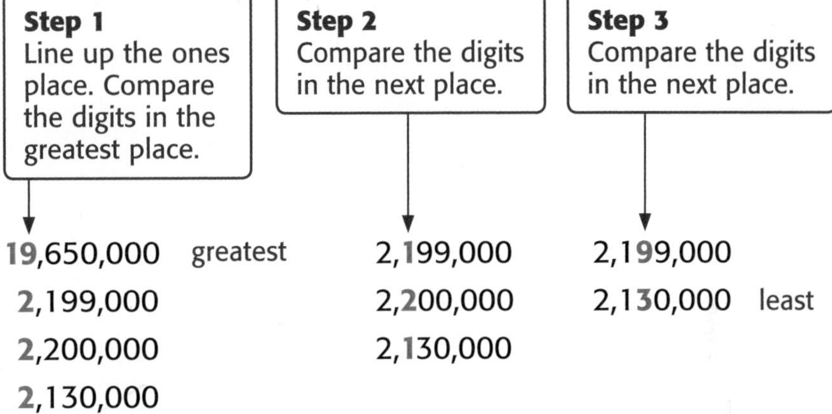

Step 1
Line up the ones place. Compare the digits in the greatest place.
Step 2
Compare the digits in the next place.
Step 3
Compare the digits in the next place.
19,650,000 greatest
2,199,000
2,200,000
2,130,000
2,199,000
2,200,000
2,130,000
2,199,000
2,130,000 least

The numbers ordered from greatest to least are 19,650,000; 2,200,000; 2,199,000; and 2,130,000.

So, the order is the United States, Canada, Brazil, and India.

CHECK What You Know

Order the numbers from greatest to least. See Examples 1 and 2 (pp. 32–33)

1. 3,456; 4,356; 3,465; 6,543
2. 52,482; 50,023; 56,028; 63,340
3. 87,035; 80,562; 78,035; 79,003
4. 145,099; 154,032; 145,004; 159,023
5. **Measurement** Order the lakes shown in the table from greatest to least surface area.

California Lakes	
Lake	**Surface Area (acres)**
Clear Lake	43,785
Lake Almanor	27,064
Lake Tahoe	123,520
Shasta Lake	29,500
Trinity Lake	16,400

Source: worldatlas.com

6. **Talk About It** When ordering whole numbers, explain what you do when the digits in the same place have the same value.

Practice and Problem Solving

See page R3.

Order the numbers from greatest to least. See Examples 1 and 2 (pp. 32–33)

7. 2,004; 1,906; 2,006; 1,507

8. 3,521; 3,512; 1,243; 3,306

9. 79,920; 82,234; 97,902; 90,125

10. 12,378; 12,783; 12,873

11. 138,023; 138,032; 139,006; 183,487

12. 258,103; 248,034; 285,091; 248,934

13. 6,052,264; 6,025,264; 6,052,462

14. 12,345,678; 1,234,567; 123,456,789

15. Rank the following cities in California from least to greatest population.

California Population	
City	**Population**
Bakersfield	283,936
Freemont	202,373
Glendale	201,326
Huntington Beach	195,305

Source: U.S. Census Bureau

16. Order the cars from most expensive to least expensive.

Most Expensive Cars	
Car	**Price**
Bugatti Veyron 16.4	$1,192,057
Leblanc Mirabeau	$645,084
Pagani Zonda Roadster	$667,321
Saleen S7	$555,000

Source: Forbes

Real-World PROBLEM SOLVING

Data File The gray whale is California's state marine mammal. The table shows the gray and other whale migration distances and populations.

17. Order the migration distances of the whales from least to greatest.

18. Order the whale populations from least to greatest.

Whales

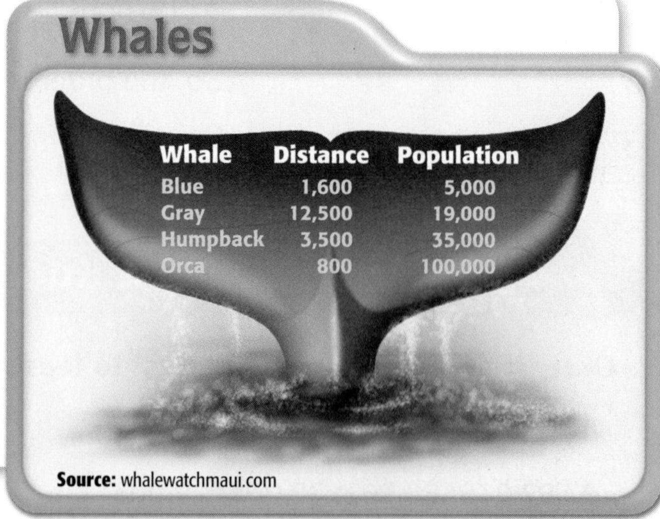

Whale	Distance	Population
Blue	1,600	5,000
Gray	12,500	19,000
Humpback	3,500	35,000
Orca	800	100,000

Source: whalewatchmaui.com

H.O.T. Problems

19. OPEN ENDED Write three numbers that are greater than 750,000 but less than 760,000.

20. NUMBER SENSE Use the digits 2, 3, 4, and 9 to create four numbers. Order them from least to greatest.

21. WRITING IN MATH Write a real-word problem in which you would order three numbers from least to greatest.

Math Online Self-Check Quiz at ca.gr4math.com

Greater Number Game

Compare Whole Numbers

Get Ready!

Players: 2 players

You will need: 40 index cards

Get Set!

Each player gets 20 index cards. Separate the cards into 2 piles of 10. On each card in the first pile, write a number in standard form that has no more than 4 digits. Next, write the expanded form of each number on one of the cards in the second pile.

Go!

- Combine both sets of cards.
- Shuffle and deal the cards.
- Place your cards face down. Turn over the top card at the same time as your partner.
- The person who turns over the greatest number takes both cards. If the cards are equal, keep turning over cards until a player can take the cards.
- Play until one person has all the cards.

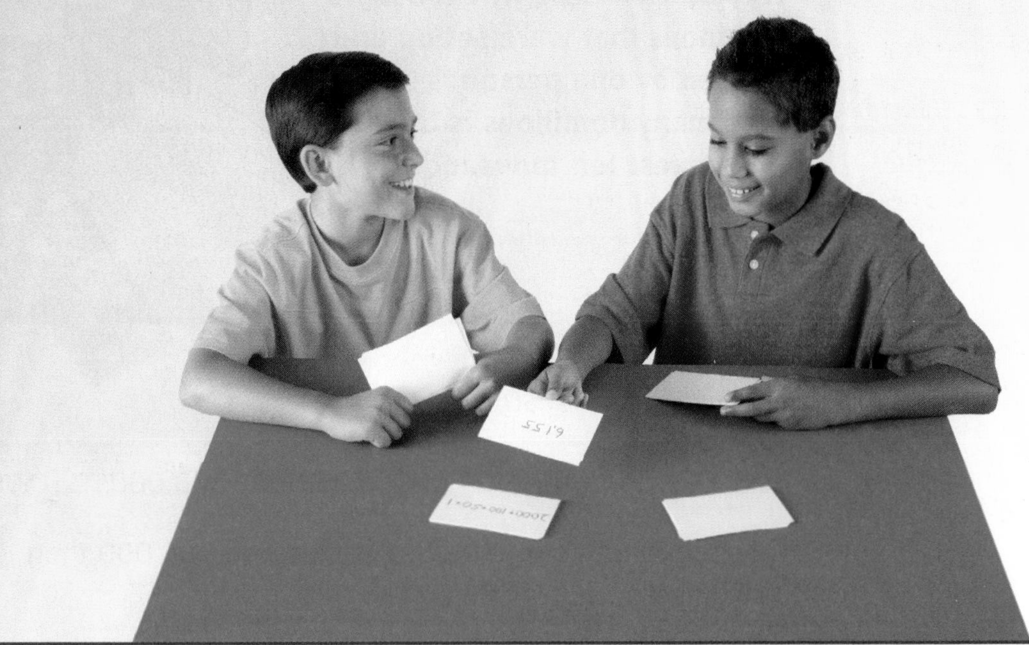

1-6 Round Whole Numbers

MAIN IDEA

I will round whole numbers through the millions.

Standard 4NS1.3 Round whole numbers through the millions to the nearest ten, hundred, thousand, ten thousand, or hundred thousand.

New Vocabulary

estimate
rounding (or round)

GET READY to Learn

A certain tractor weighs 17,554 pounds. About how much does it weigh?

When you do not need an exact answer, you can **estimate** by **rounding**. You can use a number line to round.

Real-World EXAMPLES Round Whole Numbers

1 MEASUREMENT **To the nearest thousand, how much does the tractor weigh?**

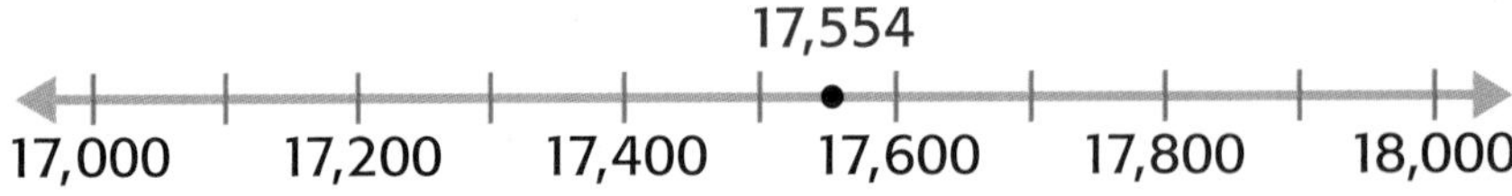

On the number line, 17,554 is closer to 18,000 than 17,000. So, round 17,554 to 18,000.

2 WORLD RECORDS **The most dominoes that were set up and toppled by one person is 303,621. How many dominoes is this to the nearest ten thousand?**

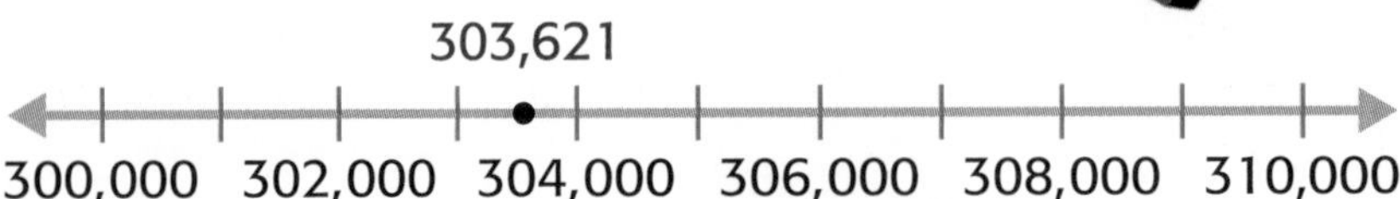

On the number line, 303,621 is closer to 300,000 than 310,000. So, round 303,621 to 300,000.

Place value can also be used to round numbers.

KEY CONCEPT — Rounding Whole Numbers

Step 1 Underline the digit to be rounded.

Step 2 Look at the digit to the right of the place being rounded.

Step 3 If the digit is 4 or less, do not change the underlined digit. If the digit is 5 or greater, add 1 to the underlined digit.

Step 4 Replace all digits after the underlined digit with zeros.

Real-World EXAMPLE — Round Whole Numbers

3 FARMERS There are 422,800 farmers in California. How many farmers is this to the nearest thousand?

You need to round 422,800 to the nearest thousand.

Step 1 Underline the digit in the place to be rounded. In this case, the 2 in the thousands place is to be rounded. 422,800

Step 2 Look at the digit to the right of the underlined digit, which is 8. 422,800

Step 3 Since this digit is greater than 5, add 1 to the underlined digit. 423,800

Step 4 Replace all digits after the underlined digit with zeros. 423,000

To the nearest thousand, 422,800 is rounded to 423,000.

Remember
Check your answer to make sure it is reasonable.

Check

The number line shows that the answer is correct.

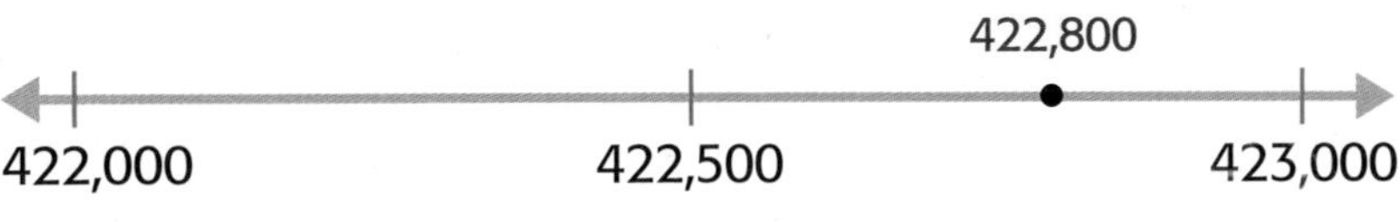

Personal Tutor at ca.gr4math.com

Round each number to the given place-value position. See Examples 1–3 (pp. 36–37)

1. 927; ten
2. 934; hundred
3. 4,282; thousand
4. 43,032; ten thousand
5. 593,205; hundred thousand
6. 709,385; thousand
7. The largest house made out of playing cards used 91,800 cards. To the nearest thousand, how many cards were used?
8. Talk About It Write the smallest number that you can round to the thousands place to get 8,000. Explain.

Practice and Problem Solving

See page R3.

Round each number to the given place-value position. See Examples 1–3 (pp. 36–37)

9. 568; ten
10. 396; ten
11. 297; hundred
12. 148,245; hundred
13. 4,752; thousand
14. 493,580; thousand
15. 519,158; hundred thousand
16. 791,275; hundred thousand
17. 77,690; hundred
18. 95,230; thousand
19. 190,236; hundred thousand
20. 303,985; ten
21. **Measurement** Earth's highest peak is Mount Everest. It is 29,028 feet high. Is this about 30,000 feet high? Explain.
22. **Measurement** The highest point in California is Mount Whitney. It is 14,494 feet high. Is this about 20,000 feet high? Explain.

Real-World PROBLEM SOLVING

Literature The graphic shows the number of characters that are in the longest novel in the world.

23. Round this number to the nearest hundred thousand.
24. To which place would this number be rounded if the rounded number was 14,156,100?

Source: *Guinness Book of World Records*

Math Online Self-Check Quiz at ca.gr4math.com

H.O.T. Problems

25. OPEN ENDED Write five numbers that would round to 50,000.

26. FIND THE ERROR Amanda and Jamal round 83,275,925 to the hundred thousands place. Who is correct? Explain.

Amanda
80,000,000

Jamal
83,300,000

27. WRITING IN MATH Create a real-world problem that involves rounding a number and results in an answer of 670,000.

Standards Practice

28 Which shows the correct order from least to greatest? (Lesson 1-5)

A 1245; 2451; 5412; 4152

B 2124; 4215; 4512; 5214

C 5214; 4512; 4215; 2124

D 2512; 2215; 4124; 4421

29 Yuma, Arizona, is the sunniest place in the world. Round Yuma's average hours of sunlight each year to the nearest thousand. (Lesson 1-6)

Top Two Sunniest Places	
Location	**Hours of Sunlight Each Year**
Yuma, Arizona	4127
Phoenix, Arizona	4041

F 4000 **H** 4200

G 4100 **J** 5000

Spiral Review

Order the numbers from greatest to least. (Lesson 1-5)

30. 685; 700; 660 **31.** 1,363; 1,468; 1,333 **32.** 12,009; 12,090; 12,900

Compare. Use >, <, or =. (Lesson 1-4)

33. 163 ● 165 **34.** 16,094 ● 16,090 **35.** 1,866 ● 1,866

36. The tallest mountain in the United States is 20,320 feet tall. Round this number to the nearest thousand. (Lesson 1-3)

1-7 Problem-Solving Investigation

MAIN IDEA I will choose the best strategy to solve a problem.

Standard 4MR1.1 Analyze problems by identifying relationships, distinguishing relevant from irrelevant information, sequencing and prioritizing information, and observing patterns. **Standard 4NS3.0 Students solve problems involving addition,** subtraction, multiplication, and division **of whole numbers** and understand the relationships among the operations.

P.S.I. TEAM +

TORY: My family is going on vacation to Mexico. Before we go, we have to trade our dollars for Mexican pesos. For every dollar we will get about 11 pesos.

YOUR MISSION: Find about how many pesos Tory's family will get for $8.

Understand

You know that one dollar is about 11 pesos.

You need to find about how many pesos they will get for $8.

Plan

For every 1 dollar, they get 11 pesos. Make a table to solve the problem.

Solve

Dollars	$1	$2	$3	$4	$5	$6	$7	$8
Pesos	11	22	33	44	55	66	77	88

+11 +11 +11 +11 +11 +11 +11

The pattern is to add 11. You can also solve this using multiplication. $8 \times 11 = 88$.
The family can expect to get about 88 pesos for $8.

Check

There is a second pattern in the table. When the digit in the dollar row is changed to pesos, the dollar digit is repeated twice. For example, $5 is 55 pesos. $8 is 88 pesos follows this pattern.

So, the answer is correct.

Mixed Problem Solving

EXTRA PRACTICE
See page R4.

Use the *four-step plan* to solve.

1. **Measurement** A black bear weighs 25 pounds more than a gorilla. Use the information in the table to find how much a black bear weighs.

Large Animal Weights	
Animal	**Weight (pounds)**
Gorilla	400
Black bear	■
Lion	440

2. A robin can fly 20 miles in one hour. An eagle can fly 40 miles in one hour. How many hours would it take for a robin to fly as far as an eagle flies in 3 hours?

3. Jade has 3 sticker sheets with 6 stickers on each sheet. How many stickers does she have in all?

4. A watch costs $34. A pair of sunglasses costs $6. How much change could you expect to receive if you bought one of each item above and paid with a $50 bill?

5. A video game store buys used video games for $10 each. Vivian wants a new video game for $77. How many used games must she sell to buy the new game?

6. Lee wants a motorized scooter. He earns $8 a week, and already has $11. How many weeks will he have to save all of his money to buy the scooter?

7. Leticia earns $20 each time she babysits. How many times will she need to babysit to earn $120?

8. Turi burns about 350 calories for every hour he skis. The last time he skied, he burned 1,200 calories. Did he ski over 3 hours? Explain.

9. Jack's basketball games are 4 quarters that are each 8 minutes long. Is it possible for Jack to play 35 minutes in a game? How do you know?

10. Xavier saved three $10 bills, six $5 bills, and twelve $1 bills. Does he have enough money to buy this MP3 player?

11. **WRITING IN MATH** Refer to Exercise 11. Suppose Xavier has 5 bills and the total is $37. Explain the steps you would take to find which bills he has.

Creatures Under the Sea

Earth's oceans are filled with many different sea creatures. Of these creatures in the ocean, marine mammals such as whales, dolphins, seals, and sea lions are the most skilled divers. Both sperm whales and elephant seals can stay underwater for almost two hours. That's a long time to hold your breath!

Population of Pacific Coast Marine Mammals

Species	Estimated Population
California sea lion	111,016
Gray whale	20,869
Hawaiian monk seal	1,300
Northern fur seal	988,000
Pacific harbor seal	131,826
Spinner dolphin	631,000
Spotted dolphin	731,000

Source: National Biological Service

 Real-World Math

Use the information on page 42 to solve each problem.

1. Which marine mammal species has the greatest population? Write in expanded and word forms.

2. There are about 20,000 blue whales. Your friend tells you that there are more blue whales than gray whales. Is your friend right? Explain.

3. A humpback whale can eat up to 9,000 pounds of food a day. Is this more or less than a blue whale eats? How much more or less?

4. A sea lion can dive 400 feet. Some seals can dive 5,314 feet. Dolphins can dive up to 1,000 feet. List these dives from greatest to least.

5. You are told that there are about 132,000 Pacific harbor seals. Is this true when you round to the nearest thousand? Explain.

6. Which animal populations, when rounded to the nearest thousand, have a one in the thousands place?

Did You Know?

A blue whale eats about 7,500 pounds of food each day.

CHAPTER 1

Study Guide and Review

FOLDABLES™ Study Organizer

GET READY to Study

Be sure the following Key Vocabulary words and Key Concepts are written in your Foldable.

Place Value and Number Sense
Place Value through Hundred Thousands | Place Value through Millions | Compare, Order, and Round Whole Numbers

BIG Ideas

Place Value

- A **place-value** chart shows the value of the digits in a number. (pp. 17–19 and 22–25)

Thousands			Ones		
hundreds	tens	ones	hundreds	tens	ones
	2	1,	8	3	3

Read and Write Numbers (pp. 17–19 and 22–25)

- **Standard form:** 21,833
- **Word form:** twenty-one thousand, eight hundred thirty-three
- **Expanded form:** 20,000 + 1,000 + 800 + 30 + 3

Compare Numbers (pp. 28–30)

- To compare numbers, use **is greater than (>)**, **is less than (<)**, or **is equal to (=)**.

123 > 122 478 < 874 925 = 925

Key Vocabulary

estimate (p. 36)
is greater than (>) (p. 28)
is less than (<) (p. 28)
place value (p. 17)
rounding (p. 36)

Vocabulary Check

Choose the vocabulary word that completes each sentence.

1. When you do not need an exact answer, you can ___?___.
2. To help you read and write numbers, you can use ___?___.
3. When you do not need an exact answer, you can estimate by ___?___.
4. The ___?___ of the 7 in 7,495 is the thousands.
5. The symbol > is used to show that a number is ___?___ another number.
6. The symbol < is used to show that a number is ___?___ another number.

Math Online Vocabulary Review at ca.gr4math.com

Lesson-by-Lesson Review

1-1 Place Value Through Hundred Thousands (pp. 17–19)

Example 1
Write 5,789 in three different ways.

Thousands			Ones		
hundreds	tens	ones	hundreds	tens	ones
		5,	7	8	9

Standard form: 5,789

Word form: five thousand, seven hundred eighty-nine

Expanded form: 5,000 + 700 + 80 + 9

Write each number in word form and in expanded form.

7. 18,045 **8.** 94,804

9. Write *four hundred thirty thousand, two hundred fifty-six* in standard form and in expanded form.

Write the value of the underlined digit.

10. $1\underline{9}0{,}843$ **11.** $84{,}\underline{2}99$

12. The Petrified Forest National Park in northeast Arizona is 93,533 acres. Write this number in word form and in expanded form.

1-2 Place Value Through Millions (pp. 22–25)

Example 2
Write *nine million, three hundred seventy-two thousand, five hundred* in standard form and expanded form.

Word form: nine million, three hundred seventy-two thousand, five hundred

Standard form: 9,372,500

Expanded form: 9,000,000 + 300,000 + 70,000 + 2,000 + 500

Write each number in standard form and in expanded form.

13. two thousand, six hundred ninety-seven

14. nine million, four hundred six thousand, two hundred seventy-one

15. León has a baseball card collection of 4,826 cards. He sells 215 cards to another collector. How many cards does he have left? Write in word form and in expanded form.

1-3 Problem-Solving Skill: The Four-Step Plan (pp. 26–27)

Example 3
Dorota saves $2 each week. How much will she save after 2 months?

Understand Dorota saves $2 each week. You need to find out how much money will she save after 2 months.

Plan There are 4 weeks in 1 month. Use repeated addition to find out how much money she has saved after 2 months.

Solve First, find out how much she saved in one month.

$2	1 week
$2	1 week
$2	1 week
+ $2	1 week
$8	

Now, find the amount saved in two months.

$8	1 month
+ $8	1 month
$16	

So, Dorota will save $16 after 2 months.

Check Count by two's 8 times.
2, 4, 6, 8, 10, 12, 14, 16

So, the answer is correct.

Solve. Use the *four-step plan*.

16. Cynthia earns 5 points at the library for each book she reads. She wants to earn 75 points in order to win the grand prize. How many books does she need to read?

17. Rafael has $72. He wants to buy the bike shown. How much more money does he need?

18. Kristina earned $22 dollars babysitting. She owes her mom $17. How much will Kristina have left after she pays her mom?

19. Trent has to read a book for class by Friday. It is Tuesday and he has 60 pages left to read. If he reads 20 pages a night for the next 3 nights, will he finish the book? Explain.

20. Presta's family is going to the mountains 280 miles away. The family's car can go 25 miles on a gallon of gas, and the gas tank holds 10 gallons. Can they travel to the mountains without stopping to fill up the gas tank? Explain.

1-4 Compare Whole Numbers (pp. 28–30)

Example 4
Compare 1,278 ● 1,500.
Use >, <, or =.

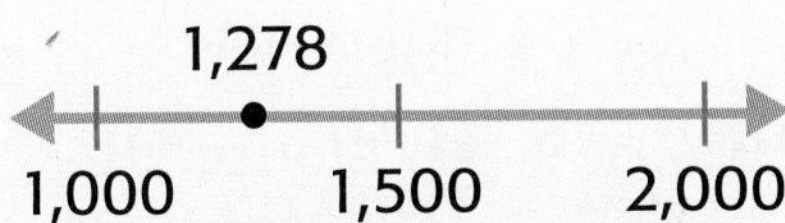

1,500 is to the right of 1,278.
So, 1,500 is greater than 1,278.
1,278 is less than 1,500.
Therefore, 1,278 < 1,500.

Compare. Use <, >, or =.

21. 25,689 ● 25,679

22. 54,820 ● 58,240

23. 109,050 ● 109,050

24. 234,461 ● 234,641

25. Supriya ate 2,142 calories on Monday. On the same day her brother ate 2,111 calories. Who had more calories on Monday?

1-5 Order Whole Numbers (pp. 32–34)

Example 5
Order 54,282; 65,820; and 52,466 from greatest to least.

First, line up the ones place. Compare the digits in the greatest place.

54,282
65,820 ← greatest
52,466

Then, compare the digits in the next place.

54,282
52,466

4 > 2. So, 54,282 is the next greatest number.

The numbers ordered from greatest to least are 65,820; 54,282; and 52,466.

Order the numbers from greatest to least.

26. 12,378; 12,784; 12,837

27. 138,023; 138,032; 139,006

28. 456,980; 612,701; 611,036

29. The table shows the population of the three states with the largest land area. Order these states from greatest to least population.

State	Population
Alaska	655,435
California	35,893,799
Texas	22,490,022

Source: infoplease.com

1-6 Round Whole Numbers (pp. 36–39)

Example 6
Round 587 to the nearest ten.

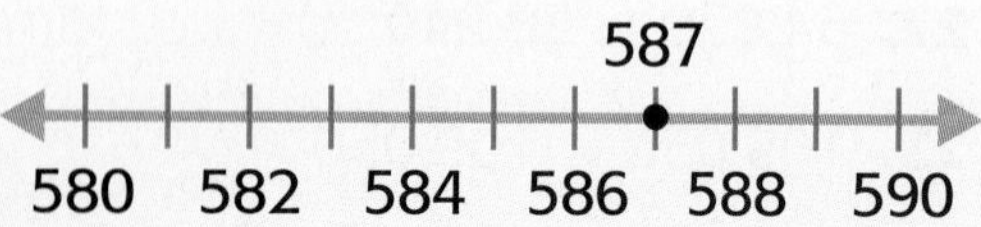

On the number line, 587 is closer to 590 than 580. Therefore, round 587 to 590.

Round each number to the given place-value position.

30. 874; hundred

31. 12,025; ten thousands

32. 617,589; ten thousands

33. 547,203; thousands

34. In 1790, the population of the United States was 3,929,214. To the nearest million, what was the population in 1790?

1-7 Problem-Solving Investigation: Choose a Strategy (pp. 40–41)

Example 7
Each time Esteban goes to the grocery store for his grandmother, she gives him $4. He has $12. How many times has Esteban gone to the grocery store?

Esteban has $12, and he gets $4 each time he goes to the store. You need to find how many times he has gone to the store. Use addition.

$4	1 trip
$4	1 trip
+ $4	1 trip
$12	

So, Esteban has gone to the store 3 times.

Use the four-step plan to solve.

35. Lindsay earns $5 for every A she gets on her report card and $3 for every B. On her last report card, she received a total of $19 for 5 subjects. How many As and Bs did she get?

36. Precious spends 35 hours in school every five-day week. How many five-day weeks will she have been in school if she has been in school for 175 hours?

37. In 1916, Jeannette Rankin of Montana became the first woman elected to Congress. Use rounding to estimate how many years ago the first woman was elected to Congress.

CHAPTER 1

Chapter Test

For Exercises 1 and 2, tell whether each statement is *true* or *false*.

1. The four steps of the four-step problem-solving plan in order are Plan, Understand, Solve, Check.

2. The standard form of nine hundred seventy is 970.

Write the value of the underlined digit.

3. 1<u>8</u>,765

4. <u>3</u>01,936

5. Students voted on their favorite frozen yogurt flavors. The results are shown. Order the results from most favorite to least favorite.

Flavor	Number of Students
Vanilla	410
Chocolate	240
Strawberry	99
Chocolate chip	401

6. STANDARDS PRACTICE Which of these is 7,201,446?

   A seven thousand, two hundred one, four hundred forty-six

   B seven million, two hundred one thousand, four hundred forty-six

   C seven hundred two thousand, one hundred forty-six

   D seven million, two hundred ten thousand, four hundred forty-six

Order the numbers from greatest to least.

7. 1,002; 1,037; 1,200; 1,102

8. 7,613; 7,702; 8,045; 7,499

9. A computer costs $1,295. Round this price to the nearest hundred.

Compare. Use <, >, or =.

10. 6,782 ● 6,702

11. 2,487 ● 2,784

12. STANDARDS PRACTICE What is 7,620,113 rounded to the nearest hundred thousand?

   F 7,600,000

   G 7,620,000

   H 7,700,000

   J 8,000,000

13. Sora earned a score of 98 on a test. Ryan earned a score of 89. Who earned a higher score?

Write each number in word form.

14. 3,476

15. 97,602

16. WRITING IN ▶MATH Andrew rounded 647,963 to the nearest hundred thousand. Is his answer correct? Explain.

700,000

Math Online Chapter Test at ca.gr4math.com

CHAPTER 1

California Standards Practice

Cumulative, Chapter 1

Standards Example

As of 2004, the population of California was thirty-five million, eight hundred ninety-three thousand, seven hundred ninety-nine. What is this number in standard form?

A 35,389,997 **C** 35,893,799

B 35,398,907 **D** 35,983,997

Read the Question

You need to find the number in standard form.

Solve the Question

A place-value chart helps you understand how the number is written in standard form.

Millions			Thousands			Ones		
hundreds	tens	ones	hundreds	tens	ones	hundreds	tens	ones
	3	5,	8	9	3,	7	9	9

The answer is C.

Choose the best answer.

1 **What is the standard form for sixteen million, three hundred twenty-seven thousand, four hundred three?**

A 16,237,340 **C** 16,372,430

B 16,327,403 **D** 16,723,043

2 **What is 54,678,491 rounded to the nearest hundred thousand?**

F 54,000,000

G 54,600,000

H 54,680,000

J 54,700,000

More California Standards Practice
For practice by standard, see pages CA1–CA43.

3 **A health club mailed coupons to four neighborhoods. The number of coupons mailed out is shown.**

Health Club Coupons	
Neighborhood	**Number of Coupons**
The Meadows	12,550
The Hills	12,638
Blackwood	12,450
The Fields	12,745

Which neighborhood received the least number of coupons?

A The Meadows **C** Blackwood

B The Hills **D** The Fields

---

4 **What is 724,385 rounded to the nearest hundred?**

F 700,000 **H** 724,300

G 720,400 **J** 724,400

---

5 **The estimated cost of Shen's new pickup truck is twenty-eight thousand, six hundred seventy-two dollars. What is this number rounded to the nearest thousand?**

A \$28,000 **C** \$29,000

B \$28,700 **D** \$29,700

---

6 **Which number is 1000 less than 25,387,226?**

F 25,377,226 **H** 25,396,226

G 25,386,226 **J** 26,286,226

---

7 **What is \$3,876,342 rounded to the nearest million?**

A \$3,800,000 **C** \$4,000,000

B \$3,900,000 **D** \$4,100,000

---

8 **The estimated cost to build a new baseball stadium is ninety-four million dollars. What is this number in standard form?**

F \$90,400 **H** \$94,000,000

G \$94,000 **J** \$94,400,000

---

9 **Which is the value of the digit 9 in 349,865?**

A 90 **C** 9000

B 900 **D** 90,000

---

10 **Which symbol makes the following true?**

12,935,374 ■ 12,953,748

F > **H** =

G < **J** +

CHAPTER 2 Addition and Subtraction

BIG Idea What is addition? What is subtraction?

Addition is an operation on two or more numbers that tells how many in all. Subtraction is an operation on two numbers that tells how many are left when some are taken away.

Example Celeste and her parents are painting a fence. The fence has three sides, with the fourth being their house. To find the total length of the fence, use addition.

$$\begin{array}{r} \scriptstyle 1 \\ 25 \\ 30 \\ +\ 25 \\ \hline 80 \end{array}$$

The total length of the fence is 80 feet.

What will I learn in this chapter?

- Use addition properties and subtraction rules.
- Estimate sums and differences.
- Determine when to estimate or find an exact answer.
- Add and subtract whole numbers, including multi-digit numbers.

Key Vocabulary

Commutative Property of Addition

Associative Property of Addition

estimate

Student Study Tools at ca.gr4math.com

FOLDABLES™ Study Organizer

Make this Foldable to help you organize information about addition and subtraction. Begin with one sheet of 11″ × 17″ paper.

1. **Fold** lengthwise about 3″ from the bottom.

2. **Fold** the paper in thirds.

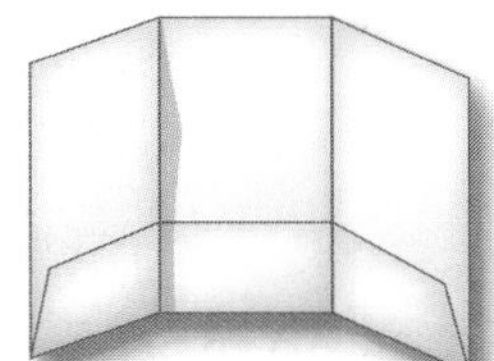

3. **Open** and staple to form 3 pockets.

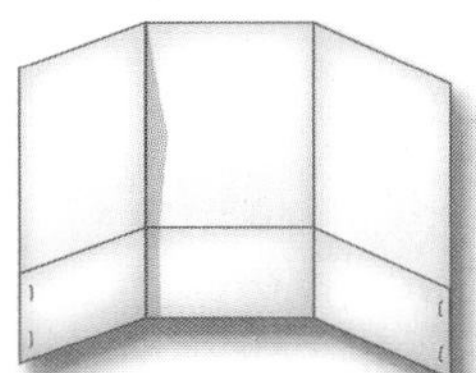

4. **Label** as shown. Place 2 index cards in each pocket.

ARE YOU READY for Chapter 2?

You have two ways to check prerequisite skills for this chapter.

Option 2

Math Online Take the Chapter Readiness Quiz at ca.gr4math.com.

Option 1

Complete the Quick Check below.

QUICK Check

Estimate. Round to the tens. (Lesson 1–6)

1. $65 + 23$

2. $58 + 31$

3. $\$64 - \$21$

4. 98 − 22

5. \$60 + \$29

6. 88 − 26

7. Kavel wants to buy a pair of swimming goggles and a snorkel. Kavel has \$22. About how much more money does he need to buy the items?

Add. (Prior grade)

8. $24 + 47$

9. $36 + 57$

10. $67 + 24$

11. \$56 + \$25

12. 46 + 78

13. \$89 + \$53

14. Zita read an 82-page book. Then she read a 69-page book. How many pages did she read in all?

Subtract. (Prior grade)

15. $26 - 9$

16. $\$31 - \$7$

17. $47 - 19$

18. 42 − 19

19. 64 − 27

20. \$73 − \$45

21. Minho took 34 photographs on Monday and some more on Tuesday. He took 71 photographs in all. How many did Minho take on Tuesday?

2-1 Algebra: Addition Properties and Subtraction Rules

MAIN IDEA

I will use addition properties and subtraction rules to add and subtract.

Standard 4AF1.0 Students use and interpret variables, mathematical symbols, and **properties to** write and **simplify expressions and sentences.**

New Vocabulary

Commutative Property of Addition

Associative Property of Addition

Identity Property of Addition

GET READY to Learn

Carlos and his mom are buying the items shown. Does the order in which the cashier scans the items change the total cost?

The following properties apply to addition.

KEY CONCEPTS — Addition Properties

Words **Commutative Property of Addition** The order in which numbers are added does not change the sum.

Examples $4 + 1 = 5 \qquad 1 + 4 = 5$

Words **Associative Property of Addition** The way in which numbers are grouped when added does not change the sum.

Examples $(5 + 2) + 3 \to 7 + 3 \to 10 \qquad 5 + (2 + 3) \to 5 + 5 \to 10$

Parentheses ( ) show which numbers are added first.

Words **Identity Property of Addition** The sum of any number and 0 is the number.

Examples $8 + 0 = 8 \qquad 0 + 8 = 8$

EXAMPLE Use Addition Properties

1 ALGEBRA Complete 0 +  **= 6. Identify the property used.**

Zero is added to a number, and the sum is 6. So, the missing number is 6. $0 + 6 = 6$.

This is the Identity Property of Addition.

EXAMPLE Use Addition Properties to Add

Remember

Use parentheses ( ) to show the two numbers you are adding first.

2 **Find (22 + 14) + 16.**

(22 + 14) + 16	Commutative Property of Addition
22 + (14 + 16)	Associative Property of Addition
22 + 30	Add 14 and 16.
52	Add 22 and 30.

Online **Personal Tutor at** ca.gr4math.com

The following rules apply to subtraction.

KEY CONCEPTS — Subtraction Rules

Words	When you subtract 0 from any number, the result is the number.
Examples	6 − 0 = 6 4 − 0 = 4
Words	When you subtract any number from itself, the result is 0.
Examples	6 − 6 = 0 5 − 5 = 0

EXAMPLE Use Subtraction Rules

3 **ALGEBRA Find the missing number in 10 − ■ = 10.**

When you subtract 0 from 10, the result is 10.

10 − 0 = 10 So, the missing number is 0.

CHECK What You Know

Copy and complete each number sentence. Identify the property or rule. See Examples 1–3 (pp. 55–56)

1. 19 − ■ = 19

2. (5 + ■) + 2 = 5 + (9 + 2)

3. 74 + 68 = ■ + 74

Add mentally. See Example 2 (p. 56)

4. 12 + 13 + 28

5. 21 + 16 + 19

6. 24 + 17 + 36

7. 

Which subtraction rule is like the opposite of the Identity Property of Addition? Explain your reasoning.

Math Online Extra Examples at ca.gr4math.com

Practice and Problem Solving

Copy and complete each number sentence. Identify the property or rule. See Examples 1–3 (pp. 55–56)

8. $(\blacksquare + 8) + 7 = 9 + (8 + 7)$
9. $4 + 3 + 1 = 3 + 1 + \blacksquare$
10. $\blacksquare + 0 = 9$

11. $5 - \blacksquare = 0$
12. $7 + (1 + 8) = (7 + \blacksquare) + 8$
13. $15 - \blacksquare = 15$

Add mentally. See Example 2 (p. 56)

14. $17 + 24 + 13$
15. $35 + 22 + 15$
16. $13 + 11 + 27$

17. $22 + 16 + 28$
18. $14 + 33 + 26$
19. $31 + 22 + 29$

20. **Measurement** There are 24 minutes left in Asia's class. Then she has 2 more classes before lunch that are each 35 minutes. How many minutes does Asia have before lunch?

21. **Measurement** Paco has 75 minutes before practice. He cleans his room for 40 minutes and reads for 30 minutes. Can he do both of these activities before his baseball game? Explain.

Write a number sentence. Then identify the property or rule used.

22. Susan ate 8 hot dogs and 12 apples in a month. Amelia ate 12 hot dogs and 8 apples in a month. Who ate more?

23. Carla has 7 triangles, 3 squares, and 9 circles. Ethan has 3 circles, 7 squares, and 9 triangles. Who has more shapes?

H.O.T. Problems

24. **OPEN ENDED** Copy and complete the number sentence $(23 + \blacksquare) + 19 = 23 + (\blacksquare + 19)$. Can any number complete the number sentence? Explain.

25. **FIND THE ERROR** Trey and Mika are showing an example of the Identity Property of Addition. Who is correct? Explain.

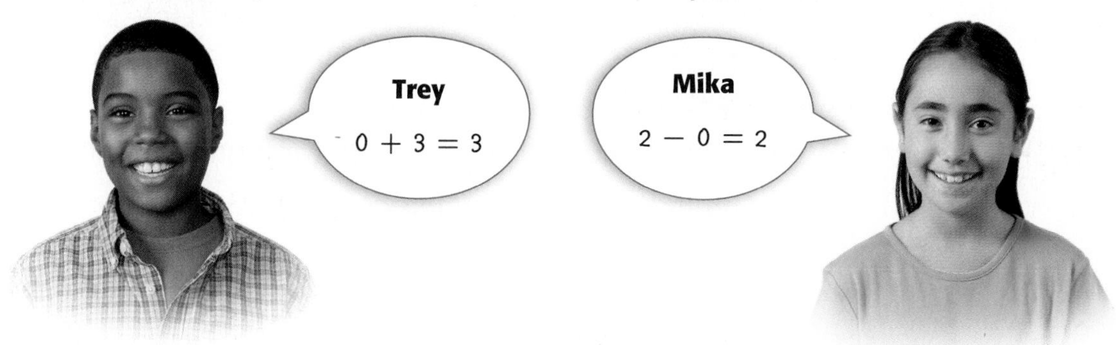

26. **WRITING IN ▶MATH** Explain how you could group $775 + 639 + 225$ to find the sum mentally.

2-2 Estimate Sums and Differences

MAIN IDEA

I will estimate sums and differences of numbers.

4NS3.1

Demonstrate an understanding of, and the ability to use, standard algorithms for the addition and subtraction of multidigit numbers.

New Vocabulary

estimate

Natalie has been saving her money so that she can buy snowboarding equipment. She wants to buy the items shown. About how much money does she need?

Sometimes you do not need an exact answer. When the word *about* is used in a problem, you can find an estimate. An **estimate** is an answer close to the exact answer.

Real-World EXAMPLE Estimate Sums

1 **MONEY** **About how much money does Natalie need to buy a snowboard and boots? Round to the tens place.**

Round each amount to the nearest tens place. Then add.

$119	rounds to →	$120
+ $ 67	rounds to →	+ $ 70
		$190

So, Natalie needs to save about $190.

When estimating, you can also round to the nearest hundred, thousand, or ten thousand.

Remember

To review the rounding rules, see Lesson 1-6 (p. 37).

EXAMPLE Estimate Sums

2 **Estimate 2,342 + 637. Round to the hundreds place.**

Round to the nearest hundreds place. Then add.

2,342	rounds to →	2,300
+ 637	rounds to →	+ 600
		2,900

So, 2,342 + 637 is about 2,900.

Remember

When adding or subtracting money, the dollar sign $ needs to be placed in the answer.

EXAMPLE Estimate Differences

3 Estimate $75.43 − $32.89. Round to the tens place.

Round each amount to the nearest ten dollars then subtract.

$75.43	rounds to →	$80.00
− $32.89	rounds to →	− $30.00
		$50.00

So, $75.43 − $32.89 is about $50.00.

Real-World EXAMPLE Estimate Differences

4 MEASUREMENT The table shows two road tunnels in California. About how much longer is Transbay Tube than Caldecott? Round to the thousands place.

California Tunnels

Tunnel's Name	Length (ft)
Caldecott	10,991
Transbay Tube	19,008

Source: answers.com

Round each length to the nearest thousand. Then subtract.

19,008	rounds to →	19,000
− 10,991	rounds to →	− 11,000
		8,000

So, the Transbay Tube is about 8,000 feet longer.

Online **Personal Tutor at** ca.gr4math.com

CHECK What You Know

Estimate. Round to the indicated place value. **See Examples 1–4 (pp. 58–59)**

1. 312 + 27; tens
2. 1,561 + 305; hundreds
3. $21.75 + $73.14; tens
4. 383 − 122; hundreds
5. $74.50 − $52.74; tens
6. 37,215 − 6,972; thousands
7. The Davis family will buy the camping equipment shown. About how much will the equipment cost?

Camping Equipment

Item	Cost
Family-size tent	$399
Camping stove	$179

8. **Talk About It** Estimate 829 + 1,560 to the nearest hundred and the nearest thousand. Compare both estimates to the actual sum. What do you notice?

Practice and Problem Solving

EXTRA PRACTICE
See page R4.

Estimate. Round to the indicated place value. See Examples 1–4 (pp. 58–59)

9. \$455 + \$22; tens

10. 624 + 53; tens

11. 2,647 + 256; hundreds

12. \$772 − \$593; hundreds

13. \$63.84 + \$27.25; tens

14. \$35.46 + \$42.68; tens

15. 985 − 639; tens

16. \$34.89 − \$23.63; ones

17. \$68.60 − \$33.26; tens

18. \$20,425 + \$47,236; thousands

19. 27,629 − 5,364; thousands

20. \$48,986.26 − \$7,664.90; thousands

21. The largest NBA arena can seat 22,076 people. Suppose two games are sold out. About how many people will attend the two games?

22. Luz is going to buy a car that costs \$18,460 new and \$15,788 used. About how much money would Luz save if she bought the car used?

23. **Measurement** A mountain climber is climbing Mt. Everest. It is 29,035 feet tall. About how many feet will the climber have traveled after going up and down the mountain?

24. Jupiter and Saturn are the two largest planets in our solar system. Jupiter is 88,846 miles across and Saturn is 74,898 miles across. What is the approximate difference in the distance across these two planets?

Real-World PROBLEM SOLVING

Architecture This table shows the tallest buildings in the world.

25. About how much taller is the Sears Tower than the Jin Mao Building?

26. Estimate the difference between the height of the Taipai 101 Building and the Empire State Building.

27. About how much taller is Petronas Towers than the Empire State Building?

Tallest Buildings in the World

Building	Location	Height (ft)
Taipai 101	Taiwan	1,669
Petronas Towers	Malaysia	1,482
Sears Tower	United States	1,450
Jin Mao Building	China	1,381
CITIC Plaza	China	1,282
Shun Hing Square	China	1,259
Empire State Building	United States	1,250

Source: *The Ultimate Book of Lists*

Math Online Self-Check Quiz ca.gr4math.com

H.O.T. Problems

28. OPEN ENDED Write two numbers that when rounded to the thousands place have an estimated sum of 10,000.

29. NUMBER SENSE If both addends are rounded down, will the sum of the numbers be greater or less than the actual sum? Explain.

30. WRITING IN MATH When rounding to estimate the sum or difference of numbers, explain a situation where less exact answers would be better than more exact answers.

Standards Practice

31 What number completes the number sentence below? **(Lesson 2-1)**

$(24 + \blacksquare) + 18 = 24 + (36 + 18)$

A 18 **C** 36

B 24 **D** 38

32 The Casey family traveled last week. They drove 182 miles on Friday, 138 miles on Saturday, and 119 miles on Sunday. Approximately how many miles did they travel? **(Lesson 2-2)**

F 200 miles **H** 320 miles

G 300 miles **J** 400 miles

Spiral Review

Algebra Copy and complete each number sentence. Identify the property or rule. (Lesson 2-1)

33. $35 - \blacksquare = 35$

34. $(57 + \blacksquare) + 36 = 57 + (25 + 36)$

Round each number to the given place-value position. (Lesson 1-6)

35. 354; ten

36. 4,396; thousand

37. 257,468; hundred

Compare. Use >, <, or =. (Lesson 1-4)

38. 8,650 ● 8,623

39. 44,068 ● 44,086

40. 248,632 ● 284,632

41. Jameson's basketball team scored a total of 58 points. Jameson scored 18 points, and his sister scored 12 points. How many points did the rest of the team score? **(Lesson 1-3)**

42. Teresa's cell phone bill is $32.45 each month. About how much money does she spend on cell phone service every two months? **(Lesson 1-3)**

2-3 Problem-Solving Skill

MAIN IDEA I will determine when to estimate or find an exact answer.

Standard 4NS1.4 Decide when a rounded solution is called for and explain why such a solution may be appropriate.
Standard 4MR2.5 **Indicate the relative advantages of exact and approximate solutions to problems** and give answers to a specified degree of accuracy.

Keith and his brother are going to build a tree house. They will need $12 for nails, $95 for tools, and $46 for wood. About how much money do they need to build the tree house?

Understand

What facts do you know?

- Nails cost $12.
- Tools cost $95.
- Wood costs $46.

What do you need to find?

- Find about how much money they need to build the tree house.

Plan

Since the question asks about how much money is needed, you can estimate the sum.

Solve

Round each amount to each greatest place value. Then add.

$12	→	$ 10	
$95	→	$100	← Round each number to its greatest place value.
+ $46	→	+ $ 50	
		$160	

So, about $160 is needed to build the tree house.

Check

Look back at the problem. Suppose the question asked for an exact answer.

```
   1
  $12
  $95
+ $46
 $153
```

Since $153 is close to $160, an estimate of $160 is correct.

ANALYZE the Skill

Refer to the problem on the previous page.

1. Why does it make sense to round in this situation?

2. Suppose it costs $16 for nails, $109 for tools, and $62 for wood. What would a good estimate be? Explain.

3. Why did the boys round each dollar amount up?

4. Why is it a good idea to round up when dealing with money even if the number would be rounded down?

PRACTICE the Skill

See page R5.

Tell whether an estimate or exact answer is needed. Then solve.

5. Determine if Doris, Anessa, and Jaleesa have more than 110 CDs.

Name	CDs Owned
Doris	21
Anessa	42
Jaleesa	33

6. Samuel bought a smoothie for $3.65 and paid with a $5 bill. About how much change should he get back?

7. A theater can hold 200 people. Two groups rented out the theater. The first group has 92 people and the other has 107 people. Are there enough seats for everyone? Explain.

8. Carissa pays $2.10 each day for lunch. Her money is in an account that is deducted each time she buys a lunch. There are 6 days until the end of the school year and her account has $12.75 in it. How much money will she get back at the end of the year?

9. Jacob is taking a test at school. The question is shown below. What is the answer?

753,029 + 608,243

10. Tracy is allowed to watch 2 hours of television each night. About how much television does she watch in a year?

11. **Measurement** Rodney needs to measure the distance around his garden. How much fencing should Rodney buy?

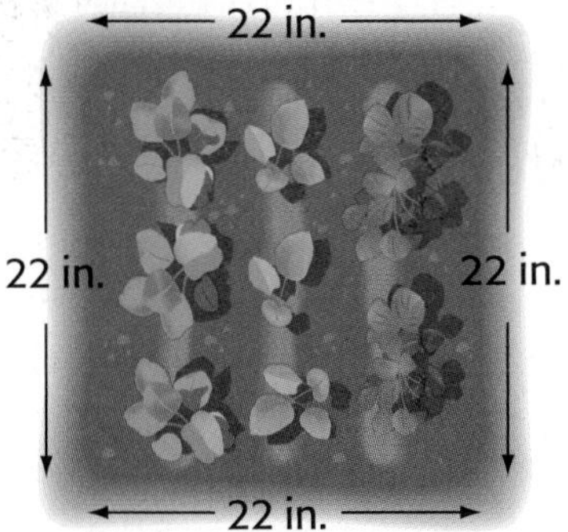

12. **WRITING IN MATH** A newspaper stated that the population of California was 33,871,600. Explain why this is probably an estimate.

2-4 Add Numbers

GET READY to Learn

Hands-On Mini Activity

The model shows 135 + 127.

1. Estimate 135 + 127.

2. To find 135 + 127, is it necessary to regroup the ones? How do you know?

3. Is it necessary to regroup the tens? How do you know?

Hundreds	Tens	Ones
1	3	5
+ 1	2	7

MAIN IDEA

I will add numbers, including multidigit numbers.

Standard 4NS3.1 **Demonstrate an understanding of, and the ability to use, standard algorithms for the addition** and subtraction **of multidigit numbers.**

When you add whole numbers, it may be necessary to regroup.

EXAMPLE **Add Whole Numbers**

1 **Add 6,824 + 349.**

Estimate 6,824 → 6,800; + 349 → + 300; 7,100

Vocabulary Link

prefixes The prefix *re-* means *again.* Example: *regroup* means *to group again.*

Step 1 Add ones.

$$\begin{array}{r} {\scriptstyle 1} \\ 6{,}824 \\ +\ 349 \\ \hline 3 \end{array}$$

4 + 9 = 13
Regroup 13 ones as 1 ten and 3 ones.

Step 2 Add tens.

$$\begin{array}{r} {\scriptstyle 1} \\ 6{,}824 \\ +\ 349 \\ \hline 73 \end{array}$$

1 + 2 + 4 = 7

Step 3 Add hundreds.

$$\begin{array}{r} {\scriptstyle 1\ 1} \\ 6{,}824 \\ +\ 349 \\ \hline 173 \end{array}$$

8 + 3 = 11
Regroup 11 hundreds as 1 thousand and 1 hundred.

Step 4 Add thousands.

$$\begin{array}{r} {\scriptstyle 1\ 1} \\ 6{,}824 \\ +\ 349 \\ \hline 7{,}173 \end{array}$$

6 + 1 = 7

Check for Reasonableness

The estimate is 7,100. Since 7,173 is close to the estimate, the answer is reasonable. ✓

Real-World EXAMPLE Add Multi-Digit Numbers

2 **TICKETS** **Weekend ticket sales for a school play are shown in the table. What was the total?**

Ticket Sales	
Day	**Amount**
Saturday	\$273.75
Sunday	\$97.75

Estimate

$$\begin{array}{rcr} \$273.75 & \rightarrow & \$270 \\ \underline{+\ \$97.75} & \rightarrow & \underline{+\ \$100} \\ & & \$370 \end{array}$$

Step 1 Add pennies.

$$\begin{array}{r} {\scriptstyle 1} \\ \$273.75 \\ \underline{+\ \$\ 97.75} \\ 0 \end{array}$$

5 + 5 = 10
Regroup 10 pennies as 1 dime and 0 pennies.

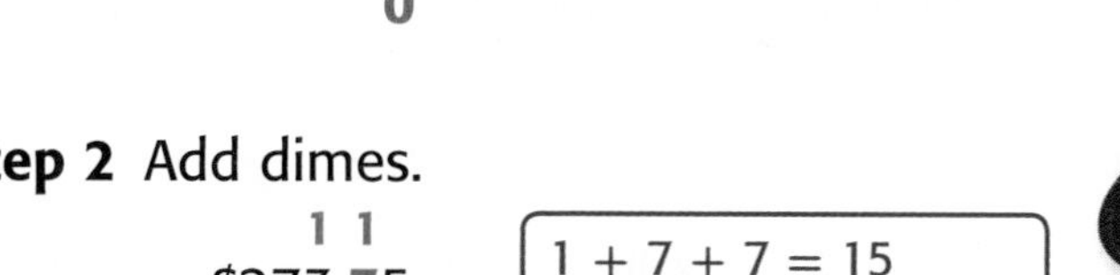

Step 2 Add dimes.

$$\begin{array}{r} {\scriptstyle 1\ 1} \\ \$273.75 \\ \underline{+\ \$\ 97.75} \\ 50 \end{array}$$

1 + 7 + 7 = 15
Regroup 15 dimes as 1 dollar and 5 dimes.

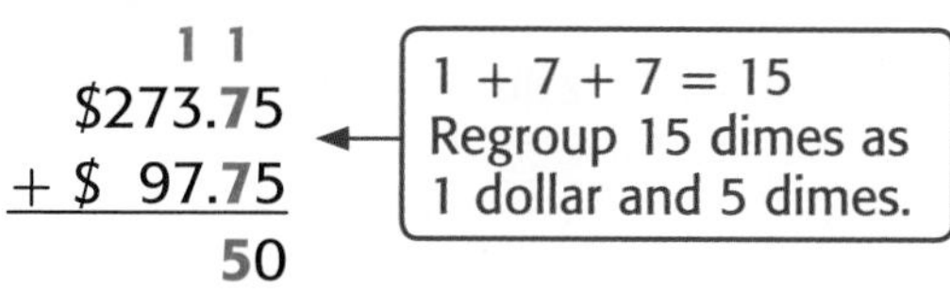

Step 3 Add ones.

$$\begin{array}{r} {\scriptstyle 1\ 1\ 1} \\ \$273.75 \\ \underline{+\ \$\ 97.75} \\ 1.50 \end{array}$$

1 + 3 + 7 = 11
Regroup 11 ones as 1 ten and 1 one.

Remember

When adding and subtracting decimals, the decimal point is brought straight down.

Step 4 Add tens.

$$\begin{array}{r} {\scriptstyle 1\ 1\ 1\ 1} \\ \$273.75 \\ \underline{+\ \$\ 97.75} \\ 71.50 \end{array}$$

1 + 7 + 9 = 17
Regroup 17 tens as 1 hundred and 7 tens.

Step 5 Add hundreds.

$$\begin{array}{r} {\scriptstyle 1\ 1\ 1\ 1} \\ \$273.75 \\ \underline{+\ \$\ 97.75} \\ \$371.50 \end{array}$$

1 + 2 = 3

So, the total ticket sales were \$371.50.

Check for Reasonableness

The estimate is \$370. Since \$371.50 is close to the estimate, the answer is reasonable. ✓

Online Personal Tutor at ca.gr4math.com

CHECK What You Know

Find each sum. Check your work by estimating. See Examples 1 and 2 (pp. 64–65)

1. 397 + 84
2. 1,592 + 429
3. \$29.71 + \$ 8.64
4. \$293.80 + \$ 82.53
5. Mr. Russo's class is collecting bottles to recycle. The class collected 178 bottles in March and 236 bottles in April. How many bottles were collected?
6. **Talk About It** Explain why it is important to line up digits in numbers when you add.

Practice and Problem Solving

EXTRA PRACTICE See page R5.

Find each sum. Check your work by estimating. See Examples 1 and 2 (pp. 64–65)

7. 364 + 58
8. 290 + 693
9. 6,742 + 975
10. 8,346 + 7,208
11. \$238.24 + \$ 73.46
12. 82,828 + 4,789
13. \$371.78 + \$823.70
14. \$6,937.82 + \$ 478.16

Real-World PROBLEM SOLVING

Data File The table shows the miles of roads for various counties in California.

15. How many miles of roads are in Siskiyou and San Francisco Counties?
16. How many miles of roads are in Los Angeles, Orange, and San Bernardino Counties?
17. Which has more miles of roads, Los Angeles or the total of the rest of the counties listed? Explain.

California Roads

County	Miles of Roads
Alpine	287
Los Angeles	21,253
Mendocino	1,860
Orange	6,457
San Bernardino	10,223
San Francisco	963
Siskiyou	3,424

Source: www.ca.gov

H.O.T. Problems

18. **OPEN ENDED** Write two 5-digit addends whose sum would give an estimate of 60,000.
19. **WRITING IN MATH** Explain why an addition problem that has 4-digit addends could have a 5-digit sum.

CHAPTER 2

Mid-Chapter Check

Lessons 2-1 through 2-4

Algebra Copy and complete each number sentence. Identify the property or rule. (Lesson 2-1)

1. 136 + 0 = ■

2. (4 + ■) + 7 = 4 + (2 + 7)

3. 58 + 98 = ■ + 58

Write a number sentence. Then identify the property or rule. (Lesson 2-1)

4. Andrea's pencil box has 9 pencils, 5 pencil-top erasers, and 3 red pens. Max's pencil box has 5 pencils, 3 pencil-top erasers, and 9 red pens. Whose pencil box contains more items? Explain.

5. **STANDARDS PRACTICE** What number completes the number sentence below? (Lesson 2-1)

(21 + ■) + 12 = 21 + (17 + 12)

A 11 **C** 17

B 12 **D** 21

Estimate. Round to the indicated place value. (Lesson 2-2)

6. $22.35 + $63.14; tens

7. 567 − 203; hundreds

8. 5,825 − 551; hundreds

9. **STANDARDS PRACTICE** About how many miles did a soccer team travel during the weekend? (Lesson 2-2)

Distance Traveled	
Day	**Distance (miles)**
Friday	146
Saturday	175
Sunday	206

F 400 miles **H** 600 miles

G 500 miles **J** 700 miles

Tell whether an estimate or exact answer is needed. Then solve. (Lesson 2-3)

10. Alejandra needs to make a fence in her yard for her puppy. She wants it to be square. One side measures 20 feet. How much fence should she buy?

Find each sum. Check for reasonableness. (Lesson 2-4)

11. $\begin{array}{r} 28{,}180 \\ +\ 7{,}233 \\ \hline \end{array}$

12. $\begin{array}{r} 63{,}456 \\ +\ 37{,}425 \\ \hline \end{array}$

13. Gina's brother is starting college in the fall. The cost of tuition for one year will be $5,491. All the other expenses for the year will cost $10,065. What will the total cost of one year of college be for Gina's brother? (Lesson 2-4)

14. **WRITING IN MATH** Explain how you could add 175 + 139 + 225 mentally. (Lesson 2-1)

Math Activity for 2-5
Subtract Numbers

When subtracting whole numbers, you may need to regroup.

MAIN IDEA
I will explore how to subtract whole numbers.

Standard 4NS3.1 Demonstrate an understanding of, and the ability to use, standard algorithms for the addition and subtraction of multidigit numbers.
Standard 4MR2.3 Use a variety of methods, such as words, numbers, symbols, charts, graphs, tables, diagrams, and models, to explain mathematical reasoning.

You Will Need
base-ten blocks

Animation
ca.gr4math.com

ACTIVITY **Use models to subtract 421 − 241.**

Step 1 **Model 421.**
Use base-ten blocks to model 421.

Hundreds	Tens	Ones

Step 2 **Subtract the ones.**
Subtract.

$$\begin{array}{r} 421 \\ -\ 241 \\ \hline 0 \end{array}$$

Step 3 **Subtract the tens.**
Since you cannot take 4 tens from 2 tens, you need to regroup. Regroup one hundreds flat as 10 tens. You now have 12 tens.

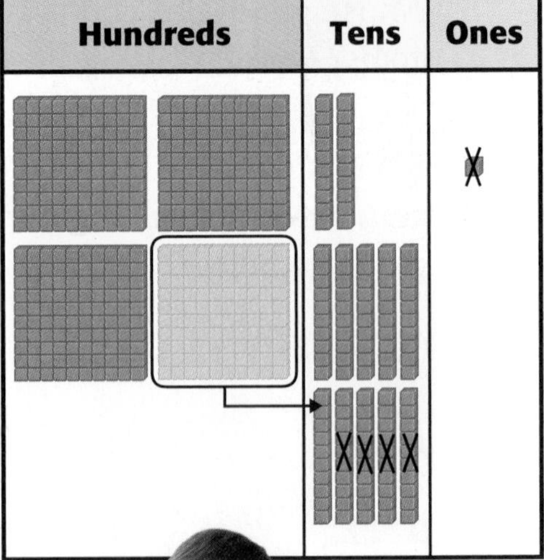

$$\begin{array}{r} {\scriptstyle 3\,12} \\ \not{4}\not{2}1 \\ -\ 241 \\ \hline 80 \end{array}$$

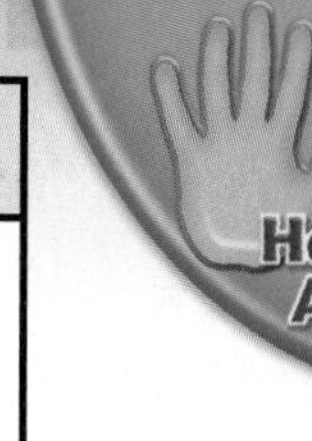

Step 4 **Subtract the hundreds.**

Take 2 hundreds flats away from the 3 hundreds flats.

```
 3 12
 4̶2̶1  ←— minuend
– 241  ←— subtrahend
  180  ←— difference
```

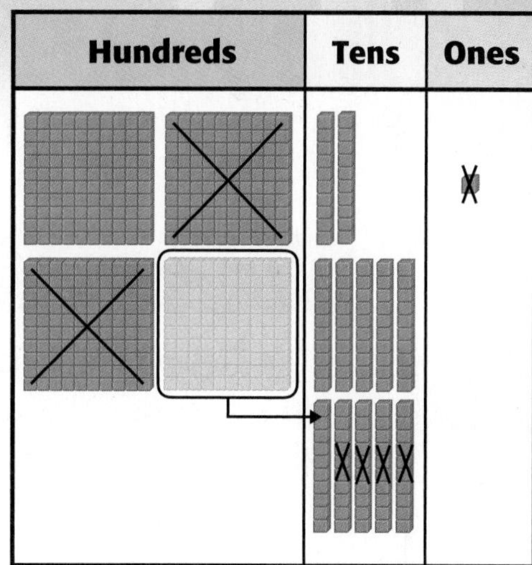

Check

You can use addition to check your subtraction.

$$\begin{array}{r} 421 \\ -\ 241 \\ \hline 180 \end{array} \qquad \begin{array}{r} 180 \\ +\ 241 \\ \hline 421 \end{array}$$

So, the answer is correct. ✓

Think About It

1. How did you subtract 241 from 421 using base-ten blocks?
2. Describe how you regrouped the tens place.

CHECK What You Know

Subtract. Check by adding.

3. 357 − 98

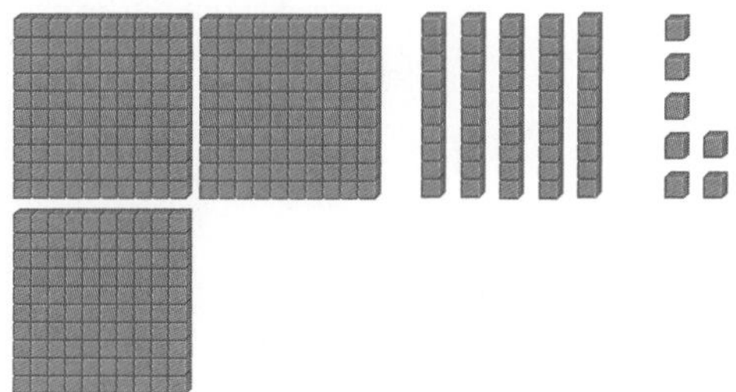

4. 679 − 345

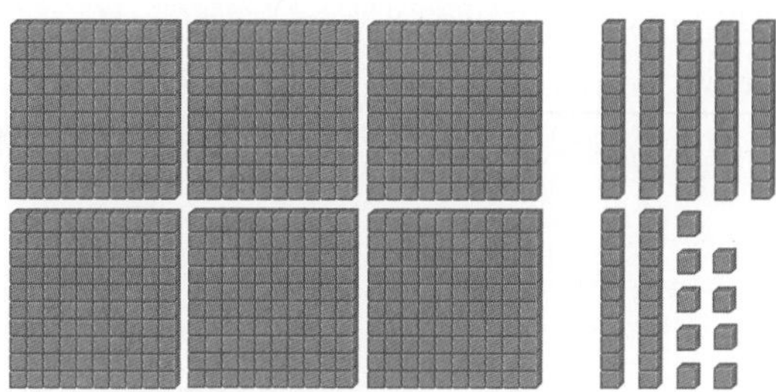

5. 287 − 195
6. 525 − 385
7. 632 − 248
8. 727 − 469
9. 861 − 593
10. 948 − 729
11. WRITING IN ▶MATH Why is it important to line up the digits in each place-value position when subtracting?

2-5 Subtract Numbers

GET READY to Learn

The Trevino family is moving to a new city. They have driven 957 miles out of the 3,214 miles that they need to travel. How many more miles do they need to drive?

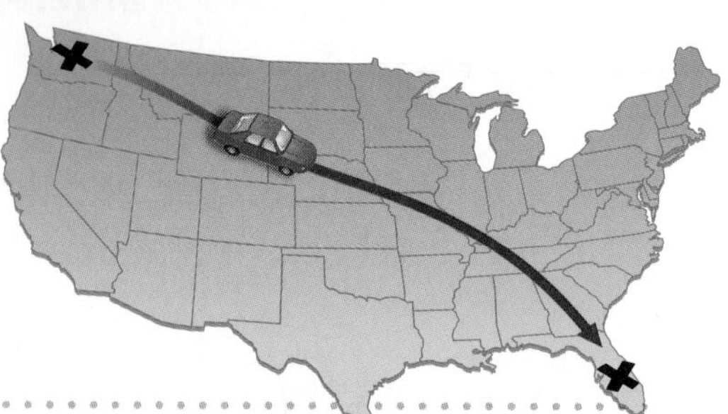

MAIN IDEA

I will subtract multidigit numbers.

Demonstrate an understanding of, and the ability to use, standard algorithms for the addition and **subtraction of multidigit numbers.**

Subtraction of whole numbers is similar to addition of whole numbers in that you may need to regroup.

Real-World EXAMPLE — Subtract Whole Numbers

1 MEASUREMENT Find 3,214 − 957 to find how many miles the Trevino family needs to travel.

Estimate 3,214 − 957 → 3,200 − 1,000 = 2,200

Step 1 Subtract ones.

Regroup a ten as 10 ones.

$$\begin{array}{r} {\scriptstyle 0\,14} \\ 3{,}2\not{1}\not{4} \\ -\ 957 \\ \hline 7 \end{array}$$

Step 2 Subtract tens.

Regroup a hundred as 10 tens.

$$\begin{array}{r} {\scriptstyle 10} \\ {\scriptstyle 1\,\not{0}\,14} \\ 3{,}\not{2}\not{1}\not{4} \\ -\ 957 \\ \hline 57 \end{array}$$

Step 3 Subtract hundreds.

Regroup a thousand as 10 hundreds.

$$\begin{array}{r} {\scriptstyle 11\,10} \\ {\scriptstyle 2\,\not{1}\,\not{0}\,14} \\ \not{3}{,}\not{2}\not{1}\not{4} \\ -\ 957 \\ \hline 257 \end{array}$$

Step 4 Subtract thousands.

$$\begin{array}{r} {\scriptstyle 11\,10} \\ {\scriptstyle 2\,\not{1}\,\not{0}\,14} \\ \not{3}{,}\not{2}\not{1}\not{4} \\ -\ 957 \\ \hline 2{,}257 \end{array}$$

Check You can use addition to check your subtraction.

$$\begin{array}{r} 3{,}214 \\ -\ 957 \\ \hline 2{,}257 \end{array} \qquad \begin{array}{r} 2{,}257 \\ +\ 957 \\ \hline 3{,}214 \end{array}$$

The answer is correct and close to the estimate. ✓

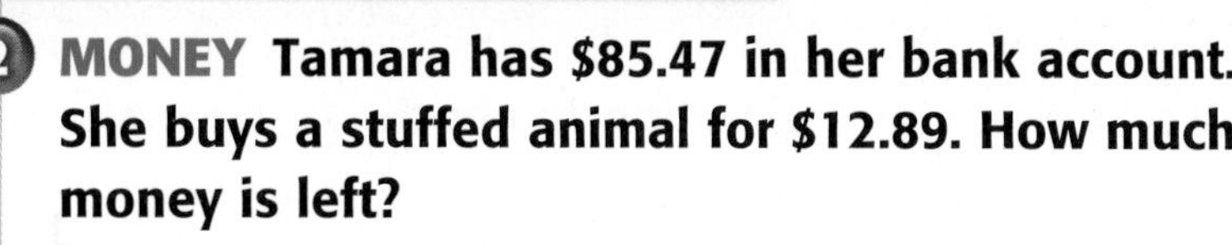

Real-World EXAMPLE Subtract Money

2 MONEY Tamara has $85.47 in her bank account. She buys a stuffed animal for $12.89. How much money is left?

Estimate

$85.47 → $85
− $12.89 → − $13
$72

Step 1 Subtract pennies.

3 17
$85.47
− $12.89
58

Regroup a dime as 10 pennies.

Step 2 Subtract dimes.

13
4 3 17
$85.47
− $12.89
58

Regroup a one dollar as 10 dimes.

Step 3 Subtract dollars.

13
4 3 17
$85.47
− $12.89
2.58

Step 4 Subtract ten dollars.

13
4 3 17
$85.47
− $12.89
$72.58

Check

$85.47 → $72.58
− $12.89 → + $12.89
$72.58 → $85.47

The answer is correct and close to the estimate. ✓

Online Personal Tutor at ca.gr4math.com

CHECK What You Know

Subtract. Use addition or estimation to check. See Examples 1 and 2 (pp. 70–71)

1. 526 − 403

2. $9.37 − $7.29

3. 2,962 − 845

4. $47.64 − $22.09

5. Kerri had $95.13 in her bank account. She bought her mom a bottle of perfume for her birthday for $25.76. How much money does she have left?

6. Talk About It Explain how to check the answer to a subtraction problem by using addition.

Practice and Problem Solving

EXTRA PRACTICE
See page R5.

Subtract. Use addition or estimation to check. See Examples 1 and 2 (pp. 70–71)

7. 479 − 292

8. \$924 − \$837

9. \$5.24 − \$2.46

10. \$9.86 − \$3.39

11. 4,273 − 365

12. 8,845 − 627

13. \$5,751 − \$4,824

14. \$647.79 − \$427.88

15. \$832.67 − \$570.49

16. 39,536 − 18,698

17. Ramon is buying a DVD that costs \$14.89, a book that costs \$15.58, and pays \$2.06 in tax. If he hands the cashier \$40, how much change will he get back?

18. Mount Everest is 29,035 feet tall. From base camp at 17,600 feet, a climber hiked 2,300 feet. How much farther does the climber have before reaching the top of the mountain?

Real-World PROBLEM SOLVING

History This table shows information about former Presidents of the United States.

United States Presidents

President	Born	Year became President	Death
John Adams	1732	1797	1801
James K. Polk	1795	1845	1849
Harry S. Truman	1884	1945	1972
John F. Kennedy	1917	1961	1963
Ronald Reagan	1911	1981	2004

19. Who was older when he became President, John Adams or Harry S. Truman?

20. Who was the youngest person on this list to become President? How old was he?

21. How old was Ronald Reagan when John F. Kennedy died?

H.O.T. Problems

22. WHICH ONE DOESN'T BELONG? Which subtraction problem does not require regrouping?

67,457 − 40,724

70,639 − 39,607

89,584 − 57,372

95,947 − 26,377

23. **WRITING IN MATH** Write a real-world problem that involves subtraction and regrouping to solve. The numbers used in the problem must have at least three digits.

Make a Big Difference

Subtract Multi-Digit Numbers

Get Ready!

Players: 2 players

You will need: paper and pencil, 0–9 spinner

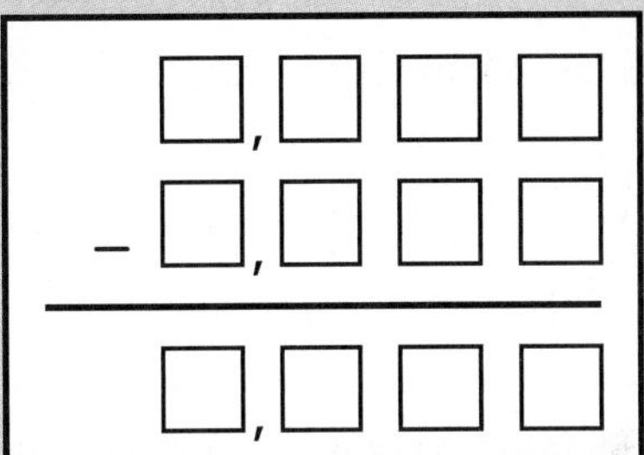

Get Set!

Make a game sheet like the one shown. Divide a spinner into ten equal sections. Label 0–9.

Go!

- Player 1 spins the spinner. Both players write that digit in a box of their choice on their game sheets.
- Continue until all eight boxes are filled. Then find the difference.
- Compare the differences. The player with the greatest difference scores 1 point.
- If the differences are equal, both players score 1 point.
- Continue playing until one player scores 5 points.

2-6 Problem-Solving Investigation

MAIN IDEA I will choose the best strategy to solve a problem.

Standard 4MR1.1 **Analyze problems by identifying relationships, distinguishing relevant from irrelevant information, sequencing and prioritizing information,** and observing patterns. Standard 4NS3.0 **Students solve problems involving addition,** subtraction, multiplication, and division **of whole numbers** and understand the relationships among the operations.

MARCO: I am downloading music. So far, I have downloaded 4 albums. Each album has 14 songs.

YOUR MISSION: Find how many songs Marco has downloaded.

Understand Marco has downloaded 4 albums, and each album has 14 songs. Find how many songs Marco has downloaded.

Plan You can organize the information in a table and use repeated addition to find how many songs Marco has downloaded.

Solve Start with 14, the number of songs on the first album. Then continue to add 14 for each additional album.

$$\begin{array}{r} 14 \\ +\ 14 \\ \hline 28 \end{array}$$ ← first album, second album

$$\begin{array}{r} \scriptstyle 1 \\ 28 \\ +\ 14 \\ \hline 42 \end{array}$$ ← third album

$$\begin{array}{r} 42 \\ +\ 14 \\ \hline 56 \end{array}$$ ← fourth album

Albums	Songs
1	14
2	28
3	42
4	56

So, he downloaded a total of 56 songs.

Check Look back at the problem. $56 - 14 = 42$, $42 - 14 = 28$, $28 - 14 = 14$, and $14 - 14 = 0$. The answer is correct.

Mixed Problem Solving

Use any strategy to solve each problem.

1. Mrs. Thomas had $85. She bought a toaster. She now has $43. How much was the toaster?

2. **Measurement** The Nile River is 4,145 miles long. The Mississippi River is 405 miles shorter than the Nile River. How long is the Mississippi River?

3. Rosana has $9 left over after buying a movie ticket. If she buys a soft pretzel, what other item can she buy?

Movie Palace	
Item	**Cost**
Small soda	$3.75
Large soda	$5.50
Soft pretzel	$4.75
Medium popcorn	$5.75

4. Alonso has 139 comic books. Maggie has 72 comic books. Do they have a total of about 200 comic books? Explain.

5. A piñata is $36, and party decorations are $18. A gift is $28. About how much is spent altogether?

6. Prem is thinking of three numbers from 1 to 10. The sum of the numbers is 14. Find the numbers.

7. Marcel earns $5 a week for doing his chores. About how many weeks will he have to save his money in order to buy the sports equipment below?

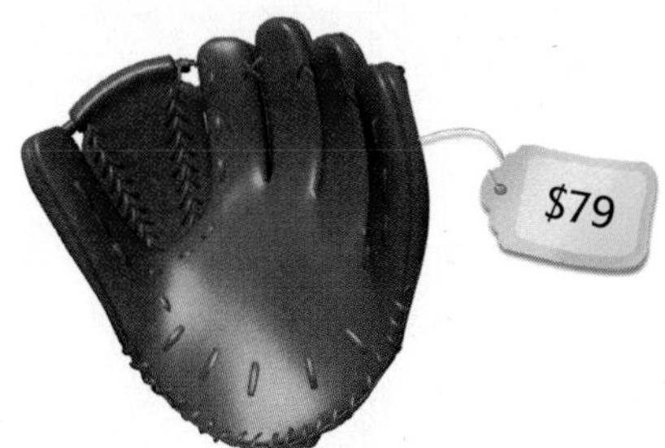

8. Greta earns $5 each week walking dogs. Her cell phone bill each month is $15. How much does she have left after paying her cell phone bill for a month that has four weeks?

9. There are 58 third graders and 62 fourth graders going on a field trip. Each bus can carry 40 people. How many buses are needed?

10. **Measurement** About how much farther does the willow warbler migrate than the barn swallow?

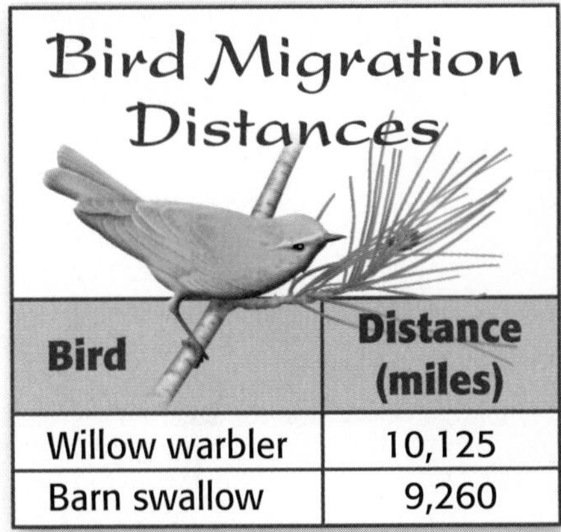

Bird Migration Distances

Bird	Distance (miles)
Willow warbler	10,125
Barn swallow	9,260

11. **WRITING IN ▶MATH** Juan bowls 132 in his first game. He bowls 148 in his second game. The answer is 280. What is the question?

Problem Solving in History

GROWING Cities

Before the California Gold Rush in 1849, San Francisco and Los Angeles were settlements of less than 1,000 people. During the Gold Rush, San Francisco's population greatly increased.

This caused prices to rise. Food became very expensive. A visitor to San Francisco paid $2 for a slice of buttered bread, $3 for an egg, and sometimes $5 for a glass of water! Los Angeles grew more slowly than San Francisco. Its population did not start to increase greatly until much later. Today, the population of Los Angeles is 10 million. San Francisco's population is 752,000.

Populations of San Francisco and Los Angeles 1850–1900

Year	San Francisco	Los Angeles
1850	21,000	3,530
1860	56,802	11,333
1870	149,473	15,309
1880	233,956	33,392
1890	298,997	50,395
1900	342,782	102,479

Standard NS3.1 Demonstrate an understanding of and the ability to use standard algorithms for the addition and subtraction of multidigit numbers.

Real-World Math

Use the information on page 76 to answer each question.

1. Your friend says that there were at least 200,000 people living in Los Angeles and San Francisco in 1870. Is your friend correct? Explain.

2. In what years was the combined population of San Francisco and Los Angeles more than 300,000?

3. What was the estimated total population of San Francisco and Los Angeles in 1900? Round to the nearest thousand.

4. Suppose you lived in San Francisco in 1860. You had $16. Did you have enough money to buy both an egg and a slice of buttered bread for 3 people? Explain.

5. How many years did it take for the population of San Francisco to reach 298,997 from the first year of the Gold Rush?

6. How much greater was the population of San Francisco than Los Angeles in 1870?

7. During what ten-year time period did San Francisco's population increase the most?

Did You Know?

Some foods were cheap during the Gold Rush. A pound of bacon sometimes cost 1 penny!

2-7 Subtract Across Zeros

MAIN IDEA

I will subtract multidigit numbers, when some digits are zero.

Standard 4NS3.1

Demonstrate an understanding of, and the ability to use, standard algorithms for the addition and **subtraction of multidigit numbers.**

GET READY to Learn

The bar graph shows the number of movies produced by five countries. What is the difference in the greatest and least number of movies produced?

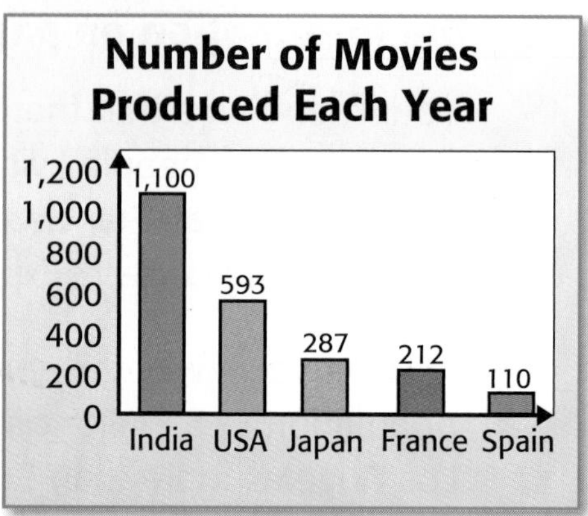

Source: *The Top 10 of Everything 2006*

Subtraction that involves digits that are zeros has the same steps as subtraction that involves digits that are not zeros.

Real-World EXAMPLE Subtract Across Zeros

1 MOVIES Refer to the graph. How many more movies does India produce than Spain?

Step 1 Subtract ones.

$$\begin{array}{r} 1{,}100 \\ -110 \\ \hline 0 \end{array}$$

0 − 0 = 0

Step 2 Subtract tens.

$$\begin{array}{r} 0\,10 \\ 1{,}\cancel{1}\cancel{0}0 \\ -110 \\ \hline 90 \end{array}$$

Regroup 1 hundred as 10 tens.
10 − 1 = 9

Step 3 Subtract hundreds.

$$\begin{array}{r} 10 \\ 0\,\cancel{0}\,10 \\ \cancel{1},\cancel{1}\cancel{0}0 \\ -110 \\ \hline 990 \end{array}$$

Regroup 1 thousand as 10 hundreds.
10 − 1 = 9

Step 4 Subtract thousands.

$$\begin{array}{r} 10 \\ 0\,\cancel{0}\,10 \\ \cancel{1},\cancel{1}\cancel{0}0 \\ -110 \\ \hline 990 \end{array}$$

0 − 0 = 0

So, India produces 990 more movies a year than Spain.

Check 990 + 110 = 1,100. So, the answer is correct. ✓

Real-World EXAMPLE Subtract Across Zeros

2 **MONEY** **Lucy's dad spent $100.89. He bought a radio and a video game. The cost of the radio was $48.52. What was the cost of the video game?**

Remember

When you subtract, start at the place farthest to the right.

Step 1 Subtract pennies.

```
  $100.89
- $ 48.52
        7
```

9 − 7 = 2

Step 2 Subtract dimes.

```
  $100.89
- $ 48.52
       37
```

8 − 5 = 3

Step 3 Subtract ones.

```
      9
   0 1010
  $100.89
- $ 48.52
     2.37
```

Regroup 1 hundred as 10 tens. Regroup one of the tens as 10 ones. 10 − 8 = 2

Step 4 Subtract tens.

```
      9
   0 1010
  $100.89
- $ 48.52
    52.37
```

9 − 4 = 5

Step 5 Subtract hundreds.

```
      9
   0 1010
  $100.89
- $ 48.52
   $52.37
```

0 − 0 = 0

So, the cost of the video game was $52.37.

Online Personal Tutor at ca.gr4math.com

CHECK What You Know

Subtract. Use addition to check. See Examples 1 and 2 (pp. 78–79)

1. 309 − 57

2. 608 − 45

3. $7.07 − $5.35

4. 903 − 791

5. 2,006 − 536

6. $80.05 − $44.23

7. On Saturday, there were 1,000 balloons at a hot air balloon festival. On Sunday, there were 150 balloons. How many more balloons were there on Saturday than on Sunday?

8. Talk About It Look at the problem below. Explain where you would start regrouping to find the difference.

```
  66,000
- 23,475
```

Practice and Problem Solving

EXTRA PRACTICE
See page R6.

Subtract. Use addition to check. See Examples 1 and 2 (pp. 78–79)

9. 408 − 36

10. 805 − 75

11. 604 − 492

12. \$5.02 − \$1.30

13. \$7.08 − \$2.22

14. 809 − 566

15. \$80.01 − \$69.30

16. 9,006 − 7,474

17. 8,007 − 4,836

18. \$93.00 − \$52.25

19. 30,070 − 14,021

20. Ava guessed that there were 1,007 marbles in a jar for a contest. There were actually 972 marbles in the jar. How far off was Ava's guess?

21. Measurement Oscar hiked one and a half miles or 7,920 feet. If Sato hiked two miles or 10,560 feet, how many more feet did Sato hike?

Real-World PROBLEM SOLVING

Travel The length of paved and unpaved roads in four countries is shown.

Countries' Roads	
Country	**Length (miles)**
France	555,506
Australia	504,307
Spain	412,463
Russia	330,814

22. How many more miles of road does Australia have than Spain?

23. Which two countries have the biggest difference in miles of roads? France and Australia, Australia and Spain, or Spain and Russia?

H.O.T. Problems

24. OPEN ENDED Identify a number that results in a 3-digit answer when 35,475 is subtracted from it.

25. FIND THE ERROR Jim and Sabrina are solving the subtraction problem shown. Who is correct? Explain.

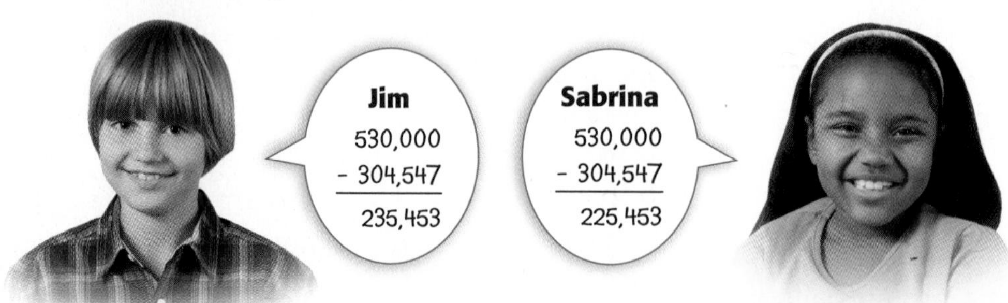

26. WRITING IN MATH Explain how you would regroup to subtract 3,406 from 5,000.

Standards Practice

27 There were 4668 people at the fair on Saturday and 3816 people on Sunday. How many more people were at the fair on Saturday?
(Lesson 2-5)

A 842 **C** 942

B 852 **D** 952

28 34,007 − 21,829
(Lesson 2-7)

F 12,178

G 12,912

H 13,108

J 13,112

Spiral Review

Solve. (Lesson 2-6)

29. Measurement On Friday, Nida drove 178 miles. On Saturday, she drove 129 miles. On Sunday, she drove 205 miles. How many miles did she drive in the three days?

30. Henri is going to buy a football that costs $10.65, a shirt that costs $8.96, and a hat that costs $6.45. If he has $30, about how much change can he expect to get back?

Subtract. Use addition or estimation to check. (Lesson 2-5)

31. 952 − 624

32. $89.61 − $12.58

33. 19,034 − 1,617

Find each sum. Check your work by estimating. (Lesson 2-4)

34. 6,922 + 24,367

35. $87.38 + $22.53

36. 36,640 + 14,255

For Exercises 37–39, use the table shown. (Lesson 1-3)

Area of Great Lakes	
Lake	**Area (square miles)**
Erie	9,922
Huron	23,011
Michigan	22,316
Ontario	7,320
Superior	31,698

37. What is the difference between the lakes with the greatest and least area?

38. Which two lakes have the least difference in area?

39. Is the combined area of Lake Erie and Lake Michigan greater than the area of Lake Superior?

Study Guide and Review

FOLDABLES Study Organizer GET READY to Study

Be sure the following Key Vocabulary words and Key Concepts are written in your Foldable.

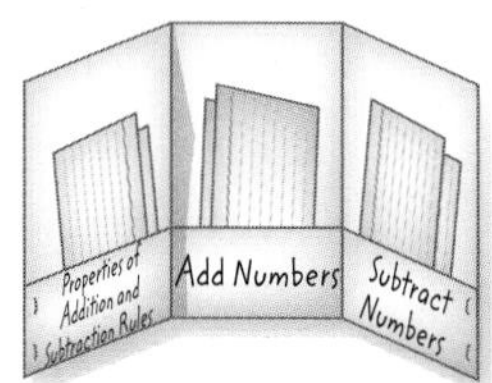

BIG Ideas

Addition Properties and Rules (p. 55)

- Addition Properties and subtraction rules can help you to add and subtract.

Estimate Sums and Differences (p. 58)

3,678	rounds to	4,000
+ 1,295	rounds to	+ 1,000
		5,000

7,418	rounds to	7,000
− 2,557	rounds to	− 3,000
		4,000

Add and Subtract Numbers (p. 64, p. 70)

- To add or subtract numbers, add or subtract each place, starting with the place farthest to the right. Regroup when needed.

```
   1 1          8 13
  3,752         9,368
+   481       −   827
  4,233         8,541
```

Key Vocabulary

Associative Property of Addition (p. 55)

Commutative Property of Addition (p. 55)

estimate (p. 58)

Vocabulary Check

Complete each sentence with the correct vocabulary word.

1. The number sentence $3 + 7 = 7 + 3$ represents the ___?___ .
2. If you do not need an exact answer, you can ___?___ .
3. Using the ___?___ , you can change the grouping without changing the sum.
4. Using the ___?___ , the order in which numbers are added does not change the sum.
5. When the word "about" is used in a problem, you should find a(n) ___?___ .

Lesson-by-Lesson Review

2-1 Algebra: Addition Properties and Subtraction Rules (pp. 55–57)

Example 1
Complete 4 + ■ = 6 + 4. Identify the property or rule.

The right side of the sentence shows 6 + 4. The left side shows a 4. So, the missing number is 6.

$$4 + 6 = 6 + 4$$

This is the Commutative Property of Addition.

Copy and complete each number sentence. Identify the property or rule.

6. ■ + 0 = 11 **7.** 12 − ■ = 12

8. (■ + 9) + 2 = 9 + (9 + 2)

9. 5 + 4 + 3 = 4 + 3 + ■

10. Lamont has 3 pencils and 2 pens. Aida has 2 pencils and 3 pens. Who has more writing utensils? Identify the property used.

2-2 Estimate Sums and Differences (pp. 58–61)

Example 2
Estimate 1,352 + 487. Round to the hundreds place.

Round. Then add.

1,352	rounds to →	1,400
+ 487	rounds to →	+ 500
		1,900

So, 1,352 + 487 is about 1,900.

Example 3
Estimate $53.52 – $27.87. Round to the tens place.

Round. Then subtract.

$53.52	rounds to →	$50.00
− $27.87	rounds to →	− $30.00
		$20.00

So, $53.52 − $27.87 is about $20.00

Estimate. Round to the indicated place value.

11. $5.19 + $3.68; ones

12. 3,436 + 597; hundreds

13. 8,728 − 6,493; thousands

14. $17.89 − $12.63; ones

15. Neka wants to buy a book that costs $12.99 and a bookmark that costs $3.75. Approximately how much will these items cost?

16. Derek is 3,285 days old. Tionna is 4,015 days old. About how much older is Tionna?

2-3 Problem-Solving Skill: Estimate or Exact Answer (pp. 62–63)

Example 4
Jenelle and her sister are going to build a bookcase. They will need $9 for nails, $18 for tools, and $38 for wood. About how much money do they need to build the bookcase?

Understand

What facts do you know?
- Nails cost $9.
- Tools cost $18.
- Wood costs $38.

What do you need to find?
- Find about how much money they need to build the bookcase.

Plan Since the question asks about how much money is needed, you can estimate the sum.

Solve

$ 9	→	$10
$18	→	$20
+ $38	→	+ $40
		$70

So, about $70 is needed to build the bookcase.

Check Look back at the problem. If the question asked for an exact answer, the result would be $9 + $18 + $38 or $65. Since $70 is close to $65, you know that an estimate of $70 makes sense.

17. There are 365 days in a year. Tess's younger brother is 3 years old. About how many days old is he?

18. Benton needs to buy the items shown. He has $20. Does Benton have enough money?

19. Admission to a water park is $21 for adults and $14 for children. How much will admission cost for two adults and three children?

20. Rebeca will go to the park when her chores are complete. How many minutes before she will go to the park?

21. Chet has $7.50 in change after buying skates for $62.50 and a helmet for $22. How much money did he have?

2-4 Add Numbers (pp. 64–66)

Example 5
Add 714 + 249.

Step 1 Add ones.

```
   1
  714
+ 249
    3
```

$4 + 9 = 13$
Regroup 13 ones as 1 ten and 3 ones.

Step 2 Add tens.

```
   1
  714
+ 249
   63
```

$1 + 1 + 4 = 6$

Step 3 Add hundreds.

```
  1
  714
+ 249
  963
```

$7 + 2 = 9$

Find each sum. Check your work by estimating.

22. 564 + 308

23. 2,875 + 496

24. \$46.91 + \$ 8.72

25. \$64.67 + \$52.37

26. 61,248 + 47,229

27. 82,267 + 21,037

28. **Measurement** Rick drove 12,363 miles in his new car the first year he owned it. He drove 15,934 miles in his car the second year he owned it. How many miles did Rick drive these two years?

2-5 Subtract Numbers (pp. 70–72)

Example 6
Subtract 4,274 – 857.

Step 1 Subtract ones.

```
       6 14
  4, 2 7 4
  –  8 5 7
         7
```

Regroup 1 ten as 10 ones.

Step 2 Subtract each place.

```
  3 12 6 14
  4, 2 7 4
  –  8 5 7
  3, 4 1 7
```

Regroup if necessary.

Subtract. Use addition or estimation to check.

29. 478 – 293

30. 872 – 694

31. 5,524 – 2,346

32. \$547.51 – \$432.26

33. 7,367 – 2,128

34. 73,979 – 63,485

35. **Measurement** A moose weighs 1,820 pounds. A camel weighs 1,521 pounds. How much more does a moose weigh than a camel?

Study Guide and Review

2-6 Problem-Solving Investigation: Choose a Strategy (pp. 74–75)

Example 7
Naomi had $125. She bought rollerblades. She now has $19. How much were the rollerblades?

Understand Naomi had $125. She now has $19. You need to find the cost of the rollerblades.

Plan Solve $125 – $19 to find the cost of the rollerblades.

Solve

```
   115
  $125
– $ 19
  $106
```

So, the cost was $106.

Check $19 + $106 = $125.
So, the answer is correct.

Use any strategy to solve.

36. Jase earned $125 last month for delivering newspapers. He will earn $185 this month. How much money will Jase earn from delivering newspapers for the two months?

37. Measurement A cheetah can run up to 71 miles per hour. A horse can run up to 45 miles per hour. Suppose both animals ran at these speeds for two hours. How much further would a cheetah have run?

38. Measurement The highest elevation in the United States is 20,320 feet. The second highest elevation is 14,494. What is the difference in these heights?

2-7 Subtract Across Zeros (pp. 78–81)

Example 8
Find 2,005 – 593.

Step 1 Subtract ones.

```
  2,005   ←  5 – 3 = 2
–   593
      2
```

Step 2 Subtract each place.

```
    9
  1 10 10
  2, 0 0 5   ←  Regroup.
–   5 9 3
  1, 4 1 2
```

Subtract. Use addition to check.

39. 300 – 206

40. $8.00 – $3.92

41. 4,008 – 642

42. $90.04 – $ 5.31

43. 8,000 – 3,836

44. $1,300.75 – $1,195.32

45. Mr. Acosta had $2,003.25 in his bank account. He bought a laptop computer for $1,299.75. How much money does he have left?

CHAPTER 2

Chapter Test

For Exercises 1–3, tell whether each statement is *true* or *false*.

1. Always start with the ones place when subtracting.

2. When asked to find the sum, you are to subtract.

3. To regroup means to add again.

Copy and complete each number sentence. Identify the property or rule.

4. ■ + 73 + 79 = 73 + 79 + 65

5. ■ − 389 = 0

6. 2 + (3 + 9) = (2 + ■) + 9

7. **STANDARDS PRACTICE** What number completes the number sentence below?

   23 + ■ = 23 + 17

   A 17 **C** 36

   B 23 **D** 38

Estimate. Round to the indicated place value.

8. 5,364 + 482; hundreds

9. 89,325 − 80,236; ten thousands

Tell whether an estimate or exact answer is needed. Then solve.

10. Mr. Murphy had $192. He bought a watch. He now has $76. How much was the watch?

11. **STANDARDS PRACTICE** What is the sum of 212,048 and 37,251?

    F 249,299

    G 289,299

    H 289,399

    J 299,289

Subtract. Use addition or estimation to check

12. $\begin{array}{r} 612 \\ -\ 430 \\ \hline \end{array}$

13. $\begin{array}{r} 8{,}547 \\ -\ 6{,}391 \\ \hline \end{array}$

14. $\begin{array}{r} 4{,}005 \\ -\ 273 \\ \hline \end{array}$

15. $\begin{array}{r} 6{,}007 \\ -\ 317 \\ \hline \end{array}$

16. Ivana had $87.10 in her bank account. She bought her sister a doll for her birthday for $15.27. How much money did she have left in her account?

17. **Measurement** The lengths of the longest rivers in the world are shown in the table.

World's Longest Rivers	
River	**Length (miles)**
Nile	4,145
Amazon	4,000
Mississippi-Missouri	3,740

    Find the difference in length of the Nile and the Mississippi-Missouri Rivers.

18. **WRITING IN MATH** Explain how you would regroup to subtract 2,317 from 4,000.

CHAPTER 2

California Standards Practice

Cumulative, Chapters 1–2

Standards Example

Roger has $50. He buys a kite for $22.50 and string for $3.95. Round to the nearest dollar to find about how much money Roger has left.

A $20 **C** $23

B $22 **D** $30

Read the Question

You need to estimate the cost of each item and then subtract.

Solve the Question

Round each amount to the nearest dollar. Then add.

$22.50	rounds to →	$23
+ $ 3.95	rounds to →	+ $ 4
		$27

So, the total cost of the items is about $27. Since $50 – $27 = $23, Roger has $23 left.

So, the answer is C.

 **Personal Tutor at** ca.gr4math.com

Choose the best answer.

1 **Melinda buys a journal that costs $7.95. She hands the clerk $10. How much change will she receive?**

A $1.95 **C** $2.95

B $2.05 **D** $3.05

2 **The local zoo had 1295 visitors on Tuesday and 1523 visitors on Wednesday. How many visitors did the zoo have on the two days?**

F 228 **H** 2818

G 2808 **J** 2908

More California Standards Practice
For practice by standard, see pages CA1–CA43.

3 What number makes this number sentence true?

$(6 + 7) + 9 = 6 + (7 + \blacksquare)$

A 6
C 9
B 7
D 21

4 What is $79.59 rounded to the nearest dollar?

F $70
H $80
G $79
J $100

5 Kayla used a clothing catalog to make a list of what she needs for summer.

Kayla's Wish List

Item	Cost
Shorts	$19.95
T-shirt	$14.99
Hooded sweatshirt	$34.99
Sneakers	$42.95

If Kayla orders all the clothing items, about how much will she spend?

A $70
C $130
B $100
D $150

6 Silvio says his street address has a 3 in the hundreds place. Which of the following could be his address?

F 1368
H 2437
G 1483
J 3865

7 A local bike shop sold 134,304 bike helmets in one year. What is the number rounded to the nearest ten thousand?

A 100,000
C 134,300
B 130,000
D 150,000

8 What is the standard form for twelve million, two hundred thirty-five thousand, one hundred twelve?

F 12,203,512
H 12,335,012
G 12,235,112
J 12,535,112

9 Which number is 10,000 more than 456,987?

A 356,987
C 460,000
B 457,987
D 466,987

10 Which is the value of the digit 5 in 1,853,742?

F 50
H 50,000
G 500
J 500,000

CHAPTER 3 Algebra: Use Addition and Subtraction

BIG Idea What are expressions and equations?

An **expression** is a combination of variables, numbers, and at least one operation. An **equation** is a sentence that contains an equals sign (=), showing that two expressions are equal.

Example A tiger can live *x* years in the wild and 5 years longer in a zoo. The equation below can be used to find how long a tiger can live in the wild if it lives 20 years in a zoo.

$$\underbrace{x}_{\text{years in wild}} + 5 = \underbrace{20}_{\text{years in zoo}}$$

What will I learn in this chapter?

- Write and find the value of expressions.
- Write and solve equations.
- Find and use a rule to write an equation.
- Balance addition and subtraction equations.
- Identify extra and missing information.

Key Vocabulary

expression
variable
parentheses
equation
balance

Student Study Tools at ca.gr4math.com

FOLDABLES™ Study Organizer

Make this Foldable to help you organize information about using addition and subtraction in algebra. Begin with a piece of 11″ × 17″ paper.

1. **Fold** lengthwise 3″ from the bottom.
2. **Fold** the paper in half.
3. **Open** and staple on either side to form pockets.
4. **Label** as shown. Take notes on index cards.

ARE YOU READY for Chapter 3?

You have two ways to check prerequisite skills for this chapter.

Option 2

Math Online Take the Chapter Readiness Quiz at ca.gr4math.com.

Option 1

Complete the Quick Check below.

QUICK Check

Find the missing number. (Prior grade)

1. 8 + ■ = 11 **2.** ■ + 5 = 9 **3.** 6 + ■ = 15

4. 13 − ■ = 7 **5.** ■ − 4 = 8 **6.** 18 − ■ = 16

7. Use the number sentence 12 + 15 + ■ = 36 to find how many books Tony read in August.

Summer Reading Club	
Month	**Number of Books Read**
June	12
July	15
August	■

8. What property is illustrated by 6 + 5 = 5 + 6?

Find the value of each expression. (Prior grade)

9. 8 + 1 + 6 **10.** 7 + 2 − 3 **11.** 2 + 10 − 6

12. 11 + 6 − 6 **13.** 12 − 3 + 4 **14.** 16 + 4 − 10

Identify a pattern. Then find the next number in the pattern. (Prior grade)

15. 3, 6, 9, 12, 15 **16.** 7, 12, 17, 22, 27 **17.** 23, 19, 15, 11, 7

18. Each baseball uniform needs 3 buttons. Copy and complete the table to find how many buttons are needed for 12 uniforms.

Uniforms	3	6	9	12
Buttons	9	18	27	■

Addition and Subtraction Expressions

GET READY to Learn

Lia has 3 baseball cards. Her friend gave her some more. You can show the number of cards Lia now has by using the expression below.

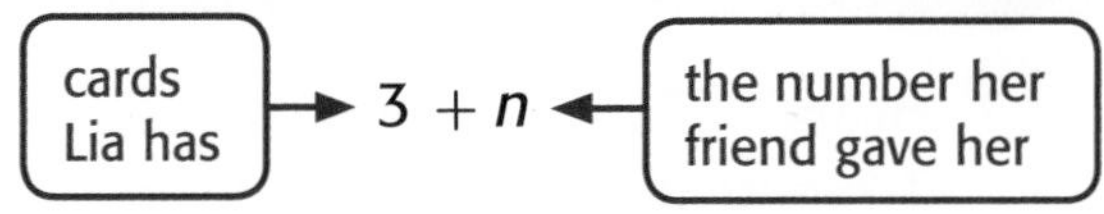

MAIN IDEA

I will write and find the value of expressions.

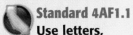

Standard 4AF1.1 Use letters, boxes, or other symbols **to stand for any number in simple expressions** or equations **(e.g., demonstrate an understanding and the use of the concept of a variable).**

New Vocabulary

expression
variable
parentheses

An **expression** like $3 + n$ is a combination of variables, numbers, and at least one operation. A **variable** is a letter or symbol that represents an unknown value. You can find the value of an expression if you know the value of the variable.

Real-World EXAMPLE — Find Value of an Expression

1 **ALGEBRA If Lia's friend gives her 5 baseball cards, how many cards will she have?**

You need to find the value of $3 + n$ when $n = 5$.

$3 + \mathbf{n}$ Write the expression.

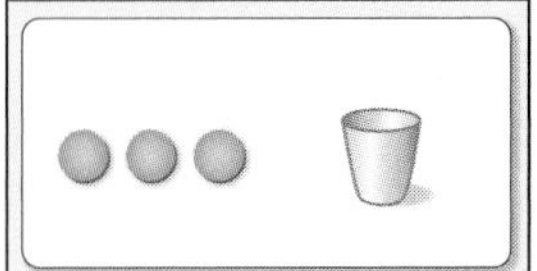

$3 + \mathbf{5}$ Replace n with 5.

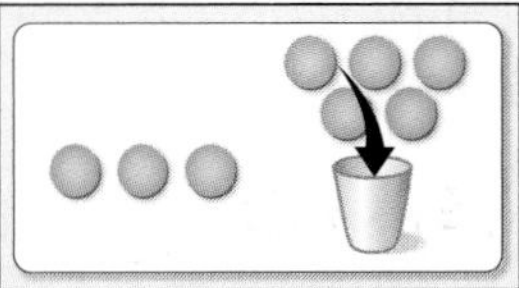

8 Add 3 and 5.

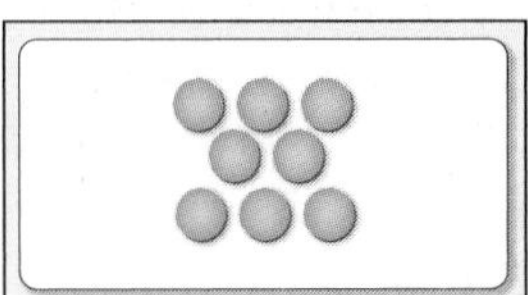

So, the value of $3 + n$ when $n = 5$ is 8.
Lia will have 8 baseball cards.

Some expressions contain parentheses, ( ). The **parentheses** tell you which operation to perform first.

EXAMPLE **Find the Value of an Expression**

Find the value of $12 - (r + 2)$ if $r = 7$.

$12 - (r + 2)$	Write the expression.
$12 - (7 + 2)$	Replace r with 7.
$12 - 9$	Find $(7 + 2)$ first.
3	Next, find $12 - 9$.

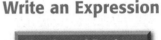

Real-World EXAMPLE **Write an Expression**

Remember

Remember that any letter or symbol can represent a variable.

3 ALGEBRA Latisha made 3 fewer baskets than Felisa. Write an expression for the number of baskets Latisha made.

Words	3 fewer baskets than Felisa
Variable	Define a variable. Let k represent the baskets Felisa made.
Expression	$k - 3$

So, Latisha made $k - 3$ baskets.

Online Personal Tutor at ca.gr4math.com

CHECK What You Know

Find the value of each expression if $x = 4$ and $m = 8$. See Examples 1 and 2 (pp. 93–94)

1. $x + 2$

2. $19 - m$

3. $8 - (x + 1)$

Write an expression for each situation. See Example 3 (p. 94)

4. two more than k

5. 44 minus y

6. the sum of 17 and z

Measurement The length of a condor is 7 inches more than the length of a bald eagle.

7. Define a variable. Then write an expression for the situation.

8. If a bald eagle is 12 inches, what is the length of a condor?

9. Talk About It Describe a situation that could be represented by $x - 6$.

Practice and Problem Solving

EXTRA PRACTICE
See page R6.

Find the value of each expression if $y = 9$ and $b = 5$. See Examples 1 and 2 (pp. 93–94)

10. $y + 2$
11. $b + 9$
12. $y - 4$
13. $11 - b$
14. $y + 20$
15. $14 + b$
16. $8 - b$
17. $12 - y$
18. $(y - 3) + 7$
19. $15 - (b + 1)$
20. $(y + 8) - 5$
21. $b + (17 - 9)$

Write an expression for each situation. See Example 3 (p. 94)

22. three more than t

23. the sum of d and six

24. ten subtracted from m

25. the difference of x and fifty-six

Pablo had 3 cats. One of the cats had kittens. See Example 3 (p. 94)

26. Define a variable. Then write an expression for the number of cats Pablo has now.

27. If the one cat has 4 kittens, how many cats will Pablo have?

Cole has 5 fewer soccer cards than his brother. See Example 3 (p. 94)

28. Define a variable. Then write an expression for the number of cards Cole has.

29. If Cole's brother has 15 cards, how many cards does Cole have?

Real-World PROBLEM SOLVING

Data File The Golden Gate Bridge is about 2 miles long and connects San Francisco with Marin County. The cost for a car to cross the bridge is $5.

30. A toll booth worker collects $25 in 10 minutes. In the next 10 minutes, another d dollars is collected. Write an expression for the amount of money collected in 20 minutes.

31. How much money was collected if $d = \$30$?

Bridges

H.O.T. Problems

32. **WHICH ONE DOESN'T BELONG?** Identify the expression that does not belong with the other three. Explain your reasoning.

3 − m	2 + 5	4 − x	k + 1

33. **WRITING IN MATH** Explain when to use a variable.

Algebra Activity for 3-2

Addition and Subtraction Equations

An **equation** is a sentence like $4 + 5 = 9$ that contains an equals sign ($=$), showing that two expressions are equal. Equations sometimes have a variable.

$4 + x = 9$ $\qquad$ $10 - m = 6$ $\qquad$ $k - 1 = 7$

When you find the value of the variable that makes the equation true, you **solve** the equation.

MAIN IDEA

I will explore addition and subtraction equations.

Standard 4AF1.1 Use letters, boxes, or other symbols **to stand for any number in** simple expressions or **equations.**

Standard 4MR2.3 Use a variety of methods, such as words, numbers, symbols, charts, graphs, tables, diagrams, **and models, to explain mathematical reasoning.**

You Will Need

counters

cups

1 Solve $n + 3 = 5$.

Step 1 **Model the expression on the left side.**

To model $n + 3$, use a cup to show n and 3 counters.

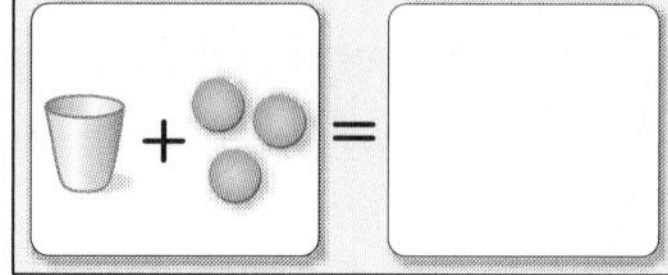

Step 2 **Model the expression on the right side.**

Place 5 counters on the right to show 5. An equals sign shows that both sides are the same.

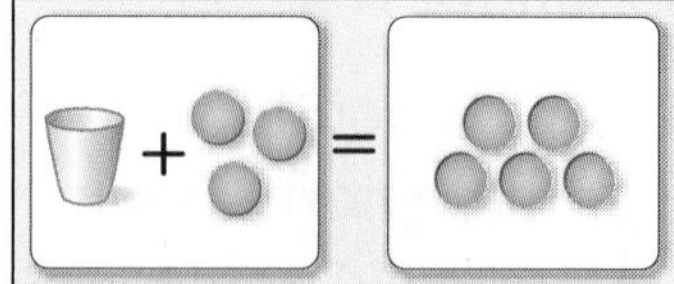

Step 3 **Find the value of n.**

Put enough counters in the cup so that the number of counters on each side of the equals sign is the same.

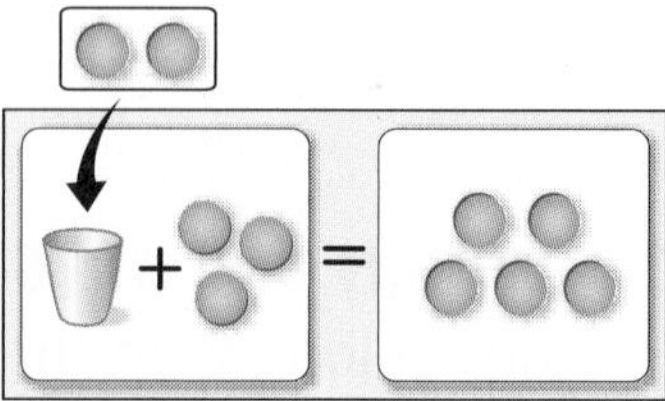

The value of n that makes $n + 3 = 5$ true is 2. So, $n = 2$.

Hands-On Activity

You can also use counters to model equations involving subtraction.

ACTIVITY

2 Solve $x - 4 = 2$.

Step 1 Model $x - 4 = 2$.

Use a cup and counters to show $x - 4 = 2$

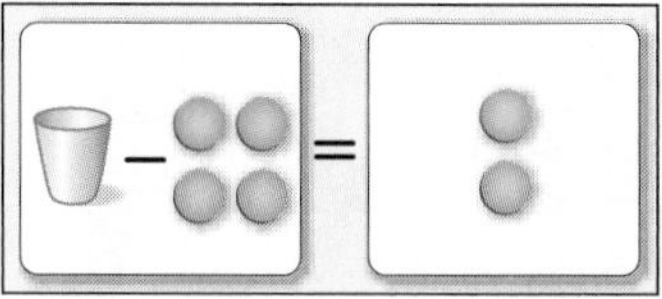

Step 2 Find the value of x.

Think: How many counters need to be placed in the cup so that when 4 are taken away 2 will be left?

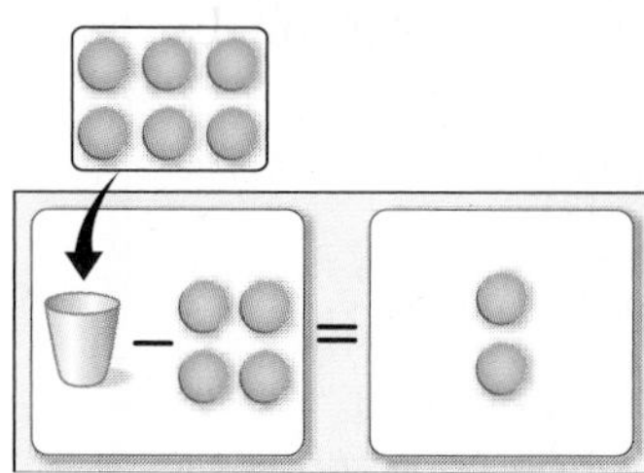

The number of counters in the cup is the variable.
So, the value of x that makes this equation true is 6. So, $x = 6$.

Think About It

1. How would you model $k + 2 = 9$?

2. What is the value of k in $k + 2 = 9$?

3. Explain how to check your answer.

CHECK What You Know

Write an equation for each model. Then find the value of n.

4.

5.

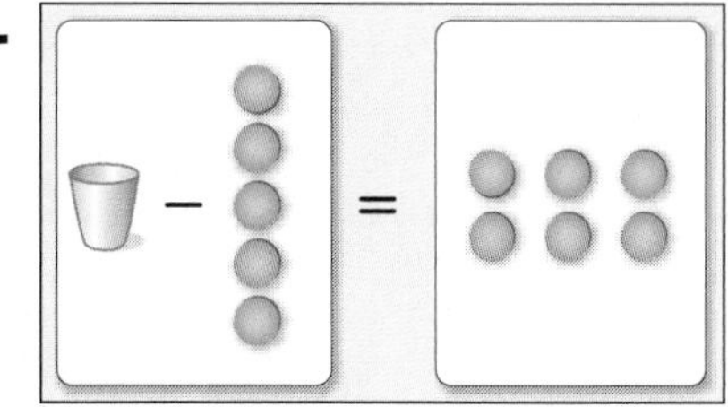

Use models to solve each equation.

6. $b + 3 = 8$ **7.** $f - 6 = 8$ **8.** $h - 5 = 12$ **9.** $k + 9 = 19$

10. WRITING IN ▶MATH Explain the difference between an expression and an equation. Give an example of each.

3-2 Solve Equations Mentally

MAIN IDEA

I will solve addition and subtraction equations mentally.

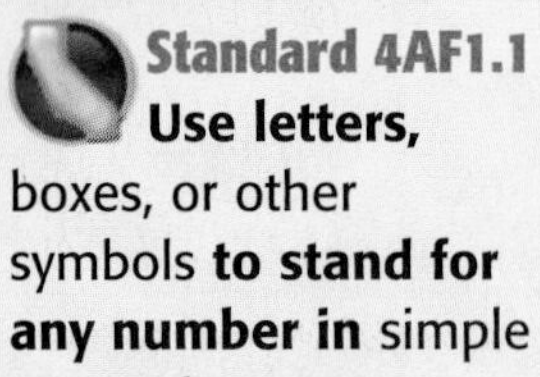

Standard 4AF1.1 Use letters, boxes, or other symbols **to stand for any number in** simple expressions or **equations (e.g., demonstrate an understanding and the use of the concept of a variable).**

New Vocabulary

equation
variable
solve

GET READY to Learn

Sashi downloaded 4 songs on Monday. After she downloaded some more songs on Tuesday, she had a total of 9 songs. How many songs did she download on Tuesday?

In the previous Explore activity, you solved equations using models. Equations can also be solved mentally.

Real-World EXAMPLE — Solve Addition Equations

1 MUSIC How many songs did Sashi download on Tuesday?

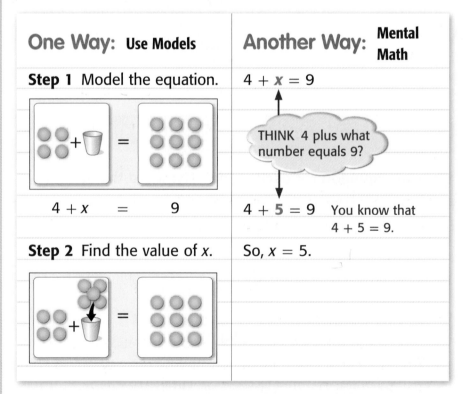

One Way: **Use Models**	Another Way: **Mental Math**
Step 1 Model the equation.	$4 + x = 9$
$4 + x \quad = \quad 9$	THINK 4 plus what number equals 9?
	$4 + 5 = 9$ You know that $4 + 5 = 9$.
Step 2 Find the value of x.	So, $x = 5$.

So, $x = 5$. Sashi downloaded 5 songs on Tuesday.

Remember

When you find the value of the variable that makes the equation true, you solve the equation.

EXAMPLE Solve Subtraction Equations

2 Solve $18 - y = 13$ mentally.

$18 - y = 13$ 18 minus what number equals 13?

$18 - 5 = 13$ You know that $18 - 5 = 13$.

$y = 5$

So, the value of y is 5.

Real-World EXAMPLE

3 ALGEBRA Garcia had 9 video games. He bought some more video games and now has a total of 12. How many video games did he buy?

Write and solve an equation.

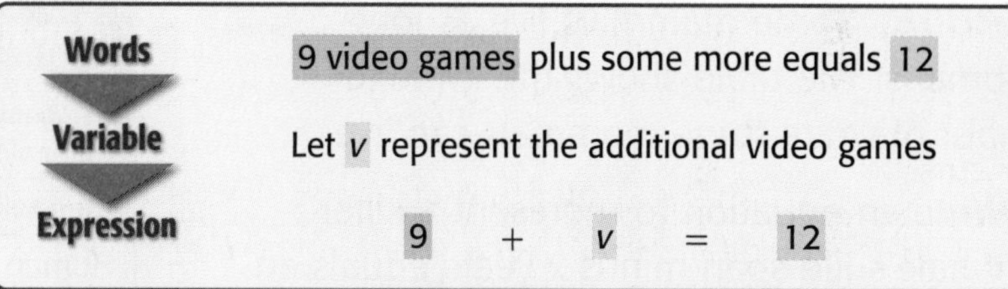

Words
9 video games plus some more equals 12
Variable
Let v represent the additional video games
Expression
9 + v = 12

$9 + v = 12$ 9 plus what number equals 12?

$9 + 3 = 12$ You know that $9 + 3 = 12$.

$v = 3$

So, $v = 3$. Garcia bought 3 more video games.

Online **Personal Tutor at** ca.gr4math.com

CHECK What You Know

Solve each equation mentally. See Examples 1 and 2 (pp. 98–99)

1. $5 + c = 11$

2. $k + 9 = 17$

3. $13 + n = 20$

4. $8 - h = 4$

5. $14 - f = 9$

6. $m - 12 = 12$

7. Keisha scored 14 points in the first half of a basketball game. At the end of the game, she had a total of 36 points. Write and solve an equation to find how many points she scored in the second half of the game. See Example 3 (p. 99)

8. Talk About It Explain how to solve $k - 3 = 12$.

Practice and Problem Solving

EXTRA PRACTICE See page R7.

Solve each equation mentally. See Examples 1 and 2 (pp. 98–99)

9. $1 + a = 4$ **10.** $d + 4 = 6$ **11.** $6 + f = 10$

12. $h + 8 = 15$ **13.** $k + 10 = 17$ **14.** $9 + n = 20$

15. $4 - b = 2$ **16.** $m - 5 = 6$ **17.** $7 - r = 2$

18. $w - 8 = 12$ **19.** $9 = 15 - y$ **20.** $11 = z - 12$

Write and solve an equation for each situation. See Example 3 (p. 99)

21. A number plus 8 equals 19.

22. The sum of 11 and a number is 35.

23. Nine subtracted from a number equals 12.

24. Fifteen less than a number is 15.

Real-World PROBLEM SOLVING

Science Some mammals live as long as humans. The table shows the average number of years some mammals can live.

Mammals that Live the Longest

Mammal	Years Lived
Killer whale	90
Blue whale	80
Human	76
African elephant	70
Gorilla	35

Source: *Scholastic Book of World Records*

25. Write an equation to represent a killer whale's life span minus x years equals an African elephant's life span. Then find the value of x.

26. Write an equation to represent a human's life span plus another mammal's life span (y) equals 111. Then find the value of y. Which animal does the variable y stand for?

H.O.T. Problems

27. FIND THE ERROR Caleb and Adriana say that the two equations have the same solution for n. Are they correct? Explain.

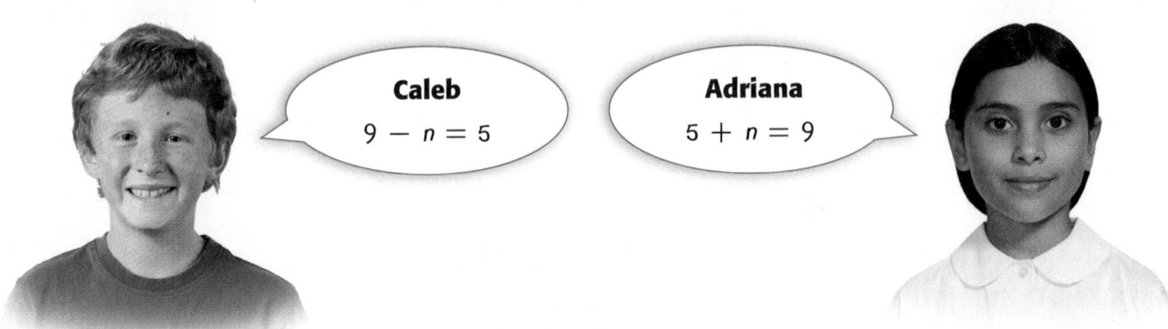

28. WRITING IN ▶MATH Write one or two sentences explaining how to solve an equation mentally.

Ready, Set, Solve!

Solve Equations

Get Ready!

Players: 2 players

Get Set!

Cut each index card in half. Then label with the equations and numbers shown.

Go!

- Shuffle the equation cards. Then spread them out, face up, on the table.
- Shuffle the number cards and place them in a pile face down.
- Player 1 selects a number card.
- Players race to find the equation that matches the number.
- The player who finds the equation first keeps the pair.
- Player 2 takes a turn by selecting a number card. Continue playing until all of the matches are made. The player with the most cards wins.

You will need: 10 index cards

equation cards

$4 - n = 3$	$n + 5 = 7$	$6 + n = 9$
$12 - n = 8$	$n - 3 = 2$	$7 + n = 13$
$18 - n = 11$	$n + 9 = 17$	$n - 6 = 3$
$n + 15 = 25$		

number cards

1	2	3
4	5	6
7	8	9
10		

3-3 Problem-Solving Skill

MAIN IDEA I will identify extra and missing information.

Standard 4MR1.1 **Analyze problems by** identifying relationships, **distinguishing relevant from irrelevant information,** sequencing and prioritizing information, and observing patterns. **Standard 4AF1.1** **Use letters,** boxes, or other symbols **to stand for any number in** simple expressions or **equations (e.g., demonstrate an understanding and the use of the concept of a variable).**

Trina is making friendship bracelets to sell for \$2 each. Last week, she sold 63 bracelets. Two weeks ago, she sold 21 bracelets. How many more bracelets did Trina sell last week than two weeks ago?

Understand

What facts do you know?

- Trina sells friendship bracelets for \$2 each.
- She sold 63 bracelets last week.
- She sold 21 bracelets two weeks ago.

What do you need to find?

- Find how many more bracelets Trina sold last week than two weeks ago.

Plan

Once you identify the information needed to solve the problem you can write an equation. Look for any extra information.

Solve

Subtract 21 from 63. You do not need to know how much the bracelets cost. This is extra information.

$$\underbrace{63}_{\text{last week}} - \underbrace{21}_{\text{two weeks ago}} = n$$

$$42 = n$$

So, Trina sold 42 more bracelets last week than the week before.

Check

Look back at the problem. Check the subtraction with addition. Since $21 + 42 = 63$, the answer is correct.

ANALYZE the Skill

Refer to the problem on the previous page.

1. Explain why you do not need to know the cost of the bracelets.
2. Suppose the problem did not include how many bracelets were sold last week. Could you solve it? Explain.
3. If you need to find the difference in profit between the two weeks, is there enough information to solve the problem?
4. Find the difference in profit between the two weeks.

PRACTICE the Skill

EXTRA PRACTICE
See page R7.

Identify any missing or extra information. Then solve if possible.

5. Chango the monkey eats four apples and three bananas for lunch every day. He eats at 12:30 P.M. How much fruit does he eat for lunch in a week?
6. Nidia asked her classmates to name their favorite flavor of ice cream. Chocolate received 14 votes, which is 5 more votes than vanilla. How many students liked vanilla?
7. Sheri and two friends want to go to a movie. The movie starts at 2 P.M. How much will admission cost?

8. **Measurement** Each day, Zoe trains each of her horses for 30 minutes, then rides them for 20 minutes. How much time does Zoe spend with her horses in one day?
9. Julia wants to buy the fish aquarium supplies shown. How much change will she get back?

Scuba Diver
$5
ROCKS
$2

10. Three fourth-grade classes are going on a field trip. How many students are going on a field trip?
11. James and Donna have $18. Each pack of baseball cards costs $3. There are 8 cards in each pack. How many packs can they buy?
12. The Video Depot is having a sale on DVDs. The cost is $27 for 3. How many DVDS can Edgar buy?
13. **WRITING IN ▸MATH** Explain how you identified any *extra or missing* information in Exercise 12.

3-4 Algebra: Find a Rule

MAIN IDEA

I will find a rule and use the rule to write an equation.

Standard 4AF1.5

Understand that an equation such as $y = 3x + 5$ is a prescription for determining a second number when a first number is given.

GET READY to Learn

Mr. Mathis put the following input number into his number machine and got the output number shown.

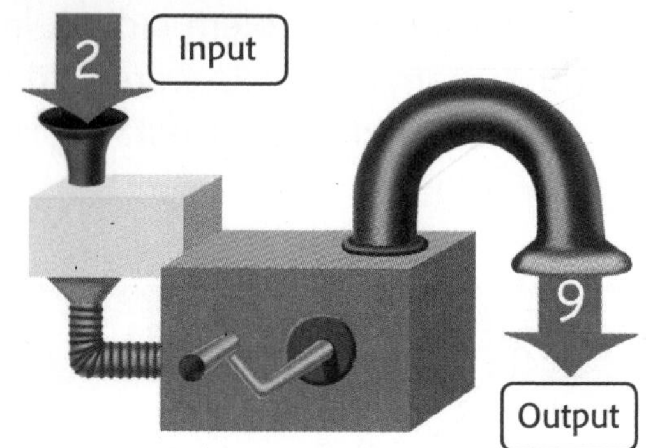

The numbers from the number machine above form a pattern. You can write an equation to describe and extend a pattern.

EXAMPLES Find an Addition Rule

1 Write an equation that describes the pattern in the table.

Input (x)	Output (y)
2	9
4	11
6	13
8	■
10	■
12	■

Pattern: $2 + \mathbf{7} = 9$
$4 + \mathbf{7} = 11$
$6 + \mathbf{7} = 13$

Rule: Add 7.

Equation: $x + 7 = y$

(x = input, y = output)

2 Use the equation to find the next three numbers.

Find the next three numbers when the input (x) is 8, 10, and 12.

$x + 7 = y$	$x + 7 = y$	$x + 7 = y$
$\mathbf{8} + 7 = 15$	$\mathbf{10} + 7 = 17$	$\mathbf{12} + 7 = 19$

So, the next three numbers in the pattern are 15, 17, and 19.

Remember

Always check to make sure the equation works for each pair of numbers in the table.

Real-World EXAMPLE Find a Subtraction Rule

3 **ALGEBRA A pizza shop offers $3 off any order $10 or over. Write an equation that describes the pattern. Then use the equation to find the next three costs.**

Input (c)	Output (d)
$11	$8
$12	$9
$14	$11
$16	■
$18	■
$20	■

Identify the rule and write it as an equation.

Rule: Subtract 3.

Equation: $c - \$3 = d$

input (points to c) output (points to d)

Find the next three numbers when the input (c) is $16, $18, and $20.

$c - \$3 = d$ $c - \$3 = d$ $c - \$3 = d$

$\mathbf{\$16} - \$3 = \$13$ $\mathbf{\$18} - \$3 = \$15$ $\mathbf{\$20} - \$3 = \$17$

So, the next three amounts are $13, $15, and $17.

Online Personal Tutor at ca.gr4math.com

CHECK What You Know

Write an equation that describes the pattern. Then use the equation to find the next three numbers.

See Examples 1–3 (pp. 104–105)

1.

Input (a)	5	9	13	17	21	25
Output (b)	9	13	17	■	■	■

2.

Input (m)	11	16	21	26	31	36
Output (n)	2	7	12	■	■	■

3. The amounts a bus company charges to take students on a field trip are shown. How much would it cost for 30, 40, and 50 students to go on a field trip?

Students	Cost ($)
10	$60
20	$70
30	■
40	■
50	■

4. **Talk About It** Explain what you should do if you test a number in an equation and it does not work.

Math Online Extra Examples at ca.gr4math.com

Practice and Problem Solving

EXTRA PRACTICE
See page R7.

Write an equation that describes the pattern. Then use the equation to find the next three numbers. See Examples 1–3 (pp. 104–105)

5.

Input (*f*)	3	6	9	12	15	18
Output (*h*)	6	9	12	■	■	■

6.

Input (*s*)	2	6	10	14	18	22
Output (*t*)	15	19	23	■	■	■

7.

Input (*v*)	16	22	28	34	40	46
Output (*w*)	5	11	17	■	■	■

8.

Input (*g*)	14	19	24	29	34	39
Output (*h*)	9	14	19	■	■	■

Create an input/output table for each equation.

9. $y + 4 = z$ **10.** $t + 11 = v$ **11.** $a - 7 = c$ **12.** $g - 10 = h$

Real-World PROBLEM SOLVING

Money The table shows what a taxi company charges (*c*) for every *m* miles traveled.

Input (*m*)	Output (*c*)
10	$12
15	$17
20	■
25	■
30	■

13. Use the table to write an equation for this situation.

14. Find the costs of a 20-mile, 25-mile, and 30-mile trip.

15. Use the equation you wrote for Exercise 13 to find the cost of a 60-mile trip.

16. Write an equation for *m* miles traveled and $4 charged for each trip.

17. Create a table for the equation in Exercise 15. How much would a 40-mile trip cost?

H.O.T. Problems

18. OPEN ENDED Write a real-world situation that can be represented by the table.

Input (*h*)	1	2	3	4	5
Output (*m*)	$10	$20	■	■	■

19. WRITING IN MATH Explain how the pattern of the input numbers is related to the pattern of the output numbers.

CHAPTER 3

Mid-Chapter Check

Lessons 3-1 through 3-4

Find the value of each expression if $x = 2$ and $m = 8$. (Lesson 3-1)

1. $x + 3$

2. $18 - m$

3. $m - (1 + 4)$

4. $(m - 2) + x$

Write an expression for each situation. (Lesson 3-1)

5. three more than k

6. the sum of 27 and z

Amado has 13 more books than Sara. (Lesson 3-1)

7. Define a variable. Then write an expression for the number of books Amado has.

8. If Sara has 8 books, how many does Amado have?

Solve each equation mentally. (Lesson 3-2)

9. $7 + c = 11$

10. $m - 4 = 12$

11. **STANDARDS PRACTICE** Which number will make the equation true? (Lesson 3-2)

$$67 + y = 121$$

A 54

B 56

C 64

D 68

Write and solve the equation for the situation. (Lesson 3-2)

12. A number plus 7 equals 19. What is the number?

Identify any missing or extra information. Then solve. (Lesson 3-3)

13. Raekwon bought his lunch every day this week. How much did he spend on lunches this week?

14. Dakota is buying a basketball for $12 and an air pump for $5. She wants to buy a baseball for $6. After purchasing the basketball and pump, the cashier gives Dakota $3. How much money did Dakota give the cashier?

15. **STANDARDS PRACTICE** Identify the equation that describes the pattern. (Lesson 3-4)

Input (a)	16	19	22	25	28	31
Output (b)	9	12	15	■	■	■

F $16 - 7 = b$

G $a + 6 = b$

H $a - 7 = b$

J $b + 6 = a$

16. Write an equation to describe the pattern. Then use the equation to find the next three numbers in the pattern. (Lesson 3-4)

Input (f)	3	6	9	12	15	18
Output (h)	7	10	13	■	■	■

17. **WRITING IN MATH** Explain how the pattern of the input numbers is related to the pattern of the output numbers. (Lesson 3-4)

Problem-Solving Investigation

MAIN IDEA I will choose the best strategy to solve a problem.

Standard 4MR2.3 **Use a variety of methods, such as words, numbers,** symbols, charts, graphs, **tables,** diagrams, and models, **to explain mathematical reasoning.** Standard 4NS3.0 **Students solve problems involving addition,** subtraction, multiplication, and division **of whole numbers** and understand the relationships among the operations.

P.S.I. TEAM +

TASHA: My soccer team is raising money by having a car wash. We earn $36 each hour by washing cars.

YOUR MISSION: Find how much money Tasha's soccer team will make in 5 hours.

Understand The soccer team earns $36 each hour. You need to find how much money the team will make in 5 hours.

Plan You can make a table that shows how much the team will earn in 1, 2, 3, 4, and 5 hours.

Solve The table shows how much money the team earns in 1, 2, 3, 4, and 5 hours.

Hours	1	2	3	4	5
Money	$36	$72	$108	$144	$180

+36 +36 +36 +36

So, Tasha's soccer team will make $180 in 5 hours.

Check Look back at the problem. Start with $180. Subtract $36 five times.

$180 − **$36** = $144
$144 − **$36** = $108
$108 − **$36** = $72
$72 − **$36** = $36
$36 − **$36** = $0

So, you know the answer is correct.

Mixed Problem Solving

See page R8.

Use any strategy shown below to solve. Tell what strategy you used.

PROBLEM-SOLVING STRATEGIES
- Draw a picture.
- Look for a pattern.
- Make a table.

1. Gigi is planting flowers in her garden in the pattern shown. How many daisies will she have if she plants 24 flowers?

2. Luis is setting up square tables for a party. One person can sit at each side of a table. He connects the tables together to form one long table. He invited 9 friends. How many tables does he need for everyone, including himself?

3. Copy and find a number pattern.

   15, 20, 18, 23, 21, ■, ■, ■

4. Misu wants to buy juice, a fruit cup, and a salad for lunch. She has $5. How much change will she get back?

LUNCH MENU
Juice....... $1
Milk .... 50¢
Fruit cup.. 50¢
Salad........ $2
Spaghetti.. $2

5. **Measurement** Jorge rode his bike to school, which is 2 miles away. After school, he rode to his friend's house, which is 1 mile from school. Then he rode home. If he rode a total of 4 miles, how far does he live from his friend?

6. Miko made 2 bowls of fruit punch for a family reunion. Each bowl fills 24 glasses. There are 12 family members at the reunion. How many glasses of punch can each person get?

7. Victor wants to buy CDs that cost $12 each. He has $40. How many CDs can he buy?

8. Liza is making a scrapbook. She is making the pattern shown as a border for one of the pages. How many bones will she need to glue to the page if she uses 36 shapes in all?

9. Darnell has baseball practice four days a week. Practice lasts for two hours each day. How many hours does he practice in four weeks?

10. **WRITING IN MATH** Niles's bedtime was 8:00 P.M. in first grade. It was 8:30 P.M. in second grade and 9:00 P.M. in third grade. The answer is 10:00 P.M. What is the question?

3-6 Balanced Equations

MAIN IDEA

I will balance addition and subtraction equations.

Standard 4FS2.1 Know and understand that equals added to equals are equal.

New Vocabulary

balance

GET READY to Learn

Hands-On Mini Activity

Step 1 Place two plates next to each other as shown. Think of each plate as one side of an equation.

Step 2 Place 1 dime on each plate.

Step 3 Add 2 nickels to the left plate.

Step 4 Place 1 dime on the right plate.

Step 5 Compare the total value of the coins on each side.

1. Are the values on each plate equal?
2. Remove a dime from each plate. What are the new values? Are they equal?
3. Add 2 nickels to the left plate and 2 dimes to the right plate. Are the new values equal?
4. What must you do to the left side so the two sides are equal?

By adding the same number to each side of an equation, the equality does not change. When the two sides of an equation remain equal, the equation remains **balanced**.

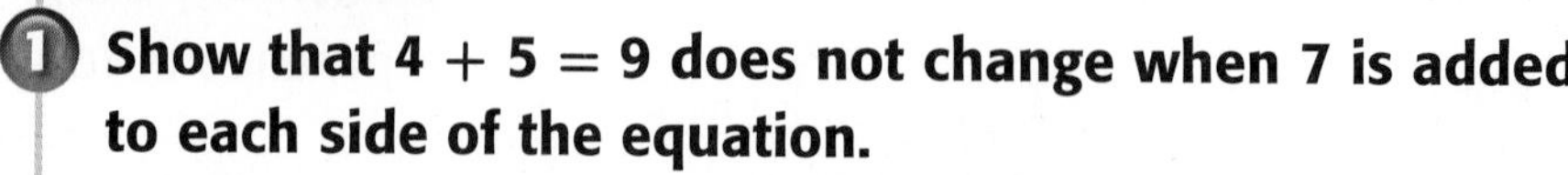

EXAMPLE Balance Equations

1. **Show that $4 + 5 = 9$ does not change when 7 is added to each side of the equation.**

$4 + 5 = 9$	Write the equation.
$4 + 5 + 7 = 9 + 7$	Add 7 to each side.
$16 = 16$	$16 = 16$

So, when you add 7 to each side, the equality does not change.

By subtracting the same number from each side of an equation, the equation remains balanced.

EXAMPLE Balance Equations

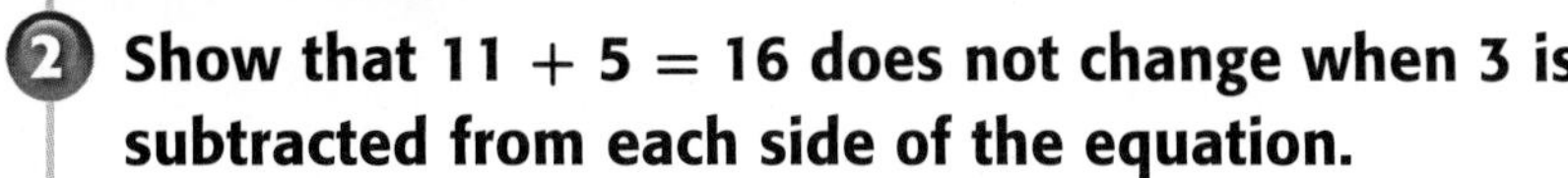

2 Show that 11 + 5 = 16 does not change when 3 is subtracted from each side of the equation.

$11 + 5 = 16$	Write the equation.
$11 + 5 - \mathbf{3} = 16 - \mathbf{3}$	Subtract 3 from each side.
$13 = 13$	13 = 13.

So, when you subtract 3 from each side, the equality does not change.

You can find missing numbers in equations.

Remember

To keep an equation in balance, add or subtract the same number from each side.

EXAMPLE Find Missing Numbers

3 Find the missing number in 25 + 3 = 12 + 13 + ■.

$25 + 3 = 12 + 13 + ■$	Write the equation.
$25 + 3 = 12 + 13 + ■$	You know that 25 = 12 + 13.

The same number must be added to each side to keep the equation balanced. So, the missing number is 3.

Online **Personal Tutor at** ca.gr4math.com

Show the equality is not changed. See Examples 1 and 2 (pp. 110–111)

1. $15 + 3 = 18$
$15 + 3 + 8 = 18 + 8$

2. $23 = 12 + 11$
$23 - 9 = 12 + 11 - 9$

Find the missing number in each equation. See Example 3 (p. 111)

3. $17 + 7 = 17 + ■$

4. $23 + 9 = 13 + 10 + ■$

5. Measurement Refer to the table. Who should stand on each side of a tug-of-war rope so both sides have equal weight?

Student	Weight (lb)
Mitch	65
Brandon	72
Chelsea	65
LaBron	72

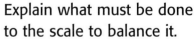

6. Talk About It Explain what must be done to the scale to balance it.

Practice and Problem Solving

EXTRA PRACTICE
See page R8.

Show the equality is not changed. See Examples 1 and 2 (pp. 110–111)

7. $21 = 17 + 4$
$21 + 5 = 17 + 4 + 5$

8. $14 + 5 = 19$
$14 + 5 - 4 = 19 - 4$

9. $29 + 12 = 41$
$29 + 12 - 7 = 41 - 7$

10. $38 = 20 + 18$
$38 + 7 = 20 + 18 + 7$

Find the missing number in each equation. See Example 3 (p. 111)

11. $23 + 9 = 23 + ■$

12. $47 + 8 = 47 + ■$

13. $38 + 5 = 18 + 20 + ■$

14. $55 + 6 = 33 + 22 + ■$

15. **Measurement** On the left side of a balance are weights of 3 ounces and 5 ounces. On the right side is a weight of 5 ounces. What must be added to the right side make the sides equal?

16. Yoshi rolls two number cubes and gets a 5 and a 4. Cristina rolls the number cubes and gets a 3 and a 6. If Yoshi rolls a total of 5 on her next roll, what does Cristina need to roll to tie her?

Real-World PROBLEM SOLVING

Money The table shows the amount of money earned by students who have different jobs.

Making Money

Student	Job	Money Earned per Week
Aisha	Wash car	\$15
Horacio	Deliver newspapers	\$30
Kelsey	Babysitting	\$24
Libby	Household chores	\$10
Antonio	Lawn mowing	\$45

17. The sum of Aisha's and Horacio's weekly earnings equals the weekly earnings of another student. Write an equation for this situation.

18. The equation shows the amounts of money earned by Aisha and Libby. Which job does Libby need to do to earn the same amount as Aisha?

Aisha Libby
\$15 + \$30 + \$24 = \$45 + ■

H.O.T. Problems

19. **OPEN ENDED** Write an example of two expressions that form a balanced equation.

20. **WRITING IN ▸MATH** Explain how to find the missing number in the equation $38 + 7 = 18 + 20 + ■$.

Standards Practice

21 Which equation describes the pattern in the table? **(Lesson 3-4)**

Input (m)	25	28	31	34
Output (n)	16	19	22	25

A $n - 9 = m$

B $9 - n = m$

C $m - 9 = n$

D $9 - m = n$

22 Which expression balances the equation? **(Lesson 3-6)**

$$17 + 8 + 2 = 12 + 5 + \blacksquare$$

F $6 + 7$

G $1 + 10$

H $13 - 5$

J $14 - 4$

Spiral Review

For Exercises 23 and 24, identify any missing or extra information. Then solve if possible. (Lesson 3-5)

23. Kamal wants to play tennis. The team practices 4 times each week. Kamal has $30. Does he have enough money to buy the equipment shown?

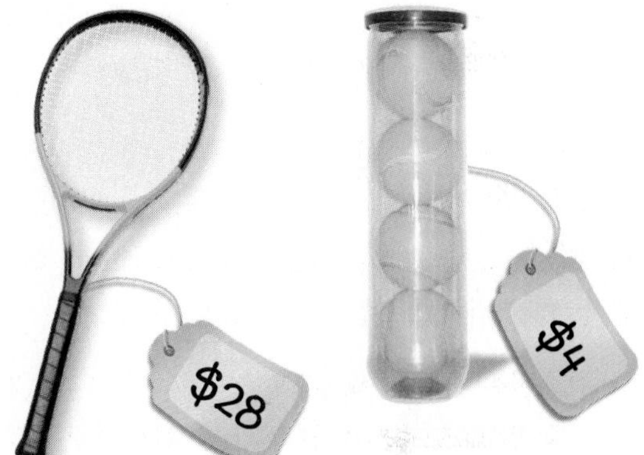

24. Measurement Santiago wakes up at 7:30 A.M. to exercise. He jogs 30 minutes a day. How many minutes does he jog in a week?

Write an equation that describes the pattern. Then use the equation to find the next three numbers. (Lesson 3-4)

25.

Input (a)	Output (b)
3	11
5	13
7	■
9	■
11	■

26.

Input (m)	Output (n)
21	16
18	13
15	■
12	■
9	■

Solve each equation mentally. (Lesson 3-2)

27. $8 + c = 15$

28. $k - 12 = 10$

29. $25 + r = 52$

Round each number to the given place-value position. (Lesson 1-6)

30. 568; ten

31. 35,406; thousand

Do Flying Squirrels Really Fly?

There are 36 types of flying squirrels. Southern flying squirrels and northern flying squirrels are found in the United States. These squirrels do not actually fly. They glide from tree to tree. These animals climb as high as 30 feet into trees. Then they use their hind legs to push off from branches.

Flying squirrels build their nests in trees, where they collect nuts and berries. They store up to 15,000 nuts in a season. What an appetite.

Southern Flying Squirrel Facts

Length of Body, including Tail . . . . 14 inches
Length of Tail . . . . 6 inches
Weight of Adult . . . . 3 ounces
Life Span . . . . 5 years

How Far Flying Squirrels Glide

Height of Squirrel in Tree (ft)	5	10	15	20
Distance of Glide (ft)	11	16	21	26

Standard 4AF1.1 **Use letters,** boxes, or other symbols **to stand for any number in** simple expressions or **equations (e.g., demonstrate an understanding and the use of the concept of a variable).**

Did You Know?
Some flying squirrels can glide as far as 1,500 feet!

Real-World Math

Use the information on pages 114 and 115 to solve each problem.

1. What is the length of a southern flying squirrel's body? Write and find the value of an expression.

2. The length of a northern squirrel's body, including the tail, is 16 inches. Its tail is the same length as a southern squirrel's tail. Write and find the value of an expression to find the length of the northern squirrel's body.

3. A southern squirrel lives to be 8 years old. How many years did this squirrel live beyond its average life span? Write and find the value of an expression.

4. Write a rule that describes how far a flying squirrel will glide when it jumps from a given height.

5. Suppose a squirrel jumps from a tree that is 25 feet tall. How far will the squirrel glide?

6. A squirrel jumps from a tree that is 30 feet tall. Will it glide farther than 40 feet? Explain.

7. What is the difference in gliding distances of a squirrel that jumps from a 40-foot tree than a squirrel that jumps from a 50-foot tree?

CHAPTER 3 Study Guide and Review

FOLDABLES Study Organizer GET READY to Study

Be sure the following Key Vocabulary words and Key Concepts are written in your Foldable.

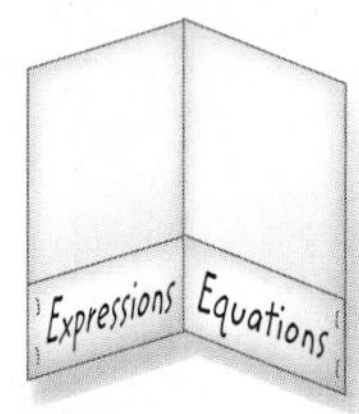

BIG Ideas

Expressions

- An **expression** is a combination of variables, numbers, and at least one operation. The symbols are called **variables**. (p. 96)

$$g - 3$$

Equations

- An **equation** is a sentence that contains an equals sign (=), showing that two expressions are equal. (p. 96)

$$y + 8 = 17$$

- An equation can be used to describe the pattern in a table. (p. 104)

Input (x)	8	10	15	26	28
Output (y)	12	14	19	■	■

Rule: Add 4.

Equation: $x + 4 = y$

Key Vocabulary

balanced (p. 110)
equation (p. 96)
expression (p. 93)
parentheses (p. 94)
variable (p. 93)

Vocabulary Check

Choose the vocabulary word that completes each sentence.

1. $6 + b$ is a(n) ___?___ .
2. A(n) ___?___ is a symbol used to represent a number.
3. $9 + h = 19$ is a(n) ___?___ .
4. When both sides of an equal sign are the same, we say the equation is ___?___ .
5. $6 - 2 = 4$ is a(n) ___?___ .
6. In the expression $2 + (7 - 3)$ you should do what is in the ___?___ first.
7. The x in the expression $x + 7$ is a ___?___ .
8. The equation $7 \times 2 = 10 + 4$ is ___?___ .
9. $y + 18$ is a(n) ___?___ .

Lesson-by-Lesson Review

3-1 Addition and Subtraction Expressions (pp. 93–95)

Example 1
What is the value of $5 + n$ if $n = 2$?

$5 + n$ Write the expression.

$5 + 2$ Replace n with 2.

7 Add 5 and 2.

Example 2
Find the value of $13 - (r + 3)$ if $r = 8$.

$13 - (r + 3)$ Write the expression.

$13 - (8 + 3)$ Replace r with 8.

$13 - 11$ Add $(8 + 3)$ first.

2 Subtract $13 - 11$.

Find the value of each expression if $y = 9$ and $b = 5$.

10. $y + 3$

11. $12 + b$

12. $(y - 2) + 6$

13. $14 - (b + 2)$

Write an expression for each situation.

14. five more than t

15. the sum of d and four

16. seven subtracted from m

Hayden's score was 15 more than Mario's.

17. Define a variable. Then write an expression for Hayden's score.

18. If Mario's score was 60, what was Hayden's score?

3-2 Solve Equations Mentally (pp. 98–100)

Example 3
Solve $4 + s = 10$ mentally.

$4 + s = 10$ 4 plus what equals 10?

$4 + 6 = 10$ $4 + 6 = 10$

$s = 6$

Example 4
Solve $18 - y = 12$ mentally.

$18 - y = 12$ 18 minus what equals 12?

$18 - 6 = 12$ $18 - 6 = 12$

$y = 6$

Solve each equation mentally.

19. $k + 10 = 18$

20. $w - 8 = 11$

21. $7 - b = 3$

22. $h + 9 = 15$

Write and solve an equation for each situation.

23. A number plus 7 equals 19. What is the number?

24. Five subtracted from a number equals 12. What is the number?

3-3 Problem-Solving Skill: Missing and Extra Information

(pp. 102–103)

Example 5
Troy's family went to the local zoo at 12 P.M. There are two adults and two children. Admission is $12 for adults and $5 for children. How much did it cost for Troy's family to go to the zoo?

Understand You know that there are two adults and two children in Troy's family. Zoo admission is $12 for adults and $5 for children. You need to find the cost for Troy's family to go to the zoo.

Plan Identify the information needed to solve the problem. Look for any extra or missing information.

Solve Add the costs of the admissions. You do not need to know what time Troy's family went to the zoo.

$\$12 + \$12 + \$5 + \$5 = \$34$

So, the cost for Troy's family to go to the zoo is $34.

Check Look back at the problem. You can check addition with subtraction.

$\$34 - \$12 - \$12 - \$5 - \$5 = \$0$

So, the answer is correct.

Identify any missing or extra information. Then solve if possible.

25. The table shows the points Camille scored in a basketball game. How many points did she score in the second half of the game?

first half	second half	total
12 points	x	26 points

26. The Cougars scored 36 points and defeated the Falcons by 12 points. How many points did the Falcons score?

27. A pet frog is two years old. It eats four times a week. If there are 365 days in a year, how many days old is the frog?

28. Deepak has football practice at 4 P.M. five days a week. How many minutes does Deepak practice in two weeks?

29. Chandra spent 23 minutes riding a bus to get home from school. When she got home she read a book for 35 minutes. What time did she leave school?

3-4 Algebra: Find a Rule (pp. 104–106)

Example 6

Write an equation that describes the pattern in the table. Then use the equation to find the next three numbers.

Input (m)	Output (n)
12	2
17	7
22	12
27	■
32	■
37	■

First, write an equation.

Pattern: $12 - \mathbf{10} = 2$
$17 - \mathbf{10} = 7$
$22 - \mathbf{10} = 12$

Rule: Subtract 10.

Equation: $m - 10 = n$

Then use the equation to find the next three numbers.

Find the next three numbers when the input (m) is 27, 32, and 37.

$m - 10 = n$

$27 - 10 = 17$

$32 - 10 = 22$

$37 - 10 = 27$

So, the next three numbers in the pattern are 17, 22, and 27.

Write an equation to describe the pattern. Then use the equation to find the next three numbers.

30.

Input (v)	Output (w)
15	6
21	12
27	18
33	■
39	■
45	■

31.

Input (g)	Output (h)
15	21
20	26
25	31
30	■
35	■
40	■

32.

Input (a)	Output (b)
11	7
13	9
15	11
17	■
19	■
21	■

3-5 Problem-Solving Investigation: Choose a Strategy (pp. 108–109)

Example 7

Kendra's aunt will fly 457 miles to Seattle. What is the approximate round-trip distance Kendra's aunt will fly to Seattle and back?

First, round 457 to the nearest hundred.

457 rounds to 500.

Now, add to find the round-trip distance.

$$\begin{array}{r} 500 \\ +\ 500 \\ \hline 1{,}000 \end{array}$$

So, Kendra's aunt will fly approximatley 1,000 miles.

The sum of 457 + 457 is 914. Since the exact answer is close to the estimate, the estimate is correct.

Use any strategy to solve.

33. Collin had 40 marbles in his collection. He gave away 12 and bought 8 more. How many marbles does he have now?

34. Lucas is collecting coupons to raise funds for his school. The first week he collects 525. The second week he collects 600. He collects 675 in the third week. If this pattern continues, how many should he collect the 7th week?

35. Karina has $27 and Jessica has $48. Do they have enough money to buy two concert tickets that cost a total of $82? Explain.

3-6 Balanced Equations (pp. 110–113)

Example 8
Find the missing number in
39 + 8 = 23 + 16 + ■.

39 + 8 = 23 + 16 + ■ Write the equation.

39 + 8 = 23 + 16 + ■ 23 + 16 = 39

The same number must be added to each side to keep the equation balanced. So, the missing number is 8.

Find the missing number in each equation.

36. 13 + 2 = 9 + 4 + ■

37. 18 + 5 = 12 + 6 + ■

38. 29 + 7 = 16 + 13 + ■

39. Mora has 3 quarters and 2 dimes. Peggy has 9 dimes. How much must Peggy get in order to have the same amount as Mora?

CHAPTER 3

Chapter Test

For Exercises 1–3, tell whether each statement is *true* or *false*.

1. The parentheses tell you which operation to perform first.

2. An expression is a math statement without numbers and symbols.

3. A letter or symbol that can represent any value is called a variable.

Write an expression for each situation.

4. thirty subtracted from h

5. the difference of x and twenty-six

6. the sum of m and 13

7. eight more than n

Solve each equation mentally.

8. $13 + n = 25$

9. $m - 12 = 22$

10. Justice rode his bike for 35 minutes on Monday, 20 minutes on Tuesday, and 44 minutes on Saturday. Did he spend more than an hour riding his bike on Monday and Tuesday? Identify any missing or extra information.

11. **STANDARDS PRACTICE** Which number would make the equation true?

$$17 + y = 20$$

A 2 **C** 37

B 3 **D** 33

Find the value of each expression if $y = 10$ and $b = 4$.

12. $14 - (b + 1)$

13. $b + (18 - y)$

14. $y + (b + 7)$

Write and solve an equation for each situation.

15. Fifteen less than a number equals 30. What is the number?

16. The sum of 21 and a number is 36. What is the number?

17. Fifty minus a number is 43. What is the number?

18. **STANDARDS PRACTICE** Which sign would go in the box to make the number sentence true?

$$26 \; \square \; 13 = 13$$

F + **H** ×

G − **J** ÷

19. Karl and Ginger are playing a boardgame. Karl has spun a 3, 6, and 5. Ginger has spun a 4 and a 5. What number does Ginger have to spin in order to be tied with Karl?

20. Kai is 7 years older than Sophia. Solve $t - 7 = 32$ to find the age of Kai.

21. **WRITING IN MATH** Explain why you sometimes need to use a variable when writing an expression.

CHAPTER 3

California Standards Practice

Cumulative, Chapters 1–3

Standards Example

What is the value of $14 - (n + 3)$ if $n = 6$?

A 23

B 18

C 6

D 5

Read the Question

You need to find the value of n in $14 - (n + 3)$ if $n = 6$.

Solve the Question

Replace the value of n in the expression. Then find the value of the expression.

$14 - (n + 3)$	Write the expression.
$14 - (6 + 3)$	Replace n with 6.
$14 - 9$	Add $6 + 3$ first.
5	Next, subtract $14 - 9$.

The value of $14 - (n + 3)$ when $n = 6$ is 5. So, the answer is D.

Personal Tutor at ca.gr4math.com

Choose the best answer.

1 **What is the value of the expression below if $n = 12$?**

$$24 + (n - 8)$$

A 4

B 12

C 28

D 44

2 **Kim has saved $59 to buy a bicycle helmet. She does not have enough money yet to buy the helmet. Let h represent the amount she still needs to buy the helmet. Which expression shows how much the helmet costs?**

F $59 + h$

G $59 - h$

H $h - 59$

J $h + (59 + h)$

3 **Which equation describes the pattern below?**

Input (x)	Output (y)
2	7
4	9
6	11
8	13

A $x - 3 = y$ **C** $x - 5 = y$

B $x + 3 = y$ **D** $x + 5 = y$

4 **Mark added 5 baseball cards to his collection. Now he has 62 cards. Which equation shows how many cards he had before?**

F $62 + 5 = c$ **H** $62 - 5 = c$

G $5 - c = 62$ **J** $5 + 62 = c$

5 **What is the value of y in the equation below?**

$$y + 27 = 48$$

A 20 **C** 32

B 21 **D** 75

6 **Rigo has $2008 in his bank account. If he buys a laptop for $1299, how much money will he have left?**

F $1819 **H** $819

G $1291 **J** $709

7 **A total of 8297 visitors attended a museum on Saturday and Sunday. If 5129 visitors attended on Saturday, how many visitors attended on Sunday?**

A 3086 **C** 3618

B 3168 **D** 3816

8 **What number makes this number sentence true?**

$$(9 + 3) + 8 = 9 + (3 + \blacksquare)$$

F 21 **H** 8

G 9 **J** 3

9 **Which rule describes the pattern?**

Input (c)	Output (d)
12	19
19	26
28	35
37	44

A Add 5. **C** Add 8.

B Add 7. **D** Add 9.

10 **Sonia hiked two miles. If one mile equals 5280 feet, how many feet did she hike?**

F 10,065 feet **H** 10,560 feet

G 10,506 feet **J** 10,650 feet

CHAPTER 4 Statistics: Data and Graphs

BIG Idea What are data and graphs?

Data is a set of collected information. When data is displayed in a **graph**, it is easier to read and interpret data.

Example The graph shows the number of children in the United States. About 35 million children are 5 to 13 years old.

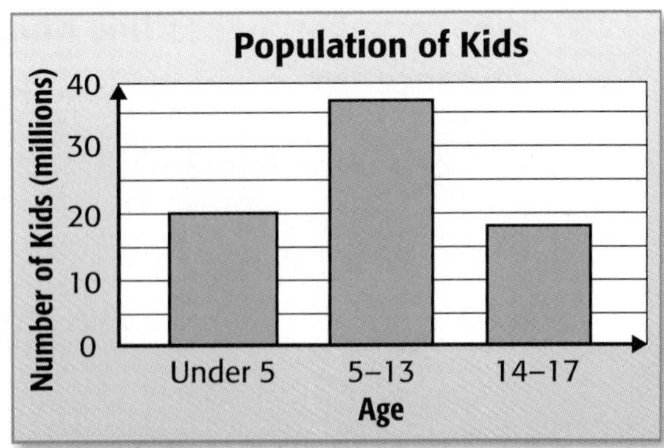

What will I learn in this chapter?

- Collect and represent data on a number line, and in graphs, tables, and charts.
- Read and interpret data.
- Identify the mode, median, and outliers of a set of data.
- Solve problems by making a table.

Key Vocabulary

data
mode
median
bar graph
line graph

Student Study Tools
at ca.gr4math.com

FOLDABLES™ Study Organizer

Make this Foldable to help organize information about data and graphs. Begin with three sheets of $8\frac{1}{2}'' \times 11''$ paper.

1. **Stack** the paper about 3 inches apart.

2. **Roll** up the bottom so all tabs are the same size.

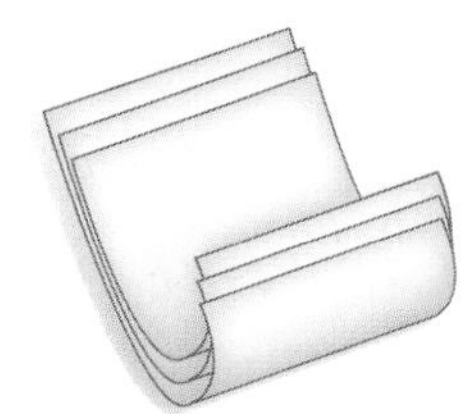

3. **Crease** and staple along the fold as shown.

4. **Label.** Take notes as you move through the chapter.

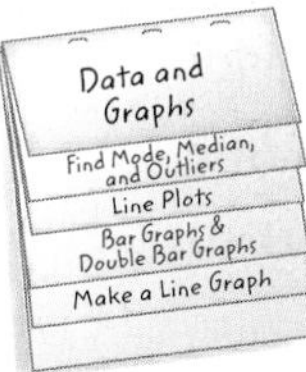

ARE YOU READY for Chapter 4?

You have two ways to check prerequisite skills for this chapter.

Option 2

Math Online Take the Chapter Readiness Quiz at ca.gr4math.com.

Option 1

Complete the Quick Check below.

QUICK Check

Order from *least* to *greatest*. (Lesson 1-5)

1. 12, 17, 19, 15, 13 **2.** 87, 56, 72, 34, 94 **3.** 31, 60, 23, 87, 91

Show each set of numbers on a number line. (Lesson 1-4)

4. 0, 2, 5, 8, 9 **5.** 20, 23, 25, 27, 30

Add or subtract. (Lessons 2-4 and 2-5)

6. $\begin{array}{r} 22 \\ +\ 34 \\ \hline \end{array}$ **7.** $\begin{array}{r} 64 \\ +\ 13 \\ \hline \end{array}$ **8.** $\begin{array}{r} 43 \\ -\ 29 \\ \hline \end{array}$ **9.** $\begin{array}{r} 59 \\ -\ 34 \\ \hline \end{array}$

Find the value of *n*.

10. $36 + 45 = n$ **11.** $64 - 12 = n$

Use the graph to answer each question. (Prior grade)

12. How many more students like art than gym?

13. How do the number of students who like music and gym compare to the number of students who like art?

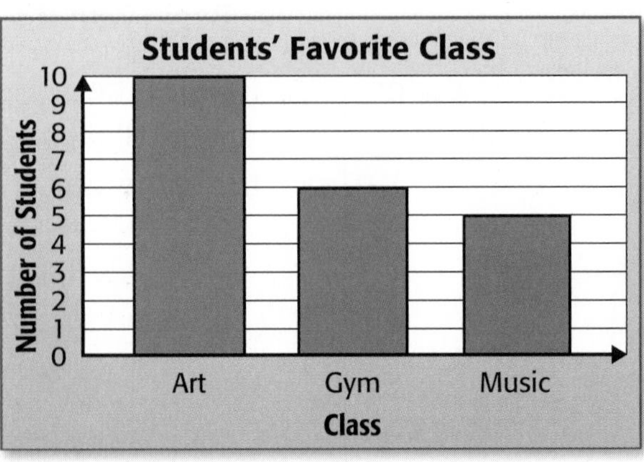

Collect and Organize Data

GET READY to Learn

Ms. Alvarez asked each of her students, "What is your favorite after-school activity?" The results are shown.

Playing a Sport	Reading	Watching T.V.
Staci	Alita	Julian
Eric	Sue	Chen
Melisa	Omar	Sarita
Kensey	Nicolas	
Alano		

MAIN IDEA

I will take a survey, and collect and organize data.

Standard 4SDAP1.1 **Formulate survey questions; systematically collect and represent data on** a number line; and coordinate graphs, **tables, and charts.**

New Vocabulary

survey
data
tally chart
frequency table

Ms. Alvarez took a survey. A **survey** is a way to collect **data** or information that answers a question. You can use a **tally chart** or a **frequency table** to record data.

Real-World EXAMPLE Organize Data

1 SCHOOL **Look at the data Ms. Alvarez collected. Organize the data in a tally chart and a frequency table.**

Step 1 Draw a table with two columns. Include a title.

Step 2 List each activity in the first column.

Step 3 Use tally marks or numbers to record the results.

Tally Chart

Favorite After School Activities	
Activity	Tally
Playing a sport	𝍸
Reading	||||
Watching T.V.	|||

Each tally mark represents a student.

Frequency Table

Favorite After School Activities	
Activity	Frequency
Playing a sport	5
Reading	4
Watch T.V.	3

Numbers are used to record the results.

Online Personal Tutor at ca.gr4math.com

You can take a survey and collect and represent data on charts and tables.

Hands-On Mini Activity

Step 1 Formulate or create a survey question you can ask your classmates. An example is shown.

What type of pet is your favorite?

a) Dog b) Cat

c) Fish d) I do not like pets.

Step 2 Create a tally chart to record your results.

Step 3 Ask the question to each of your classmates. Organize the data as you collect it.

Step 4 Use the information on your tally chart to create a frequency table.

Analyze the data.

1. Write two sentences that describe your survey results.

2. Were the survey results what you expected? Explain.

Remember

The tally marks used to represent a value of 5 are 𝍸, not IIIII.

CHECK What You Know

1. The data shows the ways Mrs. Jackson's students travel to school. Organize the data in a tally chart. See Example 1 (p. 127)

How Do You Travel to School?	
Method	**Frequency**
Bicycle	3
Bus	6
Car	9
Walk	5

2. Mary lists all of the fish in her fish tank. Organize the data below in a frequency table. See Example 1 (p. 127)

Mary's Fish Tank	
angelfish	damsel
angelfish	damsel
angelfish	damsel
clown fish	eel
clown fish	eel

3. Refer to Exercise 1. What is the most popular way to travel to school? What is the least popular? See Example 1 (p. 127)

4. Talk About It What are three different questions that you could use to conduct a survey?

Practice and Problem Solving

Organize each set of data in a tally chart. See Example 1 (p. 127)

5. Mr. Ortega records the type of pizza that his science club members like.

Favorite Type of Pizza		
cheese	cheese	sausage
cheese	pepperoni	sausage
cheese	pepperoni	
cheese	pepperoni	

6. Elisa took a survey to find out which movie to rent for her party.

Type of Movie	
action	comedy
action	comedy
action	comedy
animated	comedy

Organize each set of data in a frequency table. See Example 1 (p. 127)

7. Measurement Damián recorded the temperatures in one week.

Weekly Temperatures	
Temperature (°F)	Days
70–75	||
76–80	|||
81–85	|
86–90	|

8. A survey was taken to see how students spend their time at recess.

Recess Activities		
kickball	drawing	swing
kickball	drawing	swing
kickball	swing	tag
kickball	swing	tag
drawing	swing	tag

For Exercises 9–12, use the tally chart that shows items sold at a school store.

Items Sold at School Store	
Item	Tally
Eraser	𝍸
Bottle of glue	
Pencil	𝍸 |||
Scissors	|

9. Which item was the top seller? How many were sold?

10. Which item sold once?

11. How many items were sold altogether?

12. Organize the data in a frequency table.

H.O.T. Problems

13. OPEN ENDED Explain how a frequency table differs from a tally chart. How are they alike?

14. WRITING IN MATH Suppose you are collecting and organizing data about the population of your city. Would it be better to use a frequency table or a tally chart? Explain.

4-2 Find Mode, Median, and Outliers

GET READY to Learn

The largest spider in the world is almost one foot long. Look at the table. Which spider's length appears most often? Which length is in the middle?

World's Largest Spiders	
Spider	**Length (in.)**
Goliath birdeater	11
Slate red ornamental	9
King baboon	8
Salmon pink birdeater	10
Colombian giant redleg	8

Source: *Scholastic Book of World Records*

MAIN IDEA

I will identify the mode, median, and outliers of a set of data.

Standard 4SDAP1.2

Identify the mode(s) for sets of categorical data and **the mode(s), median, and any apparent outliers for numerical data sets.**

New Vocabulary

mode
median
outlier

The **mode** of a set of data is the number or numbers that occur(s) most often. If no number occurs more than once, there is no mode. The **median** is the number in the middle when the numbers have been arranged from least to greatest.

Real-World EXAMPLE — Mode and Median

1 **SCIENCE Use the spider data above. What are the mode and the median of the data?**

To find the mode, find the number that occurs most often.

11, 9, **8**, 10, **8** ← 8 appears twice

So, the mode is 8.

To find the median, first arrange the numbers in order from least to greatest. Then, find the middle number.

8, 8, **9**, 10, 11 ← 9 is the middle number

So, the median is 9.

Personal Tutor at ca.gr4math.com

An **outlier** is an item of data that is either much larger or much smaller than the rest of the data. A data set may not have outliers.

Remember

In some cases, when no numbers repeat in a data set, there is no mode.

Real-World EXAMPLE Identify Outliers

2 **MOVIES** **What is the outlier of the data?**

Movie Tickets Sold							
Day	Sun.	Mon.	Tues.	Wed.	Thurs.	Fri.	Sat.
Tickets	285	110	232	236	235	252	306

Look for the number that is either much larger or much smaller than the rest of the data items.

The number of tickets sold on Monday was 110. The number 110 is an outlier because it is much less than the other data items, which were between 235 and 306.

CHECK What You Know

Find the mode and median of the set of data. Identify any outliers. See Examples 1 and 2 (pp. 130–131)

1.

Shells Found on a Beach	
Name	**Shells Found**
Margo	9
Eva	7
Chris	9
Sondra	8
Louis	7

2.

Fish Caught While Camping	
Day	**Fish Caught**
Monday	3
Tuesday	6
Wednesday	2
Thursday	4
Friday	7

3.

Tall Mammals							
Mammal	Antelope	Camel	Gorilla	Giraffe	Okapi	Wallaby	Takin
Height (ft)	6	7	5	18	5	3	4

The table shows the time spent studying by 4th grade students each day.

Time Spent Studying					
Day	Mon.	Tues.	Wed.	Thurs.	Fri.
Time (min)	15	20	18	40	10

4. Identify the outlier.

5. Talk About It Give a possible explanation for an outlier in this situation.

Practice and Problem Solving

Find the mode and median of the set of data. Identify any outliers. See Examples 1 and 2 (pp. 130–131)

6.

Pints of Strawberries Sold	
Day	**Pints Sold**
Monday	18
Tuesday	14
Wednesday	11
Thursday	16
Friday	3

7.

Faces Painted at a Fair	
Day	**Faces Painted**
Wednesday	8
Thursday	23
Friday	25
Saturday	24
Sunday	28

8.

Scores in Golf Tournament	
Player	**Scores**
Trisha	58
Marita	42
Aashi	64
Ted	49
Ciro	56

9.

Arts Festival Visitors	
Day	**Visitors**
A	46
B	40
C	35
D	12
E	40

10.

Theme Park Ticket Prices							
Theme Park	A	B	C	D	E	F	G
Adult Ticket	$39	$59	$49	$45	$20	$50	$35

11.

Average High Temperatures for Each Month (°F)							
Month	August	September	October	November	December	January	February
Temp. (°F)	85	78	68	50	45	42	45

12. Look at Exercise 10. What is the difference in cost of one adult ticket for parks C and G?

13. **Measurement** Look at Exercise 11. How much warmer was it in August than in September?

Real-World PROBLEM SOLVING

Science The table at the right shows the number of rings for five planets.

Planets with Rings	
Planet	**Rings**
Uranus	11
Jupiter	1
Saturn	1,000
Neptune	6
Earth	0

Source: nineplanets.org

14. Identify the mode and median of the data.

15. Identify the outlier.

16. How many more rings does Saturn have than Uranus? Neptune?

Math Online **Self-Check Quiz at** ca.gr4math.com

H.O.T. Problems

17. FIND THE ERROR Jasmine and Greg are finding the median of the data set 34, 51, 49, 27, and 38. Who is correct? Explain.

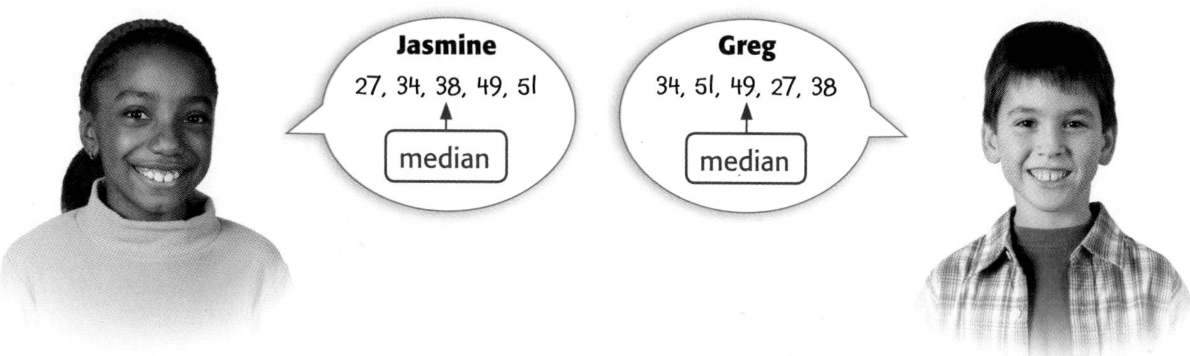

18.  **WRITING IN ►MATH** Explain a way that you can remember the difference between median and mode.

Standards Practice

19 Which sentence best descibes the data? **(Lesson 4-1)**

Favorite Animals	
Animal	**Number of Students**
Dolphin	||||
Elephant	||
Lion	~~||||~~
Snake	|||

A Thirteen students were surveyed.

B Lions are the least popular.

C Elephants are most popular.

D Three students like snakes.

20 What is the median of the data set? **(Lesson 4-2)**

Math Test Scores	
Student	**Score**
Angela	89
Carmen	93
Edgardo	85
Rafiq	78
Justin	89

F 78

G 85

H 89

J 93

Spiral Review

21. Ms. Smith recorded the jersey sizes for the girls' volleyball team. Organize the information in a frequency table. **(Lesson 4-1)**

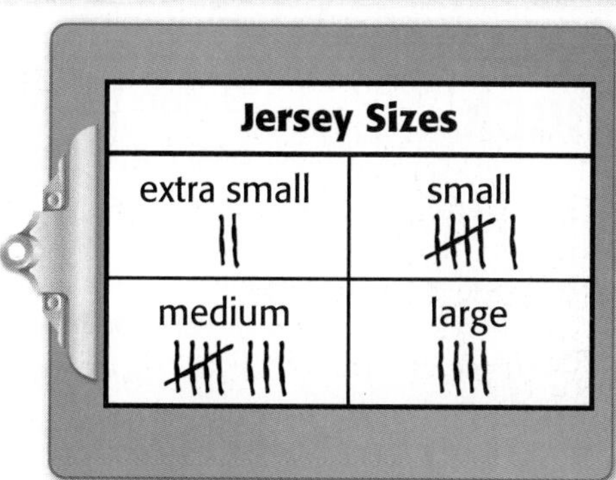

Jersey Sizes	
extra small ||	small ~~||||~~ |
medium ~~||||~~ |||	large ||||

22. Find the missing number in the equation $12 + 15 + 7 = 27 + \blacksquare$. **(Lesson 3-6)**

4-3 Problem-Solving Strategy

MAIN IDEA I will solve problems by making a table.

Standard 4MR2.3 Use a variety of methods, such as words, numbers, symbols, charts, graphs, **tables,** diagrams, and models, **to explain mathematical reasoning.** Standard 4NS3.0 **Students solve problems involving addition,** subtraction, **multiplication, and division of whole numbers and understand the relationships among the operations.**

The music club at Steven's school is going to a concert. There are 2 teachers going to the concert for every 9 students going. If there are 16 teachers going, how many students are going to the concert?

Understand

What facts do you know?

- There are 2 teachers going for every 9 students going to the concert.
- The total number of teachers going is 16.

What do you need to find?

- Find how many students are going to the concert.

Plan

You can make a table to solve the problem.

Solve

Make a table to show that there are 2 teachers going for every 9 students going.

+2 +2 +2 +2 +2 +2 +2

Teachers	2	4	6	8	10	12	14	16
Students	9	18	27	36	45	54	63	72

+9 +9 +9 +9 +9 +9 +9

So, 72 students are going to the concert.

Check

Divide the total number of teachers by the number of teachers per group.

$16 \div 2 = 8$

There are 8 groups. There are 9 students in each group. So, there are $8 \times 9 = 72$ students going altogether. The answer is correct.

ANALYZE the Strategy

Refer to the problem on the previous page.

1. Explain how a table was used to find the number of students going to the concert.
2. What pattern is shown on the table?
3. Suppose 1 teacher was going for every 3 students. How many teachers would be going on the trip?
4. Refer to Exercise 3. Check your answer. How do you know that it is correct?

PRACTICE the Strategy

See page R9.

Solve. Use the *make a table* strategy.

5. **Algebra** Kenya's school day is 6 hours long. Copy and complete the table to find if her school day is more or less than 300 minutes.

Hours	1	2	3	4	5	6
Minutes	60	120	■	■	■	■

6. Malik buys a \$2 lunch every day at school. How many lunches can Malik purchase for \$17?
7. Martín sold some of his old toys on the Internet. The cost of shipping each item is shown. If he paid \$32 in shipping, how many of his toys did he ship?

8. Jenna scored 24 points in her last basketball game. She made 2 baskets for every 5 shots she took. If one basket is equal to 2 points, how many shots did she take for the entire game?
9. Elki received her first paycheck from a job. She earns \$150 every 2 weeks. How many weeks will it take her to earn more than \$1,000?
10. The state sales tax is \$7 for every \$100 spent on certain items. Takara's mother spends \$21 in tax at the grocery store. What was the total cost of all the items she purchased?
11. **Algebra** Don spends 40 minutes on homework every night. How many minutes of homework does he complete in a week?

Day	Time Spent on Homework (min)
Monday	40
Tuesday	80
Wednesday	120
Thursday	■
Friday	■

12. **WRITING IN MATH** Explain why the *make a table* strategy is a good problem-solving strategy to use for Exercise 10.

Line Plots

MAIN IDEA

I will represent and interpret data in a line plot.

Standard 4SDAP1.3 **Interpret one-** and two-**variable data graphs to answer questions about a situation.**

Standard 4SDAP1.2 **Identify** the mode(s) for sets of categorical data and **the mode(s), median, and any apparent outliers for numerical data sets.**

New Vocabulary

line plot

GET READY to Learn

Vijay went camping in Redwood State Park. He recorded the number of elk he saw in a tally chart.

Elk Observed	
Day	**Tally**
Monday	||
Tuesday	~~||||~~
Wednesday	||||
Thursday	||
Friday	||||
Saturday	~~||||~~ ||
Sunday	||

You have used tally charts and frequency tables to show data. A **line plot** is a way to show data using Xs above a number line.

Real-World EXAMPLE Make a Line Plot

1 SCIENCE **Represent Vijay's elk data in a line plot.**

Step 1 Draw and label a number line.

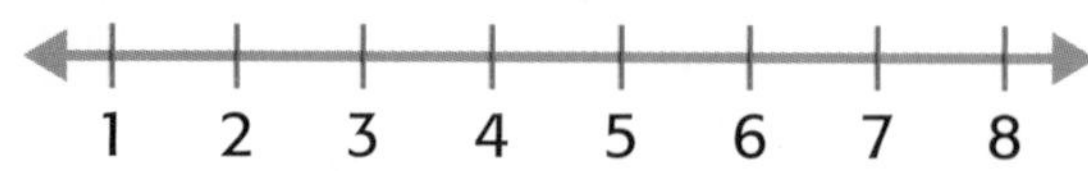

Step 2 Mark an X above the number line to show each data item. Add a title.

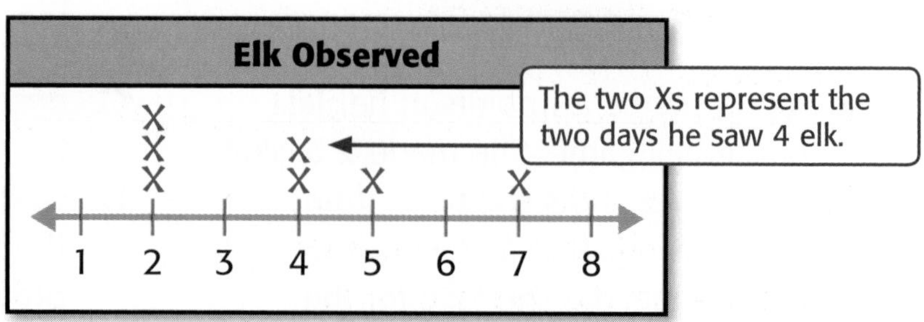

Online Personal Tutor at ca.gr4math.com

You can also read a line plot to answer questions about the data.

Read a Line Plot

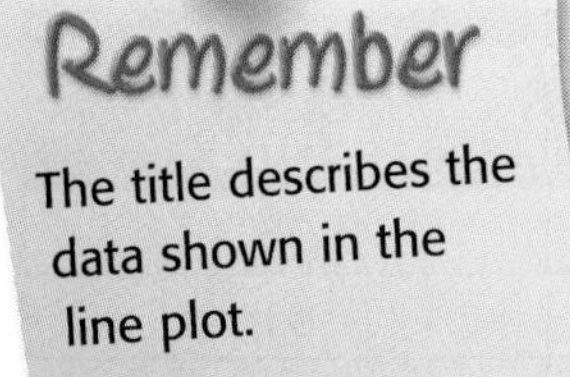

Remember
The title describes the data shown in the line plot.

2 READING Bianca's class took part in a reading competition. The results are shown below. Identify the mode, median, and any outliers for the data set.

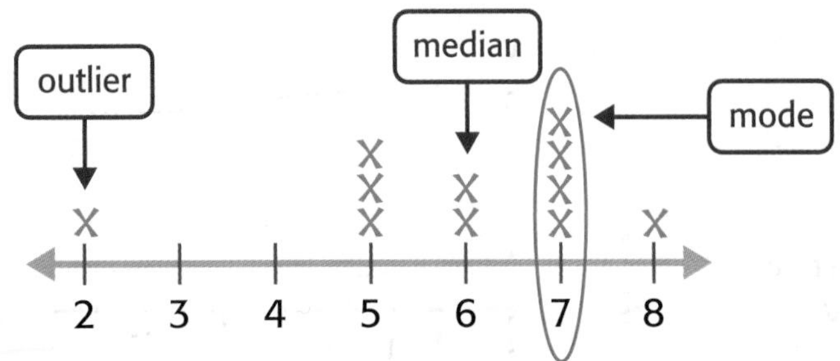

So, the mode is 7, the median is 6, and 2 is an outlier.

CHECK What You Know

Organize each set of data in a line plot. See Example 1 (p. 136)

1.

Ages of Students			
11	11	10	12
10	11	11	11
10	11	11	10

2.

Time Spent on Chores	
Student	**Time (hr)**
Mac	3
Julio	1
Tala	2
Anil	3

Identify the mode, median, and any outliers for each data set. See Example 2 (p. 137)

3.

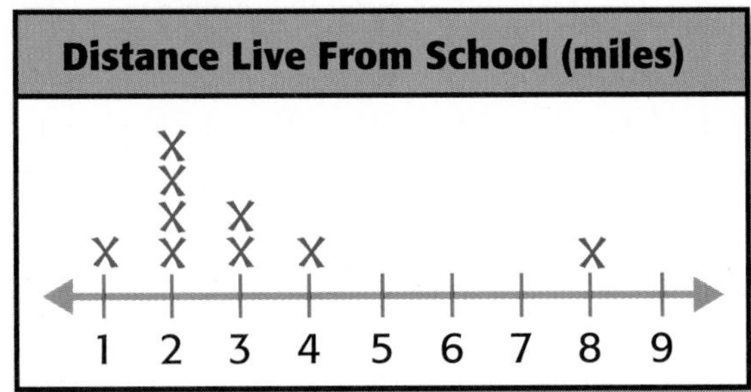

4. **Time Spent on Homework (min)**

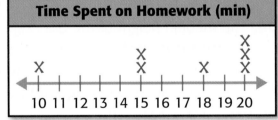

10 11 12 13 14 15 16 17 18 19 20

The line plot shows weekly allowances.

5. What is the most money a person receives?

6. Talk About It Sumi's weekly allowance is $4. Should she use the line plot to convince her parents to increase her allowance? Explain.

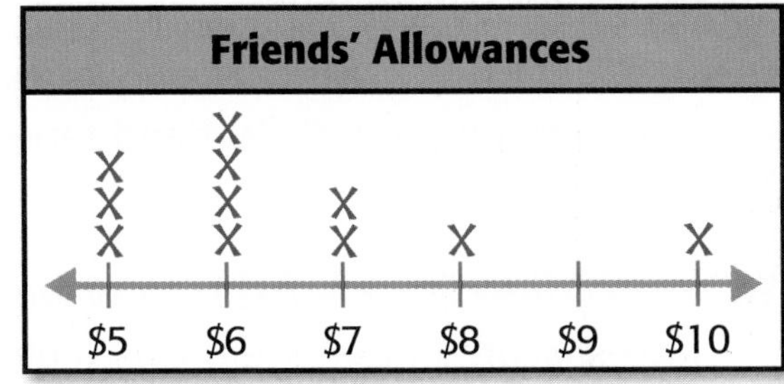

Practice and Problem Solving

EXTRA PRACTICE
See page R9.

Organize each set of data in a line plot. See Example 1 (p. 136)

7.

Crickets Caught	
Day	**Crickets**
Monday	6
Tuesday	3
Wednesday	8
Thursday	6
Friday	6

8.

Test Scores	
Student	**Score**
Darin	95
Janna	91
Grace	90
Arnoldo	95
Lali	86

9.

Points Scored per Game			
4	4	6	10
8	3	4	5
6	5	2	4

10.

Magazine Subsciptions Sold			
12	15	9	16
11	10	12	8
15	11	10	11

Identify the mode, median, and any outliers for each data set. See Example 2 (p. 137)

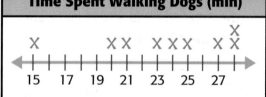

11. **Time Spent Walking Dogs (min)**

15 17 19 21 23 25 27

12.

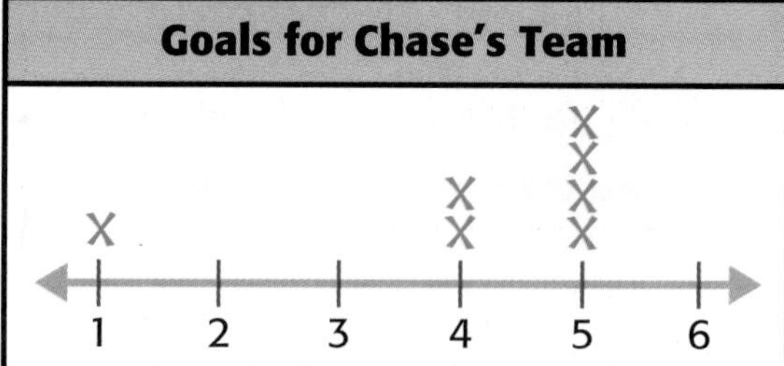

Real-World PROBLEM SOLVING

Measurement Mr. Simmons recorded the height of each player on his basketball team.

13. How many players are 58 inches tall?

14. The median height of the Los Angeles Clippers is 80 inches. Compare this height to the median height of the players on Mr. Simmons's team.

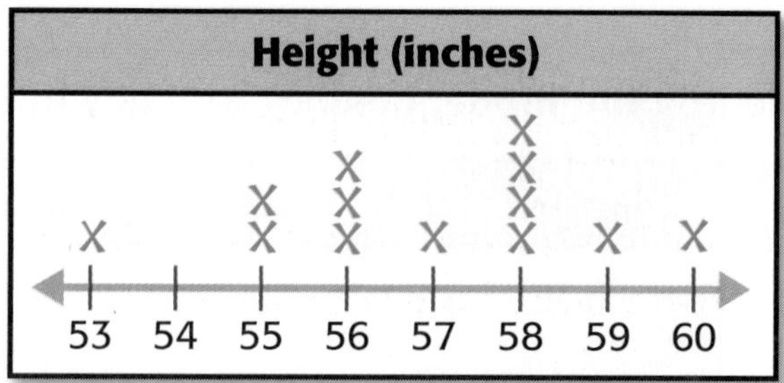

H.O.T. Problems

15. OPEN ENDED Create a survey question to ask your classmates. Ask your question. Collect and represent the data on a line plot.

16. WRITING IN ▶MATH How would the median change if the lowest score in Exercise 8 was replaced with 93?

CHAPTER 4

Mid-Chapter Check

Lessons 4-1 through 4-4

1. Organize the set of data in a tally chart and in a frequency table. (Lesson 4-1)

Sandwiches for a Picnic		
Peanut butter	Ham	Turkey
Turkey	Turkey	Peanut butter
Ham	Ham	Ham

For Exercises 2 and 3, use the tally chart below. (Lesson 4-1)

Where Do You Read?	
Place	**Tally**
Outside	𝍸 I
Bedroom	𝍸 II
Library	𝍸
Living room	III

2. Where do most students like to read?

3. How many students read in their bedroom or at the library?

4. **STANDARDS PRACTICE** What is the mode of the data set {4, 5, 8, 8, 4, 3, 4}? (Lesson 4-2)

A 3 **C** 5

B 4 **D** 8

5. Find the mode and median of the data. Identify any outliers. (Lesson 4-2)

Movies Rented During a Week					
Day	1	2	3	4	5
Movies	29	58	62	55	64

Solve. Use the *make a table* strategy. (Lesson 4-3)

6. One stamp costs 39¢. If Miguel spends \$1.95 on stamps, how many stamps did he purchase?

7. It costs \$32 for 2 admissions to a museum. Ebony and her father invite 10 friends for opening night. At this rate, how much would it cost for everyone to go to the museum?

8. **STANDARDS PRACTICE** What is the mode of the set of data shown in the line plot below? (Lesson 4-4)

Favorite Numbers

Number	1	2	3	4	5
X's	XX	XXX	XX		XX

F 1 **H** 3

G 2 **J** 5

9. Organize the set of data in a line plot.

Time it Takes to Walk Home (min)			
10	11	12	15
12	15	8	7
10	8	10	9

10. **WRITING IN MATH** Explain the difference between median and mode.

4-5 Bar and Double Bar Graphs

GET READY to Learn

The graph shows the amount of time four astronauts spent in space during a single mission. You can use the graph to compare the time spent in space.

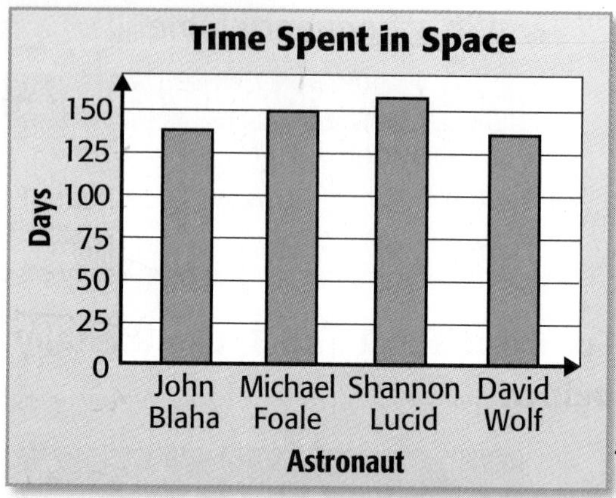

Source: *Time for Kids*

MAIN IDEA

I will use bar graphs to answer questions about a situation.

Standard 4SDAP1.3

Interpret one- and two-variable data graphs to answer questions about a situation.

New Vocabulary

double bar graph

A bar graph allows you to compare data easily.

Real-World EXAMPLES Read Bar Graphs

BOOKS The bar graph shows the most and least popular types of books at a school library.

1 What is the most popular type of book?

To find the most popular type of book, look for the longest bar.

Sports books are most popular.

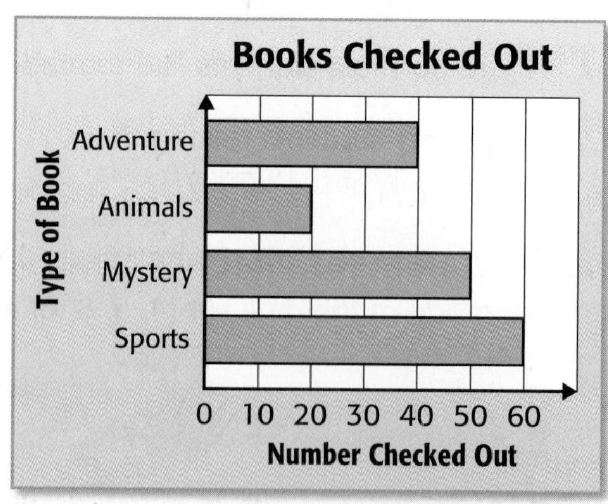

2 How many sports and animal books were checked out?

60 sports books and 20 animal books were checked out.

$60 + 20 = 80$

So, there were 80 sports and animal books checked out.

A **double bar graph** displays two sets of related data using bars of different colors and heights.

Real-World EXAMPLE Read Double Bar Graphs

Remember

When reading a double bar graph, always look at the scale and the key.

3 **SCHOOL Students are selling magazines for a fundraiser. About how many students will sell magazines in the second grade?**

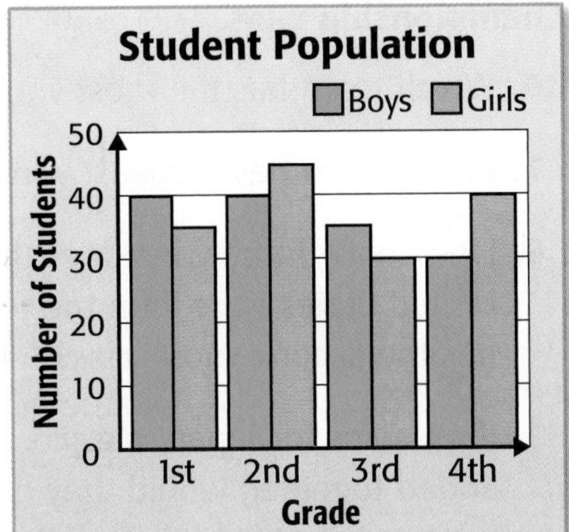

There are about 40 boys and about 45 girls in the second grade.

$40 + 45 = 85$

So, about 85 students will sell magazines in second grade.

Online Personal Tutor at ca.gr4math.com

CHECK What You Know

For Exercises 1–4, use the graphs shown. See Examples 1–3 (p. 140–141)

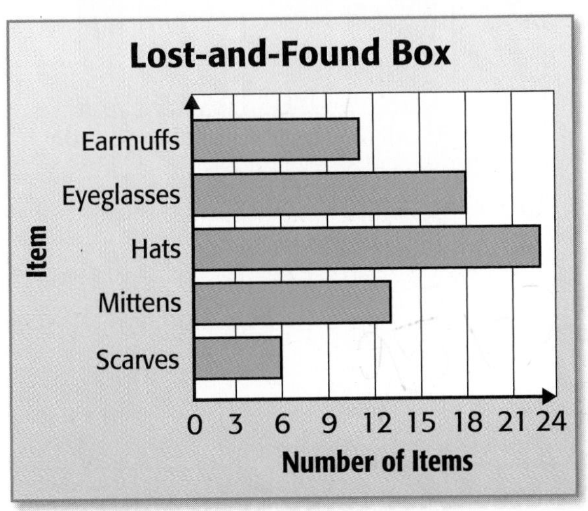

Learning to Play Instruments

Boys Girls

Students: 0, 2, 4, 6, 8, 10

Clarinet, Drum, Flute, Guitar, Trumpet

Instrument

1. What is the most common item in the lost-and-found box?

2. How many more eyeglasses are in the box than scarves?

3. What is the least popular instrument for boys?

4. What is the total number of students surveyed?

5. 

Describe when you would use a bar graph and a double bar graph to display sets of data.

Practice and Problem Solving

For Exercises 6–9, use the bar graph that shows the number of Little League Championship wins. See Examples 1–2 (p. 140)

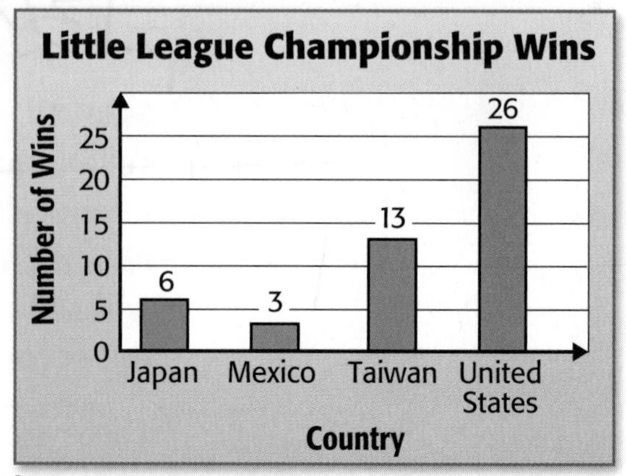

Source: *Scholastic Book of World Records*

6. Which team has the most wins?

7. Which team has the least wins?

8. How many more wins does the United States have than the team that has the second most wins?

9. If the wins for Japan, Mexico, and Taiwan were added together, would they have as many wins as the United States? Explain.

For Exercises 10–13, use the double bar graph that shows the number of tickets sold for a high school play. See Example 3 (p. 141)

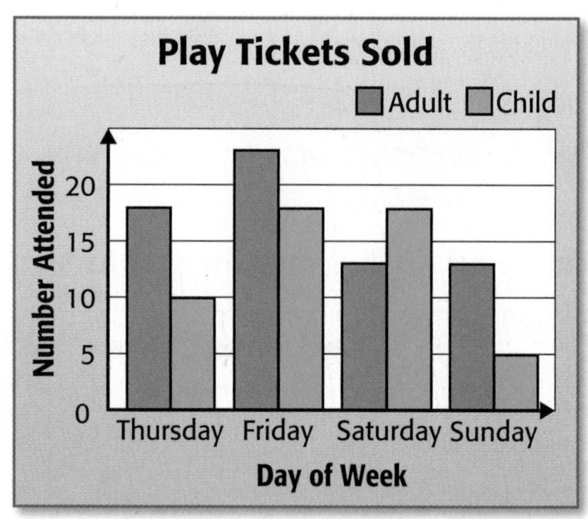

10. Which day had the highest total attendance?

11. Did more adults or children attend on Friday?

12. About how many adults attended?

13. Suppose adult tickets cost $4 and children tickets cost $2. On which day was more than $100 made in ticket sales?

H.O.T. Problems

14. **WRITING IN MATH** The graph shows the value of stocks for three companies. Write 2 sentences that describe the data.

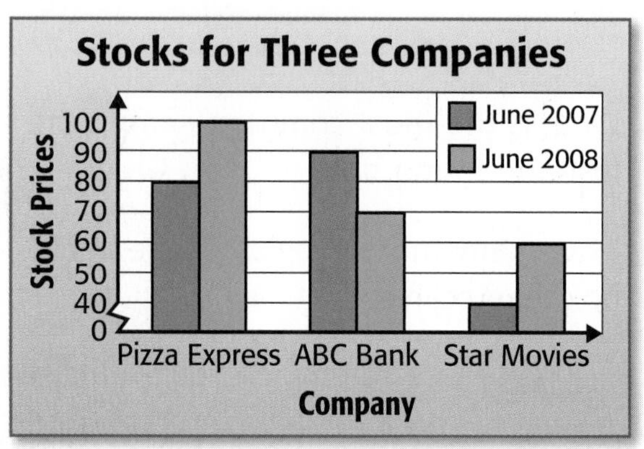

15. **OPEN ENDED** Describe a set of data that could not be shown in a double bar graph.

Math Online Self-Check Quiz at ca.gr4math.com

Graph Race

Create a Bar Graph

You will need: 0–5 number cube, grid paper

Get Ready!

Players: 2 players

Get Set!

Draw a bar graph on grid paper as shown.

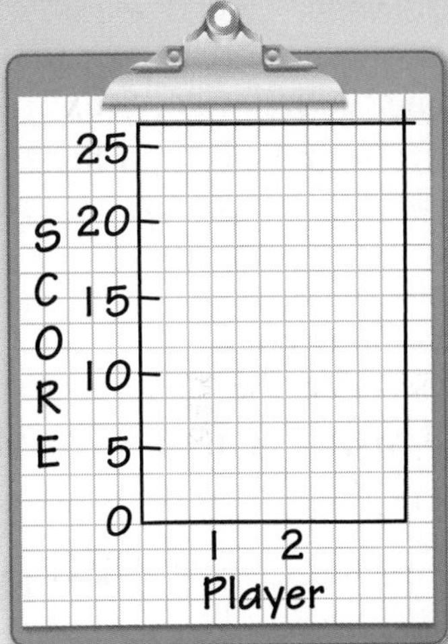

Go!

- Highest number goes first.
- Player 1 rolls the number cube and graphs the number on the bar graph.
- Player 2 rolls the number cube and graphs the number on the bar graph.
- Player 1 rolls the number cube again and adds the result to his or her previous amount. If a 0 is rolled, it is Player 2's turn.
- Play continues until a player's bar goes over 25. That player wins.

Extend

Statistics Activity for 4-5

Make Double Bar Graphs

Double bar graphs are used to compare two sets of related data.

MAIN IDEA

I will display data in double bar graph.

Standard 4SDAP1.1 Formulate survey questions; **systematically collect and represent data on a** number line; and **coordinate graphs,** tables, and charts.

Standard 4MR2.3 **Use a variety of methods, such as** words, numbers, symbols, charts, **graphs, tables,** diagrams, and models, **to explain mathematical reasoning.**

You Will Need

colored pencils

graph paper

Animation

ca.gr4math.com

ACTIVITY

Step 1 **Collect data.**

Create a frequency table that shows the number of minutes you and a partner spend studying or doing homework each day over the span of a school week.

Time Spent Studying/Homework		
Day	Student 1	Student 2
Mon.		
Tues.		
Wed.		
Thurs.		
Fri.		

Step 2 **Create a graph.**

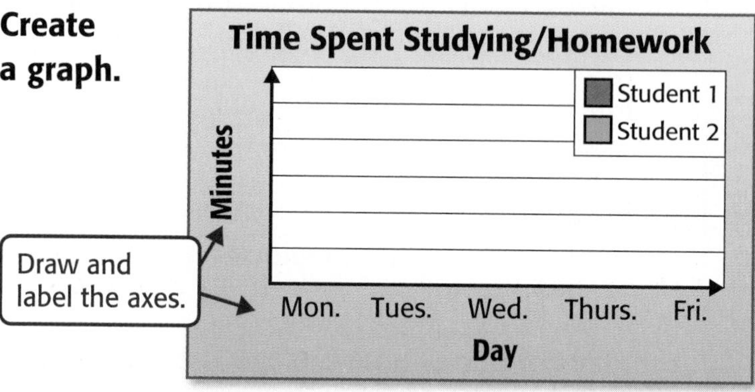

Draw two axes and label them. Write a title at the top. Choose a color for each set of data and make a **key**.

Step 3 **Choose a scale.**

The scale should include the least and the greatest number from your data.

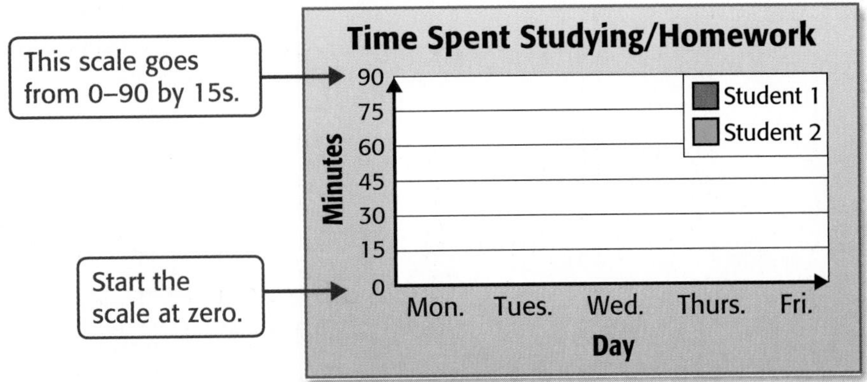

Step 4 **Draw bars.**

Draw the bars for your data on the graph. Then draw the bars for your partner's data on the graph.

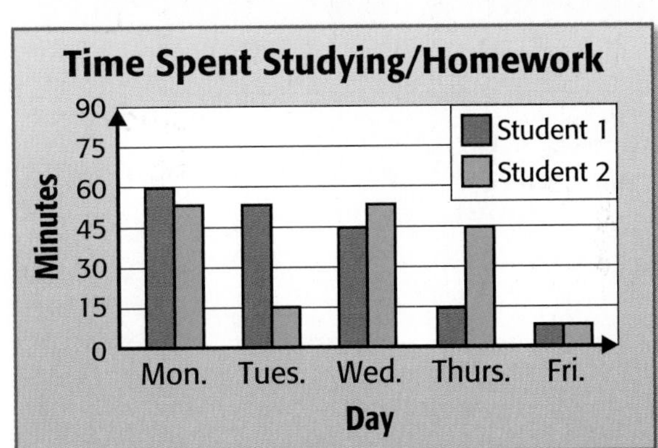

Think About It

1. Tell how you can use a double bar graph to compare data.

2. Explain how you choose a scale and intervals.

CHECK What You Know

Represent each set of data in a double bar graph.

3.

Books Read		
Month	Miki	Alicia
May	3	2
June	5	6
July	4	5
August	6	4

4.

Allowance		
Age	Morgan	Eli
7	$2	$0
8	$3	$1
9	$4	$3
10	$5	$5

5. WRITING IN ▶MATH Look at Exercises 3 and 4. Write a comparison sentence that describes the data.

Problem Solving in Science

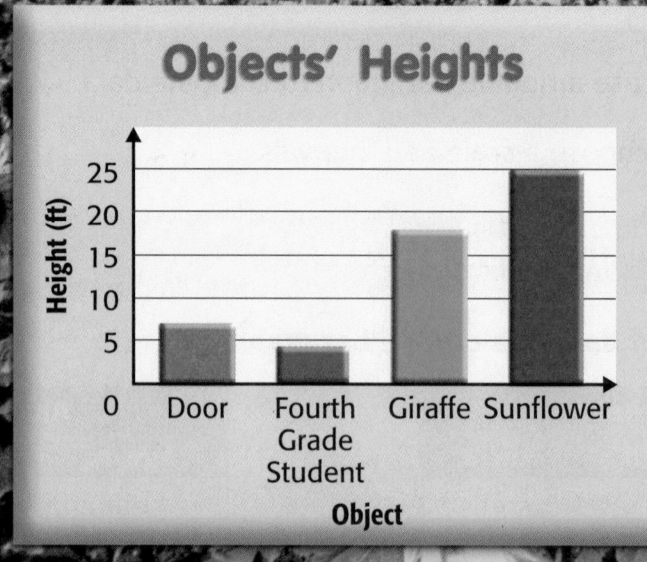

Standard 4SDAP1.3 **Interpret one-** and two-**variable data graphs to answer questions about a situation.**

Sunflowers are giants in the plant world. The tallest sunflower grew to a total height of 25 feet 5 inches. The size of the largest sunflower head is 32 inches across. This is almost three feet across!

Sunflowers can be used for decoration, but they are also an important source of food.

Sunflower oil is a valued and healthy vegetable oil. In addition, sunflower seeds are enjoyed as a healthy, tasty snack and nutritious ingredient in many foods.

Did You Know?

The shortest sunflower on record measured just over 2 inches tall.

Real-World Math

Use the information on pages 146 and 147 to solve each problem.

1. What is the tallest object on the bar graph? How tall is this object?
2. What is the difference in height of a sunflower and a giraffe?
3. What is the shortest object on the bar graph? How tall is this object?
4. Look at Exercise 3. Explain how you found the answer.
5. What is the difference between the tallest and shortest objects on the bar graph?
6. The height of how many fourth grade students equals the height of a sunflower?

4-6 Problem-Solving Investigation

MAIN IDEA I will choose the best strategy to solve a problem.

Standard 4MR2.3 **Use a variety of methods, such as words, numbers,** symbols, charts, graphs, **tables,** diagrams, and models, **to explain mathematical reasoning.** Standard 4NS2.1 Estimate and **compute the sum** or difference **of** whole numbers and **positive decimals to two places.**

P.S.I. TEAM +

TAO: I take the subway to get to school and back. Each round trip costs $1.50. My subway card has a value of $10.

YOUR MISSION: Find how many round trips Tao can make with $10.

Understand

Each round trip costs $1.50. Tao's subway card has a value of $10. Find out how many round trips he can make.

Plan

Organize the data in a table to solve the problem.

Solve

For each round trip, the total cost increases by $1.50.

Trips	1	2	3	4	5	6	7
Cost	$1.50	$3	$4.50	$6	$7.50	$9	$10.50

+1.50 +1.50 +1.50 +1.50 +1.50 +1.50

Tao's card has a value of $10. He cannot make a seventh trip because after making 6 trips he has only $1 left. This is not enough for another trip. So, he can make 6 trips to school and back.

Check

Use a set of play money that is in piles of $1.50. Add the money until you have more than $10.

Mixed Problem Solving

See page R10.

Use any strategy to solve.

1. Mrs. Vargas is making costumes for a play. She needs 4 buttons for each costume. Copy and complete the table to find how many buttons she will need for 14 costumes.

Costumes	Buttons
1	4
2	8
4	16
6	24
8	32
10	40
12	■
14	■

2. It costs $12 for 2 admissions to miniature golf. Marcus wants to invite 9 friends. At this rate, how much would it cost for 10 people?

3. **Measurement** The Castros drove 64 miles to a water park. The Brinkleys drove 81 miles. The Klines drove 19 miles. How much farther did the Castros have to drive than the Klines?

4. Ricardo has to mail 27 party invitations. The invitations come in packs of 8 that cost $3.50. How much will he spend on invitations?

5. Pete spends 30 minutes a night reading. About how many hours does he spend reading each month?

6. Tomas has $49. He wants to buy as many video games as he can. How many can he get at the yard sale?

7. Dawn mows the lawn the first and second weeks of the month. Ana mows the lawn the third and fourth weeks. Each person gets paid $6 for each mow. There are 19 weeks in which the lawn needs mowed. Who will make more money?

8. Paz is making granola bars for her scout meeting. There are 8 girls in her troop. If she makes 2 dozen granola bars, how many will each girl get?

9. During a basketball game, Faith and Brandy each scored 4 points. Maria and Jo each scored 7 points. Dena scored 12 points. Find the total points scored by this team.

10. **WRITING IN MATH** Explain when to use the *make a table* strategy to solve a word problem.

4-7 Interpret Line Graphs

GET READY to Learn

Lindsey and Jaden are measuring the growth of a flower. The graph shows the growth of the flower over four months. Find how tall the flower grew in four months.

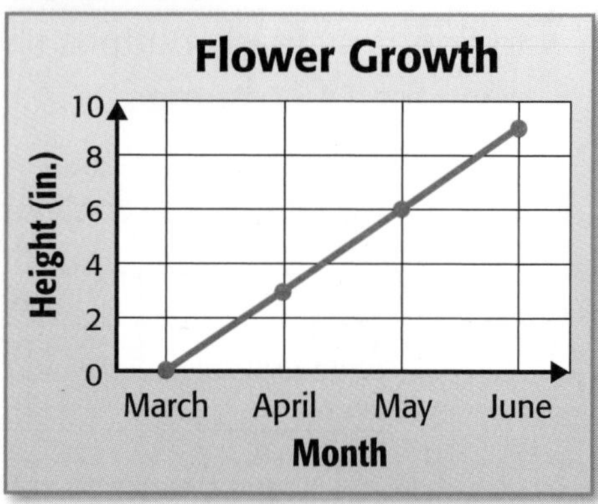

MAIN IDEA

I will interpret data in a line graph.

Standard 4SDAP1.3
Interpret one- and two-**variable data graphs to answer questions about a situation.**

New Vocabulary

line graph

A **line graph** shows how data changes over time. You can use a line graph to make predictions about future events.

Real-World EXAMPLE Interpret a Line Graph

1 **FLOWERS Refer to the graph above. How tall did the flower grow in four months?**

Find the fourth month shown on the graph. The fourth month is June.

Move up to find where the point is located on the graph. Then compare the height of the point to the scale on the left.

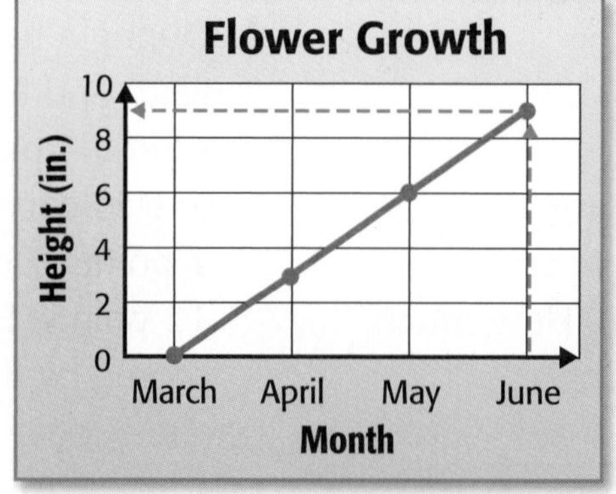

The point is located between 8 and 10 on the graph's scale. So, the plant grew 9 inches in four months.

Real-World EXAMPLE Interpret a Line Graph

2 **MEASUREMENT The graph shows the growth of a baby panda over four weeks. How much weight did the baby panda gain between the first week and the fourth week?**

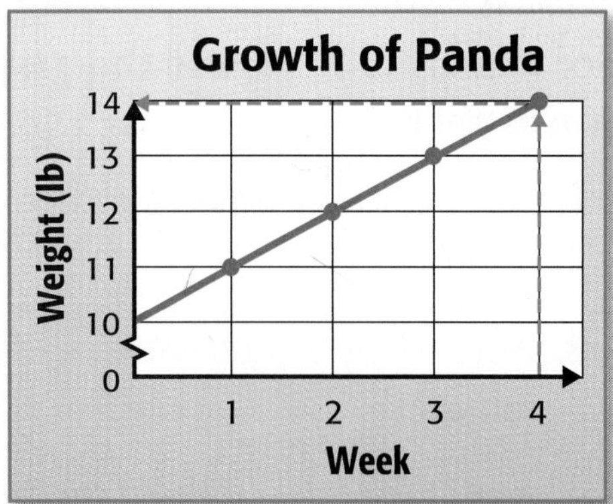

You need to subtract the panda's weight at week 1 from its weight at week 4.

During week one, the panda weighed 11 pounds. During week four, the panda weighed 14 pounds.

$14 - 11 = 3$

So, the baby panda gained 3 pounds between the first week and the fourth week.

CHECK What You Know

For Exercises 1–5, use the line graph. See Examples 1 and 2 (pp. 150–151)

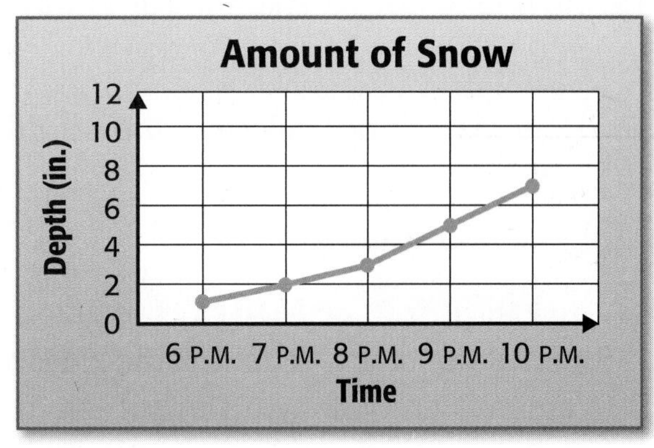

1. At what time is the least amount of snow on the ground?
2. How much snow is on the ground at 8:00 P.M.?
3. How many more inches of snow were on the ground at 9 P.M. than at 6 P.M.?
4. How many fewer inches of snow were on the ground at 7 P.M. than at 10 P.M.?
5. How much snow fell over the 4-hour period shown on the graph?
6. **Talk About It** Predict how much snow will be on the ground at midnight.

Practice and Problem Solving

See page R10.

For Exercises 7–11, use the graph that shows the number of words read. See Examples 1 and 2 (pp. 150–151)

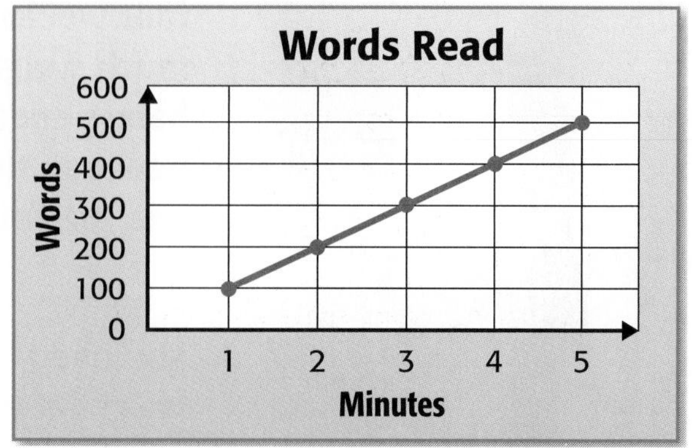

7. How many words were read in two minutes?

8. How many words were read in five minutes?

9. At this rate, how many words will be read in six minutes?

10. How many fewer words were read in two minutes than in four minutes?

11. How many more words were read in five minutes than in one minute?

For Exercises 12–16, use the graph that shows the distance a car travels. See Examples 1 and 2 (pp. 150–151)

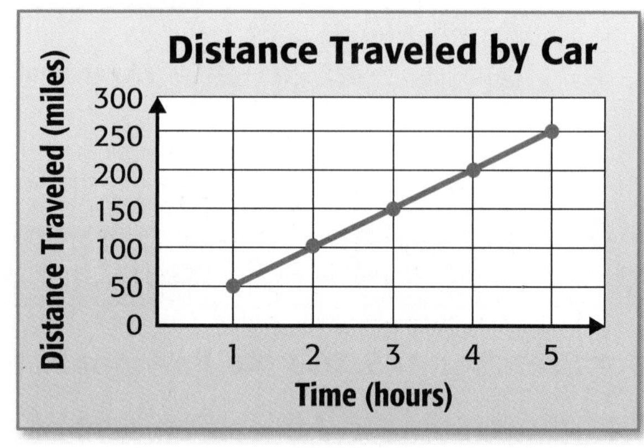

12. How many miles did the car travel in two hours?

13. How many miles did the car travel in three hours?

14. What distance did the car travel between two and four hours?

15. How long does it take the car to travel 200 miles?

16. How many more miles did the car drive in five hours than in two hours?

H.O.T. Problems

17. **WRITING IN MATH** The graph shows the rate of a submarine's descent underwater. Write two sentences that describe the data.

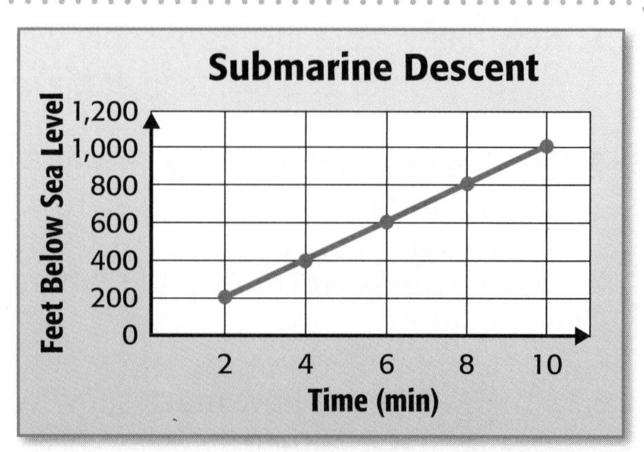

18. **OPEN ENDED** Give an example of a set of data that is best represented in a line graph.

Standards Practice

19 Roberto's change in height over a three-year period is shown on the line graph to the right.

Which of the following frequency tables did he use to make this graph? **(Lesson 4-7)**

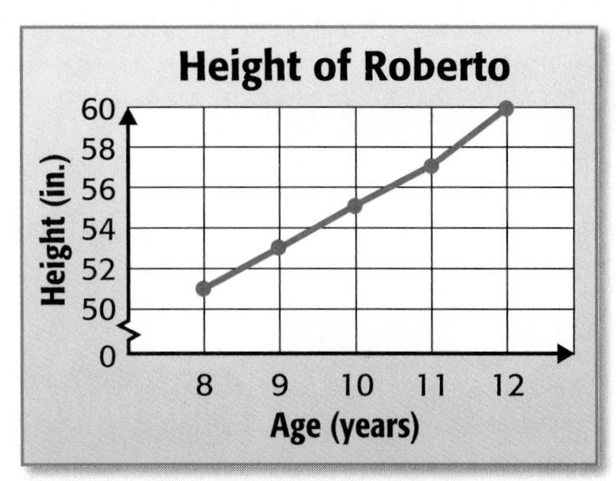

A

Roberto's Height	
Age	**Height (in.)**
8	50
9	51
10	52
11	53
12	54

B

Roberto's Height	
Age	**Height (in.)**
8	51
9	53
10	55
11	57
12	59

C

Roberto's Height	
Age	**Height (in.)**
8	51
9	53
10	55
11	57
12	60

D

Roberto's Height	
Age	**Height (in.)**
8	52
9	54
10	56
11	58
12	60

Spiral Review

20. Measurement A black bear weighs 425 pounds. A lion weighs 400 pounds. A gorilla weighs 440 pounds. Order these animals from greatest to least weight. **(Lesson 4-6)**

For Exercises 21–23, use the graph shown.
(Lesson 4-5)

21. Name the planet that has about 31 moons.

22. About how many more moons does Saturn have than Uranus?

23. Estimate the total number of moons.

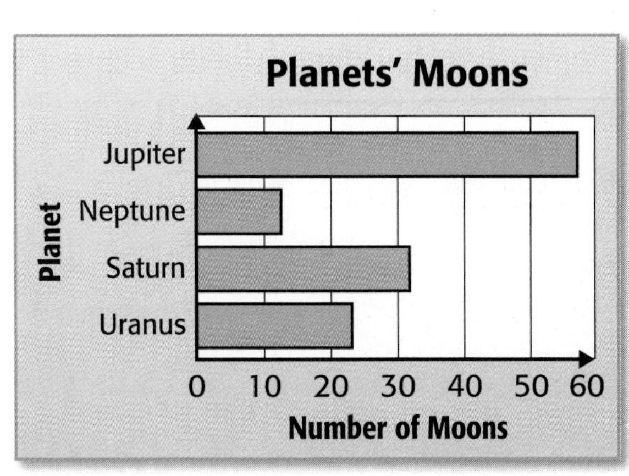

Extend

Statistics Activity for 4-7

Make a Line Graph

In the following activity, you will collect and represent data in a line graph.

MAIN IDEA

I will represent data in a line graph.

Standard 4SDAP1.1 Formulate survey questions; systematically collect and **represent data on a** number line; and **coordinate graphs,** tables, and charts.

Standard 4MR2.3 Use a variety of methods, such as words, numbers, symbols, charts, **graphs, tables,** diagrams, and models, **to explain mathematical reasoning.**

You Will Need

colored pencils
grid paper
newspaper

Animation
ca.gr4math.com

ACTIVITY

Step 1 Collect data.

Collect weather data from one day. Record the temperatures in a table like the one shown.

Time	Temperature (°F)
9 A.M.	
10 A.M.	
11 A.M.	
12 P.M.	
1 P.M.	

Step 2 Create a graph.

Draw two axes and label them. Then write a title at the top of the graph. Choose an appropriate scale for your graph.

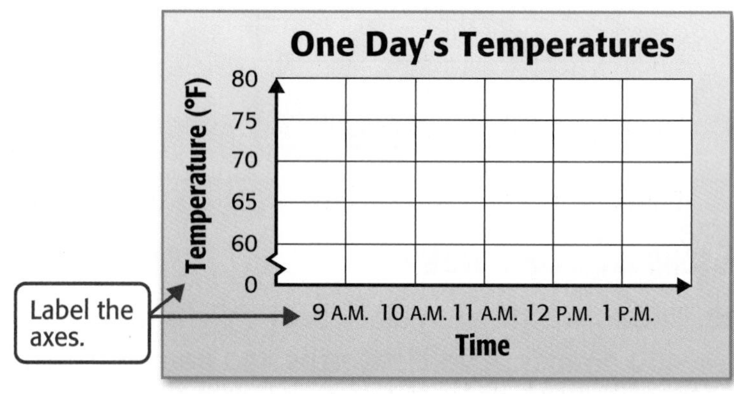

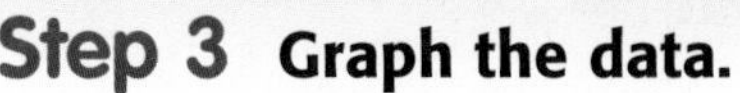

Step 3 Graph the data.

Above 9 A.M., place a point at the correct temperature. For example, if the high was 60, then place a point at 60. Continue graphing the rest of the data. An example is shown.

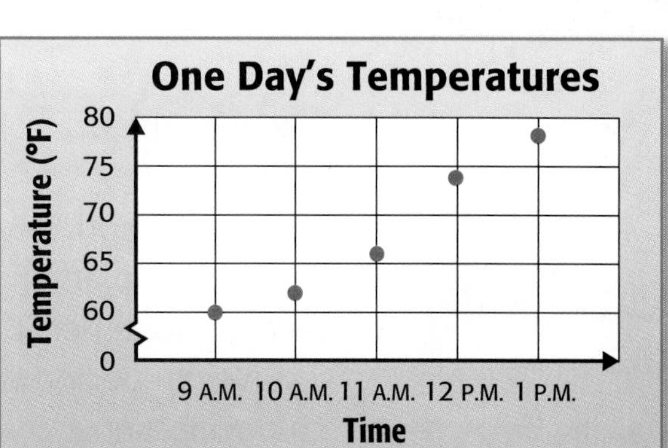

Step 4 Draw a line.

Connect the points with straight lines.

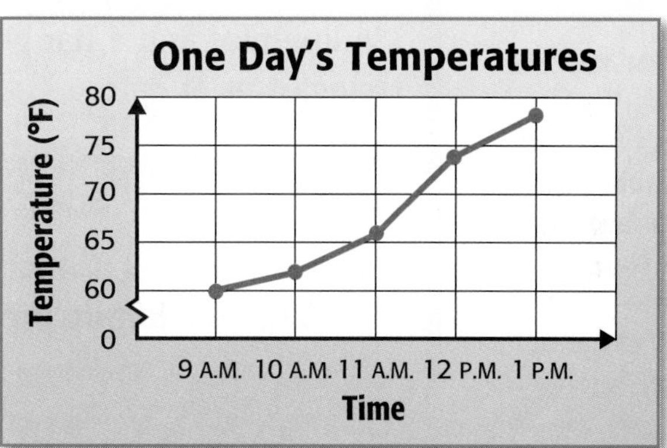

Think About It

1. Describe how a line graph shows how data changes over time.
2. Explain how you labeled the axes and chose a scale for the data.

CHECK What You Know

Represent each data set in a line graph.

3.

Plant Growth	
Week	**Height (in.)**
1	1
2	2
3	3
4	5
5	8

4.

One Day's Temperatures	
Time	**Temperature (°F)**
12 P.M.	62°
1 P.M.	65°
2 P.M.	72°
3 P.M.	66°
4 P.M.	64°

5. **WRITING IN MATH** Give an example of a set of data that is best displayed in a line graph.

4-8 Analyze Graphs

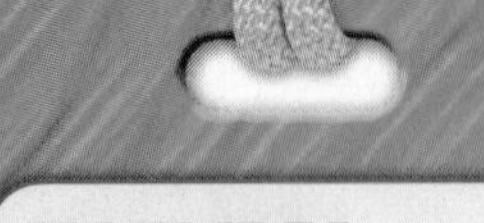

MAIN IDEA

I will use graphs to display different kinds of data.

Standard 4SDAP1.3 **Interpret one-** and two-**variable data graphs to answer questions about a situation.**

Standard 4SDAP1.1 **Formulate survey questions; systematically collect and represent data on a number line; and coordinate graphs, tables and charts.**

GET READY to Learn

The Brooks and Sanchez families are planning a vacation together. They take a survey to decide where to go on vacation.

A line plot and a bar graph can be used to display a single set of data.

Real-World EXAMPLE Analyze a Line Plot

1 **VACATIONS** **Which trip do more of the Brooks and Sanchez family members prefer to take?**

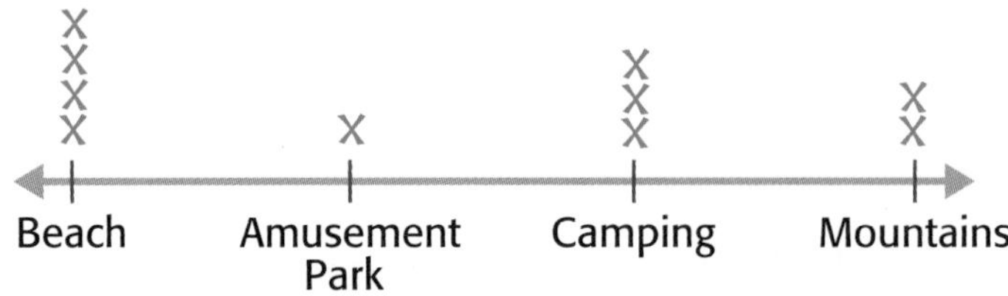

More family members prefer to go to the beach.

Real-World EXAMPLE Analyze a Bar Graph

2 **VACATIONS** **The bar graph shows the families' favorite beach activities. Which activity is the most popular?**

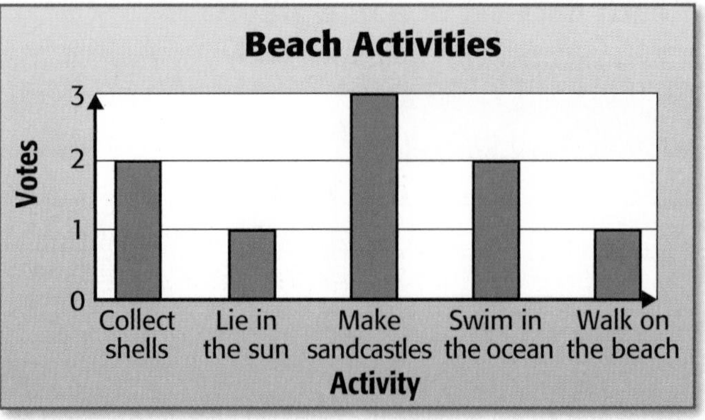

So, the most popular activity is making sandcastles.

A line graph is the best way to display change over time.

Real-World EXAMPLE **Analyze a Line Graph**

3 **VACATIONS The families enjoy temperatures in the 70s. Find which time of day would be best for visiting the beach.**

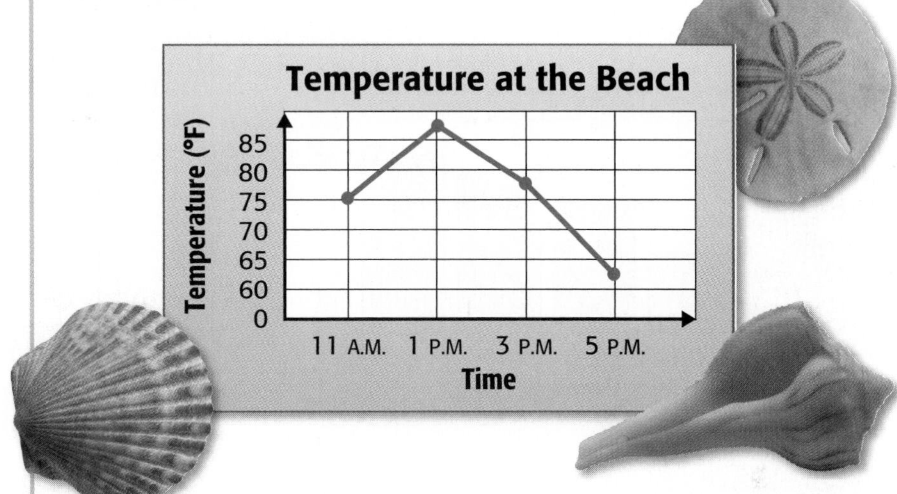

So, the families would enjoy visiting the beach between 11 A.M. and 12 P.M. or between 3 P.M. and 4 P.M.

Online **Personal Tutor at** ca.gr4math.com

Remember

Each type of graph can display different types of data.

You can make a graph to analyze the results of a survey.

Hands-On Mini Activity

Step 1 Create a survey question.

Step 2 Conduct your survey, recording the results in a tally chart.

Step 3 Display the survey results in either a line plot, bar graph, or line graph.

Use your graph to answer each question.

1. Explain why you chose the type of graph you made to display your data results.

2. Write two sentences that describe the data in your graph.

3. What are the most and least popular answers to your survey questions? How many classmates gave each?

CHECK What You Know

For Exercises 1–3, use each graph. See Examples 1–3 (pp. 156–157)

1. What was the average amount of time an American spent watching movies in 2006?

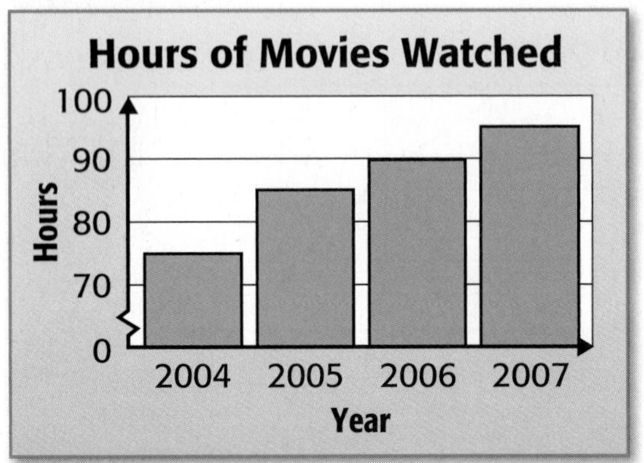

2. About how many more people were at the pool at 1 P.M. than at 4 P.M.?

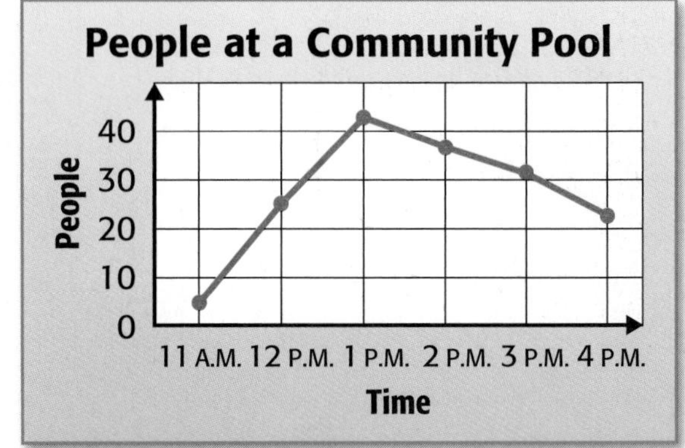

3. The line plot shows the coins Julieta has. How many coins does she have in all?

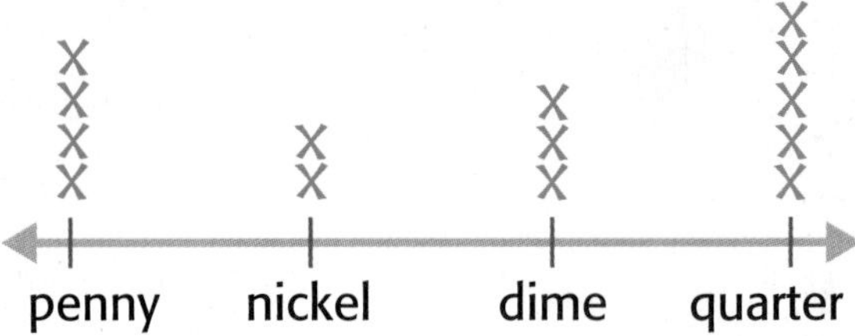

4. Talk About It Describe two different survey questions whose results could be displayed in a line plot.

Practice and Problem Solving

EXTRA PRACTICE See page R11.

For Exercises 5–9, use the bar graph that shows the type of radio music dog owners play for their dogs while they are not home.
See Examples 1–3 (pp. 156–157)

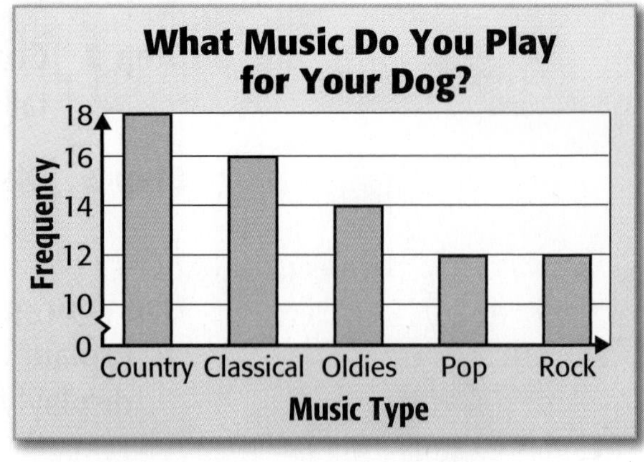

5. What was the most popular type of music?

6. How many dogs listen to oldies?

7. What is the total number of dogs that listen to pop and rock music?

8. How many more dogs listen to classical than rock music?

9. What two types of music do the same number of dogs listen to?

For Exercises 10–13, use the line plot that shows the number of raisins in a snack box. See Examples 1–3 (pp. 156–157)

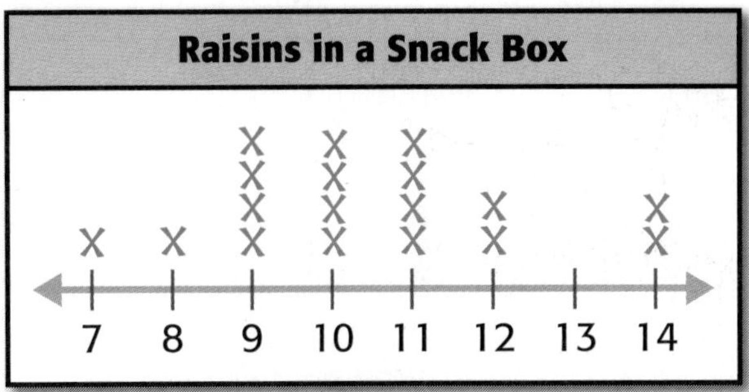

10. How many boxes had 13 raisins?

11. What is the greatest number of raisins in a box?

12. What number of raisins occurred most often?

13. How many boxes of raisins were examined?

Real-World PROBLEM SOLVING

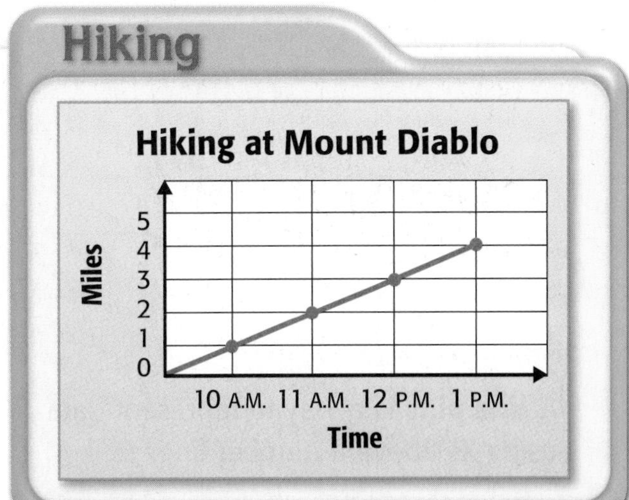

Data File Becky, Rico, and Sam are hiking and camping at Mount Diablo State Park.

14. How many miles were hiked between 10 A.M. and 1 P.M.?

15. At this rate, would the group hike six miles by 3 P.M.? Explain.

16. Suppose the group went hiking the next day at Annadel State Park and hiked twice the total miles that they hiked the day before. Create a possible line graph to show how much they hiked.

H.O.T. Problems

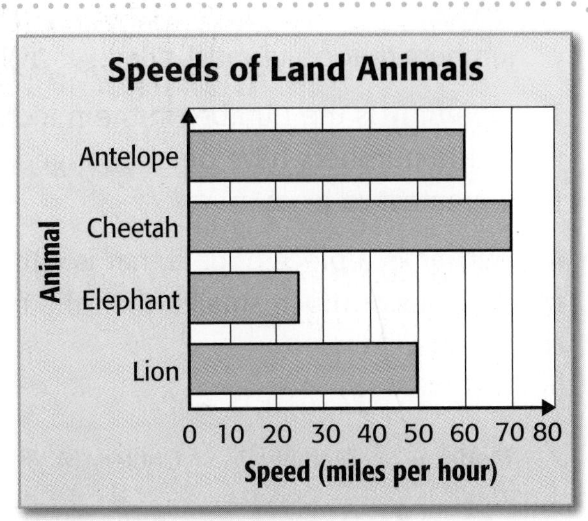

Source: www.worldalmanacforkids.com

17. OPEN ENDED Write one sentence that describes the data in the bar graph.

18. CHALLENGE Which animal can run twice as fast as the elephant? Explain.

19. WRITING IN MATH Choose one graph on pages 158–159 and write a problem in which addition needs to be used to find the answer. Tell which graph you used.

CHAPTER 4

Study Guide and Review

Be sure the following Key Vocabulary words and Key Concepts are written in your Foldable.

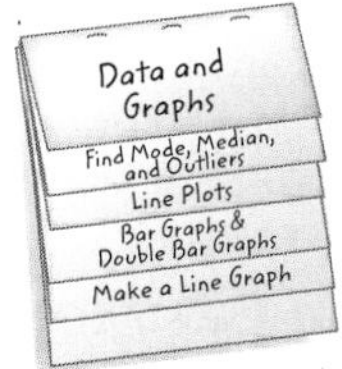

BIG Ideas

Displaying Data

- A **line plot** is a way to represent data using Xs above a number line. (p. 136)
- A **bar graph** allows you to compare data easily by looking at the bar heights. (p. 140)
- A **line graph** shows how data changes over time. (p. 150)

Mode, Median, and Outliers

- The **mode** of a set of data is the number or numbers that occur most often. (p. 130)
- The **median** is the number in the middle when the numbers have been arranged from greatest to least. (p. 130)
- An **outlier** is a piece of data that is either much larger or much smaller than the rest of the data. (p. 131)

14, 6, 8, 7, 6

Mode: 6   Median: 7   Outlier: 14

Key Vocabulary

bar graph (p. 140)
data (p. 127)
line graph (p. 150)
median (p. 130)
mode (p. 130)

Vocabulary Check

Match each phrase with the correct vocabulary word above.

1. A survey is a way to collect ____?____ .
2. The number in the middle of a set of data is the ____?____ .
3. It is easy to compare data by using the bars on a ____?____ .
4. In the data set (8, 7, 4, 6, 8), the ____?____ is 8.
5. A ____?____ shows how data changes over time.
6. In the data set (1, 4, 7, 9, 11), the ____?____ is 7.
7. A double ____?____ compares two sets of related data.
8. Graphs show ____?____ in different ways.

Math Online Vocabulary Review at ca.gr4math.com

Lesson-by-Lesson Review

4-1 Collect and Organize Data (pp. 127–129)

Example 1
Organize the data shown in a tally chart and frequency table.

Favorite Sports		
basketball	basketball	track
basketball	softball	volleyball
basketball	softball	volleyball
basketball	softball	volleyball
basketball	track	volleyball

Favorite Sports	
Sport	**Tally**
Softball	|||
Track	||
Basketball	~~||||~~ |
Volleyball	||||

Favorite Sports	
Sport	**Frequency**
Softball	3
Track	2
Basketball	6
Volleyball	4

Organize the data shown in a tally chart and frequency table.

9. Family members were asked what they wanted to do after dinner.

After Dinner Activity		
nap	read	game
game	nap	read
game	game	read
read	game	game

10. Fourth graders voted for Student Council President.

Votes for President		
Tom	Monica	Lamar
Monica	Tom	Tom
Tom	Monica	Monica
Lamar	Monica	Lamar

4-2 Find Mode, Median, and Outliers (pp. 130–133)

Example 2
Find the mode and median for the data set 50, 50, 51, 53, 95. Identify any outliers.

Order from least to greatest.

50, 50, 51, 53, 95

The mode occurs most often: 50.
The median is the number in the middle: 51.
The outlier is the number that lies outside of the data: 95.

Find the mode and median of the set of data. Identify any outliers.

11. Hours of practice each week: 3, 8, 2, 4, 3

12. Wild birds seen at a state park: 54, 17, 15, 16, 15

13. The number of students in Mr. Parker's class who brought lunches this week: 8, 6, 5, 7, 17

4-3 Problem-Solving Strategy: Make a Table (pp. 134–135)

Example 3
Students are going on a class trip. There are 140 students going, and 28 students fit on each bus. How many buses are needed?

Understand

You know that 140 students are going, and each bus holds 28 students. Find the number of buses needed.

Plan You can make a table.

Solve

Bus	Students
1	28
2	56
3	84
4	112
5	140

+28 +28 +28 +28

So, 5 buses are needed.

Check Use subtraction to check.

$$
\begin{array}{rl}
140 & \\
-\ 28 & \text{one bus} \\
\hline
112 & \\
-\ 28 & \text{one bus} \\
\hline
84 & \\
-\ 28 & \text{one bus} \\
\hline
56 & \\
-\ 28 & \text{one bus} \\
\hline
28 & \\
-\ 28 & \text{one bus} \\
\hline
0 &
\end{array}
$$

Subtracting 28 from 140 five times equals 0. So, the answer makes sense.

Solve the problems using a table.

14. **Algebra** Jordan has to read a 125-page book by Friday. It is Sunday, and Jordan plans to read 25 pages each night. Will he finish reading the book by Friday? Explain.

Day	Pages Read
Sunday	25
Monday	50
Tuesday	75
Wednesday	■
Thursday	■

15. There are 26 cars waiting on the on-ramp to the freeway. A green light lets 2 cars on at a time. How many lights will it take before all the cars enter the freeway?

16. At Riverside Elementary, there are 346 students in the school who take the bus each day.

1 bus = 40 students

What is the least number of buses the school will need to transport children to and from the school?

17. Thirty-six students are going whitewater rafting. Each raft will hold 7 students. How many more students will be needed to fill each raft with 7 people?

4-4 Line Plots (pp. 136–138)

Example 4
Organize the information from the frequency table in a line plot.

Children at the Park				
1	5	6	6	3
3	2	3	4	2
2	4	5	2	
6	3	6	7	
7	2	1	6	
5	6	6	5	

Children at the Park

1	2	3	4	5	6	7
XX	XXXXX	XXXX	XX	XXXX	XXXXXXXX	XX

Organize each set of data in a line plot.

18.

Phone Calls Made Each Day	
Day	**Calls**
Monday	3
Tuesday	2
Wednesday	5
Thursday	7
Friday	4

19.

Canned Goods Collected Each Month			
27	26	24	24
30	33	28	26
25	29	30	28

4-5 Bar and Double Bar Graphs (pp. 140–142)

Example 5
About how many rolls of wrapping paper did the third grade sell?

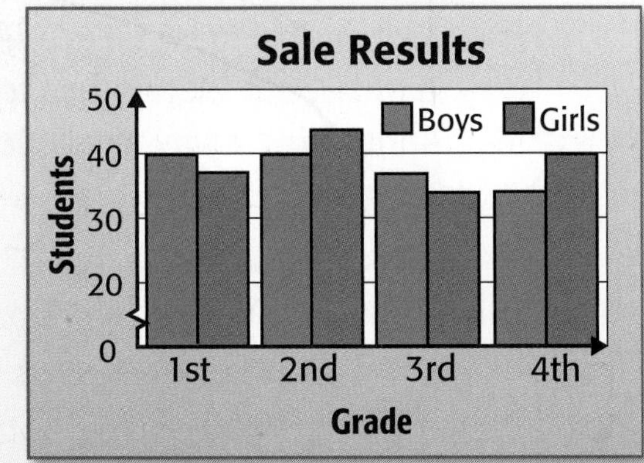

35 + 40 = 75
So, about 75 rolls of wrapping paper were sold.

For Exercises 20 and 21, use the graph.

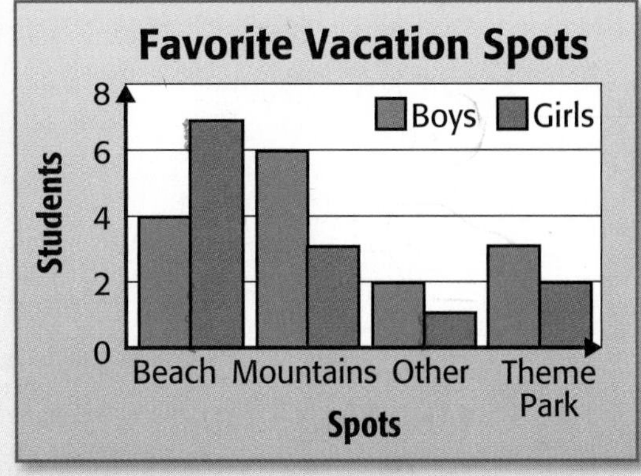

20. What is the most popular spot?

21. What is the difference in number of students who liked the most popular and least popular vacation spots?

4-6 Problem-Solving Investigation: Choose a Strategy (pp. 148–149)

Example 6
Pia wants to earn $75. If she earns $15 each time she babysits, how many times will she have to babysit in order to earn $75?

Understand

Pia earns $15 each time she babysits. She wants to earn $75. Find the number of days Pia needs to babysit to earn $75.

Plan Organize the data in a table to solve the problem.

Solve

Day	Money Earned
1	$15
2	$30
3	$45
4	$60
5	$75

Pia will have to babysit 5 times to earn $75.

Check $75 – $15 = $60
$60 – $15 = $45
$45 – $15 = $30
$30 – $15 = $15
$15 – $15 = $0

Subtracting $15 from $75 five times equals 0. So, the answer makes sense.

Use any strategy to solve.

22. Marcos has 19 baseball hats. Rashid has 5 more than Marcos. Shelly has 2 less than Rashid. How many baseball hats does Shelly have?

23. Geometry What 4 shapes could come next in the pattern?

24. The sum of two numbers is 14. The difference between those same two numbers is 0. What are the two numbers?

25. Geometry What shape could be tenth in the pattern if it continues?

26. Grant's favorite video game takes him 132 minutes to win. Each level takes Grant about 22 minutes to clear. About how many levels does his video game have?

27. Doria works at a sandwich shop. There are 3 different kinds of bread and 5 different kinds of meat to choose from. How many different sandwiches can be made using one bread and one meat?

4-7 Interpret Line Graphs (pp. 150–153)

Example 7
Measurement The graph shows hourly temperature data. Find the warmest and coldest temperature.

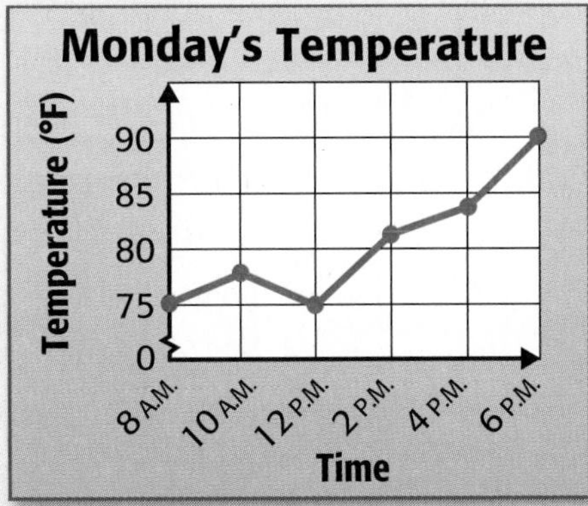

The warmest temperature occurs at the highest point on the graph. So, the warmest temperature is 90° F.

The coldest temperature occurs at the lowest point on the graph. So, the lowest temperature is 75° F.

Example 8
Measurement Use the graph above. What temperature occurs twice?

Look for the points on the graph that represent the same temperature.

A temperature of 75° F occurs at 8 A.M. and 12 P.M.

So, the temperature that occurs twice is 75° F.

Measurement For Exercises 28–30, use the line graph below.

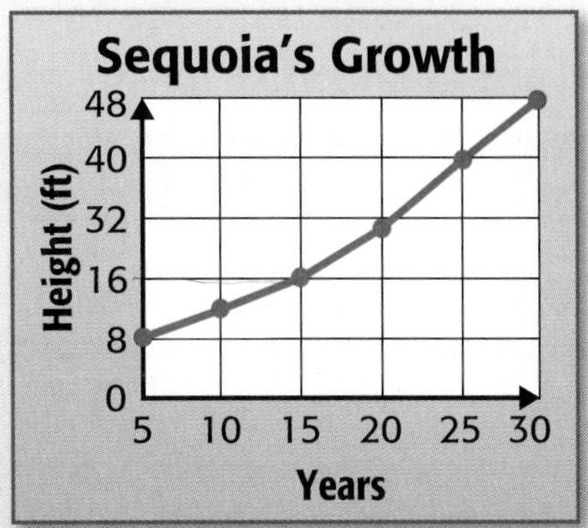

28. What was the highest height the tree reached?

29. How old was the tree when it was 16 feet tall?

30. How tall was the tree when it was 25 years old?

Measurement For Exercises 31–32, use the line graph that shows the distance traveled by a riverboat.

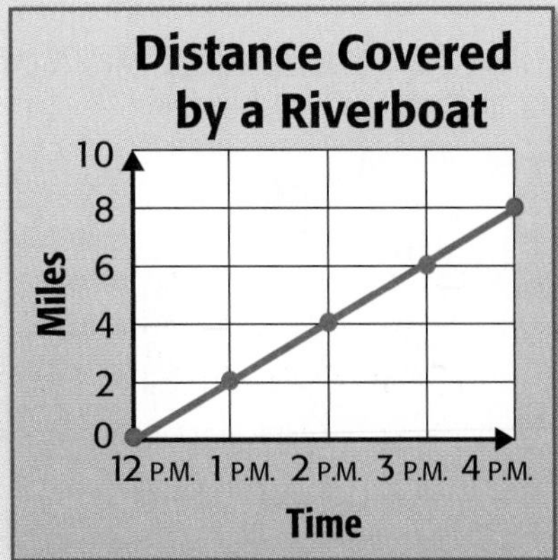

31. How many miles were traveled altogether?

32. How many more miles were traveled at 4 P.M. than at 1 P.M.?

4-8 Analyze Graphs (pp. 156–159)

Example 9

The line plot shows the snowfall for one week. What was the total amount of snowfall for the week?

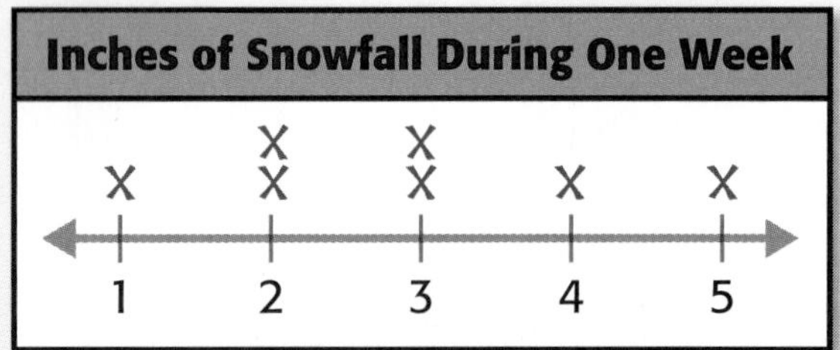

To find the total amount of snowfall, add the value of each X.

$1 + 2 + 2 + 3 + 3 + 4 + 5 = 20$

So, the amount of snow that fell in one week was 20 inches.

Example 10

The bar graph shows the amount of time spent playing different sports. Which sport was played twice as long as another sport?

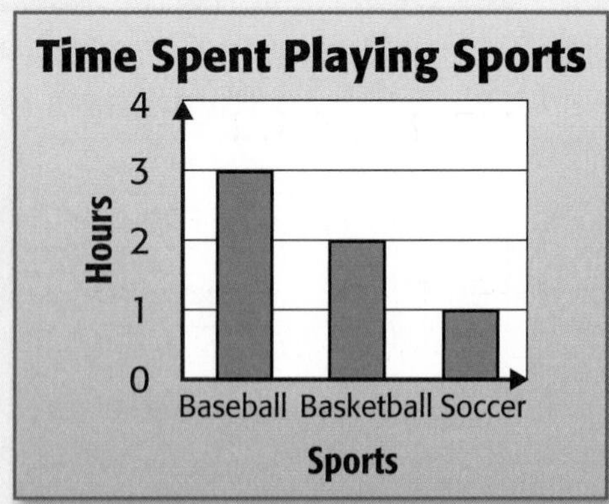

Basketball was played for 2 hours. Soccer was played for one hour. So, basketball was played twice as long as soccer. $1 \times 2 = 2$.

Measurement For Exercises 33–35, use the graph that shows the weights of mammals.

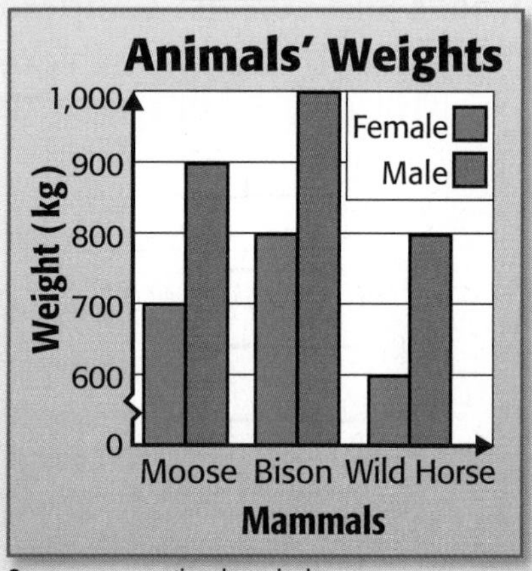

Source: www.nationalzoo.si.edu

33. About how much does a female moose weigh?

34. About how much less does a female bison weigh than a male bison?

35. About how much more does a male moose weigh than a male wild horse?

For Exercises 36 and 37, use the line plot that shows the ages of Mario's friends.

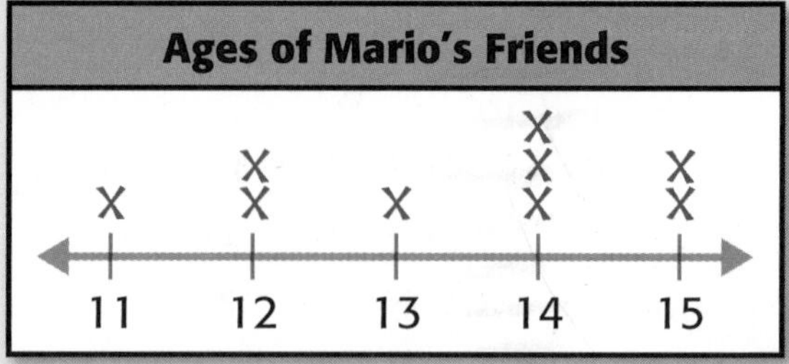

36. What is the mode for the data set?

37. What is the median?

Chapter 4 Chapter Test

For Exercises 1–3, tell whether each statement is *true* or *false*.

1. A double bar graph displays two sets of related data using bars of different colors and heights.

2. A line graph can not be used to make predictions about future events.

3. A line plot is used to display double sets of data.

Find the mode and median of each set of data.

4. 1, 9, 4, 1, 2

5. 12, 10, 15, 10, 11

6. **STANDARDS PRACTICE** Identify the median of the data below.

One-Mile Race Times	
Name	**Minutes**
Rosie	11
Michael	7
Erica	11
Janu	9
Nicole	8

A 7 minutes
B 8 minutes
C 9 minutes
D 11 minutes

Make a table to solve each problem.

7. A car needs an oil change every 3 months. Joe's car has had 4 oil changes so far. How many months have passed?

8. How much money will Kendall save if he saves $35 a month for a year?

For Execises 9 and 10, use the line graph that shows the distance traveled by a dragonfly.

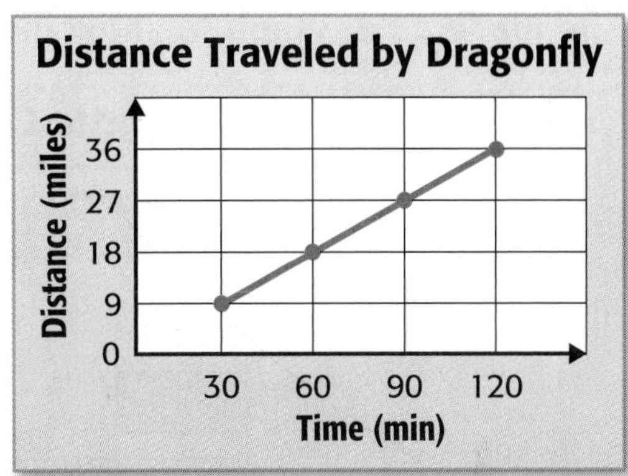

9. How many miles does a dragonfly travel in an hour?

10. At this rate, how many miles will a dragonfly travel in three hours?

11. **STANDARDS PRACTICE** A set of data has a mode of 1, a median of 2, and an outlier of 7. What is the data?

F 7, 7, 2, 1, 2, 7, 1
G 2, 1, 7, 2, 2, 2, 2
H 3, 2, 1, 2, 1, 7, 1
J 1, 7, 2, 1, 1, 1, 1

12. **WRITING IN MATH** Write two sentences that describe the data below.

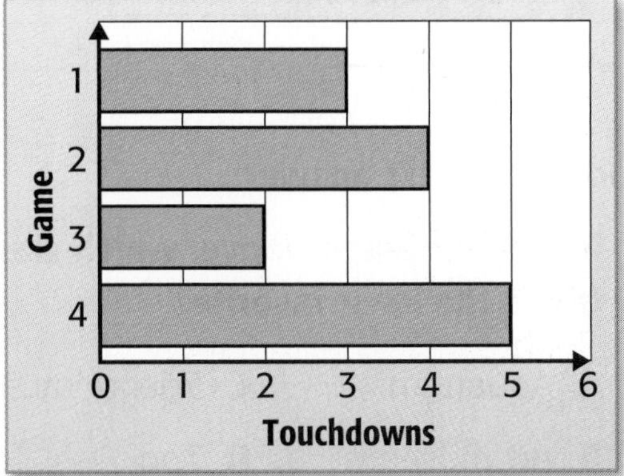

CHAPTER 4 California Standards Practice

Cumulative, Chapters 1–4

Standards Example

Marla asked her class about their favorite class trip. She made a bar graph to show the results.

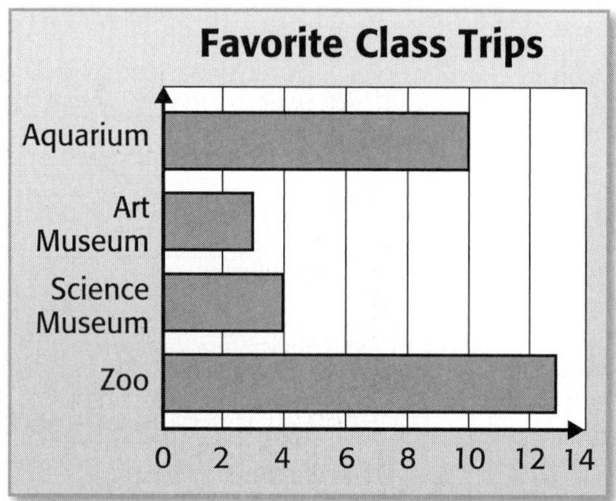

How many more students prefer going to the zoo than to the science museum?

A 3 **C** 7

B 6 **D** 9

Read the Question

Find how many more students prefer going to the zoo than the science museum. To do this, subtract.

Solve the Question

$13 - 4 = 9$

So, the answer is D.

 **Personal Tutor at** ca.gr4math.com

Choose the best answer.

1 **In the bar graph above, which class trip is the least favorite?**

A Aquarium **C** Science museum

B Art museum **D** Zoo

2 **What is the median of the data set {3, 5, 7, 2, 2, 4, 6}?**

F 3 **H** 5

G 4 **J** 6

3 **Ron sold lemonade at soccer practice. On which two days did he sell the least amount of lemonade?**

Lemonade Sales	
Day	**Tally**
Monday	𝍸 ||||
Tuesday	||||
Wednesday	𝍸 |
Thursday	||||
Friday	𝍸 |||

A Monday and Friday

B Wednesday and Friday

C Tuesday and Thursday

D Thursday and Friday

4 **What is 736,249 rounded to the nearest hundred?**

F 736,000 **H** 736,250

G 736,200 **J** 740,000

5 **What is the median of the shoe sizes shown in the data set {6, 4, 5, 8, 5}?**

A 3 **C** 5

B 4 **D** 6

6 **What is the value of the digit 9 in 169,328,457?**

F 900,000 **H** 90,000,000

G 9,000,000 **J** 900,000,000

7 **Which number is represented by n?**

$$924 - n = 388$$

A 536 **C** 1204

B 646 **D** 1312

8 **The table shows the number of visitors at the history museum. How many visitors went to the history museum in April and June?**

History Museum	
Month	**Number of Visitors**
March	3459
April	2763
May	6284
June	4375

F 1612 **H** 7032

G 6038 **J** 7138

9 **9485 − 6208 = ▢**

A 15,693 **C** 3277

B 15,267 **D** 3183

10 **What is the mode of the data shown in the line plot?**

Favorite Colors

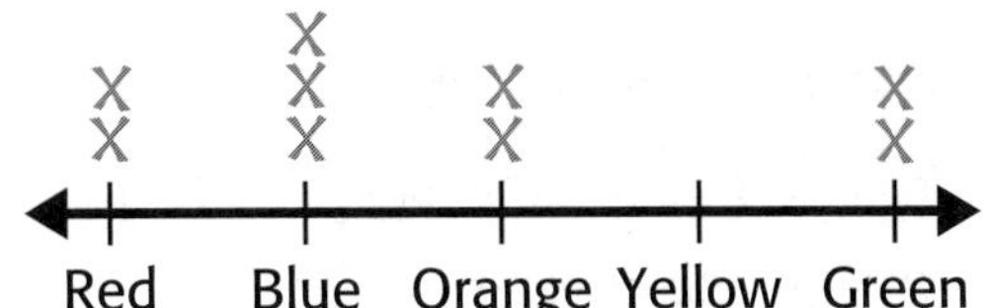

F Red **H** Orange

G Blue **J** Green

CHAPTER 5

Multiplication and Division Facts

BIG Idea What are multiplication and division?

Multiplication means to find the total of equal groups.
Division means to separate an amount into equal groups.

Example Two years on Earth is about one year on Mars. Andrés is 10 years old. If he lived on Mars, he would be 10 ÷ 2 or 5 years old.

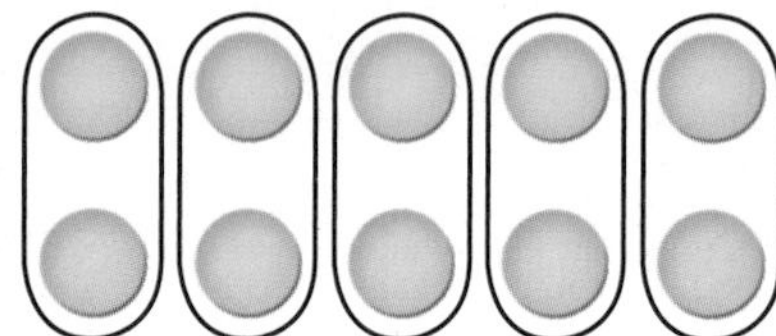

10 ÷ 2 means to separate 10 into equal groups of 2.
10 ÷ 2 = 5

What will I learn in this chapter?

- Use multiplication and division properties.
- Understand how multiplication and division are related.
- Multiply and divide facts through 12.
- Identify factors and multiples.
- Choose an operation to solve problems.

Key Vocabulary

Commutative Property of Multiplication
Associative Property of Multiplication
factor
multiple
Distributive Property of Multiplication

Student Study Tools at ca.gr4math.com

FOLDABLES™
Study Organizer

Make this Foldable to help you organize information about multiplication and division. Begin with four sheets of $8\frac{1}{2}'' \times 11''$ paper.

1. **Stack** 4 sheets of paper. Place each sheet $\frac{3}{4}$ inch apart.

2. **Roll** up the edges, so all tabs are the same size.

3. **Crease** and staple along the fold.

4. **Label** the tabs with the topics from the chapter.

Multiplication and Division Facts
Properties
Facts Through 5
Facts Through 10
Multiply by 11 and 12
Multiply Three Numbers
Factors & Multiples
Prime & Composite Numbers

ARE YOU READY for Chapter 5?

You have two ways to check prerequisite skills for this chapter.

Option 2

Math Online Take the Chapter Readiness Quiz at ca.gr4math.com.

Option 1

Complete the Quick Check below.

QUICK Check

Algebra Complete each number sentence. (Lesson 3-2)

1. $4 + 4 + 4 = \blacksquare$
2. $6 + 6 + \blacksquare + 6 = 24$
3. $9 + 9 + 9 = 3 \times \blacksquare$
4. $11 + 11 + 11 + 11 = \blacksquare \times 11$
5. Write the multiplication fact modeled by the array at the right.

Copy each array. Then circle equal groups of 3. (Prior grade)

6. ☆☆☆☆
☆☆☆☆
☆☆☆☆
7. ☾☾☾☾☾☾
☾☾☾☾☾☾
☾☾☾☾☾☾
☾☾☾☾☾☾
8. Marcia has 15 action figures. If Marcia places the figures in 3 equal rows, how many figures will be in each row?

The number patterns below are formed by skip counting. Copy and complete each pattern. (Prior grade)

9. 2, 4, 6, ■, 10, ■, 14
10. 4, 8, 12, ■, 20, 24, ■
11. 5, ■, 15, 20, ■, 30, ■
12. ■, 18, 27, ■, 45, 54, ■
13. Write a number pattern that involves skip counting. Describe the pattern.

Math Activity for 5-1

Meaning of Multiplication and Division

MAIN IDEA

I will use models to explore the meaning of multiplication and division.

Standard 4NS3.0 **Students solve problems involving** addition, subtraction, **multiplication, and division of whole numbers** and understand the relationships among the operations.

Standard 4MR3.3 **Develop generalizations of the results obtained and apply them in other circumstances.**

You Will Need
counters
cups

Concepts in Motion
Animation
ca.gr4math.com

You can use models to help you understand the meaning of multiplication and division.

ACTIVITY

1 Find 3 × 4.

Step 1 **Model 3 × 4.**

To model 3 × 4, arrange counters in an array with 3 rows and 4 columns.

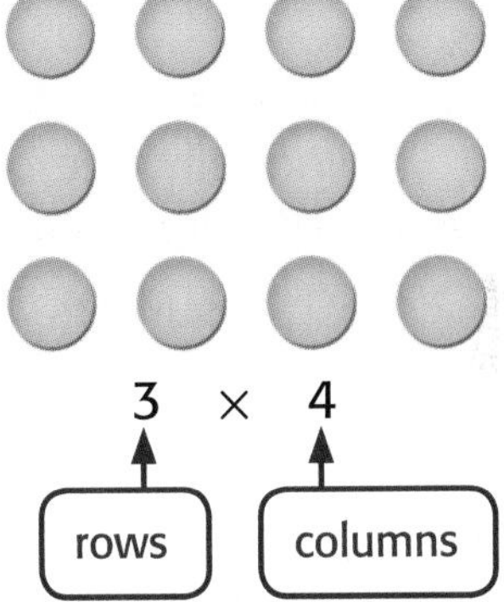

Step 2 **Use repeated addition to find 3 × 4.**

Add 3 rows of 4 counters.

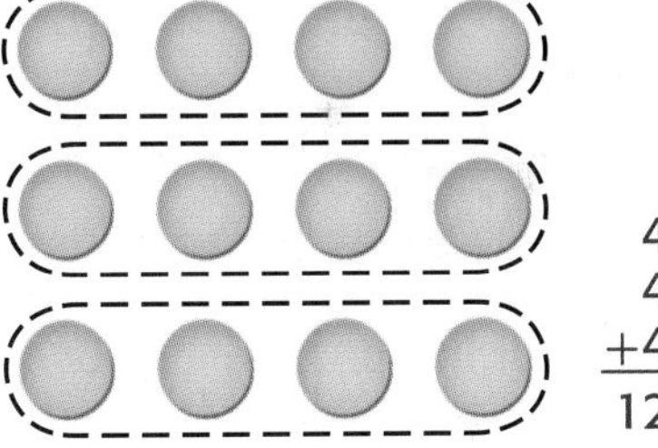

Step 3 **Make the connection.**

Multiplication and repeated addition result in the same answer.

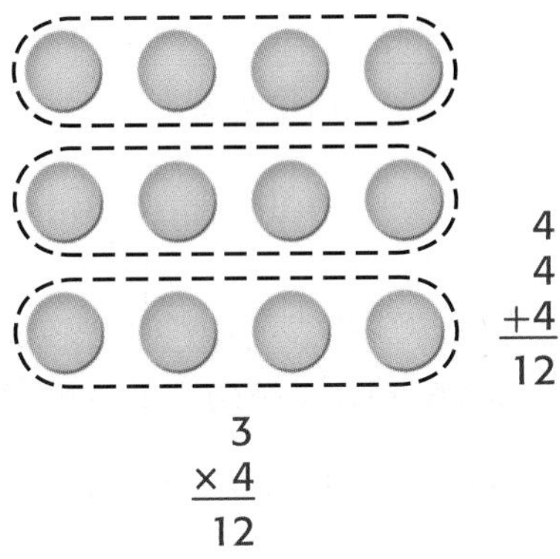

So, 3 (factor) × 4 (factor) = 12 (product).

ACTIVITY

2 Find 15 ÷ 3.

Step 1 Model 15 ÷ 3.

Use 15 counters. Put the counters in 3 rows since the divisor is 3.

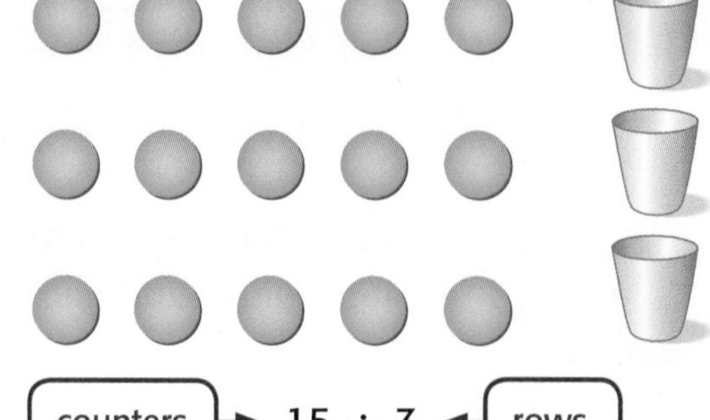

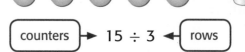

counters → 15 ÷ 3 ← rows

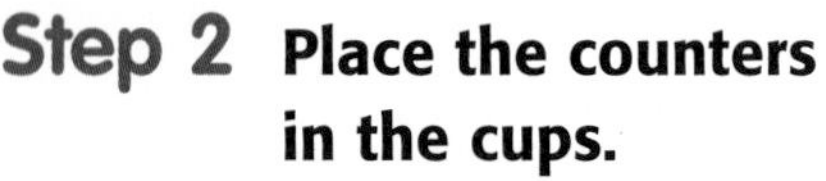

Step 2 Place the counters in the cups.

Divide the counters equally one by one into the cups until all 15 counters are gone.

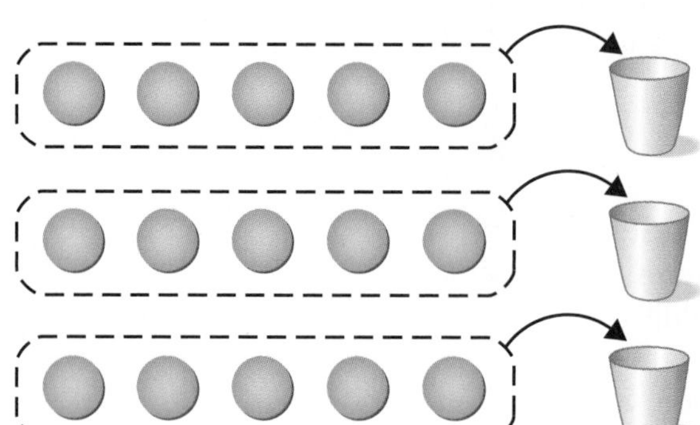

Step 3 Find 15 ÷ 3.

There are 5 counters in each cup.

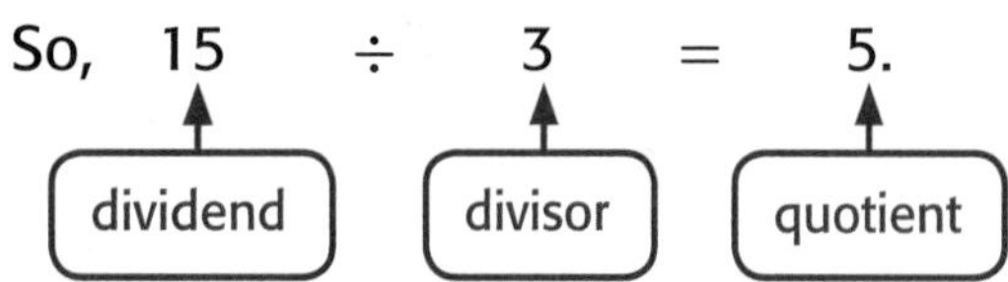

So, 15 ÷ 3 = 5.

Think About It

1. How would you model 2 × 8?

2. How would you model 10 ÷ 5?

CHECK What You Know

Use models to multiply or divide.

3. 3 × 7

4. 6 ÷ 3

5. 6 × 8

6. 24 ÷ 6

7. **WRITING IN MATH** Explain how to model 4 groups of 9. Write a number sentence to show the total amount in 4 groups of 9.

Relate Multiplication and Division

MAIN IDEA

I will understand how multiplication and division are related.

Standard 4NS3.0 Students solve problems involving addition, subtraction, **multiplication, and division of whole numbers and understand the relationships among the operations.**

Standard 4MR2.3 Use a variety of methods, such as words, **numbers,** symbols, charts, graphs, tables, diagrams, **and models, to explain mathematical reasoning.**

New Vocabulary

fact family

GET READY to Learn

Latanya and her father are baking. Her father asks her how many eggs they have. The eggs in the carton are arranged in an array.

You can write related multiplication and division sentences to describe the array of eggs.

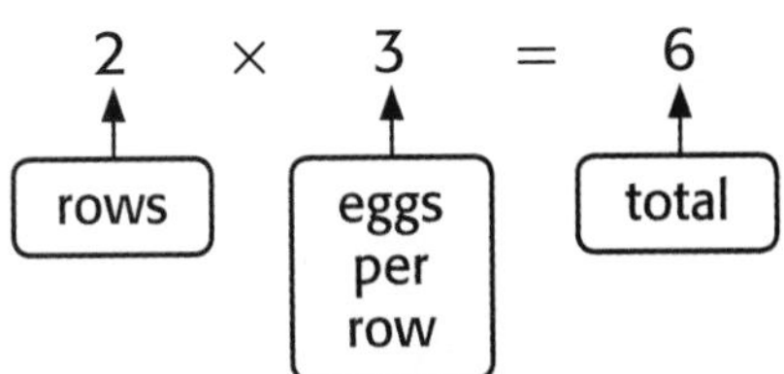

3 × 2 = 6

rows — eggs per row — total

6 ÷ 3 = 2

total — eggs per row — rows

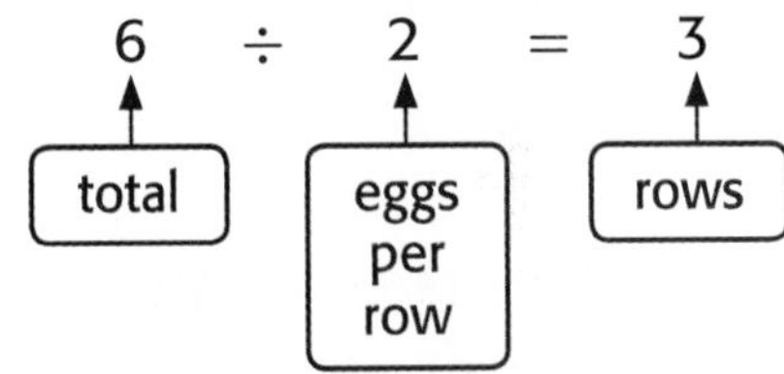

The number sentences above show a fact family. A **fact family** is a set of four related multiplication and division facts that use the same three numbers.

EXAMPLE **Write a Fact Family**

1 **Write a fact family for the array.**

There are 3 rows, 4 columns, and a total of 12 objects.

$3 \times 4 = 12$ $4 \times 3 = 12$

$12 \div 3 = 4$ $12 \div 4 = 3$

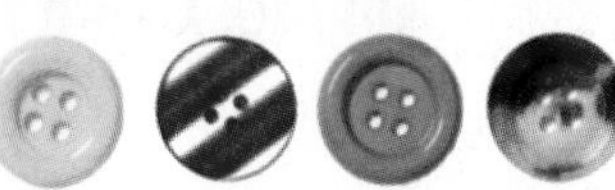

You can use a related multiplication fact to help you divide.

Remember

An array is a set of objects or symbols that are displayed in rows and columns.

Real-World EXAMPLE — Use Related Facts

2 BOOKS **Vanesa has 36 books to put on 4 shelves. The same number of books will be placed on each shelf. How many books will be on each shelf?**

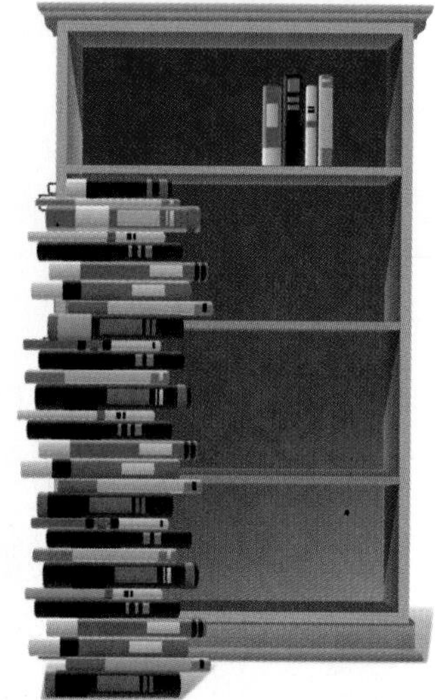

Find 36 ÷ 4. You can use a related multiplication fact to help you divide.

36 ÷ 4 = ■

What number times 4 is 36?

36 ÷ 4 = 9

So, Vanesa will place 9 books on each shelf.

Online **Personal Tutor at** ca.gr4math.com

CHECK What You Know

Write a fact family for each array or set of numbers. See Example 1 (p. 175)

1.

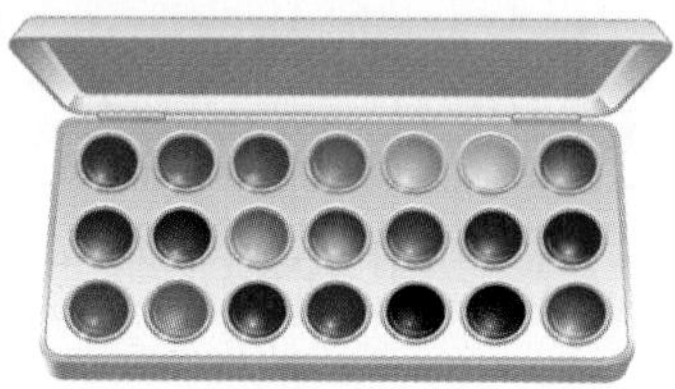

2.

3. 6, 8, 48

4. 3, 12, 4

Algebra Copy and complete each fact family. See Example 1 (p. 175)

5. 3 × 6 = ■   6 × ■ = 18

18 ÷ ■ = 3   18 ÷ 3 = ■

6. 5 × 7 = ■   ■ × 5 = 35

35 ÷ ■ = 7   35 ÷ 7 = ■

Algebra Divide. Use a related multiplication fact. See Example 2 (p. 176)

7. 22 ÷ 2 = ■

8. 27 ÷ 9 = ■

9. Ed wants to equally share 18 grapes among himself and two friends. How many grapes will each get?

10. Talk About It How are multiplication and division related? Use examples to support your answer.

Math Online **Extra Examples at** ca.gr4math.com

Practice and Problem Solving

EXTRA PRACTICE
See page R11.

Write a fact family for each array or set of numbers. See Example 1 (p. 175)

11. 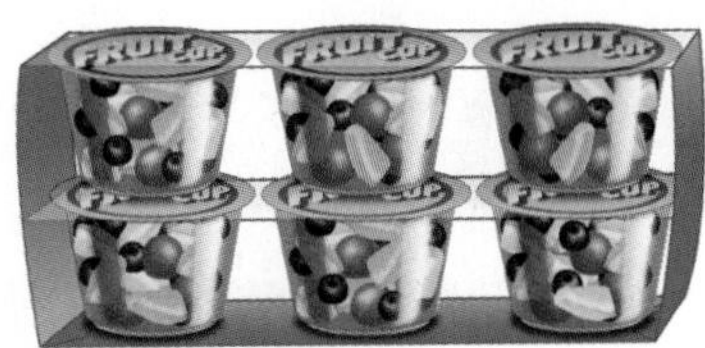

12. 

13. 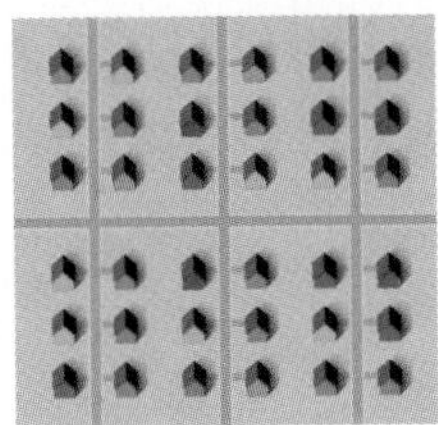

14. 

15. 6, 9, 54

16. 7, 8, 56

17. 9, 11, 99

18. 11, 12, 132

Algebra Copy and complete each fact family. See Example 1 (p. 175)

19. $4 \times 8 = ■$ $■ \times 4 = 32$ $32 \div ■ = 8$ $32 \div 8 = ■$

20. $■ \times 9 = 72$ $9 \times 8 = ■$ $72 \div ■ = 8$ $72 \div 8 = ■$

Algebra Divide. Use a related multiplication fact. See Example 2 (p. 176)

21. $18 \div 2 = ■$

22. $36 \div 6 = ■$

23. $63 \div 7 = ■$

24. $64 \div 8 = ■$

Real-World PROBLEM SOLVING

Data File The California quail became California's state bird in 1931.

25. The California quail gathers in groups, or coveys, of 10 to 20 birds. Suppose there are three coveys of 10 birds. How many quails are there in all?

26. The California quail can lay 6 to 16 eggs at a time. Suppose 18 eggs are found in different nests. There are 6 eggs in each nest. How many nests contained eggs?

Quail

H.O.T. Problem

27. WRITING IN MATH Explain how fact families and multiplication facts can help you solve division problems.

5-2 Algebra: Multiplication and Division Properties

MAIN IDEA

I will use multiplication and division properties.

Standard 4AF1.0 Students use and interpret variables, mathematical symbols, and **properties to** write and **simplify** expressions and **sentences.**

New Vocabulary

Commutative Property of Multiplication

Associative Property of Multiplication

Identity Property of Multiplication

Zero Property of Multiplication

GET READY to Learn

The table shows Jenny and Cliff's chores. Jenny earns \$3 for each chore and Cliff earns \$2 for each chore. How much does each person earn for completing chores?

Jenny \$3 per chore	Sanson \$2 per chore
Pack lunches	Set table
Take out trash	Clean room
Laundry	Walk dog
Clean room	Wash dishes
	Sweep floor

Multiplication also has properties similar to addition.

KEY CONCEPTS Multiplication Properties

Commutative Property of Multiplication

When multiplying, the order of the factors does not change the product.

$3 \times 2 = 6$
$2 \times 3 = 6$

Associative Property of Multiplication

The way in which the factors are grouped does not change the product.

$(5 \times 2) \times 3 = 30$
$5 \times (2 \times 3) = 30$

Identity Property of Multiplication

When any number is multiplied by 1, the product is that number.

$4 \times 1 = 4$

Zero Property of Multiplication

When any number is multiplied by 0, the product is 0.

$3 \times 0 = 0$

EXAMPLE Identify Properties

1 Identify the property shown by $8 \times 1 = 8$.

A number is multiplied by 1, and the product is that number. This is the Identity Property of Multiplication.

EXAMPLE Use Properties

2 **Complete $(4 \times 3) \times 2 = 4 \times (\blacksquare \times 2)$. Identify the property used.**

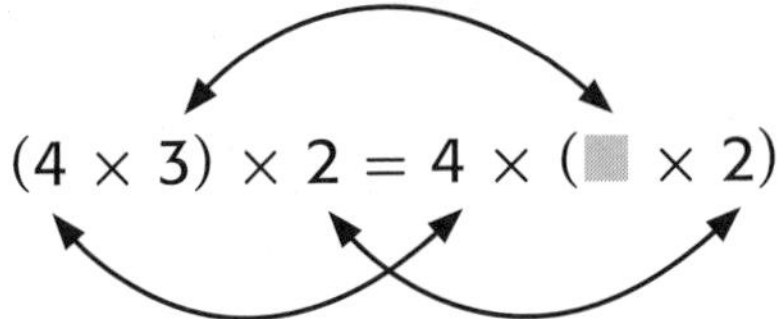

$(4 \times 3) \times 2 = 4 \times (\blacksquare \times 2)$

A 3 completes the number sentence. The way in which the factors are grouped does not change the product. This is the Associative Property of Multiplication.

Online Personal Tutor at ca.gr4math.com

The following facts can help you with division.

Remember

Quotient is the name of the answer for division problems.

KEY CONCEPTS — Division Facts

Zeros in Division

When you divide 0 by any number other than 0, the quotient is 0. $0 \div 5 = 0$

It is not possible to divide a number by 0. ~~$7 \div 0$~~

Ones in Division

When you divide any number by 1, the quotient is always the dividend. $8 \div 1 = 8$

When you divide any number by itself, the quotient is always 1. This is true for all numbers except 0. $9 \div 9 = 1$

Real-World EXAMPLE Use a Division Rule

3 **There are 9 party favors and 9 guests. How many party favors will each guest get?**

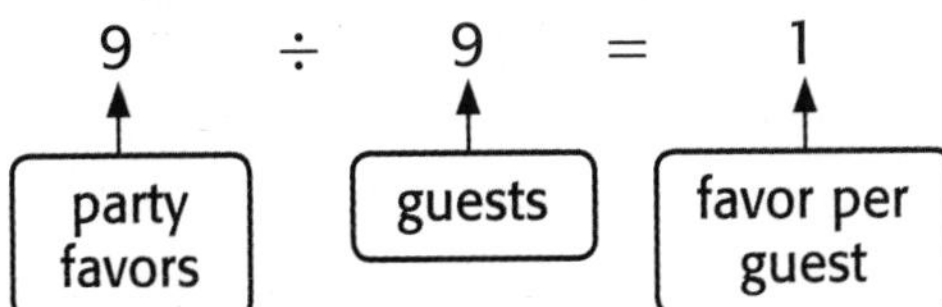

$9 \div 9 = 1$

party favors — guests — favor per guest

According to the rule, a non-zero number divided by the same number is 1. So, each guest will get 1 party favor.

What You Know

Identify the property shown by each number sentence.
See Examples 1–3 (pp. 178–179)

1. $12 \times 0 = 0$ **2.** $8 \times 5 = 5 \times 8$ **3.** $6 \div 1 = 6$

Algebra **Copy and complete each number sentence. Identify the property used.** See Example 2 (p. 174)

4. $7 \times ■ = 7$ **5.** $(7 \times 2) \times 3 = 7 \times (■ \times 3)$ **6.** $5 \div ■ = 1$

7. Brenda has 4 rows of 6 stickers. What is another way she can arrange the stickers? Write a number sentence.

8. Talk About It Explain why the Identity Property of Multiplication uses 1 while the Identity Property of Addition uses 0.

Practice and Problem Solving

Identify the property shown by each number sentence.
See Examples 1–3 (pp. 178–179)

9. $10 \div 10 = 1$ **10.** $6 \times (3 \times 4) = (6 \times 3) \times 4$ **11.** $8 \times 0 = 0$

12. $0 \div 12 = 0$ **13.** $(6 \times 3) \times 4 = (6 \times 4) \times 3$ **14.** $22 \times 1 = 22$

Algebra **Copy and complete each number sentence. Identify the property used.** See Example 2 (p. 179)

15. $3 \div ■ = 1$ **16.** $■ \times 8 = 8 \times 4$ **17.** $■ \div 11 = 0$

18. $3 \times (■ \times 6) = (3 \times 3) \times 6$ **19.** $15 \times ■ = 15$ **20.** $28 \times ■ = 0$

Real-World PROBLEM SOLVING

Hiking Write a number sentence for each situation. Then solve.

21. On their first hiking trip, Tamika and Brian hiked 7 miles a day. They hiked for 5 days. Kurt and Suki hiked 5 miles a day. How many days did it take Kurt and Suki to hike the same distance as Tamika and Brian?

22. On their second trip, Tamika and Brian hiked twice as long as they did on their first trip. How many days will Kurt and Suki need to hike to go the same distance as Tamika and Brian?

H.O.T. Problems

23. **OPEN ENDED** Using the same three numbers, write two different multiplication expressions with a product of 60.

24. **NUMBER SENSE** When finding the value of the expression $(2 \times 9) \times 5$, is it easier to find 2×9 or 2×5 first? Explain.

25. **WRITING IN ▸MATH** Marcie thinks it is easier to find $(7 \times 6) \times 2$ than to find $7 \times (6 \times 2)$. What property tells her that the number sentences are equal? Why might Marcie think it is easier to find the answer to the first number sentence?

Standards Practice

26 Luther's photo album has 6 pages with 8 photos on each page. Identify the number sentence that describes this situation. (Lesson 5-2)

A $8 \times 6 = 6 \times 8$

B $8 \times 6 > 6 \times 8$

C $8 \times 6 < 6 \times 8$

D $8 \times 8 > 6 \times 6$

27 Which number sentence is in the same fact family as $42 \div 7 = ■$? (Lesson 5-1)

F $7 + ■ = 42$

G $■ - 7 = 42$

H $7 \times ■ = 42$

J $42 \times 7 = 42$

Spiral Review

Algebra. Divide. Use a related multiplication fact. (Lesson 5-1)

28. $12 \div 3 = ■$

29. $16 \div 4 = ■$

30. $20 \div 5 = ■$

For Exercises 31 and 32, use the graph. (Lesson 4-8)

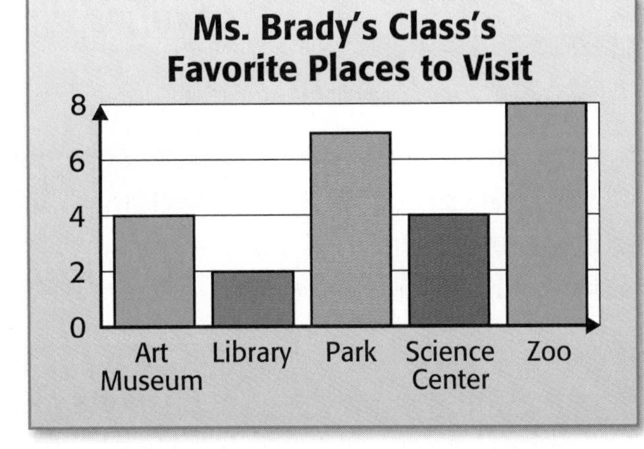

31. What is the most and least favorite place to visit?

32. Identify which two places to visit received a difference in votes of 5.

33. Fernando's two dogs eat 3 cups of food each day. How much food do his dogs eat in a week? Identify any extra or missing information. Then solve, if possible. (Lesson 3-3)

5-3 Multiply and Divide Facts Through 5

MAIN IDEA

I will recognize multiplication and division facts 0 through 5.

Standard 4NS3.0 Students solve problems involving addition, subtraction, **multiplication, and division of whole numbers** and understand relationships among the operations.

Standard 4MR2.3 Use a variety of methods, such as words, numbers, symbols, charts, graphs, tables, diagrams, **and models, to explain mathematical reasoning.**

GET READY to Learn

Charlotte is competing in a 3-mile race. Every 4 laps equals 1 mile. How many laps does she need to complete to finish the race?

To find the number of laps that Charlotte needs to complete, multiply. There are different strategies that can be used to multiply.

Real-World EXAMPLE Multiply

1 **How many laps does Charlotte need to complete in order to finish the race?**

You need to find 3×4.

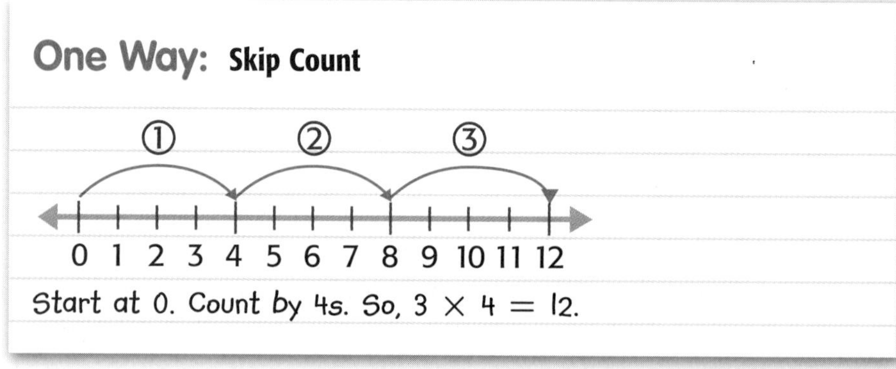

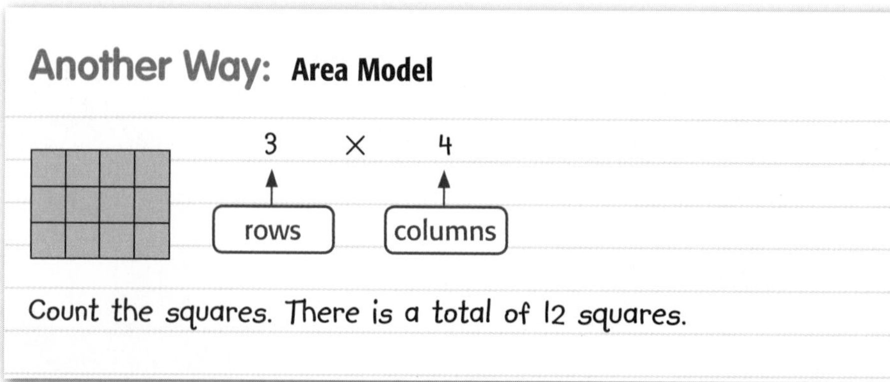

Another Way: Area Model
3 × 4
rows
columns
Count the squares. There is a total of 12 squares.

So, Charlotte must complete 12 laps in order to achieve a distance of 3 miles.

Online Personal Tutor at ca.gr4math.com

There are different strategies to use when finding division facts.

Real-World EXAMPLE Divide

2 **Omari has football practice 3 days a week. He drinks a sports drink during each practice. Suppose 12 sports drinks come in a package. How many weeks will a package of sports drinks last?**

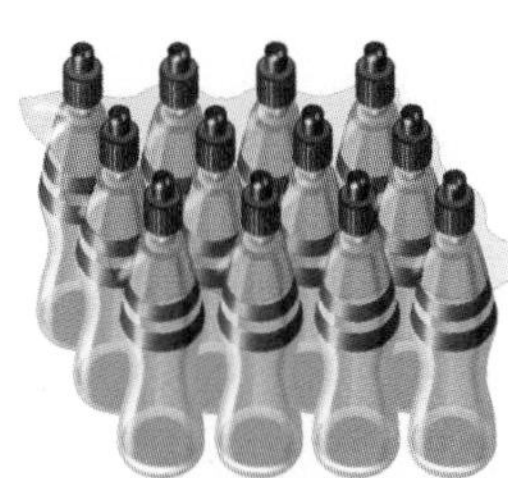

You need to find 12 ÷ 3.

Remember

You can also draw pictures, use a times table, or use models to help divide.

One Way: Repeated Subtraction

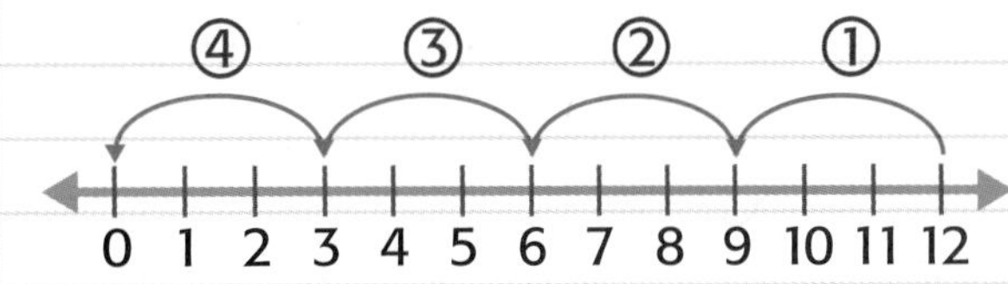

Start at 12. Count back by 3s until you reach 0. Count the number of times you subtracted. 12 ÷ 3 = 4

Another Way: Related Facts

12 ÷ 3 = ■

THINK 3 × ■ = 12?

12 ÷ 3 = 4

So, one package of sports drinks will last 4 weeks.

CHECK What You Know

Multiply or divide. See Examples 1 and 2 (pp. 182–183)

1. 5×3

2. 9×0

3. 1×5

4. 2×8

5. 6 ÷ 2

6. 24 ÷ 3

7. $5\overline{)10}$

8. $4\overline{)28}$

9. Nancy's dog gets 3 treats each day. There are 36 treats in a box. How many days will the treats last?

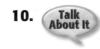

10. Talk About It What multiplication fact can help you find 9 ÷ 3? Explain.

Practice and Problem Solving

EXTRA PRACTICE
See page R12.

Multiply or divide. See Examples 1 and 2 (pp. 182–183)

11. $\begin{array}{r} 5 \\ \times\ 6 \\ \hline \end{array}$ **12.** $\begin{array}{r} 2 \\ \times\ 3 \\ \hline \end{array}$ **13.** $\begin{array}{r} 9 \\ \times\ 2 \\ \hline \end{array}$ **14.** $\begin{array}{r} 8 \\ \times\ 4 \\ \hline \end{array}$

15. 7×1 **16.** 3×7 **17.** 9×5 **18.** 4×11

19. $8 \div 1$ **20.** $10 \div 2$ **21.** $12 \div 3$ **22.** $32 \div 4$

23. $2\overline{)24}$ **24.** $3\overline{)33}$ **25.** $4\overline{)40}$ **26.** $5\overline{)60}$

Algebra Complete each number sentence.

27. $2 \times ■ = 2$ **28.** $■ \times 5 = 35$ **29.** $33 \div ■ = 11$ **30.** $■ \div 5 = 10$

Algebra Solve.

31. If ☆ = 3, then what is ☆☆☆☆☆☆☆ ?

32. If         = 45, then what is  ?

33. There are 5 sets of paint in an art class. There are 25 students in the art class. How many students share each set of paint?

34. Fumiko has 6 packs of baseball cards. There are 5 cards in each pack. How many baseball cards does Fumiko have?

Real-World PROBLEM SOLVING

Technology The number of computers in classrooms is increasing. The results of a recent study are shown to the right.

http://
One computer for every 4 students in a classroom.

35. There are 5 computers in a fourth grade classroom. The number of students per computer matches the results of the study. How many students are in this classroom?

36. There are 24 students in Mr. Montoya's class. The number of computers per student matches the results of the study. How many computers are in Mr. Montoya's class?

H.O.T. Problems

37. OPEN ENDED Write three 2-digit numbers that are divisible by 2.

38. WHICH ONE DOESN'T BELONG? Identify the number expression that does not belong with the other three. Explain.

2×4	$24 \div 3$	3×4	$8 \div 1$

39. WRITING IN MATH Write a real-world problem that can be represented by $55 \div 5$.

Standards Practice

40 George scored 21 points during a basketball game. He scored three times as many points as Darien. Which number sentence shows a related fact that can be used to find how many points Darien scored? **(Lesson 5-2)**

A $7 + 3 = 10$

B $21 \div 7 = 3$

C $21 \div 3 = 7$

D $3 \times 7 = 21$

41 Which number is missing from the number sentence? **(Lesson 5-3)**

$$45 \div \blacksquare = 9$$

F 2

G 3

H 4

J 5

Spiral Review

Algebra Copy and complete each number sentence. Identify the property used. (Lesson 5-2)

42. $8 \div \blacksquare = 1$

43. $\blacksquare \times 5 = 5 \times 4$

44. $\blacksquare \div 12 = 0$

Algebra Copy and complete each fact family. (Lesson 5-1)

45. $4 \times 7 = \blacksquare$ $\quad 7 \times \blacksquare = 28$

$28 \div \blacksquare = 7$ $\quad 28 \div 7 = \blacksquare$

46. $8 \times 9 = \blacksquare$ $\quad \blacksquare \times 8 = 72$

$72 \div \blacksquare = 8$ $\quad 72 \div 9 = \blacksquare$

47. The number of children who visited a science museum is shown in the table. About how many children visited the museum during the weekend? **(Lesson 2-3)**

Museum Visitors							
Day	Mon.	Tues.	Wed.	Thur.	Fri.	Sat.	Sun.
Visitors	325	279	312	348	441	519	495

Problem-Solving Skill

MAIN IDEA I will choose an operation to solve a problem.

Standard 4MR3.3 Develop generalizations of the results obtained and apply them in other circumstances.
Standard 4NS3.0 Students solve problems involving addition, subtraction, **multiplication,** and division **of whole numbers** and understand the relationships among the operations.

There are 9 rows on the Twisted Zipper roller coaster. Each row has 4 seats. What operation do you need to use to find how many people can ride the roller coaster at a time?

Understand

What facts do you know?

- There are 9 rows.
- There are 4 seats per row.

What do you need to find?

- The operation you should use to find how many people can ride the roller coaster at a time.

Plan

There are groups with the same number in each group. So, multiply the number of rows by the number of seats per row.

Solve

Multiply to find the answer.

$4 \times 9 = 36$

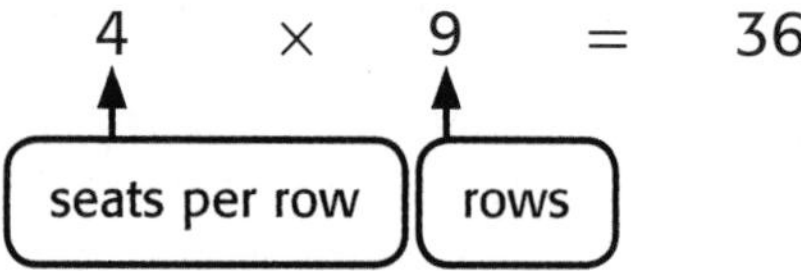

So, 36 people can ride the roller coaster at a time.

Check

Look back at the problem. Find 4×9 another way to see if you get the same answer. You can use an array.

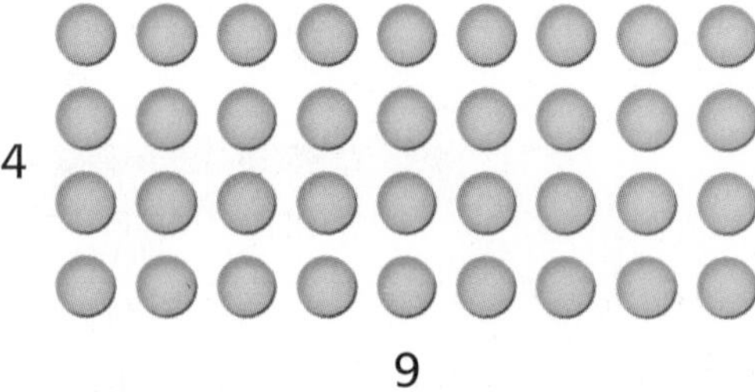

$4 \times 9 = 36$. So, the answer is correct.

ANALYZE the Skill

Refer to the problem on the previous page.

1. Explain why you multiplied 9 and 4 to find the answer.
2. What operation can be used to check the answer?
3. If 6 people can sit in each row, how many people could ride in all?
4. Refer to Exercise 3. How do you know the answer is correct?

PRACTICE the Skill

See page R12.

Tell which operation you would use to solve each problem. Then solve.

5. Fatima completed 28 problems for her math homework on Tuesday. She completed 17 more on Thursday than on Tuesday. How many problems did she complete on Thursday?
6. There are three jugglers in a circus. Each juggler can juggle 5 balls at a time. How many balls will they need for their act if they all perform at the same time?
7. A page from Dana's album is shown. Dana puts the same number of stickers on each page. She has 11 pages of stickers. How many stickers does she have in all?

8. Park Street School has 98 students and West Glenn School has 64 students who have perfect attendance. How many more students have perfect attendance at Park Street School?
9. The bar graph shows how long certain animals sleep. The koala sleeps 6 hours more than which animal?

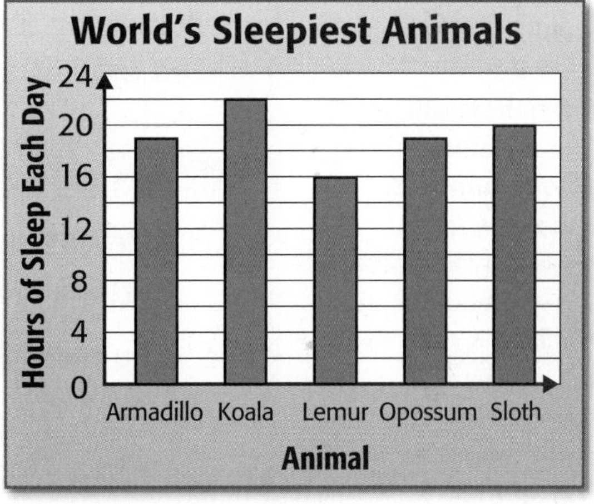

10. Use the graph above. How many more hours does a sloth sleep than a lemur?
11. Corey and his 2 friends earned $12 for doing yard work. How much money will each person get paid if they share the money evenly?
12. A lizard eats 6 crickets each day. How many crickets does it eat in one week?
13. **WRITING IN MATH** Explain how you chose an operation for Exercise 12.

5-5 Multiply and Divide Facts Through 10

MAIN IDEA

I will recognize multiplication and division facts through 10.

Standard 4NS3.0 Students solve problems involving addition, subtraction, **multiplication, and division of whole numbers** and understand relationships among the operations.
Standard 4MR3.2 Note the method of deriving the solution and demonstrate a conceptual understanding of the derivation by solving similar problems.

Lorenzo is storing his friends' phone numbers in his cell phone. Each number has 7 digits. How many number buttons did Lorenzo press if he has 9 friends?

You can find how many number buttons Lorenzo pressed by multiplying. Two multiplication strategies that you can use are area models and related facts.

Real-World EXAMPLE Multiply

1. **PHONES Each number has 7 digits. How many number buttons did Lorenzo press if he has 9 friends?**

You need to find 7 × 9.

One Way: Area Model	Another Way: Related Fact
Make an area model.	Think of a related fact.
(9 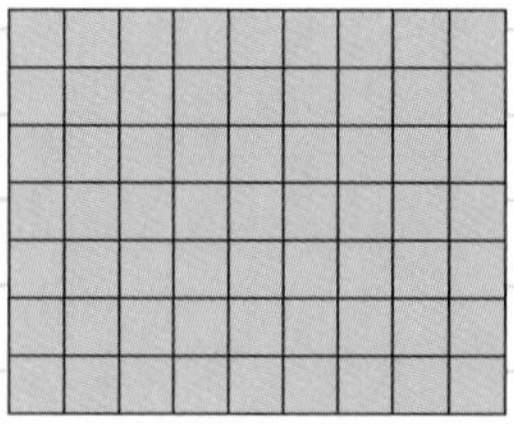 columns by 7 rows area model) 7 × 9 rows columns	7 × 9 = ■ THINK ■ ÷ 7 = 9? 63 ÷ 7 = 9 7 × 9 = 63
There are 63 squares in all. So, 7 × 9 = 63.	

So, Lorenzo must press 63 number buttons.

Real-World EXAMPLE Divide

2 **TELEVISION Carolyn noticed that 9 minutes of commercials play during a 30-minute television program. How many 30-minute shows did Carolyn watch during a weekend if she watched 54 minutes of commercials?**

> **Remember**
>
> The factors in a multiplication problem become the divisor and quotient in the related division problem.

Each television program has 9 minutes of commercials. Divide 54 by 9 to find how many 30-minute shows Carolyn watched. You can use a related multiplication fact.

$54 \div 9 = \blacksquare$

THINK What times 9 is 54?

$54 \div 9 = 6$

So, Carolyn watched 6 thirty-minute shows.

Check The area model shows 54 squares in rows of 9. Count the number of rows.

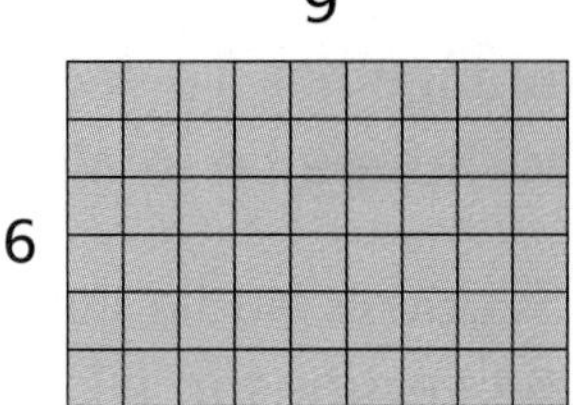

So, $54 \div 9 = 6$. ✓

Online Personal Tutor at ca.gr4math.com

CHECK What You Know

Multiply or divide. See Examples 1 and 2 (pp. 188–189)

1. $\begin{array}{r} 9 \\ \times 8 \\ \hline \end{array}$

2. $\begin{array}{r} 10 \\ \times 7 \\ \hline \end{array}$

3. 6×4

4. 8×8

5. $49 \div 7$

6. $60 \div 6$

7. $8\overline{)48}$

8. $10\overline{)100}$

9. Linda sold 8 magazine subscriptions to make money for her school. Each magazine subscription costs $9. How much money did Linda collect?

10. 

What do you notice when you multiply 10 and a number? Explain an easy method for finding a product when 10 is one of the factors.

Practice and Problem Solving

EXTRA PRACTICE
See page R12.

Multiply or divide. **See Examples 1 and 2 (pp. 188–189)**

11. $\begin{array}{r} 6 \\ \times 6 \\ \hline \end{array}$

12. $\begin{array}{r} 10 \\ \times 8 \\ \hline \end{array}$

13. $\begin{array}{r} 7 \\ \times 7 \\ \hline \end{array}$

14. $\begin{array}{r} 6 \\ \times 7 \\ \hline \end{array}$

15. 9×4

16. 10×5

17. 6×8

18. 10×10

19. $30 \div 6$

20. $42 \div 7$

21. $72 \div 8$

22. $90 \div 10$

23. $7\overline{)70}$

24. $9\overline{)63}$

25. $8\overline{)56}$

26. $10\overline{)80}$

27. Juliana played 9 holes of miniature golf. Her total score was 54. Suppose she got the same score on each hole. What was Juliana's score per hole?

28. While on vacation, Felipe sent 42 postcards to his friends. How many friends did he send to if he sent 7 postcards to each person?

Real-World PROBLEM SOLVING

Fruit Oranges are the fruit of a citrus tree originally from southeast Asia. Oranges grow in different sizes and colors. Most oranges have 10 sections inside.

29. Nadia bought 2 oranges for each member of her family. Nadia has 4 family members. Each orange has 10 sections. How many sections will there be in all?

30. Suppose Nadia cuts 6 oranges in half. She finds that there are 54 sections in all. If there are the same number of sections in each orange, how many sections are in each orange?

H.O.T. Problems

31. OPEN ENDED Write three number sentences that each contain the number 6 and have a product greater than 40.

32. NUMBER SENSE Explain why the fact family of 7 and 49 only has two number sentences.

33. CHALLENGE The product of two numbers is 24. The sum of the numbers is 11. What are the two numbers?

34. WRITING IN MATH Is the quotient of $135 \div 9$ greater than or less than the quotient of $153 \div 9$? Explain how you know without finding the quotients.

CHAPTER 5

Mid-Chapter Check

Lessons 5-1 through 5-5

Write a fact family for each set of numbers. (Lesson 5-1)

1. 7, 28, 4

2. 3, 24, 8

Divide. Use a related multiplication fact. (Lesson 5-1)

3. $18 \div 2$

4. $20 \div 5$

5. $33 \div 3$

6. $36 \div 4$

7. **STANDARDS PRACTICE** Which number sentence is in the same fact family as $63 \div 7 = \blacksquare$? (Lesson 5-1)

A $7 + \blacksquare = 63$

B $\blacksquare - 7 = 63$

C $7 \times \blacksquare = 63$

D $63 \times 7 = \blacksquare$

Identify the property shown by each number sentence. (Lesson 5-2)

8. $15 \times 0 = 0$

9. $9 \times 3 = 3 \times 9$

Algebra Copy and complete each number sentence. Identify the property used. (Lesson 5-2)

10. $5 \div \blacksquare = 1$

11. $7 \times \blacksquare = 0$

Multiply or divide. (Lesson 5-3)

12. $20 \div 5$

13. 4×3

14. Emmett brushes his teeth 3 times a day. How many times does Emmett brush his teeth in one week?

Algebra Complete each number sentence. (Lesson 5-3)

15. $\blacksquare \times 5 = 45$

16. $3 \times \blacksquare = 3$

17. **STANDARDS PRACTICE** Which number is missing from the number sentence? (Lesson 5-3)

$$27 \div \blacksquare = 9$$

F 2

G 3

H 4

J 5

Tell which operation you would use to solve each problem. Then solve. (Lesson 5-4)

18. Lance walked 4 dogs on Monday. He walked twice that many on Tuesday. How many dogs did he walk on Tuesday?

19. Each row of the stadium can hold 9 people. Diana reserved 3 rows for her family. How many people in Diana's family will be at the stadium?

Multiply or divide. (Lesson 5-5)

20. 10×6

21. $56 \div 7$

22. **WRITING IN MATH** Does the Associative Property work with division? Explain how you know.

Problem Solving in History

Did you know that soda was invented by doctors? Many people thought that the mineral water in natural springs had healing powers. In 1767, a doctor invented the first glass of carbonated water, which came to be known as "soda water."

About 80 years later, pharmacy owners and scientists began to add flavors to soda water. It was renamed "soda pop" in 1861. Soon, Americans could buy soda in bottles from grocery stores and vending machines. These drinks are still very popular.

1815

first soda fountain invented

1886

pharmacy owner sells 9 sodas per day at 5¢ each

1894

soda sells in cases of 24 bottles

Standard 4NS3.0 **Students solve problems involving addition, subtraction, multiplication, and division of whole numbers** and understand the relationships among the operations.

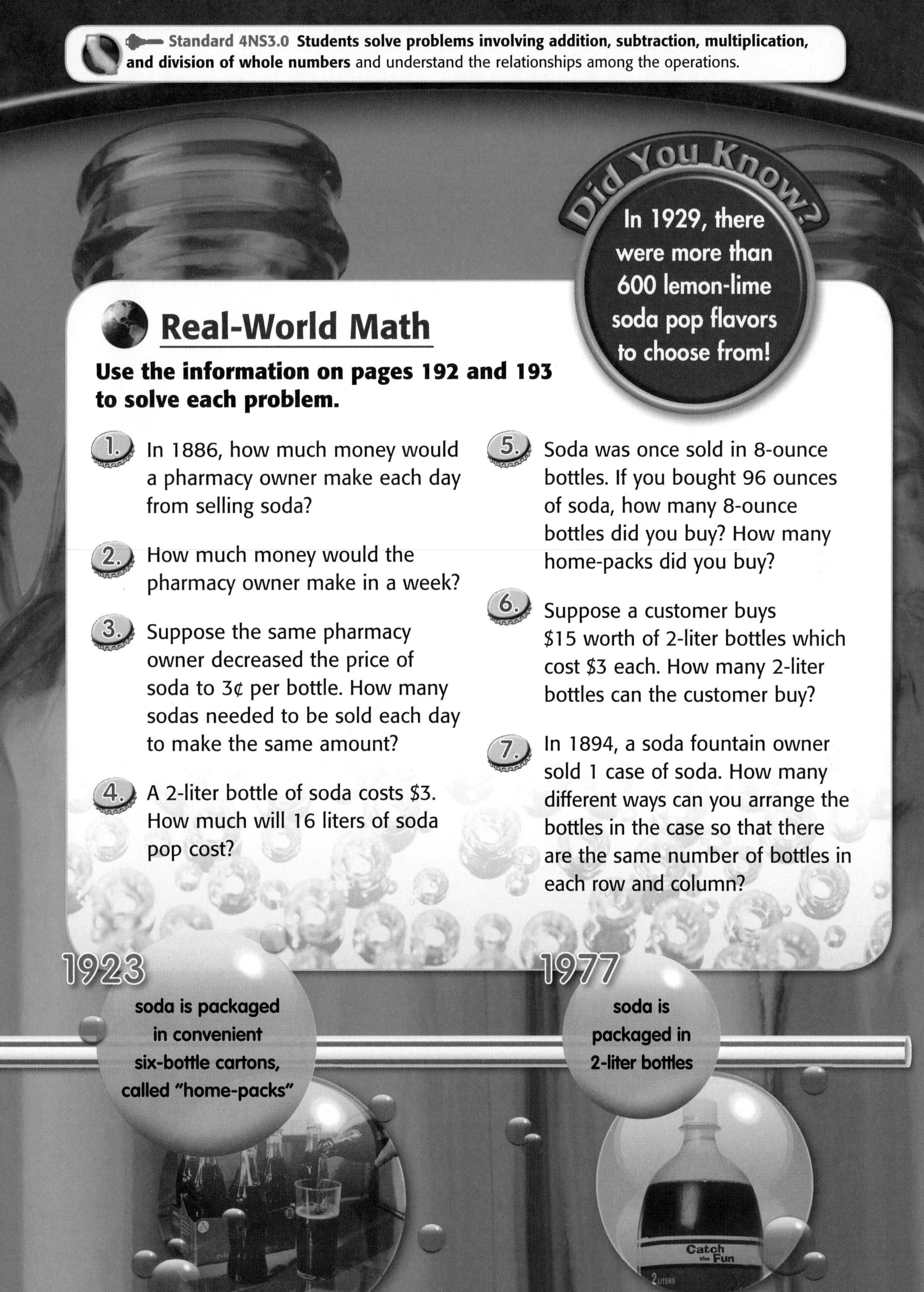

Did You Know? In 1929, there were more than 600 lemon-lime soda pop flavors to choose from!

Real-World Math

Use the information on pages 192 and 193 to solve each problem.

1. In 1886, how much money would a pharmacy owner make each day from selling soda?

2. How much money would the pharmacy owner make in a week?

3. Suppose the same pharmacy owner decreased the price of soda to 3¢ per bottle. How many sodas needed to be sold each day to make the same amount?

4. A 2-liter bottle of soda costs $3. How much will 16 liters of soda pop cost?

5. Soda was once sold in 8-ounce bottles. If you bought 96 ounces of soda, how many 8-ounce bottles did you buy? How many home-packs did you buy?

6. Suppose a customer buys $15 worth of 2-liter bottles which cost $3 each. How many 2-liter bottles can the customer buy?

7. In 1894, a soda fountain owner sold 1 case of soda. How many different ways can you arrange the bottles in the case so that there are the same number of bottles in each row and column?

1923 soda is packaged in convenient six-bottle cartons, called "home-packs"

1977 soda is packaged in 2-liter bottles

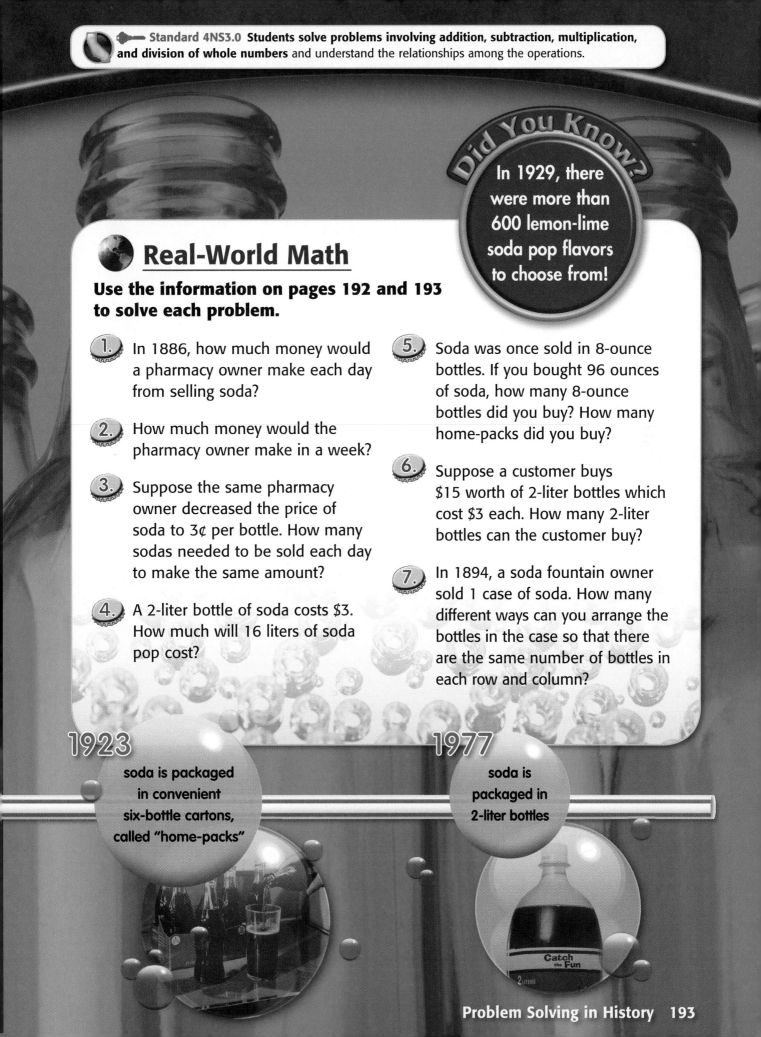

5-6 Multiply with 11 and 12

I will recognize multiplication facts for 11 and 12.

4NS3.0 Students solve problems involving addition, subtraction, **multiplication, and division of whole numbers** and understand relationships among the operations.

Standard 4MR3.3 Develop generalizations of the results obtained and apply them in other circumstances.

New Vocabulary

Distributive Property of Multiplication

One day, a florist receives 7 orders for a dozen roses. How many roses does the florist need to make the 7 bouquets?

To multiply larger numbers, the Distributive Property of Multiplication is helpful. The **Distributive Property of Multiplication** says that you can multiply the addends of a number and then add the products.

Real-World EXAMPLE Multiply

1 How many roses does the florist need to make 7 bouquets?

There are 12 roses in one dozen. So, you need to find 7×12.

Think of 7×12 as $(7 \times 10) + (7 \times 2)$.

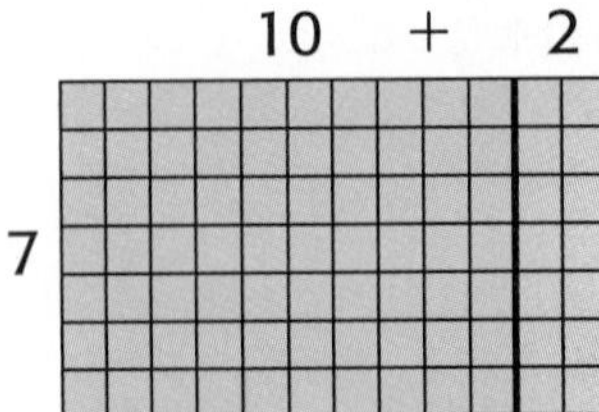

$$\begin{aligned} 7 \times 12 &= (7 \times 10) + (7 \times 2) \\ &= 70 + 14 \\ &= 84 \end{aligned}$$

So, 84 roses are needed to make 7 bouquets.

You can use a related multiplication fact to find the quotient in a division problem.

Remember When solving a word problem, think about the facts you know and what you need to find.

Real-World EXAMPLE Divide

2 MOVIES Shaun and 10 of his friends went to a movie. The total cost for the 11 movie tickets was $66. How much did each ticket cost?

You know that 11 tickets cost $66.
Use a related multiplication fact to help you find $66 ÷ 11.

Shaun + 10 friends

$66 ÷ 11 = ■

THINK 11 × ■ = $66?
11 × $6 = $66

$66 ÷ 11 = $6

So, each ticket cost $6.

Check The area model shows that $6 × 11 = $66.

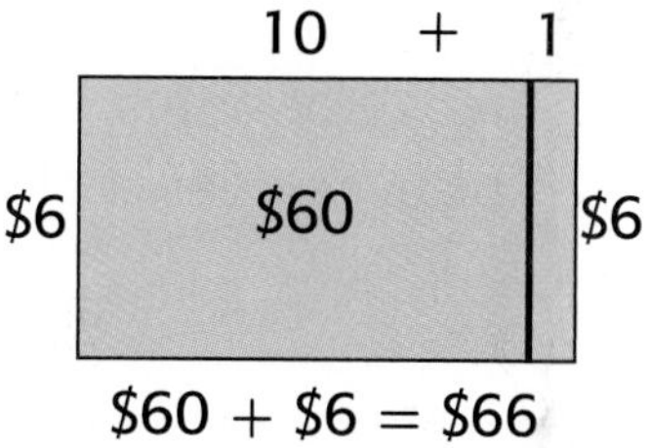

$60 + $6 = $66

So, $66 ÷ 11 = $6 is correct. ✓

Online Personal Tutor at ca.gr4math.com

CHECK What You Know

Multiply or divide. See Examples 1 and 2 (pp. 194–195)

1. $\begin{array}{r} 11 \\ \times\ 9 \\ \hline \end{array}$

2. $\begin{array}{r} 10 \\ \times\ 12 \\ \hline \end{array}$

3. 4 × 11

4. 6 × 12

5. 88 ÷ 11

6. 108 ÷ 9

7. $11\overline{)121}$

8. $12\overline{)132}$

9. There are 8 cartons of eggs on a grocery store shelf. Each carton contains one dozen eggs. How many eggs are on the shelf?

10. Talk About It How would you use two smaller area models to find 9 × 12? Draw the area models.

Practice and Problem Solving

EXTRA PRACTICE See page R13.

Multiply or divide. See Examples 1 and 2 (pp. 194–195)

11. 11×5 **12.** 12×5 **13.** 11×7 **14.** 12×8

15. 2×11 **16.** 12×7 **17.** 11×10 **18.** 12×12

19. $44 \div 11$ **20.** $72 \div 6$ **21.** $99 \div 11$ **22.** $120 \div 10$

23. $12\overline{)48}$ **24.** $11\overline{)66}$ **25.** $12\overline{)84}$ **26.** $11\overline{)110}$

Algebra **Find the value of each number sentence if**  **= 12 and** ☺ **= 11.**

27. ♥ × 6 **28.** 8 × ☺ **29.** 132 ÷ ☺ **30.** 144 ÷ 

Compare. Write >, <, or =.

31. 11 × 8 ■ 6 × 12 **32.** 132 ÷ 12 ■ 99 ÷ 9 **33.** 12 × 10 ■ 11 × 11

34. A piano has 88 keys. An octave, or range of notes, is 8 keys. How many octaves does a piano have?

35. Mrs. Hanson has 12 grandchildren. She gives each grandchild $10. How much money does she give in all?

Real-World PROBLEM SOLVING

Animals The table gives expected life spans for some animals when they live in the wild.

36. Identify the two animals that have life spans of 60 months.

37. What is the life span of a Tasmanian devil in months?

38. How many more months is a platypus expected to live than a koala?

39. A mongoose is 7 years old. How many months longer is it expected to live?

40. Find the difference between a mongoose's life span and a toucan's life span in months.

Animal Life Spans

Animal	Years
Bat	5 years
Gerbil	5 years
Koala	8 years
Mongoose	12 years
Platypus	10 years
Toucan	6 years
Tasmanian devil	8 years

H.O.T. Problems

41. OPEN ENDED Write three number sentences. Each should contain the number 12, a one-digit number as the other factor, and a product less than 60.

42. WHICH ONE DOESN'T BELONG? Identify the number sentence that does not belong with the other three. Explain.

9×11	$99 \div 9$	11×9	$88 \div 11$

43. WRITING IN MATH Write a problem about a real-world situation that involves finding the product of 6 and 12.

Standards Practice

44 In which number sentence does 8 make the number sentence true? **(Lesson 5-5)**

A $36 \div \blacksquare = 4$

B $42 \div \blacksquare = 6$

C $56 \div \blacksquare = 7$

D $81 \div \blacksquare = 9$

45 Look at the problem below.

$$\square = \triangle \times 12$$

If $\triangle = 10$, what is $\square$? **(Lesson 5-6)**

F 120 **H** 132

G 121 **J** 143

Spiral Review

Multiply or divide. (Lesson 5-5)

46. 7×5 **47.** 8×9 **48.** $64 \div 8$ **49.** $10\overline{)90}$

Tell which operation you would use to solve each problem. Then solve. (Lesson 5-4)

50. There are 108 cotton balls in a bag. Each student needs 9 cotton balls for an art project. How many students will get the cotton balls?

51. There are 24 rocks in Hatsu's rock collection. She wants to display her rocks in an array. Identify 3 possible ways to display the rocks.

Algebra Complete each number sentence. (Lesson 5-3)

52. $3 \times \blacksquare = 3$ **53.** $\blacksquare \times 4 = 28$ **54.** $22 \div \blacksquare = 11$ **55.** $\blacksquare \div 4 = 10$

Problem-Solving Investigation

MAIN IDEA I will choose the best strategy to solve a problem.

Standard 4MR1.1 **Analyze problems by identifying relationships, distinguishing relevant from irrelevant information, sequencing and prioritizing information, and observing patterns.** Standard 4NS3.0 **Students solve problems involving addition, subtraction, multiplication, and division of whole numbers and understand the relationships among the operations.**

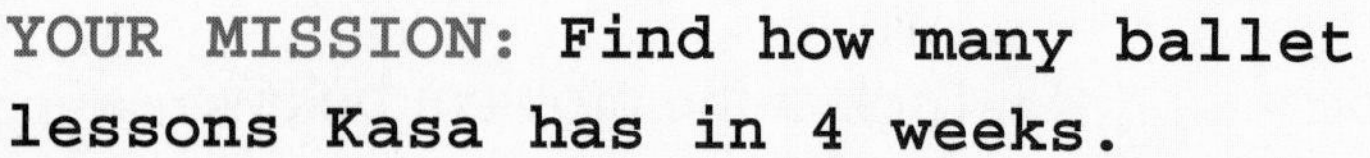

KASA: I go to ballet lessons every week. I dance 2 hours during every lesson. I dance a total of 6 hours each week.

YOUR MISSION: Find how many ballet lessons Kasa has in 4 weeks.

Understand	Kasa dances 2 hours during each lesson. She dances a total of 6 hours each week. Find how many lessons she has in 4 weeks.
Plan	Divide the number of hours Kasa practices each week by the number of hours each lesson lasts. Then multiply by 4, the number of weeks..
Solve	$\underbrace{6}_{\text{hours per week}} \div \underbrace{2}_{\text{hours per lesson}} = \underbrace{3}_{\text{lessons per week}}$ So, Kasa has 3 ballet lessons each week. $\underbrace{3}_{\text{lessons per week}} \times \underbrace{4}_{\text{weeks}} = \underbrace{12}_{\text{lessons in 4 weeks}}$ So, Kasa has 12 ballet lessons in 4 weeks.
Check	Look back at the problem. Check your answer by dividing the number of lessons in 4 weeks by the number of weeks. $12 \div 4 = 3$. Then, multiply the number of hours per lesson by the number of lessons each week. $2 \times 3 = 6$. So, the answer is correct.

Mixed Problem Solving

See page R13.

Use the make a table strategy or choose an operation to solve each problem.

PROBLEM-SOLVING STRATEGIES

- Make a table.
- Choose an operation

1. Mr. and Mrs. Lopez are putting square tiles on the floor in their bathroom. They can fit 6 rows of 4 tiles in the bathroom. How many tiles do they need to buy?

2. A teacher gives quizzes that are each worth 15 points. If the teacher gives 5 quizzes, how many points are all of the quizzes worth?

3. Marisol has 7 books from the library. She gets 5 new books and returns 3 books. How many library books does she have now?

4. Raheem is playing a game at a carnival. He needs to earn 400 points to win a large stuffed animal. He has thrown 4 out of his 5 darts. Is it possible for him to win the 400 point prize? If so, how many points does he still need?

5. A scout troop went hiking on the trail shown below. They hiked 4 miles an hour. How long did they hike?

6. Wesley needs to finish reading a book before Monday. He started reading the 44-page book on Thursday. How many pages will he need to read each day if he reads an equal number of pages each day?

7. Twenty students want to raise money for new playground equipment. They need $2,200. Copy and complete the table to find out how much money each student needs to raise.

New Playground Equipment	
Money per Student	**Total Raised**
$90	$1,800
$95	$1,900
$100	$2,000
$105	■
■	■

8. **WRITING IN MATH** Tell which problem-solving strategy you used to solve Exercise 7. Explain how you used this strategy when solving Exercise 7.

5-8 Multiply Three Numbers

GET READY to Learn

There are 2 baseball cards in each pack. There are 6 packs in each box. If Raul buys 3 boxes for his collection, how many cards will he have?

MAIN IDEA

I will multiply 3 factors.

Standard 4AF1.0

Students use and interpret variables, mathematical symbols, and **properties to write and simplify** expressions and **sentences.**

In Lesson 2-1, you learned to use the Associative Property of Addition to add more than 2 numbers. You can use the Associative Property of Multiplication to multiply more than two numbers.

Real-World EXAMPLE Associative Property

1 TRADING CARDS **How many baseball cards will Raul have?**

You need to find $2 \times 6 \times 3$. There are two ways to group the numbers.

One Way	Another Way
Multiply 2×6 first.	Multiply 6×3 first.
$2 \times 6 \times 3$	$2 \times 6 \times 3$
$(2 \times 6) \times 3$	$2 \times (6 \times 3)$
12×3	2×18
36	36

Remember

To review the Associative Property of Multiplication, see Lesson 5-2 (p. 178).

So, Raul will have 36 baseball cards.

CHECK What You Know

Multiply. See Example 1 (p. 200)

1. $3 \times 1 \times 5$

2. $2 \times 2 \times 3$

3. $3 \times 5 \times 3$

4. $6 \times 2 \times 3$

5. $4 \times 2 \times 7$

6. $3 \times 4 \times 8$

7. Art supply paint comes in a box that contains 3 sets of 8 bottles of paint. An art teacher ordered 2 boxes. How many bottles of paint were ordered?

8. Talk About It Identify the order that makes it easiest to multiply the factors in the number sentence $9 \times 6 \times 2$. Explain.

Practice and Problem Solving

See page R13.

Multiply. See Example 1 (p. 200)

9. $6 \times 1 \times 5$

10. $2 \times 2 \times 7$

11. $5 \times 7 \times 2$

12. $10 \times 2 \times 5$

13. $3 \times 9 \times 3$

14. $2 \times 6 \times 7$

15. $4 \times 3 \times 7$

16. $2 \times 9 \times 4$

17. $5 \times 1 \times 12$

Algebra Copy and complete each number sentence.

18. $4 \times ■ \times 1 = 12$

19. $2 \times 6 \times ■ = 60$

20. $■ \times 3 \times 4 = 24$

Algebra Compare. Write >, <, or =.

21. $4 \times 2 \times 9$ ● $7 \times 4 \times 2$

22. $5 \times 2 \times 8$ ● $6 \times 2 \times 6$

Algebra Find the value of each number sentence if ☼ = 2, ☺ = 3, and ☆ = 4.

23. $5 \times 1 \times$ ☆

24. $6 \times$ ☼ $\times 9$

25. ☺ $\times 12 \times$ ☆

26. $10 \times$ ☼ $\times$ ☆

27. Gabriel is training for a race. He jogs 2 miles a day. He jogs this distance 4 days a week. How many miles will he jog in 6 weeks?

28. **Measurement** Blanca bikes 2 miles to her grandfather's house and 2 miles back to her house 5 times each month. How many miles does she bike?

29. **Measurement** For one week, 4 inches of snow fell every morning and 3 inches fell every night. Was this enough snow to cover a bench that is 4 feet tall? Explain.

30. Helen borrowed 12 books from the library. The books are due in 4 weeks. If she reads 2 books 2 days a week, will she have enough time to read all of the books? Explain.

Real-World PROBLEM SOLVING

Animals Did you know that pigs are very intelligent animals? They are considered to be smarter than dogs. More information about farm animals is shown to the right.

DOWN ON THE FARM

A pig has an average of 8 piglets per litter.

A chicken lays an average of 3 eggs per week.

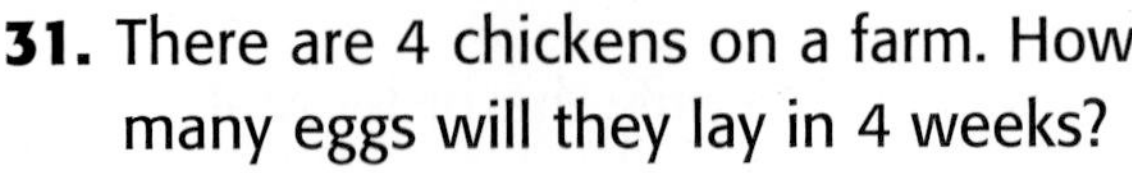

31. There are 4 chickens on a farm. How many eggs will they lay in 4 weeks?

32. Use the number sentence $2 \times 3 \times \blacksquare = 30$ to find how many weeks it will take 2 chickens to lay 30 eggs.

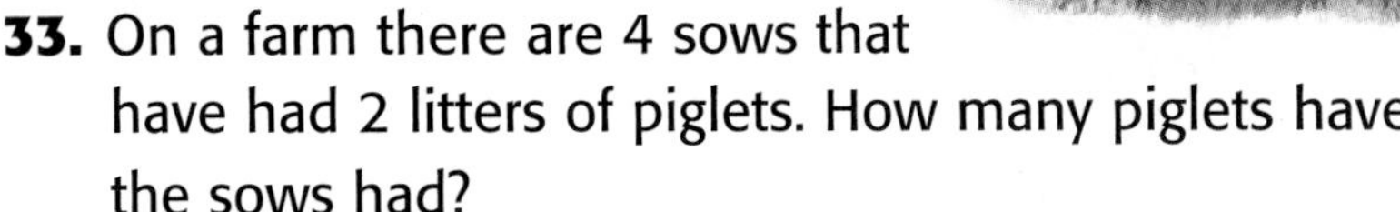

33. On a farm there are 4 sows that have had 2 litters of piglets. How many piglets have the sows had?

34. How many weeks would it take 2 chickens to have more eggs than the number of piglets that were mentioned in Exercise 33?

H.O.T. Problems

35. OPEN ENDED Copy and complete $2 \times 11 \times \blacksquare > 4 \times 9 \times 3$ to make a true sentence.

36. FIND THE ERROR Jamil and Denise are finding $4 \times \blacksquare \times 7 = 56$. Who is correct? Explain.

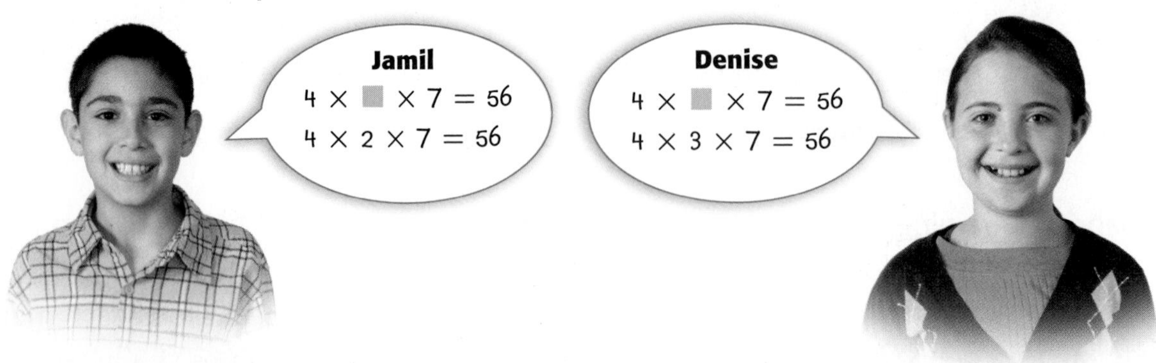

37. CHALLENGE Identify 4 factors that result in a product of 24.

38. WRITING IN ▶MATH Manuel has 24 marbles in his collection. He wants to store his marbles in 2 cases. If the marbles are displayed in even rows and columns, what arrays could the marbles be displayed in?

Multiplication Bingo

Multiplication Facts

Get Ready!

Players: 3 or more players

You will need: 6 index cards

Get Set!

Make a game board like the one shown. Label each square with a number that can be found on a multiplication table. Cut each index card in half, and label each card with a number from 1 to 12.

6	27	12	9
36	18	10	45
8	54	32	15
72	144	16	81

Go!

- Shuffle the cards. Place them face down in a stack on the table.
- Player 1 chooses a card.
- Players look at the game board to find a number that results from multiplying the number on the card times any other number. Color 1 square if it contains a product of the number.
- Player 2 chooses a card.
- Play continues the same way.
- The first player that colors 4 squares in a row, column, or diagonally wins.

5-9 Factors and Multiples

MAIN IDEA

I will find factors and multiples of whole numbers.

Standard 4NS4.1 Understand that many whole numbers break down in different ways (e.g. 12 = 4 × 3 = 2 × 6 = 2 × 2 × 3).

Standard 4MR2.3 Use a variety of methods, such as words, numbers, symbols, charts, graphs, **tables,** diagrams, **and models, to explain mathematical reasoning.**

New Vocabulary

factor

multiple

GET READY to Learn

Mrs. Navarro is arranging desks in her classroom. There are 24 desks. How many ways can she arrange the desks so that the number of desks in each row is the same?

Two or more numbers that are multiplied together to form a product are called **factors**. To find the different arrangements of desks, think about the factors of 24.

Real-World EXAMPLE Identify Factors

1 SCHOOL How many ways can Mrs. Navarro arrange the desks in her classroom?

Think of number pairs that result in a product of 24.

$1 \times 24 = 24$

$2 \times 12 = 24$

$3 \times 8 = 24$

$4 \times 6 = 24$

THINK There are 4 more arrays:
24 × 1 8 × 3
12 × 2 6 × 4

The factors of 24 are 1, 2, 3, 4, 6, 8, 12, and 24. So, the desks can be arranged in eight ways.

A **multiple** of a number is the product of that number and any whole number. For example, 15 is a multiple of 5 since $3 \times 5 = 15$.

EXAMPLE Identify Multiples

2 Identify the first 5 multiples of 7.

On a multiplication table, look across the row for 7, or down the column for 7. All of the numbers listed in the row or the column are multiples of 7.

Remember

The first multiple of a number is always zero.

×	0	1	2	3	4	5	6	7	8	9	10	11	12
0	0	0	0	0	0	0	0	0	0	0	0	0	0
1	0	1	2	3	4	5	6	7	8	9	10	11	12
2	0	2	4	6	8	10	12	14	16	18	20	22	24
3	0	3	6	9	12	15	18	21	24	27	30	33	36
4	0	4	8	12	16	20	24	28	32	36	40	44	48
5	0	5	10	15	20	25	30	35	40	45	50	55	60
6	0	6	12	18	24	30	36	42	48	54	60	66	72
7	0	7	14	21	28	35	42	49	56	63	70	77	84
8	0	8	16	24	32	40	48	56	64	72	80	88	96
9	0	9	18	27	36	45	54	63	72	81	90	99	108
10	0	10	20	30	40	50	60	70	80	90	100	110	120
11	0	11	22	33	44	55	66	77	88	99	110	121	132
12	0	12	24	36	48	60	72	84	96	108	120	132	144

So, the first five multiples of 7 are 0, 7, 14, 21, and 28.

CHECK What You Know

Find all of the factors of each number. See Example 1 (p. 204)

1. 6 **2.** 10 **3.** 12 **4.** 36

Identify the first five multiples for each number. See Example 2 (p. 205)

5. 2 **6.** 4 **7.** 9 **8.** 12

9. Elena is baking muffins in the pan shown at the right. How many muffins will Elena make if she uses 1, 2, 3, or 4 pans?

10. Talk About It Explain the relationship between factors and multiples.

Practice and Problem Solving

EXTRA PRACTICE
See page R14.

Find all of the factors of each number. See Example 1 (p. 204)

11. 4 **12.** 7 **13.** 14 **14.** 20

15. 28 **16.** 30 **17.** 35 **18.** 42

Identify the first five multiples for each number. See Example 2 (p. 205)

19. 1 **20.** 3 **21.** 5 **22.** 6

23. 7 **24.** 8 **25.** 9 **26.** 11

Identify all of the factors that are related to each array.

27. 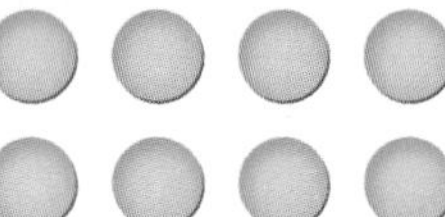

28. 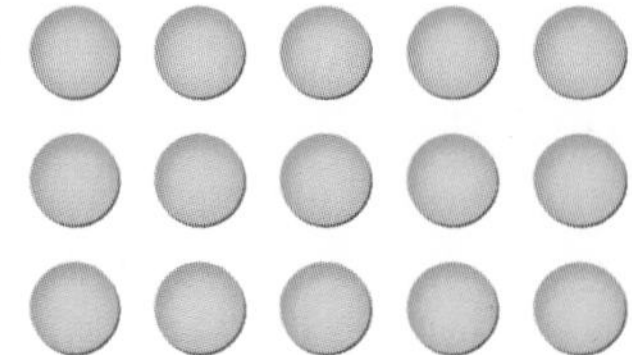

29. A chameleon eats 6 crickets a day. How many crickets does a chameleon eat in one week? in 8, 9, 10, and 11 days?

30. Pedro walks his dog 3 times a day. How many times does Pedro walk his dog in one week? in 10, 11, or 12 days?

31. There are 50 stars on the American flag. One way the stars can be arranged is a 5×10 array. Identify two more ways to arrange the stars.

32. There are 24 cans of soup on a shelf. One way the cans can be displayed is in a 4×6 array. Identify two more ways the cans can be displayed.

Real-World PROBLEM SOLVING

Science A certain comet can be seen every 6 years.

33. How old is a person who has seen the comet 4, 5, 6, or 7 times if they first saw the comet when they were 6 years old?

34. Warren is 10 years old. Warren's dad is 38 years old, and his mom is 36 years old. What is the total of the most number of times Warren and his parents could have seen the comet?

35. Suppose the comet can be seen every 4 years. Would your answer to Exercise 34 change? Explain.

H.O.T. Problems

36. OPEN ENDED List three numbers that have 2 and 3 as factors.

37. CHALLENGE Identify the number less than 144 with the most factors.

38. WRITING IN ▸MATH A fourth grade class is having a class picture taken for the yearbook. There are 24 students in the class. Explain why standing in 1 row of 24 is not the best way for the students to be arranged for the picture.

Standards Practice

39 Which number will make the number sentence true? **(Lesson 5-8)**

$3 \times \blacksquare \times 4 = 108$

A 7

B 8

C 9

D 10

40 Which number has more than 6 factors? **(Lesson 5-9)**

F 6

G 12

H 15

J 36

Spiral Review

Multiply. **(Lesson 5-8)**

41. $2 \times 7 \times 3$

42. $3 \times 5 \times 4$

43. $11 \times 5 \times 2$

For Exercises 44 and 45, use the picture at the right. Identify the operation you used. **(Lesson 5-7)**

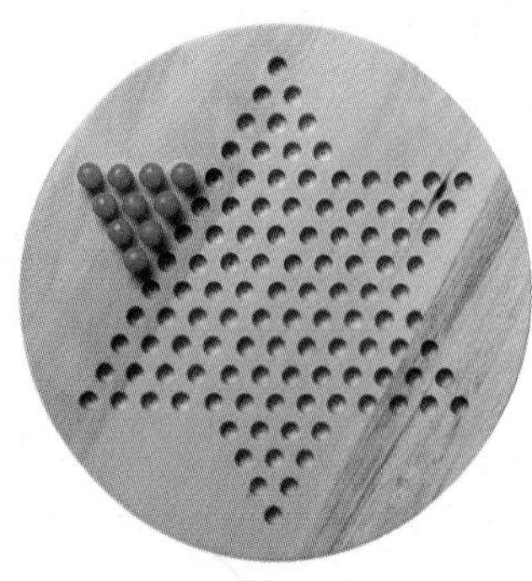

44. There are 5 people who want to play the game shown. How many marbles do they need in all?

45. There are 30 marbles on the game board at the start of a game. How many players are there?

Algebra Find the value of each if ☆ = 11 and ☼ = 12. **(Lesson 5-6)**

46. ☆ × 6

47. 132 ÷ ☼

48. ☼ × ☆

5-10 Prime and Composite Numbers

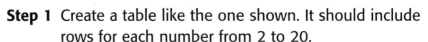

GET READY to Learn

Hands-On Mini Activity

MAIN IDEA

I will determine if a number is prime or composite.

Standard 4NS4.2 Know that numbers such as 2, 3, 4, 7, and 11 do not have any factors except for 1 and themselves and that such numbers are called prime numbers.

New Vocabulary

composite number

prime number

Animation
ca.gr4math.com

Materials: base-ten blocks

Step 1 Create a table like the one shown. It should include rows for each number from 2 to 20.

Number of Squares	Rectangle Formed	Dimensions of Each Rectangle
2		1 × 2
3		1 × 3
4		1 × 4, 2 × 2
5		1 × 5
6		1 × 6, 2 × 3
⋮		
20		

Step 2 Any number of squares can be arranged into one or more different rectangles. A 1 × 3 rectangle is the same as a 3 × 1 rectangle. Use base-ten blocks to help you complete the table.

1. Which numbers have more than one rectangle formed?
2. Which numbers have only one rectangle formed?
3. For the numbers that have only one rectangle formed, what do you notice about the shape of these rectangles?

The squares in the activity can be used to identify prime and composite numbers.

Vocabulary Link
composite
Everyday Use a combination of many things

Math Use a number that has more than two factors

KEY CONCEPT Prime and Composite Numbers

Definition	Examples
Prime Number A whole number with exactly two distinct factors, 1 and itself.	2, 3, 7, 11
Composite Number A whole number with more than two factors.	4, 6, 10, 18
Neither Prime nor Composite 1 has only one factor.	0, 1

EXAMPLES Identify Composite and Prime Numbers

Tell whether each number is *prime, composite*, or *neither*.

1 **18**

Find the factors of 18.

1×18
2×9
3×6

Factors of 18: 1, 2, 6, 9, 18. Since 18 has more than two factors, it is a composite number.

2 **23**

Find the factors of 23.

1×23

Factors of 23: 1, 23. Since 23 has exactly two distinct factors, it is a prime number.

CHECK What You Know

Tell whether each number is *prime, composite,* or neither.
See Examples 1 and 2 (p. 209)

1. 5 **2.** 15 **3.** 21 **4.** 31

5. Is there a way to place 29 books on shelves so that each shelf has the same number of books, with more than one book on each shelf?

6. Talk About It Identify the smallest prime number. Explain how you know this is the smallest prime number.

Practice and Problem Solving

EXTRA PRACTICE See page R14.

Tell whether each number is *prime, composite,* or *neither.* See Examples 1 and 2 (p. 209)

7. 0 **8.** 1 **9.** 3 **10.** 4

11. 7 **12.** 11 **13.** 14 **14.** 22

15. 25 **16.** 29 **17.** 36 **18.** 41

19. What prime number is greater than 20 and less than 25?

20. What two prime numbers are greater than 30 and less than 40?

21. Ken is planting vegetables in his garden. He has 20 seeds. Determine whether 20 is a prime or composite number. If it is composite, list all of the ways Ken can arrange the seeds in even rows.

22. Mrs. Evans has 13 pictures to hang on a wall. Is there any way she can arrange the pictures so that the same number of pictures is in each row? Tell whether 13 is a composite or prime number. Explain.

Real-World PROBLEM SOLVING

Art There is a lot of math in a quilt.

23. Susana is making a quilt by sewing together square pieces of fabric. She has 36 fabric squares. How many ways can she create a quilt that has the same number of squares in each row and each column?

24. Barrington is working on making a quilt using 47 fabric squares. Can he use all of the fabric squares to make a quilt that has the same number of squares in the rows and columns, other than making a 1×47 quilt? Explain.

H.O.T. Problems

25. OPEN ENDED Write five numbers less than 20 that are not composite.

26. WRITING IN MATH The numbers 17, 31, and 37 are prime numbers. Reversing the order of the digits to make 71, 13, and 73 also results in prime numbers. Does this always work with 2-digit prime numbers? Explain.

 Math Online **Self-Check Quiz at** ca.gr4math.com

Standards Practice

27 Which is *not* a multiple of 6?
(Lesson 5-9)

A 12 **C** 36

B 24 **D** 49

28 Which is a prime number?
(Lesson 5-10)

F 4 **H** 8

G 5 **J** 9

Spiral Review

Identify the first five multiples for each number. (Lesson 5-9)

29. 3 **30.** 5 **31.** 8 **32.** 11

Algebra **Copy and complete each number sentence.** (Lesson 5-8)

33. $2 \times \blacksquare \times 3 = 12$ **34.** $3 \times 4 \times \blacksquare = 36$ **35.** $\blacksquare \times 2 \times 4 = 72$

Solve. Identify the operation you used. (Lesson 5-4)

36. Mr. Fox is tiling his bathroom floor with square tiles. There will be 9 rows of tiles with 8 tiles in each row. How many tiles are needed to tile the floor?

Write an equation that describes the pattern. Then use the equation to find the next three numbers in the pattern. (Lesson 3-4)

37.

Input (a)	Output (b)
2	7
6	11
10	■
14	■
18	■

38.

Input (m)	Output (n)
15	6
18	9
21	■
24	■
27	■

Write and solve an equation for each situation. (Lesson 3-2)

39. A number plus 6 equals 13. What is the number?

40. The sum of 17 and a number is 29. What is the number?

41. Eight subtracted from a number equals 4. What is the number?

42. A number minus 5 equals 17. What is the number?

Chapter 5 Study Guide and Review

Be sure the following Key Vocabulary words and Key Concepts are written in your Foldable.

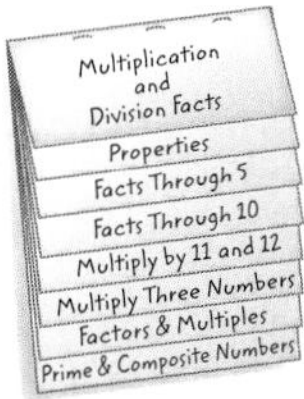

BIG Ideas

Relate Multiplication and Division (p. 175)

- A **fact family** is a set of four related multiplication and division facts.

$3 \times 4 = 12 \quad 4 \times 3 = 12$

$12 \div 4 = 3 \quad 12 \div 3 = 4$

Multiplication Properties (pp. 178–179)

$3 \times 4 = 4 \times 3$	Commutative Property
$3 \times 0 = 0$	Zero Property
$3 \times 1 = 3$	Identity Property
$3 \times (4 \times 2) = (3 \times 4) \times 2$	Associative Property

Factors and Multiples (pp. 204–205)

- Two or more numbers that are multiplied together to form a product are called **factors**.

factors of 6: 1, 2, 3, and 6

- A **multiple** of a number is the product of that number and any whole number.

multiples of 7: 0, 7, 14, 21, …

Key Vocabulary

Associative Property of Multiplication (p. 178)
Commutative Property of Multiplication (p. 178)
Distributive Property of Multiplication (p. 194)
factor (p. 204)
multiple (p. 205)

Vocabulary Check

Complete each sentence with the correct vocabulary word.

1. Two or more numbers that are multiplied together to form a product are called ___?___.
2. The ___?___ says that the order of the factors does not change the product when multiplying.
3. The ___?___ says that you can multiply the addends of a sum by a number and then add the products.
4. A(n) ___?___ of a number is the product of that number and any whole number.

 Math Online Vocabulary Review at ca.gr4math.com

Lesson-by-Lesson Review

5-1 Relate Multiplication and Division (pp. 175–177)

Example 1
Write a fact family for the array.

$2 \times 4 = 8$
$4 \times 2 = 8$
$8 \div 4 = 2$
$8 \div 2 = 4$

Example 2
Write a fact family for the numbers 3, 5, and 15.

$3 \times 5 = 15$ $5 \times 3 = 15$

$15 \div 3 = 5$ $15 \div 5 = 3$

Write a fact family for each array or set of numbers.

5. 3, 7, 21 **6.** 9, 5, 45

7.

8.

5-2 Algebra: Multiplication and Division Properties (pp. 178–181)

Example 3
Identify the property shown by $9 \times 1 = 9$.

A number is multiplied by 1, and the product is the number. This is the Identity Property of Multiplication.

Example 4
Complete $(5 \times 2) \times 3 = 5 \times (■ \times 3)$. Identify the property used.

$(5 \times 2) \times 3 = 5 \times (\mathbf{2} \times 3)$

The way in which the factors are grouped does not change the product.

This is the Associative Property of Multiplication.

Identify the property shown by each number sentence.

9. $12 \div 12 = 1$ **10.** $3 \times 6 = 6 \times 3$

Algebra Copy and complete each number sentence. Identify the property used.

11. $5 \div ■ = 1$ **12.** $■ \div 14 = 0$

13. David has soccer practice for 3 hours each night. Sofia has softball practice for 2 hours each night. Will David and Sofia practice for the same amount of time in 5 nights? Use a multiplication property to justify your answer.

Study Guide and Review

5-3 Multiply and Divide Facts Through 5 (pp. 182–185)

Example 5
Find 4 × 5.

You can use an area model to find 4 × 5.

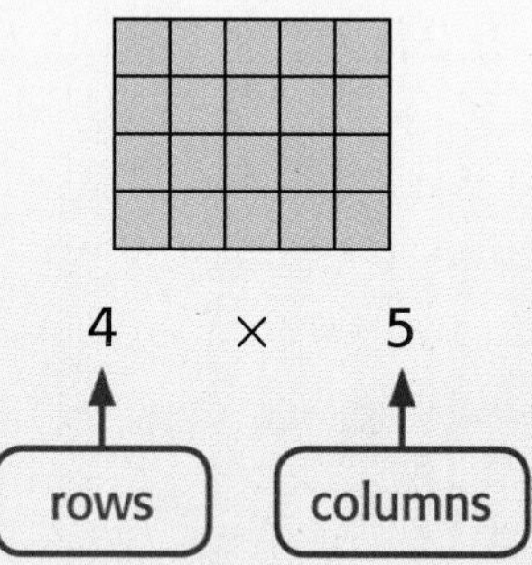

Count the squares. There is a total of 20 squares.

Multiply or divide.

14. 4 × 4 **15.** 5 × 3

16. 6 ÷ 3 **17.** $9\overline{)18}$

Algebra Complete each number sentence.

18. ■ × 3 = 6 **19.** 4 × ■ = 32

20. 56 ÷ ■ = 8 **21.** 44 ÷ ■ = 11

22. Algebra If ☆ = 2, then what is ☆ + ☆ + ☆ + ☆ + ☆ ?

5-4 Problem-Solving Skill: Choose an Operation (pp. 186–187)

Example 6
There are 9 rows on the bleachers. Each row holds 10 people. How many people can sit in the bleachers at once?

There are 9 rows with 10 seats per row. Find how many people can sit in the bleachers at a time.

Multiply the number of rows by the number of seats.

9 × 10 = 90

(9: rows; 10: seats per row)

So, 90 people can sit on the bleachers. Since 90 ÷ 10 = 9, the answer is correct.

Tell which operation you would use to solve each problem. Then solve.

23. Loretta spent $60 on 10 tickets for a concert. How much was each ticket?

24. Moses's vacation is 2 weeks long. Nina's vacation is 3 weeks longer than Moses's. How long is Nina's vacation?

25. A bus ticket costs $4.50. Gavin paid for it with $10. How much change should he get back?

26. There are 5 members in the band who play the drums. Three times as many members play the flute. How many band members play the flute?

5-5 Multiply and Divide Facts Through 10 (pp. 188–190)

Example 7
Find 4 × 7.

Make an area model to represent 4 × 7.

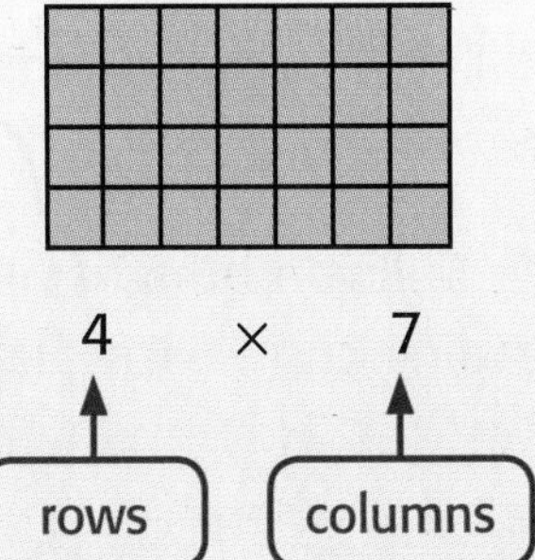

There is a total of 28 squares.

So, 4 × 7 = 28.

Multiply or divide.

27. 4 × 8 **28.** 9 × 6

29. 10 ÷ 2 **30.** 90 ÷ 9

31. Spencer sold 9 magazine subscriptions to make money for his club. Each magazine subscription costs $7. How much money did Spencer collect?

32. Mr. Dunn has 6 rows of desks in his classroom. There are 5 desks in each row. How many desks are in Mr. Dunn's classroom?

5-6 Multiply with 11 and 12 (pp. 194–197)

Example 8
Marina has scored 9 points on each of 11 quizzes. How many points has she scored in all?

Think of 9 × 11 as (9 × 10) + (9 × 1).

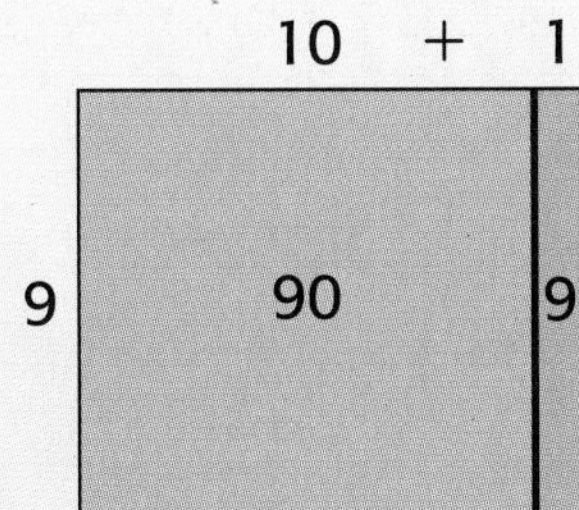

9 × 11 = (9 × 10) + (9 × 1)
= 90 + 9
= 99

So, Marina has scored 99 points.

Multiply or divide.

33. 72 ÷ 8 **34.** 12 × 6

35. 12)84 **36.** 12 × 9

Compare. Write >, <, or =.

37. 108 ÷ 12 ■ 88 ÷ 8

38. 12 × 6 ■ 8 × 10

39. 36 ÷ 3 ■ 6 × 2

40. Kirsten's parents go to the grocery store once a week. How many times do they go to the grocery store in one year?

5-7 Problem-Solving Investigation: Choose a Strategy (pp. 198–199)

Example 9
Carlo wants to buy a frozen yogurt. The flavors of yogurt are vanilla, chocolate, or strawberry. The yogurt comes in a dish or on a cone. How many choices does he have?

Understand

What facts do you know?

- The yogurt flavors are vanilla, chocolate, and strawberry.
- Yogurt comes in a dish or on a cone.

What do you need to find?

- How many yogurt choices Carlo has.

Plan Make a table.

Solve

Flavor	Cone	Dish
Vanilla	X	X
Chocolate	X	X
Strawberry	X	X

Carlo has 6 choices for his yogurt.

Check There are 3 flavors and two choices for each flavor. So, Carlo has 6 choices. The answer is correct.

Use the *make a table* strategy or choose an operation to solve each problem.

41. Amy wants to buy two dolls. Each doll costs $16. What is the total cost of the dolls?

42. Mr. Sullivan bought pizza for the reading club. Each pizza had 10 slices. How many pizzas did he buy if there were 120 slices?

43. Twyla worked five days in one week. She worked 40 hours during that week. She worked the same number of hours each day. How many hours did she work each day?

44. Conchita has 25 math problems for homework each day. Copy and complete the table to find how many problems she completes in five days.

Day	Problems Completed
1	25
2	50
3	75
4	■
5	■

45. Bradley has 3 tap dancing lessons each week. Each lesson is 2 hours long. How many hours of lessons will Bradley have completed in 4 weeks?

5-8 Multiply Three Numbers (pp. 200–203)

Example 10
Find 3 × 5 × 4.

You need to find 3 × 5 × 4.

One Way	Another Way
Multiply 3 × 5 first.	Multiply 5 × 4 first.
3 × 5 × 4	3 × **5 × 4**
(**3 × 5**) × 4	3 × (**5 × 4**)
15 × 4	3 × 20
60	60

So, 3 × 5 × 4 = 60.

Multiply.

46. 6 × 2 × 3 **47.** 2 × 4 × 9

48. 2 × 8 × 4 **49.** 5 × 1 × 11

Algebra Copy and complete each number sentence.

50. ■ × 7 × 3 = 42

51. 4 × ■ × 3 = 108

52. Jason goes to the park for 2 hours a day, 5 days a week. How many hours will he spend in the park in a month?

5-9 Factors and Multiples (pp. 204–207)

Example 11
Find all of the factors of 6.

Think of number pairs that result in a product of 6.

1 × 6

2 × 3

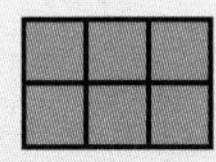

So, the factors of 6 are 1, 2, 3, and 6.

Example 12
Identify the first 5 multiples of 4.

Multiples of 4: 0, 4, 8, 12, 16, 20, 24, …

The first five multiples of 4 are 0, 4, 8, 12, and 16.

Find all of the factors of each number.

53. 8 **54.** 12

55. 16 **56.** 28

Identify the first five multiples for each number.

57. 3 **58.** 5

59. 8 **60.** 10

61. Lora is arranging her 18 snow globes on a shelf. Write the different ways she can arrange the snow globes.

62. Glenn reads 11 pages in his book each day. How many pages will he read in one week? in 9, 10, or 11 days?

5-10 Prime and Composite Numbers (pp. 208–211)

Example 13
Tell whether the number 16 is *prime*, *composite*, or *neither*.

Find the factors of 16.

1 × 16

2 × 8

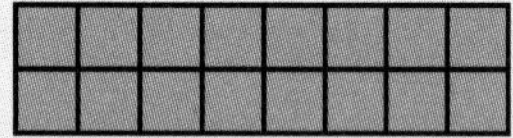

4 × 4

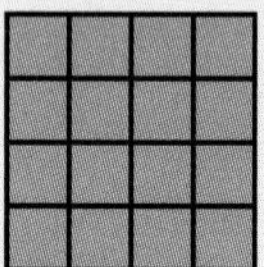

Factors of 16: 1, 2, 4, 8, 16

Since 16 has more than two factors, it is a composite number.

Example 14
Tell whether the number 17 is *prime*, *composite*, or *neither*.

Find the factors of 17.

1 × 17

Factors of 17: 1, 17

Since 17 has exactly 2 distinct factors, it is a prime number.

Tell whether each number is *prime*, *composite*, or neither.

63. 1 **64.** 14

65. 20 **66.** 31

67. 35 **68.** 43

69. What prime number is greater than 30 and less than 35?

70. What prime number is greater than 50 and less than 55?

71. Emily has 8 posters to hang. Tell whether 8 is a prime or composite number. If it is composite, list all of the ways Emily can arrange the posters in even rows.

72. Jolon is arranging 7 airplane models on a shelf. Tell whether 7 is a prime or composite number. If it is composite, list all of the ways Jolon can arrange the models in even rows.

73. A theatre can seat 100 people. Tell whether 100 is a prime or composite number. If it is composite, list all of the ways the seats can be arranged.

CHAPTER 5

Chapter Test

For Exercises 1–3, tell whether each statement is *true* or *false*.

1. A number that has more than two factors is a composite number.
2. Factors are numbers that do not divide into a whole number evenly.
3. A prime number has exactly 2 factors, 1 and the number itself.

Algebra Compare. Write >, <, or =.

4. $2 \times 7 \times 3$ ■ $8 \times 3 \times 4$
5. $5 \times 3 \times 9$ ■ $4 \times 2 \times 5$
6. There are 5 boxes of paints on an art store shelf. Each box contains one dozen colors. How many paint colors are on the shelf?

Find all of the factors of each number.

7. 27
8. 36
9. **STANDARDS PRACTICE** Which number will make the number sentence true?

$4 \times$ ■ $\times 5 = 180$

A 7 **C** 9
B 8 **D** 10

10. Write a fact family for the array.

Algebra Find the value of each number sentence if ♥ = 5 and ☺ = 10.

11. ♥ $\times 8$
12. ☺ $\div 5$

Copy and complete each number sentence. Identify each property shown.

13. ■ $\times 7 = 7 \times 4$
14. ■ $\div 12 = 0$
15. Identify all of the factors related to the array.

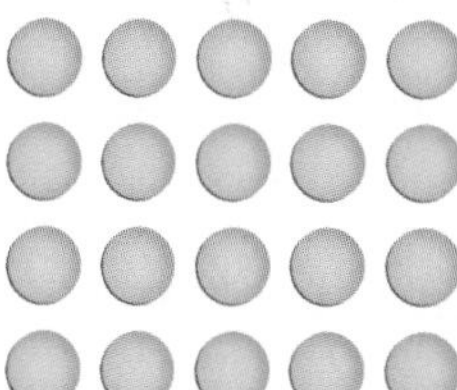

Identify the first five multiples for each number.

16. 7
17. 9

Multiply.

18. $6 \times 3 \times 12$
19. $4 \times 2 \times 7$

Divide.

20. $33 \div 11$
21. $36 \div 6$
22. **STANDARDS PRACTICE** Which number has more than 6 factors?

F 6 **H** 15
G 12 **J** 64

23. **WRITING IN MATH** Explain how multiplication and division are related.

CHAPTER 5

California Standards Practice

Cumulative, Chapters 1–5

Standards Example

Jen has 24 swimming trophies. She wants to arrange an equal number on 4 shelves of a bookcase. How many trophies will she place on each shelf?

A 8 **C** 4

B 6 **D** 3

Read the Question

You need to find an equal number of trophies that will fit on 4 shelves. Divide $24 \div 4$.

Solve the Question

To help you divide, think about a related multiplication fact.

$4 \times 6 = 24$ and $6 \times 4 = 24$

So, $24 \div 4 = 6$.

The answer is B.

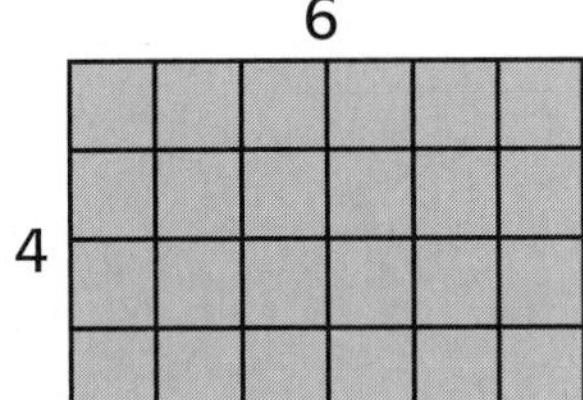

Personal Tutor at ca.gr4math.com

Choose the best answer.

1 **Mrs. Park has 35 students. She puts 7 students in each group. How many groups are there?**

A 4 **C** 6

B 5 **D** 7

2 **The school cafeteria has 100 seats. Each table seats 10 students. How many tables are in the cafeteria?**

F 8 **H** 80

G 10 **J** 800

3 **Which of the following is a prime number?**

A 2 **C** 6
B 4 **D** 8

---

4 **The table below shows the number of miles Neil biked during June. About how many miles did he bike in all?**

Neil's Biking Distance for June	
Week	**Number of Miles**
1	39
2	52
3	46
4	53

F 150 miles **H** 190 miles
G 175 miles **J** 210 miles

---

5 **Which statement is true?**

A The only factors of 3 are 1 and 3.
B The only factors of 4 are 1 and 4.
C The only factors of 6 are 1 and 6.
D The only factors of 10 are 1 and 10.

---

6 **Which of the following has the greatest value?**

F 297,503 **H** 457,650
G 329,450 **J** 479,350

---

7 **Which number is represented by *n*?**

$$43 - n = 24$$

A 18 **C** 27
B 19 **D** 67

---

8 **Which of these is another way to write the product of 12 × 5?**

F $1 \times 6 \times 5$ **H** $3 \times 6 \times 5$
G $2 \times 6 \times 5$ **J** $6 \times 6 \times 5$

---

9 **Which of these is another way to write the number 3,003,013?**

A three million, 3 hundred, thirteen
B three million, 3 thousand, thirteen
C three hundred thousand, thirteen
D thirty million, thirty thousand, thirteen

---

10 **Ajay surveyed 35 students about their favorite sport. He made a table to show his results.**

Favorite Sport	
Sport	**Number of Students**
Baseball	9
Basketball	8
Football	12
Soccer	6

How many more students prefer football and baseball than basketball and soccer?

F 6 **H** 8
G 7 **J** 9

Chapter 6 Algebra: Use Multiplication and Division

BIG Idea How are equations used to solve problems?

Example Karen has 54 rubber balls. She wants to divide them equally among 6 friends. Write and solve an equation to find the number of rubber balls each friend will get.

friends		number of balls each gets		total number of balls	
6	×	d	=	54	Think 6 times what number equals 54?
6	×	9	=	54	
		d	=	9	You know that $6 \times 9 = 54$.

The value of d is 9. So, each friend will get 9 balls.

What will I learn in this chapter?

- Write and find the value of expressions.
- Write and solve equations.
- Find and use a rule to write an equation.
- Balance multiplication and division equations.
- Solve problems by working backward.

Key Vocabulary

expression

order of operations

equation

Student Study Tools at ca.gr4math.com

FOLDABLES™ Study Organizer

Make this Foldable to help you organize information about using multiplication and division in algebra. Begin with a sheet of 11″ × 17″ paper.

1. **Fold** a 3″ tab along one side as shown.

2. **Fold** again into thirds. Glue the ends of the pockets closed.

3. **Label** as shown. Take notes on index cards. Store the note cards in the correct pockets.

ARE YOU READY for Chapter 6?

You have two ways to check prerequisite skills for this chapter.

Option 2

Math Online Take the Chapter Readiness Quiz at ca.gr4math.com.

Option 1

Complete the Quick Check below.

QUICK Check

Find the missing number. (Lesson 3-1)

1. 3 + ■ = 11

2. ■ + 7 = 15

3. 8 + ■ = 13

4. 12 − ■ = 6

5. ■ − 5 = 4

6. 18 − ■ = 9

Write an equation for each situation. Then solve. (Lesson 3-2)

7. Ramona folded 7 pieces of origami on Saturday. After she folded more origami on Sunday, she had a total of 14 pieces of origami. How many pieces of origami did she fold on Sunday?

8. Mike read 12 pages of a book on Wednesday. After he read more pages on Thursday, he read a total of 25 pages. How many pages did he read on Thursday?

Write an equation to describe the pattern. Then use the equation to find the next three numbers. (Lesson 3-4)

9.

Input (a)	3	6	9	12	15	18
Output (b)	8	11	14	■	■	■

10.

Input (m)	15	21	27	33	39	45
Output (n)	7	13	19	■	■	■

11. Adamo is 12 years old. He is 6 years older than his younger sister Sayra. Copy and complete the table to find how old Sayra will be when Adamo is 32 years old.

Input (a)	12	16	20	24	28	32
Output (b)	6	10	14	■	■	■

6-1 Multiplication and Division Expressions

MAIN IDEA

I will write and find the value of multiplication and division expressions.

Standard 4AF1.1 Use letters, boxes, or other symbols **to stand for any number in simple expressions** or equations **(e.g., demonstrate an understanding and the use of the concept of a variable).**

Review Vocabulary

expression a combination of variables, numbers, and at least one operation; *Example:* $n + 3$; $4 \times n$

GET READY to Learn

Danielle has 4 cans of tennis balls. The total number of balls can be represented by the expression below.

cans → $4 \times n$ ← balls per can

Finding the value of multiplication and division expressions is similar to finding the value of addition and subtraction expressions.

Real-World EXAMPLE Find Value of an Expression

1 ALGEBRA If there are 3 balls in each can, what is the total number of tennis balls? Find the value of $4 \times n$ if $n = 3$.

$4 \times n$	Write the expression.
4×3	Replace n with 3.
12	Multiply 4 and 3.

So, the value of the expression is 12. Danielle has a total of 12 tennis balls.

Recall that you perform the operations inside parentheses first.

EXAMPLE Find the Value of an Expression

2 Find the value of $2 \times (15 \div x)$ if $x = 5$.

$2 \times (15 \div x)$	Write the expression.
$2 \times (15 \div 5)$	Replace x with 5.
2×3	Find $(15 \div 5)$ first.
6	Next, find 2×3.

Remember

When a number and a variable appear together as in $3y$, it means *multiply*.

Example: $3y = 3 \times y$

You can write expressions for real-world situations.

Real-World EXAMPLE Write an Expression

3 Owen has *d* dollars to buy airplane models. Write an expression for the number of models Owen can buy with his money.

Write an expression.

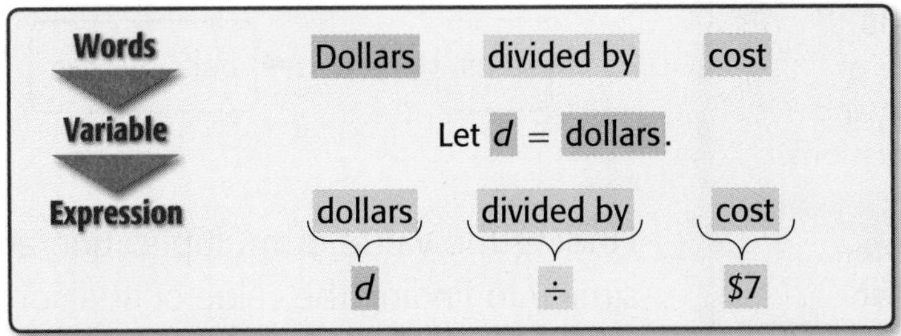

Words
Dollars divided by cost
Variable
Let d = dollars.
Expression
dollars divided by cost
d ÷ $7

So, the number of airplane models Owen can buy is $d \div \$7$.

Online Personal Tutor at ca.gr4math.com

CHECK What You Know

Find the value of each expression if $a = 3$ and $c = 6$. See Examples 1 and 2 (p. 225)

1. $2a$ **2.** $c \div a$ **3.** $(15 \div a) \times 6$

Write an expression for each situation. See Example 3 (p. 226)

4. 9 times n

5. n multiplied by 12

6. a number divided by 8

7. 24 divided by a number

For Exercises 8 and 9, use the following information. See Example 3 (p. 226)
Tobias has four times as much money as Kyle.

8. Define a variable. Then write an expression for the amount of money Tobias has.

9. If Kyle has $8, how much money does Tobias have?

10. Talk About It How do you find the value of $9 \times (y \div 4)$ when $y = 20$?

Practice and Problem Solving

EXTRA PRACTICE
See page R14.

Find the value of each expression if $f = 10$ and $g = 5$.
See Examples 1 and 2 (p. 225)

11. $6g$

12. $f \times 7$

13. $f \div 5$

14. $g \div 5$

15. gf

16. $f \div g$

17. $4 \times (f \div 2)$

18. $(f \div g) \times 9$

19. $(f \times g) \div 5$

Write an expression for each situation. See Example 3 (p. 226)

20. n multiplied by 5

21. the product of 2 and a number

22. 8 divided by n

23. 18 divided by a number

A teacher has 7 boxes of pens. Each box contains 8 pens. See Example 3 (p. 226)

24. Define a variable. Then write an expression for the number of pens the teacher has.

25. If the teacher bought 2 more boxes of pens, how many pens will the teacher have?

Eduardo has 5 CDs with 9 songs on each of them. See Example 3 (p. 226)

26. Define a variable. Then write an expression for the number of songs that are on the CDs.

27. If Eduardo lets a friend borrow 2 of his CDs, how many songs will be on the CDs he has left?

Real-World PROBLEM SOLVING

Data File The state mammal of California is the grizzly bear.

28. Write an expression for the total length of any given number of bears.

29. **Measurement** Find the total length of 4 male bears.

State Mammal

The "Bear" Facts
Maximum running speed ... 35 mph
Maximum length .... 7 feet
Maximum weight .... 1,500 pounds
Length of front claws .... 5 inches
Source: enchantedlearning.com

H.O.T. Problems

30. **OPEN ENDED** Write a division expression that has a value of 3 if $n = 7$.

31. **WRITING IN MATH** Write a problem that uses the expression $(4 \times n) \div 7$.

6-2 Problem-Solving Strategy

MAIN IDEA I will solve problems by working backward.

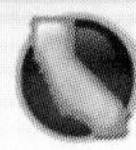

Standard 4MR1.1 **Analyze problems by identifying relationships, distinguishing relevant from irrelevant information, sequencing and prioritizing information, and observing patterns.** Standard 4NS3.0 **Students solve problems involving** addition, **subtraction,** multiplication, and division **of whole numbers and understand the relationships among the operations.**

Currently there are 25 students in the chess club. Last October, 3 students joined. Two months before that, in August, 8 students joined. How many students were in the club originally?

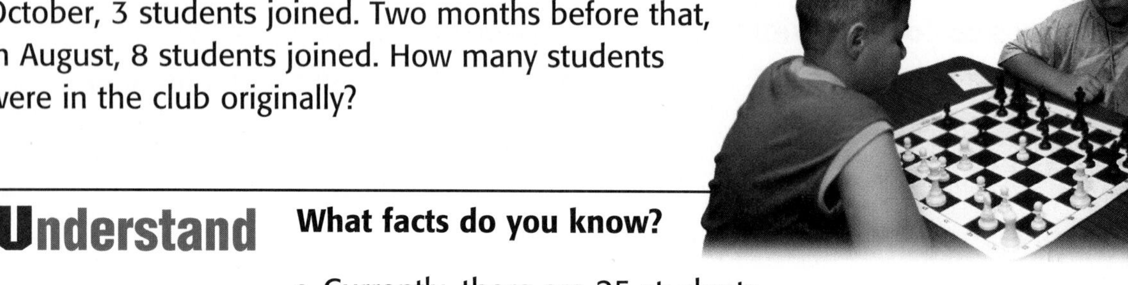

Understand

What facts do you know?

- Currently, there are 25 students in the club.
- 3 students joined in October.
- 8 students joined in August.

What do you need to find?

- The number of students that were in the club originally.

Plan

Work backward to solve the problem.

Solve

Work backward and use inverse operations. Start with the end result and subtract the students who joined the club.

$$\begin{array}{r} 25 \\ -\ 3 \\ \hline 22 \end{array}$$

25 ← students in the club now
3 ← students who joined in October

$$\begin{array}{r} 22 \\ -\ 8 \\ \hline 14 \end{array}$$

8 ← students who joined in August

So, there were 14 students in the club originally.

Check

Look back at the problem. A total of 3 + 8 or 11 students joined the club. So, if there were 14 students originally, there would be 14 + 11 or 25 students in the club now. The answer is correct.

ANALYZE the Strategy

Refer to the problem on the previous page.

1. Explain why an 8 was subtracted from the number of students that are in the chess club now.

2. Suppose there are 28 students in the chess club now. How many students were in the club originally?

3. Suppose 2 students moved away. How would you find the number of students in the club originally?

4. Look back at Exercise 3. Check your answer. How do you know it is correct? Show your work.

PRACTICE the Strategy

EXTRA PRACTICE
See page R15.

Solve. Use the *work backward* strategy.

5. Garrett went ice skating. He paid $6 for admission. Then he bought a bowl of soup for $2 and a hot cocoa for $1. Garrett now has $11. How much money did he have originally?

6. **Measurement** Jamila completed her homework at 5:30 P.M. Use the table to find how long Jamila worked on her homework.

Jamila's Activities
Dismissed 3 P.M.
Walked home 15 minutes
Ate snack 15 minutes
Watched T.V. 1 hour

7. Claudio and his family are going on vacation. He packs 3 more shirts than shorts, 2 more socks than shirts, and 4 pairs of shorts. How many shirts, shorts, and socks did he pack?

8. On a farm, there are 7 more horses than chickens. There are 3 times as many cows as horses. The number of chickens is shown. How many cows are there?

9. **Measurement** Yoki jogged 15 miles in a week. She jogged 2 miles on Monday. She jogged twice as many miles on Wednesday. She jogged 3 miles on Thursday. How many miles did she jog on the other days?

10. Mateo is thinking of a number. He adds 6, divides by 2, subtracts 1, and multplies by 7. The result is 28. What is Mateo's number?

11. WRITING IN MATH Refer to Exercise 8. Explain how you used the *work backward* strategy to find the solution.

6-3 Order of Operations

GET READY to Learn

Tabitha has 3 cats. Two of her cats each had a litter of kittens with 4 kittens in each litter. Tabitha found good homes for 6 of the kittens. How many cats does Tabitha still have?

has 3 cats		2 litters of 4 kittens		found homes for 6
3	+	(2 × 4)	−	6

To find the value of an expression with more than one operation, you need to follow the rules for the **order of operations**.

MAIN IDEA

I will use the order of operations to find the value of expressions.

Standard 4AF1.2 Interpret and evaluate mathematical expressions that now use parentheses.

Standard 4AF1.3 Use parentheses to indicate which operation to perform first when writing expressions containing more than two terms and different operations.

New Vocabulary

order of operations

KEY CONCEPT — Order of Operations

1. Do the operations in the parentheses first.
2. Multiply and divide in order from left to right.
3. Add and subtract in order from left to right.

EXAMPLE Use the Order of Operations

1 Find 3 + (2 × 4) − 6 to find how many cats Tabitha still has.

$3 + (2 \times 4) - 6$	Write the expression.
$3 + 8 - 6$	Parentheses first. $(2 \times 4) = 8$
$3 + 8 - 6$	There is no multiplication or division, so move to next step.
$11 - 6$	Add and subtract from left to right. $3 + 8 = 11$ and $11 - 6 = 5$
5	

So, Tabitha has 5 cats left.

You can use the order of operations to find the value of an expression with variables.

Remember

If an expression has no parentheses ( ), go to the next step.

EXAMPLE **Use the Order of Operations**

2 **Find the value of $3x + 5y - 4$, when $x = 5$ and $y = 7$.**

Follow the order of operations.

$3x + 5y - 4 = 3 \times 5 + 5 \times 7 - 4$ $x = 5$ and $y = 7$.

$= 15 + 35 - 4$ Multiply from left to right.

$= 50 - 4$ Add and subtract from left to right.

$= 46$ Subtract.

Online **Personal Tutor at** ca.gr4math.com

CHECK What You Know

Find the value of each expression. **See Examples 1 and 2 (pp. 230–231)**

1. $(7 + 1) \times 3 - 5$

2. $(8 - 5) \div 3 + 2$

3. $13 + 4 - (7 \times 2)$

4. $5(m + 3)$, if $m = 2$

5. $3r - (5 \times 2) + 6$, if $r = 4$

6. $2x - 3y + 2$, if $x = 7$ and $y = 4$

7. $4p + (3 \times 8) \div 6$, if $p = 2$

8. $7w + 5v - 1$, if $w = 3$ and $v = 6$

For Exercises 9 and 10, use the supplies that Sancho and his mom bought for a school project.

GLUE $2
$2
MARKERS $4

9. Write an expression that can be used to find the total cost of the supplies.

10. Find the total cost of the supplies.

11. **Talk About It** What operation would you do first in $6 + (14 \div 7)$? Explain your reasoning.

Practice and Problem Solving

EXTRA PRACTICE See page R15.

Find the value of each expression. See Examples 1 and 2 (pp. 230–231)

12. $(5 + 4) \times 7 - 3$

13. $(6 - 2) \div 4 + 1$

14. $8 \times (14 - 8) + 7$

15. $16 \div (7 - 3) - 2$

16. $6 \times (8 - 5) + 9$

17. $(8 + 6) \div (12 - 5)$

18. $8(n - 4)$, if $n = 9$

19. $9(2 + g)$, if $g = 6$

20. $7m - (6 \div 2) + 3$, if $m = 3$

21. $(4 + 6) - 5h + 8$, if $h = 2$

22. $4x \div (8 - 4) - 5 + 3w$, if $x = 7$ and $w = 2$

23. $t + 3r \div 5 \times (5 - 2)$, if $t = 6$ and $r = 5$

Write and find the value of an expression for each situation.

24. Veronica has $12. She will babysit 6 hours over the weekend. She gets paid $3 each hour. How much money will she have after she babysits?

25. **Measurement** Todd walked 2 miles a day for 4 days and 3 miles on the fifth day. How many miles did he walk?

26. A person's heart rate while exercising can be found with the expression $(220 - a) \times 7 \div 10$, where a is the person's age. Find the heart rate of a 20-year-old person who is exercising.

27. To change a temperature from degrees Celsius to degrees Fahrenheit, use the expression $(c \times 9) \div 5 + 32$. What is the temperature in degrees Fahrenheit if it is 5 in degrees Celsius?

Real-World PROBLEM SOLVING

Entertainment Jude and Diego are going to the movies. The ticket and food prices are shown. They each get a student discount of $2 off a ticket.

28. Diego bought snacks for the movies. Use $6 – $2 + $5 + $3 to find the total cost of his ticket and snacks.

29. Which snacks did Diego buy?

30. Diego had $20. He paid for Jude's ticket. Can you use $20 – 2 × ($6 – $2) – $5 – $3 to find how much change Diego received? Explain.

ACTIVITY

2 **Solve $n \div 2 = 3$.**

Step 1 **Model the equation.**

In $n \div 2 = 3$, the variable n is unknown. Use a cup to represent n. The expression $n \div 2$ means to divide a cup into 2 equal parts. Think of the top view of a cup.

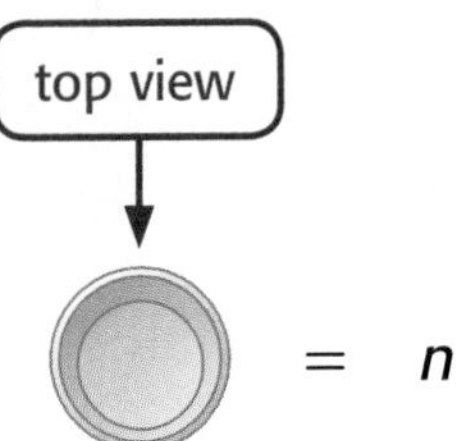

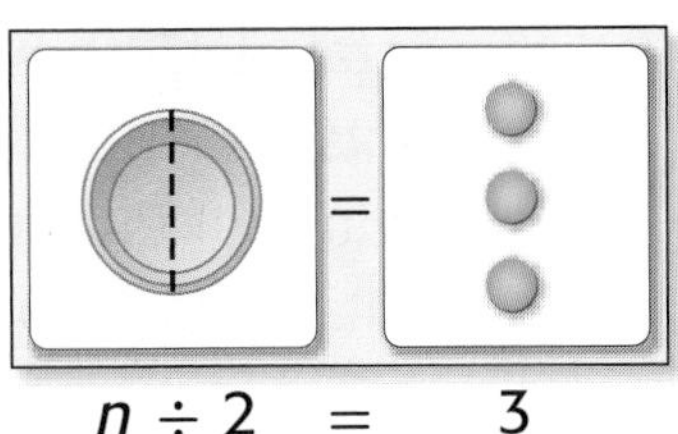

$n \div 2 = 3$

Step 2 **Find the value of *n*.**

Since $n \div 2 = 3$, each 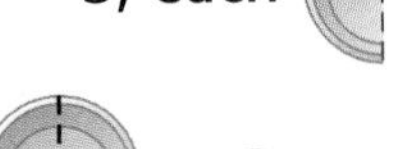 = 3.

So, 2 parts = 6.

So, the value of n is 6.

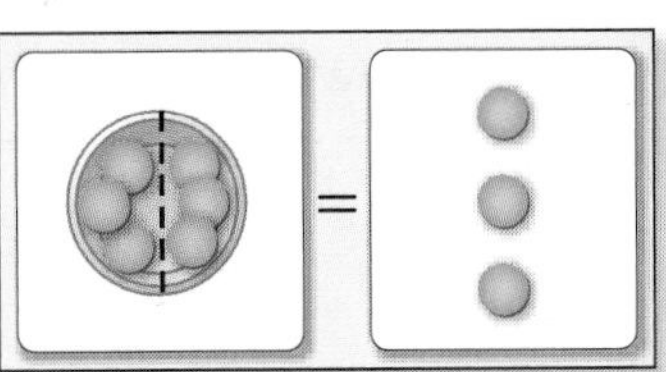

$n \div 2 = 3$

$6 \div 2 = 3$

Think About It

1. How do you model $2 \times y = 10$?

2. Use your model to solve $2 \times y = 10$.

CHECK What You Know

Write an equation for each model. Then solve.

3. 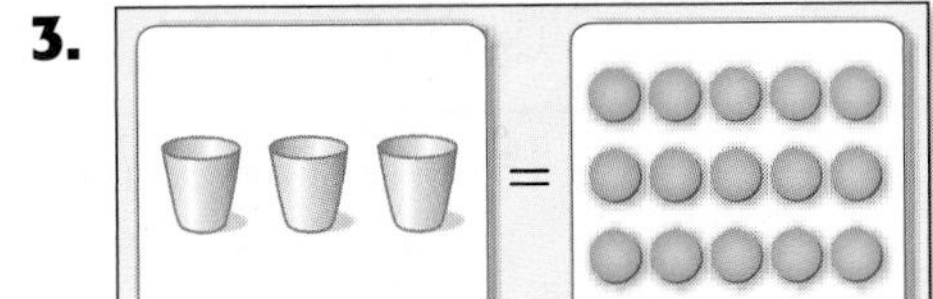

4. 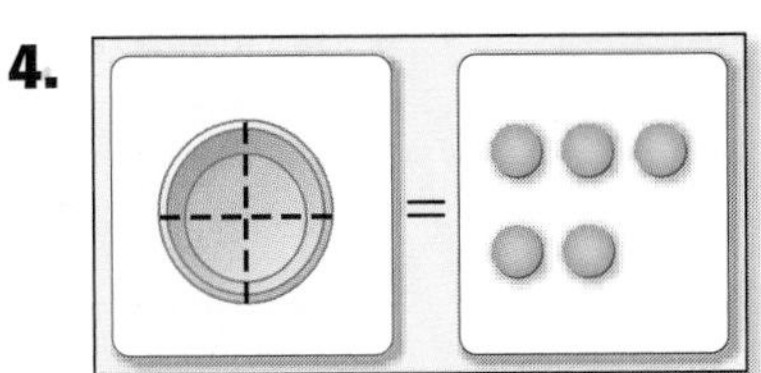

Model each equation. Then solve.

5. $6 \times r = 12$

6. $2 \times m = 14$

7. $w \div 4 = 4$

8. $z \div 2 = 9$

9. **WRITING IN MATH** Explain how to check your answer.

6-4 Solve Equations Mentally

MAIN IDEA

I will solve multiplication and division equations mentally.

Standard 4AF1.1 Use letters, boxes, or other symbols **to stand for any number in** simple expressions or **equations (e.g., demonstrate an understanding and the use of the concept of a variable).**

GET READY to Learn

Kelly is planting tomatoes. She has 3 rows of plants with a total of 15 tomato plants. What is the number of tomato plants in each row?

3 rows	how many per row		equal	15?
3	$\times$	v	$=$	15

To solve an equation like $3 \times v = 15$, you can use a model or mental math.

Real-World EXAMPLE **Solve Multiplication Equations**

1. **GARDENS Solve $3 \times v = 15$ to find how many tomato plants are in each row.**

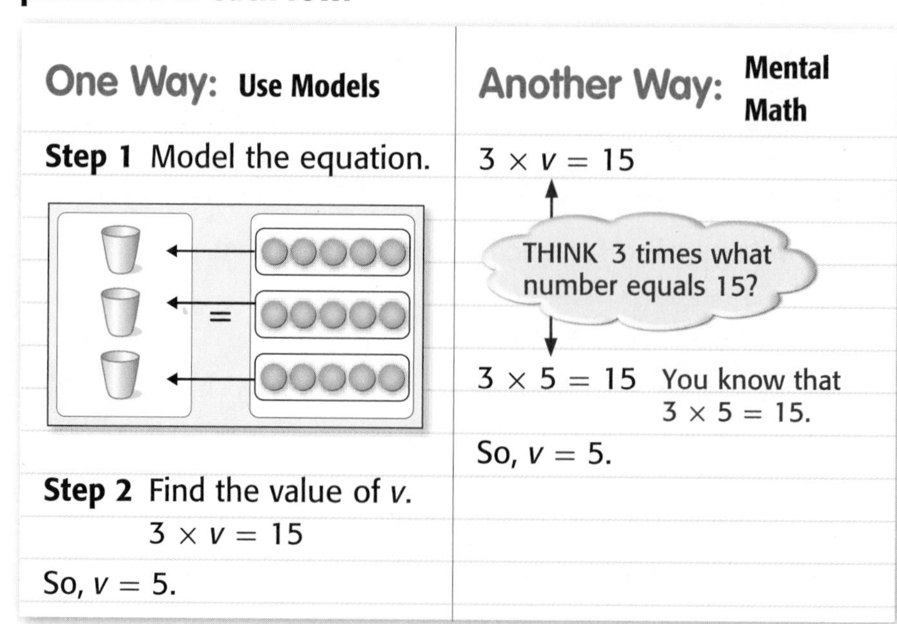

One Way: Use Models	**Another Way: Mental Math**
Step 1 Model the equation.	$3 \times v = 15$
	THINK 3 times what number equals 15?
	$3 \times 5 = 15$ You know that $3 \times 5 = 15$.
	So, $v = 5$.
Step 2 Find the value of v. $3 \times v = 15$	
So, $v = 5$.	

Division equations can also be solved mentally.

Remember

Related facts can help you find the value of variables in expressions.

EXAMPLE Solve Division Equations

2 Solve $d \div 3 = 7$.

$d \div 3 = 7$	What number divided by 3 equals 7?
$21 \div 3 = 7$	You know that $21 \div 3 = 7$.
$d = 21$	

So, the value of d is 21.

Real-World EXAMPLE Write and Solve Equations

3 Five friends went fishing. They each caught the same number of fish. A total of 30 fish were caught. Write and solve an equation to find how many fish each person caught.

Write and solve an equation.

Words	5 friends caught 30 fish
Variable	Let f = number of fish caught per person.
Expression	$5 \times f = 30$

$5 \times f = 30$	5 times what number equals 30?
$5 \times 6 = 30$	You know that $5 \times 6 = 30$.
$f = 6$	

So, $f = 6$. Each person caught 6 fish.

Online Personal Tutor at ca.gr4math.com

CHECK What You Know

Solve each equation mentally. See Examples 1 and 2 (pp. 236–237)

1. $2 \times k = 6$

2. $c \times 8 = 32$

3. $48 \div g = 8$

Write and solve an equation to find the number. See Example 3 (p. 237)

4. A number times 4 equals 36. What is the number?

5. Talk About It How would you solve $10 \div a = 2$ mentally?

Practice and Problem Solving

EXTRA PRACTICE
See page R15.

Solve each equation mentally. See Examples 1 and 2 (pp. 236–237)

6. $3 \times p = 9$

7. $6 \times h = 42$

8. $4 \times g = 48$

9. $5 \times k = 50$

10. $a \times 5 = 25$

11. $t \times 12 = 60$

12. $36 \div m = 4$

13. $49 \div z = 7$

14. $81 \div n = 9$

15. $100 \div b = 10$

16. $y \div 7 = 9$

17. $r \div 12 = 11$

Write an equation for each situation. Then solve. See Example 3 (p. 237)

18. A number multiplied by 11 equals 33. What is the number?

19. 5 times a number equals 45. Find the number.

20. A number divided by 6 equals 4. Find the number.

21. 121 divided by a number equals 11. What is the number?

22. Mr. Ruiz is 4 times as old as Rodolfo. Mr. Ruiz is 48 years old. What is Rodolfo's age?

23. Ayana dribbled a basketball for 12 minutes, which is 6 times as long as Luke. How long did Luke dribble the ball?

Real-World PROBLEM SOLVING

Measurement The table shows the activities offered at a camp.

24. Casandra went horseback riding for three hours. She covered d miles at a speed of 10 miles each hour. Write and solve a division equation to find the length of the horse trail.

25. The length of the horse trail is 5 times as long as the length of the bike trail. Write and solve a division equation to find the length of the bike trail.

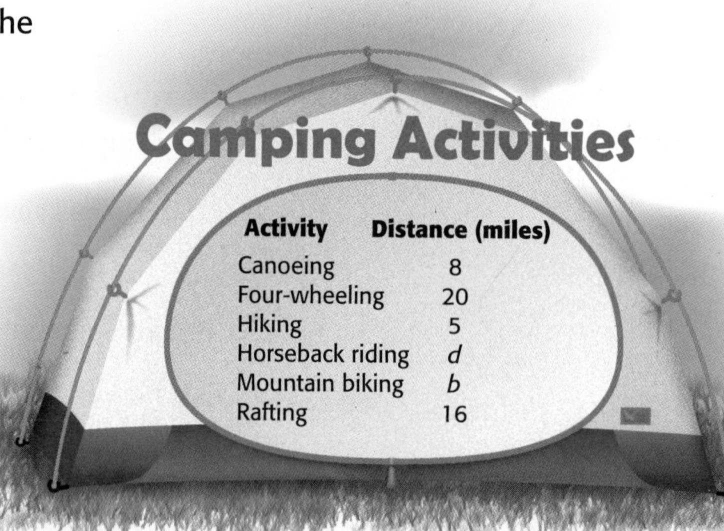

Camping Activities

Activity	Distance (miles)
Canoeing	8
Four-wheeling	20
Hiking	5
Horseback riding	d
Mountain biking	b
Rafting	16

H.O.T. Problems

26. **OPEN ENDED** Write one multiplication equation and one division equation that both have a variable whose value is 6.

27. **WRITING IN MATH** Write a word problem for $10 \div f = 5$.

CHAPTER 6

Mid-Chapter Check

Lessons 6-1 through 6-4

Find the value of each expression if $a = 2$ and $c = 5$. (Lesson 6-1)

1. $30 \div c$
2. $(14 \div a) \times c$

3. STANDARDS PRACTICE What is the value of the expression below if $a = 3$? (Lesson 6-1)

$$15 - (a + 5)$$

A 4

B 7

C 20

D 26

Write an expression for each situation. (Lesson 6-1)

4. 7 times n

5. 36 divided by a number

6. **Measurement** Mala has a piano lesson at 4:30 P.M. It takes 15 minutes to get to her lesson and 5 minutes to warm up. What time should she leave home to be ready for her lesson on time? (Lesson 6-2)

7. José and his mom bought the pet supplies shown. They received a discount of \$1 off each toy. Find the value of $2 \times (\$2 - \$1) + \$6$ to find the total cost of the supplies. (Lesson 6-3)

Find the value of each expression. (Lesson 6-3)

8. $15 - 3 \times (4 + 1)$

9. $21 \div (6 - 3) + 7$

Solve each equation mentally. (Lesson 6-4)

10. $c \times 4 = 32$

11. $56 \div g = 8$

Write and solve an equation for each situation. (Lesson 6-4)

12. A number times 5 equals 35. What is the number?

13. 54 divided by a number equals 9. What is the number?

14. Conrado downloaded 56 songs onto his digital music player in a week. He downloaded the same number of songs each day. Write and solve an equation to find how many songs he downloaded each day.

15. STANDARDS PRACTICE Which number is represented by n? (Lesson 6-4)

$$8 \times n = 40$$

F 5

G 6

H 32

J 48

16. WRITING IN ▶MATH Write a real-world problem for the equation $22 \div f = 11$. (Lesson 6-4)

6-5 Problem-Solving Investigation

MAIN IDEA I will choose the best strategy to solve a problem.

Standard 4MR1.1 **Analyze problems by identifying relationships, distinguishing relevant from irrelevant information, sequencing and prioritizing information, and observing patterns.** Standard 4NS3.0 **Students solve problems involving addition,** subtraction, **multiplication,** and division **of whole numbers and understand the relationships among the operations.**

P.S.I. TEAM +

MATT: I take 30-minute guitar lessons two times a week. How many minutes do I have guitar lessons in six weeks?

YOUR MISSION: Find how many minutes Matt has guitar lessons in six weeks.

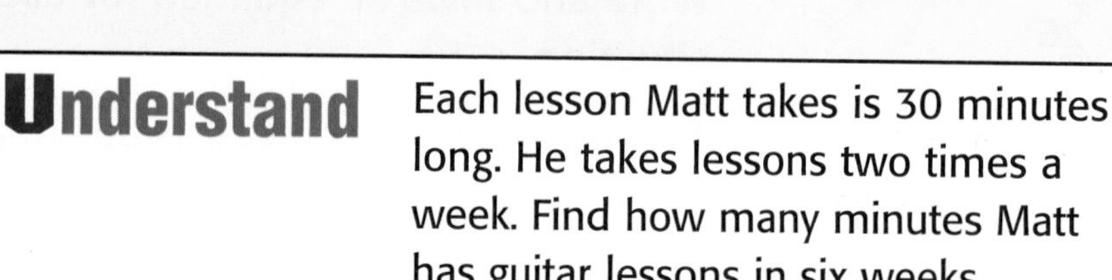

Understand Each lesson Matt takes is 30 minutes long. He takes lessons two times a week. Find how many minutes Matt has guitar lessons in six weeks.

Plan You can use a table to help you solve the problem.

Solve First, find how many minutes Matt has lessons each week.

$$\begin{array}{rl} 30 & \text{lesson 1} \\ +30 & \text{lesson 2} \\ \hline 60 & \text{minutes per week} \end{array}$$

Now use a table to find how many minutes Matt has lessons in six weeks.

Week	1	2	3	4	5	6
Time (min)	60	120	180	240	300	360

+60 +60 +60 +60 +60

So, Matt has lessons 360 minutes in six weeks.

Check Look back at the problem. Subtract 60 from 360 six times. The result is 0. So, the answer is correct.

Mixed Problem Solving

Use any strategy shown below to solve. Tell which strategy you used.

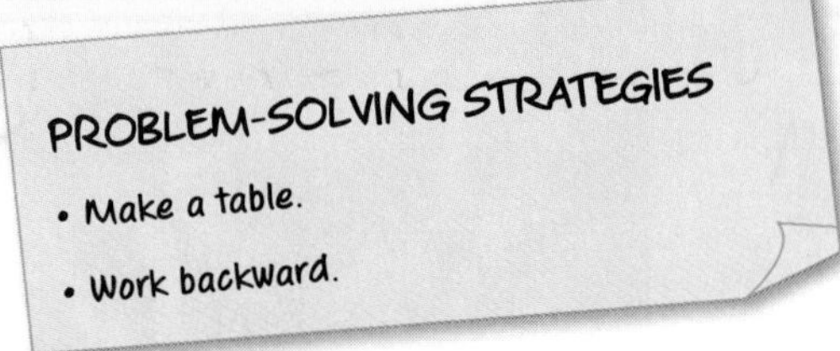

1. A plant grew 3 inches in the first month. The second month it grew twice as many inches. It grew a total of 18 inches in three months. How many inches did it grow during the third month?

2. A zoo has twice as many lions as cheetahs. There are 3 more tigers than cheetahs. The number of lions is shown below. How many of each cat are there?

3. Jonas is 9 years old. His sister is 7 years old. How old were they when Jonas was twice his sister's age?

4. Seki is making breakfast. He and his two brothers each have 2 eggs. His sister has 1 egg. How many eggs should he cook?

5. Tommy and his two friends each have $15 to go bowling. It costs each boy $3 to rent shoes and $5 for each game. What is the total amount of money left if they each play two games?

6. Nolan gets $5 each week for his allowance. Camila gets $15 each week for mowing the lawn. How much money will Nolan make when Camilla makes $75?

Camila	Nolan
$15	$5
$30	$10
$45	$15
$60	■
$75	■

7. There are about 4 weeks in a month and 12 months in a year. About how many weeks are there in 2 years?

8. Vicki collects stickers. She bought 12 at the store. She traded 2 large stickers for 6 small stickers. She gave her sister 8 stickers. She now has 38 stickers. How many did she have originally?

9. Tia wants to rent 2 movies and 3 video games for 2 days. She has $20. How much change will she receive?

10. **WRITING IN ▶MATH** Santos has 28 action figures. They are lined up in four equal rows. The answer is $n \times 4 = 28$. What is the question?

6-6 Algebra: Find a Rule

MAIN IDEA

I will find and use a rule to write an equation.

Standard 4AF1.5

Understand that an equation such as $y = 3x + 5$ is a prescription for determining a second number when a first number is given.

GET READY to Learn

Tracy rakes yards to earn money. If she rakes 2 yards a day, she earns $12. If she rakes 4 yards, she earns $24. If she rakes 6 yards, she earns $36. How much money will she earn if she rakes 10 yards?

You can write an equation to describe and extend a pattern.

Real-World EXAMPLES Find a Multiplication Rule

1 MONEY Write an equation that describes the amount of money Tracy earns.

Show the information in a table. Then look for the pattern that describes the rule.

Yards Raked	Amount Earned ($)
Input (a)	Output (b)
2	12
4	24
6	36
8	■
10	■
12	■

Patterns: $2 \times 6 = 12$
$4 \times 6 = 24$
$6 \times 6 = 36$

Rule: Multiply by 6.

Equation: $a \times 6 = b$

input (a) output (b)

2 Use the equation to find how much money Tracy will earn if she rakes 8, 10, and 12 yards.

$a \times \$6 = b$ $8 \times \$6 = \$48$

$a \times \$6 = b$ $10 \times \$6 = \$60$

$a \times \$6 = b$ $12 \times \$6 = \$72$

So, Tracy will earn $48, $60, and $72.

Remember

Always check to make sure the rule works for each number in the table.

Real-World EXAMPLES Find a Division Rule

3 MONEY The cost of crackers is shown. Write an equation that describes the pattern.

Total Cost ($)	Boxes of Crackers
Input (g)	Output (h)
4	1
8	2
12	3
16	
20	
24	

Look for the pattern that describes the rule.

Pattern: $4 \div \mathbf{4} = 1$
$6 \div \mathbf{4} = 2$
$12 \div \mathbf{4} = 3$

Rule: Divide by 4.

Equation: $g \div 4 = h$

input ↑ g ouput ↑ h

4 Use the equation to find how many boxes you get for $16, $20, or $24.

$g \div \mathbf{4} = h$ | $g \div \mathbf{4} = h$ | $g \div \mathbf{4} = h$
$\$16 \div \mathbf{4} = 4$ | $\$20 \div \mathbf{4} = 5$ | $\$24 \div \mathbf{4} = 6$

So, $16, $20, or $24 will buy 4, 5, or 6 boxes of crackers.

Online Personal Tutor at ca.gr4math.com

CHECK What You Know

Write an equation that describes the pattern. Then use the equation to find the next three numbers. See Examples 1–4 (pp. 242–243)

1.

Input (w)	2	4	6	8	10	12
Output (v)	12	24	36			

2.

Input (x)	16	24	32	40	48	56
Output (y)	2	3	4			

3. The table shows the cost of movie tickets. How many tickets will you get for $72? See Examples 1–4 (pp. 242–243)

Total Cost	Input (c)	$12	$24	$36	$48	$60	$72
Tickets	Output (t)	2	4	6			

4. **Talk About It** How are a rule and an equation alike? How are they different?

Practice and Problem Solving

EXTRA PRACTICE See page R16.

Write an equation that describes each pattern. Then use the equation to find the next three numbers. See Examples 1–4 (pp. 242–243)

5.

Input (m)	1	3	5	7	9	11
Output (n)	5	15	25	■	■	■

6.

Input (b)	2	4	6	8	10	12
Output (c)	14	28	42	■	■	■

7.

Input (j)	3	9	15	21	27	33
Output (k)	1	3	5	■	■	■

8.

Input (e)	10	20	30	40	50	60
Output (f)	2	4	6	■	■	■

9. A local sports team sells \$6 tickets for \$3, \$8 tickets for \$4, and \$10 tickets for \$5. Write a rule and equation to find the cost of a \$20 ticket.

10. The admission for an art museum costs \$5 per person. Make a table to find how much it would cost for 2, 3, 4, 5, and 6 people to attend the exhibit.

Real-World PROBLEM SOLVING

Art Lydia makes bead necklaces. The table shows the relationship between the number of blue beads and green beads Lydia uses.

Blue Beads	Green Beads
Input (j)	Output (k)
3	1
9	3
15	5
21	■
27	■
33	■

11. Write an equation that describes the relationship between green beads and blue beads.

12. How many green beads does Lydia need if she is using 36 blue beads?

13. How many beads does Lydia have in all if she has 9 green beads?

H.O.T. Problems

14. **OPEN ENDED** Create a table that shows inputs and outputs. Choose a multiplication or division rule for the table. Then choose 6 input numbers and find the output numbers.

15. **CHALLENGE** Can both an addition equation and a multiplication equation be written for the number pattern in the table to the right? Explain.

Input (m)	Output (n)
1	2
2	4
3	6

16. **WRITING IN MATH** Write a problem about a real-world situation that involves a pattern. What equation describes the pattern?

Equation Race

Solve Equations

Get Ready!

Players: 2 players

You will need: 16 index cards

Get Set!

Label 16 index cards as shown.

$n \div 9 = 7$	$n \div 11 = 10$	
$15 \div n = 3$	$n \div 8 = 6$	$35 \div n = 5$
$24 \div n = 12$	$n \div 4 = 9$	$144 \div n = 12$
$12 \times n = 108$	$n \times 9 = 18$	$8 \times n = 64$
$5 \times n = 45$	$n \times 4 = 40$	$3 \times n = 36$
$n \times 7 = 42$	$n \times 11 = 22$	

Go!

- Shuffle the cards. Then spread out the cards face down.
- Player 1 turns over one equation card.
- Both players use mental math to solve the equation.
- The first player to correctly solve the equation gets 1 point.
- Player 2 turns over another equation card. Repeat steps until all of the cards have been used.
- The player with the most points wins.

Problem Solving in Science

Ready, Set, Click!

The first photographers had difficult jobs. They carried separate pieces of film in large metal containers. Each container was 12 inches wide and 16 inches long!

Taking a picture was first a chemical process. Today, taking a picture is a digital process, too. Digital cameras take pictures like a television records images.

There are now many different types of cameras that are affordable. Some cameras that scientists have invented are only used once. There are many different kinds of these cameras, including digital disposable cameras.

Did You Know?

The digital camera revolution started in 1981.

Standard 4AF1.1 **Use** letters, **boxes,** or other symbols **to stand for any number in simple expressions** or equations **(e.g., demonstrate an understanding and the use of the concept of a variable).**

Real-World Math

Use the table below to answer each problem.

1. Describe a pattern in the table. Use the pattern to find how much a camera costs if the price of a package is $40.
2. Cesar buys two digital cameras, a package of outdoor cameras, and three flash cameras. Write an expression to show how much money he spends. Then solve.
3. Suppose you buy a package of outdoor cameras and a flash camera. If you pay with $30, how much change will you get?
4. Which two cameras cost the same as one underwater camera?
5. If you buy 2 packages of underwater cameras, you get a $3 discount. How much money will you spend?
6. You spend $65 on two packages of cameras. What kind of cameras did you buy?
7. Hanna has $30. Identify two ways she can spend her money on individual cameras without having any change.

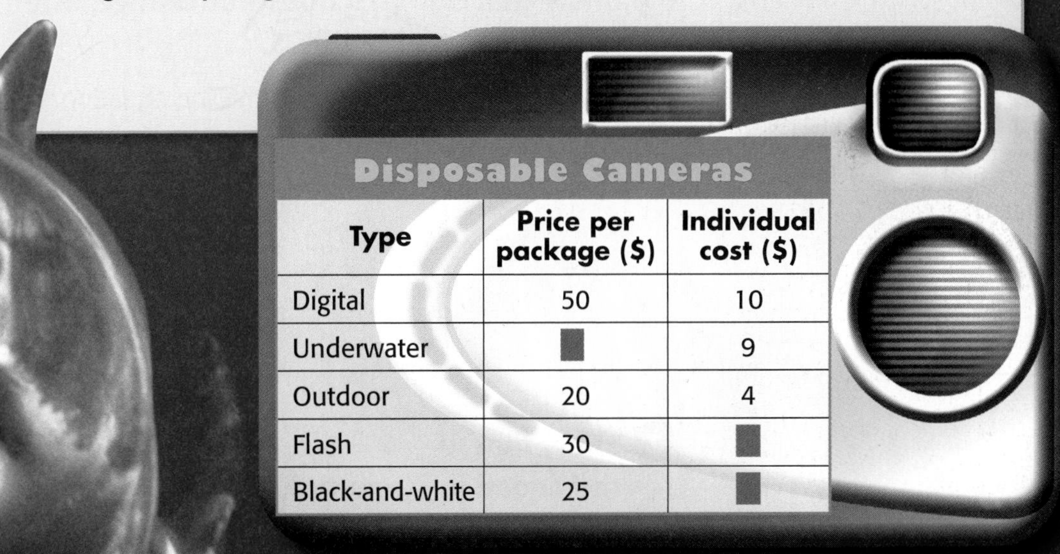

Disposable Cameras

Type	Price per package ($)	Individual cost ($)
Digital	50	10
Underwater	■	9
Outdoor	20	4
Flash	30	■
Black-and-white	25	■

6-7 Balanced Equations

GET READY to Learn

The model shows the equation $3n = 9$. Notice that each cup is matched with 3 counters. If you divide both of the cups and the counters by 3, you get $n = 3$.

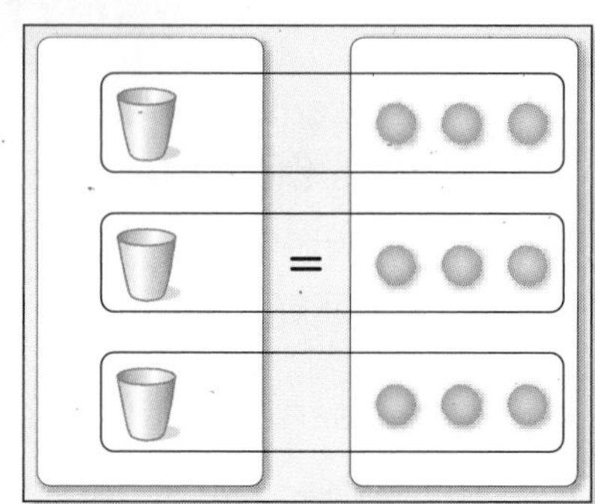

MAIN IDEA

I will balance multiplication and division equations.

Standard 4AF2.2 Know and understand that equals multiplied by equals are equal.

If you multiply or divide each side of an equation by the same number, the equality does not change.

EXAMPLES Balanced Equations

1 Show that $5g = 15$ does not change when each side of the equation is divided by 5.

$5g = 15$	Write the equation.
$5g \div \mathbf{5} = 15 \div \mathbf{5}$	Divide each side by 5.
$g = 3$	So, $g = 3$.

Check $5g = 15$

$5 \times 3 = 15$	Replace g with 3.
$15 = 15$ ✓	

2 Show that $w \div 4 = 3$ does not change when each side of the equation is multiplied by 4.

$w \div 4 = 3$	Write the equation.
$w \div 4 \times \mathbf{4} = 3 \times \mathbf{4}$	Multiply each side by 4.
$w = 12$	So, $w = 12$.

Check $w \div 4 = 3$

$12 \div 4 = 3$	Replace w with 12.
$3 = 3$ ✓	

Online Personal Tutor at ca.gr4math.com

You can can apply the idea of balanced equations to help you find missing numbers in equations.

EXAMPLES Find Missing Numbers

3 Find the missing number in $3 \times 2 \times 7 = 6 \times$ ■.

$3 \times 2 \times 7 = 6 \times$ ■ Write the equation.

$3 \times 2 \times 7 = 6 \times$ ■ You know that $3 \times 2 = 6$.

Each side of the equation must be multiplied by the same number to keep the equation balanced.
So, the missing number is 7.

4 Find the missing numbers in $3 \times 8 \div 4 = 24 \div$ ■.

$3 \times 8 \div 4 = 24 \div$ ■ Write the equation.

$3 \times 8 \div 4 = 24 \div$ ■ You know that $3 \times 8 = 24$.

Each side of the equation must be divided by the same number to keep the equation balanced.
So, the missing number is 4.

CHECK What You Know

Show the equality is not changed. See Examples 1 and 2 (p. 248)

1. $3r = 12$
$3r \div 3 = 12 \div 3$

2. $m \div 4 = 5$
$m \div 4 \times 4 = 5 \times 4$

Find the missing number in each equation.
See Examples 3 and 4 (p. 249)

3. $2 \times 2 \times 6 = 4 \times$ ■

4. $2 \times 6 \div 3 = 12 \div$ ■

5. Lisa and Percy each raised money for a charity by jumping rope. The graphic shows how much they raised in the first hour. Did they raise the same amount of money? Explain.

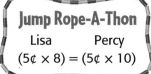

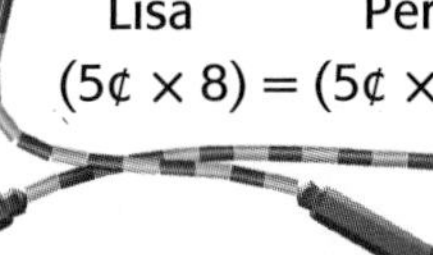

Jump Rope-A-Thon
Lisa Percy
(5¢ × 8) = (5¢ × 10)

6. Talk About It If $w \div 5 = u \div 5$, what do you know about w and u?

Practice and Problem Solving

Show the equality is not changed. See Examples 1 and 2 (p. 248)

7. $8w = 24$
$8w \div 8 = 24 \div 8$

8. $6y = 36$
$6y \div 6 = 36 \div 6$

9. $a \div 7 = 3$
$a \div 7 \times 7 = 3 \times 7$

10. $s \div 9 = 5$
$s \div 9 \times 9 = 5 \times 9$

Find the missing number in each equation. See Examples 3 and 4 (p. 249)

11. $2 \times 4 \times 6 = 8 \times \blacksquare$

12. $6 \times 2 \times 3 = 12 \times \blacksquare$

13. $3 \times 6 \div 9 = 18 \div \blacksquare$

14. $4 \times 9 \div 6 = 36 \div \blacksquare$

15. $4 \times \blacksquare \times 2 = 30 - 6$

16. $25 \div 5 \times 2 = 2 \times \blacksquare + 2$

17. Suzie will jog 2 miles twice each week for 4 weeks. Her father will jog 8 miles each week. How many weeks must Suzie's father jog in order to jog the same distance?

18. Jaya earns $4 each hour she babysits. She babysat 2 hours each week for 3 weeks. Bob earns $8 each time he washes a car. How many cars must Bob wash to earn the same amount Jaya earned?

Real-World PROBLEM SOLVING

Measurement Nari and Trevor are packed for a ski trip.

19. Nari's suitcase weighs 50 pounds. How many outfits did she pack?

$$\underbrace{24 \text{ lb}}_{\text{equipment}} + \underbrace{(\blacksquare \times 6 \text{ lb})}_{\text{outfits}} + \underbrace{(4 \times 2 \text{ lb})}_{\text{coats}} = 50 \text{ lb}$$

20. Trevor's suitcase weighs 60 pounds. How many coats did he pack?

$$\underbrace{24 \text{ lb}}_{\text{equipment}} + \underbrace{(4 \times 6 \text{ lb})}_{\text{outfits}} + \underbrace{(\blacksquare \times 4 \text{ lb})}_{\text{coats}} = 60 \text{ lb}$$

Items to Pack

Item	Weight
Ski outfit	6
Winter coat	4
Ski equipment	24

H.O.T. Problems

21. OPEN ENDED Write an example of two expressions that involve multiplication and a balanced equation.

22. WRITING IN ▸MATH Explain how to apply the idea of balanced equations to find the missing number in the equation $3 \times 4 \times 6 = 12 \times \blacksquare$.

Standards Practice

23 Which equation can be used to describe the pattern in the table? **(Lesson 6-6)**

Input (*m*)	Output (*n*)
1	3
3	9
5	15
7	21
9	27

A $m + 3 = n$

B $m + 6 = n$

C $m \times 3 = n$

D $n \times 3 = m$

24 What number makes this number sentence true? **(Lesson 6-7)**

$$(12 - 6) \times 7 = 6 \times \blacksquare$$

F 5

G 6

H 7

J 8

25 If $3 + 2 = 5$ and $4 \times 6 = 24$, what number is missing in $(3 + 2) \times \blacksquare = 5 \times (4 \times 6)$? **(Lesson 6-7)**

A 5

B 12

C 24

D 30

Spiral Review

Write an equation that describes each pattern. Then use the equation to find the next three numbers. **(Lesson 6-6)**

26.

Input (*w*)	30	24	18	12	6	0
Output (*v*)	10	8	6	■	■	■

27.

Input (*r*)	1	3	5	7	9	11
Output (*s*)	5	15	25	■	■	■

28. Winnie spends $2 for lunch each school day. Winnie was absent 2 days in 4 weeks. Write an expression to show how much money she spends on lunches during 4 weeks of school. **(Lesson 6-5)**

Write an equation for each situation. Then solve. **(Lesson 6-4)**

29. The product of a number and 7 equals 49. What is the number?

30. 132 divided by a number equals 11. What is the number?

CHAPTER 6

Study Guide and Review

FOLDABLES Study Organizer GET READY to Study

Be sure the following Key Vocabulary words and Key Concepts are written in your Foldable.

BIG Ideas

Expressions (p. 225)

- To find the value of an **expression**, replace the variable with a value and simplify.

The value of $36 \div x$, if $x = 9$, is 4.

Order of Operations (p. 230)

- To find the value of an expression follow the **order of operations**.

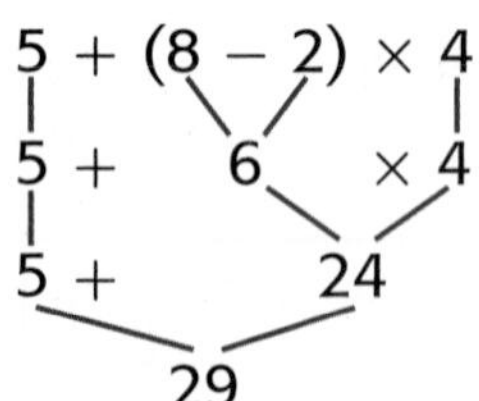

Equations (p. 236)

- Equations can be solved mentally.

$3 \times \mathbf{n} = 12$ 3 times what is 12?

$3 \times \mathbf{4} = 12$ $3 \times 4 = 12$

$n = 4$

So, the value of n is 4.

Key Vocabulary

expression (p. 225)
order of operations (p. 230)
equation (p. 234)

Vocabulary Check

Choose the vocabulary word that completes each sentence.

1. The ___?___ is a set of rules used to find the value of an expression.
2. A number sentence like $(3 \times b) + 7 = 4 \times 7$ is a(n) ___?___.
3. A(n) ___?___ is a combination of variables, numbers, and at least one operation.
4. A statement like $18 \div n + 3$ is a(n) ___?___.
5. ___?___ tells you to perform the operation in parentheses first.
6. A number sentence with an equals sign showing that two expressions are equal is a(n) ___?___.

Lesson-by-Lesson Review

6-1 Multiplication and Division Expressions (pp. 225–227)

Example 1
Find the value of $5 \times n$ if $n = 3$.

$5 \times n$	Write the expression.
5×3	Replace n with 3.
15	Multiply 5 and 3.

Example 2
Find the value of $3 \times (12 \div x)$ if $x = 6$.

$3 \times (12 \div x)$	Write the expression.
$3 \times (12 \div 6)$	Replace x with 6.
3×2	Find $(12 \div 6)$ first.
6	Multiply 3×2.

Find the value of each expression if $f = 4$ and $g = 6$.

7. $f \times 3$

8. $g \div 2$

9. $24 \div (g \times 2)$

10. $(16 \div f) \times g$

Write an expression for each situation.

11. a number divided by 7

12. 32 divided by a number

13. Terri has 4 times as many coins as Kuni. If Kuni has 7 coins, how many do they have in all?

6-2 Problem-Solving Strategy: Work Backward (pp. 228–229)

Example 3
Ernesto bought a football for \$6, a hat for \$12, and he gave his brother \$3. He has \$8 left. How much money did he have originally?

Work backward.

\$8	Ernesto has \$8.
+ \$6	Add the cost of the football.
\$14	
+ \$12	Add the cost of the hat.
\$26	
+ \$3	Ernesto gave \$3 to his brother
\$29	So, Ernesto had \$29 originally.

14. Kendrick and Belinda walk to school. Kendrick walks 5 minutes to Belinda's house. Then they walk 10 minutes to school. They arrive at school at 8:30 A.M. What time does Kendrick leave his house?

15. Fred woke up and took a 5-minute shower. Then he ate breakfast, which took 1 hour. Next, he went to the park for 2 hours. When he came home, he ate lunch at 11:30 A.M. What time did Fred wake up?

Study Guide and Review

6-3 Order of Operations (pp. 230–233)

Example 4
Find the value of $5 + (3 \times 4) - 7$.

$5 + (3 \times 4) - 7$	Write the expression.
$5 + 12 - 7$	Parentheses first.
$5 + 12 - 7$	No multiplication or division.
$17 - 7$	Add and subtract from left to right.
10	

So, the value is 10.

Find the value of each expression.

16. $(7 - 4) \div 3$

17. $10 - 2 \times (4 + 1)$

18. $(2 \times 3) + (17 - 8)$

19. $5 + 2 \times 4$

20. $3 \div 3 + 7 - 3$

21. $21 \div 7 + 5 \times 4$

22. Tara walks her dog 2 blocks, which takes 30 minutes. How long will it take Tara to walk her dog 4 blocks, including a stop at the park for 15 minutes?

6-4 Solve Equations Mentally (pp. 236–238)

Example 5
Solve $3 \times v = 27$.

$3 \times v = 27$ 3 times what equals 27?

$3 \times 9 = 27$ You know that $3 \times 9 = 27$.

$v = 9$

Example 6
Solve $32 \div d = 4$.

$32 \div d = 4$ 32 divided by what equals 4?

$32 \div 8 = 4$ You know that $32 \div 4 = 8$.

$d = 8$

Solve each equation mentally.

23. $3 \times k = 12$

24. $c \times 6 = 48$

25. $12 \times z = 60$

26. $p \div 5 = 9$

27. $n \div 8 = 7$

28. $27 \div m = 3$

Write an equation for each situation. Then solve.

29. A number times 7 equals 56. What is the number?

30. 81 divided by a number equals 9. What is the number?

31. Elias had $10. He bought 5 packs of trading cards. Find the price of each pack of cards.

6-5 Problem-Solving Investigation: Choose a Strategy (pp. 240–241)

Example 7

Jonah has 3 different types of books. He has twice as many mysteries as animal books. He has 3 fewer sports books than animal books. He has 16 mysteries. How many animal and sports books does he have?

Understand

Jonah has 3 types of books. He has twice as many mysteries as animal books. He has 3 fewer sports books than animal books. He has 16 mysteries. Find how many animal and sports books he has.

Plan You can use the *four-step plan* to solve the problem.

Solve Find how many animal and sports books Jonah has.

16	÷	2	=	8
mysteries				animal
8	−	3	=	5
animal				sports

Check Jonah has 8 animal books because $8 \times 2 = 16$ mystery books. He has 5 sports books because $5 + 3 = 8$ animal books. The answer is correct.

Use any strategy to solve.

32. Each child in Ms. Flores's class will receive 4 pencils, 2 notebooks, and 3 pens. There are 18 children in her class. How many of each item will she need in all?

33. **Measurement** Suppose the animals listed in the table traveled at the speeds shown for 2 hours. How much farther will a barracuda travel than a whale in that amount of time?

Sea Animal's Swim Speeds

Animal	Speed (mph)
Barracuda	30
Dolphin	25
Whale	20

34. Kenisha let Andy borrow 4 markers. Then Douglas borrowed 3 markers. Kenisha has 17 markers left. How many did she have originally?

35. Bart and Oya went to a county fair. Bart rode 4 rides for every 2 rides that Oya rode. How many rides did Oya ride if Bart rode 24?

36. A number is divided by 3. Next, 5 is added to the quotient. Then, the sum is multiplied by 4. The result is 32. What is the number?

6-6 Algebra: Find a Rule (pp. 242–245)

Example 8
Write an equation that describes the pattern in the table.

Input (g)	Output (h)
5	1
10	2
15	3

Pattern: $5 \div 5 = 1$

$10 \div 5 = 2$

$15 \div 5 = 3$

Rule: Divide by 5.

Equation: $g \div 5 = h$

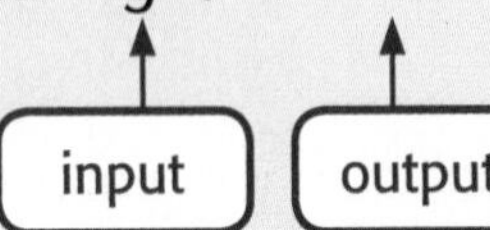

Write an equation that describes the pattern. Then use the equation to find the next three numbers.

37.

Input (m)	Output (n)
1	7
3	21
5	35
7	■
9	■
11	■

38.

Input (x)	Output (y)
9	3
18	6
27	9
36	■
45	■
54	■

6-7 Balanced Equations (pp. 248–251)

Example 9
Show that $9h = 72$ does not change when each side is divided by 9.

$9h = 72$	Write the equation.
$9h \div 9 = 72 \div 9$	Divide each side by 9.
$h = 8$	$8 = 8$

Check

$9h = 72$	
$9 \times 8 = 72$	Replace h with 8.
$72 = 72$	

Show the equality is not changed.

39. $7t = 21$
$7t \div 7 = 21 \div 7$

40. $p \div 6 = 5$
$p \div 6 \times 6 = 5 \times 6$

41. Hernando walked a dog twice a day, 3 days a week, for two weeks. His sister walked the dog 6 times each week. How many weeks must his sister walk the dog in order to equal the number of times he walked the dog?

CHAPTER 6

Chapter Test

For Exercises 1 and 2, tell whether each statement is *true* or *false*.

1. When finding the value of $3 + 2 \times 4$, the first step is to multiply.

2. An example of an equation is $2 + x = 7$.

3. **STANDARDS PRACTICE** Find the value of the expression.

$$9 \times (5 - 3) \div 3$$

A 6 **C** 8

B 7 **D** 9

4. Leah downloaded 3 songs onto her digital music player on Monday. She downloaded 2 times as many on Wednesday. She now has 21 songs. How many did she have originally?

Find the value of each expression.

5. $81 \div 9 \times (6 - 4)$

6. $8 \times 3 \div (5 + 7)$

7. **Measurement** An object on Earth weighs 6 times what it would weigh on the moon. An object weighs 72 pounds on Earth. Write and solve a multiplication equation to find the weight of the object on the Moon.

Solve each equation mentally.

8. $m \div 10 = 12$ **9.** $6 \times a = 54$

10. The product of a number and 12 is 84. Write an equation to find the number.

11. **STANDARDS PRACTICE** Which equation describes the pattern?

Input (j)	Output (k)
8	1
24	3
40	5
56	7
72	9

F $j - 7 = k$ **H** $j \div 8 = k$

G $j \div 7 = k$ **J** $k + 7 = j$

12. The ski club is having a car wash. They make $5 for each car they wash. Write a rule and an equation to find how much money they will make if they wash 4 cars.

Show the equality is not changed.

13. $5g = 35$
$5g \div 5 = 35 \div 5$

14. $n \div 8 = 12$
$n \div 8 \times 8 = 12 \times 8$

15. **WRITING IN ▸MATH** Explain how to find the missing number in the equation $(9 \times 4) \div ■ = 60 \div 10$.

CHAPTER 6

California Standards Practice

Cumulative, Chapters 1–6

Standards Example

Which equation can be used to describe the pattern in the table?

Input (x)	Output (y)
1	4
2	8
3	12
4	16
5	20
6	24

A $x \times 3 = y$ **C** $x \times 4 = y$

B $x + y = 5$ **D** $y \div 2 = x$

Read the Question

You need to find the equation that describes the pattern in the table.

Solve the Question

Each output (y) value is four times each input (x) value.

So, the rule is to multiply the input value (x) by 4. So, the answer is $x \times 4 = y$, or answer choice C.

Personal Tutor at ca.gr4math.com

Choose the best answer.

1 **Which equation can be used to describe the pattern in the table?**

Input (x)	1	2	3	4	5	6
Output (y)	5	7	9	11	13	15

A $y = 3x + 3$ **C** $y = 2x + 3$

B $y = 2x - 5$ **D** $y = 2x - 1$

2 **Annie spent $18 on school supplies. She has $42 left to spend on clothes. Which equation can be used to find how much money Annie had before she went shopping? Let m = money.**

F $m + 42 = 18$ **H** $m - 18 = 42$

G $m = 42 - 18$ **J** $m + 18 = 42$

3 **Which number is represented by c?**

$$12 \times c = 108$$

A 5 **C** 8

B 6 **D** 9

---

4 **What is the value of the expression below if $d = 9$?**

$$36 \div (d - 3)$$

F 3 **H** 6

G 4 **J** 9

---

5 **Lanu bought four books. Each book cost $6. Lanu has $16 left. Which equation can be used to find how much money he had before he went shopping? Let m = money.**

A $m - (4 \times \$6) = \$16$

B $(4 \times \$6) - m = \$16$

C $(4 \times \$6) - \$16 = m$

D $\$16 - (4 \times m) = \$6$

---

6 **What number goes in the box to make this number sentence true?**

$$(8 - 5) \times 9 = 3 \times \square$$

F 3 **H** 8

G 5 **J** 9

---

7 **Which number is 100,000 more than 873,496?**

A 773,496 **C** 883,496

B 874,496 **D** 973,496

---

8 **The table shows the visitors at Wyatt Park. How many total visitors came to the park in May and July?**

Wyatt Park	
Month	**Visitors**
May	6,453
June	7,782
July	8,134
August	7,996

F 14,235 **H** 14,587

G 14,449 **J** 15,916

---

9 **What is the value of the expression?**

$$(57 + 7) \div (2 \times 4)$$

A 6 **C** 8

B 7 **D** 9

---

10 **Tonisha's family has 2 newspapers delivered to their house each day. When they came back from a trip, there were 14 newspapers. Which equation can be used to find the number of days they were gone?**

F $14 \div 2 = d$ **H** $14 - d = 2$

G $14 + d = 2$ **J** $14 \times 2 = d$

CHAPTER 7 Multiply by One-Digit Numbers

BIG Idea How do you multiply by one-digit numbers?

Multiply each digit by the one-digit number, starting with the ones place. Regroup when necessary.

Example A great white shark can swim 2,900 miles on a single meal. If a great white shark eats 3 meals a day, it could swim 2,900 × 3 or 8,700 miles.

$$\begin{array}{rl} 2{,}900 & \\ \times \quad 3 & \\ \hline 6{,}000 & \text{Multiply } 3 \times 2{,}000. \\ +\ 2{,}700 & \text{Multiply } 3 \times 900. \\ \hline 8{,}700 & \text{Add the partial products.} \end{array}$$

What will I learn in this chapter?

- Multiply multiples of 10, 100, and 1,000.
- Estimate products using rounding.
- Multiply a multi-digit number by a one-digit number.
- Determine reasonable answers.

Key Vocabulary

multiply
estimate
product
Distributive Property of Multiplication

Student Study Tools at ca.gr4math.com

FOLDABLES™ Study Organizer

Make this Foldable to help you organize information about multiplying by one-digit numbers. Begin with one sheet of 11″ × 17″ paper.

1. **Fold** the short sides so they meet in the middle.
2. **Fold** the top to the bottom.
3. **Unfold** and cut to make four tabs.
4. **Label** each tab as shown.

ARE YOU READY for Chapter 7?

You have two ways to check prerequisite skills for this chapter.

Option 2

Math Online Take the Chapter Readiness Quiz at ca.gr4math.com.

Option 1

Complete the Quick Check below.

QUICK Check

Multiply. Use models if needed. (Lessons 5-3 and 5-5)

1. 2×3 **2.** $4 \times \$4$ **3.** 5×6 **4.** $7 \times \$8$

5. 9×4 **6.** 8×3 **7.** $\$7 \times 5$ **8.** 9×9

9. Evan's photo album has 8 pages of pictures. How many photos are in Evan's album if the same number of photos are on each page?

Identify the place value of the underlined digit. (Lesson 1-1)

10. 1,<u>6</u>30 **11.** $<u>5</u>,367 **12.** 20,4<u>9</u>5 **13.** $<u>8</u>9,196

14. Measurement Mount Everest's tallest peak is 29,035 feet. It is the highest point on Earth. Identify the place value of each digit in 29,035.

Round each number to its greatest place value. (Lesson 1-6)

15. 26 **16.** $251 **17.** 4,499 **18.** $33,103

19. There are 1,366 students at Sunrise Elementary School. Approximately how many students attend the school?

Multiples of 10, 100, and 1,000

GET READY to Learn

The whale shark is the world's largest fish. Its mouth is 5 feet long, and each foot contains 600 teeth. How many teeth does a whale shark have?

MAIN IDEA

I will multiply multiples of 10, 100, and 1,000 using basic facts and patterns.

Preparation for Standard

4NS3.2 Demonstrate an understanding of, and the ability to use, standard algorithms for multiplying a multidigit number by a two-digit number and for dividing a multidigit number by a one-digit number; use relationships between them to simplify computations and to check results.

You can use basic facts and number patterns to multiply.

Real-World EXAMPLE Multiples of 100

1 **ANIMALS How many teeth does a whale shark have?**

You need to find 5×600. Use basic facts and patterns.

$5 \times 6 = 30$ 5 × 6 ones = 30 ones = 30

$5 \times 60 = 300$ 5 × 6 tens = 30 tens = 300

$5 \times 600 = 3{,}000$ 5 × 6 hundreds = 30 hundreds = 3,000

So, a whale shark has 3,000 teeth. Notice that this answer is 5×6 with two zeros at the end.

EXAMPLE Multiples of 1,000

2 **Find $3 \times 7{,}000$.**

$3 \times 7 = 21$ 3 × 7 ones = 21 ones = 21

$3 \times 70 = 210$ 3 × 7 tens = 21 tens = 210

$3 \times 700 = 2{,}100$ 3 × 7 hundreds = 21 hundreds = 2,100

$3 \times 7{,}000 = 21{,}000$ 3 × 7 thousands = 21 thousands = 21,000

So, $3 \times 7{,}000$ is 21,000. Notice that this answer is 3×7 with three zeros at the end.

When you know basic facts and number patterns, you can multiply mentally.

Real-World EXAMPLE Multiply Mentally

Remember

As the number of zeros in a factor increases, the number of zeros in the product increases.

3 **MEASUREMENT The weight of a fire truck is 8 × 4,000 pounds. What is its weight in pounds?**

To find its weight, you need to find 8 × 4,000.

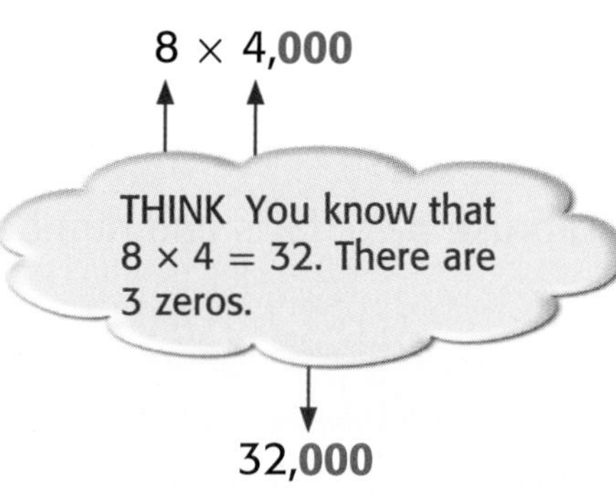

8 × 4,000
THINK You know that 8 × 4 = 32. There are 3 zeros.
32,000

8 × 4,000 = 32,000. So, the weight of the fire truck is 32,000 pounds.

Online **Personal Tutor at** ca.gr4math.com

CHECK What You Know

Multiply. Use basic facts and patterns. See Examples 1 and 2 (p. 263)

1. 2 × 1
2 × 10
2 × 100
2 × 1,000

2. 6 × 8
6 × 80
6 × 800
6 × 8,000

3. 7 × 9
7 × 90
7 × 900
7 × 9,000

Multiply. Use mental math. See Example 3 (p. 264)

4. 3 × 20

5. 8 × 600

6. 9 × 9,000

7. A zookeeper is in charge of feeding an anteater. Each day the anteater eats 5 × 6,000 ants. How many ants must the zookeeper give the anteater each day?

8. Talk About It What is the product of 4 and 5,000? Explain why there are more zeros in the product than in the factors in the problem.

Practice and Problem Solving

EXTRA PRACTICE
See page R17.

Multiply. Use basic facts and patterns. See Examples 1 and 2 (p. 263)

9. 5 × 3
5 × 30
5 × 300
5 × 3,000

10. 3 × 4
3 × 40
3 × 400
3 × 4,000

11. 2 × 9
2 × 90
2 × 900
2 × 9,000

12. 6 × 7
6 × 70
6 × 700
6 × 7,000

13. 9 × 1
9 × 10
9 × 100
9 × 1,000

14. 8 × 5
8 × 50
8 × 500
8 × 5,000

Multiply. Use mental math. See Example 3 (p. 264)

15. 4 × 30

16. 6 × 40

17. 7 × 200

18. 4 × 500

19. 3 × 9,000

20. 9 × 6,000

Algebra Copy and complete.

21. If 6 × ■ = 42,
then 60 × ■ = 4,200.

22. If 5 × 7 = ■,
then 50 × ■ = 3,500.

23. Mr. Singh's car payments are $300 a month. How much money will he pay in 6 months?

24. Mia's cell phone plan includes 2,000 monthly minutes. How many minutes does she get over 6 months?

Real-World PROBLEM SOLVING

Travel The Williams family is going to a theme park.

25. Admission tickets cost $30 for each person. What is the total cost for the 5 family members for one day?

26. The cost for each person to eat for one week is $100. Find the total cost for the family to eat for one week.

27. Suppose each family member goes on 70 rides during the week. How many rides will they go on altogether?

H.O.T. Problems

28. OPEN ENDED Write two multiplication expressions that have a product of 20,000.

29. WRITING IN ▶MATH How would you find 1 × 10,000? What is 1 × 10,000?

7-2 Problem-Solving Skill

MAIN IDEA I will decide whether an answer to a problem is reasonable.

Standard 4MR3.1 Evaluate the reasonableness of the solution in the context of the original situation.

Preparation for Standard 4NS3.2 Demonstrate an understanding of, and the ability to use, standard algorithms for multiplying a multidigit number by a two-digit number and for dividing a multidigit number by a one-digit number; use relationships between them to simplify computations and to check results.

Odell donated 3 cases of dog treats to a dog shelter. Each case has 900 treats. The dogs eat 2,500 treats each month. Odell says he has donated enough treats for more than one month. Is his claim reasonable?

Understand

What facts do you know?

- 3 cases of treats were donated.
- Each case has 900 treats.
- The animals eat 2,500 treats each month.

What do you need to find?

- Is it reasonable to say that the 3 cases of treats will last longer than one month?

Plan

Find 3 × 900. Then determine if the amount is reasonable.

Solve

3 × 900

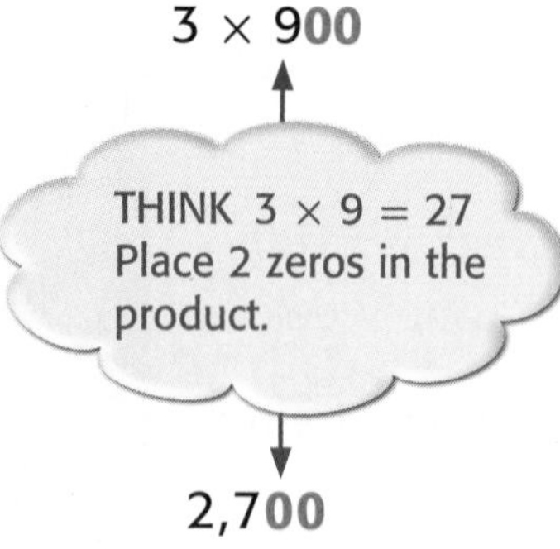
THINK 3 × 9 = 27
Place 2 zeros in the product.

2,700

Since 2,700 > 2,500, it is reasonable to say that the three cases will last longer than one month.

Check

You can add to check the multiplication.

900 + 900 + 900 = 2,700

So, the answer is correct.

ANALYZE the Skill

Refer to the problem on the previous page.

1. Explain why 3 is multiplied by 900 to decide if Odell was being reasonable.
2. Explain why there are 2 zeros at the end of the product of 3 and 900.
3. Look back at the example. What would make Odell's claim *not* reasonable?
4. Suppose Odell donates 5 cases of treats. Is it reasonable to believe the treats will last 2 months? Explain.

PRACTICE the Skill

See page R17.

Decide whether each answer is reasonable. Explain your reasoning.

5. Ben delivers 40 newspapers each day. Is 400 a reasonable estimate for the number of newspapers Ben delivers each week?
6. The calendar shows the number of days each month Olivia rides her bike.

September

Sun	Mon	Tues	Wed	Thurs	Fri	Sat
					1	2
3 (B)	4	5	6	7	8	9
10 (B)	11	12	13 (B)	14	15	16 (B)
17	18	19	20	21	22 (B)	23
24 (B)	25	26	27	28 (B)	29	30 (B)

Each time she rides her bike, she travels 10 miles. Is it reasonable to say that Olivia will bike more than 500 miles in 6 months?

7. Jay makes $40 a week doing yard work. He is saving his money to buy a laptop computer that costs $400. He has already saved $120. Is it reasonable to say that Jay will save enough money to buy the laptop in 6 weeks?
8. **Measurement** The distance from Ian's home to the museum is 2,640 yards. Is it reasonable to say that Ian's home is more than 9,000 feet away from the museum?
9. Kiri spends 60 minutes a week walking to school. Is it reasonable to say that she spends 240 minutes walking to school in four weeks?
10. The table below shows the number of pennies collected by four children.

Pennies Collected

Child	Number of Pennies
Myron	48
Teresa	52
Veronica	47
Warren	53

Is it reasonable to say that the children collected about 200 pennies in all?

11. **WRITING IN ▸MATH** Write a problem where $180 would be a reasonable answer.

7-3 Use Rounding to Estimate Products

GET READY to Learn

The fastest passenger train in the world actually floats above its track. This train in China can travel up to 267 miles per hour. About how far can the train travel in 3 hours?

MAIN IDEA

I will estimate products by rounding.

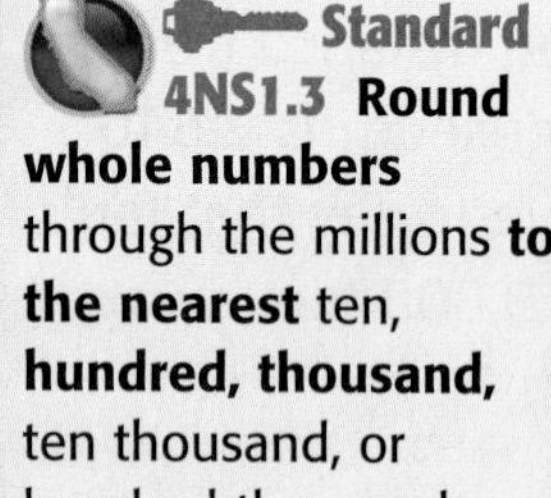

Standard 4NS1.3 **Round whole numbers** through the millions **to the nearest** ten, **hundred, thousand,** ten thousand, or hundred thousand.

New Vocabulary

estimate

To **estimate** products, round factors to their greatest place.

Real-World EXAMPLE Estimate Products

1 TRAVEL **About how far can the train travel in 3 hours?**

Estimate 3×267. Round the larger factor to its greatest place. Then use basic facts and patterns to multiply.

3×267

↓ THINK 267 rounds to 300.

$\mathbf{3} \times \mathbf{3}00 = 900$

So, the train can travel about 900 miles in 3 hours. Since 267 was rounded up, the estimated product is greater than the actual product.

EXAMPLE Estimate Larger Products

2 **Estimate $8 \times 2{,}496$.**

First round, then multiply using basic facts and patterns.

$8 \times 2{,}496$

↓ THINK 2,496 rounds to 2,000.

$\mathbf{8} \times \mathbf{2},000 = 16{,}000$

So, $8 \times 2{,}496$ is about 16,000.
Since 2,496 was rounded down, the estimated product is less than the actual product.

You can also estimate products involving money.

Remember

- When you round up, the estimated product is greater than the actual product.
- When you round down, the estimated product is less than the actual product.

Real-World EXAMPLE — Estimate Money

3 **MONEY Ava's older brother is going to a four-year college. The cost of his tuition is $8,562 each year. About how much will 4 years of college tuition cost?**

You need to estimate $4 \times \$8,562$.

First round, then multiply.

$$4 \times \$8,562$$
$$\downarrow$$
$$4 \times \$9,000 = \$36,000$$

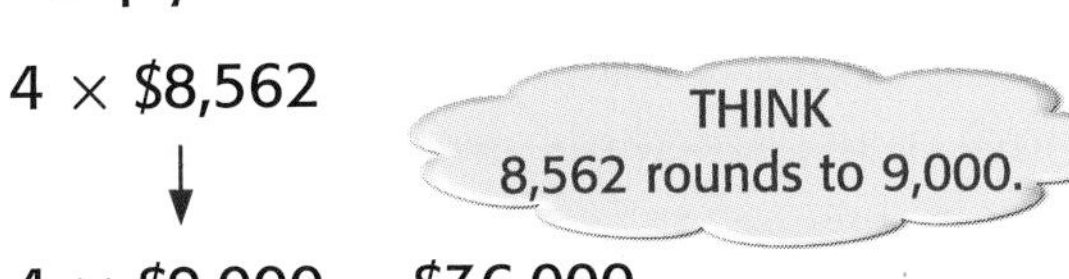
THINK
8,562 rounds to 9,000.

So, tuition will cost about $36,000.

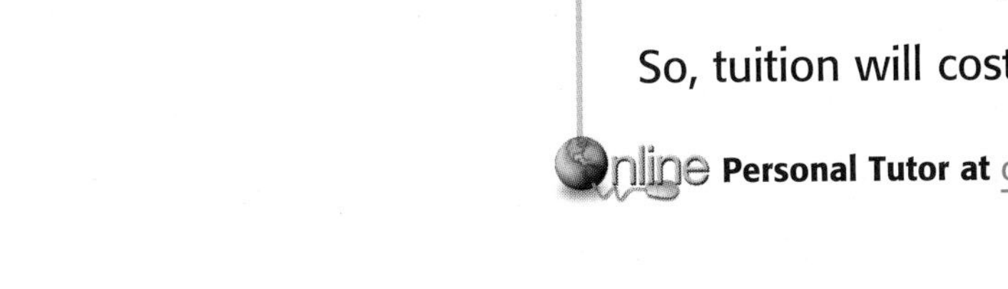

Personal Tutor at ca.gr4math.com

CHECK What You Know

Estimate each product. Then tell if the estimate is *greater than* or *less than* the actual product. See Examples 1–3 (pp. 268–269)

1. 449×5

2. $\$870 \times 9$

3. $3,293 \times 3$

4. $7 \times \$1,395$

5. $6 \times 5,500$

6. $9 \times \$7,420$

For Exercises 7 and 8, use the data at the right.

7. Mr. and Mrs. Rivera are planning to go on an African safari. They have saved $1,125 a year for 8 years. If the trip costs $9,830, do they have enough money saved for the trip? Explain.

8. **Talk About It** Suppose Mr. and Mrs. Rivera saved $1,499 a year for 8 years. Why would an estimated answer be misleading for the amount saved?

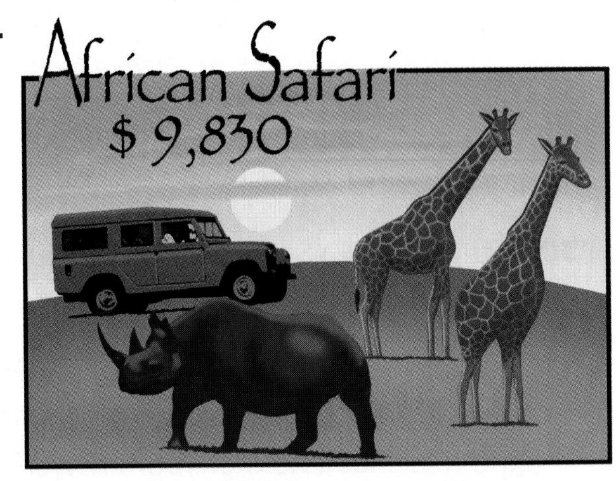
African Safari
$ 9,830

Practice and Problem Solving

Estimate each product. Then tell if the estimate is *greater than* or *less than* the actual product. See Examples 1–3 (pp. 268–269)

9. 562×6

10. 896×2

11. 729×8

12. 949×4

13. 2 × \$438

14. 8 × \$647

15. 5 × \$355

16. 7 × \$450

17. 7 × 1,125

18. 3 × 5,489

19. 9 × 3,500

20. 6 × 8,816

21. 4 × \$6,502

22. 7 × \$8,856

23. 9 × \$9,498

24. 7 × \$9,310

25. There are 24 students in each class at Watson Elementary School. About how many students are there if there are 8 classes?

26. The round-trip distance from Los Angeles to San Diego is 242 miles. Mr. Chen travels this distance 6 days a week. About how many miles does he travel each week?

Real-World PROBLEM SOLVING

Entertainment Toby and Lena like to go to the arcade. They earn points toward prizes.

27. Toby went to the arcade 2 times. He earned 5,150 points each time. What is the biggest prize Toby can get?

28. How many toy cars could Toby get with his points?

29. Lena went to the arcade 7 times. She earned 9,050 points each time. What are the two largest prizes she can get?

H.O.T. Problems

30. NUMBER SENSE Explain how you can tell if your estimated answer is more or less than the exact answer to a multiplication problem.

31. WRITING IN MATH Suppose you need to find the exact answer to 4 × \$189. How can you use estimation to check the reasonableness of your answer?

Estimation Station

Estimate Products

Get Ready!

Players: 2 players
You will need: spinner, 1 number cube, 2 whiteboards

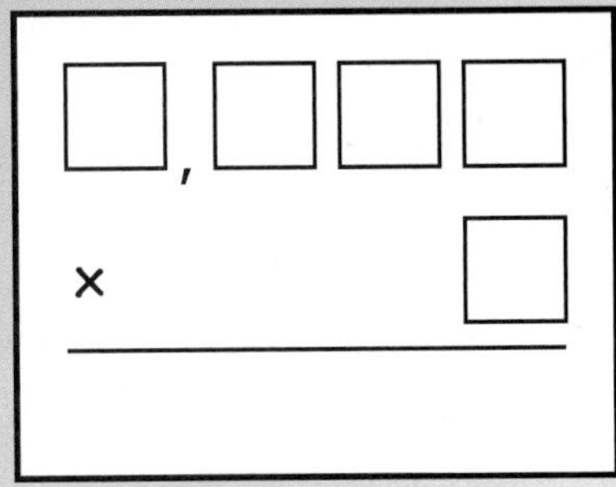

Get Set!

Each player makes a spinner and a game board as shown.

Go!

- Player 1 rolls the number cube to find a one-digit factor. Record the number in the second row on the game board.
- Player 1 then spins to find out how many digits will be in the second factor.
- Player 1 rolls the number cube to find the digits in the second factor. Record each digit.
- Player 1 estimates the product and gets 1 point if the estimate is correct.
- Player 2 takes a turn.
- Continue playing. The player who earns 10 points first wins.

7-4 Multiply Two-Digit Numbers

GET READY to Learn

Hands-On Mini Activity

Materials: base-ten blocks

Base-ten blocks can be used to explore multiplying two-digit numbers. In this activity, you will find 4×13.

Step 1 Model 4 groups of 13.

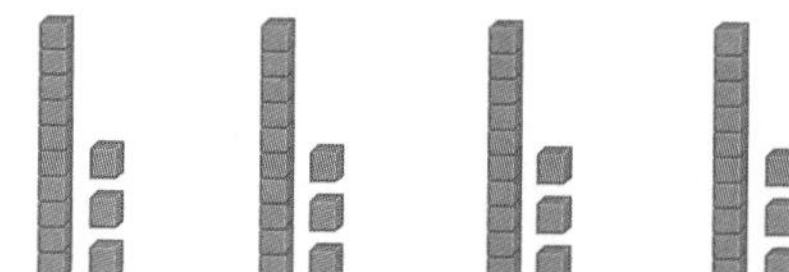

Step 2 Combine the tens and ones. Regroup 12 ones as 1 ten and 2 ones.

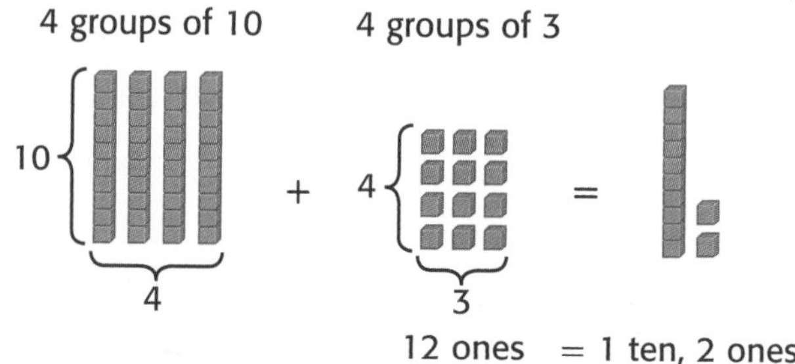

Step 3 Add the partial products.

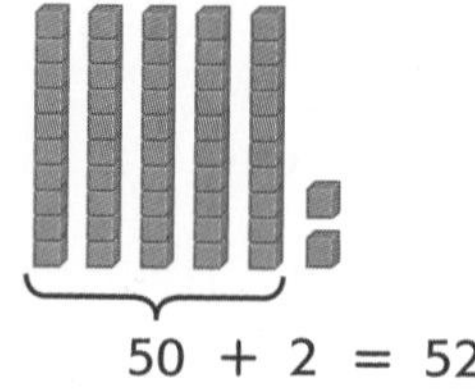

So, $4 \times 13 = 52$.

Find each product. Use base-ten blocks.

1. 3×18 **2.** 4×19 **3.** 3×21

4. Multiplication is a shortcut for which operation?

5. When is it necessary to regroup in a multiplication problem? When is regrouping not needed?

MAIN IDEA

I will multiply a two-digit number by a one-digit number.

Preparation for Standard 4NS3.2 Demonstrate an understanding of, and the ability to use, standard algorithms for multiplying a multidigit number by a two-digit number and for dividing a multidigit number by a one-digit number; use relationships between them to simplify computations and to check results.

Standard 4MR2.1 Use estimation to verify the reasonableness of calculated results.

Concepts in Motion

Animation
ca.gr4math.com

Using place-value models is not the only way to multiply a two-digit number by a one-digit number.

EXAMPLE Multiply with Regrouping

Find 6 × 38. Estimate $6 \times 38 \longrightarrow 6 \times 40 = 240$

Remember

To review the Distributive Property of Multiplication, see Lesson 5-6 (p. 194).

One Way: Distributive Property

$$6 \times 38 = (6 \times 30) + (6 \times 8)$$
$$= 180 + 48$$
$$= 228$$

Another Way: Partial Products

38	
× 6	
48	Multiply 6 × 8.
+ 180	Multiply 6 × 30.
228	Add the partial products.

	30	8
6	180	48

180 + 48 = 228

Another Way: Paper and Pencil

Step 1 Multiply the ones.		Step 2 Multiply the tens.	
4		4	
38	6 × 8 = 48	38	6 × 3 = 18
× 6	Regroup 48 ones	× 6	Add the
8	as 4 tens and 8 ones.	228	regrouped tens, 4.

Check for reasonableness

The product, 228, is close to the estimate, 240. ✓

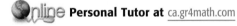

Personal Tutor at ca.gr4math.com

CHECK What You Know

Multiply. Check for reasonableness. See Example 1 (p. 273)

1. 23 × 2

2. 42 × 2

3. 8 × \$98

4. Haley can fit 25 books on each of 5 shelves. How many books will fit in all?

5. Talk About It Explain how to find 6 × 37.

Practice and Problem Solving

EXTRA PRACTICE
See page R18.

Multiply. Check for reasonableness. See Example 1 (p. 273)

6. $\begin{array}{r} 33 \\ \times\ 2 \\ \hline \end{array}$

7. $\begin{array}{r} \$24 \\ \times\ 2 \\ \hline \end{array}$

8. $\begin{array}{r} 11 \\ \times\ 7 \\ \hline \end{array}$

9. $\begin{array}{r} 13 \\ \times\ 3 \\ \hline \end{array}$

10. 2 × $27

11. 4 × 29

12. 5 × 18

13. 7 × $36

14. 6 × 52

15. 8 × 75

16. 4 × $83

17. 9 × 99

18. Will makes $4 an hour shampooing dogs at a pet shop. Last month he worked 26 hours. How much money did Will earn?

19. If a sales tax is 7 cents for each dollar that is spent on any item, how much sales tax is charged for a badminton set that costs $35?

Real-World PROBLEM SOLVING

Data File The California Caverns are located in Mountain Ranch, California.

20. The Diaz family has 5 members. How much would it cost for the family to go on a walking tour?

21. The Diaz family has $475. Is this enough to go on the Mammoth Cave Expedition? Explain.

22. Find the total cost of 5 walking tours and 3 gemstone minings.

Source: caverntours.com

H.O.T. Problems

23. **OPEN ENDED** Write two problems that result in a product of 120.

24. **WHICH ONE DOESN'T BELONG?** Which multiplication problem does not belong with the other three? Explain.

$\begin{array}{r} 12 \\ \times 8 \\ \hline \end{array}$	$\begin{array}{r} 22 \\ \times 4 \\ \hline \end{array}$	$\begin{array}{r} 52 \\ \times 2 \\ \hline \end{array}$	$\begin{array}{r} 33 \\ \times 3 \\ \hline \end{array}$

25. **WRITING IN ▸MATH** How do you use partial products to find 6 × 42?

 Math Online **Self-Check Quiz at** ca.gr4math.com

Mid-Chapter Check

Lessons 7-1 through 7-4

Multiply. Use basic facts and patterns.
(Lesson 7-1)

1. 3 × 4
3 × 40
3 × 400
3 × 4,000

2. 12 × 5
12 × 50
12 × 500
12 × 5,000

3. Toshi needs 292 toothpicks for a project. A box holds 150 toothpicks. Is it reasonable to buy 2 boxes? Explain. **(Lesson 7-2)**

4. Mara and Billy bought 6 bags of balloons for a party. Is it reasonable to say they will have more than 75 balloons? **(Lesson 7-2)**

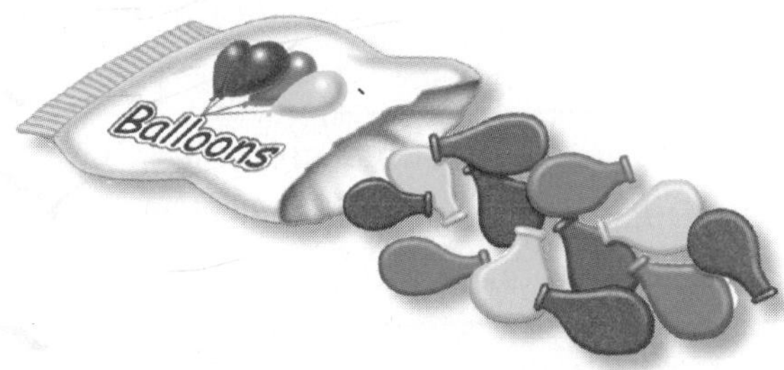

Estimate each product. (Lesson 7-3)

5. 3 × 252

6. 5 × 7,493

7. **STANDARDS PRACTICE** Jada pays $1875 a year in car payments. About how much money will she pay in 5 years? **(Lesson 7-3)**

A $5000 **B** $7500

C $9375 **D** $10,000

8. Juan plans to read 264 pages a month to complete his book in 6 months. About how many pages are in his book? **(Lesson 7-3)**

9. Measurement Each gallon of paint covers about 350 square feet. Ann estimated that 3 gallons of paint would be enough to cover 1,400 square feet. Will Ann have enough paint? Explain.

Multiply. Check for reasonableness.
(Lesson 7-3)

10. $\begin{array}{r} 43 \\ \times\ 2 \\ \hline \end{array}$

11. $\begin{array}{r} \$51 \\ \times\ 3 \\ \hline \end{array}$

12. 9 × 62

13. 8 × 47

14. There are 24 pencils in a package. How many pencils will you have if you buy 6 packages? **(Lesson 7-4)**

15. **STANDARDS PRACTICE** There are 27 boxes of markers in the art room. If each box holds 8 markers, how many markers are in the art room? **(Lesson 7-4)**

F 106 **H** 216

G 166 **J** 226

16. **WRITING IN MATH** Cassie got the following problem wrong on her math test. Explain what she did wrong. **(Lesson 7-4)**

$$\begin{array}{r} {}^{5} \\ 47 \\ \times\ 8 \\ \hline 326 \end{array}$$

Problem-Solving Investigation

MAIN IDEA I will choose the best strategy to solve a problem.

Standard 4MR1.1 **Analyze problems by identifying relationships, distinguishing relevant from irrelevant information, sequencing and prioritizing information,** and observing patterns. **Preparation for Standard 4NS3.3** Solve problems involving multiplication of multidigit numbers by two-digit numbers.

P.S.I. TEAM +

ISABEL: I am making punch for a party. One bowl of punch serves 35 guests. I am going to make four bowls of punch.

YOUR MISSION: Find how many guests will be served by four bowls.

Understand	One bowl of punch serves 35 guests. Isabel is making four bowls of punch. Find how many guests will be served by four bowls of punch.
Plan	Use the *four-step plan* and write a number sentence. Multiply the number of guests served by one bowl of punch by the number of bowls being made.
Solve	You need to find $35 \times 4 = \blacksquare$. $\begin{array}{r} 35 \\ \times\ 4 \\ \hline 20 \\ +120 \\ \hline 140 \end{array}$ 20 Multiply 4×5. +120 Multiply 4×30. 140 Add. 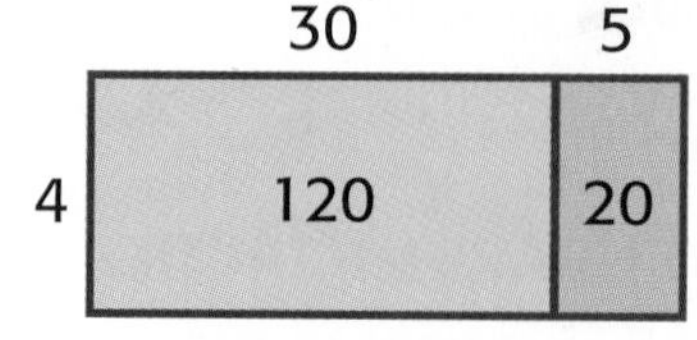 30 5 4 120 20 $120 + 20 = 140$ So, four bowls of punch will serve 140 guests.
Check	Look back at the problem. You can use repeated addition to check your answer. $35 + 35 + 35 + 35 = 140.$ So, the answer is correct.

Mixed Problem Solving

Use any strategy shown below to solve. Tell what strategy you used.

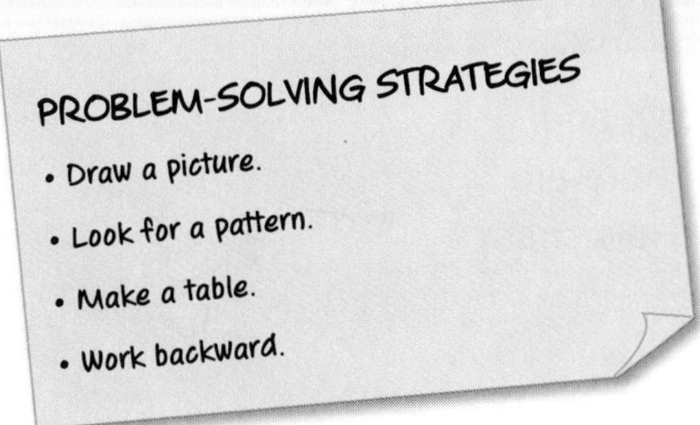

1. There are 12 members in each scout troop. Make a table to find out how many members will attend a meeting if there are 10, 11, 12, or 13 scout troops attending.

2. Nate is trying to choose 3 items from the menu below. What are 3 possible combinations Nate could choose?

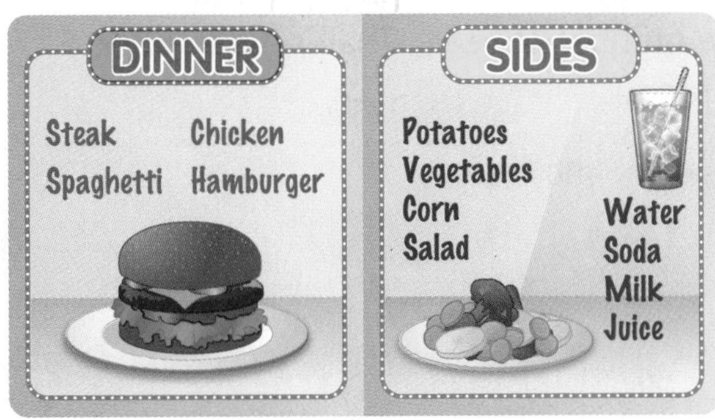

3. Kishi is choosing an outfit to wear to school. She has 3 shirts, 2 pants, and 3 shoes to choose from. How many different outfits does she have to choose from?

4. Four bears eat 2,000 ants per day. How many ants will 2 bears eat in one day?

5. There are 18 stickers on each sheet. There are five sheets in one pack. How many stickers are in one pack?

6. **Algebra** Copy and complete the pattern below. Describe the pattern.

   100, 200, 400, ■, 1,600, ■, 6,400

7. **Geometry** If this pattern is repeated, identify the 18th shape in the pattern.

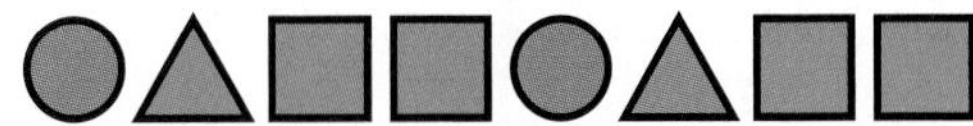

8. A wall has an animal poster to the right of a car poster. A space poster is last. A music poster is to the left of the space poster. What is the order of the 4 posters?

9. Emma now has $32. She earned $12 babysitting and she received $5 for her allowance. How much money did she have originally?

10. The Turner family played miniature golf. What is the total cost if 2 adults and 3 children played 18 holes of golf?

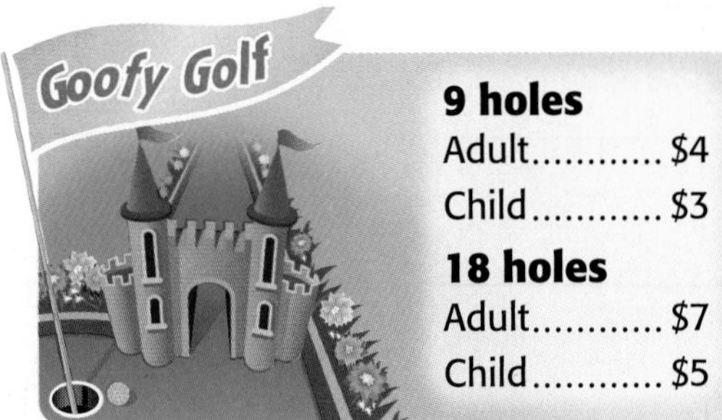

11. **WRITING IN MATH** Look at Exercise 9. Identify the strategy you used. Explain how you used this strategy to solve the problem.

7-6 Multiply Multi-Digit Numbers

MAIN IDEA

I will multiply a three-digit number by a one-digit number.

Preparation for Standard

4NS3.2 Demonstrate an understanding of, and the ability to use, standard algorithms for multiplying a multidigit number by a two-digit number and for dividing a multidigit number by a one-digit number; use relationships between them to simplify computations and to check results.

Standard 4MR2.1

Use estimation to verify the reasonableness of calculated results.

GET READY to Learn

Today is Laura's birthday, and she is nine years old. There are 365 days in one year. How many days old is Laura?

You multiply multi-digit numbers the same way you multiply a two-digit number by a one-digit number.

Real-World EXAMPLE Partial Products

1 TIME How many days old is Laura?

To find how many days old Laura is, multiply the number of days in a year by the number of years. That is, find 365×9. You can use partial products.

Estimate $9 \times 365 \longrightarrow 9 \times 400 = 3{,}600$

365	
× 9	
45	Multiply 9×5.
540	Multiply 9×60.
+ 2,700	Multiply 9×300.
3,285	Add the partial products.

	300 +	60 +	5
9	2,700	540	45

2,700
540
+ 45
3,285

So, Laura is 3,285 days old.

Check for reasonableness

The product, 3,285, is close to the estimate, 3,600. ✓

Remember

Always check for reasonableness.

3 × $1,175
↓
3 × $1,000 = $3,000

Since $3,525 is close to $3,000, the answer is reasonable.

You can also use an algorithm to multiply.

EXAMPLE Multiply Money

2 **Find 3 × $1,175.**

Step 1 Multiply the ones.

```
      1
 $1,175
 ×    3
      5
```

3 × 5 ones = 15
Regroup 15 ones as 1 ten and 5 ones.

Step 2 Multiply the tens.

```
    21
 $1,175
 ×    3
     25
```

3 × 7 tens = 21 tens
Add the regrouped tens.
21 tens + 1 ten = 22 tens
Regroup 22 tens as 2 hundreds and 2 tens.

Step 3 Multiply the hundreds.

```
    21
 $1,175
 ×    3
    525
```

3 × 1 hundred = 3 hundreds
Add the regrouped hundreds.
3 hundreds + 2 hundreds = 5 hundreds

Step 4 Multiply the thousands.

```
    21
 $1,175
 ×    3
 $3,525
```

3 × 1 thousand = 3 thousands

	$1,000	+ $100	+ $70	+ $5
3	$3,000	$300	$210	$15

```
  $3,000
    $300
    $210
 +   $15
  $3,525
```

Online Personal Tutor at ca.gr4math.com

CHECK What You Know

Multiply. Check for reasonableness. See Examples 1 and 2 (pp. 278–279)

1. 135
× 2

2. 532
× 6

3. 2 × $2,957

4. 7 × 7,832

5. A vacation costs $1,389 for one person. What is the total cost of this vacation for a family of four?

6. Talk About It Explain why it is a good idea to estimate answers to multiplication problems.

Practice and Problem Solving

EXTRA PRACTICE
See page R18.

Multiply. Check for reasonableness. See Examples 1 and 2 (pp. 278–279)

7. $\$168 \times 2$

8. 313×3

9. 252×2

10. $\$338 \times 3$

11. 238×4

12. 819×5

13. $\$781 \times 5$

14. 340×6

15. $7 \times \$4{,}160$

16. $7 \times 5{,}611$

17. $8 \times 6{,}328$

18. $9 \times \$5{,}679$

19. $8 \times 7{,}338$

20. $7 \times 8{,}469$

21. $9 \times \$9{,}927$

22. $9 \times 8{,}586$

Algebra Find the value of each expression if $n = 8$.

23. $n \times 295$

24. $737 \times n$

25. $n \times \$2{,}735$

26. $7{,}372 \times n$

Compare. Use >, <, or =.

27. 4×198 ● 3×248

28. 7×385 ● 6×457

29. Ms. Gomez buys 8 cases of seeds at the school plant sale. If there are 144 packages of seeds in each case, how many packages of seeds has she bought?

30. **Measurement** On average 1,668 gallons of water are used by each person in the United States daily. How much water is used by one person in a week?

Real-World PROBLEM SOLVING

Science The rainforests are the richest, oldest, and most productive ecosystems on Earth. Animals such as anacondas, iguanas, monkeys, and parrots live in rainforests.

31. A four-square-mile section of rainforest has 125 mammals. How many mammals would live in an area 3 times that size?

32. Rainforest land that is used to raise cattle is worth $60 an acre. Rainforest land that is used for its plants is worth $2,400 an acre. Find the difference in worth of 5 acres of land used to raise cattle compared to the same amount of land used for its plants.

H.O.T. Problems

33. OPEN ENDED Write a four-digit number and a one-digit number whose product is greater than 6,000 and less than 6,200.

34. FIND THE ERROR Roberta and Camden are finding 362 × 2. Who is correct? Explain.

35. WRITING IN ▸MATH Write a real-world problem that involves multiplying a three-digit by a one-digit number, and regrouping.

Standards Practice

36 Approximately how long would 6 train cars be? **(Lesson 7-4)**

A 300 ft **C** 330 ft

B 324 ft **D** 360 ft

37 There are 1440 minutes in a day. How many minutes are in 7 days? **(Lesson 7-6)**

F 7880

G 9880

H 10,080

J 11,080

Spiral Review

Multiply. Check for reasonableness. **(Lesson 7-4)**

38. 3 × 21 **39.** 5 × 34 **40.** 8 × $72

Estimate each product. **(Lesson 7-3)**

41. 2 × 265 **42.** 3 × 849 **43.** 7 × 5,513

44. There are 26 students, 1 teacher, and 4 parents going on a field trip. Each car can hold 4 people. Is it reasonable to say that 7 cars will allow every person to go on the field trip? Explain. **(Lesson 7-2)**

Problem Solving in Science

EMPERORS OF THE ICE

There are 17 different types of penguins. Emperor penguins are the tallest and heaviest penguins. An Emperor penguin is over 3 feet tall and can weigh from 42 to 101 pounds. The average Emperor penguin weighs 66 pounds and can swim 15 miles per hour.

About 200,000 pairs of Emperor penguins live in 40 different groups in Antarctica. Penguins huddle together to share their body heat during the cold winter temperatures and bitter winds.

Did You Know?

Emperor penguins usually dive 60 to 70 feet. An average dive lasts 3 to 6 minutes.

Preparation for Standard 4NS3.3 Solve problems involving multiplication of multidigit numbers by two-digit numbers.

Real-World Math

Use the information on pages 282 and 283 to solve each problem.

1. Suppose that eight average-sized Emperor penguins are standing together. What is their total weight?

2. Six penguins of varying weights are standing together. What is the least they can weigh? the most?

3. Suppose a penguin's dive lasts 4 minutes. How many times did its heart beat during the dive?

4. How many miles can a penguin swim in 3 hours?

5. Suppose it takes a penguin 3 minutes to walk from its resting place to the place where it dives. What is a reasonable number of times its heart beats in these three minutes before it dives?

6. Based on the following table, estimate how many times a penguin's heart beats after completing all of the activities listed for two minutes each.

PENGUIN HEARTBEAT

Activity	Heartbeat (beats per minute)
Resting	65
Before a dive	180–200
Hitting the water	100
Diving	20
Returning to surface	200

7-7 Multiply Across Zeros

GET READY to Learn

The cost of Iván's braces is about \$108 each month for 4 years. How much money will his parents pay after 6 months?

MAIN IDEA

I will multiply multidigit numbers with zeros by a one-digit number.

Preparation for Standard 4NS3.2 Demonstrate an understanding of, and the ability to use, standard algorithms for multiplying a multidigit number by a two-digit number and for dividing a multidigit number by a one-digit number; use relationships between them to simplify computations and to check results.

Standard 4MR2.1 Use estimation to verify the reasonableness of calculated results.

You can use partial products or the Distributive Property to multiply across zeros.

Real-World EXAMPLE — Multiply Across Zeros

1 MONEY How much will Iván's parents pay for his braces?

Multiply the cost of each month by 6. That is, find 6 × \$108.

Estimate 6 × \$108 → 6 × \$100 = \$600

The model shows 6 × \$108.

	\$100	+ \$8
6	6 × \$100	6 × \$8

← 6 × 0 = 0, so there is no space in the rectangle for that product.

One Way: Distributive Property	Another Way: Partial Products
6 × \$108 =	\$108
(6 × \$100) + (6 × \$8)	× 6
= \$600 + \$0 + \$48	\$ 48 6 × \$8
= \$648	\$ 0 6 × \$0
	\$600 6 × \$100
	\$648 Add the partial products.

So, Iván's parents will pay \$648 after 6 months.

Check for reasonableness

The answer, \$648, is close to the estimate, \$600. ✓

You can also use an algorithm to multiply.

Real-World EXAMPLE Multiply Across Zeros

2 **TREES If three trees are each 2,025 years old, what is the total age of the trees?**

Estimate $3 \times 2{,}025 \rightarrow 3 \times 2{,}000 = 6{,}000$

Step 1 Multiply the ones.

$$\begin{array}{r} {}^{1} \\ 2{,}025 \\ \times \quad 3 \\ \hline 5 \end{array}$$

3×5 ones $= 15$ ones

Regroup 15 ones as 1 ten and 5 ones.

Step 2 Multiply the tens.

$$\begin{array}{r} {}^{1} \\ 2{,}025 \\ \times \quad 3 \\ \hline 75 \end{array}$$

3×2 tens $= 6$ tens

Add the regrouped tens.

6 tens + 1 ten = 7 tens

Step 3 Multiply the hundreds.

$$\begin{array}{r} {}^{1} \\ 2{,}025 \\ \times \quad 3 \\ \hline 075 \end{array}$$

3×0 hundreds $= 0$ hundreds

Step 4 Multiply the thousands.

$$\begin{array}{r} {}^{1} \\ 2{,}025 \\ \times \quad 3 \\ \hline 6{,}075 \end{array}$$

3×2 thousands $= 6$ thousands

So, the total age of the trees is 6,075 years.

Check for Reasonableness

The answer, 6,075, is close to the estimate, 6,000. ✓

Online **Personal Tutor at** ca.gr4math.com

CHECK What You Know

Multiply. Check for reasonableness. **See Examples 1 and 2 (pp. 284–285)**

1. $\begin{array}{r} 303 \\ \times 3 \\ \hline \end{array}$

2. $\begin{array}{r} \$507 \\ \times \quad 6 \\ \hline \end{array}$

3. $\begin{array}{r} 908 \\ \times \quad 8 \\ \hline \end{array}$

4. $2 \times 1{,}073$

5. $7 \times \$3{,}102$

6. $9 \times 7{,}004$

7. Valerie jogs 3 miles every day. If there are 5,280 feet in a mile, how many feet does she run in one day?

8. Talk About It Explain how to find the product of 4 and 2,008.

Practice and Problem Solving

EXTRA PRACTICE
See page R19.

Multiply. Check for reasonableness. See Examples 1 and 2 (pp. 284–285)

9. $\begin{array}{r} 201 \\ \times\ 2 \\ \hline \end{array}$

10. $\begin{array}{r} \$402 \\ \times\ 3 \\ \hline \end{array}$

11. $\begin{array}{r} 709 \\ \times\ 5 \\ \hline \end{array}$

12. $\begin{array}{r} 904 \\ \times\ 9 \\ \hline \end{array}$

13. 2 × $1,108

14. 4 × 6,037

15. 3 × 8,504

16. 5 × $9,082

17. 6 × 4,005

18. 6 × 6,007

19. 7 × $8,009

20. 9 × 9,002

Algebra **Copy and complete each table.**

21.

Rule: Multiply by 4.	
Input	Output
607	■
1,085	■
3,009	■
5,104	■
8,006	■

22.

Rule: Multiply by 6,008.	
Input	Output
2	■
3	■
5	■
7	■
8	■

23. **Measurement** A city in Africa is one of the wettest places in the world. It receives 405 inches of rain each year. How many inches of rain would it receive in 5 years?

24. An elementary school is collecting money to donate to the Special Olympics. About $103 is collected each month. How much money is collected over the 9 months of the school year?

Real-World PROBLEM SOLVING

Health The bar graph shows the time people spend on certain activities in one year.

25. How many times will a person laugh in 3 years?

26. How many dreams does a person have in five years?

27. How many telephone calls does a family of 4 make in one year?

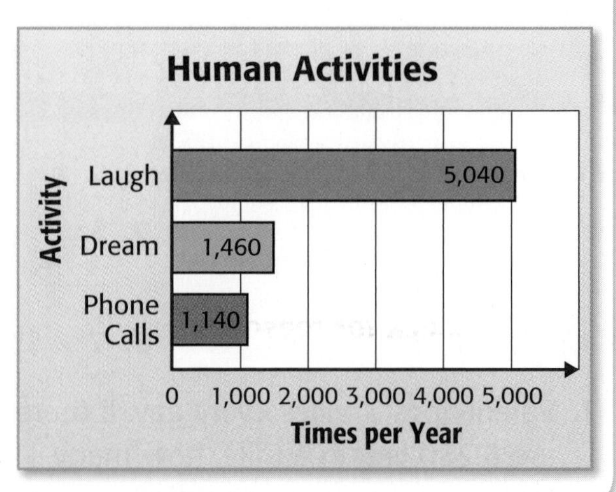

H.O.T. Problems

28. OPEN ENDED Copy and complete ■,005 × ■ = ■,0 ■5.

29. FIND THE ERROR Silvia and Dexter are finding 3 × 6,005. Who is correct? Explain.

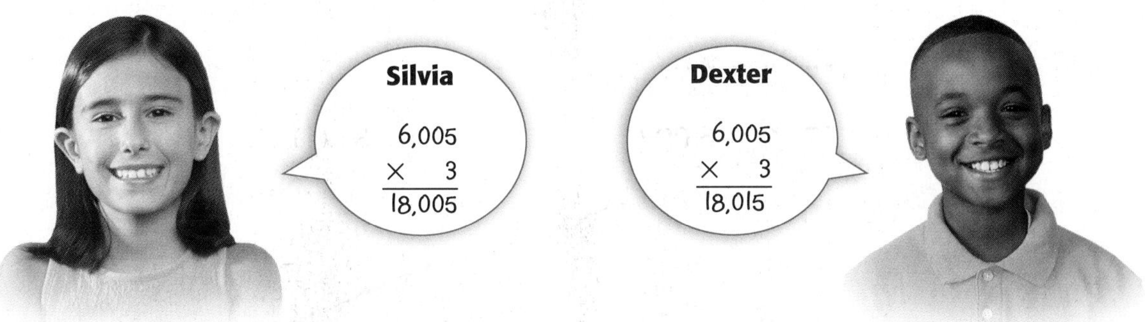

30. WRITING IN ►MATH Write a real-world problem that involves multiplying a 4-digit number with a zero in the hundreds place by a 1-digit number.

Standards Practice

31 There are 245 boxes of canned juice in a warehouse. If there are 6 cans of juice in each box, how many cans of juice are in the warehouse? **(Lesson 7-6)**

A 1240

B 1440

C 1470

D 1480

32 The weights of zoo animals are shown below. **(Lesson 7-7)**

Animals' Weights	
African elephant	14,432 pounds
White rhinoceros	7937 pounds
Hippopotamus	5512 pounds
Giraffe	3527 pounds
American bison	2205 pounds

A zoo has 6 American bison. What is the total weight of the bison?

F 12,200 lb **H** 13,200 lb

G 12,230 lb **J** 13,230 lb

Spiral Review

Multiply. Check for reasonableness. (Lessons 7-4 and 7-6)

33. 4 × 65 **34.** 7 × $327 **35.** 9 × 1,948

36. Suppose the pattern 7, 12, 17, 22, 27, ... continues until there is a total of 12 numbers. Find the sum of the last two numbers. **(Lesson 7-5)**

CHAPTER 7

Study Guide and Review

FOLDABLES Study Organizer GET READY to Study

Be sure the following Key Vocabulary words and Key Concepts are written in your Foldable.

Estimate Products	Multiply Two-Digit Numbers
Multiply Three-Digit Numbers	Multiply Across Zeros

BIG Ideas

Multiply Multiples of 10, 100, and 1,000

Use basic facts and patterns. (p. 263)

$3 \times 7 = 21$	3×7 ones
$3 \times 70 = 210$	3×7 tens
$3 \times 700 = 2{,}100$	3×7 hundreds
$3 \times 7{,}000 = 21{,}000$	3×7 thousands

Estimate Products (p. 268)

$4 \times 192 \rightarrow 4 \times 200 = 800$

Multiply by One-Digit Numbers (p. 272)

There are many ways you can multiply.

	3,000 +	500 +	0 +	2
6	18,000	3,000	0	12

$$\begin{array}{r} 18{,}000 \\ 3{,}000 \\ 0 \\ +\ \ 12 \\ \hline 21{,}012 \end{array}$$

$$\begin{array}{r} {}^{3\ 1}\ \ \ \ \\ 3{,}502 \\ \times\ \ \ \ 6 \\ \hline 21{,}012 \end{array}$$

Multiply the ones, tens, hundreds, and thousands. Regroup as needed.

Key Vocabulary

Distributive Property of Multiplication (pp. 194, 273)

estimate (pp. 36, 268)

multiply (pp. 170, 263)

product (p. 268)

Vocabulary Check

Choose the vocabulary word that completes the sentence.

1. When you do not need an exact answer you can ___?___.
2. Finding the product means you need to ___?___.
3. The ___?___ says that you can multiply the addends of a number and then add the products.
4. To ___?___ products, round factors to their greatest place.
5. When two factors are multiplied together, the result is a(n) ___?___ .
6. You need to ___?___ to find the total of equal groups.

Lesson-by-Lesson Review

7-1 Multiples of 10, 100, and 1,000 (pp. 263–265)

Example 1
Find 7 × 6,000.

Use basic facts and patterns to find 7 × 6,000.

7 × 6 = 42	7 × 6 ones
7 × 60 = 420	7 × 6 tens
7 × 600 = 4,200	7 × 6 hundreds
7 × 6,000 = 42,000	7 × 6 thousands

So, 7 × 6,000 = 42,000.
Notice that this answer is 7 × 6 with three zeros added to the end.

Multiply. Use basic facts and patterns.

7. 2 × 50 **8.** 4 × 90

9. 5 × 400 **10.** 8 × 600

11. 6 × 3,000 **12.** 9 × 7,000

13. **Measurement** One ton is equal to 2,000 pounds. How many pounds are equal to 7 tons?

7-2 Problem-Solving Skill: Reasonable Answers (pp. 266–267)

Example 2
Andrés walks 40 miles each month. Is it reasonable to say that he will walk more than 300 miles in 6 months? Explain.

Andrés walks 40 miles each month. Find if it is reasonable to say he will walk more than 300 miles in 6 months. Find 6 × 40 and then compare.

6 × 4 = 24

6 × 40 = 240

240 < 300. So, it is not reasonable to say Andrés will walk more than 300 miles in 6 months.

14. Jaime's family eats 12 cups of fruit each week. Is 200 a reasonable estimate for the number of cups of fruit they will eat each month? Explain.

15. There are 8 party bags. Each bag contains the items shown. Is it reasonable to say that the bags will have 75 items in all? Explain.

16. Ahmik donates $200 each month to the local homeless shelter. Is it reasonable to say that he will give more than $3,000 a year? Explain.

Study Guide and Review

7-3 Use Rounding to Estimate Products (pp. 268–271)

Example 3
Estimate 4 × 8,596.

First round. Then use basic facts and patterns to multiply.

4 × 8,596

THINK 8,596 rounds to 9,000.

4 × 9,000 = 36,000

So, 4 × 8,596 is about 36,000.

Estimate each product. Then tell if the estimate is *greater than* or *less than* the actual product.

17. 5 × 248

18. 7 × 584

19. 1,478 × 4

20. 9,385 × 8

21. About how many children play football if there are 9 teams of 18 children?

22. Rob can read a 240-page book in a week. About how many pages can he read in 6 weeks?

7-4 Multiply Two-Digit Numbers (pp. 272–274)

Example 4
Tania has four decks of 52 cards. How many cards does Tania have?

Find 4 × 52.

Step 1 Multiply the ones.

$$\begin{array}{r} 52 \\ \times\ 4 \\ \hline 8 \end{array} \quad 4 \times 2 = 8$$

Step 2 Multiply the tens.

$$\begin{array}{r} 52 \\ \times\ 4 \\ \hline 208 \end{array} \quad 4 \times 5 = 20$$

	50	+ 2
4	200	8

$$\begin{array}{r} 200 \\ +\ 8 \\ \hline 208 \end{array}$$

So, Tania has 208 cards.

Multiply. Check for resonableness.

23. 62 × 7

24. 77 × 9

25. 35 × 3

26. 88 × 5

27. Measurement A kangaroo can jump as far as 44 feet in a single jump. What distance would three jumps of this size cover?

28. Paulo watched 7 movies in one month. Each movie was 120 minutes long. How many minutes did Paulo watch movies during this month?

7-5 Problem-Solving Investigation: Choose a Strategy (pp. 276–277)

Example 5
Dominic is making dinner. Setting the table and preparing a salad will take 15 minutes each. Making the entree will take 1 hour. If dinner is to be served at 6:00 P.M., what time does he need to start preparing dinner?

Use the *work backward* strategy.

6 P.M.	end result
− 1 hour	entree
5 P.M.	
−15 minutes	salad
4:45 P.M.	
−15 minutes	set table
4:30 P.M.	

So, Dominic needs to start at 4:30 P.M.

Use any strategy to solve.

29. There are 11 fish in an aquarium. Three of the fish are yellow. There are twice as many blue fish as yellow fish. The rest of the fish are red. How many red fish are there?

30. Adelina earns $35 a day for babysitting. She earns a total of $315. How many days did she babysit?

31. Katelyn is going to rent a movie last. She is going to the post office second. She is going to the pet store before the post office. She is going to the library before she rents a movie. In what order is she completing her errands?

7-6 Multiply Multi-Digit Numbers (pp. 278–281)

Example 6
Find $1,276 × 4.

Step 1
Multiply ones.

$$\begin{array}{r} {}^{2} \\ \$1,276 \\ \times \quad 4 \\ \hline 4 \end{array}$$

Step 2
Multiply tens.

$$\begin{array}{r} {}^{3\,2} \\ \$1,276 \\ \times \quad 4 \\ \hline 04 \end{array}$$

Step 3
Multiply hundreds.

$$\begin{array}{r} {}^{1\ \,3\,2} \\ \$1,276 \\ \times \quad 4 \\ \hline 104 \end{array}$$

Step 4
Multiply thousands.

$$\begin{array}{r} {}^{1\ \,3\,2} \\ \$1,276 \\ \times \quad 4 \\ \hline \$5,104 \end{array}$$

Multiply. Check for resonableness.

32. 6 × 109

33. 8 × 854

34. $\begin{array}{r} 4,355 \\ \times \quad 3 \\ \hline \end{array}$

35. $\begin{array}{r} 5,820 \\ \times \quad 7 \\ \hline \end{array}$

36. An average hen lays 228 eggs in one year. How many eggs does a hen lay in four years?

37. There are 365 days in one year. Kevin is 9 years old. How many days old is Kevin?

7-7 Multiply Across Zeros (pp. 284–287)

Example 7

The cost for one person to go skiing for two days is $109. What is the cost for a family of five to go skiing for two days?

You need to find the product of $109 × 5.

Step 1 Multiply the ones.

```
    4
 $109
×   5
    5
```

5 × 9 ones = 45 ones
Regroup 45 ones as 4 tens

Step 2 Multiply the tens.

```
    4
 $109
×   5
   45
```

5 × 0 tens = 0 tens
Add the regrouped tens.
0 tens + 4 tens = 4 tens

Step 3 Multiply the hundreds.

```
    4
 $109
×   5
 $545
```

5 × 1 hundred = 5 hundreds

	$100	+ $9
5	$500	$45

$500 + $45 = $545

So, the cost is $545.

Multiply. Check for reasonableness.

38. 107 × 2

39. 205 × 4

40. 409 × 6

41. 603 × 7

42. 8 × 906

43. 5 × 6,009

Algebra Find the value of *y*.

44. $3 \times 207 = y$

45. $y = 7 \times 4{,}081$

Algebra Copy and complete the table.

46.

Rule: Multiply by 6.	
Input	**Output**
307	■
1,009	■
4,708	■
6,003	■
9,002	■

47. Measurement A truck driver covered the distance shown in the table below. How many miles did he cover in 5 weeks?

Distance Covered	
Week	**Distance (miles)**
1	3,008
2	3,008
3	2,805
4	2,805
5	2,805

CHAPTER 7

Chapter Test

Multiply. Use basic facts and patterns.

1. 5 × 4
5 × 40
5 × 400
5 × 4,000

2. 9 × 6
9 × 60
9 × 600
9 × 6,000

Multiply. Use mental math.

3. 2 × 60

4. 4 × 50

5. 6 × 800

6. 8 × 9,000

7. School supplies cost $30. Is it reasonable for 9 students to purchase supplies with $300? Explain.

8. **STANDARDS PRACTICE**
Which pair of numbers best completes the equation?

□ × 100 = ⬭

A 65 and 650

B 65 and 6,500

C 605 and 6,500

D 650 and 6,500

9. Fiona makes $25 a day babysitting. Is it reasonable to say she will have more than $200 at the end of a week? Explain.

Estimate each product.

10. 4 × 657

11. 7 × 9,431

Multiply.

12. 5 × 64

13. 9 × 75

14. Hakeem takes 60 minute tennis lessons twice a week. How many minutes of tennis lessons does Hakeem take in four weeks?

Algebra Find the value of each expression if $n = 6$.

15. $n \times 827$

16. $3,285 × n

Multiply.

17. 4 × 226

18. 8 × 591

Algebra Copy and complete.

19. If 3 × ■ = 21,
then 30 × ■ = 2,100.

20. If 8 × ■ = 48,
then 80 × ■ = 4,800.

21. **STANDARDS PRACTICE**
A plane carries 234 passengers. If the plane makes 4 trips a day, how many passengers is the plane transporting a day?

F 826

G 926

H 936

J 981

22. **WRITING IN ▸MATH** Joshua does not understand why 4,200 is not the correct estimate for 681 × 7. Explain.

CHAPTER 7 California Standards Practice

Cumulative, Chapters 1–7

What is the total number of sheets of paper in 6 packages?

A 300 **C** 3000

B 600 **D** 30,000

Read the Question

You need to find number of sheets of paper in 6 packages.

Solve the Question

$6 \times 5 = 30$ 6×5 ones $= 30$ ones $= 30$

$6 \times 50 = 300$ 6×5 tens $= 30$ tens $= 300$

$6 \times 500 = 3000$ 6×5 hundreds $= 30$ hundreds $= 3000$

So, $6 \times 500 = 3000$.
The answer is C.

 **Personal Tutor at** ca.gr4math.com

Choose the best answer.

1 Cora has 20 rolls of pennies. If 50 pennies are in each roll, how many pennies does she have?

A 200 **C** 2000

B 1000 **D** 10,000

2 Samir earns $22 each week mowing lawns. How much will he earn in 4 weeks?

F $75 **H** $88

G $80 **J** $125

More California Standards Practice
For practice by standard, see pages CA1–CA43.

3 Joel is going on a three-day biking trip. The daily cost is $46. How much will the trip cost?

A $92
B $128
C $138
D $460

---

4 What is the value of x?

$$(12 \div 3) \times (6 - 3) = x$$

F 1
G 9
H 12
J 24

---

5 The bar graph shows Connor's savings for the month of April.

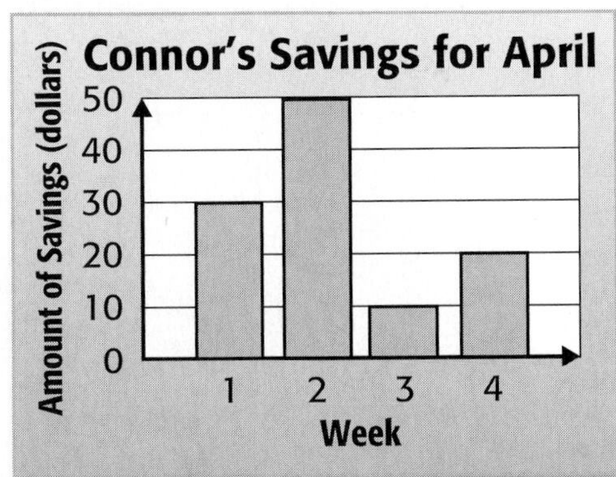

Which week did Connor save more than $30?

A Week 1
B Week 2
C Week 3
D Week 4

---

6 Find n if $38 + n = 107$.

F 68
G 69
H 79
J 145

---

7 The table shows the number of miles the Lin family drove over three days.

Day	Miles
Tuesday	176
Wednesday	228
Thursday	132

Approximately about how many miles did the Lin family drive in the three days?

A 300 miles
B 400 miles
C 500 miles
D 600 miles

---

8 The Marshall School has 8 classrooms. Each classroom has 22 desks. How many desks does the school have?

F 160
G 166
H 176
J 180

---

9 Adult admission to the aquarium is $9. On Tuesday, 345 adults visited the aquarium. How much money did the aquarium collect on Tuesday?

A $3000
B $3105
C $3200
D $4000

---

10 $4800 - 3254 = \blacksquare$

F 1546
G 1556
H 1666
J 1667

CHAPTER 8 Multiply by Two-Digit Numbers

How do you multiply by a two-digit number?

You can use area models and partial products.

Example During recycling week, 15 students collected 12 pounds of recyclable items each. The model shows that 15 × 12 or 180 pounds of recyclable items were collected.

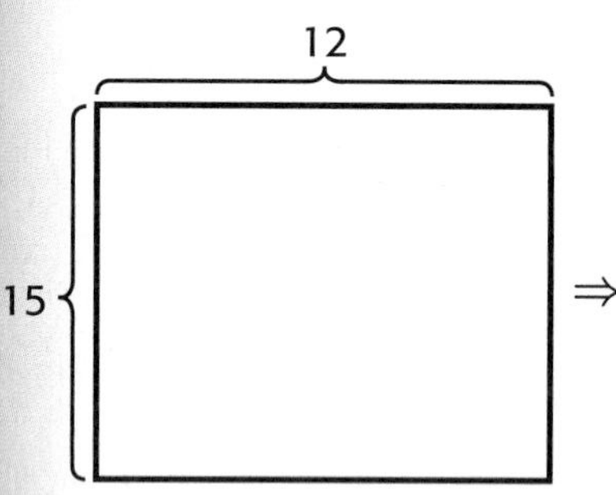

⇒

	10	2
10	100	20
5	50	10

$$\begin{array}{r} 15 \\ \times 12 \\ \hline 100 \\ 20 \\ 50 \\ +10 \\ \hline 180 \end{array}$$

What will I learn in this chapter?

- Multiply by multiples of ten.
- Estimate products by rounding.
- Multiply by two-digit numbers.
- Multiply multi-digit numbers by a two-digit number.
- Solve problems by acting them out.

Key Vocabulary

Distributive Property of Multiplication
estimate
factor
multiple
product

Student Study Tools at ca.gr4math.com

FOLDABLES™
Study Organizer

Make this Foldable to help you organize information about multiplying by two-digit numbers. Begin with 3 sheets of $8\frac{1}{2}'' \times 11''$ paper.

1. **Stack** the paper so that the sheets are $\frac{3}{4}$ inch apart.
2. **Roll** up the edges so tabs are the same size.
3. **Crease** and staple along the fold as shown.
4. **Label** the tabs as shown.

ARE YOU READY for Chapter 8?

You have two ways to check prerequisite skills for this chapter.

Option 2

Math Online Take the Chapter Readiness Quiz at ca.gr4math.com.

Option 1

Complete the Quick Check below.

QUICK Check

Round to the given place. (Lesson 1-6)

1. 604; nearest hundred

2. 2,188; nearest thousand

3. 85,888; nearest ten-thousand

4. 681,002; nearest hundred thousand

5. The students raised $6,784 for a new playground. To the nearest thousand, about how much money did the students raise?

Add. (Lesson 2-4)

6. 759 + 307

7. 5,138 + 507

8. 9,290 + 812

9. 6,005 + 8,204

10. 34,068 + 6,055

11. 242,607 + 480,196

Write the multiplication expression for each model. Then multiply. (Lesson 5-2)

12. 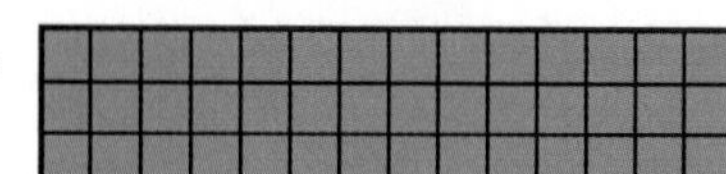

13. 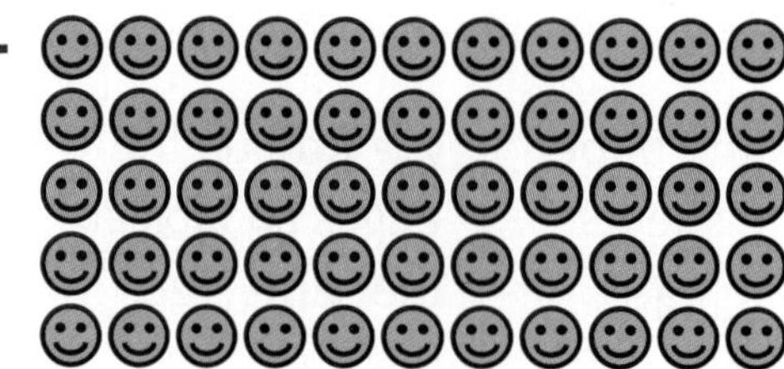

Multiply. (Lesson 7-4)

14. 36×7

15. 40×9

16. 86×5

8-1 Multiply by Tens

GET READY to Learn

Rita took 20 pictures at her family reunion. She printed the pictures so that each of her 25 family members could have them. How many pictures did Rita print?

MAIN IDEA

I will multiply a whole number by a multiple of ten.

Standard 4NS3.3 Solve problems involving the multiplication of multidigit numbers by two-digit numbers.

Standard 4NS3.2 Demonstrate an understanding of, and the ability to use, standard algorithms for multiplying a multidigit number by a two-digit number and for dividing a multidigit number by a one-digit number; use relationships between them to simplify computations and to check results.

When you multiply a two-digit number by a multiple of ten such as 20, 30, 40, ..., the digit in the ones place is always a zero.

Real-World EXAMPLE Multiply by Tens

1 PHOTOGRAPHS How many pictures did Rita print?

You need to find 25×20.

One Way: Use Properties

25×20	Write the problem.
$25 \times (10 \times 2)$	Think of 20 as 10×2.
$25 \times (2 \times 10)$	Commutative Property of Multiplication
$(25 \times 2) \times 10$	Associative Property of Multiplication
50×10	Multiply. $25 \times 2 = 50$
500	Mental Math

Another Way: Use Paper and Pencil

Step 1 Multiply the ones.	**Step 2** Multiply the tens.
$\begin{array}{r} 25 \\ \times\ 20 \\ \hline 0 \end{array}$ ← 0 ones × 25 = 0	$\begin{array}{r} 25 \\ \times\ 20 \\ \hline 500 \end{array}$ ← 2 tens × 25 = 50 tens

So, Rita printed 500 pictures.

Real-World EXAMPLE Multiply by Tens

2 **MUSIC An electronics store has 30 digital music players in stock that cost $125 each. How much do the digital music players cost altogether?**

Step 1 Multiply the ones.

$$\begin{array}{r} \$125 \\ \times\ 30 \\ \hline 0 \end{array}$$ ← 0 ones × 125 = 0

Step 2 Multiply the tens.

$$\begin{array}{r} \$125 \\ \times\ 30 \\ \hline \$3{,}750 \end{array}$$ ← 3 tens × 125 = 375 tens

So, the music players cost a total of $3,750.

Check

Think of 30 × 125 as 3 × 10 × 125.

30 × $125	Write the problem.
(3 × 10) × $125	Think of 30 as 3 × 10.
(10 × 3) × $125	Commutative Property
10 × (3 × $125)	Associative Property
10 × $375	Multiply. 3 × $125 = $375.
$3,750	Mental Math

So, the answer is correct. ✓

Online **Personal Tutor at** ca.gr4math.com

Remember

When you multiply a number by a multiple of ten, the digit in the ones place is always zero.

CHECK What You Know

Multiply. See Examples 1 and 2 (pp. 299–300)

1. $\begin{array}{r} 36 \\ \times\ 10 \\ \hline \end{array}$

2. $\begin{array}{r} 53 \\ \times\ 30 \\ \hline \end{array}$

3. $\begin{array}{r} 79 \\ \times\ 80 \\ \hline \end{array}$

4. $255× 20

5. $389 × 40

6. $518 × 70

7. Latasha bikes 20 miles every week. There are 52 weeks in a year. How many miles does she bike in a year?

8. Talk About It Joey is finding 40 × 67. Explain why he can think of 40 × 67 as 4 × 10 × 67.

Practice and Problem Solving

EXTRA PRACTICE See page R19.

Multiply. See Examples 1 and 2 (pp. 299–300)

9. 15×20

10. 27×30

11. 46×40

12. 53×60

13. 80 × 80

14. 94 × 90

15. $275 × 10

16. $312 × 30

17. $381 × 50

18. $457 × 50

19. $564 × 70

20. $698 × 80

21. If 7 × 29 = 203, then what is 70 × 29?

22. If 3 × 52 = 156, then what is 30 × 52?

23. Baby robins eat 14 feet of earthworms each day. How many feet of worms does a baby robin eat in 20 days?

24. Mozart could learn a piece of music in 30 minutes. How long would it take him to learn 15 pieces of music?

Real-World PROBLEM SOLVING

Birds Hummingbirds feed every 10 minutes. They fly about 25 miles per hour and flap their wings 60 to 80 times each second.

25. What is the least number of times a hummingbird will flap its wings in 15 seconds?

26. What is the greatest number of times it will flap its wing in 15 seconds?

27. How many minutes have passed if a hummingbird has eaten 45 times?

28. If a hummingbird flies a total of 20 hours, how far did it fly?

H.O.T. Problems

29. OPEN ENDED Create a number sentence with two 2-digit factors whose product has 3 zeros.

30. WHICH ONE DOESN'T BELONG? Identify the multiplication problem that does not belong with the other three. Explain.

15 × 30	28 × 20	41 × 21	67 × 40

31. WRITING IN ▶MATH How many zeros would be in the product of 50 and 60? Explain.

8-2 Estimate Products

GET READY to Learn

Did you know that a hamster sleeps more than half the day? It sleeps about 14 hours each day. About how many hours does it sleep in 3 weeks?

MAIN IDEA

I will estimate products by rounding.

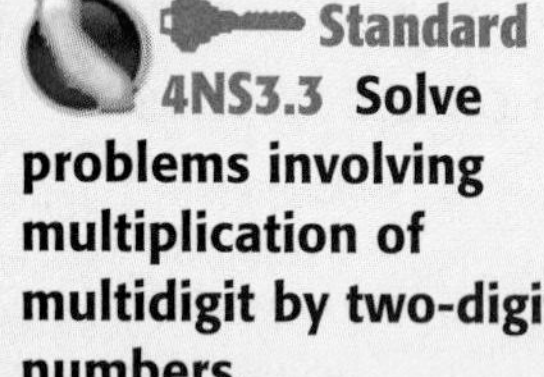

Standard 4NS3.3 Solve problems involving multiplication of multidigit by two-digit numbers.

Standard 4NS1.3 Round whole numbers through the millions to the nearest ten, hundred, thousand, ten thousand, or hundred thousand.

Review Vocabulary

estimate When you do not need an exact answer, you can estimate. **(Lesson 1–6)**

The word *about* tells you to estimate. When you estimate the product of two two-digit factors, it is helpful to round them both.

Real-World EXAMPLES Estimate Products

1 ANIMALS A hamster sleeps 14 hours each day. About how many hours does a hamster sleep in 3 weeks?

There are 21 days in 3 weeks. So, estimate 21×14.

Step 1 Round each factor to the nearest ten.

$$\begin{array}{r} 21 \\ \times\ 14 \\ \hline \end{array} \longrightarrow \begin{array}{r} 20 \\ \times\ 10 \\ \hline \end{array}$$

21 rounds to 20.
14 rounds to 10.

Step 2 Multiply.

$$\begin{array}{r} 20 \\ \times\ 10 \\ \hline 200 \end{array}$$

$0 \text{ ones} \times 20 = 0$
$1 \text{ ten} \times 20 = 20 \text{ tens}$

So, a hamster sleeps about 200 hours in 21 days or 3 weeks. Since both factors were rounded down, the estimate is less than the actual product.

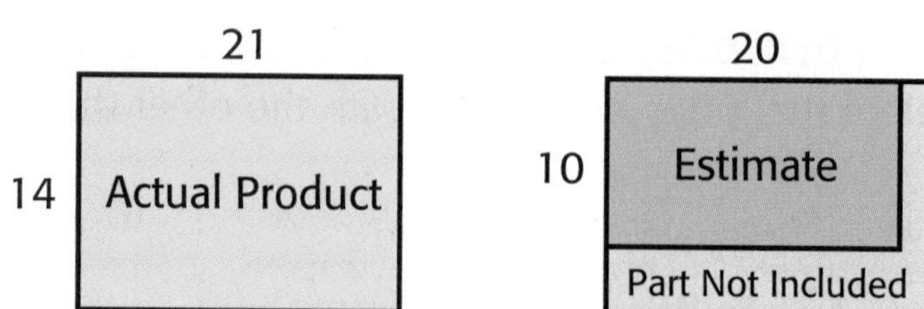

Personal Tutor at ca.gr4math.com

Real-World EXAMPLES Estimate Products

2 **MEASUREMENT Tonya spends 35 minutes playing at the park each day. About how many minutes does she play at the park in a year?**

There are approximately 365 days in a year. So, you need to estimate 365 × 35.

Step 1 Round each factor to its greatest place.

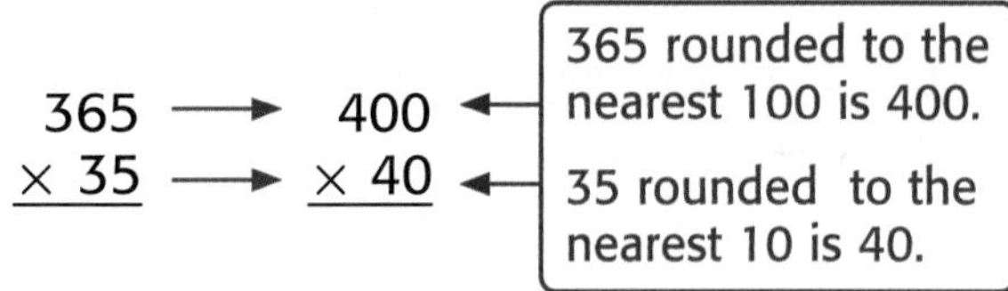

Remember

If one factor is rounded up and one factor is rounded down, it will not be obvious whether the estimate is greater or less than the actual product.

Step 2 Multiply.

$$\begin{array}{r} 400 \\ \times\ 40 \\ \hline 16{,}000 \end{array}$$

So, Tonya spends about 16,000 minutes playing at the park in a year. Since both factors were rounded up, the estimate is greater than the actual product.

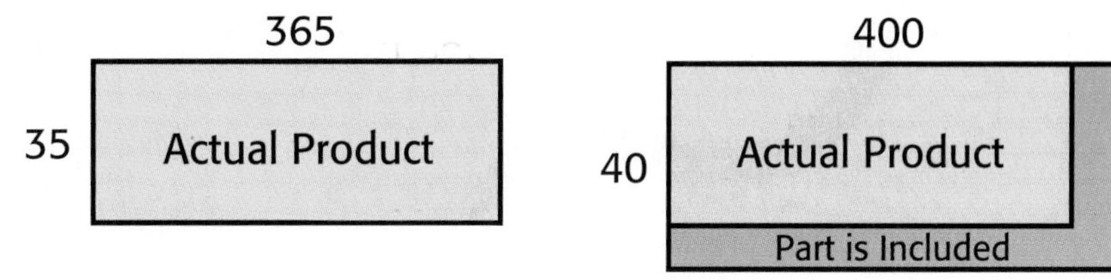

CHECK What You Know

Estimate. Tell whether the estimate is greater or less than the actual product. See Examples 1 and 2 (pp. 302–303)

1. $\begin{array}{r} 34 \\ \times\ 12 \\ \hline \end{array}$

2. $\begin{array}{r} 57 \\ \times\ 25 \\ \hline \end{array}$

3. $376 × 17

4. 525 × 43

5. The average person makes about 22 phone calls each week. About how many phone calls is this each year?

6. Talk About It Explain how you know if an estimated product is more or less than the actual product.

Practice and Problem Solving

EXTRA PRACTICE
See page R19.

Estimate. Tell whether the estimate is greater or less than the actual product. See Examples 1 and 2 (pp. 302–303)

7. $\begin{array}{r} 28 \\ \times\ 25 \\ \hline \end{array}$

8. $\begin{array}{r} 43 \\ \times\ 14 \\ \hline \end{array}$

9. $\begin{array}{r} \$56 \\ \times\ 37 \\ \hline \end{array}$

10. $\begin{array}{r} 58 \\ \times\ 29 \\ \hline \end{array}$

11. $\begin{array}{r} 64 \\ \times\ 41 \\ \hline \end{array}$

12. $\begin{array}{r} 79 \\ \times\ 55 \\ \hline \end{array}$

13. $\begin{array}{r} \$91 \\ \times\ 64 \\ \hline \end{array}$

14. $\begin{array}{r} 94 \\ \times\ 82 \\ \hline \end{array}$

15. $234 × 11

16. 352 × 37

17. 489 × 86

18. 535 × 42

19. 678 × 56

20. 739 × 84

21. 891 × 78

22. 919 × 92

23. An antelope can run 55 miles per hour. About how many miles would it travel if it ran a total of 12 hours?

24. Karena averages 16 points in each basketball game. About how many points will she score in 14 games?

25. A certain type of millipede has 750 legs. About how many legs would 12 of these millipedes have?

26. About how many pounds of fruit would the average American eat in 11 years?

Food Eaten Each Year

Type of Food	Amount (lb)
Fresh fruit	127
Fresh vegetables	148
Milk and cream	205

Source: *The Top 100 of Everything*

Real-World PROBLEM SOLVING

Data File People rushed to California in search of gold in 1849. This is called the California Gold Rush.

History

- A wind wagon was used by some people as transportation to California.
- It could travel 15 miles per hour.

27. About how many miles would the wind wagon travel over 7 days traveling 8 hours each day?

28. People paid up to $100 for a glass of water on the trail to California. If it cost $93 for 1 glass, about how much would 12 glasses of water cost?

H.O.T. Problems

29. OPEN ENDED Identify two factors that have an estimated product of 2,000.

30. NUMBER SENSE Estimate 51 × 39 and 84 × 45. Which is closer to its actual product? Explain your reasoning.

31. WRITING IN ▶MATH Write a real-world problem that involves estimating the product of two 2-digit numbers.

Standards Practice

32 What is the total length of 35 anacondas? **(Lesson 8-1)**

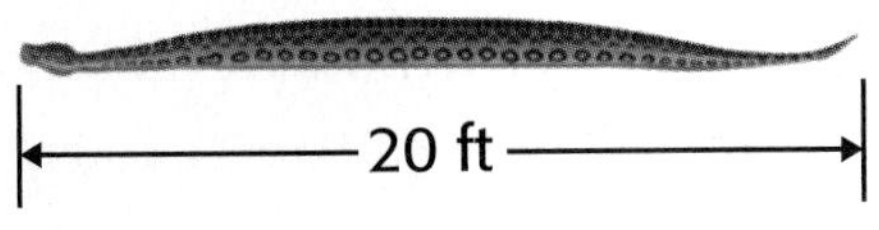

A 600 feet

B 700 feet

C 800 feet

D 900 feet

33 There are 365 days in a year. Which is the best estimate of the number of days in 12 years? **(Lesson 8-2)**

F 7000

G 6000

H 5000

J 4000

Spiral Review

Multiply. (Lesson 8-1)

34. 27 × 10

35. 43 × 50

36. \$96 × 70

Multiply. Check for reasonableness. (Lesson 7-7)

37. 1,006 × 3

38. 4,065 × 6

39. 7,040 × 9

40. Write an equation that describes the pattern. Then use the equation to find the next three numbers. **(Lesson 6-6)**

Input (*w*)	1	3	5	7	9	11
Output (*v*)	4	12	20	■	■	■

41. Arthur earns \$20 for every lawn he mows. He mows 12 houses twice a month. He has been mowing for 3 months. How much money does he make in 1 month? Identify any extra or missing information. Then solve.

Write the value of the underlined digit. (Lesson 1-2)

42. 189,3$\underline{9}$7

43. $\underline{2}$,670,830

44. 34,7$\underline{9}$1,028

8-3 Problem-Solving Strategy

MAIN IDEA I will solve a problem by acting it out.

Standard 4MR2.3 Use a variety of methods, such as words, numbers, symbols, charts, graphs, tables, diagrams, **and models, to explain mathematical reasoning.** **Standard 4NS3.0 Students solve problems involving addition,** subtraction, multiplication, and division **of whole numbers** and understand the relationships among the operations.

Sonoda has 6 coins in his bank. The coins equal 65¢. What combination of coins does he have in his bank?

Understand

What facts do you know?

- Sonoda has 6 coins.
- The value of the 6 coins is 65¢.

What do you need to find?

- Find the coins Sonoda has in his bank.

Plan

You can use play money to act out different combinations of 65¢.

Solve

One way to make 65¢ is with 2 quarters, 1 dime, and 1 nickel. But, that is only 4 coins. You need 2 more coins.

Take 1 quarter and exchange it for 2 dimes and 1 nickel. The value stays the same, and the number of coins increases to 6.

So, Sonoda has 1 quarter, 3 dimes, and 2 nickels.

Check

Look back at the problem.

$$\begin{aligned} & \text{1 quarter} + \text{3 dimes} + \text{2 nickels} \\ = & (1 \times 25¢) + (3 \times 10¢) + (2 \times 5¢) \\ = & 25¢ + 30¢ + 10¢ \\ = & 65¢ \end{aligned}$$

So, the answer is correct.

ANALYZE the Strategy

Refer to the problem on the previous page.

1. If Sonoda has a few coins that total 55¢, what is the least amount of coins he can have?

2. Suppose Sonoda had 60¢ in his bank. What 5 coins would he have?

3. Suppose Sonoda found 3 coins on the sidewalk. The coins total $1. What coins did Sonoda find? Explain.

4. Describe another strategy you could use to solve this problem.

PRACTICE the Strategy

See page R20.

Solve. Use the *act it out* strategy.

5. Angelo's father is 30 years old. This is 10 years older than twice Angelo's age. How old is Angelo?

6. Ellen needs to visit 3 Web sites for a homework assignment. In how many different ways can she visit the Web sites?

7. There are five people at a party, and each person has shaken hands with every other person. How many handshakes took place among the five people?

8. **Geometry** Can 12 toothpicks be used to form 4 squares that are the same size and same shape?

9. Berta, Maya, and Zach are in different checkout lines at a store. Berta has 3 more people in front of her than are in front of Maya. There are 2 times as many people in front of Zach as there are in front of Maya. The total number of people in front of the girls is 11. How many people are in front of each person?

10. **Geometry** How many different rectangles can you make using all of the squares shown below?

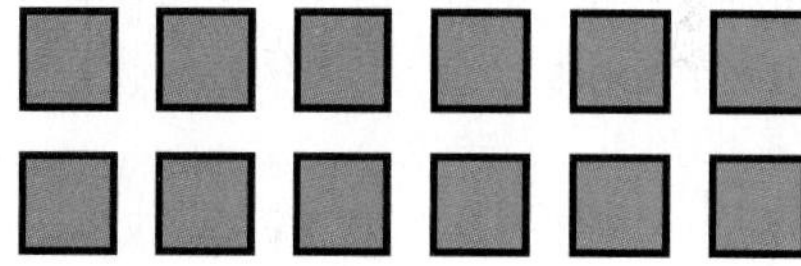

11. List five different money combinations that equal 34¢.

12. Jamaica has 8 coins with a value of $1. What coins does she have?

13. Dane needs to set up tables for his nine family members and himself to eat dinner. The square tables will seat one person on each side. Explain how Dane can arrange six square tables in a rectangle so that there is one seat for each person with no extra seats.

14. **WRITING IN MATH** When should the *act it out* strategy be used to solve a problem? Explain.

Math Activity for 8-4

Multiply Two-Digit Numbers

MAIN IDEA

I will explore multiplying by two-digit numbers.

Preparation for Standard 4NS3.3 Solve problems involving multiplication of multidigit numbers by two-digit numbers.

Standard 4MR2.3 Use a variety of methods, such as words, numbers, symbols, charts, graphs, tables, diagrams, **and models, to explain mathematical reasoning.**

You Will Need
colored pencils
graph paper

In Lesson 5-6, you learned that the **Distributive Property of Multiplication** allows you to break apart factors to find a product. You can use the Distributive Property to multiply two-digit numbers.

KEY CONCEPT — Distributive Property

To multiply a sum by a number, multiply each addend by the number and add the products.

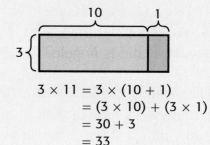

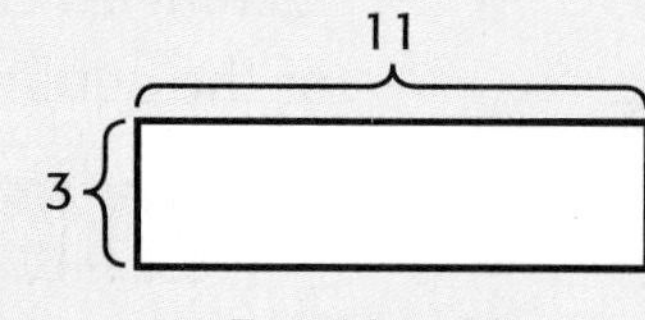

$3 \times 11 = 33$

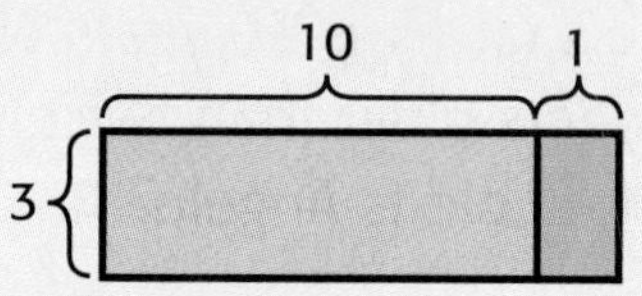

$$\begin{aligned}3 \times 11 &= 3 \times (10 + 1)\\ &= (3 \times 10) + (3 \times 1)\\ &= 30 + 3\\ &= 33\end{aligned}$$

ACTIVITY **Find 12 × 15.**

Step 1 **Draw a rectangle.**

Draw a rectangle on graph paper. Use 12 and 15 as the dimensions.

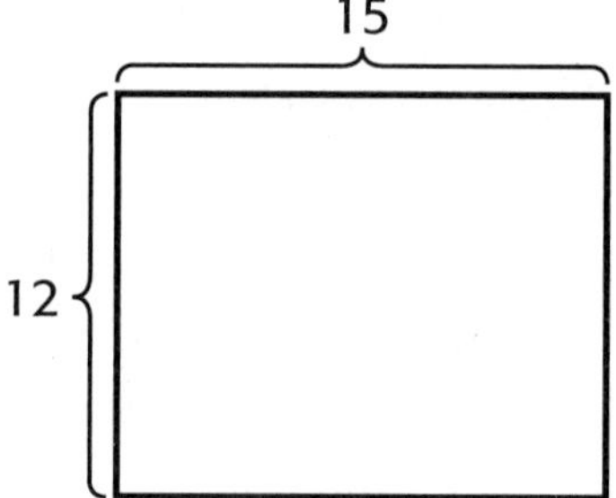

Step 2 **Separate the tens and ones.**

First, break up the 15 as 10 and 5. Next, break up the 12 as 10 and 2.

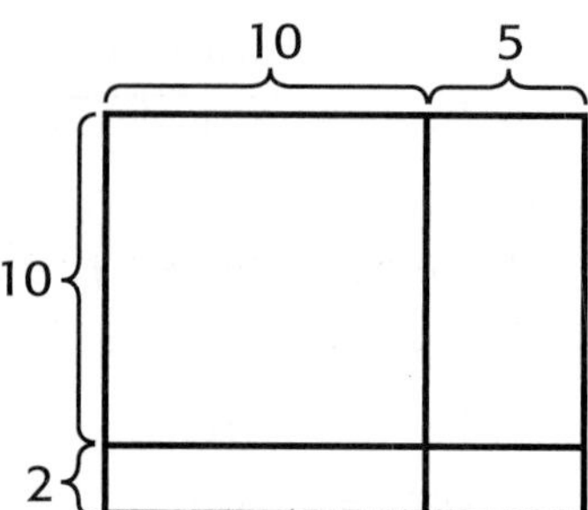

Step 3 **Find each product. Then add.**

10 × 10	=	100
10 × 5	=	50
2 × 10	=	20
2 × 5	=	+ 10
		180

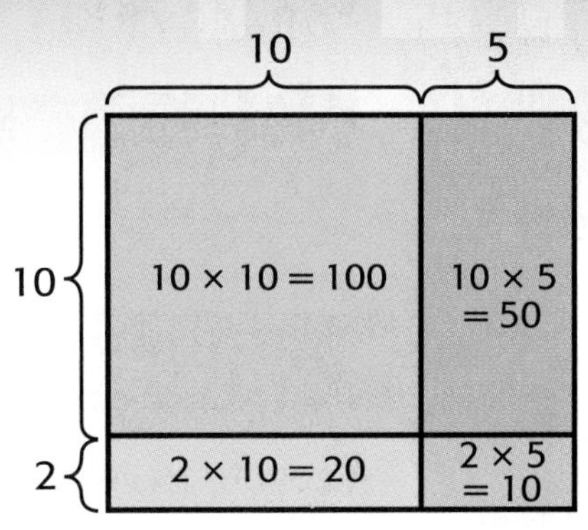

Step 4 **Make the connection.**
Distributive Property

$$12 \times 15 = (10 \times 15) + (2 \times 15)$$
$$= (10 \times 10) + (10 \times 5) + (2 \times 10) + (2 \times 5)$$
$$= 100 + 50 + 20 + 10$$
$$= 180$$

Partial Products

15	
× 12	
10	2 × 5
20	2 × 10
50	10 × 5
+ 100	10 × 10
180	Add partial products.

Think About It

1. How would you use the Distributive Property to find 12 × 18?

CHECK What You Know

Write the multiplication sentence for each area model. Multiply.

2.

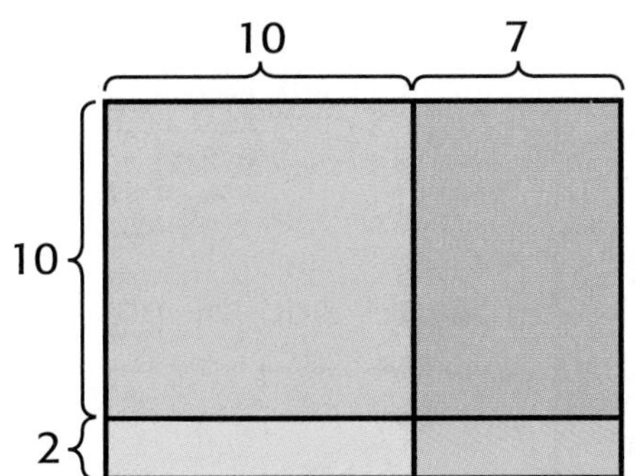

3.

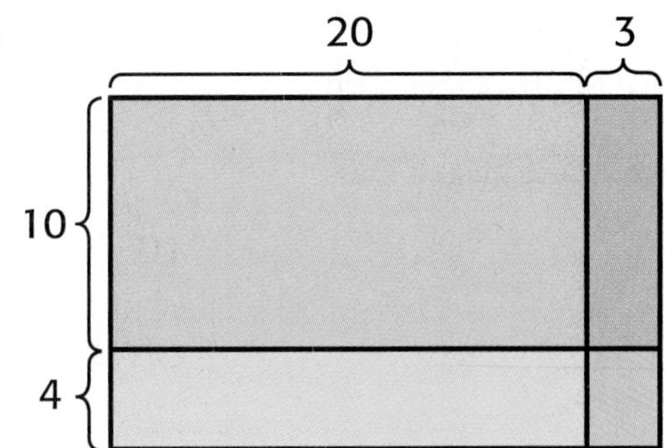

Multiply. Use an area model and the Distributive Property.

4. 12 × 10

5. 14 × 18

6. 25 × 28

7. WRITING IN ►MATH Explain how to find 16 × 19.

8-4 Multiply Two-Digit Numbers

MAIN IDEA

I will multiply two-digit numbers.

Preparation for Standard 4NS3.2 Demonstrate an understanding of, and the ability to use, standard algorithms for multiplying a multidigit number by a two-digit number and for dividing a multidigit number by a one-digit number; use the relationships between them to simplify computations and to check results.

Preparation for Standard 4NS3.3 Solve problems involving multiplication of multidigit numbers by two-digit numbers.

GET READY to Learn

A coyote travels 27 miles per hour. How far would a coyote travel in 12 hours?

There is more than one way to multiply two-digit numbers.

Real-World EXAMPLE

1 **MEASUREMENT A coyote travels 27 miles each hour. Multiply 27 × 12 to find how far a coyote can travel in 12 hours.**

One Way: Partial Products

27	
× 12	
14	Multiply 2 × 7.
40	Multiply 2 × 20.
70	Multiply 10 × 7.
+ 200	Multiply 10 × 20.
324	Add partial products.

	20	7
10	200	70
2	40	14

Another Way: Paper and Pencil

Step 1 Multiply the ones.

$$\begin{array}{r} {\scriptstyle 1} \\ 27 \\ \times\ 12 \\ \hline 54 \end{array} \leftarrow 2 \times 27$$

Step 2 Multiply the tens.

$$\begin{array}{r} {\scriptstyle 1} \\ 27 \\ \times\ 12 \\ \hline 54 \\ 270 \end{array} \begin{array}{l} \leftarrow 2 \times 27 \\ \leftarrow 10 \times 27 \end{array}$$

Step 3 Add the products.

$$\begin{array}{r} {\scriptstyle 1} \\ 27 \\ \times\ 12 \\ \hline 54 \\ +270 \\ \hline 324 \end{array} \leftarrow \text{Add.}$$

So, a coyote can travel 324 miles in 12 hours.

Real-World EXAMPLE Multiply Money

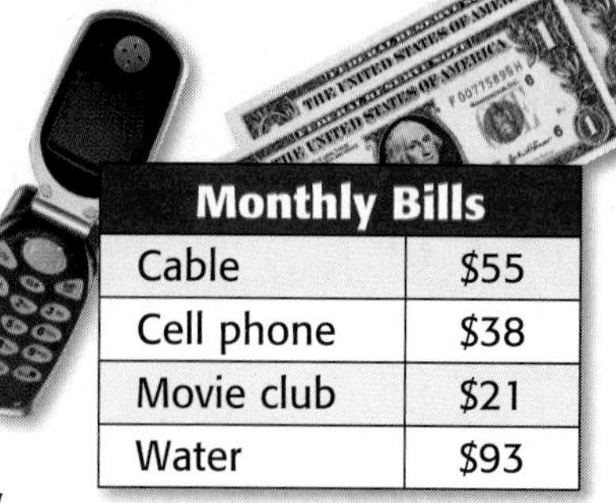

2 **EXPENSES Heidi's monthly bills are shown. How much does she spend on her cell phone service in 2 years?**

Monthly Bills	
Cable	$55
Cell phone	$38
Movie club	$21
Water	$93

Heidi's cell phone bill is $38. There are 24 months in 2 years. So multiply $38 by 24 to find how much she spends in 2 years.

Remember

Make an estimate to check the reasonableness of the answer.

Estimate $40 \times 20 = 800$

Step 1 Multiply the ones.

$$\begin{array}{r} \$38 \\ \times\ 24 \\ \hline 152 \end{array} \leftarrow 4 \times 38$$

Step 2 Multiply the tens.

$$\begin{array}{r} \$38 \\ \times\ 24 \\ \hline 152 \\ +\ 760 \end{array} \leftarrow 20 \times 38$$

Step 3 Add the products.

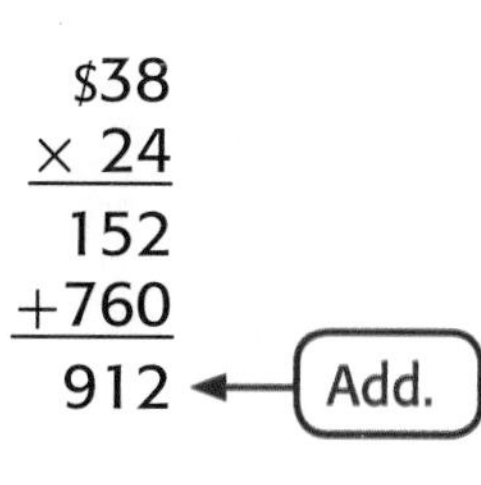

$$\begin{array}{r} \$38 \\ \times\ 24 \\ \hline 152 \\ +760 \\ \hline 912 \end{array} \leftarrow \text{Add.}$$

Check $600 + 160 + 120 + 32 = 912$

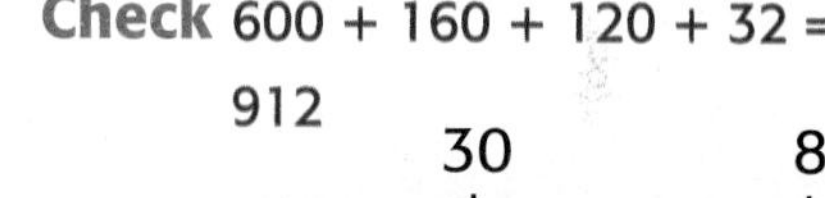

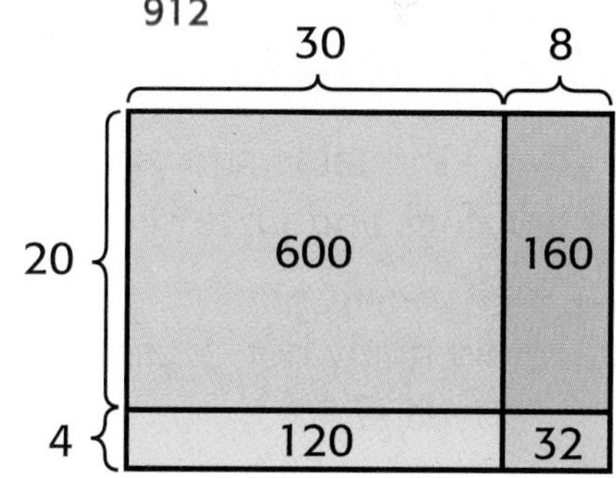

So, the cost of cell phone service for 2 years is $912.

Check for Reasonableness

912 is close to the estimate of 800. The answer is reasonable. ✓

Online **Personal Tutor at** ca.gr4math.com

CHECK What You Know

Multiply. See Examples 1 and 2 (pp. 310–311)

1. $\begin{array}{r} 35 \\ \times\ 24 \\ \hline \end{array}$

2. $\begin{array}{r} \$57 \\ \times\ 42 \\ \hline \end{array}$

3. 92×81

4. A farmer plants 35 rows of tomatoes. There are 25 plants in each row. How many plants are there altogether?

5. Talk About It Explain the steps needed to find the product of 23 and 56.

Practice and Problem Solving

EXTRA PRACTICE See page R20.

Multiply. See Examples 1 and 2 (pp. 310–311)

6. 19×15

7. 36×24

8. 42×38

9. 52×47

10. 54×51 ($)

11. 68×46 ($)

12. 74×63 ($)

13. 82×49 ($)

14. 47 × 24

15. 64 × 46

16. 83 × 67

17. 91 × 78

18. Bamboo plants can grow up to 36 inches in a day. How many inches could they grow in 3 weeks?

19. Josie earns about 28 points on each quiz she takes. How many points will Josie earn on 12 quizzes?

20. A greyhound dog can jump a distance of 27 feet. How many feet will a greyhound travel if it jumps 12 times?

21. Each day, enough paper is recycled in the U.S. to fill 15 miles of train boxcars. How many miles of boxcars could be filled over 25 days?

Real-World PROBLEM SOLVING

Food The table shows the average amount of hot dogs and pizza slices each person eats per year.

Amount of Food Eaten Each Year

Food	Number
Hot dog	60
Slice of pizza	46

Source: amusingfacts.com

22. How many hot dogs will a person eat in 11 years?

23. How many slices of pizza will a person eat in 12 years?

24. How many more hot dogs than pizza slices will a person eat in 15 years?

H.O.T. Problems

25. **OPEN ENDED** Copy and complete the multiplication problem to make a true sentence.

$$20 \times \blacksquare\blacksquare = \blacksquare00$$

26. **WHICH ONE DOESN'T BELONG?** Identify the multiplication problem that does not belong with the other three. Explain.

22 × 15 | \$45 × 28 | 37 × 18 | \$66 × 25

27. **WRITING IN ▶MATH** Explain why the product of two 2-digit numbers can never be two digits.

CHAPTER 8

Mid-Chapter Check

Lessons 8-1 through 8-4

Multiply. (Lesson 8-1)

1. 38×30

2. 52×20

3. John jogs 30 miles every week. There are 52 weeks in a year. How many miles does John jog in a year? (Lesson 8-1)

4. **STANDARDS PRACTICE** What is the total length of 30 newborn Florida alligators? (Lesson 8-1)

10 in.

A 200 inches **C** 400 inches

B 300 inches **D** 500 inches

Estimate. Tell whether the estimate is greater or less than the actual product. (Lesson 8-2)

5. 24×14

6. $\$37 \times 21$

7. **STANDARDS PRACTICE** There are 365 days in a year. Which is the best estimate of the number of days in 19 years? (Lesson 8-2)

F 4000 days **H** 7000 days

G 5000 days **J** 8000 days

8. The average person sends about 25 emails a month. About how many emails is this each year? (Lesson 8-2)

Solve. Use the *act it out* strategy. (Lesson 8-3)

9. Talia's mother is 40 years old. This is 13 years older than three times Talia's age. How old is Talia?

10. Emil has 4 coins in his pocket equaling 41¢. What combination of coins does he have in his pocket?

Multiply. (Lesson 8-4)

11. 27×13

12. 45×14

13. $\$67 \times 42$

14. 77×53

15. **Measurement** A person breathes 95 gallons of air every hour. How many gallons of air does a person breathe in one day? (Lesson 8-4)

16. **WRITING IN MATH** Mae is finding the product to the multiplication problem shown below. How many zeros will the product have? Explain.

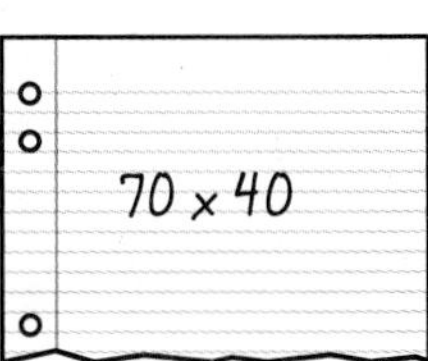

8-5 Multiply Three-Digit Numbers by Two-Digit Numbers

MAIN IDEA

I will multiply a three-digit number by a two-digit number.

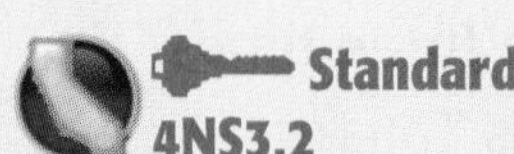

Standard 4NS3.2 **Demonstrate an understanding of, and the ability to use, standard algorithms for multiplying a multidigit number by a two-digit number** and for dividing a multidigit number by a one-digit number; use the relationships between them to simplify computations and to check results.

Standard 4NS3.3 **Solve problems involving multiplication of multidigit by two-digit numbers.**

GET READY to Learn

Rose uses about 275 minutes on her cell phone each month. How many minutes does she use in a year?

You can multiply 3-digit numbers by 2-digit numbers.

Real-World EXAMPLE

1 PHONES How many minutes does Rose use in a year?

There are 12 months in 1 year. So, multiply the number of minutes each month by 12. Find 275 × 12.

Estimate 300 × 10 = 3,000.

Step 1 Multiply 275 by 2.

$$\begin{array}{r} {}^{1\,1} \\ 275 \\ \times\ 12 \\ \hline 550 \end{array} \leftarrow \boxed{2 \times 275}$$

Step 2 Multiply 275 by 1 ten.

$$\begin{array}{r} {}^{1\,1} \\ 275 \\ \times\ 12 \\ \hline 550 \\ 2{,}750 \end{array} \leftarrow \boxed{10 \times 275}$$

Step 3 Add the products.

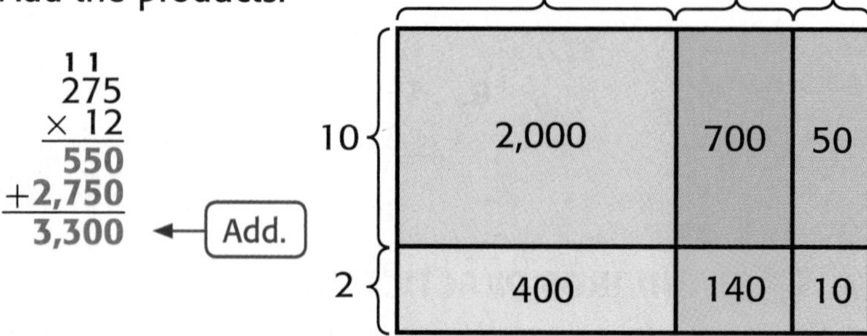

So, Rose uses 3,300 minutes in a year.

Check for Reasonableness

Since 3,300 is close to the estimate, the answer is reasonable. ✓

Real-World EXAMPLE

2 **MONEY A school bought 25 of the computers shown. What was the total cost?**

You need to multiply \$749 by 25.

Estimate \$700 × 30 = \$21,000.

Step 1 Multiply \$749 by 5.

$$\begin{array}{r} {}^{4} \\ \$749 \\ \underline{\times\ 25} \\ \$3{,}745 \end{array} \leftarrow \boxed{\$749 \times 5}$$

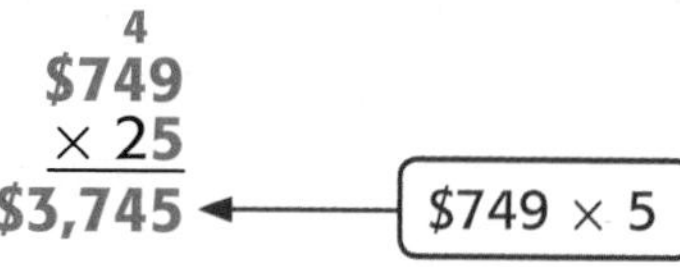

Remember

You may need to regroup when multiplying the ones, tens, and hundreds.

Step 2 Multiply \$749 by 20.

$$\begin{array}{r} {}^{1} \\ {}^{4} \\ \$749 \\ \underline{\times\ 25} \\ \$3{,}745 \\ \$14{,}980 \end{array} \leftarrow \boxed{\$749 \times 20}$$

Step 3 Add the partial products.

$$\begin{array}{r} {}^{1} \\ {}^{4} \\ \$749 \\ \underline{\times\ 25} \\ \$3{,}745 \\ \underline{+\$14{,}980} \\ \$18{,}725 \end{array} \leftarrow \boxed{\text{Add.}}$$

So, the product of \$749 and 25 is \$18,725.

Check for Reasonableness

Since \$18,725 is close to the estimate, the answer is reasonable. ✓

Personal Tutor at ca.gr4math.com

CHECK What You Know

Multiply. See Examples 1 and 2 (pp. 314–315)

1. $\begin{array}{r} 135 \\ \underline{\times\ 18} \end{array}$

2. $\begin{array}{r} 340 \\ \underline{\times\ 32} \end{array}$

3. \$703 × 89

4. A herd of elephants can travel 50 miles a day. At this rate, how far would a herd travel in a year?

5. **Talk About It** Explain how to find the product of 56 and 945.

Practice and Problem Solving

EXTRA PRACTICE
See page R20.

Multiply. See Examples 1 and 2 (pp. 314–315)

6. 106×12

7. 248×24

8. 283×33

9. 362×35

10. 467×41

11. 489×53

12. $\$508 \times 59$

13. $\$632 \times 66$

14. $770 × 71

15. $862 × 87

16. $901 × 96

17. $934 × 97

18. Every second, 630 steel cans are recycled. How many cans are recycled in 1 minute?

19. A city in Hawaii receives 451 inches of rainfall each year. How much rainfall will this city receive in 35 years?

20. The average hen lays 257 eggs each year. There are 22 hens on a farm. How many eggs will they lay in 3 years?

21. Canada's foggiest community is the city of Argentia. It has 206 days of fog each year. How many days of fog will occur in 12 years?

Real-World PROBLEM SOLVING

Sports The table shows facts about balls used in sports.

22. How many dimples are on a dozen golf balls?

23. How many stitches do 75 baseballs have?

24. Find the difference in the number of dimples on 25 golf balls and the number of stitches on 25 baseballs.

Sports Ball Facts

Ball	Fact
Golf ball	450 dimples
Baseball	108 stitches
Soccer ball	32 panels

25. **FIND THE ERROR** Michelle and Alberto are finding 351 × 26. Who is correct? Explain.

Michelle

$$\begin{array}{r} 351 \\ \times\ 26 \\ \hline 9{,}126 \end{array}$$

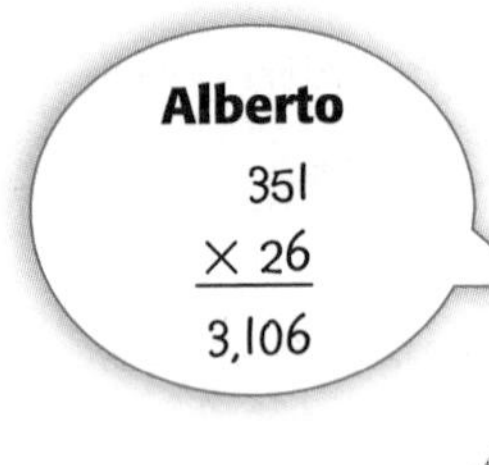

26. **WRITING IN MATH** Write a real-world problem that involves multiplying a 3-digit number by a 2-digit number.

Math Online Self-Check Quiz at ca.gr4math.com

Standards Practice

27 While riding in a car, Denzel counted 17 blue cars on a highway in 1 minute. At this rate, how many blue cars will Denzel see in 45 minutes? **(Lesson 8-4)**

A 360

B 400

C 765

D 775

28 There are 24 hours in a day and 365 days in a year. How many hours are in a year? **(Lesson 8-5)**

F 2190

G 7440

H 8000

J 8760

Spiral Review

Multiply. (Lesson 8-4)

29. $\begin{array}{r} 34 \\ \times\ 10 \\ \hline \end{array}$

30. $\begin{array}{r} 55 \\ \times\ 49 \\ \hline \end{array}$

31. $\begin{array}{r} \$272 \\ \times\ 66 \\ \hline \end{array}$

32. The tables shown need to be joined together so that 20 students can sit down for a student council meeting. Two people can sit on each side of a table. Draw a picture to show how the tables should be arranged. **(Lesson 8-3)**

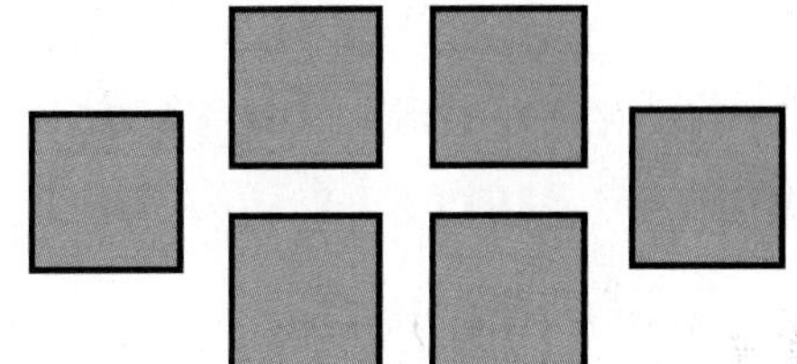

Estimate. Tell whether the estimate is greater or less than the actual product. (Lesson 8-2)

33. $\begin{array}{r} 26 \\ \times\ 17 \\ \hline \end{array}$

34. $\begin{array}{r} 61 \\ \times\ 33 \\ \hline \end{array}$

35. $\begin{array}{r} \$87 \\ \times\ 75 \\ \hline \end{array}$

Find the value of each expression. (Lesson 6-3)

36. $24 \div (3 + 5) - 2$

37. $4 \times (11 - 4) + 6$

38. $(9 + 6) \div (10 - 7)$

Find all of the factors of each number. (Lesson 5-9)

39. 8

40. 11

41. 24

42. 36

43. For every 4 magazines Avery sells, he receives $2. Use the table to find how much money he will raise if he sells 20 magazines. **(Lesson 4-3)**

Magazines Sold	4	8	12	16	20
Money	$2	$4	$6	■	■

WALLS WITH HISTORY

Humans have built forts all over the world for thousands of years. Most forts are rectangles. There are more than 136 forts in the United States. Some forts can hold hundreds to thousands of people, while others hold less than 100. The Alamo, a fort in Texas, protected 189 soldiers. The fort protected them for 13 days against an army of 6,000 soldiers!

Some forts like Sutter's Fort are now museums or state parks. However, other forts like Fort Knox in Kentucky are still used by the military today.

FAMOUS FORTS IN THE UNITED STATES

Fort	Location	Size of Main Building
Fort McIntosh	(Georgia)	33 yds by 33 yds
The Alamo	(Texas)	148 ft by 159 ft
Stone Fort at Harper's Ferry	(West Virginia)	40 ft by 100 ft
Sutter's Fort	(California)	64 ft by 35 ft
Fort Clatsop	(Oregon)	50 ft by 50 ft

Standard 4NS3.3 **Solve problems involving multiplication of multidigit numbers by one-digit numbers.**

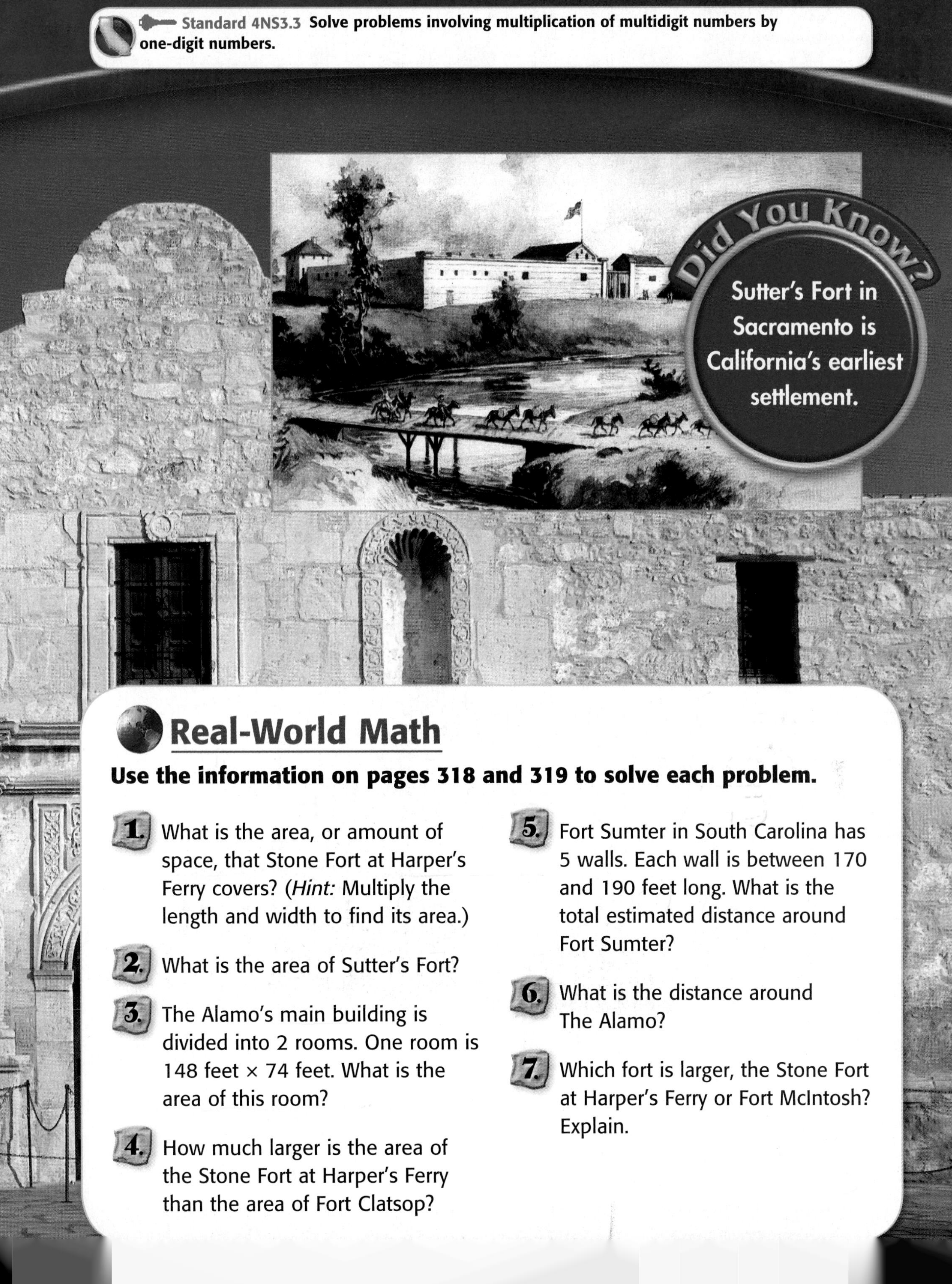

Real-World Math

Use the information on pages 318 and 319 to solve each problem.

1. What is the area, or amount of space, that Stone Fort at Harper's Ferry covers? (*Hint:* Multiply the length and width to find its area.)
2. What is the area of Sutter's Fort?
3. The Alamo's main building is divided into 2 rooms. One room is 148 feet × 74 feet. What is the area of this room?
4. How much larger is the area of the Stone Fort at Harper's Ferry than the area of Fort Clatsop?
5. Fort Sumter in South Carolina has 5 walls. Each wall is between 170 and 190 feet long. What is the total estimated distance around Fort Sumter?
6. What is the distance around The Alamo?
7. Which fort is larger, the Stone Fort at Harper's Ferry or Fort McIntosh? Explain.

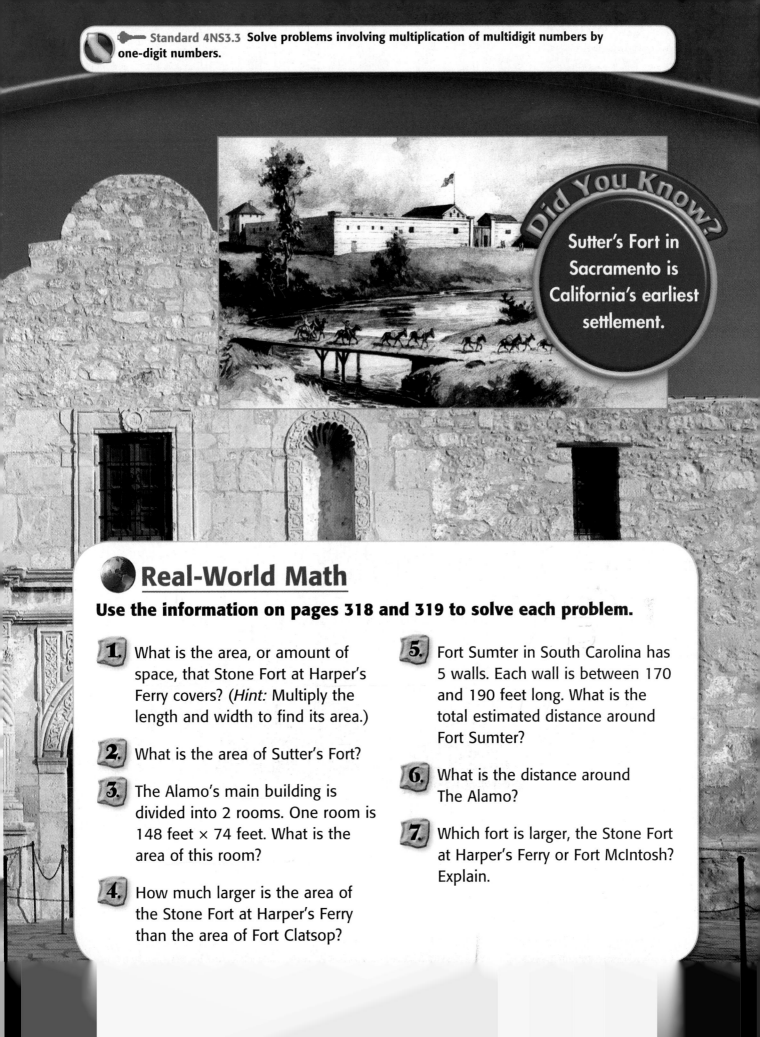

8-6 Problem-Solving Investigation

MAIN IDEA I will choose the best strategy to solve a problem.

Standard 4MR1.1 **Analyze problems by identifying relationships, distinguishing relevant from irrelevant information, sequencing and prioritizing information, and observing patterns.** Standard 4NS3.0 **Students solve problems involving addition,** subtraction, multiplication and division **of whole numbers** and understand the relationships among the operations.

P.S.I. TEAM +

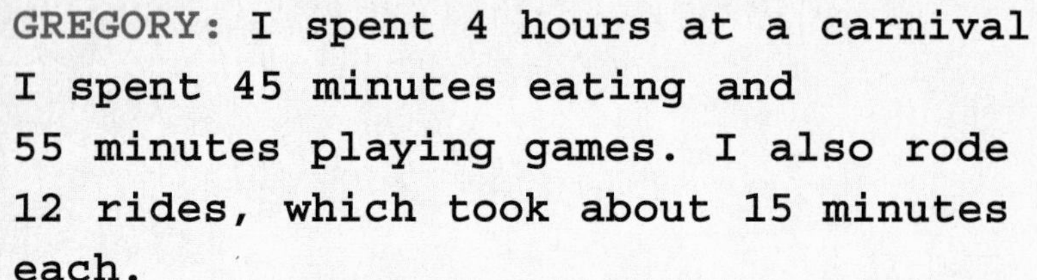

GREGORY: I spent 4 hours at a carnival. I spent 45 minutes eating and 55 minutes playing games. I also rode 12 rides, which took about 15 minutes each.

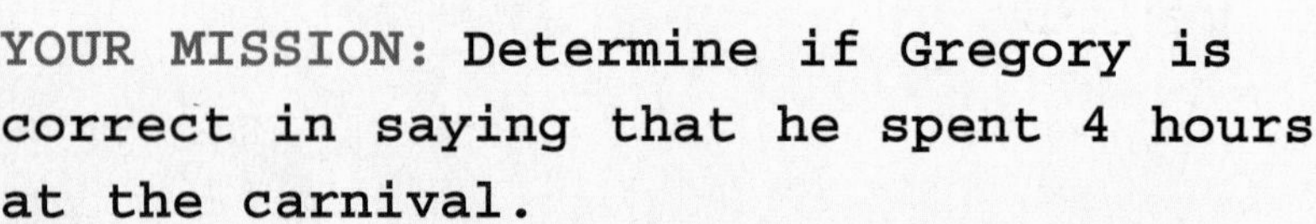

YOUR MISSION: Determine if Gregory is correct in saying that he spent 4 hours at the carnival.

Understand	You know the amount of time Gregory spent at the carnival and on each activity. Find if he is correct.
Plan	Solve a multi-step problem. Find the total number of minutes spent on activities and compare to 4 hours.
Solve	First, change hours to minutes. Then compare the two amounts of time.
Check	Look back at the problem. Use subtraction to check amount of time spent on carnival activities. 280 – 180 – 55 – 45 = 0. So, Gregory was not correct.

Solve work:

time Gregory said he spent at carnival	time spent riding rides	time spent on carnival activities
60 minutes	15	
60 minutes	× 12	45 minutes
60 minutes	30	55 minutes
+ 60 minutes	+ 150	+ 180 minutes
240 minutes	180	280 minutes

Since 240 minutes does not equal 280 minutes, Gregory is not correct.

Mixed Problem Solving

See page R21.

Use any strategy shown below to solve. Tell what strategy you used.

PROBLEM-SOLVING STRATEGIES
- Make a table.
- Choose an operation.
- Work backward.
- Act it out.

1. A coach bought 5 pizzas. Each pizza has 12 slices. There are 18 players on the team. Is it reasonable to say that each player can eat 3 slices? Explain.

2. At 6:00 A.M. the temperature was 45°F. At 12:00 P.M. the temperature was 55°F. At 8:00 P.M. the temperature was 49°F. Create a number sentence to show the changes in temperatures.

3. **Measurement** Javon hikes the trail shown below 3 times a week. Is it reasonable to say that he hikes more than 20 miles in one month? Explain.

4. Sergio is thinking of two numbers that have a sum of 16 and a product of 48. What are the two numbers?

5. Carson is counting the money in his piggy bank. He has 57¢. He has 3 kinds of coins and 9 coins in all. What coins does he have?

6. Taru has 13 trophies. Three of the trophies are for swimming. She has two times as many soccer trophies as swimming trophies. The rest of the trophies are for tennis. How many tennis trophies does she have?

7. Edmundo has $35.48 saved and needs to buy the items. Does he have enough money?

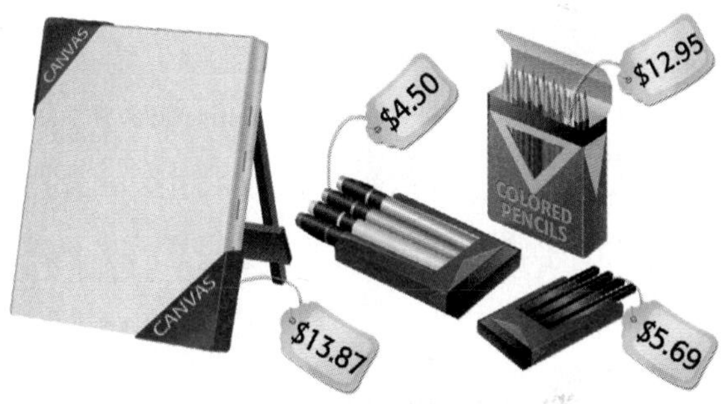

8. Betty has 12 vases to make gifts for her family. Each vase will need ribbon that costs 30¢ and beads that cost $1. She estimates she will spend $15. Is her estimate reasonable? Explain.

9. Every teacher at Elmwood Elementary is provided with 3,000 sheets of paper. How many sheets of paper do the 40 teachers have altogether?

10. **WRITING IN MATH** Isaac is baking four batches of bran muffins. There are 12 muffins in each batch. The answer is 144 muffins. What is the question?

8-7 Multiply Greater Numbers

GET READY to Learn

Suppose 7,275 visitors go to a certain zoo every week. How many visitors go to the zoo in a year?

MAIN IDEA

I will multiply four- and five-digit numbers by a two-digit number.

Standard 4NS3.3 Demonstrate an understanding of, and the ability to use, standard algorithms for multiplying a multidigit number by a two-digit number and for dividing a multidigit number by a one-digit number; use the relationships between them to simplify computations and to check results.

Standard 4MR2.1 Use estimation to verify the reasonableness of calculated results.

You can multiply multi-digit numbers by two-digit numbers.

Real-World EXAMPLE

1 ZOOS If 7,275 visitors go to a zoo every week, how many visitors go to the zoo in a year? Find 7,275 × 52.

Estimate 7,000 × 50 = 350,000.

Step 1 Multiply the ones. Regroup if necessary.

```
    1 1
  7,275
×    52
 14,550  ← 7,275 × 2
```

Step 2 Multiply the tens.

```
  1 3 2
    1 1
  7,275
×    52
 14,550
363,750  ← 7,275 × 2
```

Step 3 Add the partial products. Check for reasonableness.

```
   1 3 2
     1 1
   7,275
 ×    52
  14,550
+363,750
 378,300  ← Add.
```

So, the zoo gets 378,300 visitors in a year.

Check for Reasonableness

Since 378,300 is close to the estimate, the answer is reasonable. ✓

Real-World EXAMPLE

2 **SPORTS A stadium in California can seat 45,050 fans. There are 81 home games in a season. What is the greatest number of fans that can attend the home games in one season?**

You need to find 45,050 × 81.

Estimate 50,000 × 80 = 4,000,000.

Remember

Write a zero in the ones place when you multiply the tens.

Step 1 Multiply the ones.

```
  45,050
×     81
  45,050  ← 45,050 × 1
```

Step 2 Multiply the tens.

```
   4 4
  45,050
×     81
  45,050
3,604,000  ← 45,050 × 80
```

Step 3 Add the partial products.

```
    4 4
   45,050
 ×     81
   45,050
+ 3,604,000
  3,649,050  ← Add.
```

So, 3,649,050 fans can attend all of the home games.

Check for Reasonableness

3,649,050 is close to the estimate. The answer is reasonable. ✓

Online **Personal Tutor at** ca.gr4math.com

CHECK What You Know

Multiply. See Examples 1 and 2 (pp. 322–323)

1. 1,360 × 29

2. 7,251 × 58

3. $23,973 × 41

4. An average professional baseball player earns $15,750 per game. How much money does a player earn in a month in which 23 games are played?

5. Talk About It How is multiplying a 3-digit number by a 2-digit number like multiplying a 5-digit number by a 2-digit number?

Practice and Problem Solving

EXTRA PRACTICE
See page R21.

Multiply. See Examples 1 and 2 (pp. 322–323)

6. 1,418 × 12

7. 2,983 × 24

8. 4,166 × 35

9. 6,873 × 39

10. 8,316 × 14

11. 9,809 × 67

12. $13,820 × 21

13. $17,846 × 26

14. $25,067 × 30

15. $29,452 × 38

16. $30,824 × 43

17. $37,525 × 48

18. **Measurement** Gabrielle rides her bike 2 miles a day. In one mile there are 5,280 feet. How many feet does she ride her bike in 2 weeks?

19. **Measurement** If a cow produces 2,305 gallons of milk each year, how many gallons of milk do 75 cows produce in a year?

Real-World PROBLEM SOLVING

Measurement The map shows distances between some cities in the United States.

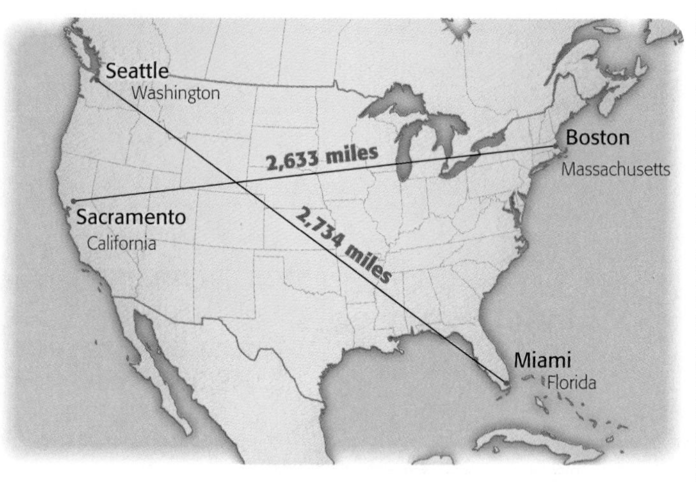

20. Sandra traveled round trip from Sacramento, California, to Boston, Massachusetts, 6 times during the summer months. How many miles did she travel altogether?

21. Marcos traveled round trip from Miami, Florida, to Seattle, Washington, 8 times. How many miles did he travel altogether?

H.O.T. Problems

22. **OPEN ENDED** Create a multiplication exercise that has a product greater than 1,000,000.

23. **NUMBER SENSE** Is the product of 11 and 1,000 greater or less than 10,000? How can you tell without multiplying?

24. **WRITING IN ▸ MATH** What is the greatest number of digits a product could have if a 2-digit factor is multiplied by a 5-digit number? Explain.

Math Online **Self-check Quiz at** ca.gr4math.com

Greatest Products

Multiply Multi-Digit Numbers

Get Ready!

Players: 2

You will need: 6 number cubes labeled 0–5, paper and pencil

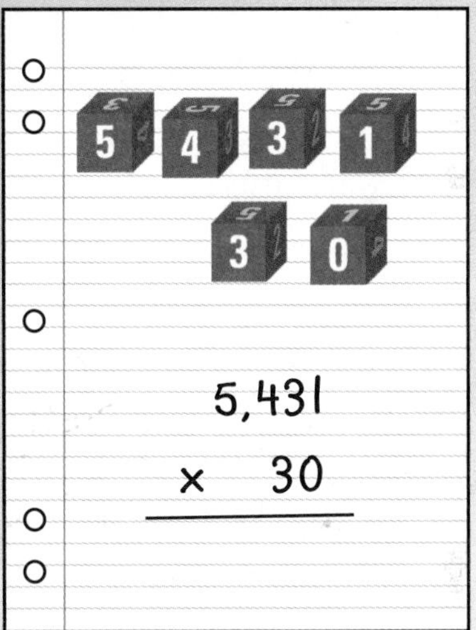

Get Set!

Each player should have a sheet of notebook paper.

Go!

- Player 1 rolls all 6 number cubes.
- Player 1 uses the number cubes to create a problem that involves multiplying a 4-digit number by a 2-digit number.
- Player 1 can arrange the digits in any place value and then find the product of the 2 factors.
- Player 2 takes a turn.
- The player who creates the greatest product earns 1 point.
- The player to earn 5 points first wins.

CHAPTER 8

Study Guide and Review

FOLDABLES™ Study Organizer GET READY to Study

Be sure the following Key Vocabulary words and Key Concepts are written in your Foldable.

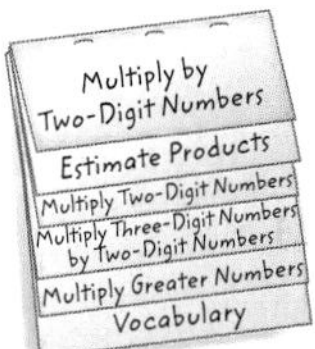

BIG Ideas

Estimate Products (p. 302)

Round each factor, then multiply.

```
  36 ──►    40  ◄─ 36 rounds to 40.
× 28 ──►  × 30  ◄─ 28 rounds to 30.
         1,200
```

Multiply by two-digit numbers. (p. 310)

```
   178    Multiply the ones,
 ×  34    tens, and hundreds.
   712    Regroup as needed.
+5,340
 6,052    Add the partial products.
```

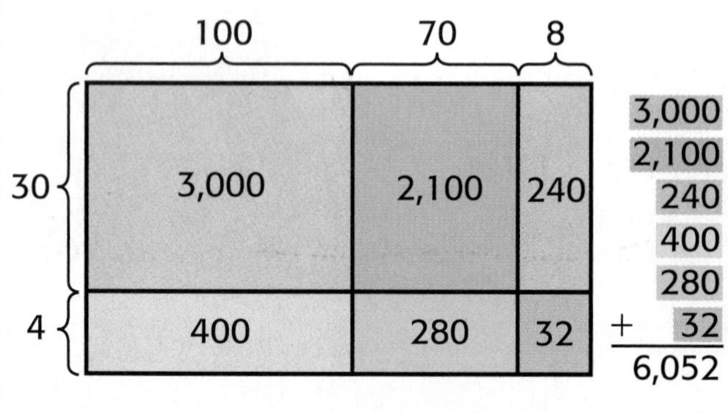

Key Vocabulary

Distributive Property of Multiplication (p. 308)

estimate (p. 302)

factor (p. 299)

multiple (p. 299)

product (p. 299)

Vocabulary Check

1. A number that is close to an exact value is a(n) ___?___.

2. The numbers 1, 2, 3, and 6 are ___?___ of the number 6.

3. A(n) ___?___ of a number is the product of that number and any whole number.

4. The ___?___ allows you to multiply a sum by a number by multiplying each addend by the number and adding the products.

5. A(n) ___?___ is a number that divides into a whole number evenly.

6. A number is a(n) ___?___ of its factors.

Math Online **Vocabulary Review at** ca.gr4math.com

Lesson-by-Lesson Review

8-1 Multiply by Tens (pp. 299–301)

Example 1
A football coach is ordering 30 jerseys for his football team. The jerseys cost $29 each. What will the total cost of the jerseys be?

Step 1 Multiply the ones.

$$\begin{array}{r} 29 \\ \times\ 30 \\ \hline 0 \end{array} \leftarrow \boxed{0 \text{ ones} \times 29 = 0}$$

Step 2 Multiply the tens.

$$\begin{array}{r} 29 \\ \times\ 30 \\ \hline 870 \end{array} \leftarrow \boxed{3 \text{ tens} \times 29 = 87 \text{ tens}}$$

So, the total cost will be $870.

Multiply.

7. $\begin{array}{r} 90 \\ \times\ 90 \\ \hline \end{array}$ **8.** $\begin{array}{r} 34 \\ \times\ 80 \\ \hline \end{array}$

9. $28 × 40 **10.** $45 × 30

11. Jeremy reads the number of books shown in a month. How many books will he read in 2 years?

12. There are 30 students in each class. There are 27 classrooms. How many students are there?

8-2 Estimate Products (pp. 302–305)

Example 2
Estimate 33 × 18.

Step 1 Round each factor to the nearest ten.

$$\begin{array}{r} 33 \\ \times 18 \\ \hline \end{array} \rightarrow \begin{array}{r} 30 \\ \times 20 \\ \hline \end{array} \leftarrow \boxed{\begin{array}{l} \text{Round 33 to 30.} \\ \text{Round 18 to 20.} \end{array}}$$

Step 2 Multiply.

$$\begin{array}{r} 30 \\ \times\ 20 \\ \hline 600 \end{array} \leftarrow \boxed{\begin{array}{l} 0 \text{ ones} \times 30 = 0 \\ 2 \text{ tens} \times 30 = 60 \text{ tens} \end{array}}$$

So, 33 × 18 is about 600.

Estimate. Tell whether the estimate is greater or less than the actual product.

13. $\begin{array}{r} 82 \\ \times 38 \\ \hline \end{array}$ **14.** $\begin{array}{r} \$76 \\ \times 24 \\ \hline \end{array}$

15. $244 × 31 **16.** 482 × 49

17. 371 × 66 **18.** 527 × 84

19. Aleta makes $12 an hour. She worked 28 hours this week. About how much money will she make?

8-3 Problem-Solving Strategy: Act It Out (pp. 306–307)

Example 3

Elvio has 6 coins in his pocket equaling 72¢. What combination of coins does he have in his pocket?

Understand

What facts do you know?

- Elvio has 6 coins in his pocket.
- The value of the coins is 72¢.

What do you need to find?

- The coins Elvio has.

Plan Act out the problem.

Solve One way to make 72¢ is with 1 fifty-cent piece, 2 dimes, and 2 pennies. You need one more coin.

Take the fifty-cent piece and exchange it for 2 quarters.

The value of the coins stays the same, and the number of coins increases to six.

So, Elvio has 2 quarters, 2 dimes, and 2 pennies.

Check The answer makes sense for the facts given in the problem. You have 6 coins that have a total value of 72¢.

20. There are cartons of milk in 10 rows of 8. You remove 4 cartons from each of 5 rows. How many cartons are left?

21. Jewel is painting a pattern on a bowl in art class. She is using the shapes below to form the pattern. How many ways can Jewel arrange the shapes to form a repeating pattern if she uses each shape once?

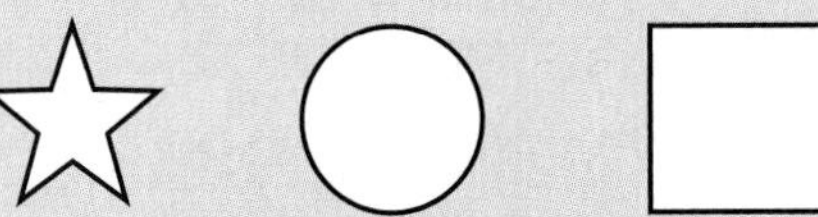

22. Joan saved $8 the first week, three times that the second week, and $14.75 the third week. How much did she save in three weeks?

23. **Geometry** Look at the pattern below. How many squares are needed to make the 6th figure in the pattern shown?

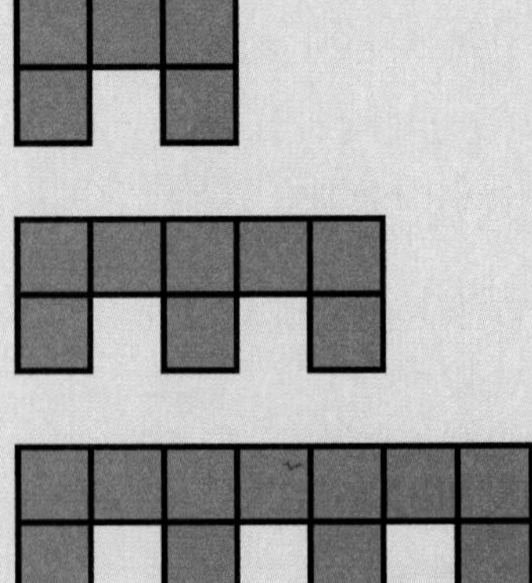

24. Can nine toothpicks be used to make four triangles that are the same size and same shape?

8-4 Multiply Two-Digit Numbers (pp. 310–312)

Example 4
Julio scores 18 points in each basketball game. If there are 14 games in a season, how many points will Julio score?

Multiply the number of games by the number of points scored in each game.

$$\begin{array}{r} {}^{3} \\ 18 \\ \times 14 \\ \hline 72 \\ +\,180 \\ \hline 252 \end{array}$$

72 ← Multiply the ones.
+ 180 ← Multiply the tens.
252 ← Add.

So, Julio will score 252 points.

Multiply.

25. $\begin{array}{r} 63 \\ \times\ 46 \\ \hline \end{array}$

26. $\begin{array}{r} 26 \\ \times 34 \\ \hline \end{array}$

27. $\begin{array}{r} \$72 \\ \times\ 49 \\ \hline \end{array}$

28. $\begin{array}{r} \$55 \\ \times\ 41 \\ \hline \end{array}$

29. 37 × 68

30. 89 × 53

31. $19 × 72

32. 95 × 84

33. Measurement Kittens can run up to 31 miles per hour. At this rate, how much distance would a kitten cover in a day?

8-5 Multiply Three-Digit Numbers by Two-Digit Numbers (pp. 314–317)

Example 5
Find 803 × 42.

Estimate $800 × 40 = $32,000

$$\begin{array}{r} {}^{1}\ \ \ \\ \$803 \\ \times\ 42 \\ \hline 1{,}606 \\ +32{,}120 \\ \hline \$33{,}726 \end{array}$$

1,606 ← Multiply the ones.
+32,120 ← Multiply the tens.
$33,726 ← Add.

Check for Reasonableness
Since $33,726 is close to the estimate, the answer is reasonable. ✓

Multiply.

34. $\begin{array}{r} 712 \\ \times\ 87 \\ \hline \end{array}$

35. $\begin{array}{r} 841 \\ \times\ 96 \\ \hline \end{array}$

36. $\begin{array}{r} 367 \\ \times\ 71 \\ \hline \end{array}$

37. $\begin{array}{r} 670 \\ \times\ 87 \\ \hline \end{array}$

38. $705 × 88

39. $234 × 45

40. 103 × 33

41. 632 × 35

42. A school bought 35 microscopes at $125 each for its science lab. What was the total cost?

43. If a person makes $625 each week, how much will that person have made after one year?

Study Guide and Review

8-6 Problem-Solving Investigation: Choose a Strategy (pp. 320–321)

Example 6
A theater can seat 785 people. There are 23 performances in a month. Is it reasonable to say that more than 20,000 people can attend the performances in a month?

Multiply 785 by 23. Then compare.

```
    11
    21
   785
 ×  23
 2,355  ← Multiply the ones.
+15,700 ← Multiply the tens.
 18,055 ← Add the products.
```

Since 18,055 < 20,000, it is not reasonable to say that more than 20,000 people can attend the performances in a month.

Use any strategy to solve.

44. By the end of the year, Lolita wants to read 50 books. If she reads 3 books each month, for the 9 months she is in school, will she reach her goal?

45. Elan has a $20 bill. He wants to buy a ball cap that costs $17.50. What will his change be?

46. Toni wants to save enough money to buy a tennis racket for $75. She earns $5 a week for doing chores. Is it reasonable to say that Toni will have enough money to buy the tennis racket in 3 months? Explain.

8-7 Multiply Greater Numbers (pp. 322–325)

Example 7
One of the fastest planes in the world can fly up to 5,329 miles per hour. At this rate, how far would this plane fly in 24 hours?

```
      1
    113
   5,329
 ×    24
  21,316
+106,580
 127,896 ← Add.
```

So, this plane would fly 127,896 miles in 24 hours.

Multiply.

47. 1,418 × 14

48. 2,983 × 21

49. 13,720 × 31

50. 17,946 × 25

51. $24,017 × 30

52. $39,402 × 48

53. **Measurement** Leela's grandparents live 35 miles away. There are 5,280 feet in one mile. How many feet did she travel?

CHAPTER 8

Chapter Test

Multiply.

1. $\begin{array}{r} 26 \\ \times 10 \\ \hline \end{array}$

2. $\begin{array}{r} 43 \\ \times 30 \\ \hline \end{array}$

3. 89 × 33

4. 82 × 91

5. Elio jogs for 30 minutes each time he exercises. If he exercises 18 times in a month, how many minutes will he jog?

Estimate.

6. 152 × 47

7. 439 × 81

8. Shannon is reading a book that has about 18 pages in each chapter. The book has 12 chapters. About how many pages does the book have?

Solve. Use the *act it out* strategy.

9. Lina buys bread for $3.75 at the store. She gives the cashier $4. List three combinations of coins she could receive as change.

10. **STANDARDS PRACTICE** A school needs to buy 475 math books for its fourth grade students. Each book costs $85. What will the total cost be?

A $40,000 **C** $45,000

B $40,375 **D** $53,150

11. Roxana brought 6 dozen snacks for her birthday party at school. Each person got 3 snacks. How many people are in her class? Explain your answer.

Multiply.

12. 107 × 12

13. 258 × 24

14. $\begin{array}{r} 1,324 \\ \times \quad 12 \\ \hline \end{array}$

15. $\begin{array}{r} 2,831 \\ \times \quad 24 \\ \hline \end{array}$

16. **Measurement** The table shows how many miles Ari biked each week of a month. At this rate, how many miles will Ari bike in a year?

Distance Biked	
Week	**Miles**
1	12
2	14
3	8
4	10

17. A store has 275 boxes of oranges. Each box costs $12. What will the total cost be?

18. **STANDARDS PRACTICE** There are 24 hours in a day. There are 365 days in a year. How many hours are there in a year?

F 9560

G 8760

H 8670

J 8000

19. **WRITING IN MATH** What is the greatest number of digits a product could have if a 4-digit number is multiplied by a 3-digit number? Explain.

CHAPTER 8

California Standards Practice

Cumulative, Chapters 1–8

Standards Example

Miguela mowed 54 lawns over the summer. She charged $23 a lawn. How much money did she earn over the summer?

A $1242 **C** $1132

B $1232 **D** $124

Read the Question

You need to multiply 54 by $23 to find the amount of money earned.

Solve the Question

Step 1 Multiply the ones.

```
   54
 ×$23
 $162 ← 3 × 54
```

Step 2 Multiply the tens. Then add the partial products.

```
    54
  ×$23
  $162 ← 3 × 54
+$1080 ← 20 × 54
 $1242 ← Add.
```

So, Miguela earned $1,242.
The answer is A.

Online Personal Tutor at ca.gr4math.com

Choose the best answer.

1 **Blake planted 12 rows of corn. Each row had 15 corn plants. How many corn plants will he have in all?**

A 170 **C** 225

B 180 **D** 240

2 **What number makes this equation true?**

$$30 \times \blacksquare = 27{,}000$$

F 90 **H** 800

G 240 **J** 900

More California Standards Practice
For practice by standard, see pages CA1–CA43.

3 **To raise money for new art supplies, 24 students walked 10 miles each. How many miles did they walk?**

A 240 **C** 1200

B 480 **D** 2400

4 **Talli read 38 pages in a book each day for 11 days. About how many pages did she read in all?**

F 800 **H** 400

G 550 **J** 300

5 **If Sean buys all the items, about how much will he spend?**

Baseball Equipment

Item	Cost
mitt	\$39.99
bat	\$34.99
ball	\$19.99
T-shirt	\$12.95

A \$80 **C** \$100

B \$90 **D** \$120

6 **Emanuel has 72 photos. His photo album holds 6 pictures on a page. How many pages will he use?**

F 12 **H** 9

G 10 **J** 8

7 **Leslie surveyed 30 students about their favorite kind of books.**

Favorite Kind of Books

Kind	Tally
Adventure	~~IIII~~ ~~IIII~~
Science fiction	~~IIII~~ III
Mystery	~~IIII~~ IIII
Poetry	III

Which 2 kinds of books do 19 students enjoy reading most?

A Adventure and science fiction

B Science fiction and mystery

C Mystery and adventure

D Poetry and science fiction

8 **While playing a board game, Vera scored 10 points on her first turn. At the end of the game, she had a total of 38 points. Which equation describes her points?**

F $p - 10 = 38$

G $10 + p = 38$

H $10 + 38 = p$

J $10 - p = 38$

9 **Mrs. Wilson bought 175 stamps. Each stamp costs 39 cents. How much did she spend on stamps?**

A \$68.25 **C** \$72.50

B \$70.25 **D** \$73.50

CHAPTER 9 Divide by One-Digit Numbers

BIG Idea How do you divide by a one-digit number?

Divide each digit of the dividend by the divisor.

Example A toll worker on the Golden Gate Bridge collected $75 in tolls. How many cars passed through the toll booth if the toll cost is $5 per car?

$$\begin{array}{r} 15 \\ 5\overline{)75} \\ -5\downarrow \\ \hline 25 \\ -25 \\ \hline 0 \end{array}$$

For each place, divide, multiply, subtract, and compare. Then bring down the next digit in the dividend.

So, 15 cars have passed through the toll booth.

What will I learn in this chapter?

- Divide two- or three-digit numbers by a one-digit number.
- Divide multi-digit numbers by a one-digit number.
- Estimate quotients.
- Solve problems by using the *guess and check* strategy.

Key Vocabulary

dividend **remainder**
divisor **compatible numbers**
quotient

Student Study Tools at ca.gr4math.com

FOLDABLES™ Study Organizer

Make this Foldable to help you organize information about dividing by one-digit numbers. Begin with 5 sheets of 11″ × 17″ paper.

1. **Fold** one sheet in half widthwise.
2. **Open** and fold the bottom to form a pocket. Glue.
3. **Repeat** Steps 1 and 2 four times. Glue the back of one folder to the front of another.
4. **Label** the pockets as shown. Place an index card in each pocket.

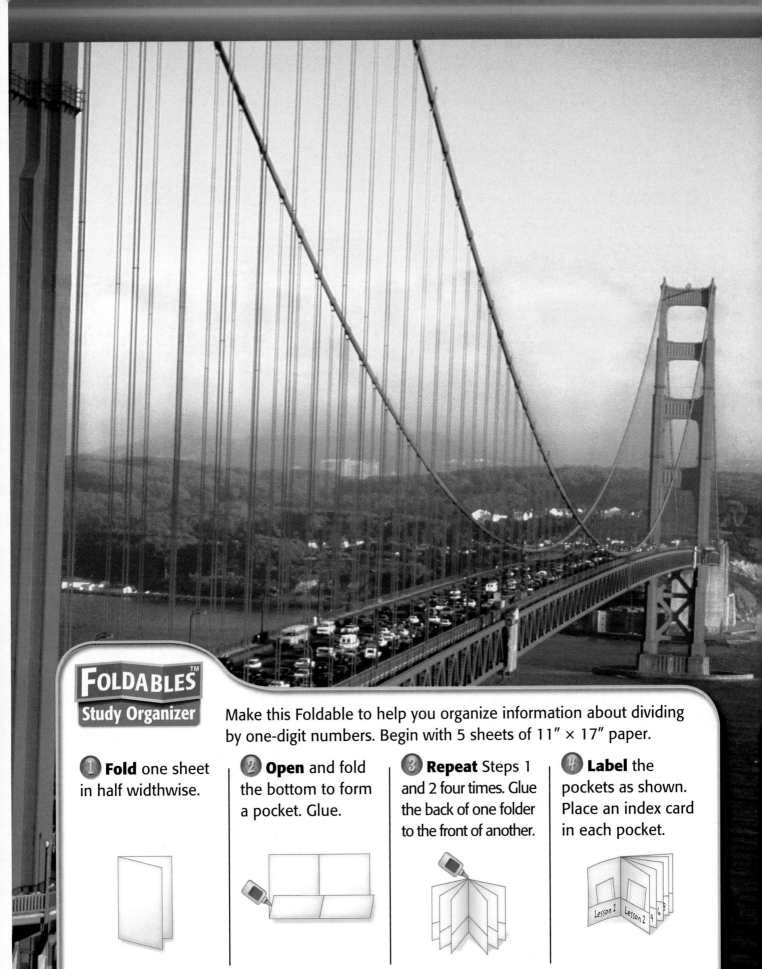

ARE YOU READY for Chapter 9?

You have two ways to check prerequisite skills for this chapter.

Option 2

Math Online Take the Chapter Readiness Quiz at ca.gr4math.com.

Option 1

Complete the Quick Check below.

QUICK Check

Subtraction. **(Prior grade)**

1. $\begin{array}{r} 25 \\ -\ 6 \\ \hline \end{array}$ **2.** $\begin{array}{r} 42 \\ -\ 8 \\ \hline \end{array}$ **3.** $\begin{array}{r} 67 \\ -\ 29 \\ \hline \end{array}$ **4.** $\begin{array}{r} 93 \\ -\ 54 \\ \hline \end{array}$

5. 24 − 15 **6.** 31 − 17 **7.** 50 − 23 **8.** 86 − 49

9. There are 81 pages in Gerardo's book. He has read 38 pages. How many pages are left to read?

Divide. **(Lesson 5-5)**

10. $2\overline{)3}$ **11.** $4\overline{)5}$ **12.** $6\overline{)7}$ **13.** $8\overline{)9}$

14. 4 ÷ 3 **15.** 7 ÷ 5 **16.** 9 ÷ 6 **17.** 9 ÷ 7

18. Sharon has $32. She wants to buy CDs that cost $8 each. How many can she buy?

Round each number to its greatest place value. **(Lesson 1-6)**

19. 269 **20.** $2,513 **21.** 14,895 **22.** 56,071

23. There are 2,515 mammals at a zoo and 3,496 animals that are not mammals at the zoo. About how many animals are there in all?

Explore

Math Activity for 9-1
Model Division

MAIN IDEA

I will explore dividing by one-digit numbers.

Standard 4MR2.3 Use a variety of methods, such as words, numbers, symbols, charts, graphs, tables, diagrams, **and models, to explain mathematical reasoning.**

Preparation for Standard 4NS3.3 Solve problems involving multiplication of multidigit numbers by two-digit numbers.

You Will Need
base-ten blocks

New Vocabulary

dividend
divisor
quotient
remainder

In division, the **dividend** is the number that is being divided. The **divisor** is the number that divides the dividend. The **quotient** is the result.

quotient
divisor)dividend

ACTIVITY

1 Find 39 ÷ 3.

Step 1 Model the dividend, 39.

Use 3 tens and 9 ones to show 39.

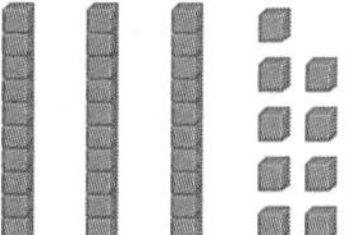

Step 2 Divide the tens.

The divisor is 3. So, divide the tens into 3 equal groups. There is a ten in each group.

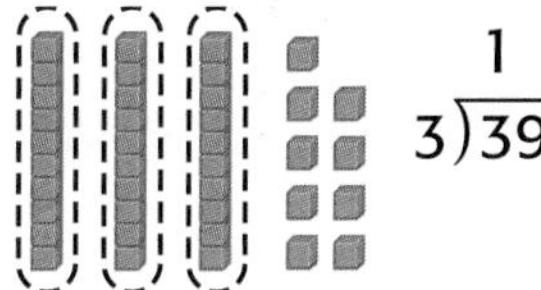

Step 3 Divide the ones.

Divide the ones into 3 equal groups. There are 1 ten and 3 ones in each group.
So, 39 ÷ 3 = 13.

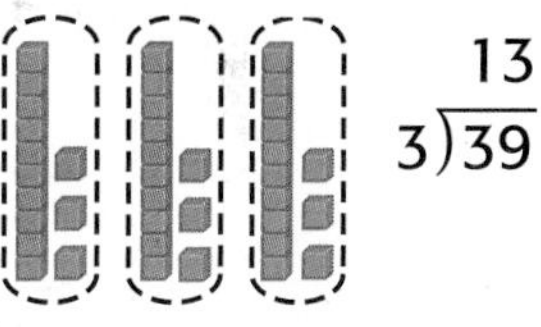

Hands-On Activity

ACTIVITY

2 **Find 68 ÷ 5.**

Step 1 **Model the dividend 68.**

Use 6 tens and 8 ones to show 68.

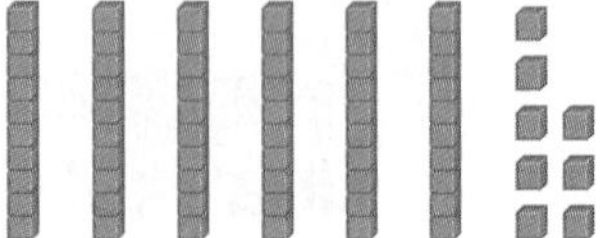

Step 2 **Divide the tens.**

The divisor is 5. So, divide the tens into 5 equal groups. There is a ten in each group.

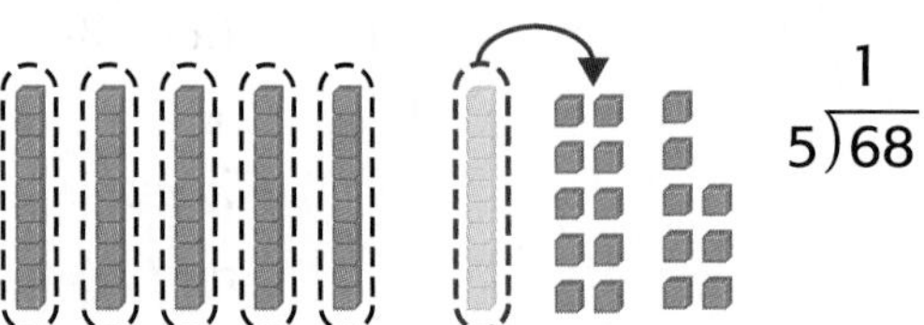

Regroup one ten as ten ones.

$5\overline{)68}$ with quotient 1

Step 3 **Divide the ones.**

Divide the ones into 5 equal groups. There is 1 ten and 3 ones in each group. There are 3 ones left over. The 3 is the **remainder**.
So, 68 ÷ 5 = 13R3.

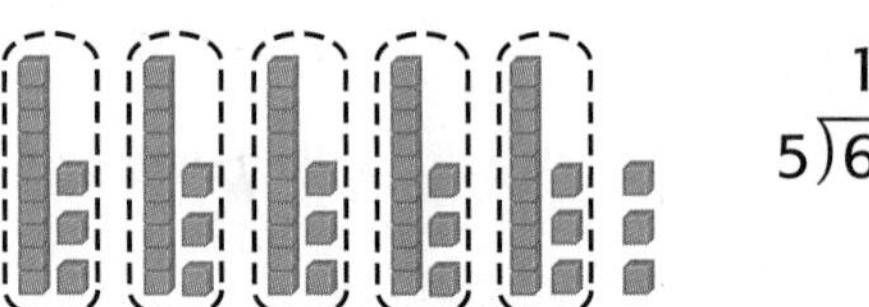

$5\overline{)68}$ with quotient 13R3

Think About It

1. How would you use base-ten blocks to find 58 ÷ 4?

2. Explain what it means to have a remainder when dividing.

CHECK What You Know

Write the division expression shown by each model. Then divide.

3.

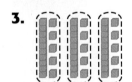

4.

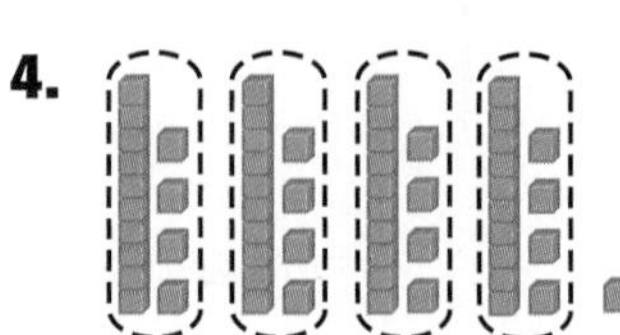

Use models to find each quotient.

5. 36 ÷ 2 **6.** 48 ÷ 3 **7.** 57 ÷ 4 **8.** 77 ÷ 5

9. WRITING IN ▶MATH Explain how to use models to find 79 ÷ 6.

9-1 Division with Remainders

MAIN IDEA

I will carry out division with and without remainders.

Preparation for Standard

4NS3.2 Demonstrate an understanding of, and the ability to use, standard algorithms for multiplying a multidigit number by a two-digit number and for dividing a multidigit number by a one-digit number; use relationships between them to simplify computations and to check results.

GET READY to Learn

Mr. Hein's class is going to a natural history museum. Each seat on the bus can hold 2 people. There are 28 students and 8 adults. How many seats are needed?

You have used models to divide. You can also use paper and pencil.

Real-World EXAMPLE

1 SCHOOL How many bus seats are needed for the field trip?

There are 36 people. Each seat holds 2 people. Find $36 \div 2$.

Step 1 Divide the tens.

```
2)36
  ↓
```

Can 3 tens be divided equally into groups of 2?

```
  1
2)36
```

There is one ten in each group. Put 1 in the quotient over the tens place.

Step 2 Multiply, subtract, and compare.

```
  1
2)36
 -2
  1
```

Multiply. $2 \times 1 = 2$

Subtract. $3 - 2 = 1$

Compare. $1 < 2$

Step 3 Bring down the ones.

```
  1
2)36
 -2↓
  16
```

Bring down 6 ones.

16 ones in all.

Step 4 Divide the ones.

```
  18
2)36
 -2↓
  16
 -16
   0
```

Divide. $16 \div 2 = 8$

Put 8 in the quotient over the ones place.

Multiply. $2 \times 8 = 16$

Subtract. $16 - 16 = 0$

Compare. $0 < 2$

So, 18 seats are needed.

You can interpret the remainder in division problems.

Remember

To check a division answer, multiply the quotient by the divisor.

$$\begin{array}{r} 18 \\ \times\ 4 \\ \hline 72 \\ +\ 2 \\ \hline 74 \end{array}$$ ← Add the remainder.

Real-World EXAMPLE Division with Remainders

2 MONEY Manuel has $74. He wants to buy 4 comic books that each cost the same amount. How much will each book cost?

Manuel has $74. Each comic book costs the same amount. So, divide $74 by 4 to find how much each book will cost.

Step 1 Divide the tens.

$$\begin{array}{r} 1 \\ 4\overline{)\$74} \\ -4 \\ \hline 3 \end{array}$$

Divide. 7 ÷ 4 = 1
So, put 1 in the quotient over the tens place.
Multiply. 4 × 1 = 4
Subtract. 7 − 4 = 3
Compare. 3 < 4

Step 2 Divide the ones.

$$\begin{array}{r} 18 \text{ R2} \\ 4\overline{)\$74} \\ -4\downarrow \\ \hline 34 \\ -32 \\ \hline 2 \end{array}$$

Bring down the ones.
Divide. 34 ÷ 4 = 8
Put 8 over the ones place.
Multiply. 4 × 8 = 32
Subtract. 34 − 32 = 2
Compare. 2 < 4
Remainder = 2

So, each comic book will cost a little more than $18.

Check The model shows that $74 ÷ 4 is a little more than $18.

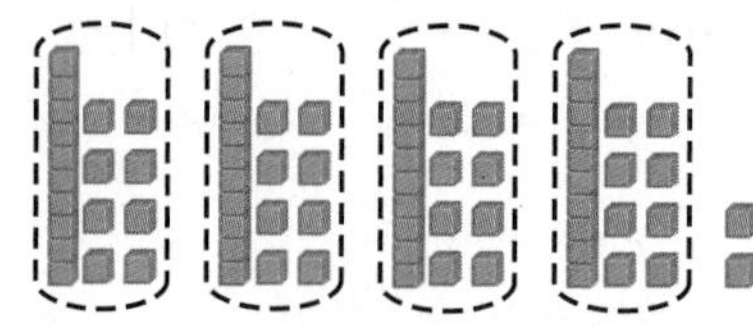

 **Personal Tutor at** ca.gr4math.com

CHECK What You Know

Divide. Check each answer. See Examples 1 and 2 (pp. 339–340)

1. $2\overline{)26}$ **2.** $3\overline{)36}$ **3.** $5\overline{)59}$ **4.** $8\overline{)84}$

5. 93 ÷ 3 **6.** 84 ÷ 4 **7.** 61 ÷ 2 **8.** 86 ÷ 3

9. There are 4 zookeepers to feed 85 animals. If each zookeeper feeds the same number of animals, will all of the animals be fed by the 4 zookeepers? Explain.

10. Talk About It Why is the remainder always less than the divisor?

Practice and Problem Solving

EXTRA PRACTICE See page R21.

Divide. Check each answer. See Examples 1 and 2 (pp. 339–340)

11. $2\overline{)28}$ **12.** $4\overline{)48}$ **13.** $3\overline{)33}$ **14.** $2\overline{)26}$

15. $5\overline{)53}$ **16.** $6\overline{)67}$ **17.** $7\overline{)73}$ **18.** $9\overline{)96}$

19. $93 \div 3$ **20.** $84 \div 4$ **21.** $64 \div 2$ **22.** $69 \div 3$

23. $79 \div 2$ **24.** $91 \div 4$ **25.** $77 \div 3$ **26.** $99 \div 4$

27. Marlene makes $4 an hour babysitting. If she earned $48, how many hours did she babysit?

28. Seven scouts need to sell 75 boxes of cookies. Each scout gets the same number of boxes. How many boxes will be left to sell?

Real-World PROBLEM SOLVING

Science There are many different insects and worms on Earth.

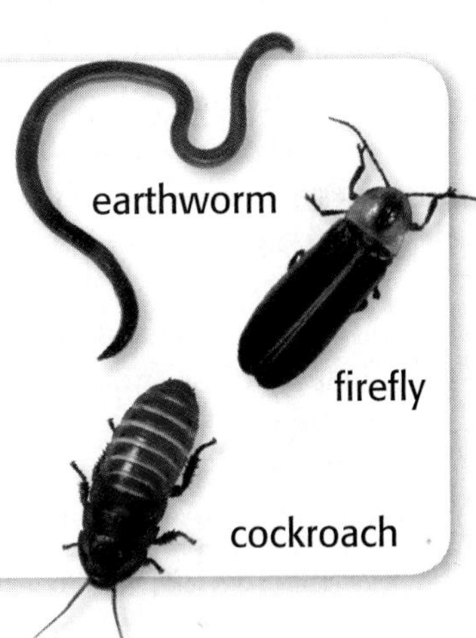

29. The lifespan of a firefly is 7 days. How many fireflies have a total lifespan of 77 days?

30. A cockroach can travel 3 miles per hour. How long would it take the cockroach to travel 32 miles?

H.O.T. Problems

31. **OPEN ENDED** Identify a two-digit dividend that will result in a quotient with a remainder of 1 when the divisor is 4.

32. **FIND THE ERROR** Kate and Yutaka found $46 \div 4$. Who is correct? Explain.

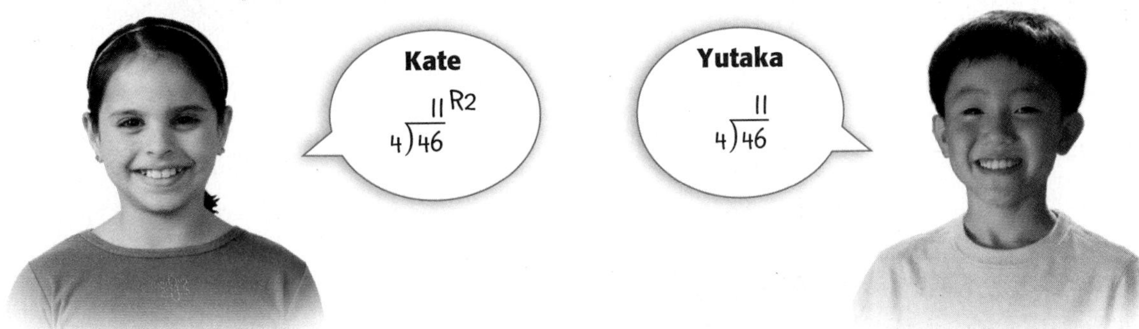

33. **WRITING IN MATH** When you divide a number by 6, can the remainder be 6? Explain.

9-2 Divide Multiples of 10, 100, and 1,000

GET READY to Learn

A certain amusement park has 5 entrances. If 1,500 people entered the amusement park and separated into equal lines, how many people are in each line?

MAIN IDEA

I will use basic facts and patterns to divide mentally.

Standard 4NS3.2

Demonstrate an understanding of, and the ability to use, standard algorithms for multiplying a multidigit number by a two-digit number and for **dividing a multidigit number by a one-digit number; use relationships between them to simplify computations and to check results.**

You can find patterns when dividing multiples of 10. Using patterns makes it easy to divide multiples of 10.

Real-World EXAMPLE Divide Multiples of 10

1 AMUSEMENT PARKS How many people are in each line at the amusement park?

You need to divide 1,500 people into 5 equal groups. Find $1{,}500 \div 5$.

One Way: Use a Multiplication Pattern

$5 \times 3 = 15$	→	$15 \div 5 = 3$
$5 \times 30 = 150$	→	$150 \div 5 = 30$
$5 \times 300 = 1{,}500$	→	$1{,}500 \div 5 = 300$

Another Way: Use a Basic Fact

The basic fact for $1{,}500 \div 5$ is $15 \div 5$.

$15 \div 5 = 3$ ← basic fact
$150 \div 5 = 30$
$1{,}500 \div 5 = 300$

So, there are 300 people in each line.

Remember

Multiplication can be used to check division.

EXAMPLE Divide Multiples of 10

2 **Find the quotient of 2,400 and 4.**

One Way: Use a Multiplication Pattern

$4 \times 6 = 24$	→	$24 \div 4 = 6$
$4 \times 60 = 240$	→	$240 \div 4 = 60$
$4 \times 600 = 2{,}400$	→	$2{,}400 \div 4 = 600$

Another Way: Use a Basic Fact

The basic fact for $2{,}400 \div 4$ is $24 \div 4$.

$24 \div 4 = 6$ ← basic fact

$240 \div 4 = 60$

$2{,}400 \div 4 = 600$

So, $2{,}400 \div 4$ is 600.

Online Personal Tutor at ca.gr4math.com

CHECK What You Know

Copy and complete each set of patterns. See Examples 1 and 2 (pp. 342–343)

1. $12 \div 4 = ■$
$120 \div 4 = ■$
$1{,}200 \div 4 = ■$

2. $\$36 \div 6 = ■$
$\$360 \div 6 = ■$
$\$3{,}600 \div 6 = ■$

3. $45 \div 9 = ■$
$450 \div 9 = ■$
$4{,}500 \div 9 = ■$

Divide. Use patterns. See Examples 1 and 2 (pp. 342–343)

4. $\$400 \div 2$

5. $1{,}600 \div 4$

6. $\$3{,}200 \div 8$

For Exercise 7, use the information to the right.

7. There are 4 members of a family planning a weekend camping trip. How much will the trip cost for each person?

Family Vacation

Item	Total Cost
Campsite rental cost	$50
Camping supplies	$75
Food	$75

8. 

What basic fact will help you find the quotient of 4,200 and 7?

Practice and Problem Solving

EXTRA PRACTICE See page R22.

Copy and complete each set of patterns. See Examples 1 and 2 (pp. 342–343)

9. $12 \div 2 =$ ■
$120 \div 2 =$ ■
$1{,}200 \div 2 =$ ■

10. $\$28 \div 7 =$ ■
$\$280 \div 7 =$ ■
$\$2{,}800 \div 7 =$ ■

11. $54 \div 9 =$ ■
$540 \div 9 =$ ■
$5{,}400 \div 9 =$ ■

12. $\$36 \div 4 =$ ■
$\$360 \div 4 =$ ■
$\$3{,}600 \div 4 =$ ■

13. $42 \div 6 =$ ■
$420 \div 6 =$ ■
$4{,}200 \div 6 =$ ■

14. $\$72 \div 8 =$ ■
$\$720 \div 8 =$ ■
$\$7{,}200 \div 8 =$ ■

Divide. Use patterns. See Examples 1 and 2 (pp. 342–343)

15. $200 \div 5$
16. $\$600 \div 3$
17. $800 \div 2$
18. $900 \div 3$
19. $\$1{,}400 \div 7$
20. $4{,}500 \div 5$
21. $6{,}300 \div 9$
22. $\$6{,}400 \div 8$
23. $\$3{,}500 \div 5$
24. $1{,}600 \div 8$
25. $5{,}400 \div 6$
26. $\$8{,}100 \div 9$

27. The cost of a used car is $3,200. If the payments are spread over 8 months, what is the payment each month?

28. The Nair family collected 2,400 pennies. The pennies will be divided evenly among the 4 children. How many dollars did each child get?

Real-World PROBLEM SOLVING

Measurement Animals migrate due to factors such as climate and food availability. The table shows a few migration distances.

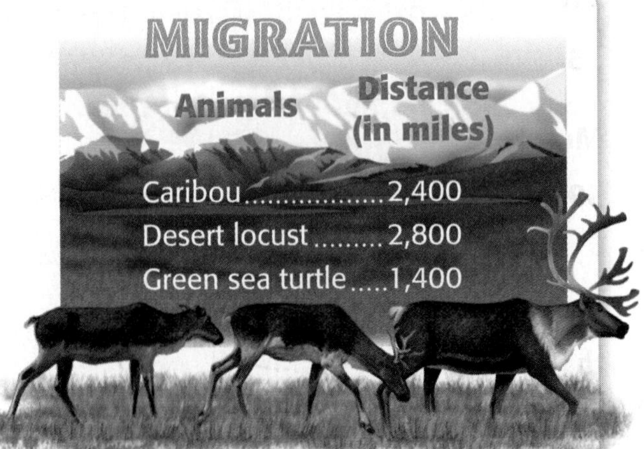

MIGRATION

Animals	Distance (in miles)
Caribou	2,400
Desert locust	2,800
Green sea turtle	1,400

29. Suppose a group of green sea turtles travel 7 miles a day, how many days will the migration take?

30. Suppose a swarm of desert locusts travel 7 miles per hour. They travel 10 hours per day. How many days will the migration take?

31. A herd of caribou migrated the distance shown in 8 months. If they traveled the same distance each month, how many miles did the herd travel each month?

H.O.T. Problems

32. NUMBER SENSE Without actually dividing, tell which has the greater quotient, $1,500 \div 3$ or $2,400 \div 6$? Explain.

33. WRITING IN ▶MATH Explain how you would know that the quotient of $600 \div 2$ is a 3-digit number.

Standards Practice

34 Rosita read a 75-page book in 5 days. She read the same number of pages each day. How many pages did she read each day? (Lesson 9-1)

A 5

B 10

C 15

D 150

35 Antoine went to his sister's college graduation. There were 1200 students graduating. They were separated equally into 4 sections of the auditorium. How many students were seated in each section? (Lesson 9-2)

F 3

G 30

H 300

J 3000

Spiral Review

Divide. Check each answer. (Lesson 9-1)

36. $2\overline{)37}$

37. $5\overline{)49}$

38. $7\overline{)81}$

Multiply. (Lesson 8-7)

39. $1,672 \times 18$

40. $4,061 \times 39$

41. $9,544 \times 65$

For Exercises 42–44, use the table. It shows the life spans of reptiles. Choose the best operation. Then solve. (Lesson 5-4)

42. How many years will three generations of Galapagos turtles live?

43. How much longer can an American alligator live than a komodo dragon?

44. Which animal lives 90 years longer than the boa constrictor?

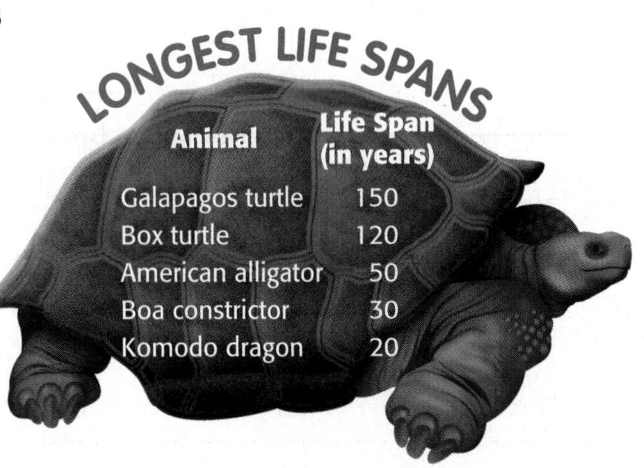

LONGEST LIFE SPANS

Animal	Life Span (in years)
Galapagos turtle	150
Box turtle	120
American alligator	50
Boa constrictor	30
Komodo dragon	20

9-3 Problem-Solving Strategy

MAIN IDEA I will solve problems by using the *guess and check* strategy.

Standard 4MR1.1 Analyze problems by identifying relationships, distinguishing relevant from irrelevant information, sequencing and prioritizing information, and observing patterns. Standard 4NS3.0 **Students solve problems involving addition, subtraction,** multiplication, and division **of whole numbers and understand the relationships among the operations.**

Ruben bought 3 gifts for his sisters. Two of the gifts cost the same. The other gift costs \$3 more than the other two. If the total amount of money spent was \$27, how much did each gift cost?

Understand	**What facts do you know?** • There are 3 gifts, and two gifts cost the same. • One gift is \$3 more than the other two. • Ruben spent \$27 on all 3 gifts. **What do you need to find?** • The cost of each gift.
Plan	You can guess and check to solve the problem.
Solve	Use gift + gift + (gift + \$3) = \$27 and make logical guesses. Start with numbers smaller than \$10 because \$10 × 3 = \$30 and the total is less than \$30. Try \$9. \$9 + \$9 + (\$9 + \$3) = \$30 No, too large. Try \$8. \$8 + \$8 + (\$8 + \$3) = \$27 Yes So, two gifts cost \$8 each and the third gift costs \$8 + \$3, or \$11.
Check	Subtract the cost of each gift from the total cost. First gift: \$27 − \$8 = \$19 Second gift: \$19 − \$8 = \$11 Third gift: \$11 − \$11 = \$0 So, the answer is correct.

ANALYZE the Strategy

Refer to the problem on the previous page.

1. Explain why gift + gift + (gift + \$3) is used to solve the equation.
2. Explain why the first guess was \$9 instead of a smaller number.
3. Suppose Ruben spent \$39 on the gifts. How much does each gift cost?
4. Explain how you found the answer to Exercise 3.

PRACTICE the Strategy

EXTRA PRACTICE See page R22.

Solve. Use the *guess and check* strategy.

5. Kendra took photographs at the park. She photographed 20 dogs and owners in all. If there was a total of 64 legs, how many dogs and owners were there?
6. Corrine is making twice as much fruit punch as lemonade. She is making 12 gallons total. How many gallons will be fruit punch and how many will be lemonade?
7. **Measurement** Theo lives twice as far from Cassidy as Jarvis. How far do Theo and Jarvis live from Cassidy?

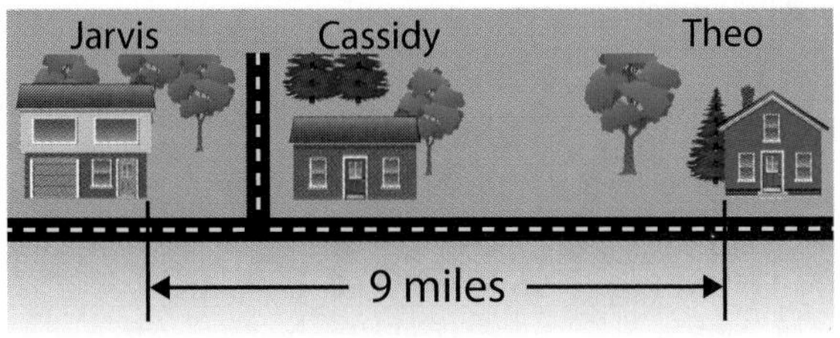

8. The total number of tickets sold for a play was 450. On Friday, 150 tickets were sold. Fifty more tickets sold on Saturday than on Sunday. How many tickets sold on Saturday and Sunday?
9. At a zoo gift shop, Jeffrey bought two of the items shown. He gave the cashier \$20, and received \$4 in change. Which two items did he buy?

10. Ahmed and Marco collect miniature cars. Marco has 37 fewer cars than Ahmed. They have 249 cars altogether. How many cars does each boy have?
11. Mirna's basketball team has played 14 games. They have lost and tied an equal number of times. They have won 5 times as many games as they have lost. How many games have they won, lost, and tied?
12. **WRITING IN MATH** Explain what it means to solve a problem by *guess and check.*

9-4 Estimate Quotients

GET READY to Learn

Circuses have been around for more than 200 years. They sometimes travel by train. Suppose a circus travels 642 miles in 8 hours. *About* how many miles per hour did the train travel?

MAIN IDEA

I will estimate quotients.

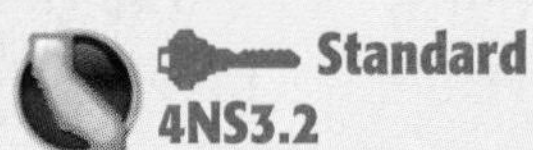
Standard 4NS3.2

Demonstrate an understanding of, and the ability to use, standard algorithms for multiplying a multidigit number by a two-digit number and for **dividing a multidigit number by a one-digit number; use relationships between them to simplify computations and check results.**

New Vocabulary

compatible numbers

There are different ways to estimate quotients. One way is to use compatible numbers. **Compatible numbers** are numbers that are easy to divide mentally.

Real-World EXAMPLE — Estimate Quotients

1 TRAVEL **Estimate the quotient of 642 and 8 to find how fast the train is traveling.**

One Way: Compatible Numbers	Another Way: Basic Facts
642 ÷ 8	642 ÷ 8
642 is close to 640. 640 and 8 are compatible numbers because they are easy to divide mentally.	What basic multiplication fact is close to the numbers in the problem?
	8 × 8 = 64
640 ÷ 8 = 80 8 × 8 = 64	8 × 80 = 640
	So, 640 ÷ 8 = 80.

So, the circus train is traveling about 80 miles per hour.

Check

You know that 640 ÷ 8 = 80 because 8 × 80 = 640. ✓

Online **Personal Tutor at** ca.gr4math.com

Real-World EXAMPLE Estimate Quotients

2 DOLLS Isabella has 6 dolls in her doll collection. The collection is worth $1,168. Each doll is worth the same amount of money. About how much is each doll worth?

You need to estimate $1,168 ÷ 6.

One Way: Compatible Numbers	Another Way: Basic Facts
$1,168 ÷ 6	$1,168 ÷ 6
$1,168 is close to $1,200. $1,200 and 6 are compatible numbers because they are easy to divide mentally.	What basic multiplication fact is close to the numbers in the problem?
$1,200 ÷ 6 = $200	6 × 2 = 12 6 × 20 = 120 6 × 200 = 1,200
	So, $1,200 ÷ 6 = $200.

So, each doll is worth about $200.

Check

You know that $1,200 ÷ 6 = $200 because 6 × $200 = $1,200. ✓

CHECK What You Know

Estimate. Check your estimate. See Examples 1 and 2 (pp. 348–349)

1. 161 ÷ 4

2. $424 ÷ 6

3. 715 ÷ 8

4. 2,660 ÷ 9

5. $5,643 ÷ 8

6. 8,099 ÷ 9

7. On Saturday, 1,164 people saw a movie at Upcity Theater. There were a total of 4 movie screens with the same number of people in each audience. About how many people watched each screen?

8. Talk About It Explain how to estimate $4,782 ÷ 6.

Practice and Problem Solving

EXTRA PRACTICE
See page R22.

Estimate. Check your estimate. See Examples 1 and 2 (pp. 348–349)

9. $123 \div 3$

10. $\$244 \div 6$

11. $162 \div 2$

12. $345 \div 7$

13. $\$538 \div 6$

14. $415 \div 6$

15. $\$1,406 \div 7$

16. $2,431 \div 8$

17. $\$2,719 \div 9$

18. $4,187 \div 7$

19. $\$7,160 \div 9$

20. $8,052 \div 9$

21. Tran earned 806 points on 9 tests. If he earned about the same number of points on each test, about how many points did he earn on each test?

22. **Measurement** Gloria ran 1,575 miles in 8 months. If she runs the same number of miles each month, about how many miles does she run each month?

Real-World PROBLEM SOLVING

Data File You can go hut hiking in Yosemite National Park. Hut hiking involves hiking and spending the night in huts instead of tents.

23. The total cost for the 5 members in the Valdez family to hut hike for 6 days is $2,475. About how much does it cost for each family member?

24. Harold needs to climb a 361-foot hill to get to the next hut. About how many yards away is he from the next hut? (*Remember:* 3 feet = 1 yard)

H.O.T. Problems

25. **OPEN ENDED** The estimated quotient of a division sentence is 200. What could the division sentence be?

26. **WRITING IN MATH** Estimate $5,425 \div 6$ using $5,400 \div 6$. Is the estimate greater than or less than the actual quotient? Explain.

CHAPTER 9

Mid-Chapter Check

Lessons 9-1 through 9-4

Divide. Check each answer. (Lesson 9-1)

1. $92 \div 3$

2. $37 \div 2$

3. Gwen earns $5 an hour delivering newspapers. If she earned $35 this week, how many hours did she spend delivering newspapers? (Lesson 9-1)

4. **STANDARDS PRACTICE** Gabriel solved the problem below. Which expression could be used to check his answer? (Lesson 9-1)

$$136 \div 5 = 27 \text{ R}1$$

A $(27 \times 1) + 5$

B $(27 \times 5) + 1$

C $(27 + 5) \times 1$

D $(27 + 1) \times 5$

Copy and complete each set of patterns. (Lesson 9-2)

5. $42 \div 7 = \blacksquare$
$420 \div 7 = \blacksquare$
$4{,}200 \div 7 = \blacksquare$

6. $25 \div 5 = \blacksquare$
$250 \div 5 = \blacksquare$
$2{,}500 \div 5 = \blacksquare$

Divide. Use patterns. (Lesson 9-2)

7. $150 \div 5$

8. $600 \div 2$

9. Jairo has 200 minutes left on his cell phone plan for the last five days of the month. If Jairo uses the same number of minutes each day, how many minutes can Jairo use his cell phone each day?

Solve. Use the *guess and check* strategy. (Lesson 9-3)

10. Patricia and Ashley collect stamps. Patricia has 13 more stamps than Ashley. Together they have 229 stamps. How many stamps does each girl have?

11. Dion bought three of the items shown below. He gave the cashier $10 and received $5.50 in change. Which three items did he buy?

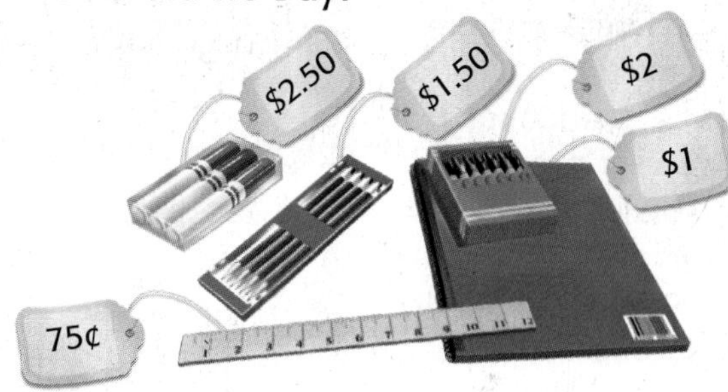

Estimate. Check your estimate. (Lesson 9-4)

12. $156 \div 3$

13. $182 \div 9$

14. **STANDARDS PRACTICE** Vikas drove 325 miles in five hours. Approximately how many miles did Vikas drive each hour? (Lesson 9-4)

F 60

G 64

H 68

J 70

15. WRITING IN MATH (Lesson 9-4) If you estimate $4{,}225 \div 6$ using $4{,}200 \div 6$, is the estimate greater or less than the actual quotient? Explain.

9-5 Two-Digit Quotients

MAIN IDEA

I will divide a two-digit dividend by a one-digit number.

Standard 4NS3.2 **Demonstrate an understanding of, and the ability to use, standard algorithms for** multiplying a multidigit number by a two-digit number and for **dividing a multidigit number by a one-digit number;** use relationships between them to simplify computations and to check results. **Standard 4MR2.1 Use estimation to verify the reasonableness of calculated results.**

GET READY to Learn

More than 75% of the world's geysers are found in Yellowstone National Park. Suppose one of Yellowstone's geysers erupts every 7 minutes, how many times does it erupt in 95 minutes?

Recall that to divide a two-digit number by a one-digit number, you need to divide the tens, then divide the ones.

Real-World EXAMPLE Two-Digit Quotients

1 How many times does the geyser erupt in 95 minutes?

The geyser erupts every 7 minutes. You need to find the number of times it erupts in 95 minutes. So, find 95 ÷ 7.

Estimate 95 ÷ 7 ⟶ 100 ÷ 10 = 10

Step 1 Divide the tens.

```
   1
7)95
 -7
  2
```

Divide. 9 ÷ 7 = 1
Put 1 in the quotient over the tens place.
Multiply. 7 × 1 = 7
Subtract. 9 − 7 = 2
Compare. 2 < 7

Step 2 Divide the ones.

```
  13 R4
7)95
 -7↓
  25
 -21
   4
```

Bring down the ones.
Divide. 25 ÷ 7 = 3
Put 3 in the quotient over the ones place.
Multiply. 7 × 3 = 21
Subtract. 25 − 21 = 4
Compare. 4 < 7
The remainder is 4.

So, the geyser will erupt about 13 times in 95 minutes.

Check for reasonableness

13 is close to the estimate. The answer is reasonable. ✓

Sometimes it is not possible to divide the first digit of the dividend by the divisor.

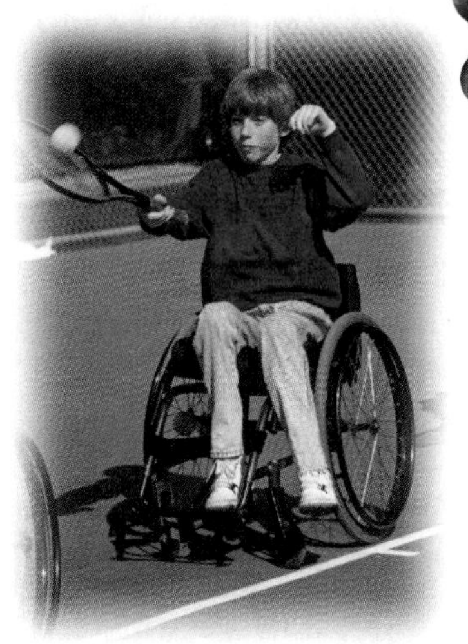

Real-World EXAMPLE Divide with Remainders

2 **SPORTS A tennis coach has 125 tennis balls. There are 4 members on the team. How many balls does each player get for practice if each player gets the same number of balls?**

There are 125 tennis balls and 4 team members. Divide 125 by 4 to find how many balls each player gets.

Estimate $125 \div 4 \longrightarrow 120 \div 4 = 30$, so about 30 balls per person

Step 1 Estimate to place the first digit.

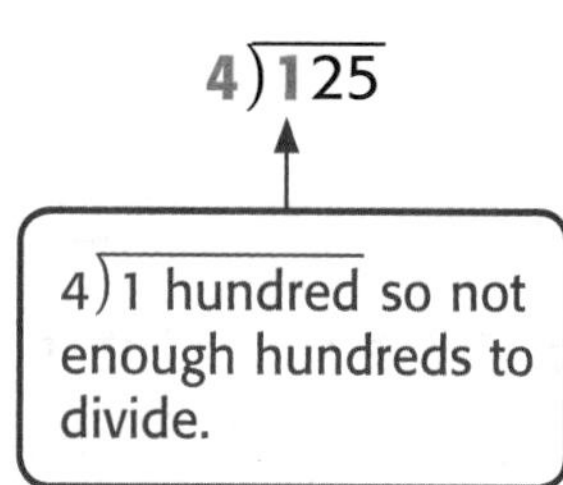

4)125
4)1 hundred so not enough hundreds to divide.

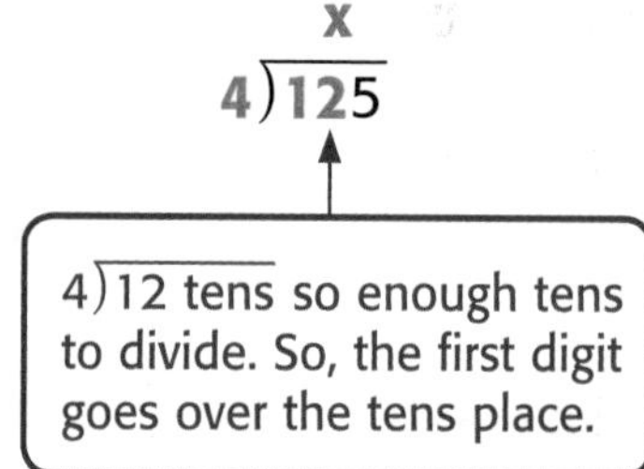

x
4)125
4)12 tens so enough tens to divide. So, the first digit goes over the tens place.

Step 2 Divide the tens.

```
   3
4)125
 -12
   0
```

Divide. $12 \div 4 = 3$
Put 3 in the quotient over the tens place.
Multiply. $4 \times 3 = 12$
Subtract. $12 - 12 = 0$
Compare. $0 < 4$

Remember

When a real-world problem has a remainder, you have to interpret the remainder.

Step 3 Divide the ones.

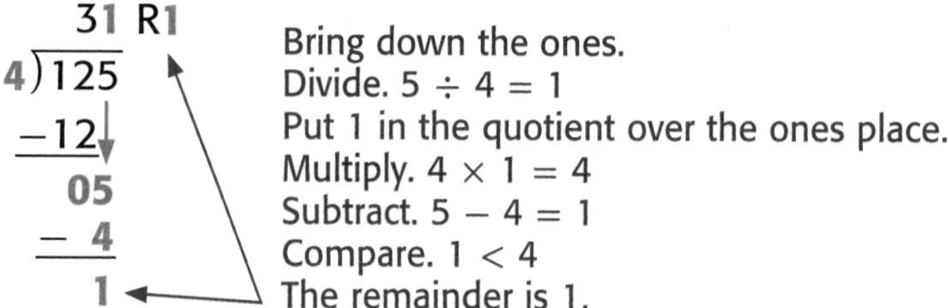

```
  31 R1
4)125
 -12↓
   05
  - 4
    1
```

Bring down the ones.
Divide. $5 \div 4 = 1$
Put 1 in the quotient over the ones place.
Multiply. $4 \times 1 = 4$
Subtract. $5 - 4 = 1$
Compare. $1 < 4$
The remainder is 1.

So, each team member gets 31 balls.

Check for reasonableness

The answer is close to the estimate. So, it is reasonable. ✓

Online **Personal Tutor at** ca.gr4math.com

CHECK What You Know

Divide. Use estimation to check. See Examples 1 and 2 (pp. 352–353)

1. $2\overline{)33}$ **2.** $4\overline{)56}$ **3.** $5\overline{)71}$

4. $179 \div 3$ **5.** $387 \div 4$ **6.** $697 \div 7$

7. Holden and Alma earned $32 by doing yard work in their neighborhood. They will share their money equally. How much money will each person get?

8. Talk About It: Estimation is one method that can be used to check division answers. Identify another method.

Practice and Problem Solving

EXTRA PRACTICE See page R23.

Divide. Use estimation to check. See Examples 1 and 2 (pp. 352–353)

9. $2\overline{)37}$ **10.** $3\overline{)64}$ **11.** $4\overline{)79}$ **12.** $5\overline{)82}$

13. $7\overline{)74}$ **14.** $6\overline{)91}$ **15.** $2\overline{)151}$ **16.** $3\overline{)286}$

17. $387 \div 5$ **18.** $493 \div 5$ **19.** $567 \div 6$ **20.** $682 \div 7$

21. $694 \div 7$ **22.** $783 \div 8$ **23.** $795 \div 8$ **24.** $883 \div 9$

25. There are 78 campers at a summer camp. There are 6 campers per cabin. How many cabins are there?

26. Carlo has $46 to spend on trading cards. If each pack of cards cost $3, how many packages can he buy?

Real-World PROBLEM SOLVING

Recycling Every month, Americans throw out enough bottles and jars to fill up a giant skyscraper. All of these jars are recyclable.

27. When one aluminum can is recycled, enough energy is saved to run a television for 3 hours. How many cans need to be recycled to run a television for 75 hours?

28. Most Americans use 7 trees a year in products that are made from trees. How old is a person who has used 85 trees?

Math Online Self-Check Quiz at ca.gr4math.com

H.O.T. Problems

29. OPEN-ENDED When Kira's father's age is divided by Kira's age, you get a quotient of 13 R1. Identify one possibility for their ages.

30. FIND THE ERROR Amber and Paul are finding 53 ÷ 3. Who is correct? Explain.

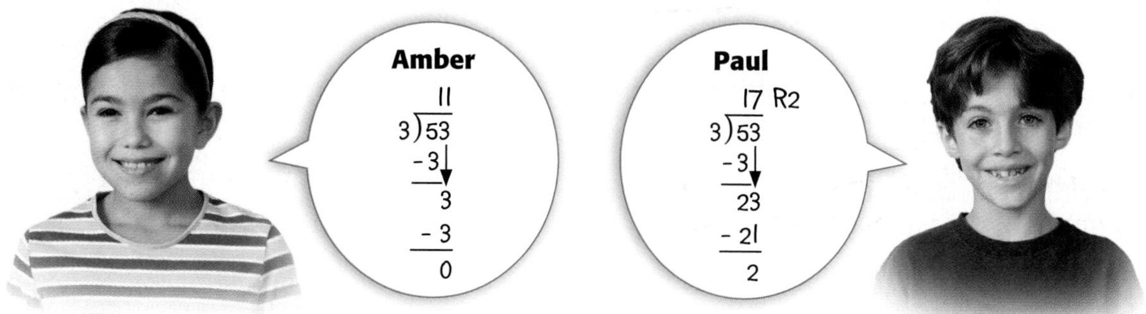

31. WRITING IN ►MATH Write a division problem that requires regrouping and has a remainder in the quotient. Give to a classmate to solve.

Standards Practice

32 Martín biked 78 miles in 5 days. About how many miles did he bike each day? **(Lesson 9-4)**

A 14 **C** 18

B 16 **D** 20

33 Raj ran 54 feet during a football game. If there are 3 feet in one yard, how many yards did he run? **(Lesson 9-5)**

F 17 **H** 19

G 18 **J** 20

Spiral Review

Estimate. Check your estimate. **(Lesson 9-4)**

34. 139 ÷ 2 **35.** \$449 ÷ 5 **36.** 562 ÷ 7 **37.** \$805 ÷ 9

38. Pablo works at an animal hospital. Last week he took care of 49 birds and snakes. He took care of four birds for every three snakes. How many of each animal did he take care of? **(Lesson 9-3)**

Divide. Use patterns. **(Lesson 9-2)**

39. \$600 ÷ 3 **40.** 2,400 ÷ 4 **41.** 4,900 ÷ 7 **42.** 4,800 ÷ 8

43. Jerry was given 3 CDs from his friends, 4 from his parents, and 1 from his sister. He now has 38. How many did he have originally? **(Lesson 6-3)**

9-6 Problem-Solving Investigation

MAIN IDEA I will choose the best strategy to solve a problem.

Standard 4MR1.1 **Analyze problems by identifying relationships, distinguishing relevant from irrelevant information, sequencing and prioritizing information, and observing patterns.** Standard 4NS3.0 **Students solve problems involving addition, subtraction,** multiplication, and division **of whole numbers** and understand the relationships among the operations.

P.S.I. TEAM +

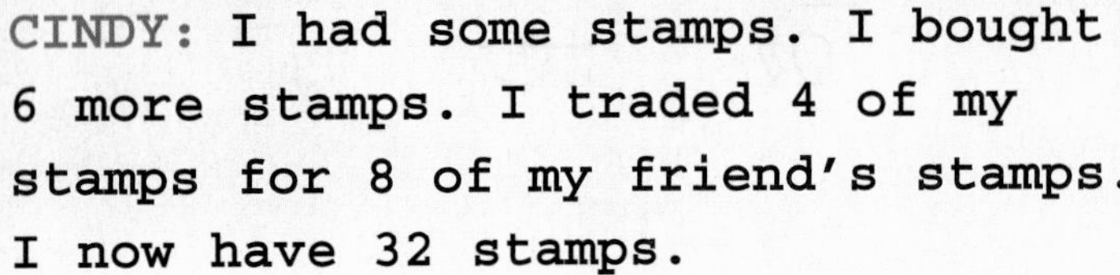

CINDY: I had some stamps. I bought 6 more stamps. I traded 4 of my stamps for 8 of my friend's stamps. I now have 32 stamps.

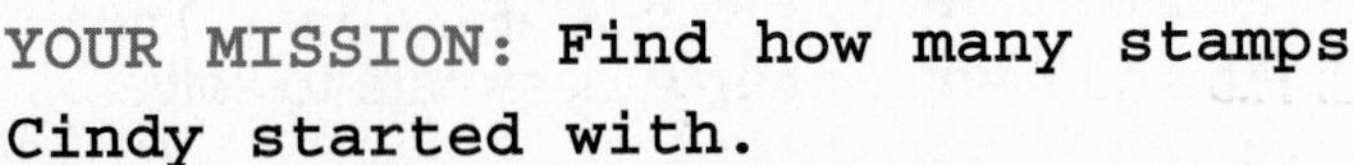

YOUR MISSION: Find how many stamps Cindy started with.

Understand You know that Cindy bought 6 stamps. She traded 4 stamps for 8 stamps. She now has 32 stamps. You need to find the number of stamps Cindy started with.

Plan You need to find how many stamps Cindy started with. So, the work backward strategy is a good choice.

Solve Start with the end result, then work backward.

End result →	32	stamps Cindy has now
	− 8	stamps Cindy received from a friend
	24	
	24	
	+ 4	stamps Cindy gave to a friend
	28	
	28	
	− 6	stamps Cindy bought
	22	

Check Look back at the problem. Cindy gained 14 stamps and lost 4. This means she has 10 more stamps then she started with. If she now has 32 stamps, then she started with 22 stamps. The answer is correct.

Mixed Problem Solving

Use any strategy shown below to solve. Tell what strategy you used.

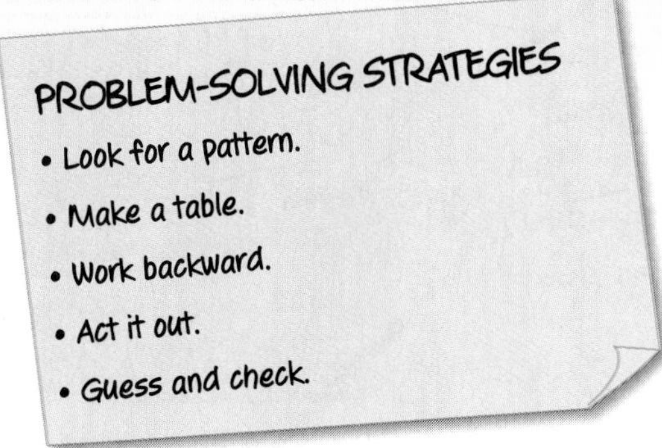

1. Ellis rode his bike to and from his cousin's home over the weekend. His cousin lives 5 miles away. If Ellis rode a total of 20 miles, how many times did he visit his cousin?

2. What is the next number in the pattern 2, 5, 11, 23, ■?

3. Judie and her dad caught 63 fish over the summer. The license allowed them to keep fish longer than 8 inches. Only 2 out of every 5 fish were long enough to keep. About how many did they keep?

4. Alvin buys 2 pairs of jeans, 2 pairs of shoes, 3 T-shirts, and 2 dress shirts for school. How much did he spend?

5. There are 24 cars in a parking lot. There are twice as many 4-door cars as 2-door. How many of each are there?

6. **Measurement** Lucy the Great Dane eats the amount of dog food shown each day. Roscoe the Pug eats 1 cup for every 2 that Lucy eats each day. How much food does Roscoe eat in a week?

7. A worker at an arcade is handing out 30 tokens for a party. There are more than 6 people at the party. The tokens are shared equally among the people. After the tokens are handed out, 6 are left. How many people are at the party? How many tokens does each person get?

8. Anoki has 5 coins that total 62¢. What are the coins?

9. Selena is going to a birthday party at 12 P.M. She needs to complete the activities shown before the party starts. What time should Selena start to get ready?

Activity	Time
Shower/get ready	30 minutes
Eat breakfast	30 minutes
Chores	2 hours
Pick up Felix and go	30 minutes

10. **WRITING IN ►MATH** Identify the probelm-solving strategy you used to solve Exercise 9. Explain how you used the strategy to solve the problem.

9-7 Three-Digit Quotients

GET READY to Learn

There are 678 people in line to ride a roller coaster. Each coaster car holds 6 people. How many coaster cars are needed so that everyone in line rides the coaster once?

MAIN IDEA

I will divide a three-digit dividend by a one-digit number.

Standard 4NS3.2 **Demonstrate an understanding of, and the ability to use, standard algorithms for** multiplying a multidigit number by a two-digit number and for **dividing a multidigit number by a one-digit number;** use relationships between them to simplify computations and check results.

Finding a quotient like 678 ÷ 6 is similar to dividing a two-digit number by a one-digit number.

Real-World EXAMPLE **Three-Digit Quotients**

1 **ROLLER COASTERS** **How many coaster cars are needed?**

Divide 678 by 6 to find the number of coaster cars needed.

Estimate $678 \div 6 \longrightarrow 700 \div 7 = 100$

Step 1 Divide the hundreds.

$$\begin{array}{r} 1 \\ 6\overline{)678} \\ -6 \\ \hline 0 \end{array}$$

Divide. $6 \div 6 = 1$
Put 1 in hundreds place.
Multiply. $6 \times 1 = 6$
Subtract. $6 - 6 = 0$
Compare. $0 < 6$

Step 2 Divide the tens.

$$\begin{array}{r} 11 \\ 6\overline{)678} \\ -6\downarrow \\ \hline 07 \\ -6 \\ \hline 1 \end{array}$$

Bring down the tens.
Divide. $7 \div 6 = 1$
Put 1 in the tens place.
Multiply. $6 \times 1 = 6$
Subtract. $7 - 6 = 1$
Compare. $1 < 6$

Step 3 Divide the ones.

$$\begin{array}{r} 113 \\ 6\overline{)678} \\ -6\downarrow \\ \hline 07 \\ -6\downarrow \\ \hline 18 \\ -18 \\ \hline 0 \end{array}$$

Bring down the ones.
Divide.
Divide. $18 \div 6 = 3$
Put 3 in ones place.
Multiply. $6 \times 3 = 18$
Subtract. $18 - 18 = 0$
Compare. $0 < 6$

So, 113 coaster cars are needed.

When dividing three-digit numbers, you can have a remainder like you sometimes have when dividing two-digit numbers.

Always start a division problem by dividing the greatest place value.

Real-World EXAMPLE — Three-Digit Quotients with Remainders

2 MEASUREMENT A roller coaster takes about 2 minutes to travel its track. How many feet does the coaster travel in one minute?

The coaster travels 985 feet in 2 minutes. To find how far it travels in 1 minute, divide 985 by 2.

Estimate $985 \div 2 \longrightarrow 1{,}000 \div 2 = 500$

$$\begin{array}{r} 492 \text{ R1} \\ 2\overline{)985} \\ -8 \\ \hline 18 \\ -18 \\ \hline 05 \\ -4 \\ \hline 1 \end{array}$$

THINK A remainder of 1 tells you that the quotient is just over 492.

So, the roller coaster travels a little more than 492 feet each minute.

Check for reasonableness
The answer, a little more than 492, is close to the estimate. So, it is reasonable. ✓

Online Personal Tutor at ca.gr4math.com

CHECK What You Know

Divide. Use estimation to check. See Examples 1 and 2 (pp. 358–359)

1. $2\overline{)286}$

2. $3\overline{)345}$

3. $4\overline{)492}$

4. $745 \div 2$

5. $679 \div 3$

6. $917 \div 4$

7. Measurement A tug-of-war team weighs a total of 774 pounds. The 6 members on the team weigh the same amount. How much does each person weigh?

8. Talk About It How would you mentally figure out how many digits the quotient of $795 \div 5$ will have? Explain your reasoning.

Practice and Problem Solving

EXTRA PRACTICE
See page R23.

Divide. Use estimation to check. See Examples 1 and 2 (pp. 358–359)

9. $2\overline{)324}$ **10.** $3\overline{)585}$ **11.** $5\overline{)775}$ **12.** $6\overline{)696}$

13. $7\overline{)847}$ **14.** $7\overline{)973}$ **15.** $2\overline{)573}$ **16.** $3\overline{)787}$

17. 849 ÷ 2 **18.** 994 ÷ 4 **19.** 1,863 ÷ 3 **20.** 3,974 ÷ 4

21. A coach ordered 6 soccer goals for $678. How much did each goal cost?

22. Britney needs to finish reading a book in 3 days. If the book is 348 pages long, how many pages does she need to read each day?

23. Maria is making friendship necklaces. She needs 2 feet of ribbon for each necklace. How many necklaces can she make if she has 439 feet of ribbon?

24. The students at Kennedy Elementary School have collected 926 cans of food that are going to be divided equally among 4 shelters. How many cans will be given to each shelter?

Real-World PROBLEM SOLVING

Architecture The White House is the official home and workplace of the President of the United States. President Theodore Roosevelt gave the White House its name, based on its color.

25. Measurement It takes 570 gallons of paint to paint the outside of the White House. If the number of gallons used to paint each of its 4 sides is equal, how many gallons of paint are used on each side?

26. There are 132 rooms and 6 floors in the White House. If each floor has the same number of rooms how many rooms would each floor have?

H.O.T. Problems

27. OPEN ENDED Write a division problem that results in a quotient that is greater than 200 and less than 250.

28. WHICH ONE DOESN'T BELONG? Identify the problem that will have a quotient less than 100.

$2\overline{)478}$ $3\overline{)264}$ $4\overline{)652}$ $5\overline{)815}$

29. CHALLENGE Find $3\overline{)4,275}$.

30. WRITING IN ▶MATH Write a real-world division problem that involves dividing a 3-digit number by a 1-digit number that results in a 2-digit quotient with a remainder.

Standards Practice

31 There are 6 rows of vegetables in Ian's garden. If there is a total of 96 plants, how many plants are in each row? **(Lesson 9-5)**

A 13 **C** 15

B 14 **D** 16

32 Catalina is putting some photos in an album. If she has 192 photos, and four photos fit on one page, how many pages does she need? **(Lesson 9-7)**

F 46 **H** 48

G 47 **J** 49

Spiral Review

33. The numbers shown are called *triangular numbers*. Find the next two triangular numbers **(Lesson 9-6)**

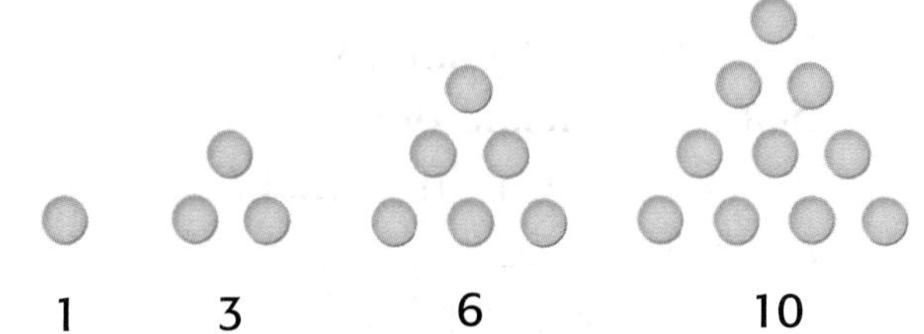

Divide. **(Lesson 9-5)**

34. $2\overline{)56}$ **35.** $3\overline{)72}$ **36.** $5\overline{)86}$ **37.** $8\overline{)93}$

Estimate. **(Lesson 9-4)**

38. 2,750 ÷ 4 **39.** $3,643 ÷ 6 **40.** 7,199 ÷ 9

9-8 Quotients with Zeros

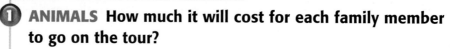

GET READY to Learn

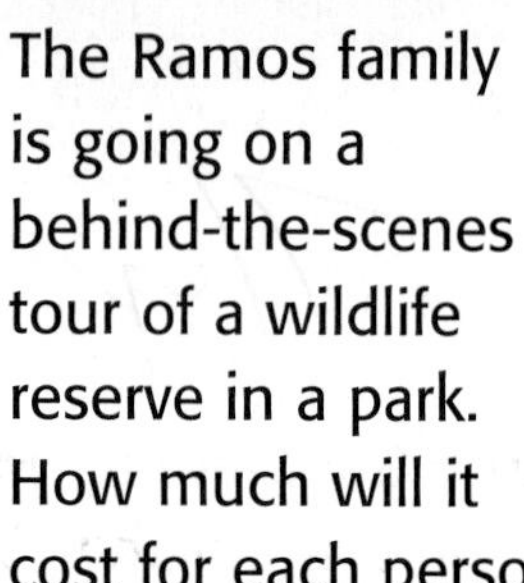

The Ramos family is going on a behind-the-scenes tour of a wildlife reserve in a park. How much will it cost for each person?

Cost of Tour	
Number of People	Cost ($)
3	$327

MAIN IDEA

I will divide with zeros in the quotients.

Standard 4NS3.2

Demonstrate an understanding of, and the ability to use, standard algorithms for multiplying a multidigit number by a two-digit number and for **dividing a multidigit number by a one-digit number;** use relationships between them to simplify computations and check results.

In division, a quotient will sometimes contain zeros.

Real-World EXAMPLE — Divide Greater Numbers

1 ANIMALS How much it will cost for each family member to go on the tour?

You need to find $327 ÷ 3.

Step 1 Divide the hundreds.

```
   $1
3)$327
  -3
   0
```

Divide. 3 ÷ 3 = 1
Put 1 in hundreds place.
Multiply. 3 × 1 = 3
Subtract. 3 − 3 = 0
Compare. 0 < 3

Step 2 Divide the tens.

```
   $10
3)$327
  -3↓
   02
  -0
    2
```

Bring down the tens.
Divide. Since 2 < 3, there is not enough to divide. So, put 0 in the tens place.
Multiply. 3 × 0 = 3
Subtract. 2 − 0 = 2
Compare. 0 < 3

Step 3 Divide the ones.

```
   $109
3)$327
  -3↓
   02
   -0↓
    27
   -27
     0
```

Bring down the ones.
Divide. 27 ÷ 3 = 9
Put 9 in the ones place.
Multiply. 3 × 9 = 27
Subtract. 27 − 27 = 0
Compare. 0 < 3

So, it will cost each family member $109.

Real-World EXAMPLE — Divide with Remainders

2 **VACATIONS The Kincaids have to drive a total of 415 miles to get to and from Dolphin Cove. How far is it to Dolphin Cove?**

The total distance the Kincaids will travel is 415 miles. To find the distance to Dolphin Cove, divide 415 by 2.

Estimate $415 \div 2 \longrightarrow 400 \div 2 = 200$

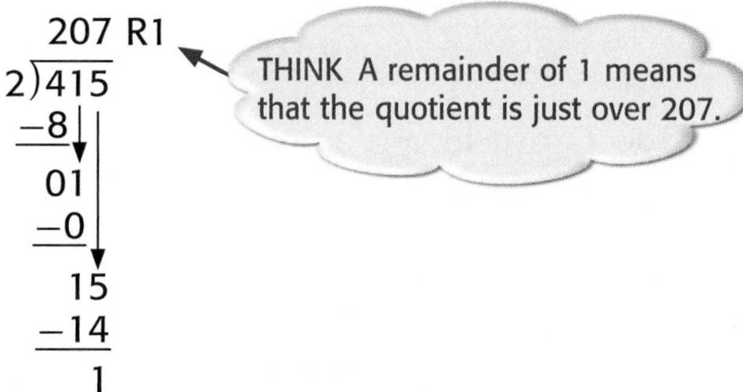

207 R1
2)415
−8
01
−0
15
−14
1
THINK A remainder of 1 means that the quotient is just over 207.

Remember

Remember to divide, multiply, subtract, and compare. Then bring down the next number in the dividend.

So, the distance to Dolphin Cove is a little more than 207 miles.

Check for reasonableness

The quotient, 207 R1, is close to the estimate. So, the answer is reasonable. ✓

CHECK What You Know

Divide. Use estimation to check. See Examples 1 and 2 (pp. 362–363)

1. $2\overline{)212}$

2. $3\overline{)\$627}$

3. $4\overline{)416}$

4. $617 \div 2$

5. $\$913 \div 3$

6. $825 \div 4$

7. Clara's total score for 3 games of bowling is 312. If Clara earned the same score for each game, what was her score for each game?

8. Talk About It Explain how to find the quotient of $624 \div 3$.

Practice and Problem Solving

EXTRA PRACTICE See page R24.

Divide. Use estimation to check. See Examples 1 and 2 (pp. 362–363)

9. $2\overline{)214}$ **10.** $3\overline{)327}$ **11.** $5\overline{)\$545}$ **12.** $6\overline{)648}$

13. $7\overline{)742}$ **14.** $8\overline{)\$824}$ **15.** $2\overline{)417}$ **16.** $3\overline{)622}$

17. $613 ÷ 3 **18.** 837 ÷ 4 **19.** 1,819 ÷ 2 **20.** $2,929 ÷ 3

21. There are 412 toys to be put on 4 shelves at a toy store. If the same number of toys fit on each shelf, how many toys fit on each shelf?

22. There are 408 students at a school. There are 4 lunch periods. If there are the same number of students in each lunch period, how many students are in each period?

Real-World PROBLEM SOLVING

Treasure Geocaching is an outdoor treasure hunting game in which participants use a Global Positioning System to hide and seek "treasures" all over the world. The "treasures" are usually toys or trinkets.

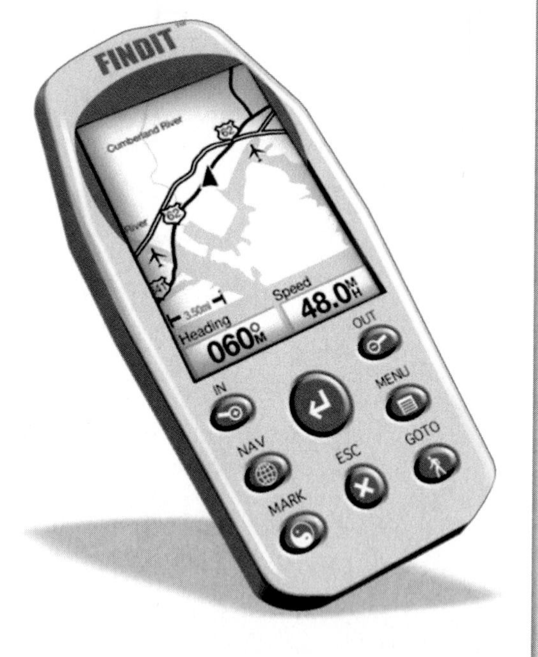

23. Chad is saving his money to buy a Global Positioning System receiver so that he can go geocaching. He has 2 months to save $215. How much money does he need to save each month?

24. Some of the treasures have been hidden on mountains. If the treasure is 325 feet away, how many yards away is it? (*Remember:* 3 feet = 1 yard)

H.O.T. Problems

25. OPEN ENDED Identify a 3-digit dividend that will result in a 3-digit quotient that has a zero in the tens place when the divisor is 6.

26. WRITING IN MATH Explain how an estimate could help you remember to write a zero in a quotient that results in a 2-digit quotient with a remainder.

Math Online Self-Check Quiz at ca.gr4math.com

Division Shuffle

Division of Multi-Digit Numbers

Get Ready!

Players: 2 players

You will need: 5 index cards, 2 white boards, 2 dry erase markers

___)___ ___ ___

Get Set!

- Cut each index card in half. Label each card with one number so that the cards are labeled 0 through 9.

Go!

- Shuffle and then place the cards face down on the table.
- Both players draw a division symbol on their dry erase boards.
- Player 1 draws four cards, and then turns them over one at a time. After each card is turned over, Players 1 and 2 write each number in any blank on their dry erase boards.
- After all of the numbers are recorded, Players 1 and 2 find and check the quotients.
- The player that has the greatest quotient gets 1 point.
- Continue playing until a player earns 5 points. Reshuffle the cards if needed.

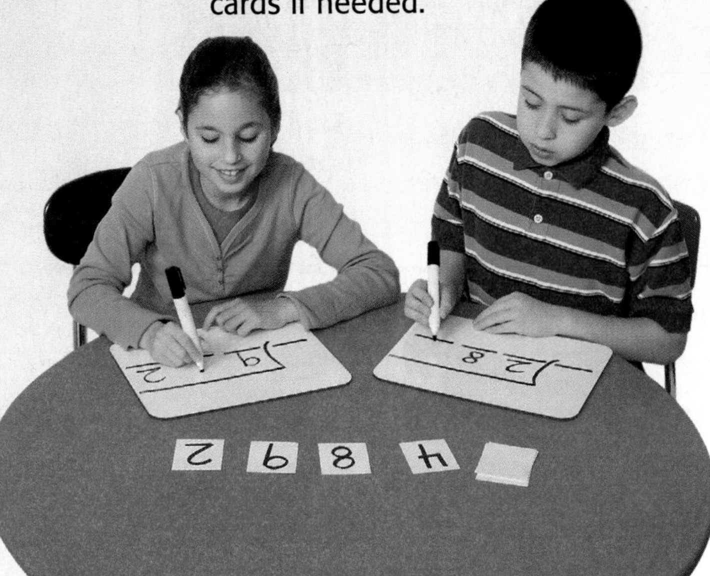

Problem Solving in Science

A DESERT SAFARI

The Sahara desert in Africa is 800–1,200 miles wide and 3,000 miles long. Animals like elephants, giraffes, lions, and chimpanzees live in or near this desert. Many African desert animals can also be found in zoos, where they are protected and fed.

Some animals, such as the elephant, are very large. An average elephant weighs 12,250 pounds, and its trunk weighs 400 pounds!

Food Eaten by Zoo Animals

Animal	Number	Daily Food (lb)
Hippo	6	900
Elephant	10	1,600
Giraffe	6	360
Lion	7	218
Camel	5	94
Hyena	8	144
Chimpanzee	9	117
Flamingo	8	1

Standard 4NS3.4 Solve problems involving division of multidigit numbers by one-digit numbers.

Real-World Math

Use the information on page 366 to solve each problem.

1. Suppose each camel eats the same amount of food. About how much food would one camel eat in one week?

2. A visitor travels the Sahara desert from east to west in 10 days and travels the same amount each day. How many miles does the visitor travel each day?

3. Suppose each elephant eats the same amount of food. How much food do four elephants eat in a day?

4. How many ounces of food does each flamingo eat per day? (*Hint*: 1 pound = 16 ounces)

5. Does a hyena or a chimpanzee eat more each day? Explain.

6. How much more do three elephants eat than three hippos?

7. How much food is eaten each day by one giraffe, one hyena, and one lion? Order these animals in order from greatest to least with respect to the amount of food each eats.

Did You Know?

The African elephant is the largest land mammal.

9-9 Divide Greater Numbers

MAIN IDEA

I will divide four- and five-digit dividends by a one-digit number.

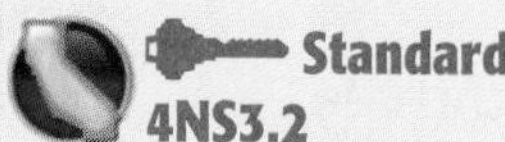

Standard 4NS3.2

Demonstrate an understanding of, and the ability to use, standard algorithms for multiplying a multidigit number by a two-digit number and for **dividing a multidigit number by a one-digit number;** use relationships between them to simplify computations and check results.

GET READY to Learn

One of the largest holes in the world is a copper mine. It is 5,808 feet wide. How many yards wide is the hole?

You can use the same process to divide larger numbers that you use with smaller numbers.

Real-World EXAMPLE Divide Greater Numbers

1 **MEASUREMENT How many yards wide is the copper mine?**

The mine is 5,808 feet wide. There are 3 feet in 1 yard. So, to find the width in yards, divide 5,808 by 3.

Step 1 Divide the thousands.

```
   1
3)5,808
 -3
  2
```

Divide. $5 \div 3 = 1$
Put 1 in thousands place.
Multiply. $3 \times 1 = 3$
Subtract. $5 - 3 = 2$

Compare. $2 < 3$

Step 2 Divide the hundreds.

```
   19
3)5,808
 -3↓
  28
 -27
   1
```

Bring down the hundreds.
Divide. $28 \div 3 = 9$
Multiply. $3 \times 9 = 27$
Put 9 in hundreds place.
Subtract. $28 - 27 = 1$

Compare. $1 < 3$

Step 3 Divide each place.

```
  1,936
3)5,808
 -3↓
  28
 -27↓
    10
    -9↓
     18
    -18
      0
```

For each place, divide, multiply, subtract, compare, and bring down the next digit to form a new number to be divided.

So, the copper mine is 1,936 yards wide.

Real-World EXAMPLE Divide Greater Numbers

2 **MONEY The largest gold nugget ever found was in California. It weighed 195 pounds and was worth $43,534 at the time it was found. Suppose that 4 people found it, sold it, and divided the money evenly. How much money would each person get?**

Divide $43,534 by 4 to find out how much money each person will get.

Estimate $43,534 ÷ 4 ⟶ $40,000 ÷ 4 = $10,000

Remember

For each place, divide, multiply, subtract, compare, and bring the next digit in the dividend directly down to form a new number to be divided.

Step 1 Divide the ten thousands.

```
    $1
 4)$43,534
   -4
    0
```

Divide 4 ÷ 4 = 1
Put 1 in the quotient over the ten thousands place.

Multiply. 4 × 1 = 4
Subtract. 4 − 4 = 0
Compare. 0 < 4

Step 2 Divide the thousands.

```
    $10
 4)$43,534
   -4↓
    03
   -0
     3
```

Bring down the thousands.
Divide. 3 ÷ 4 = 0
Put 0 in the quotient over the thousands place.

Multiply. 4 × 0 = 0
Subtract. 3 − 0 = 3
Compare. 3 < 4

Step 3 Divide each place.

```
    $10,883 R2
 4)$43,534
   -4↓
    03
   -0↓
     35
    -32↓
      33
     -32↓
       14
      -12
        2
```

For each place, divide, multiply, subtract, and compare. Then bring down the next digit in the dividend.

So, each person would get just over $10,883.

Personal Tutor at ca.gr4math.com

CHECK What You Know

Divide. Use estimation to check. See Examples 1 and 2 (pp. 368–369)

1. $2\overline{)2,764}$ **2.** $3\overline{)\$6,163}$ **3.** $5\overline{)8,045}$

4. $60,436 \div 4$ **5.** $\$81,497 \div 6$ **6.** $98,193 \div 8$

7. An art museum hosted an exhibit. One day, 6,414 people attended the exhibit during the 6 hours it was open. If the same number of people attend each hour, how many people attend each hour?

8. Talk About It Explain how dividing a 5-digit dividend by a 1-digit divisor is similar to dividing a 3-digit dividend by a 1-digit divisor. How is it different?

Practice and Problem Solving

EXTRA PRACTICE See page R24.

Divide. Use estimation to check. See Examples 1 and 2 (pp. 368–369)

9. $2\overline{)2,418}$ **10.** $3\overline{)3,428}$ **11.** $4\overline{)\$4,228}$ **12.** $5\overline{)7,465}$

13. $6\overline{)8,802}$ **14.** $8\overline{)\$9,597}$ **15.** $7\overline{)70,248}$ **16.** $8\overline{)92,072}$

17. $\$58,413 \div 4$ **18.** $59,561 \div 6$ **19.** $184,932 \div 2$ **20.** $\$291,387 \div 3$

21. Kirby bought a used car for $3,626. He plans on paying for it in two years. How much will he pay each year?

22. **Measurement** The farthest distance a pumpkin has ever been thrown is 4,434 feet. How many yards is this?

Real-World PROBLEM SOLVING

Measurement The map shows distances between cities in the United States.

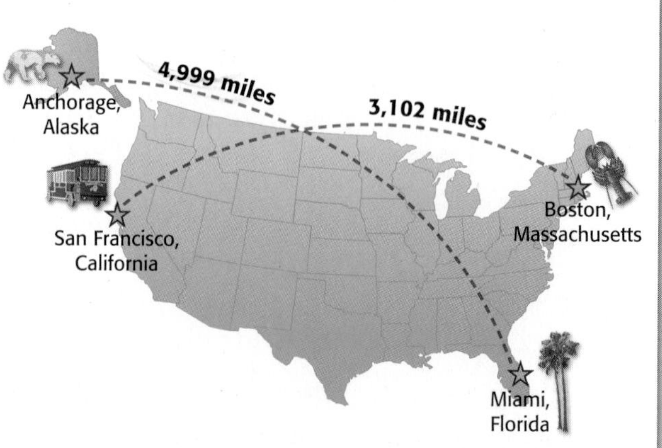

23. The Regan family is driving cross country for a vacation. They are driving from San Francisco, California, to Boston, Massachusetts. If they drive an equal distance each day, how many miles will they travel each day if they make the trip in 6 days?

24. The Collins family is moving to Miami, Florida, from Anchorage, Alaska. If they drive an equal distance each day, about how many miles would they travel each day if they make the trip in 8 days?

H.O.T. Problems

25. OPEN ENDED Write a division problem that involves dividing a 5-digit number by a 1-digit number. The quotient must be between 1,000 and 1,200.

26. CHALLENGE Divide 218,376 by 2.

27. WRITING IN ▶MATH How many digits would be in the quotient of 12,495 ÷ 5? Explain how you know.

Standards Practice

28 The map shows the distance in feet to the treasure.

Find 318 ÷ 3 to find how many yards it is from X to the treasure. **(Lesson 9-8)**

A 104

B 105

C 106

D 107

29 Rodrigo's horse ate 3150 pounds of food in 3 months. How many pounds of food did it eat each month? **(Lesson 9-9)**

F 1025 pounds

G 1050 pounds

H 1500 pounds

J 1550 pounds

Spiral Review

Divide. Use estimation to check. (Lesson 9-8)

30. $3\overline{)624}$ **31.** $4\overline{)\$824}$ **32.** $5\overline{)537}$

Divide. Use estimation to check. (Lesson 9-7)

33. $2\overline{)468}$ **34.** $3\overline{)\$645}$ **35.** $4\overline{)872}$

36. Janise bought the items shown to the right. If the shirts are equal in price and the total cost was $80, how much did each item cost? **(Lesson 9-6)**

37. Algebra Find the value of $n \times 317$ if $n = 4$. **(Lesson 7-6)**

CHAPTER 9

Study Guide and Review

FOLDABLES™ Study Organizer GET READY to Study

Be sure the following Key Vocabulary words and Key Concepts are written in your Foldable.

BIG Ideas

Division of Multi-Digit Numbers (p. 358)

- Divide a multi-digit number by a one-digit number.

```
    $234
 2)$468
  −4↓
   06
  − 6↓
    08
   − 8
     0
```

For each place, divide, multiply, subtract, and compare. Then bring down the next digit in the dividend.

Estimate Quotients (p. 348)

- You can use compatible numbers to estimate quotients.

$722 \div 9$

THINK 722 is close to 720. 720 and 9 are compatible numbers because they are easy to divide mentally.

$720 \div 9 = 80 \quad 9 \times 8 = 72$

Key Vocabulary

compatible numbers (p. 348)
dividend (p. 337)
divisor (p. 337)
quotient (p. 337)
remainder (p. 338)

Vocabulary Check

Complete each sentence with the correct vocabulary word.

1. The number that is left over in a division problem is the ___?___ .
2. The number that divides the dividend is the ___?___ .
3. The number you are dividing is the ___?___ .
4. ___?___ are numbers that are easy to divide mentally.
5. The result of a division problem is the ___?___ .
6. In the division problem $4\overline{)136}$, the number 136 is the ___?___ .

Math Online Vocabulary Review at ca.gr4math.com

Lesson-by-Lesson Review

9-1 Division with Remainders (pp. 339–341)

Example 1

Find 59 ÷ 3.

```
   19 R2
 3)59
  -3↓
   29
  -27
    2
```

For each place, divide, multiply, subtract, and compare.

Then bring down the next digit in the dividend.

Check

```
   19
 ×  3
   57
 +  2
   59
```

So, the answer is correct. ✓

Divide.

7. $5\overline{)53}$ **8.** $6\overline{)67}$

9. 91 ÷ 4 **10.** 77 ÷ 3

11. Christy has 37 books. She wants to put them evenly on her 4 shelves. How many books will she not be able to fit?

12. Rafael wants to earn $40 for a new pair of skates. If he earns $6 an hour for yard work, how many hours will he have to work to have the money for the skates?

9-2 Divide Multiples of 10, 100, and 1,000 (pp. 342–345)

Example 2

Find 1,600 ÷ 4.

Use patterns to divide.

16 ÷ 4 = 4

160 ÷ 4 = 40

1,600 ÷ 4 = 400

So, 1,600 ÷ 4 = 400.

Check

Use addition to check.

```
   400
   400
   400
 + 400
 1,600
```

So, the answer is correct. ✓

Divide.

13. 27 ÷ 9 = ■
270 ÷ 9 = ■
2,700 ÷ 9 = ■

14. 49 ÷ 7 = ■
490 ÷ 7 = ■
4,900 ÷ 7 = ■

15. 900 ÷ 3 **16.** 1,800 ÷ 9

17. 3,600 ÷ 4 **18.** 4,900 ÷ 7

19. 6,400 ÷ 8 **20.** 7,200 ÷ 9

21. Chuck collected 150 shells during his five days of vacation. If Chuck collected the same number of shells each day, how many shells did he collect each day?

9-3 Problem-Solving Strategy: Guess and Check (pp. 346–347)

Example 3
Opal and Steve collect coins. Opal has 32 more coins than Steve. They have 146 coins altogether. How many coins does each person have?

Understand

What facts do you know?

- Opal has 32 more coins than Steve.
- They have 146 coins altogether.

What do you need to find?

- The number of coins each person has.

Plan You can guess and check to solve the problem.

Solve Make logical guesses.

$146 \div 2 = 73$, so Opal will have more than 73, and Steve will have less than 73.

Check Think of 2 addends that have a difference of about 30, and a sum of about 150.

Try 90 + 60. $90 + 60 = 150$

The sum is too high. Try smaller numbers until you find the correct answer.

The correct answer is 89 and 57 because $89 + 57 = 146$

Solve. Use the *guess and check* strategy.

22. Juanita made a vegetable tray. There are 2 times more cucumber slices than tomato slices and 4 times more carrot slices than cucumber slices. If there are 5 tomato slices, how many slices of carrots and cucumbers are there?

23. Toru bought a CD and a DVD. The CD cost $5 less than the DVD, and the total was $29. How much was each item?

24. There are rabbits, ponies, and goats at a petting zoo. There are eight times as many goats as ponies. There are six more rabbits than ponies. The number of ponies is shown. Find how many rabbits and goats.

25. Etta is buying a sweater and a pair of pants. The sweater cost $12 more than the pants. The total cost will be $84. What is the cost of each clothing item?

9-4 Estimate Quotients (pp. 348–350)

Example 4
Find 273 ÷ 9.

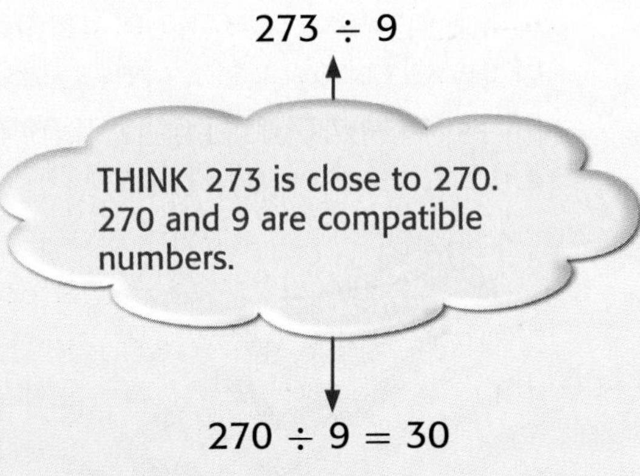

273 ÷ 9
THINK 273 is close to 270. 270 and 9 are compatible numbers.
270 ÷ 9 = 30

So, 273 ÷ 9 is about 30.

Estimate.

26. \$254 ÷ 5 **27.** 634 ÷ 7

28. 5,571 ÷ 8 **29.** 7,218 ÷ 9

30. **Measurement** A roller coaster car made it to the bottom of a 318-foot hill in 5 seconds. About how many feet did the car travel each second?

31. A skate park has \$3,225 to spend on 8 new ramps. About how much can be spent on each ramp?

9-5 Two-Digit Quotients (pp. 352–355)

Example 5
Find 95 ÷ 4.

Step 1 Divide the tens.

```
  2      Divide. 9 ÷ 4 = 2
4)95     Put 2 in the quotient.
 -8      Multiply. 4 × 2 = 8
  1      Subtract. 9 − 8 = 1
         Compare. 1 < 4
```

Step 2 Divide the ones.

```
  23 R3  Bring down the ones.
4)95     Divide. 15 ÷ 4 = 3
 -8↓     Put 3 in the quotient.
  15     Multiply. 4 × 3 = 12
 -12     Subtract. 15 − 12 = 3
   3     Compare. 3 < 4
         Remainder = 3
```

So, 95 ÷ 4 = 23 R3.

Divide.

32. 3)86 **33.** 6)96

34. 87 ÷ 4 **35.** 95 ÷ 3

36. There are 85 crayons in Miranda's crayon box. She wants to share them equally with two of her friends. How many crayons will Miranda and her friends each get? How many will be left over?

37. Garcia placed his baseball cards into 3 envelopes. He ended up with 17 cards in each envelope and 2 left over. How many cards did Garcia have to begin with?

9-6 Problem-Solving Investigation: Choose a Strategy (pp. 356–357)

Example 6
There are 1,323 students trying out for basketball teams. Is it reasonable to say that more than 150 teams will be formed if there are nine players on each team?

Understand

There are 1,323 students trying out for basketball teams. Nine players will be on each team.

Will there be more than 150 teams formed?

Plan Divide the number of students trying out by the number of players per team.

Solve Divide 1,323 by 9.

```
    147
9)1,323
 -9↓
  42
 -36↓
   63
  -63
    0
```

There will be 147 teams. So, it is not reasonable to say there will be more than 150 teams.

Check Use multiplication to check.

$90 \times 147 = 1{,}323$

So, the answer is correct.

Use any strategy to solve.

38. Frida had 3 pencils. Then her teacher gave her some of the packs of pencils shown. Now Frida has 11 pencils. How many packs of pencils did the teacher give Frida?

39. Each hand in the human body has 27 bones. There are 6 more bones in the fingers than in the wrist. There are 3 fewer bones in the palm than in the wrist. How many bones are in the fingers and wrist?

40. One banner is made using three sheets of paper. How many different banners can be made using red, yellow, and black paper one time each if the paper is placed in a row?

41. What number is missing from the pattern 2, 7, 12, 17, ■?

42. A number is divided by 5. Next, 4 is subtracted from the quotient. Then, 6 is added to the difference. The result is 10. What is the number?

9-7 Three-Digit Quotients (pp. 358–361)

Example 7
Find 426 ÷ 4.

Estimate 426 ÷ 4 → 400 ÷ 4 = 100

```
  106 R2
4)426
 -4
  02
 - 0
  26
 -24
   2
```

For each place, divide, multiply, subtract, and compare.

Then bring down the next digit in the dividend.

So, 426 ÷ 4 = 106 R2.

Check for reasonableness
The quotient, 106 R2, is close to the estimate. So, the answer is reasonable. ✓

Divide.

43. 3)787

44. 994 ÷ 4

45. There are 7 teachers and 147 students in the 4th grade. If the same number of students are in each class, how many students will be in each class?

46. There are 1,035 cars in the airport parking lot. The lot has 9 rows of parked cars. How many cars are in each row if the same number of cars are in each row?

47. Explain how to check Exercise 46 to be sure your answer is correct.

9-8 Quotients with Zeros (pp. 362–365)

Example 8
Find $416 ÷ 2.

```
  $208
2)$416
  -4
   01
  -0
   16
  -16
    0
```

For each place, divide, multiply, subtract, and compare.
Then bring down the next digit in the dividend.

So, $416 ÷ 2 = $208.

Divide.

48. 2)217

49. 3)621

50. 817 ÷ 4

51. 925 ÷ 3

52. 436 students ride the bus home each day. The school has 8 buses. How many students fit on each bus?

53. Tamera wants to fit all of her 749 marbles into 7 jars. How many should she put in each jar?

Study Guide and Review

9-9 Divide Greater Numbers (pp. 368–371)

Example 9
Find 6,213 ÷ 3.

Estimate 6,213 ÷ 3 ⟶ 6,000 ÷ 3 = 2,000

Step 1 Divide the thousands.

$$\begin{array}{r} 2 \\ 3\overline{)6,213} \\ -6 \\ \hline 0 \end{array}$$

Step 2 Divide the hundreds.

$$\begin{array}{r} 20 \\ 3\overline{)6,213} \\ -6\downarrow \\ \hline 02 \\ -\ 0 \\ \hline 2 \end{array}$$

Step 3 Divide each place.

$$\begin{array}{r} 2,071 \\ 3\overline{)6,213} \\ -6 \\ \hline 02 \\ -\ 0 \\ \hline 21 \\ -21 \\ \hline 03 \\ -\ 3 \\ \hline 0 \end{array}$$

For each place, divide, multiply, subtract, and compare. Then bring down the next digit in the dividend.

So, 6,213 ÷ 3 = 2,071.

Check for reasonableness
The quotient, 2,071, is close to the estimate. So the answer is correct ✓

Divide.

54. $3\overline{)\$6,597}$

55. $5\overline{)8,802}$

56. 79,561 ÷ 6

57. \$91,387 ÷ 8

58. Candice is making bows. She uses a 9-inch piece of ribbon for each bow. How many bows can she make with 1,827 inches of ribbon?

59. There is a total of 3,915 people attending three shows of an orchestra concert. How many people are attending each show if the same number of people attend each show?

60. There are 1,440 students who attend a school. There are four lunch periods. If the same number of students eat during each lunch period, how many students eat during each lunch period?

61. Measurement A 5-kilometer race is about 16,404 feet long. How many yards long is the race? *Remember*: 3 feet = 1 yard

CHAPTER 9

Chapter Test

For Exercises 1 and 2, decide whether each statement is *true* or *false*.

1. A quotient is the number being divided.

2. In the problem 62 ÷ 2, the number 2 is the divisor.

Divide. Check each answer.

3. $2\overline{)45}$

4. 73 ÷ 4

5. **STANDARDS PRACTICE** There are 5,280 feet in a mile. Since 1 yard equals 3 feet, how many yards are in one mile?

   A 1760 yd **C** 1780 yd
   B 1770 yd **D** 1790 yd

Copy and complete each set of patterns.

6. 24 ÷ 4 = ■
   240 ÷ 4 = ■
   2,400 ÷ 4 = ■

7. 18 ÷ 2 = ■
   180 ÷ 2 = ■
   1,800 ÷ 2 = ■

Divide. Use patterns.

8. $3,200 ÷ 4

9. 5,400 ÷ 6

10. Three members of the Cotter family are flying to Washington, D.C., for vacation. The total cost of the tickets is $1,250. About how much was each person's ticket?

Divide. Use estimation to check.

11. $5\overline{)410}$

12. 863 ÷ 3

13. Sara earned the same score on her last 2 tests. Her total score was 184. What was her score on each of the 2 tests?

Divide. Use estimation to check.

14. $2\overline{)417}$

15. $929 ÷ 3

16. **Measurement** The Toshiro family is moving across the country. They will drive a total of 2,835 miles over 7 days. If they drive the same distance each day, how far will they drive each day?

Divide. Use estimation to check.

17. $2\overline{)46,302}$

18. 62,932 ÷ 7

19. A family is buying a boat. They hope to have it paid off in 3 years. How much do they have to pay each year to reach their goal?

20. **STANDARDS PRACTICE**

   60,436 ÷ 4

   F 15,109 **H** 15,110
   G 15,108 **J** 15,111

21. **WRITING IN MATH** How many digits would be in the quotient of 12,795 ÷ 5? Explain how you know.

CHAPTER 9

California Standards Practice

Cumulative, Chapters 1–9

Standards Example

Rosa has 130 photos. Her photo album has space for 6 photos on a page. About how many pages will she need for her photos?

A 13 **C** 20

B 19 **D** 24

Read the Question

You need to find a close estimate for the number of pages Rosa will need.

Solve the Question

Use basic facts.

$130 \div 6$

What basic multiplication fact is close to the numbers in the problem?

$6 \times 2 = 12$

$6 \times 20 = 120$

So, Rosa needs about 20 pages.
The answer is C.

Personal Tutor at ca.gr4math.com

Choose the best answer.

1 **Josh has 81 toy cars to share equally among 3 friends. How many toy cars will each friend receive?**

A 18 **C** 30

B 27 **D** 37

2 **Which number is represented by *n*?**

$$n + 938 = 1456$$

F 518 **H** 528

G 522 **J** 594

3 **The soccer team has 144 water bottles in 6 boxes. How many water bottles are in each box?**

A 20 **C** 24

B 22 **D** 25

4 **Which number makes each equation true?**

$$54 \div 6 = \square$$
$$540 \div 60 = \square$$
$$5400 \div 600 = \square$$

F 6 **H** 60

G 9 **J** 90

5 **How many students live 8 or more miles from school?**

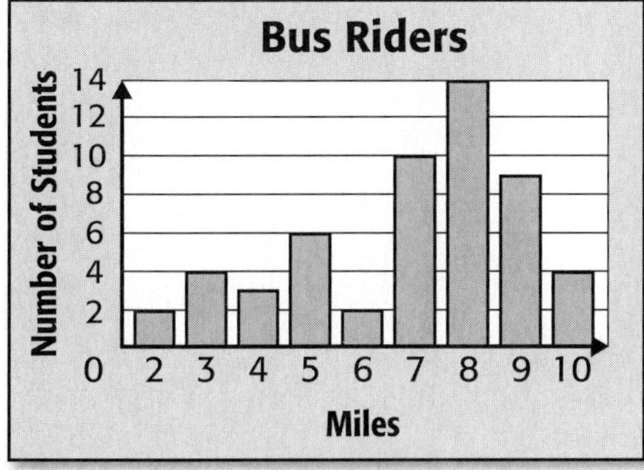

A 25 **C** 27

B 26 **D** 28

6 **Which of the following has the least value?**

F 45,034,653 **H** 45,689,236

G 45,073,542 **J** 45,856,494

7 $4\overline{)1378}$

A 433 R2 **C** 344

B 344 R2 **D** 354

8 **The bar graph shows the number of cans students collected.**

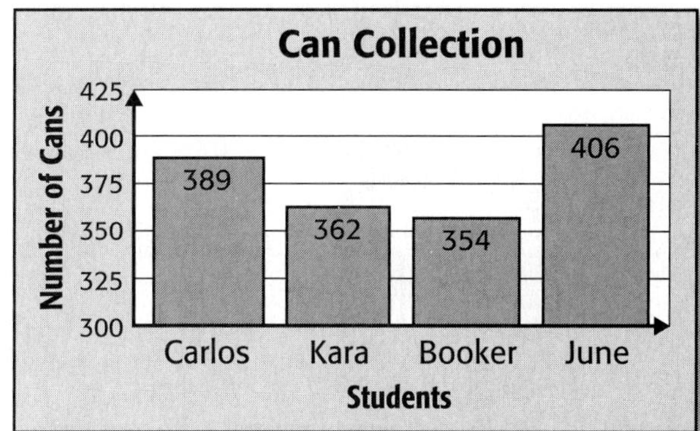

Which 2 students collected a sum of cans that is less than 750?

F Carlos and Kara

G Booker and Carlos

H June and Booker

J Kara and June

9 **Which is the best estimate for $351 \div 5$?**

A 6 **C** 60

B 7 **D** 70

10 **What is the mode of {2, 3, 3, 3, 5, 5, 7}?**

F 2 **H** 5

G 3 **J** 7

CHAPTER 10 Geometry

What are solid and plane figures?

A **solid figure**, or 3-dimensional figure, is a figure with length, width, and height. A **plane figure**, or 2-dimensional figure, is a figure with length and width.

Example Plane and solid figures are often found in traffic signs.

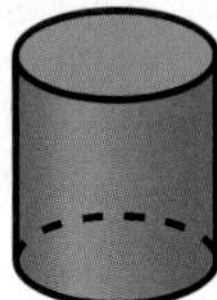

What will I learn in this chapter?

- Identify, describe, and classify solid and plane figures.
- Identify lines, line segments, rays, and angles.
- Identify parts of circles.
- Identify and make nets.
- Solve problems by looking for a pattern.

Key Vocabulary

solid figure
plane figure
line
angle
circle

Student Study Tools at ca.gr4math.com

FOLDABLES™ Study Organizer

Make this Foldable to help you organize information about geometry. Begin with 10 sheets of notebook paper.

1. **Staple** the sheets of notebook paper together to form a booklet.

2. **Cut** a tab as shown. On the third page, make the tab longer, and so on.

3. **Write** the chapter title on the cover. Label each tab with a lesson number.

ARE YOU READY for Chapter 10?

You have two ways to check prerequisite skills for this chapter.

Option 2

Math Online Take the Chapter Readiness Quiz at ca.gr4math.com.

Option 1

Complete the Quick Check below.

QUICK Check

Identify each solid figure. (Prior grade)

1. 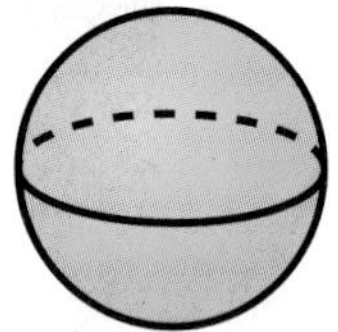

2. 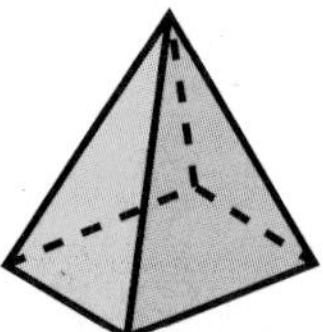

3. 

4. Identify the solid figure the two objects at the right represent.

How many straight sides does each figure have? (Prior grade)

5. 

6. 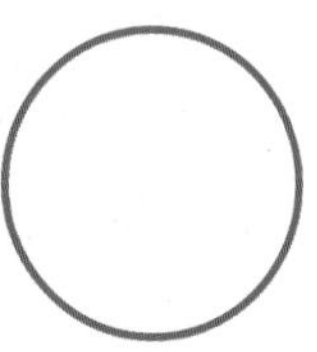

7. 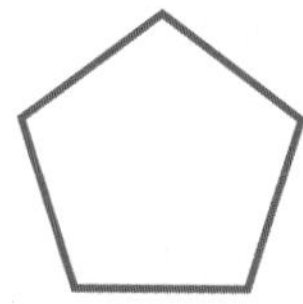

8. The musical instrument at right resembles a triangle. How many sides does the instrument have?

Tell how many right angles each figure has. (Prior grade)

9. 

10. 

11. 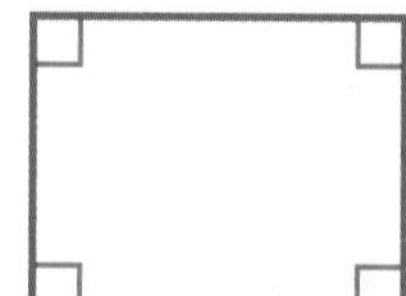

12. Explain how you know whether an angle is a right angle.

10-1 Solid Figures

GET READY to Learn

A dog crate is shown. It resembles a solid figure. A **solid figure** is a 3-dimensional figure with length, width, and height.

MAIN IDEA

I will identify and describe solid figures, and identify and draw nets.

Standard 4MG3.6 Visualize, describe, and make models of geometric solids in terms of the number and shape of faces, edges, and vertices; interpret two-dimensional representations of three-dimensional objects; and draw patterns (of faces) for a solid that, when cut and folded, will make a model of the solid.

New Vocabulary

solid figure
face
edge
vertex
net

- A **face** is a flat side.
- Two faces meet at an **edge**.
- A **vertex** is where three or more faces meet.

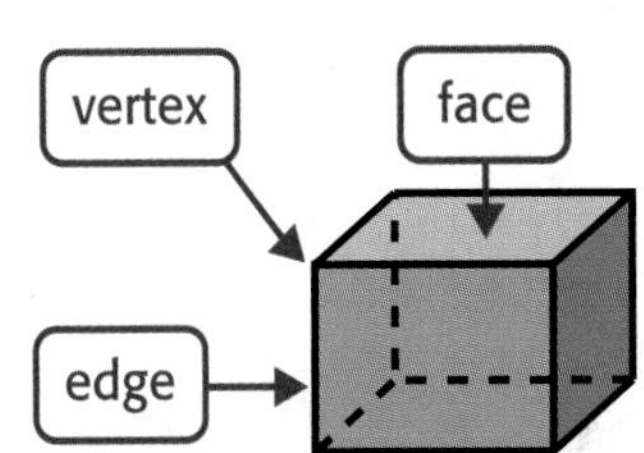

KEY CONCEPT — Solid Figures

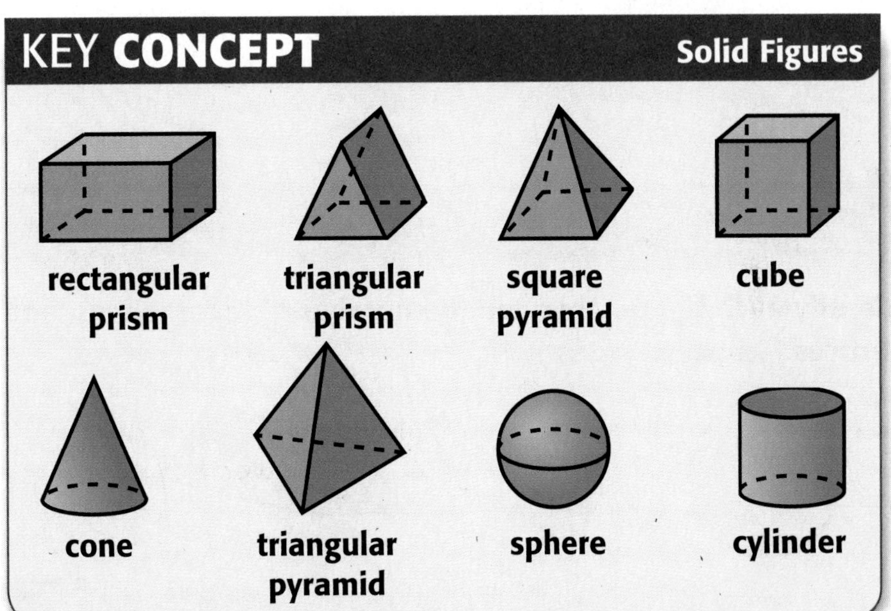

Real-World EXAMPLE — Identify Solid Objects

1 Identify the shape of the gift box. Then tell the number of faces, edges, and vertices.

The gift box is a rectangular prism.
It has 6 faces, 12 edges, and 8 vertices.

Online Personal Tutor at ca.gr4math.com

A **net** is a 2-dimensional figure that can be folded to make a solid figure.

Hands-On Mini Activity

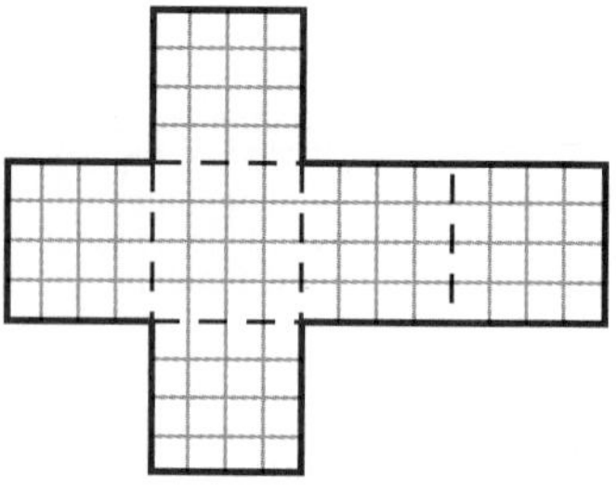

Step 1 Using grid paper, draw and cut out the net shown.

Step 2 Fold along the dotted lines. Tape the edges.

Step 3 Identify the solid.

Remember

A prism has rectangular sides. A pyramid has triangular sides.

1. Draw another net that could be used to form a cube.
2. Identify the solid figure the net shown at the right makes.
3. Explain how you can identify a shape from its net without folding the paper.

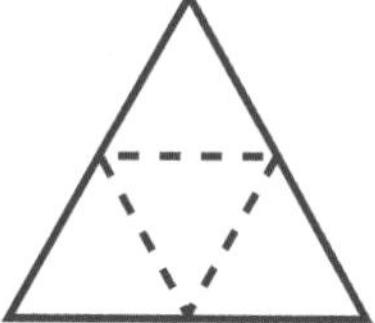

CHECK What You Know

Identify each figure. Then tell the number of faces, edges, and vertices. See Example 1 (p. 385)

1.

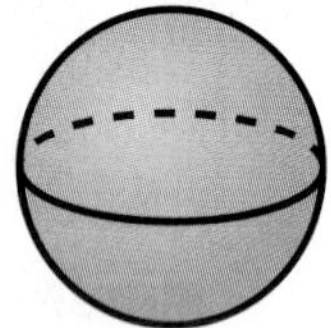

2.

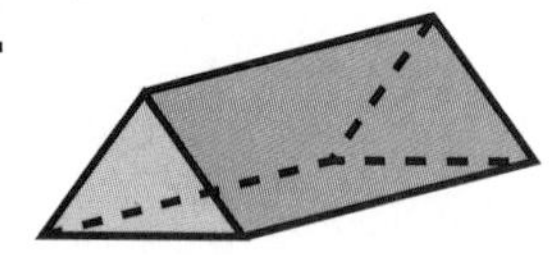

3.

Identify the solid figure each net makes.

4.

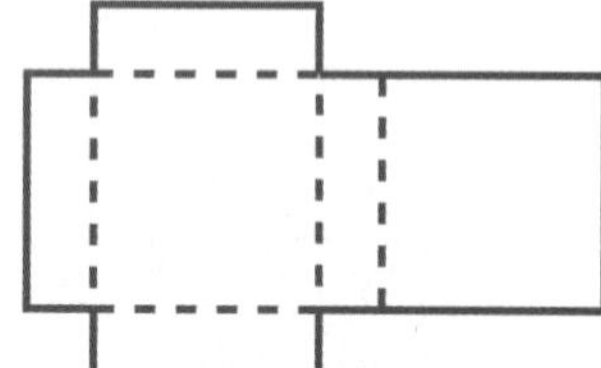

5.

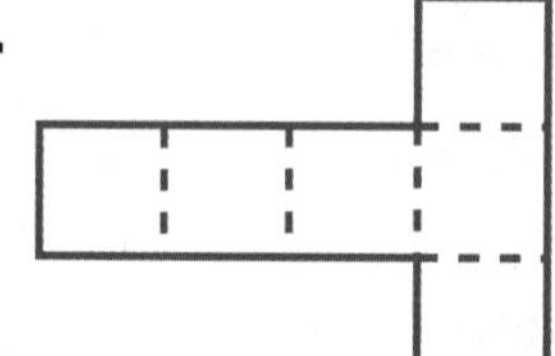

6.

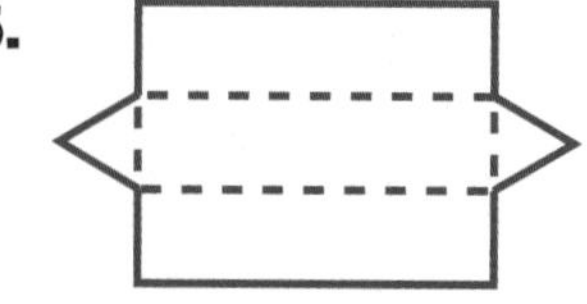

7. Name two solid figures that have 6 faces.

8. Talk About It Compare a triangular prism and a triangular pyramid.

Practice and Problem Solving

See page R24.

Identify each figure. Then tell the number of faces, edges, and vertices.
See Example 1 (p. 385)

9. 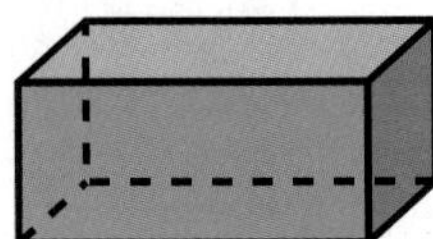

10. 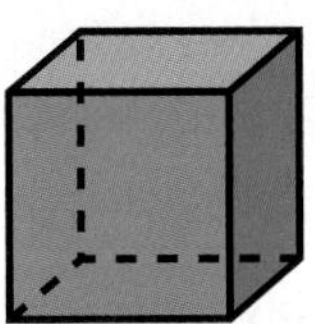

11. 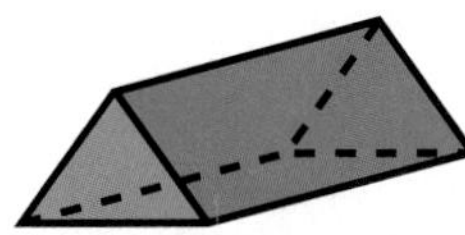

12. 

13. 

14. 

Identify the solid figure each net makes.

15. 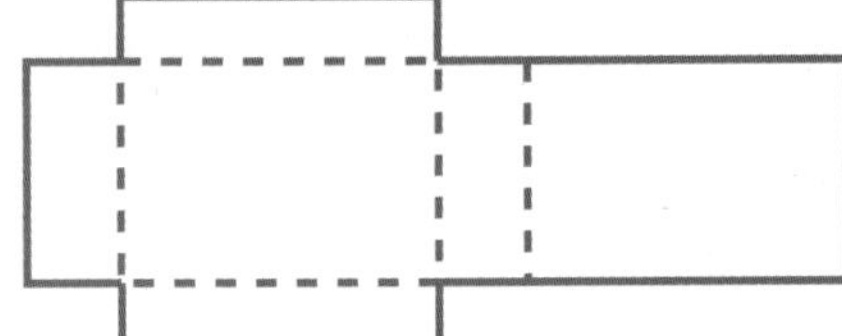

16. 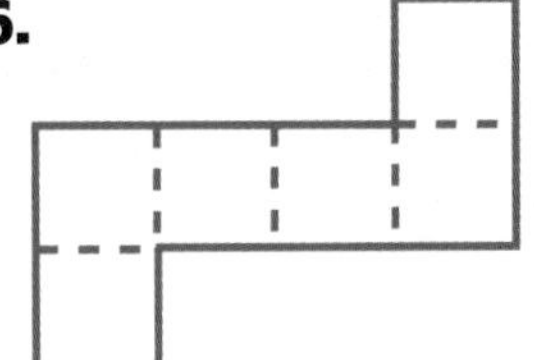

17. 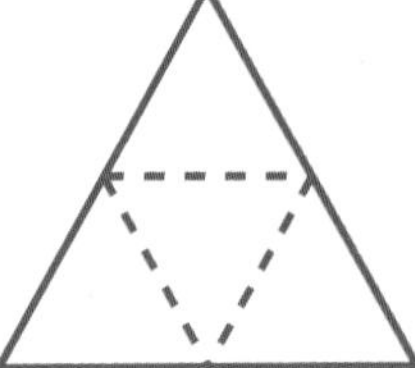

18. 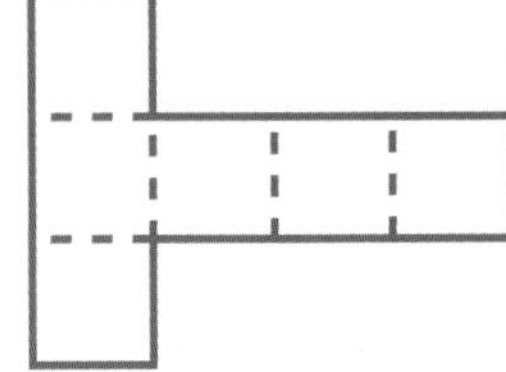

19. 

20. 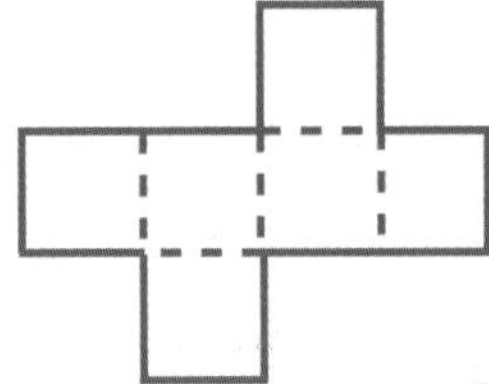

21. This solid has 4 faces, 6 edges, and 4 vertices. What solid is it?

22. This solid can be made using 2 circles and 1 large rectangle. What solid is it?

H.O.T. Problems

23. **OPEN ENDED** Draw any solid. Then describe its faces, edges, and vertices.

24. **WHICH ONE DOESN'T BELONG?** Identify the figure that does not belong with the other three.

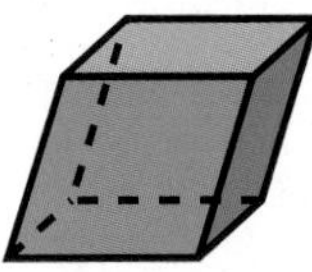

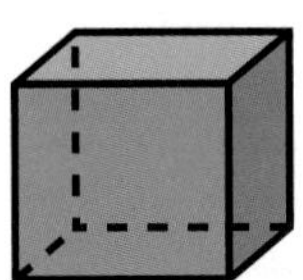

25. **WRITING IN MATH** How are a cone and cylinder alike? How are they different?

10-2 Plane Figures

GET READY to Learn

These are traffic signs that you may see every day. What shapes are the signs?

SPEED 20

MAIN IDEA

I will identify, describe, and classify plane figures.

Standard 4MG3.0 Students demonstrate an understanding of plane and solid **geometric objects and use this knowledge to** show relationships and **solve problems.**

New Vocabulary

plane figure
polygon
sides
triangle
quadrilateral
pentagon
hexagon
octagon

The shapes of the signs are plane figures. A **plane figure** is a 2-dimensional figure with length and width. **Polygons** are closed plane figures that have three or more line segments called **sides**.

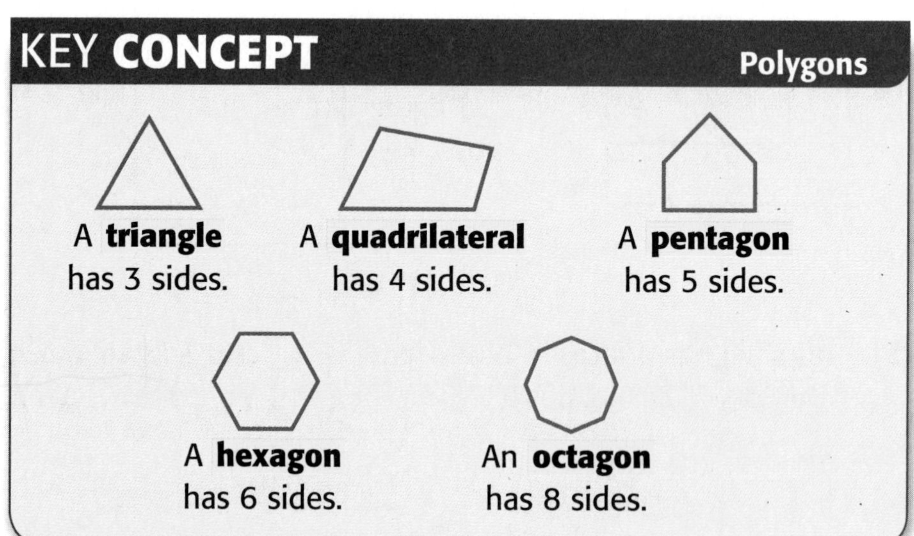

KEY CONCEPT
Polygons
A triangle has 3 sides.
A quadrilateral has 4 sides.
A pentagon has 5 sides.
A hexagon has 6 sides.
An octagon has 8 sides.

Real-World EXAMPLE Identify a Polygon

1 SPORTS Identify the shape of home plate.

Look at the shape of the home plate. It has 5 sides.

So, this figure is a pentagon.

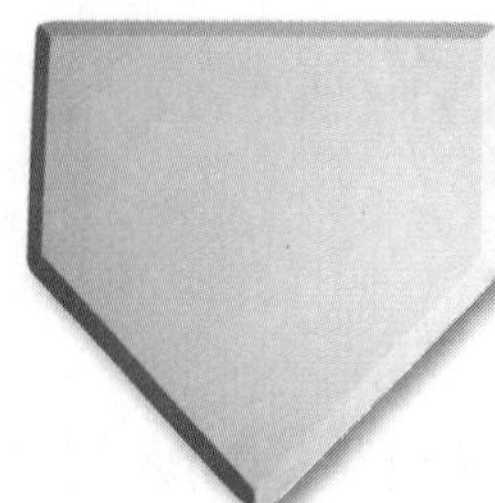

A circle is not a polygon because it does not have straight sides. Other shapes are not polygons as well.

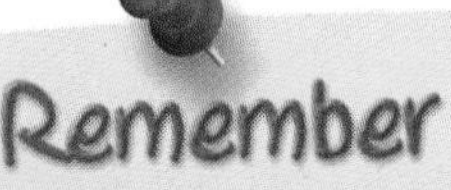

Remember

Polygons have straight sides only, not curved sides.

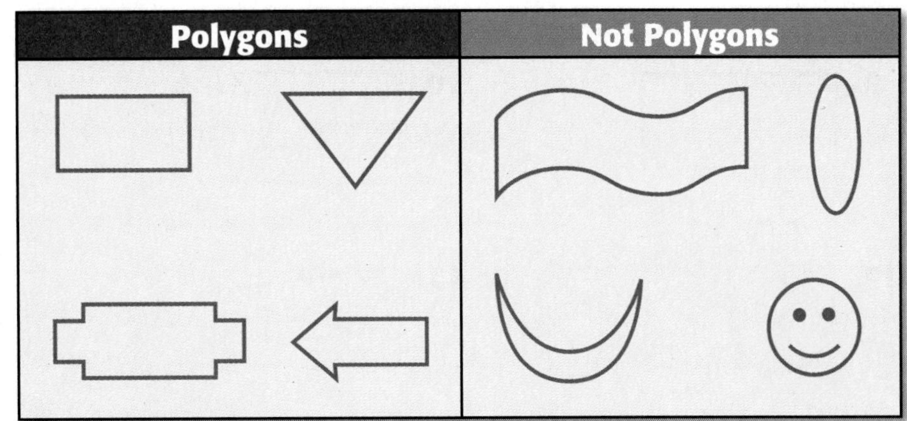

EXAMPLES Identify a Polygon

Tell whether each shape is a polygon.

2 

The figure has curved sides. It is not a polygon.

3 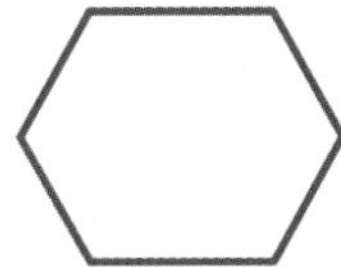

The figure has 6 sides. The sides are straight. So, it is a polygon.

Online Personal Tutor at ca.gr4math.com

CHECK What You Know

Identify each polygon. See Example 1 (p. 388)

1. 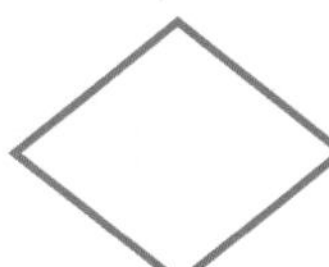

2. 

3. 

Tell whether each shape is a polygon. See Examples 2 and 3 (p. 389)

4. 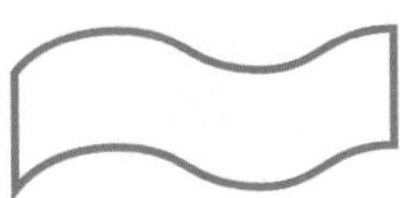

5. 

6. 

7. Identify two polygons on the soccer ball.

8. 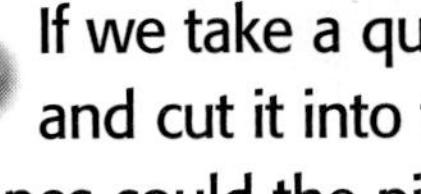

If we take a quadrilateral and cut it into two pieces, what shapes could the pieces be?

Practice and Problem Solving

See page R25.

Identify each polygon. See Example 1 (p. 388)

9. 

10. 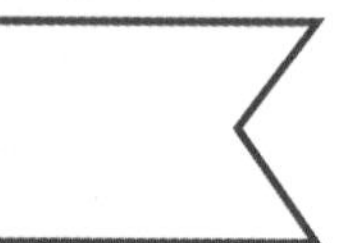

11. 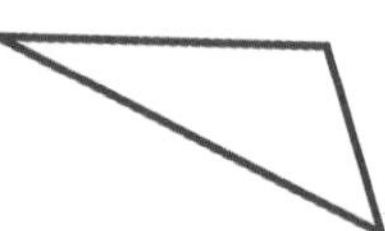

12. 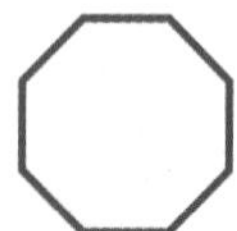

13. 

14. 

Tell whether each shape is a polygon. See Examples 2 and 3 (p. 389)

15. 

16. 

17. 

18. 

19. 

20. 

Identify two polygons in each real-world object.

21. 

22. 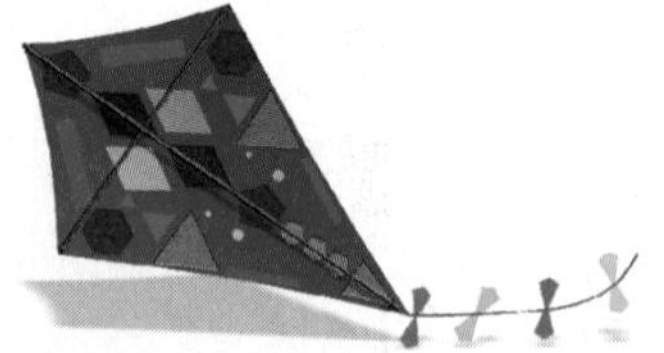

Real-World PROBLEM SOLVING

Art Polygons and other shapes are used in the painting *Castle and Sun.*

23. Name two polygons in the painting.

24. Is the sun a polygon? Explain.

25. What polygon is in the painting most often?

26. What polygon in the painting has the most sides?

H.O.T. Problems

27. OPEN ENDED Draw and identify a polygon.

28. FIND THE ERROR Carlota and Gabe are drawing a polygon. Who is correct? Explain.

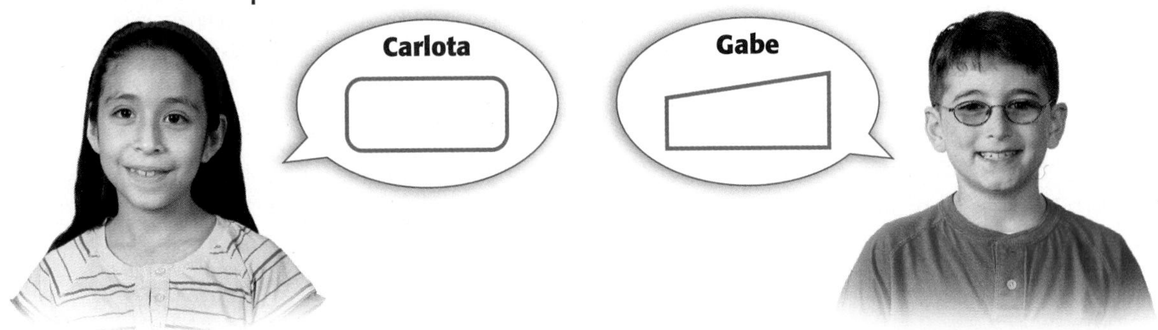

29. WRITING IN ▸MATH Write about a real-world object that is made up of polygons.

Standards Practice

30 Which figure can form a cube when folded on the dotted lines without overlapping? (Lesson 10–1)

A
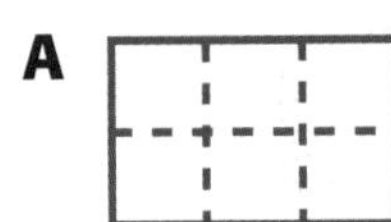

C
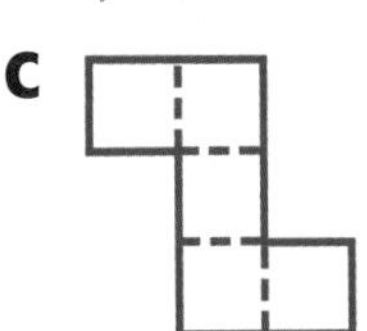

B

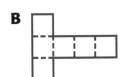

D
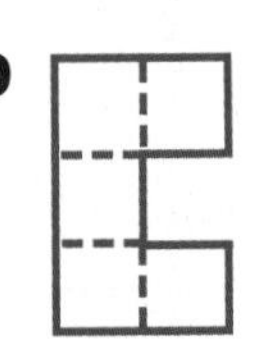

31 Which statement about these figures is true? (Lesson 10-2)

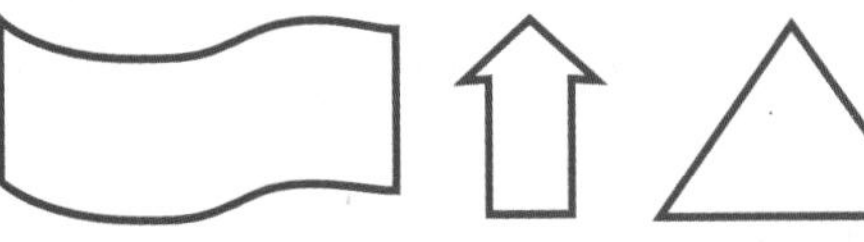

F There is one polygon.

G These are all polygons.

H There are two polygons.

J None of these are polygons.

Spiral Review

Identify each figure. Then tell the number of faces, edges, and vertices. (Lesson 10-1)

32.

33.
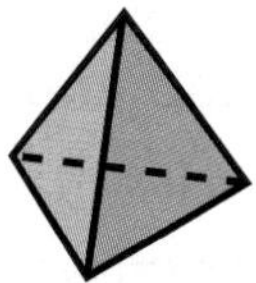

Divide. Use estimation to check. (Lesson 9-9)

34. 1,549 ÷ 3 **35.** \$2,484 ÷ 5 **36.** $7\overline{)13{,}504}$ **37.** $9\overline{)\$36{,}429}$

10-3 Problem-Solving Strategy

MAIN IDEA I will solve problems by looking for a pattern.

Standard 4MR1.1 **Analyze problems by** identifying relationships, distinguishing relevant from irrelevant information, sequencing and prioritizing information, and **observing patterns.** Standard 4MG3.0 **Students demonstrate an understanding of plane** and solid **geometric objects and use this knowledge to** show relationships and **solve problems.**

Amado is helping his dad put tile on a table top. They are laying the tiles in a pattern. They have run out of tiles and need to buy more. What color of tiles need to be purchased to complete the table?

Understand	**What facts do you know?** • You know the tiles form a pattern. • You know they need to buy more tiles. **What do you need to find?** • Find the tile colors that need to be purchased.
Plan	Look for a pattern. Then continue your pattern to find the missing tiles.
Solve	There are two rows of tile and the tiles repeat red, green, blue, and yellow.  In the first row, the missing tiles are blue and green. In the second row, the missing tiles are red, blue, and yellow. So, Amado and his father need 2 blue, 1 green, 1 red, and 1 yellow tile.
Check	Look back at the problem. The answer makes sence for the facts given. So, the answer is correct.

ANALYZE the Strategy

Refer to the problem on the previous page.

1. How do you identify a pattern in a problem-solving situation?

2. If Amado and his dad used 36 tiles, how many tiles would they use of each color?

3. Suppose Amado and his dad laid 3 more rows of tiles. How many green tiles would they need in all?

4. Look back at Exercise 3. Check your answer. Explain how you know the answer is correct.

PRACTICE the Strategy

EXTRA PRACTICE See page R25.

Solve. Use the *look for a pattern* strategy.

5. Draw the next three shapes in the pattern below.

6. **Algebra** Copy and complete the table. What might be the pattern?

Input (g)	Output (h)
6	24
8	32
5	20
3	■
■	36

7. Claudia will arrive at the airport on the first plane after 9 A.M. Planes arrive every 45 minutes after 6 A.M. When will Claudia's plane arrive?

8. Marta gathered 8 seashells on the first day, 20 on the second day, and 32 on the third day. If the pattern continues, how many shells will she gather on the fifth day?

9. Describe a pattern below. Then find the missing number.

2, 4, 8, ■, 32

10. Two hikers take turns carrying a backpack during a hike. The first hiker starts carrying the pack. They change every 3 miles. They have hiked 14 miles so far. How many times have they changed? Who has the pack now?

11. A pattern of figures is shown below. Draw the next two figures that might follow.

12. A border on a scrapbook page has a repeating design that shows a triangle, a pentagon, and a hexagon. Draw the first eight figures in the pattern.

13. **WRITING IN MATH** Create a pattern with geometric shapes. Give it to a classmate and see if he or she can continue your pattern.

10-4 Lines, Line Segments, and Rays

GET READY to Learn

Farmers often plant crops like corn in rows. The rows resemble line segments.

MAIN IDEA

I will identify, describe, and classify lines, line segments, and rays.

Standard 4MG3.1 Identify lines that are parallel and perpendicular.

New Vocabulary

line
ray
endpoint
line segment
parallel
intersecting
perpendicular

KEY CONCEPTS — Lines, Rays, Segments

Words	Model
A **line** is a straight set of points that extend in opposite directions without ending.	A B line *AB* or $\overleftrightarrow{AB}$
A **ray** is a part of a line that has one **endpoint** and extends in one direction without ending.	endpoint A B ray *AB* or $\overrightarrow{AB}$
A **line segment** is a part of a line between two endpoints.	endpoint A B $\overline{AB}$

EXAMPLES Identify Lines, Rays, or Line Segments

Identify each figure.

1 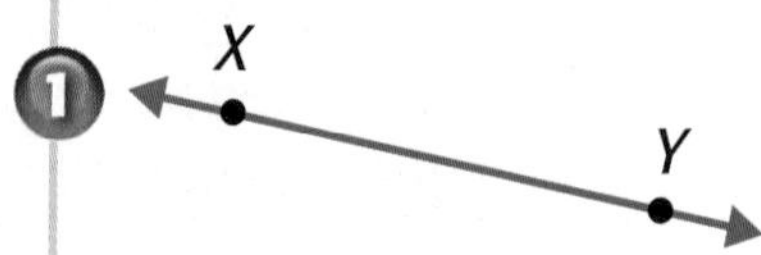

The figure extends in opposite directions without ending. Line *XY* or $\overleftrightarrow{XY}$.

2 

This figure has one endpoint and extends in one direction without ending. Ray *AB* or $\overrightarrow{AB}$.

Math Online **Extra Examples at** ca.gr4math.com

You can describe lines, rays, and line segments by the way they meet or cross each other.

Remember

The symbol || means parallel. The symbol ⊥ means perpendicular. The symbol ⌝ means right angle.

KEY CONCEPTS — Types of Lines

Words **Parallel** lines are always the same distance apart. They do not meet.

Model

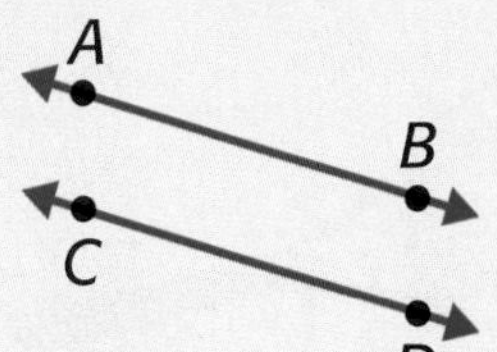

line *AB* is parallel to line *CD*

$\overleftrightarrow{AB} \parallel \overleftrightarrow{CD}$

Words Lines that meet or cross each other are called **intersecting** lines.

Model

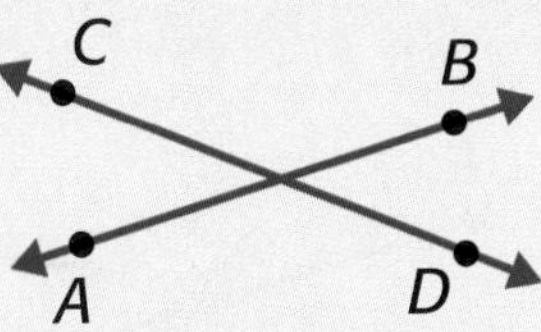

line *AB* intersects line *CD*

$\overleftrightarrow{AB}$ intersects $\overleftrightarrow{CD}$

Words Lines that meet or cross each other to form right angles are called **perpendicular** lines.

Model

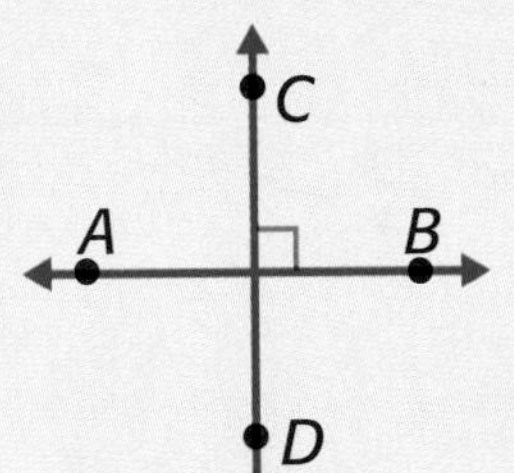

line *AB* is perpendicular to line *CD*

$\overleftrightarrow{AB} \perp \overleftrightarrow{CD}$

EXAMPLE Describe Lines

3 Describe the figure.

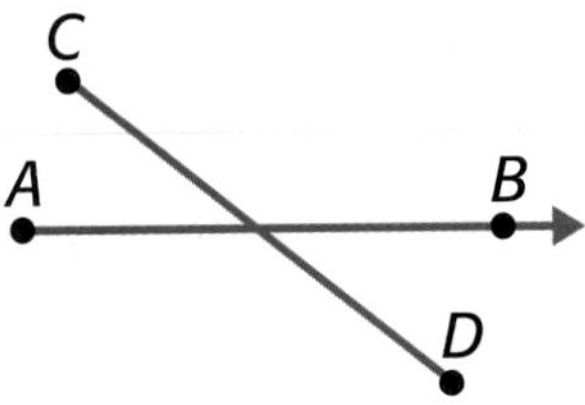

The figure shows ray *AB* and line segment *CD*. Notice that ray *AB* intersects line segment *CD*.

$\overrightarrow{AB}$ intersects $\overline{CD}$.

Online Personal Tutor at ca.gr4math.com

CHECK What You Know

Identify each figure. See Examples 1 and 2 (p. 394)

1. Q R

2.

3. A C

4. Describe the line segments formed on a tennis racquet. See Example 3 (p. 395)

5. Talk About It List a real-world example for a line segment, parallel lines, and intersecting lines.

Practice and Problem Solving

EXTRA PRACTICE See page R25.

Identify each figure. See Examples 1 and 2 (p. 394)

6.

7.

8.

Describe the figure. See Example 3 (p. 395)

9. B F D E

10.

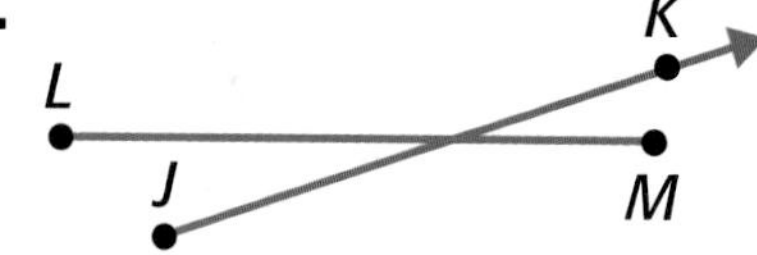

11.

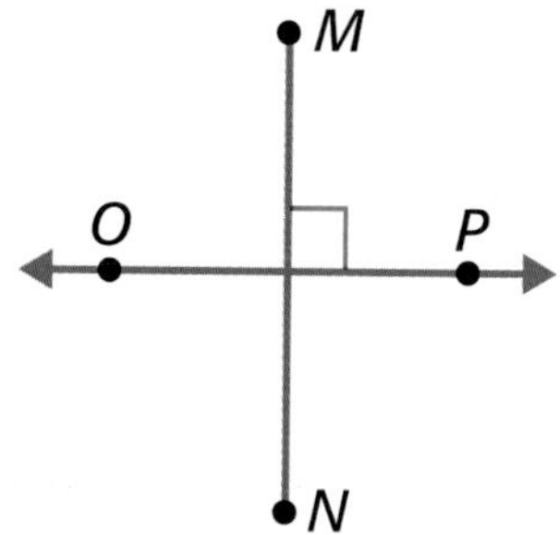

Real-World PROBLEM SOLVING

Geography On a map, streets resemble line segments. Use the map to the right to answer Exercises 12–15.

12. Identify two streets that are parallel to Oak Street.

13. Tell whether Center Street and Johnston Street are parallel, intersecting, or perpendicular lines. Explain.

14. Identify two streets that are parallel.

15. Are there any streets that are intersecting? Explain.

Pine St
Stephenson St
School St
Queen St
Johnston St
Oak St
Oak St
Center St
Church St
Main St

H.O.T. Problems

OPEN ENDED Draw an example of each figure described.

16. ray *CD*

17. $\overleftrightarrow{DE} \parallel \overleftrightarrow{FG}$

18. $\overline{RS}$ intersecting $\overline{TU}$

REASONING Tell whether each statement is *true* or *false*.

19. If two lines are parallel, they are the same distance apart.

20. If two lines are parallel, they are also perpendicular.

21. **WRITING IN ►MATH** Can you draw two lines on a sheet of paper that are both parallel and perpendicular? Explain.

Standards Practice

22 The figure below has five sides. What is it called? (Lesson 10-2)

A hexagon

B triangle

C octagon

D pentagon

23 Which figure shows parallel lines? (Lesson 10-4)

F

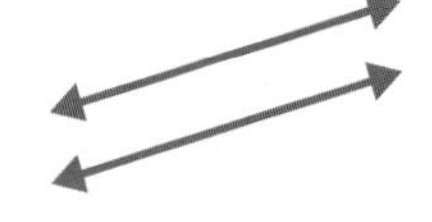

H

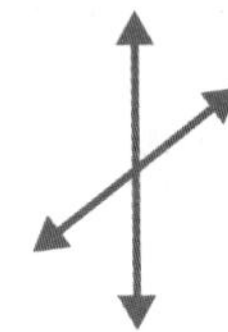

G

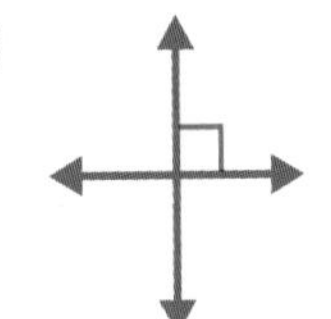

J

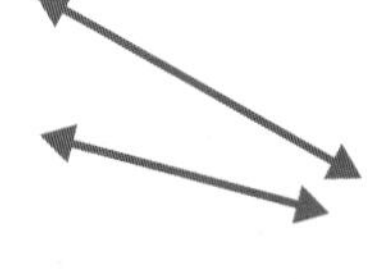

Spiral Review

For Exercises 24 and 25, use the table. (Lesson 10-3)

24. Mr. Ito's class is playing a game. The table shows how many playing pieces are needed. Copy and complete the table.

25. Explain how to find the number of pieces needed if you know the number of students playing.

Game Pieces Needed

Students	Number of Pieces
4	36
7	63
■	72
9	■
10	90

Identify each polygon. (Lesson 10-2)

26.

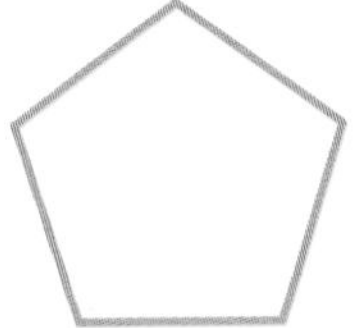

27.

28.

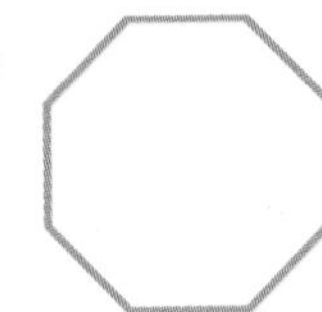

10-5 Angles

MAIN IDEA

I will identify, describe and classify angles.

Standard 4MG3.5 Know the definitions of a right angle, an acute angle, and an obtuse angle. Understand that 90°, 180°, 270°, and 360° are associated, respectively, with $\frac{1}{4}$, $\frac{1}{2}$, $\frac{3}{4}$ and full turns.

New Vocabulary

angle
right angle
acute angle
obtuse angle

GET READY to Learn

Brent's teacher assigned ten problems for homework. Brent started his homework at 4:00 P.M. He completed it at the time shown. How far has the minute hand turned?

An **angle** is a figure made from two rays that have the same endpoint. Angles are measured in degrees (°).

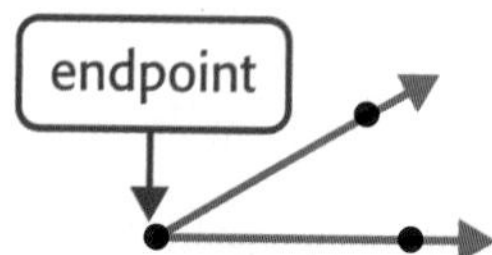

KEY CONCEPT — Turns and Angles

90° — $\frac{1}{4}$ turn

180° — $\frac{1}{2}$ turn

270° — $\frac{3}{4}$ turn

360° — full turn

Real-World EXAMPLE — Turns and Angles

1 **MEASUREMENT Refer to the clock above. Write how far the minute hand has turned in degrees and as a fraction.**

Compare the angle shown on the clock to the angles shown in the Key Concept box.

So, the angle shown on the clock is 90° or a $\frac{1}{4}$ turn.

Remember

A corner, like the corners on a desk, is a right angle.

KEY CONCEPT — Types of Angles

A **right angle** measures 90°. A right angle is formed by perpendicular rays.

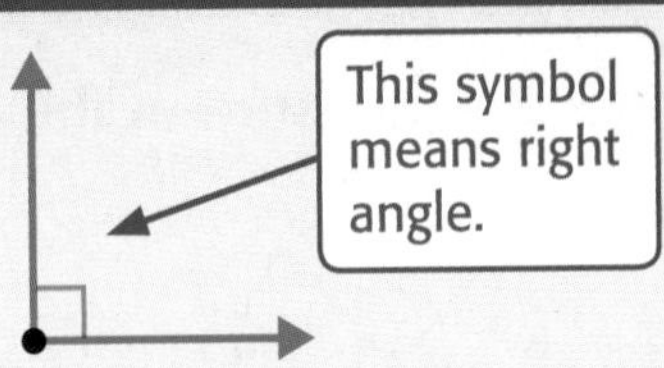
This symbol means right angle.

An **acute angle** measures greater than 0° and less than 90°.

An **obtuse angle** measures greater than 90°, but less than 180°.

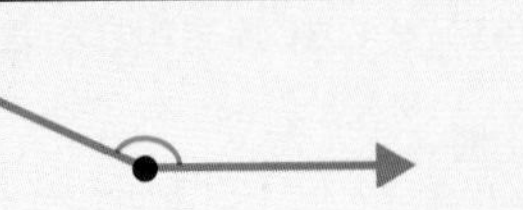

EXAMPLES Classify an Angle

Classify each angle as *right*, *acute*, or *obtuse*.

2 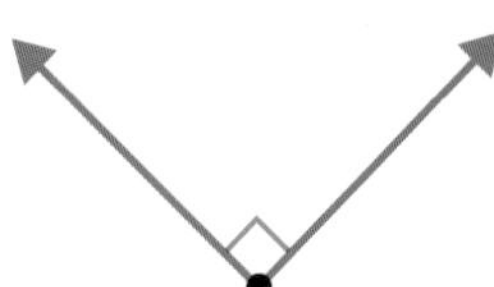

The angle is 90°.
So, it is a right angle.

3 

The angle is greater than 90° and less than than 180°.
So, it is an obtuse angle.

Online Personal Tutor at ca.gr4math.com

CHECK What You Know

Write the measure of each angle in degrees and as a fraction. See Example 1 (p. 398)

1. 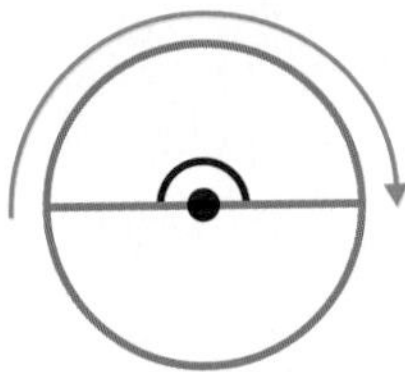

2. 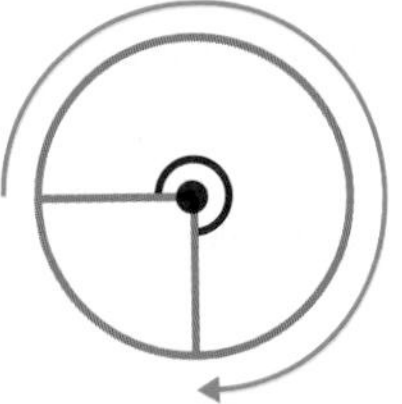

3. 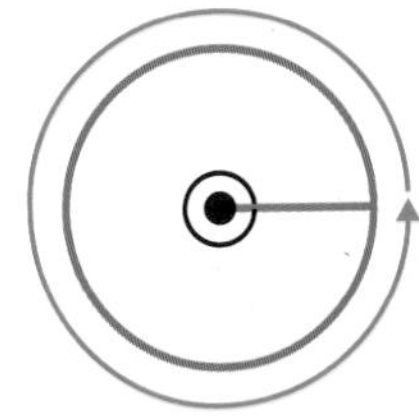

Classify each angle as *right*, *acute*, or *obtuse*. See Examples 2 and 3 (p. 399)

4. 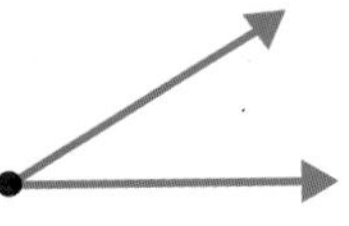

5. 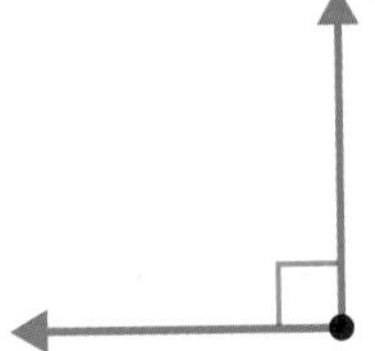

6. 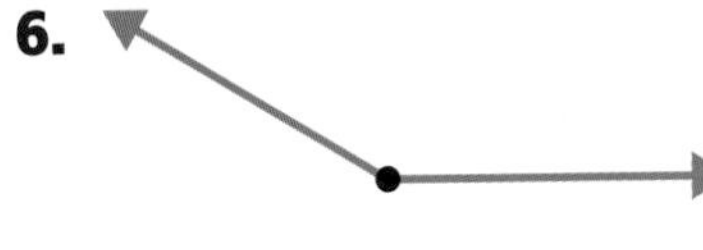

7. Talk About It Describe an *acute*, *obtuse* and *right angle*.

Practice and Problem Solving

EXTRA PRACTICE
See page R26.

Write the measure of the angle in degrees and as a fraction of a full turn. See Example 1 (p. 398)

8. 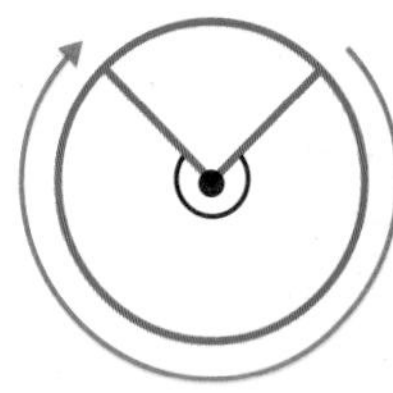

9. 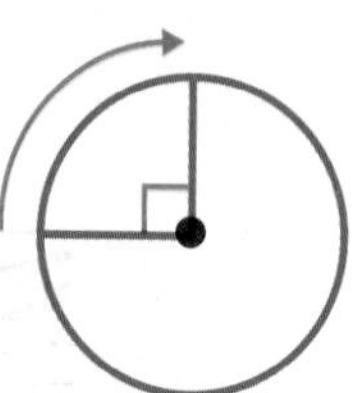

10. 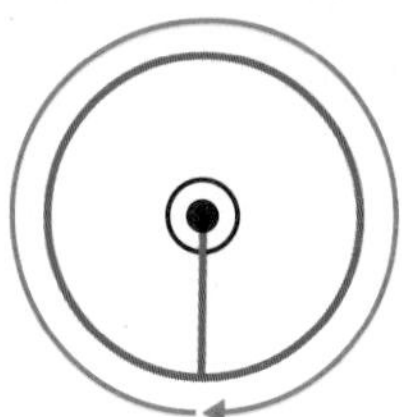

Classify each angle as *right, acute,* or *obtuse*. See Examples 2 and 3 (p. 399)

11.

12. 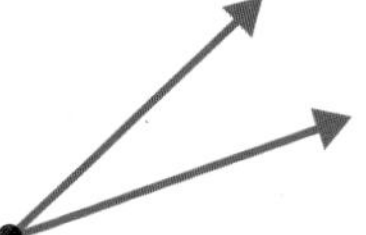

13. 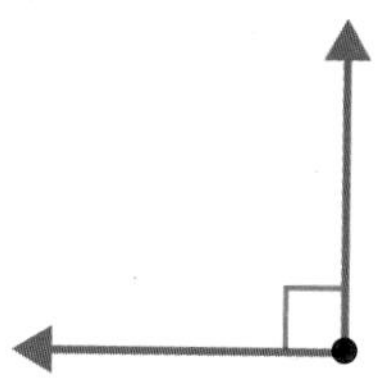

14. 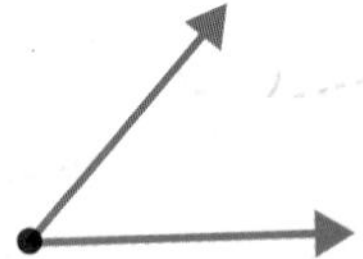

15. 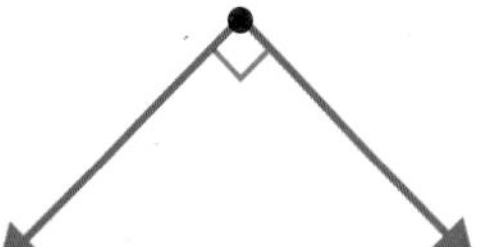

16. 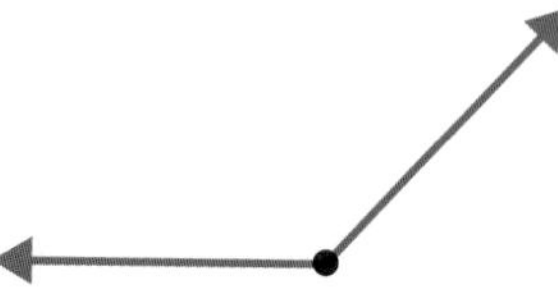

17. The timer is set to 30 minutes. How many degrees will the dial have turned when the timer goes off?

18. Classify the angle shown on the gas gauge below.

Real-World PROBLEM SOLVING

Geography A compass can be used to find direction. The arrow on a compass always faces north.

19. If you are facing north and turn west, what angle could be drawn to represent your movement?

20. You are facing east and are told to turn 180°. What direction will you be facing? Write the angle your body has turned as a fraction?

H.O.T. Problems

21. OPEN ENDED Draw three different acute angles.

22. WRITING IN MATH Choose three objects in your classroom that have angles. Classify each angle as *acute*, *obtuse*, or *right*.

CHAPTER 10 Mid-Chapter Check

Lessons 10-1 through 10-5

Identify each figure. Then tell the number of faces, edges, and vertices. (Lesson 10-1)

1. 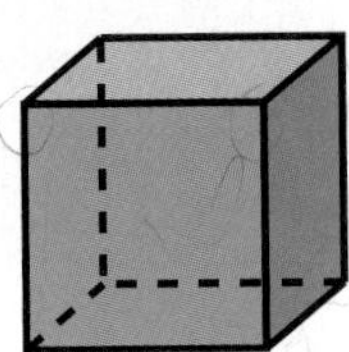

2. 

3. Identify the solid figure the net would make. (Lesson 10-1)

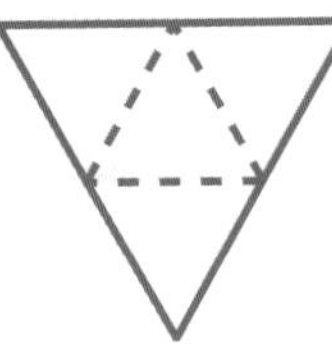

Identify each polygon. (Lesson 10-2)

4. 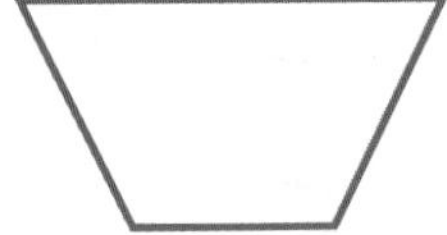

5. 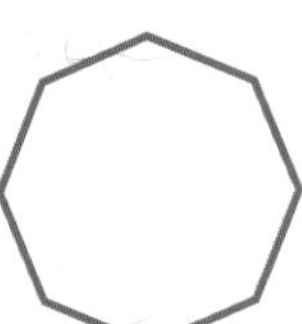

6. **STANDARDS PRACTICE** Look at the figures below. (Lesson 10-2)

 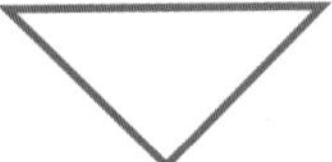 

Which statement is true?

A There is 1 polygon.

B These are all polygons.

C There are 2 polygons.

D None of these are polygons.

7. Identify two polygons on the bird house. (Lesson 10-2)

8. **STANDARDS PRACTICE** What is the figure called? (Lesson 10-2)

F hexagon

G triangle

H octagon

J pentagon

For Exercises 9 and 10, solve. Use the *look for a pattern* strategy. (Lesson 10-3)

9. Describe a pattern in 3, 9, 27, ■, 243. Then find the missing number.

10. A ferry leaves the harbor every 35 minutes. The first ferry leaves at 6:30 A.M. Davion plans on taking the first ferry after 8 A.M. When will his ferry leave?

Identify each figure. (Lesson 10-4)

11. A B

12. C D

Write the measure of each angle in degrees and as a fraction. (Lesson 10-5)

13. 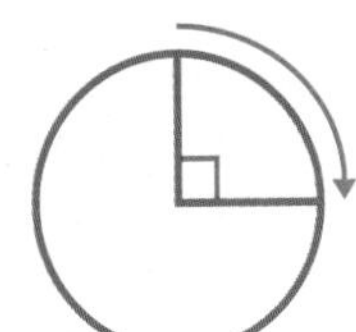

14. 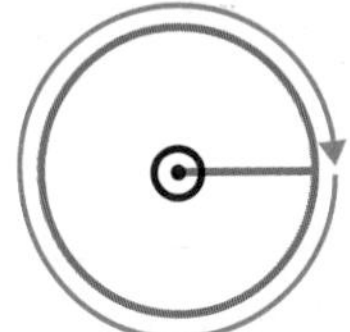

15. **WRITING IN MATH** Can a figure be a polygon and a solid? Explain.

Problem-Solving Investigation

MAIN IDEA I will choose the best strategy to solve a problem.

Standard 4MR2.3 **Use a variety of methods, such as words,** numbers, symbols, charts, graphs, tables, diagrams, **and models, to explain mathematical reasoning.** Standard 4MG3.0 **Students demonstrate an understanding of plane** and solid **geometric objects and use this knowledge to** show relationships and **solve problems.**

P.S.I. TEAM +

ARTURO: **I have the five puzzle pieces shown. I need to form a square using all of the pieces.**

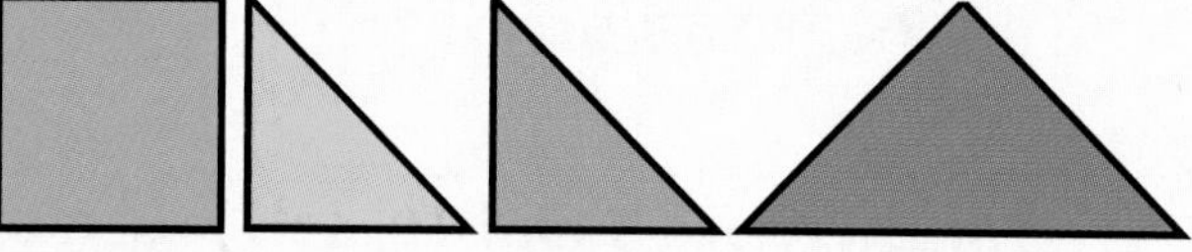

YOUR MISSION: **Arrange the five puzzle pieces to form a square.**

Understand	You know there are five puzzle pieces. Find how to arrange the pieces to form a square.
Plan	Use the *act it out* strategy. Trace the pieces and cut them out of paper. Then arrange the polygons in different ways to figure out how they will form a square.
Solve	Arrange the pieces in different ways until you form a square. 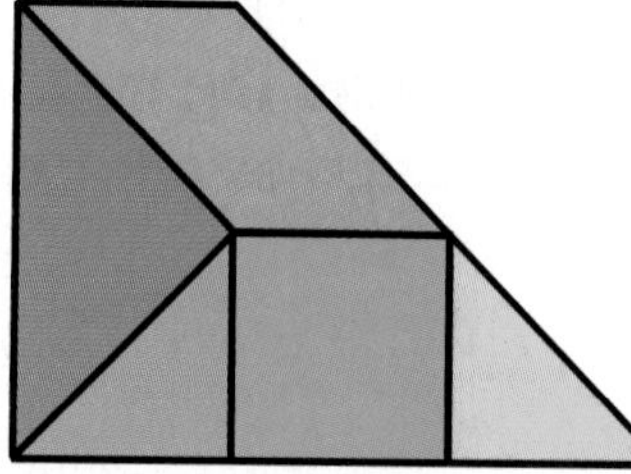 
Check	Look back at the problem. The figure formed by the pieces is a square because it is a rectangle that has four equal sides. So, the answer is correct.

Mixed Problem Solving

See page R26.

Use any strategy shown below to solve. Tell what strategy you used.

PROBLEM-SOLVING STRATEGIES
- Make a table.
- Act it out.
- Guess and check.
- Look for a pattern.

1. Keli can run 3 miles in 36 minutes. She plans to improve her time by running 1 mile one minute faster every 2 weeks. Is it reasonable to say that Keli will be able to run 3 miles in 25 minutes in 3 weeks? Explain.

2. Identify four bills worth $50 using $1, $5, $10, and $20 bills.

3. Draw the possible next three figures in the pattern below.

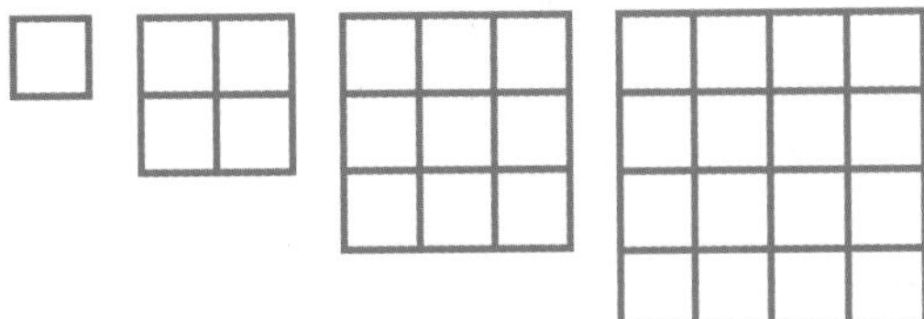

4. Pilar had 8 trading cards. She then bought some packs with 6 cards in each pack. Pilar now has 44 cards. How many packs did she buy?

5. Kareem has $20. He wants to buy the items shown. Will he have enough money? Explain. (Lesson 1-3)

$9 $8 $4

6. Kala wants to download 12 songs on her digital music player. She only has 5 minutes to download the songs. If it takes 30 seconds for Kala to download one song, will she have enough time to download all of the songs? Explain.

7. Suppose the polygons below repeat to form a pattern. How many sides might the ninth polygon have?

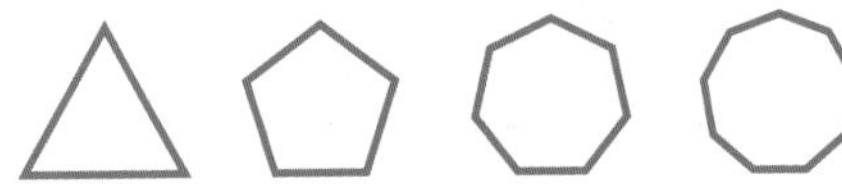

8. Mason has $12. He earns $5 every week for doing chores. Is it reasonable to say that Mason will be able to buy a skateboard that costs $60 in 10 weeks? Explain.

9. A number is multiplied by 2. Then 4 is subtracted from the product. The result is 8. What was the original number?

10. During football practice, Emilio is running drills. He runs 20 yards forward and then 10 yards backward starting at one goal line. How many sets will it take him to reach the other goal line 100 yards away?

11. WRITING IN MATH Look at Exercise 7. Which problem-solving strategy did you use to find the answer? Explain how you used this strategy to solve the problem.

10-7 Triangles

MAIN IDEA

I will identify, describe, and classify triangles.

Standard 4MG3.7 Know the definitions of different triangles (e.g. equilateral, isosceles, scalene) and identify their attributes.

New Vocabulary

isosceles triangle
equilateral triangle
scalene triangle
right triangle
acute triangle
obtuse triangle

GET READY to Learn

This sandwich is cut in half. What figure does each half resemble?

There are many different types of triangles. You can classify triangles by the lengths of their sides.

KEY CONCEPT — Classify Triangles by Sides

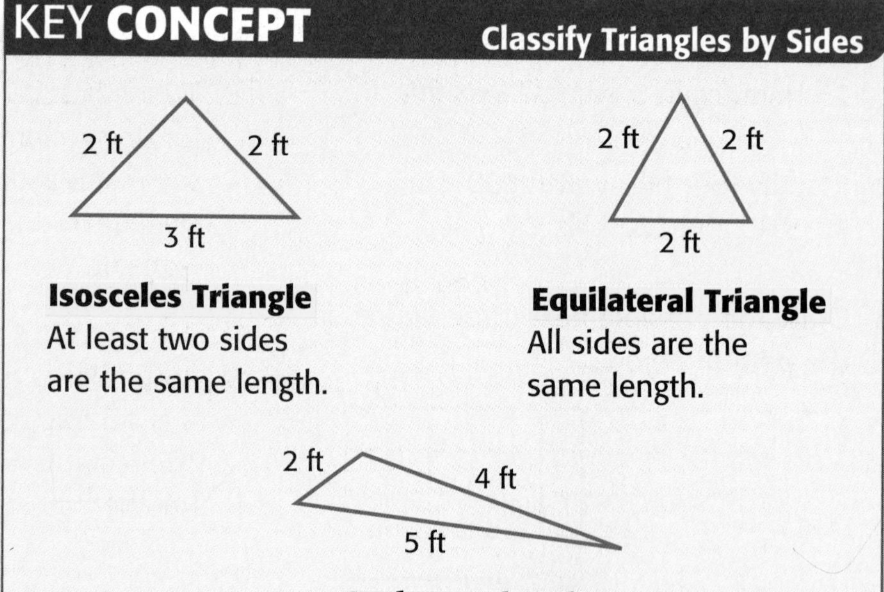

Isosceles Triangle
At least two sides are the same length.

Equilateral Triangle
All sides are the same length.

Scalene Triangle
No sides are the same length.

EXAMPLE Classify by Sides

1. **Classify the triangle. Use *isosceles, equilateral,* or *scalene*.**

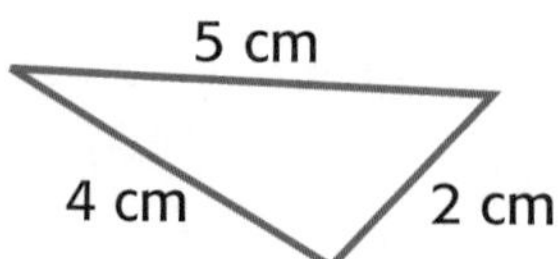

Since no sides are the same length, the triangle is scalene.

Triangles can also be classified by the measure of their angles.

Remember

In a right triangle, two sides are perpendicular to each other.

KEY CONCEPT — Classify Triangles by Angles

A **right triangle** has one right angle.

An **acute triangle** has three angles that are less than 90°.

An **obtuse triangle** has one obtuse angle.

EXAMPLE — Classify by Sides and Angles

2 Classify the triangle. Use *isosceles, equilateral,* or *scalene* and *acute, right,* or *obtuse.*

All of the sides are the same length, the triangle is equilateral. The triangle has three angles that are less than 90°, so it is also acute.

Online **Personal Tutor at** ca.gr4math.com

CHECK What You Know

Classify each triangle. Use *acute, right,* or *obtuse* and *isosceles, equilateral,* or *scalene.* See Examples 1 and 2 (pp. 404–405)

1.

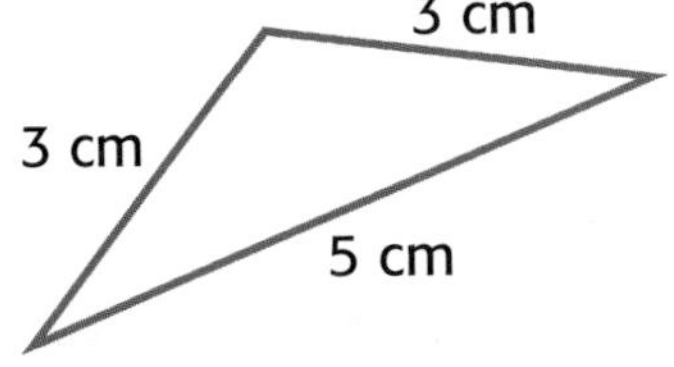

2.

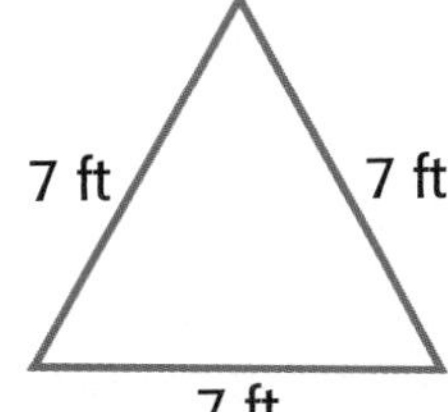

3.

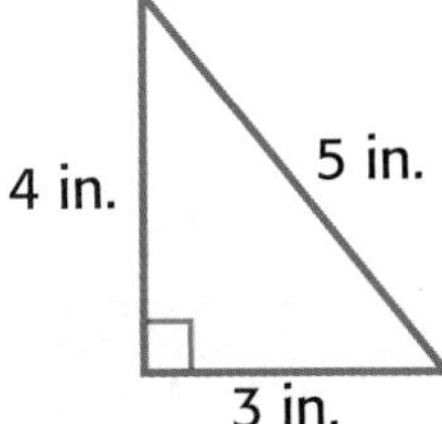

4. Rex has a pennant hanging in his room. What type of triangle is the pennant?

5. Talk About It — Two sides of an equilateral triangle measure 3 feet. What is the measure of the third side? Explain.

Practice and Problem Solving

EXTRA PRACTICE
See page R26.

Classify each triangle. Use *acute, right,* or *obtuse* and *isosceles, equilateral,* or *scalene.* See Examples 1 and 2 (pp. 404–405)

6.

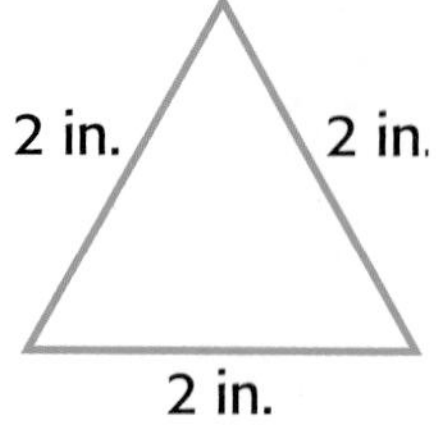

7.

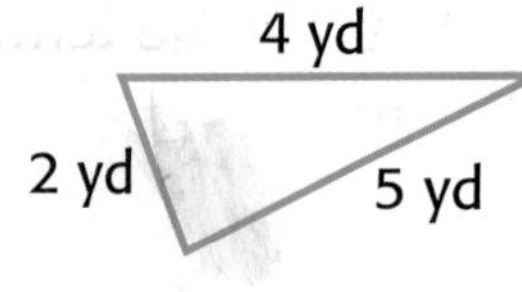

8.

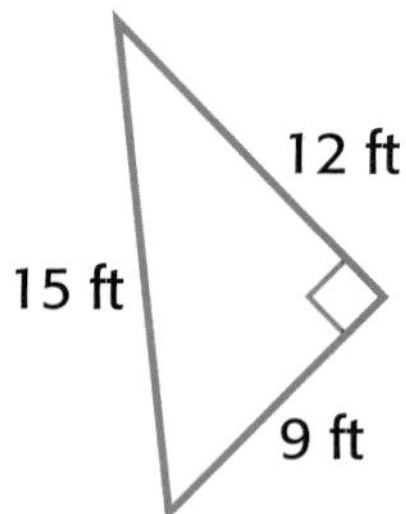

9.

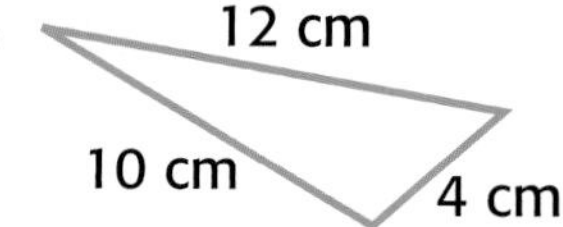

10.

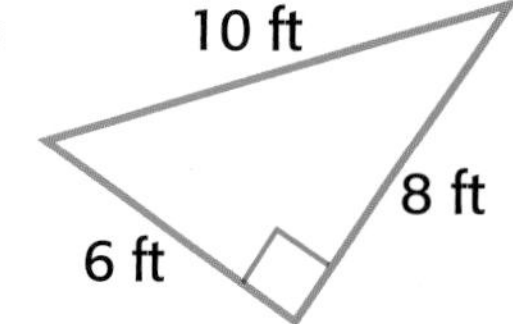

11.

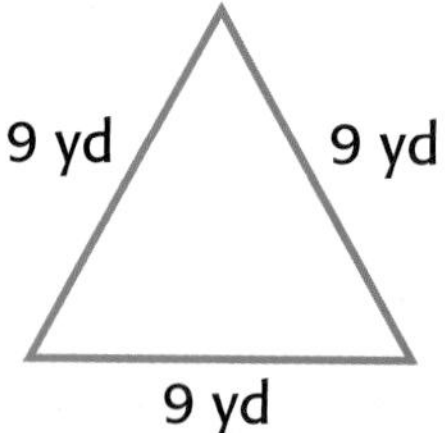

Draw an example of each triangle.

12. right scalene triangle

13. obtuse isosceles triangle

14. Describe the triangle formed by the ladder and the wall.

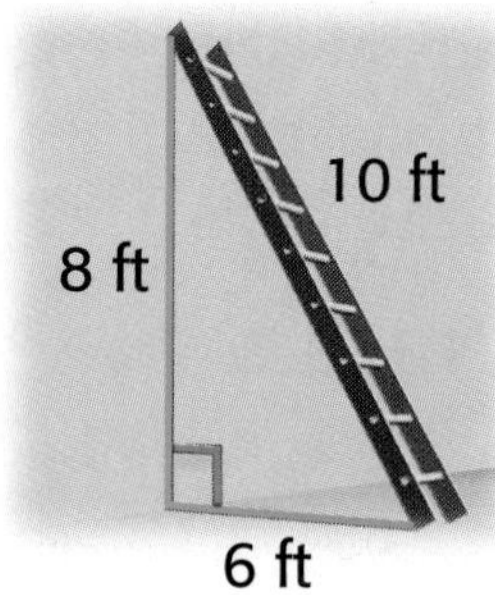

15. Classify the triangle on the wedge of cheese.

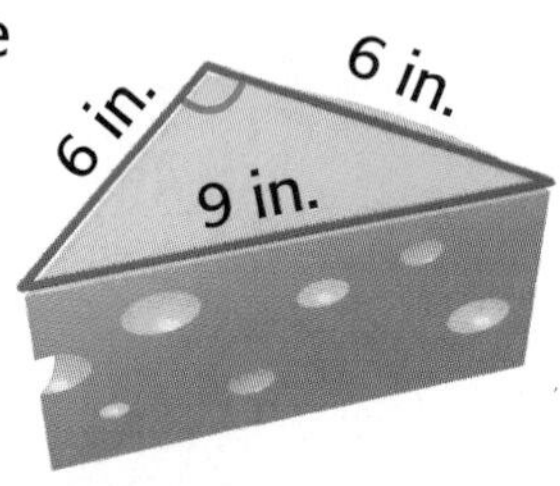

16. Shonda draws an equilateral triangle with 2 sides that equal 12 inches in length when added together. What is the length of the third side?

17. Measurement Ross draws an isosceles triangle with sides 5 centimeters and 3 centimeters. What could the measure of the third side be?

18. Algebra Copy and complete the table.

Polygon	Triangle	Square	Pentagon	Hexagon	Octagon
Number of Triangles in Polygon	1	2	3	■	■
Number of Sides in Polygon	3	4	■	6	8

H.O.T. Problems

19. **OPEN ENDED** Draw a triangle. Describe it in as many ways as you can.

20. **WHICH ONE DOESN'T BELONG?** Identify the term that does not belong with the other three. Explain.

right | obtuse | scalene | acute

21. **WRITING IN ▶MATH** Can an equilateral triangle be obtuse? Explain your answer.

Standards Practice

22 In the figure, which two angles appear to be obtuse? **(Lesson 10-5)**

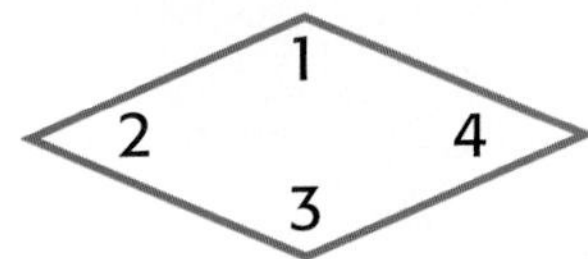

A Angles 1 and 2

B Angles 1 and 3

C Angles 1 and 4

D Angles 2 and 4

23 What kind of triangle always has 3 acute angles and 3 sides the same length? **(Lesson 10-7)**

F isosceles

G right

H equilateral

J scalene

Spiral Review

24. Suppose the pattern at the right was extended to 30 shapes in all. How many pentagons and octagons would there be? **(Lesson 10-6)**

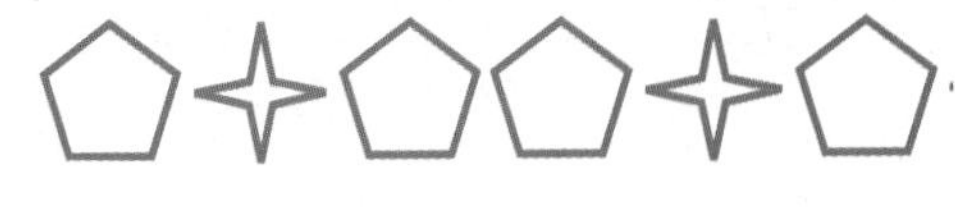

Classify each angle as *right, acute,* or *obtuse.* **(Lesson 10-5)**

25. 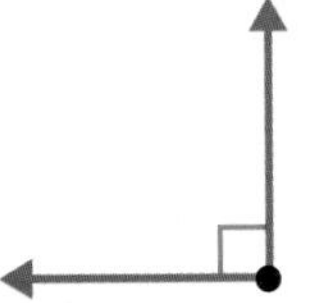

26. 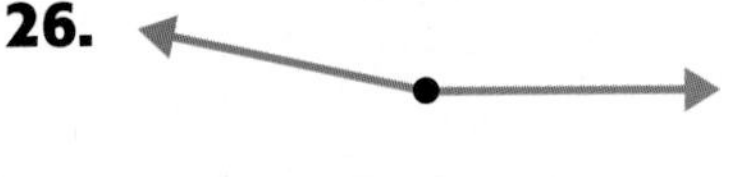

27. 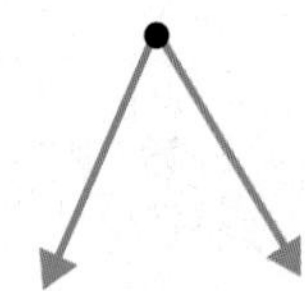

Identify the first five multiples for each number. **(Lesson 5-9)**

28. 3 **29.** 5 **30.** 8 **31.** 11

Problem Solving in Art

Garden Art

Four-Sided Pyramid

The Sculpture Garden in Washington, D.C., is filled with many shapes. It has 17 large sculptures. Many of these sculptures are made of different solid figures. For example, the *Four-Sided Pyramid* is made of concrete cubes. It is around 32 feet tall and 33 feet wide.

Another sculpture in this garden, *Cluster of Four Cubes,* is made of four metal cubes that spin in the breeze. These cubes are about 9 feet high in the air. *Moondog* is a metal sculpture that has triangles, hexagons, and pentagons in its shape. It is so large you can walk under it!

Did You Know?

There are 624 cubes in the *Four-Sided Pyramid.*

Standard 4MG3.6 Visualize, **describe,** and make models of **geometric solids in terms of the number and shape of faces, edges, and vertices;** interpret two-dimensional representations of three-dimensional objects; and draw patterns of a solid that, when cut and folded, will make a model of the solid.

Cluster of Four Cubes

Moondog

Real-World Math

Use the artwork *Moondog, Four-Sided Pyramid,* and *Cluster of Four Cubes* to solve each problem.

1. What geometric shape does the *Four-Sided Pyramid* resemble?
2. How many faces, edges, and vertices does the *Four-Sided Pyramid* have?
3. How many edges does one cube in *Cluster of Four Cubes* have?
4. Can you see a rectangle in the picture of *Moondog*? Explain.
5. How many equilateral triangles do you see in the picture of *Moondog*?
6. All the edges of the *Four-Sided Pyramid* are equal. What kind of triangles make up the faces? How many triangles are there?
7. Suppose one face of a cube on *Cluster of Four Cubes* is cut diagonally. What kind of triangle will it make?

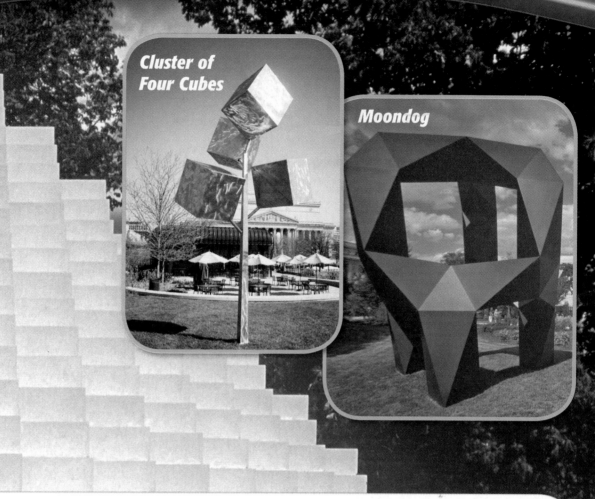

10-8 Quadrilaterals

GET READY to Learn

There are many quadrilaterals in these fields. How can you describe some of the different figures?

MAIN IDEA

I will identify, describe, and classify quadrilaterals.

Standard 4MG3.8 Know the definitions of different quadrilaterals (e.g. rhombus, square, rectangle, parallelogram, trapezoid).

New Vocabulary

rectangle
square
rhombus
parallelogram
trapezoid

All quadrilaterals have 4 sides and 4 angles.

KEY CONCEPT — Quadrilaterals

A **rectangle** has 4 right angles, with opposite sides equal and parallel.

A **square** has 4 right angles, with opposite sides parallel. All sides are equal in length.

A **rhombus** has 4 equal sides and opposite sides are parallel.

These marks show equal sides.

A **parallelogram** has opposite sides equal in length and parallel.

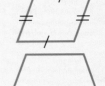

A **trapezoid** has exactly 1 pair of parallel sides.

EXAMPLE — Classify a Quadrilateral

1 Classify the quadrilateral in as many ways as possible.

It can be classified as a parallelogram, rectangle, square, and rhombus.

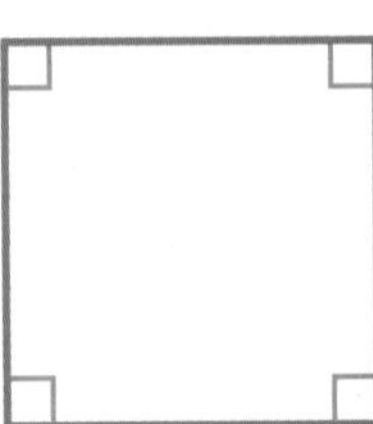

Many real-world objects have the shapes of quadrilaterals.

Real-World EXAMPLES Real-World Shapes

2 VIDEO GAMES Write the type of quadrilateral that best describes the game controller.

The game controller has one pair of parallel sides. So, it has the shape of a trapezoid.

3 Identify the shape outlined in the sculpture.

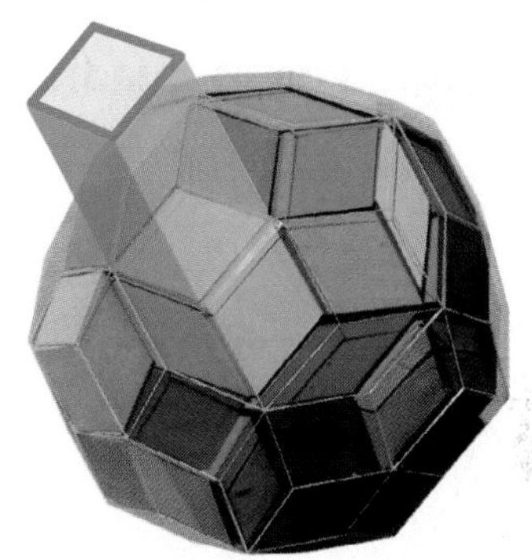

The opposite sides of the shape are equal and parallel. So, the shape is a parallelogram.

Online **Personal Tutor at** ca.gr4math.com

CHECK What You Know

Classify each quadrilateral in as many ways as possible.

See Example 1 (p. 410)

1. 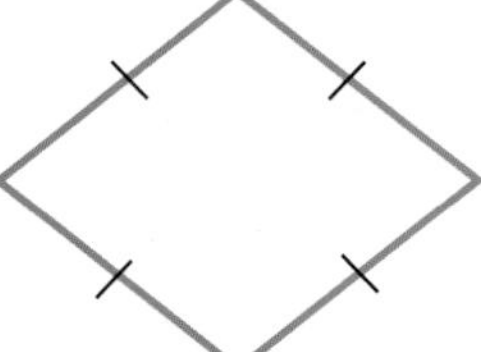

2. 

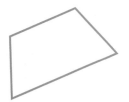

3. 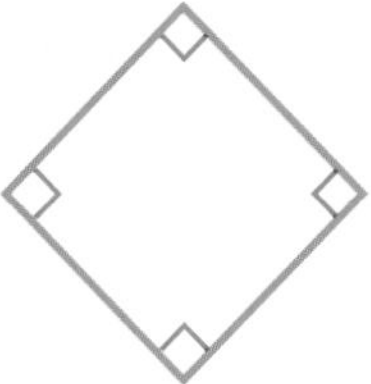

Write the type of quadrilateral that best describes the shape.

See Examples 2–3 (p. 411)

4. 

5. 

6. 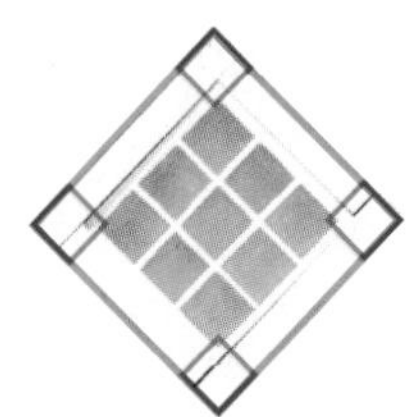

7. Talk About It How are a square and a rhombus alike? How are they different?

Practice and Problem Solving

EXTRA PRACTICE See page R27.

Classify each quadrilateral in as many ways as possible.
See Example 1 (p. 410)

8. 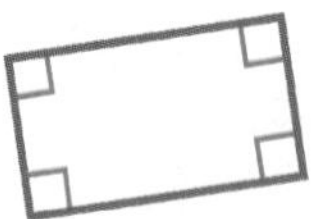

9. 

10. 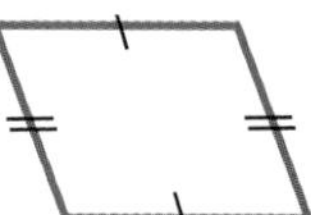

11. 

12. 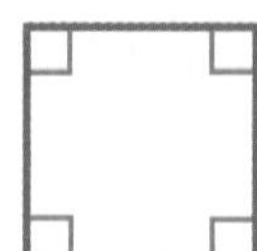

13. 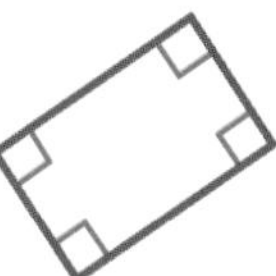

Write the type of quadrilateral that best describes the shape.
See Examples 2 and 3 (p. 411)

14. 

15. 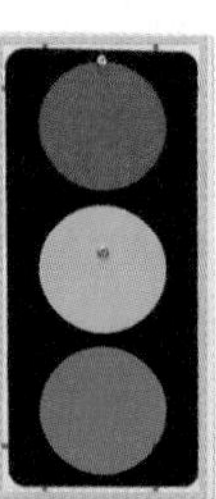

16. 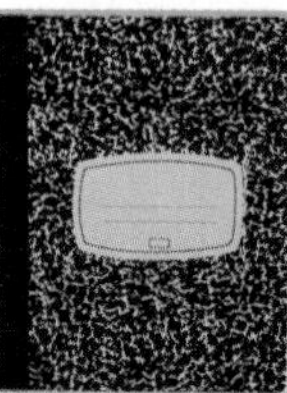

17. 

18. 

19. 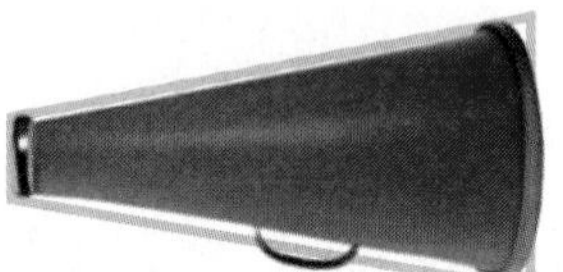

20. A quadrilateral has 4 sides with opposite sides parallel and 4 right angles. Two sides are longer than the others. What is the quadrilateral?

21. Phillip draws a quadrilateral. It has all 4 sides the same length. Its opposite sides are parallel. What quadrilateral did he draw?

H.O.T. Problems

22. OPEN ENDED Draw two quadrilaterals that can be classified as parallelograms.

REASONING Tell whether each statement is *true* or *false.*

23. A rhombus is a square

24. A rectangle is a parallelogram

25. WRITING IN ▸MATH True or false: All squares are rectangles, but not all rectangles are squares. Explain.

Shape Up

Draw Polygons

You will need: 10 index cards

Get Ready!

Players: 2

Get Set!

Cut the cards in half. Then label the cards with the terms shown.

polygon	perpendicular
quadrilateral	right angle
triangle	acute angle
pentagon	obtuse angle
hexagon	straight angle
line	rectangle
ray	square
line segment	rhombus
parallel	parallelogram
intersecting	trapezoid

Go!

- Shuffle the cards. Then spread the cards face down on the table.
- Player 1 turns over a card and draws an example of the polygon.
- If Player 1 cannot draw the polygon, Player 2 is given a chance to draw the polygon.
- Player 2 keeps the card if he or she can draw the polygon. If he or she cannot, the card is put back.
- Player 2 selects a card.
- Continue playing until all cards are gone. The player who collects the most cards wins.

10-9 Parts of a Circle

MAIN IDEA

I will identify parts of a circle.

Standard 4MG3.2 Identify the radius and diameter of a circle.

New Vocabulary

circle
center
diameter
radius

GET READY to Learn

A flying disc and a music CD look like a circle. What other objects look like circles?

A **circle** is a plane figure in which all points are the same distance from a point called the **center**. The parts of a circle are below.

KEY CONCEPTS — Parts of a Circle

Words
A line segment that connects the center of a circle to a point on the circle is a **radius** of the circle.

Model

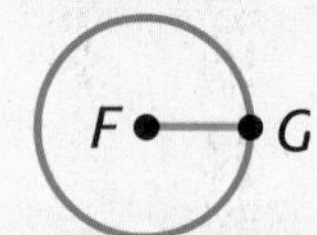

$\overline{FG}$ is the radius.

Words
A line segment that connects two points on a circle and goes through the center of a circle is a **diameter** of a circle.

Model

The diameter is twice the radius.

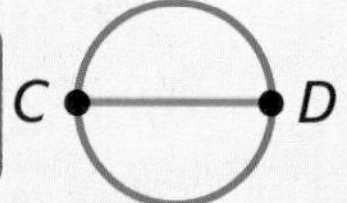

$\overline{CD}$ is the diameter.

Real-World EXAMPLES Parts of a Circle

ENTERTAINMENT **Identify the part of the circle.**

The line segment connects two points on the circle and goes through the center. This is a diameter.

The line segment connects the center of the circle to one point on the circle. This is a radius.

Parts of a circle can be identified using letters.

EXAMPLES Parts of a Circle

3 **Identify the part of the circle that is represented by *C*.**

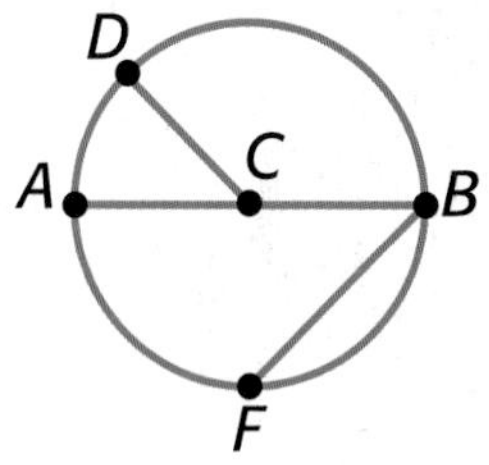

C is the point from which all points on the circle are the same distance.

So, *C* is the center of the circle.

4 **Identify the part of the circle that is represented by $\overline{DC}$.**

$\overline{DC}$ is a line segment that connects the center of the circle to a point on the circle.

So, $\overline{DC}$ is a radius.

Online **Personal Tutor at** ca.gr4math.com

CHECK What You Know

Identify the part of the circle. See Examples 1 and 2 (p. 414)

1. 

2. 

3. 

Identify the parts of the circle. See Examples 3 and 4 (p. 415)

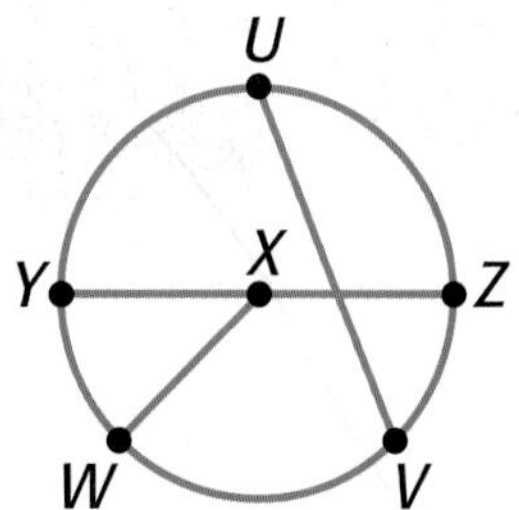

4. $\overline{YX}$

5. $\overline{YZ}$

6. *X*

7. **Measurement** A plate has a diameter of 16 centimeters. A second plate has a radius of 10 centimeters. Which plate is larger? Explain.

8. Talk About It Explain the difference between diameter and radius of a circle.

Practice and Problem Solving

EXTRA PRACTICE See page R27.

Identify the part of the circle. See Examples 1 and 2 (p. 414)

9. 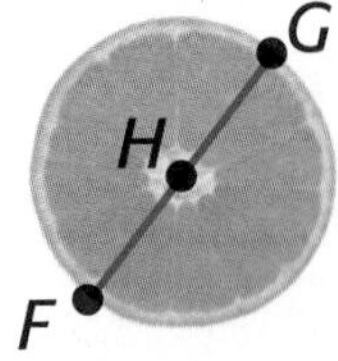

10. 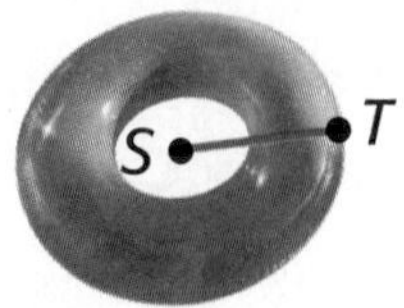

11. 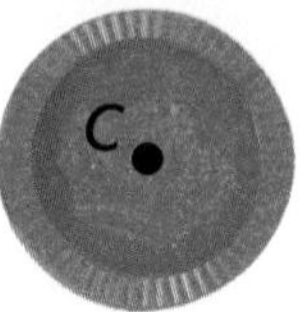

12. 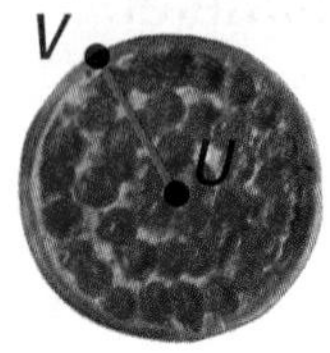

13. 

14. 

Identify the parts of the circle. See Examples 3 and 4 (p. 415)

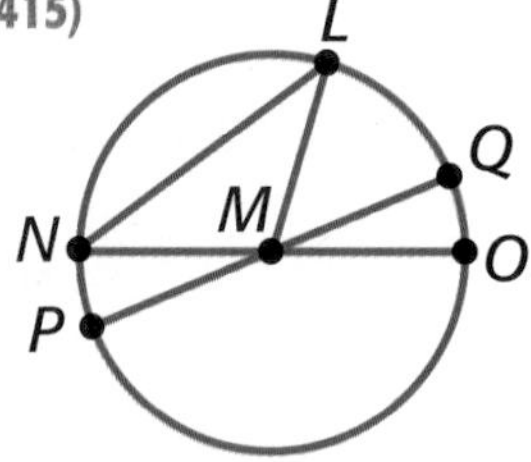

15. $\overline{LM}$

16. $\overline{NM}$

17. M

18. $\overline{ON}$

19. $\overline{ML}$

20. $\overline{PQ}$

21. The diameter of Tariq's dart board is 18 inches. What is the radius of the dart board?

22. Leigh can choose between two circular paths to walk on at a park. Which path should Leigh choose if she wants to get as much exercise as possible?

Path Distances	
Path	**Distance**
1	radius = 60 yds
2	diameter = 110 yds

H.O.T. Problems

23. REASONING What is the measure of the diameter in the circle shown? Explain.

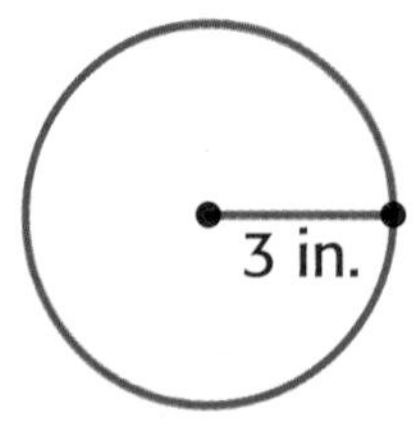

24. OPEN ENDED Draw an object in your classroom that represents a circle. Label all of the circle's parts.

25. WRITING IN MATH How can you find the center point of a circle when you know the diameter?

Math Online Self-Check Quiz at ca.gr4math.com

Standards Practice

26 Which drawing best represents a figure that has only one pair of parallel lines? **(Lesson 10-8)**

A 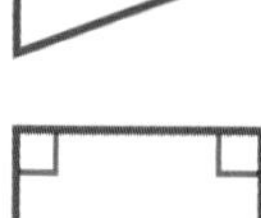

B 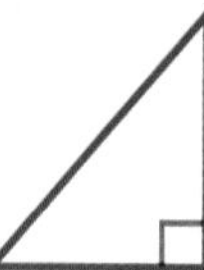

C 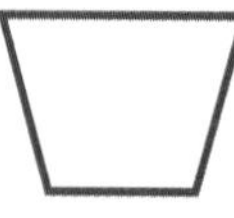

D 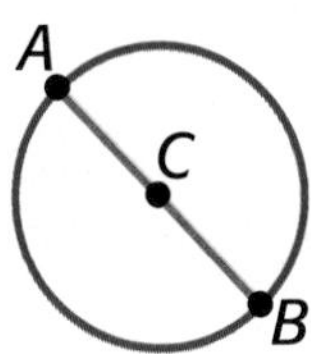

27 Look at the circle with center *C*. The line segment *AB* is **(Lesson 10-9)**

A C B

F a center.

G a radius.

H a diameter.

J a circumference.

Spiral Review

Classify each quadrilateral in as many ways as possible. (Lesson 10-8)

28. 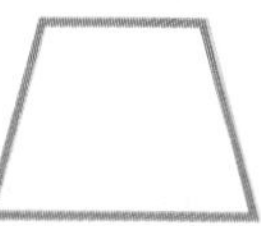

29. 

30. 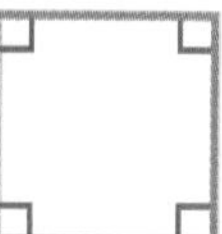

Classify each triangle. Use *acute, right,* or *obtuse* and *isosceles, equilateral,* or *scalene.* (Lesson 10-7)

31. 

32. 

33. 

34. As a plant cell grows, it divides in half. One cell divides into two cells. Then the two cells divide into four cells and so on. How many cells will there be after the fifth division? **(Lesson 10-3)**

Copy and complete each set of patterns. (Lesson 9-2)

35. $16 \div 8 = \blacksquare$
$160 \div 8 = \blacksquare$
$1{,}600 \div 8 = \blacksquare$

36. $\$48 \div 6 = \blacksquare$
$\$480 \div 6 = \blacksquare$
$\$4{,}800 \div 6 = \blacksquare$

37. $81 \div 9 = \blacksquare$
$810 \div 9 = \blacksquare$
$8{,}100 \div 9 = \blacksquare$

Estimate each product. (Lesson 8-2)

38. 32×18

39. 48×22

40. $\$52 \times 18$

41. Algebra If $a = 3$, what is the value of $a + 6$? **(Lesson 3-1)**

CHAPTER 10 Study Guide and Review

FOLDABLES™ Study Organizer GET READY to Study

Be sure the following Key Vocabulary words and Key Concepts are written in your Foldable.

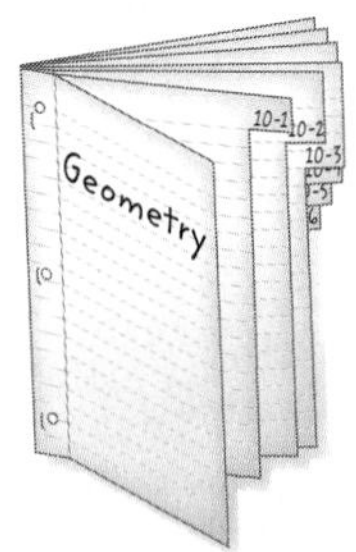

BIG Ideas

- A **solid figure** is a 3-dimensional figure with length, width, and height. (p. 385)

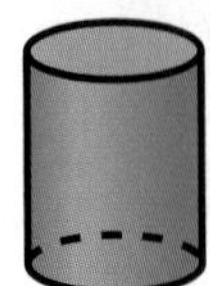  

- A **plane figure** is a 2-dimensional figure with length and width. (p. 388)

  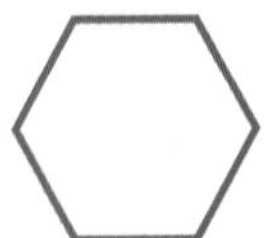

- **Parts of circles** (p. 414)

  V is the center.

  $\overline{UV}$ is the radius.

  $\overline{WX}$ is the diameter.

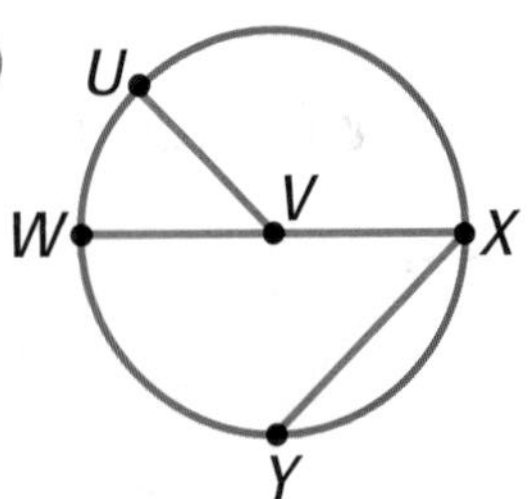

Key Vocabulary

angle (p. 398)
circle (p. 414)
line (p. 394)
plane figure (p. 388)
solid figure (p. 385)

Vocabulary Check

Decide which vocabulary word best completes each sentence.

1. A(n) ___?___ is a plane figure where all the points are the same distance from the center.
2. A(n) ___?___ is a 3-dimensional figure with length, width, and height.
3. A(n) ___?___ is a straight set of points that extend in opposite directions without ending.
4. A(n) ___?___ is a figure made from two rays that have the same endpoint.
5. A(n) ___?___ is a 2-dimensional figure with length and width.

Lesson-by-Lesson Review

10-1 Solid Figures (pp. 385–387)

Example 1

Identify the shape of the cooking pot. Then tell the number of faces, edges, and vertices.

The cooking pot is a cylinder.

It has 2 faces, 0 edges, and 0 vertices.

Identify each figure. Then tell how many faces, edges, and vertices it has.

6.  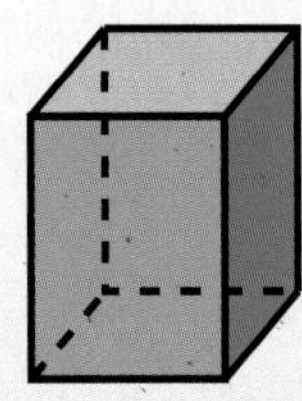

7. 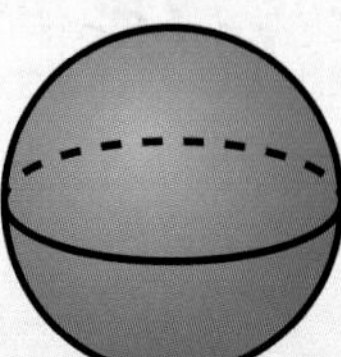

8. Identify the solid figure the net would make.

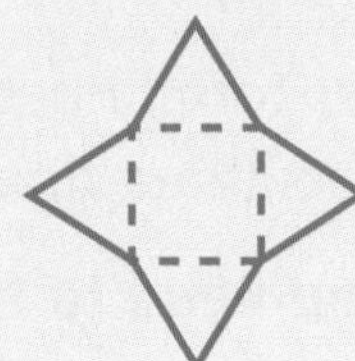

10-2 Plane Figures (pp. 388–391)

Tell whether each shape is a polygon.

Example 2

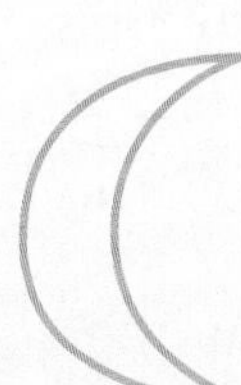

The moon has curved sides. So, it is not a polygon.

Example 3

This figure has 8 sides. The sides are straight. So, it is a polygon.

Identify each polygon.

9. 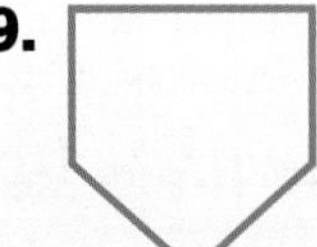

10. 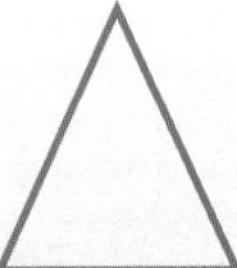

11.

12. 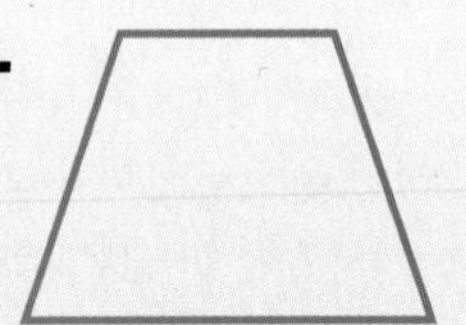

Tell whether the shape is a polygon.

13. 

14. 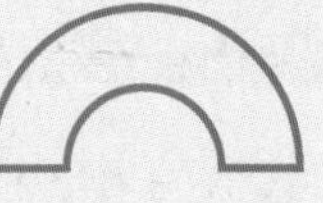

10-3 Problem-Solving Strategy: Look for a Pattern (pp. 392–393)

Example 4
Bruce is creating a pattern on a bowl in art class. There is enough space on the bowl for the pattern to repeat three times. How many stars will he make?

Understand

What facts do you know?

- The figures form a pattern that repeats three times.

What do you need to find?

- The number of stars Bruce will make.

Plan Look for a pattern to solve.

Solve The pattern is sun, star, moon, sun, star, moon. There are 2 stars in the pattern before it repeats.

So, the number of stars Bruce will make after the pattern repeats three times is 2×3 or 6.

Check The answer makes sense for the facts given. The answer is correct.

15. Describe a pattern below. Then find the missing number.

45, 36, 27, ■, 9

16. Copy and complete the pattern. What might be the next two figures in this pattern?

17. Algebra Copy and complete the table. What is the pattern?

Input (x)	Output (y)
8	40
4	20
9	45
7	■
■	15

18. Nell jogged for 8 minutes on Monday. Then she jogged for 13 minutes on Tuesday. She jogged for 18 minutes on Wednesday. How many minutes will Nell jog on Sunday?

19. The pattern below can also be shown as 1, 4, 7, 10. Draw the next two possible figures. What are the next two numbers?

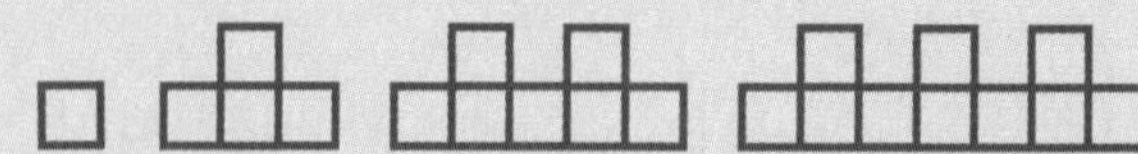

20. Describe a pattern below. Then find the missing number.

1, 3, 7, 15, ■

10-4 Lines, Line Segments, and Rays (pp. 394–397)

Example 5
Describe the figure.

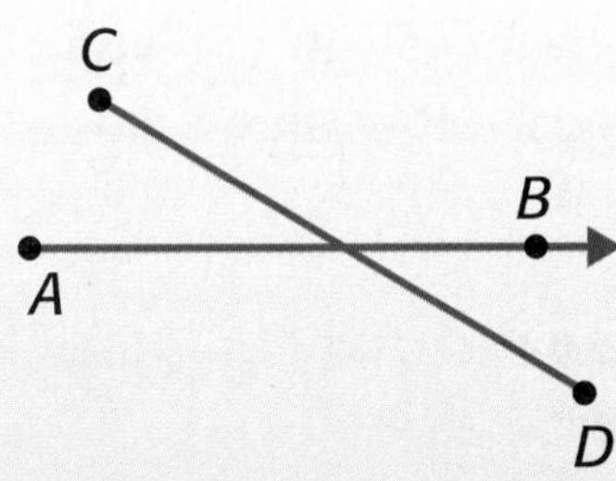

The figure shows ray *AB* and line segment *CD*. Notice that ray *AB* intersects line *CD*.

$\overrightarrow{AB}$ intersects $\overline{CD}$.

Identify each figure.

21. **22.**

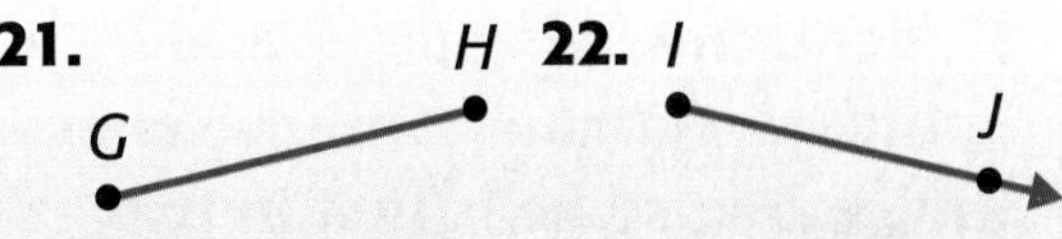

Describe the figure.

23. **24.**

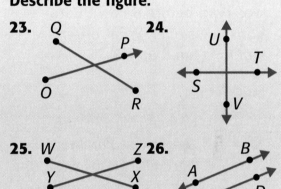

25. **26.**

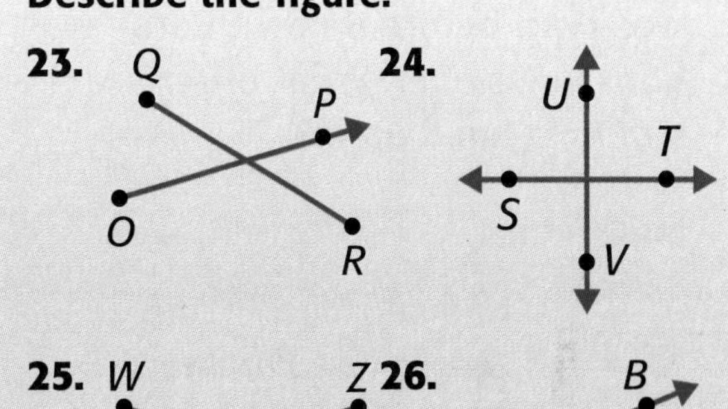

10-5 Angles (pp. 398–400)

Example 6
Write the measure of the angle shown below in degrees and as a fraction of a full turn.

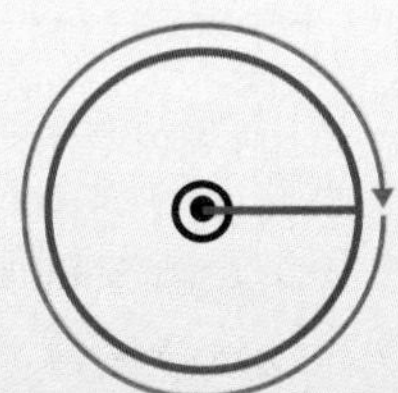

The angle shown is 360° or a full turn.

Write the measure of each angle in degrees and as a fraction of a full turn.

27. **28.**

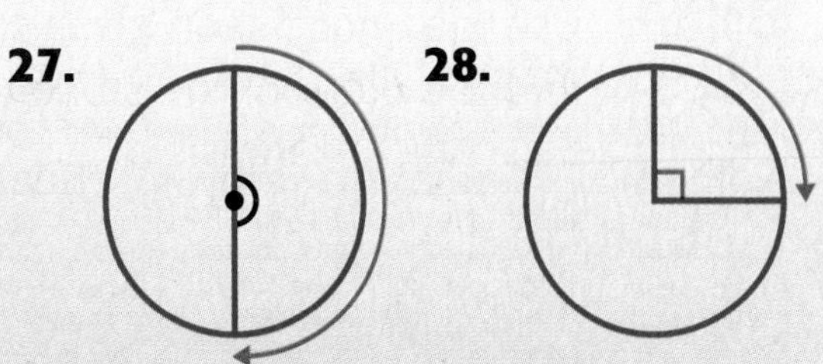

Classify each angle as *right, acute,* or *obtuse*.

29.

30.

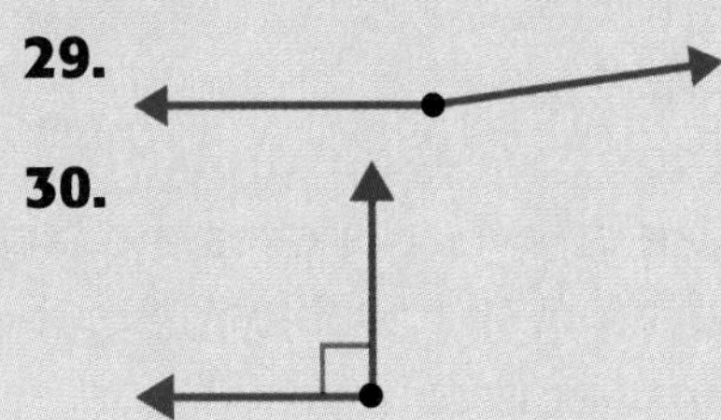

10-6 Problem-Solving Investigation: Choose a Strategy (pp. 402–403)

Example 7

Students are lining up according to birthdays. Nathan's birthday is in September, so he is first in line. Beatriz was born in December. Ruby was born before Beatriz. Carlie was born in October. What order are the students lined up in?

Understand

Nathan is first in line. Beatriz was born in December. Ruby was born before Beatriz. Carlie was born in October.

What order are the students lined up in?

Plan Work backward to solve the problem.

Solve Use the information given to find the order of the students.

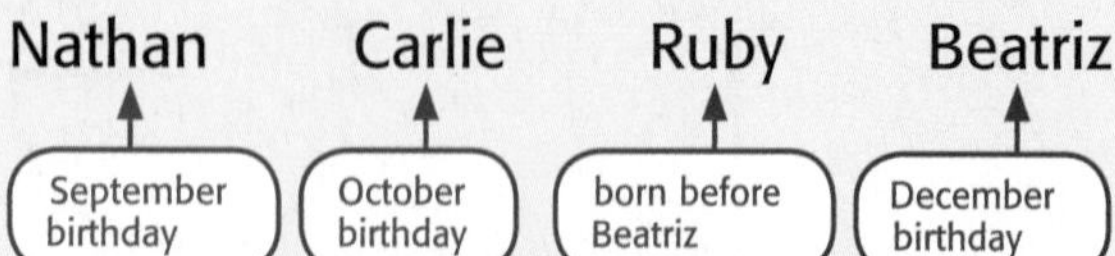

So, the order of the students is Nathan, Carlie, Ruby, and Beatriz.

Check Look back at the problem. The answer matches the facts given in the problem. So, the answer is correct.

Use any strategy to solve.

31. Kaga works as a tour guide. He earned $457 in July and $865 in August. How much did he earn in all?

32. Draw the next two possible figures in the pattern.

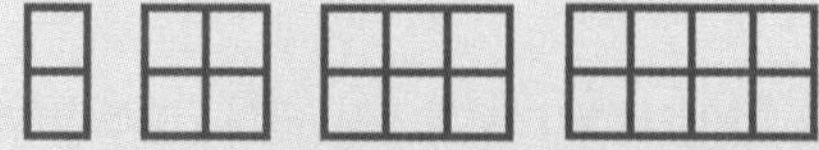

33. Patty rounds a number to the nearest hundred and gets 200. What is the least number it could be? the greatest number?

34. Algebra Copy and complete the table. What is the pattern?

Input (x)	Output (y)
3	30
6	60
9	90
12	■
■	150

35. Logan has 7 jars of coins. Each jar has 35 coins. How many coins does Logan have?

36. Viviana watches four movies every month. Each movie is two hours long. Is it reasonable to say that Viviana watches about 100 hours of movies a year?

10-7 Triangles (pp. 404–407)

Example 8
Classify each triangle. Use *acute, right,* or *obtuse* and *isosceles, equilateral,* or *scalene*.

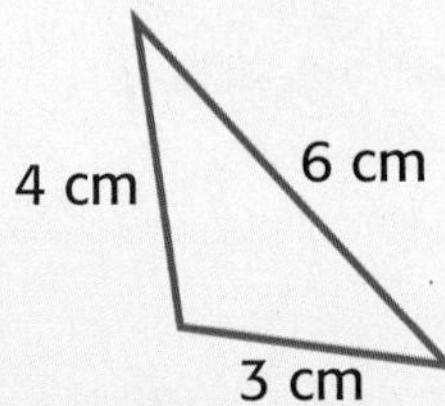

Since no sides are the same length, the triangle is scalene.

The triangle has one obtuse angle, so it is obtuse.

Classify each triangle. Use *acute, right,* or *obtuse* and *isosceles, equilateral,* or *scalene*.

37. 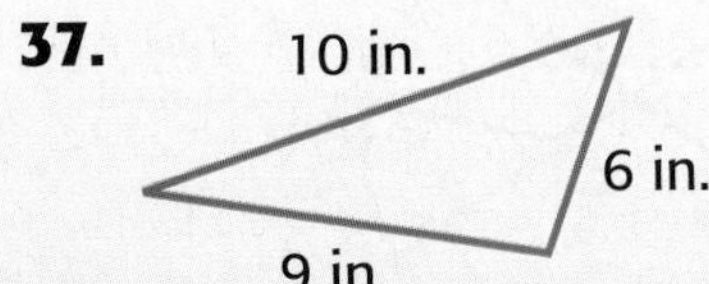

38. 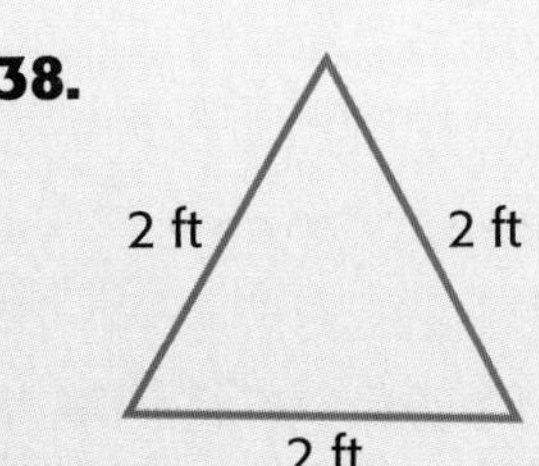

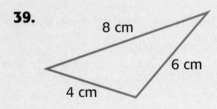

39. 8 cm, 6 cm, 4 cm

10-8 Quadrilaterals (pp. 410–412)

Example 9
Classify the quadrilateral in as many ways as possible.

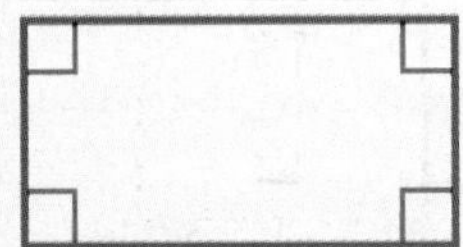

The figure has parallel sides. So, it is a parallelogram.

It has 4 right angles. So, it is a rectangle.

Classify each quadrilateral in as many ways as possible.

40.

41. 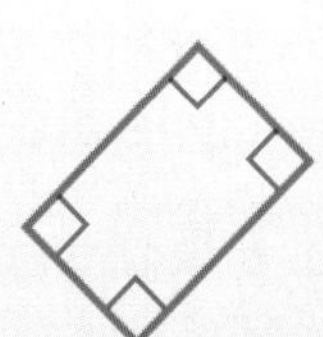

42. 

43. 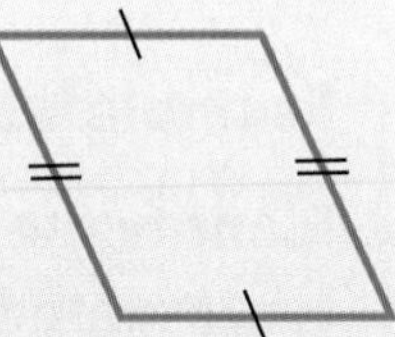

44. 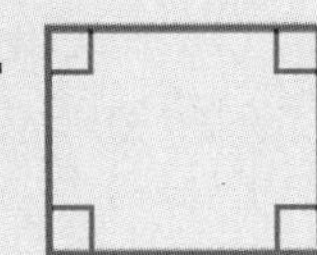

45. 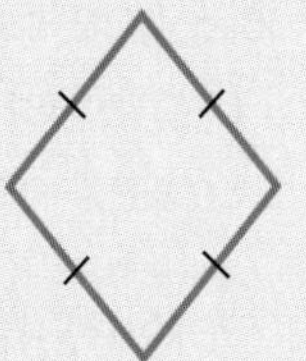

10-9 Parts of a Circle (pp. 414–417)

Identify the part of the circle.

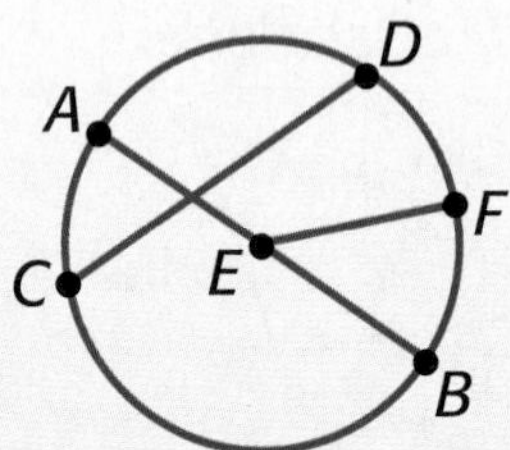

Example 10

Identify the part of the circle that is represented by $\overline{AB}$.

$\overline{AB}$ is a line segment that goes through the center of a circle.

So, $\overline{AB}$ is a diameter.

Example 11

Identify the part of the circle that is represented by *E*.

E is a point from which all points on the circle are the same distance.

So, *E* is the center of the circle.

Example 12

Identify the part of the circle that is represented by $\overline{EF}$.

$\overline{EF}$ is a line segment that connects the center of the circle to a point on the circle.

So, $\overline{EF}$ is a radius.

Identify the part of the circle.

46.

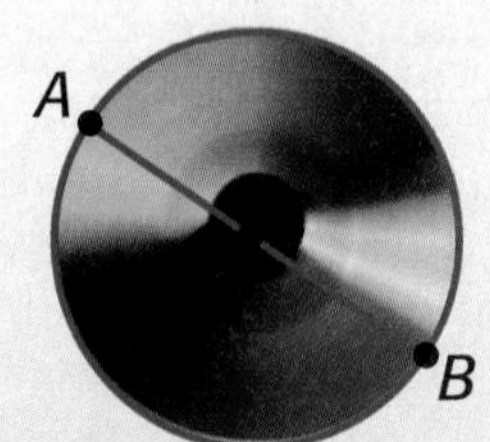

47.

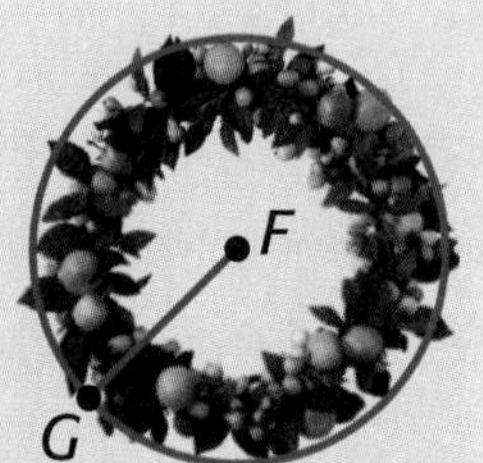

Identify the parts of the circle.

48. *W*

49. $\overline{UV}$

50. $\overline{WX}$

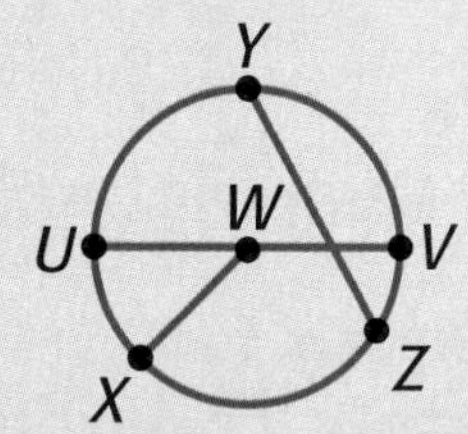

51. Measurement Liana has two toy planes. The first plane is on a string that is 12 feet long. The second plane can go in a circle that has a diameter of 22 feet. Which plane can make a larger circle in the air? Explain.

Chapter 10 Chapter Test

For exercises 1–3, decide whether each statement is *true* or *false*.

1. A circle is a plane figure in which all points are the same distance from a fixed point.

2. A trapezoid has 2 pairs of parallel sides.

3. An obtuse triangle has two obtuse angles.

4. **Measurement** One plate has a diameter of 12 centimeters. A second plate has a radius of 7 centimeters. Which plate is larger? Explain.

Classify each quadrilateral in as many ways as possible.

5. 

6. 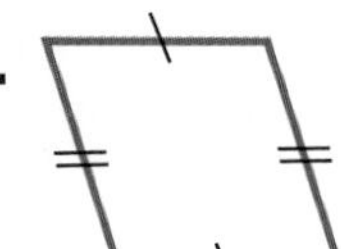

7. **STANDARDS PRACTICE** Look at the circle with center *C*.

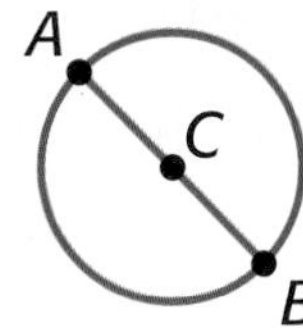

The line segment $\overline{AC}$ appears to be

A a center.

B a radius.

C a diameter.

D a circumference.

Classify each triangle. Use *acute, right,* or *obtuse* and *isosceles, equilateral,* or *scalene.*

8. 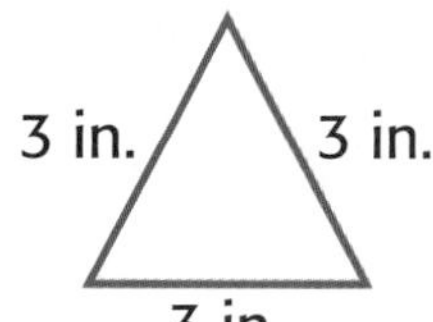

9. 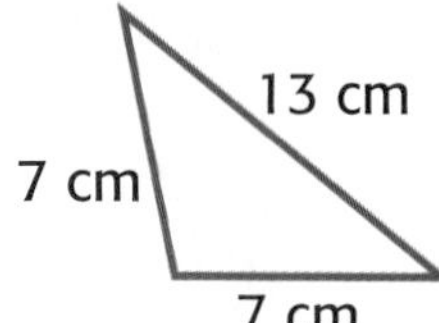

Classify each angle as *right, acute,* or *obtuse.*

10. 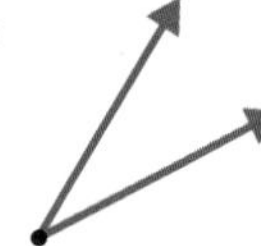

11. 

12. Draw the next two possible figures in the pattern below.

13. **STANDARDS PRACTICE** In the figure below, which two angles appear to be acute?

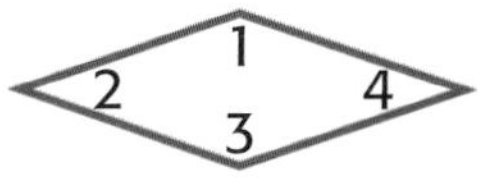

F Angles 1 and 2

G Angles 1 and 3

H Angles 1 and 4

J Angles 2 and 4

14. **WRITING IN MATH** Is it possible to draw an isosceles triangle that is acute? Explain. Draw a picture to support your answer.

CHAPTER 10

California Standards Practice

Cumulative, Chapters 1–10

Standards Example

Which figure can form a square pyramid when folded on the dotted lines without overlapping?

A 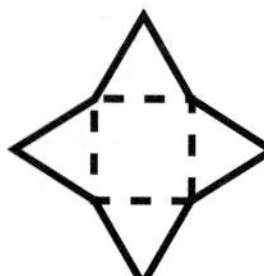

C 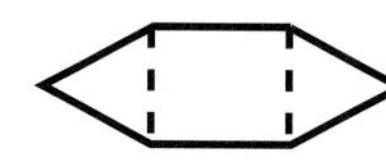

B 

D 

Read the Question

Identify the figure that will form a pyramid when folded.

Solve the Question

A square pyramid has a square base and triangular sides. The only figure that has a square base and triangles as faces is choice A.
So, the answer is A.

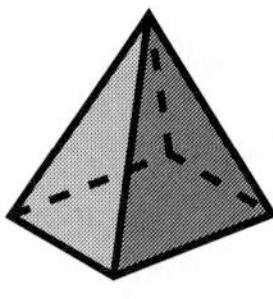

Personal Tutor at ca.gr4math.com

Choose the best answer.

1 **Which figure below has exactly one pair of parallel sides?**

A rectangle

B square

C trapezoid

D rhombus

2 **Look at the figure. Which of the following best describes the figure?**

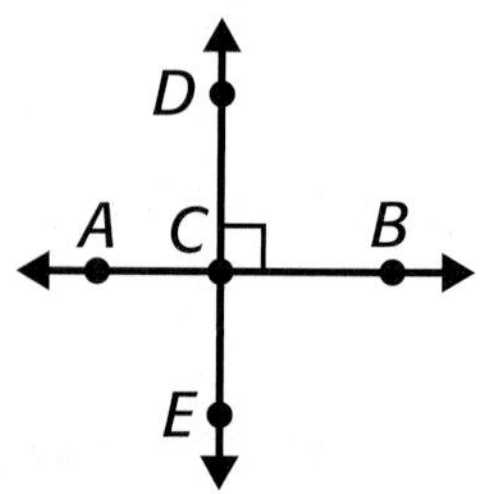

F rays

G line segments

H perpendicular lines

J parallel lines

For practice by standard, see pages CA1–CA43.

3 **Which is the best estimate for $426 \div 7$?**

A 50   **C** 70

B 60   **D** 80

---

4 **Which object below has the shape of a triangle?**

F

H

G

J

---

5 **What is the name of the figure for the net shown below?**

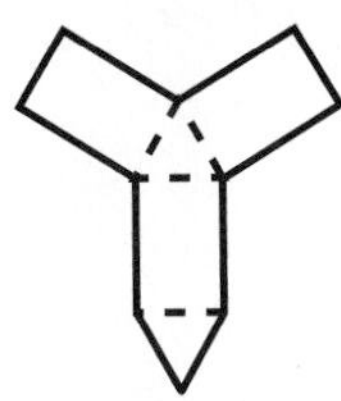

A rectangular prism

B square pyramid

C triangular prism

D cube

---

6 **What kind of triangle is shown below?**

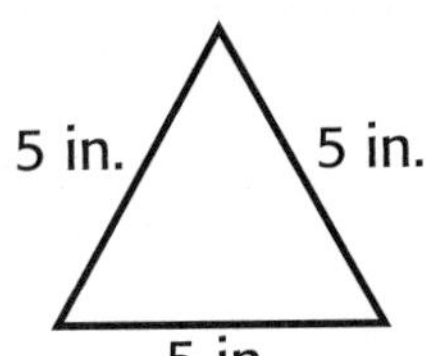

F scalene   **H** isosceles

G right   **J** equilateral

---

7 **Which line segment is the diameter?**

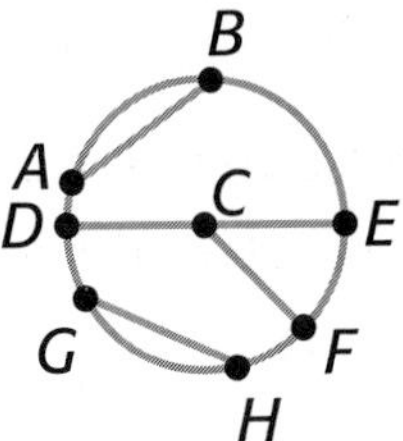

A $\overline{AB}$ **C** $\overline{GH}$

B $\overline{CF}$ **D** $\overline{DE}$

---

8 **Classify the angle.**

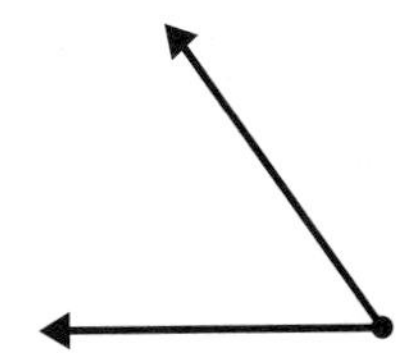

F straight   **H** obtuse

G acute   **J** right

---

9 **Gigi has 4 boxes filled with books. Each box can hold 24 books. How many books does she have?**

A 68   **C** 96

B 88   **D** 120

---

10 **What is the value of x?**

$$(15 \div 3) \times (10 - 4) = x$$

F 5   **H** 30

G 11   **J** 35

CHAPTER 11 Geometry and Measurement

BIG Idea What is perimeter?

Perimeter is the distance around a closed figure.

Example To find the perimeter of the cow pasture, you can add the lengths of the sides of the fence.

$$\begin{array}{r} 225 \text{ yd} \\ 225 \text{ yd} \\ 150 \text{ yd} \\ +\ 150 \text{ yd} \\ \hline 750 \text{ yd} \end{array}$$

So, the perimeter of the pasture is 750 yards.

What will I learn in this chapter?

- Identify congruent figures.
- Identify figures that have bilateral and rotational symmetry.
- Understand and use formulas to find perimeter and area.
- Relate perimeter and area.
- Solve problems by working simpler problems.

Key Vocabulary

congruent
line symmetry
perimeter
area
complex figure

Student Study Tools at ca.gr4math.com

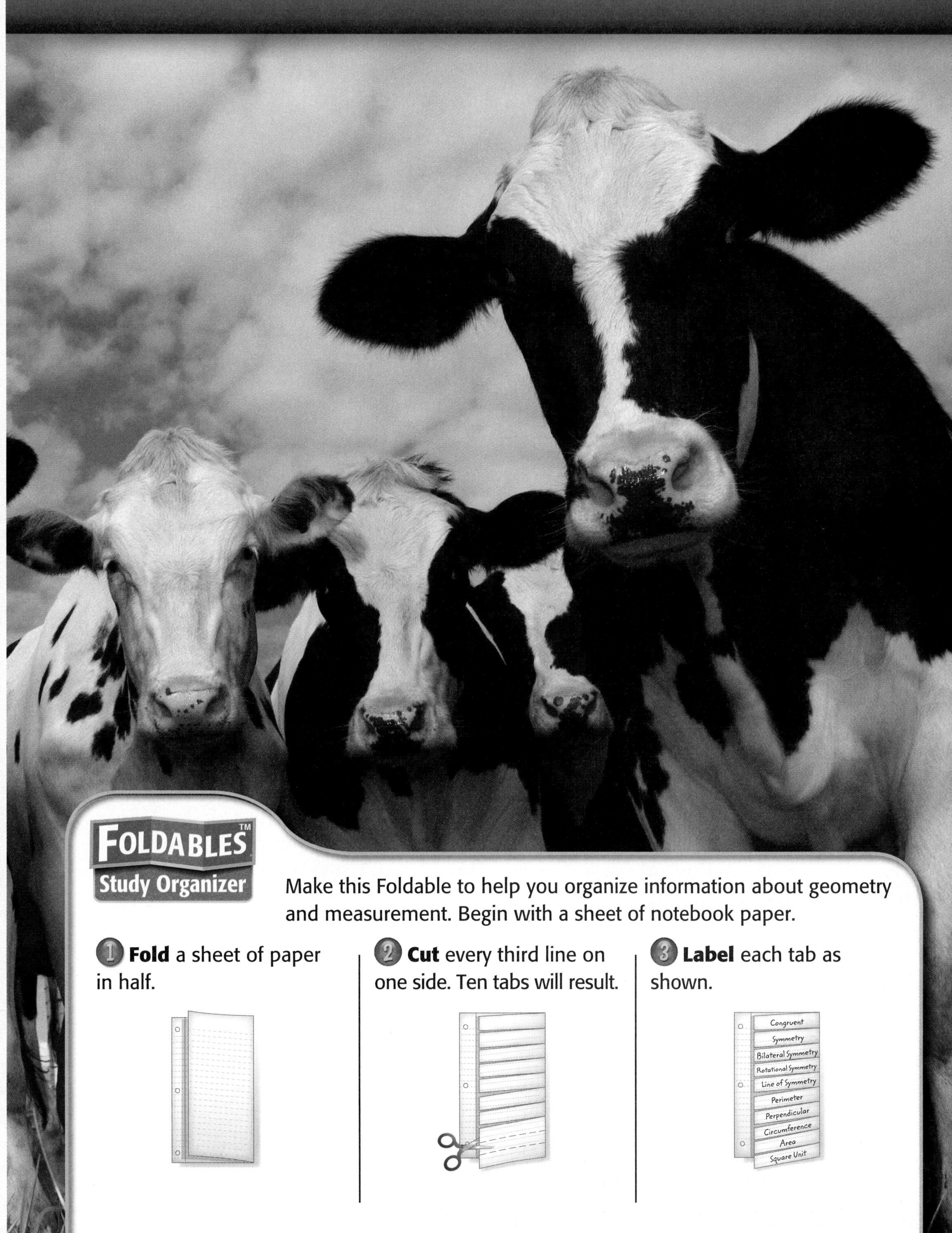

FOLDABLES™ Study Organizer

Make this Foldable to help you organize information about geometry and measurement. Begin with a sheet of notebook paper.

1. **Fold** a sheet of paper in half.

2. **Cut** every third line on one side. Ten tabs will result.

3. **Label** each tab as shown.

ARE YOU READY for Chapter 11?

You have two ways to check prerequisite skills for this chapter.

Option 2

Math Online Take the Chapter Readiness Quiz at ca.gr4math.com.

Option 1

Complete the Quick Check below.

QUICK Check

Tell whether each figure is divided in half by the dashed line. Write *yes* or *no*. (Prior grade)

1. 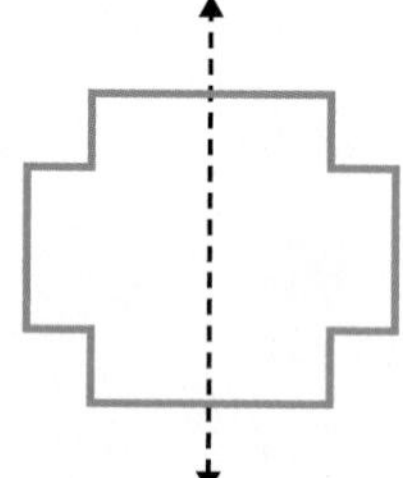

2. 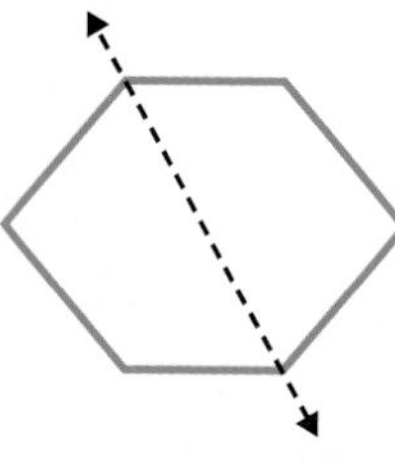

3. 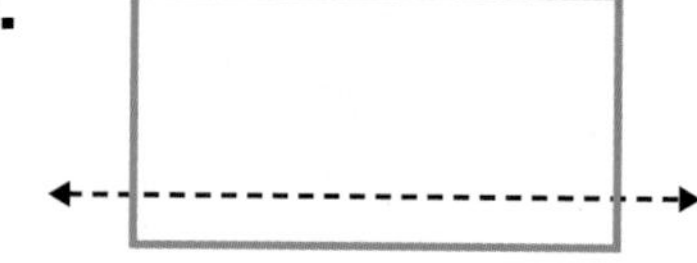

4. Jon is sharing his sandwich with his brother. Is the sandwich divided in half?

Find the value of each expression. (Lesson 3-1)

5. $8 + 14 + 8 + 14$

6. $9 + 16 + 9 + 16$

7. 15×7

8. 12×6

9. $(2 \times 7) + (2 \times 14)$

10. $(2 \times 13) + (2 \times 9)$

Identify each polygon. (Lesson 10-2)

11. 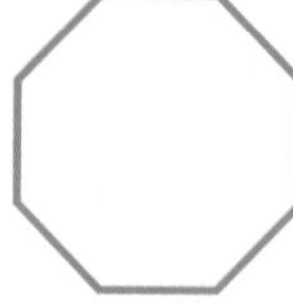

12. 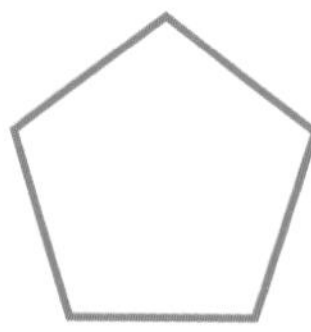

13. 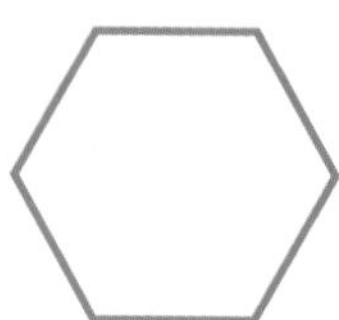

14. Peyton is looking in a kaleidoscope. Identify two of the polygons that can be seen.

Geometry: Congruent

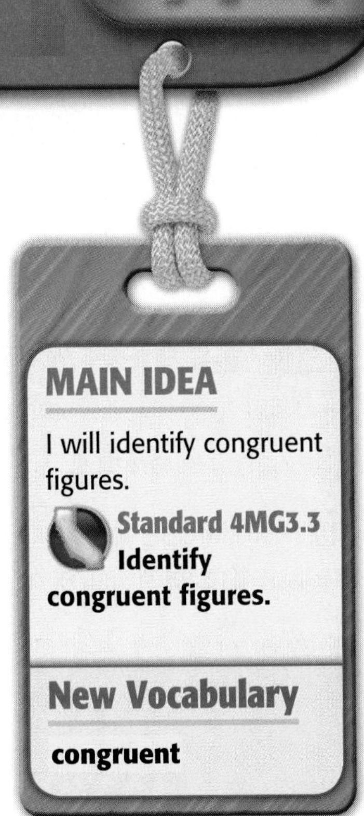

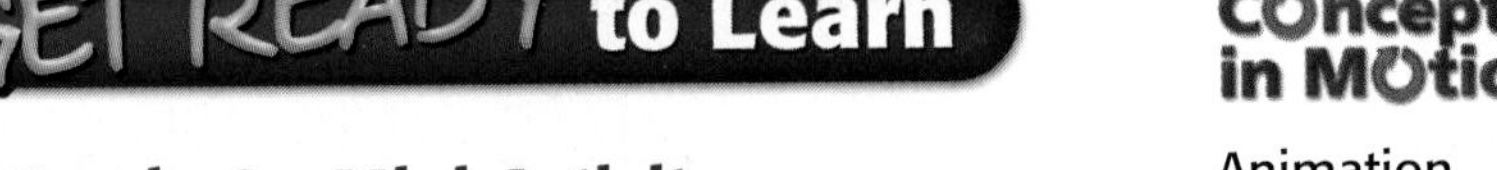

Concepts in Motion
Animation
ca.gr4math.com

Hands-On Mini Activity

Materials geomirror and pattern blocks

Step 1 Place a geomirror and a hexagon pattern block onto a sheet of paper.

Step 2 Look into the geomirror from the left side. Trace the figure you see reflected onto the right side.

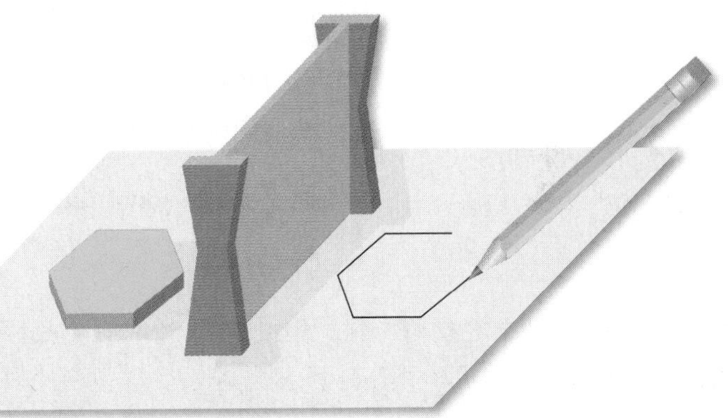

Step 3 Repeat the steps using two other pattern blocks. What do you notice about the size and shape of each pair of figures?

Review Vocabulary

hexagon a figure with six sides (Lesson 10-2)

trapezoid a quadrilateral with one pair of parallel sides (Lesson 10-8)

When figures have the same size and shape, they are **congruent**.

EXAMPLES Identify Congruent Figures

Tell whether the figures appear to be congruent. Write *yes* or *no*.

1

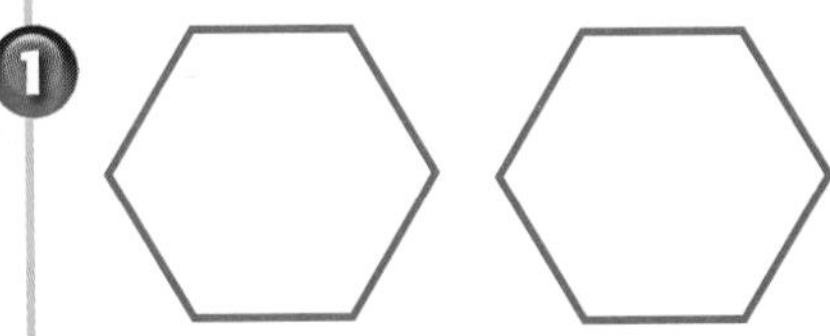

The hexagons appear to have the same size and shape. They are congruent.

2

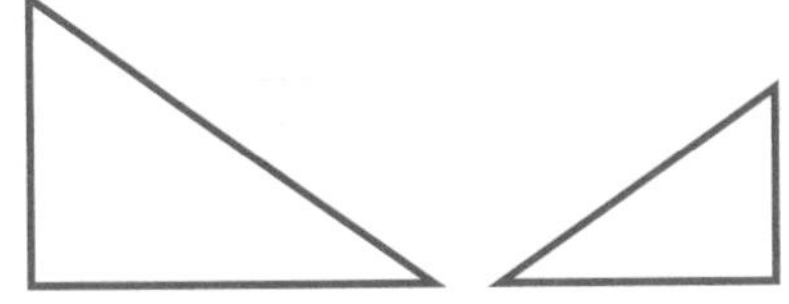

The triangles appear to have the same shape, but have a different size. So, they are not congruent.

Real-World EXAMPLE — Identify Congruent Figures

3 SCHOOL The diagrams show the shapes and sizes of two classrooms. Are the classrooms congruent? Explain.

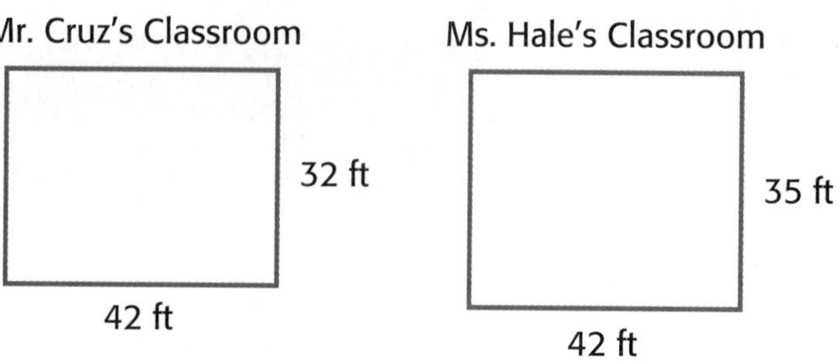

Both classrooms have the same shape. They are rectangles.

Both classrooms have the same length, but Ms. Hale's classroom has a greater width. So, they are not the same size.

Since the classrooms have different sizes, they are not congruent.

CHECK What You Know

Tell whether the figures appear to be congruent. Write *yes* or *no*. See Examples 1–3 (pp. 431–432)

1.

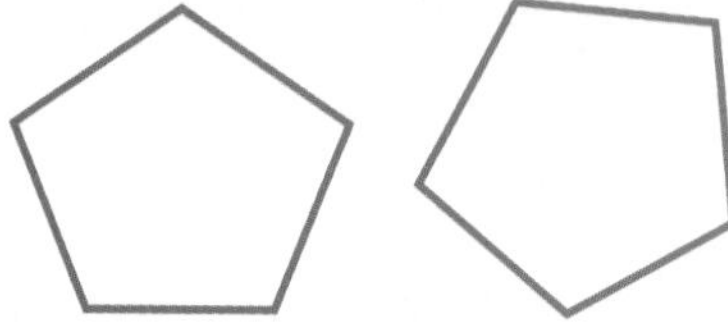

2.

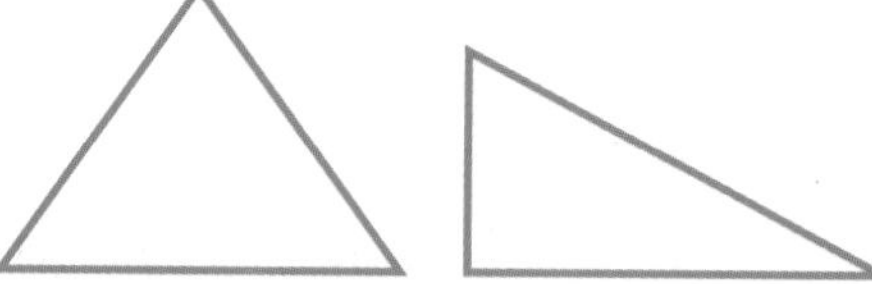

3. How many of the kitchen tiles appear to be congruent to the tile labeled E?

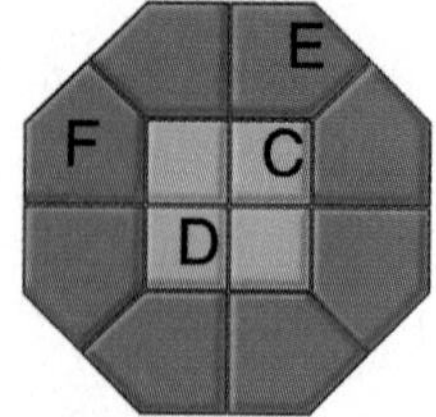

4. In the birdhouse, do the windows and door appear to be congruent? Explain.

5. Talk About It: Look around your classroom. Name two objects that appear to be congruent and two objects that are not congruent.

Math Online Extra Examples at ca.gr4math.com

Practice and Problem Solving

See page R27.

Tell whether the figures appear to be congruent. Write *yes* or *no*. See Examples 1–3 (pp. 431–432)

6.

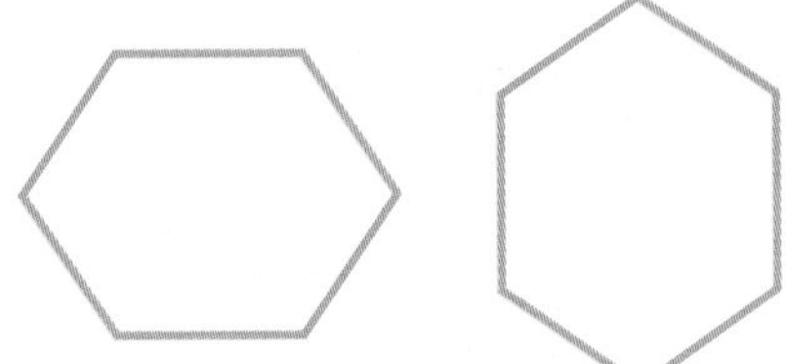

7.

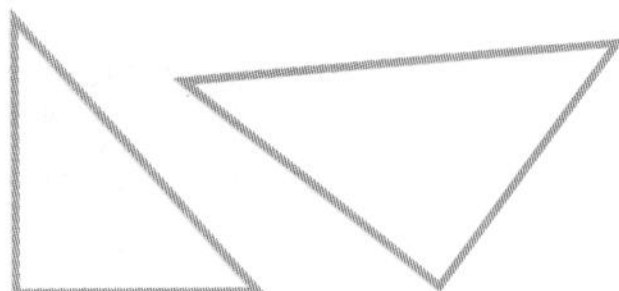

8.

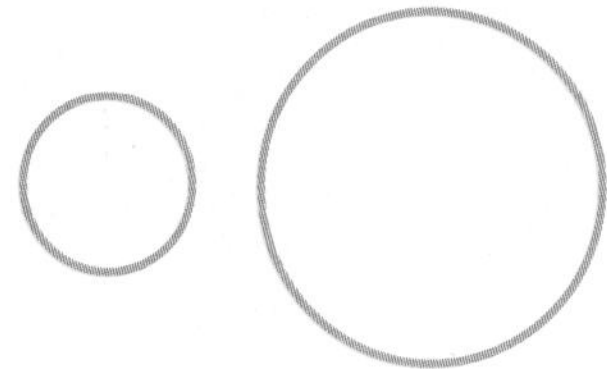

9.

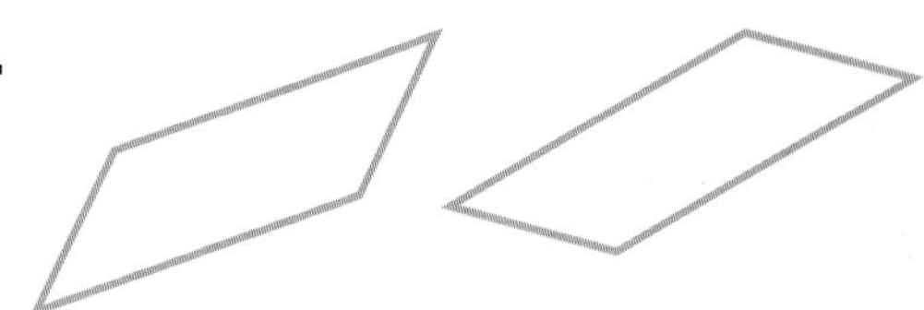

10. Tell whether the cells on a honeycomb are congruent.

11. Which figures on a soccer ball are congruent?

12. **Measurement** The television in Sabina's room is 30 inches wide and 24 inches long. His neighbor has the same television. If his neighbor's television is 30 inches wide, how long is it?

13. **Measurement** One of Paloma's picture frames is 5 inches wide and 7 inches long. She has another picture frame that is the same size. If it is 7 inches long, how wide is it?

H.O.T. Problems

14. **OPEN ENDED** Create two rectangles. Tell whether they are congruent or not congruent. Explain.

15. **FIND THE ERROR** Derek and Jacinto are comparing their slices of pizza. Who is correct? Explain.

16. **WRITING IN MATH** Are all squares with one side measuring 5 inches congruent? Explain your reasoning.

11-2 Geometry: Symmetry

GET READY to Learn

A butterfly uses its wings to fly. Look at the left side and the right side of the butterfly. When a butterfly folds its wings in half, will the two parts match?

MAIN IDEA

I will identify figures that have bilateral and rotational symmetry.

Standard 4MG3.4 Identify figures that have bilateral and rotational symmetry.

New Vocabulary

line symmetry
line of symmetry
bilateral symmetry
rotational symmetry

A figure has **line symmetry** if it can be folded so that the two parts of the figure match, or are congruent. This is also called **bilateral symmetry**. The fold line is a **line of symmetry**.

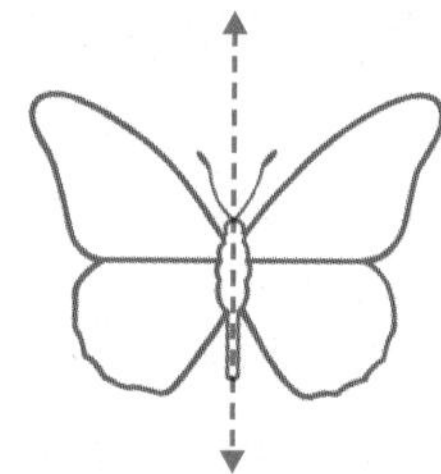

1 line of symmetry

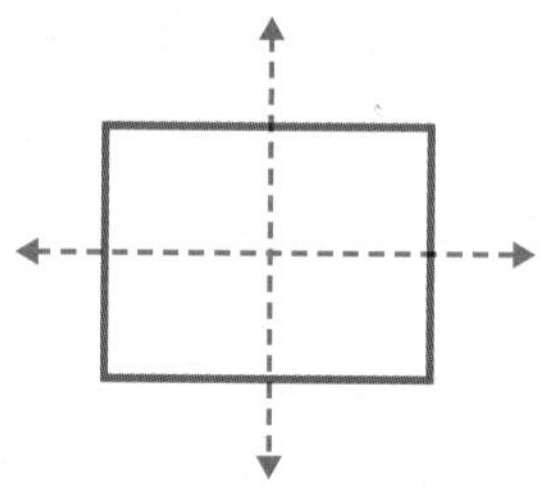

2 lines of symmetry

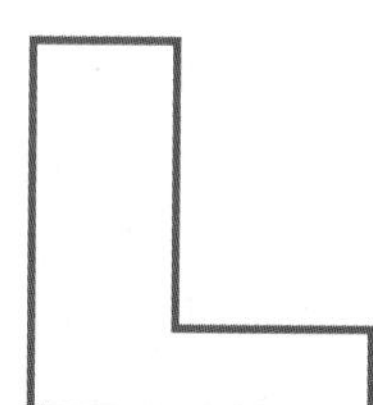

no lines of symmetry

EXAMPLES

Tell whether each figure has line symmetry. Write *yes* or *no*. Then tell how many lines of symmetry the figure has.

1 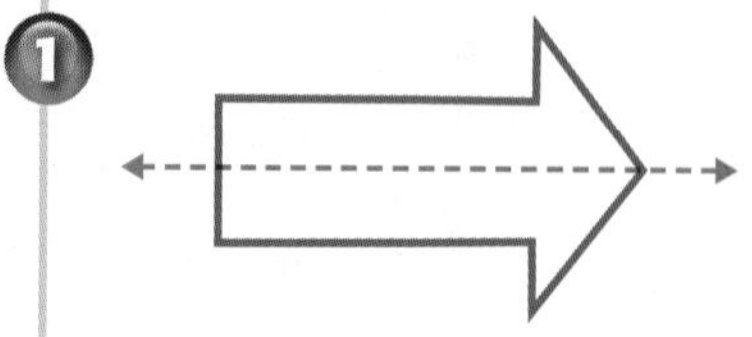

Yes; the figure has 1 line of symmetry.

2 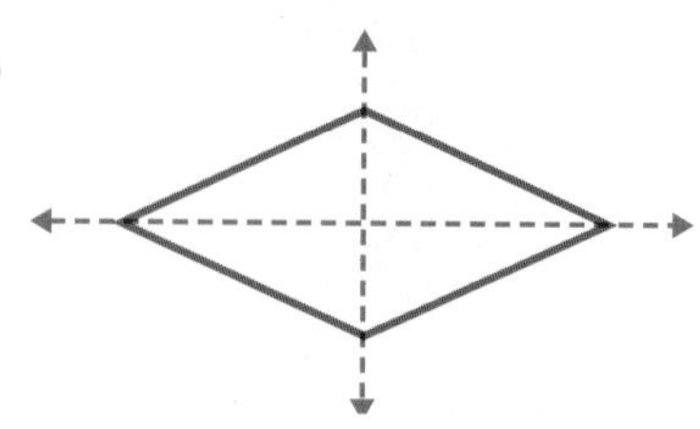

Yes; the figure has 2 lines of symmetry.

When a figure fits exactly over itself after being rotated 180° or less, it has **rotational symmetry**.

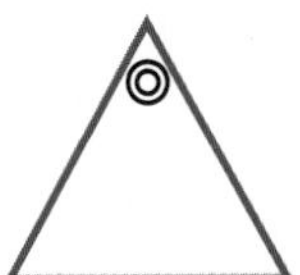
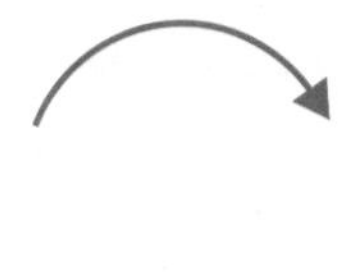
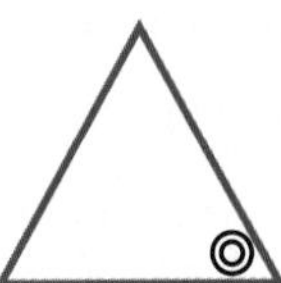
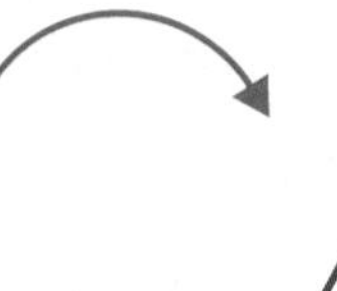
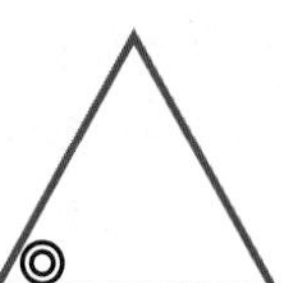

An equilateral triangle has rotational symmetry because it is the same after each rotation.

EXAMPLE Identify Rotational Symmetry

3 Tell whether the figure has rotational symmetry.

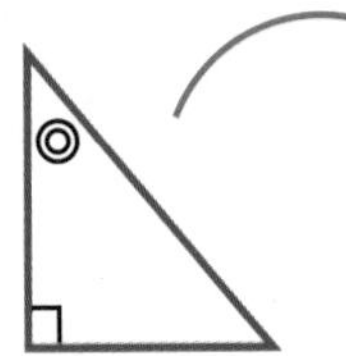
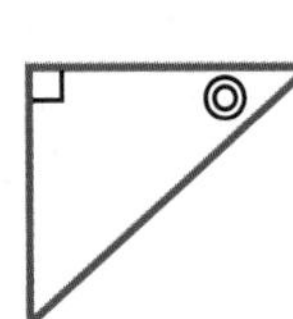
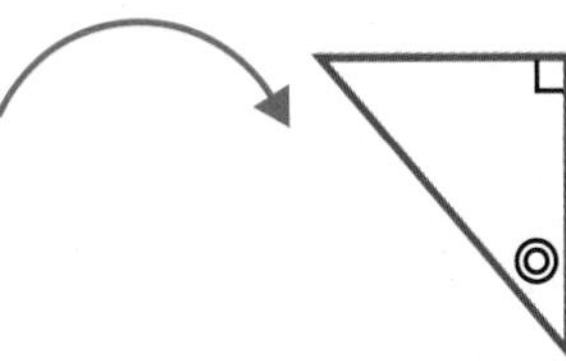

The right triangle does not look like it did before the turn. So, it does not have rotational symmetry.

Online **Personal Tutor at** ca.gr4math.com

CHECK What You Know

Tell whether each figure has line symmetry. Write *yes* or *no*. Then tell how many lines of symmetry the figure has.
See Examples 1 and 2 (p. 434)

1.

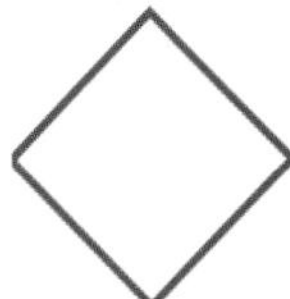

2.

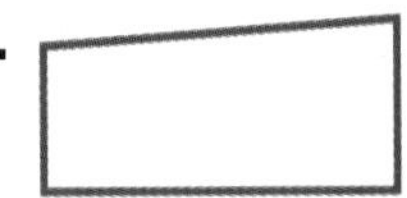

Tell whether the figure has rotational symmetry. Write *yes* or *no*. See Example 3 (p. 435)

3.

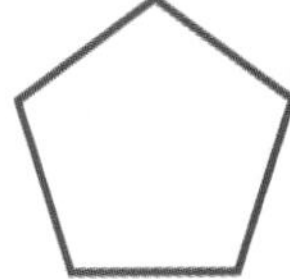

4.

5. Tell whether the snowflake shown at the right has rotational symmetry. Explain.

6. Talk About It Do you think that a figure with bilateral symmetry can also have rotational symmetry? Draw a picture to explain your reasoning.

Practice and Problem Solving

Tell whether each figure has line symmetry. Write *yes* or *no*. Then tell how many lines of symmetry the figure has.

See Examples 1 and 2 (p. 434)

7. 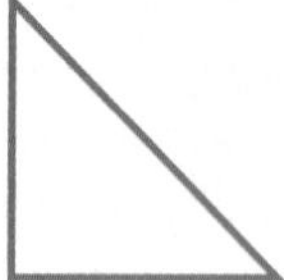

8. 

9. 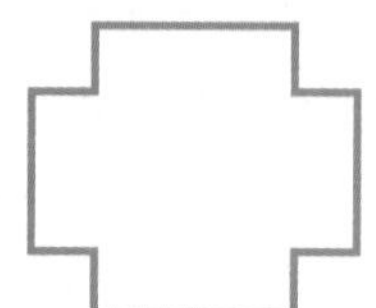

10. 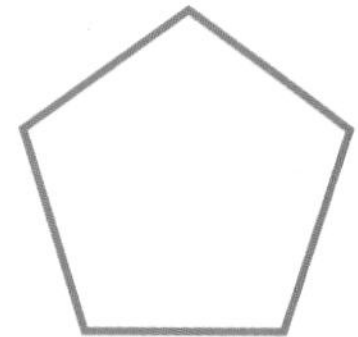

Tell whether the figure has rotational symmetry. Write *yes* or *no*. See Example 3 (p. 435)

11. 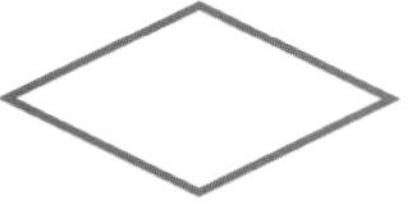

12. 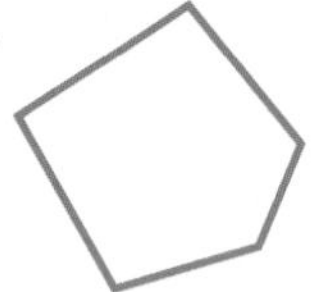

13. 

14. 

15. Does the letter C have symmetry? If it does, tell how many lines of symmetry the letter has.

16. Does a square have symmetry? If is does, tell how many lines of symmetry the shape has.

Tell whether the line is a line of symmetry. Write *yes* or *no*.

17. 

18. 

19. 

Real-World PROBLEM SOLVING

Art Lines of symmetry can be seen in many pieces of art work such as cultural masks.

20. Sketch the mask shown and show the line of symmetry.

21. Using a sheet of grid paper, create half of a cultural mask. Then, switch papers with another student. Complete the image of the cultural mask you now have.

22. Does the cultural mask you created have rotational symmetry?

Math Online Self-Check Quiz at ca.gr4math.com

H.O.T. Problems

23. OPEN ENDED Design a plane figure that has more than 3 lines of symmetry.

24. WRITING IN ▶MATH How many lines of symmetry do you think a circle has? Explain.

Standards Practice

25 Which figure appears to be congruent to the square shown? (Lesson 11-1)

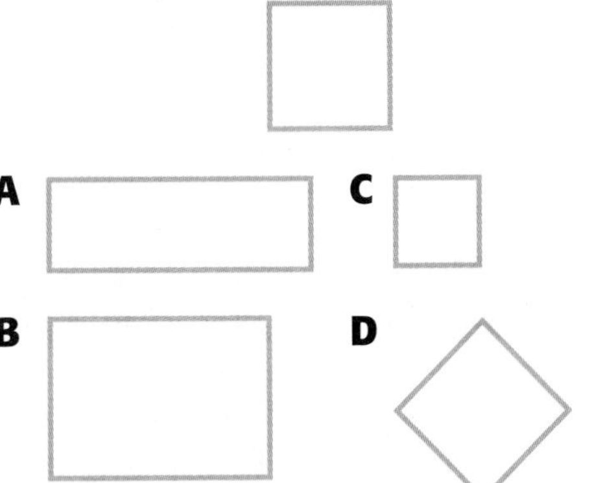

26 Which drawing best represents a figure with one line of symmetry? (Lesson 11-2)

F

H 

G

J 

Spiral Review

Tell whether the figures appear to be congruent. Write *yes* or *no*. (Lesson 11-1)

27. 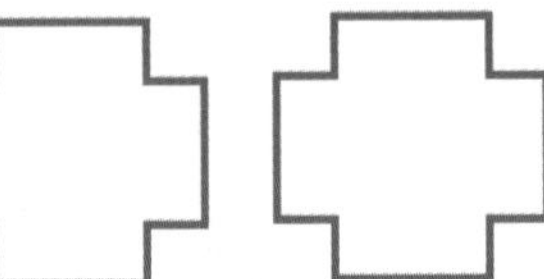

28. 

29. 

In the circle at the right point *R* is the center. Identify the parts of the circle. (Lesson 10-9)

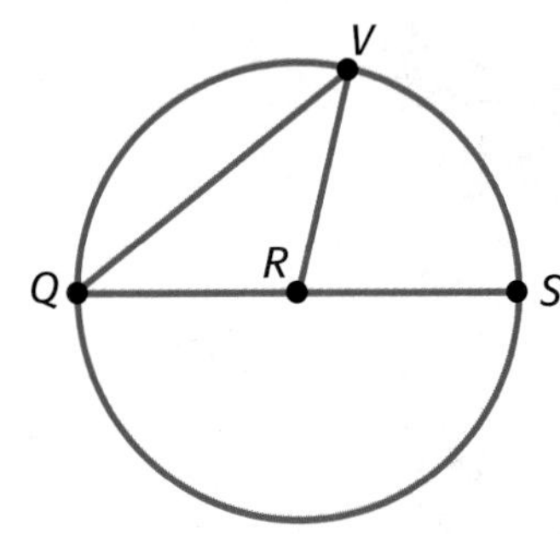

30. $\overline{RS}$

31. $\overline{QS}$

32. $\overline{RV}$

33. Eliza made $36,587 last year. Is it reasonable to say that Eliza made more than $3,000 each month? Explain. (Lesson 7-2)

11-3 Measurement: Perimeter

GET READY to Learn

Berto is walking around a park on the path shown. How far did Berto walk?

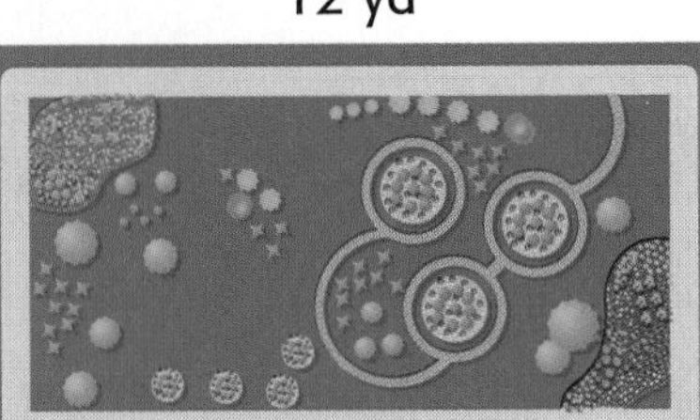

The distance around a figure is called the **perimeter**.

KEY CONCEPT — Perimeter of a Rectangle

Words Perimeter equals the sum of the lengths of the sides. Perimeter also equals 2 times length plus 2 times width.

Formula $P = \ell + \ell + w + w$

$P = (2 \times \ell) + (2 \times w)$

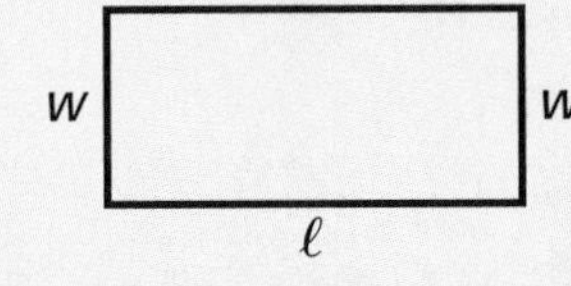

MAIN IDEA

I will find the perimeter of a polygon.

Standard 4MG1.4 **Understand and use formulas to solve problems involving perimeters** and areas **of rectangles and squares.** Use those formulas to find the areas of more complex figures by dividing the figures into basic shapes.

Standard 4AF1.4 **Use and interpret formulas to answer questions about quantities and their relationships.**

New Vocabulary

perimeter

Find Perimeter

1 **DISTANCE** **How far did Berto walk?**

One Way: Use Addition	**Another Way:** Use the Formula
Add the measures of all of the sides of the figure.	Multiply the length and the width by 2. Then add.
$P = 12 + 12 + 6 + 6$	$P = (2 \times \ell) + (2 \times w)$
$P = 36$	$P = (2 \times 12) + (2 \times 6)$
	$P = 24 + 12$ or 36

So, Berto walked 36 yards.

You can use addition or a formula to find the perimeter of a square.

EXAMPLE Find Perimeter

2 **Find the perimeter of a square with side lengths of 6 inches.**

There is more than one way to find the perimeter of a square.

6 in.

6 in. 6 in.

6 in.

One Way: Use Addition	**Another Way:** Use the Formula
Add the measures of all of the sides of the figure.	Multiply the length of one side by 4 because there are 4 sides of equal length.
$P = 6 + 6 + 6 + 6$ $P = 24$	$P = 4 \times \text{side length}$ $P = 4 \times 6$ $P = 24$

So, the perimeter of the square is 24 inches.

Online Personal Tutor at ca.gr4math.com

CHECK What You Know

Find the perimeter of each square or rectangle. See Examples 1 and 2 (pp. 438–439)

1. 8 cm, 8 cm, 8 cm, 8 cm

2. 7 in., 4 in., 4 in., 7 in.

3. 5 cm, 5 cm, 5 cm, 5 cm

4. Luis made a drawing of his room. His drawing is shown. What is the perimeter of Luis's room?

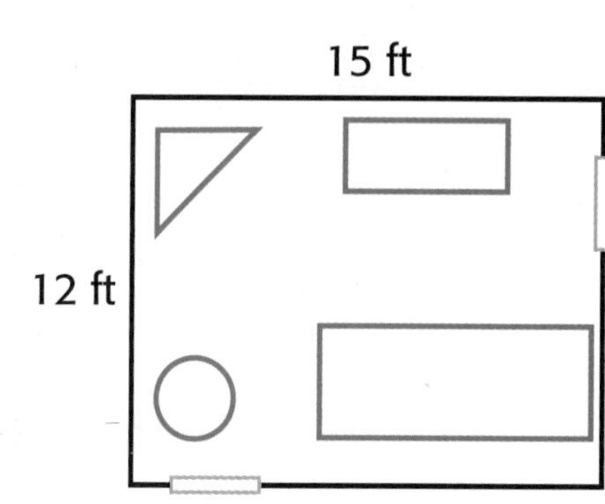

5. **Measurement** What is the perimeter of a square with side lengths of 4 inches?

6. Talk About It Explain the two ways to find the perimeter of a rectangle. What are the two ways to find the perimeter of a square?

Practice and Problem Solving

EXTRA PRACTICE See page R28.

Find the perimeter of each square or rectangle. See Examples 1 and 2 (pp. 438–439)

7.

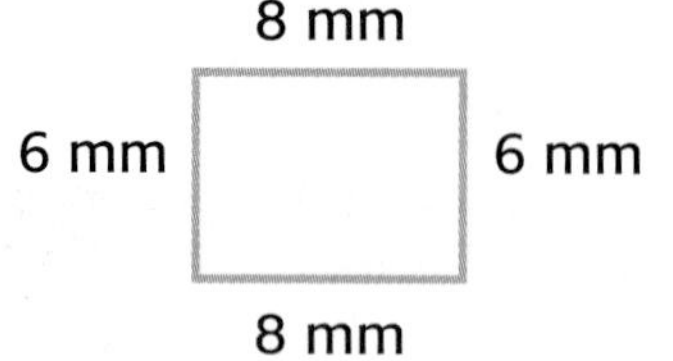

8.

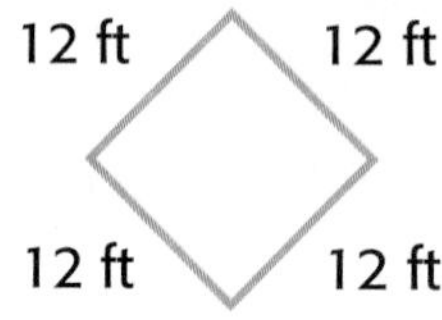

9.

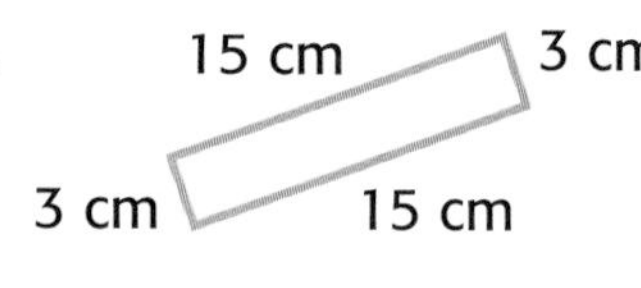

10.

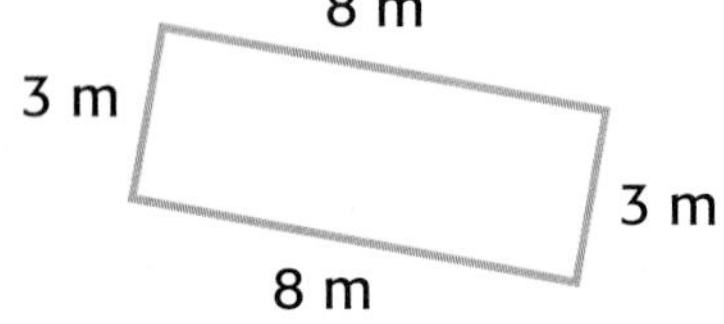

11.

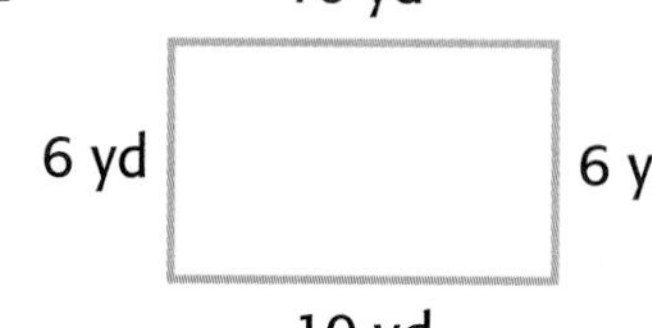

12.

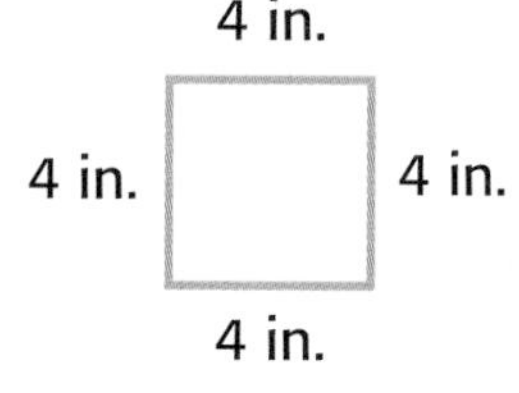

Find the perimeter of each rectangle in units.

13.

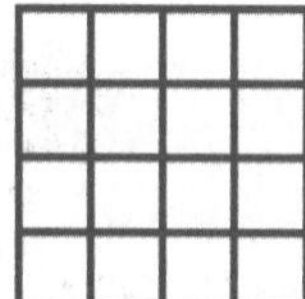

14.

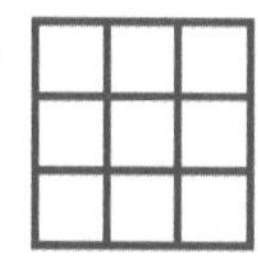

15.

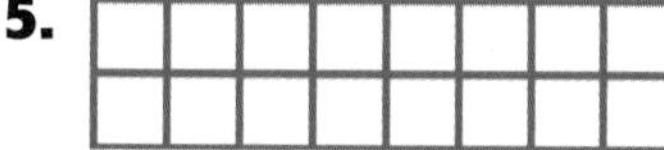

16. **Measurement** A baseball diamond is shaped like a square. Each side is 90 feet long. What is the total distance around the baseball diamond?

17. A family is installing a rectangular fence. Their yard is 82 feet long and 45 feet wide. How many feet of fencing will they need?

Real-World PROBLEM SOLVING

Social Science The Parthenon is an ancient building in Athens, Greece. It has a rectangular base measuring about 228 feet by 101 feet.

18. What is the perimeter of the base of the Parthenon?

19. If you doubled the length of each side of the base of the Parthenon, is the perimeter doubled?

H.O.T. Problems

20. **OPEN ENDED** Locate a four-sided figure in your classroom. Find its perimeter. What formula did you use to find the perimeter?

21. **WRITING IN MATH** Suppose you double the side length of the square. Will the perimeter also double? Explain.

Math Online Self-Check Quiz at ca.gr4math.com

CHAPTER 11 Mid-Chapter Check

Lessons 11-1 through 11-3

Tell whether the figures appear to be congruent. Write *yes* or *no*. (Lesson 11-1)

1. 

2. 

3. **Measurement** Tanika's swimming pool is 8 feet wide and 12 feet long. Tanika's neighbor has the same pool. If the pool is 12 feet long, how wide is it? (Lessson 11-1)

Tell whether each figure has line symmetry. Write *yes* or *no*. Then tell how many lines of symmetry the figure has. (Lesson 11-2)

4. 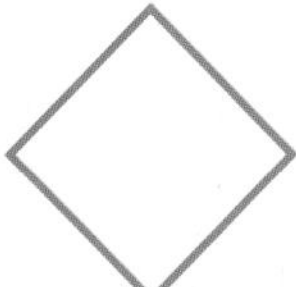

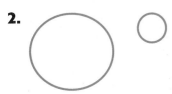

5. 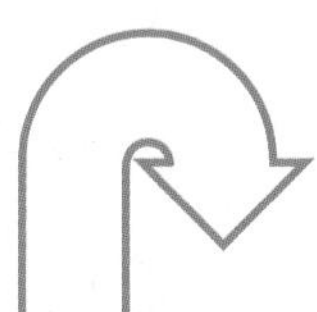

6. **STANDARDS PRACTICE** How many lines of symmetry does this figure have? (Lesson 11-2)

A 0

B 1

C 2

D 3

Find the perimeter of each square or rectangle. (Lesson 11-3)

7. 9 cm, 4 cm

8. 5 in., 5 in.

9. What is the perimeter of the rectangle below in units? (Lesson 11-3)

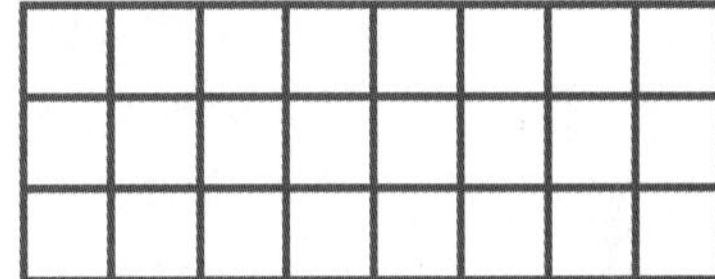

10. **Measurement** Kaya's family needs a fence in their yard for her new puppy. All four sides of the yard measure 20 yards. What is the perimeter needed for the fence? (Lesson 11-3)

11. **STANDARDS PRACTICE** What is the perimeter of the square shown? (Lesson 11-3)

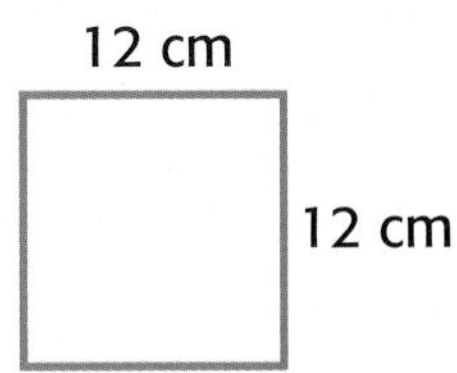

F 24 cm

G 36 cm

H 48 cm

J 60 cm

12. **WRITING IN ▶MATH** Can the formula for finding the perimeter of a rectangle be used to find the perimeter of a square? Explain.

11-4 Problem-Solving Strategy

MAIN IDEA I will solve problems by solving a simpler problem.

Standard 4MR1.2 **Determine when and how to break a problem into simpler parts.** Standard 4NS3.0 **Students solve problems involving addition,** subtraction, **multiplication,** and division **of whole numbers** and understand the relationships among the operations.

Pearl is painting a backdrop that is 30 feet long and 12 feet wide for a play. The backdrop needs two coats of paint. She has two cans of paint. Each can covers 400 square feet. You can use the formula Area = length × width to determine if Pearl has enough paint.

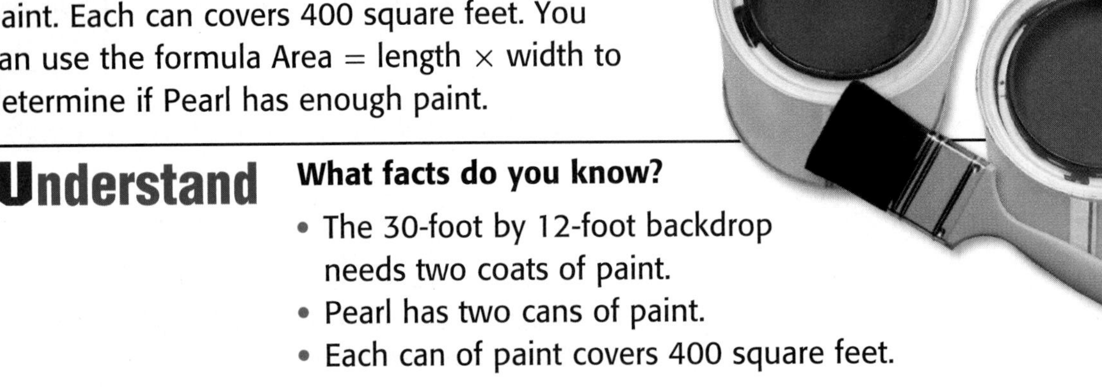

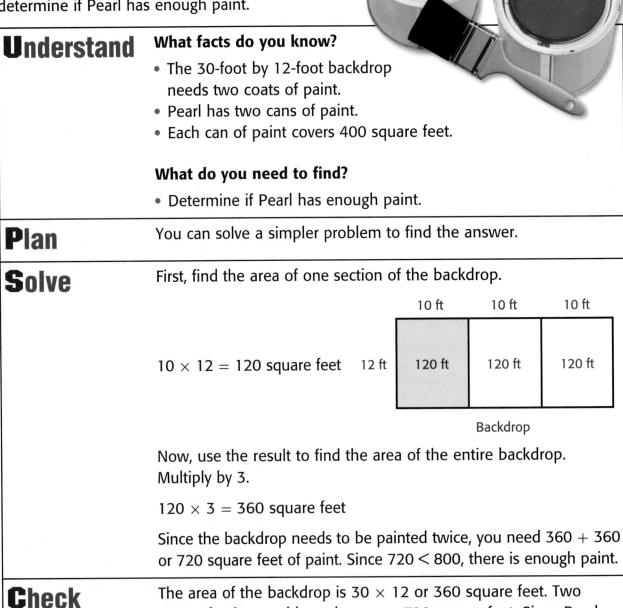

Understand

What facts do you know?

- The 30-foot by 12-foot backdrop needs two coats of paint.
- Pearl has two cans of paint.
- Each can of paint covers 400 square feet.

What do you need to find?

- Determine if Pearl has enough paint.

Plan

You can solve a simpler problem to find the answer.

Solve

First, find the area of one section of the backdrop.

$10 \times 12 = 120$ square feet

	10 ft	10 ft	10 ft
12 ft	120 ft	120 ft	120 ft

Backdrop

Now, use the result to find the area of the entire backdrop. Multiply by 3.

$120 \times 3 = 360$ square feet

Since the backdrop needs to be painted twice, you need $360 + 360$ or 720 square feet of paint. Since $720 < 800$, there is enough paint.

Check

The area of the backdrop is 30×12 or 360 square feet. Two coats of paint would need to cover 720 square feet. Since Pearl has enough paint to cover 800 square feet, the answer is correct.

ANALYZE the Strategy

Refer to the problem on the previous page.

1. Explain why 10 × 12 was the first step in finding the area of the backdrop.

2. Explain the steps that were taken to find the amount of paint needed to cover the backdrop twice.

3. Suppose each can of paint covers 350 square feet. Would she have enough to cover the backdrop twice? Explain.

4. Look back at Exercise 3. Explain how you found the answer.

PRACTICE the Strategy

EXTRA PRACTICE
See page R28.

Solve. Use the *solve a simpler problem* strategy.

5. Marcos is making three tile pictures. He uses 310 green tiles to make each picture. He uses 50 fewer red tiles than green tiles for each picture. How many red and green tiles does he use in all?

6. **Measurement** Ling is putting up a wallpaper border on three walls that are 14 feet long and 12 feet tall. How many feet of wallpaper border will she use if she puts the border only at the top of the wall?

7. Violeta sells twice as much orange juice as lemonade. She charges $1.50 for each. She sold 10 cups of lemonade. How much did she earn in all?

8. A basketball coach is going to buy 16 basketballs. What will be the total cost of the basketballs?

9. Jerome's CD has 16 songs, and each song is 3 minutes long. Ana's CD has 14 songs, and each song is 4 minutes. Whose CD plays longer and by how much?

10. Five gardeners spent 260 hours in all planting trees. One of the gardeners spent 40 hours. The rest spent the same amount of time. How many hours did each spend on planting trees?

11. Marian is placing 72 photographs in an album. She will put the same number of photos on each of 6 pages. She can put 4 pictures in each row. How many rows will be on each page?

12. WRITING IN MATH Explain how you solved Exercise 11.

11-5 Measurement: Area

MAIN IDEA

I will find the area of rectangles and squares.

Standard 4MG1.4 Understand and use formulas to solve problems involving perimeters and **areas of rectangles and squares.** Use those formulas to find the areas of more complex figures by dividing the figures into basic shapes.

Standard 4MG1.1 Measure the area of rectangular shapes by using appropriate units, such as square centimeter (cm^2), **square meter** (m^2), **square kilometer** (km^2), **square inch** ($in.^2$), **square yard** ($yd.^2$), or **square mile** ($mi.^2$).

New Vocabulary

area
square units

GET READY to Learn

The Perez family wants to put the sandbox shown in their backyard. What is the area of the sandbox?

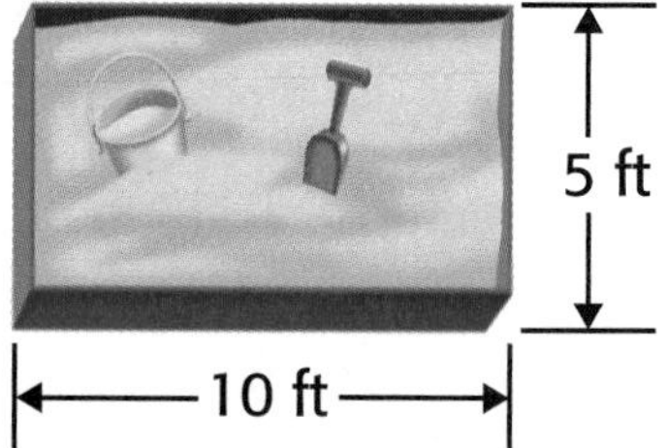

Area is the number of square units needed to cover a region or figure without any overlap. It is measured in **square units**.

Real-World EXAMPLE — Area of a Rectangle

1 SANDBOX Find the area of the sandbox.

One Way: Count	Another Way: Multiply
10 ft by 5 ft grid. There are 50 square feet.	Multiply the length times the width to find the area. A = length × width $A = \ell \times w$ = 10 feet × 5 feet = 50 square feet

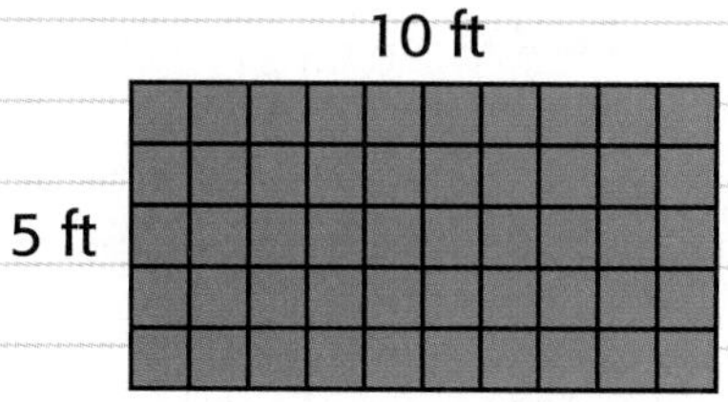

So, the area of the sandbox is 50 square feet.

KEY CONCEPT — Area of a Rectangle

Words To find the area of a rectangle, multiply the length by the width.

Formula $A = \ell \times w$

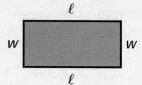

(Rectangle labeled ℓ, w, w, ℓ)

You can also find the area of a square.

KEY CONCEPT — Area of a Square

Words To find the area of a square, multiply the length of one side s by itself.

Formula $A = s \times s$

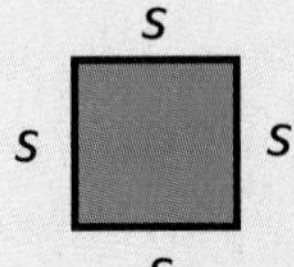

Real-World EXAMPLE — Area of a Square

2 **PICTURES What is the area of the picture if its sides are 4 inches in length?**

A = side × side	Formula
A = 4 in. × 4 in.	Replace s with 4.
A = 16 square inches	Multiply.

The area of the picture is 16 square inches.

Online **Personal Tutor at** ca.gr4math.com

CHECK What You Know

Find the area of each square or rectangle. **See Examples 1 and 2 (pp. 444–445)**

1. 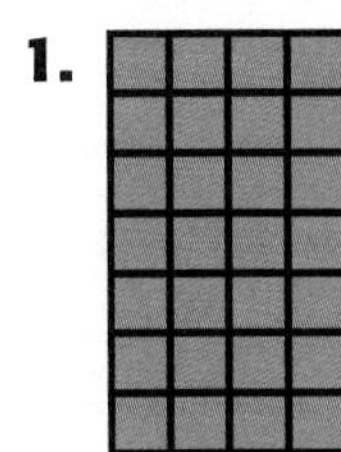

2. 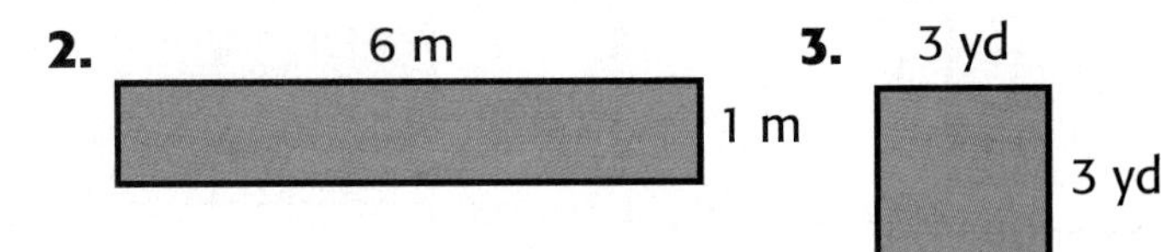

3.

4. Mr. Malone is hanging a picture on a wall. The picture frame has a length of 12 inches and a width of 9 inches. How much wall space will the picture need?

5. **Talk About It** Explain two ways to find the area of a rectangle. What are the two ways to find the area of a square?

Practice and Problem Solving

EXTRA PRACTICE
See page R29.

Find the area of each square or rectangle. See Examples 1 and 2 (pp. 444–445)

6. 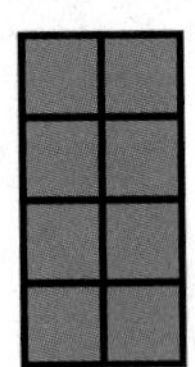

7. 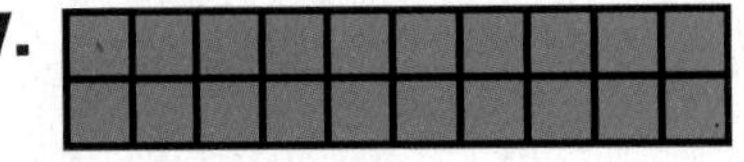

8. 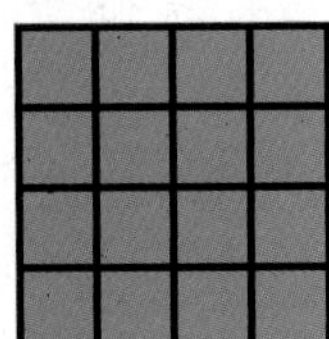

9. 6 m
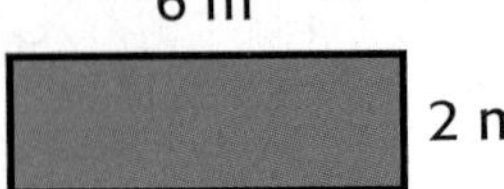
2 m

10. 8 km
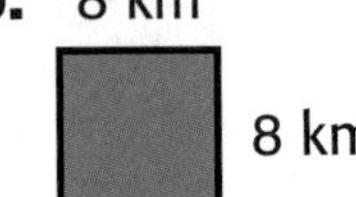
8 km

11. 10 yd
2 yd

12. Measurement Each child in Mrs. Chan's class has a rectangular desk that is 15 inches long and 32 inches wide. What is the area of each student's desk?

13. Measurement Ricky's computer monitor is a rectangle with an area of 180 square inches. The length is 15 inches. What is the perimeter of the monitor?

14. Measurement A car is 15 feet long and 6 feet wide. It is parked on a rectangular driveway with an area of 112 square feet. How much of the driveway is *not* covered by the car?

15. Measurement A rectangular playground is 40 meters by 10 meters. Its area will be covered with shredded tires. Each bag of shredded tires covers 200 square meters and costs $30. Find the total cost for this project.

H.O.T. Problems

16. OPEN ENDED Draw three rectangles that each have an area of 36 square inches, but have different perimeters.

NUMBER SENSE The area and the measure of one side of each square or rectangle is given. Find the missing sides.

17. 6 in.
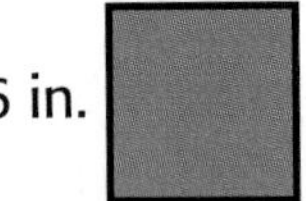
Area = 36 square inches

18. 4 m

Area = 36 square meters

19. 1 cm
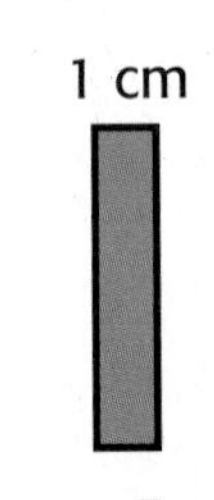
Area = 5 square centimeters

20. WRITING IN MATH A square has sides measuring 3 feet. If the sides of a square are doubled, will the area also double? Explain.

 Math Online Self-Check Quiz at ca.gr4math.com

Area Guess

Find Area of Rectangles

Get Ready!

Players: 2 players

You will need: 2 metric rulers with centimeters

Get Set!

Each player makes a copy of the table shown.

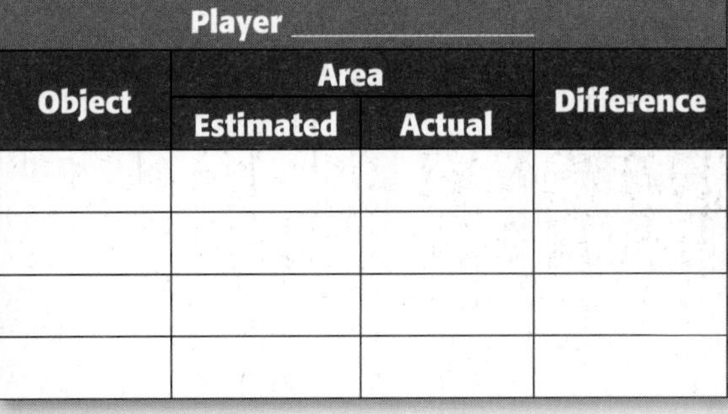

Player ______			
Object	Area		Difference
	Estimated	Actual	

Go!

- Each player selects four objects in the classroom that have a rectangular surface.
- Each player estimates the area of the objects selected to the nearest square centimeter.
- Find the exact measurements and the exact areas of the objects.
- Find the differences between the estimated areas and the actual areas of the objects.
- Find the sum of the four differences.
- The player who has the least difference between the estimated and actual areas wins.

Measurement Activity for 11-5

Perimeter and Area

In this activity, you will explore whether or not rectangles with the same area can have different perimeters.

MAIN IDEA

I will explore perimeter and area.

Standard 4MG1.2 Recognize that rectangles that have the same area can have different perimeters.

Standard 4MG1.3 Understand that rectangles that have the same perimeter can have different areas.

You Will Need

grid paper

ACTIVITY Relate Perimeter and Area

Step 1 Draw rectangles.

Draw the following rectangles on grid paper.

- 1 unit by 24 units
- 2 units by 12 units
- 3 units by 8 units
- 4 units by 6 units

Step 2 Copy and complete the table.

Find the perimeter and area of the rectangles. Record the information on your table.

Figure	Perimeter	Area
Rectangle 1	■ units	■ square units
Rectangle 2	■ units	■ square units
Rectangle 3	■ units	■ square units
Rectangle 4	■ units	■ square units

Step 3 Examine your table.

What similarities and differences do you notice among the rectangles?

Is it possible for rectangles with the same area to have different perimeters?

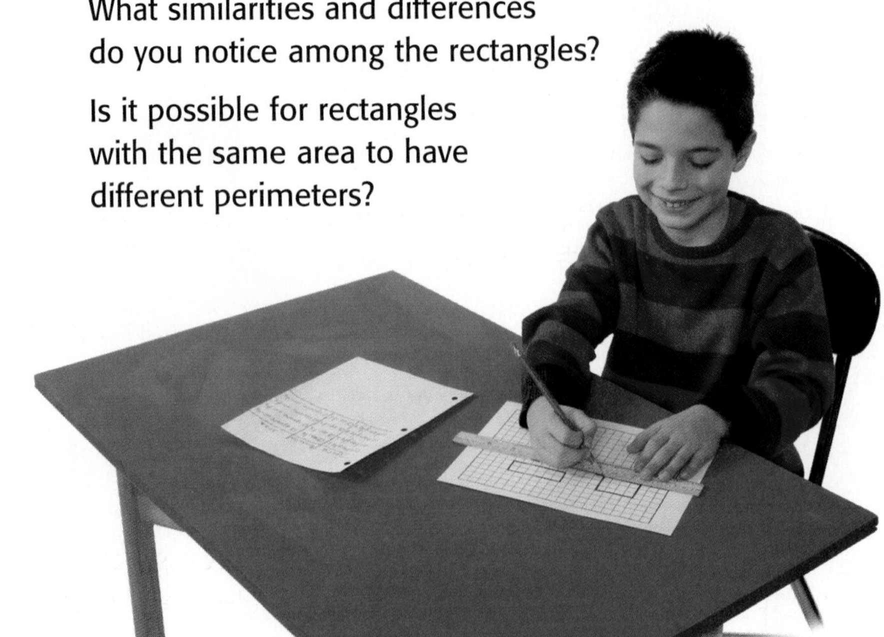

Animation
ca.gr4math.com

Think About It

1. Explain the difference between area and perimeter.

2. Is it possible to draw a rectangle that has an area of 24 square units and a perimeter of 24 units? Explain.

3. Is there a relationship between the area and the perimeter of a rectangle? Explain.

4. Look at the rectangles that you drew. What do you notice about the shape of the rectangle that has the greatest perimeter?

CHECK What You Know

Find the perimeter and area for each square or rectangle.

5.

6. 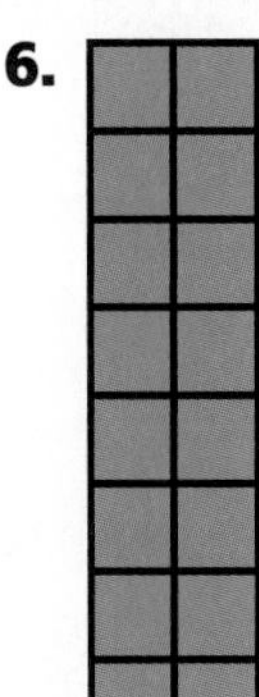

7.

8. What do the figures in Exercises 5–7 have in common? How do these figures differ?

9. Draw two rectangles that have the same areas and the same perimeters.

10. Can rectangles that have the same perimeter have different areas? Explain.

11. WRITING IN ▸MATH If a figure has a greater perimeter than another, does it also have a greater area? Explain your thinking.

Tide Pool Ecosystems

Tide pools are rocky areas on the edge of an ocean that are filled with sea water. Many plants and animals live there. Some animals that can be found in tide pools are starfish, mussels, and crabs. Kelp and other sea plants are also found in tide pools.

Life is tough for plants and animals that live in tide pools. Parts of the shore are covered and then uncovered as tides go in and out. The plants and animals that live in tide pools must avoid being washed away by waves, keep from drying out in the sun, and avoid predators. The tide pool ecosystem is the hardest ecosystem to recreate in an aquarium.

mussel

crab

starfish

Standard MG1.4 Understand and use formulas to solve problems involving perimeters and areas of rectangles and squares. Use those formulas to find the areas of more complex figures by dividing the figures into basic shapes.

Aquariums

Front Capacity (gal)	Side Length (in.)	Dimensions Width (in.)
20	24	12
25	30	12
30	36	18
40	48	12

Real-World Math

Use the information on pages 450 and 451 to solve each problem.

1. Which organisms in the photo have bilateral symmetry?
2. Which organisms in the photo have rotational symmetry?
3. How many lines of symmetry does the starfish have?
4. What is the perimeter of the front side of a 20-gallon aquarium?
5. What is the perimeter of the front side of a 30-gallon aquarium?
6. What is the perimeter of the front side of a 40-gallon aquarium?
7. What is the area of the front side of a 40-gallon aquarium?
8. Find the area of the front side of a 25-gallon aquarium. What is its perimeter? Which is greater?

Did You Know?

A starfish can grow back an arm if it loses one.

11-6 Problem-Solving Investigation

MAIN IDEA I will choose the best strategy to solve a problem.

Standard 4MR1.1 **Analyze problems by identifying relationships, distinguishing relevant from irrelevant information, sequencing and prioritizing information, and observing patterns.** 4NS3.0 **Students solve problems involving addition,** subtraction, **multiplication,** and division **of whole numbers** and understand the relationships among the operations.

P.S.I. TEAM +

LYNN: It takes me 4 minutes to jog one block in my neighborhood.

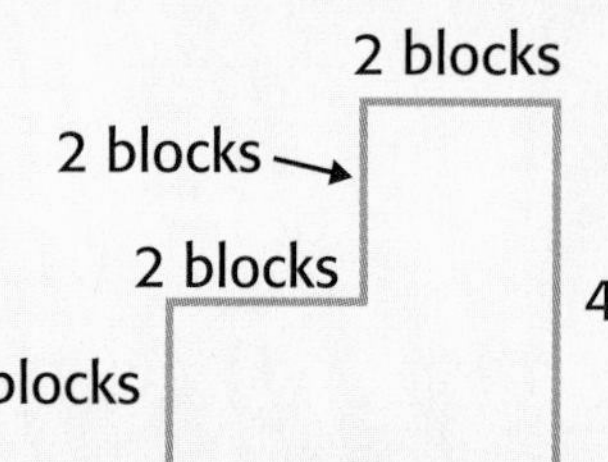

YOUR MISSION: Find how long it takes Lynn to jog the route in her neighborhood.

Understand	It takes Lynn 4 minutes to jog one block. Find how many minutes it takes her to jog the route shown.
Plan	You can use number sentences to solve the problem.
Solve	First, find the total number of blocks Lynn jogs. $\underbrace{2 + 2 + 2 + 2 + 4 + 4}_{\text{Add the distances}} = \underbrace{16}_{\text{Total blocks}}$ So, she jogs 16 blocks. Use number sentences to find how long it takes to jog the route. $\underbrace{4}_{\text{Minutes per block}} \times \underbrace{16}_{\text{Total blocks}} = \underbrace{64}_{\text{Total minutes}}$ So, Lynn jogs for 64 minutes.
Check	To check your work, estimate an answer: $4 \times 20 = 80$. Since 64 is close to 80, the answer is correct.

Mixed Problem Solving

See page R29.

Use any of the strategies shown below to solve. Tell what strategy you used.

PROBLEM-SOLVING STRATEGIES
- Act it out.
- Guess and check.
- Look for a pattern.
- Work a simpler problem.

1. **Measurement** A lion cub's weight is shown. An older lion weighs three times as much as the cub. How much do the lions weigh altogether?

2. **Measurement** The temperature when Jake got up was 45°F. By recess, the temperature had risen 8°F. Then, at bedtime, the temperature had fallen 4°F. What was the temperature when Jake went to bed?

3. Four numbers between 1 and 9 have a sum of 23. Use each number once. What are the numbers?

4. A movie theater has 18 screens. About 212 people go to each movie on a Friday. If all the screens are showing a movie at the same time on Friday, about how many people are in the theater?

5. The table shows the amount of vegetables sold at a grocery store every four weeks. Is it reasonable to say that the store sells about 300 vegetables every week?

Vegetable	Amount
Corn	396
Onions	316
Tomatoes	489

6. Alak brought 25 trading cards to a hobby show. He received three cards for one card in three trades. Then he gave 2 cards for one card in two trades. How many cards does Alak have now?

7. Pedro bought 3 pencils for 75¢. How much would 10 pencils cost?

8. Describe the pattern below. Then find the missing number.

   20, 200, 2,000, ■, 200,000

9. **Measurement** Clarissa has 4 pictures that are the size of the one shown. How much space will they take up in her photo album?

5 in.

3 in.

10. **WRITING IN ▸MATH** Look back at Exercise 9. Explain how you solved the problem.

11-7 Measurement: Area of Complex Figures

GET READY to Learn

Drew is staying at a hotel that has the swimming pool shown. Drew wants to know the area of the pool. How can he find the area?

MAIN IDEA

I will find the area of complex figures.

Standard 4MG1.4 Understand and use formulas to solve problems involving perimeters and **areas of rectangles and squares. Use those formulas to find the areas of more complex figures by dividing the figures into basic shapes.**

New Vocabulary

complex figure

A **complex figure** is made up of two or more shapes. To find the area of a complex figure, break the figure into smaller parts.

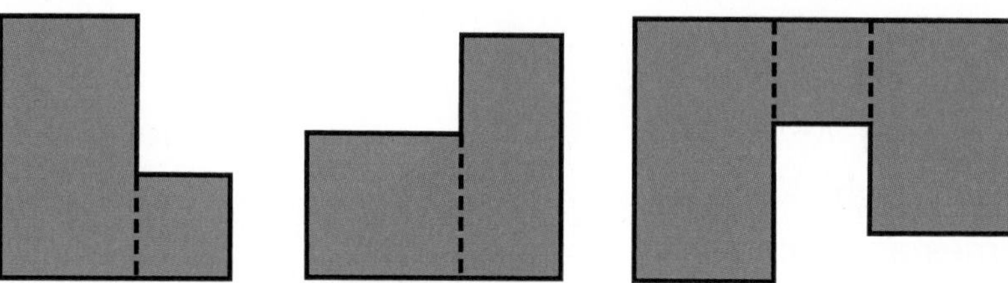

Real-World EXAMPLE

Area of a Complex Figure

1 **POOLS** **Find the area of the swimming pool at Drew's hotel.**

Step 1 Break up the figure into smaller parts. Look for rectangles and squares.

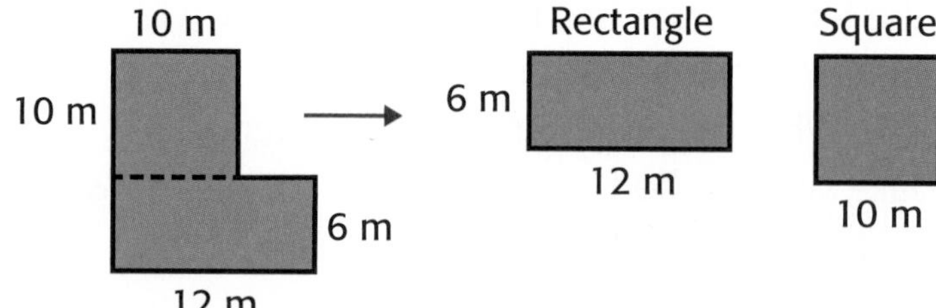

Step 2 Find the area of each part.

Rectangle

$A =$ length $\times$ width

$A = \ell \times w$

$A = 12 \text{ m} \times 6 \text{ m}$

$A = 72$ square meters

Square

$A =$ side $\times$ side

$A = s \times s$

$A = 10 \text{ m} \times 10 \text{ m}$

$A = 100$ square meters

Step 3 Add the areas.

The area is $72 + 100$ or 172 square meters.

EXAMPLE Area of a Complex Figure

2 **Find the area of the complex figure.**

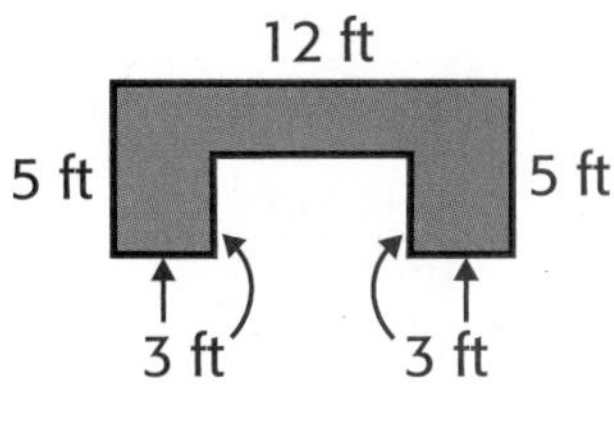

Step 1 Break up the figure into smaller parts. Look for rectangles and squares. This figure can be broken into 1 rectangle and 2 squares.

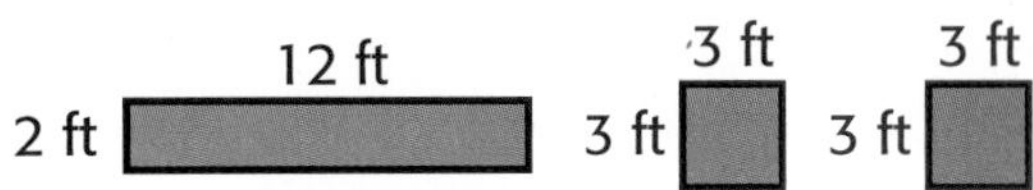

Step 2 Find the area of each part.

Rectangle	**Square**
A = length × width	A = side × side
A = 12 ft × 2 ft	A = 3 ft × 3 ft
A = 24 square feet	A = 9 square feet

Step 3 Add the areas.
24 + 9 + 9 = 42

So, the area of the figure is 42 square feet.

Online **Personal Tutor at** ca.gr4math.com

CHECK What You Know

Find the area of each figure. See Examples 1 and 2 (pp. 454–455)

1.

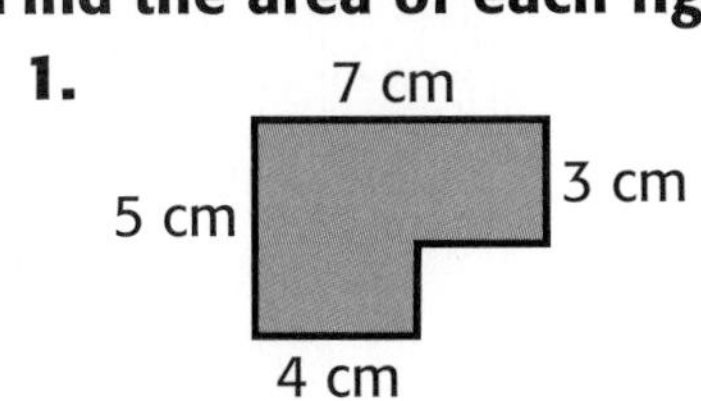

2.

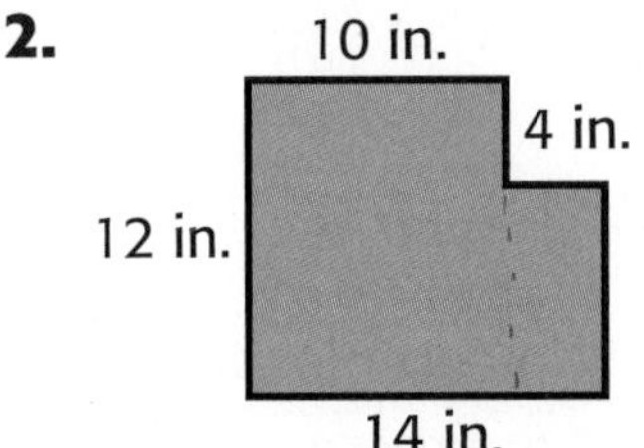

3.

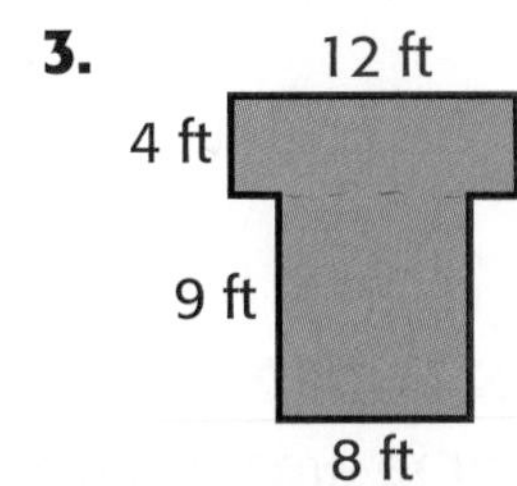

4. What is the area of the garden shown at the right?

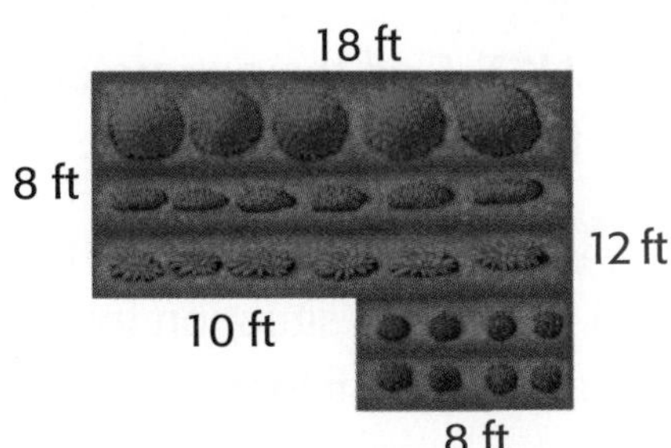

5. Talk About It Refer to Exercise 4. When finding the area of the garden, what two shapes did you look for?

Practice and Problem Solving

EXTRA PRACTICE
See page R29.

Find the area of each figure. See Examples 1 and 2 (pp. 454–455)

6.

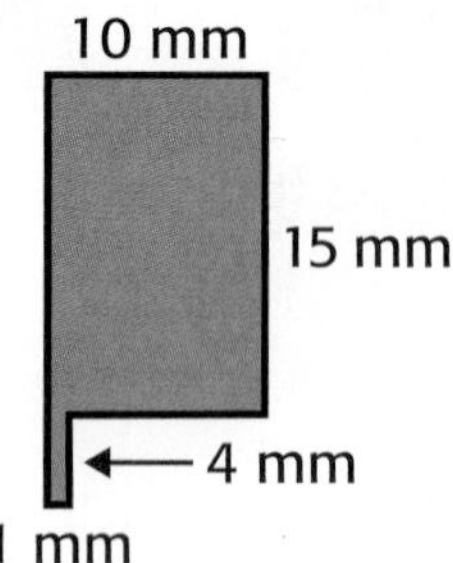

7.

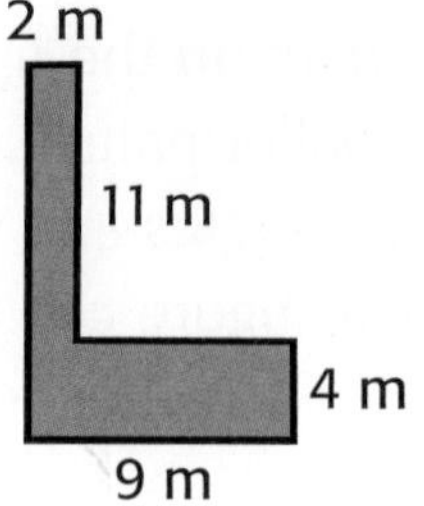

8.

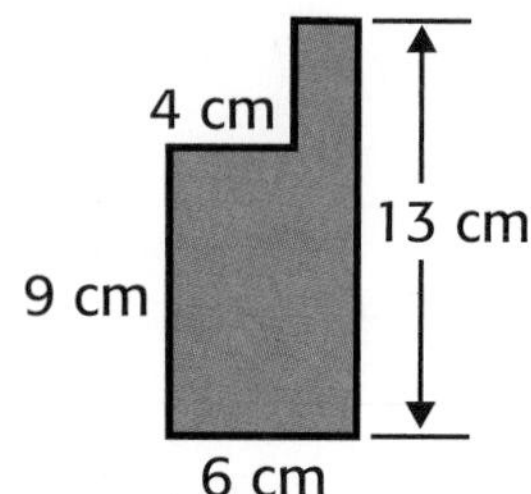

9.

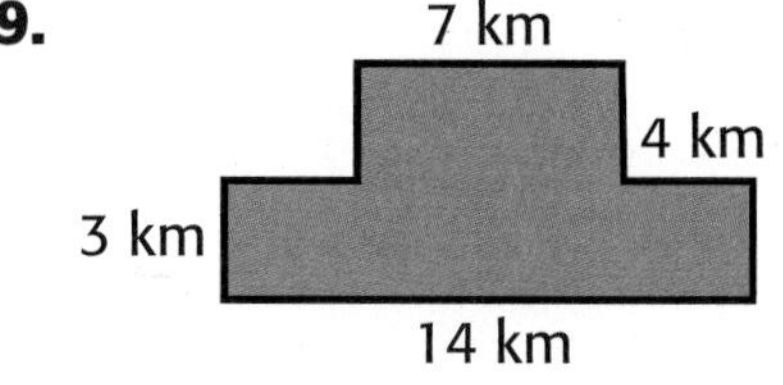

10.

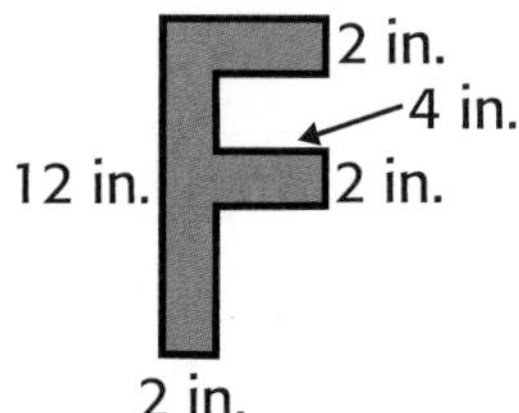

11.

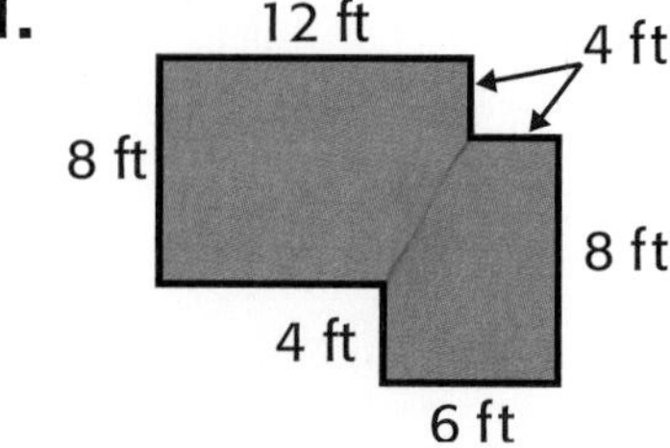

12. Courtney is playing miniature golf. What is the area of the entire figure?

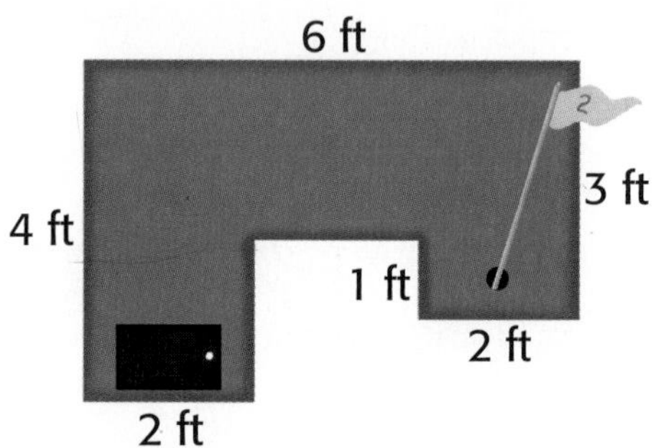

13. What is the area of the desktop?

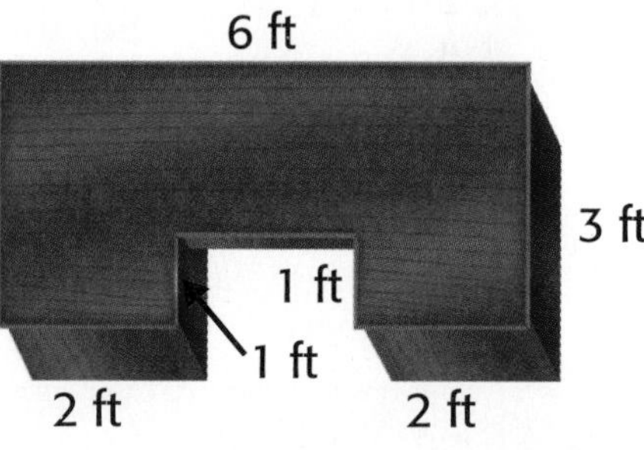

H.O.T. Problems

14. OPEN ENDED Draw and label two complex figures that have the same area but have different perimeters.

15. CHALLENGE Find the perimeter and area of the shaded figure in units.

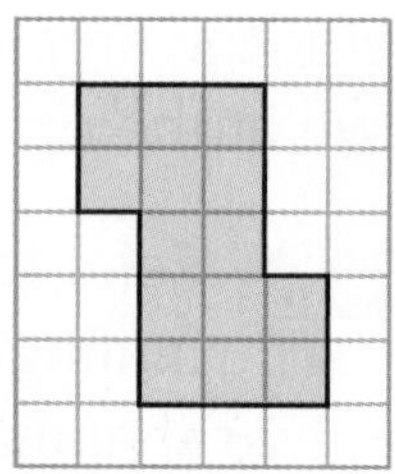

16. WRITING IN MATH Create a word problem about a real-world situation involving perimeter and area of a complex figure.

 Math Online Self-Check Quiz at ca.gr4math.com

Standards Practice

17 Which equation below represents the area (A) of the square in square inches? **(Lesson 11-5)**

7 in.

A $7 = A \times 7$

B $A = (2 \times 7) + (2 \times 7)$

C $A = 7 \times 7$

D $A = 7 \times 4$

18 Which statement about the figure is true? **(Lesson 11-7)**

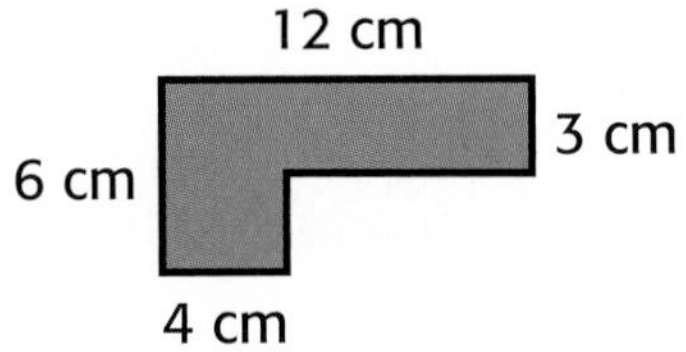

F The area is equal to the perimeter.

G The perimeter is greater than the area.

H The perimeter 38 centimeters.

J The area is 48 square centimeters.

Spiral Review

19. The sum of two numbers is 26. One number is four more than the other. What are the two numbers? **(Lesson 11-6)**

20. Bobby is mowing a lawn that is rectangular in shape. The lawn is 35 feet wide and 75 feet long. What is the area of the lawn? **(Lesson 11-5)**

Find the perimeter of each square or rectangle. **(Lesson 11-3)**

21. 6 cm

6 cm

22.

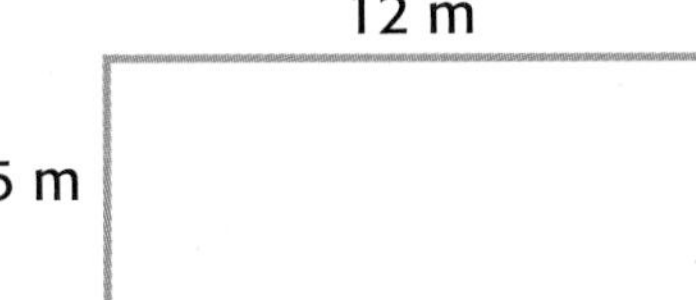

23. Pia plays 32 minutes each soccer game and has 15 games during the season. Her older sister plays 28 minutes each soccer game and has 18 games in her season. How many more minutes does Pia's sister play than Pia? **(Lesson 7-6)**

Find the value of each expression. **(Lesson 6-3)**

24. $(9 + 11) \times 5 - 10$

25. $(23 - 5) \div 3 + 8$

26. $2 + 30 - (5 \times 5)$

27. **Algebra** Copy and complete $6 \times (\blacksquare \times 5) = (6 \times 4) \times 5$. Identify the property used. **(Lesson 5-2)**

Study Guide and Review

FOLDABLES™ Study Organizer GET READY to Study

Be sure the following Key Vocabulary words and Key Concepts are written in your Foldable.

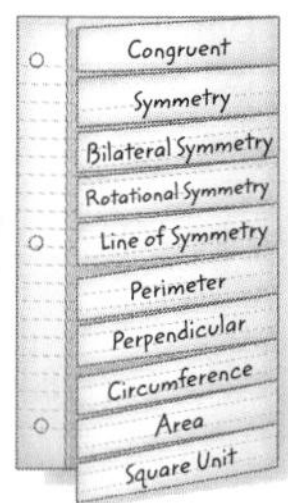

BIG Ideas

Congruent Figures (pp. 429–430)

Two figures are **congruent** if they have the same size and shape.

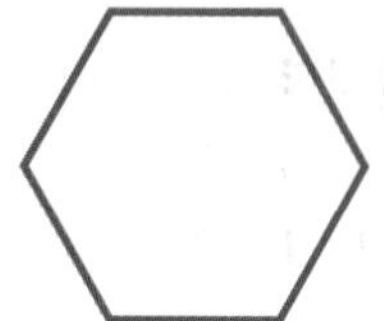

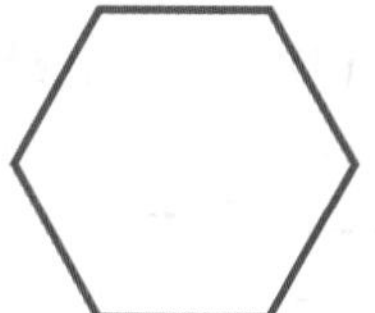

Line Symmetry (p. 432)

A figure has **line symmetry** if it can be folded so that two parts are congruent.

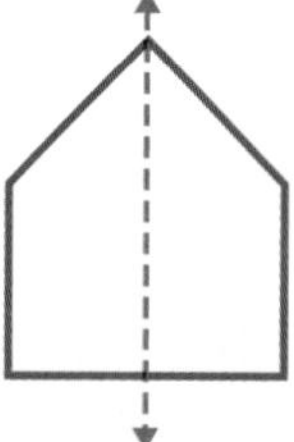

Perimeter and Area (pp. 436 and 443)

- Perimeter is the sum of the lengths of the sides of a figure.
- Area of a rectangle = length × width
- Area of a square = side × side

Key Vocabulary

area (p. 449)
complex figure (p. 454)
congruent (p. 431)
line symmetry (p. 434)
perimeter (p. 438)

Vocabulary Check

Choose the vocabulary word that completes each sentence.

1. The distance around a figure is the ___?___.
2. If two figures have the same size and shape, they are ___?___.
3. A figure has ___?___ if it can be folded so that the two parts of the figure match.
4. ___?___ refers to the number of square units needed to cover a region or figure.
5. A ___?___ is a shape that is made up of two or more basic shapes.

Math Online Vocabulary Review at ca.gr4math.com

Lesson-by-Lesson Review

11-1 Geometry: Congruent (pp. 431–433)

Example 1
The diagrams show the shapes and sizes of two tables. Are the tables congruent? Explain.

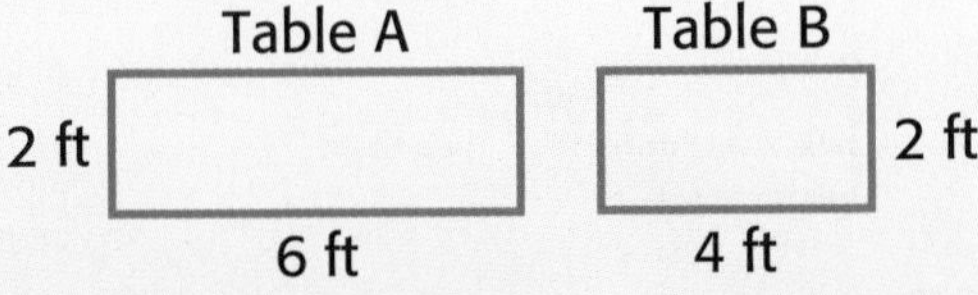

Both tables have the same width but do not have the same length.

Since the tables have different sizes, they are not congruent.

Tell whether the figures appear to be congruent. Write *yes* or *no*.

6. 

7. 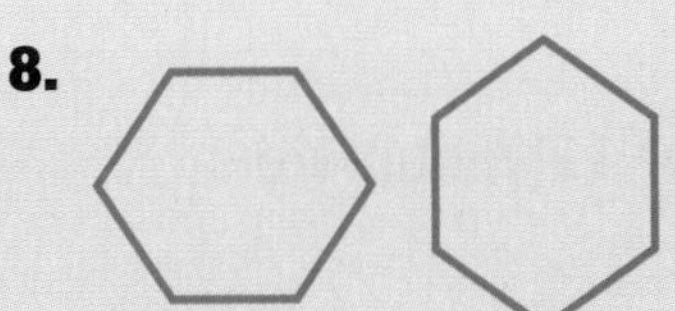

8.

11-2 Geometry: Symmetry (pp. 434–437)

Example 2
Tell whether each figure has line symmetry. Then tell how many lines of symmetry the figure has.

The figure has 0 lines of symmetry.

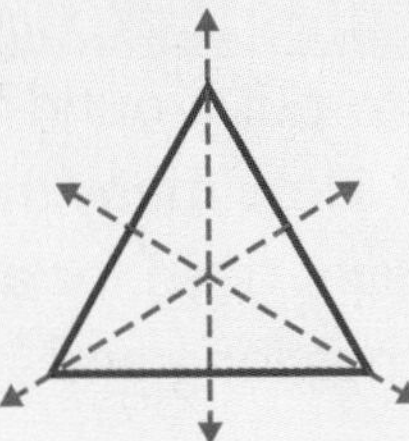

The figure has 3 lines of symmetry.

Tell whether each figure has line symmetry. Write *yes* or *no*. Then tell how many lines of symmetry the figure has.

9. **10.**

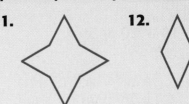

Tell whether the figure has rotational symmetry. Write *yes* or *no*.

11. **12.**

11-3 Measurement: Perimeter (pp. 438–440)

Example 3
Find the perimeter of the rectangle.

12 in.
8 in. | 8 in.
12 in.

$P = 2\ell + 2w$
$P = (2 \times 12) + (2 \times 8)$
$P = 24 + 16$ or 40 inches

Example 4
Find the perimeter of the square.

3 cm

$P = 4 \times s$
$P = 4 \times 3$ or 12 centimeters

Find the perimeter of each square or rectangle.

13. 15 cm, 3 cm

14. 6 yd, 6 yd

15. **Measurement** A poster has a length of 24 inches and its width is 12 inches. What is the perimeter of the poster?

11-4 Problem-Solving Strategy: Solve a Simpler Problem (pp. 442–443)

Example 5
Find the perimeter of the first floor of the house shown below.

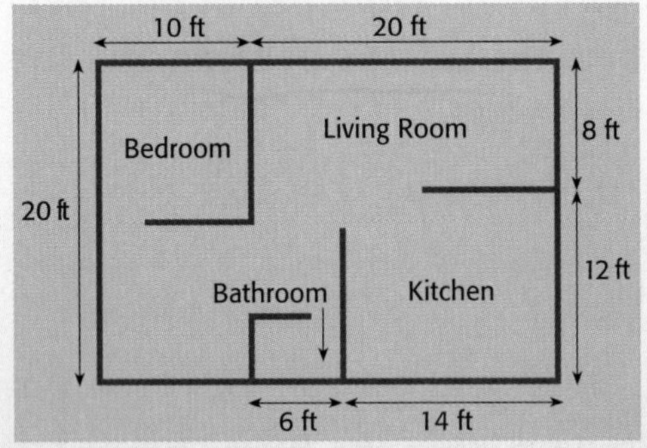

Find the total length first. Then multiply by the width.

Length = 10 + 20 or 30 ft
Width = 20 ft

$P = \ell + \ell + w + w$
$P = 30 + 30 + 20 + 20$
$P = 60 + 40$ or 100 feet

16. **Measurement** Mr. and Mrs. Lobo are building a fence around their rectangular yard that is 16 ft long and 14 ft wide. How much fence will they need?

17. Melisa ran two laps around the track. How many feet did she run?

440 ft
220 ft

18. **Measurement** Oliver is buying string to put around the edges of a poster. How many inches of string will Oliver need for a poster that is 44 inches long and 28 inches wide?

11-5 Measurement: Area (pp. 444–447)

Example 6
Find the area of a rectangle that is 7 meters by 4 meters.

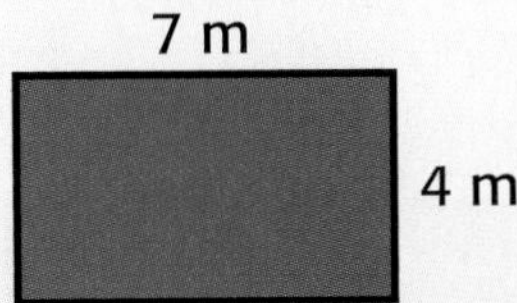

To find the area, multiply the length and the width.

$A = \ell \times w$
$A = 7$ meters $\times$ 4 meters
$A = 28$ square meters

So, the area of the rectangle is 28 square meters.

Example 7
What is the area of a square with sides that are 5 inches in length?

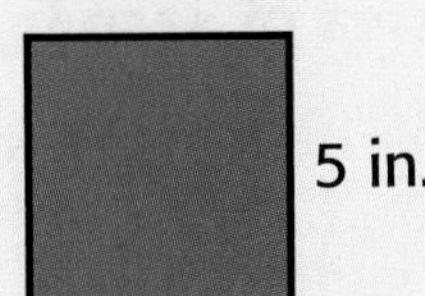

To find the area, multiply the side length by itself.

$A = s \times s$
$A = 5$ inches $\times$ 5 inches
$A = 25$ square inches

So, the area of the square is 25 square inches.

Find the area of each square or rectangle.

19. 

20. 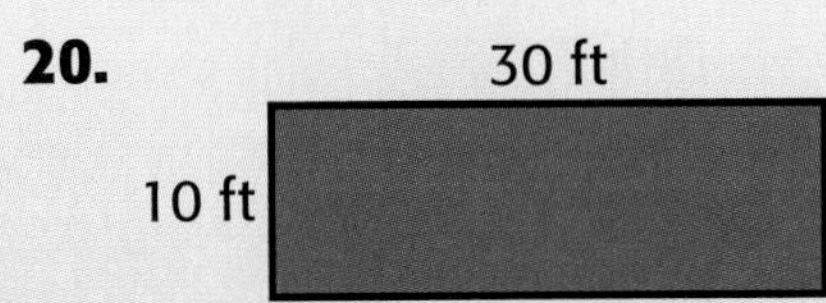

21. 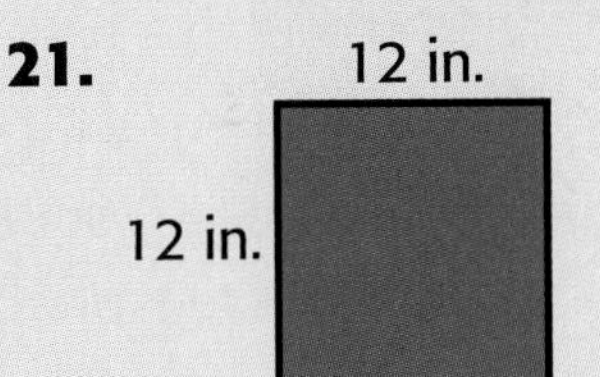

Algebra The area and the measure of one side of each square or rectangle is given. Find the missing side.

22. 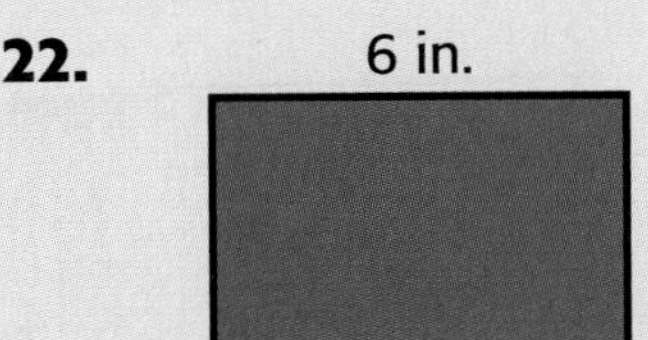

Area = 24 square inches

23. 8 ft

Area = 64 square feet

24. Rodolfo's table tennis table has an area of 45 square feet. The length is 9 feet. What is the perimeter of the table tennis table?

11-6 Problem-Solving Investigation: Choose a Strategy (pp. 452–453)

Example 8
Mr. Palmer is buying a cover for his pool table. Is it reasonable to say that a cover with an area of 30 square feet will be large enough to cover his pool table?

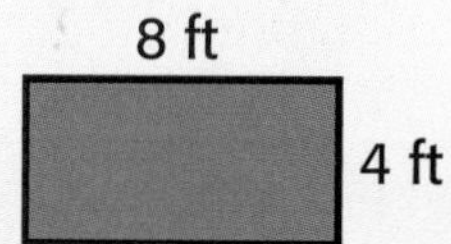

$A = \ell \times w$

$A = 8 \text{ feet} \times 4 \text{ feet}$

$A = 32 \text{ square feet}$

The pool table has an area of 32 square feet. Since $30 < 32$, it is not reasonable to say that the cover is large enough.

Use any strategy to solve.

25. Mindy is mowing the lawn. What area does she have to mow?

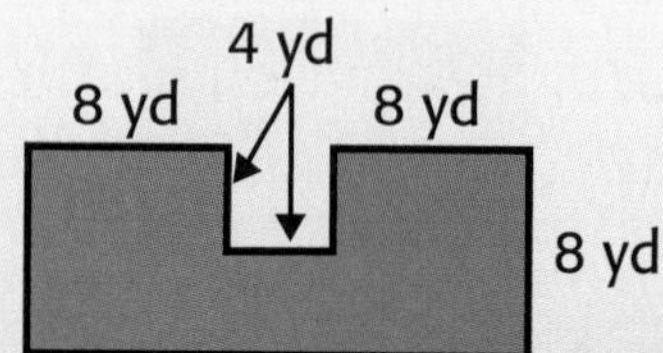

26. Measurement What is the total area of the three squares below?

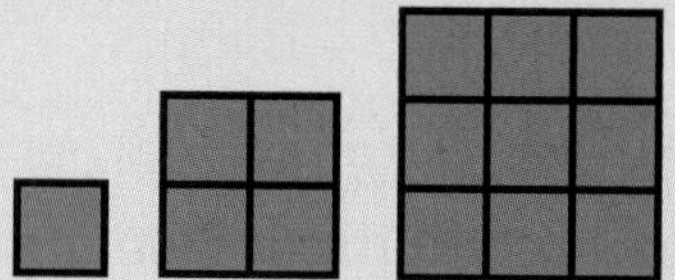

11-7 Measurement: Area of Complex Figures (pp. 454–457)

Example 9
Find the area of the complex figure.

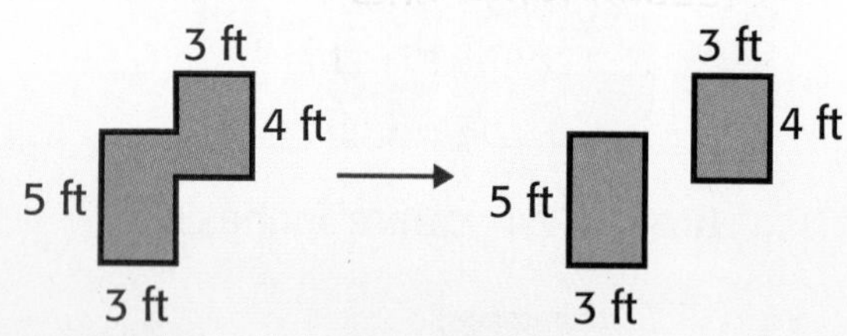

This figure can be broken into 2 rectangles.

$A = 5 \times 3$ $\quad$ $A = 3 \times 4$

$A = 15$ $\quad$ $A = 12$

$15 + 12 = 27$

So, the area is 27 square feet.

Find the area of each figure.

27.

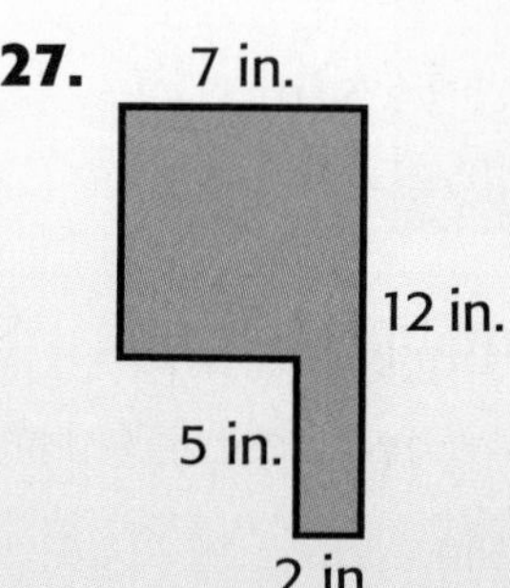

28.

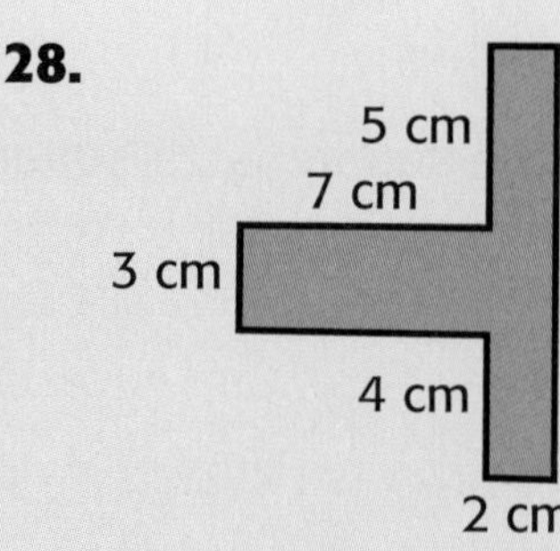

CHAPTER 11 Chapter Test

For Exercises 1 and 2, tell whether each statement is *true* or *false*.

1. To find the area of a complex figure, break the figure into smaller parts.

2. Figures that have the same size and shape are congruent.

Find the area of each figure.

3.

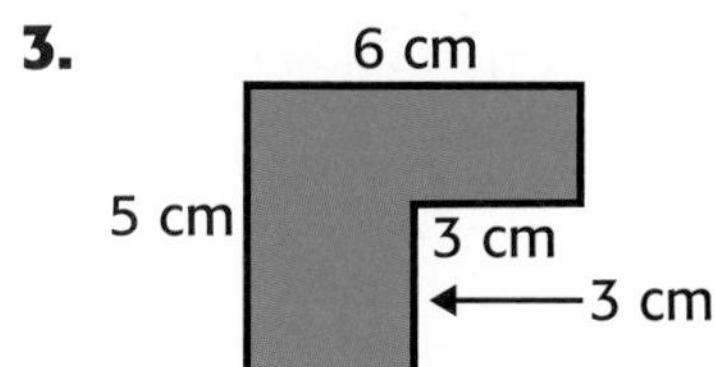

4.

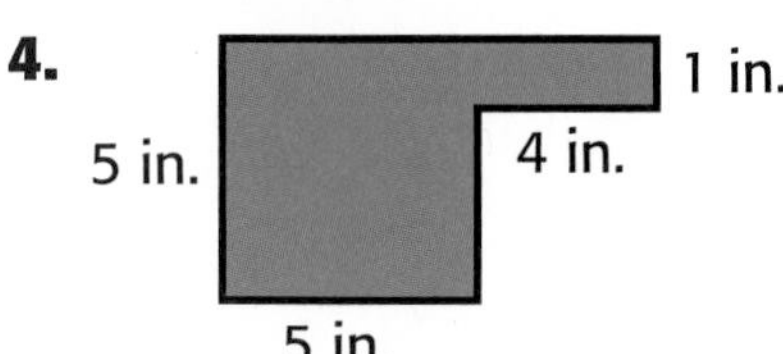

5. Tessa is helping her father build a tree house. The floor is to have an area of 24 square feet. If the length of the floor is 6 feet, what is the width?

6. **STANDARDS PRACTICE** Which statement about the rectangle is true?

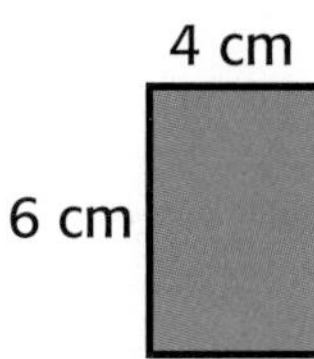

A The area is equal to the perimeter.

B The area is less than the perimeter.

C The perimeter is 20 centimeters.

D The area is 10 square centimeters.

7. Find the area of the rectangle.

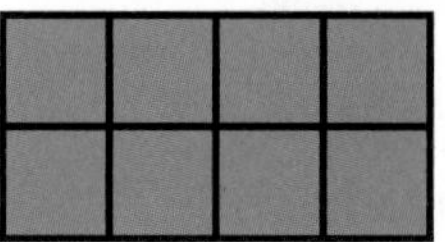

8. Brett had to paint 3 walls. Each wall was 9 feet tall and 12 feet long. How much wall area did he paint?

9. Which figure has the greater perimeter?

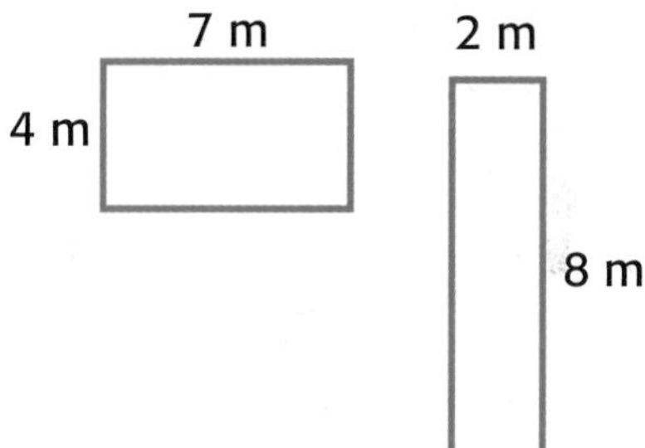

Tell how many lines of symmetry each letter has.

10. Y

11. H

12. **STANDARDS PRACTICE** Which equation represents the area (A) of the square in square inches?

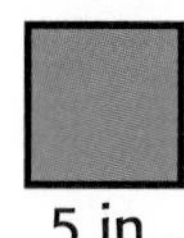

F $5 = A \times 5$

G $A = 5 \times 5$

H $A = (2 \times 5) + (2 \times 5)$

J $A = 5 \times 4$

13. **WRITING IN MATH** Do all squares have the same number of lines of symmetry? Explain.

CHAPTER 11

California Standards Practice

Cumulative, Chapters 1–11

Standards Example

The Dawson family's living room is shown. What is the area of the living room?

8 ft
10 ft
4 ft
4 ft

A 112 square feet **C** 48 square feet

B 64 square feet **D** 28 square feet

Read the Question

You need to find the area of the living room.

Solve the Question

Find the area of each shape. Then add the areas.

Area of Rectangle

$A = \ell \times w$

$A = 8$ feet $\times$ 6 feet

$A = 48$ square feet

Area of Square

$A = s \times s$

$A = 4$ feet $\times$ 4 feet

$A = 16$ square feet

48 square feet + 16 square feet = 64 square feet

So, the area of the living room is 64 square feet. The answer is B.

Personal Tutor at ca.gr4math.com

Choose the best answer.

1 **What is the perimeter of a square that has an area of 64 square feet?**

A 8 feet **C** 24 feet

B 16 feet **D** 32 feet

2 **Which shape has bilateral symmetry?**

F ⌂ **H** △

G ▭ **J** ♡

3 **Hannah plans to put a fence around her yard.**

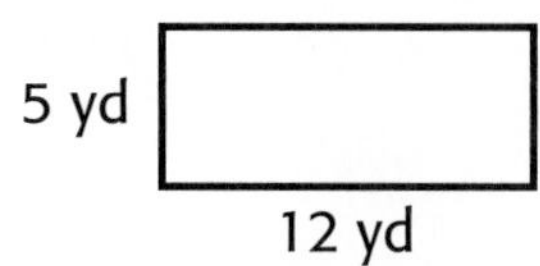

What is the perimeter of the yard?

A 28 yards
B 32 yards
C 34 yards
D 46 yards

4 **Which triangle appears to be congruent to the one shown at the right?**

F

G

H 

J 

5 **What is the value of the expression?**

$$(72 - 9) \div (7 \times 1)$$

A 7
B 8
C 9
D 56

6 **Julius collected 640 cans. Mark said he collected 10 times the number Julius collected. How many cans did Mark collect?**

F 640
G 6000
H 6400
J 64,000

7 **Identify the angle shown below.**

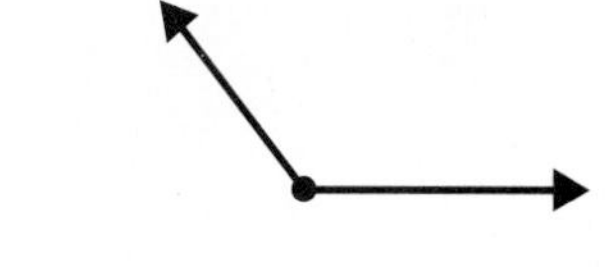

A right
B obtuse
C acute
D scalene

8 $6\overline{)2124}$

F 354
G 364
H 454
J 464

9 **Which pair of figures appear to be congruent?**

A

B

C

D

10 **Nita plans to tile her bathroom floor, which is shown. The tiles are 1 foot long and 1 foot wide. How many tiles will she need?**

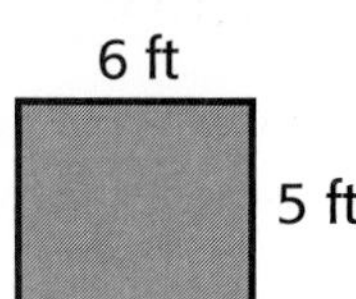

F 11 tiles
G 25 tiles
H 26 tiles
J 30 tiles

CHAPTER 12 Algebra and Graphing

BIG Idea What is a function?

A **function** is a relationship where one quantity depends upon another quantity.

Example Lia practices for 2 hours each week. The total hours she practices depends upon the number of weeks.

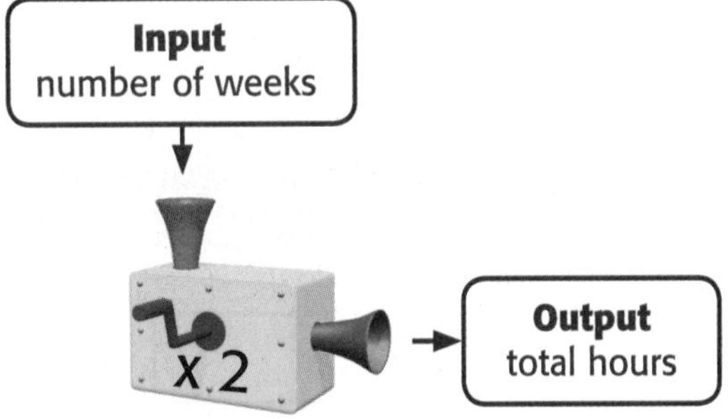

What will I learn in this chapter?

- Understand and use negative numbers.
- Locate and name points on a coordinate grid.
- Complete function tables.
- Draw points to show linear relationships.
- Solve problems by using logical reasoning.

Key Vocabulary

coordinate

ordered pair

origin

***x*-axis**

***y*-axis**

Student Study Tools at ca.gr4math.com

FOLDABLES™ Study Organizer

Make this Foldable to help you organize information about algebra and graphing. Begin with three sheets of $8\frac{1}{2}'' \times 11''$ paper.

1. **Stack** the paper slightly apart as shown.

2. **Fold** the bottom up to form tabs. Crease.

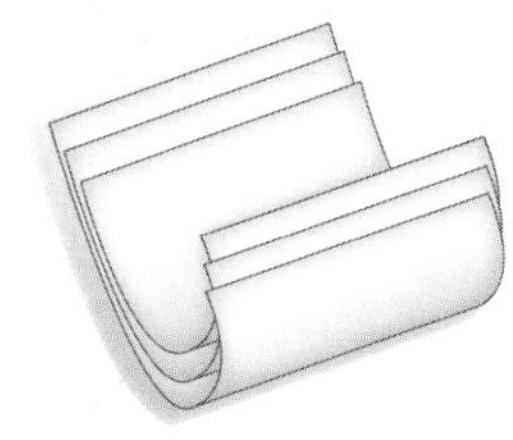

3. **Staple** along the crease.

4. **Label** with the topics from the chapter as shown.

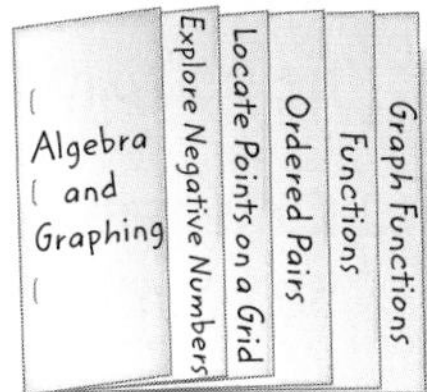

ARE YOU READY for Chapter 12?

You have two ways to check prerequisite skills for this chapter.

Option 2

Math Online Take the Chapter Readiness Quiz at ca.gr4math.com.

Option 1

Complete the Quick Check below.

QUICK Check

Graph each set of numbers on a number line. (Lesson 1-5)

1. 5, 0, 2, 4, 6

2. 1, 3, 9, 7, 0

Find the value of each expression if $a = 4$ and $c = 8$. (Lesson 6-1)

3. $a \times 2$

4. $c \div a$

5. $(16 \div a) \times 6$

6. $(c \div a) \times 7$

Copy and complete each table. Then describe the rule. (Lessons 3-4 and 6-6)

7.

Input	Output
2	10
3	11
5	13
7	■
9	■

8.

Input	Output
12	2
24	4
36	6
42	■
54	■

For Exercises 9–11, use the graph. It shows the amount of money Yao earns to babysit 1, 2, 3, and 4 children. (Lesson 12-6)

9. How much does Yao earn per child?

10. How much more money will he earn if he babysits 4 children than 2 children?

11. If the pattern continues, how much will he earn if he babysits 5 children?

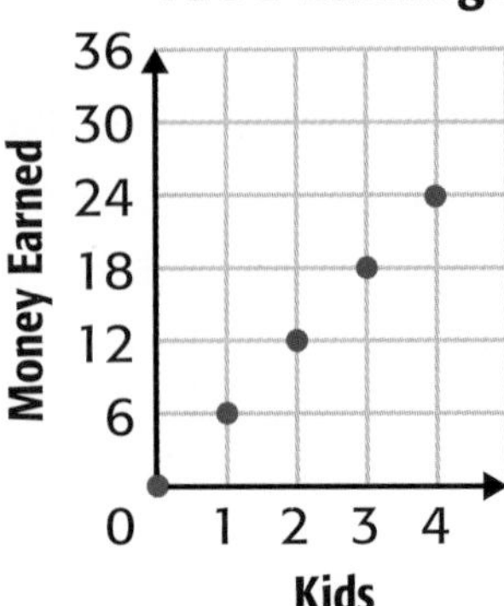

12-1 Negative Numbers

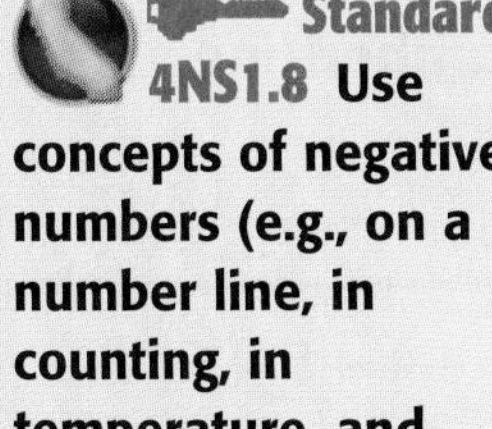

MAIN IDEA

I will understand and use negative numbers.

Standard 4NS1.8 **Use concepts of negative numbers (e.g., on a number line, in counting, in temperature, and in "owing").**

New Vocabulary

positive number
negative number

GET READY to Learn

Clara is recording temperature data for a science project. Which temperatures are above zero? Which temperatures are below zero?

Weekday Low Temperatures	
Day	**Low Temperature**
Monday	+5°F
Tuesday	−2°F
Wednesday	−1°F
Thursday	+4°F
Friday	−3°F

The numbers +5 and +4 are **positive numbers**. They can be written with or without a + sign. The numbers −2, −1, and −3 are **negative numbers**. A negative number has a − sign.

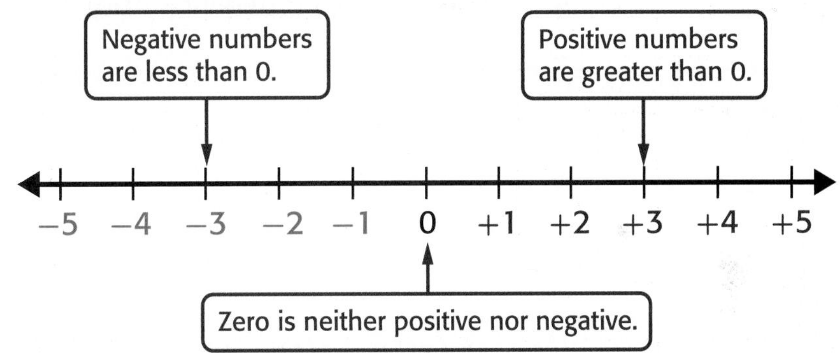

Real-World EXAMPLES Write Negative Numbers

Write the number that represents each situation.

1. **WEATHER 4 degrees below zero**
The temperature is below zero. The number is –4.

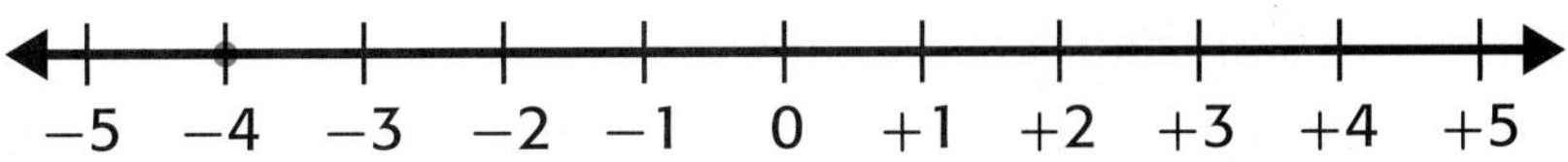

2. **FOOTBALL a gain of 3 yards**
The word *gain* means an increase. The number is +3 or 3.

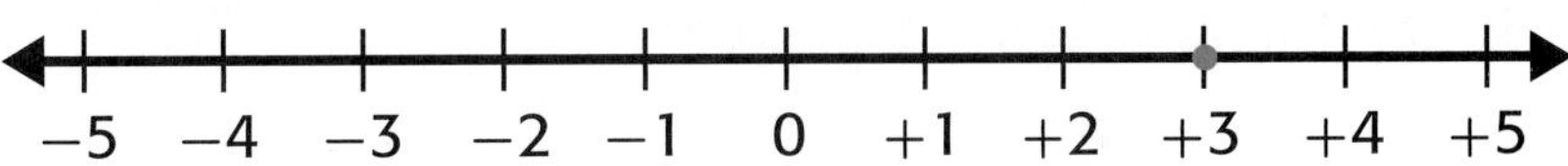

Remember

The value of numbers increases on a number line as you move further to the right.

For each negative number, there is a positive number the same distance from 0. These pairs are called *opposites.*

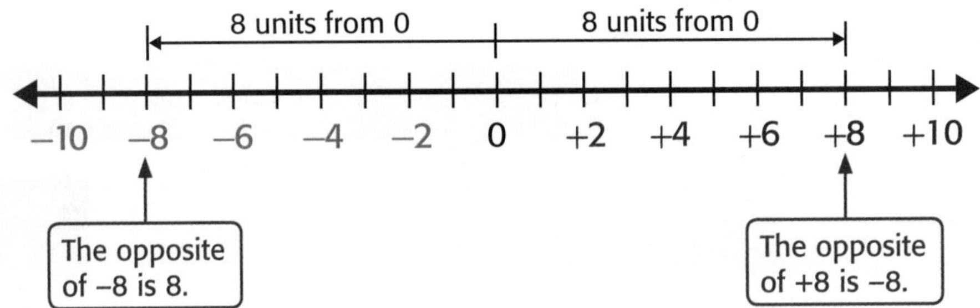

EXAMPLE Identify Numbers

3 **Write the number of each letter on the number line.**

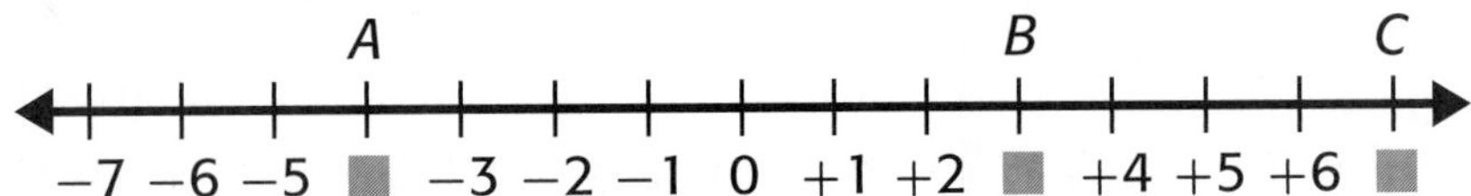

A is the same distance from zero as +4. So, *A* is −4.

B is between +2 and +4. So, *B* is +3.

C is after +6. So, *C* is +7.

Online Personal Tutor at ca.gr4math.com

CHECK What You Know

Write the number that represents each situation. Then show the number on a number line. See Examples 1 and 2 (p. 469)

1. move 12 steps forward

2. move back 3 spaces

3. remove $15 from a bank

4. 5 degrees above 0

5. Write the number that identifies each letter on the number line. See Example 3 (p. 470)

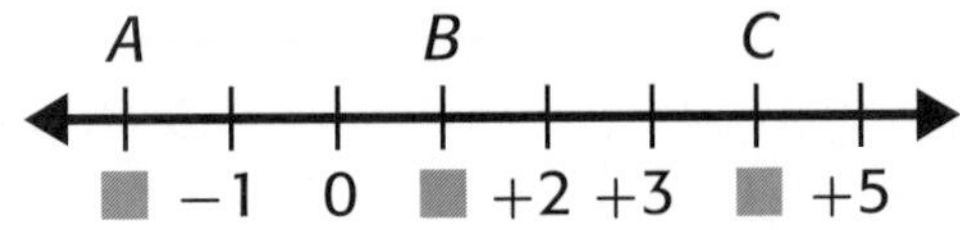

6. The outside temperature this morning was −6°F. Now, it is 12 degrees warmer. Use a number line to find the current temperature.

7. Talk About It How is a Fahrenheit thermometer like a number line?

Practice and Problem Solving

Write the number that represents each situation. Then show the number on a number line. See Examples 1 and 2 (p. 469)

8. a loss of 6 yards

9. cut 10 seconds off a running time

10. receive $68

11. earn $15

12. 12 feet below sea level

13. speed decreased by 5 miles per hour

14. owes $7

15. scored 14 points

Write the number of each letter on the number line. See Example 3 (p. 470)

16.

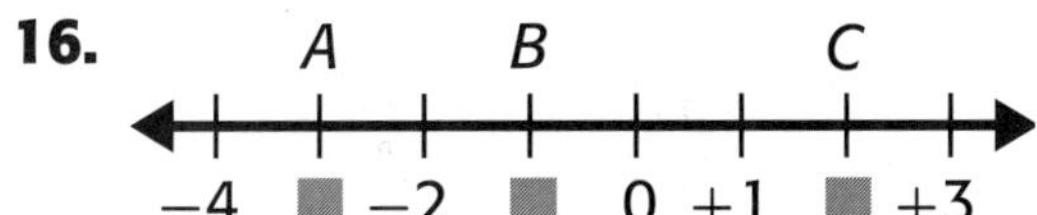

17.

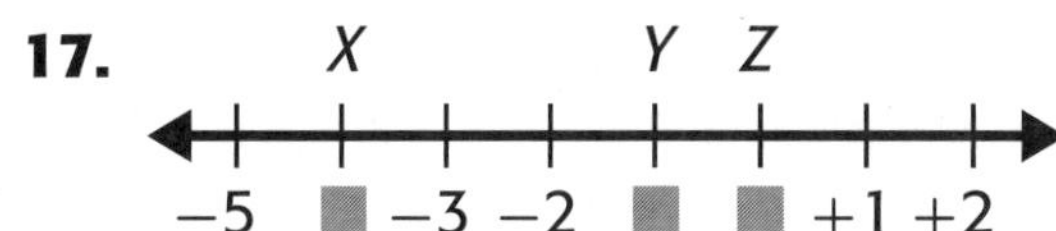

18. Corbin owes his friend $2. The next day he receives his allowance of $5. If Corbin returns the money to his friend, how much money will he have?

19. Destiny draws a number line. She starts at point *Z* and moves 12 units to the right. She stops on −1. What number did she start from?

Real-World PROBLEM SOLVING

Entertainment The table shows possible items that can be captured when playing a video game. Use a number line to find the score after capturing each set of items.

Object	Points
	+10
	−3
	+8
	−5

20. Pot of Gold, Rainbow, Shamrock, Rainbow

21. Shamrock, Key, Pot of Gold, Shamrock

22. What two items will you need to capture to lose the points gained from capturing a rainbow?

H.O.T. Problems

23. OPEN ENDED Refer to Exercises 20–22. List 3 items in which the player's score would be greater than 14. Include at least one negative number.

24. WRITING IN MATH Write about a real-world situation in which negative numbers are used.

12-2 Find Points on a Grid

GET READY to Learn

The map gives the locations of several students' homes and their school. From the school, Dave lives 5 units right and 3 units up. This can be written as (5, 3).

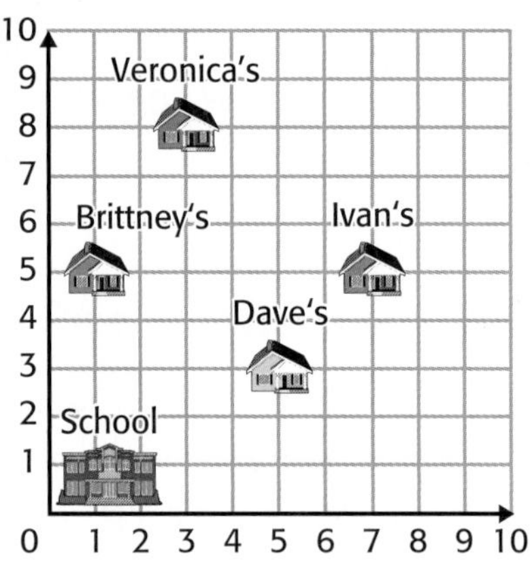

MAIN IDEA

I will use ordered pairs to find and name points on a grid.

Preparation for Standard 4MG2.1

Draw the points corresponding to linear relationships on graph paper (e.g., draw 10 points on the graph of the equation $y = 3x$ and connect them by using a straight line).

New Vocabulary

- coordinate plane
- origin
- *x*-axis
- *y*-axis
- ordered pair
- coordinates

The map shown above is an example of a coordinate plane. A **coordinate plane** is formed when two number lines intersect at their zero points. The lines are perpendicular.

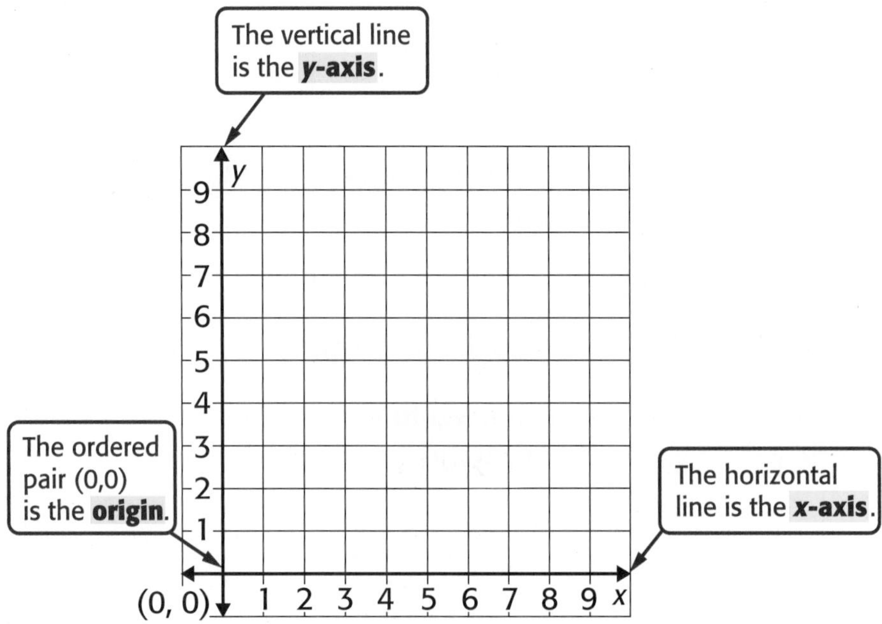

Vocabulary Link

The prefix *quad-* means *four.*

The point (5, 3) is an example of an **ordered pair**. The numbers in an ordered pair are called **coordinates**. The coordinates give the location of the point.

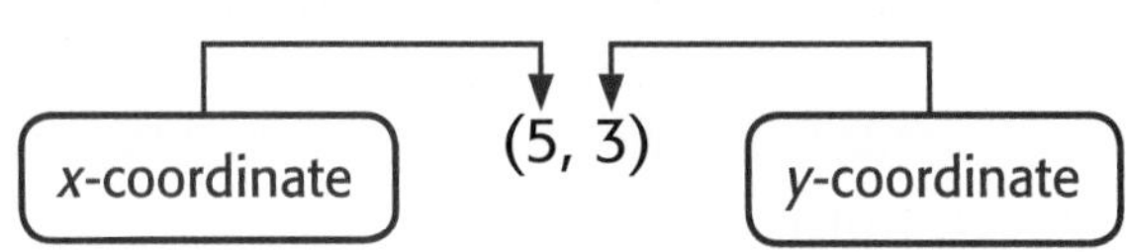

Real-World EXAMPLE Find Ordered Pairs

1 A map of a zoo is shown. Identify the animal that is located at (5, 4).

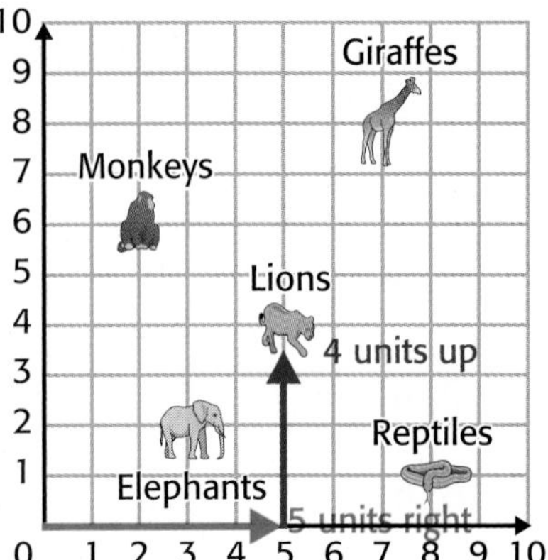

To find (**5**, **4**), start at (0, 0). Move right **5** units. Then, move up **4** units. The ordered pair (**5**, **4**) locates the lions.

Online Personal Tutor at ca.gr4math.com

Some graphs have four regions called *quadrants*. Notice that the numbers below and to the left of zero are negative.

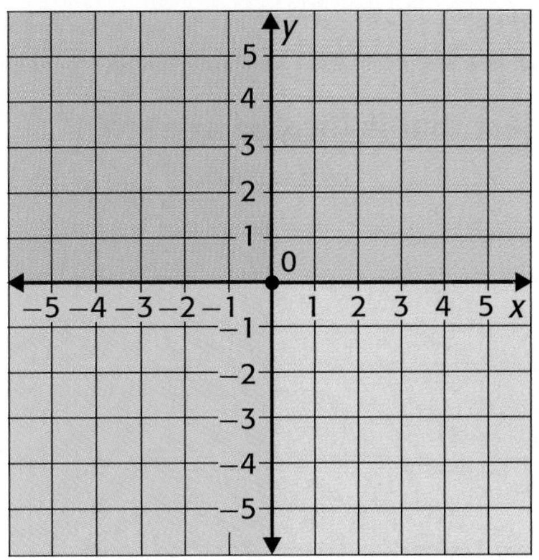

Four Quadrants

EXAMPLE Find Ordered Pairs

2 Identify the letter located at (−4, 3).

To find (**−4**, **3**), start at (0, 0). The −4 tells you to move **4** units to the left. The 3 tells you to move **3** units up. The ordered pair (**−4**, **3**) locates the letter *D*.

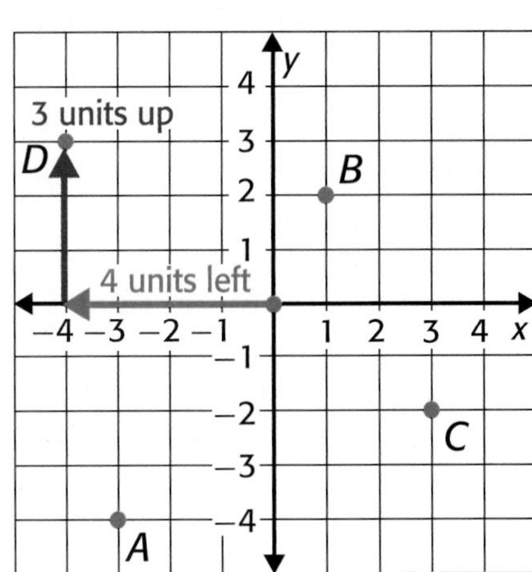

CHECK What You Know

Identify the building that is located at each ordered pair. See Examples 1 and 2 (p. 473)

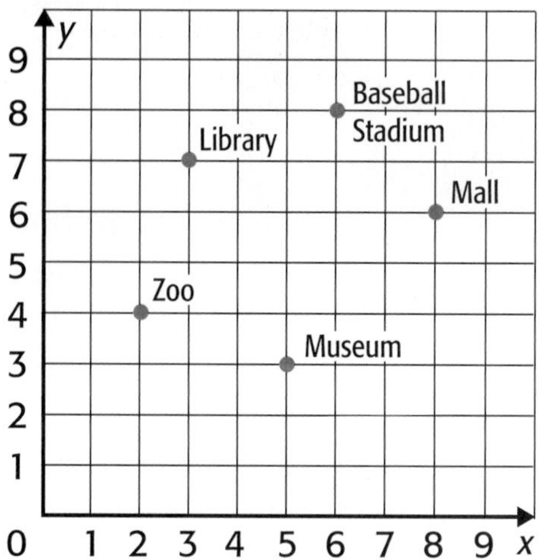

1. (6, 8)
2. (3, 7)
3. (2, 4)
4. (8, 6)
5. Talk About It — How does an ordered pair name a location?

Practice and Problem Solving

EXTRA PRACTICE See page R30.

Identify the object that is located at each ordered pair. See Examples 1 and 2 (p. 473)

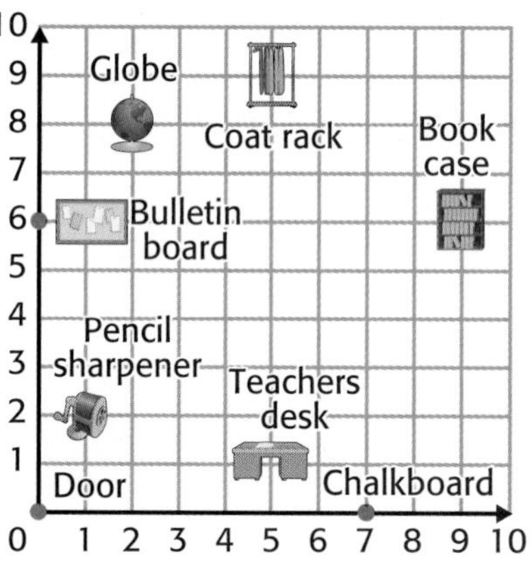

6. (9, 6)
7. (2, 8)
8. (5, 1)
9. (1, 2)
10. Describe how to move from the ordered pairs for pencil sharpener to coat rack.

Real-World PROBLEM SOLVING

Data File Map makers use latitude and longitude lines to find locations. These lines form a coordinate grid.

11. What city can be found near 37°N and 120°W?
12. What latitude and longitude lines are near Santa Cruz?
13. Name two other cities on this map and their lines of latitude and longitude.

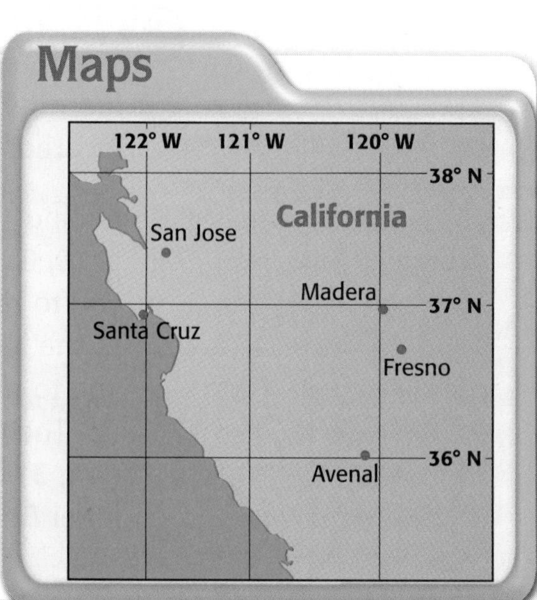

H.O.T. Problems

14. OPEN ENDED Draw a picture of your classroom on grid paper. Draw the location of your desk on the grid. What is the ordered pair for your location?

15. WHICH ONE DOESN'T BELONG? Identify which of the ordered pairs does not belong with the other three. Explain your reasoning.

(4, 1) | (−6, −3) | (3, 4) | (2, 5)

16. WRITING IN ▶MATH How is the location of (2, 4) different from the location of (−2, −4)? Explain.

Standards Practice

17 Which symbol below is located at −2 on the number line below? **(Lesson 12-1)**

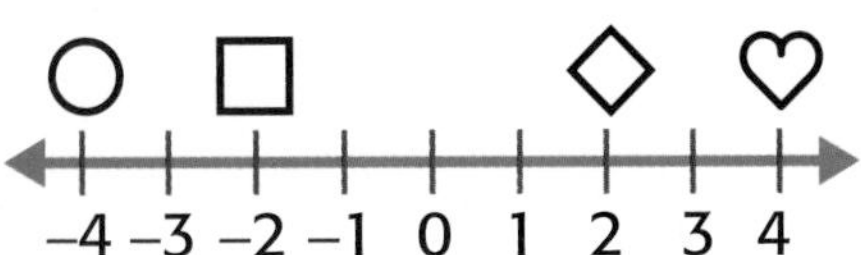

A □

B ○

C ♡

D ◇

18 Which ordered pair is graphed? **(Lesson 12-2)**

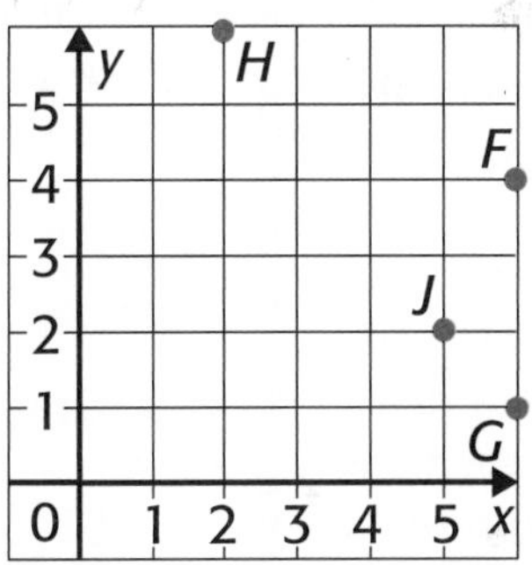

F (2, 5)

G (4, 3)

H (5, 4)

J (5, 2)

Spiral Review

19. The outside temperature this morning was −2°F. Now, it is 5 degrees cooler. Use a number line to find the current temperature. **(Lesson 12-1)**

Find the area of each figure. (Lesson 11-7)

20.

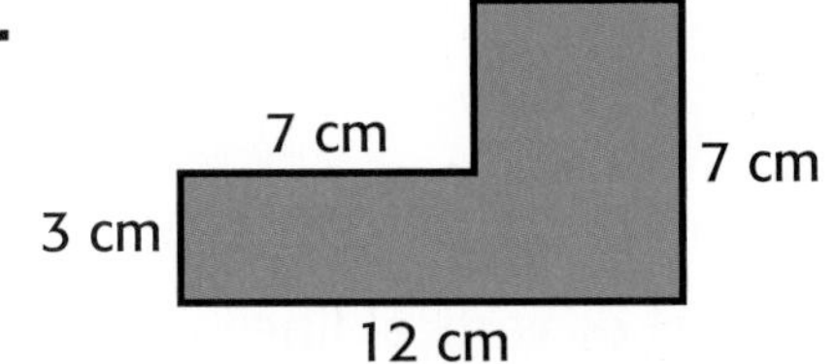

21.

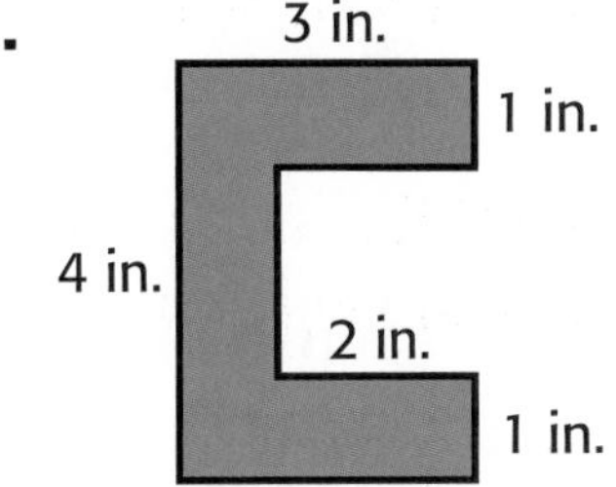

12-3 Graph Ordered Pairs

MAIN IDEA

I will graph ordered pairs and find the lengths of line segments on a coordinate grid.

Standard 4MG2.2 Understand that the length of a horizontal line segment equals the difference of the *x*-coordinates.

Standard 4MG2.3 Understand that the length of a vertical line segment equals the difference of the *y*-coordinates.

New Vocabulary

graph

GET READY to Learn

Brock and Bala are on a treasure hunt. What ordered pair gives the directions to the location of the treasure?

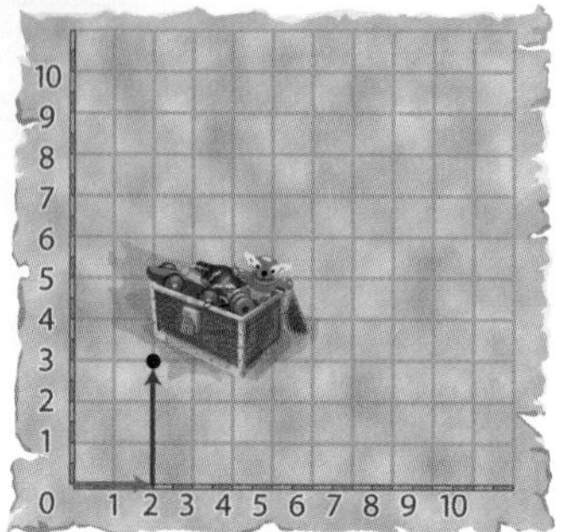

The map above shows the graph of point *T* at (2, 3). This is the location of the treasure. You can graph any ordered pair.

EXAMPLE Graph Ordered Pairs

1 Graph point *B* at (–3, 4).

Step 1 Start at (0, 0).

Step 2 The *x*-coordinate is **–3**. So, move 3 units to the left.

Step 3 The *y*-coordinate is **4**. So, move 4 units up.

Step 4 Graph a point at (**–3**, **4**). Label it *B*.

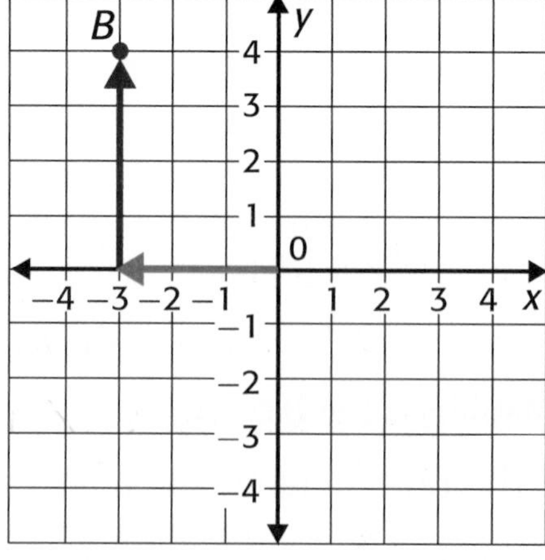

Personal Tutor at ca.gr4math.com

You can find the length of a horizontal or vertical line segment on a grid.

KEY CONCEPT — Length of Line Segments

- The length of a vertical line segment equals the difference of the *y*-coordinates.
- The length of a horizontal line segment equals the difference of the *x*-coordinates.

Remember

To find horizontal and vertical distances between ordered pairs, you can also count the number of units between points.

EXAMPLES — Length of Line Segments

Find the length of the line segment between each set of ordered pairs.

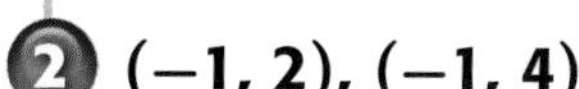

2 (−1, 2), (−1, 4)

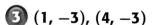

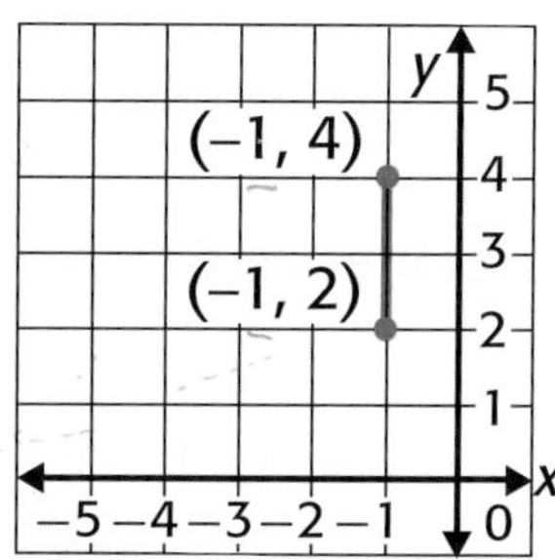

The line segment is vertical. Subtract the *y*-coordinates.

4 − 2 or 2

The length is 2 units.

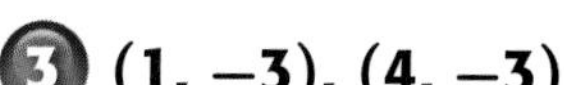

3 (1, −3), (4, −3)

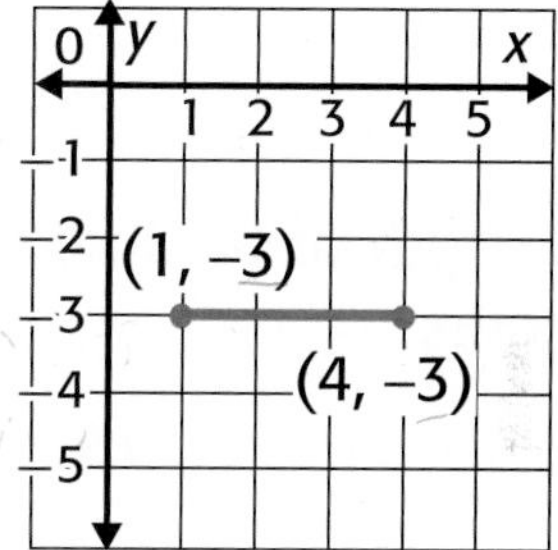

The line segment is horizontal. Subtract the *x*-coordinates.

4 − 1 or 3

The length is 3 units.

CHECK What You Know

Copy the grid. Then, graph and label each point on the grid. See Example 1 (p. 476)

1. point *A:* (3, 4) **2.** point *B:* (−1, 3)

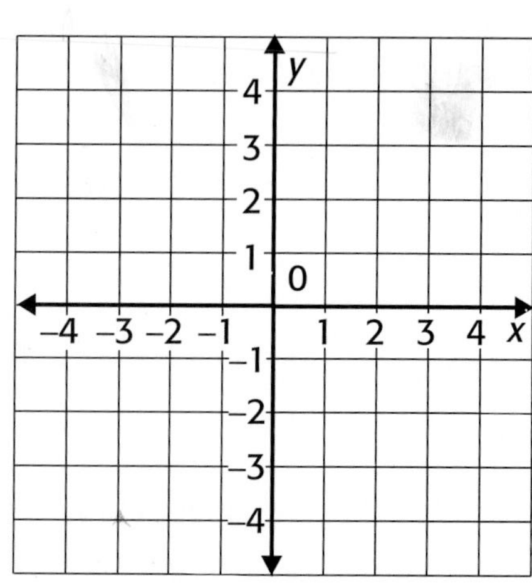

Find the length of the line segment between each set of ordered pairs.

See Examples 2 and 3 (p. 477)

3. (4, 7), (4, 12) **4.** (4, −2), (6, −2)

5. 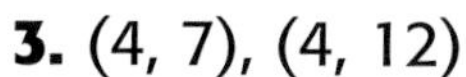 How do you find the length of a vertical or horizontal line segment?

Practice and Problem Solving

EXTRA PRACTICE
See page R30.

Copy the grid. Then, graph and label each point on the grid. See Example 1 (p. 476)

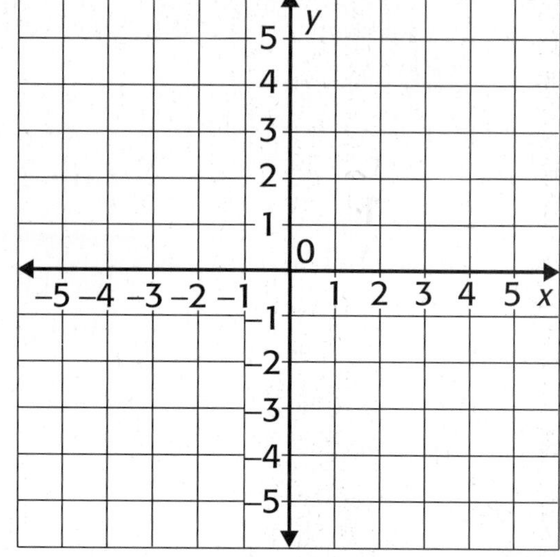

6. point *A:* (5, –2)
7. point *B:* (–3, 0)
8. point *C:* (3, 1)
9. point *D:* (–4, –4)
10. point *E:* (0, 5)
11. point *F:* (–2, 1)
12. point *G*: (–1, –3)
13. point *H*: (0, –4)

Find the length of the line segment between each set of ordered pairs. See Examples 2 and 3 (p. 477)

14. (5, 9), (5, 3)
15. (1, 0), (7, 0)
16. (–1, 7), (–1, 0)
17. (–4, 6), (–4, 2)

18. **Geometry** Three corners of a square on a coordinate plane are located at (2, 1), (2, 4), and (5, 1). What is the ordered pair of the fourth corner?

19. **Geometry** Four corners of a rectangle on a coordinate plane are located at (–1, 0), (–1, 5), (–4, 0), and (–4, 5). Find the area of this figure.

For Exercises 20 and 21 use a coordinate grid that has 4 quadrants.

20. Your house is located at a map's center, (0, 0). Your friend's house is located 4 blocks east and 2 blocks north of your house. What are the coordinates of your friend's house?

21. Your school is located at a map's center, (0, 0). To get home, you walk 3 blocks west and 1 block south. What are the coordinates of your house?

H.O.T. Problems

22. **OPEN ENDED** Write two ordered pairs that are the ends of a horizontal line segment.

23. **WRITING IN ▸MATH** Explain two ways to find the length of a vertical line segment.

Mid-Chapter Check

CHAPTER 12

Lessons 12-1 through 12-3

Write the number that represents each situation. Then show the number on a number line. (Lesson 12-1)

1. Pati read 3 more pages of her book.
2. Caleb spent $8 on a video game.

Write the number of each letter on the number line. (Lesson 12-1)

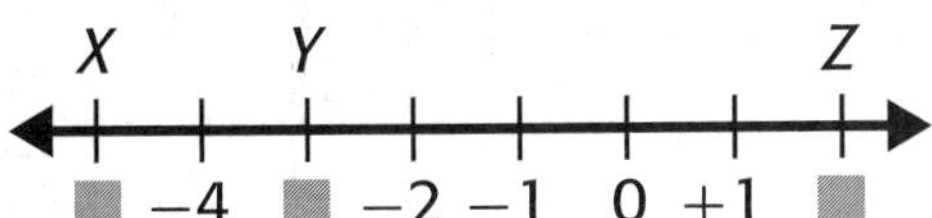

3. X
4. Z

5. **STANDARDS PRACTICE** Which symbol is located at 4? (Lesson 12-1)

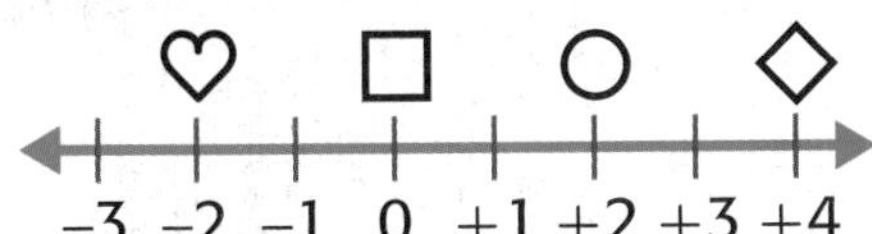

A □ **C** ○

B ♡ **D** ◇

For Exercises 6 and 7, identify the letter located at each ordered pair. (Lesson 12-2)

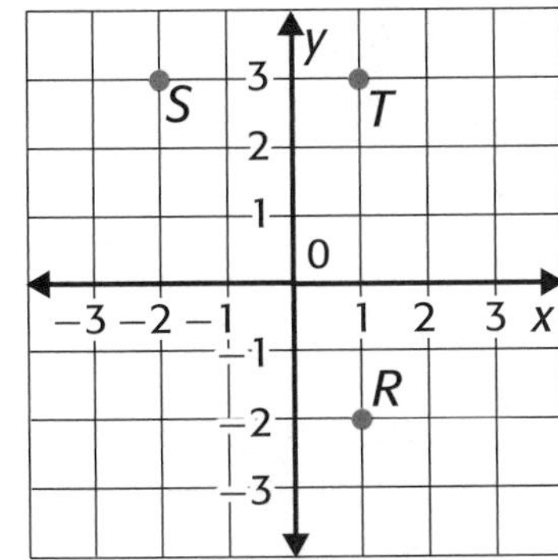

6. (−2, 3)
7. (1, −2)

8. **STANDARDS PRACTICE** Which ordered pair is graphed? (Lesson 12-2)

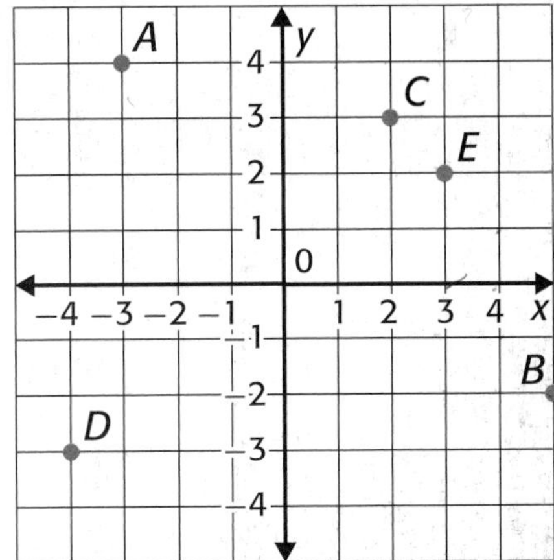

F (3, 4) **H** (3, 1)

G (2, 3) **J** (5, 2)

For Exercises 9 and 10, use the grid above. (Lesson 12-2)

9. Describe how to move from point A to point C.
10. Describe two ways to move from point B to point E.

Find the length of the line segment between each set of ordered pairs. (Lesson 12-3)

11. (7, 4), (7, 14)
12. (−2, 4), (−2, 7)
13. **WRITING IN MATH** Explain two real-world situations where negative numbers are necessary.

Problem Solving in Geography

atitude and Longitude

The coordinate grid system of latitude and longitude is used to find exact locations on Earth.

Latitude measures the north-south position of locations on Earth. Longitude measures the east-west position of locations on Earth. You can learn the basics of latitude and longitude using a four-quadrant grid system. The Equator represents 0 on the x-axis. A line called the Prime Meridian represents 0 on the y-axis.

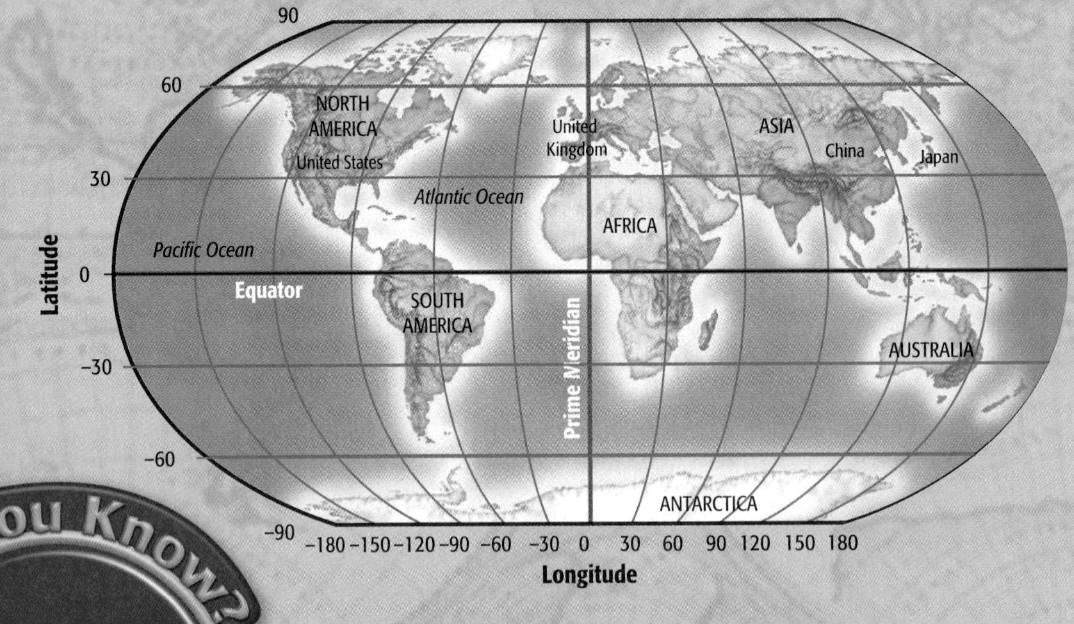

ou Know?

e length of Equator is 901 miles.

Standard 4MG2.0 Students use two-dimensional coordinate grids to represent points and graph lines and simple figures.

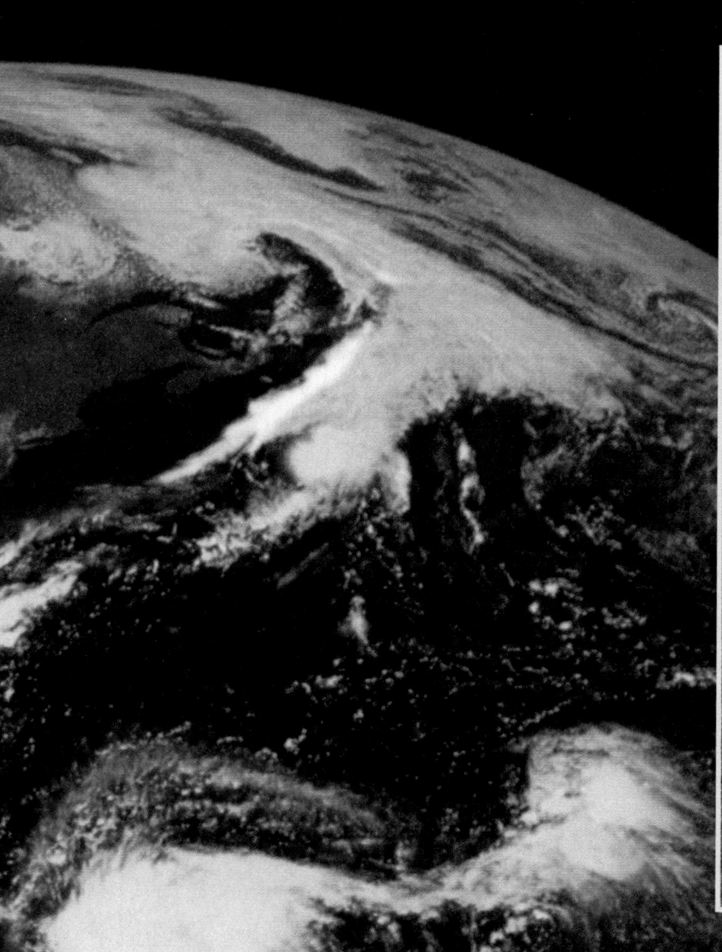

Outside the Royal Observatory in Greenwich, United Kingdom, are brass strips set in the ground and walls marking the exact site of the line of the Prime Meridian.

Real-World Math

Use the information on page 480 to solve each problem.

1. What continent is located at (30, 0)?
2. What ocean is located at (−60, 30)?
3. What continent is located at (120, −30)?
4. Identify one coordinate that represents North America.
5. What continent is closest to the point (0, 0)?
6. Suppose you are at coordinate (−60, 0). If you fly 60 units north and 150 units east, which continent would you land in?

Problem-Solving Strategy

MAIN IDEA I will solve problems using logical reasoning.

Standard 4MR1.1 **Analyze problems by identifying relationships, distinguishing relevant from irrelevant information, sequencing and prioritizing information,** and observing patterns. Standard 4SDAP1.1 Formulate survey questions; **systematically collect and represent data on** a number line; and coordinate graphs, **tables,** and charts.

Bella, Devan, Carl, and Jill live on Ash, Pine, Maple, and Oak Streets. Bella lives on Ash. Devan does not live on Pine. Carl lives on Maple. What street does Jill live on?

Understand

What facts do you know?

- The four students live on Ash, Pine, Maple, and Oak Streets.
- Bella lives on Ash Street.
- Devan does not live on Pine Street.
- Carl lives on Maple Street.

What do you need to find?

- Find what street Jill lives on.

Plan

You can use logical reasoning and a table to solve the problem.

Solve

- Bella lives on Ash and Carl lives on Maple. So, Jill cannot live on either of these streets.
- Devan does not live on Pine Street. He must live on Oak Street.

	Ash	Maple	Pine	Oak
Bella	✓	X	X	X
Devan	X	X	X	✓
Carl	X	✓	X	X
Jill	X	X	✓	X

So, Jill must live on Pine Street.

Check

Look back at the problem. The answer makes sense for the facts given in the problem. So, the answer is correct.

ANALYZE the Strategy

Refer to the problem on the previous page.

1. Explain how eliminating options helped to solve the problem.
2. Suppose Bella lives on Pine. Devan does not live on Ash. Carl lives on Oak. What streets do the four students live on?
3. Why do you think a table was used in solving the problem?
4. Look back at Exercise 3. Check your answer. How do you know that it is correct?

PRACTICE the Strategy

See page R31.

Solve. Use *logical reasoning*.

5. Three dogs are named Max, Sam, and Rufus. One is a collie, one is a spaniel, and one is a pug. Sam is not the collie. The spaniel's name is the longest. What are the names of each dog?
6. Hector arranges the cards in a row. The 2 is between the two odd numbered cards. The 4 has no card to its left. The 3 has cards on both sides. What is the order?

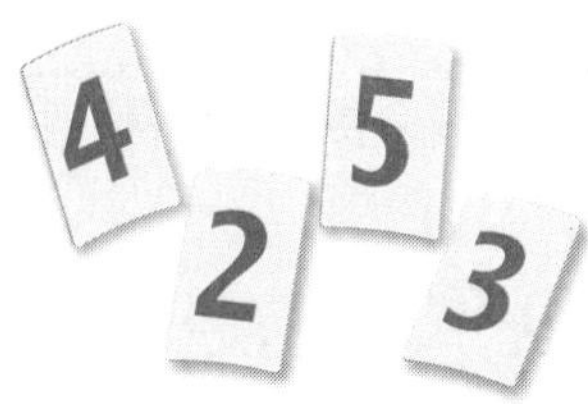

7. There are 4 people in a line. Kenzo is at the end. Juan is second in line. Carla is in front of Kenzo. Amy is first. What is the order of the people?
8. Manuella, Danny, and Tyson are wearing red, blue, and yellow T-shirts. Manuella is wearing red, and Danny is not wearing blue. What color T-shirt is each person wearing?
9. Jesse, Kata, Romeo, and Sheldon play basketball. Their numbers are 5, 7, 9, and 12. Jesse's number equals the number of letters in his name. Kata's is a two-digit number, while Romeo's number is not a prime number. What is Sheldon's number?
10. Lizzy has dogs, birds, and fish. She has twice as many dogs as birds. She has three more fish than dogs. She has two birds. How many dogs and fish does she have?

11. Copy and complete the puzzle below. Use the digits 1, 2, 3, and 4 so that each row and column has each digit listed one time.

2	■	■	1
1	4	■	2
3	■	2	4
4	■	■	3

12. **WRITING IN MATH** Explain what it means to use logical reasoning.

12-5 Functions

MAIN IDEA

I will complete function tables.

Standard 4AF1.5

Understand that an equation, such as $y = 3x + 5$, is a prescription for determining a second number when a first number is given.

New Vocabulary

function

GET READY to Learn

The table shows the number of tacos four students have eaten. Each student is going to eat 2 more tacos. How many tacos will each student have eaten after eating 2 more tacos?

Tacos Eaten	
Name	**Number**
Reed	2
Suni	4
Kenna	3
Darren	1

The number of tacos each student will eat depends on the amount he or she has already eaten. A relationship where one number depends on another number is a **function**.

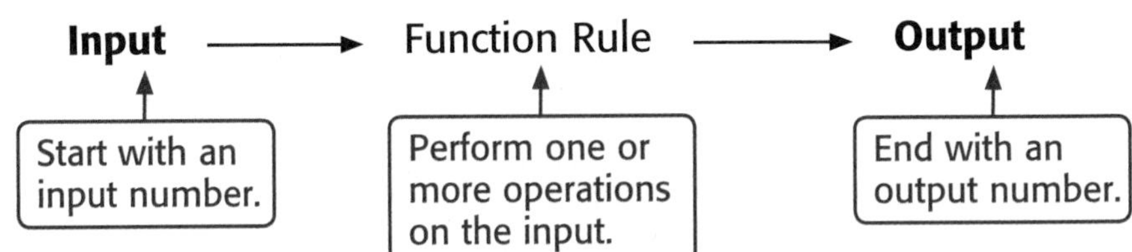
Input
Function Rule
Output
Start with an input number.
Perform one or more operations on the input.
End with an output number.

You can show the input, output, and function rule in a table.

Real-World EXAMPLE Complete a Function Table

1 **FOOD How many tacos will each student have eaten after eating 2 more?**

Make a table to find how many tacos each student will have eaten after eating 2 more tacos. Add 2 to each input to find each output.

Rule: Add 2.		
Input: Number Eaten	**Rule: + 2**	**Output: Total Eaten**
2	2 + 2	4
4	4 + 2	6
3	3 + 2	5
1	1 + 2	3

Review Vocabulary

variable a letter or symbol that represents an unknown value **(Lesson 3-1)**

Online **Personal Tutor at** ca.gr4math.com

Rules can be used to complete function tables. The input values are given by x. The output values are given by y.

Remember

A variable is a letter or symbol that represents an unknown value. Look back to Lesson 3-1 to review variables.

EXAMPLES Complete a Function Table

Replace x with the input numbers to find the output numbers.

2 $y = 7x$

The rule $y = 7x$ means to multiply x by 7 to get y.

Rule: Multiply by 7.		
Input (x)	**Rule: $y = 7x$**	**Output (y)**
2	7×2	14
4	7×4	28
6	7×6	42
8	7×8	56

3 $y = 3x + 4$

First, multiply x by 3. Then, add 4 to the product to get y.

Rule: Multiply by 3 then add 4.	
Input (x)	**Output (y)**
2	10
4	16
6	22

CHECK What You Know

Copy and complete each function table. See Examples 1–3 (pp. 484–485)

1.

Rule: Subtract 2.		
Input (x)	**Rule: $y = x - 2$**	**Output (y)**
2	2 – 2	0
3	3 – 2	1
4	4 – 2	2
5	■	■
6	■	■

2.

Rule: $2x + 1 = y$	
Input (x)	**Output (y)**
1	3
2	5
3	7
4	■
5	■

3. Talk About It — Explain how to find y when you are given that $x = 2$ and the rule is $y = 5x$.

Practice and Problem Solving

EXTRA PRACTICE
See page R31.

Copy and complete each function table. See Examples 1–3 (pp. 484–485)

4.

Rule: Multiply by 2.		
Input (x)	Rule: $y = 2x$	Output (y)
0	2×0	0
2	2×2	4
4	2×4	8
6	■	■
8	■	■

5.

Rule: Divide by 4, then add 5.		
Input (x)	Rule: $y = x \div 4 + 5$	Output (y)
16	$16 \div 4 + 5$	9
24	$24 \div 4 + 5$	11
28	$28 \div 4 + 5$	12
32	■	■
36	■	■

6.

Rule: Subtract 4	
Input (x)	Output (y)
5	1
6	2
9	5
12	■
16	■

7.

Rule: $y = 3x$	
Input (x)	Output (y)
5	15
7	21
8	24
9	■
10	■

8.

Rule: $y = 2x + 3$	
Input (x)	Output (y)
1	5
2	7
3	9
4	■
6	■

9. The owner of a clothing store makes a $10 profit for each T-shirt sold. Make a function table to show the profits earned if 2, 4, 6, 8, or 10 T-shirts are sold.

10. Tickets for a minor league baseball game regularly cost $6. Today, if you buy one ticket, a second is free. Make a function table to show the price for 2, 4, 6, 8, or 10 attendees.

H.O.T. Problems

11. OPEN ENDED Create two function tables in which the inputs and outputs are the same, but the rules are different.

12. REASONING What would be the rule for an input value of 3 and an output value of 8?

13. WRITING IN MATH Explain how to find x when you are given y in the rule $y = x \div 3$.

Outputs Add Up

Using Functions

Get Ready!

Players: 2 players

You will need: 5 index cards and 2 number cubes

Get Set!

Label each index card as shown.

y = 3x + 5

y = 2x + 12

y = 3x + 3

y = 2x - 2

y = 3x - 8

Go!

- Shuffle the cards and place them face down on your desk. Player 1 rolls both number cubes and records the numbers rolled on a sheet of paper.
- Player 2 then rolls both number cubes and records the numbers rolled on a sheet of paper.
- Next, Player 1 turns over a card. Both players use the numbers they rolled as two inputs (x) for the function in order to find two outputs (y).
- Finally, both players add their outputs. The player with the highest output is the winner.
- Place the index card at the bottom of the pile and play again.

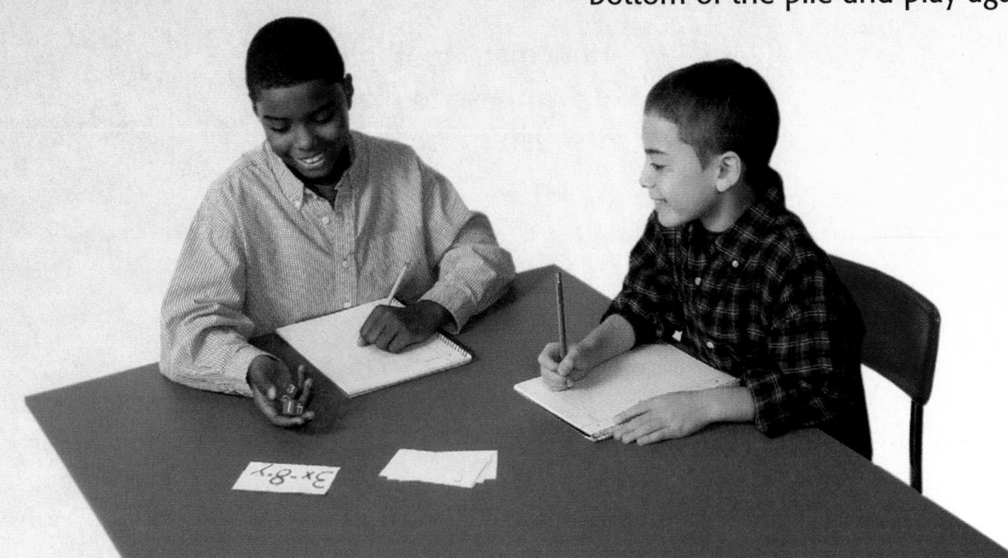

Algebra Activity for 12-6

Graph Functions

In the following activity, you will use toothpicks to make squares to see if there is a relationship between the number of toothpicks used and the number of squares formed.

MAIN IDEA

I will graph functions.

Standard 4MG2.1 Draw the points corresponding to linear relationships on graph paper.
Standard 4MR2.3 Use a variety of methods, such as words, numbers, symbols, charts, graphs, tables, diagrams, **and models, to explain mathematical reasoning.**

You Will Need
toothpicks

Animation
ca.gr4math.com

ACTIVITY Graph a Function

Step 1 Create a table.

Copy the table shown.

Input (x) Squares	Output (y) Toothpicks	(Input, Output)
1	4	(1, 4)
2	7	(2, 7)
3	■	(■, ■)
4	13	(4, 13)
5	■	(■, ■)

Step 2 Make squares.

Using toothpicks, make 1 square and then 2 squares as shown.

Step 3 Record data.

How many toothpicks did you use to make 1 square? 2 squares?

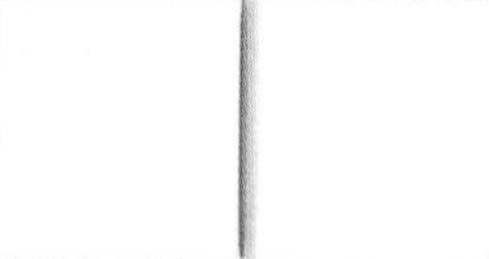

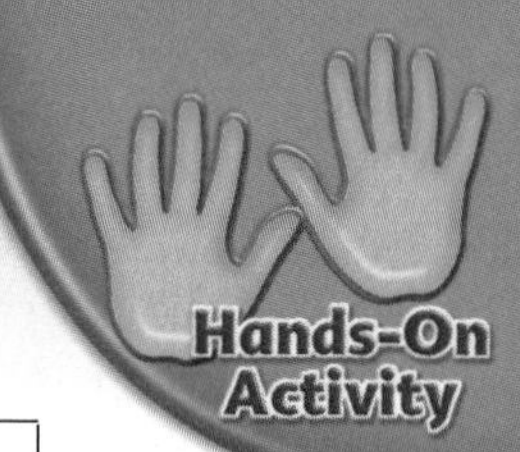

Step 4 **Make more squares.**

Repeat Steps 2 and 3 for 3, 4, and 5 squares.

Step 5 **Graph the function.**

Graph the ordered pairs from the table on a grid like the one shown.

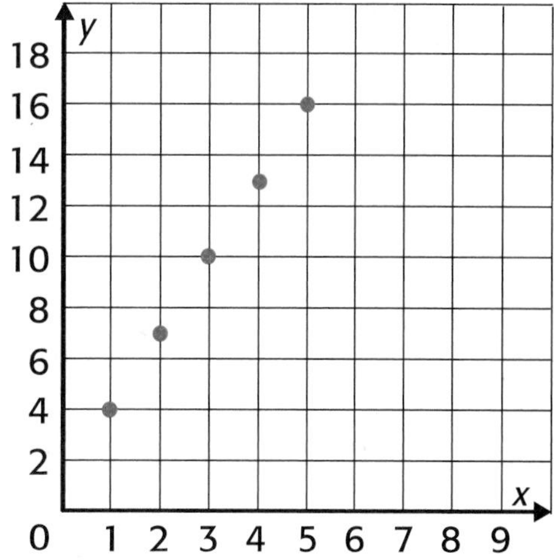

Think About It

1. Describe the pattern in the input and output values.

2. What is the rule that describes the function?

3. What will be the ordered pair for 6 squares? 7 squares?

4. Describe how the points appear on the graph.

CHECK What You Know

Copy and complete each function table. Then graph the function.

5.

Rule: $y = 2x$		
Input (x) Dimes	Output (y) Nickels	(x, y)
1	2	(1, 2)
2	4	(2, 4)
3	6	(3, 6)
4	■	■
5	■	■

6.

Rule: $y = x \div 3$		
Input (x) Feet	Output (y) Yards	(x, y)
3	1	(3, 1)
6	2	(6, 2)
9	3	(9, 3)
12	■	■
15	■	■

7. **WRITING IN MATH** How can you use the graph of a function to find (x, y) values?

12-6 Graph Functions

GET READY to Learn

MAIN IDEA

I will graph functions.

Standard 4MG2.1 Draw the points corresponding to linear relationships on graph paper (e.g., draw 10 points on the graph of the equation $y = 3x$ and connect them by using a straight line).

Troy's parents give him \$2 for every A he earns on his report card. The function table shows how much Troy will earn if he gets 1, 2, 3, or 4 As.

Input (x)	Output (y)
Number of As	Money Earned
1	\$2
2	\$4
3	\$6
4	\$8

The rule is to multiply by 2. This rule can be written as $y = 2x$. In the Explore Activity, you learned to graph functions.

EXAMPLE Graph a Function

1 Graph the function $y = 2x$. Then use the graph to find how much Troy will get if he earns 6 As.

Step 1 Write the ordered pairs. Then graph.

Input (x)	Output (y)	Ordered Pair
Number of As	Money Earned	(x, y)
1	\$2	(1, 2)
2	\$4	(2, 4)
3	\$6	(3, 6)
4	\$8	(4, 8)

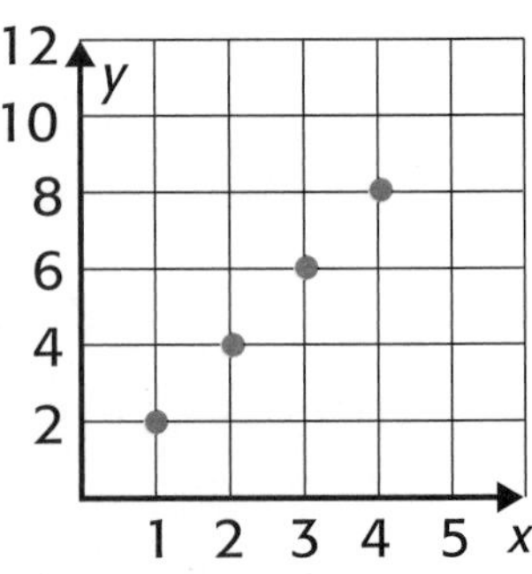

Step 2 Extend the pattern in the graph by drawing a straight line. The straight line will help you see the pattern.

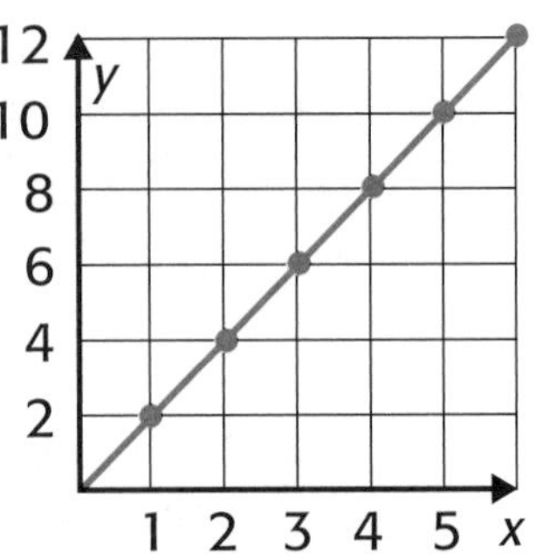

So, if Troy earns 6 As, he will receive \$12.

EXAMPLE Graph a Function

2 **Draw ten points on the graph of the function $y = 2x + 1$.**

Complete a table to find the ordered pairs. Then graph the ordered pairs. Connect the points with a straight line.

Input (x)	Output (y)	(x, y)
0	1	(0, 1)
1	3	(1, 3)
2	5	(2, 5)
3	7	(3, 7)
4	9	(4, 9)
5	11	(5, 11)
6	13	(6, 13)
7	15	(7, 15)
8	17	(8, 17)
9	19	(9, 19)

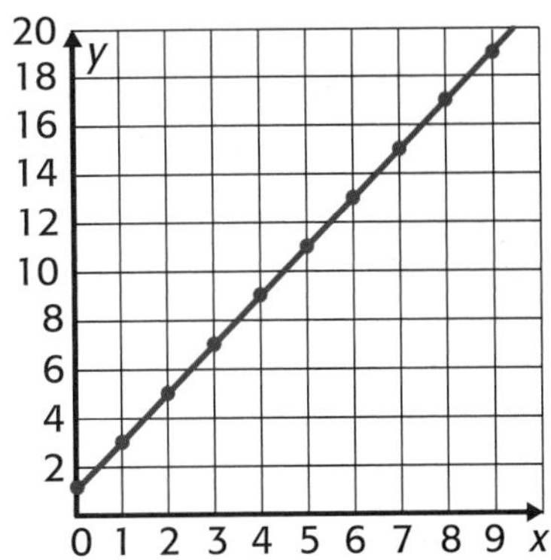

Online Personal Tutor at ca.gr4math.com

CHECK What You Know

Graph ten points on the graph of the function. See Examples 1–2 (pp. 490–491)

1. $y = 5x$

2. $y = 2x + 3$

3. $y = 3x - 2$

4. Dina reads 4 times faster than Rey. The rule can be written as $y = 4x$. The function table shows the time Rey and Dina spend reading. Create a graph to show the number of minutes Dina reads if Rey reads for 10 minutes.

Input (x) Minutes Rey Reads	Output (y) Minutes Dina Reads	(x, y)
1	4	(1, 4)
2	8	(2, 8)
3	12	(3, 12)
4	16	(4, 16)

5. Talk About It Is the ordered pair (5, 14) on the graph of the function $y = 2x + 4$? What about the ordered pair (5, 12)? How do you know?

Practice and Problem Solving

EXTRA PRACTICE
See page R31.

Graph ten points on the graph of the function. See Examples 1–2 (pp. 490–491)

6. $y = 1x$

7. $y = 6x$

8. $y = 1x + 6$

9. $y = 2x - 1$

10. $y = 4x + 2$

11. $y = 5x - 3$

12. An adult blue whale's heartbeat can be as slow as 5 beats per minute. The rule can be written as $y = 5x$. The function table shows the number of heartbeats that take place at this rate over time. Create a graph to show the number of heartbeats that occur in 10 minutes.

Input (x)	Output (y)	
Number of Minutes	Number of Heartbeats	(x, y)
1	5	(1, 5)
2	10	(2, 10)
3	15	(3, 15)
4	20	(4, 20)

13. Laine gives \$3 of her weekly allowance to a charity. The rule can be written as $y = 3x$. The function table shows the amount of money Laine has given to a charity after a certain number of weeks. Create a graph to show the amount of money given to charity after 10 weeks.

Input (x)	Output (y)	
Weeks	Amount to Charity	(x, y)
1	3	(1, 3)
2	6	(2, 6)
3	9	(3, 9)
4	12	(4, 12)

H.O.T. Problems

14. OPEN ENDED Create a function rule with two steps that results in a positive number. Graph ten points of the function. Then connect the points on the graph.

15. NUMBER SENSE Create a function to solve the following problem. D'Angelo gets \$12 a week for an allowance. He is saving his money to buy a football jersey of his favorite professional player. If the jersey costs \$75, how many weeks will it take for him to have enough money?

16. WRITING IN ▶MATH Explain the difference in the graphs of $y = 2x$ and $y = 4x$.

Math Online Self-Check Quiz at ca.gr4math.com

Standards Practice

17 Justina used this table to find the total cost of different numbers of tickets to a water park.

Ticket Prices				
Tickets	3	6	9	12
Total Cost	\$9	\$18	\$27	\$36

Based on the information in the table, how would Justina find the price of 1 ticket? **(Lesson 12-5)**

A Multiply the number of tickets by 2.

B Multiply the price of tickets by 2.

C Divide the number of tickets by 3.

D Divide the price of 3 tickets by 3.

18 Melanie graphed three points on a grid. The 3 points were all on a straight line.

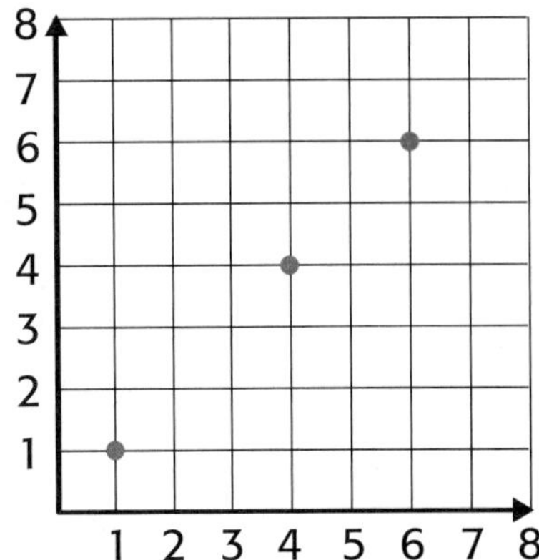

If she graphs another point on the line, what could be its coordinates? **(Lesson 12-6)**

F (3, 3) **H** (9, 8)

G (8, 9) **J** (4, 5)

Spiral Review

Copy and complete each function table. **(Lesson 12-5)**

19.

Rule: $y = 7x$	
Input (x)	Output (y)
3	21
6	42
2	14
10	■
0	■

20.

Rule: $y = x \div 4$	
Input (x)	Output (y)
8	2
12	3
20	5
24	■
48	■

21.

Rule: $y = 2x + 7$	
Input (x)	Output (y)
2	11
8	23
5	17
12	■
1	■

22. Jenna, Theo, and Elisa have different birthday months. The birthday months are September, December, and April. Jenna was born in the spring. Elisa was not born in September. What is each person's birthday month? **(Lesson 12-4)**

Divide. Use estimation to check. **(Lesson 9-7)**

23. $2\overline{)236}$ **24.** $3\overline{)345}$ **25.** $5\overline{)865}$

12-7 Problem-Solving Investigation

MAIN IDEA I will solve problems by choosing the best strategy.

Standard 4MR1.1 Analyze problems by identifying relationships, distinguishing relevant from irrelevant information, sequencing and prioritizing information, and observing patterns. Standard 4AF1.5 Understand that an equation such as $y = 3x + 5$ is a prescription for determining a second number when a first number is given.

P.S.I. TEAM +

AIDEN: I have a video game system. Games cost $20. Felice has a different video game system. Her games cost $15. How many video games can we each buy if we each have $60?

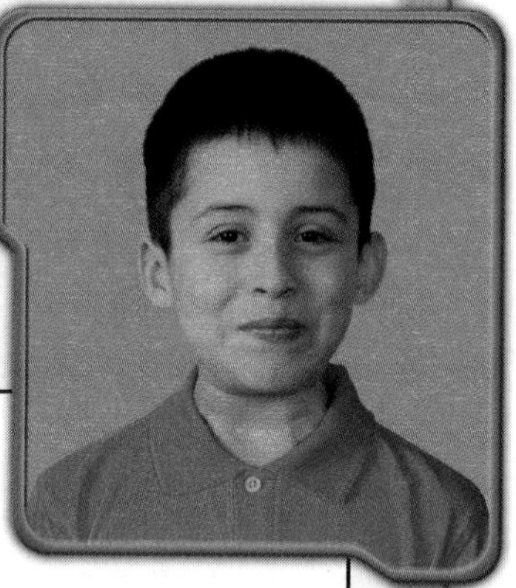

YOUR MISSION: Find out how many games each person can buy.

Understand Games for Aiden's game system cost $20. Games for Felice's game system cost $15. Each has $60 to spend on video games. Find how many games each person can buy.

Plan Organize the data in a table to show the number of games and the total amount of money spent.

Solve

Aiden	
Rule: $y = 20x$	
Games	Total ($)
1	20
2	40
3	60

Felice	
Rule: $y = 15x$	
Games	Total ($)
1	15
2	30
3	45
4	60

Since Aiden's games cost more, he can buy only 3, but Felice can buy 4.

Check Look back at the problem. Since $20 \times 3 = 60$ and $15 \times 4 = 60$, you know that the answer is correct.

Mixed Problem Solving

See page R32.

Use any strategy shown below to solve. Tell what strategy you used.

PROBLEM-SOLVING STRATEGIES
- Act it out.
- Guess and check.
- Look for a pattern.
- Work a simpler problem.
- Use logical reasoning.

1. Keisha and Marco went hiking from 9:30 A.M. until 12:00 P.M. After lunch, they hiked for another hour and 40 minutes. How many minutes did they spend hiking?

2. For every day at school that no students are absent, a teacher put 3 marbles in a jar. If the jar holds 426 marbles, how many days of no absences will it take to fill the jar?

3. A roller coaster car carries 32 people every 10 minutes. There are 572 people in line in front of Ruben. About how long will it take for him to ride the roller coaster?

4. A family spends $22 on tickets for a community play.

If there are two adults, how many children are with them?

5. Dora took 9 photos with her camera. She takes 2 more photos each day for a week. How many more days does she need to take photos to have 30?

6. Sally gave a cashier $25 for two CDs. They cost the same amount. She got $3 back. How much did each CD cost?

7. April's birthday party is being held at an arcade. Each guest will be given 16 tokens to play games. Copy and complete the table to find how many tokens are needed for 12 guests.

Guests	Tokens
2	32
4	64
6	96
8	128
10	■
12	■

8. A concert hall has 13 rows of seats. The hall has a total of 221 seats. Write a number sentence that could be used to find the number of seats in each row.

9. Myron has 2 red marbles for every one green marble. He has three times as many blue marbles as red marbles. Myron has four red marbles. How many green and blue marbles does he have?

10. **WRITING IN ▸MATH** Identify the problem-solving strategy you used to find the answer to Exercise 9. Explain how you found the answer.

Chapter 12 Study Guide and Review

FOLDABLES Study Organizer GET READY to Study

Be sure the following Key Vocabulary words and Key Concepts are written in your Foldable.

BIG Ideas

Coordinate Plane (p. 472)

- The **coordinates** of an **ordered pair** give the location of a point.

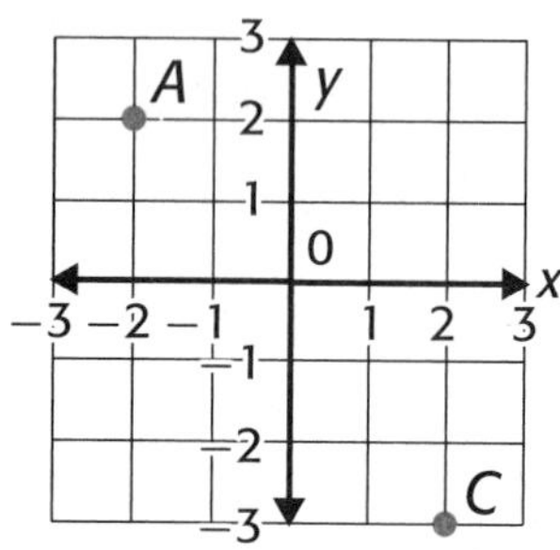

Point C is located at $(2, -3)$.

Function Tables (p. 484)

- Use rules to complete function tables.

Rule: Multiply by 2.		
Input (x)	Rule: $\times 2$	Output (y)
1	$1 \times 2 = 2$	2
2	$2 \times 2 = 4$	4
3	$3 \times 2 = 6$	6

Key Vocabulary

coordinates (p. 472)
ordered pair (p. 472)
origin (p. 472)
***x*-axis** (p. 472)
***y*-axis** (p. 472)

Vocabulary Check

Choose the vocabulary word that completes each sentence.

1. (3, 5) is an example of a(n) ___?___ .
2. The vertical axis on a coordinate plane is the ___?___ .
3. A number in an ordered pair is called a(n) ___?___ .
4. The ordered pair (0, 0) is the ___?___ .
5. The horizontal axis on a coordinate plane is the ___?___ .
6. A(n) ___?___ plane is formed when two number lines intersect at their zero points.
7. To find an ordered pair, you start at the ___?___ .

Math Online Vocabulary Review at ca.gr4math.com

Lesson-by-Lesson Review

12-1 Negative Numbers (pp. 469–471)

Example 1
Dawn lost her lunch money. Her friend let her borrow $2. Now Dawn owes her friend $2. Write the number that represents the money owed. Then show the number on a number line.

The word *owes* implies a *loss.*

The number is −2. Place a point at −2.

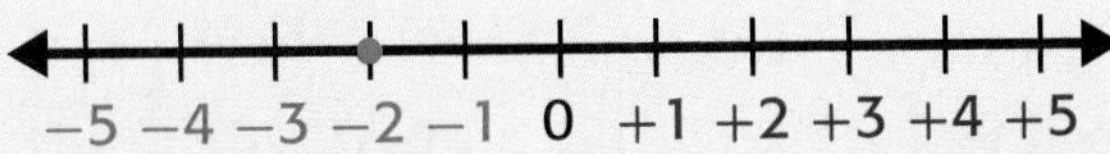

Write the number that represents each situation. Then show the number on a number line.

8. Shannon cut 20 seconds off his running time.

9. Marcel received $18 for his birthday.

Write the number of each letter on the number line.

10. A B C D

−4 ■ −2 ■ ■ +1 ■ +3

12-2 Find Points on a Grid (pp. 472–475)

Example 2
Identify the letter that is located at (3, −2).

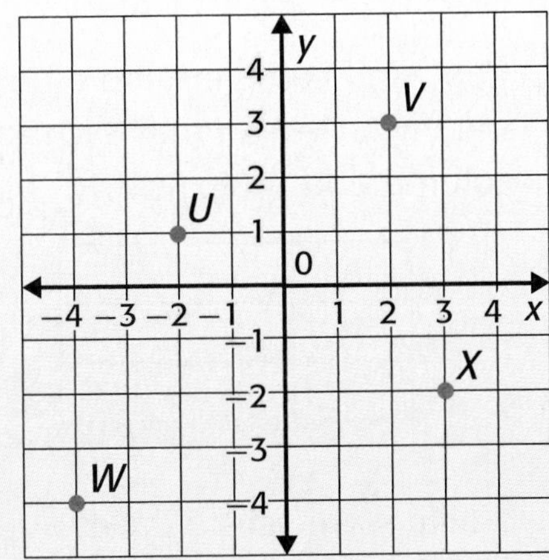

Start at (0, 0). The 3 tells you to move 3 units to the right. The −2 tells you to move 2 units down. The letter *X* is located at (3, −2).

Identify the letter that is located at each ordered pair.

11. (−3, 2)

12. (1, 4)

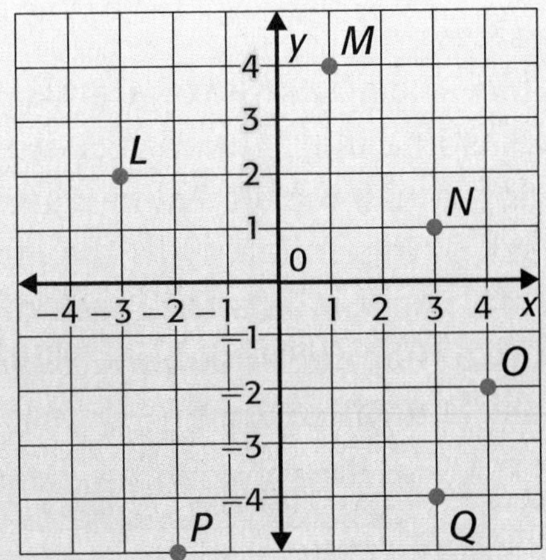

13. Describe how to move from *L* to *Q*.

12-3 Graph Ordered Pairs (pp. 476–478)

Example 3
Graph point *A* at (4, –2).

Start at (0, 0). Move 4 units to the right. Move 2 units down. Graph a point and label it *A*.

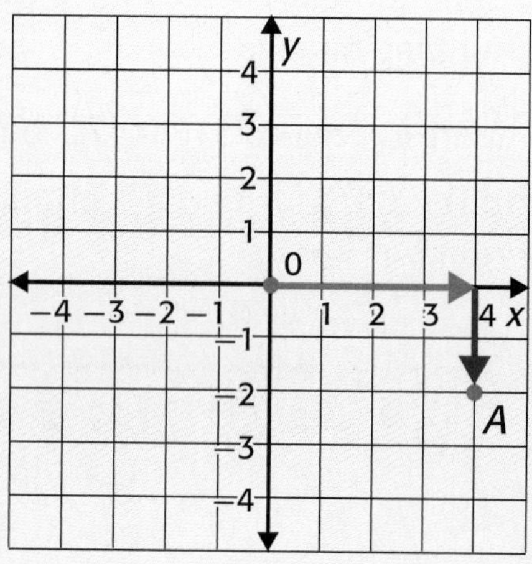

Graph and label each point on a grid.

14. point *A*: (–2, 5)

15. point *B*: (0, –4)

16. point *C*: (1, 2)

17. point *D*: (–3, –3)

Find the length of the segment between each set of ordered pairs.

18. (2, 1), (2, 7) **19.** (–4, –5), (–9, –5)

20. (3, 4), (3, 12) **21.** (2, –8), (7, –8)

12-4 Problem-Solving Strategy: Use Logical Reasoning (pp. 482–483)

Example 4
Fabio, Vijay, and Grace are wearing masks in a play. The masks are a cat, a dog, and a rabbit. Fabio wears the mask of the animal with the longest name. Grace wears the mask of the animal that does not bark. Which mask is each wearing?

	Cat	Dog	Rabbit
Fabio	✗	✗	✓
Vijay	✗	✓	✗
Grace	✓	✗	✗

22. Copy and complete the puzzle. Use the digits 1–9 so that each row and column add up to 15.

8	1	■
■	5	7
4	■	2

23. A bike store sells bicycles and tricycles. There are a total of 19 wheels. There are 8 bikes in all. What is one possible combination of bicycles and tricycles that could be in the store?

12-5 Functions (pp. 484–487)

Example 5
Create a function table for the rule $y = 3x + 1$.

The rule $y = 3x + 1$ means to multiply x by 3 and then add 1.

Rule: $y = 3x + 1$	
Input (x)	Output (y)
2	7
4	13
6	19
8	25
10	31

24. Copy and complete function table.

Rule: $y = 6x - 4$	
Input (x)	Output (y)
1	2
3	14
6	32
9	■
12	■

12-6 Graph Functions (pp. 490–493)

Example 6
Graph the function $y = x \div 2$.

Find and graph the ordered pairs.

Input (x)	Output (y)
2	1
4	2
6	3
8	4

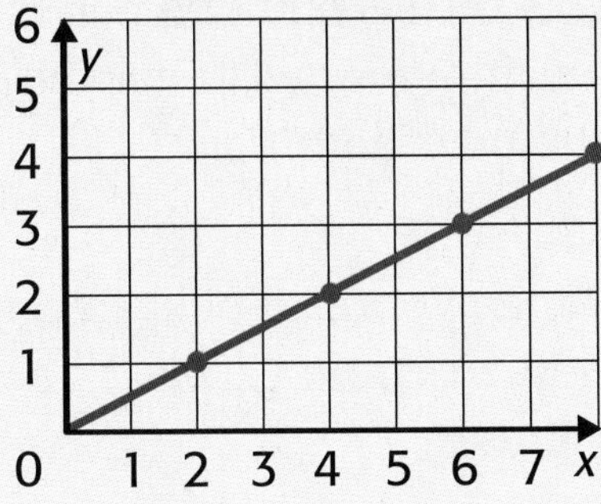

Graph ten points on the graph of the function.

25. $y = 3x$

26. $y = x \div 3$

27. $y = x \div 2 + 3$

28. $y = 4x - 4$

29. The function table shows ordered pairs for the rule $y = 2x$. Create a graph to show 10 ordered pairs for the rule $y = 2x$.

Input (x)	Output (y)	Ordered Pair (x, y)
2	4	(2, 4)
4	8	(4, 8)
6	12	(6, 12)
8	16	(8, 16)
10	20	(10, 20)

12-7 Problem-Solving Investigation: Choose a Strategy (pp. 494–495)

Example 7
Silvio wants to win a carnival prize that is worth 200 points. Silvio earns 20 points for each game he plays. How many games will he have to play?

Understand

What facts do you know?

- Silvio wants to win a prize that is worth 200 points.
- Silvio earns 20 points each time he plays a game.

What do you need to find?

- The number of games Silvio needs to play to win.

Plan To find the answer, organize the data in a table.

Solve The rule is $y = 20x$.

Rule: $y = 20x$	
Input (x)	Output (y)
1	20
2	40
3	60
⋮	⋮
9	180
10	200

So, Silvio needs to play 10 games to win the prize.

Check Since $20 \times 10 = 200$, the answer is correct.

Use any strategy to solve.

30. Draw the next three figures in the pattern shown below.

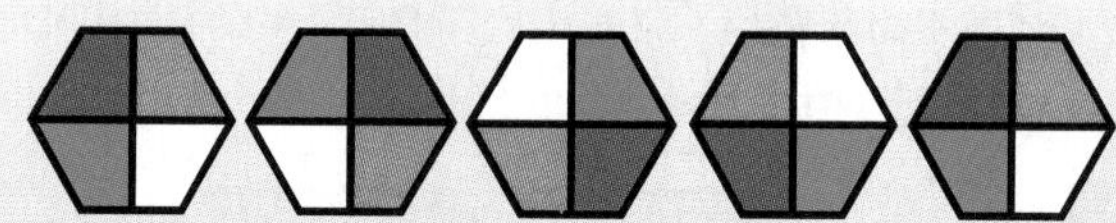

31. Michael has seven coins that total $1.50. What are the coins?

32. A zookeeper is in charge of feeding the bears, giraffes, lions, and monkeys. The bears are fed before the monkeys but after the lions. The giraffes are fed last. Copy and complete the chart to show the feeding schedule of the animals.

	7:00	7:15	7:30	7:45
Bears	✗	✓	✗	✗
Giraffes	✗	✗	✗	✓
Lions	✓	✗	✗	✗
Monkeys	✗	✗	✓	✗

33. Emily has $85 to spend on clothes. She wants to buy two sweaters that cost $50 each. If she buys one, she gets the second one half off. How much money will Emily have left if she buys both?

34. Roberta's watch beeps every hour. How many times will it beep in 5 days?

CHAPTER 12

Chapter Test

1. Copy and complete the table.

Rule: $y = 7x$	
Input (x)	**Output (y)**
5	35
6	42
7	49
8	■

Identify the letter at each ordered pair.

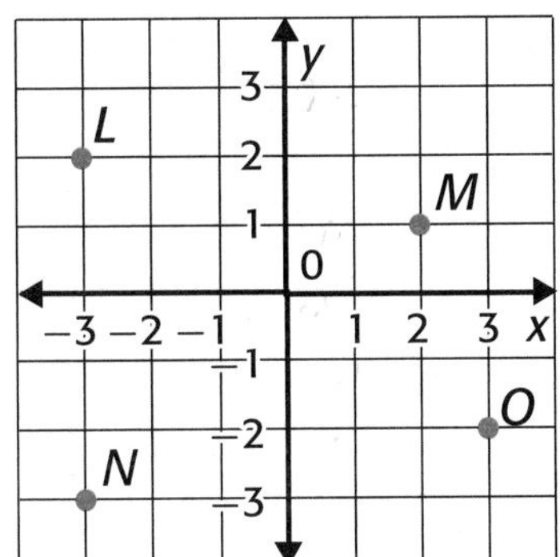

2. (−3, 2)

3. (3, −2)

Use the graph above. Write the order pair for each letter.

4. Letter *M*

5. Letter *N*

6. STANDARDS PRACTICE Find the distance between the points.

A 1 unit

B 2 units

C 3 units

D 4 units

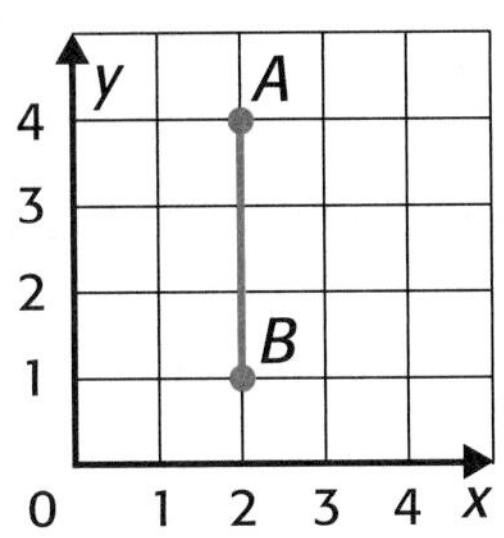

7. Cards numbered 2, 3, 4, and 5 are in a row. The 4 is between odd cards. The 2 has no cards to its right. The 5 is surrounded. What is their order?

Graph ten points on the graph of the function.

8. $y = 3x + 1$

9. $y = 4x - 2$

10. STANDARDS PRACTICE Ira graphed three points on the grid. They appear to be forming a line.

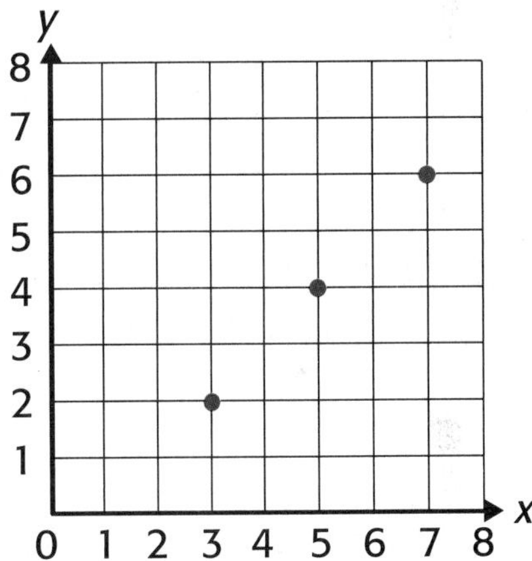

If Ira graphs another point on the line, what could its coordinates be?

F (8, 6)

G (8, 8)

H (8, 9)

J (9, 8)

Write the number that represents each situation.

11. put $50 in the bank

12. 12 degrees below zero

13. WRITING IN MATH Identify which of the ordered pairs does not belong with the other three. Explain.

(0, 4), (2, 4), (0, 3), (4, 4)

CHAPTER 12

California Standards Practice

Cumulative, Chapters 1–12

Standards Example

Mira made a map of her neighborhood. Identify the building that is located at (7, 2).

A Mira's house **C** Park

B Bank **D** School

Mira's Neighborhood

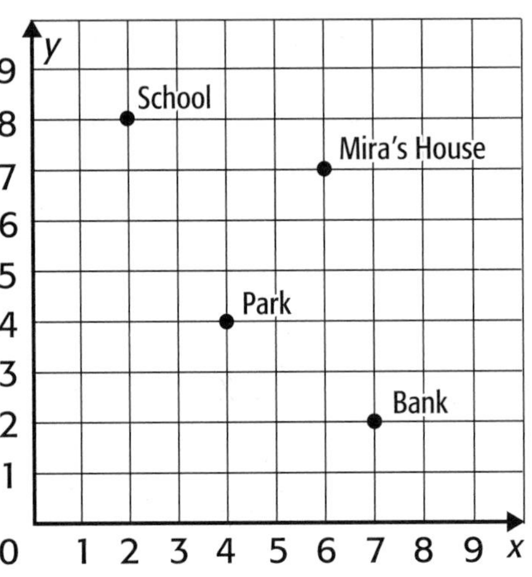

Read the Question

Identify the building that is located at (7, 2).

Solve the Question

To find (7, 2), start at (0, 0). Move right 7 units. Then, move up 2 units. The ordered pair (7, 2) locates a bank. The answer is B.

Choose the best answer.

1 **The points are on the same line.**

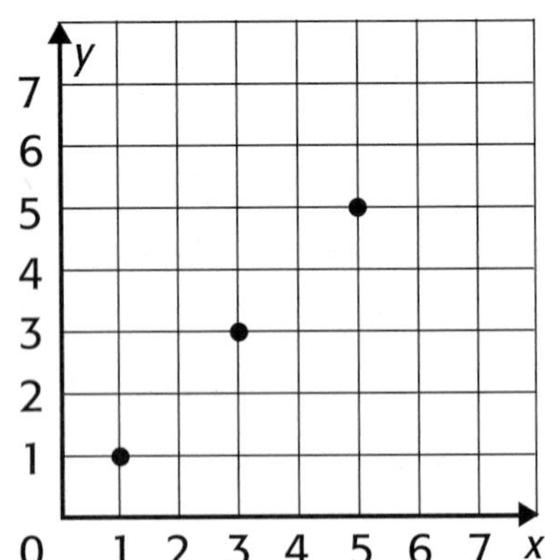

If Bart graphs another point on the line, what could be its ordered pair?

A (4, 5) **C** (6, 5)

B (5, 6) **D** (7, 7)

2 **Find the length of the segment between the points.**

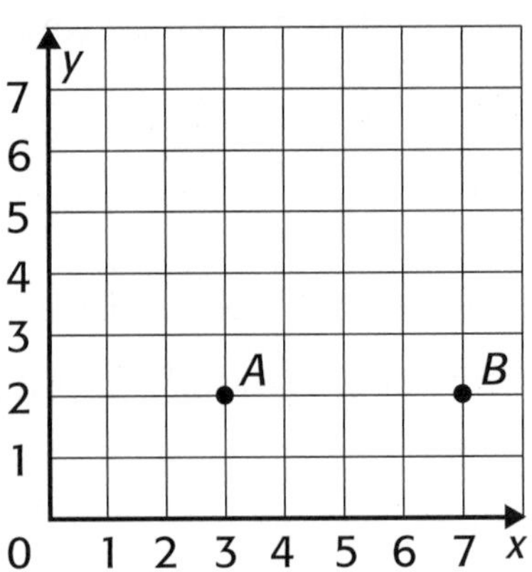

F 1 unit **H** 3 units

G 2 units **J** 4 units

More California Standards Practice
For practice by standard, see pages CA1–CA43.

3 **The numbers in the pattern decrease by the same amount each time. What are the next three numbers?**

20, 16, 12, 8, 4, ■, ■, ■

A 0, –4, –8 **C** 0, 1, 2

B 0, –2, –4 **D** 0, 4, 8

4 **How can you find the number of units from Point *K* to point *L*?**

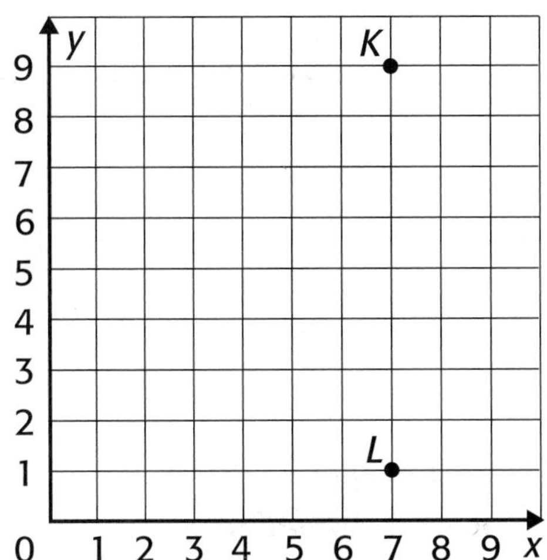

F Subtract 7 – 1. **H** Add 1 + 9.

G Subtract 9 – 1. **J** Add 9 + 7.

5 **What kind of a triangle is shown?**

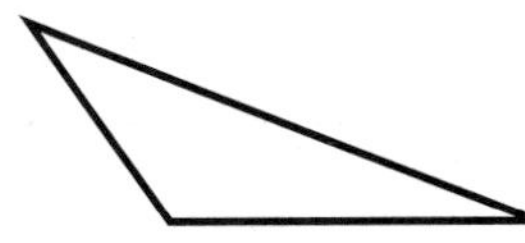

A obtuse **C** right

B acute **D** isosceles

6 **Which is the graph of $y = 2x$?**

F
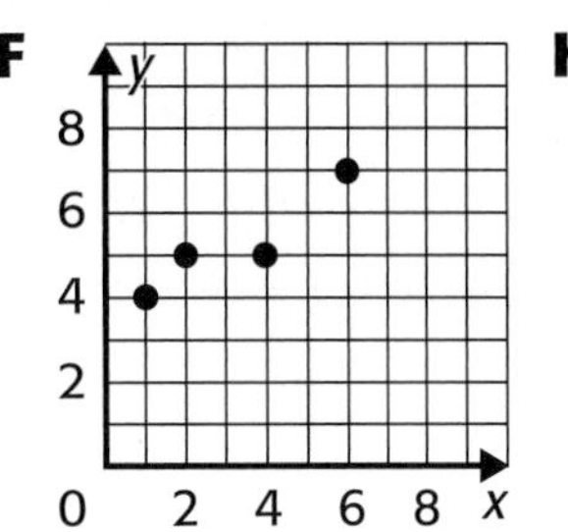

H
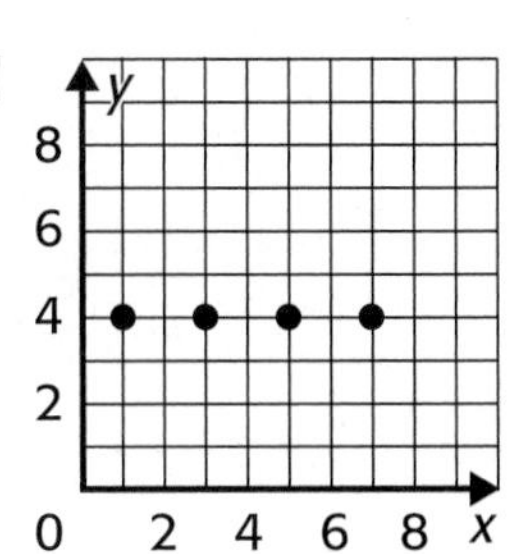

G
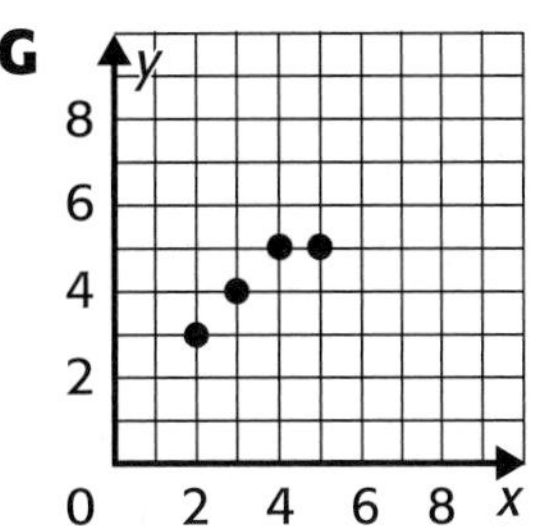

J
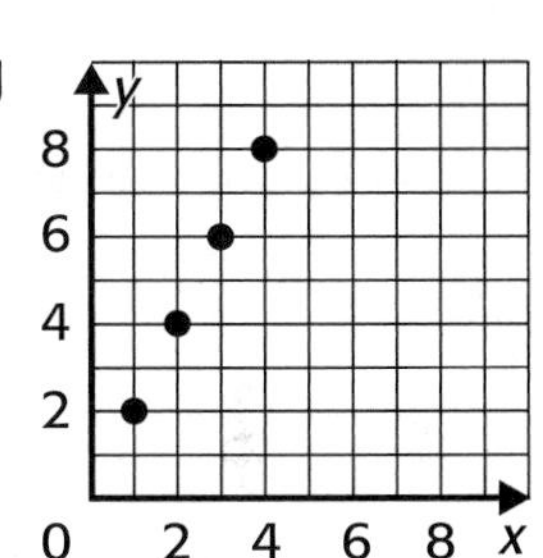

7 **A rectangle has an area of 28. Which of the following could not be its dimensions?**

A 7×4 **C** 14×2

B 9×3 **D** 28×1

8 **Which symbol is located at –6?**

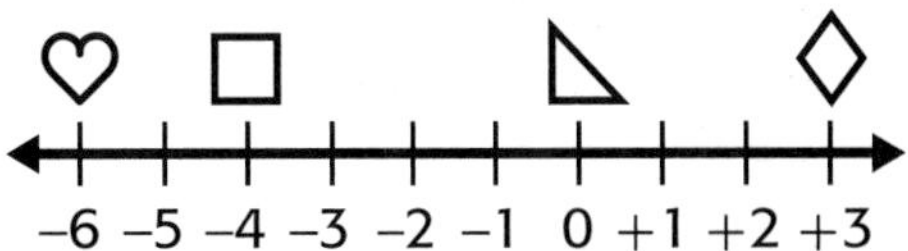

F □ **H** ◺

G ♡ **J** ◇

9 **Which of these is another way to write the product 9×7?**

A $1 \times 3 \times 7$ **C** $2 \times 9 \times 7$

B $2 \times 7 \times 7$ **D** $3 \times 3 \times 7$

CHAPTER 13

Fractions

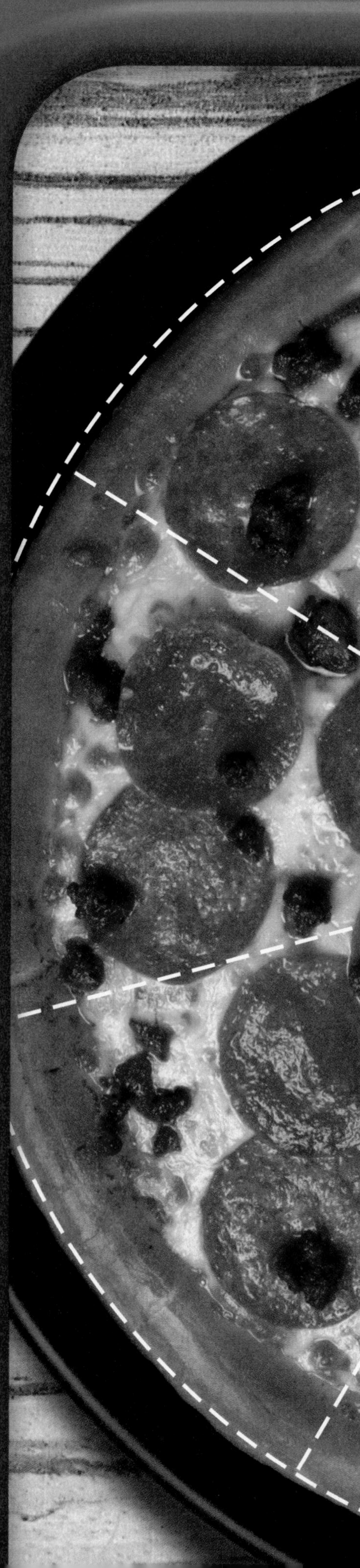

BIG Idea What is a fraction?

A **fraction** is a number that names part of a whole or part of a set.

Example If you have a pizza that is cut into eight pieces, each piece would be *one-eighth* or *one of eight* pieces.

or

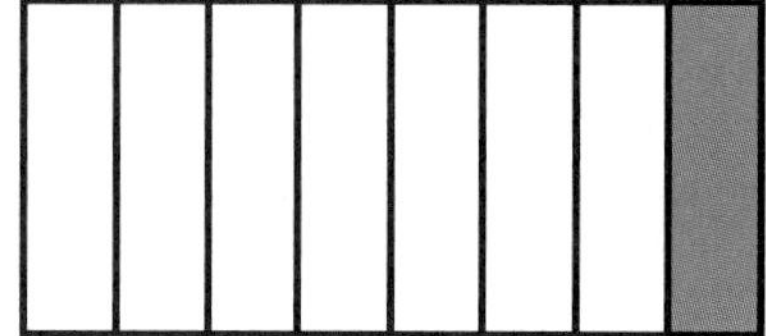

What will I learn in this chapter?

- Identify, read, and write fractions.
- Identify and find equivalent fractions.
- Compare and order fractions.
- Add and subtract like fractions.
- Solve problems by drawing a picture.

Key Vocabulary

fraction

numerator

denominator

equivalent fractions

mixed number

Student Study Tools at ca.gr4math.com

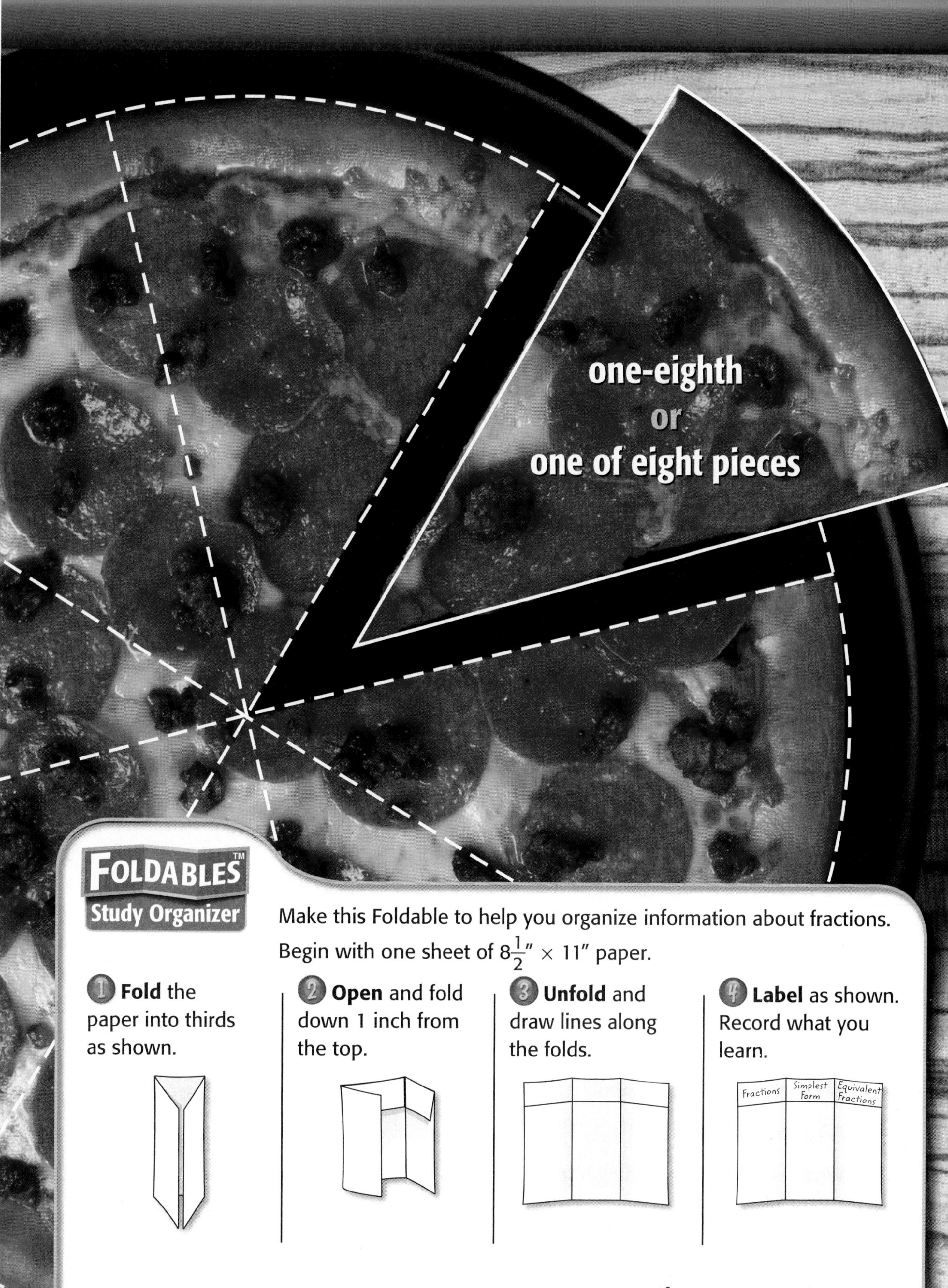

FOLDABLES™
Study Organizer

Make this Foldable to help you organize information about fractions. Begin with one sheet of $8\frac{1}{2}'' \times 11''$ paper.

1. **Fold** the paper into thirds as shown.
2. **Open** and fold down 1 inch from the top.
3. **Unfold** and draw lines along the folds.
4. **Label** as shown. Record what you learn.

ARE YOU READY for Chapter 13?

You have two ways to check prerequisite skills for this chapter.

Option 2

Math Online Take the Chapter Readiness Quiz at ca.gr4math.com.

Option 1

Complete the Quick Check below.

QUICK Check

Write the word that names the equal parts in each whole. Write *halves*, *thirds*, *fourths*, and *fifths*.
(Prior grade)

1. 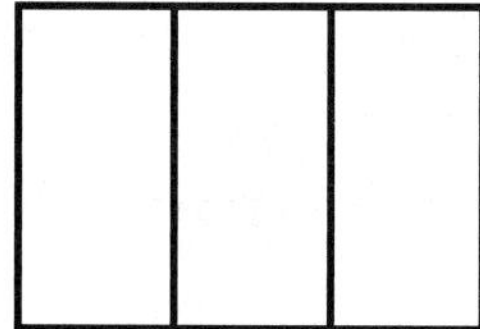

2. 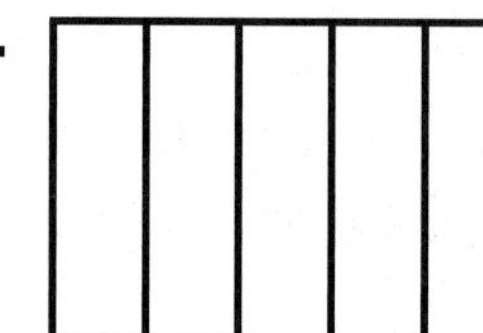

3. 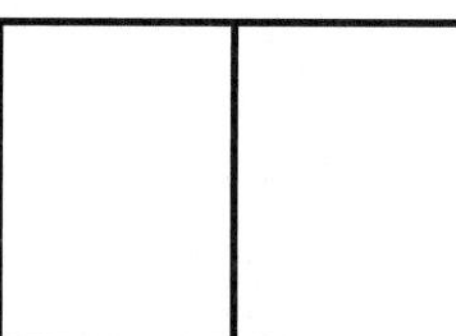

4. 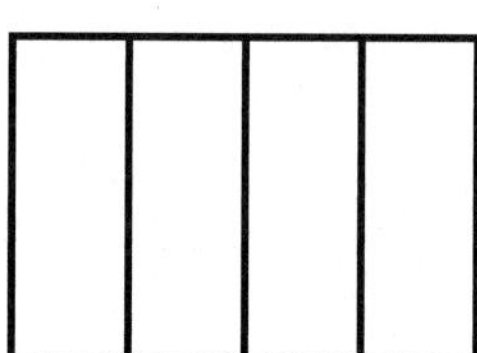

Divide. **(Lesson 5-5)**

5. 16 ÷ 4 **6.** 48 ÷ 8 **7.** 24 ÷ 3 **8.** 36 ÷ 6

9. 72 ÷ 9 **10.** 64 ÷ 8 **11.** 42 ÷ 6 **12.** 56 ÷ 8

13. Tyree downloaded 120 songs in 10 days. He downloaded the same number of songs each day. How many songs did he download each day?

List the factors of each number. **(Lesson 5-9)**

14. 12 **15.** 30 **16.** 45 **17.** 21

18. What factor of 36 is missing from 1, 2, 3, 4, 6, ■, 12, 18, 36?

13-1 Parts of a Whole

GET READY to Learn

Some of the pieces of pizza have pepperoni. Some have just cheese. You can use a fraction to describe the pizza and the toppings.

MAIN IDEA

I will identify, write, and read fractions for parts of a whole.

Standard 4NS1.5 Explain different interpretations of fractions, for example, parts of a whole, parts of a set, and division of whole numbers by whole numbers; explain equivalence of fractions.

Standard 4NS1.7 Write the fraction represented by a drawing of parts of a figure; represent a given fraction by using drawings; and relate a fraction to a simple decimal on a number line.

New Vocabulary

fraction
numerator
denominator

A **fraction** is a number that names part of a whole or part of a set. In a fraction, the **numerator** tells the number of equal parts. The **denominator** tells the number of equal parts in all.

pieces with pepperoni → 3 ← numerator
total number of pieces → 4 ← denominator

Real-World EXAMPLE

1 **FOOD Suppose Molly and her mom made the pizza shown. What fraction of the pizza is pepperoni?**

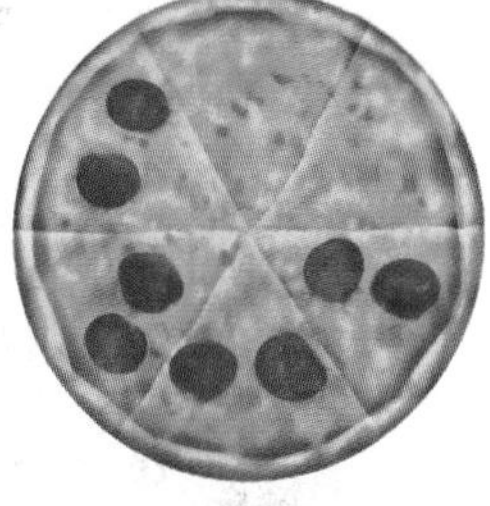

Write pepperoni slices → $\frac{4}{6}$ ← total slices in all

Read *four-sixths* or *four divided by six*

So, $\frac{4}{6}$ of the whole pizza is pepperoni.

EXAMPLE Write and Read Fractions

2 **What fraction of the figure is shaded?**

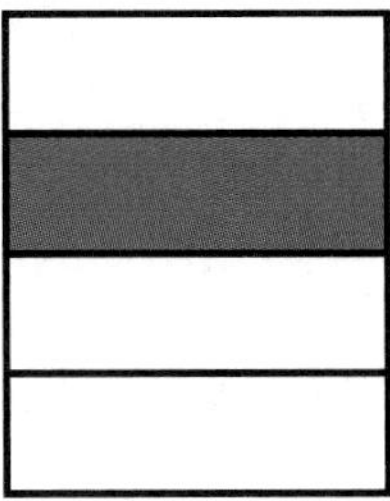

Write parts shaded → $\frac{1}{4}$ ← total equal parts in all

Read *one-fourth* or *one divided by four*

So, $\frac{1}{4}$ of the whole figure is shaded.

You can use different pictures to show the same part of a whole.

Real-World EXAMPLE **Draw a Fraction Model**

> **Remember**
>
> The denominator is always the bottom number in a fraction. Remember that **d** in **d**enominator could stand for **d**own.

3 **GARDENS The students at Watson Elementary School are making a garden. They will plant vegetables in $\frac{1}{3}$ of the whole garden. Draw a picture to show this fraction.**

One Way: **Use a Rectangle**	Another Way: **Use a Circle**
vegetables / other / other	vegetables / other / other
Divide a rectangle into 3 equal parts. Shade one part to show one-third.	Divide a circle into 3 equal parts. Shade one part to show one-third.

Online **Personal Tutor at** ca.gr4math.com

CHECK What You Know

Write the fraction that names part of the whole. See Examples 1 and 2 (p. 507)

1. 

part left

2. 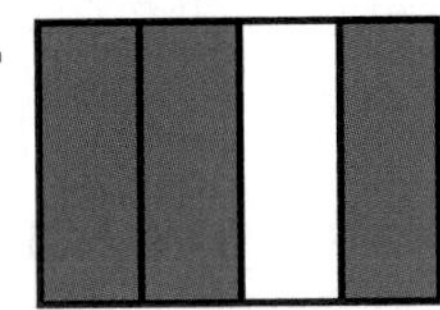

part shaded

3. 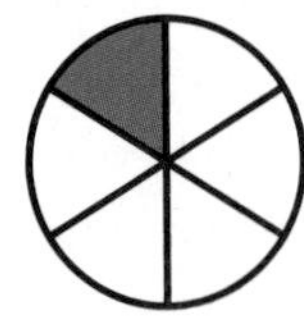

part not shaded

Draw a picture and shade part of it to show the fraction. See Example 3 (p. 508)

4. $\frac{1}{4}$ **5.** $\frac{2}{3}$ **6.** $\frac{5}{8}$

7. A birthday cake is cut into 8 equal pieces. Arnaldo ate one piece. The guests ate the remaining pieces. What fraction of the whole cake did the guests eat?

8. Talk About It What part of a fraction is the denominator? What does the denominator mean?

Practice and Problem Solving

See page R32.

Write the fraction that names part of the whole. See Examples 1 and 2 (p. 507)

9. 
part left

10. 
part filled

11. 
part filled

12. 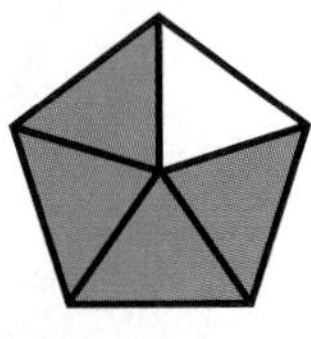
part shaded

13. 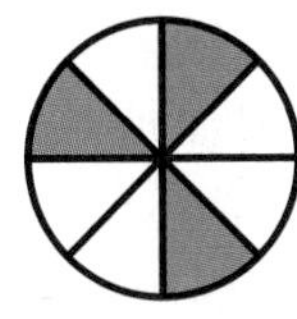
part not shaded

14. 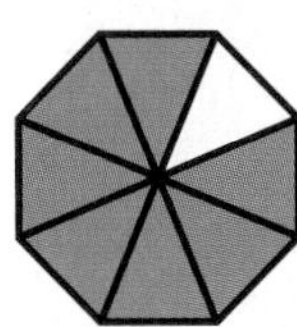
part not shaded

Draw a picture and shade part of it to show the fraction. See Example 3 (p. 508)

15. $\frac{3}{5}$ **16.** $\frac{3}{6}$ **17.** $\frac{7}{8}$ **18.** $\frac{4}{10}$

Alphabet flags are used by ships at sea to send short messages. Write the fraction for the part of each flag that is blue.

19. 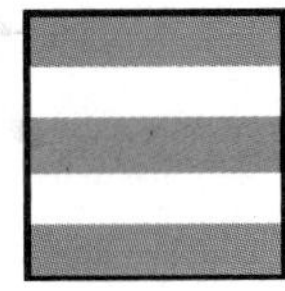
Letter C

20. 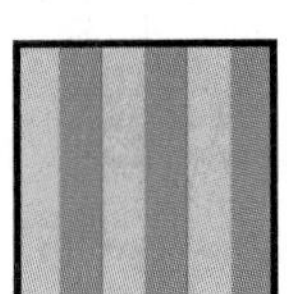
Letter G

21. 
Letter N

22. 
Letter Z

For Exercises 23–25, use the recipe shown.

23. What is the total number of cups of ingredients needed to make one batch of the party mix?

24. What fraction of the ingredients is pretzels?

25. What fraction of the ingredients are peanuts and raisins?

Recipe for: Party Mix
1 cup peanuts
3 cups rice cereal
2 cups pretzels
2 cups raisins
Makes: one batch

H.O.T. Problems

26. OPEN ENDED Name two different real-world items that can show the fraction $\frac{2}{3}$.

27. WRITING IN MATH If the denominator of $\frac{2}{5}$ was increased from 5 to 10, would it be greater or less than $\frac{2}{5}$? Explain.

13-2 Parts of a Set

MAIN IDEA

I will identify, read, write, and model fractions for parts of a set.

Standard 4NS1.5 Explain different interpretations of fractions, for example, parts of a whole, **parts of a set, and division of whole numbers by whole numbers;** explain equivalence of fractions.

Standard 4NS1.7 Write the fraction represented by a drawing of parts of a figure; represent a given fraction by using drawings; and relate a fraction to a simple decimal on a number line.

GET READY to Learn

A set of toy cars has two red cars, one green car, and one blue car. What fraction of the cars is green?

A set is a group of objects. In Lesson 13-1, you learned to use a fraction to name part of a whole. Fractions can also be used to name part of a set.

Real-World EXAMPLE

1 CARS What fraction of the set of cars is green?

Write green cars → $\frac{1}{4}$ ← numerator
total cars → ← denominator

Read *one-fourth* or *one divided by four*

So, $\frac{1}{4}$ of the set of cars is green.

EXAMPLE Write and Read Fractions

2 What fraction of the set of stars is *not* green?

Write stars *not* green → $\frac{2}{5}$
total stars →

Read *two-fifths* or *two divided by five*

So, $\frac{2}{5}$ of the set of stars are *not* green.

Online Personal Tutor at ca.gr4math.com

You have learned that fractions can be used to name part of a whole and part of a set. Another way of looking at fractions is as division of whole numbers by whole numbers.

Remember

Recall that a quotient is the answer to a division problem.

Real-World EXAMPLE Fraction as a Quotient

3 FOOD Tammy and three friends went to a pancake breakfast. They ordered and shared three pancakes equally. What part of the pancakes did each receive?

Draw a picture to show the division.

1 1 / 1 2 2 3 / 2 3 3 4 / 4 4

Three pancakes are divided among 4 people. So, each person receives 3 divided by 4 or $\frac{3}{4}$ of the pancakes.

CHECK What You Know

Write the fraction for the part of the set that is yellow. Then write the fraction for the part that is *not* yellow. See Examples 1 and 2 (p. 510)

1. 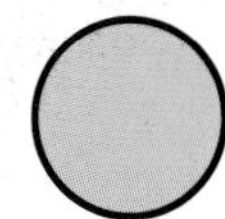 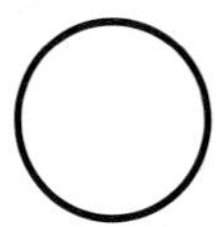

2. 

Write the fraction that names the part of the set of vegetables.
See Examples 1 and 2 (p. 510)

3. *not* red peppers

4. *not* corn

5. *not* green peppers

6. Five chimpanzees are sharing four bananas equally. What part of the bananas does each receive?
See Example 3 (p. 511)

7. Talk About It Explain what the following sentence means. Three-fifths of a set of animals are dogs.

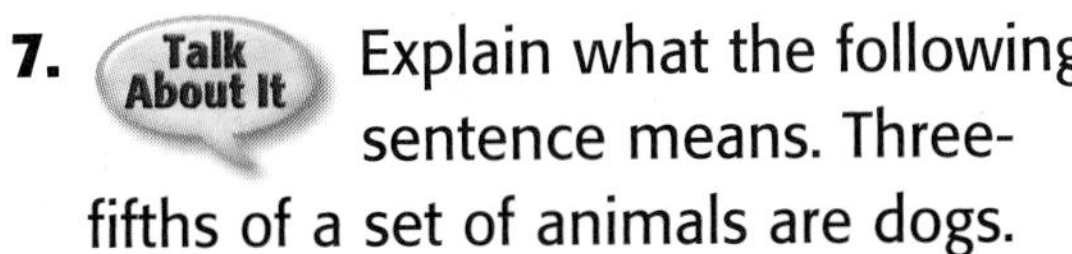

Practice and Problem Solving

See page R32.

Write the fraction for the part of the set that is blue. Then write the fraction for the part that is *not* blue. See Examples 1 and 2 (p. 510)

8.    

9. 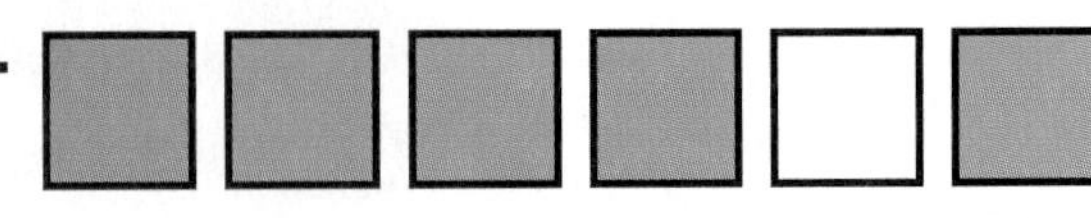

10. 

11. 

Write the fraction that names the part of the set of shapes. See Example 2 (p. 510)

12. *not* circles

13. *not* squares

14. *not* triangles

15. *not* red

16. *not* yellow

17. *not* blue

18. Eight people are sharing five apples equally. What part of the apples does each receive? See Example 3 (p. 511)

19. Twelve elephants are sharing nine bales of hay equally. What part of the bales of hay does each receive? See Example 3 (p. 511)

Real-World PROBLEM SOLVING

Data File The state marine mammal of California is the gray whale.

20. Suppose 10 gray whales are traveling together. If 4 of the whales are adult females and 3 are babies, what fraction is adult males?

21. Gray whales can dive for 30 minutes at a time. Write the fraction that names the part of an hour a gray whale can dive.

H.O.T. Problems

22. **OPEN ENDED** Draw a set of objects that shows the fraction $\frac{3}{5}$.

23. **FIND THE ERROR** Three-eighths of a set of fruit is oranges. What part is *not* oranges? Who is correct, Sonja or Jairo?

24. **WRITING IN ▶MATH** Write a problem that involves identifying a fraction that describes part of a group.

Standards Practice

25 Which figure shows $\frac{2}{5}$? **(Lesson 13-1)**

A

C

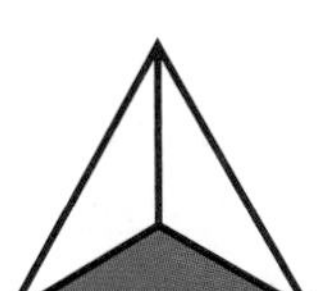

B

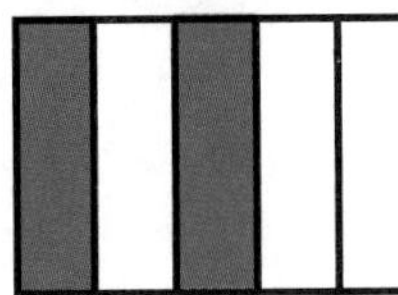

D

26 Stephen walks his dog 4 days each week. His brother walks the dog the other days. What fraction names the number of days Stephen's brother walks the dog? **(Lesson 13-2)**

F $\frac{3}{7}$

G $\frac{1}{2}$

H $\frac{4}{7}$

J $\frac{3}{4}$

Spiral Review

Draw a picture and shade part of it to show the fraction. **(Lesson 13-1)**

27. $\frac{2}{5}$

28. $\frac{1}{6}$

29. $\frac{4}{10}$

Graph ten points on the graph of the function. **(Lesson 12-6)**

30. $y = 2x + 1$

31. $y = x - 1$

32. Maurice has two penpals. He sends each penpal three letters each month. Is it reasonable to say that Maurice will write more than 75 letters in one year? Explain. **(Lesson 7-2)**

13-3 Problem-Solving Strategy

MAIN IDEA I will solve problems by drawing a picture.

Standard 4MR2.3 Use a variety of methods, such as words, numbers, symbols, charts, graphs, tables, diagrams, **and models, to explain mathematical reasoning.** Standard 4NS1.7 Write the fraction represented by a drawing of parts of a figure; **represent a given fraction by using drawings;** and relate a fraction to a simple decimal on a number line.

Brandi and her mom are at a pet store. The pet store has 15 reptiles. One-third of the reptiles are turtles. Two are snakes, and the rest are lizards. How many of each reptile are there?

Understand

What facts do you know?

- There are 15 reptiles at the store.
- One-third are turtles.
- Two are snakes.
- The rest are lizards.

What do you need to find?

- Find the number of each reptile.

Plan

Draw a picture to solve the problem.

Solve

- Draw 15 circles. Since the fraction $\frac{1}{3}$ is used, place the circles in 3 equal groups.
- To show the turtles, shade $\frac{1}{3}$ of the circles. That is, one of the three equal groups. So, there are 5 turtles. There are 2 snakes, so shade 2 circles to show the snakes.
- There are 8 circles not shaded. This is the number of lizards.

snakes

So, there are 5 turtles, 2 snakes, and 8 lizards at the pet store.

Check

Look back at the problem. 5 turtles + 2 snakes + 8 lizards = 15 reptiles. The pet store has 15 reptiles. So, the answer is correct.

ANALYZE the Strategy

Refer to the problem on the previous page.

1. Explain why you used 15 circles.
2. You know that $\frac{1}{3}$ of the reptiles are turtles. Explain why 5 boxes were shaded to show the number of turtles.
3. If the pet store had 24 reptiles, how many of the reptiles would be lizards?
4. Check your answer to Exercise 3. How do you know that it is correct?

PRACTICE the Strategy

EXTRA PRACTICE See page R33.

Solve. Use the *draw a picture* strategy.

5. There are three trees in a backyard. The second tree is half as tall as the first. The third tree is taller than the second tree and shorter than the first tree. The total height of the trees is 24 feet. Find the height of each tree.

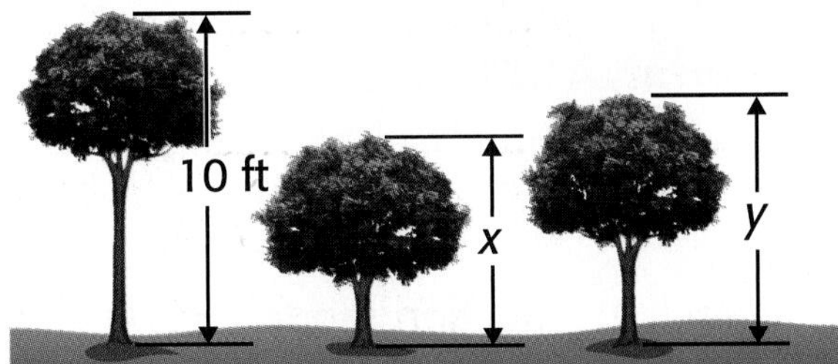

6. Pam and three other students are waiting in a line. Lakita is ahead of Pam. Sanjay is third in line. Rob is behind Sanjay. In what order are the students standing?

7. Emil bought his mom a dozen roses. Some of the roses are shown below. The rest are white. Which color were there the most of? How many roses were that color?

8. There are 22 students in Ms. Lane's class. Half of them packed their lunches. Eight students are buying pizza. The rest are buying salads. How many students are buying salads?

9. The table shows how long Adam and Kenya rode their bikes. Who biked longer? How much longer?

Biking Schedule	
Name	**Time Spent Biking**
Adam	$\frac{1}{3}$ of an hour
Kenya	15 minutes

10. There are 16 books on a shelf. One-fourth of the books are about animals. Two are adventure. The rest are mystery. How many are mystery books?

11. **WRITING IN MATH** Look back at Exercise 10. Explain how you used the *draw a picture* strategy to solve the problem.

Explore

Math Activity for 13-4

Equivalent Fractions

MAIN IDEA

I will identify equivalent fractions.

Standard 4NS1.5 Explain different interpretations of fractions, for example, parts of a whole, parts of a set, and division of whole numbers by whole numbers; **explain equivalence of fractions** (see Standard 4.0).

Standard 4MR2.3 Use a variety of methods, such as words, **numbers,** symbols, charts, graphs, tables, diagrams, and **models, to explain mathematical reasoning.**

You Will Need

fraction models

New Vocabulary

equivalent fractions

Concepts in Motion

Animation

ca.gr4math.com

Fractions that represent the same amount are **equivalent fractions**.

ACTIVITY

1 Identify two fractions that are equivalent to $\frac{1}{3}$.

Step 1 Model $\frac{1}{3}$.

Start with 1 whole. Then, use the $\frac{1}{3}$ fraction model to show $\frac{1}{3}$.

1		
$\frac{1}{3}$		

Step 2 Find a fraction equivalent to $\frac{1}{3}$.

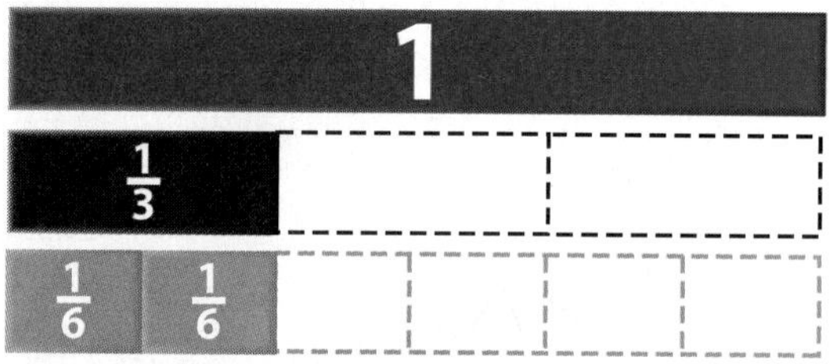

Using $\frac{1}{6}$ fraction models, place them below the $\frac{1}{3}$ fraction model. How many $\frac{1}{6}$ fraction models are used?

1					
$\frac{1}{3}$					
$\frac{1}{6}$	$\frac{1}{6}$				

Step 3 Find another fraction equivalent to $\frac{1}{3}$.

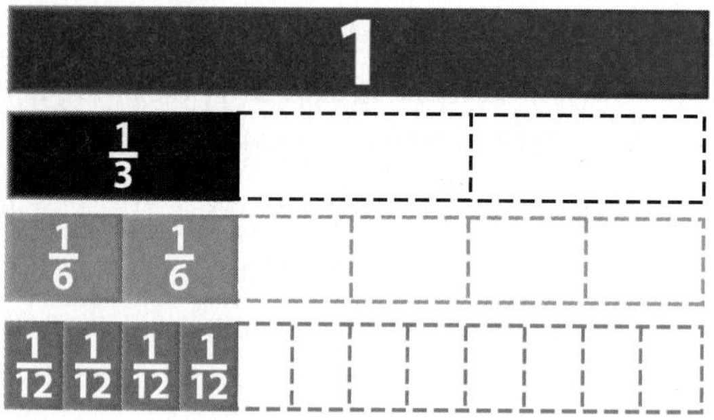

Use $\frac{1}{12}$ fraction models to equal the length of the $\frac{1}{3}$ fraction model. Count the number of $\frac{1}{12}$ fraction models.

1											
$\frac{1}{3}$											
$\frac{1}{6}$	$\frac{1}{6}$										
$\frac{1}{12}$	$\frac{1}{12}$	$\frac{1}{12}$	$\frac{1}{12}$								

So, $\frac{1}{3}$, $\frac{2}{6}$, and $\frac{4}{12}$ are equivalent fractions.

ACTIVITY

Hands-On Activity

2 **Identify equivalent fractions.**

Step 1 Draw three identical number lines that show zero and one.

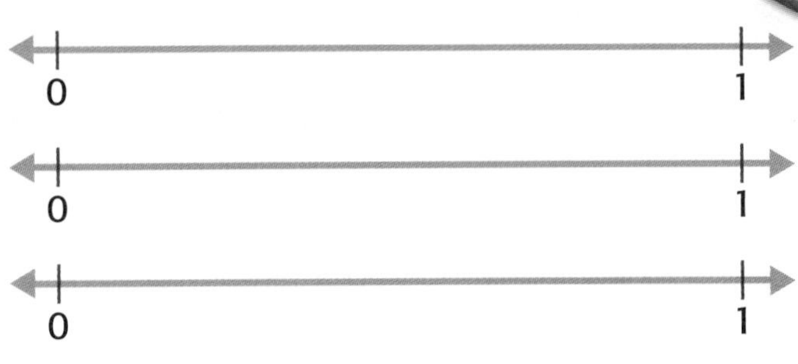

Step 2 Divide the first number line into fourths. Divide the second number line into eighths. Divide the third number line into sixteenths.

Notice that $\frac{1}{4} = \frac{2}{8} = \frac{4}{16}$.

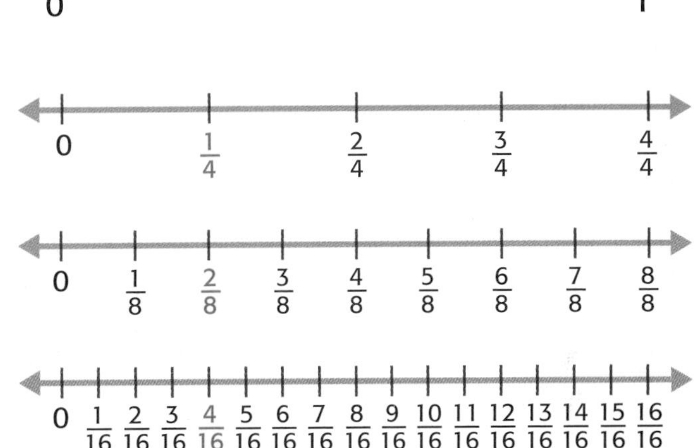

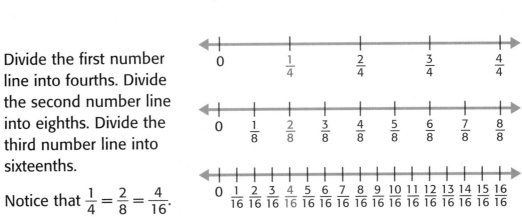

Think About It

1. **Algebra** Copy and complete $\frac{1}{3} = \frac{■}{9} = \frac{■}{15}$.
2. Refer to Activity 2. Find two fractions equivalent to $\frac{3}{4}$.

CHECK What You Know

Determine whether each pair of fractions is equivalent. Use fraction models or number lines.

3. $\frac{2}{4}$ and $\frac{6}{12}$
4. $\frac{6}{8}$ and $\frac{5}{10}$
5. $\frac{2}{3}$ and $\frac{3}{5}$
6. $\frac{9}{12}$ and $\frac{3}{4}$

Find two equivalent fractions for each fraction. Use fraction models or number lines.

7. $\frac{1}{5}$
8. $\frac{2}{6}$
9. $\frac{4}{8}$
10. $\frac{2}{12}$
11. **WRITING IN MATH** Explain what it means for two fractions to be equivalent.

13-4 Equivalent Fractions

MAIN IDEA

I will find equivalent fractions.

Standard 4NS1.5 Explain different interpretations of fractions, for example, parts of a whole, parts of a set, and division of whole numbers by whole numbers; **explain equivalence of fractions.**

New Vocabulary

equivalent fractions

GET READY to Learn

Megan has 8 fish in an aquarium. Four fish are green. So, Megan says that $\frac{4}{8}$ of the fish are green. Megan could use another fraction to represent $\frac{4}{8}$.

The fraction models below show that $\frac{4}{8}$ is the same as $\frac{1}{2}$. Fractions that name the same number are **equivalent fractions**.

1							
$\frac{1}{2}$							
$\frac{1}{8}$	$\frac{1}{8}$	$\frac{1}{8}$	$\frac{1}{8}$				

EXAMPLE Find Equivalent Fractions

1 **Find three fractions that are equivalent to $\frac{4}{8}$.**

To find equivalent fractions, you can use multiplication or division.

Vocabulary Link

prefixes The prefix *equi-* means *equal*.

One Way: Multiply		Another Way: Divide	
$\frac{4 \times 2}{8 \times 2} = \frac{8}{16}$	Multiply the numerator and the denominator by the same number, 2.	$\frac{4 \div 2}{8 \div 2} = \frac{2}{4}$ $\frac{2 \div 2}{4 \div 2} = \frac{1}{2}$	Divide the numerator and the denominator by the same number, 2.

So, $\frac{8}{16}$, $\frac{2}{4}$, or $\frac{1}{2}$ could be used to represent $\frac{4}{8}$.

Online Personal Tutor at ca.gr4math.com

CHECK What You Know

Write the fraction for the part that is shaded. Then find an equivalent fraction. See Example 1 (p. 518)

1. 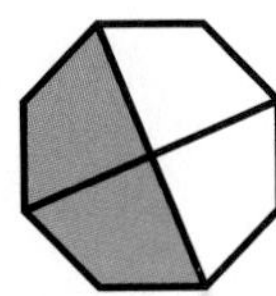

2. 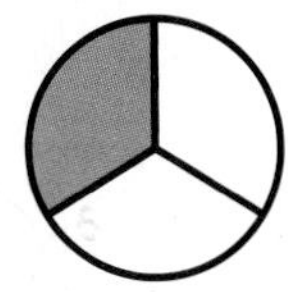

3. 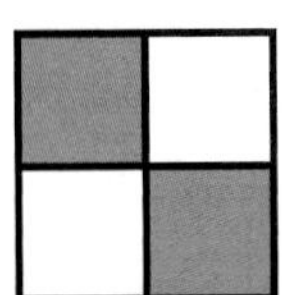

Find an equivalent fraction for each fraction. See Example 1 (p. 518)

4. $\frac{1}{4}$ **5.** $\frac{4}{6}$ **6.** $\frac{1}{5}$ **7.** $\frac{8}{10}$ **8.** $\frac{1}{3}$

9. Javier has 4 juice boxes. Three are grape flavored. Write two fractions that describe the part of the juice boxes that is grape.

10. Talk About It Tell why $\frac{3}{4}$, $\frac{6}{8}$, and $\frac{9}{12}$ are equivalent fractions. Give an example of another set of three equivalent fractions.

Practice and Problem Solving

Write the fraction for the part that is shaded. Then find an equivalent fraction. See Example 1 (p. 518)

11. 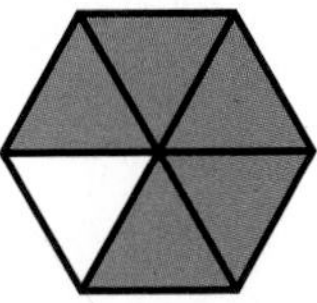

12. 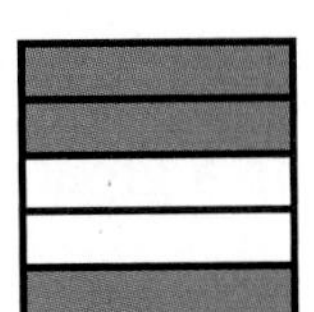

13. 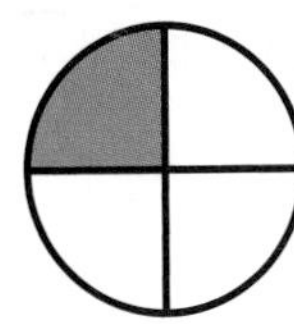

14. 

15. 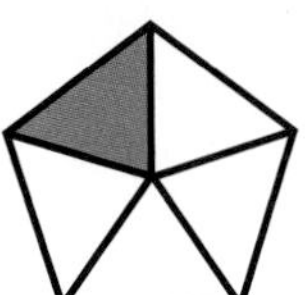

16. 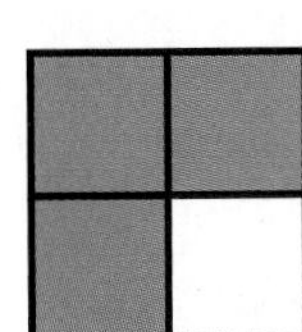

Find an equivalent fraction for each fraction. See Example 1 (p. 518)

17. $\frac{2}{7}$ **18.** $\frac{2}{5}$ **19.** $\frac{6}{10}$ **20.** $\frac{2}{12}$ **21.** $\frac{2}{3}$

22. $\frac{6}{8}$ **23.** $\frac{1}{2}$ **24.** $\frac{9}{18}$ **25.** $\frac{1}{6}$ **26.** $\frac{12}{20}$

27. A roller coaster has 16 cars. Six of the cars are green. Write two fractions for the part of the cars that is green.

28. **Measurement** Lucas ran $\frac{1}{2}$ mile. Candace ran $\frac{4}{6}$ mile. Did they run the same distance? Explain.

Algebra **Find the value of x.**

29. $\frac{3}{4} = \frac{12}{x}$

30. $\frac{2}{5} = \frac{x}{25}$

31. $\frac{8}{12} = \frac{x}{3}$

32. $\frac{8}{64} = \frac{1}{x}$

Real-World PROBLEM SOLVING

Science Giraffes grow to a height of about 20 feet. Their neck is about $\frac{2}{5}$ their total height. Giraffes spend about $\frac{5}{6}$ of a day eating.

33. What fraction of a day does a giraffe spend eating? Write another fraction that represents this amount.

34. What fraction of the total height is the length of a giraffe's neck? Write a fraction equivalent to this fraction.

35. Giraffes often sleep $\frac{1}{2}$ of an hour each day. Write two fractions that represent the same amount of time.

36. What is the height of the giraffe in inches?

H.O.T. Problems

37. **OPEN ENDED** Write a fraction equivalent to $\frac{2}{5}$. Write a fraction equivalent to $\frac{3}{6}$. Which fraction represents a greater amount? Explain.

38. **FIND THE ERROR** Rachel and Miguel are finding a fraction equivalent to $\frac{6}{18}$. Who is correct? Explain.

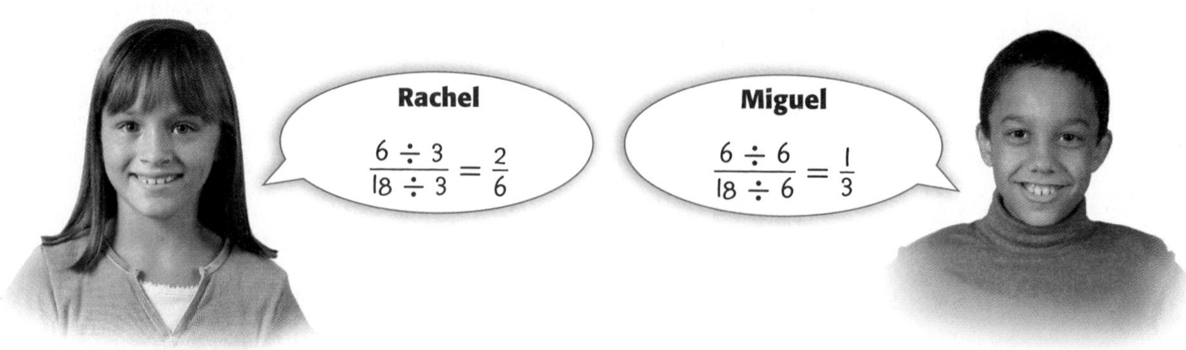

Rachel
$\frac{6 \div 3}{18 \div 3} = \frac{2}{6}$
Miguel
$\frac{6 \div 6}{18 \div 6} = \frac{1}{3}$

39. **CHALLENGE** Identify a fraction that is equivalent to $\frac{25}{100}$.

40. **WRITING IN ▸MATH** Can you always find an equivalent fraction for a fraction? Explain.

CHAPTER 13 Mid-Chapter Check

Lessons 13-1 through 13-4

Write the fraction that names the shaded part of the whole. (Lesson 13-1)

1. 

2. 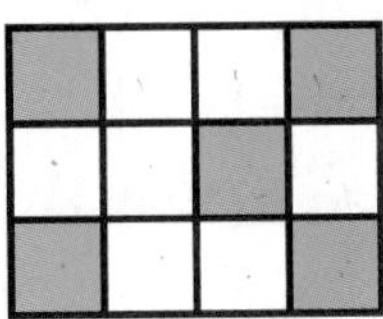

Draw a picture and shade part of it to show the fraction. (Lesson-13-1)

3. $\frac{1}{8}$

4. $\frac{3}{7}$

5. The flag of Italy is shown. What fraction of the flag is green? (Lesson 13-1)

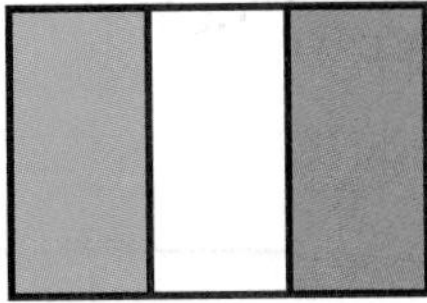

6. **STANDARDS PRACTICE** What fraction of the hearts is shaded? (Lesson 13-2)

A $\frac{4}{10}$

B $\frac{1}{2}$

C $\frac{5}{9}$

D $\frac{6}{10}$

7. Draw a picture that represents the statement below. (Lesson 13-2)

Three of the five leaves are shaded.

8. There are 3 red apples, 6 green apples, and 1 yellow apple on a table. Of the apples, what fraction is green? (Lesson 13-2)

Write the fraction that names the part of the set of smile faces. (Lesson 13-2)

9. red

10. green

11. Janey is planting 12 trees in her yard. There are 5 maple trees and the rest are oak. What fraction of the trees is oak? (Lesson 13-3)

12. Galeno spent $\frac{1}{2}$ of his money on a movie ticket and $\frac{1}{4}$ of his money on a snack. He had \$8 before the movie. How much money does he have now? (Lesson 13-3)

Find an equivalent fraction for each fraction. (Lesson 13-4)

13. $\frac{1}{3}$

14. $\frac{4}{5}$

Algebra **Find the value of *x*.** (Lesson 13-4)

15. $\frac{1}{2} = \frac{3}{x}$

16. $\frac{4}{5} = \frac{x}{10}$

17. Yang's mom used 12 of the 20 stamps she had bought. Yang said that she used $\frac{3}{5}$ of the stamps. Is Yang correct? Explain. (Lesson 13-4)

18. **WRITING IN MATH** Is $\frac{1}{4}$ of the rectangle green? Explain why or why not. (Lesson 13-1)

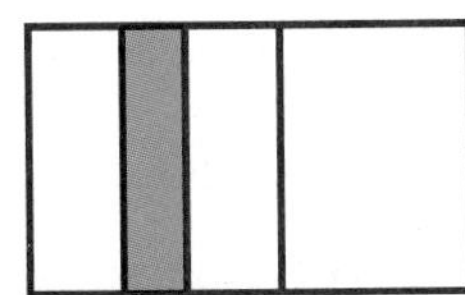

13-5 Simplest Form

MAIN IDEA

I will write a fraction in simplest form.

Standard 4NS1.5 Explain different interpretations of fractions, for example, parts of a whole, parts of a set, and **division of whole numbers by whole numbers; explain equivalence of fractions.**

New Vocabulary

simplest form

GET READY to Learn

There are 12 questions on a quiz. Tomas got 8 out of 12 or $\frac{8}{12}$ of the questions correct. Some of the fractions equivalent to $\frac{8}{12}$ are $\frac{2}{3}$ and $\frac{4}{6}$.

Name: Tomas

1. true
2. true
3. false
4. producer
5. consumer
6. carnivore
7. omnivore
8. herbivore
9. carnivore
10. omnivore
11. decomposer
12. herbivore

Among the equivalent fractions $\frac{2}{3}$, $\frac{4}{6}$, and $\frac{8}{12}$, the fraction $\frac{2}{3}$ is in **simplest form** because its numerator and denominator have no common factor other than 1.

Fractions in Simplest Form				
$\frac{1}{2}$	$\frac{2}{3}$	$\frac{3}{4}$	$\frac{3}{7}$	$\frac{5}{8}$

Fractions NOT in Simplest Form				
$\frac{2}{4}$	$\frac{4}{6}$	$\frac{8}{10}$	$\frac{8}{12}$	$\frac{16}{24}$

To change a fraction into its simplest form, you can divide both the numerator and the denominator by the greatest common factor.

EXAMPLE Write a Fraction in Simplest Form

1 Write $\frac{8}{12}$ in simplest form.

Step 1 Find the common factors.

Factors of 8: 1, 2, 4, 8

Factors of 12: 1, 2, 3, 4, 6, 12

Common factors: 1, 2 and 4

Step 2 Divide by the greatest common factor, 4.

$$\frac{8 \div 4}{12 \div 4} = \frac{2}{3}$$

The numbers 2 and 3 have no common factor other than 1.

So, $\frac{8}{12}$ in simplest form is $\frac{2}{3}$.

Review Vocabulary

factor numbers that are multiplied to give a product; *Example:* 2 and 3 are factors of 6 **(Lesson 7-1)**

To change a fraction into simplest form, you can also divide by common factors.

Real-World EXAMPLE

2 ANIMALS Koala bears sleep for up to 18 hours each day. What part of a day do koalas sleep? Write your answer in simplest form.

Step 1 Write a fraction.

$\frac{18}{24}$ ← hours sleep each day; ← total hours in a day

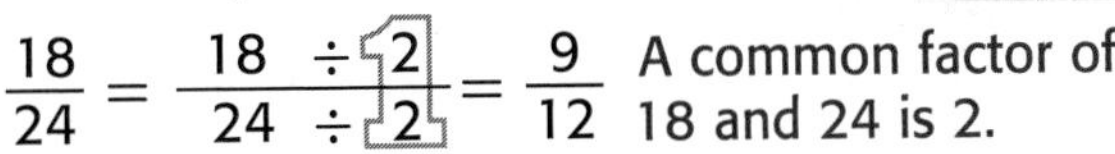

Step 2 Divide by common factors.

$\frac{18}{24} = \frac{18 \div 2}{24 \div 2} = \frac{9}{12}$ A common factor of 18 and 24 is 2.

$\frac{9}{12} = \frac{9 \div 3}{12 \div 3} = \frac{3}{4}$ A common factor of 9 and 12 is 3.

So, $\frac{18}{24}$ simplifies to $\frac{3}{4}$. Koalas sleep up to $\frac{3}{4}$ of a day.

Remember

Divide until the numerator and the denominator have no common factor other then 1.

Online Personal Tutor at ca.gr4math.com

KEY CONCEPT — Simplest Form

One Way	Divide the numerator and denominator by the greatest common factor.
Another Way	Divide the numerator and denominator by common factors until the only common factor is 1.

CHECK What You Know

Write each fraction in simplest form. If it is in simplest form, write *simplest form*. See Example 1 (p. 522)

1. $\frac{2}{4}$
2. $\frac{6}{10}$
3. $\frac{5}{6}$
4. $\frac{18}{30}$
5. Daniela read for 24 minutes. What fraction of an hour did she read? Write simplest form. See Example 2 (p. 523)
6. 

How do you know that $\frac{4}{5}$ is in simplest form?

Practice and Problem Solving

EXTRA PRACTICE See page R33.

Write each fraction in simplest form. If it is in simplest form, write *simplest form*. See Example 1 (p. 522)

7. $\frac{2}{10}$ **8.** $\frac{3}{12}$ **9.** $\frac{7}{20}$ **10.** $\frac{6}{9}$ **11.** $\frac{4}{16}$

12. $\frac{10}{15}$ **13.** $\frac{18}{27}$ **14.** $\frac{24}{40}$ **15.** $\frac{32}{42}$ **16.** $\frac{42}{56}$

Measurement What part of one day is each amount of time? Write as a fraction in simplest form. See Example 2 (p. 523)

17. 9 hours **18.** 16 hours **19.** 20 hours

Algebra Find the value of x to simplify each fraction.

20. $\frac{15}{45} = \frac{x}{3}$ **21.** $\frac{16}{28} = \frac{4}{x}$ **22.** $\frac{20}{36} = \frac{x}{9}$

Write as a fraction in simplest form.

23. Six of the 16 marbles in a bag are yellow. What fraction of the marbles is yellow?

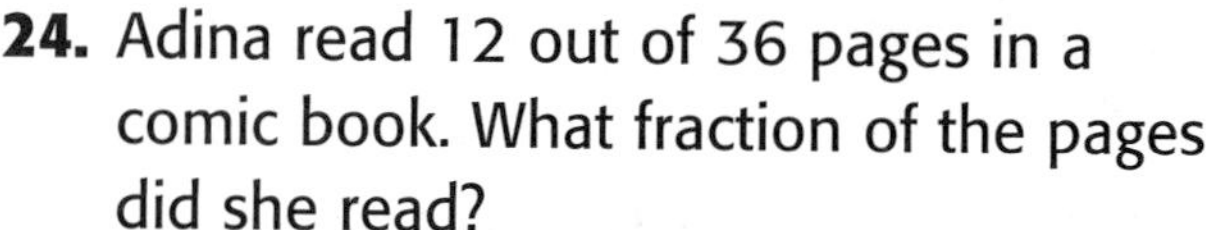

24. Adina read 12 out of 36 pages in a comic book. What fraction of the pages did she read?

Measurement The table lists the length of some objects in a classroom. What part of a foot is each object? Write as a fraction in simplest form. See Example 2 (p. 523)

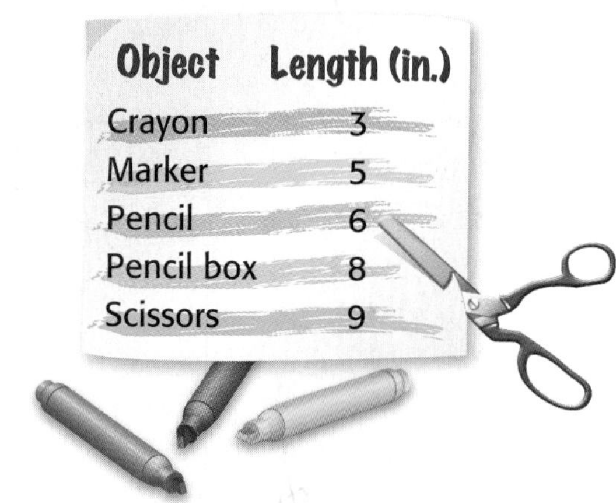

Object	Length (in.)
Crayon	3
Marker	5
Pencil	6
Pencil box	8
Scissors	9

25. pencil **26.** crayon

27. scissors **28.** pencil box

H.O.T. Problems

29. OPEN ENDED Write three factions that are in simplest form.

30. WHICH ONE DOESN'T BELONG? Identify the fraction that does not belong with the other three. Explain your reasoning.

$\frac{2}{3}$ $\frac{6}{15}$ $\frac{1}{2}$ $\frac{11}{12}$

31. WRITING IN MATH The simplest form of $\frac{6}{15}$ is $\frac{2}{5}$. How can you use multiplication to show that they name the same amount?

Fractions Made Simple

Fractions in Simplest Form

Get Ready!

Players: 2

You will need: 10 index cards

Get Set!

Cut each index card in half. Then label each card with one fraction as shown.

$\frac{2}{4}$	$\frac{3}{6}$	$\frac{5}{10}$	$\frac{7}{14}$
$\frac{2}{6}$	$\frac{3}{9}$	$\frac{5}{15}$	$\frac{7}{21}$
$\frac{3}{12}$	$\frac{4}{16}$	$\frac{6}{24}$	$\frac{8}{32}$
$\frac{2}{10}$	$\frac{3}{15}$	$\frac{5}{25}$	$\frac{7}{35}$
$\frac{2}{12}$	$\frac{3}{18}$	$\frac{5}{30}$	$\frac{6}{36}$

Go!

- Shuffle the cards. Then spread out the cards face down on the table.
- Player 1 turns over 1 card and must write the fraction in simplest form. If player 1 is correct, Player 1 keeps the card. If Player 1 is incorrect, the card is put back.
- Player 2 takes a turn.
- Play continues in the same way. The player with the most cards wins.

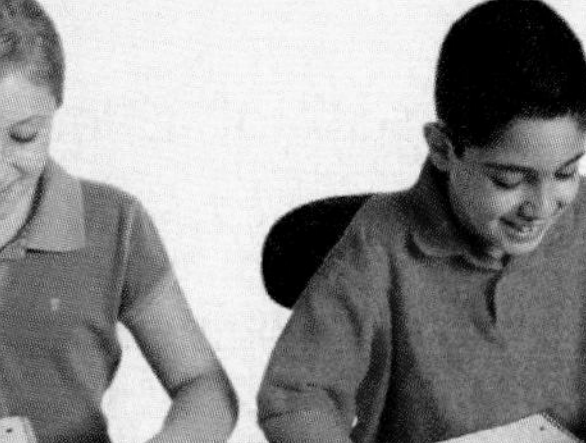

13-6 Problem-Solving Investigation

MAIN IDEA I will choose the best strategy to solve a problem.

Standard 4MR2.2 Apply strategies and results from simpler problems to more complex problems. **Standard 4NS1.7** Write the fraction represented by a drawing of parts of a figure; **represent a given fraction by using drawings;** and relate a fraction to a simple decimal on a number line.

P.S.I. TEAM +

ANICA: My class visited the zoo. I learned that one-sixth of the animals at the zoo are reptiles. There are 420 animals at the zoo. How many animals are reptiles?

YOUR MISSION: Find how many animals are reptiles.

Understand There are 420 animals at a zoo. One-sixth of the animals are reptiles. Find how many animals are reptiles.

Plan Solve a simpler problem. First, find one-sixth of a smaller number. Then multiply to find one-sixth of 420.

Solve First, find one-sixth of 42.

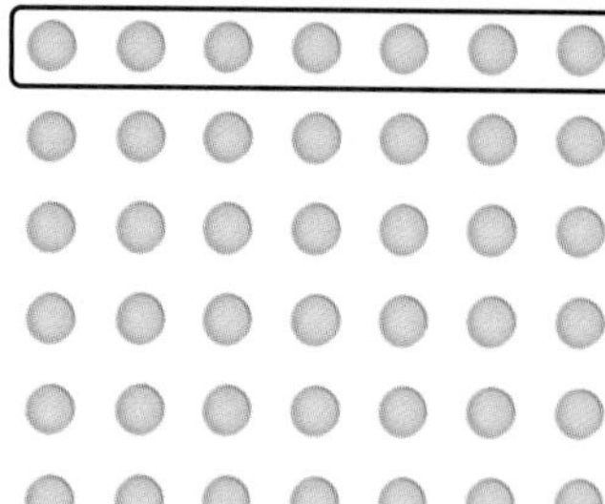

There are 42 counters in 6 equal rows. One of the six equal groups is circled.

So, one-sixth of 42 equals 7. Now multiply.

$$\begin{array}{r} 42 \\ \times\ 10 \\ \hline 420 \end{array}$$

THINK What number can you multiply 42 by to equal 420? Then multiply 7 by the same number.

$$\begin{array}{r} 7 \\ \times\ 10 \\ \hline 70 \end{array}$$

So, 70 of the animals at the zoo are reptiles.

Check Since $70 \times 6 = 420$, then 70 is one-sixth of 420. The answer is correct.

Mixed Problem Solving

EXTRA PRACTICE
See page R34.

Use any strategy shown below to solve. Tell what strategy you used.

PROBLEM-SOLVING STRATEGIES

- Guess and check.
- Look for a pattern.
- Work a simpler problem.
- Use logical reasoning.
- Draw a picture.

1. A chef wants to cook an 8-pound turkey. It takes 20 minutes per pound to fully cook. What time should the chef start cooking the turkey if it needs to be done at 5:00 P.M?

2. After Malcolm buys three packages of stickers like the one shown, the number of stickers in his collection will double. How many stickers will he have?

3. Dario and three of his friends shared the cost of renting a rowboat. It cost $12 an hour and they used the boat for 3 hours. How much did each friend pay?

4. A geometric pattern is shown. What could be the next figure in the pattern?

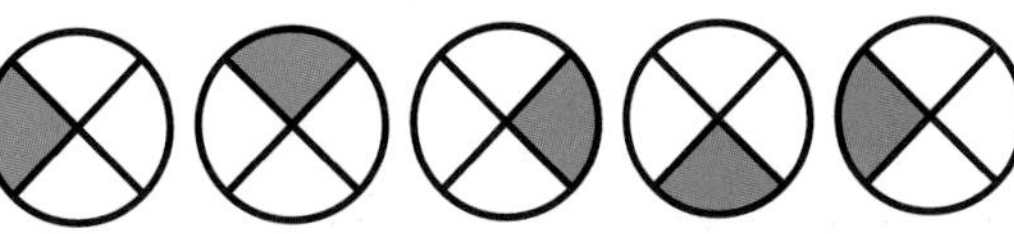

5. Mei has some coins. She has 3 more quarters than nickels and 2 more dimes than quarters. If Mei has 4 nickels, how much money does she have?

6. A customer buys small, medium, and large sweatshirts. The total cost is $68. How many of each size were bought?

7. Daisy exercises for 30 minutes 2 times a day. If she keeps up this schedule for 30 days, how many minutes will she exercise in all?

8. Randall's goal is to run one mile the first week and double the number of miles each week for the next 6 weeks. How many miles will he run the sixth week?

9. Find the area of the fifth figure in the pattern of squares shown.

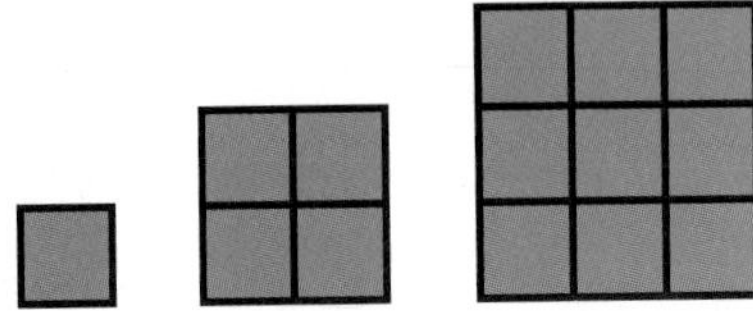

10. **WRITING IN MATH** Write a few sentences to explain what it means to solve a problem by solving a simpler problem.

Compare and Order Fractions

GET READY to Learn

Ramon has an insect collection. The table shows the lengths of four insects in his collection. Which is longer, a field cricket or a whirligig beetle?

Insect	Length (in.)
Mosquito	$\frac{1}{4}$
Field Cricket	$\frac{5}{8}$
Whirligig Beetle	$\frac{3}{8}$
Lightning Bug	$\frac{1}{2}$

MAIN IDEA

I will compare and order simple fractions.

Standard 4NS1.9 Identify on a number line the relative position of positive fractions, positive mixed numbers, and positive decimals to two decimal places.

You can compare fractions, you can use models, number lines, and equivalent fractions.

Real-World EXAMPLES Compare Fractions

1 SCIENCE Which insect is longer, a field cricket or a whirligig beetle?

You can use models to compare $\frac{5}{8}$ and $\frac{3}{8}$.

$\frac{5}{8}$ Field cricket

$\frac{3}{8}$ Whirligig beetle

The models show that $\frac{5}{8} > \frac{3}{8}$.

So, the field cricket is longer than the whirligig beetle.

2 SCIENCE Which is longer, a mosquito or lightning bug?

You need to compare $\frac{1}{4}$ and $\frac{1}{2}$.

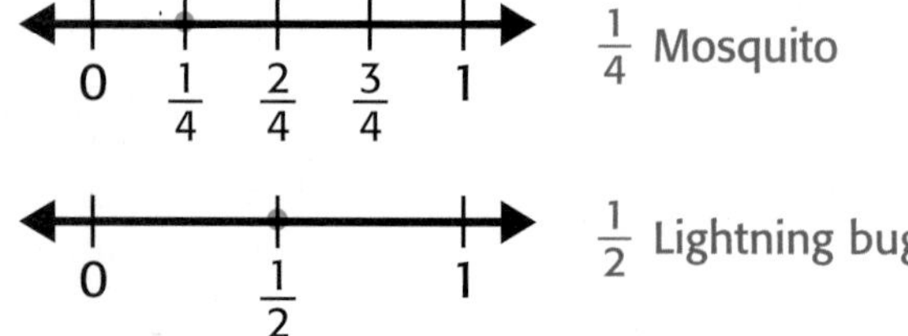

So, the lightning bug is longer than the mosquito.

EXAMPLE Order Fractions

3 **Order $\frac{2}{3}$, $\frac{1}{2}$, and $\frac{7}{12}$ from least to greatest.**

One Way: Number Lines	Another Way: Equivalent Fractions
Use a number line.	Find equivalent fractions with the same denominator.
0 ... $\frac{2}{3}$ ... 1	$\frac{2 \times 4}{3 \times 4} = \frac{8}{12}$ $\frac{1 \times 6}{2 \times 6} = \frac{6}{12}$
0 ... $\frac{1}{2}$ ... 1	Compare the numerators. Order from least to greatest.
0 ... $\frac{7}{12}$ ... 1	$\frac{6}{12}, \frac{7}{12}, \frac{8}{12}$
$\frac{1}{2} < \frac{7}{12} < \frac{2}{3}$	$\frac{1}{2}, \frac{7}{12}, \frac{2}{3}$

So, the order from least to greatest is $\frac{1}{2}, \frac{7}{12}, \frac{2}{3}$.

Online Personal Tutor at ca.gr4math.com

CHECK What You Know

Compare. Write <, >, or =. See Examples 1 and 2 (p. 528)

1. 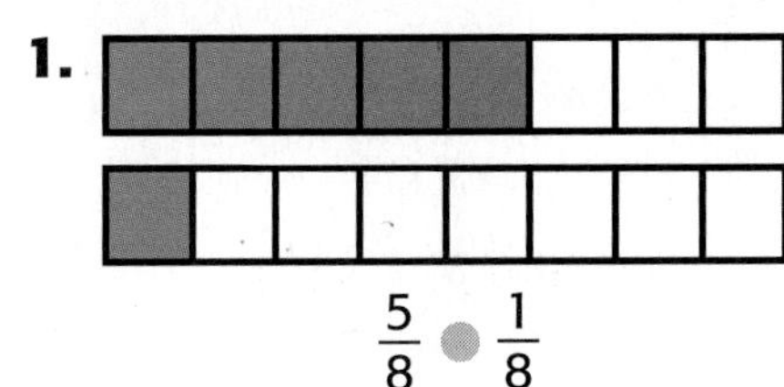

$\frac{5}{8}$ ● $\frac{1}{8}$

2. 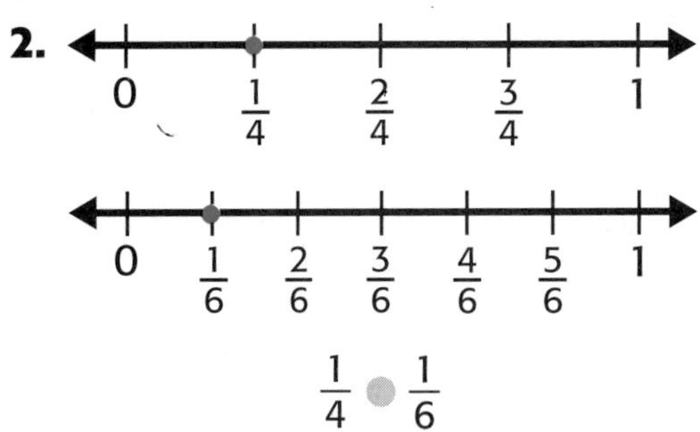

$\frac{1}{4}$ ● $\frac{1}{6}$

3. $\frac{3}{4}$ ● $\frac{1}{2}$

4. $\frac{3}{6}$ ● $\frac{3}{4}$

Order from least to greatest. See Example 3 (p. 529)

5. $\frac{3}{8}, \frac{2}{6}, \frac{4}{8}$

6. $\frac{1}{16}, \frac{7}{8}, \frac{3}{4}$

7. Griff worked for $\frac{1}{3}$ of an hour. Sasha worked for $\frac{3}{12}$ of an hour. Who worked longer?

8. 

Explain how to compare the fractions $\frac{7}{12}$ and $\frac{2}{6}$.

Practice and Problem Solving

EXTRA PRACTICE
See page R34.

Compare. Write <, >, or =. See Examples 1 and 2 (p. 528)

9.

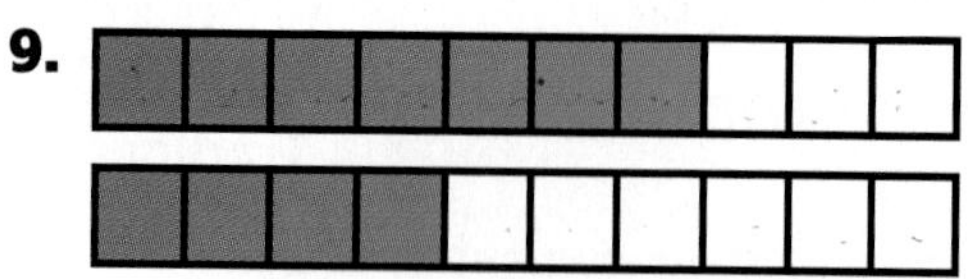

$\frac{7}{10} \bullet \frac{4}{10}$

10.

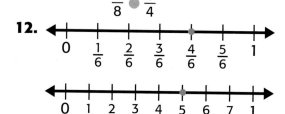

$\frac{4}{8} \bullet \frac{1}{4}$

11.

0, $\frac{1}{3}$, $\frac{2}{3}$, 1

0, $\frac{1}{6}$, $\frac{2}{6}$, $\frac{3}{6}$, $\frac{4}{6}$, $\frac{5}{6}$, 1

$\frac{2}{3} \bullet \frac{5}{6}$

12.

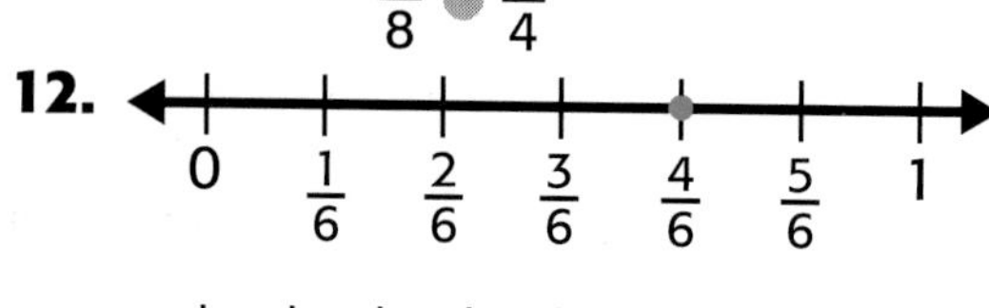

0, $\frac{1}{8}$, $\frac{2}{8}$, $\frac{3}{8}$, $\frac{4}{8}$, $\frac{5}{8}$, $\frac{6}{8}$, $\frac{7}{8}$, 1

$\frac{4}{6} \bullet \frac{5}{8}$

13. $\frac{2}{6} \bullet \frac{1}{3}$

14. $\frac{3}{5} \bullet \frac{5}{6}$

15. $\frac{4}{5} \bullet \frac{8}{10}$

16. $\frac{2}{3} \bullet \frac{5}{9}$

17. $\frac{4}{10} \bullet \frac{1}{2}$

18. $\frac{5}{8} \bullet \frac{2}{3}$

Order from least to greatest. See Example 3 (p. 529)

19. $\frac{4}{6}, \frac{1}{3}, \frac{3}{3}$

20. $\frac{3}{4}, \frac{2}{3}, \frac{7}{8}$

21. $\frac{3}{10}, \frac{3}{4}, \frac{3}{5}$

22. Which meat makes up most of Mr. Collin's sandwich?

23. Allison took a survey. Find the favorite weekend activity.

Favorite Weekend Activities

Activity	Fraction of Friends
Movie	$\frac{2}{6}$
Mall	$\frac{1}{4}$
Basketball	$\frac{5}{12}$

ADMIT ONE ADMIT ONE

24. Vani ate $\frac{1}{4}$ of the carrots in the bag. Enrique ate $\frac{3}{12}$ of the carrots in the bag. Who ate more carrots?

25. Suzanne studied $\frac{2}{3}$ hour on Saturday and $\frac{1}{6}$ hour on Sunday. Which day did she study longer?

26. The table shows how much time each student needs to finish an art project. Does Simón need more or less time than Phil? Explain.

Student	Time
Simón	$\frac{4}{12}$ hour
Phil	$\frac{3}{4}$ hour

H.O.T. Problems

27. OPEN ENDED Write three fractions that are *not* greater than $\frac{1}{2}$.

28. WHICH ONE DOESN'T BELONG? Identify the set of fractions that does not belong with the other three sets. Explain.

$\frac{1}{4}, \frac{5}{8}, \frac{15}{16}$	$\frac{2}{9}, \frac{1}{3}, \frac{1}{2}$	$\frac{2}{5}, \frac{1}{2}, \frac{7}{10}$	$\frac{3}{4}, \frac{1}{2}, \frac{2}{12}$

29. CHALLENGE Identify a fraction that is greater than $\frac{150}{300}$.

30. WRITING IN ► MATH Explain how to decide if $\frac{3}{4}$ is greater than or less than $\frac{3}{5}$.

Standards Practice

31 What fraction is best represented by point M on the number line? **(Lesson 13-5)**

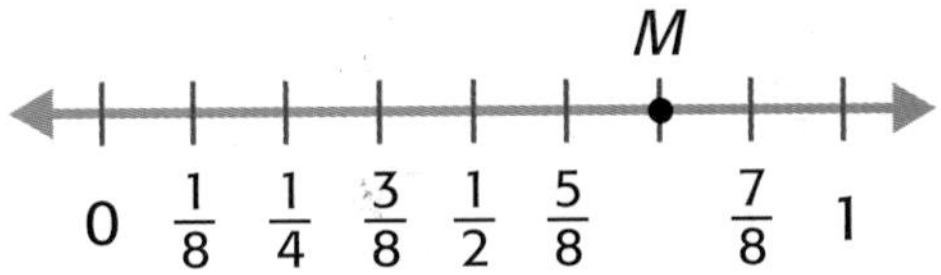

A $\frac{1}{4}$

B $\frac{3}{8}$

C $\frac{1}{2}$

D $\frac{3}{4}$

32 Which set of fractions is ordered from greatest to least? **(Lesson 13-7)**

F $\frac{3}{5}, \frac{6}{15}, \frac{2}{10}$

G $\frac{2}{10}, \frac{3}{5}, \frac{6}{15}$

H $\frac{2}{10}, \frac{6}{15}, \frac{3}{5}$

J $\frac{6}{15}, \frac{3}{5}, \frac{2}{10}$

Spiral Review

33. The sum of two prime numbers is 10. What are the numbers? **(Lesson 13-6)**

Write each fraction in simplest form. **(Lesson 13-5)**

34. $\frac{6}{20}$ **35.** $\frac{4}{16}$ **36.** $\frac{3}{27}$

37. Toya has 8 coins in her piggy bank. One-fourth of the coins are quarters. Three of the coins are dimes. The rest of the coins are pennies. How many pennies does Toya have? **(Lesson 13-3)**

Find each product. **(Lesson 7-4)**

38. 37×4 **39.** 51×7 **40.** 85×9

No BONES about it . . .

Every human has a skeleton made up of bones. Your skeletal system is very important. Not only does it protect your internal organs but it also allows you to stand up and walk. Without a skeleton you would be nothing but skin and guts!

Humans are born with 350 bones in their body. But, by the time you are 25, you will only have about 200 bones. This is because some of the bones join together to make a single bone.

The smallest bone is in the ear. It can be as small as $\frac{1}{10}$ of an inch. The largest bone, the femur, is located in the thigh. It is about $\frac{1}{4}$ of your height.

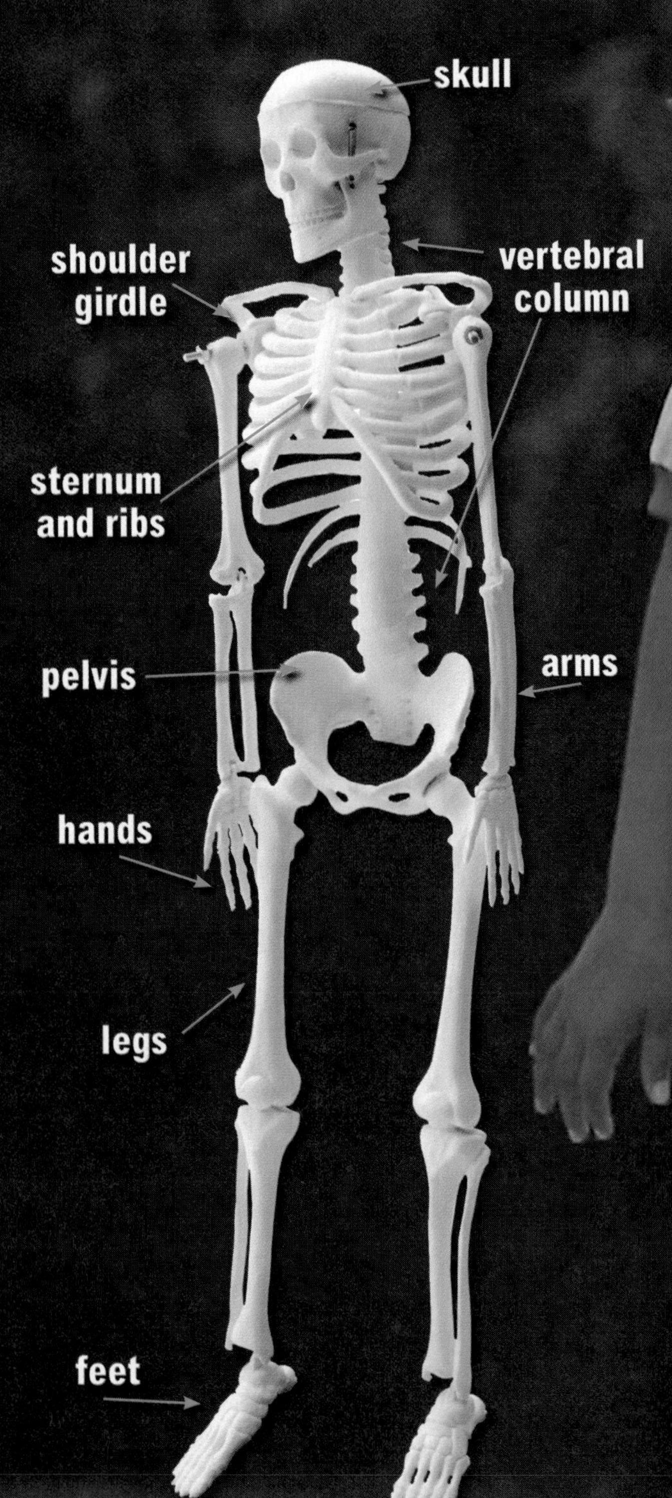

Did You Know?

Of the bones in your skeleton, about $\frac{3}{20}$ are found in your spine.

Standard 4NS1.5 **Explain different interpretations of fractions, for example, parts of a whole, parts of a set, and division of whole numbers by whole numbers; explain equivalence of fractions.**

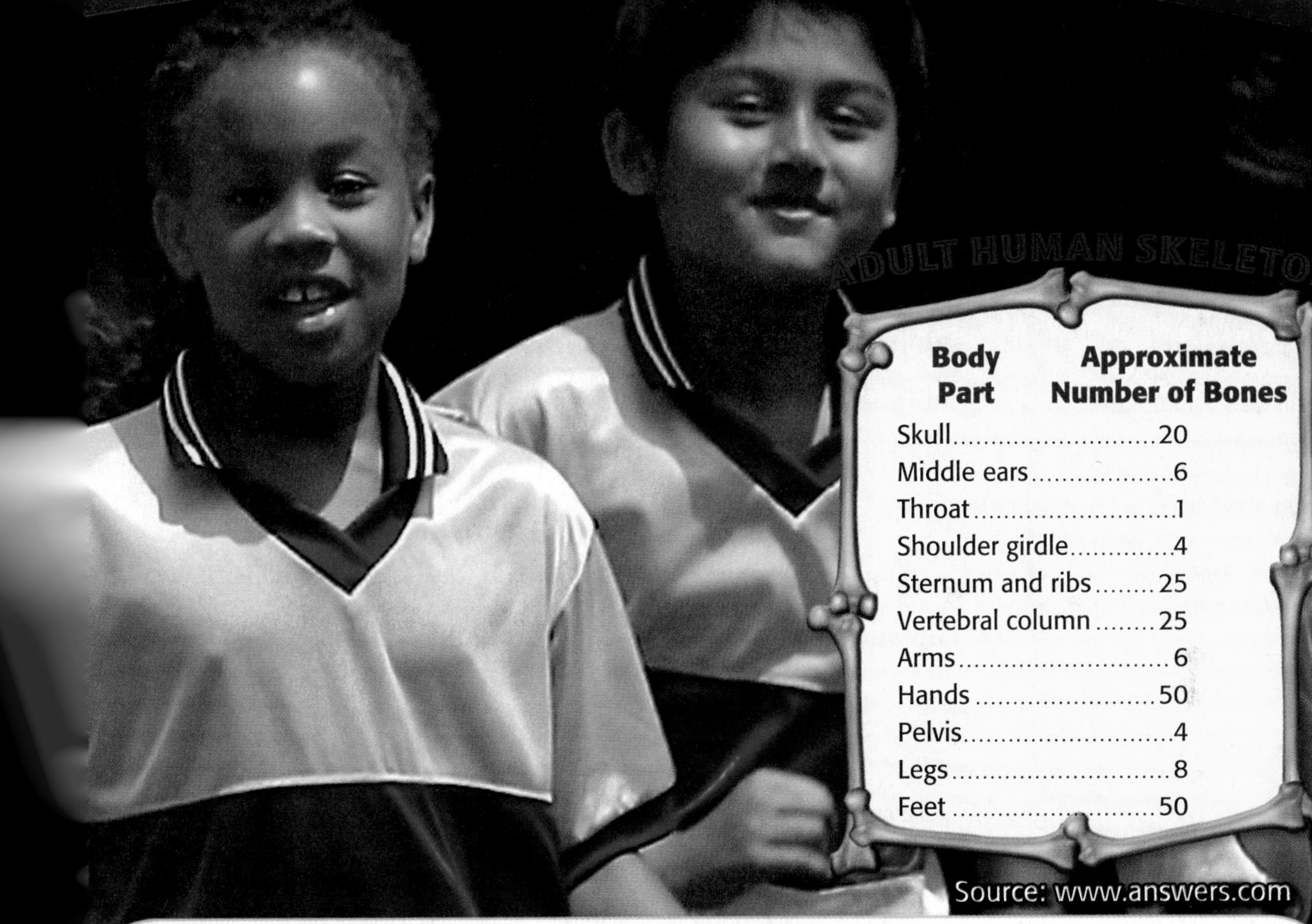

ADULT HUMAN SKELETON

Body Part	Approximate Number of Bones
Skull	20
Middle ears	6
Throat	1
Shoulder girdle	4
Sternum and ribs	25
Vertebral column	25
Arms	6
Hands	50
Pelvis	4
Legs	8
Feet	50

Source: www.answers.com

Problem Solving

Use the information on pages 532–533 to solve each problem.

1. What fraction of the bones in an adult human is located in the skull? Write in simplest form.
2. Which two body parts contain $\frac{1}{2}$ of the bones in an adult human? Explain your reasoning.
3. Which body part contains $\frac{1}{25}$ of the bones in an adult human?
4. What fraction of the bones at birth does a human have when an adult?
5. Are more bones located in the skull or in the spine?
6. The backbone is approximately 28 inches. What fraction of a foot is 28 inches? Write as a mixed number.
7. CHALLENGE Use your height to find the length of your femur in inches.

13-8 Add and Subtract Like Fractions

GET READY to Learn

Pablo spent $\frac{2}{6}$ of an hour on a jigsaw puzzle. Conrad spent $\frac{1}{6}$ of an hour on the puzzle. How much time did they spend working on the puzzle in all?

MAIN IDEA

I will add and subtract fractions.

Reinforcement of Grade 2

3NS3.2 Add and subtract simple fractions (e.g., determine that $\frac{1}{8} + \frac{3}{8}$ is the same as $\frac{1}{2}$).

New Vocabulary

like fractions

The fractions $\frac{2}{6}$ and $\frac{1}{6}$ have the same denominators. They are called **like fractions**. You can add like fractions.

KEY CONCEPTS — Add Fractions

Words To add fractions with like denominators, add the numerators and keep the same denominator.

Example $\frac{3}{5} + \frac{1}{5} = \frac{3+1}{5} = \frac{4}{5}$

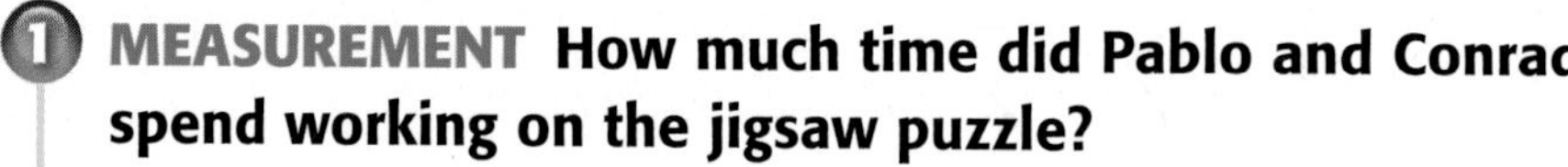

Real-World EXAMPLE — Add Fractions

1 MEASUREMENT **How much time did Pablo and Conrad spend working on the jigsaw puzzle?**

Step 1 Add the numerators. Keep the same denominator.

$$\frac{2}{6} + \frac{1}{6} = \frac{2+1}{6}$$
$$= \frac{3}{6}$$

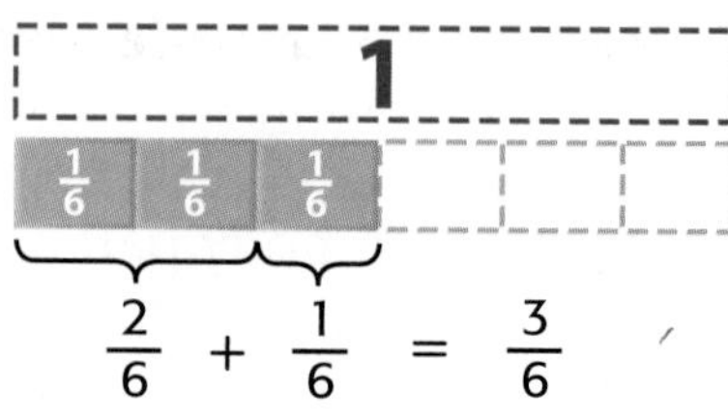

Step 2 Write in simplest form.

$$\frac{3 \div 3}{6 \div 3} = \frac{1}{2}$$

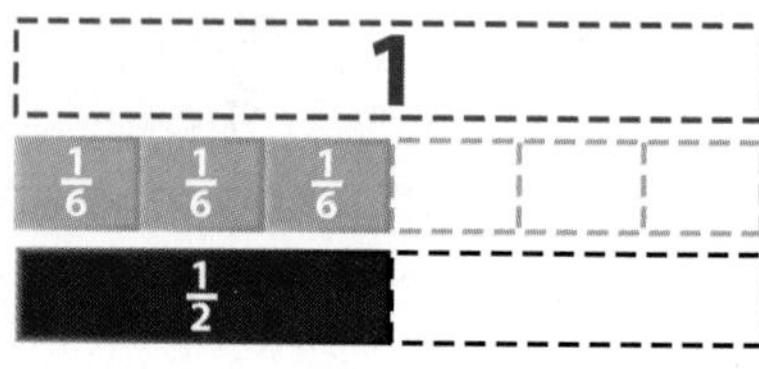

So, they spent $\frac{1}{2}$ of an hour on the puzzle.

You can also subtract fractions with like denominators.

Always write the sum or difference of two fractions in simplest form.

KEY CONCEPT — **Subtract Fractions**

Words To subtract fractions with like denominators, subtract the numerator and keep the same denominator.

Example $\frac{3}{6} - \frac{2}{6} = \frac{3-2}{6} = \frac{1}{6}$

Real-World EXAMPLE — **Subtract Fractions**

2 **Liliana jogged $\frac{5}{8}$ of a mile on Monday and $\frac{3}{8}$ of a mile on Tuesday. How much farther did she jog on Monday?**

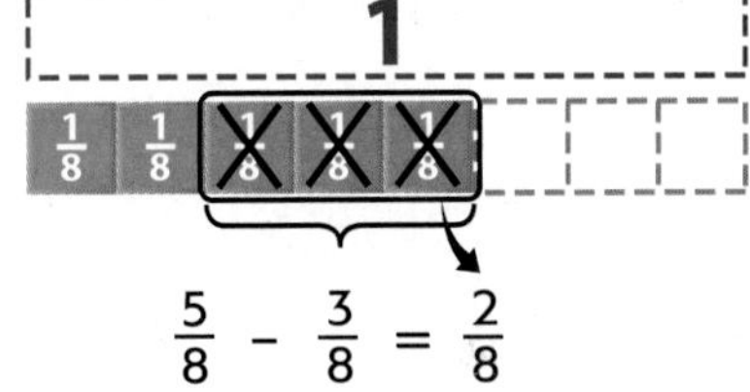

You need to subtract $\frac{5}{8}$ and $\frac{3}{8}$.

$\frac{5}{8} - \frac{3}{8} = \frac{2}{8}$ Subtract numerators. Keep the same denominator.

$\frac{2 \div 2}{8 \div 2} = \frac{1}{4}$ Write the answer in simplest form.

Online **Personal Tutor at** ca.gr4math.com

CHECK What You Know

Find each sum or difference. Write in simplest form. See Examples 1 and 2 (pp. 534–535)

1. $\frac{2}{4} + \frac{1}{4}$

2. $\frac{3}{5} + \frac{1}{5}$

3. $\frac{4}{7} + \frac{3}{7}$

4. $\frac{9}{12} - \frac{5}{12}$

5. $\frac{7}{10} - \frac{3}{10}$

6. $\frac{4}{6} - \frac{3}{6}$

7. Ann ate 2 slices of the pizza, and Teresa ate 3 slices of the pizza. What is the difference in the amount of pizza that the children ate written as a fraction?

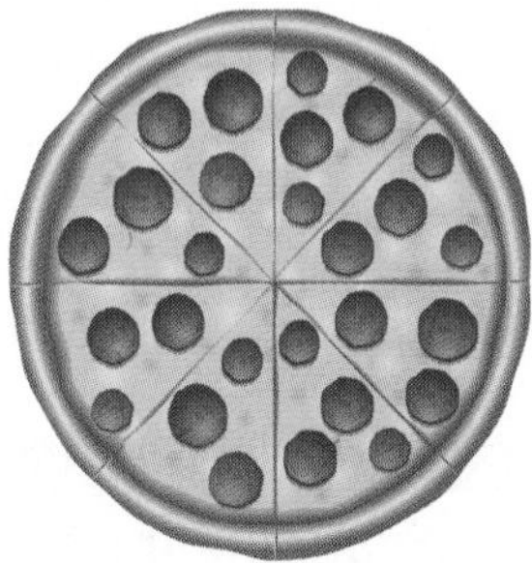

8. 

Explain how to add $\frac{3}{12}$ and $\frac{4}{12}$.

Practice and Problem Solving

EXTRA PRACTICE See page R34.

Find each sum or difference. Write in simplest form. See Examples 1 and 2 (pp. 534–535)

9. $\frac{1}{3} + \frac{1}{3}$

10. $\frac{2}{6} + \frac{3}{6}$

11. $\frac{3}{8} + \frac{1}{8}$

12. $\frac{5}{9} + \frac{2}{9}$

13. $\frac{3}{10} + \frac{7}{10}$

14. $\frac{2}{5} + \frac{1}{5}$

15. $\frac{7}{8} - \frac{2}{8}$

16. $\frac{6}{7} - \frac{3}{7}$

17. $\frac{5}{6} - \frac{4}{6}$

18. $\frac{9}{10} - \frac{6}{10}$

19. $\frac{6}{7} - \frac{2}{7}$

20. $\frac{11}{12} - \frac{4}{12}$

21. Virginia had $\frac{18}{24}$ of the pictures left on her roll of film. Then she took $\frac{7}{24}$ of the pictures. What fraction of pictures does she have left?

22. Kenji fed his dog $\frac{3}{18}$ of the treats in a box of dog treats on Monday. He fed his dog $\frac{2}{18}$ of the treats on Tuesday. What fraction of the treats is left?

23. Dan used $\frac{3}{12}$ of a pack of golf balls. Then he used $\frac{2}{12}$ of the pack of golf balls. What fraction of balls does he have left?

24. Marcela ate $\frac{4}{10}$ of a box of crackers last week. Then she ate $\frac{2}{10}$ of the box of crackers this week. What fraction of the box of crackers did Marcela eat?

Real-World PROBLEM SOLVING

Entertainment Fractions can be found in games.

25. Of the checkers on the board, $\frac{11}{20}$ belong to Evita. What fraction of the checkers on the board belongs to Desiree?

26. Refer to your answer in Exercise 25. Evita captures some of Desiree's checkers. Desiree now has $\frac{5}{20}$ left. How many checkers did Evita take?

H.O.T. Problems

27. OPEN ENDED Write two fractions whose sum is greater than 1.

28. WRITING IN MATH Write a real-world problem that involves adding fractions and has an answer of 1.

Math Online Self-Check Quiz at ca.gr4math.com

Standards Practice

29 Identify the improper fraction below that is NOT equivalent to the mixed number that is shown. (Lesson 13-8)

A $\frac{5}{2}$

B $\frac{10}{4}$

C $\frac{15}{6}$

D $\frac{20}{7}$

30 Abe spent $\frac{1}{4}$ of an hour doing his homework and $\frac{2}{4}$ of an hour watching TV. Which equation shows what fraction of an hour he spent on both activities? (Lesson 13-9)

F $\frac{1}{4} + \frac{2}{4} = \frac{3}{8}$

G $\frac{1}{4} + \frac{2}{4} = \frac{12}{8}$

H $\frac{1}{4} + \frac{2}{4} = \frac{3}{4}$

J $\frac{1}{4} + \frac{2}{4} = \frac{12}{4}$

Spiral Review

Order from least to greatest. (Lesson 13-7)

31. $\frac{1}{8}, \frac{2}{6}, \frac{3}{8}$

32. $\frac{4}{15}, \frac{2}{5}, \frac{1}{3}$

33. $\frac{7}{16}, \frac{5}{8}, \frac{3}{4}$

Write each fraction in simplest form. (Lesson 13-5)

34. $\frac{4}{6}$

35. $\frac{3}{9}$

36. $\frac{2}{12}$

37. $\frac{12}{16}$

38. Mr. Gonzalez is planting a garden. He can plant 5 rows of 6 vegetables, 4 rows of 7 vegetables, or 3 rows of 9 vegetables. Which garden layout would allow him to plant the most vegetables? (Lesson 13-3)

Identify each polygon. (Lesson 10-2)

39.

40.

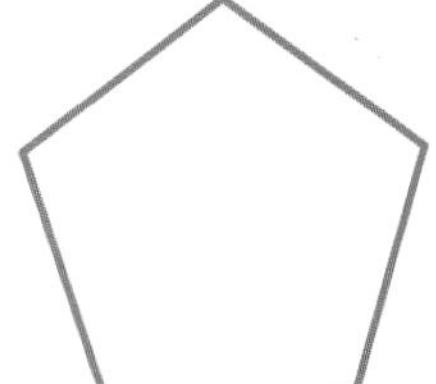

41.

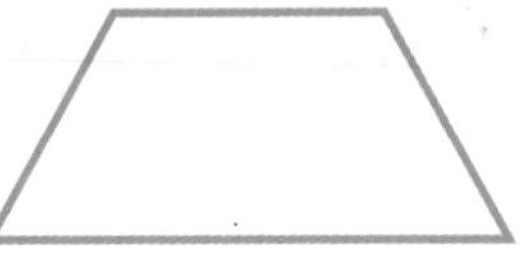

Find the missing number in each equation. (Lesson 3–6)

42. ■ + 11 = 25 + 11

43. 15 + 12 = 15 + ■

44. 9 + 11 + 18 = 20 + ■

13-9 Mixed Numbers

MAIN IDEA

I will write mixed numbers and improper fractions.

Standard 4NS1.5 **Explain different interpretations of fractions, for example,** parts of a whole, parts of a set, and **division of whole numbers by whole numbers;** explain equivalents of fractions.

Standard 4NS1.9 **Identify on a number line the relative position of positive fractions, positive mixed numbers,** and positive decimals to two decimal places.

New Vocabulary

mixed number

improper fraction

GET READY to Learn

Nyoko is selling pies at a bake sale. Each pie has 5 slices. Each slice of pie is sold separately. There are 7 slices left. What fraction of the pies are left?

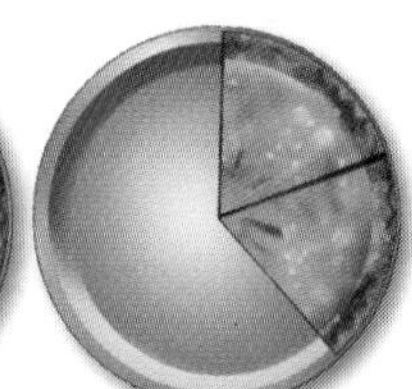

A **mixed number** has a whole number part and a fraction part. An **improper fraction** has a numerator that is greater than or equal to its denominator.

Mixed Numbers	Improper Fractions
$1\frac{1}{2}$ $2\frac{3}{4}$ $3\frac{5}{6}$	$\frac{3}{2}$ $\frac{11}{4}$ $\frac{23}{6}$

Real-World EXAMPLE

1 **FOOD What fraction of a pie does Nyoko have left?**

Each pie has 5 slices. There are 7 slices left.

One Way: Mixed Number	Another Way: Improper Fraction
Count the wholes and the parts.	Count the parts.
$\frac{5}{5} + \frac{2}{5} = 1\frac{2}{5}$ (whole, part)	$\frac{7}{5}$

So, $1\frac{2}{5}$ or $\frac{7}{5}$ of a pie is left.

You can change from a mixed number to an improper fraction. You can also change from an improper fraction to a mixed number.

EXAMPLES Mixed Number to Improper Fraction

2 Write $1\frac{3}{8}$ as an improper fraction.

$1\frac{3}{8} = 1 + \frac{3}{8}$ Write the mixed number as the sum of a whole and part.

$= \frac{8}{8} + \frac{3}{8}$ Write the whole number as a fraction.

$= \frac{8 + 3}{8}$ Add.

$= \frac{11}{8}$

Remember

The fraction bar stands for *divided by*. So, $\frac{11}{8}$ means *11 divided by 8*.

3 Write $\frac{11}{8}$ as a mixed number.

Divide the numerator by the denominator.

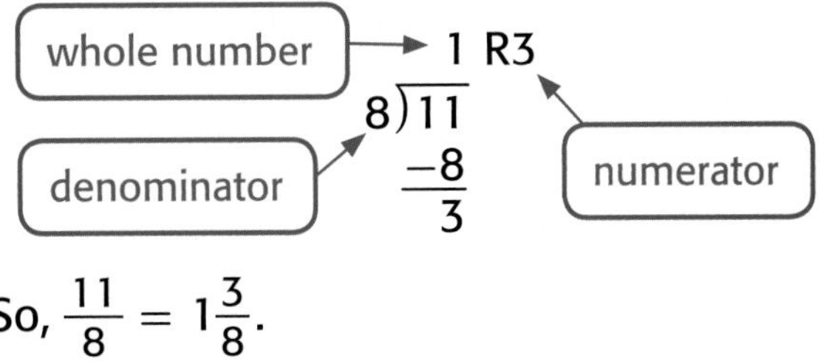

So, $\frac{11}{8} = 1\frac{3}{8}$.

Online Personal Tutor at ca.gr4math.com

You can show improper fractions and mixed numbers on a number line.

EXAMPLE Use a Number Line

4 Identify point *A* as a mixed number and improper fraction.

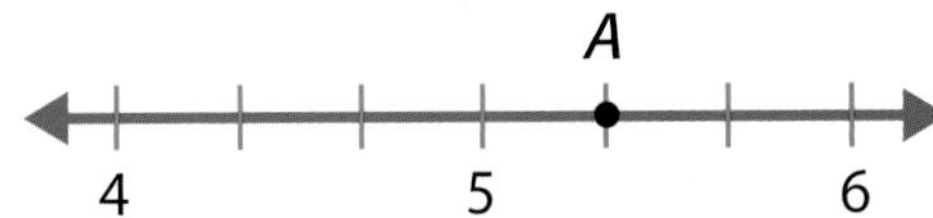

Each interval on the number line is one-third. So, point *A* is $5\frac{1}{3}$.

A

4 5 $5\frac{1}{3}$ 6

$5\frac{1}{3} = \frac{3}{3} + \frac{3}{3} + \frac{3}{3} + \frac{3}{3} + \frac{3}{3} + \frac{1}{3}$

$= \frac{3 + 3 + 3 + 3 + 3 + 1}{3} = \frac{16}{3}$

So, Point *A* is $5\frac{1}{3}$ or $\frac{16}{3}$.

CHECK What You Know

Write a mixed number and an improper fraction for each model.
See Example 1 (p. 538)

1. 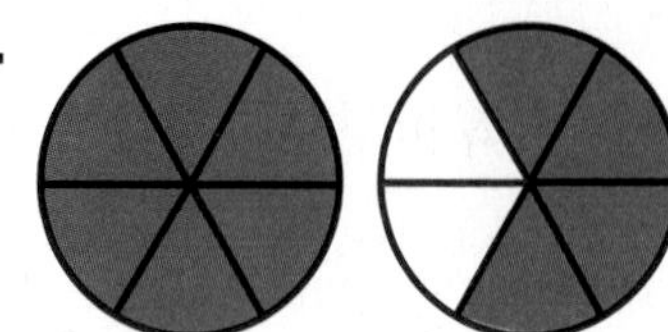

2. 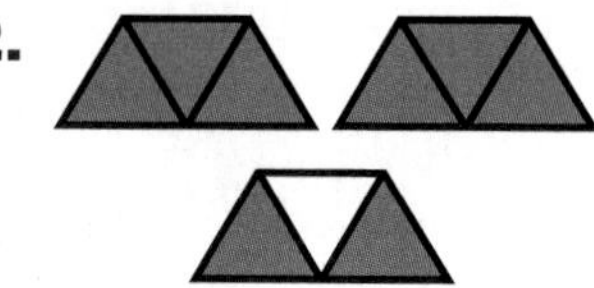

3. 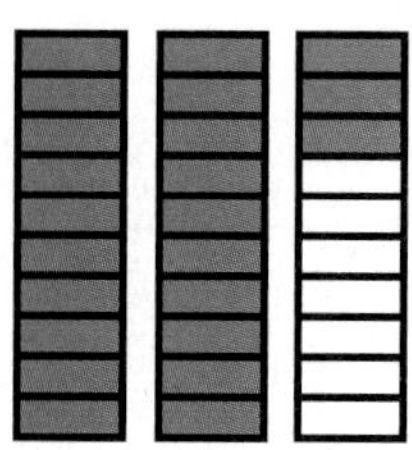

Write each as an improper fraction or a mixed number. See Examples 2 and 3 (p. 539)

4. $1\frac{2}{5}$ **5.** $2\frac{3}{4}$ **6.** $\frac{9}{4}$ **7.** $\frac{13}{3}$

Identify each point. Write as a mixed number and an improper fraction. See Example 4 (p. 539)

8. 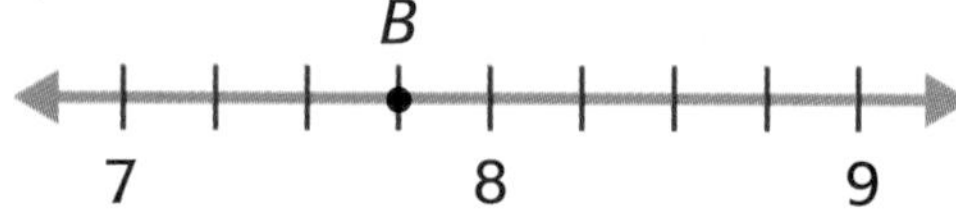

9. 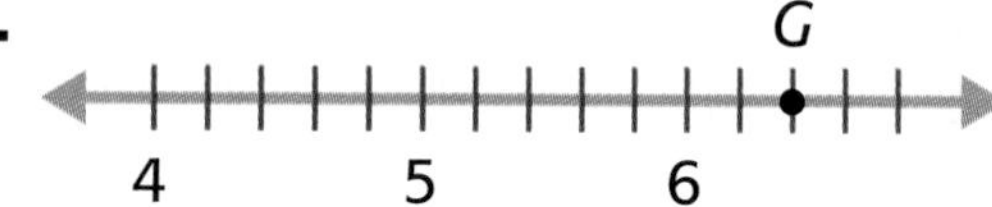

10. Andrew has $1\frac{3}{8}$ orange slices and Sheri has $1\frac{4}{16}$ orange slices. Who has more orange slices?

11. 

Explain how to compare $2\frac{3}{5}$ and $\frac{17}{5}$.

Practice and Problem Solving

EXTRA PRACTICE
See page R35.

Write a mixed number and an improper fraction for each model.
See Example 1 (p. 538)

12. 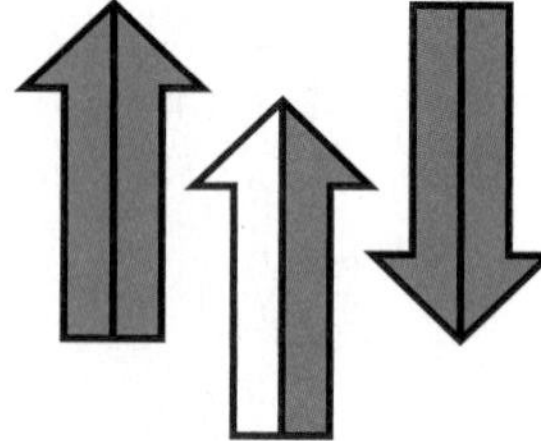

13. 

14. 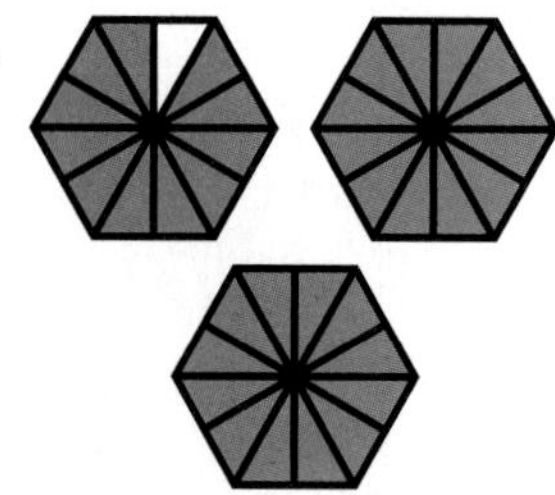

Write each as a improper fraction or a mixed number. See Example 2 (p. 539)

15. $1\frac{3}{4}$ **16.** $2\frac{7}{10}$ **17.** $6\frac{7}{8}$ **18.** $8\frac{5}{8}$

19. $\frac{7}{3}$ **20.** $\frac{17}{5}$ **21.** $\frac{45}{8}$ **22.** $\frac{50}{6}$

Identify each point. Write as a mixed number and an improper fraction. See Example 4 (p. 539)

23.

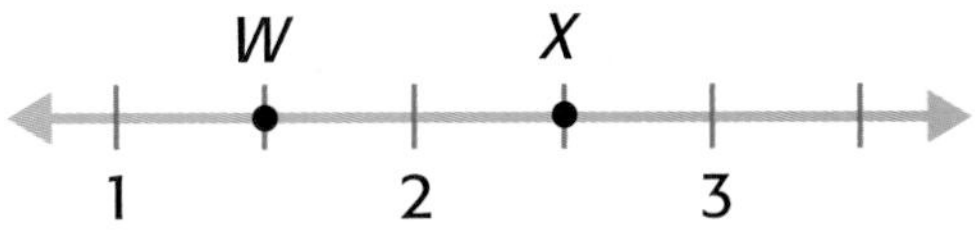

24.

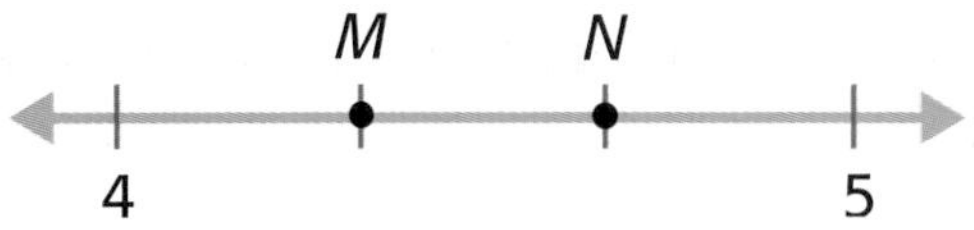

25. Ray needs $1\frac{1}{2}$ cups of flour for pancakes and $1\frac{3}{4}$ cups of sugar for banana bread. Does Ray need more sugar or more flour?

26. Elio drank $2\frac{3}{5}$ cups of water after the first half of the soccer match and $2\frac{4}{6}$ cups of water after the second half. When did he drink more water?

Real-World PROBLEM SOLVING

Travel A diagram of a horseback riding tour is shown. There are resting stops along the trail.

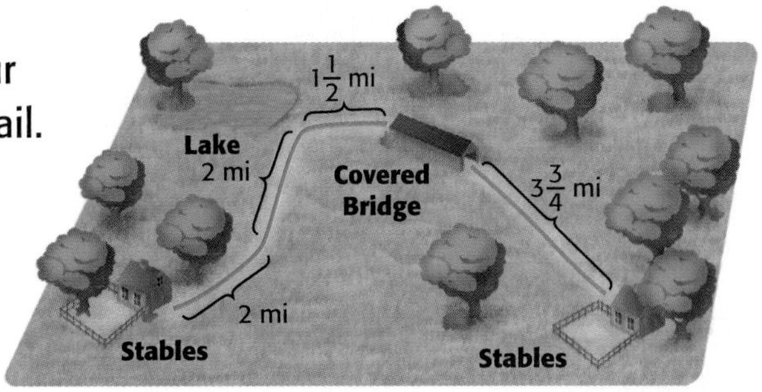

27. Joaquin and his family started at the stables on the left. They are at the covered bridge. How many miles of the trail have they traveled?

28. Joaquin reached the end of the trail in 2 hours and 15 minutes. Write the amount of time he spent on the trail as an improper fraction in simplest form.

H.O.T. Problems

29. OPEN ENDED Name an improper fraction that can be written as a whole number.

30. FIND THE ERROR Heather and Wesley are writing $4\frac{3}{5}$ as an improper fraction. Who is correct? Explain.

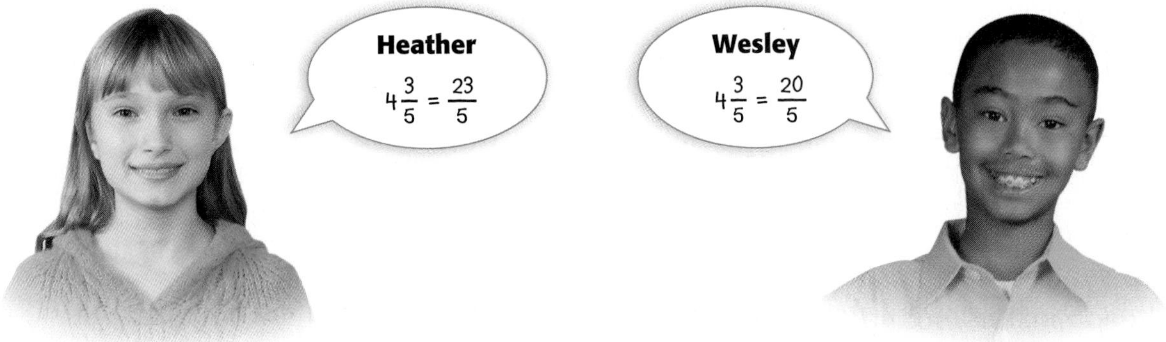

31. WRITING IN MATH Compare a fraction, mixed number, and improper fraction.

CHAPTER 13

Study Guide and Review

FOLDABLES™ Study Organizer GET READY to Study

Be sure the following Key Vocabulary words and Key Concepts are written in your Foldable.

Fractions	Simplest Form	Equivalent Fractions

BIG Ideas

- A **fraction** names part of a whole or part of a set. (p. 507)

  $\frac{4}{5}$ ← numerator (4), ← denominator (5)

- **Equivalent fractions** represent the same amount. (p. 518)

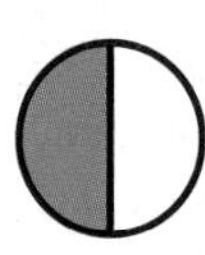

$\frac{1}{2}$

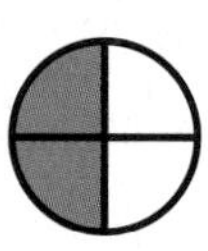

$\frac{2}{4}$

$\frac{4}{8}$

- To add fractions with like denominators, add the numerators and keep the same denominator. (p. 534)

  $$\frac{4}{8} + \frac{3}{8} = \frac{4+3}{8} = \frac{7}{8}$$

- To subtract fractions with like denominators, subtract the numerators and keep the same denominator. (p. 535)

  $$\frac{4}{8} - \frac{3}{8} = \frac{4-3}{8} = \frac{1}{8}$$

Key Vocabulary

denominator (p. 507)
equivalent fractions (p. 518)
fraction (p. 507)
mixed number (p. 534)
numerator (p. 507)

Vocabulary Check

Complete each sentence with the correct vocabulary word.

1. In the fraction $\frac{3}{4}$, the 4 is the ___?___.
2. A number that names part of a whole or part of a set is a(n) ___?___.
3. A(n) ___?___ has a whole number part and a fraction part.
4. In the fraction $\frac{3}{4}$, the 3 is the ___?___.
5. Fractions that represent the same amount are ___?___.
6. In a fraction, the ___?___ is the top number and the ___?___ is the bottom number.

Math Online Vocabulary Review at ca.gr4math.com

Lesson-by-Lesson Review

13-1 Parts of a Whole (pp. 507–509)

Example 1
What fraction of the figure is shaded?

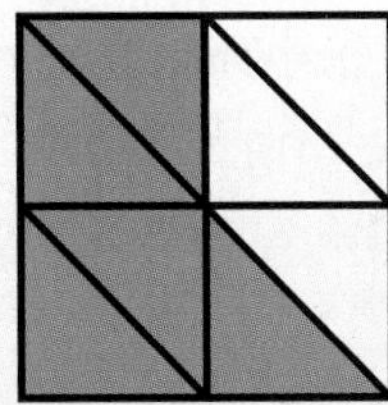

Write parts shaded ⟶ $\frac{5}{8}$
total parts in all ⟶

Read *five-eighths* or
five divided by eight

So, $\frac{5}{8}$ of the figure is shaded.

Write the fraction that names part of the whole.

7. part shaded

8. part shaded

Draw a picture and shade part of it to show the fraction.

9. $\frac{2}{3}$

10. $\frac{5}{6}$

11. What fraction of the waffle is missing?

13-2 Parts of a Set (pp. 510–513)

Example 2
What fraction of the crayons shown is *not* red?

Write crayons not red ⟶ $\frac{3}{5}$
total crayons ⟶

Read *three-fifths* or
three divided by five

So, $\frac{3}{5}$ of the crayons are *not* red.

Write the fraction that names the part of the set of shapes.

12. *not* purple

13. *not* green

14. *not* orange

15. *not* red

16. *not* yellow

17. *not* a sun

18. There are five cars. Two-fifths of the cars are blue. Draw a picture to show the set.

CHAPTER 13 Study Guide and Review

13-3 Problem-Solving Strategy: Draw a Picture (pp. 514–515)

Example 3
Frank has 24 crayons. Of them, $\frac{1}{3}$ are blue. Four are yellow, and the rest are green. How many crayons are green?

Understand

What facts do you know?

- There are 24 crayons.
- $\frac{1}{3}$ are blue.
- 4 are yellow.
- The rest are green.

What do you need to find?

Find how many crayons Frank has of each color.

Plan Draw a picture.

Solve Divide 24 equal parts. Shade $\frac{1}{3}$ to show the blue crayons. Shade 4 to show the yellow crayons.

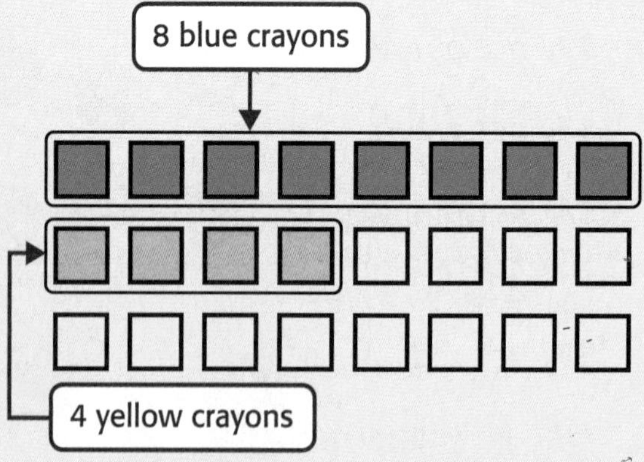

There are 12 parts left. So, 12 of the crayons are green.

Check Since $8 + 4 + 12 = 24$ crayons, the answer makes sense.

19. The 24 students in Ms. Cameron's class are working on final art projects. One-half of them are painting. Eight of the students are making a clay sculpture. The rest of the students are making sketches. How many students are making sketches?

20. Serefina took part in the activities listed. How long did she eat a snack?

Serefina's Activities	
Activity	**Time Spent**
Read a book	$\frac{1}{2}$ of an hour
Watch TV	20 minutes
Eat a snack	rest of the hour

21. Of 15 cars, 7 are blue and $\frac{1}{5}$ are red. The rest of the cars are black. How many cars are black?

22. Jeff had 28 grapes. He ate $\frac{1}{2}$ of them for lunch. Then he ate 10 more as a snack. How many are left?

23. Marisa has a marble collection. One-fourth of her 16 marbles are blue. Her red marbles are shown below. The rest of the marbles are green. How many of the marbles are green?

13-4 Equivalent Fractions (pp. 518–520)

Example 4

Find two fractions equivalent to $\frac{4}{6}$.

One Way: Multiply

$\frac{4 \times 2}{6 \times 2} = \frac{8}{12}$ Multiply the numerator and the denominator by the same number, 2.

Another Way: Divide

$\frac{4 \div 2}{6 \div 2} = \frac{2}{3}$ Divide the numerator and the denominator by the same number, 2.

So, $\frac{8}{12}$ and $\frac{2}{3}$ are equivalent to $\frac{4}{6}$.

Find an equivalent fraction for each fraction.

24. $\frac{1}{5}$ **25.** $\frac{1}{3}$ **26.** $\frac{1}{4}$

27. $\frac{6}{8}$ **28.** $\frac{7}{14}$ **29.** $\frac{9}{12}$

Write an equivalent fraction for each amount.

30. Dave hit 4 out of 8 baseballs.

31. Tionne's team won 9 out of 12 tennis matches.

32. Lara ate 4 out of 8 carrot sticks.

13-5 Simplest Form (pp. 522–525)

Example 5

Write $\frac{4}{12}$ in simplest form.

Step 1 Find the common factors.

factors of 4: 1, 4, 2

factors of 12: 1, 2, 3, 4, 6,12

common factors: 2 and 4

Step 2 Divide by the greatest common factor, 4.

$\frac{4}{12} \times \frac{4}{4} = \frac{1}{3}$ The numbers 1 and 3 have no common factor other than 1.

So, $\frac{4}{12}$ in simplest form is $\frac{1}{3}$.

Write each fraction in simplest form. If it is in simplest form, write *simplest form*.

33. $\frac{2}{10}$ **34.** $\frac{6}{9}$ **35.** $\frac{1}{2}$

36. $\frac{18}{20}$ **37.** $\frac{1}{4}$ **38.** $\frac{10}{15}$

Measurement What part of one day is each amount of time? Write as a fraction in simplest form.

39. 6 hours **40.** 60 minutes

Algebra Find the value of x to simplify each fraction.

41. $\frac{12}{20} = \frac{x}{5}$ **42.** $\frac{4}{36} = \frac{1}{x}$

43. $\frac{10}{25} = \frac{x}{5}$ **44.** $\frac{12}{27} = \frac{4}{x}$

13-6 Problem-Solving Investigation: Choose a Strategy (pp. 526–527)

Example 6
Charlie runs track daily and records his time in seconds. In the last four days he has recorded the following times:

27, 24, 21, 18

If his pattern continues, what should his next two times be?

Understand

You know that Charlie's last four running times are 27, 24, 21, and 18. You need to find Charlie's next two running times.

Plan Look for a pattern in the times. Then extend to solve the problem.

Solve Notice that each of Charlie's times goes down by three. So, the pattern is subtract 3.

27, 24, 21, 18, 15, 12
−3 −3 −3 −3 −3

So, Charlie's next two times will be 15 and 12 seconds.

Check You can use addition to check.

$12 + 3 = 15$
$15 + 3 = 18$

So, the answer is correct.

Use any strategy to solve.

45. Shane has to pitch in 24 baseball games. Create a table to show how many games he will have to pitch in each week of the 3 month season.

46. Kellie earned \$35 a day for chopping wood. If she earned a total of \$245, how many days did she chop wood?

47. Draw the next possible figure in the pattern.

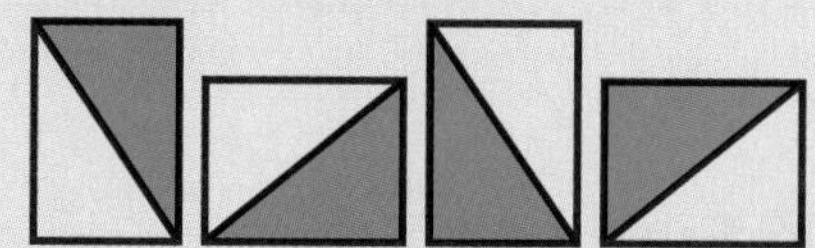

48. Darius has 5 coins that total 86¢. What are the coins?

49. Dale, Luanda and Renee each play one sport. Dale does not play soccer. Renee does not play football or volleyball. Luanda does not play football. What sport does each play?

50. There are 12 balloons. One-third of the balloons are red. The blue balloons are shown below. The rest of the balloons are yellow. How many of the balloons are yellow?

13-7 Compare and Order Fractions (pp. 528–531)

Example 7

Dakota has a red and a blue pencil. The red pencil is $\frac{1}{2}$ of a foot long. The blue pencil is $\frac{3}{8}$ of a foot long. Which pencil is longer?

You can use number lines to compare the length of the pencils.

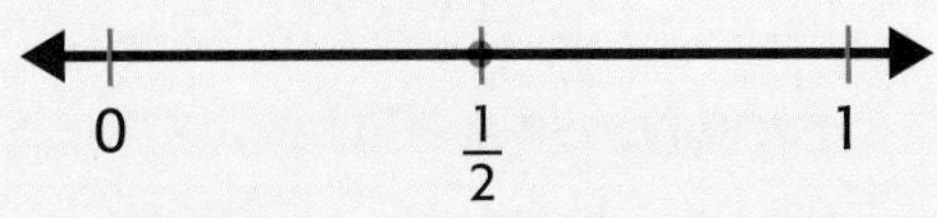

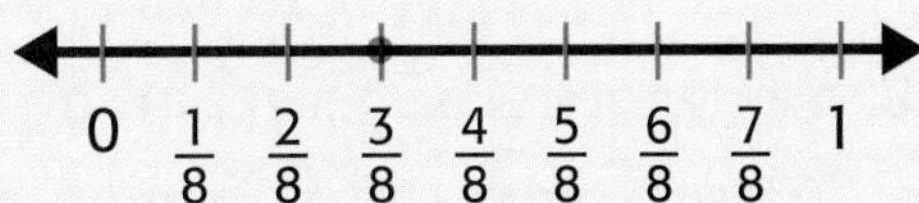

So, the red pencil is longer than the blue pencil.

Example 8

Order $\frac{1}{2}$, $\frac{1}{5}$, and $\frac{3}{10}$ from least to greatest.

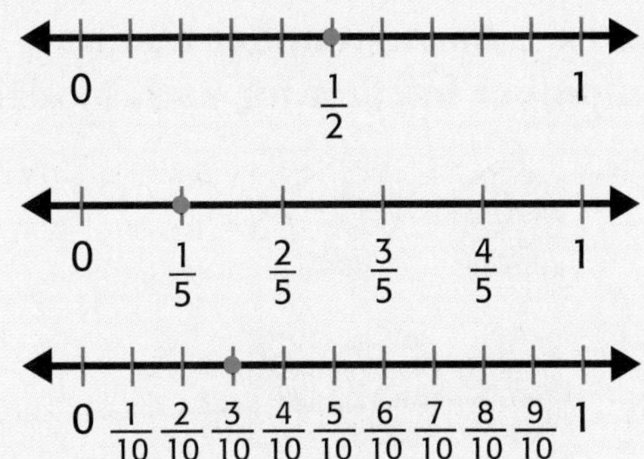

The farther to the right on the number line, the greater the fraction.

So, the order from least to greatest is $\frac{1}{5}$, $\frac{3}{10}$, $\frac{1}{2}$.

Compare. Write <, >, or =.

51.

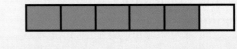

52.

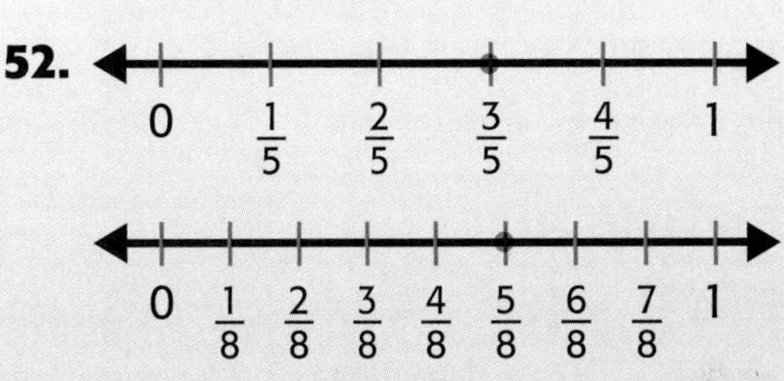

$\frac{3}{5}$ ● $\frac{5}{8}$

53. $\frac{4}{5}$ ● $\frac{8}{10}$

54. $\frac{6}{6}$ ● $\frac{5}{6}$

55. $\frac{3}{8}$ ● $\frac{2}{3}$

56. $\frac{4}{8}$ ● $\frac{1}{4}$

Order from the least to the greatest.

57. $\frac{2}{3}, \frac{3}{7}, \frac{4}{35}$

58. $\frac{1}{4}, \frac{3}{16}, \frac{7}{8}$

59. $\frac{2}{3}, \frac{3}{4}, \frac{1}{2}$

60. $\frac{1}{3}, \frac{9}{21}, \frac{2}{7}$

61. Patrick took $\frac{3}{4}$ of an hour to finish a test. José took $\frac{3}{8}$ of an hour to finish. Who took longer to take the test?

62. The Butler family took a vote on which movie to rent. $\frac{2}{6}$ of the family members voted for an action movie, $\frac{8}{12}$ of the family members voted for a comedy movie. Which movie received more votes?

Study Guide and Review

13-8 Add and Subtract Like Fractions (pp. 534–537)

Example 9

Find $\frac{3}{12} + \frac{4}{12}$.

Add the numerators. Keep the same denominator.

$$\frac{3}{12} + \frac{4}{12} = \frac{7}{12}$$

Example 10

Find $\frac{3}{4} - \frac{1}{4}$.

Subtract the numerators. Keep the same denominator.

$$\frac{3}{4} - \frac{1}{4} = \frac{2}{4}$$

$$\frac{2 \div 2}{4 \div 2} = \frac{1}{2}$$ Write the answer in simplest form.

Find each sum or difference. Write in simplest form.

63. $\frac{2}{6} + \frac{1}{6}$ **64.** $\frac{5}{10} + \frac{3}{10}$

65. $\frac{14}{18} - \frac{5}{18}$ **66.** $\frac{11}{12} - \frac{6}{12}$

67. Elroy listened to $\frac{7}{15}$ of the songs on his new CD on Saturday. He listened to $\frac{4}{15}$ of the songs on Sunday. What fraction of the songs on his CD did he listen to?

68. Sari wrote $\frac{2}{5}$ of her report on Tuesday and $\frac{1}{5}$ of her report on Wednesday. How much of her report does she have left to write?

13-9 Mixed Numbers (pp. 538–541)

Example 11

A fourth grade class had a pizza party. The amount of pizza eaten can be represented as $3\frac{1}{5}$. Write the amout of the pizza eaten as an improper fraction.

$$3\frac{1}{5} = \frac{5}{5} + \frac{5}{5} + \frac{5}{5} + \frac{1}{5}$$

$$= \frac{5 + 5 + 5 + 1}{5}$$

$$= \frac{16}{5}$$

So, $3\frac{1}{5} = \frac{16}{5}$.

Write a mixed number and an improper fraction for each model.

69.  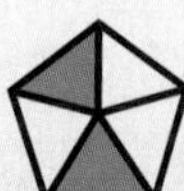

70. 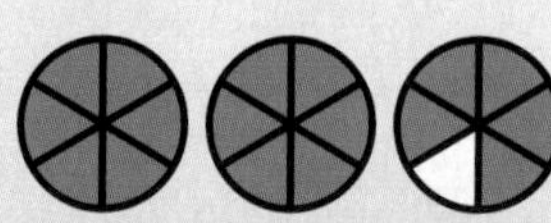

Write each as an improper fraction or a mixed number.

71. $\frac{18}{4}$ **72.** $\frac{32}{8}$

73. $2\frac{3}{4}$ **74.** $3\frac{7}{8}$

Chapter 13 Chapter Test

For Exercises 1 and 2, tell whether each statement is *true* or *false*.

1. An improper fraction has a numerator that is less than its denominator.

2. To find an equivalent fraction, multiply or divide the numerator and denominator by the same number.

Write each fraction in simplest form.

3. $\frac{3}{12}$

4. $\frac{24}{40}$

Find an equivalent fraction for each fraction.

5. $\frac{1}{5}$

6. $\frac{1}{3}$

7. Madison and Alan each ate the amount of apple pie shown. How much of one whole apple pie is left if the shaded parts represent pieces of pie?

8. **STANDARDS PRACTICE** Which fraction is NOT equivalent to the shaded area of the circle?

A $\frac{1}{2}$

B $\frac{2}{4}$

C $\frac{4}{8}$

D $\frac{7}{12}$

Compare. Write <, >, or =.

9. $\frac{2}{4}$ ● $\frac{3}{4}$

10. $\frac{4}{10}$ ● $\frac{1}{2}$

Write each mixed number as an improper fraction.

11. $2\frac{3}{4}$

12. $4\frac{5}{12}$

13. There are 12 fish in Ricardo's aquarium. One-half of the fish are goldfish. Four of the fish are tetras. The rest of the fish are rainbowfish. How many of the fish are rainbowfish?

Find each sum or difference. Write in simplest form.

14. $\frac{3}{10} + \frac{4}{10}$

15. $\frac{4}{15} + \frac{6}{15}$

16. $\frac{11}{12} - \frac{4}{12}$

17. $\frac{13}{18} - \frac{5}{18}$

18. Abby read $\frac{3}{10}$ of a book on Saturday. Then she read $\frac{4}{10}$ of the book on Sunday. What fraction of the book does Abby still have to read?

19. **STANDARDS PRACTICE** Identify the improper fraction below that is NOT equivalent to $2\frac{4}{5}$.

F $\frac{28}{10}$

G $\frac{42}{15}$

H $\frac{5}{14}$

J $\frac{56}{20}$

20. **WRITING IN MATH** Explain how $\frac{2}{7}$ and $\frac{6}{21}$ are equivalent fractions.

CHAPTER 13

California Standards Practice

Cumulative, Chapters 1–13

Standards Example

Kathryn walked $\frac{2}{5}$ of a mile in the morning and $\frac{1}{5}$ of a mile in the afternoon. Which model shows the fraction of a mile Kathryn walked in all?

A 

C 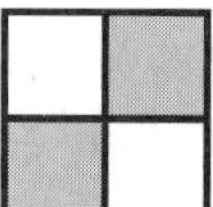

B 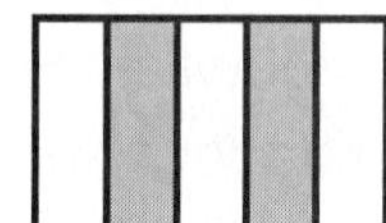

D 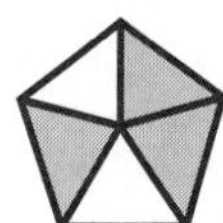

Read the Question

You need to find which model shows the fraction of a mile Kathryn walked in all.

Solve the Question

Find the distance Kathryn walked in all.

$$\frac{2}{5} + \frac{1}{5} = \frac{2 + 1}{5} = \frac{3}{5}$$

Kathryn walked $\frac{3}{5}$ of a mile on Wednesday. Look for a model that shows 3 out of 5 parts shaded. So, the answer is D.

Online **Personal Tutor at** ca.gr4math.com

Choose the best answer.

1 **Which model shows $\frac{1}{6} + \frac{3}{6}$?**

 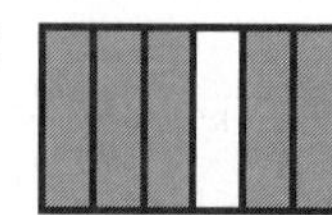

D 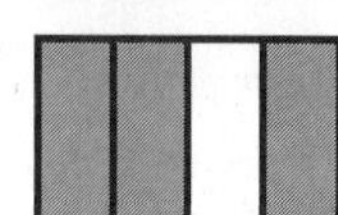

2 **Santos read a 280-page book in 7 days. He read the same number of pages each day. How many pages did he read each day?**

F 30

G 36

H 40

J 42

More California Standards Practice
For practice by standard, see pages CA1–CA43.

3 **What fraction is best represented by point *N* on the number line?**

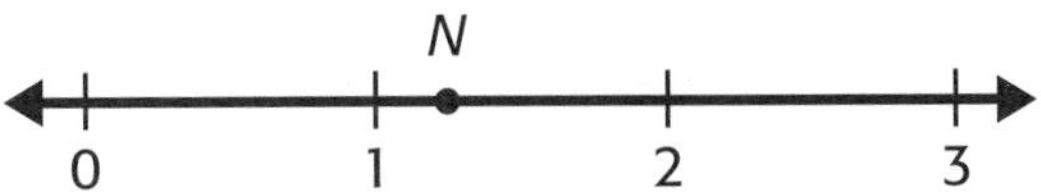

A $\frac{3}{4}$

B $1\frac{1}{4}$

C $1\frac{3}{4}$

D $2\frac{1}{4}$

---

4 **Which set of fractions is in order from least to greatest?**

F $\frac{6}{10}, \frac{4}{5}, \frac{1}{2}$

G $\frac{4}{5}, \frac{1}{2}, \frac{6}{10}$

H $\frac{1}{2}, \frac{4}{5}, \frac{6}{10}$

J $\frac{1}{2}, \frac{6}{10}, \frac{4}{5}$

---

5 **Vara jogged $2\frac{3}{5}$ miles. Write $2\frac{3}{5}$ as an improper fraction.**

A $\frac{13}{10}$

B $\frac{10}{5}$

C $\frac{12}{5}$

D $\frac{13}{5}$

---

6 **The model is shaded to show which fraction?**

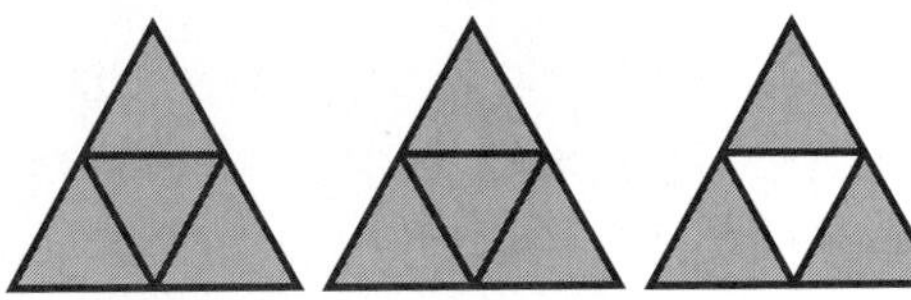

F $2\frac{1}{3}$

G $2\frac{2}{3}$

H $2\frac{3}{4}$

J $3\frac{1}{3}$

---

7 **What is the value of the expression below if $c = 4$?**

$$21 - (c + 7)$$

A 7

B 10

C 11

D 32

---

8 **The cafeteria has 24 tables. Each table has 8 seats. How many people can sit in the cafeteria?**

F 32

G 172

H 192

J 240

---

9 **Which of the following is represented by the model?**

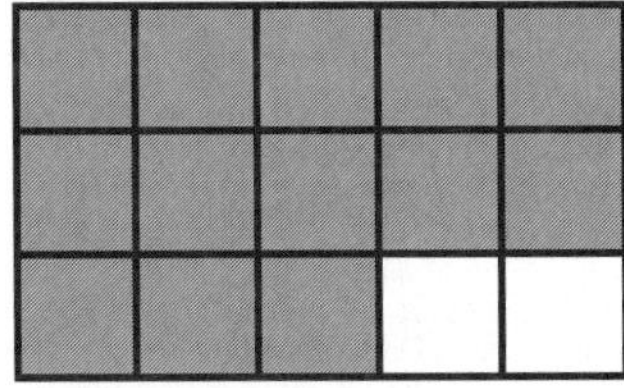

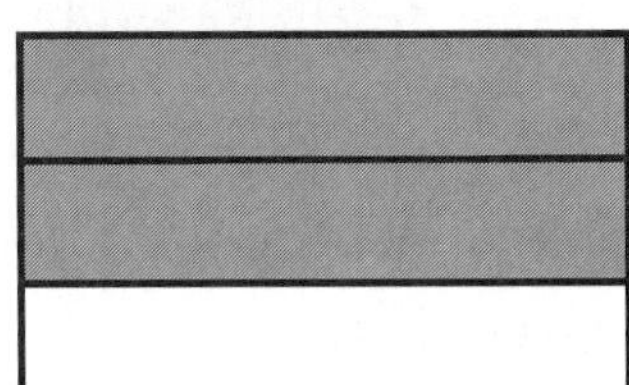

A $\frac{2}{13} > \frac{1}{3}$

B $\frac{2}{3} > \frac{13}{15}$

C $\frac{1}{3} = \frac{2}{3}$

D $\frac{13}{15} > \frac{2}{3}$

---

10 **Which number is 100,000 more than 32,769,201?**

F 32,769,201

G 32,779,201

H 32,869,201

J 42,769,201

CHAPTER 14 Decimals

BIG Idea What are decimals?

Decimals are numbers that use place value and a decimal point to show part of a whole.

Example There are 10 dimes in a dollar. One dime is $\frac{1}{10}$ of a dollar. There are 100 pennies in a dollar. One penny is $\frac{1}{100}$ of a dollar.

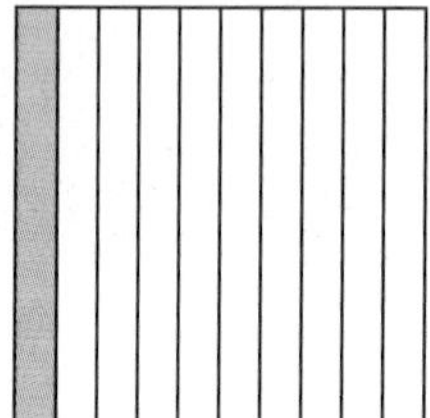

One dime is $\frac{1}{10}$ of a dollar.

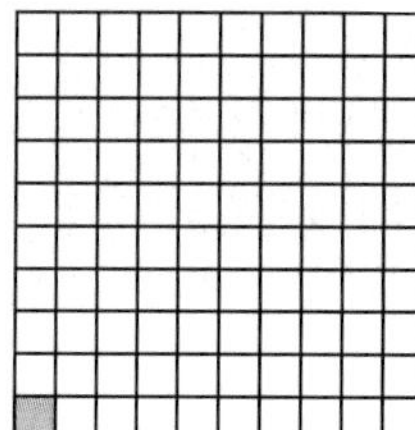

One penny is $\frac{1}{100}$ of a dollar.

What will I learn in this chapter?

- Identify, read, write, and model decimals.
- Relate decimals, fractions, and mixed numbers.
- Compare and order decimals.
- Solve problems by making a model.

Key Vocabulary

decimal

decimal point

tenth

hundredth

Student Study Tools at ca.gr4math.com

FOLDABLES™ Study Organizer

Make this Foldable to help you organize information about decimals. Begin with one sheet of 11″ × 17″ paper.

1 **Fold** the short sides so they meet in the middle.

2 **Fold** again so the top meets the bottom.

3 **Unfold** and cut as shown to make four tabs.

4 **Label** the outside of each tab as shown.

ARE YOU READY for Chapter 14?

You have two ways to check prerequisite skills for this chapter.

Option 2

Math Online Take the Chapter Readiness Quiz at ca.gr4math.com.

Option 1

Complete the Quick Check below.

QUICK Check

Write a fraction to describe the part that is green. (Lesson 13-1)

1. 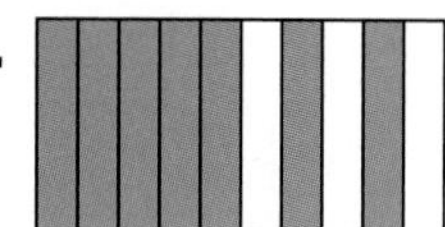

2. 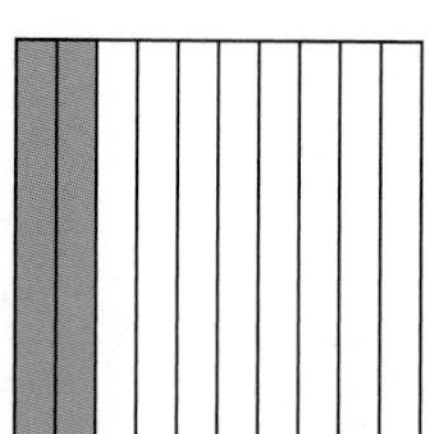

3. 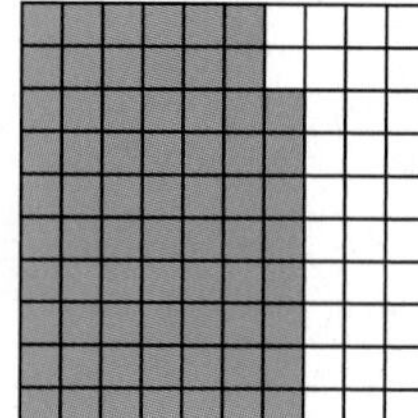

Write each as a fraction. (Lessons 13-1 and 13-2)

4. four tenths

5. eight tenths

6. twenty hundredths

7. On Tuesday, seven-tenths of an inch of rain fell. Write the amount of rain that fell as a fraction.

Algebra Copy and complete. (Lesson 13-4)

8. $\frac{1}{5} = \frac{■}{10}$

9. $\frac{4}{5} = \frac{■}{10}$

10. $\frac{1}{2} = \frac{■}{10}$

11. $\frac{1}{4} = \frac{■}{100}$

12. $\frac{2}{5} = \frac{■}{100}$

13. $\frac{1}{2} = \frac{■}{100}$

14. In Salvador's aquarium, $\frac{4}{10}$ of the fish are yellow and $\frac{6}{10}$ are blue. Are there more blue or yellow fish in Salvador's aquarium? Explain how you know.

Math Activity for 14-1

Fractions and Decimals

MAIN IDEA

I will model tenths and hundredths.

 **Standard 4NS1.6 Write tenths and hundredths in decimal and fraction notations** and know the fraction and decimal equivalents for halves and fourths.

Standard 4MR2.3 Use a variety of methods, such as words, numbers, symbols, charts, graphs, tables, diagrams, **and models, to explain mathematical reasoning.**

You Will Need
tenths grid
hundredths grid

A fraction shows part of a whole. A decimal also shows a part of a whole. A **decimal** is a number that uses place value, numbers, and a decimal point to show part of a whole.

one whole

$\frac{1}{1} = 1.0$

decimal point

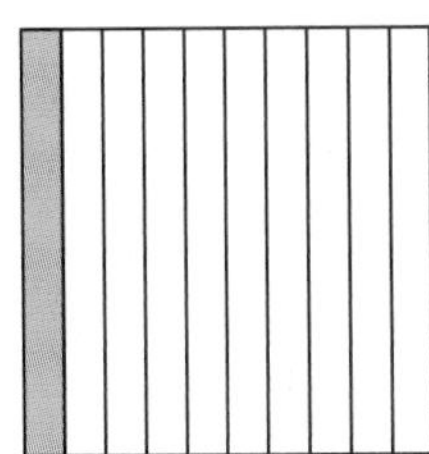

one **tenth**

$\frac{1}{10} = 0.1$

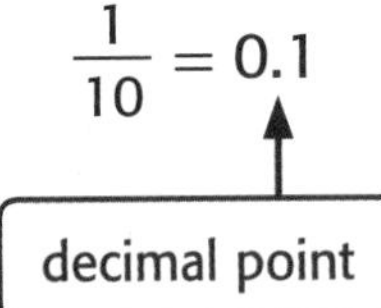

decimal point

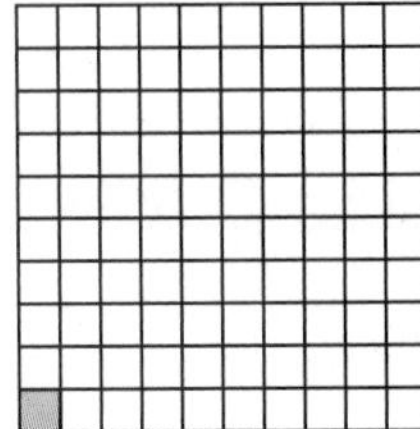

one **hundredth**

$\frac{1}{100} = 0.01$

decimal point

ACTIVITY

1 Model 4 tenths.

Step 1 Use a tenths grid.
Shade in 4 of the 10 parts to show 4 tenths.

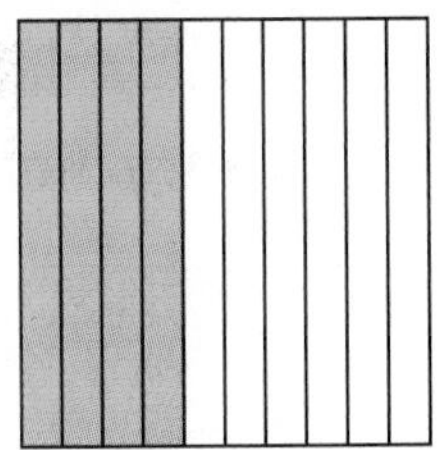

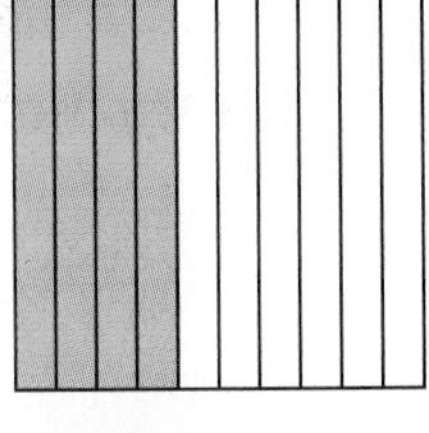

Step 2 Use a hundredths grid.
Shade 40 of the 100 parts to show 40 hundredths.

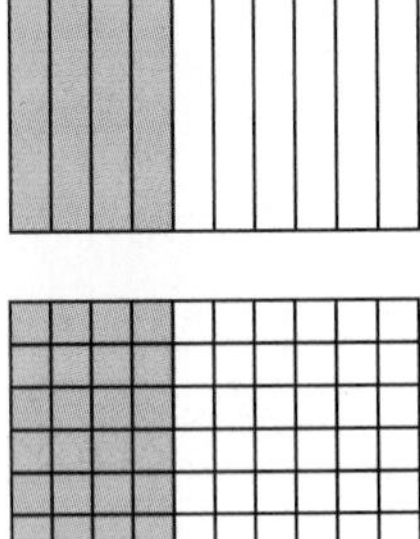

Step 3 Compare.
Compare the grids. Write the fraction for each shaded part.

Step 4 Write decimals.
How is 4 tenths written as a decimal?
How is 40 hundredths written as a decimal?

Animation
ca.gr4math.com

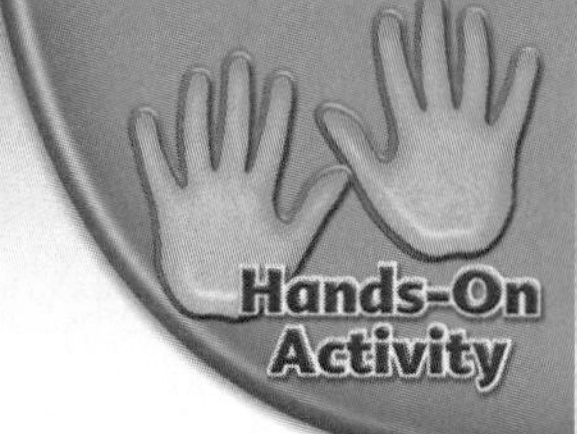

ACTIVITY

2 Model 77 hundredths.

Step 1 Use a hundredths grid.
Shade 77 of the 100 parts to show 77 hundredths.

Step 2 Use a tenths grid.
Shade 77 hundredths on the tenths grid.

Step 3 Compare.
Compare the grids. Should a tenths grid be used to show 77 hundredths? Why or why not?

Think About It

1. Do $\frac{4}{10}$, $\frac{40}{100}$, 0.4, and 0.40 represent the same number? Explain.

2. Is 0.02 greater than 0.2? Support your answer with models.

3. Is 0.3 greater than 0.30? Explain.

CHECK What You Know

Write a fraction and a decimal for each shaded part.

4. 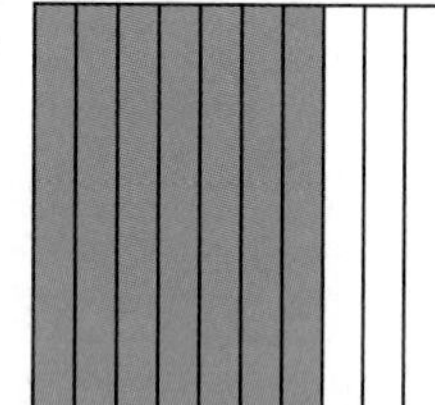

5. 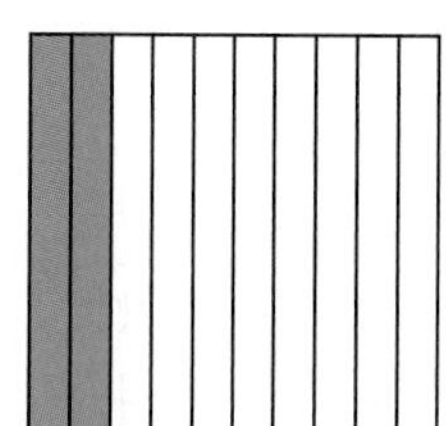

6. 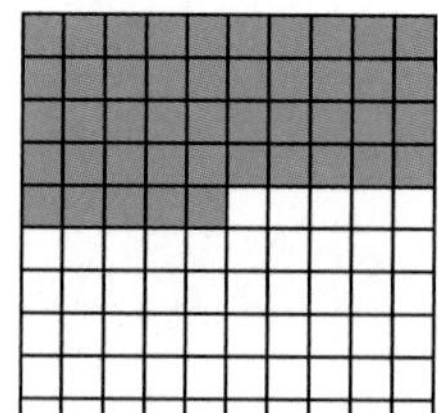

7. 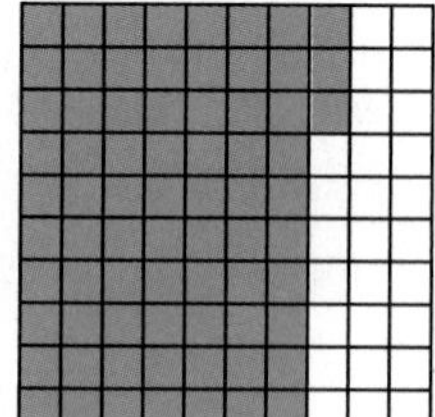

Draw a model of each fraction using a tenths or hundredths grid.

8. $\frac{1}{10}$ **9.** $\frac{3}{10}$ **10.** $\frac{60}{100}$ **11.** $\frac{82}{100}$

Draw a model of each decimal using a tenths or hundredths grid.

12. 0.5 **13.** 0.75 **14.** 0.3 **15.** 0.25

16. WRITING IN ►MATH Explain how to write a fraction with a denominator of 10 as a decimal.

14-1 Tenths and Hundredths

MAIN IDEA

I will identify, read, and write tenths and hundredths as decimals and fractions.

Standard 4NS1.6 **Write tenths and hundredths in decimal and fraction notations** and know the fraction and decimal equivalents for halves and fourths (i.e., $\frac{5}{10} = 0.5$ or 0.50; $\frac{7}{4} = 1\frac{3}{4} = 1.75$).

New Vocabulary

decimal
decimal point
tenth
hundredth

GET READY to Learn

It costs 85 cents for a child to ride the Sacramento light rail system. Can you write this part of a dollar as a fraction and as a decimal?

A **decimal** is a number that uses place value, and a **decimal point** to show part of a whole.

EXAMPLE Read and Write Decimals

1 **MONEY** **Write 85 cents as a fraction and as a decimal.**

The amount 85 cents means 85 pennies out of 1 dollar.

One Way: Model

Draw a hundredths model. Shade 85 out of 100 parts to show 85 cents.

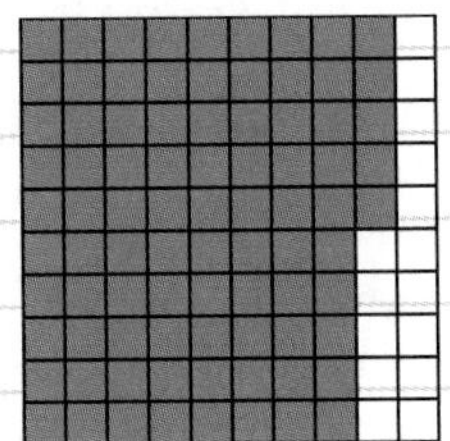

Read eighty-five hundredths

Write $\frac{85}{100}$ or 0.85

Another Way: Place Value

Hundreds	Tens	Ones	Tenths	Hundredths
		0.	8	5

Read eighty-five hundredths

Write $\frac{85}{100}$ or 0.85

Some decimals can be written as **tenths** and **hundredths**.

EXAMPLE Write Tenths and Hundredths

2 **Write $\frac{5}{10}$ as two different decimals.**

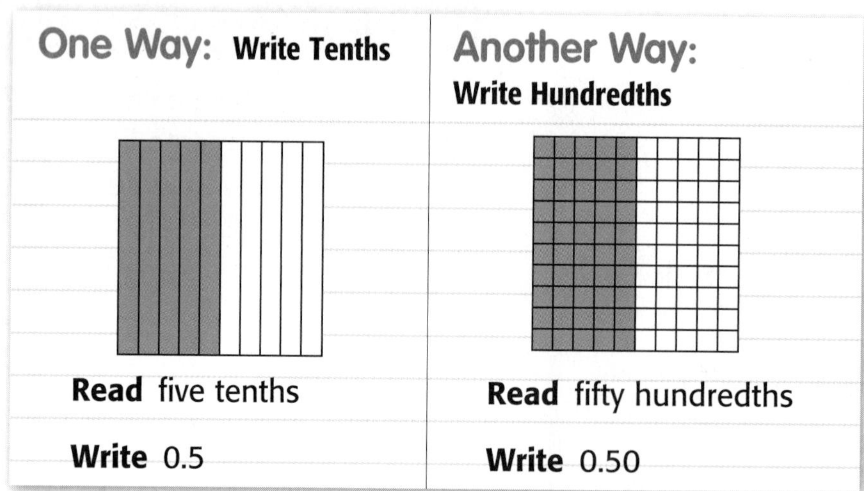

One Way: Write Tenths
Read five tenths
Write 0.5
Another Way: Write Hundredths
Read fifty hundredths
Write 0.50

The decimals 0.5 and 0.50 are equivalent decimals.

Online **Personal Tutor at** ca.gr4math.com

CHECK What You Know

Write a fraction and a decimal for each shaded part. See Example 1 (p. 557)

1. 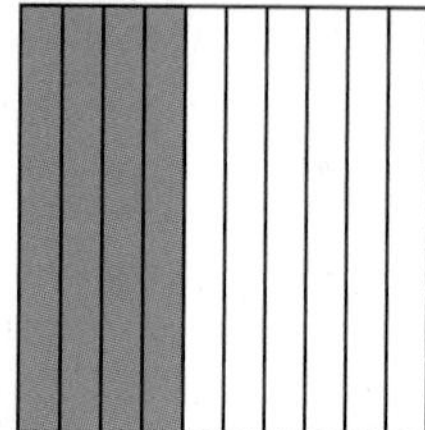

2. 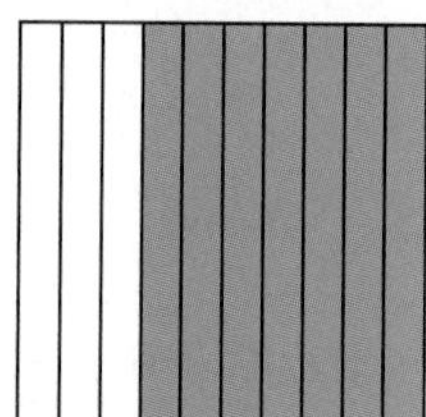

3. 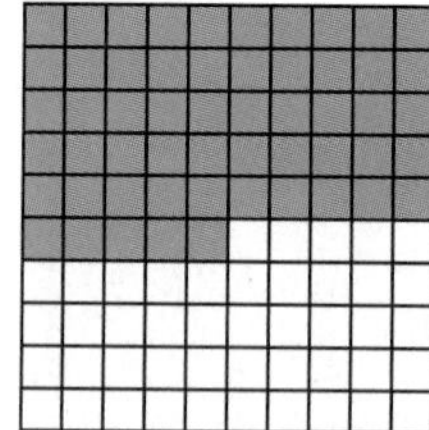

Write as a fraction and as a decimal. See Example 1 (p. 557)

4. one tenth

5. twenty-five hundredths

6. seven hundredths

Write each fraction as a decimal. See Example 2 (p. 558)

7. $\frac{6}{10}$

8. $\frac{9}{10}$

9. $\frac{10}{100}$

10. $\frac{69}{100}$

11. **Measurement** A baby owl weighs about twenty-three hundredths of a kilogram. Write this amount as a fraction and decimal.

12. **Talk About It** Shade all of the boxes along the outer edge of a hundredths grid. Write a fraction and decimal for the shaded area part. Why is it not 0.40?

Practice and Problem Solving

EXTRA PRACTICE
See page R35.

Write a fraction and a decimal for each shaded part. See Example 1 (p. 557)

13. 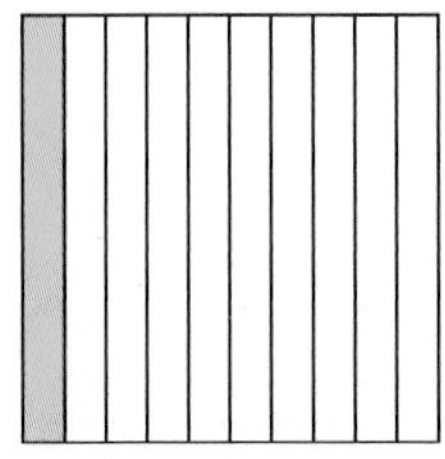

14. 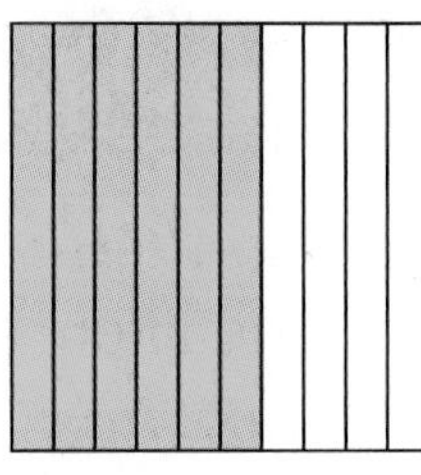

15. 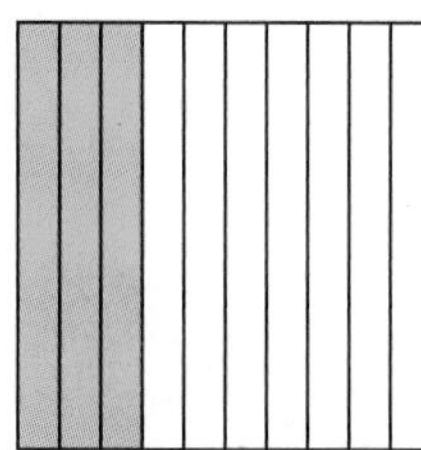

16. 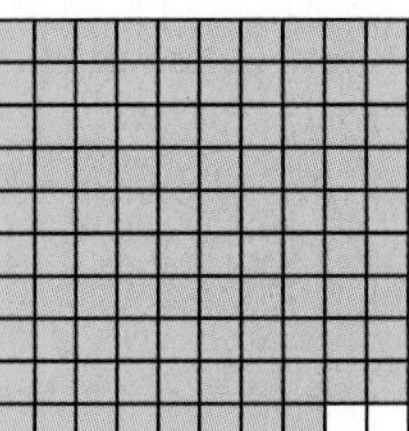

17. 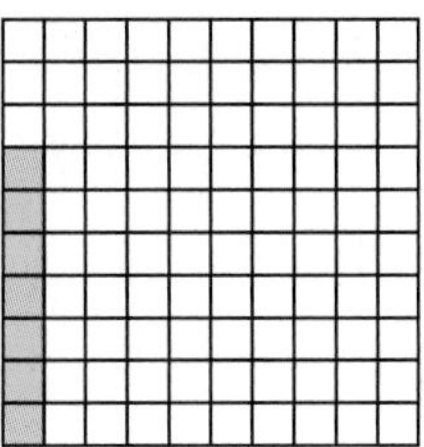

18. 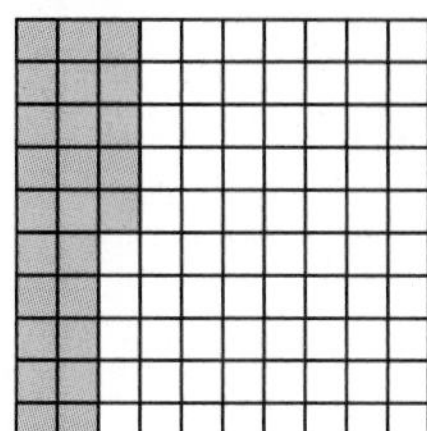

Write as a fraction and as a decimal. See Example 1 (p. 557)

19. sixty-two hundredths

20. two tenths

21. thirty-five hundredths

22. eight tenths

23. fourteen hundredths

24. six tenths

Write each fraction as a decimal. See Example 2 (p. 558)

25. $\frac{22}{100}$

26. $\frac{2}{100}$

27. $\frac{2}{10}$

28. $\frac{50}{100}$

29. $\frac{75}{100}$

30. $\frac{80}{100}$

31. Measurement On Monday, it snowed $\frac{6}{10}$ of an inch of snow.

32. Measurement A car traveled $\frac{3}{10}$ of a mile in 18 seconds.

33. Each state has a representation of $\frac{2}{100}$ in the U.S. Senate.

34. Cody learned that $\frac{4}{10}$ of the students in his class are left handed.

H.O.T. Problems

35. OPEN ENDED Write a fraction whose decimal value is between $\frac{2}{10}$ and $\frac{25}{100}$. Write the fraction and its equivalent.

36. CHALLENGE Decide whether the following sentence is true or false. Explain. The fraction $\frac{6}{1,000}$ equals 0.006.

37. WRITING IN ▸MATH Write a summary statement about decimals equivalent to fractions that have denominators of 10 and 100.

14-2 Relate Mixed Numbers and Decimals

MAIN IDEA

I will identify, read, and write decimals greater than 1.

Standard 4NS1.6 **Write tenths and hundredths in decimal and fraction notation** and know the fraction and decimal equivalents for halves and fourths (e.g., $\frac{1}{2} = 0.5$ or 0.50; $\frac{7}{4} = 1\frac{3}{4} = 1.75$).

Review Vocabulary

mixed number a number named by a whole number and a fraction; *Example:* $2\frac{1}{2}$ (Lesson 13–7)

GET READY to Learn

Giant saguaro (*sah-WAH-ro*) cacti are found in California, Arizona, and Mexico. A saguaro's growth is slow. It takes about 30 years for one to grow $2\frac{5}{10}$ feet tall and start flowering.

A mixed number like $2\frac{5}{10}$ is a fraction greater than one. You can write mixed numbers as decimals.

EXAMPLE Mixed Numbers as Decimals

1 **Write $2\frac{5}{10}$ as a decimal.**

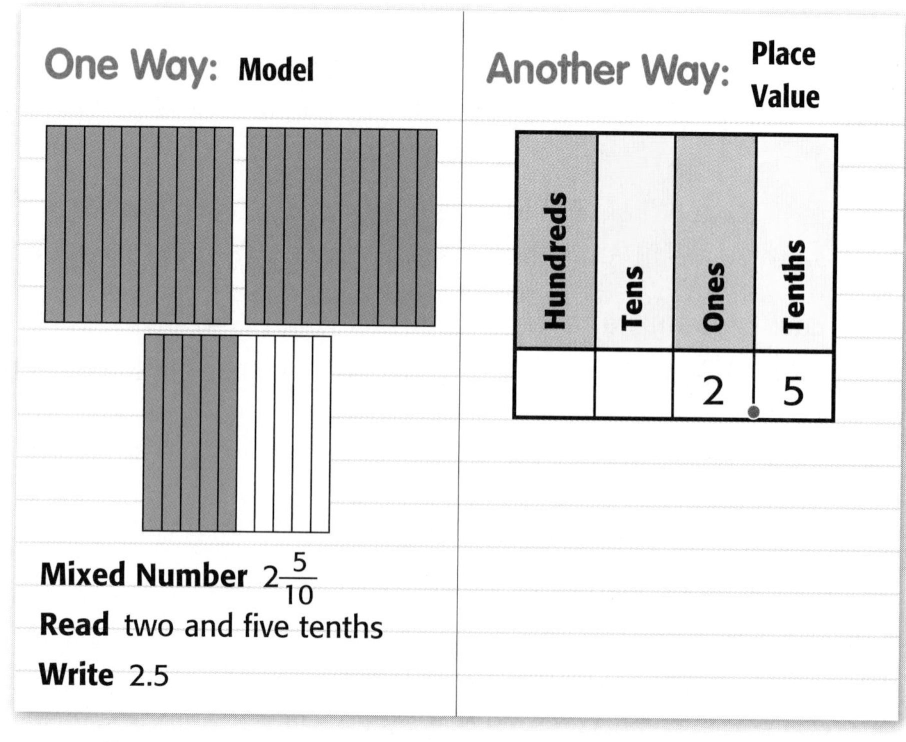

Mixed Number $2\frac{5}{10}$

Read two and five tenths

Write 2.5

So, $2\frac{5}{10}$ as a decimal is 2.5.

Remember
When reading a decimal, the word "and" represents the decimal.

Real-World EXAMPLE

2 **MEASUREMENT** **The length of an iguana is $1\frac{9}{100}$ yards. Write $1\frac{9}{100}$ as a decimal.**

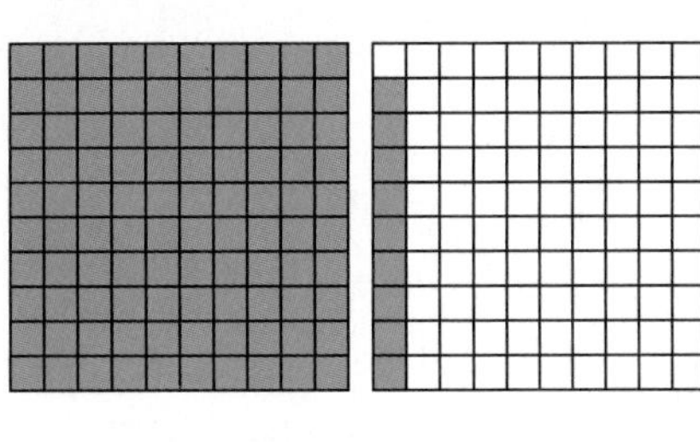

Hundreds	Tens	Ones	Tenths	Hundredths
		1.	0	9

Mixed Number $1\frac{9}{100}$

Read one and nine hundredths

Write 1.09

Online **Personal Tutor at** ca.gr4math.com

CHECK What You Know

Write each as a mixed number and decimal. See Examples 1 and 2 (pp. 560–561)

1.

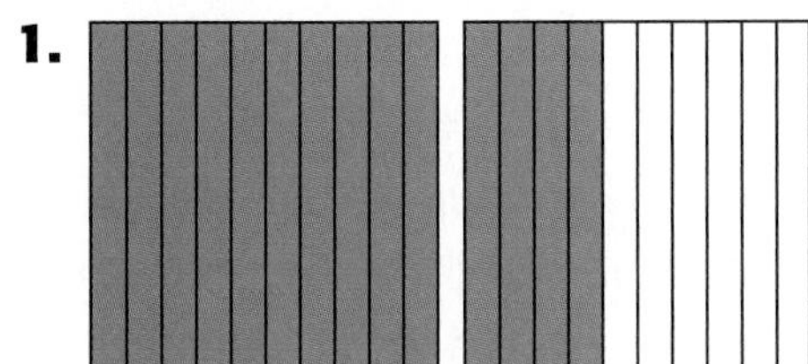

2.

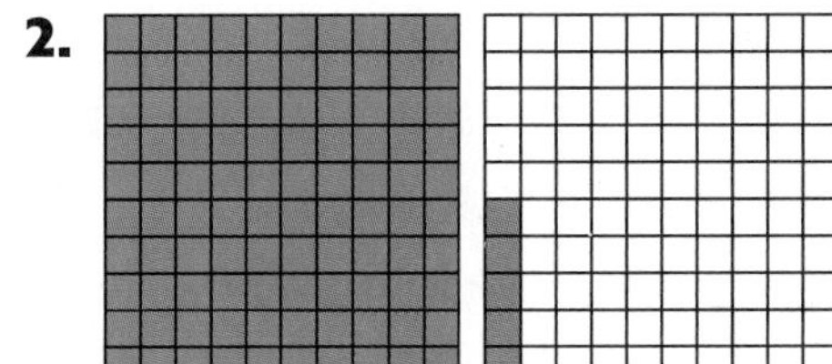

3. twelve and three tenths

4. twelve and three hundredths

5. three and six tenths

6. sixteen and thirty-two hundredths

Write each as a decimal. See Examples 1 and 2 (pp. 560–561)

7. $5\frac{3}{10}$

8. $12\frac{5}{10}$

9. $6\frac{50}{100}$

10. $24\frac{8}{100}$

11. Jodi ran the 100-meter dash in 14.6 seconds. Tyra ran the 100-meter dash in 14.64 seconds. Write each girl's time as a mixed number.

12. Talk About It Do $8\frac{5}{10}$, $8\frac{1}{2}$, and 8.5 name the same amount? Explain your reasoning.

Practice and Problem Solving

EXTRA PRACTICE See page R35.

Write each as a mixed number and decimal. See Examples 1 and 2 (pp. 560–561)

13. 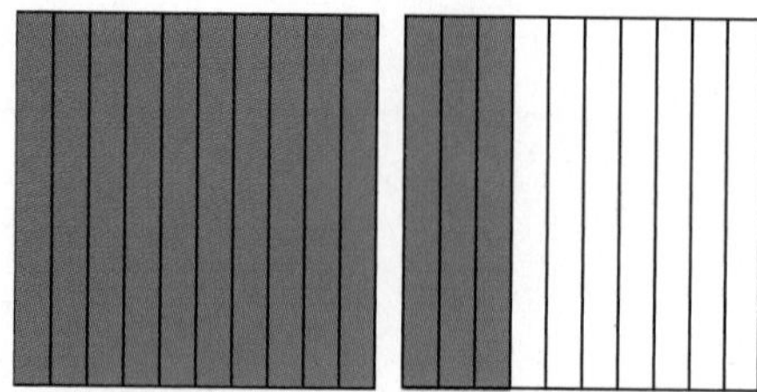

14. 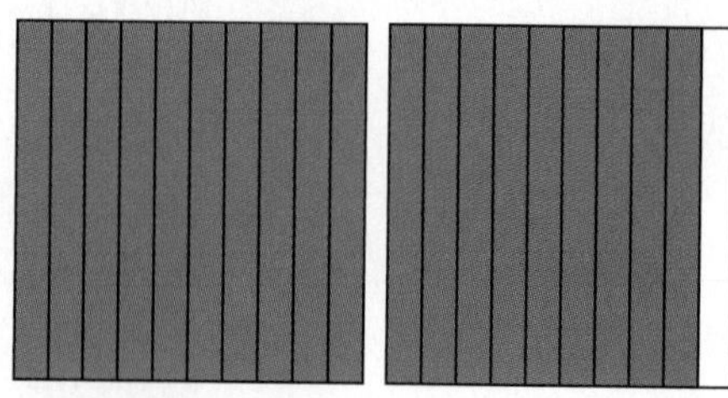

15. 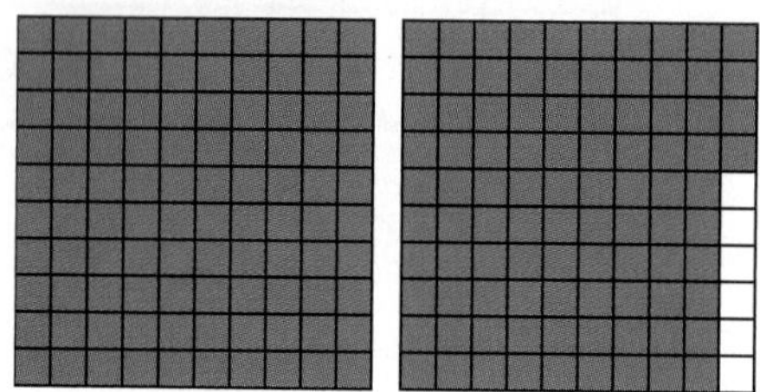

16. 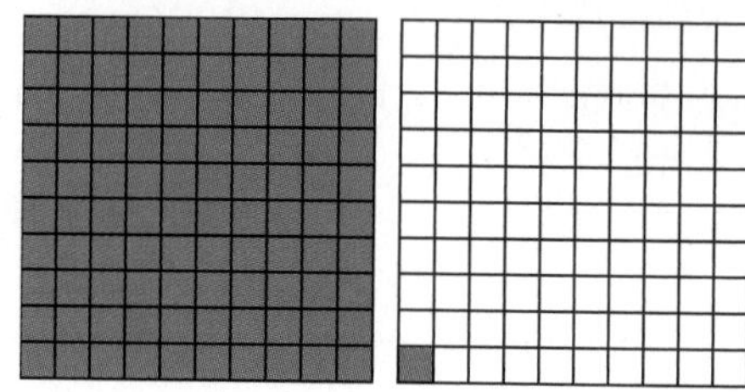

17. one and five tenths

18. sixteen and seven tenths

19. nineteen and one hundred hundredths

20. fifty-six and one hundredth

Write each as a decimal. See Examples 1 and 2 (pp. 560–561)

21. $2\frac{5}{10}$

22. $6\frac{6}{10}$

23. $50\frac{1}{10}$

24. $78\frac{8}{10}$

25. $10\frac{16}{100}$

26. $60\frac{2}{100}$

27. $5\frac{25}{100}$

28. $22\frac{75}{100}$

29. **Measurement** Aaron has grown $3\frac{4}{10}$ feet since he was born. Write a decimal to show how many feet Aaron has grown.

30. **Measurement** Coastal Plains received 5.52 inches of rain. Write a mixed number to show the number of inches Coastal Plains received.

31. **Measurement** Kevin lives $2\frac{6}{10}$ miles from the library. Write a decimal to show how many miles Kevin lives from the library.

32. **Measurement** A moose is one of the world's tallest mammals. Write a decimal to show how tall a moose is.

33. **Measurement** Ramona's paper airplane flew 3.05 meters. Write a mixed number to show how many meters the airplane flew.

Math Online Self-Check Quiz at ca.gr4math.com

H.O.T. Problems

34. OPEN ENDED Write a mixed number and decimal that are less than five and eight tenths.

35. FIND THE ERROR Brianna and Nick are writing $2\frac{3}{4}$ as a decimal. Who is correct? Explain your reasoning.

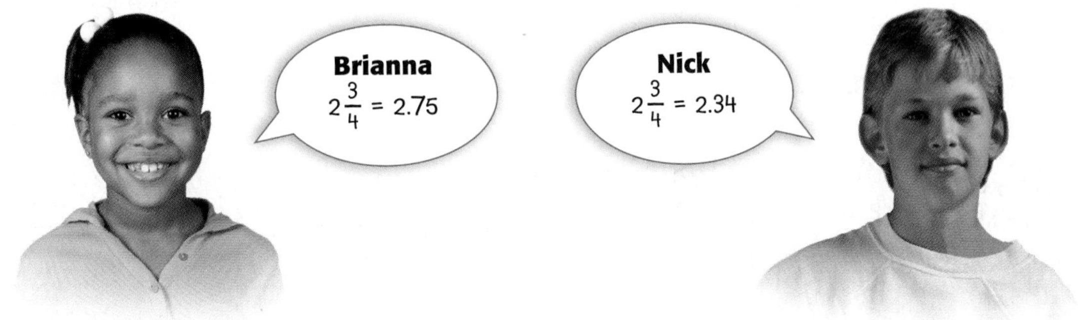

36. WRITING IN ▸MATH Are $2\frac{4}{8}$ and 2.5 equivalent? Explain.

Standards Practice

37 Which number represents the shaded parts of the figure? (Lesson 14-1)

A 0.04

B 0.4

C 4.0

D 4.4

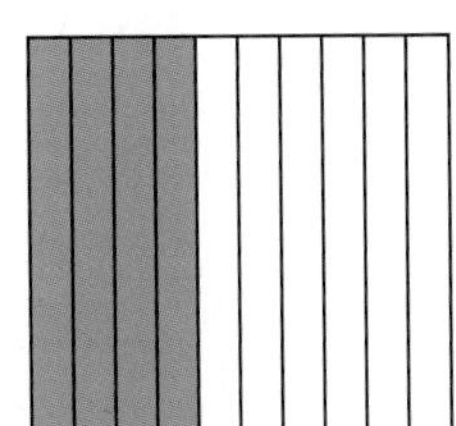

38 Which of the following is seven and seven hundredths? (Lesson 14-2)

F 0.77

G 7.07

H 7.7

J $7\frac{7}{10}$

Spiral Review

Write as a fraction and as a decimal. (Lesson 14-1)

39. five tenths

40. fifty-six hundredths

Find each sum or difference. Write in simplest form. (Lesson 13-9)

41. $\frac{7}{12} + \frac{3}{12}$

42. $\frac{2}{4} + \frac{1}{4}$

43. $\frac{8}{10} - \frac{6}{10}$

44. $\frac{8}{16} - \frac{4}{16}$

45. Justino has read $\frac{3}{10}$ of a book. He then reads $\frac{2}{10}$ more. How much of the book is left to read?

14-3 Problem-Solving Strategy

MAIN IDEA I will solve problems by making a model.

Standard 4MR2.3 **Use a variety of methods, such as words, numbers,** symbols, charts, graphs, tables, diagrams, **and models, to explain mathematical reasoning.** Standard 4NS3.0 **Students solve problems involving addition, subtraction, multiplication and division of whole numbers and understand the relationships among the operations.**

Luisa's mom has asked her to find seating for 22 guests for her birthday party. They have an oval table that can seat 10 people. They also have square tables that each seat 4 people. How many square tables are needed to seat the guests?

Understand

What facts do you know?

- An oval table seats 10 people.
- There will be 22 guests altogether.
- Each square table seats 4 people.

What do you need to find?

- The number of square tables needed to seat the guests.

Plan

You can make a model to see how many tables are needed.

Solve

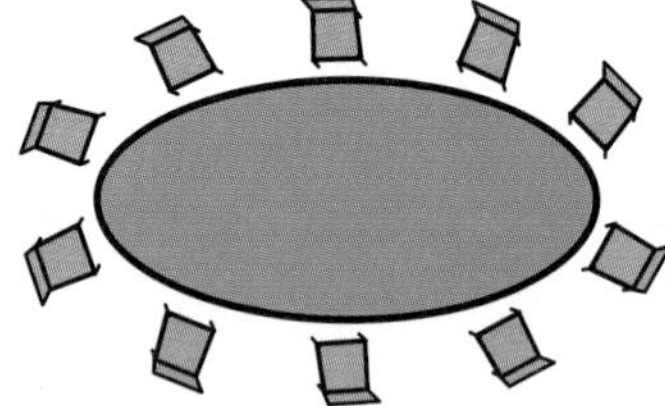

The oval table can seat 10 people.
$22 - 10 = 12$

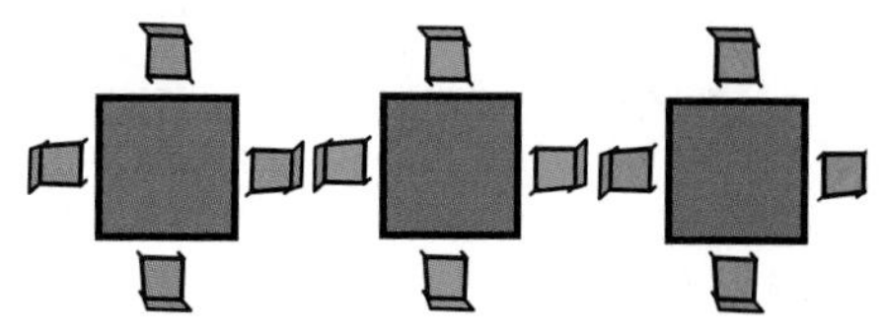

12 people will sit at square tables.
$12 - 12 = 0$

So, three is the fewest number of square tables needed to seat the guests.

Check

Look back at the problem. The fewest number of square tables needed is 3. This makes sense because $22 - 10 - (3 \times 4) = 0$. So, the answer is correct.

ANALYZE the Strategy

Refer to the problem on the previous page.

1. Explain how a model was used to find the fewest number of tables.

2. Explain another strategy you could use to solve Luisa's problem.

3. Suppose there were 30 guests. How many square tables would be needed?

4. Look back to Exercise 3. Check your answer. How do you know that it is correct? Show your work.

PRACTICE the Strategy

Solve. Use the *make a model* strategy.

5. Eileen opened 8 boxes of clay for her project. Each box had 4 sticks of gray clay and half as many sticks of red clay. How many sticks of clay were there in all?

6. Cesar is making a model of the longest bridge in the table for a school project. The scale he is using is one inch equals 200 feet. How many inches long will the model be?

Bridges	
Bridge	**Length (ft)**
Golden Gate	4,200
New Carquinez Straight	3,478
Oakland Bay	2,310

7. Katia is painting her living room. The room has 3 walls that are 16 feet long and 9 feet tall. A gallon of paint covers 150 square feet. How many gallons should she buy to cover all 3 walls?

8. Every day Marvin runs 3,200 meters around the school track. How many times does he run around the track?

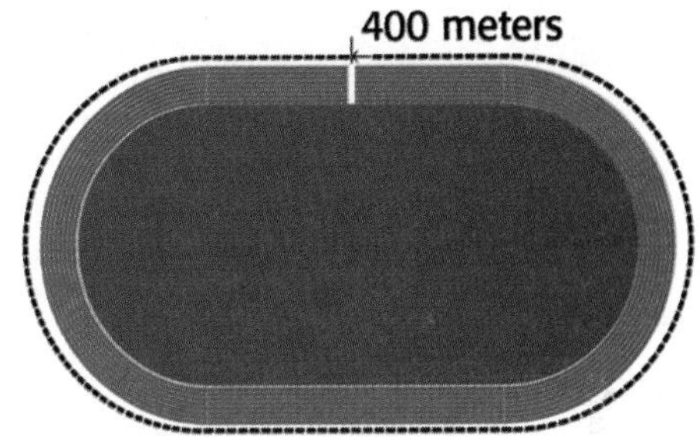

9. Mariana rode her bike 5 miles. Then she went back to get her brother. They rode together for 17 miles. How far did Mariana go altogether?

10. A volleyball court measures 18 meters by 9 meters. A basketball court measures 29 meters by 15 meters. How many volleyball courts could be placed in a basketball court?

11. **WRITING IN MATH** The bottom layer of a triangular-shaped display has 4 boxes. There is one less box in each layer. There are four layers. The answer is 10. What is the question?

Compare and Order Decimals

GET READY to Learn

The table shows the results from a skateboarding competition. Who has the higher score, Nitika or Elise?

Skateboarding Results

Name	Score
Nitika	79.7
Selma	79.2
Kenyi	78.9
Elise	79.5
Jane	78.8

MAIN IDEA

I will compare and order decimals.

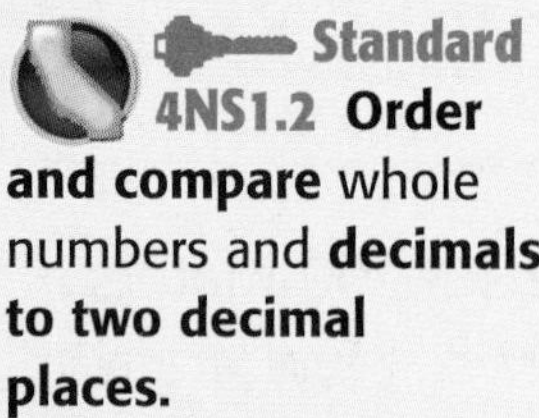

Standard 4NS1.2 **Order and compare** whole numbers and **decimals to two decimal places.**

Standard 4NS1.9 **Identify on a number line** the relative position of positive fractions, positive mixed numbers, and **positive decimals to two decimal places.**

Vocabulary Link

order

Everyday Use select desired items

Math Use to arrange in a logical pattern

To compare decimals, you can use a number line or place value.

Real-World EXAMPLE Compare Decimals

1 **SCORES Who has the higher score, Nitika or Elise?**

Nitika has a score of 79.7, while Elise has a score of 79.5.

One Way: Number Line

79.5 79.7

79.2 80.0

79.0 79.4 79.6 79.8

79.7 is to the right of 79.5.
So, 79.7 > 79.5.

Another Way: Place Value

Line up the decimal points. Then compare the digits in each place value position.

Tens	Ones	Tenths	Hundredths
7	9	7	0
7	9	5	0

In the tenths place, 7 > 5.
So, 79.7 is greater than 79.5.

You can also order decimals.

EXAMPLE Order Decimals

2 Order 9.86, 9.8, 9.92, and 9.09 from greatest to least.

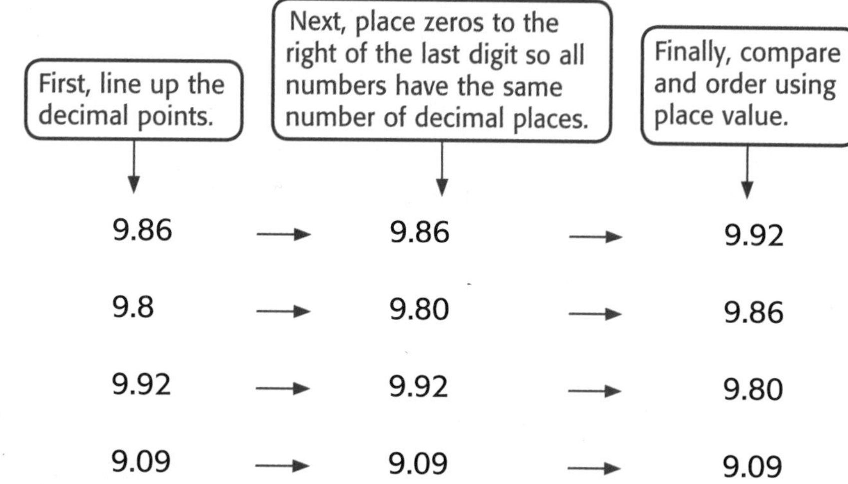

First, line up the decimal points.
Next, place zeros to the right of the last digit so all numbers have the same number of decimal places.
Finally, compare and order using place value.
9.86 → 9.86 → 9.92
9.8 → 9.80 → 9.86
9.92 → 9.92 → 9.80
9.09 → 9.09 → 9.09

The order from greatest to least is 9.92, 9.86, 9.8, and 9.09.

Online Personal Tutor at ca.gr4math.com

CHECK What You Know

Compare. Write $>$, $<$, or $=$. See Example 1 (p. 566)

1. 0.2 ● 0.6
2. 12.07 ● 1.207
3. 5.60 ● 5.6
4. 3.25 ● 32.5
5. 2.5 ● 2.50
6. 178.6 ● 1.786

Order from greatest to least. See Example 2 (p. 567)

7. 3.2, 4.5, 3.9, 4.1
8. 0.12, 1.2, 1.21, 12.0
9. 6.5, 5.6, 6.52, 5.62
10. 5.7, 5.2, 4.7, 6.3
11. 23.5, 235.0, 0.235, 2.35
12. 2.4, 4.27, 4.2, 2.47

13. **Measurement** Five friends are going to different summer camps. The table shows the distance between each camp and their hometown. Order the distances from least to greatest.

Traveling to Camp	
Name	**Distance (mi)**
Bill	64.25
Deng	42.5
Nia	3.28
Antón	64.87
Irena	42.35

14. Who traveled the greatest distance?

15. **Talk About It** Tell how to order 5.5, 5.3, 5.4, and 5.0 from greatest to least.

Practice and Problem Solving

EXTRA PRACTICE See page R36.

Compare. Write >, <, or =. See Example 1 (p. 566)

16. 0.74 ● 7.4 **17.** 16.33 ● 16.3 **18.** 0.56 ● 0.58 **19.** 0.8 ● 0.80

20. 1 ● 0.09 **21.** 0.90 ● 0.9 **22.** 82.6 ● 82.60 **23.** 1.06 ● 1.05

Order from greatest to least. See Example 2 (p. 567)

24. 0.4, 0.42, 0.54 **25.** 0.08, 0.80, 0.82 **26.** 12.5, 1.25, 12.05

27. 19.62, 19.56, 19.60 **28.** 0.5, 0.55, 0.6 **29.** 68.16, 81.6, 68.1

30. **Measurement** The table shows the amount of rainfall for Berkeley, California. Which month had the most rainfall?

Month	Rainfall (in.)
January	5.13
February	4.08
March	4.75
April	4.62

31. **Measurement** The table shows the distances Quinn biked. Did he bike more the first weekend or the last weekend?

Distance Biked in July	
Weekend	**Distance (mi)**
1	3.25
2	3.5
3	3
4	3.6

32. Marlon averages 5.6 rebounds per game. Tina averages 5.9 rebounds per game. Nim averages 4.3 rebounds per game. Who averages the most rebounds? Explain.

33. **Measurement** Rita ran the 100-meter dash four times, which is timed in seconds. Her times were 16.25, 15.36, 16.55, and 15.23. What was her slowest time?

H.O.T. Problems

34. **OPEN ENDED** Draw a number line that contains two whole numbers. Divide the number line in tenths. Identify the location of three decimals on the number line.

35. **NUMBER SENSE** What number is halfway between 4.36 and 4.48 on a number line?

36. **WRITING IN ▸MATH** Write a real-world problem about comparing or ordering decimals.

Math Online Self-Check Quiz at ca.gr4math.com

CHAPTER 14

Mid-Chapter Check

Lessons 14-1 through 14-4

Write a fraction and a decimal for each shaded part. (Lesson 14-1)

1. 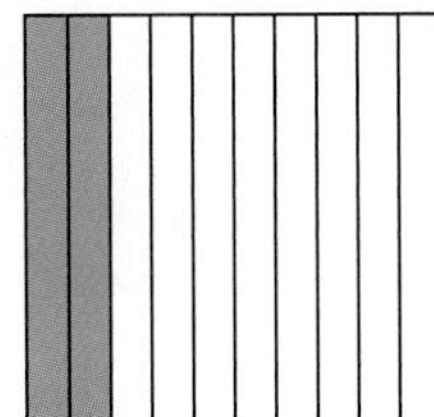

2. 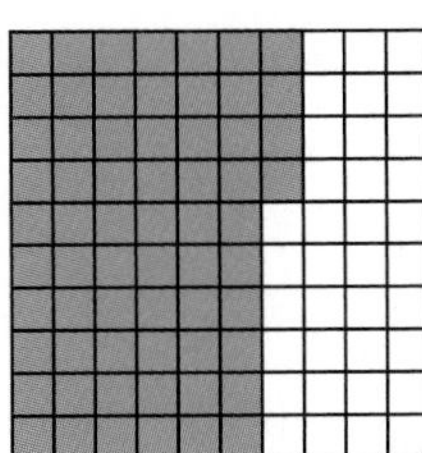

Write each fraction as a decimal. (Lesson 14-1)

3. $\frac{7}{10}$

4. $\frac{34}{100}$

Write as a fraction and as a decimal. (Lesson 14-1)

5. three fourths

6. one fifth

7. **STANDARDS PRACTICE** Which of the following is six and six hundredths? (Lesson 14-1)

A 0.66

B 6.06

C 6.6

D $6\frac{6}{10}$

Write each as a decimal. (Lesson 14-2)

8. $9\frac{1}{4}$

9. $10\frac{3}{5}$

10. $7\frac{1}{5}$

11. $2\frac{3}{4}$

Write each as a mixed number and decimal. (Lesson 14-2)

12. seven and three fourths

13. two and six tenths

14. **STANDARDS PRACTICE** Which number represents the shaded parts of the figure? (Lesson 14-2)

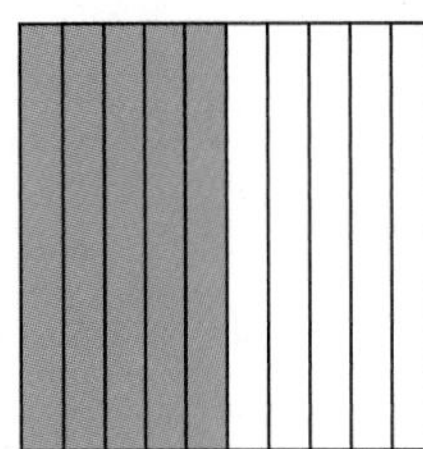

F 0.05

G 0.5

H 5.0

J 5.5

Solve. Use the *make a model* strategy. (Lesson 14-3)

15. Dasan has 18 coins. One half are nickels. One third are dimes. The rest are quarters. How much are Dasan's coins worth?

Compare. Write $>$, $<$, or $=$. (Lesson 14-4)

16. 3.7 ● 3.2

17. 13.09 ● 1.309

18. 6.4 ● 6.4

19. 13.09 ● 130.9

Order from greatest to least. (Lesson 14-4)

20. 1.2, 2.5, 1.9, 2.1

21. 0.32, 3.2, 1.31, 13.0

22. **WRITING IN MATH** Explain why $\frac{3}{10}$ and $\frac{30}{100}$ are equal.

14-5 Problem-Solving Investigation

MAIN IDEA I will choose the best strategy to solve a problem.

Standard 4MR1.1 **Analyze problems by identifying relationships, distinguishing relevant from irrelevant information, sequencing and prioritizing information, and observing patterns.** Standard 4NS3.0 **Students solve problems involving addition, subtraction, multiplication,** and division **of whole numbers** and understand the relationships among the operations.

P.S.I. TEAM +

SANDEEP: My father and I each ate $\frac{1}{4}$ of a pizza. My brother ate 1 more slice than I did and twice as many as my mother. She ate 2 slices.

YOUR MISSION: Find the number of slices of pizza Sandeep's family ate.

Understand	You know how much pizza each person ate. Find the total number of slices of pizza the family ate.
Plan	Use logical reasoning to determine the answer.
Solve	Start with what is known. • Mother: 2 slices • Brother: twice as much as his mother or $2 \times 2 = 4$ slices • Sandeep: 1 less slice than his brother or 3 slices • Father: 3 slices So, Sandeep's family ate $2 + 4 + 3 + 3 = 12$ slices of pizza.
Check	Look back at the problem. Sandeep and his father → $\frac{1}{4}$ of $12 = 3$ Sandeep's brother → $3 + 1 = 4$ Sandeep's mother → $4 \div 2 = 2$. $3 + 3 + 4 + 2 = 12$. So, the answer is correct.

Mixed Problem Solving

See page R36.

Use any strategy shown below to solve. Tell what strategy you used.

PROBLEM-SOLVING STRATEGIES
- Look for a pattern.
- Work a simpler problem.
- Use logical reasoning.
- Draw a picture.
- Make a model.

1. Gina cut an apple into 8 slices and ate 3 of them. Rudy cut an apple into 4 slices and ate 2 of them. If the apples were the same size, who ate more?

2. Sarah's dad gave her the money shown. He gave $7 to each of her two brothers. He had $16 left. How much money did Sarah's dad start with?

3. Craig paid $75 for a snowboard that he used 32 times. Diego paid twice as much as Craig but used his board 82 times. Who got a better deal per use? Explain.

4. Felicia is building a garden. The garden will have an area of 48 square feet. Give three possible dimensions in whole numbers.

5. What is the rule for the pattern shown? What number comes next?

   5, 13, 10, 18, 15, . . .

6. **Measurement** Adriano's driveway is rectangular in shape. The area of the driveway is 345 square feet. The length is shown. What is the width of the driveway?

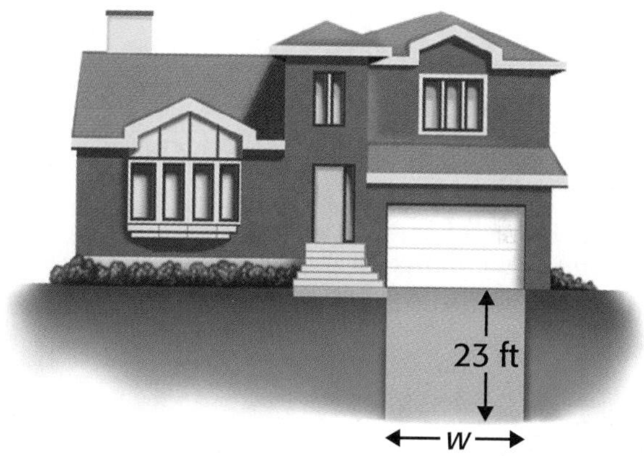

7. Paige and Mustafa were in a snow skiing competition. Paige earned a score of 88.6, while Mustafa earned a score of 88.59. Who won? Explain.

8. Alani started her homework at 4:25 P.M. She stopped at 5:15 P.M. to eat dinner. She started her work again at 5:50 P.M. She then worked another 15 minutes and finished. How many minutes did she do her homework?

9. **WRITING IN MATH** The sum of Roman and his younger sister's age together equals 24. Roman's age is twice the amount of his sister's. How old is Roman and his sister? Explain how you found your answer.

14-6 Fraction and Decimal Equivalents

GET READY to Learn

Nicole and Austin's family is driving to Eureka, California. Nicole says that the odometer shows they have driven 0.5 mile. Austin says $\frac{1}{2}$ mile. Can they both be correct?

MAIN IDEA

I will learn about fraction and decimal equivalents.

Standard 4NS1.6 Write tenths and hundredths in decimal and fraction notation and know the fraction and decimal equivalents for halves and fourths (e.g., $\frac{1}{2} = 0.5$ or 0.50; $\frac{7}{4} = \frac{13}{4} = 1.75$).

Standard 4NS1.7 Write the fraction represented by a drawing of parts of a figure; represent a given fraction by using drawings; **and relate a fraction to a simple decimal on a number line.**

New Vocabulary

decimal equivalent

When a fraction and a decimal name the same amount, they are fraction and **decimal equivalents**.

EXAMPLE Fraction and Decimal Equivalents

1 Determine whether 0.5 and $\frac{1}{2}$ are equivalent.

The models show that 0.5 and $\frac{1}{2}$ name the same amount.

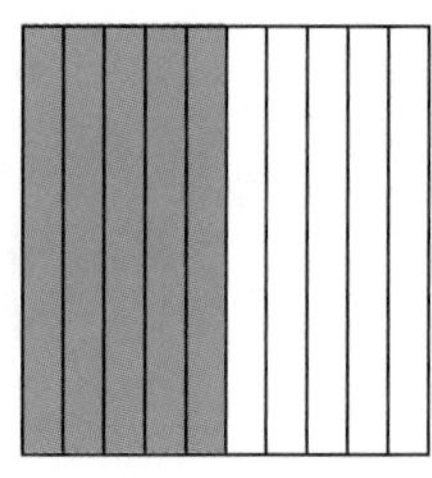

$0.5 = \frac{5}{10} = \frac{1}{2}$

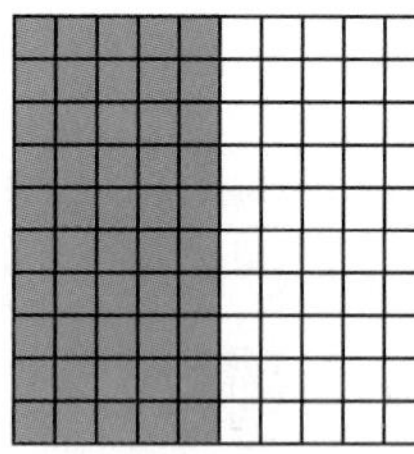

$0.50 = \frac{50}{100} = \frac{1}{2}$

The number lines also show that they name the same amount.

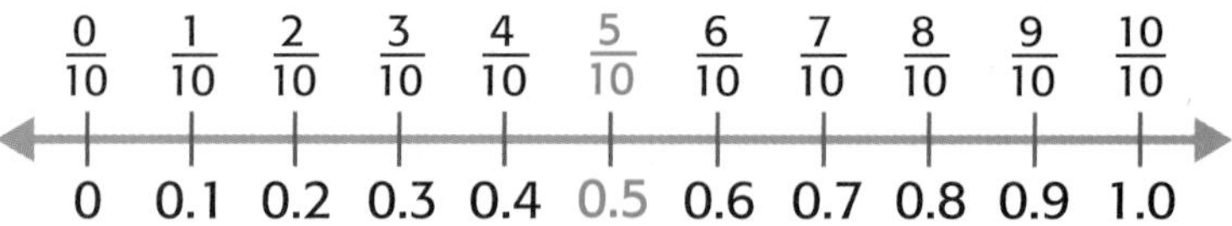

So, 0.5 and $\frac{1}{2}$ are equivalent.

To find a decimal that is equivalent to a fraction, it helps to write the fraction with a denominator of 10 or 100.

EXAMPLE Find Fraction and Decimal Equivalents

2 Write a fraction and decimal to describe the shaded part of the model.

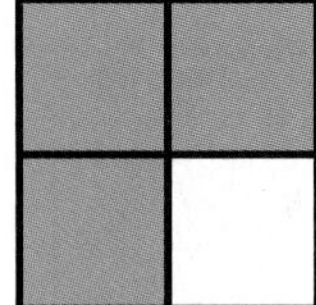

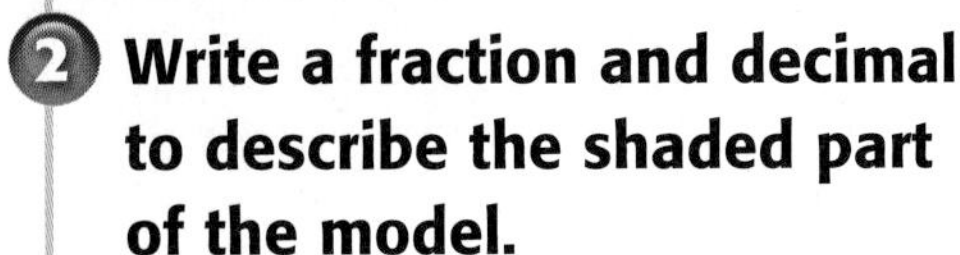

$\frac{3 \times 25}{4 \times 25} = \frac{75}{100}$ ← THINK What number can you multiply the denominator by to get 100?

$\frac{75}{100} = 0.75$ Write $\frac{75}{100}$ as a decimal.

So, $\frac{3}{4}$ and 0.75 describe the shaded part of the model.

Here are some common fraction and decimal equivalents.

KEY CONCEPT Fraction-Decimal Equivalents

$\frac{1}{2} = 0.5$	$\frac{1}{4} = 0.25$	$\frac{2}{4} = 0.5$	$\frac{3}{4} = 0.75$
$\frac{1}{5} = 0.2$	$\frac{2}{5} = 0.4$	$\frac{3}{5} = 0.6$	$\frac{4}{5} = 0.8$

CHECK What You Know

Write a fraction and decimal to describe the shaded part of each model. See Examples 1 and 2 (pp. 572–573)

1. 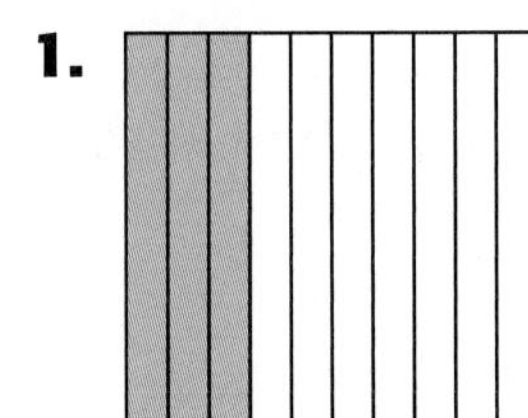

2. 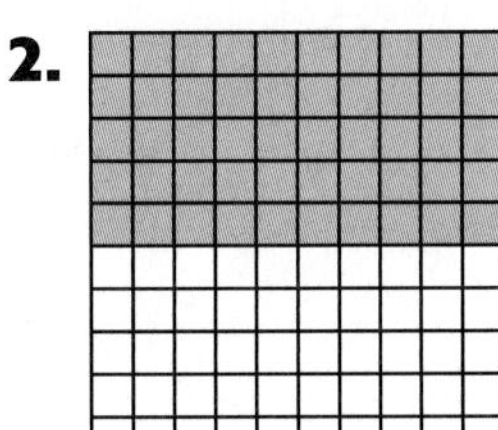

3. 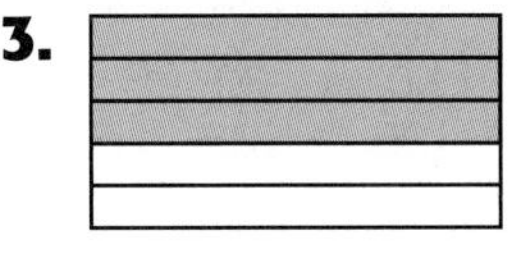

4. 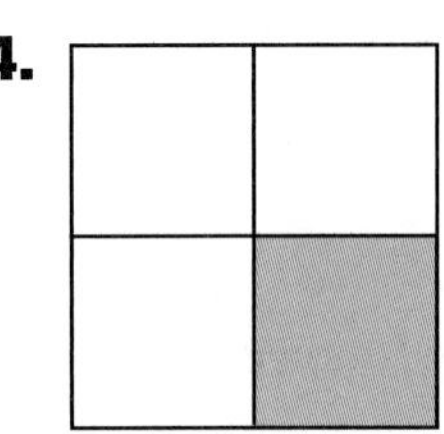

Write each fraction as a decimal. See Example 2 (p. 573)

5. $\frac{6}{10}$

6. $\frac{6}{100}$

7. $\frac{2}{4}$

8. $\frac{4}{5}$

9. Lupe got 20 out of 25 questions correct on a quiz. Write her score as a decimal and a fraction.

10. 

What do you notice about $\frac{3}{4}$, $\frac{6}{8}$, and $\frac{12}{16}$?

Practice and Problem Solving

See page R37.

Write a fraction and decimal to describe the shaded part of each model. See Examples 1 and 2 (pp. 572–573)

11. 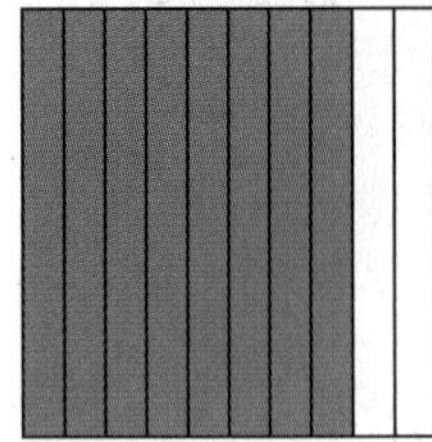

12. 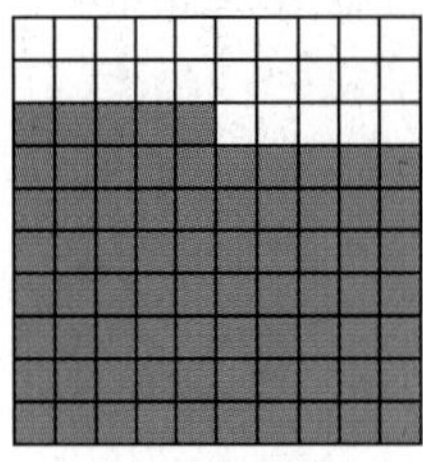

13. 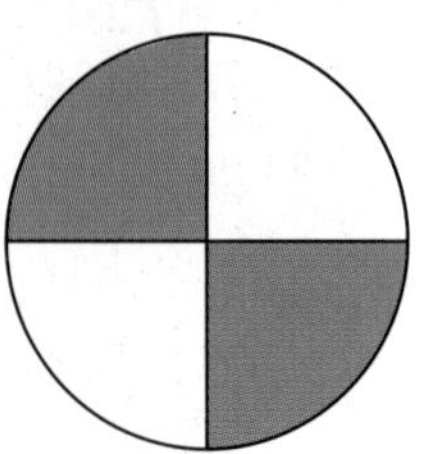

14. 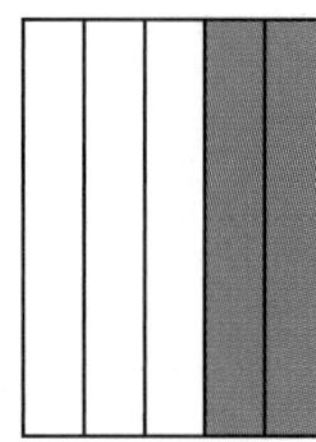

15. 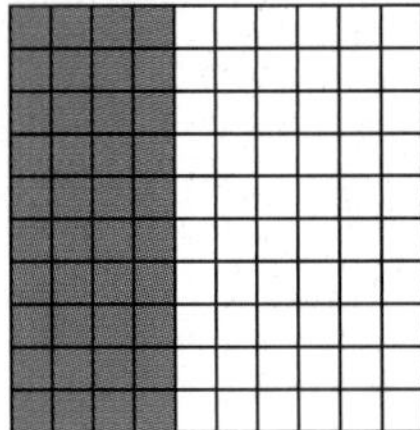

16. 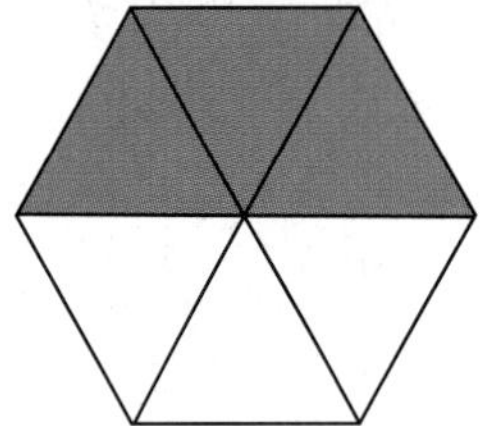

17. 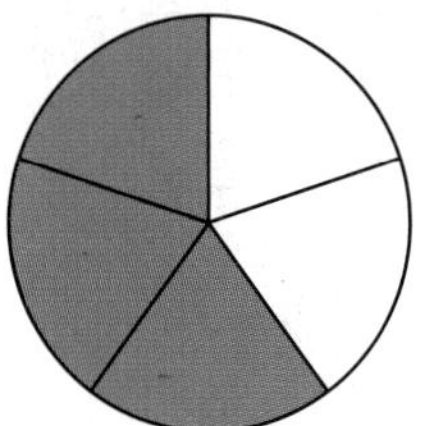

18. 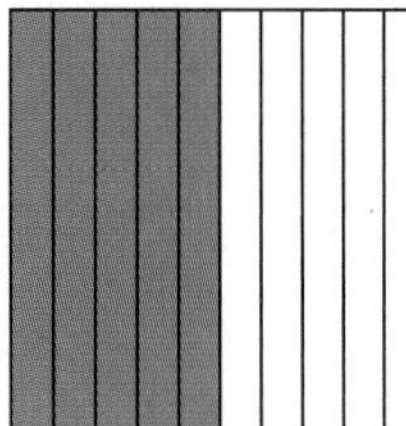

Write each fraction as a decimal. See Example 2 (p. 573)

19. $\frac{78}{100}$

20. $\frac{4}{10}$

21. $\frac{3}{5}$

22. $\frac{35}{100}$

23. $\frac{1}{4}$

24. $\frac{4}{5}$

25. $\frac{7}{25}$

26. $\frac{1}{10}$

Recreate the number line using decimal equivalents. See Example 1 (p. 572)

27. 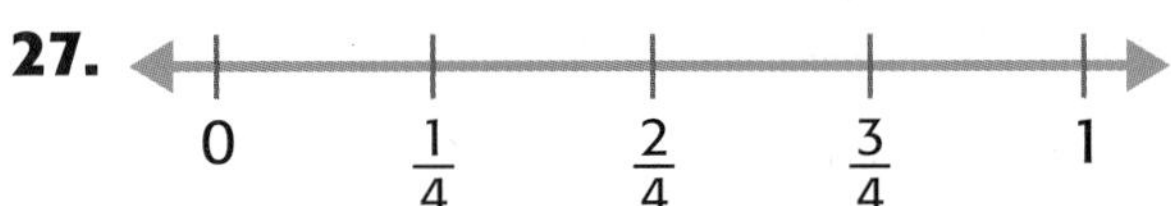

28. 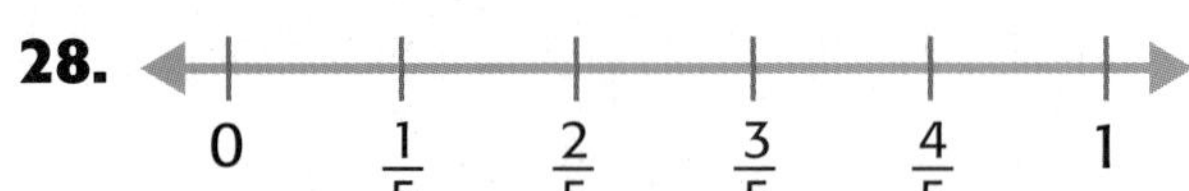

29. 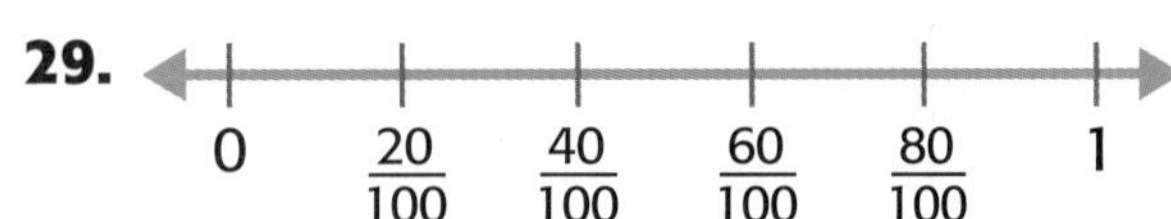

30. 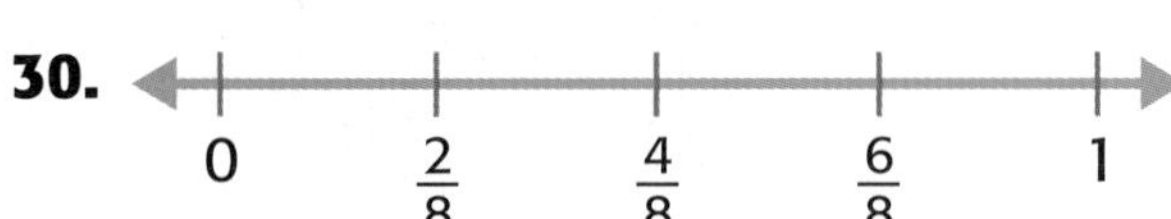

Write each amount as a fraction and a decimal.

31. **Measurement** Diana swam 3 out of 4 laps, which is almost a mile.

32. Vince read 6 out of 10 pages in a chapter of a book.

33. Robin ate 8 out of her 10 orange slices.

34. Cathy has completed 18 out of 20 math problems.

35. Maya has painted 1 out of 4 walls of her bedroom.

36. Jack has opened 3 out of 10 of his birthday presents.

H.O.T. Problems

37. OPEN ENDED Create a model and shade in a fraction of it. Write two fractions and a decimal to describe the shaded area of the model.

38. CHALLENGE Talia collects stuffed frogs. She has 25 frogs, and $\frac{2}{25}$ of them are multicolored. The rest are green. How many green frogs are in her collection? Explain how you found your answer.

39. WRITING IN MATH Leonardo is completing $0.\blacksquare = \frac{5}{50}$. Explain how he can find the correct answer.

Standards Practice

40 Look at the number line and detemine which order of numbers correctly shows the location of the points. (Lesson 14-4)

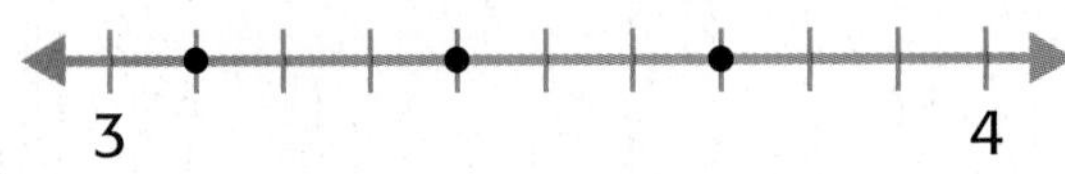

A 3.1, 3.3, $3\frac{7}{10}$

B 3.1, $3\frac{4}{10}$, 3.7

C 3.01, 3.04, $3\frac{7}{100}$

D $3\frac{1}{10}$, 3.1, $3\frac{4}{10}$

41 Which of the number sentences is false? (Lesson 14-6)

F $\frac{1}{4} = 0.25$

G $0.5 = \frac{4}{8}$

H $1.2 = 1\frac{1}{4}$

J $0.2 = 0.20$

Spiral Review

42. Elliott's age and his brother's age have a sum of 15. Elliott's age is twice as much as his brother's. How old are the boys? (Lesson 14-5)

Compare. Write >, <, or =. (Lesson 14-4)

43. 0.70 ● 0.07 **44.** 8.75 ● 8.7 **45.** 19.70 ● 19.7

Identify these quadrilaterals as square, rhombus, rectangle, parallelogram, or trapezoid. (Lesson 10-7)

46.

47.

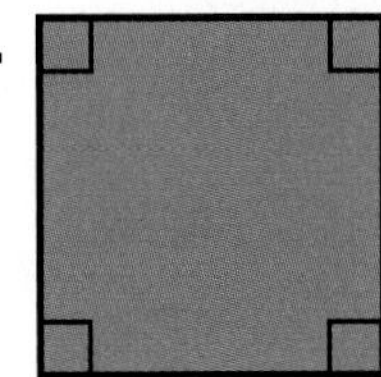

Estimate. Check your estimate. (Lesson 9-4)

48. 153 ÷ 3 **49.** 347 ÷ 5 **50.** 5,618 ÷ 8

Problem Solving in Music

Decimal Note-ation

Like numbers, musical notes are a universal language. Musical notes are based on fractions. The most common musical notes include whole, half, quarter, eighth, and sixteenth notes. These values represent the duration of the notes. The durations of the notes are not specific; they are relative to the other notes. For example, a one-eighth note is twice as long as a one-sixteenth note, a one-fourth note is twice as long as a one-eighth note, and so on.

Did You Know?

Beethoven was the first musician to use the one-hundred twenty-eighth note.

Standard 4NS1.6 Write tenths and hundredths in decimal and fraction notations and know the fraction and decimal equivalents for halves and fourths.

Musical Notes and Equivalent Fractions		
Note	**Notation**	**Fractional Equivalent**
Whole		$\frac{1}{1}$
Half		$\frac{1}{2}$
Quarter		$\frac{1}{4}$

Real-World Math

Use table above to answer each problem.

Write the value of each musical note as a decimal.

1.

2.

3. 

4. Refer to Exercises 1–3. Draw a number line that shows these values.

Write the value of each musical note as a mixed number. Then write each mixed number as a decimal.

5. 

6. 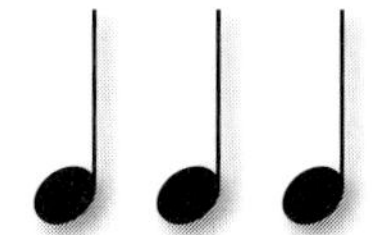

7. 

8. Draw three musical notes that represent a value of 2.5.

9. Draw four musical notes that represent a value of $2\frac{1}{4}$.

14-7 Decimals, Fractions, and Mixed Numbers

GET READY to Learn

The table shows the number of inches Walter has grown over four years. At what age did Walter grow the most inches? the fewest inches?

Walter's Change in Growth	
Age	**Growth (in.)**
7	2.5
8	$2\frac{1}{4}$
9	2.0
10	$2\frac{3}{4}$

MAIN IDEA

I will compare and order decimals, fractions, and mixed numbers.

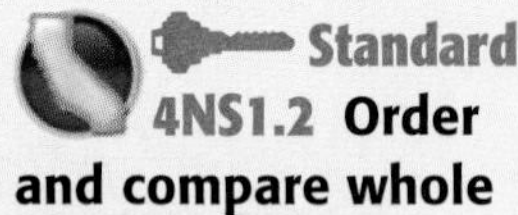

Standard 4NS1.2 Order and compare whole numbers and decimals to two decimal places.

Standard 4NS1.9 Identify on a number line the relative position of positive fractions, positive mixed numbers, and positive decimals to two decimal places.

To compare fractions and decimals, you can write the fractions as decimals and then compare.

Real-World EXAMPLE

1 MEASUREMENT At what age did Walter grow the most inches? the fewest inches?

Step 1 Write $2\frac{1}{4}$ and $2\frac{3}{4}$ as decimals.

$2\frac{1}{4} = 2.25$ $\quad\quad$ $2\frac{3}{4} = 2.75$

Step 2 Compare 2.5, $2\frac{1}{4}$, 2.0, and $2\frac{3}{4}$.

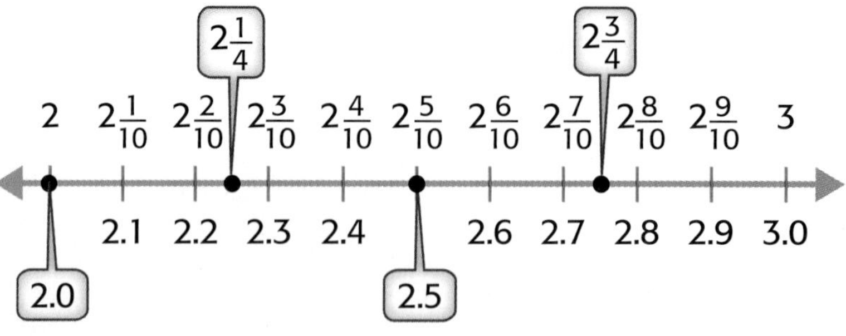

The order from greatest to least is $2\frac{3}{4}$, 2.5, $2\frac{1}{4}$, and 2.0.

So, Walter grew the most when he was 10 and the least when he was 9.

Online Personal Tutor at ca.gr4math.com

Use a number line to compare. Write <, >, or =. See Example 1 (p. 578)

1. 1.25 ● $1\frac{1}{4}$ **2.** 9.2 ● $9\frac{2}{10}$ **3.** $3\frac{3}{100}$ ● 3.3 **4.** 6.6 ● $6\frac{5}{10}$

Use a number line to order from greatest to least. See Example 1 (p. 578)

5. 6.34, $6\frac{1}{4}$, 6.5, $6\frac{21}{100}$ **6.** $6\frac{1}{5}$, 6.48, $6\frac{4}{10}$, 6.12

7. Which plant food produced a plant with highest growth? Explain.

Plant Food	Feed Me!	Magic Touch	Feed Booster	Garden Growth
Plant Growth (in.)	$3\frac{7}{10}$	3.1	$3\frac{1}{2}$	3.36

8. Talk About It Is the number sentence $5.5 = 5\frac{3}{6} = \frac{44}{8}$ true? Explain.

Practice and Problem Solving

EXTRA PRACTICE See page R37.

Use a number line to compare. Write <, >, or =. See Example 1 (p. 578)

9. 7 ● $6\frac{9}{10}$ **10.** 3.03 ● $3\frac{3}{100}$ **11.** $\frac{16}{4}$ ● 4 **12.** 8.2 ● 8

13. 5.3 ● 5.03 **14.** $4\frac{1}{10}$ ● 4.1 **15.** 12.5 ● $12\frac{2}{5}$ **16.** 15.36 ● 15.4

Use a number line to order from greatest to least. See Example 1 (p. 578)

17. $10\frac{1}{2}$, 10.9, $10\frac{36}{100}$, 10.75 **18.** 5.71, $5\frac{67}{100}$, $4\frac{5}{10}$, 4.75

19. $\frac{5}{10}$, $\frac{3}{4}$, 0.38, $\frac{25}{100}$, $\frac{1}{1}$ **20.** $\frac{4}{5}$, 2.25, $2\frac{3}{4}$, 2.77

Write the letter that represents each mixed number or decimal.
See Example 1 (p. 578)

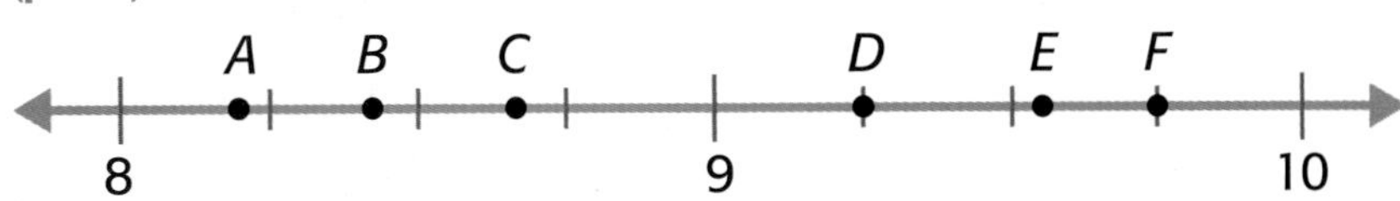

21. $9\frac{6}{10}$ **22.** 8.2 **23.** $8\frac{2}{5}$ **24.** $9\frac{1}{4}$

25. The table to the right shows the amount of rainfall Capitol City received during three months. Order the amounts of rain received from greatest to least.

Month	Rainfall (in.)
March	$2\frac{89}{100}$
April	3.25
May	$3\frac{2}{10}$

H.O.T. Problems

26. **FIND THE ERROR** Alicia and Leonardo are identifying the number point *C* represents. Who is correct? Explain.

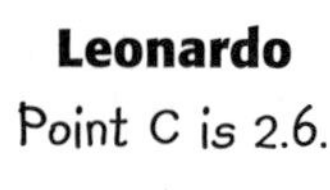

27. **WHICH ONE DOESN'T BELONG?** Identify the number that does not belong with the others. Explain.

three and five tenths	$3 + 0.5$	$3\frac{1}{2}$	3.05

Standards Practice

28 Which fraction means the same as 0.25? (Lesson 14-6)

A $\frac{2}{10}$

B $\frac{1}{4}$

C $\frac{2}{5}$

D $\frac{5}{10}$

29 Which letter represents the number closest to 3.6? (Lesson 14-7)

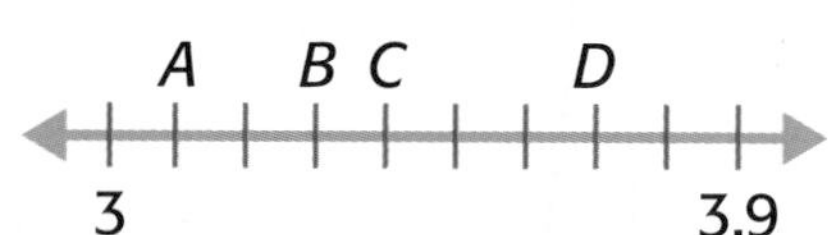

F *A*

G *B*

H *C*

J *D*

Spiral Review

Write each fraction as a decimal. (Lesson 14-6)

30. $\frac{4}{10}$

31. $\frac{35}{100}$

32. $\frac{4}{5}$

33. Enrico went to a movie. It started at 3:25 P.M. and lasted 135 minutes. What time was the movie over? (Lesson 14-5)

Order from greatest to least. (Lesson 14-4)

34. 1.5, 1.8, 1.2, 2.1

35. 3.2, 2.3, 3.23, 2.32

36. 7.8, 8.78, 7.88, 8.7

Math Online Self-Check Quiz at ca.gr4math.com

Fraction and Decimal Game

Compare Decimals to Fractions

Get Ready!

Players: 2

You Will Need: 10 index cards

Get Set!

On each index card, write a statement using >, <, or =. Write 5 true statements and 5 false statements. A few examples are shown to the right.

$0.25 < \frac{1}{3}$	$0.5 > \frac{10}{20}$
$0.75 = \frac{3}{4}$	$0.8 < \frac{75}{100}$

Go!

- Shuffle the cards.
- Spread out the cards face down on a desk.
- Player 1 turns over an index card and must say whether the statement is true or false.
- Player 1 keeps the card if the answer is correct, and draws again. If Player 1 is wrong, the index card is put back. Player 2 takes a turn.
- The player who collects the most cards, wins.

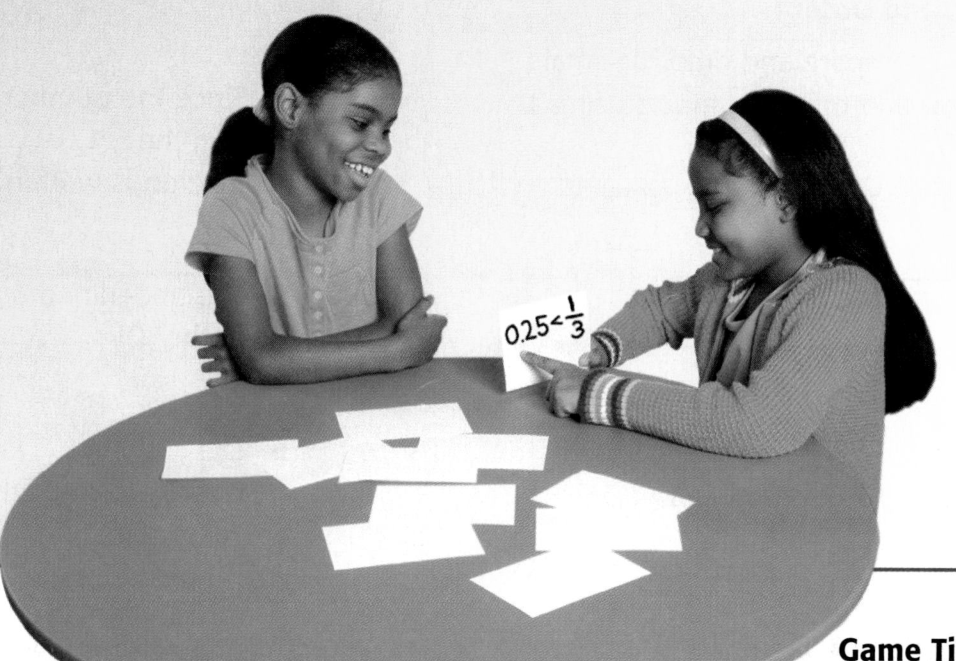

CHAPTER 14

Study Guide and Review

FOLDABLES Study Organizer GET READY to Study

Be sure the following Key Vocabulary words and Key Concepts are written in your Foldable.

BIG Ideas

Read, Write, and Model Decimals

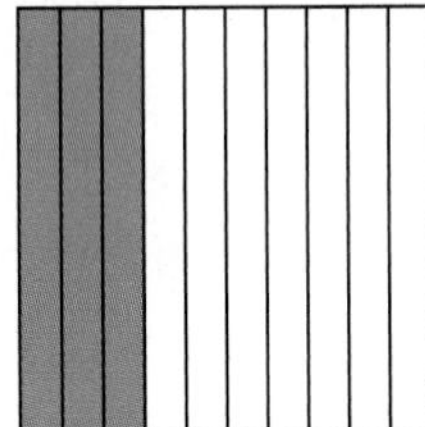

three tenths

$\frac{3}{10}$ or 0.3

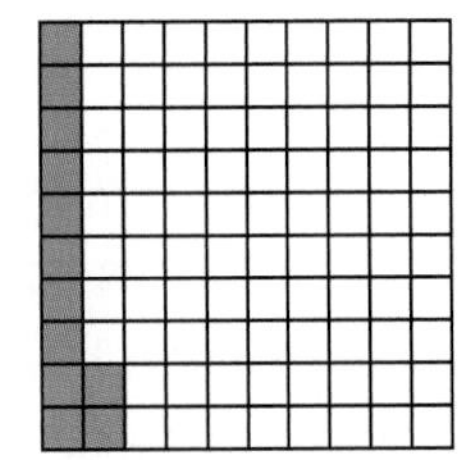

twelve hundredths

$\frac{12}{100}$ or 0.12

Compare and Order

- You can compare and order decimals, fractions, and mixed numbers using a number line.

$1\frac{25}{100} = 1.25$

$1\frac{3}{4} < 1.85$

Key Vocabulary

decimal (p. 557)
decimal point (p. 557)
hundredth (p. 558)
tenth (p. 558)

Vocabulary Check

Complete each sentence with the correct vocabulary word.

1. In 0.56, the ___?___ is between the 0 and 5.
2. A(n) ___?___ is a number that uses place value, numbers, and a decimal point to show part of a whole.
3. The underlined digit in 1.<u>3</u>6 is in the ___?___ place.
4. Since the number 0.36 has a 6 in the ___?___ place, the fraction is written as $\frac{36}{100}$.
5. The underlined digit in 0.4<u>2</u> is in the ___?___ place.
6. The ___?___ is always directly to the right of the ones place.

Math Online Vocabulary Review at ca.gr4math.com

Lesson-by-Lesson Review

14-1 Tenths and Hundredths (pp. 557–559)

Example 1

Write eight tenths as two different decimals.

Write tenths	Write Hundredths
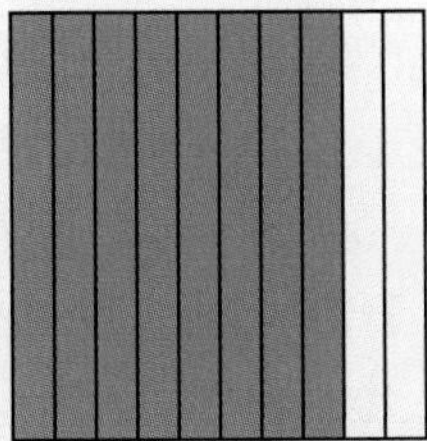	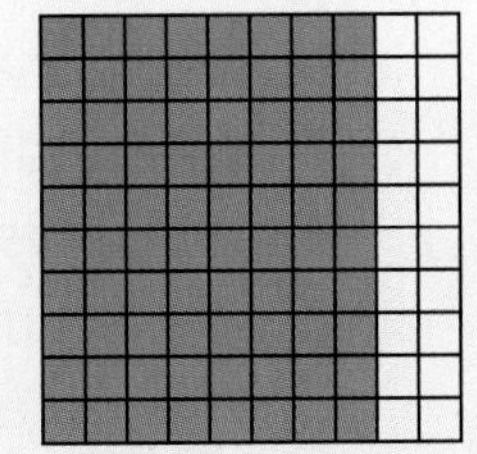
eight tenths 0.8	eighty hundredths 0.80

The decimals 0.8 and 0.80 are equivalent decimals.

7. Write a fraction and a decimal for the shaded part.

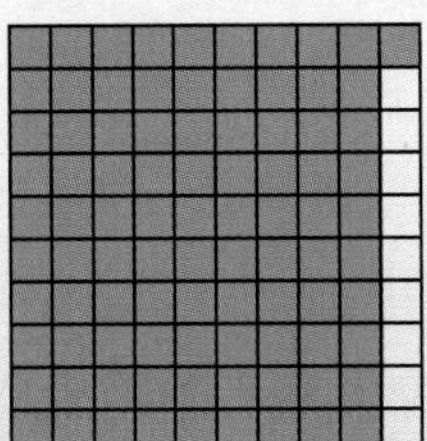

Write as a fraction and as a decimal.

8. three tenths

9. twenty-two hundredths

Write each fraction as two different decimals.

10. $\frac{1}{10}$ **11.** $\frac{60}{100}$

14-2 Relate Mixed Numbers and Decimals (pp. 560–563)

Example 2

Write $\frac{752}{100}$ as a decimal.

Hundreds	Tens	Ones	Tenths	Hundredths
		7.	5	2

Mixed Number $\frac{752}{100}$

Read seven and fifty-two hundredths

Write 7.52

Write each as a mixed number and decimal.

12. forty-six and seven tenths

13. fifty-one and three hundredths

Write each as a decimal.

14. $30\frac{3}{100}$ **15.** $7\frac{8}{10}$

16. A Burmese python is eight and twenty-three hundredths meters long. Write its length as a mixed number.

14-3 Problem-Solving Strategy: Make a Model (pp. 564–565)

Example 3
Leo jogged 3 miles from his home. Then he jogged back to his house to get his skateboard. He rode his skateboard for 2 miles. How far did Leo travel?

Understand

What facts do you know?
Leo jogged 3 miles and then jogged back to his house. He then rode his skateboard for 2 miles.

What do you need to find?
Find how far Leo traveled.

Plan You can draw a model.

Solve

3 miles

3 miles 2 miles

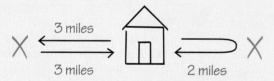

jogging route skateboard route

3 mi + 3 mi + 2 mi = 8 mi

So, Leo traveled 8 miles.

Check Look back at the problem.
Use multiplication to check.
(2 × 3) + 2
6 + 2
8

So, the answer is correct. ✓

17. There are 12 coins in a piggy bank that equal $2. What could be the coins?

18. Measurement Tía drew three squares. The first square is shown. The sides of the second square are twice as long as the sides of the first square. The sides of the third square are twice as long as the sides of the second square. Find the total perimeter of the squares.

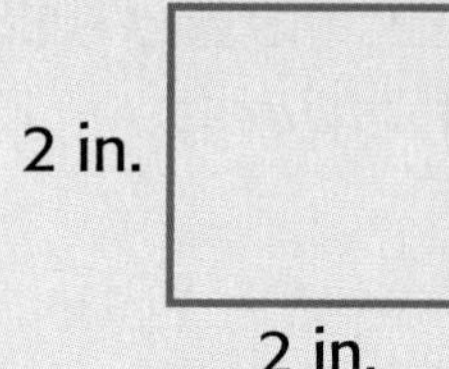

19. Raul paid $12.50 for a shirt and socks. The socks cost $1.75. How much was the shirt?

20. One fourth of 36 houses receive 1 newspaper each day. The rest of the houses receive 2 newspapers each day. How many newspapers are delivered each day?

21. Raven wants to arrange 18 square tables into one larger rectangular-shaped table with the least perimeter possible. How many tables will be in each row?

14-4 Compare and Order Decimals (pp. 566–568)

Example 4
Compare 7.26 and 7.62.

Hundreds	Tens	Ones	Tenths	Hundredths
		7	2	6
		7	6	2

Since the ones column has the same digits, compare the tenths place.

6 > 2. So, 7.62 > 7.26

Compare. Write >, <, or =.

22. 6.50 ● 6.5 **23.** 2.06 ● 2.05

24. 0.58 ● 0.59 **25.** 0.78 ● 0.87

Order from greatest to least.

26. 54.06, 54.6, 54.04, 54.4

27. 80.17, 80.2, 80.3, 80.36

28. 4.3, 4.25, 4.4, 4.56

29. India has 2.04 percent of the world's coral reefs and Fiji has 3.52 percent. Which country has a greater percentage of the world's coral reefs?

14-5 Problem-Solving Investigation: Choose a Strategy (pp. 570–571)

Example 5
What is the rule for the pattern 0, 3, 6, 9, 12, ■? What number comes next?

Each number is 3 more than the number before it.

0, 3, 6, 9, 12, ■
+3 +3 +3 +3

So, the rule is +3.

Use the rule, +3, to find the next number in the pattern. So, the next number in the pattern is 12 + 3 or 15.

Use any strategy to solve.

30. Steph is making a necklace with 15 beads. One third of the beads are red. The rest are black. How many are black?

31. Jonathan has a $20 bill. He buys a puzzle for $12.69. What will his change be?

32. Andrea pays the train fare of $2.75. What coins can Andrea use to pay for the fare using quarters, dimes, and nickels?

33. A biologist collected samples of bark from 258 trees. She took 4 samples from each tree. How many samples did she take in all?

Study Guide and Review

14-6 Fraction and Decimal Equivalents (pp. 572–575)

Write a fraction and decimal to describe the shaded area.

Example 6

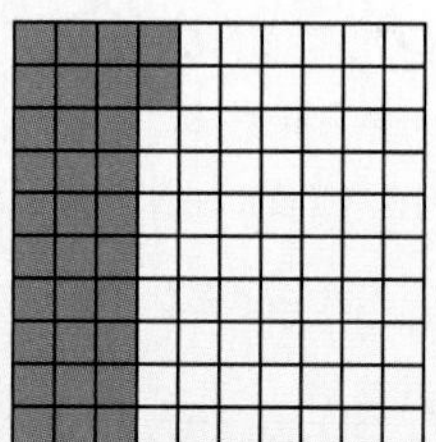

Thirty-two out of 100 squares are shaded. This is $\frac{32}{100}$ or 0.32.

Example 7

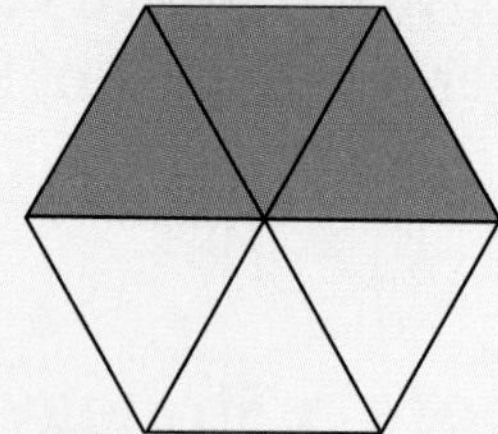

Three out of 6 triangles are shaded. This is $\frac{3}{6}$ or 0.5.

Write a fraction and decimal to describe the shaded area.

34.

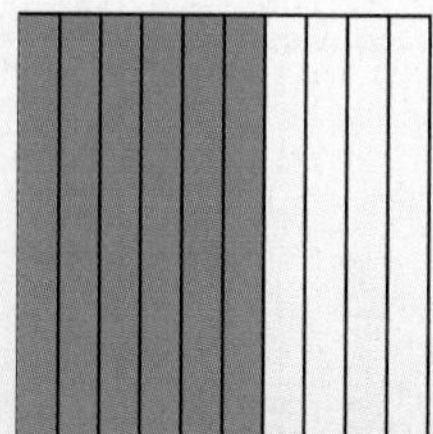

35.

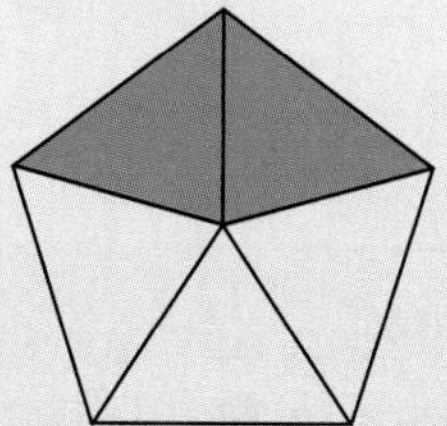

36. Della gave her brother part of a sandwich and said, "Here is your $\frac{1}{2}$ of the sandwich." Her brother said, "Actually, you ate $\frac{2}{4}$ of it." Who is correct? Explain.

14-7 Decimals, Fractions, and Mixed Numbers (pp. 578–581)

Example 8
Order 6.34, $6\frac{1}{4}$, 6.5, and $6\frac{21}{100}$ from greatest to least.

Write the fractions as decimals. Then, compare.

$6\frac{1}{4} = 6.25$ $\quad$ $6\frac{21}{100} = 6.21$

The order is 6.5, 6.34, $6\frac{1}{4}$, $6\frac{21}{100}$.

Order from greatest to least.

37. $9\frac{1}{2}$; 9.9; $9\frac{36}{100}$; 9.75

38. 54.71; $54\frac{67}{100}$; $5\frac{5}{10}$; 56.75

39. Some of the greatest distances ever jumped in a long-jump competition are $\frac{89}{10}$ meters, $\frac{895}{100}$ meters, 8.99 meters, and $\frac{896}{100}$ meters. Order these distances from greatest to least.

CHAPTER 14

Chapter Test

For Exercises 1 and 2, tell whether each statement is *true* or *false*.

1. To compare fractions and decimals, you can write the fractions as decimals and then compare.

2. Some decimals can be represented as more than one equivalent fraction.

Compare. Write <, >, or =.

3. 1.75 ● $1\frac{3}{4}$ **4.** $3\frac{2}{100}$ ● 3.2

5. Write a fraction and a decimal for the shaded part.

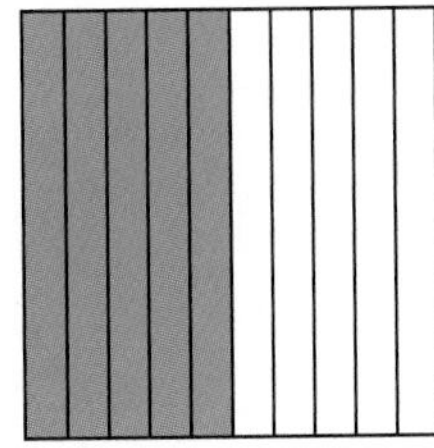

6. STANDARDS PRACTICE Which of the number sentences is false?

A $\frac{1}{4} = 0.25$ **C** $1.2 = 1\frac{1}{4}$

B $0.75 = \frac{6}{8}$ **D** $0.2 = 0.20$

7. A teacher is arranging 24 desks in a classroom in even rows. How many desks should be placed in each row so that the teacher has the smallest perimeter to walk around?

Write as a fraction and as a decimal.

8. nine tenths

9. twenty hundredths

Write each as a decimal.

10. $4\frac{7}{10}$ **11.** $18\frac{65}{100}$

Write a fraction and a decimal to describe the shaded part of the model.

12.

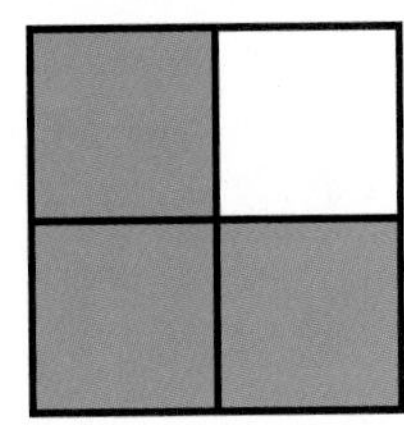

13.

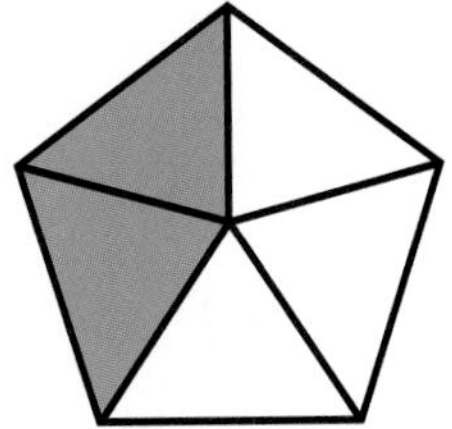

Order from greatest to least.

14. 7.8; 7.78; 8.78; 8.7

15. $\frac{3}{4}$; 2.25; $2\frac{3}{4}$; 1.75

16. 9.3; $9\frac{1}{4}$; $9\frac{3}{4}$; 9.5

17. STANDARDS PRACTICE Look at the number line. Which order of numbers correctly shows the location of the points?

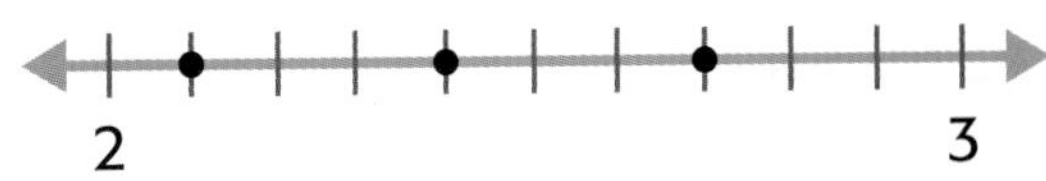

F 2.1, 2.2, $2\frac{7}{10}$ **H** 2.01, 2.04, $2\frac{7}{100}$

G 2.1, $2\frac{4}{10}$, 2.7 **J** $2\frac{1}{10}$, 2.1, $2\frac{4}{10}$

18. WRITING IN MATH Claire was given the following Exercise: $\frac{7}{10} = 0.\blacksquare$. Explain how you would find the correct answer.

CHAPTER 14 California Standards Practice

Cumulative, Chapters 1–14

Standards Example

On the number line below, what number does point *G* represent?

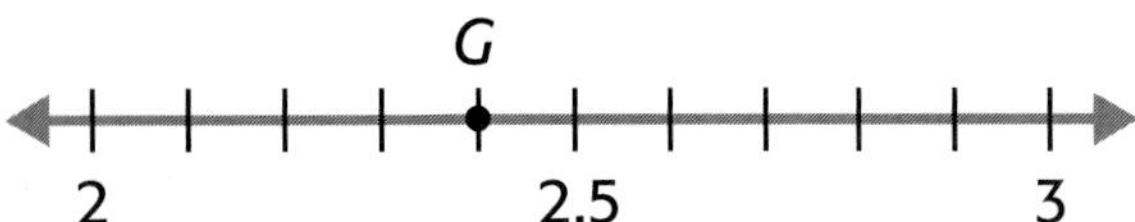

A 2.04 **C** 2.4

B 2.2 **D** 2.44

Read the Question

You need to find the number for point *G*.

Solve the Question

Look at the number line. There are 10 equal sections between 2 and 3. So, it is divided into tenths. Count to find the location of point *G*.

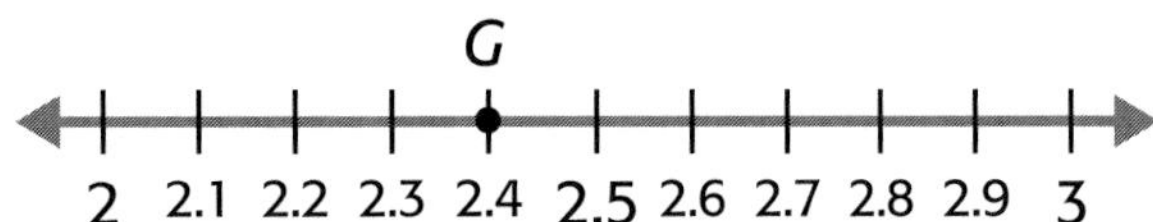

So, point *G* represents 2.4.
The answer is C.

Online Personal Tutor at ca.gr4math.com

Choose the best answer.

1 **On the number line below, what number does point *M* represent?**

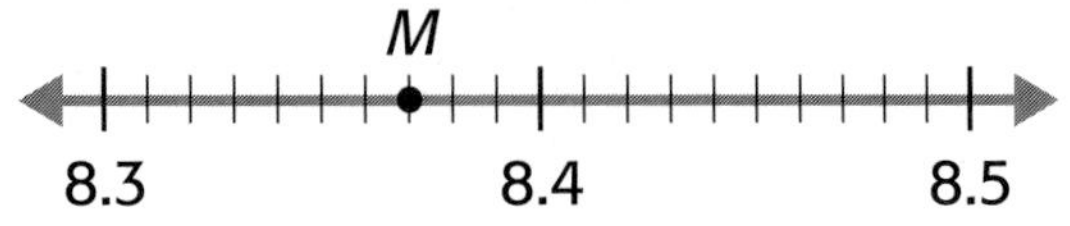

A 8.4 **C** 8.37

B 8.38 **D** 8.3

2 **Which decimal means the same as $\frac{3}{4}$?**

F 0.78

G 0.75

H 0.7

J 0.34

3 Which of the following has the greatest value?

A 11.5
B 5.11
C 1.15
D 0.51

4 Which decimal does the model show?

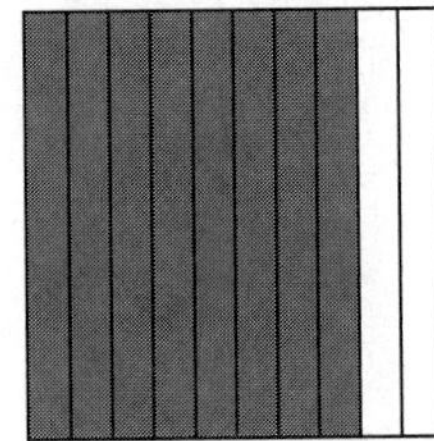

F 8
G 0.88
H 0.8
J 0.08

5 Which fraction means the same as 0.45?

A $\frac{1}{45}$
B $\frac{10}{45}$
C $\frac{45}{100}$
D $\frac{45}{10}$

6 Which list shows the decimals ordered from greatest to least?

Track Practice	
Runner	**Miles**
Andres	1.24
Kirk	1.5
Damon	1.31
Mauricio	1.45

F 1.24, 1.31, 1.45, 1.5
G 1.45, 1.5, 1.24, 1.31
H 1.31, 1.24, 1.5, 1.42
J 1.5, 1.45, 1.31, 1.24

7 Which fraction is equivalent to $\frac{3}{12}$?

A $\frac{1}{8}$
B $\frac{1}{6}$
C $\frac{1}{4}$
D $\frac{1}{3}$

8 The function table shows the input and output values for $y = 3x - 2$.

Rule: $y = 3x - 2$	
Input (x)	Output (y)
1	1
2	4
3	7
4	■

What is the missing value?

F 8
G 10
H 11
J 13

9 What is the value of the expression $(64 \div 8) \times (4 + 3)$?

A 8
B 56
C 63
D 108

10 Lena walks a dog for \$14 each walk. She walks the dog 4 times a week. How much does she earn in a week?

F \$40
G \$46
H \$56
J \$58

Decimals: Addition and Subtraction

BIG Idea How do I subtract decimals?

You can use models to subtract decimals.

Example One butterfly has a wingspan of 0.33 feet, and another has a wingspan of 0.25 feet. The model shows that the wingspan of the first butterfly is 0.33 − 0.25 or 0.08 feet longer than the other.

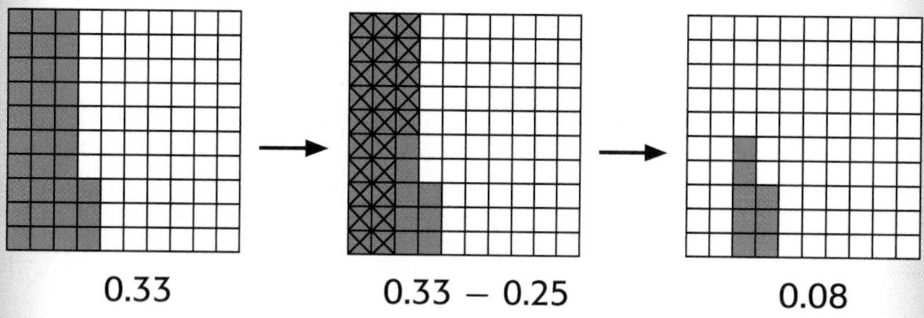

What will I learn in this chapter?

- Round decimals.
- Estimate decimal sums and differences.
- Add and subtract simple decimals.
- Solve problems by working backward.

Key Vocabulary

decimal

decimal point

estimate

sum

difference

Student Study Tools at ca.gr4math.com

FOLDABLES™
Study Organizer

Make this Foldable to help you organize information about decimals. Begin with one sheet of $8\frac{1}{2}'' \times 11''$ paper.

1. **Fold** the paper lengthwise about 3 inches from the bottom.

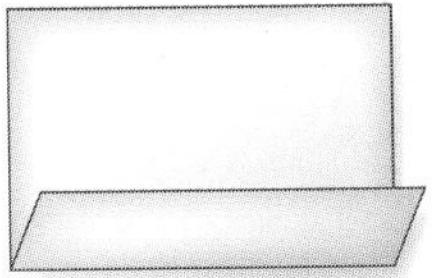

2. **Fold** the paper in thirds.

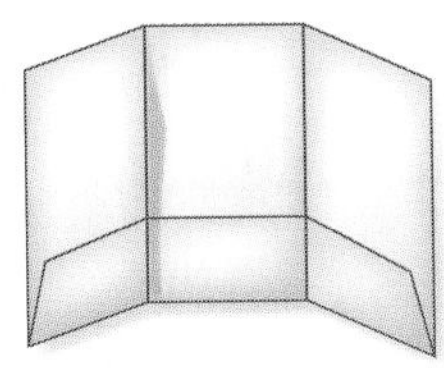

3. **Open** and staple the edges to form 3 pockets.

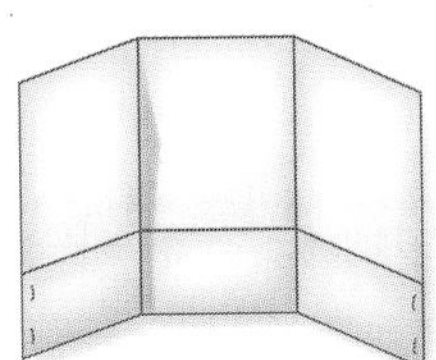

4. **Label** as shown. Place two index cards in each pocket.

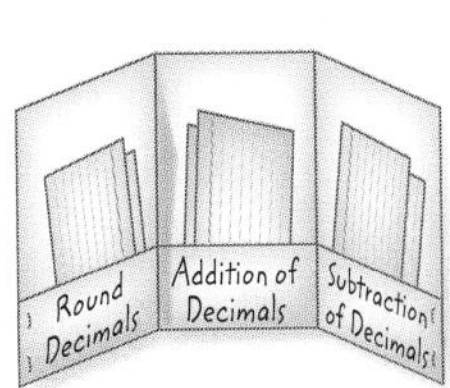

ARE YOU READY for Chapter 15?

You have two ways to check prerequisite skills for this chapter.

Option 2

Math Online Take the Chapter Readiness Quiz at ca.gr4math.com.

Option 1

Complete the Quick Check below.

QUICK Check

Round each number to the indicated place value. (Lesson 1-7)

1. 852; hundreds

2. 2,614; tens

3. 26,703; ten thousands

4. Farah has $1,363 in her bank account. To the nearest thousand, how much money does she have in her account?

Write a decimal for the shaded part of each figure. (Lesson 14-1)

5.

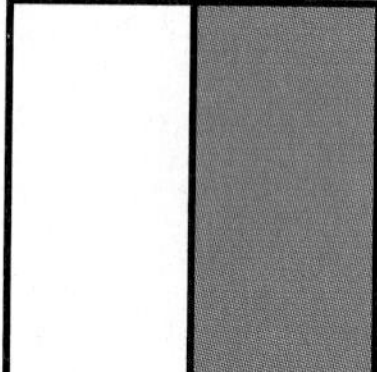

6.

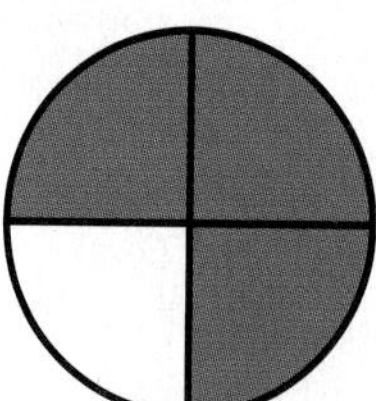

7.

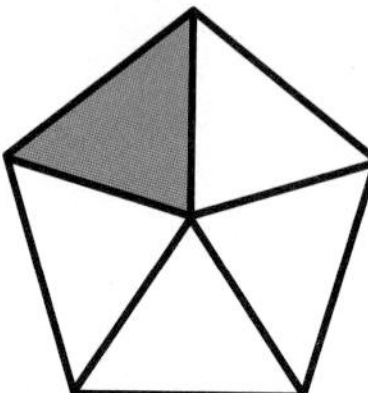

8. Tim ate part of the sandwich shown. Write a decimal to represent the amount of the sandwich Tim ate.

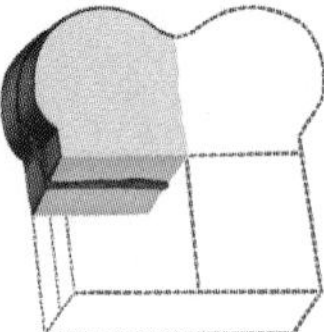

Graph each decimal on a number line. (Lesson 14-4)

9. 0.15

10. 0.38

11. 1.75

12. What decimal does the letter *D* represent?

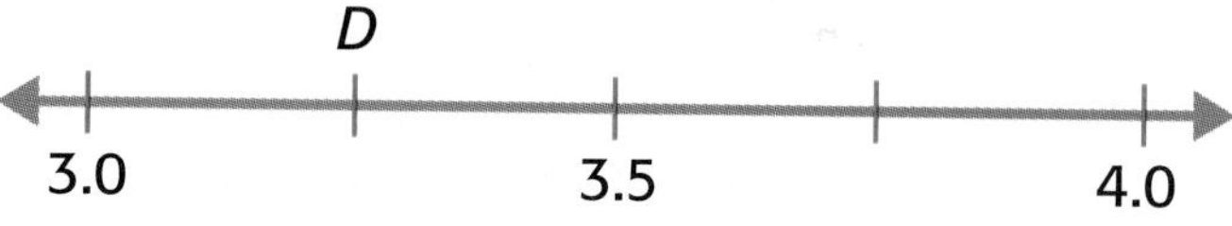

15-1 Round Decimals

MAIN IDEA

I will round decimals.

Standard 4NS2.2 **Round two-place decimals to one decimal or the nearest whole number and judge the reasonableness of the rounded answer.**

GET READY to Learn

Death Valley is a national park in California. Death Valley has 3.37 million acres of land. What is 3.37 rounded to the nearest whole number?

You can use a number line or rounding rules to round a two place decimal like 3.37.

Real-World EXAMPLE Round Decimals

1 **PARKS** **The land area of Death Valley is 3.37 million acres. Round 3.37 to the nearest whole number.**

One Way: Use a Number Line

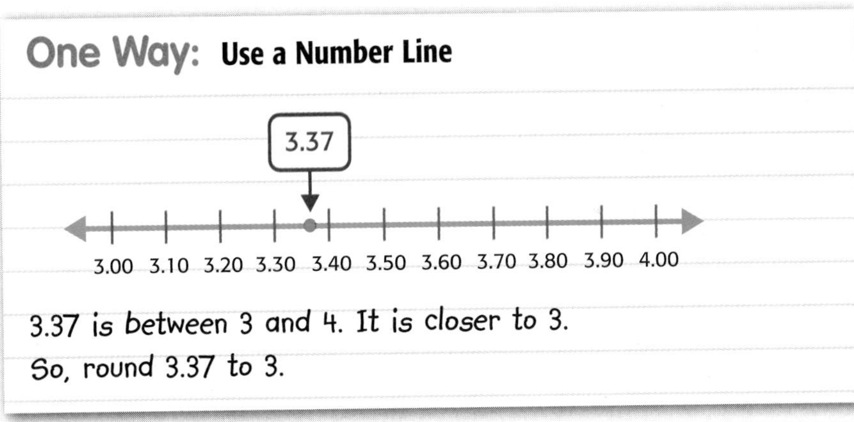

3.37 is between 3 and 4. It is closer to 3.
So, round 3.37 to 3.

Another Way: Use Rounding Rules

Use the same process that you use with rounding whole numbers.

Underline the digit to be rounded. In this case, the digit is in the ones place.

3.37

Then look at the digit to the right. Since 3 is less than 5, the digit 3 remains the same.

To the nearest whole number, 3.37 rounds to 3.

Review Vocabulary

decimal and **decimal point** A decimal is a number that uses place value and a decimal point to show part of a whole. **(Lesson 14-1)**

EXAMPLE Round Decimals

2 Round 38.52 to the nearest whole number.

Use the rounding rules.

Underline the digit to be rounded. In this case, the digit is in the ones place.

33.52

Then look at the digit to the right. Since that digit is 5, add one to the underlined digit

To the nearest whole number, 38.52 rounds to 39.

Real-World EXAMPLE Round Decimals

3 SPORTS During one golfing season, Tiger Woods had an average score of 68.41. Round this score to the nearest tenth.

Use the rounding rules.

Underline the digit to be rounded. In this case, the digit is in the tenths place.

68.41

Then look at the digit to the right. Since 1 is less than 5, the underlined digit remains the same.

To the nearest tenth, 68.41 rounds to 68.4.

Online **Personal Tutor at** ca.gr4math.com

CHECK What You Know

Round to the nearest whole number. See Examples 1 and 2 (pp. 593–594)

1. 3.24 **2.** 9.87 **3.** 36.61 **4.** 83.14

Round to the nearest tenth. See Example 3 (p. 594)

5. 4.13 **6.** 8.45 **7.** 25.94 **8.** 67.28

9. Measurement Use the table to round the length of each bird to the nearest tenth of a foot.

World's Smallest Birds

Bird	Length (feet)
Pygmy parrot	0.29
Bee hummingbird	0.20
Gouldian finch	0.33
New Zealand wren	0.29

10. Talk About It How is rounding decimals similar to rounding whole numbers? How is it different?

Practice and Problem Solving

EXTRA PRACTICE See page R37.

Round to the nearest whole number. See Examples 1 and 2 (pp. 593–594)

11. 1.54 **12.** 6.38 **13.** 31.72 **14.** 49.63

15. 54.37 **16.** 59.72 **17.** 64.26 **18.** 81.48

Round to the nearest tenth. See Example 3 (p. 594)

19. 2.58 **20.** 7.31 **21.** 37.54 **22.** 42.07

23. 55.70 **24.** 63.05 **25.** 79.49 **26.** 97.33

For Exercises 27 and 28, round to the nearest whole number.

27. One of the world's largest insects is a stick insect. It is 1.83 feet long. About how long is this insect?

28. Caley wants to buy a shirt for $22.53. About how much money will she need to buy the shirt?

29. One of the most valuable cars in the world is worth $2.29 million dollars. How much is this car worth to the nearest tenth?

30. **Measurement** Rebeca rounded the weights of various sports balls to the nearest whole number. Are her estimates reasonable? Explain.

Ball	Actual Weight (oz)	Estimate (oz)
Soccer	14.5	15
Tennis	2.1	2
Lacrosse	5.18	5

31. **Measurement** A city in the country of Peru receives only 0.09 inches of rainfall each year. Is it reasonable to say that the city receives about 1 inch of rain each year? Explain.

Real-World PROBLEM SOLVING

School Mr. Johnson is working on first quarter report cards. Use the table to the right to answer the questions.

Mr. Johnson's Class

Student	Grade
Angelo	92.52
Nara	88.27
Jena	85.46
Doug	76.81
Hoshi	84.53
Jodie	88.59

32. For Angelo to earn an A, he must achieve a 93 or above. Mr. Johnson rounds his students' grades to the nearest whole number. Will Angelo get an A? Explain.

33. To the nearest whole number, who earned a higher score, Nara or Jodie?

34. To the nearest whole number, which two students earned the same grade?

H.O.T. Problems

OPEN ENDED Give a reasonable rounded estimate for each decimal.

35. 23.81 pounds

36. 30.85 feet

37. 16.37 miles per gallon

CHALLENGE Round to the nearest tenth.

38. $1\frac{1}{4}$

39. $2\frac{3}{4}$

40. $4\frac{53}{100}$

41. **WRITING IN ▸MATH** Explain how to find the greatest decimal in tenths that rounds to 75. What is the decimal?

Standards Practice

42 Order the numbers shown from greatest to least. **(Lesson 14-7)**

A 2.46, $2\frac{1}{2}$, 2.64, $2\frac{1}{3}$

B 2.64, $2\frac{1}{2}$, $2\frac{1}{3}$, 2.46

C 2.64, $2\frac{1}{2}$, 2.46, $2\frac{1}{3}$

D $2\frac{1}{3}$, 2.46, $2\frac{1}{2}$, 2.64

43 The length of a vehicle is 205.83 inches. Find the total length to the nearest whole number. **(Lesson 15-1)**

F 200 inches

G 205 inches

H 206 inches

J 210 inches

Spiral Review

Use a number line to compare. Write <, >, or =. **(Lesson 14-7)**

44. 1.75 ● $1\frac{3}{4}$

45. $7\frac{6}{100}$ ● 7.6

46. 46.2 ● $46\frac{1}{4}$

Write a fraction and decimal to describe the shaded part of each model. **(Lesson 14-6)**

47.

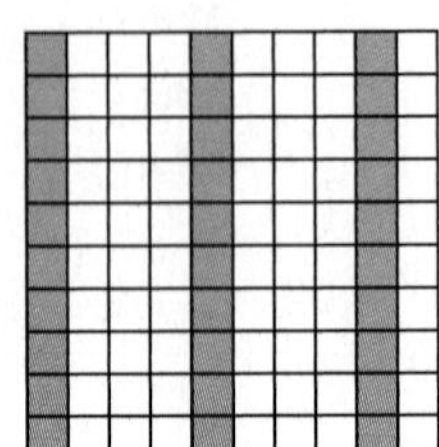

48.

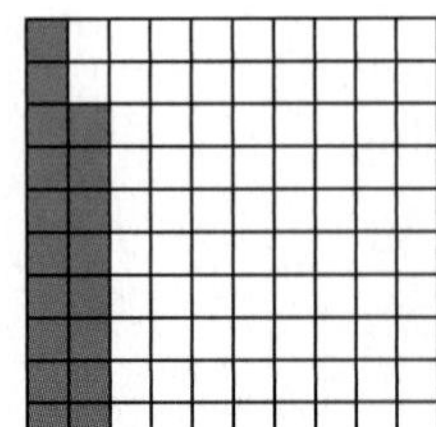

49.

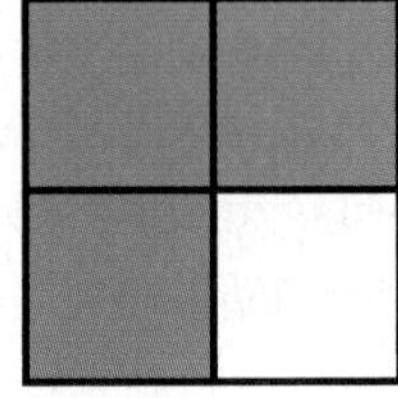

50. Alano, Sidney, and Tasha play instruments. Each student plays either the flute, the violin, or the cello. Sidney does not play the violin or the cello. Alano does not play the cello. What instruments do Alano, Sidney, and Tasha play? **(Lesson 12-3)**

Match Up

Round Decimals

You will need: 10 index cards

0.13	0.1	38.54	38.5
0.15	0.2	38.56	38.6
2.14	2.4	2.46	2.5
8.73	8.7	8.77	8.8
12.31	12.3	12.35	12.4

Get Ready!

Players: 2 players

Get Set!

Cut each index card in half. Then label each card with one decimal as shown.

Go!

- Shuffle the cards. Then spread the cards out face down.
- Player 1 turns over two cards.
- If one decimal equals the other decimal after being rounded to the tenths place, Player 1 keeps the cards. Player 1 continues by choosing two more cards.
- If one decimal does not equal the other decimal after being rounded to the tenths place, the cards are turned over and Player 2 takes a turn.
- Continue playing until all matches are made. The player with the most cards wins.

15-2 Estimate Decimal Sums and Differences

GET READY to Learn

MAIN IDEA

I will use rounding to estimate sums and differences.

Standard 4NS2.1 Estimate and compute the sum or difference of whole numbers and positive decimals to two places.

Martina is going white water rafting with her family. During their first day, they will travel 6.5 miles before lunch and 8.75 miles after lunch. About how far will they travel on their first day?

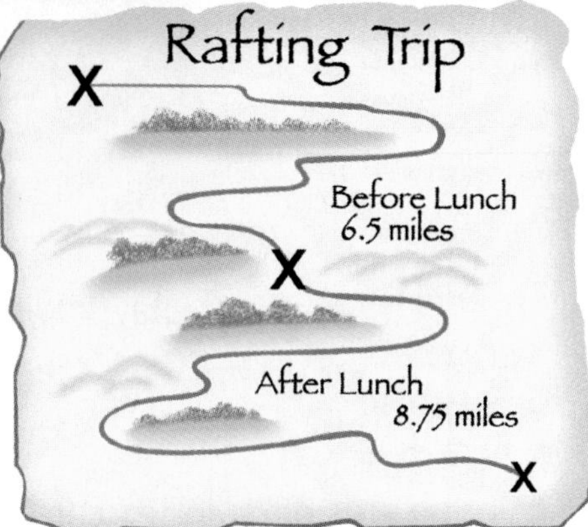

To estimate the sum of decimals, you can round each decimal to the nearest whole number and then add.

Review Vocabulary

estimate when you do not need an exact answer you can estimate **(Lesson 1-6)**

KEY CONCEPT — Estimate Decimal Sums

Words To estimate the sum of two or more decimals, round each decimal to the nearest whole number. Then add.

Example

$7.85	⟶	$8
+ $4.20	⟶	+ $4
		$12

Real-World EXAMPLE — Estimate Sums

1 TRAVEL About how far will Martina and her family travel on their first day?

You need to estimate 6.5 + 8.75.

Round each addend to the nearest whole number. Then add.

6.50	⟶	7	Round 6.50 to 7.
+ 8.75	⟶	+ 9	Round 8.75 to 9.

So, Martina and her family will travel about 16 miles.

Remember

When rounding to the nearest whole number, think about the whole number that comes before and after the number to be rounded.

KEY CONCEPT Estimate Decimal Differences

Words To estimate the difference of two decimals, round each decimal to the nearest whole number. Then subtract.

Example

$$\begin{array}{r} \$28.75 \\ -\ \$13.49 \\ \hline \end{array} \longrightarrow \begin{array}{r} \$29 \\ -\ \$13 \\ \hline \$16 \end{array}$$

Real-World EXAMPLE Estimate Differences

2 **Neela wants to buy a cell phone that costs \$37.99. She has \$45.25. About how much money will she have left to buy ring tones after she buys the phone?**

Estimate \$45.25 − \$37.99.

Round each decimal to the nearest whole number. Then subtract.

$$\begin{array}{r} \$45.25 \\ -\ \$37.99 \\ \hline \end{array} \longrightarrow \begin{array}{r} \$45 \\ -\ \$38 \\ \hline \end{array}$$

Round \$45.25 to \$45.
Round \$37.99 to \$38.

$$\begin{array}{r} \overset{3\,15}{\$4\!\!\!/\,5\!\!\!/} \\ -\ \$38 \\ \hline \$\ 7 \end{array}$$

So, Neela will have about \$7 left to buy ring tones.

 **Personal Tutor at** ca.gr4math.com

CHECK What You Know

Estimate. Round to the nearest whole number. **See Examples 1 and 2 (pp. 598–599)**

1. $\begin{array}{r} 1.5 \\ +\ 2.3 \\ \hline \end{array}$

2. $\begin{array}{r} 5.4 \\ -\ 3.61 \\ \hline \end{array}$

3. $\begin{array}{r} 24.9 \\ +\ 9.8 \\ \hline \end{array}$

4. 62.8 − 9.5

5. \$8.75 + \$3.25

6. 46.37 − 7.3

7. Hakan is running in a charity race that is 3.12 miles long. Hakan has run 1.2 miles so far. About how many miles does he have left to run?

8. **Talk About It** Explain how you could use estimation to find a reasonable sum for 2.1 and 3.3.

Practice and Problem Solving

EXTRA PRACTICE
See page R38.

Estimate. Round to the nearest whole number. See Examples 1 and 2 (pp. 598–599)

9. 2.5 + 4.8

10. 9.8 + 8.2

11. 8.5 + 11.7

12. 19.6 + 2.4

13. \$17.50 + \$6.25

14. 28.49 + 12.83

15. 9.7 − 7.2

16. 5.2 − 4.6

17. 34.5 − 5.4

18. 29.7 − 8.9

19. \$49.54 − \$25.15

20. \$78.29 − \$39.85

Algebra Estimate by rounding to the nearest whole number. Then compare. Use >, <, or =.

21. 18.34 + 3.67 ● 12.29 + 7.95

22. 14.58 − 6.91 ● 21.62 − 12.19

23. The hawk moth is the fastest flying insect. It can fly up to 33.3 miles per hour. A hornet can fly up to 13.3 miles per hour. About how much faster can the moth fly than the hornet?

24. Amit is buying some action figures for \$12.29. He is also buying a pack of trading cards for \$1.25. If he pays with a 20 dollar bill, about how much change will he get back?

25. Oscar is 4.3 feet tall. The giant ragwood plant is 8.9 feet tall. Is 8 – 4 a reasonable estimate of the difference in Oscar's and the plant's height to the nearest whole number? Explain.

26. On Monday, Paco ran one mile in 7.58 minutes. On Tuesday, he ran one mile in 8.23 minutes. Is 7.6 + 8.2 a reasonable estimate of the combined times to the nearest tenth? Explain.

Real-World PROBLEM SOLVING

Science The table to the right shows the speeds in which planets travel during their orbits, or trips around the sun.

Orbital Speeds of Planets

Planet	Speed (miles per second)
Mercury	29.75
Venus	21.76
Earth	18.51
Mars	14.51
Jupiter	8.12

27. To the nearest whole number, what is the difference between the fastest and slowest orbital speeds of the planets listed?

28. About how much faster does Mercury travel than Earth?

29. Earth's orbital speed is faster than two other planets on the table. About how much faster does Earth travel than each of these planets?

H.O.T. Problems

30. OPEN ENDED Write an addition and a subtraction problem that involves decimals and results in an estimated answer of $12?

31. CHALLENGE Estimate 32.4 + 21.5 + 17.95 to the nearest whole number.

32. WRITING IN ▸MATH Explain how you would estimate the difference of 9 and 5.52.

Standards Practice

33 The deepest plant root is 393.7 feet deep. What is the depth of the root rounded to the nearest whole number? **(Lesson 15-1)**

A 300 feet

B 390 feet

C 394 feet

D 400 feet

34 On Friday, Noah drove 166.5 miles. On Saturday, he drove 68.4 miles. On Sunday, he drove 72.75 miles. Approximately how many miles did Noah drive in three days? **(Lesson 15-2)**

F 200 miles

G 210 miles

H 300 miles

J 310 miles

Spiral Review

Round to the nearest whole number. **(Lesson 15-1)**

35. 28.5

36. 43.4

37. 84.2

Use a number line to compare. Write >, <, or =. **(Lesson 14-7)**

38. $3 \bullet 2\frac{7}{10}$

39. $7.03 \bullet 7\frac{3}{100}$

40. $\frac{25}{5} \bullet 5$

41. Identify a pattern in the shapes at the right. Continue the pattern by drawing the next four shapes. **(Lesson 10-3)**

42. Algebra The table shows a pattern. Identify the rule. Then find the missing numbers. **(Lesson 10-3)**

Rule: ■				
Input	3	4	5	■
Output	7	9	■	13

15-3 Problem-Solving Strategy

MAIN IDEA I will solve problems by working backward.

Standard 4MR1.1 Analyze problems by identifying relationships, distinguishing relevant from irrelevant information, sequencing and prioritizing information, and observing patterns. Standard 4NS3.1 Demonstrate an understanding of, and the ability to use, standard algorithms for the addition and subtraction of multidigit numbers.

Rey has lacrosse practice in the evenings. He gets home from school and eats a snack for 15 minutes. Then he spends 1 hour doing his homework. It takes him 15 minutes to get to practice. Practice is at 5 P.M. What time does Rey get home from school?

Understand

What facts do you know?

- Rey eats a snack for 15 minutes.
- He works on homework for 1 hour.
- It takes 15 minutes to get to practice at 5 P.M.

What do you need to find?

- What time Rey gets home from school.

Plan

Work backward to solve the problem.

Solve

Start with the end result. Then work backward one step at a time.

5 P.M. − 15 minutes = 4:45 P.M.
(practice starts) (time to get to practice)

4:45 P.M. − 1 hour = 3:45 P.M.
(homework)

3:45 P.M. − 15 minutes = 3:30 P.M.
(time spent eating)

So, Rey got home from school at 3:30 P.M.

Check

Look back at the problem.
15 minutes + 1 hour + 15 minutes = 1 hour and 30 minutes.
He gets home at 3:30 P.M. One hour and 30 minutes later is 5 P.M.
The answer is correct.

ANALYZE the Strategy

Refer to the problem on the previous page.

1. Explain why 15 minutes was subtracted from 5 P.M. in the first step of solving the problem.

2. Suppose practice started at 4:30 P.M. What time would Rey get home from school?

3. Suppose it takes Rey 45 minutes to complete his homework. What time would he get home from school?

4. Look back to Exercise 3. Check your answer. How do you know it is correct? Explain.

PRACTICE the Strategy

See page R38.

Solve. Use the work backward strategy.

5. Debbie bought a movie ticket. She then let her friend borrow $3. She now has $7. How much money did she have originally?

6. Adrian volunteers at an animal shelter. It takes him 20 minutes to walk each dog shown. It takes him 15 minutes to give each dog a bath. He finished walking and bathing the dogs at 6 P.M. What time did he start?

7. A number is multiplied by 3. Next, 8 is subtracted from the product. Then, the difference is divided by 4. The result is 7. What is the number?

8. Susana jogs a mile in 8 minutes. She warms up for 10 minutes. She stretches for 5 minutes after she jogs. She jogs 2 miles, including warming up and stretching. She finishes at 8 A.M. What time does she start?

9. Nadina has two times as many pennies as dimes. The number of quarters she has is shown below. She has 4 more dimes than quarters. How much money does she have?

10. A number is divided by 3. Next, 25 is added to the quotient. Then, the sum is multiplied by 4. The result is 116. What is the number?

11. **WRITING IN ▶MATH** Explain how you used the *work backward* strategy to solve Exercise 10.

Math Activity for 15-4
Addition of Decimals

MAIN IDEA

I will use models to add decimals.

Standard 4NS2.1 Estimate and **compute the sum** or difference **of whole numbers and positive decimals to two places.**

Standard 4MR2.3 Use a variety of methods such as words, numbers, symbols, charts, graphs, tables, diagrams, and **models, to explain mathematical reasoning.**

You Will Need
grid paper
colored pencils

Animation
ca.gr4math.com

You can use grid paper to explore adding decimals.

ACTIVITY

Use models to add decimals. Find 1.5 + 0.29.

Step 1 **Model 1.5.**

To show 1.5, shade one whole 10-by-10 grid and $\frac{5}{10}$ or $\frac{50}{100}$ of a second grid.

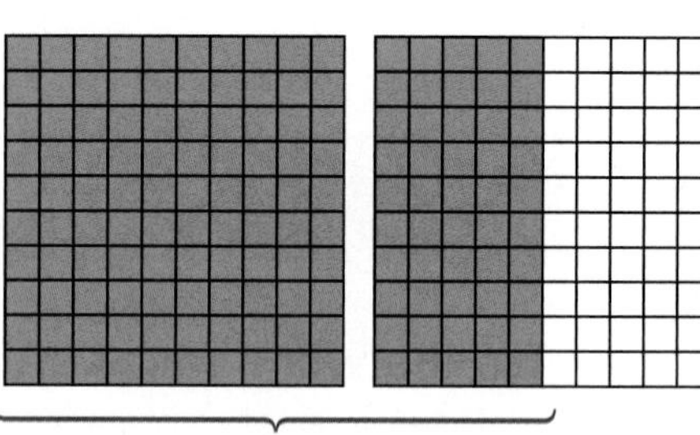

Step 2 **Model 0.29.**

To show 0.29, shade $\frac{29}{100}$ of the second grid using a different color.

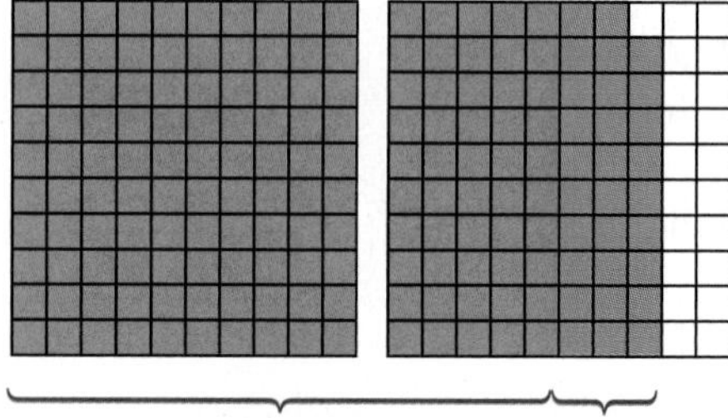

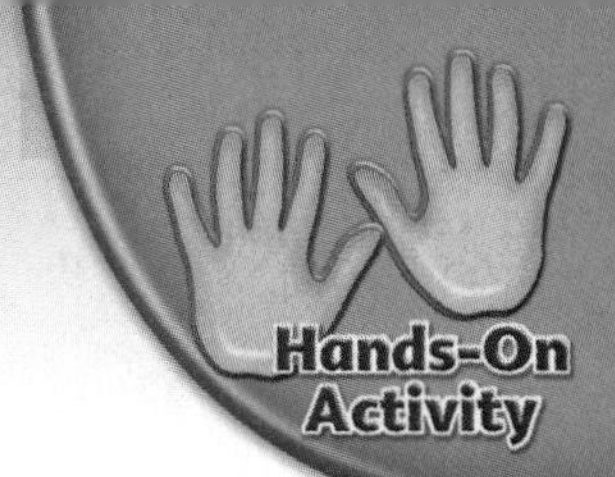

Step 3 **Add the decimals.**

Count the total number of shaded squares. Write as a decimal.

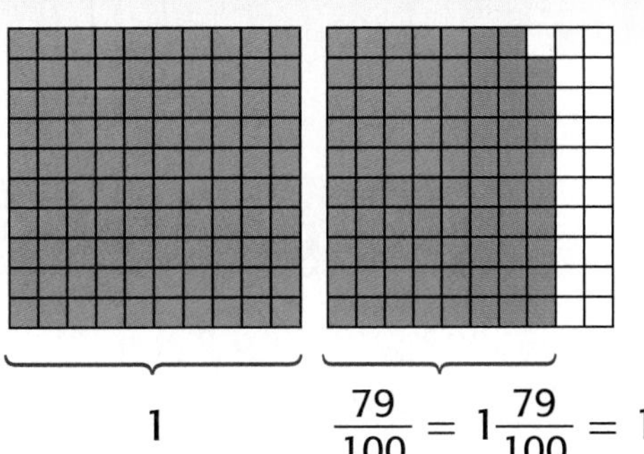

$1 \quad \frac{79}{100} = 1\frac{79}{100} = 1.79$

Think About It

1. Why did you draw two 10-by-10 grids to show 1.5?
2. Why did you shade 50 squares of the second grid?
3. Why did you shade 29 squares of the second grid?
4. How did you find the sum of the decimals?

CHECK What You Know

Add. Use the models.

5. 1.15 + 0.57

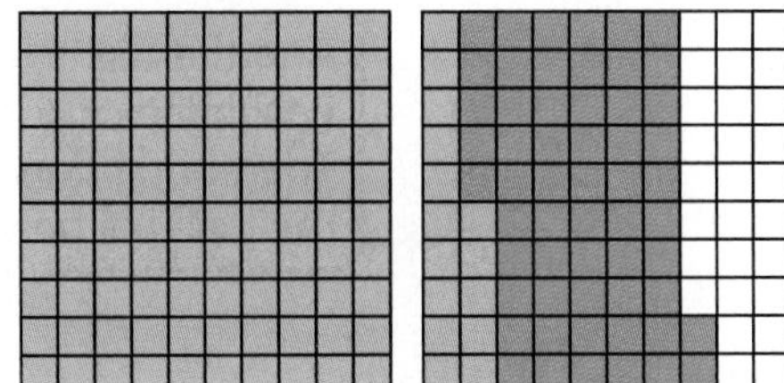

6. 0.25 + 0.46

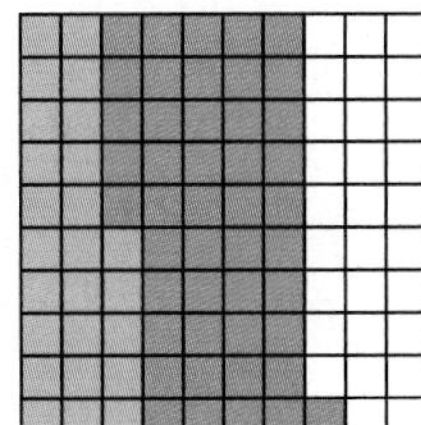

Add. Use models if needed.

7. $\begin{array}{r} 0.45 \\ +\ 0.30 \\ \hline \end{array}$

8. $\begin{array}{r} 0.16 \\ +\ 0.58 \\ \hline \end{array}$

9. $\begin{array}{r} 1.12 \\ +\ 1.50 \\ \hline \end{array}$

10. $\begin{array}{r} 0.19 \\ +\ 1.62 \\ \hline \end{array}$

11. $\begin{array}{r} 1.09 \\ +\ 1.58 \\ \hline \end{array}$

12. $\begin{array}{r} 1.42 \\ +\ 0.26 \\ \hline \end{array}$

13. 0.44 + 1.39

14. 1.28 + 2.10

15. 2.05 + 1.9

16. WRITING IN ▸MATH Write the steps to use to find 2.34 + 1.76.

15-4 Add Decimals

GET READY to Learn

Darlene practiced the flute 1.5 hours on Saturday. On Sunday, she practiced 2.33 hours. How long did she practice during the two days?

MAIN IDEA

I will add decimals.

Standard 4NS2.1 Estimate and compute the sum or difference **of whole numbers and positive decimals to two places.**

Standard 4MR2.1 Use estimation to verify the reasonableness of calculated results.

In the previous Explore Activity, you used models to add decimals. You can also use paper and pencil to add decimals.

Real-World EXAMPLE — Add Decimals

1 MEASUREMENT **How many hours did Darlene practice the flute during the two days?**

Estimate $1.5 + 2.33 \longrightarrow 2 + 2 = 4$

Step 1 Line up the decimal points.

$$\begin{array}{r} 1.50 \\ +\ 2.33 \\ \hline \end{array}$$

Write 0 in the hundredths place as a placeholder.

Step 2 Add.

$$\begin{array}{r} 1.50 \\ +\ 2.33 \\ \hline 3.83 \end{array}$$

Add the digits in each place value. Then bring down the decimal point.

So, Darlene practiced a total of 3.83 hours.

Check for reasonableness

Since 3.83 is close to the estimate of 4, the answer is reasonable. The model shows that 1.5 + 2.33 is 3.83. ✓

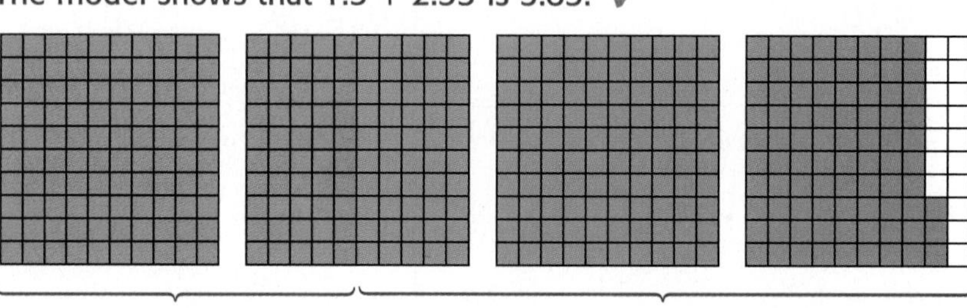

$$1\frac{50}{100} \quad + \quad 2\frac{33}{100} = 3\frac{83}{100} \text{ or } 3.83$$

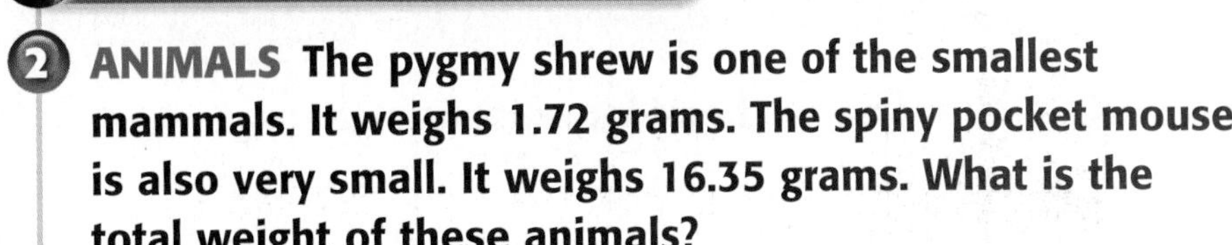

Add Decimals

2 **ANIMALS The pygmy shrew is one of the smallest mammals. It weighs 1.72 grams. The spiny pocket mouse is also very small. It weighs 16.35 grams. What is the total weight of these animals?**

You need to find 1.72 + 16.35. **Estimate** 2 + 16 = 18

Step 1 Line up the decimal points.

$$\begin{array}{r} 1.72 \\ +\ 16.35 \\ \hline \end{array}$$

Remember

Line up the decimal points before you add to make sure you are adding the same place values together.

Step 2 Add.

$$\begin{array}{r} \overset{1}{}1.72 \\ +\ 16.35 \\ \hline 18.07 \end{array}$$

Add the digits in each place value. Regroup if necessary.

So, the total weight of the mammals is 18.07 grams.

Check for reasonableness

The sum of 18.07 is close to the estimate of 18. So, the answer is reasonable. ✓

CHECK What You Know

Add. Use estimation to check for reasonableness. See Examples 1 and 2 (pp. 606–607)

1. $\begin{array}{r} 1.4 \\ +\ 0.7 \\ \hline \end{array}$

2. $\begin{array}{r} 4.72 \\ +\ 3.9 \\ \hline \end{array}$

3. $\begin{array}{r} 9.8 \\ +\ 7.33 \\ \hline \end{array}$

4. 4.82 + 6.27

5. \$25.85 + \$8.49

6. 54.90 + 38.41

For Exercises 7 and 8, use the poster shown.

7. Andre has his birthday dinner at Medieval Era, a dinner theatre with knights jousting. What is the total cost for Andre and his father?

8. Suppose Andre's mother is also going to his birthday dinner. What is the total cost?

9. **Talk About It** Why is it important to line up the decimal points before you add?

Practice and Problem Solving

EXTRA PRACTICE See page R38.

Add. Use estimation to check for reasonableness. See Examples 1 and 2 (pp. 606–607)

10. 0.7 + 0.2

11. 0.4 + 0.6

12. 2.1 + 0.39

13. 5.1 + 7.56

14. 8.76 + 6.95

15. 7.09 + 4.68

16. $9.82 + $5.33

17. $12.33 + $5.79

18. 47.28 + 36.05

19. $51.20 + $29.75

20. 3.21 + 14.7 + 9.35

21. The ostrich lays the largest bird egg in the world. It weighs 1.8 kg. The emu lays the second largest bird egg in the world. It weighs 0.82 kg. What is the combined weight of the two bird eggs?

22. Two bones in a leg are the femur and tibia. The average adult male femur is 19.88 inches long. The tibia is 16.94 inches long. How long is the average adult male's leg?

Real-World PROBLEM SOLVING

Data File The Living Desert in Palm Desert features a zoo, an animal conservation center, and a natural history museum.

23. Suppose Jamie and his mom want to camp overnight in the Living Desert. How much would it cost?

24. Heath, Rodney, and Mia go to the Living Desert on a field trip with their fourth grade class. If they bring $25, will they have enough money to enter the Living Desert?

Desert

Admission Rates

General Admission	$11.95
Seniors (62+)	$10.50
Children (Ages 3–12)	$7.50
Children under 3	Free
Overnight stay	
Adults	$79.50
Children	$49.75

H.O.T. Problems

25. **WHICH ONE DOESN'T BELONG?** Three of the decimals shown below have a sum equal to 14.04. Identify the number that does not belong with the other three.

1.15 | 2.57 | 5.03 | 6.44

26. WRITING IN MATH Explain how to find the sum of 136.28 and 264.57.

CHAPTER 15

Mid-Chapter Check

Lessons 15-1 through 15-4

Round to the nearest whole number. (Lesson 15-1)

1. 4.55

2. 25.24

3. **Measurement** A bald eagle's nest is 2.4 meters wide. How wide is its nest to the nearest whole number? (Lesson 15-1)

Round to the nearest tenth. (Lesson 15-1)

4. 8.58

5. 36.34

6. **STANDARDS PRACTICE** The height of a monster truck is 15.4 feet. What is the height of the truck rounded to the nearest whole number? (Lesson 15-1)

A 14 ft

B 15 ft

C 15.4 ft

D 16 ft

Estimate. Round to the nearest whole number. (Lesson 15-2)

7. $\begin{array}{r} 2.4 \\ +\ 3.8 \\ \hline \end{array}$

8. $\begin{array}{r} 9.4 \\ -\ 5.82 \\ \hline \end{array}$

Algebra **Estimate by rounding to the nearest whole number. Then compare. Use $>$, $<$, or $=$.** (Lesson 15-2)

9. 13.73 + 8.04 ● 9.8 + 12.52

10. 46.91 − 19.8 ● 53.4 − 20.26

11. Tamika Catchings, a WNBA player, averages 19.2 points per game. About how many points would Tamika score in two games? (Lesson 15-2)

12. A number is divided by 4. Next, 8 is added to the quotient. Then, the sum is multiplied by 2. The result is 28. What is the number? (Lesson 15-3)

13. **Measurement** Bruno is going on vacation and needs to leave for the airport at 1 P.M. What time does Bruno need to wake up? (Lesson 15-3)

Task	Time to Complete (hours)
Clean house	3.25
Eat lunch	0.75
Pack suitcase	1.5

Add. Use estimation to check for reasonableness. (Lesson 15-4)

14. 14.5 + 7.8

15. 37.08 + 19.56

16. **STANDARDS PRACTICE** Brad buys a movie ticket for \$4.75, a pretzel for \$1.50, and a soda for \$2.25. How much money did Brad spend?

F \$8.50

G \$8.75

H \$9

J \$9.25

Algebra **Describe a pattern. Then identify the missing numbers.** (Lesson 15-4)

17. 0.8, 1.6, ■, 3.2, ■, ■

18. 1.23, 3.25, ■, ■, 9.31, ■

19. **WRITING IN MATH** Tell whether 40 is a reasonable estimate for the sum of 28.4 + 14.68. Explain.

Olympic Games

The Olympic games have been taking place since ancient times.

There are currently summer and winter games. Each season occurs every four years and includes different sports. There are over one hundred summer events including cycling, gymnastics, swimming and diving, and track and field, among others. A highlight of the summer games has always been the gymnastic events. These events mix strength, agility, style, and grace. Some of the events that take place in the gymnastic competition are floor exercise, horizontal bar, parallel bars, pommel horse, rings, and vault. Gymnasts are scored on a scale of one to ten, with ten being a perfect score and very difficult to earn.

Recent Olympic Games Men's Individual Scores

Gymnast	Floor	Horse	Rings	Vault	Parallel Bars	High Bar	Total Score
Paul Hamm (U.S.)	9.73	9.70	9.59	9.14	9.84	9.84	57.84
Kim Dae-Eun (Korea)	9.65	9.54	9.71	9.41	9.78	9.73	57.82
Yang Tae-Young (Korea)	9.51	9.65	9.73	9.70	9.71	9.48	57.78

Recent Olympic Games Women's Individual Scores

Gymnast	Vault	Uneven Bars	Beam	Floor	Total Score
Carly Patterson (U.S.)	9.38	9.58	9.73	9.71	38.34
Svetlana Khorkina (Russia)	9.46	9.73	9.46	9.56	38.21
Zhang Nan (China)	9.33	9.46	9.66	9.60	38.05

* All scores have been rounded to the nearest hundredth.

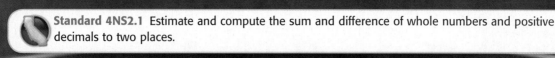

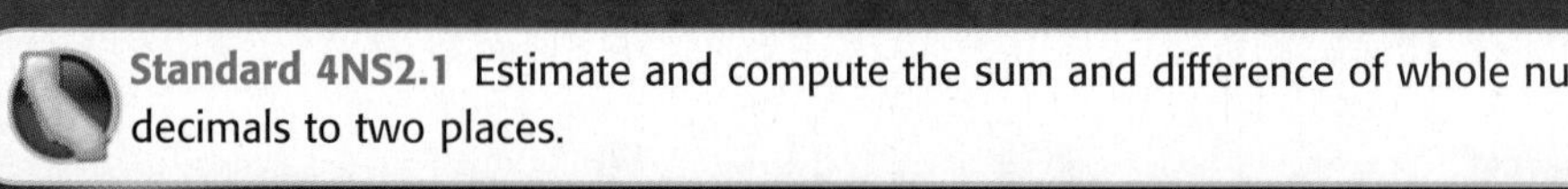
Standard 4NS2.1 Estimate and compute the sum and difference of whole numbers and positive decimals to two places.

Did You Know?
As of January 1, 1999, trampoline became a gymnastic event at the Olympic games.

Real-World Math

Use the information on the previous page to solve each problem.

1. A summer Olympic games will be taking place in London, England, in the year 2012. What years will the four previous Olympic games have been held?

2. What is the top female gymnast's total score rounded to the nearest whole number?

3. How much higher is Paul Hamm's score in the parallel bars than the vault when both scores are rounded to the nearest tenth?

4. What is the sum of Carly Patterson's two highest event scores when rounded to the nearest tenth?

5. Kim Dae-Eun's scores were higher than Paul Hamm's scores in two of the events. Identify the events. Find the difference in their scores for each event to the nearest tenth.

6. The gymnasts that earn the top three total scores win gold, silver, and bronze medals. Suppose the scores were rounded to the tenths place. Would this scoring change the medals that were given out to the male athletes? Explain.

7. Which place value would the female gymnast's scores have to be rounded to in order to have a three-way tie for gold? Explain.

15-5 Problem-Solving Investigation

MAIN IDEA I will choose the best strategy to solve a problem.

Standard 4MR1.1 **Analyze problems by identifying relationships, distinguishing relevant from irrelevant information, sequencing and prioritizing information,** and observing patterns. Standard 4SDAP1.1 Formulate survey questions; systematically collect and **represent data on a** number line; and coordinate graphs, **tables,** and charts.

P.S.I. TEAM +

JENNIFER: My friends and I all have different kinds of pets. Among the three of us, we have a lizard, a cat, a gerbil, and a snake. I do not have a cat. Rondell's pet is not a gerbil or a snake. Lorena's two pets are not lizards. My pet does not begin with the letters s or g.

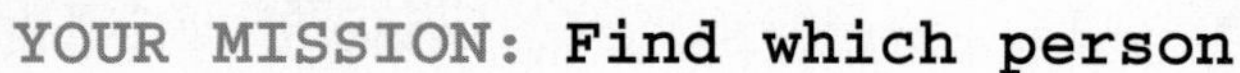

YOUR MISSION: Find which person owns each pet.

Understand You know the clues for each person's pet. You need to find which person owns each pet.

Plan Make a table to show what you know. Then use logical reasoning to find which person owns each pet.

Solve Make a table. Write a yes or a no for each fact that you are given. Once you write yes in the table, you can write no in the rest of the boxes in that row and column.

	Cat	Gerbil	Lizard	Snake
Jennifer	No	No	Yes	No
Lorena	No	Yes	No	Yes
Rondell	Yes	No	No	No

So, Jennifer owns a lizard. Lorena owns a gerbil and a snake. Rondell owns a cat.

Check Look back at the problem. The solution matches the facts given in the problem. So, the answer is correct.

Mixed Problem Solving

Use any strategy shown below to solve. Tell what strategy you used.

PROBLEM-SOLVING STRATEGIES

- Work a simpler problem.
- Use logical reasoning.
- Draw a picture.
- Make a model.
- Work backward.

1. Reina is going bowling. Which route would be the shortest? Explain.

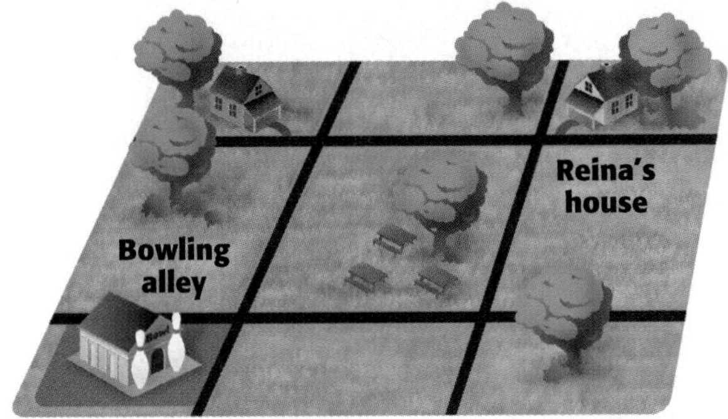

2. Students voted for a new mascot. Six out of ten students voted for a tiger. There are 300 students. How many students voted for a tiger?

3. A number is divided by 3. Then the quotient is subtracted from 20. The result is 8. What is the number?

4. Haley's comet can be seen from Earth about every 76 years. The next time it will be visible is in 2062. When was the comet's last visit?

5. Dean bought three comic books for $6. At the same price, how much would 10 comic books cost?

6. Laurie spent 30 minutes on math homework. She spent half as much time doing her science homework. She spent 5 minutes longer on her reading homework than her science homework. How much time did Laurie spend on her homework?

7. The toy car below cost $2.50. At the same price, how many toy cars can Domingo buy with $10?

8. A type of bacteria doubles in number every 12 hours. After 2 days, there are 48 bacteria. How many bacteria were there at the beginning of the first day?

9. The product of two numbers is 24. Their difference is 5. What are these two numbers?

10. Audrey biked the trail below. Find the value of y.

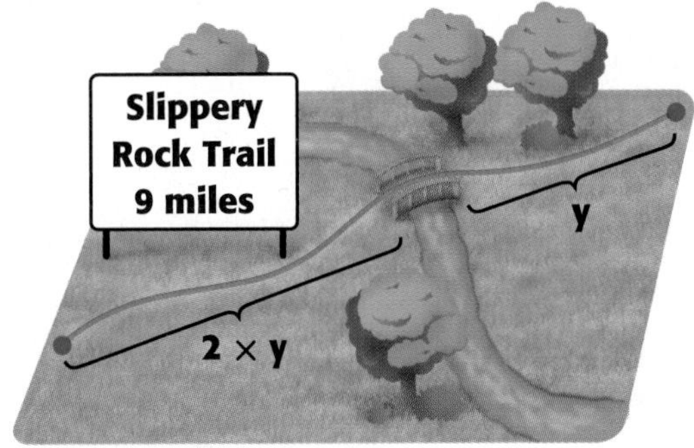

11. **WRITING IN ▶MATH** The two busiest subway systems in the world have 3.1 and 2.84 billion passengers each year. The answer is 5.94 billion. What is the question?

Math Activity for 15-6

Subtraction of Decimals

You can use grid paper to explore subtracting decimals.

ACTIVITY

Use models to find 2.75 − 1.15.

Step 1 **Model 2.75.**

To show 2.75, shade two whole grids and $\frac{75}{100}$ of a third grid.

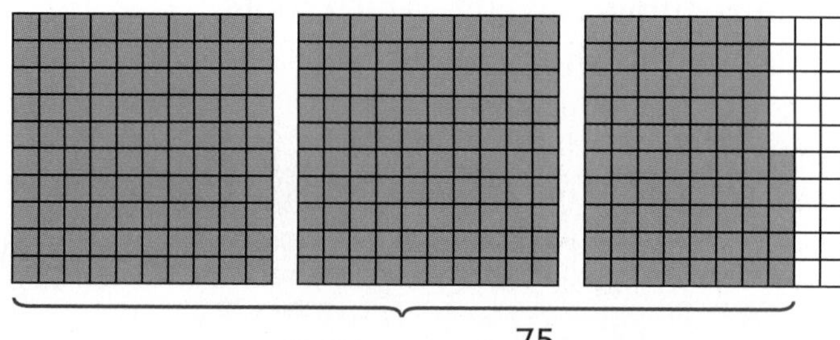

2.75 or $2\frac{75}{100}$

Step 2 **Subtract 1.15.**

To subtract 1.15, cross out 1 whole grid and 15 squares of the third grid.

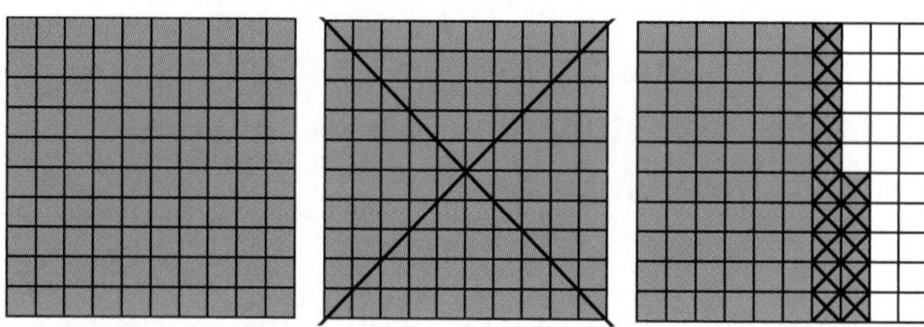

2.75 − 1.15 or $1\frac{15}{100}$

MAIN IDEA

I will use models to subtract decimals.

Standard 4NS2.1 Estimate and **compute the** sum or **difference of whole numbers and positive decimals to two places.**

Standard 4MR2.3 **Use a variety of methods, such as words, numbers,** symbols, charts, graphs, tables, diagrams, **and models, to explain mathematical reasoning.**

You Will Need
grid paper
colored pencil

Animation
ca.gr4math.com

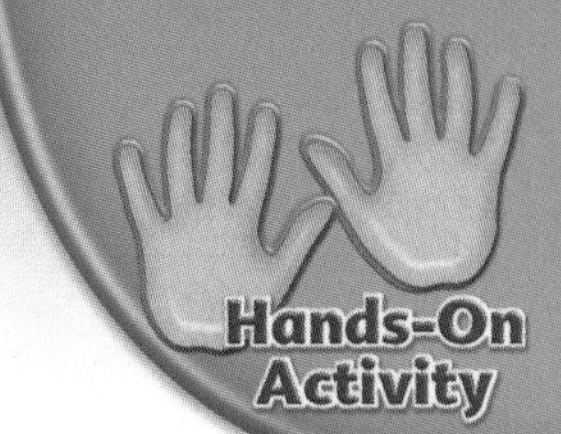

Step 3 **Find the difference.**

Count the number of shaded squares left.

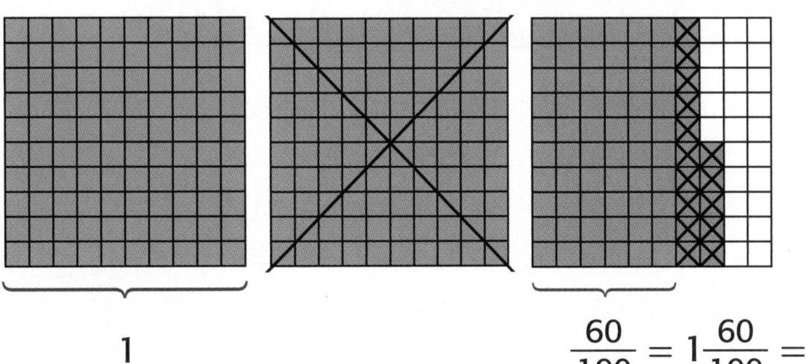

Think About It

1. How did you model 2.75?
2. How did you model subtracting 1.15 from 2.75?
3. How did you find the difference?

CHECK What You Know

Subtract. Use the models.

4. 1.46 – 0.34

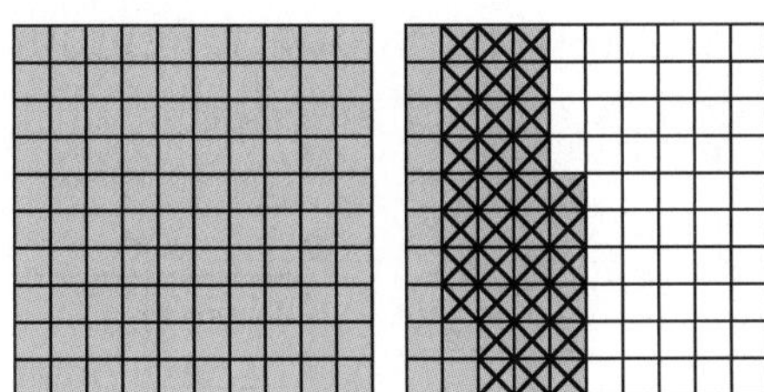

5. 2.8 – 1.23

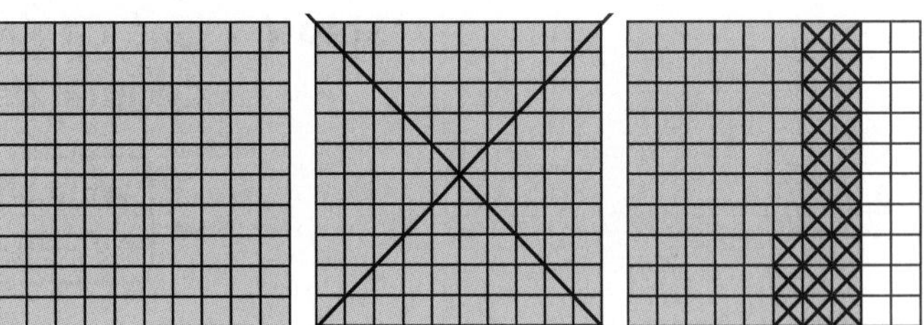

Subtract. Use models if needed.

6. $\begin{array}{r} 0.55 \\ -\ 0.29 \\ \hline \end{array}$

7. $\begin{array}{r} 0.99 \\ -\ 0.46 \\ \hline \end{array}$

8. $\begin{array}{r} 1.4 \\ -\ 1.11 \\ \hline \end{array}$

9. $\begin{array}{r} 2.6 \\ -\ 1.09 \\ \hline \end{array}$

10. $\begin{array}{r} 2.81 \\ -\ 1.29 \\ \hline \end{array}$

11. $\begin{array}{r} 3.77 \\ -\ 1.08 \\ \hline \end{array}$

12. 2.98 – 1.84

13. 3.45 – 2.73

14. 3.93 – 2.94

15. **WRITING IN ▶MATH** Explain how to find 3.46 – 2.62.

15-6 Subtract Decimals

MAIN IDEA

I will subtract decimals.

Standard 4NS2.1 Estimate and compute the sum or **difference of whole numbers and positive decimals to two places.**

Standard 4MR2.1 Use estimation to verify reasonableness of calculated results.

GET READY to Learn

Albert Einstein was a very intelligent man who made many important scientific discoveries. His brain had a mass of 1.23 kilograms. This is less than the mass of an average adult male brain, which has a mass of about 1.4 kilograms. What is the difference in mass?

In the previous Explore activity, you used models to subtract decimals. You can also use paper and pencil.

Real-World EXAMPLE — Subtract Decimals

1 MEASUREMENT **What is the difference in mass between Albert Einstein's brain and the mass of an average adult male brain?**

Estimate 1.4 − 1.23 ⟶ 1.4 − 1.2 = 0.2

Step 1 Line up the decimal points.

$$\begin{array}{r} 1.40 \\ -\ 1.23 \\ \hline \end{array}$$

Write a 0 as a placeholder.

Step 2 Subtract. Regroup if needed.

$$\begin{array}{r} \scriptsize{3\,10} \\ 1.\cancel{4}\cancel{0} \\ -\ 1.23 \\ \hline 0.17 \end{array}$$

Place the decimal point.

So, Einstein's brain had a mass of 0.17 kilogram less than the mass of an average adult male brain.

Check for reasonableness

The answer 0.17 is close to the estimate of 0.2. So, the answer is reasonable. The model shows that 1.4 − 1.23 is 0.17. ✓

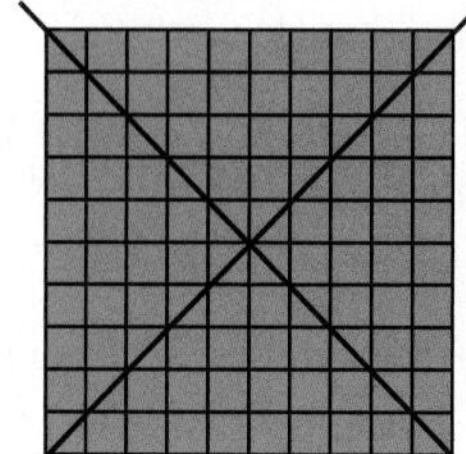

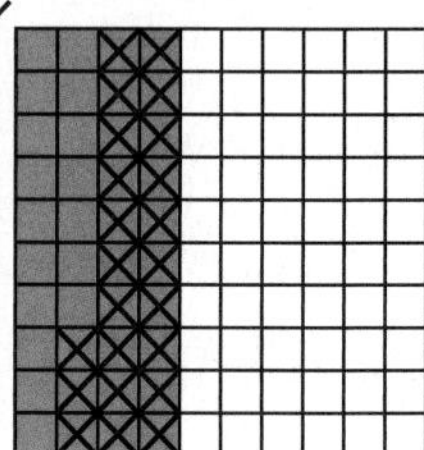

Real-World EXAMPLE Subtract Decimals

2 MEASUREMENT **The average rock python is 24.6 feet long. The average king cobra is 17.7 feet long. How much longer is the rock python than the king cobra?**

Subtract 24.6 − 17.7 to find how much longer the rock python is than the king cobra.

Estimate 24.6 − 17.7 ⟶ 25 − 18 = 7

Step 1 Line up the decimal points.

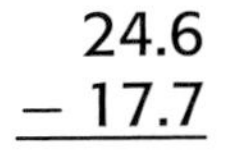

Step 2 Subtract.

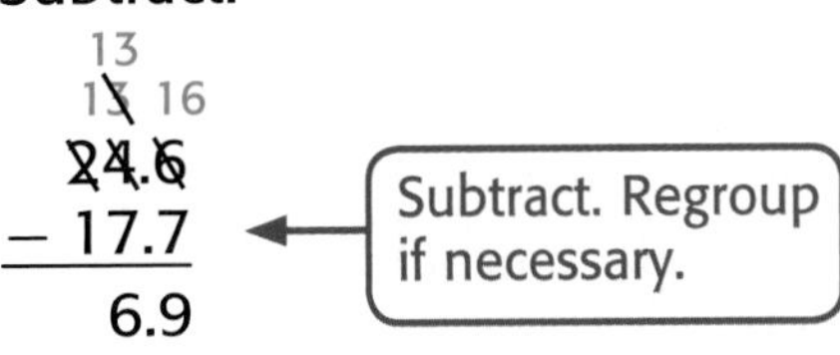

So, the average rock python is 6.9 feet longer than the average king cobra.

Check for Reasonableness

The answer, 6.9, is close to the estimate of 7. So, the answer is reasonable. ✓

Rock Python

Since 17.7 + 6.9 + 24.6, the answer is correct.

Online **Personal Tutor at** ca.gr4math.com

CHECK What You Know

Subtract. Check your answer. See Examples 1 and 2 (pp. 616–617)

1. 1.4 − 1.0

2. 0.8 − 0.49

3. \$1.67 − \$0.58

4. 4.67 − 2.36

5. \$8.72 − \$2.95

6. 25.74 − 12.08

7. The height of the tallest woman in the world is 7.58 feet. The height of the tallest man in the world is 8.92 feet. How much taller is the tallest man than the tallest woman?

8. Talk About It Explain how subtracting decimals is similar to subtracting whole numbers. How is it different?

Practice and Problem Solving

EXTRA PRACTICE See page R39.

Subtract. Check your answer. See Examples 1 and 2 (pp. 616–617)

9. 2.7 − 1.4

10. 5.5 − 3.8

11. 7.2 − 0.9

12. 4.6 − 1.45

13. 6.84 − 3.56

14. $9.67 − $7.05

15. 11.92 − 8.87

16. $19.38 − $14.55

17. 21.80 − 15.91

18. $25.09 − $12.40

19. 34.94 − 28.17

20. 56.87 − 38.05

For Exercises 21 and 22, use the table shown.

21. How many more people play tennis in the most popular state than in the least popular state?

22. What is the total number of people in Florida, Texas, and New York who play tennis?

Most Popular States for Tennis

State	Number of Players (millions)
California	3.2
Florida	1.4
Illinois	1.0
New York	1.7
Texas	1.4

Source: USTA

23. Julina is buying pet supplies. She has $25.50. She buys cat food for $8.99, a collar for $4.79, and cat toys for $3.25. How much money will Julina have left?

24. The average American eats 57.4 kilograms of fresh fruit and 67.2 kilograms of fresh vegetables each year. What is the difference in the yearly amount of fruit and vegetables an American eats?

Real-World PROBLEM SOLVING

Science The table to the right shows the heights of different dinosaurs.

25. What is the difference in height between the two shortest dinosaurs?

26. How much taller is a Tyrannosaurus than a Araucanoraptor?

27. Which two dinosaurs have a height difference of 1.45 feet?

Dinosaur Heights

Dinosaur	Height (feet)
Abrictosaurus	1.3
Araucanoraptor	2.75
Bagaceratops	1.5
Microvenator	2.5
Supersaurus	66.0
Triceratops	9.5
Tyrannosaurus	23.0

Source: dinodatabase.com

H.O.T. Problems

28. FIND THE ERROR Morgan and Lloyd are finding 46.27 − 28.16. Who is correct? Explain.

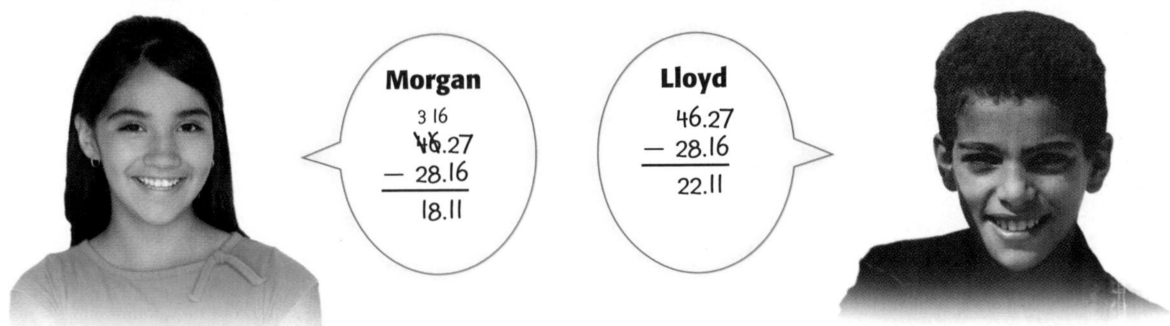

29. OPEN ENDED A whole number is subtracted from 24.84. The difference is greater than 9 and less than 10. What is the number?

Standards Practice

30 At the school store, Benito bought a package of pens for $1.34 and a set of map pencils for $2.78. What was the total cost? **(Lesson 15-4)**

A $1.44

B $3.02

C $4.02

D $4.12

31 Sandy and her father have $100. They buy a fishing pole for $39.95 and a stove for $29.39. Which additional item could they buy? **(Lesson 15-6)**

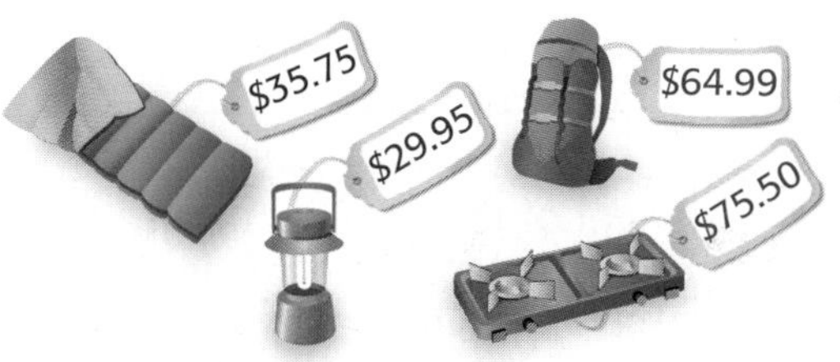

F Backpack

G Camp stove

H Lantern

J Sleeping bag

Spiral Review

Add. Use estimation to check for reasonableness. (Lesson 15-4)

32. 0.75 + 0.62

33. 4.49 + 0.76

34. 8.40 + 6.87

35. Mila volunteers at a food bank at 9 A.M. It takes 30 minutes to drive to the food bank, 20 minutes to eat breakfast, and 45 minutes to get ready in the morning. What is the latest time she can set her alarm to wake up? **(Lesson 15-3)**

Estimate. Round to the nearest whole number. (Lesson 15-2)

36. 2.5 + 4.3

37. 8.4 − 5.7

38. 22.9 + 5.4

CHAPTER 15

Study Guide and Review

FOLDABLES™ Study Organizer GET READY to Study

Be sure the following Key Vocabulary words and Key Concepts are written in your Foldable.

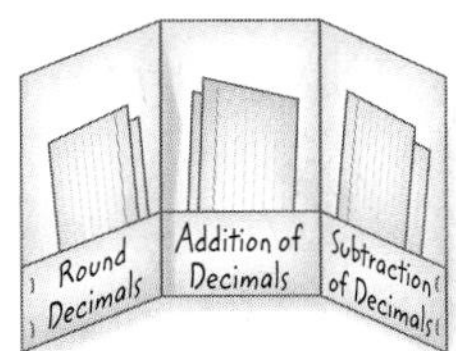

BIG Ideas

Round Decimals (p. 593)

- Round 4.36 to the nearest whole number.

4.36

Look at the digit to the right of the place you want to round to. Since it is less than 5, round down.

So, 4.36 rounds to 4.

Estimate Sums and Differences (p. 598)

- Round each addend to the nearest whole number, then add.

8.6 + 7.2 ⟶ 9 + 7 = 16

Add and Subtract Decimals (pp. 606, 616)

Find 1.27 + 0.36.	Find 0.78 – 0.45.
1.27 + 0.36 1.63	1.78 – 0.45 1.33

Key Vocabulary

decimal (pp. 557, 593)
decimal point (pp. 557, 593)
difference (pp. 70, 598)
estimate (pp. 36, 598)
sum (pp. 64, 598)

Vocabulary Check

Complete each sentence with the correct vocabulary word.

1. The answer to an addition problem is the __?__.

2. A(n) __?__ is a period separating the ones and the tenths in a number.

3. A(n) __?__ indicates about how much.

4. The answer to a subtraction problem is the __?__.

5. A(n) __?__ is a number with one or more digits to the right of the decimal point.

6. A(n) __?__ is a number that is close to an exact amount.

Lesson-by-Lesson Review

15-1 Round Decimals (pp. 593–597)

Example 1
Round 12.16 to the nearest tenth.

One Way: Use a Number Line

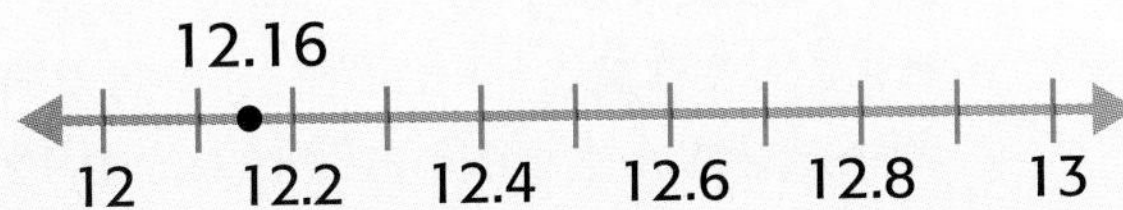

12.16
12
12.2
12.4
12.6
12.8
13

12.16 is closer to 12.2 than 12.1.

Another Way: Use Rounding Rules

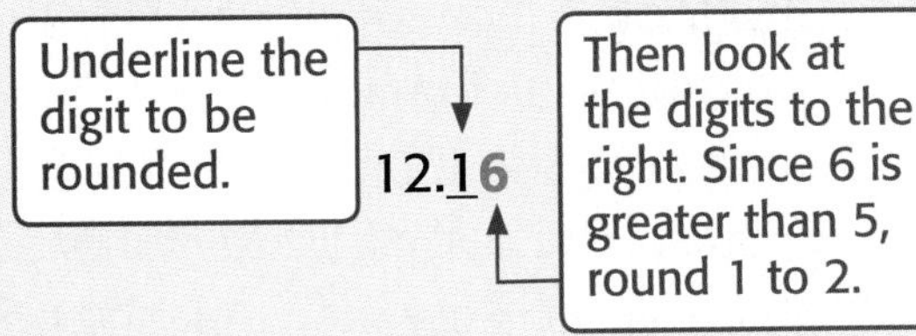

Underline the digit to be rounded.
12.16
Then look at the digits to the right. Since 6 is greater than 5, round 1 to 2.

So, round 12.16 up to 12.2.

Round to the nearest whole number.

7. 4.12 **8.** 3.65

9. 12.40 **10.** 69.95

11. **Measurement** Marni hiked 3.65 miles on Saturday. About how many miles did she hike?

12. A baby panda weighs 4.36 ounces. About how many ounces does the baby panda weigh?

13. Travis spent $5.32 at lunch. About how much did he spend?

Round to the nearest tenth.

14. 7.45 **15.** 9.81

16. 32.78 **17.** 44.54

15-2 Estimate Decimal Sums and Differences (pp. 598–601)

Example 2
Estimate 8.63 + 6.15.

$$\begin{array}{r} 8.63 \\ +\ 6.15 \\ \hline \end{array} \rightarrow \begin{array}{r} 9 \\ +\ 6 \\ \hline 15 \end{array}$$

Round 8.63 to 9.
Round 6.15 to 6.

So, 8.63 + 6.15 is about 15.

Example 3
Estimate 25.25 − 12.76.

$$\begin{array}{r} 25.25 \\ -\ 12.76 \\ \hline \end{array} \rightarrow \begin{array}{r} 25 \\ -\ 13 \\ \hline 12 \end{array}$$

Round 25.25 to 25.
Round 12.76 to 13.

So, 25.25 − 12.76 is about 12.

Estimate. Round to the nearest whole number.

18. $\begin{array}{r} 4.88 \\ +\ 14.56 \\ \hline \end{array}$ **19.** $\begin{array}{r} 35.15 \\ -\ 14.93 \\ \hline \end{array}$

20. $\begin{array}{r} 9.51 \\ +\ 7.43 \\ \hline \end{array}$ **21.** $\begin{array}{r} 99.65 \\ -\ 24.67 \\ \hline \end{array}$

22. A basketball usually costs $17.95. It is on sale for $9.99. About how much less is the sale price than the original price?

15-3 Problem-Solving Strategy: Work Backward (pp. 602–603)

Example 4

Felipe's basketball team is having a car wash. It takes 10 minutes to wash a car. Felipe's team finished washing 12 cars at 5 P.M. What time did the car wash start?

Understand

What facts do you know?

- It takes 10 minutes to wash a car.
- Felipe's team finished washing 12 cars at 5 P.M.

What do you need to find?

- The time the car wash started.

Plan Work backward.

Solve Start with the end result. Then work backward.

12	×	10	=	120
cars		minutes to wash 1 car		minutes to wash 10 cars

5 P.M. − 120 minutes = 3 P.M.

120 min = 2 hr

The car wash started at 3 P.M.

Check It took 120 minutes or 2 hours to wash the cars. Two hours before 5 P.M. is 3 P.M. So, the answer is correct.

23. A number is added to 3. The sum is multiplied by 5. The result is 45. What is the number?

24. Howard is doing his chores. He swept the floor for 20 minutes. He dusted for 10 minutes less than he swept. He cleaned his room for 45 minutes longer than he dusted. How long did it take Howard to clean his room?

25. Alana took 18 pictures of animals. She took 2 pictures of gorillas. She took twice as many pictures of penguins. She took 6 pictures of giraffes. The rest of the pictures are of sea lions. How many pictures did Alana take of sea lions?

26. Harrison, Colin, and Ruthie's favorite colors are red, blue, and green. Colin likes blue the best. Ruthie does not like green. What is Harrison's favorite color?

27. A number is divided by 7. Nine is added to the quotient. Then 5 is subtracted from the sum. The result is 9. What is the number?

15-4 Add Decimals (pp. 606–608)

Example 5
Find 2.7 + 12.38.

Step 1 Line up the decimal points.

$$\begin{array}{r} 2.70 \\ +\ 12.38 \\ \hline \end{array}$$

Place a zero in the hundredths place.

Step 2 Add.

$$\begin{array}{r} {}^{1} \\ 2.70 \\ +\ 12.38 \\ \hline 15.08 \end{array}$$

Add the digits in each place value. Regroup if necessary.

So, 2.7 + 12.38 = 15.08.

Add. Use estimation to check for reasonableness.

28. $\begin{array}{r} 3.6 \\ +\ 0.8 \\ \hline \end{array}$

29. $\begin{array}{r} 6.82 \\ +\ 4.7 \\ \hline \end{array}$

30. 5.03 + 18.9

31. 34.82 + 8.31

32. **Measurement** The first flight of an airplane covered a distance of 17.96 kilometers. The plane's second flight covered a distance of 19.57 kilometers. What is the total distance covered by the two flights?

15-5 Problem-Solving Investigation: Choose a Strategy (pp. 612–613)

Example 6
There are 27 plants in a garden. There are twice as many tomato as cucumber plants and three more pepper than cucumber plants. How many of each kind of plant is in the garden?

You can use logical reasoning to solve the problem.

There are 9 pepper plants.

There are 3 more pepper than cucumber plants. So, the number of cucumber plants is 9 − 3 or 6.

There are twice as many tomato as cucumber plants. So, the number of tomato plants is 2 × 6 or 12.

Check
9 + 6 + 12 = 27
So, the answer is correct.

Use any strategy to solve.

33. Lani is putting up a tent for camping. The tent has four corners. Each corner needs three stakes. How many stakes does Lani need?

34. Edwin is buying the books shown. How much will the books cost?

35. Use the symbols +, −, ×, or ÷ to make the following math sentence true. Use each symbol only once.

3 ■ 4 ■ 6 ■ 1 = 18

15-6 Subtract Decimals (pp. 616–619)

Example 7

A spider is one of the slowest moving animals. It travels at a speed of 1.2 miles per hour. A sloth is even slower. It travels at a speed of 0.07 miles per hour. How much faster is a spider than a sloth?

To find out how much faster a spider is than a sloth, subtract 0.07 from 1.20.

Step 1 Line up the decimal points.

$$\begin{array}{r} 1.20 \\ -\ 0.07 \\ \hline \end{array}$$

Step 2 Subtract. Regroup if needed.

$$\begin{array}{r} \scriptsize{1\,10} \\ 1.\not{2}\not{0} \\ -\ 0.07 \\ \hline 1.13 \end{array}$$

Subtract the digits in each place. Regroup.

The model shows 1.20 − 0.07 = 1.13.

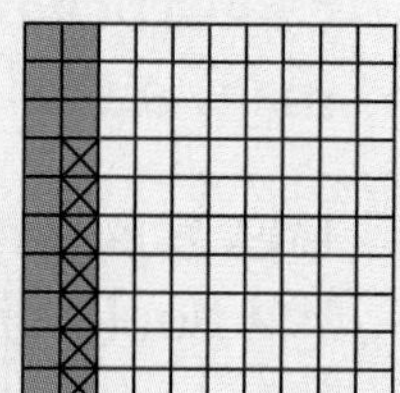

So, a spider is 1.13 miles per hour faster than a sloth.

Check

You can use addition to check.

$$\begin{array}{r} 1.13 \\ +\ 0.07 \\ \hline 1.20 \end{array}$$

So, the answer is correct. ✓

Subtract. Check your answer.

36. $\begin{array}{r} 2.6 \\ -\ 0.7 \\ \hline \end{array}$

37. $\begin{array}{r} 8.3 \\ -\ 1.5 \\ \hline \end{array}$

38. $\begin{array}{r} 6.9 \\ -\ 3.81 \\ \hline \end{array}$

39. $\begin{array}{r} 8.57 \\ -\ 5.9 \\ \hline \end{array}$

40. 26.08 − 16.4

41. 59.81 − 41.26

42. The longest space walk was 8.93 hours long. The second longest space walk was 8.48 hours long. How much longer was the longest space walk than the second longest space walk?

For Exercises 43 and 44, use the table. It shows snakes that have the longest fangs.

Snakes' Fangs	
Snake	**Fang Length (cm)**
Australian Taipan	1.8
Black Mamba	2.5
Bushmaster	3.8
Diamondback Rattlesnake	2.5
Gaboon Viper	5.1

Source: *Scholastic Book of World Records*

43. What is the difference in length of the Gaboon Viper's and Black Mamba's fangs?

44. Which two snakes have the greatest difference in length of fangs? What is the difference?

CHAPTER 15

Chapter Test

Estimate. Round to the nearest whole number.

1. 26.7 − 9.09

2. $31.56 + $5.01

3. San Francisco receives an average of 2.9 inches of rain in November. It receives an average of 3.6 inches of rain in December. About how much rainfall does San Francisco receive during these two months?

4. Eva has 4 coins. Two of the coins are the same and equal 50¢. One coin is a nickel. One coin is worth ten cents. What coins does Eva have?

Subtract. Check your answer.

5. 6.9 − 2.48

6. 74.64 − 12.8

7. Marie is 4.25 feet tall. Marie's brother is 3.5 feet tall. How much taller is Marie than her brother?

8. **STANDARDS PRACTICE** What is 67.34 rounded to the nearest tenth?

A 67
B 67.3
C 67.34
D 68

Add. Check for reasonableness.

9. 4.97 + 8.4

10. 6.26 + 29.4

Round to the nearest tenth.

11. 3.05

12. 84.72

13. Hermán rode 16.72 kilometers on his bike. After he rested, he rode another 11.35 kilometers. How many kilometers did he ride altogether?

14. **STANDARDS PRACTICE** Raymond and his father are planning a camping trip. The advertisement for a campsite is shown below.

If Raymond and his father have $45 to spend on a campsite, how many nights will they be able to stay?

F 2
G 3
H 4
J 5

Algebra **Find the missing value.**

15. $x + 1.2 = 3.6$

16. $2.8 + y = 4.5$

17. A number is subtracted from 15. The difference is multiplied by 4. Then the product is divided by 8. The result is 3. What is the number?

18. **WRITING IN MATH** Explain how to estimate 12.46 + 34.9 rounding each number to the nearest whole number.

CHAPTER 15

California Standards Practice

Cumulative, Chapters 1–15

Standards Example

Nelia biked on Monday and on Wednesday. How many miles did she bike on the two days?

Distance Biked	
Day	**Distance (mi)**
Monday	3.5
Wednesday	3.75

A 6.25 miles **C** 7.25 miles

B 6.75 miles **D** 7.75 miles

Read the Question

You need to add to find the number of miles biked.

Solve the Question

Line up the decimal points. Then add.

$$\begin{array}{r} 3.50 \\ +\ 3.75 \\ \hline 7.25 \end{array}$$

3.50 Use 0 as a placeholder.

7.25 Place the decimal point.

So, the answer is C.

Online Personal Tutor at ca.gr4math.com

Choose the best answer.

1 **Terrez drove 42.5 miles in one hour. He drove 51.3 miles in the next hour. How many miles did he drive?**

A 93.8 miles **C** 98.3 miles

B 93.9 miles **D** 938 miles

2 **Pamela is 52.6 inches tall. Roberto is 54.2 inches tall. How much taller is Roberto than Pamela?**

F 2.6 inches **H** 1.6 inches

G 2.4 inches **J** 1.4 inches

3 **Arturo bought a kite for $19.95 and string for $4.19. Which is the closest estimate of the total amount spent?**

A $20
B $22
C $24
D $25

4 **What is 35.18 rounded to the nearest tenth?**

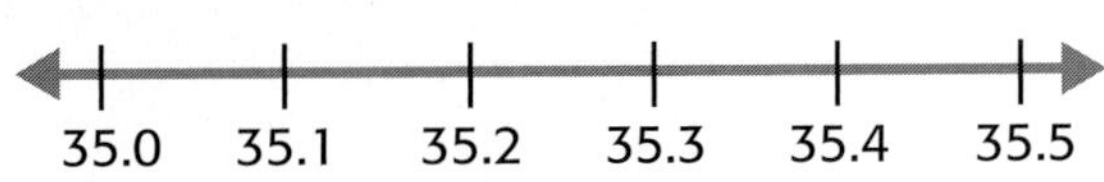

F 35.1
G 35.2
H 35.3
J 35.5

5 **Joy has $70. She buys these items.**

If she rounds each amount to the nearest whole number, about how much change should she receive?

A $10
B $15
C $18
D $20

6 **During one week, Ravi ran 4.2 miles. The following week he ran 5.75 miles. About how much farther did Ravi run the following week?**

F 1 mile
G 2 miles
H 3 miles
J 10 miles

7 **Which point on the number line is greater than 6.5 and less than 7.0?**

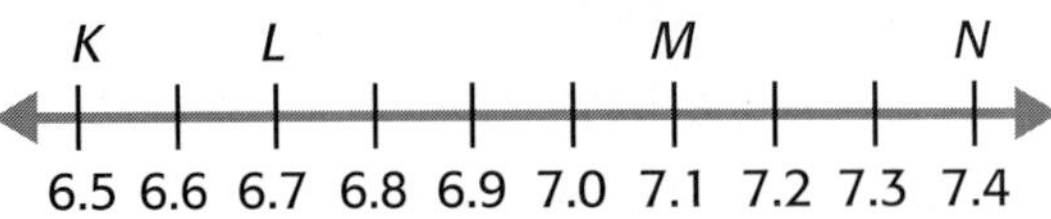

A *K*
B *L*
C *M*
D *N*

8 **Liseta earns $34.75 each week walking dogs. About how much will she earn in 3 weeks?**

F $105
G $180
H $204
J $210

9 **Which group of numbers are all prime numbers?**

A 1, 2, 4, 10
B 2, 3, 5, 7
C 1, 2, 5, 9
D 2, 3, 6, 10

10 **The table shows the number of visitors at the Pet Zoo. How many visitors went to the Pet Zoo in June and July?**

Pet Zoo	
Month	**Number of Visitors**
May	2873
June	2930
July	4382

F 5803
G 6822
H 7312
J 8331

CHAPTER 16 Probability

BIG Idea What is probability?

Probability is the chance of an event taking place. It can be described as *certain*, *likely*, *unlikely*, and *impossible*.

Example Kumar and Robert are playing a game. They each spin a spinner once. Kumar is likely to land on blue. Robert is unlikely to land on red.

Kumar

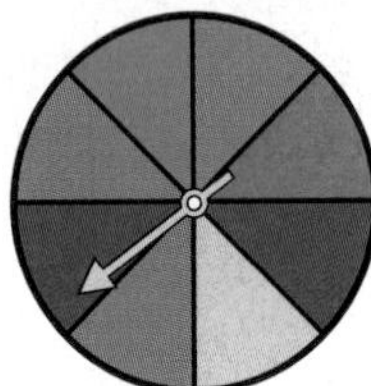

Robert

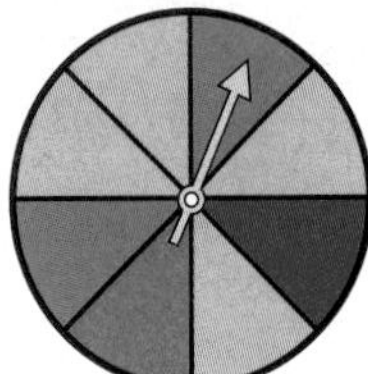

What will I learn in this chapter?

- Find and explore probability.
- Express outcomes in words, numbers, and in an organized way.
- Make predictions for probability situations.
- Solve problems by making an organized list.

Key Vocabulary

probability
outcome
prediction
tree diagram

Student Study Tools at ca.gr4math.com

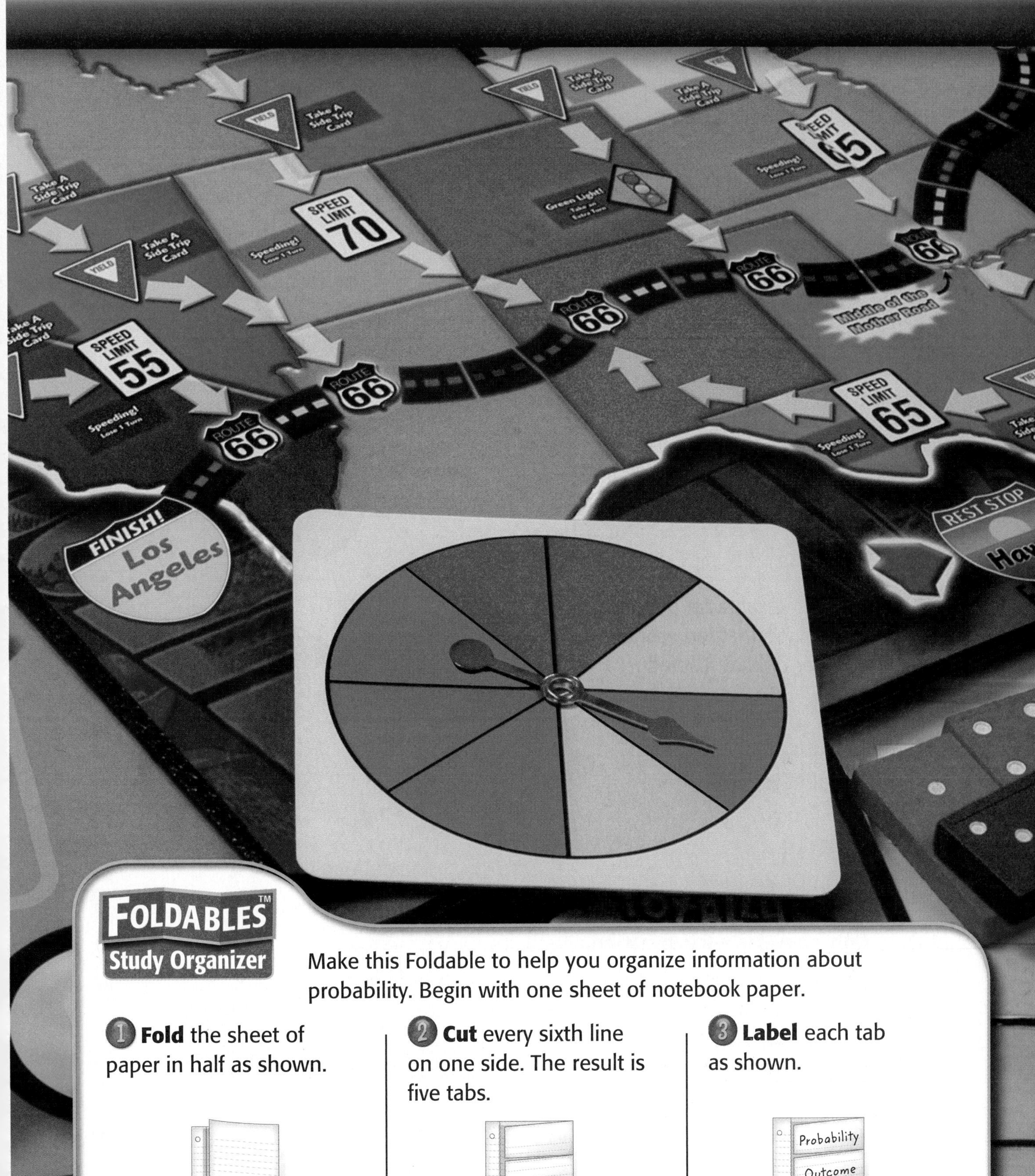

FOLDABLES™ Study Organizer

Make this Foldable to help you organize information about probability. Begin with one sheet of notebook paper.

1. **Fold** the sheet of paper in half as shown.

2. **Cut** every sixth line on one side. The result is five tabs.

3. **Label** each tab as shown.

Probability
Outcome
Favorable Outcome
Prediction
Tree Diagram

ARE YOU READY for Chapter 16?

You have two ways to check prerequisite skills for this chapter.

Option 2

Math Online Take the Chapter Readiness Quiz at ca.gr4math.com.

Option 1

Complete the Quick Check below.

QUICK Check

Write the fraction that represents the shaded area. (Lesson 13-1)

1. 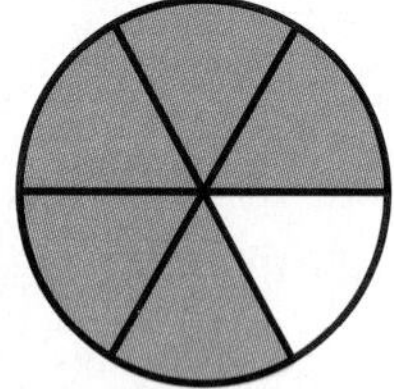

2. 

3. 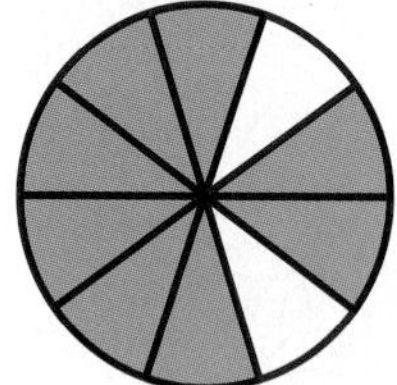

4. Lola has three Labrador puppies. Write a fraction that represents the number of black Labrador puppies.

5. What fraction of the Labrador puppies are yellow?

Make a tally chart for each situation. (Lesson 4-1)

6. Antonia took a survey to find out her friends' favorite colors.

Favorite Colors		
red	yellow	green
blue	pink	red
green	blue	pink
red	blue	blue

7. Mr. Duffy recorded the ages of the students on the basketball team.

Ages of Basketball Players		
10	11	9
9	10	11
10	9	10
10	10	10

16-1 Probability and Outcomes

GET READY to Learn

Only Sophie knew the colors of the marbles in the bag. She asked Marta to reach in and choose a marble without looking. What color do you think Marta will grab?

MAIN IDEA

I will describe probability.

Standard 4SDAP2.2 Express outcomes of experimental probability situations verbally and numerically (e.g., 3 out of 4; $\frac{3}{4}$).

Standard 4SDAP2.1 Represent all possible outcomes for a simple probability situation in an organized way (e.g., **tables,** grids, tree diagrams).

New Vocabulary

outcome

probability

An **outcome** is a result in an experiment. The chance that an outcome will occur is its **probability**. The words *certain, likely, equally likely, unlikely,* and *impossible* can describe probability.

certain to choose red

likely to choose red

equally likely to choose red or blue

unlikely to choose red

impossible to choose red

EXAMPLE Describe Outcomes

1 Describe how likely it is that Marta will choose a yellow marble from Sophie's bag.

There are 8 marbles in the bag. and 2 are yellow.

In the bag, less than half of the marbles are yellow. So, it is *unlikely* that Marta will choose a yellow marble.

Real-World EXAMPLE Describe Outcomes

2 **MONEY** **The table shows the coins Tucker has in his pocket. Suppose he drops a coin on the ground. Describe the probability that the coin he dropped is a dime.**

Coin	Frequency
Quarter	1
Dime	5
Penny	2
TOTAL	8

There are 8 coins in Tucker's pocket. Of those coins, 5 are dimes.

Since most of the coins are dimes, it is *likely* that Tucker dropped a dime.

Online **Personal Tutor at** ca.gr4math.com

CHECK What You Know

The spinner is spun. Describe the probability of each outcome. Write *certain, likely, equally likely, unlikely,* or *impossible*.

See Examples 1 and 2 (pp. 631–632)

1. odd number

2. even number

3. number less than 3

4. number greater than 9

5. prime number

6. the number 5, 11, or 13

7. The table shows the type of apples in Kali's refrigerator. Kali is going to grab an apple without looking. Describe the probability that Kali will grab a red apple.

Type of Apple	Frequency
Green	7
Red	3
Yellow	5

8. **Talk About It** Omar is reaching into the bag shown and choosing one cube without looking. Are there any colors that are more likely to be chosen? Explain.

Practice and Problem Solving

A marble is chosen from the bag without looking. Describe the probability of each outcome. Write *certain, likely, equally likely, unlikely,* or *impossible.* See Examples 1 and 2 (pp. 631–632)

9. green

10. red, yellow, or green

11. not green

The spinner is spun. Describe the probability of each outcome. Write *certain, likely, equally likely, unlikely,* or *impossible.*

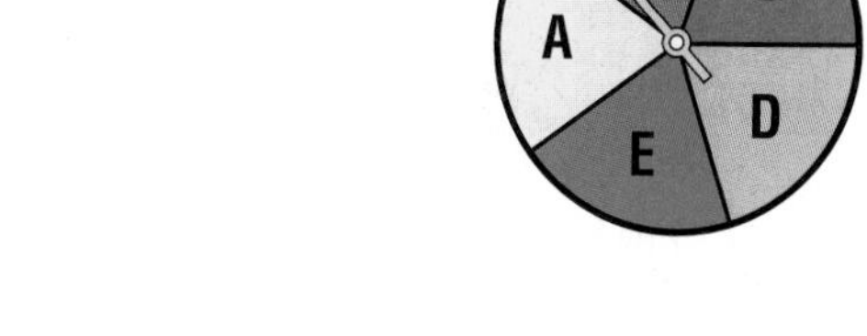

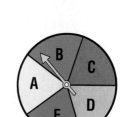

12. consonant

13. vowel

14. letter in the name LILITH

15. Sancho spun a spinner 21 times. The table shows his results.

Color	Results
Blue	卌 ||
Green	卌 卌 ||
Orange	||

Suppose Sancho spins the spinner one more time. Describe the probability that the spinner will land on orange.

16. Erin dropped a stack of 32 plastic cups. The table shows how the cups landed.

How Cup Landed	Number
	10
	18
	4

Suppose Erin drops one more cup. Describe the probability that the cup will land on its side.

Make a table to show the possible outcomes for each situation. Then, use the table to describe the probability.

17. Christopher has a bag of canned foods. He has two cans of corn, five cans of peaches, and one can of pineapple. He grabs a can out of the bag without looking. Describe the probability of Christopher grabbing a can of corn.

18. Ms. Lim is picking classroom helpers by pulling slips of paper out of a hat. Four slips of paper say "pass papers." One slip says "feed hamster." Two slips say "clean boards." Alisa pulls out a slip of paper. Describe the probability that she will pass out papers.

H.O.T. Problems

19. OPEN ENDED Make a spinner with 8 equal parts in which green is most *likely* to be landed on and so that red and blue are *unlikely* to occur.

20. FIND THE ERROR A number cube is labeled 1–6. Sue and Miguel are describing the probability that the number cube will land on an even number. Who is correct? Explain.

Sue
It is likely.

Miguel
It is equally likely.

21. WRITING IN MATH Describe a probability situation in which an outcome is certain to happen.

Standards Practice

22 Gail has $5.25. She is buying a book that costs $2.75. How much change will she receive? (Lesson 15-6)

A $2

B $2.50

C $3

D $3.25

23 Damián has a bag of 20 tiles numbered 10–29. Which is best described as *unlikely*? (Lesson 16-1)

F choosing an odd number

G choosing an even number

H choosing a 19

J choosing a composite number

Spiral Review

Subtract. Check your answer. (Lesson 15-6)

24. $\begin{array}{r} 2.3 \\ -\ 1.5 \\ \hline \end{array}$

25. $\begin{array}{r} 12.9 \\ -\ 4.6 \\ \hline \end{array}$

26. $\begin{array}{r} 36.08 \\ -\ 21.45 \\ \hline \end{array}$

27. Orlando bought 2 used video games that cost $12.95 each and paid with $30. Explain two ways to find how much change he should receive. (Lesson 15-5)

Certain Fun

Describe Probability

Get Ready!

Players: 3 players

Get Set!

Cut each index card in half. Then copy the words and pictures as shown. The pictures represent marbles in a bag.

Go!

- Player 1 shuffles the cards with pictures on them.
- Player 1 selects and turns over a picture card.
- Players 2 and 3 select a word card that describes the probability of picking the red marble out of a bag of marbles.
- The player to show the correct word card first gets a point.
- Continue playing. The first player to reach 5 points wins.

You will need: 10 index cards

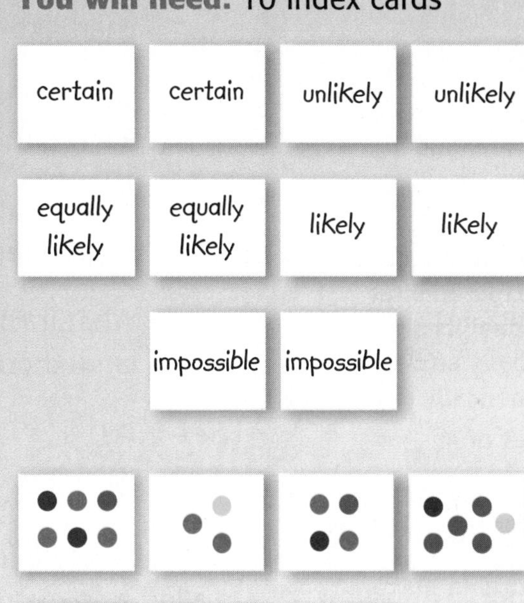

16-2 Probability and Fractions

GET READY to Learn

Hands-On Mini Activity

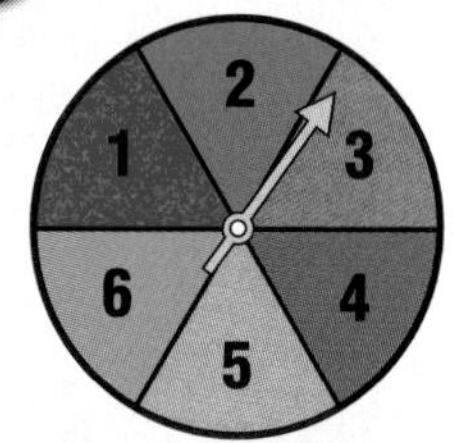

1. Make a spinner and a tally chart like the ones shown.
2. Spin the spinner 20 times. Record the results.
3. Which outcomes occurred most often? How often?
4. What fraction of the spins landed on 6?

Number	Tally
1	
2	
3	
4	
5	
6	

MAIN IDEA

I will describe probability in words and in numbers.

Standard 4SDAP2.2

Express outcomes of experimental probability situations verbally and numerically (e.g., 3 out of 4; $\frac{3}{4}$).

New Vocabulary

favorable outcome

You can use a fraction to describe probability of a desired result, called a **favorable outcome**.

KEY CONCEPT — **Probability as a Fraction**

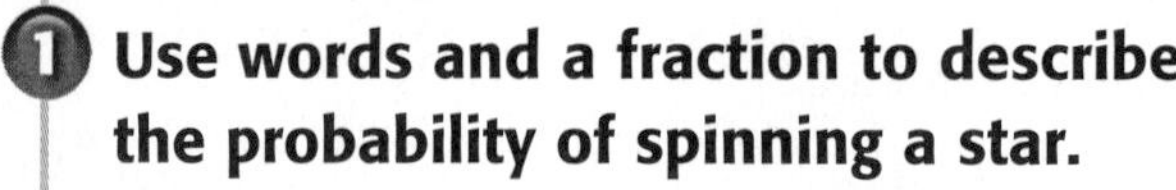

$$\text{Probability} = \frac{\text{number of favorable outcomes}}{\text{total possible outcomes}}$$

EXAMPLE Find Probability

1 Use words and a fraction to describe the probability of spinning a star.

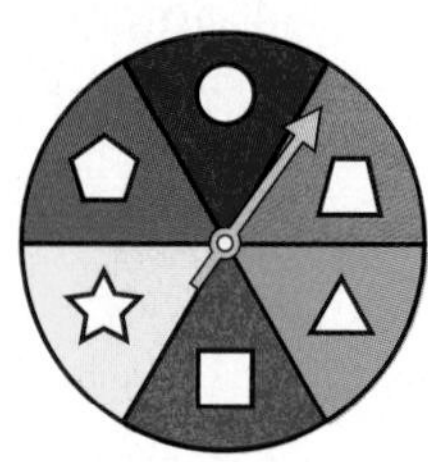

One out of six of the shapes is a star.

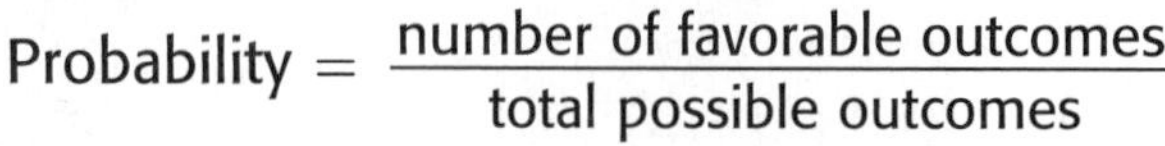

$$\text{Probability} = \frac{\text{number of favorable outcomes}}{\text{total possible outcomes}}$$

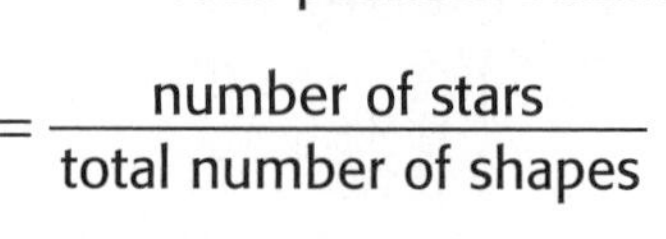

$$= \frac{\text{number of stars}}{\text{total number of shapes}}$$

$$= \frac{1}{6}$$

So, the probability of spinning a star is 1 out of 6, or $\frac{1}{6}$.

Real-World EXAMPLE   Find Probability

2 **SCHOOL Mr. Carter has a box of kick balls. The box has 3 blue, 2 purple, and 7 red kick balls. Use words and a fraction to describe the probability of a student choosing a red kick ball out of the box without looking.**

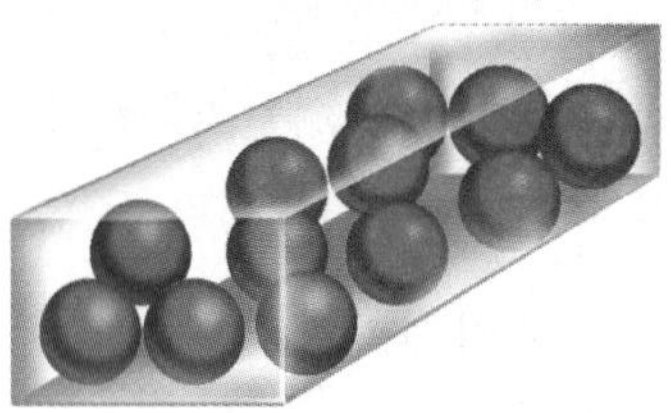

Seven out of twelve of the kick balls are red.

$$\text{Probability} = \frac{\text{number of favorable outcomes}}{\text{total possible outcomes}}$$

$$= \frac{\text{number of red kick balls}}{\text{total number kick balls}}$$

$$= \frac{7}{12}$$

So, the probability of choosing red is $\frac{7}{12}$, or 7 out of 12.

Personal Tutor at ca.gr4math.com

CHECK What You Know

The spinner is spun. Use words and a fraction to describe the probability of each outcome. **See Examples 1 and 2 (pp. 636–637)**

1. D

2. A

3. B or D

4. Z

5. vowel

6. consonant

7. *not* A or C

8. *not* B

9. Marion has a bag of marbles. If he chooses a marble from the bag without looking, what is the probability that Marion will choose a green marble? The marbles are shown at the right.

10. **Talk About It** Paulo dropped an 18-page book on the floor. Is there a greater probability that the book will open to page 8 instead of 12? Explain.

Practice and Problem Solving

EXTRA PRACTICE
See page R40.

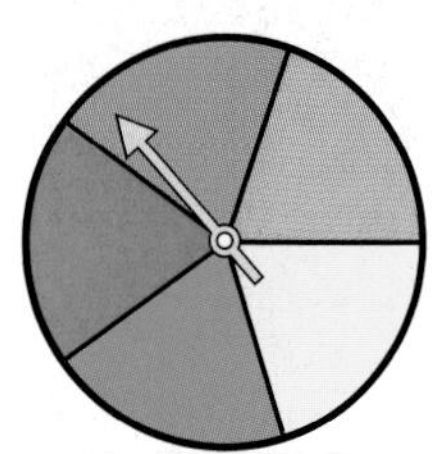

The spinner is spun. Use words and a fraction to describe the probability of each outcome. See Examples 1 and 2 (pp. 636–637)

11. yellow

12. green or blue

13. white

14. a color that is *not* green

15. red

16. a color *not* in the United States flag

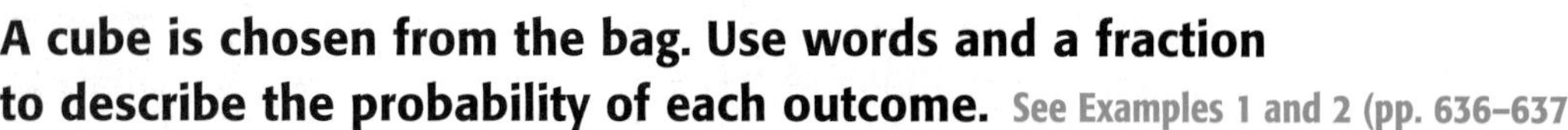

A cube is chosen from the bag. Use words and a fraction to describe the probability of each outcome. See Examples 1 and 2 (pp. 636–637)

17. red cube

18. white cube

19. yellow or red cube

20. blue, red, or yellow cube

21. green sphere

22. primary color cube

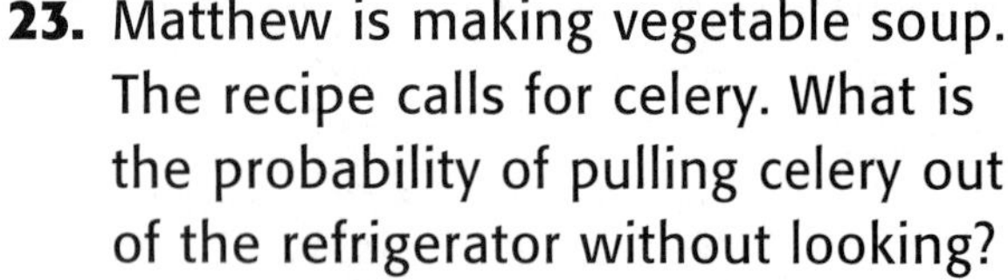

23. Matthew is making vegetable soup. The recipe calls for celery. What is the probability of pulling celery out of the refrigerator without looking?

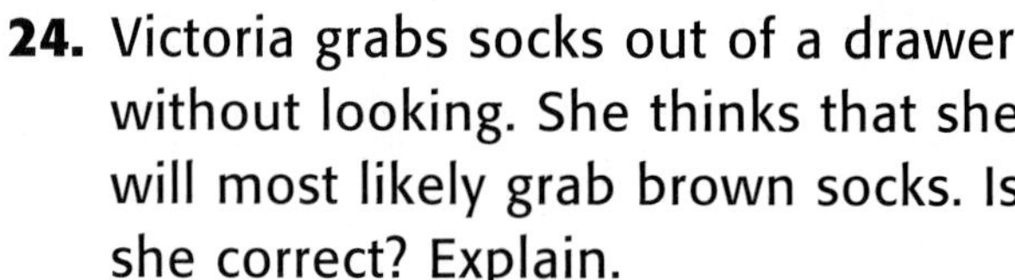

24. Victoria grabs socks out of a drawer without looking. She thinks that she will most likely grab brown socks. Is she correct? Explain.

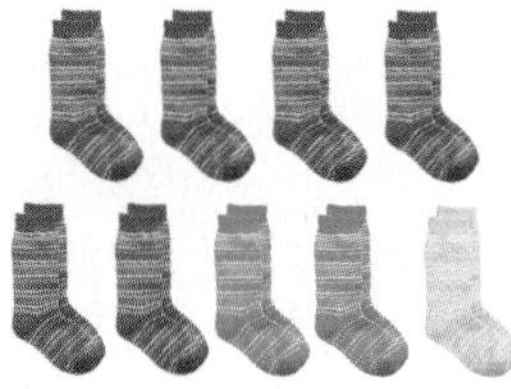

Real-World PROBLEM SOLVING

Language Arts The letters in *California* have been written on tiles and placed in a bag. Without looking, a student will choose a tile from the bag and show it to the class.

25. What is the probability of choosing each letter out of the bag?

26. What letter(s) has the greatest probability of being chosen most often?

H.O.T. Problems

27. **OPEN ENDED** Draw and label a spinner so that the probability of spinning yellow is greater than the probability of spinning green.

28. **CHALLENGE** Latoya has a bag that has 8 cubes. The probability of choosing a blue cube is $\frac{1}{4}$, a red cube is $\frac{1}{2}$, and a black cube $\frac{1}{4}$. How many of each color of cube is in the bag?

29. 

Create a real-world problem that involves probability and has an answer of $\frac{1}{4}$.

Standards Practice

30 Kylie has 7 pencils, 4 pens, 5 markers, and 9 highlighters in her backpack. If she chooses 1 item without looking, which item is she most likely to choose? (Lesson 16-1)

A pencil

B pen

C marker

D highlighter

31 If Ariana chooses 1 piece of fruit without looking, what is the probability that it will be an apple? (Lesson 16-2)

F $\frac{1}{5}$

G 2 out of 5

H 3 out of 5

J $\frac{4}{5}$

Spiral Review

A marble is chosen from the bag without looking. Describe the probability of each outcome. Write *certain, likely, equally likely, unlikely,* or *impossible.* (Lesson 16-1)

32. What is the probability of choosing a blue or yellow marble from the bag?

33. What is the probability of choosing a green marble?

Subtract. Check your answer. (Lesson 15-6)

34. \$26.78 − \$13.06

35. 64.9 − 55.17

36. 90.5 − 43.25

37. Liz has 4 coins in her pocket that total 50 cents. Two of the coins are the same. What coins does Liz have? (Lesson 12-3)

16-3 Problem-Solving Strategy

MAIN IDEA I will make an organized list to solve problems.

Standard 4MR1.1 Analyze problems by identifying relationships, distinguishing relevant from irrelevant information, sequencing and prioritizing information, and observing patterns. Standard 4SDAP2.1 Represent all possible outcomes for a simple probability situation in an organized way (e.g. tables, grids, tree diagrams).

The Burke family is going camping for the weekend. There are four children in the Burke family, Devon, Nikki, Jade, and Terrell. They will sleep in two tents, with two children in each tent. How many different combinations are possible?

Understand

What facts do you know?

- There are 4 children going camping.
- Two children will sleep in each tent.

What do you need to find?

- Find how many combinations are possible.

Plan

You can make a list of all the possible combinations. Then count the total number of different combinations.

Solve

First, write the name of one of the children. Then, write the name of another child by the first child's name. Continue to do this with each child. Do not repeat pairs.

Nikki–Jade **Jade–Terrell** **Terrell–Devon**

Nikki–Terrell **Jade–Devon**

Nikki–Devon

There are 6 different combinations that can be in each tent.

Check

Look back at the problem. There are 4 children. They can each pair up with three other children. The list shows each child's name paired with 3 other children. The answer is correct.

ANALYZE the Strategy

Refer to the problem on the previous page.

1. Suppose one of the children brings a friend camping. How does the additional child affect the possible combinations?

2. Identify another way to organize all of the possible outcomes.

3. Suppose Nikki, Jade, and Terrell go for a hike in a single file line. Make a list to show all the possible ways they can line up.

4. What is the probability that Nikki will be first in line if the children line up in random order?

PRACTICE the Strategy

See page R40.

Solve. *Make an organized list.*

5. Richard has one blue shirt and one red shirt. He has gray pants and navy pants. How many different outfits can he wear?

6. Sadie put four slips of paper into a hat. Each slip of paper has a number written on it as shown. Sadie chooses two slips of paper. How many different sums could she have?

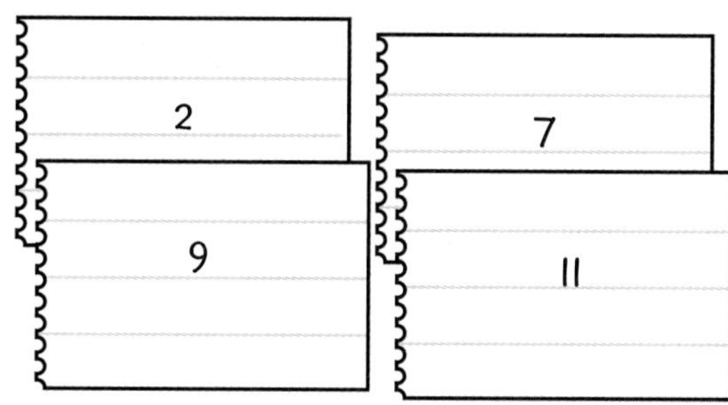

7. Yogi's mom is hanging three photographs side-by-side on a wall. How many different ways can the photographs be arranged?

8. Pari, Montana, Katie, and Leon are in line for lunch. Montana is first. How many ways could the other people be arranged behind her?

9. Jimmy put the coins shown into a piggy bank. If he chooses 2 coins at a time, what possible combinations might he choose?

10. Sandra has three animal-shaped pillows. One is a dog, another is a cat, and the third is a fish. How many different ways can she arrange her pillows?

11. Alexa needs to read a mystery, biography, or fantasy book. Then she must write a report, give a speech, or act out a scene from the book. How many different options are there?

12. **WRITING IN ▸MATH** Look back at Exercise 11. Explain how you used the *make an organized list* strategy to solve the problem.

Explore

Probability Activity for 16-4
Make Predictions

When a **prediction** is made, you think that something will happen, such as the outcome of an experiment.

MAIN IDEA

I will make predictions for a probability situation.

Standard 4MR2.3 **Use a variety of methods, such as words, numbers, symbols,** charts, graphs, **tables,** diagrams, and models, **to explain mathematical reasoning.**

Standard 4SDAP2.1 **Represent all possible outcomes for a simple probability situation in an organized way** (e.g., **tables,** grids, tree diagrams).

You Will Need

connecting cubes, transparent spinner

New Vocabulary

prediction

Animation Lab
ca.gr4math.com

ACTIVITY

Make predictions using 10 connecting cubes.

Step 1 **Get ready for the experiment.**

Make a table like the one shown. Then place 3 green, 5 red, and 2 yellow cubes in a bag.

Outcome	Prediction	Tally	Frequency
Green			
Red			
Yellow			

Step 2 **Make predictions.**

Suppose you were to choose a cube 50 times, placing the cube back into the bag each time. Predict the number of times each color will be chosen. Record your predictions in the table.

Step 3 **Experiment.**

Choose a cube without looking. Use a tally mark to record the color in the table. Repeat 49 times. Then count the tallies and record the numbers in the frequency column.

Step 4 **Examine the results.**

Examine the results of your experiment. Compare your predictions to the actual outcomes. Were your predictions reasonable?

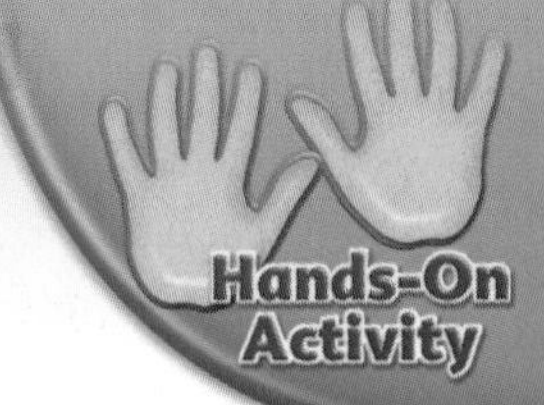

Think About It

1. Suppose one cube is chosen from the bag. What is the probability it will be green? red? yellow? Write each as a fraction.
2. Predict what color will be chosen most often if you were to choose a cube 100 times? 200 times?
3. Suppose 4 red cubes were removed from the bag and not replaced. Predict what color will be chosen most often. Explain.
4. How many cubes of each color should be placed in the bag so that each color has the same probability? Explain.

CHECK What You Know

For Exercises 5–8, use a spinner like the one shown.

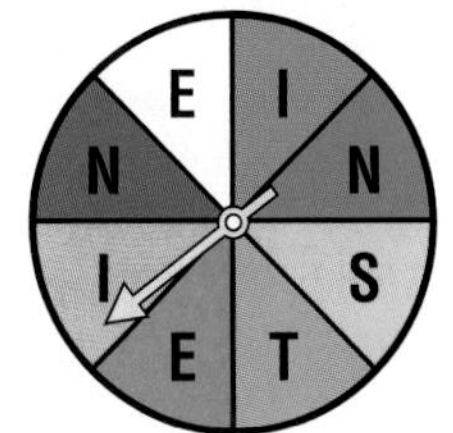

5. If you spin the spinner 40 times, which letter(s) would you predict the spinner to land on the most? Explain.
6. Copy the following table. Spin the spinner 40 times and record your results.

Outcome	Prediction	Tally	Frequency
E			
I			
N			
S			
T			

7. Examine the results. Compare your predictions to the actual outcomes. Were your predictions reasonable? Explain.
8. Use your results to make a prediction about how many times the spinner would land on E if it was spun 80 times. Explain how you made your prediction.
9. **WRITING IN ▸MATH** Create a probability experiment using a spinner. Then predict which outcome(s) would take place most often. Explain your reasoning.

16-4 Find Probability

MAIN IDEA

I will find the probability of outcomes using a grid.

Standard 4SDAP2.1 **Represent all possible outcomes for a simple probability situation in an organized way** (e.g., tables, **grids,** tree diagrams).

Standard 4SDAP2.2 **Express outcomes of experimental probability situations verbally and numerically (e.g., 3 out of 4; $\frac{3}{4}$).**

New Vocabulary

grid

GET READY to Learn

Two spinners are shown. What two-color combinations are possible when both spinners are spun at the same time?

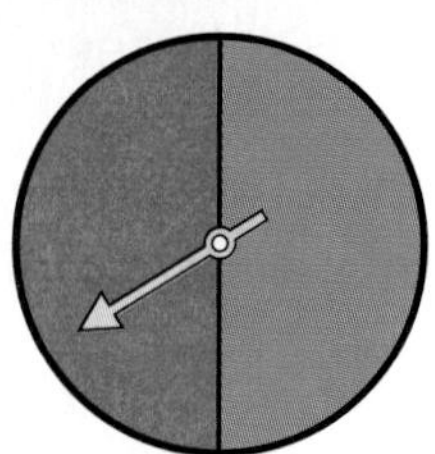

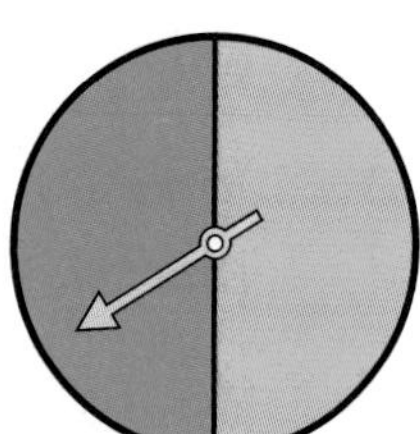

A **grid** can be used to show all of the possible outcomes of a situation. On a grid, each outcome is shown where each row and column intersect.

EXAMPLE Use a Grid

1 **The grid shows the results of spinning the spinners above. Find the probability of the first spinner landing on red and the second spinner landing on yellow.**

		Second Spinner	
		Green	**Yellow**
First Spinner	**Red**	red, green	red, yellow
	Blue	blue, green	blue, yellow

There are four possible color combinations. Red and green, red and yellow, blue and green, and blue and yellow.

One of the outcomes is red and yellow.

$$\text{Probability} = \frac{\text{favorable outcome}}{\text{total possible outcomes}}$$

$$= \frac{1}{4}$$

So, the probability is 1 out of 4, or $\frac{1}{4}$.

Online Personal Tutor at ca.gr4math.com

EXAMPLE Make and Use a Grid

2 **Create a grid to show all the possible outcomes of tossing two coins. Then find the probability of one coin landing on heads and one coin landing on tails.**

Step 1 Write the possible outcomes for each coin on the side and top of the grid.

Step 2 Write the possible outcomes for tossing two coins in the squares where each row and column intersect.

Second Coin

First Coin	heads	tails
heads	heads, heads	heads, tails
tails	tails, heads	tails, tails

There are four possible outcomes. Two of the outcomes are heads, tails. So, the probability of heads, tails is 2 out of 4 or $\frac{2}{4}$.

CHECK What You Know

Two spinners are divided into four equal parts. The grid shows the possible outcomes when each spinner is spun once.

See Examples 1 and 2 (pp. 644–645)

Second Spinner

First Spinner	Red (R)	Blue (B)	Yellow (Y)	Green (G)
Red (R)	RR	RB	RY	RG
Blue (B)	BR	BB	BY	BG
Yellow (Y)	YR	YB	YY	YG
Green (G)	GR	GB	GY	GG

1. How many possible outcomes are there?

2. What is the probability of spinning two different colors?

3. What is the probability of spinning green on the first spin?

4. Make a grid that shows the outcomes for two spinners that both have the colors green, blue, and orange. Find the probability of spinning at least one orange.

5. Talk About It Refer to Exercise 4. How could you use multiplication to find the total number of outcomes?

Practice and Problem Solving

See page R40.

One spinner is divided into four equal parts. A second spinner is divided into five equal parts. The grid shows the possible outcomes when each spinner is spun once. See Examples 1 and 2 (pp. 644–645)

6. How many possible outcomes are there?

7. What is the probability that an outcome contains numbers that are both greater than 3?

8. Find the probability of spinning the same two numbers.

Second Spinner

First Spinner	1	2	3	4
1	1, 1	1, 2	1, 3	1, 4
2	2, 1	2, 2	2, 3	2, 4
3	3, 1	3, 2	3, 3	3, 4
4	4, 1	4, 2	4, 3	4, 4
5	5, 1	5, 2	5, 3	5, 4

Make a grid to find each probability.

9. Two number cubes are numbered 1–6. Nina needs to roll a sum of 8 or greater to win a game. Find the probability that Nina will win.

10. There is one red shirt, one green shirt, and one blue shirt in a drawer. There are black and tan pants in another drawer. One shirt and pants are randomly chosen. Find the probability that a green shirt is chosen.

Real-World PROBLEM SOLVING

Nature A bush has flowers that can bloom in four different colors. Suppose it is equally likely for a bush to have any color flowers.

11. Two bushes are randomly chosen. What is the probability that at least one has blue flowers?

12. What is the probability that a bush will have the same color of flowers?

Bush 2

Bush 1	Blue (B)	Green (G)	Pink (P)	White (W)
Blue (B)	B, B	B, G	B, P	B, W
Green (G)	G, B	G, G	G, P	G, W
Pink (P)	P, B	P, G	P, P	P, W
White (W)	W, B	W, G	W, P	W, W

H.O.T. Problems

13. OPEN ENDED Draw and label two spinners with at least three different colors on each. The outcomes of spinning the spinners must include landing on red more often than any other color.

14. WRITING IN ▶MATH Look at Exercise 13. Use a grid to explain how the spinners you created land on red more often than any other color in the possible outcomes.

CHAPTER 16

Mid-Chapter Check

Lessons 16-1 through 16-4

The spinner is spun. Describe the probability of each outcome. Write *certain, likely, equally likely, unlikely,* or *impossible.* (Lesson 16-1)

1. odd number

2. a number less than 10

3. **STANDARDS PRACTICE** Tyler has a bag of tiles numbered 1–15. He will choose a tile without looking. Which of the following is impossible? (Lesson 16-1)

   A choosing an odd number

   B choosing an even number

   C choosing a 0

   D choosing a composite number

One piece of fruit is chosen without looking. Use words and a fraction to describe the probability of each outcome. (Lesson 16-2)

4. orange

5. apple or peach

6. **STANDARDS PRACTICE** If a student chooses one game piece without looking, what is the probability that it will not be purple? (Lesson 16-2)

   F $\frac{1}{7}$ **H** 5 out of 7

   G 2 out of 7 **J** $\frac{6}{7}$

7. Serena has one red shirt and one white shirt. She has one blue skirt and one black skirt. How many different outfits can she create? (Lesson 16-3)

For Exercises 8 and 9, use the grid that shows the outcome of two spinners. (Lesson 16-4)

Spinner 2

Spinner 1	Red	Yellow	Green	Blue
Red	red, red	red, yellow	red, green	red, blue
Blue	blue, red	blue, yellow	blue, green	blue, blue

8. How many outcomes are there?

9. What is the probability of spinning two different colors?

10. **WRITING IN MATH** Describe the probability of a spinner landing on B if the spinner has sections that are all labeled with C. Explain.

Problem Solving in Science

CORAL REEFS

Coral reefs are among the most diverse communities on Earth. Coral reefs can include up to 800 kinds of coral. Coral reefs can be a variety of colors, such as white, red, pink, green, blue, orange, and purple. They also provide food and shelter for about 4,000 kinds of fish and hundreds of other marine animals and plants.

Some of the marine animals that live in this habitat are sponges, fish, jellies, sea stars, crabs, lobsters, turtles, and sea snakes.

Did You Know?

Millions of plants and animals living near coral reefs have not been discovered.

Standard 4SDAP2.2 Express outcomes of experimental **probability situations verbally and numerically** (e.g., 3 out of 4; $\frac{3}{4}$).

Real-World Math

Use the information below to solve each problem.

Riley is going scuba diving in a coral reef. There are three blue fish, seven yellow fish, one sea turtle, and two eels that are visible in the reef.

1. What animal is Riley most likely to see? Explain.
2. Is Riley more likely to see a blue fish or an eel? Explain.
3. What is the probability that Riley will see an animal that has fins?
4. Use fractions to explain what animal Riley is least likely to see.
5. Tell whether there are any animals Riley is equally likely to see. Explain.
6. Describe the probabilities of seeing each animal as *certain*, *likely*, *equally likely*, *unlikely*, or *impossible*.

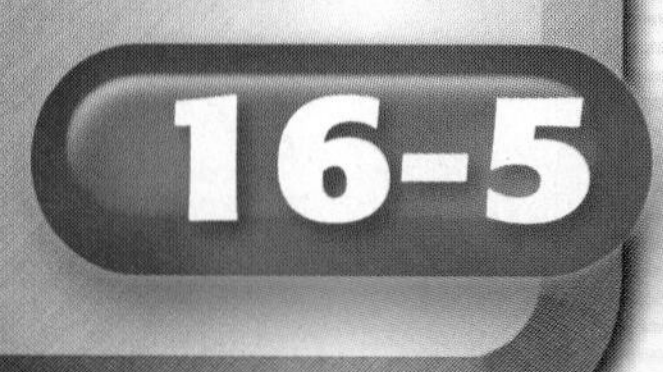

16-5 Problem-Solving Investigation

MAIN IDEA I will choose the best strategy to solve a problem.

Standard 4MR1.1 **Analyze problems by identifying relationships, distinguishing relevant from irrelevant information, sequencing, and prioritizing information, and observing patterns.** Standard 4NS3.0 **Students solve problems involving addition, subtraction, of whole numbers and understand the relationships among the operations.**

P.S.I. TEAM +

CARMEN: My family ate at a restaurant. We ordered salads for $6 each, steaks for $15 each, and sandwiches for $8 each. The total cost was $43.

YOUR MISSION: Find how many of each item was ordered.

Understand	You know the cost of each item and the total cost of the meal. Find how many of each item was ordered.
Plan	Use logical reasoning to solve the problem.
Solve	At least one of each item was ordered. Add the costs. $15 1 steak $ 6 1 salad + $ 8 1 sandwich $29 So, the cost of the other items ordered must be $43 − $29, or $14. Since $8 + $6 is the only combination of costs that equal $14, you know that another salad and another sandwich were ordered. So, they ordered 1 steak, 2 salads, and 2 sandwiches.
Check	Look back at the problem. Check your answer with addition. $6 + $6 + $8 + $8 + $15 = $43 So, the answer is correct.

Mixed Problem Solving

See page R41.

Use any strategy shown below to solve. Tell what strategy you used.

PROBLEM-SOLVING STRATEGIES

- Use logical reasoning.
- Make a model.
- Make an organized list.
- Draw a picture.
- Work backward.

1. There are 6 wagons for the fall hayride. Each wagon needs 4 horses to pull it. How many horses will it take to pull all 6 wagons?

2. There are four boys and six girls in line at a movie theater. Each is carrying two food items purchased at the concession stand. How many food items do they have in all?

3. Curtis bought the meal shown below. He paid with a $20 bill and his change was $14.25. If the fruit juice cost $1.25, how much did each taco cost?

4. Macie made 70 bracelets in 3 colors. She made 22 red bracelets and 18 blue bracelets. How many bracelets were yellow?

5. Carol, Irina, Yori, and Nora are on a relay team. The fastest girl will run last. The slowest girl will run second. Irina runs faster than Carol. Nora runs first. Irina runs slower than Yori. In What order does the team run?

6. Julie sold roses at a bike club fundraiser. Use the pattern in the table below to find how many roses she had left on Friday.

Day	Started with	Ended with
Monday	96	48
Tuesday	48	24
Wednesday	24	12
Thursday	12	6
Friday	6	■

7. Amós's baseball team needs $2,500 to pay for camp. They raised $310.35 in April and $477.67 in May. They already had $1,203.59 saved. How much do they still need to pay for camp?

8. **Measurement** An object on Earth weighs 6 times its weight on the moon. An astronaut weighs 210 pounds on Earth. How much would he or she weigh on the moon?

9. **WRITING IN MATH** There are three rock, five country, and two oldies CDs in Mrs. Link's car. The answer is $\frac{5}{10}$. What is the question?

16-6 Tree Diagrams

GET READY to Learn

Ginny and Josefina are playing with the spinner and letter tiles shown. What are all the possible combinations of spinning the spinner and choosing one letter tile from a bag without looking?

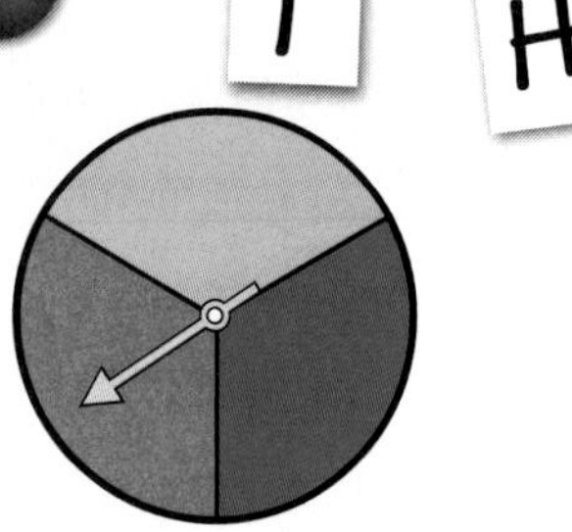

MAIN IDEA

I will use a tree diagram to show outcomes.

Standard 4SDAP2.1 **Represent all possible outcomes for a simple probability situation in an organized way** (e.g., tables, grids, **tree diagrams).**

Standard 4SDAP2.2 **Express outcomes of experimental probability situations verbally and numerically (e.g., 3 out of 4; $\frac{3}{4}$).**

New Vocabulary

tree diagram

You can use a **tree diagram** to show all possible outcomes of any event.

EXAMPLE Use a Tree Diagram

1 **How many outcomes are possible if you spin the spinner once and choose one letter tile from the bag?**

Use a tree diagram to find the possible outcomes.

List each color on the spinner. Then pair each color with a letter from the tiles.

Spinner	Tile	Outcome
red	M	red, M
	A	red, A
	T	red, T
	H	red, H
yellow	M	yellow, M
	A	yellow, A
	T	yellow, T
	H	yellow, H
blue	M	blue, M
	A	blue, A
	T	blue, T
	H	blue, H

There are 12 possible outcomes.

Online Personal Tutor at ca.gr4math.com

EXAMPLE Use a Tree Diagram

2 **Rico is tossing a coin and choosing a marble from the bag shown. What is the probability of landing on heads and choosing an orange marble?**

Coin	Marble	Outcome
heads	blue	heads, blue
	green	heads, green
	orange	heads, orange
	red	heads, red
tails	blue	tails, blue
	green	tails, green
	orange	tails, orange
	red	tails, red

There are 8 possible outcomes and one is heads, orange.

$$\text{Probability} = \frac{\text{heads, orange}}{\text{total possible outcomes}} = \frac{1}{8}$$

CHECK What You Know

Draw a tree diagram to show all possible outcomes. Then find the probability for each situation. See Examples 1 and 2 (pp. 652–653)

1. Toss a coin and spin the spinner. Find the probability of landing on heads and spinning a baseball.

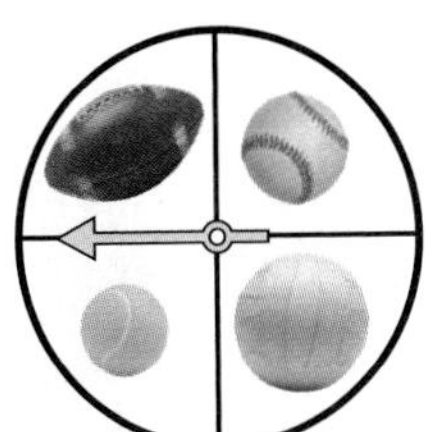

2. Toss a coin and roll a number cube numbered 1–6. Find the probability of landing on tails and landing on 3.

3. Zane is deciding what to eat for lunch. How many sandwich and drink combinations does he have to choose from?

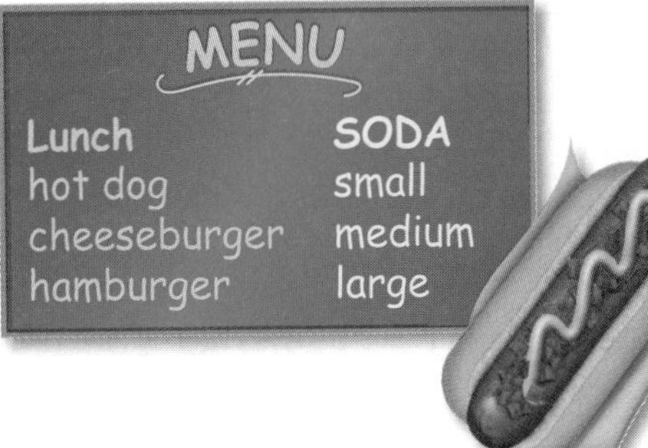

MENU
Lunch
hot dog
cheeseburger
hamburger
SODA
small
medium
large

4. Talk About It Explain how a tree diagram and an organized list are the same. How are they different?

Practice and Problem Solving

See page R41.

Draw a tree diagram to show all possible outcomes. Then find the probability for each situation. See Examples 1 and 2 (pp. 652–653)

5. Spin a spinner and roll a number cube numbered 5–10. Find the probability of landing on blue and rolling a 7.

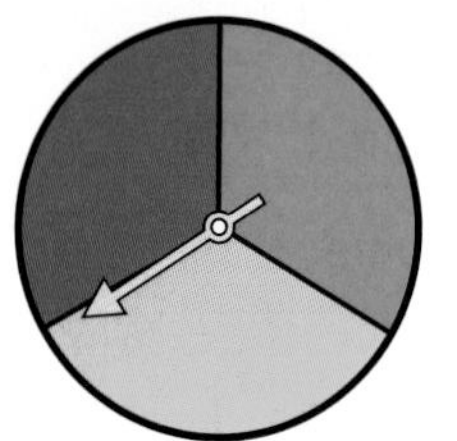

6. Tossing a coin and choosing a marble. Find the probability of green and heads.

7. Spin a spinner and roll a number cube numbered 0–5. Find the probability of a sum of 6.

8. Find the probability of randomly choosing a blue sweatshirt.

Souvenirs

Item	Color
T-shirt	blue
sweatshirt	yellow
hat	

9. Elki was randomly given a party favor. What is the probability Elki got a red ball?

Type of Toy	Color
Ball	blue
Stuffed animal	orange
Whistle	green
	yellow
	red

10. What is the probability of randomly choosing a jean jacket and a pink hat?

11. A spinner is labeled with five numbers. The probability of landing on a multiple of 2 is $\frac{0}{5}$. What does this tell you about the numbers on the spinner?

H.O.T. Problems

12. **CHALLENGE** Make a tree diagram to show all possible crust/size/topping combinations. How many combinations include a thick crust and a small size?

Crust	Size	Toppings
Thick	Small	Veggie
Thin	Medium	Meat
	Large	

13.  Can you have a probability of $\frac{3}{2}$? Explain.

Standards Practice

14 If Manuel spins the spinner twice, what are all the possible outcomes? (Lesson 16-4)

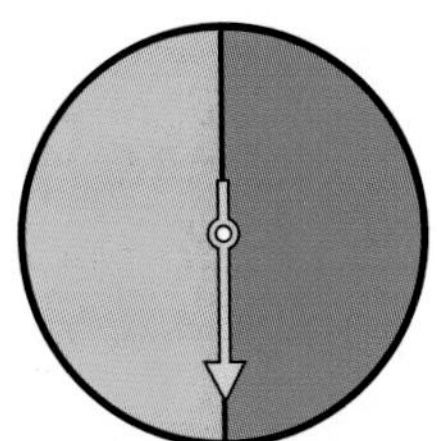

A 2 blue or 1 blue and 1 yellow

B 2 blue or 2 yellow or 1 blue and 1 yellow

C 2 blue or 1 blue and 1 yellow

D 2 blue or 2 yellow

15 A coin is tossed. What is the probability of landing on heads? (Lesson 16-6)

F $\frac{1}{4}$

G $\frac{1}{3}$

H $\frac{1}{2}$

J $\frac{2}{2}$

16 A number cube is numbered 2, 3, 5, 7, 11, and 13. What is the probability that when rolled twice, the sum of the numbers is a composite number? (Lesson 16-6)

A $\frac{3}{6}$

B $\frac{5}{36}$

C $\frac{18}{36}$

D $\frac{5}{6}$

Spiral Review

17. A basketball team won a game by 6 points. The sum of the teams' scores was 70. How many points did each team score? (Lesson 16-5)

18. Hugo has 2 quarters and 2 dimes in his pocket. Use a grid to show the possible outcomes of pulling 2 coins out of his pocket one at a time. (Lesson 16-4)

Divide. Use estimation to check. (Lesson 9-8)

19. $3\overline{)624}$

20. $2\overline{)315}$

21. $5\overline{)1{,}045}$

22. Solve the equation $5 \times k = 30$ mentally.

CHAPTER 16

Study Guide and Review

FOLDABLES Study Organizer GET READY to Study

Be sure the following Key Vocabulary words and Key Concepts are written in your Foldable.

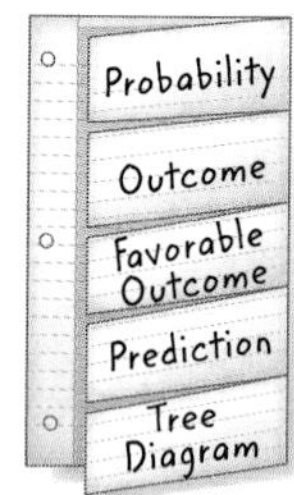

BIG Ideas

Probability (pp. 631 and 636)

- **Probability** is the chance that an **outcome** will occur. A fraction can be used to describe probability.

$$\text{Probability} = \frac{\textbf{favorable outcome}}{\text{total possible outcomes}}$$

Tree Diagrams (p. 652)

- A tree diagram shows all of the possible outcomes of any event, such as tossing two coins.

Coin 1	Coin 2	Outcome
heads	heads	heads, heads
	tails	heads, tails
tails	heads	tails, heads
	tails	tails, tails

Key Vocabulary

outcome (p. 631)
prediction (p. 642)
probability (p. 631)
tree diagram (p. 652)

Vocabulary Check

Decide which vocabulary word best completes each sentence.

1. The chance that an outcome will occur is its ___?___ .
2. A(n) ___?___ is a result.
3. A(n) ___?___ can be used to show all possible outcomes of any event.
4. The ___?___ of an event can be described as *certain, likely, equally likely, unlikely,* and *impossible*.
5. When a(n) ___?___ is made, you think something will happen.
6. You can use a(n) ___?___ to find probability.

Lesson-by-Lesson Review

16-1 Probability and Outcomes (pp. 631–635)

Example 1
A marble is chosen without looking. Describe the probability that the chosen marble will be red.

There are 10 marbles, and 6 are red.

Since more than half the marbles are red, it is likely to choose a red.

The spinner is spun. Describe the probability of each outcome. Write *certain, likely, equally likely, unlikely,* or *impossible*.

7. 3 or 5

8. even number

9. a number greater than 7

10. prime number

16-2 Probability and Fractions (pp. 636–639)

Example 2
The number cube is labeled 5–10. Use words and a fraction to describe he probability of rolling a number that is less than 7.

Two out of six of the numbers are less than 7.

$$\text{Probability} = \frac{\text{favorable outcomes}}{\text{total possible outcomes}}$$

$$= \frac{\text{a number less than 7}}{\text{all numbers}}$$

$$= \frac{2}{6}$$

So, the probability is 2 out of 6 or $\frac{2}{6}$

The spinner is spun. Use words and a fraction to describe the probability of each outcome.

11. purple

12. primary color

13. *not* blue

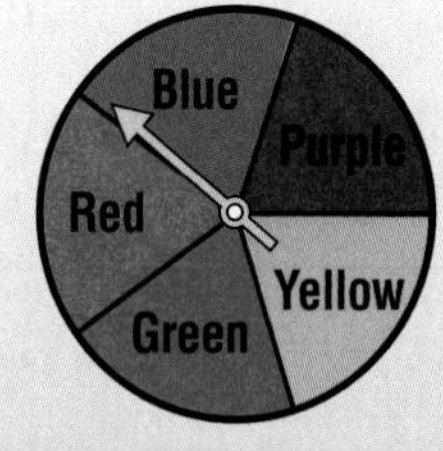

Six letter tiles are labeled S, C, H, O, O, L. One letter tile is randomly chosen. Use words and a fraction to describe the probability of each outcome.

14. O

15. C

16. vowel

17. consonant

16-3 Problem-Solving Strategy: Make an Organized List (pp. 640–641)

Example 3

Daniel, Erik, Owen, and Alek are going hiking. They will hike in pairs. How many different pairs of hiking partners are possible?

Understand

What facts do you know?

- There are four people hiking.
- They will hike in pairs.

What do you need to find?

- Find how many pairs of hiking partners are possible.

Plan Make an organized list.

Solve First, write the name of one person. Then, write the name of another person by the first person's name. Continue to do this with each person. Do not repeat pairs.

Daniel – Erik Erik – Owen

Daniel – Owen Erik – Alek

Daniel – Alek Owen – Alek

There are 6 different pairs.

Check Look back at the problem. The answer makes sense for the problem. So, the answer is correct.

Solve. Use the *make an organized list* strategy.

18. Sergio has to create a combination of three numbers for his lock. The lock has 2, 4, and 6 written on it. How many possible combinations could he choose?

19. The four toys are to be placed on a shelf. How many different ways can the toys be arranged?

20. Drake, Juliana, Carlo, and Sofia are in line for the bus. Drake is first. How many ways can the other people be arranged behind him?

21. Wendy is arranging CDs on a shelf. She has classical, country, pop, and rock CDs. How many different ways can the CDs be arranged?

22. A gardener is planting daffodil, daisy, and lily bulbs along a sidewalk. How many different ways can the three bulbs be arranged?

16-4 Find Probability (pp. 644–646)

Example 4
Each spinner is spun once. Find the probability of spinning blue and green.

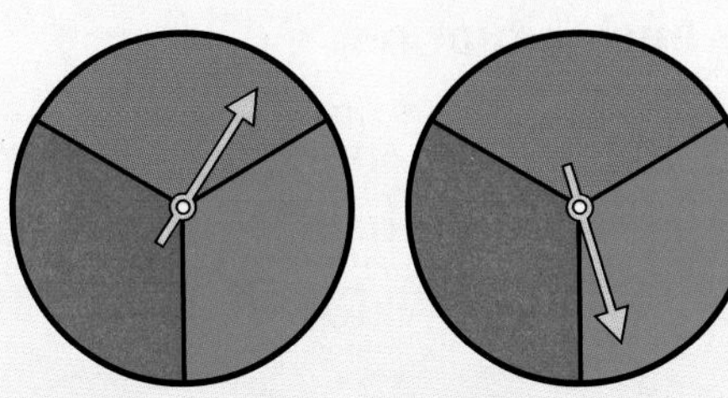

		Spinner 2		
		Red (R)	**Green (G)**	**Blue (B)**
Spinner 1	**Red (R)**	R, R	R, G	R, B
	Green (G)	G, R	G, G	G, B
	Blue(B)	B, R	B, G	B, B

$$\text{Probability} = \frac{\text{blue and green}}{\text{total possible outcomes}}$$
$$= \frac{2}{9}$$

Two spinners are divided into three equal parts. The grid shows the possible outcomes when each spinner is spun once.

		Spinner 2		
		4	**5**	**6**
Spinner 1	**1**	1, 4	1, 5	1, 6
	2	2, 4	2, 5	2, 6
	3	3, 4	3, 5	3, 6

23. How many outcomes are possible?

24. What is the probability that both numbers are less than 5?

25. Find the probability that both numbers are odd?

26. What is the probability of spinning two prime numbers?

16-5 Problem-Solving Investigation: Choose a Strategy (pp. 650–651)

Example 5
Alberto has $4.50 left after buying skates for $62.50 and a helmet for $24. How much did he have originally?

Use the work backward strategy.

$ 4.50	Change
+ $62.50	Amount for skates
$67.00	
+ $24.00	Amount for helmet
$91.00	

So, Alberto had $91 originally.

Use any strategy to solve.

27. A teacher is arranging 24 desks. If she wants to group the desks in groups of 4, how many groups will she have?

28. Peter can choose a ham or turkey sandwich. He can choose an apple or orange. How many different sandwich and fruit combinations can Peter choose?

16-6 Tree Diagrams (pp. 652–655)

Example 6
Angie can use clay or paper for an art project. Her project can be blue, green, or yellow. What are all the combinations of material and color Angie's art project can be?

Use a tree diagram.

Material	Color	Outcome
clay	blue	clay, blue
	green	clay, green
	yellow	clay, yellow
paper	blue	paper, blue
	green	paper, green
	yellow	paper, yellow

There are six possible combinations.

Example 7
Chantal is flipping two coins. What is the probability of tossing two heads?

Use a tree diagram.

Coin 1	Coin 2	Outcome
heads	heads	heads, heads
	tails	heads, tails
tails	heads	tails, heads
	tails	tails, tails

There are 4 possible outcomes. One of these outcomes is two heads. So, the probability is 1 out of 4 or $\frac{1}{4}$.

For Excercises 29 and 30, draw a tree diagram to show all possible outcomes. Then find the probability for each situation.

29. Toss a coin and spin the spinner. Find the probability landing on tails and spinning purple.

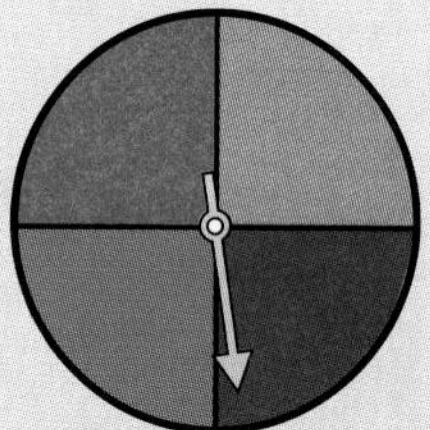

30. Choose a marble and roll a number cube numbered 1–6. Find the probability of choosing green and rolling 2.

31. Dustin randomly chooses a shirt. What is the probability of selecting a green long sleeved shirt?

Shirts	
Type	**Color**
long sleeved	blue
short sleeved	green
button up	red
	white

32. What is the probability of randomly choosing a blue or green short sleeved shirt?

Chapter 16 Chapter Test

For Exercises 1 and 2, tell whether each statement is *true* or *false*.

1. A tree diagram shows all of the possible outcomes of an event.

2. You can only use a fraction to describe the probability of a favorable outcome.

The spinner is spun. Describe the probability of each outcome. Write *certain, likely, equally likely, unlikely,* or *impossible*.

3. round object

4. sports ball

5. basketball

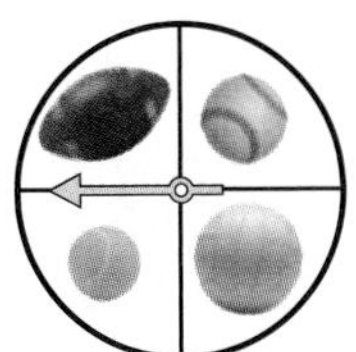

6. Draw a tree diagram to show all possible outcomes of flipping a coin and choosing one pattern block.

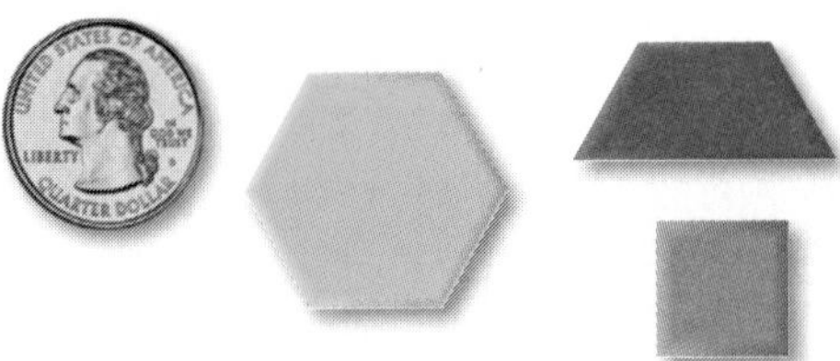

7. **STANDARDS PRACTICE** If Ana spins the spinner, what outcome is most likely?

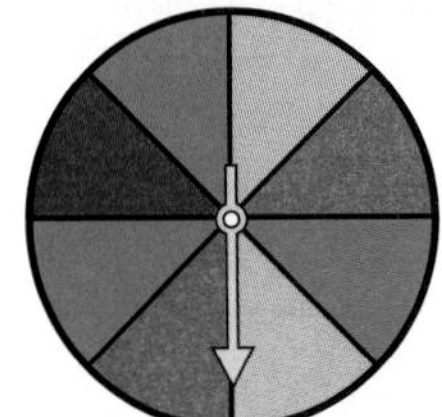

A red **C** green

B yellow **D** purple

A number cube numbered 5-10 is rolled. Use words and a fraction to describe the probability of each outcome.

8. 7, 8, or 9

9. prime number

10. number less than 7

11. Zachary purchased a video game for \$35 and a controller for \$21. How much change will he get if he pays the cashier \$60?

The two spinners are each spun once.

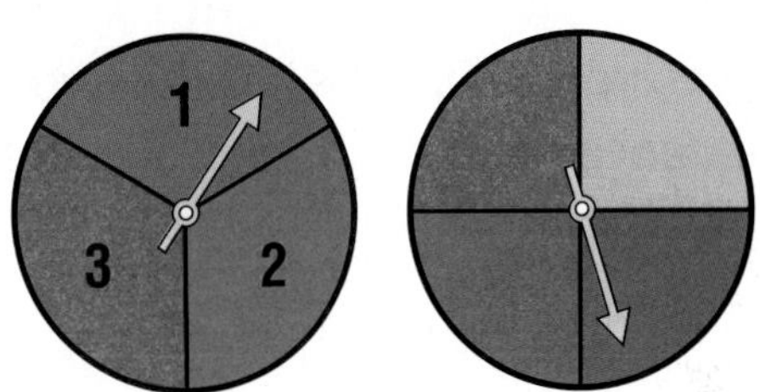

12. How many outcomes are possible?

13. What is the probability of spinning a 3 and landing on yellow?

14. **STANDARDS PRACTICE** Two coins are flipped. What is the probability that both coins will land on heads?

F $\frac{1}{4}$ **H** $\frac{3}{4}$

G $\frac{2}{4}$ **J** $\frac{4}{4}$

15. **WRITING IN MATH** Write a problem that involves probability and has an answer of $\frac{1}{3}$.

CHAPTER 16

California Standards Practice

Cumulative, Chapters 1–16

Standards Example

Mandy has a bag of marbles. Of the 14 marbles, 2 are blue, 1 is green, 8 are red, and 3 are yellow. If Mandy choses a marble without looking, which color is likely to be pulled?

A blue

B green

C red

D yellow

Read the Question

Find the color that is likely to be pulled.

Solve the Question

There are 14 marbles. Of those marbles, 8 are red. Since most of the marbles are red, it is likely that red will be chosen.

The answer is C.

Personal Tutor at ca.gr4math.com

Choose the best answer.

1 **Kari has a bag of 20 blocks. Six are blue, 4 are red, 7 are green, and 3 are yellow. If Kari chooses a block without looking, which color is most likely to be chosen?**

A blue

B green

C red

D yellow

2 **Two ribbons, one yellow and one blue, are placed in an envelope. What is the probability of choosing a yellow ribbon from the envelope without looking?**

F 2

G 1

H $\frac{1}{2}$

J $\frac{1}{4}$

3 **Admission to the amusement park is \$40 for adults and \$25 for children. How much will admission cost for 1 adult and 3 children?**

A \$90

B \$115

C \$145

D \$160

---

4 **Larisa has three pairs of pants and two sweaters.**

Larisa's Outfits	
Pants	tan, black, navy
Sweaters	red stripe, white

How many different outfits can Larisa wear?

F 3

G 5

H 6

J 12

---

5 **Nadia tossed a number cube labeled 1–6. What is the probability that she will toss an even number?**

A $\frac{1}{6}$

B $\frac{1}{5}$

C $\frac{1}{3}$

D $\frac{1}{2}$

---

6 **What is the value of the expression below if $y = 7$?**

$$84 \div (y + 5)$$

F 7

G 12

H 14

J 42

---

7 **Which is the best estimate for $323 \div 80$?**

A 4

B 5

C 40

D 50

---

8 **What kind of triangle always has 3 acute angles and 3 sides the same length?**

F right

G scalene

H isosceles

J equilateral

---

9 **What is the value of the digit 7 in 279,685?**

A 700,000

B 70,000

C 7000

D 70

---

10 **The grid shows the possible outcomes of spinning two different spinners.**

Spinner 2 (columns) / **Spinner 1** (rows)

	1	2	3	4
A	A, 1	A, 2	A, 3	A, 4
B	B, 1	B, 2	B, 3	B, 4
C	C, 1	C, 2	C, 3	C, 4
D	D, 1	D, 2	D, 3	D, 4

What is the probability of landing on B and an odd number?

F $\frac{1}{16}$

G $\frac{1}{8}$

H $\frac{1}{4}$

J $\frac{1}{2}$

Looking Ahead

to the Grade 5 Standards

Let's Look Ahead!

Add and Subtract Mixed Numbers

MAIN IDEA

I will add and subtract mixed numbers with like denominators.

Preparation for Standard

5NS2.3 Solve simple problems, including ones arising in concrete situations, involving the addition and subtraction of fractions and mixed numbers (like and unlike denominators of 20 or less), and express answers in the simplest form.

GET READY to Learn

Rosa and Myles are making one batch of lemon-orange drink. How many combined cups of orange juice and lemonade will they need?

Lemon-Orange Drink
1 3/4 c orange juice
Makes: one batch
1 1/4 c lemonade
5 1/4 c water

Mixed numbers like $1\frac{3}{4}$ and $1\frac{1}{4}$ have the same or like denominators. You can add mixed numbers with like denominators.

KEY CONCEPT — Add Mixed Numbers

To add mixed numbers with like denominators,

- First, add the fractions.
- Then add the whole numbers. Regroup and simplify if needed.

Real-World EXAMPLE

1 **MEASUREMENT** **How many combined cups of orange juice and lemonade will Rosa and Myles need?**

You need to add $1\frac{3}{4}$ and $1\frac{1}{4}$.

Step 1 Add fractions.

$$\begin{array}{r} 1\frac{3}{4} \\ +\ 1\frac{1}{4} \\ \hline \frac{4}{4} \end{array}$$

Step 2 Add whole numbers. Then regroup and simplify.

$$\begin{array}{r} 1\frac{3}{4} \\ +1\frac{1}{4} \\ \hline 2\frac{4}{4} \end{array} = 2 + 1 = 3 \qquad \left(\frac{4}{4} = 1\right)$$

So, 3 cups of orange juice and lemonade are needed.

You can also subtract mixed numbers with like denominators.

KEY **CONCEPT** — Subtract Mixed Numbers

To subtract mixed numbers with like denominators,

- First, subtract the fractions.
- Then subtract the whole numbers. Regroup and simplify if needed.

Real-World **EXAMPLE**

2 MEASUREMENT It took Len $1\frac{5}{6}$ hours to set up a tent. It took him $\frac{1}{6}$ hour to take down the tent. How many hours longer did it take to set up the tent?

You need to subtract $1\frac{5}{6} - \frac{1}{6}$.

When adding and subtracting fractions, always write the answer in simplest form.

Step 1 Subtract fractions.

$$\begin{array}{r} 1\frac{5}{6} \\ -\ \frac{1}{6} \\ \hline \frac{4}{6} \end{array}$$

Step 2 Subtract whole numbers.

$$\begin{array}{r} 1\frac{5}{6} \\ -\ \frac{1}{6} \\ \hline 1\frac{4}{6} \end{array}$$

Step 3 Simplify.

$$\begin{array}{r} 1\frac{5}{6} \\ -\ \frac{1}{6} \\ \hline 1\frac{4}{6} \end{array} = 1\frac{2}{3}$$

Rename $\frac{4}{6}$ as $\frac{2}{3}$.

So, it took Len $1\frac{2}{3}$ hours longer to set up the tent.

Check

You can use addition to check.

$$\begin{array}{r} 1\frac{4}{6} \\ +\ \frac{1}{6} \\ \hline 1\frac{5}{6} \end{array}$$

Add the mixed number and fraction with the like denominators.

So, the answer is correct. ✓

Online **Personal Tutor at** ca.gr4math.com

CHECK What You Know

Add or subtract. Write in simplest form. See Examples 1 and 2 (pp. 666–667)

1. $1\frac{1}{3} + 2\frac{1}{3}$

2. $3\frac{2}{5} + 4\frac{3}{5}$

3. $2\frac{4}{5} - 1\frac{1}{5}$

4. $3\frac{8}{9} - 2\frac{5}{9}$

5. Amal is filling a bird feeder with a mixture of $1\frac{1}{3}$ cups of sunflower seeds and $1\frac{2}{3}$ cups of corn. How much feed does Amal put in the bird feeder?

6. Talk About It Explain how to write the difference of $7\frac{5}{6}$ and $3\frac{1}{6}$ in simplest form.

Practice and Problem Solving

Add or subtract. Write in simplest form. See Examples 1 and 2 (pp. 666–667)

7. $2\frac{3}{5} + 1\frac{1}{5}$

8. $3\frac{4}{10} + 4\frac{5}{10}$

9. $2\frac{2}{8} + 4\frac{4}{8}$

10. $3\frac{4}{9} + 5\frac{5}{9}$

11. $8\frac{4}{5} - 5\frac{1}{5}$

12. $6\frac{6}{8} - 3\frac{1}{8}$

13. $9\frac{3}{4} - 4\frac{1}{4}$

14. $5\frac{7}{10} - \frac{2}{10}$

15. $6\frac{5}{12} + \frac{7}{12}$

16. $7\frac{1}{6} + \frac{1}{6}$

17. $6\frac{11}{12} - 1\frac{1}{12}$

18. $8\frac{5}{8} - 6$

Measurement **Add or subtract to solve.**

19. Antonio bought $2\frac{2}{8}$ pounds of red grapes and $\frac{5}{8}$ pounds of green grapes for a fruit salad. How many pounds of grapes did he buy in all?

20. Tate rode his bike $3\frac{2}{6}$ miles to Ali's house. They then rode to the movie theater, which was another $2\frac{3}{6}$ miles. How many miles did Tate ride in all?

Algebra **Compare. Use >, <, or =.**

21. $3\frac{1}{4} + 2\frac{1}{4}$ ● 6

22. $1\frac{3}{5} + 3\frac{2}{5}$ ● 5

23. 9 ● $5\frac{3}{10} + 4\frac{1}{10}$

24. 4 ● $7\frac{7}{12} - 3\frac{5}{12}$

25. $9\frac{8}{9} - 6\frac{5}{9}$ ● 4

26. 2 ● $3\frac{5}{8} - 2\frac{3}{8}$

27. How much taller is the second sunflower than the first sunflower?

28. The table shows how many hours Mike will sing during the school music concert on Saturday and Sunday. How long will he sing during both days?

Mike's Music Concert	
Day	**Time (h)**
Saturday	$2\frac{1}{4}$
Sunday	$1\frac{1}{4}$

Real-World PROBLEM SOLVING

Waterfalls The world's largest indoor waterfalls are listed in the table.

29. What is the difference in height between the tallest and shortest waterfall?

30. Which two waterfalls have a difference of $7\frac{3}{10}$ meters?

31. What is the difference in height of Trump Tower and the Orchid Hotel waterfalls?

Largest Indoor Waterfall	
Waterfall	**Height (m)**
International Center, Michigan	$34\frac{7}{10}$
Trump Tower, New York	$27\frac{4}{10}$
Mohegan Sun, Connecticut	$26\frac{1}{10}$
Orchid Hotel, India	$21\frac{3}{10}$

H.O.T. Problems

32. **OPEN ENDED** Write one addition and one subtraction problem involving mixed numbers that result in an answer of 5.

33. **FIND THE ERROR** Shiloh and Mario are finding the sum of $5\frac{5}{9}$ and $3\frac{2}{9}$. Who is correct? Explain.

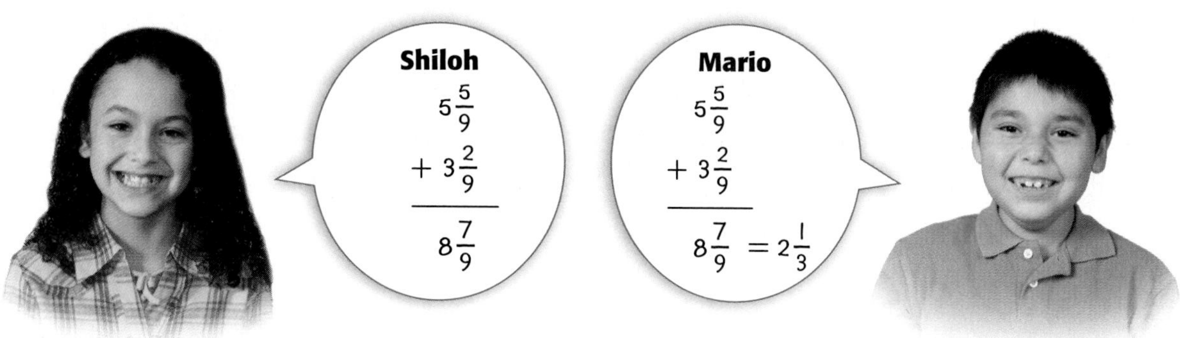

Shiloh
$5\frac{5}{9} + 3\frac{2}{9} = 8\frac{7}{9}$
Mario
$5\frac{5}{9} + 3\frac{2}{9} = 8\frac{7}{9} = 2\frac{1}{3}$

34. **WRITING IN ▶MATH** Explain how to add mixed numbers with like denominators.

Add Fractions with Unlike Denominators

MAIN IDEA

I will add fractions with unlike denominators.

Preparation for Standard

5NS2.3 Solve simple problems, including ones arising in concrete situations, involving the addition and subtraction of fractions and mixed numbers (like and unlike denominators of 20 or less), and express answers in the simplest form.

GET READY to Learn

Monica plans to buy yarn for two art projects. One project requires $\frac{1}{3}$ yards of yarn, and the other project requires $\frac{1}{2}$ yards of yarn. How much yarn does Monica need in all?

The fractions $\frac{1}{3}$ and $\frac{1}{2}$ have different or unlike denominators. You can use fraction models to add fractions with unlike denominators.

Real-World EXAMPLE

1 **ART** **Add $\frac{1}{3}$ and $\frac{1}{2}$ to find how much yarn Monica needs.**

Step 1 Model $\frac{1}{3}$ and $\frac{1}{2}$.

Using fraction models, place $\frac{1}{3}$ and $\frac{1}{2}$ under 1 whole.

1	
$\frac{1}{3}$	$\frac{1}{2}$

Step 2 Add.

Find the like fraction models that fit exactly under $\frac{1}{3} + \frac{1}{2}$.

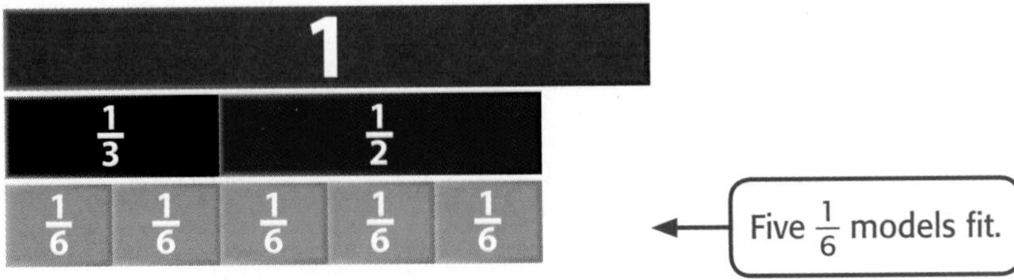

So, Monica needs $\frac{1}{3} + \frac{1}{2}$ or $\frac{5}{6}$ yards of yarn.

Online Personal Tutor at ca.gr4math.com

27. How much taller is the second sunflower than the first sunflower?

28. The table shows how many hours Mike will sing during the school music concert on Saturday and Sunday. How long will he sing during both days?

Mike's Music Concert	
Day	**Time (h)**
Saturday	$2\frac{1}{4}$
Sunday	$1\frac{1}{4}$

Real-World PROBLEM SOLVING

Waterfalls The world's largest indoor waterfalls are listed in the table.

29. What is the difference in height between the tallest and shortest waterfall?

30. Which two waterfalls have a difference of $7\frac{3}{10}$ meters?

31. What is the difference in height of Trump Tower and the Orchid Hotel waterfalls?

Largest Indoor Waterfall	
Waterfall	**Height (m)**
International Center, Michigan	$34\frac{7}{10}$
Trump Tower, New York	$27\frac{4}{10}$
Mohegan Sun, Connecticut	$26\frac{1}{10}$
Orchid Hotel, India	$21\frac{3}{10}$

H.O.T. Problems

32. OPEN ENDED Write one addition and one subtraction problem involving mixed numbers that result in an answer of 5.

33. FIND THE ERROR Shiloh and Mario are finding the sum of $5\frac{5}{9}$ and $3\frac{2}{9}$. Who is correct? Explain.

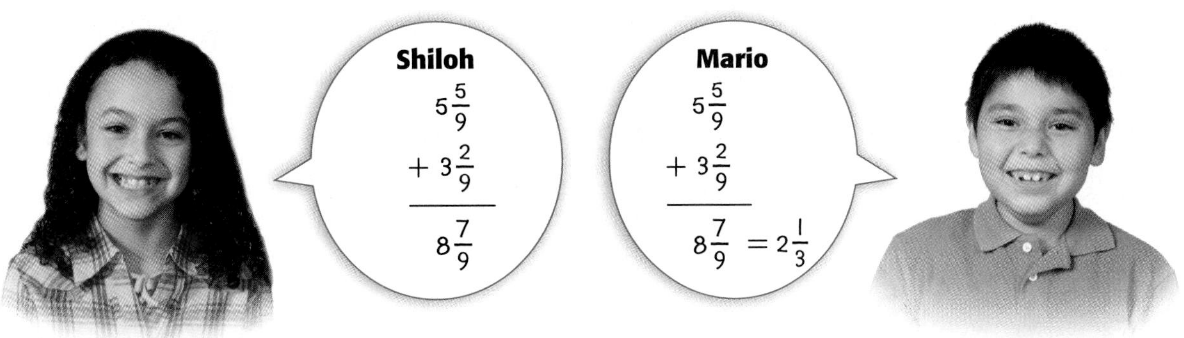

Shiloh
$5\frac{5}{9} + 3\frac{2}{9} = 8\frac{7}{9}$
Mario
$5\frac{5}{9} + 3\frac{2}{9} = 8\frac{7}{9} = 2\frac{1}{3}$

34. WRITING IN MATH Explain how to add mixed numbers with like denominators.

Add Fractions with Unlike Denominators

MAIN IDEA

I will add fractions with unlike denominators.

Preparation for Standard

5NS2.3 Solve simple problems, including ones arising in concrete situations, involving the addition and subtraction of fractions and mixed numbers (like and unlike denominators of 20 or less), and express answers in the simplest form.

GET READY to Learn

Monica plans to buy yarn for two art projects. One project requires $\frac{1}{3}$ yards of yarn, and the other project requires $\frac{1}{2}$ yards of yarn. How much yarn does Monica need in all?

The fractions $\frac{1}{3}$ and $\frac{1}{2}$ have different or unlike denominators. You can use fraction models to add fractions with unlike denominators.

Real-World EXAMPLE

1 ART Add $\frac{1}{3}$ and $\frac{1}{2}$ to find how much yarn Monica needs.

Step 1 Model $\frac{1}{3}$ and $\frac{1}{2}$.

Using fraction models, place $\frac{1}{3}$ and $\frac{1}{2}$ under 1 whole.

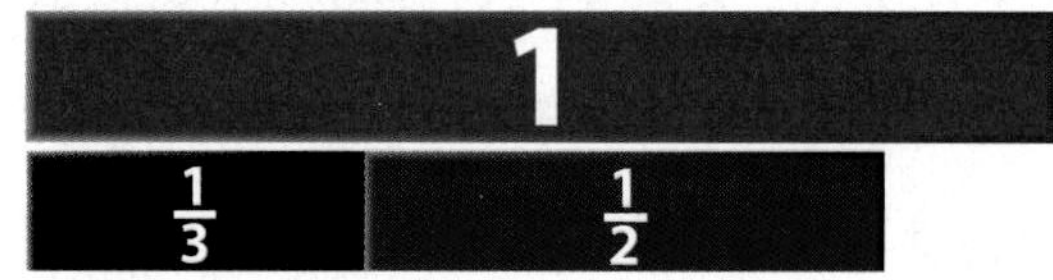

Step 2 Add.

Find the like fraction models that fit exactly under $\frac{1}{3} + \frac{1}{2}$.

1				
$\frac{1}{3}$		$\frac{1}{2}$		
$\frac{1}{6}$	$\frac{1}{6}$	$\frac{1}{6}$	$\frac{1}{6}$	$\frac{1}{6}$

Five $\frac{1}{6}$ models fit.

So, Monica needs $\frac{1}{3} + \frac{1}{2}$ or $\frac{5}{6}$ yards of yarn.

Online Personal Tutor at ca.gr4math.com

In addition to fraction models, you can use paper and pencil to add fractions with unlike denominators.

EXAMPLE **Add Fractions with Unlike Denominators**

 **MEASUREMENT A butterfly traveled $\frac{3}{4}$ mile on Monday and $\frac{5}{6}$ mile on Tuesday. How many miles did the butterfly travel in all?**

You need to find $\frac{3}{4} + \frac{5}{6}$.

Step 1 Write the problem.

$$\begin{array}{r} \frac{3}{4} \\ +\ \frac{5}{6} \\ \hline \end{array}$$

Step 2 Find equivalent fractions.

$$\begin{array}{rcr} \frac{3}{4} & \longrightarrow & \frac{9}{12} \\ +\ \frac{5}{6} & \longrightarrow & +\ \frac{10}{12} \\ \hline \end{array}$$

Write $\frac{3}{4}$ and $\frac{5}{6}$ as equivalent fractions.

Remember

Look back to Lesson 13-4 on page 518 to review how to find equivalent fractions.

Step 3 Add the fractions with like denominators. Then write the sum as a mixed number.

$$\begin{array}{rcr} \frac{3}{4} & \longrightarrow & \frac{9}{12} \\ +\ \frac{5}{6} & \longrightarrow & +\ \frac{10}{12} \\ \hline & & \frac{19}{12} = 1\frac{7}{12} \end{array}$$

So, $\frac{3}{4} + \frac{5}{6} = 1\frac{7}{12}$.

Check

The model shows $\frac{3}{4} + \frac{5}{6}$.

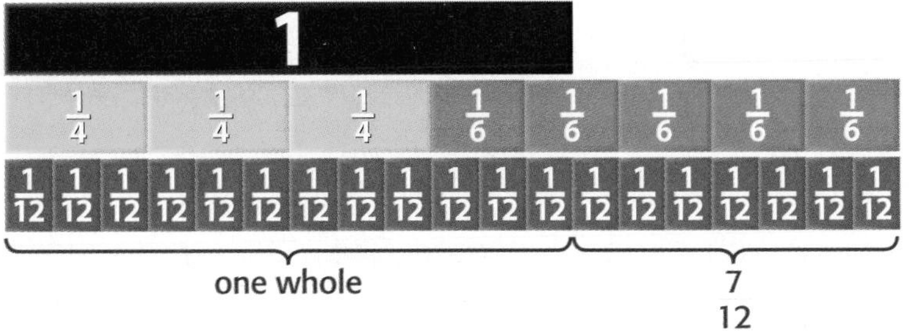

So, $\frac{3}{4} + \frac{5}{6} = 1\frac{7}{12}$. The answer is correct. ✓

CHECK What You Know

Add. Use fraction models if needed. Write in simplest form. See Examples 1 and 2 (pp. 670–671)

1. 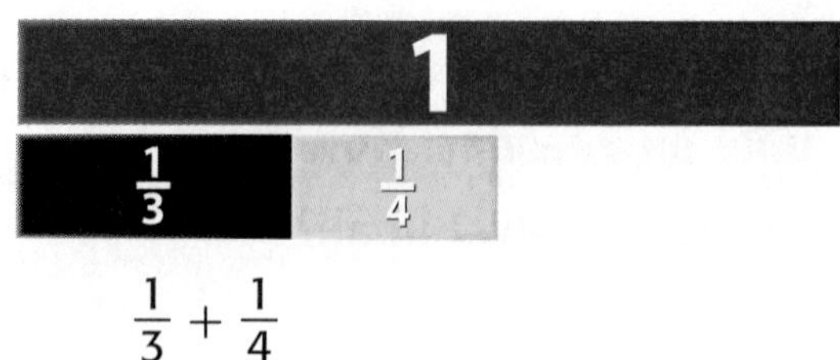

$\frac{1}{3} + \frac{1}{4}$

2. $\frac{5}{8} + \frac{3}{4}$

3. $\frac{3}{10} + \frac{3}{5}$

4. **Measurement** Crystal ran $\frac{1}{4}$ of a mile. Anita ran $\frac{5}{8}$ of a mile. How far did the girls run in all?

5. Talk About It Explain how to find the sum of $\frac{10}{12}$ and $\frac{5}{6}$.

Practice and Problem Solving

Add. Use fraction models if needed. Write in simplest form.

See Examples 1 and 2 (pp. 670–671)

6. 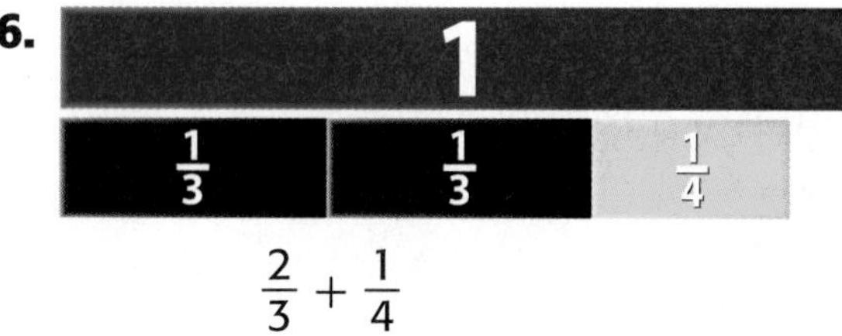

$\frac{2}{3} + \frac{1}{4}$

7. 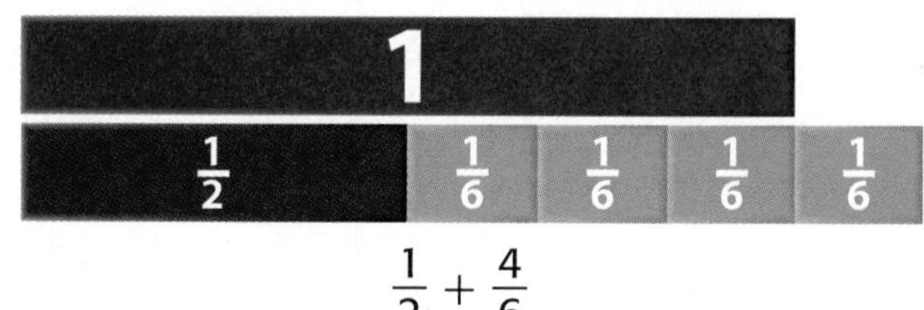

$\frac{1}{2} + \frac{4}{6}$

8. $\frac{1}{5} + \frac{3}{10}$

9. $\frac{2}{3} + \frac{1}{12}$

10. $\frac{2}{4} + \frac{7}{12}$

11. $\frac{1}{3} + \frac{1}{6}$

12. $\frac{1}{5} + \frac{1}{6}$

13. $\frac{1}{3} + \frac{5}{7}$

14. $\frac{3}{6} + \frac{1}{4}$

15. $\frac{7}{9} + \frac{2}{3}$

16. **Measurement** Ms. Jones is watering her plant with a special mixture. She mixes $\frac{2}{3}$ cup of water with $\frac{1}{6}$ cup of liquid plant food. What amount of special mixture did she make?

17. Mr. Cortez shoveled $\frac{1}{2}$ of the snow off his driveway before stopping to rest. Then he shoveled another $\frac{1}{3}$ of the snow. How much of the driveway has Mr. Cortez shoveled?

18. Stella's favorite recipe is shown below. If she makes one serving, will she be able to use a glass that holds 1 cup of liquid? Explain.

19. **Measurement** The table below shows how much paint Mr. Price needs in his art classes. How many gallons will he use in all?

Paint Supply List	
Class	**Paint (gal)**
Class 1	$\frac{1}{5}$
Class 2	$\frac{2}{3}$
Class 3	$\frac{3}{10}$

Real-World PROBLEM SOLVING

Science The table shows the sizes of various newborn animals.

20. What is the total weight of the heaviest and lightest animals listed?

21. Which two animals have a total weight of $\frac{7}{16}$ pounds?

22. What is the total weight of the alligator and the cheetah?

23. What is the total weight of all of the animals?

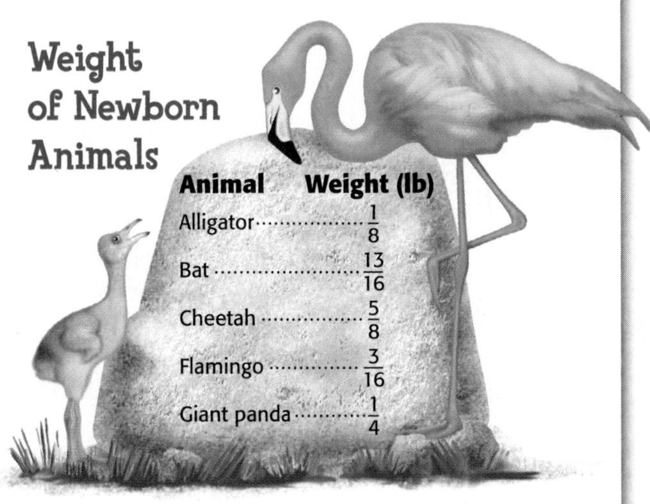

Weight of Newborn Animals

Animal	Weight (lb)
Alligator	$\frac{1}{8}$
Bat	$\frac{13}{16}$
Cheetah	$\frac{5}{8}$
Flamingo	$\frac{3}{16}$
Giant panda	$\frac{1}{4}$

H.O.T. Problems

24. **NUMBER SENSE** Is the sum of $\frac{4}{6}$ and $\frac{5}{8}$ greater or less than 1? How can you tell without adding?

25. **WHICH ONE DOESN'T BELONG?** Stacy added two of the fractions $\frac{1}{3}$, $\frac{3}{4}$, and $\frac{4}{5}$. Which fraction below cannot be a sum of the fractions Stacy added together?

$1\frac{1}{12}$ $1\frac{2}{15}$ $1\frac{5}{18}$ $1\frac{11}{20}$

26. **WRITING IN ▶MATH** Could you use 8 as a denominator to add $\frac{1}{2}$ and $\frac{3}{4}$? Explain.

Subtract Fractions with Unlike Denominators

MAIN IDEA

I will subtract fractions with unlike denominators.

Preparation for Standard

5NS2.3 Solve simple problems, including ones arising in concrete situations, involving the addition and subtraction of fractions and mixed numbers (like and unlike denominators of 20 or less), and express answers in the simplest form.

GET READY to Learn

In December, Centerville had $\frac{3}{5}$ of an inch of rain. In January, Centerville's rainfall was $\frac{1}{2}$ of an inch less than December. How much rain fell in January?

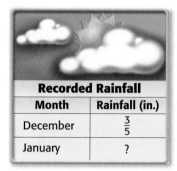

Recorded Rainfall

Month	Rainfall (in.)
December	$\frac{3}{5}$
January	?

In the previous lesson, you used fraction models to add fractions with unlike denominators. You can also use fraction models to subtract fractions with like denominators.

Real-World EXAMPLE

1 **MEASUREMENT** **How much rain fell in January?**

You need to find $\frac{3}{5} - \frac{1}{2}$.

Step 1 Model $\frac{3}{5} - \frac{1}{2}$.

Using fraction models, place $\frac{1}{2}$ under $\frac{3}{5}$.

$\frac{1}{5}$	$\frac{1}{5}$	$\frac{1}{5}$
$\frac{1}{2}$		?

This area represents the difference of the fractions.

Step 2 Find $\frac{3}{5} - \frac{1}{2}$.

Find the fraction model that fits exactly in the area that represents the difference.

$\frac{1}{5}$	$\frac{1}{5}$	$\frac{1}{5}$
$\frac{1}{2}$		$\frac{1}{10}$

One $\frac{1}{10}$ fraction model fits in the area. So, $\frac{3}{5} - \frac{1}{2} = \frac{1}{10}$.

So, $\frac{1}{10}$ of an inch of rain fell in January.

Besides fraction models, paper and pencil can be used to subtract fractions with unlike denominators.

EXAMPLE

2 MEASUREMENT This morning, $\frac{5}{6}$ of an inch of snow was on the ground. By noon, $\frac{2}{3}$ of an inch of snow melted. How much snow is left on the ground?

You need to find $\frac{5}{6} - \frac{2}{3}$.

Step 1 Write the problem.

$$\begin{array}{r} \frac{5}{6} \\ -\ \frac{2}{3} \\ \hline \end{array}$$

Step 2 Find equivalent fractions.

$$\begin{array}{r} \frac{5}{6} \\ -\ \frac{2}{3} \\ \hline \end{array} \quad \begin{array}{c} \longrightarrow \\ \longrightarrow \end{array} \quad \begin{array}{r} \frac{5}{6} \\ -\ \frac{4}{6} \\ \hline \end{array}$$

Write $\frac{5}{6}$ and $\frac{2}{3}$ as equivalent fractions.

Step 3 Subtract the fractions with like denominators.

$$\begin{array}{r} \frac{5}{6} \\ -\ \frac{2}{3} \\ \hline \end{array} \quad \begin{array}{c} \longrightarrow \\ \longrightarrow \end{array} \quad \begin{array}{r} \frac{5}{6} \\ -\ \frac{4}{6} \\ \hline \frac{1}{6} \end{array}$$

So, $\frac{1}{6}$ of an inch of snow is left on the ground.

Check

The model shows $\frac{5}{6} - \frac{2}{3}$.

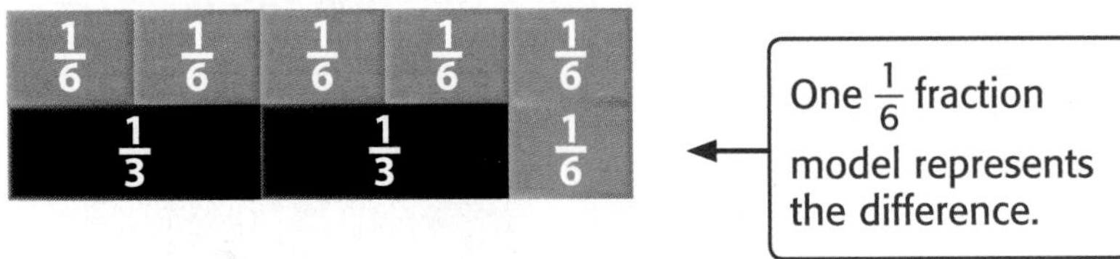

One $\frac{1}{6}$ fraction model represents the difference.

So, $\frac{5}{6} - \frac{2}{3} = \frac{1}{6}$. The answer is correct. ✓

Remember

After subtracting fractions, always look to see if the answer can be written in simplest form.

Online **Personal Tutor at** ca.gr4math.com

Subtract. Use fraction models if needed. Write in simplest form.

See Examples 1 and 2 (pp. 674–675)

1.

$\frac{1}{4}$	$\frac{1}{4}$	$\frac{1}{4}$
$\frac{1}{2}$		?

$\frac{3}{4} - \frac{1}{2}$

2. $\frac{4}{6} - \frac{1}{3}$

3. $\frac{3}{4} - \frac{1}{3}$

4. Russ poured $\frac{3}{4}$ gallon of liquid from a container that holds $\frac{7}{8}$ gallon. How much liquid is left in the container?

5. **Talk About It** Explain how to find the difference of $\frac{9}{10}$ and $\frac{1}{5}$ in simplest form.

Practice and Problem Solving

Subtract. Use fraction models if needed. Write in simplest form.

See Examples 1 and 2 (pp. 674–675)

6. 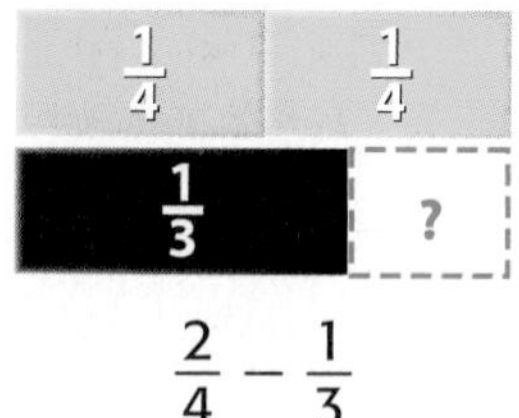

$\frac{2}{4} - \frac{1}{3}$

7. 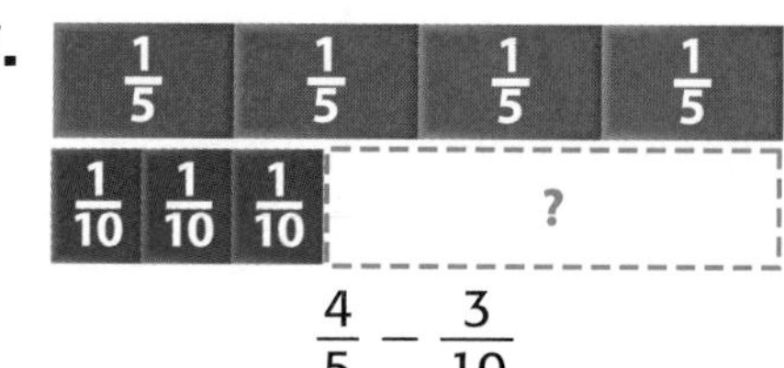

$\frac{4}{5} - \frac{3}{10}$

8. $\frac{7}{9} - \frac{1}{3}$

9. $\frac{7}{8} - \frac{3}{4}$

10. $\frac{5}{6} - \frac{1}{3}$

11. $\frac{7}{8} - \frac{1}{2}$

12. $\frac{3}{5} - \frac{1}{2}$

13. $\frac{3}{4} - \frac{1}{6}$

14. $\frac{2}{3} - \frac{1}{4}$

15. $\frac{6}{8} - \frac{1}{6}$

Algebra Copy and complete each function table.

16.

Rule: Subtract $\frac{1}{2}$.	
Input	**Output**
$\frac{3}{4}$	■
■	$\frac{5}{12}$

17.

Rule: Subtract $\frac{1}{6}$.	
Input	**Output**
$\frac{1}{4}$	■
■	$\frac{1}{12}$

18.

Rule: Subtract $\frac{1}{4}$.	
Input	**Output**
$\frac{5}{8}$	■
■	$\frac{3}{16}$

Algebra **Find the value of *x*.**

19. $\frac{2}{3} - \frac{1}{12} = \frac{x}{12}$

20. $\frac{9}{10} - \frac{6}{x} = \frac{3}{10}$

21. $\frac{11}{15} - \frac{2}{3} = \frac{x}{15}$

Measurement **Solve each problem.**

22. Paula lives $\frac{1}{4}$ mile from school. Cris lives $\frac{4}{5}$ mile from school. How much farther from school does Cris live than Paula?

23. A stew has $\frac{1}{4}$ cup of onions and $\frac{1}{2}$ cup of celery. How much more celery is in the stew than onions?

24. Selina fed her two dogs. How much more food did the big dog get than the puppy?

Dog Food Fed to Dogs	
Dog	Amount of Food (cups)
Big dog	$\frac{11}{12}$
Puppy	$\frac{1}{4}$

25. Mark swam in two races. The distances he swam are shown in the table. Which race was a farther distance? What was the difference in distance?

Race Distances	
Race	Distance (mi)
1	$\frac{5}{6}$
2	$\frac{5}{12}$

H.O.T. Problems

26. FIND THE ERROR Ella and Anthony are finding $\frac{7}{12} - \frac{1}{4}$. Who is correct? Explain.

Ella

$\frac{7}{12} - \frac{1}{4} = \frac{4}{12}$

Anthony

$\frac{7}{12} - \frac{1}{4} = \frac{4}{12} = \frac{1}{3}$

27. WHICH ONE DOESN'T BELONG? Identify the problem that does not belong with the other three. Explain.

$\frac{3}{4} - \frac{1}{4} = \frac{2}{4}$ | $\frac{7}{9} - \frac{1}{3} = \frac{4}{9}$ | $\frac{4}{5} - \frac{3}{10} = \frac{5}{10}$ | $\frac{7}{12} - \frac{1}{4} = \frac{4}{12}$

28. **WRITING IN ▸MATH** How do you find a fraction equivalent to $\frac{5}{6}$?

Statistics: Circle Graphs

MAIN IDEA

I will interpret and make circle graphs.

Preparation for Standard 5SDAP1.2 Organize and display single-variable data in appropriate graphs and representations (e.g. histogram, circle graphs) and explain which types of graphs are appropriate for various data sets.

New Vocabulary

circle graph

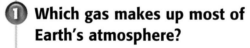

GET READY to Learn

There are a number of gases that make up Earth's atmosphere. The most common gases are oxygen and nitrogen.

A **circle graph** shows data as parts of a circle.

Real-World EXAMPLES Interpret a Circle Graph

SCIENCE The circle graph shows the gases that make up Earth's atmosphere.

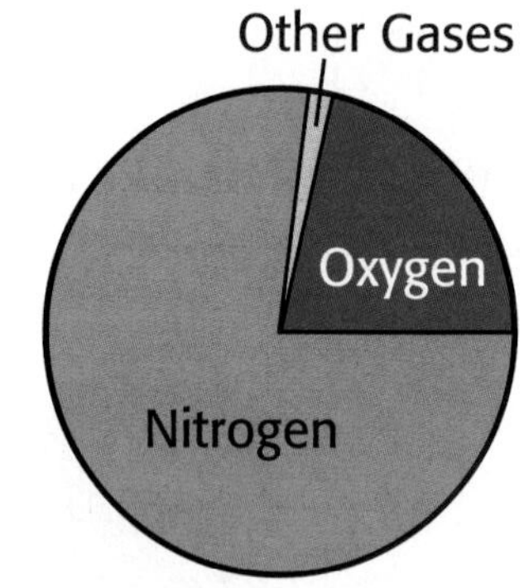

1. **Which gas makes up most of Earth's atmosphere?**

   The largest section represents the gas that makes up most of the atmosphere. This is nitrogen.

2. **What is the second most common gas in the atmosphere?**

   The second largest section represents the second most common gas in the atmosphere. This is oxygen.

3. **About what fraction of the atmosphere does each of these two gases take up?**

   Nitrogen is about $\frac{3}{4}$ of the circle. Oxygen is about $\frac{1}{4}$ of the circle. So, Earth's atmosphere is about $\frac{3}{4}$ nitrogen and about $\frac{1}{4}$ oxygen.

Real-World EXAMPLE Make a Circle Graph

Remember

When interpreting a graph:

◔ is $\frac{1}{4}$

is $\frac{1}{3}$

◑ is $\frac{1}{2}$, and

is $\frac{3}{4}$.

4 **Lisa surveyed four of her friends about their favorite hobbies. The table to the right shows the results. Make a circle graph to show the results of a survey.**

Favorite Hobbies	
Hobby	**Friends**
Cooking	1
Sports	2
Games	1

Step 1 Divide a circle into sections.

There are 4 friends. So, divide the circle into 4 sections.

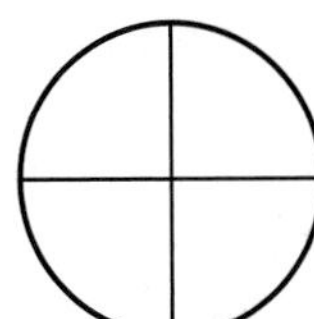

Step 2 Shade the circle.

Shade 1 section for cooking, 2 sections for sports, and 1 section for games.

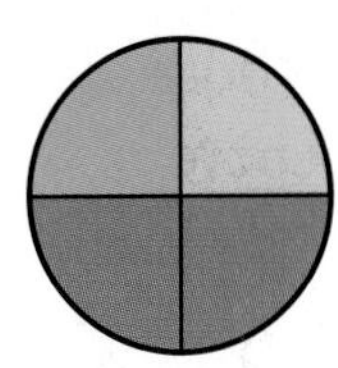

Step 3 Label the circle graph.

Label each section and write a title for the graph.

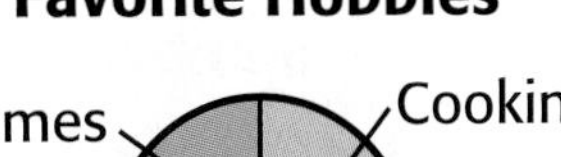

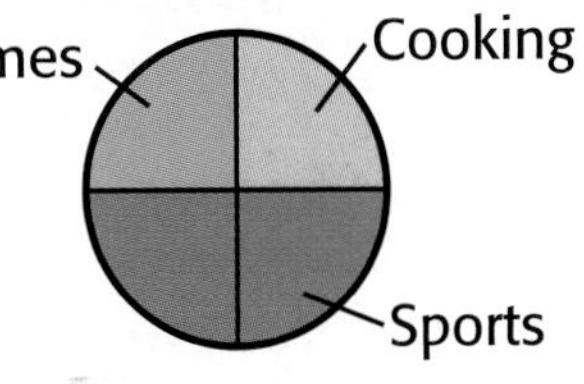

Personal Tutor at ca.gr4math.com

CHECK What You Know

For Exercises 1 and 2, use the circle graph.

See Examples 1–3 (p. 678)

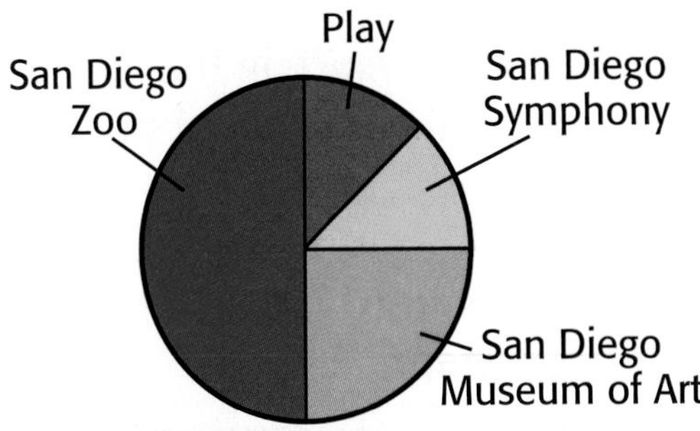

1. What was the favorite class field trip? What fraction of the class chose it?

2. Identify three field trips that a total of $\frac{3}{4}$ of the class chose.

3. Use the data in the table at the right to make a circle graph. See Example 4 (p. 679)

Topping	Students
Cheese	6
Pepperoni	11
Other	3

4. **Talk About It** Suppose you want to make a circle graph. How do you know how many sections to divide the circle into?

Practice and Problem Solving

For Exercises 5–10, use the circle graph.
See Examples 1–3 (p. 678)

Favorite Chore

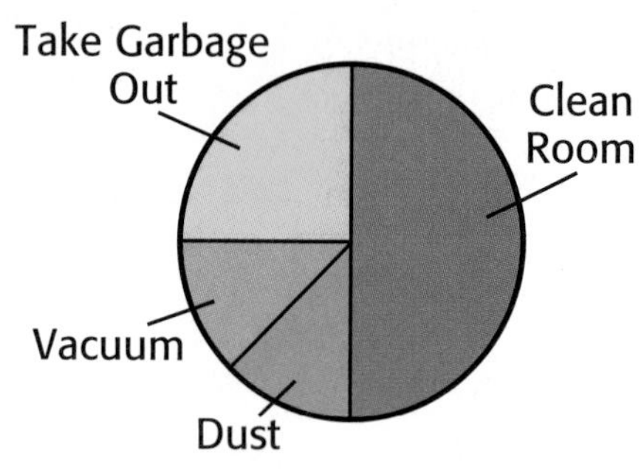

5. Identify the most favorite chore.

6. Identify the least favorite chore.

7. What fraction of students chose taking out the garbage as their favorite chore?

8. Which chore did $\frac{1}{2}$ of the students like?

9. What fraction of students chose dusting as their favorite chore?

10. One chore was chosen half as much as clean room. Identify this chore.

For Exercises 11–15, use the circle graph that shows the number of students that own a dog.
See Examples 1–3 (p. 678)

Number of Dogs per Household

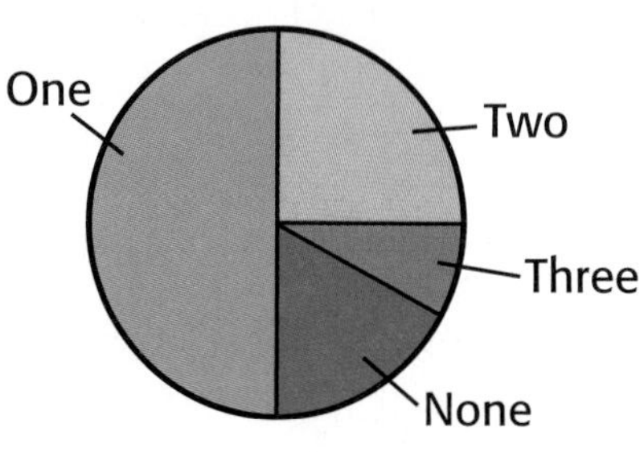

11. What fraction of students own 2 dogs?

12. What fraction of students own one dog?

13. How many dogs do most students own?

14. What is the greatest number of dogs a student owns? About what fraction of students have this number of dogs?

15. What is the difference in the fraction of students who own one dog and the fraction of students who own two dogs?

For Exercises 16 and 17, use the information in each table to create a circle graph. See Example 4 (p. 679)

16.

Students' Favorite Class	
Class	**Students**
Art	$\frac{4}{12}$
Physical education	$\frac{3}{12}$
Music	$\frac{5}{12}$

17.

Trees in the Backyard	
Trees	**Backyard**
Pine	$\frac{1}{6}$
Oak	$\frac{3}{6}$
Maple	$\frac{2}{6}$

For Exercises 18 and 19, use the information in each table to create a circle graph. See Example 4 (p. 679)

18.

Angelina's Allowance	
Activity	**Allowance ($)**
Arcade	3
Movies	5
Snacks	1
Toy	1

19.

Students' Favorite Kites	
Kites	**Students**
Birds	$\frac{3}{8}$
Airplanes	$\frac{1}{8}$
Butterflies	$\frac{2}{8}$
Colorful patterns	$\frac{2}{8}$

H.O.T. Problems

20. OPEN ENDED Survey eight of your classmates. Ask each to name his or her favorite fruit. Display the results in a circle graph.

21. FIND THE ERROR Maryann and Rashaun surveyed 6 students about their favorite colors. Then they each created a circle graph to represent their data. Who is correct? Explain.

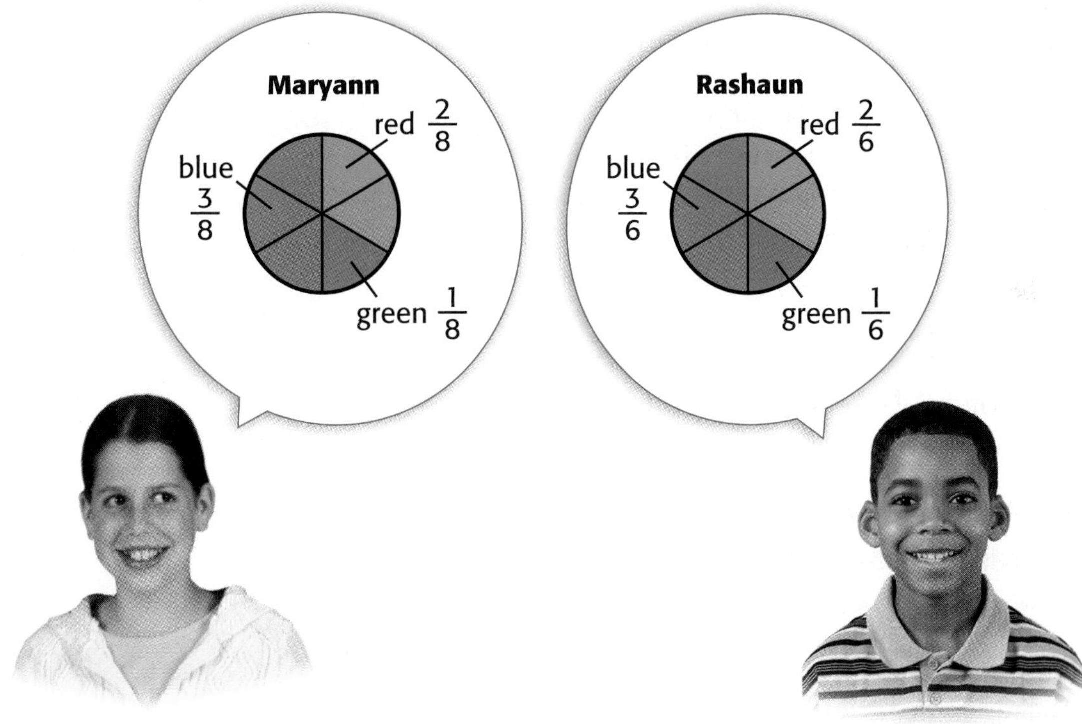

22. NUMBER SENSE Could the fraction on the blue section of the circle graph also be written as $\frac{4}{8}$? Explain.

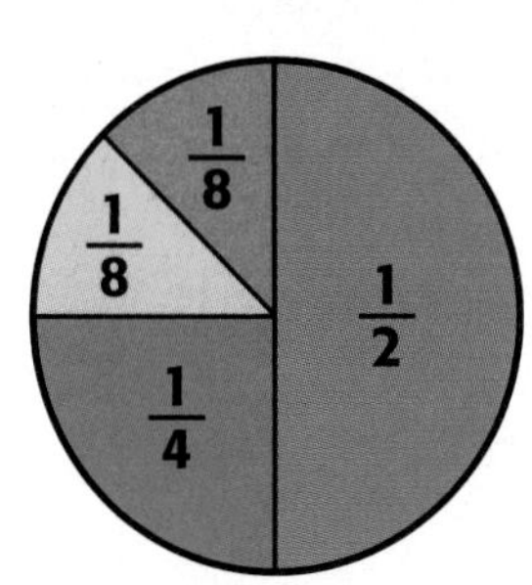

23. WRITING IN MATH Refer to Exercise 22. Explain why the largest section is labeled as $\frac{1}{2}$.

Standards Review

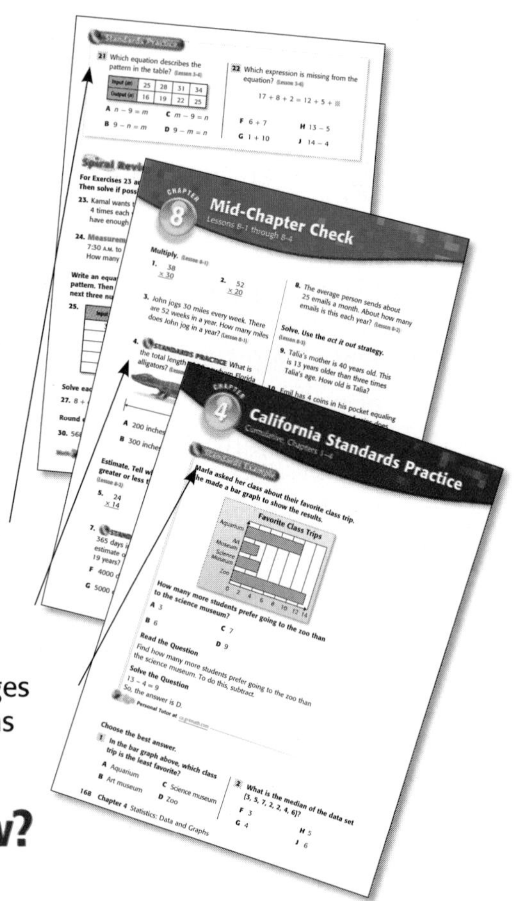

Throughout the school year, you may be required to take several tests, and you may have many questions about them. Here are some answers to help you get ready.

How Should I Study?

The good news is that you've been studying all along—a little bit every day. Here are some of the ways your textbook has been preparing you.

- **Every Day** Each lesson had practice questions that cover the California standards.
- **Every Week** The Mid-Chapter Check and Chapter Test had several practice questions.
- **Every Month** The California Standards Practice pages at the end of each chapter had even more questions similar to those on tests.

Are There Other Ways to Review?

Absolutely! The following pages contain even more practice for each California Standard.

Math Online **Additional California Standards Practice at** ca.gr4math.com

Tips for SUCCESS

Before the Test

- Go to bed early the night before the test. You will think more clearly after a good night's rest.
- Become familiar with common formulas and when they should be used.
- Think positively.

During the Test

- Read each problem carefully. Underline key words and think about different ways to solve the problem.
- Watch for key words like *not.* Also look for order words like *least*, *greatest*, *first*, and *last*.
- Answer questions you are sure about first. If you do not know the answer to a question, skip it and go back to that question later.
- Check your answer to make sure it is reasonable.
- Make sure that the number of the question on the answer sheet matches the number of the question on which you are working in your test booklet.

Whatever you do...

- Don't try to do it all in your head. If no figure is provided, draw one.
- Don't rush. Try to work at a steady pace.
- Don't give up. Some problems may seem hard to you, but you may be able to figure out what to do if you read each question carefully or try another strategy.

Multiple-Choice Questions

Incomplete shading
(A) (B) (C) (D)
Too light shading
(A) (B) (C) (D)
Correct shading
(A) (B) (C) (D)

In multiple-choice questions, you are asked to choose the best answer from four possible answers.

To record a multiple-choice answer, you will be asked to shade in a bubble that is a circle. Always make sure that your shading is dark enough and completely covers the bubble.

Standards Example

1 **The points on the coordinate grid below are on the same straight line.**

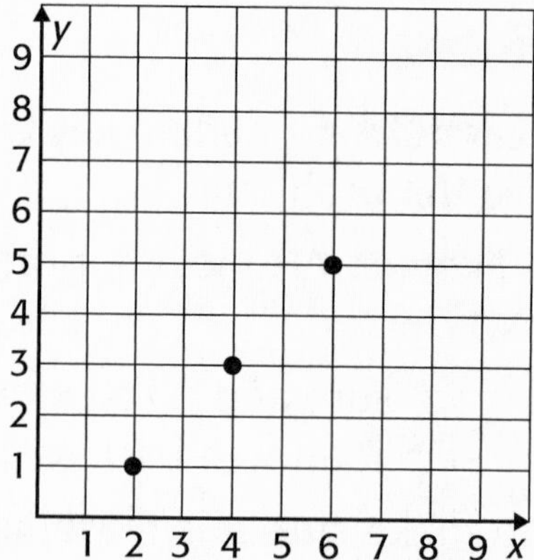

Which of the following ordered pairs represents a point that could also be on the line?

A (4, 4) **B** (7, 5) **C** (8, 6) **D** (8, 7)

Read the Problem Carefully You need to find which ordered pair could be on the line with the other points.

STRATEGY

Grids Copy the grid onto scratch paper and draw the line to check your answer.

Solve the Problem Look at the points on the grid. Visualize a line going through the points.

The line on the grid goes through each of the points. Of the ordered pairs given, the only point that falls on the line is (8, 7).

The correct choice is D.

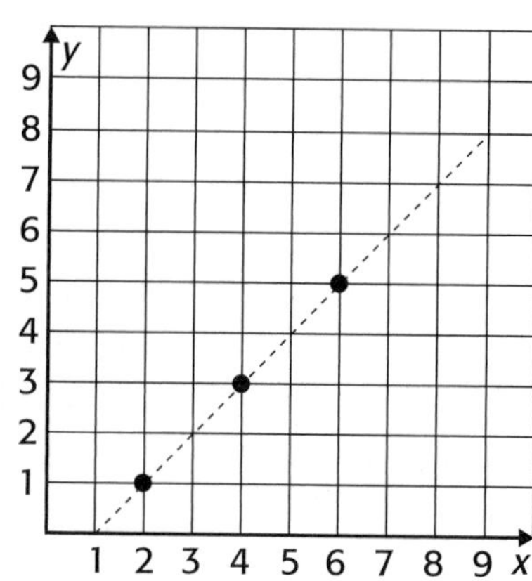

STRATEGY

Making Tables Making a table can help you sort out the information in the problem.

Standards Example

2 **Jacy surveyed his classmates to find out how many pets each of his friends has. The results are shown.**

Number of Pets		
2	3	2
0	4	3
2	1	1

What is the mode of the information?

F 1 **G** 2 **H** 3 **J** 4

Read the Problem Carefully You know how many pets each of Jacy's friends has. You are asked to find the mode.

Solve the Problem The mode is the number that occurs most often. Make a tally chart to organize the data.

Number of Pets	
0	|
1	||
2	|||
3	||
4	|

The number of pets that occurs most often is 2.

The correct choice is G.

Standards Example

3 **Which letter is located at −4 on the number line below?**

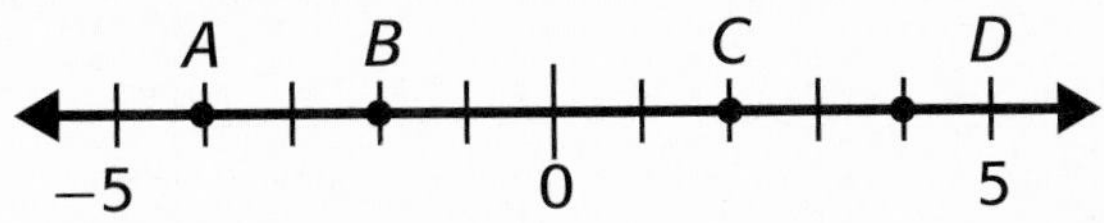

A *A* **B** *B* **C** *C* **D** *D*

STRATEGY

Elimination Can you eliminate any of the choices?

Read the Problem Carefully You are asked to find −4.

Solve the Problem Count left 4 units from 0 to find which point represents −4. Point *A* is at −4.

The correct choice is A.

Practice by Standard: Number Sense

Standard Set 1.0: Students understand the place value of whole numbers and decimals to two decimal places and how whole numbers and decimals relate to simple fractions. Students use the concepts of negative numbers.

DIRECTIONS
Choose the best answer.

QUICK Practice

1 Which of these is the number 4,008,020? (4NS1.1)

A four million, eight thousand, twenty
B four million, eighty thousand, twenty
C four thousand, eight thousand, twenty
D four billion, eight thousand, twenty

2 Which of the following has the greatest value? (4NS1.2)

F 21.3
G 18.5
H 7.19
J 6.32

3 What is 614,782 rounded to the nearest hundred? (4NS1.3)

A 600,000
B 610,000
C 614,800
D 615,000

QUICK Review

STRATEGY Use the place values of the digits in the number to read it.

How would you read the number 4,008,020?

For more help with reading whole numbers, see page 22.

STRATEGY Line the decimal points up to compare the numbers.

Which decimal has the greatest tens digit?

For more help with comparing decimals, see page 566.

STRATEGY If the digit in the tens place is 5 or more, round up. If it is 4 or less, round down.

What is the digit in the tens place? Should you round up or down to the nearest hundred?

For more help with rounding whole numbers, see page 36.

QUICK Practice

4 Which fraction represents the smallest part of a whole? **(4NS1.5)**

F $\frac{1}{10}$

G $\frac{1}{8}$

H $\frac{1}{5}$

J $\frac{1}{4}$

QUICK Review

STRATEGY Look at the denominators to compare the fractions.

Which fraction has the largest denominator?

For more help with comparing fractions, see page 528.

5 Which fraction means the same as 0.23? **(4NS1.6)**

A $\frac{23}{1}$

B $\frac{23}{10}$

C $\frac{23}{100}$

D $\frac{23}{1000}$

STRATEGY How would you read the decimal 0.23?

What are the place values of the digits 2 and 3 in 0.23? How do you read 0.23?

For more help with understanding fraction and decimal equivalents, see page 572.

6 What fraction is best represented by point *K* on this number line? **(4NS1.9)**

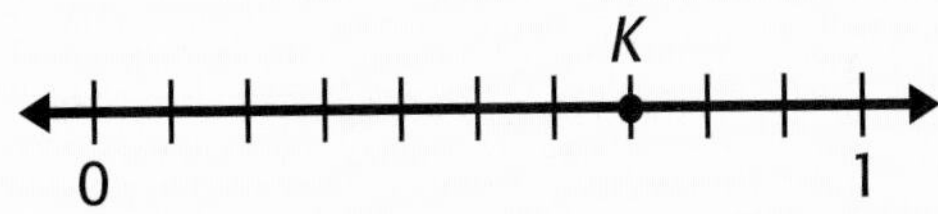

F $\frac{3}{4}$

G $\frac{7}{10}$

H $\frac{2}{3}$

J $\frac{2}{5}$

STRATEGY Count the number of dashes between 0 and 1. What does each dash represent?

What fractional part of a whole does each dash mark represent?

For more help with identifying fractions on a number line, see pages 517, 528.

Practice on Your Own

Standard Set 1.0

7 The numbers below increase by the same amount each time. What are the next three numbers in this pattern? (4NS1.8)

7, 10, 13, 16, 19, ■, ■, ■

A 21, 24, 27 **C** 22, 24, 27
B 22, 25, 28 **D** 23, 26, 29

8 Which symbol is located at −2 on the number line below? (4NS1.8)

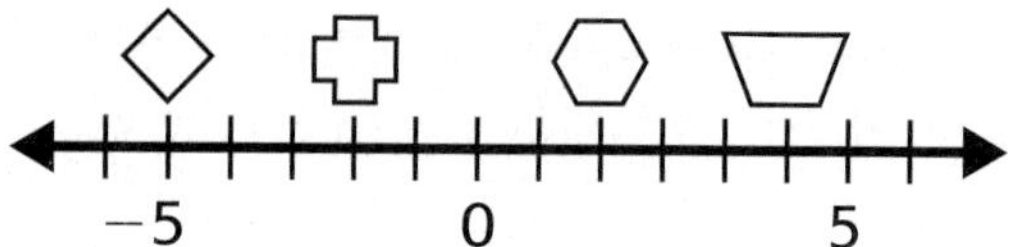

F 

G 

H 

J 

9 Which of the following has the greatest value? (4NS1.2)

A thirty thousand, eight hundred, fifty-nine

B thirty thousand, five hundred, eighty-nine

C thirty thousand, fifty-eight

D thirty thousand, five hundred, eighty-five

10 The population of a certain country is about eighty-three million people. What is this in standard form? (4NS1.1)

F 83,000

G 8,300,000

H 80,300,000

J 83,000,000

11 What is 45,715,903 rounded to the nearest thousand? (4NS1.3)

A 45,715,000

B 45,715,900

C 45,716,000

D 45,720,000

12 What fraction is represented by the shaded part of the figure below? (4NS1.7)

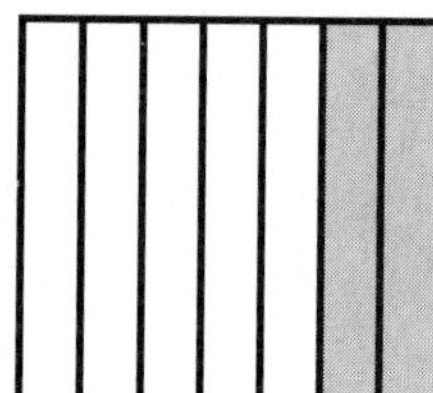

F $\frac{1}{7}$ **H** $\frac{2}{7}$

G $\frac{1}{4}$ **J** $\frac{3}{8}$

13 Which of the following means the same as 0.17? (4NS1.6)

A seven hundredths

B seventeen hundredths

C seventeen thousandths

D seven thousandths

Practice by Standard: Number Sense

Standard Set 2.0: Students extend their use and understanding of whole numbers to the addition and subtraction of simple decimals.

DIRECTIONS
Choose the best answer.

QUICK Practice

1 On Monday, Belinda practiced the piano for 42 minutes. On Tuesday, she practiced for 29 minutes, and on Wednesday she practiced for 47 minutes. About how many minutes did she spend practicing the piano all three days? (4NS2.1)

A 100 minutes
B 120 minutes
C 150 minutes
D 200 minutes

2 Raul had $15.84 in his wallet. He spent $4.79 on a package of light bulbs. About how much did he have left over after buying the light bulbs? Round your answer to the nearest dollar. (4NS2.1)

F $9
G $10
H $11
J $12

3 The total length of an insect is 1.28 centimeters. What is the length of the insect rounded to the nearest tenth? (4NS2.2)

A 1 cm
B 1.2 cm
C 1.22 cm
D 1.3 cm

QUICK Review

STRATEGY Use rounding to estimate the total number of minutes.

Round each amount of minutes to the nearest ten. Then find the sum.

For more help with estimating the sum of whole numbers, see page 58.

READING HINT The words *left over* mean subtraction. Use rounding to estimate the difference between the two amounts.

Round each amount up to the nearest whole dollar. Then subtract the amounts to estimate how much he has left over.

For more help with estimating the difference of decimals, see page 598.

STRATEGY Look at the digit in the hundredths place to know how to round.

Should you round up or down when the next digit is 8?

For more help with rounding decimals, see page 593.

QUICK Practice

4 What is the height of the tree rounded to the nearest whole number? **(4NS2.2)**

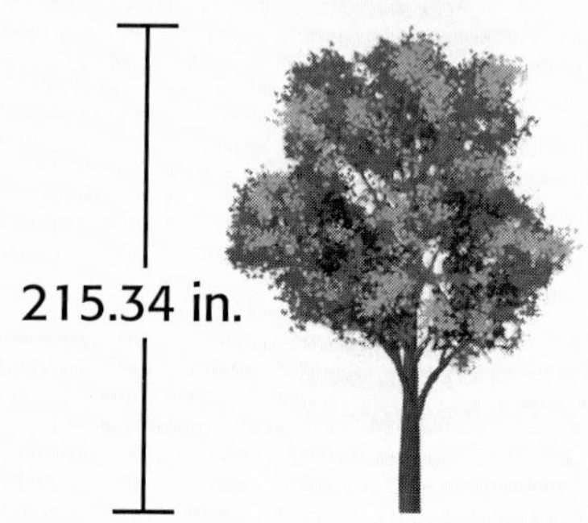

F 200 inches
G 210 inches
H 215 inches
J 220 inches

QUICK Review

STRATEGY Look to the digit one place to the right of the ones digit. If it is 5 or greater, round the ones digit up. If it is 4 or less, round down.

What is the tenths digit in 215.34?

Hundreds	Tens	Ones	Tenths	Hundredths
2	1	5	3	4

For more help with rounding decimals, see page 593.

5 Meredith wants to purchase a stapler, an ink cartridge, and a calculator for her home office.

Office Supplies	
Stapler	$9.89
Ink cartridge	$19.95
Calculator	$28.05

About how much will she spend altogether for the supplies? Round your answer to the nearest whole number. **(4NS2.1)**

A $58
B $60
C $65
D $67

STRATEGY Use rounding to estimate the total cost of the supplies.

Round the cost of each item to the nearest whole number. Then find the sum.

What is the closest ten to each number?

For more help with estimating money, see page 598.

Practice on Your Own

Standard Set 2.0

6 What is the length of the leaf rounded to the nearest whole number? (4NS2.2)

F 1 inch
G 2 inches
H 3 inches
J 4 inches

7 Levi drives a van for a delivery company. The table shows how many miles he drove each day last week.

Day	Miles
Monday	195
Tuesday	247
Wednesday	408
Thursday	353
Friday	296

About how many miles did Levi drive altogether last week? (4NS2.1)

A 1000 miles
B 1200 miles
C 1500 miles
D 1800 miles

8 Taka's cat has a tail with a length of 11.76 inches. What is the length of her cat's tail rounded to the nearet tenth? (4NS2.2)

F 12 inches
G 11.8 inches
H 11.7 inches
J 11 inches

9 Mrs. Sato spent $3.89 on apples, $8.09 on juice, and $2.99 on cereal at the grocery store. About how much did she spend altogether? Round your answer to the nearest dollar. (4NS2.1)

A $15
B $16
C $17
D $18

10 The total length of an airplane is 38.65 feet. What is the length of the airplane rounded to the nearest whole number? (4NS2.2)

F 38 feet
G 38.6 feet
H 38.7 feet
J 39 feet

11 Thomas had $35.21 in his piggy bank. He earned $14.75 for mowing his neighbor's lawn and put this in the bank. About how much did he have in the piggy bank altogether? Round your answer to the nearest dollar. (4NS2.1)

A $45
B $50
C $55
D $60

12 Jamal bought a sandwich for $4.79 and a juice for $1.15. He paid with $20. About how much change did he receive? Round your answer to the nearest dollar. (4NS2.1)

F $12
G $13
H $14
J $15

Practice by Standard: Number Sense

Standard Set 3.0: Students solve problems involving addition, subtraction, multiplication, and division of whole numbers and understand the relationships among the operations.

DIRECTIONS
Choose the best answer.

QUICK Practice	QUICK Review
1 4189 − 2785 = (4NS3.1) **A** 2414 **B** 2404 **C** 1414 **D** 1404	**STRATEGY** Line the numbers up in a vertical column and find the difference. Use borrowing from digits with larger place values if needed. For more help with subtracting whole numbers, see pages 68, 70.
2 493 ÷ 7 = (4NS3.2) **F** 7 R3 **G** 70 R3 **H** 71 **J** 71 R3	**STRATEGY** First decide how many times 7 goes into 49. Then continue to use the method for dividing whole numbers. Use the method for dividing whole numbers to find the quotient. For more help with dividing whole numbers, see page 353.
3 There are 12 teams of 14 students at the school field day. How many students are participating in field day altogether? (4NS3.3) **A** 168 **B** 154 **C** 48 **D** 26	**READING HINT** The word *of* usually indicates a multiplication problem. You can solve the problem by finding the product of 12 and 14. For more help with solving problems that involve multiplication, see pages 308, 310.

QUICK Practice

4 Lakota rode 52 miles on her bicycle in 4 hours. She rode at the same speed during these 4 hours. What was her average speed in miles per hour? **(4NS3.4)**

F 8 miles per hour

G 10 miles per hour

H 12 miles per hour

J 13 miles per hour

QUICK Review

STRATEGY Use division to find Lakota's average speed.

This problem can be solved by finding the quotient of 52 and 4.

For more help with solving problems that involve division of whole numbers, see page 352.

5 $\begin{array}{r} 3751 \\ +\ 4160 \\ \hline \end{array}$ **(4NS3.1)**

A 5413

B 6421

C 7911

D 8011

STRATEGY Use rounding to estimate the sum. Then eliminate answers that seem unreasonable.

Add the digits in each column from right to left. If the sum in a column is greater than 9, add a 1 to the next column.

For more help with adding whole numbers, see page 64.

6 There are 7 school buses at Horizon Elementary School this morning. Each bus holds the same number of students. If there are 266 students on the buses altogether, how many students are on each bus? **(4NS3.4)**

F 36

G 38

H 178

J 259

STRATEGY Use division to find the number of students on each bus.

You can solve this problem by finding the quotient of 266 and 7.

For more help with solving problems that involve division of whole numbers, see page 353.

Practice on Your Own

Standard Set 3.0

7 Simona solved the problem below. Which expression could be used to check her answer? (4NS3.2)

$$654 \div 25 = 26 \text{ R4}$$

A $(25 \times 26) \times 4$

B $(25 \times 26) + 4$

C $(25 + 26) + 4$

D $(25 + 26) \times 4$

8 There are 200 booths at a state fair. Each booth is given 5000 tickets to sell to customers. How many tickets is this in all? (4NS3.3)

F 10,000

G 100,000

H 1,000,000

J 10,000,000

9 (4NS3.1)

$$\begin{array}{r} 8543 \\ -\ 3614 \\ \hline \end{array}$$

A 4919 **C** 5919

B 4929 **D** 5929

10 $842 \div 26 =$ (4NS3.2)

F 31 **H** 32

G 31 R9 **J** 32 R10

11 There are 15 mail carriers in Meera's hometown. Each mail carrier begins the day with 12 bags of letters to deliver. How many bags of letters are there in all? (4NS3.3)

A 27 **C** 180

B 37 **D** 210

12 Rudy's heart beat 510 times in 6 minutes. His heart rate was the same each minute. How many times per minute did Rudy's heart beat? (4NS3.4)

F 85 **H** 80

G 83 **J** 78

13 There are 9 bookshelves. Each shelf has the same number of books. If there are 234 books on the shelves altogether, how many books are on each shelf? (4NS3.4)

A 24 **C** 27

B 26 **D** 28

14 A pet store had nine aquarium tanks of 36 fish each. Which expression can be used to find the total number of fish? (4NS3.3)

F $36 + 9$

G $36 - 9$

H 36×9

J $36 \div 9$

Practice by Standard: Number Sense

Standard Set 4.0: Students know how to factor small whole numbers.

DIRECTIONS
Choose the best answer.

QUICK Practice

1 Which of these is another way to write the product 8×7? (4NS4.1)

A $4 \times 3 \times 7$

B $3 \times 2 \times 7$

C $8 \times 3 \times 4$

D $4 \times 2 \times 7$

2 The ages of Christine and her siblings are shown in the table below.

Sibling	Age (years)
Christine	10
Jody	8
Kristen	15
Shawn	13
Robbie	12

Who has an age that is a prime number? (4NS4.2)

F Robbie

G Shawn

H Kristen

J Jody

3 Which is a composite number? (4NS4.2)

A 6

B 7

C 11

D 13

QUICK Review

STRATEGY Rewrite 8 as a product of two factors.

Can the number 7 be factored? Can the number 8?

For more help with factoring, see page 204.

READING HINT A *prime number* is a number that does not have any factors other than 1 and itself.

Which number only has factors of 1 and itself?

For more help with identifying prime numbers, see page 208.

READING HINT A composite number is a number that has more than two factors.

Which number has more than two factors?

For more help with identifying composite numbers, see page 208.

QUICK Practice

4 Which statement is true? (4NS4.2)

F The only factors of 14 are 1 and 14.

G The only factors of 12 are 1 and 12.

H The only factors of 11 are 1 and 11.

J The only factors of 10 are 1 and 10.

QUICK Review

STRATEGY Choose the answer choice that shows a prime number.

Which of the numbers in the answer choices is prime?

For more help with identifying prime numbers, see page 208.

5 Which of the following shows all of the factors of 18? (4NS4.1)

A 2, 3, 6, 9

B 2, 3, 6, 9, 18

C 1, 2, 3, 6, 7, 9, 18

D 1, 2, 3, 6, 9, 18

READING HINT A number is a *factor* of another number if it divides evenly into the other number.

How many ways can you multiply two numbers to get 18?

For more help with factoring numbers, see page 204.

6 Which is a prime number? (4NS4.2)

F 6

G 7

H 8

J 9

READING HINT A *prime number* is a number that does not have any factors other than 1 and itself.

Find the number that only has 1 and itself as factors.

For more help with identifying prime numbers, see page 208.

7 Which of these is another way to write 12? (4NS4.1)

A 2×4

B $2 \times 2 \times 2$

C $2 \times 2 \times 3$

D $2 \times 3 \times 3$

STRATEGY Write the number 12 as the product of its factors.

Multiply the numbers in the answer choices to see which one equals 12.

For more help with factoring numbers, see page 204.

Practice on Your Own

Standard Set 4.0

8 Which is a prime number? (4NS4.2)

F 14

G 15

H 16

J 17

9 Which statement is true? (4NS4.2)

A The only factors of 12 are 1 and 12.

B The only factors of 13 are 1 and 13.

C The only factors of 14 are 1 and 14.

D The only factors of 15 are 1 and 15.

10 Which of these is another way to write the product 15×11? (4NS4.1)

F $3 \times 5 \times 11$

G $2 \times 3 \times 5 \times 11$

H $3 \times 4 \times 5 \times 7$

J $2 \times 6 \times 11$

11 Erina swam four laps in a pool three days a week for two weeks. Which of the following represents the number of laps Erina swam? (4NS4.1)

A $4 \times 3 \times 2$

B $4 \times 3 \times 3$

C $4 \times 3 \times 4$

D $4 \times 3 \times 5$

12 The numbers of students in 4 different classrooms are shown.

Classroom Teacher	Number of Students
Mr. Perez	25
Miss Foster	27
Mrs. Simpson	29
Mr. Ramos	28

Which classroom teacher has a prime number of students in his or her classroom? (4NS4.2)

F Mr. Perez

G Miss Foster

H Mrs. Simpson

J Mr. Ramos

13 Which of these is another way to write 30? (4NS4.1)

A $2 \times 2 \times 5$

B $2 \times 3 \times 4$

C $2 \times 3 \times 5$

D $2 \times 4 \times 5$

14 Suppose Dario starts counting from 2 through 16 as shown. How many prime numbers will he count? (4NS4.2)

2, 3, 4, 5, 6, …

F 7 **H** 5

G 6 **J** 4

Practice by Standard: Algebra and Functions

Standard Set 1.0: Students use and interpret variables, mathematical symbols, and properties to write and simplify expressions and sentences.

DIRECTIONS
Choose the best answer.

QUICK Practice	QUICK Review
1 Which number is represented by *d* in the number sentence below? **(4AF1.1)** $7 \times d = 105$ **A** 14 **C** 16 **B** 15 **D** 17	**STRATEGY** Eliminate incorrect answer choices by substituting them into the number sentence. Which answer choice results in a true number sentence when you substitute it for *d*? For more help with understanding variables in an equation, see pages 234, 236.
2 What is the value of the expression below? **(4AF1.2)** $(4 \times 7) \div (3 + 1)$ **F** 5 **H** 7 **G** 6 **J** 8	**STRATEGY** Simplify within each set of parentheses first. Then perform the division. Use the order of operations to simplify the expression. For more help with evaluating numerical expressions, see page 230.
3 $4 \times (3 - 1)$ **(4AF1.3)** **A** 11 **C** 9 **B** 10 **D** 8	**STRATEGY** Remember to simplify within the parentheses first. Use the order of operations to simplify the expression. For more help with evaluating numerical expressions, see page 230.

QUICK Practice

4 Which equation below represents the area (A) of the rectangle in square meters? **(4AF1.4)**

F $A = 40 + 32$

G $A = 40 \times 32$

H $40 = A \times 32$

J $A = (2 \times 40) + (2 \times 32)$

5 The sum of a and b equals 20. If $a = 11$, which equation can be used to find b? **(4AF1.5)**

A $11 + b = 20$

B $11 - b = 20$

C $b - 11 = 20$

D $b + 20 = 11$

6 $(6 \times 7) \div (7 - 4)$ **(4AF1.2)**

F 9

G 10

H 12

J 14

QUICK Review

STRATEGY The *area* of a rectangle can be found by multiplying the length by the width.

What is the length of the rectangle? What is the width? How can you use these values to find the area?

For more help with using formulas, see page 444.

STRATEGY Represent the situation with an equation.

Write an expression for the sum of a and b and set it equal to 20. Then substitute 11 for a.

For more help with setting up equations to find unknown values, see pages 96, 98.

STRATEGY Simplify within each set of parentheses first. Then perform the division.

Use the order of operations to simplify the expression.

For more help with evaluating numerical expressions, see page 230.

Practice on Your Own

Standard Set 1.0

7 What is the value of the expression below if $m = 6$? (4AF1.2)

$$23 - (m + 9)$$

A 26
B 18
C 8
D 4

8 Look at the problem below.

$$\square + 19 = \triangle$$

If $\square = 11$, what is $\triangle$? (4AF1.5)

F 30
G 22
H 18
J 8

9 What is the value of b? (4AF1.2)

$$(18 \div 3) \times (6 - 3) = b$$

A 2
B 12
C 14
D 18

10 $12 \div (6 - 2) =$ (4AF1.3)

F 0
G 2
H 3
J 4

11 What is the value of k? (4AF1.2)

$$(15 \div 3) \times (6 + 4) = k$$

A 50
B 34
C 15
D 5

12 The formula $F = 32 + (C \times 9) \div 5$ takes a temperature in degrees Celsius (C) and tells you the temperature in degrees Fahrenheit (F). Suppose a thermometer reads 20°C. What is the temperature in degrees Fahrenheit? (4AF1.4)

F 62°F
G 68°F
H 70°F
J 73°F

13 $10 \times (7 - 3) + 5 =$ (4AF1.3)

A 36
B 45
C 60
D 72

14 $(11 \times 5) \div (4 + 1) =$ (4AF1.2)

F 7
G 9
H 11
J 15

15 The product of h and k equals 84. If $h = 12$, which equation can be used to find the value of k? (4AF1.5)

A $12 \div k = 84$
B $84 - k = 12$
C $12 \times 84 = k$
D $12 \times k = 84$

Practice by Standard: Algebra and Functions

Standard Set 2.0: Students know how to manipulate equations.

California Standards Review

DIRECTIONS
Choose the best answer.

QUICK Practice	QUICK Review
1 The letters R and H stand for numbers. If $R + 65 = H + 65$, which statement is true? (4AF2.1) **A** $R > H$ **C** $R = H$ **B** $R < H$ **D** $R = H - 65$	STRATEGY Recognize that if you add 65 to two equal numbers, the results are equal. What do you know about the two numbers R and H that must be true if $R + 65 = H + 65$? For more help with understanding that equals added to equals are equal, see page 110.
2 What number goes in the box to make this number sentence true? (4AF2.2) $(8 - 2) \times 3 = \blacksquare \times 3$ **F** 5 **H** 7 **G** 6 **J** 8	STRATEGY Recognize that if you multiply the same number by 3, the results are equal. You can solve this problem by simplifying $8 - 2$. For more help with understanding that equals multiplied by equals are equal, see page 248.
3 What number goes in the box to make this number sentence true? (4AF2.1) $89 + \blacksquare = 89 + 12$ **A** 2×2 **C** 2×4 **B** 2×3 **D** 3×4	STRATEGY Eliminate choices first that do not meet all of the requirements. Substitute each answer choice into the box to see which one results in a true number sentence. For more help with understanding that equals added to equals are equal, see page 110.

QUICK Practice

4 What number goes in the box to make this number sentence true? (4AF2.2)

$\blacksquare \div 5 = (22 + 8) \div 5$

F 30
G 18
H 10
J 6

QUICK Review

STRATEGY Recognize that if you divide the same number by 5, the results are equal.

You can solve this problem by simplifying 22 + 8.

For more help with understanding that equals divided by equals are equal, see page 248.

5 What number goes in the box to make this number sentence true? (4AF2.2)

$9 \times \blacksquare = 9 \times 7$

A 3
B 7
C 49
D 63

STRATEGY Eliminate choices first that do not meet all of the requirements.

Substitute each answer choice into the box to see which one results in a true number sentence.

For more help with understanding that equals multiplied by equals are equal, see page 248.

6 The letters C and D stand for numbers. If $C - 32 = D - 32$, which statement is true? (4AF2.1)

F $C = D$
G $C < D$
H $C = D + 32$
J $C = D - 32$

STRATEGY Recognize that if you subtract 32 from two equal numbers, the results are equal.

What do you know about the two numbers C and D that must be true if $C - 32 = D - 32$?

For more help with understanding that equals subtracted from equals are equal, see page 110.

Practice on Your Own

Standard Set 2.0

7 The letters M and N stand for numbers. If $M \times 6 = N \times 6$, which statement is true? **(4AF2.2)**

A $M > N$

B $M = N$

C $M < N$

D $M = N \div 6$

8 What number goes in the box to make this number sentence true? **(4AF2.1)**

$$\blacksquare - 9 = (3 \times 5) - 9$$

F 15

G 13

H 11

J 6

9 What number goes in the box to make this number sentence true? **(4AF2.2)**

$$81 \div \blacksquare = 81 \div 3$$

A 3

B 9

C 18

D 27

10 What expression goes in the box to make this number sentence true? **(4AF2.1)**

$$17 + 16 = 17 + \blacksquare$$

F 2×4

G 3×4

H 4×4

J 3×8

11 What number goes in the box to make this number sentence true? **(4AF2.2)**

$$\blacksquare \div 4 = (9 + 7) \div 4$$

A 4

B 8

C 12

D 16

12 What number goes in the box to make this number sentence true? **(4AF2.2)**

$$5 \times (7 - 4) = 5 \times \blacksquare$$

F 3

G 5

H 7

J 15

13 The letters Q and R stand for numbers. If $Q + 56 = R + 56$, which statement is true? **(4AF2.1)**

A $Q = R + 56$

B $Q = R - 56$

C $Q = R$

D $Q < R$

14 What expression goes in the box to make this number sentence true? **(4AF2.2)**

$$\blacksquare \times 9 = 15 \times 9$$

F 2×3

G 2×5

H 3×4

J 3×5

Practice by Standard: Measurement and Geometry

Standard Set 1.0: Students understand perimeter and area.

DIRECTIONS
Choose the best answer.

QUICK Practice

1 Which statement about the figures is true? (4MG1.2)

Figure 1

12 feet

18 feet

Figure 2

9 feet

24 feet

A They both have the same width.

B They both have the same length.

C They both have the same area.

D They both have the same perimeter.

QUICK Review

STRATEGY Compare the areas and perimeters of the two rectangles.

What is the area of each rectangle?
What is the perimeter of each rectangle?

Recall that area is the number of square units needed to cover a figure.

ℓ

w w

ℓ

Perimeter is the distance around a figure.

ℓ

w w

ℓ

For more help with recognizing that rectangles that have the same area can have different perimeters, see page 448.

QUICK Practice

2 What is the area of the rectangle below? **(4MG1.1)**

F 80 square meters

G 72 square meters

H 42 square meters

J 36 square meters

QUICK Review

STRATEGY Use the formula for the area of a rectangle, $A = \ell \times w$.

Find the area of the rectangle by multiplying the length by the width.

For more help with finding the area of a rectangle, see page 444.

3 Which statement about the figures is true? **(4MG1.3)**

Figure 1

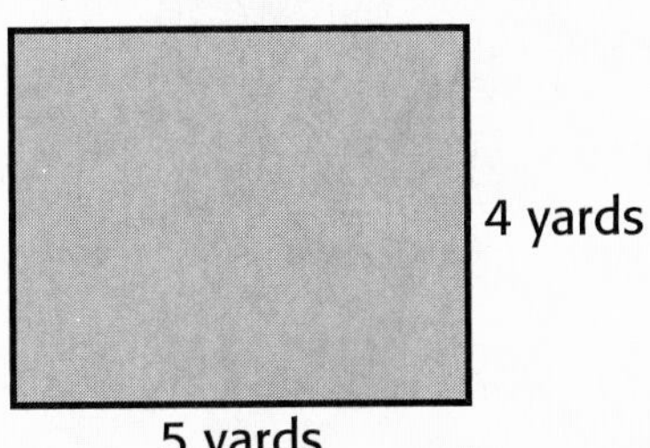

Figure 2

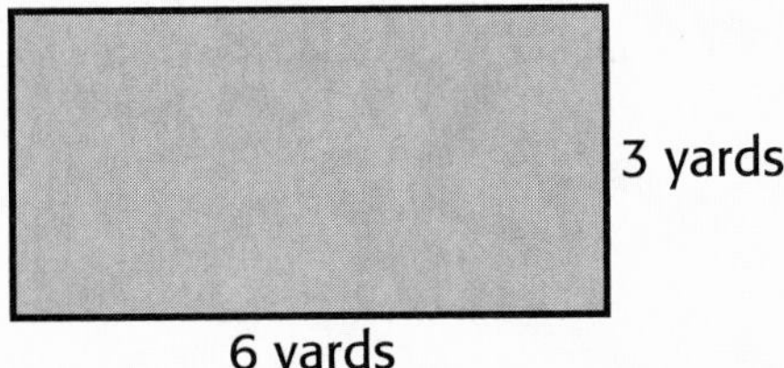

A They both have the same width.

B They both have the same length.

C They both have the same area.

D They both have the same perimeter.

STRATEGY Compare the areas and perimeters of the two rectangles.

What is the area of each rectangle?
What is the perimeter of each rectangle?

Recall the formulas for the area and perimeter of a rectangle.

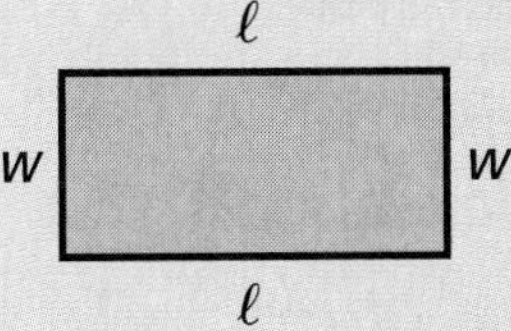

$$A = \ell \times w \qquad P = 2\ell + 2w$$

For more help with recognizing that rectangles that have the same perimeter can have different areas, see page 448.

Practice on Your Own

Standard Set 1.0

4 Mr. Romero's deck has the shape and dimensions shown below.

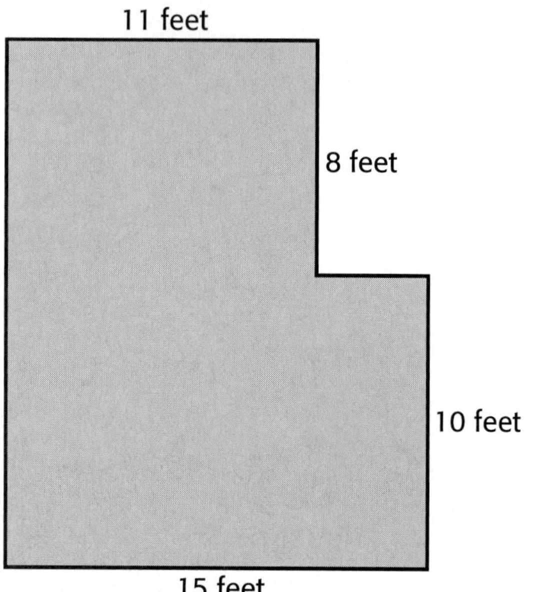

What is the area of the deck? (4MG1.4)

F 270 square feet

G 256 square feet

H 238 square feet

J 220 square feet

5 Refer to the deck in Exercise 4. Suppose Mr. Romero wants to put a railing around the perimeter of the deck. How many feet of railing will he need? (4MG1.4)

A 66 feet

B 58 feet

C 44 feet

D 42 feet

6 Which statement about the figures is true? (4MG1.3)

Figure 1

12 inches

22 inches

Figure 2

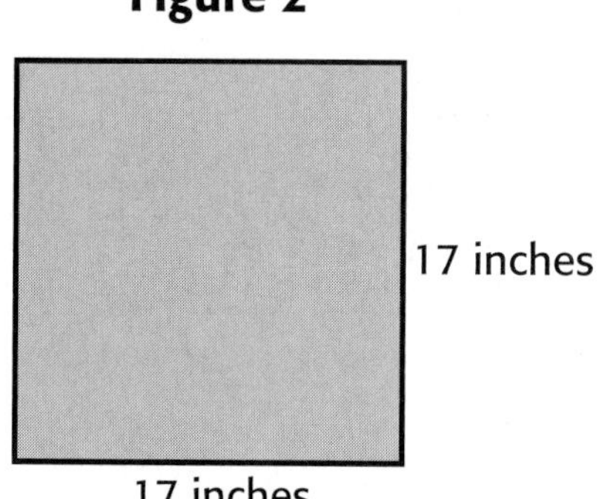

F They both have the same area.

G They both have the same perimeter.

H They both have the same length.

J They both have the same width.

7 A rectangular playground is 215 meters long and 140 meters wide. Suppose Tamika jogs around the perimeter of the playground. How far does she jog in all? (4MG1.1)

A 830 meters

B 710 meters

C 650 meters

D 625 meters

Practice by Standard: Measurement and Geometry

Standard Set 2.0: Students use two-dimensional coordinate grids to represent points and graph lines and simple figures.

California Standards Review

DIRECTIONS
Choose the best answer.

QUICK Practice

1 Miguel plotted three points on a grid. The three points appeared to be on the same line.

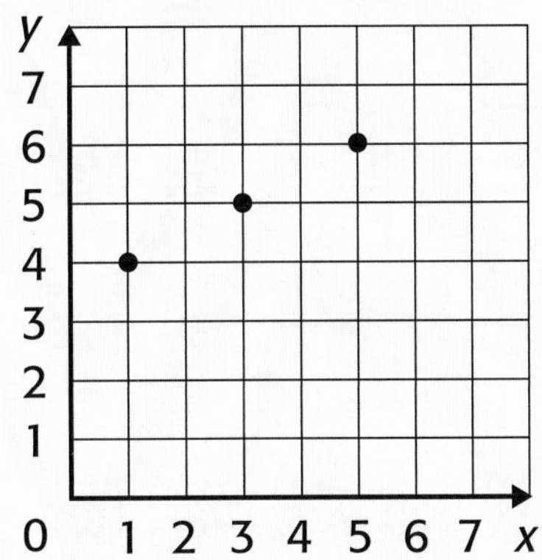

If he plots another point on the line, what could be its coordinates? (4MG2.1)

A (7, 6) **C** (6, 7)
B (7, 7) **D** (8, 7)

2 Refer to the graph in Exercise 1. If Miguel plots a point that is *not* on the line, what could be its coordinates? (4MG2.1)

F (9, 8) **H** (13, 11)
G (11, 9) **J** (15, 11)

QUICK Review

STRATEGY Imagine drawing a line through the 3 points to see what other points lie on the line.

Draw a line through the 3 points. Then plot each point on the coordinate grid. Which point lies on the line?

For more help with drawing points that correspond to linear relationships, see pages 488, 490.

STRATEGY Imagine the line through the 3 points in Exercise 1.

Which of the points given does not lie on the line?

For more help with drawing points that correspond to linear relationships, see pages 488, 490.

QUICK Practice

3 Look at the line segment shown below.

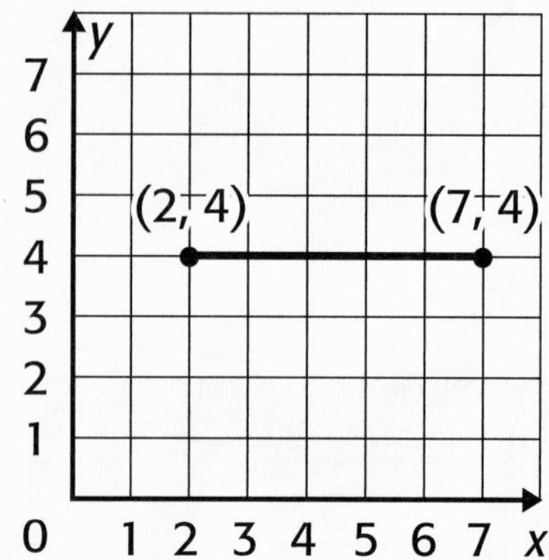

What is the length of the line segment? (4MG2.2)

A 0 units

B 3 units

C 5 units

D 6 units

QUICK Review

STRATEGY Find the difference between the *x*-coordinates of the endpoints to find the segment's length.

The length of the segment can be found by simplifying the expression 7 − 2.

For more help with finding the length of horizontal line segments, see page 477.

4 What is the length of the line segment shown on the grid? (4MG2.3)

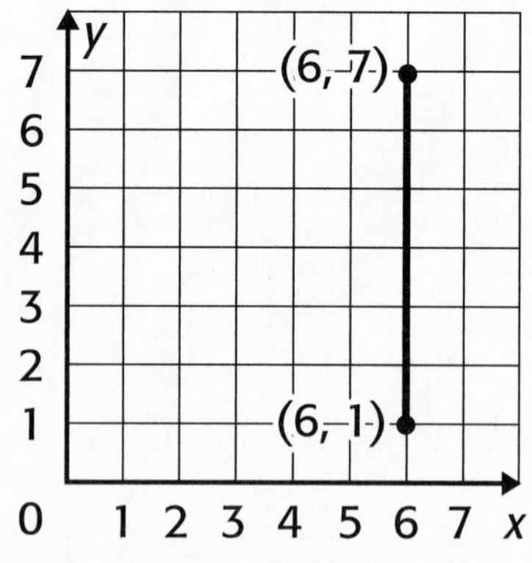

F 0 units

G 4 units

H 5 units

J 6 units

STRATEGY Find the difference between the *y*-coordinates of the endpoints to find the segment's length.

The length of the segment can be found by simplifying the expression 7 − 1.

For more help with finding the length of vertical line segments, see page 477.

Practice on Your Own

Standard Set 2.0

5 Look at the graph. Point *M* is at (2, 8). Point *N* is at (2, 3).

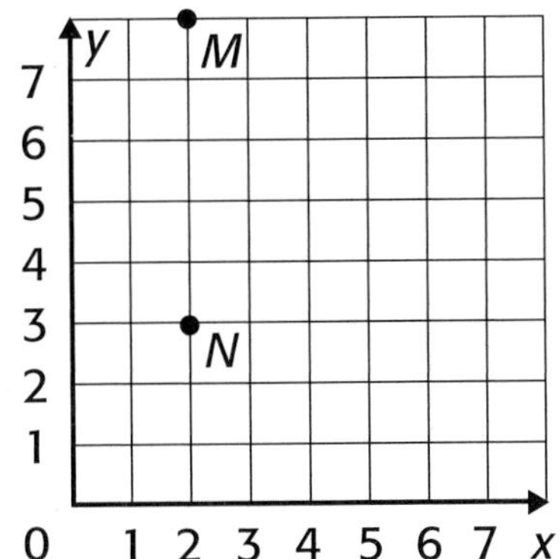

How can you find the number of units from point *M* to point *N*? **(4MG2.3)**

A Add: 8 + 3

B Add: 8 + 2

C Subtract: 8 − 3

D Subtract: 8 − 2

6 What is the length of the line segment shown on the grid? **(4MG2.2)**

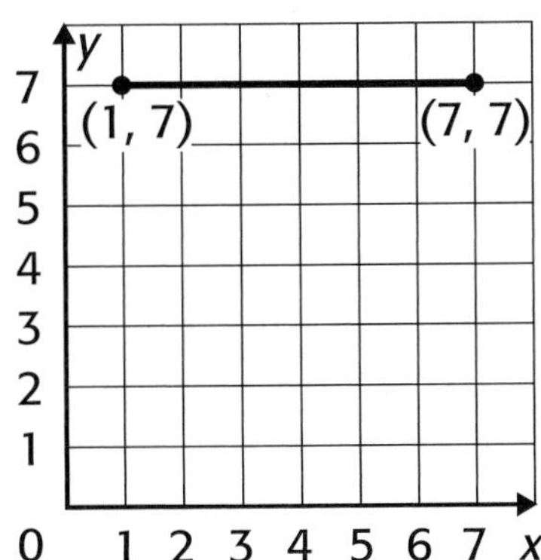

F 6 units

G 5 units

H 4 units

J 3 units

7 Three points that appear to lie on the same line are plotted on the grid.

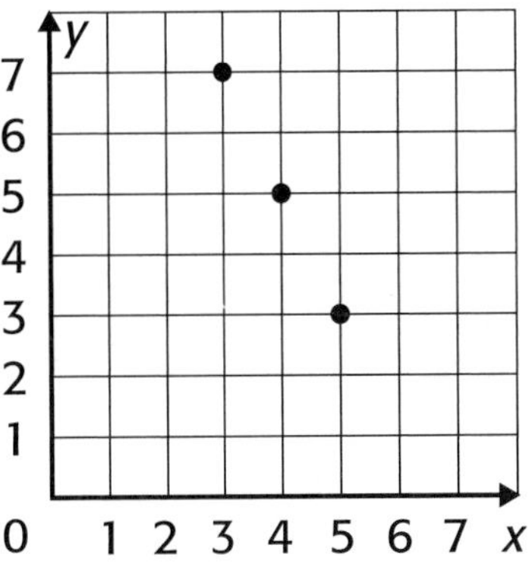

Suppose another point on the line is plotted. What could its coordinates be? **(4MG2.1)**

A (6, 1)

B (7, 1)

C (6, 2)

D (7, 2)

8 What is the length of the line segment shown on the grid? **(4MG2.3)**

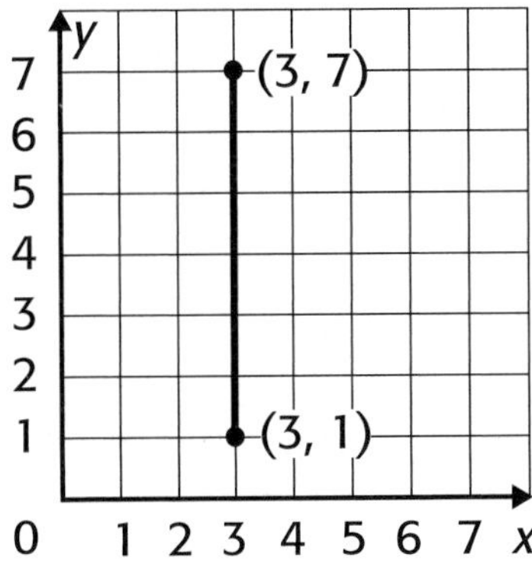

F 4 units

G 5 units

H 6 units

J 7 units

Practice by Standard: Measurement and Geometry

Standard Set 3.0: Students demonstrate an understanding of plane and solid geometric objects and use this knowledge to show relationships and solve problems.

DIRECTIONS
Choose the best answer.

QUICK Practice

1 Which figure(s) below show pairs of lines that appear to be perpendicular? (4MG3.1)

Figure 1

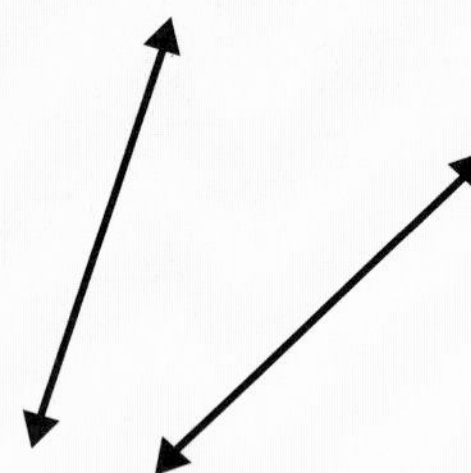

Figure 2

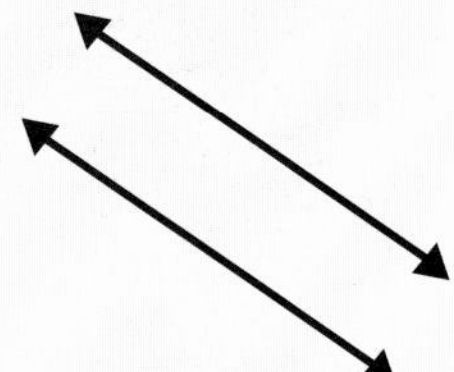

Figure 3

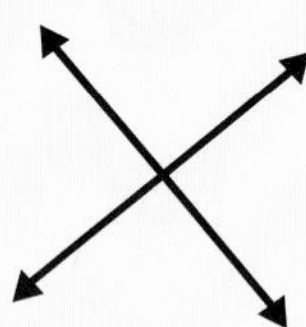

A Figure 2 only

B Figure 3 only

C Figure 1 and Figure 2

D Figure 1 and Figure 3

QUICK Review

READING HINT *Perpendicular lines* are lines that intersect to form right angles.

Which lines appear to intersect to form right angles?

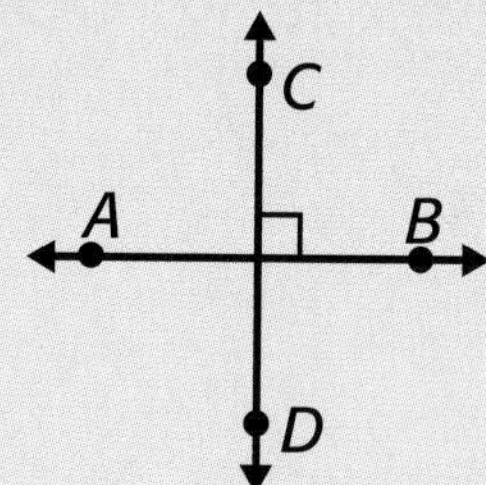

For more help with identifying perpendicular lines, see page 395.

QUICK Practice

2 Look at the circle with center *P*.

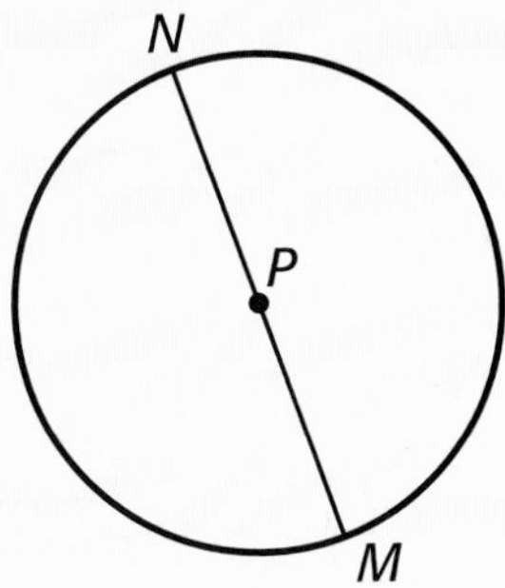

The line segment *PM* appears to be **(4MG3.2)**

F an arc.

G a perimeter.

H a radius.

J a diameter.

QUICK Review

READING HINT A radius of a circle connects its center to a point on the circle. A diameter passes through the center and connects two points on the circle.

What do you call a segment that connects the center of a circle to a point on the circle?

For more help with identifying the radius of a circle, see page 414.

3 What figure would be formed if you folded along the dotted lines? **(4MG3.6)**

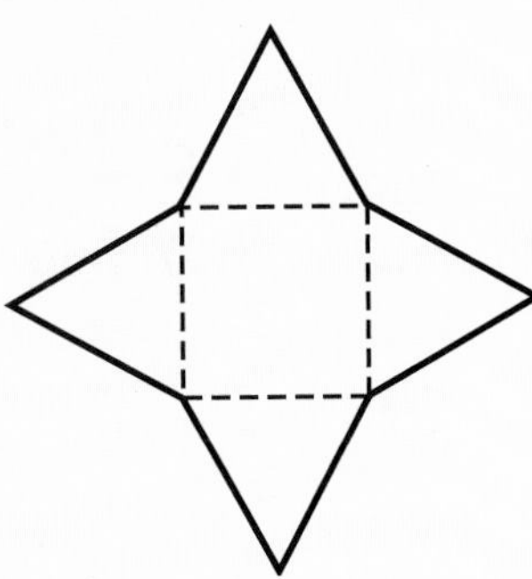

A cone

B cylinder

C prism

D pyramid

STRATEGY Imagine cutting the figure out of the paper and folding along the dotted lines. What would the folded figure look like?

The figure would have a square base and 4 triangular sides that meet at a vertex. What is the name of this three-dimensional figure?

square

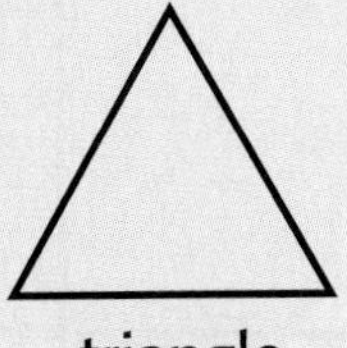
triangle

For more help with identifying nets of three-dimensional figures, see page 386.

Practice on Your Own

Standard Set 3.0

4 What kind of triangle has three sides of different lengths? (4MG3.7)

F equilateral
G isosceles
H right
J scalene

5 Which figures below appear to be congruent? (4MG3.3)

A

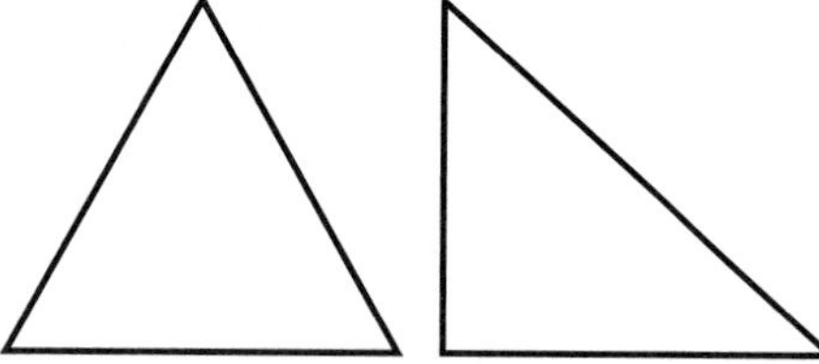

B

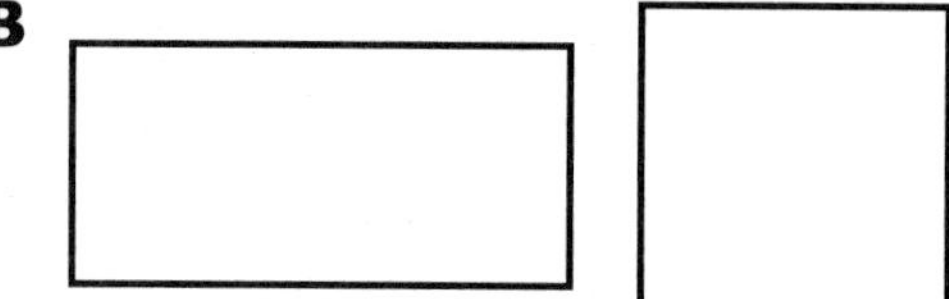

C

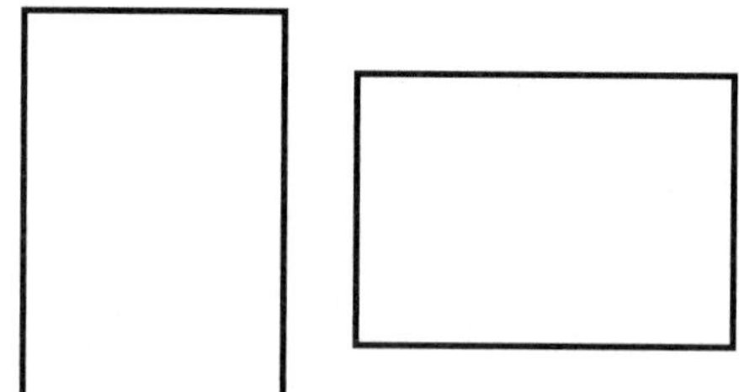

D

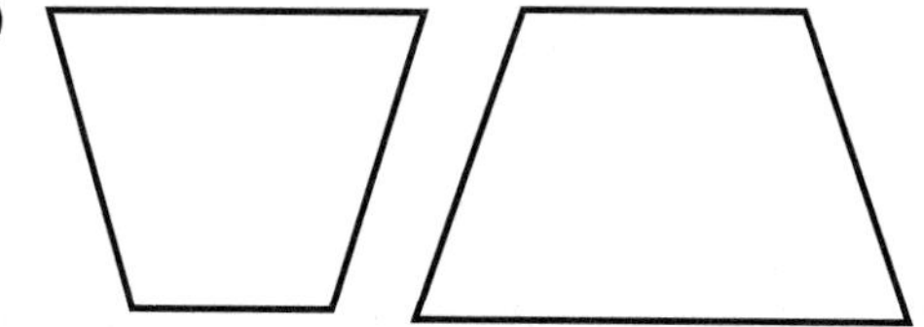

6 How many lines of symmetry does the figure below have? (4MG3.4)

F 0 **H** 2
G 1 **J** 3

7 How many degrees are there in a $\frac{1}{4}$ turn clockwise? (4MG3.5)

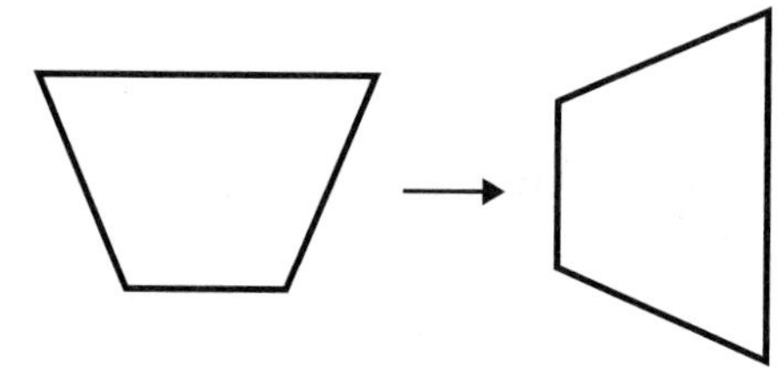

A 90° **C** 270°
B 180° **D** 360°

8 Which quadrilateral has 2 pairs of parallel opposite sides and 4 right angles? (4MG3.8)

F parallelogram
G rectangle
H square
J trapezoid

Practice by Standard: Data Analysis and Probability

Standard Set 1.0: Students organize, represent, and interpret numerical and categorical data and clearly communicate their findings.

DIRECTIONS
Choose the best answer.

QUICK Practice

1 A survey found that 7 people were in favor of building a new highway, 5 were opposed, and 3 were not sure. Which tally chart shows the correct results of the survey? (4PS1.1)

A

Survey Results	
In favor	卌
Opposed	卌 ||
Not sure	|||

B

Survey Results	
In favor	卌 ||
Opposed	卌
Not sure	||||

C

Survey Results	
In favor	卌 ||
Opposed	卌
Not sure	|||

D

Survey Results	
In favor	卌 |
Opposed	卌 ||
Not sure	||||

QUICK Review

STRATEGY Eliminate answer choices that do not show the correct tallies.

Which chart has 7 tally marks for in favor, 5 tally marks for opposed, and 3 tally marks for not sure?

Recall that data displayed in a tally chart can also be displayed in a bar graph.

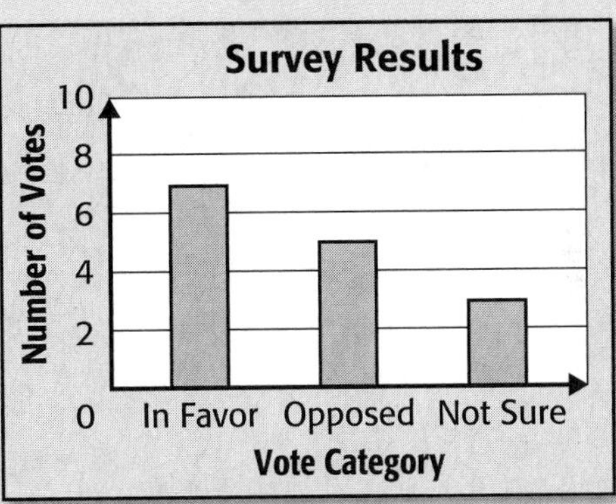

For more help with recording the outcomes of an experiment systematically, see page 127.

QUICK Practice

2 The ages of the players on Gloria's volleyball team are shown below. What is the mode of the ages? **(4PS1.2)**

8, 9, 8, 9, 9, 9, 10, 11, 10, 9, 9, 8

F 8 **H** 10

G 9 **J** 11

3 Mr. Baker asked the students in his homeroom how many books they read over the summer. The results are shown in the line plot.

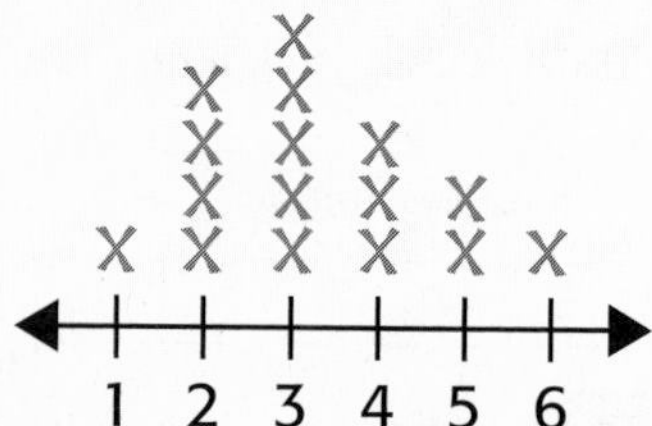

How many students read 3 books last summer? **(4PS1.3)**

A 2 **C** 4

B 3 **D** 5

4 Refer to the line plot in Exercise 3. Which number of books read appears to be an outlier? **(4PS1.2)**

F 1 book

G 5 books

H 6 books

J Not here

QUICK Review

READING HINT The *mode* of a data set is the number that occurs most frequently.

Which age is most common among the volleyball players?

For more help with finding the mode of a data set, see page 130.

STRATEGY Find the column that represents reading 3 books and count the Xs.

How many Xs are there above the number 3 in the line plot?

For more help with interpreting data displays, see page 136.

READING HINT An *outlier* is a data point that is significantly higher or lower than the rest of the data.

Does there appear to be a data point that is significantly higher or lower than the rest of the data?

For more help with identifying outliers, see page 131.

Practice on Your Own

Standard Set 1.0

5 The tally chart shows how many school subjects 14 students have to do homework for tonight.

Subjects	Tally
1	||
2	~~||||~~
3	|||
4	||
5	|

Which graph shows these results? (4PS1.1)

A

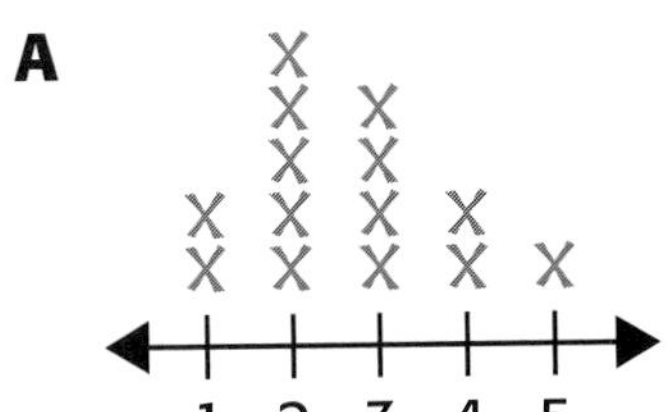

B

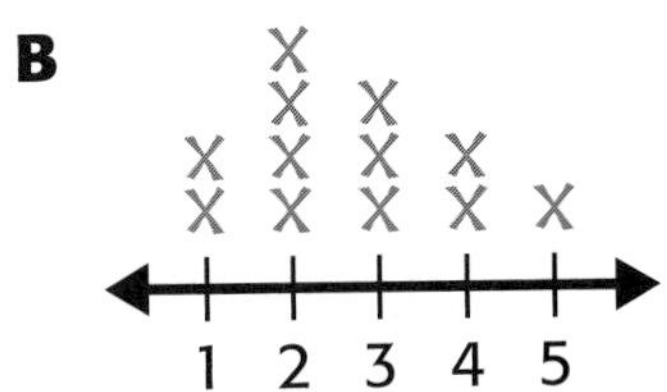

C

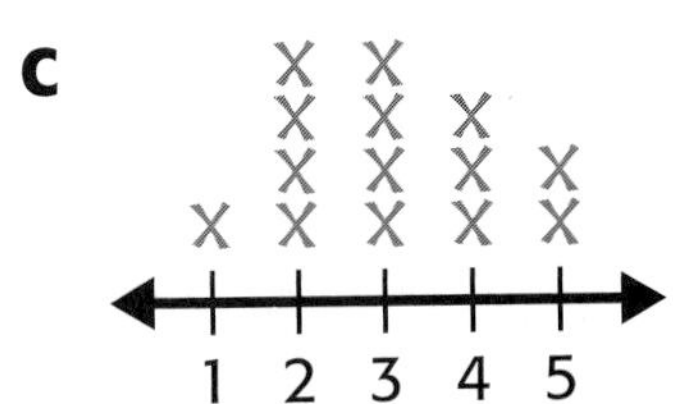

D

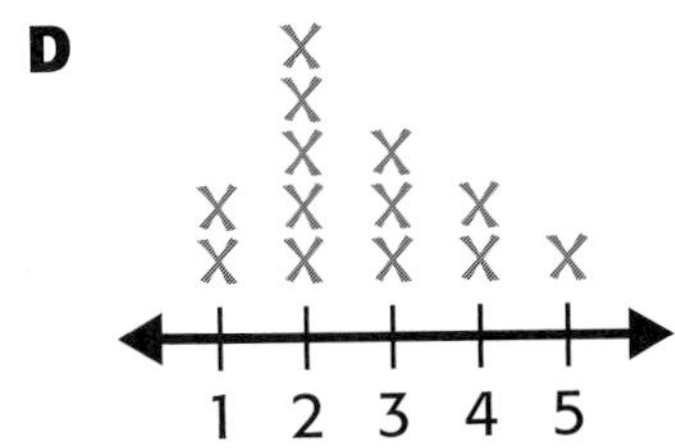

6 Refer to the tally chart in Exercise 5. What is the mode number of school subjects that the students have to do for homework for tonight? (4PS1.2)

F 1 subject

G 2 subjects

H 3 subjects

J 4 subjects

7 Refer to the bar graph below. It shows the number of absent students each day last week at Beechwood School.

How many students were absent on Wednesday of last week? (4PS1.3)

A 3

B 4

C 5

D 6

8 Refer to the bar graph in Exercise 7. What was the median number of absent students for the week? (4PS1.2)

F 3

G 4

H 5

J 6

Practice by Standard: Data Analysis and Probability

Standard Set 2.0: Students make predictions for simple probability situations.

DIRECTIONS
Choose the best answer.

QUICK Practice

1 Ben has a jar with 7 green chips, 5 red chips, 4 yellow chips, and 9 blue chips in it. If he pulls out 1 chip without looking, what color is he most likely to choose? **(4PS2.2)**

A blue
B green
C red
D yellow

QUICK Review

STRATEGY The color that has the most chips in the bag is most likely to be chosen.

What color is most common among the chips in the bag?

For more help with expressing the outcomes of probability situations verbally, see page 631.

QUICK Practice

2 Emma flips a coin and spins the spinner below.

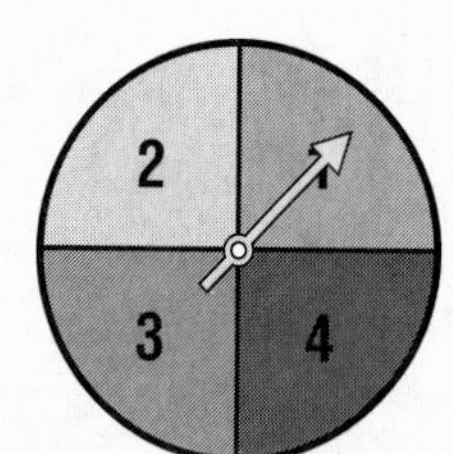

How many possible outcomes are there? **(4PS2.1)**

F 2 **H** 8
G 4 **J** 12

QUICK Review

READING HINT An *outcome* is a possible result of an experiment. For example, flipping heads and spinning a 3 is one outcome.

Draw a tree diagram to count all of the outcomes.

For more help with representing all possible outcomes of an experiment, see page 652.

QUICK Practice

3 The table shows the number of coins in a piggy bank.

Coin	Number
Penny	𝍸𝍷𝍷
Nickel	𝍷𝍷𝍷𝍷
Dime	𝍷𝍷𝍷𝍷
Quarter	𝍸

Suppose Brock selects a coin from the bank without looking. What is the probability that it will be a quarter? **(4PS2.2)**

A $\frac{1}{4}$ **C** $\frac{3}{8}$

B $\frac{3}{10}$ **D** $\frac{1}{2}$

QUICK Review

STRATEGY Divide the number of favorable outcomes by the total number of outcomes.

How many coins are there in the piggy bank? How many of them are quarters?

For more help with finding the probability of a simple event, see page 636.

QUICK Practice

4 The tree diagram shows the possible outcomes when two coins are flipped.

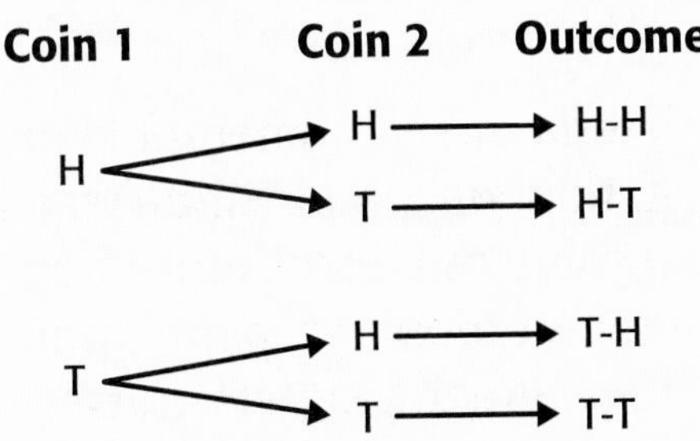

How many posible outcomes are there? **(4PS2.1)**

F 8 **H** 5

G 6 **J** 4

QUICK Review

STRATEGY Use the rightmost column of the tree diagram to count the outcomes.

The outcomes are shown in the rightmost column.

For more help with using tree diagrams to count outcomes, see page 652.

Practice on Your Own

Standard Set 2.0

5 To play a board game, each player rolls a 0–5 number cube and chooses a card at random from a deck. There is 1 red, 1 green, 1 yellow, and 1 blue card.

How many possible outcomes are there on each turn? (4PS2.1)

A 12 **C** 24
B 16 **D** 48

6 Refer to the board game in Exercise 5. What is the probability that Sonia will roll a 3 and select a yellow card on her next turn? (4PS2.2)

F 1 out of 8
G 1 out of 12
H 1 out of 16
J 1 out of 24

7 David will pick one pair of pants and one sweater to wear at random from the following choices.

Pants	Sweater
Tan Black	Red Blue Orange

How many different possible outcomes are there? (4PS2.1)

A 4 **C** 6
B 5 **D** 8

8 Each week at a summer camp, some campers are selected to be team leaders. The table shows the number of campers and team leaders during the past 3 weeks.

Team Leaders	
Campers	**Leaders**
120	12
150	15
190	19

Suppose there will be 180 campers at the summer camp next week. Which is the most reasonable number of team leaders to expect? (4PS2.2)

F 14
G 15
H 16
J 18

9 A pizzeria offers 3 different kinds of crust: thin, pan, and hand-tossed. Customers can also choose from 6 different toppings: pepperoni, sausage, green peppers, mushrooms, ground beef, and olives. Suppose Tonio wants to order a 1-topping pizza. How many different choices does he have? (4PS2.1)

A 18
B 15
C 12
D 9

Practice by Standard: Mathematical Reasoning

Standard Set 1.0: Students make decisions about how to approach problems.

DIRECTIONS
Choose the best answer.

QUICK Practice

1 Drew bought 5 packages of fruit juice for a soccer game. There are 4 cans of juice in each package. They sell for $1.89 per package. How much did he spend on fruit juice altogether? **(4MR1.1)**

A $10.20 **C** $7.56

B $9.45 **D** $7.22

2 What is the area of the figure below? **(4MR1.2)**

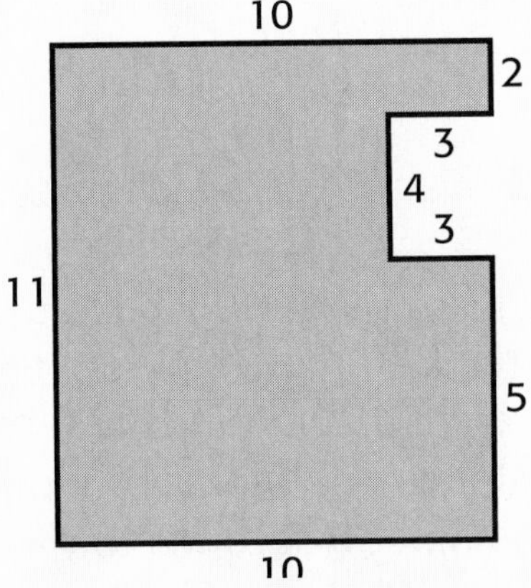

F 110 square units

G 106 square units

H 102 square units

J 98 square units

QUICK Review

STRATEGY Only use the relevant information from the statement to solve the problem.

Does it matter how many cans of juice come in each package?

For more help with distinguishing relevant from irrelevant information, see page 102.

STRATEGY Break the problem into simpler parts to make solving it easier.

How can you divide the figure into parts that are all rectangles?

For more help with breaking a problem into simpler parts, see page 442.

Practice on Your Own

Standard Set 1.0

3 Maggie collects stickers. She keeps them in a picture book with the same number of stickers on each page. The table shows the total number of stickers on different numbers of pages.

Sticker Collection	
Number of Pages	Number of Stickers
1	16
2	32
3	48
4	64
5	80
6	96
7	■
8	128

How many stickers are there on 7 pages of the book? **(4MR1.1)**

A 108 stickers

B 112 stickers

C 114 stickers

D 118 stickers

4 Refer to Maggie's sticker collection in Exercise 3. Suppose there are 8 columns of stickers on every 2 pages of the book. Each column has the same number of stickers. How many rows of stickers are there on each page? **(4MR1.2)**

F 4

G 8

H 12

J 16

5 Look at the pattern of figures below.

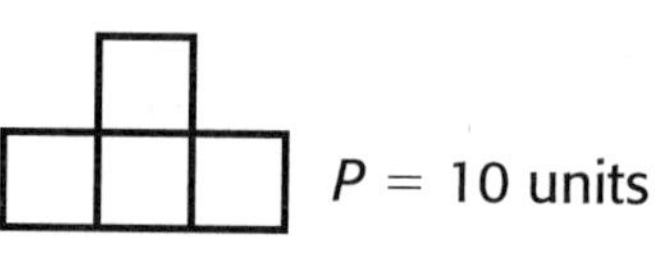

Figure 1

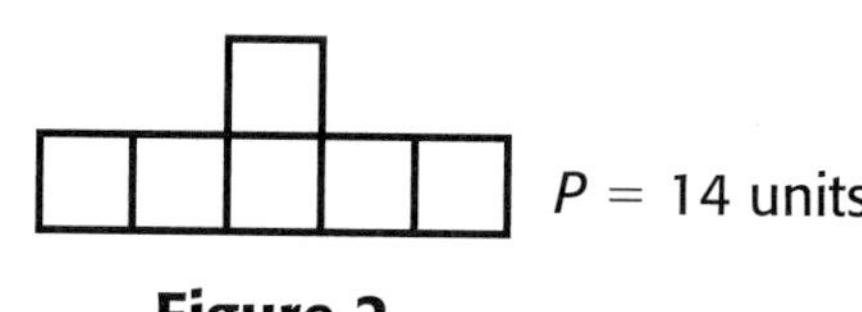

Figure 2

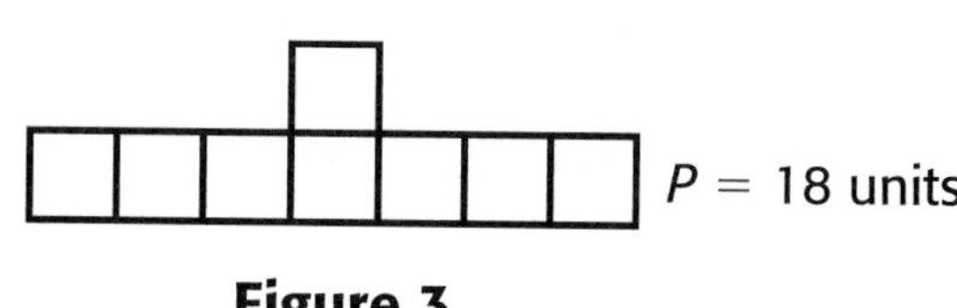

Figure 3

If the pattern is continued, what will be the perimeter of the sixth figure? **(4MR1.1)**

A 26 units

B 28 units

C 30 units

D 32 units

6 Ling ran 240 meters during recess. He weighs 120 pounds and burns 24 calories per minute while running. It took him 30 seconds to run this distance. What was Ling's average speed in meters per second? **(4MR1.1)**

F 2 meters per second

G 5 meters per second

H 8 meters per second

J 10 meters per second

Practice by Standard: Mathematical Reasoning

Standard Set 2.0: Students use strategies, skills, and concepts in finding solutions.

DIRECTIONS
Choose the best answer.

QUICK Practice

1 The sum of the angles of a quadrilateral is 360°. What is the measure of the missing angle below? **(4MR2.6)**

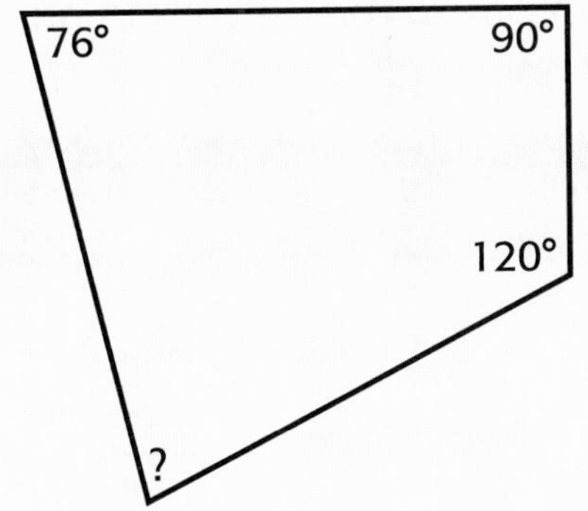

A 74° **C** 64°

B 71° **D** 61°

2 The 4th graders need to raise more than \$235 next week in the school fundraiser to win first place. Which of the following shows the amount they must raise to win first place? **(4MR2.3)**

F amount $>$ 235

G amount $<$ 235

H amount $=$ 235

J amount $=$ 235 $-$ 1

QUICK Review

STRATEGY Subtract the sum of the known angle measures from 360 to find the measure of the missing angle.

This problem can be solved by simplifying the expression $360 - (76 + 90 + 120)$.

For more help with making precise calculations, see page 62.

READING HINT The phrase *at least* means greater than or equal to.

Will the 4th graders win first place if they raise \$235? Will they win first place if they raise more than \$235?

For more help with using numbers and symbols to represent mathematical reasoning, see page 28.

Practice on Your Own

Standard Set 2.0

3 The table shows the costs of 4 items Timothy is purchasing at the grocery store. Estimate the total cost of these 4 items. **(4MR2.1)**

Grocery Shopping	
Item	**Cost**
Apples	$3.05
Bread	$2.09
Milk	$2.85
Eggs	$1.89

A $8
B $10
C $12
D $15

4 What is the area of the shaded part of the figure? **(4MR2.2)**

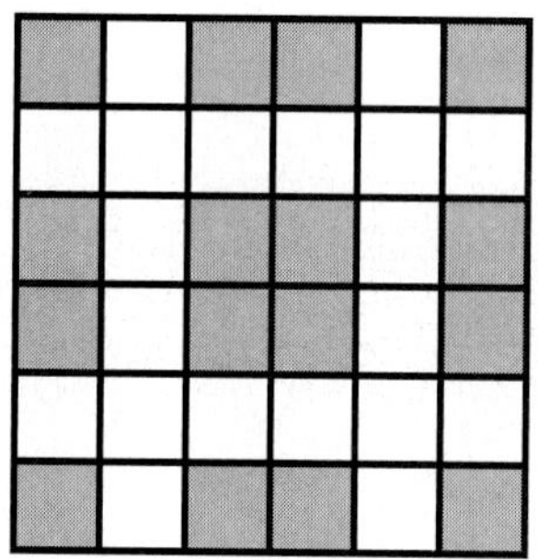

F 72 square centimeters
G 68 square centimeters
H 64 square centimeters
J 60 square centimeters

5 Dana has 12 dolls. Each doll has four different dresses. How could you find the total number of dresses? **(4MR2.4)**

A Add 4 and 12.
B Subtract 4 from 12.
C Multiply 4 by 12.
D Divide 12 by 4.

6 There are 180 players on 15 basketball teams at a tournament. Each team has the same number of players. How could you find how many players there are on each team? **(4MR2.4)**

F Add 180 and 15.
G Subtract 15 from 180.
H Multiply 15 by 180.
J Divide 180 by 15.

7 The table shows the total number of people who rode a certain bus each day last week.

Bus Riders	
Day	**Passengers**
Monday	307
Tuesday	388
Wednesday	321
Thursday	286
Friday	211

About how many people rode the bus in all last week? Round your answer to the nearest 100. **(4MR2.5)**

A 1400
B 1500
C 1600
D 1700

8 The average cat sleeps 18 hours a day. How could you find the number of hours in one day the average cat is awake? **(4MR2.4)**

F Add 18 and 24.
G Subtract 18 from 24.
H Multiply 18 by 24.
J Divide 24 by 18.

Practice by Standard: Mathematical Reasoning

Standard Set 3.0: Students move beyond a particular problem by generalizing to other situations.

DIRECTIONS
Choose the best answer.

QUICK Practice

1 José wrote the first few rows of a pattern called Pascal's Triangle. Each row has a 1 on each end. Each number is found by adding the two numbers directly above it in the previous row.

1
1 2 1
1 3 3 1
1 4 6 4 1

What is the next row in the pattern? **(4MR3.2)**

A 1 5 10 5 1

B 1 5 10 10 5 1

C 1 6 12 15 12 6 1

D 1 6 12 12 6 1

QUICK Review

STRATEGY Look for a pattern and predict the next number.

What happens to the numbers between the 1s with each term?

For more help with extending patterns, see page 392.

QUICK Practice

2 There are 53 football players traveling to an away game. The vans hold 12 people each. Coach Brown needs to find how many vans are needed altogether. How many vans will be needed? **(4MR3.1)**

F 3 vans

G 4 vans

H 5 vans

J 6 vans

QUICK Review

STRATEGY Eliminate answer choices that are not reasonable solutions.

What is the minimum number of vans that can hold 53 people?

For more help with evaluating the reasonableness of a solution, see page 266.

Practice on Your Own

Standard Set 3.0

3 In the egg toss game at the school field day, many teams are eliminated after each round.

Number of Rounds	Players Remaining
1	256
2	128
3	64
4	32
5	16
6	8

How many rounds will be needed in order to determine the winning team? (4MR3.3)

A 10

B 9

C 8

D 7

4 Coach Mata keeps track of her team's shooting statistics during the basketball season.

Shooting Statistics	
Shots Taken	Shots Made
59	20
50	17
48	16

If the team takes 75 shots in their next game, which is the most reasonable estimate for how many shots they will make? (4MR3.1)

F 30

G 25

H 20

J 15

5 Cora uses the method shown below to find the areas of triangles with different heights and base lengths.

Height: 6, Base: 4

Area: $\frac{1}{2} \times 6 \times 4 = 12$

Height: 12, Base: 10

Area: $\frac{1}{2} \times 12 \times 10 = 60$

Height: 8, Base: 4

Area: $\frac{1}{2} \times 8 \times 4 = 16$

What is the area of a triangle with a height of 8 meters and a base length of 12 meters? (4MR3.2)

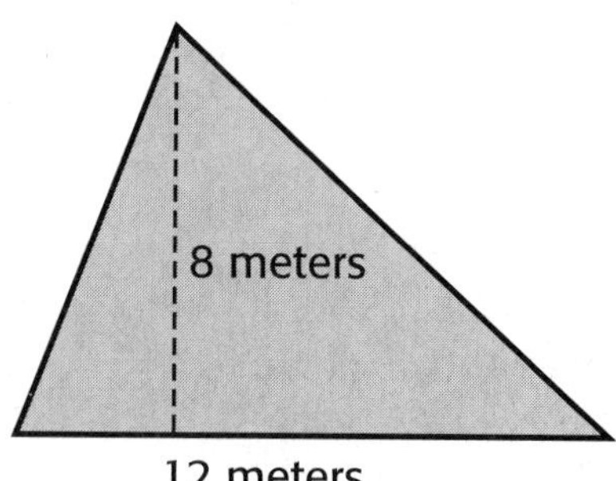

A 96 square meters

B 84 square meters

C 54 square meters

D 48 square meters

6 Jennie bought 5 gel pens priced at 89¢ each. Which would give the most reasonable estimate for the total cost of the 5 gel pens? (4MR3.1)

F 80¢ × 5

G 85¢ × 5

H 90¢ × 5

J 95¢ × 5

Practice on Your Own

7 Max created a table showing the length, width, and area of different rectangles.

Length (units)	Width (units)	Area (square units)
2	8	16
5	3	15
6	4	24
3	9	27
8	5	40

Which of the following best describes the method Max uses to find the area of a rectangle? (4MR3.2)

A Multiply the length by the width.

B Divide the length by the width.

C Add the length to the width.

D Subtract the length from the width.

8 Use Max's method from Exercise 7 to find the area of the rectangle below. (3MR3.2)

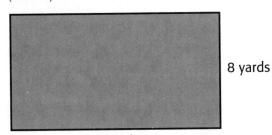

F 20 square yards

G 72 square yards

H 84 square yards

J 96 square yards

9 There are 237 students going on a field trip. The students will travel on buses that hold 48 people each. Mr. King needs to find how many buses are needed altogether. Which of the following is the most reasonable number of buses that will be needed? (4MR3.1)

A 6 buses

B 5 buses

C 4 buses

D 3 buses

10 Vanesa has a tablecloth with an area of 48 square feet. She wants to fold the tablecloth to store it in a closet. The table below shows the area of the tablecloth after each time she folds it in half.

Number of Folds	Area (square feet)
1	48
2	24
3	12
4	6
5	3
6	■

It takes Vanesa 6 folds to get the tablecloth small enough to fit on the closet shelf. What is the area after 6 folds? (4MR3.3)

F 2.5 square feet

G 2 square feet

H 1.5 square feet

J 1 square foot

Student Handbook

Built-In Workbooks

Reference

How to Use the Student Handbook

A Student Handbook is the additional skill and reference material found at the end of books. The Student Handbook can help answer these questions.

What If I Need More Practice?

You, or your teacher, may decide that working through some additional problems would be helpful. The **Extra Practice** section provides these problems for each lesson so you have ample opportunity to practice new skills.

What If I Forget a Vocabulary Word?

The **English-Spanish Glossary** provides a list of important, or difficult, words used throughout the textbook. It provides a definition in English and Spanish as well as the page number(s) where the word can be found.

What If I Need to Find Something Quickly?

The **Index** alphabetically lists the subjects covered throughout the entire textbook and the pages on which each subject can be found.

What If I Forget Measurement Conversions or Multiplication Facts?

Inside the back cover of your math book is a list of measurement conversions that are used in the book. You will also find a multiplication table inside the back cover.

Extra Practice

Lesson 1-1

Pages 17–19

Write the value of the underlined digit.

1. 1,637 **2.** 37,904 **3.** 56,572 **4.** 209,631

Write each number in word form and in expanded form.

5. 2,493 **6.** 6,319 **7.** 7,085 **8.** 9,160

9. 28,482 **10.** 71,045 **11.** 523,608 **12.** 347,281

Write each number in standard form and in expanded form.

13. fifty-six thousand, seven hundred twenty

14. two hundred thirty-four thousand, eight hundred three

Lesson 1-2

Pages 22–25

Write each number in word form and expanded form.

1. 9,005 **2.** 19,860 **3.** 26,010 **4.** 360,508

5. 408,040 **6.** 26,053,107 **7.** 730,000,520 **8.** 800,530,700

Write each number in standard form and in expanded form.

9. nine million, twenty-four thousand, ten

10. six hundred thirty-five million, eight hundred fifty-seven thousand, five

11. Write in word form and in standard form.

300,000 + 20,000 + 1,000 + 50 + 8

Lesson 1-3

Pages 26–27

Solve. Use the *four-step plan*.

1. Mrs. Beal's students earned a class party. An extra large pizza cost \$28. If she bought 3 pizzas, how much did she spend?

2. Carisa can draw 3 pictures in the morning and 3 pictures in the afternoon. If she draws for 5 days, how many pictures can she make?

3. Tom watched 45 movies this year. Each movie was two hours long. How many hours did he spend watching movies this year?

4. A basketball game has 4 quarters. If 5 players each score 2 points during each quarter, how many total points are scored?

Lesson 1-4

Pages 28–30

Compare. Use >, <, or =.

1. 9,719 ● 9,791

2. 3,780 ● 3,080

3. 34,925 ● 34,952

4. 89,629 ● 89,635

5. 47,283 ● 42,283

6. 72,036 ● 72,300

7. 325,614 ● 235,614

8. 758,438 ● 758,438

9. 7,863,403 ● 7,863,304

10. 9,604,138 ● 9,064,946

Copy and complete to make the number sentence true.

11. 4,■58 < 4,859

12. 34,199 = 3■,199

13. 214,166 > 2■4,166

14. 5,877,820 > 5,877,8■0

Lesson 1-5

Pages 32–35

Order the numbers from greatest to least.

1. 1,443; 1,434; 1,444; 1,344

2. 6,519; 6,600; 3,941; 4,872

3. 19,400; 9,400; 19,004; 10,440

4. 52,951; 49,384; 51,954; 52,865

5. 85,610; 85,185; 85,611; 85,625

6. 94,846; 49,846; 84,694; 46,948

7. 275,391; 2,086,344; 258,983

8. 361,259; 361,084; 61,999; 846,465

9. 568,208; 559,876; 59,986; 58,869

10. 768,635; 792,456; 741,056; 78,318

11. 3,849,257; 38,492,570; 38,492,057

12. 4,608,056; 4,608,942; 4,608,924

Lesson 1-6

Pages 36–39

Round each number to the given place-value position.

1. 451; hundred

2. 949; hundred

3. 4,965; thousand

4. 20,368; thousand

5. 36,801; hundred

6. 42,204; ten thousand

7. 70,988; thousand

8. 83,756; ten

9. 437,947; ten thousand

10. 455,877; ten

11. 849, 604; thousand

12. 934,567; hundred thousand

Lesson 1-7

Pages 40–41

Use the *four-step plan* to solve.

1. Lisa lives 7 miles from school. She bikes to school and back every day. How many miles does she bike in 1 school week?
2. A chicken runs 5 miles an hour. An ostrich runs 40 miles an hour. How many hours would it take a chicken to run the same distance it took an ostrich to run in two hours?
3. Aaron bought a shirt that cost $27 and a hat that cost $3. How much change will he receive if he pays with two $20 bills?
4. A bag of 15 oranges costs $20. Oranges that are sold individually cost $2. Is it cheaper to buy 15 oranges in a bag or 15 oranges sold individually? Explain.

Lesson 2-1

Pages 55–57

Copy and complete each number sentence. Identify the property or rule used.

1. $20 - \blacksquare = 0$
2. $14 + 37 = \blacksquare + 14$
3. $7 + (4 + 8) = (7 + 4) + \blacksquare$
4. $197 + 0 = \blacksquare$
5. $233 - \blacksquare = 233$
6. $72 + 9 = \blacksquare + 72$
7. $(14 + 3) + 8 = 14 + (3 + \blacksquare)$
8. $863 + 44 = \blacksquare + 863$
9. $21 + (\blacksquare + 9) = (21 + 17) + 9$
10. $541 - \blacksquare = 0$

Lesson 2-2

Pages 58–61

Estimate. Round to the indicated place value.

1. 43 + 29; tens
2. 664 + 49; tens
3. 1,329 + 755; hundreds
4. 9,488 + 2,061; thousands
5. $341.63 + $299.82; hundreds
6. 59 − 34; tens
7. 859 − 42; tens
8. 2,495 − 468; hundreds
9. $6,295 − $1,402; thousands
10. 37,423 − 18,196; ten thousands

Lesson 2-3

Pages 62–63

Tell whether an estimate or exact answer is needed. Then solve.

1. Nina bought a CD that cost \$11.99. She gave the cashier a \$20 bill. About how much change should she get back?
2. Carlos wants to buy a new football that costs \$32.50. He earns \$6.50 every week delivering newspapers. How many weeks will it take to save enough money for the ball?
3. The 29 students in Jin's science class are riding in vans on a field trip. Each van can hold 8 students. How many vans will be needed?
4. Mika spends about 45 minutes practicing the piano each day, Monday through Friday. About how many hours does she practice in four weeks?

Lesson 2-4

Pages 64–66

Find each sum. Check your work by estimating.

1. $\begin{array}{r} 456 \\ +\ 233 \\ \hline \end{array}$
2. $\begin{array}{r} \$387.96 \\ +\ \$\ \ 43.48 \\ \hline \end{array}$
3. $\begin{array}{r} 5{,}678 \\ +\ 2{,}431 \\ \hline \end{array}$
4. $\begin{array}{r} \$\ \ 67.44 \\ +\ \$384.06 \\ \hline \end{array}$
5. $\begin{array}{r} 60{,}483 \\ +\ 98{,}218 \\ \hline \end{array}$
6. $\begin{array}{r} \$328.19 \\ +\ \$673.75 \\ \hline \end{array}$
7. $\begin{array}{r} 357{,}816 \\ +\ 93{,}402 \\ \hline \end{array}$
8. $\begin{array}{r} \$9{,}456.56 \\ +\ \$\ \ 331.45 \\ \hline \end{array}$
9. $\begin{array}{r} \$6{,}789.02 \\ +\ \$4{,}351.54 \\ \hline \end{array}$

Lesson 2-5

Pages 70–73

Subtract. Use addition or estimation to check your answer.

1. $\begin{array}{r} 721 \\ -\ 563 \\ \hline \end{array}$
2. $\begin{array}{r} \$8.07 \\ -\ \$3.28 \\ \hline \end{array}$
3. $\begin{array}{r} 926 \\ -\ 644 \\ \hline \end{array}$
4. $\begin{array}{r} \$17.66 \\ -\ \$\ \ 8.19 \\ \hline \end{array}$
5. $\begin{array}{r} 9{,}663 \\ -\ 5{,}201 \\ \hline \end{array}$
6. $\begin{array}{r} \$67.41 \\ -\ \$39.83 \\ \hline \end{array}$
7. $\begin{array}{r} \$245.09 \\ -\ \$\ \ 76.25 \\ \hline \end{array}$
8. $\begin{array}{r} 55{,}788 \\ -\ 34{,}223 \\ \hline \end{array}$
9. $\begin{array}{r} 71{,}864 \\ -\ 49{,}667 \\ \hline \end{array}$

Lesson 2-6

Pages 74–75

Tell whether an estimate or exact answer is needed. Then solve.

1. Mr. Lee spent about $23 on paintbrushes, $50 dollars on paint, and $15 on colored chalk. About how much did he spend on art supplies?
2. Tia is hanging lights around her window. The window is a square with sides that are 28 inches. How many inches of lights will Tia need?
3. The cats in the animal shelter eat 18 pounds of food each day. How many pounds of food do the cats eat each week?
4. Casey has $6. He buys a sandwich for $1.85, a salad for $1.90, and milk for $0.95. About how much money will he have left?

Lesson 2-7

Pages 78–81

Subtract. Use addition to check.

1. 800 − 567
2. $4.00 − $2.98
3. 1,000 − 703
4. 3,600 − 1,695
5. 5,000 − 2,367
6. $90.00 − $48.90
7. 7,000 − 5,804
8. 6,400 − 3,166
9. 9,600 − 1,879
10. 7,000 − 4,386
11. $47.00 − $28.64
12. 8,600 − 7,621
13. $2,200 − $883.72

Lesson 3-1

Pages 93–95

Find the value of each expression if $x = 6$ and $c = 7$.

1. $c + 5$
2. $x - 3$
3. $c + 9$
4. $7 + x$
5. $c - 2$
6. $14 - x$
7. $(x - 2) + 9$
8. $16 - (c + 5)$
9. $5 + (6 + x)$

Write an expression for each situation.

10. five less than *y*
11. the sum of *b* and seventeen
12. *d* minus twenty-four
13. fifty-one subtracted from *f*

Lesson 3-2

Pages 98–101

Solve each equation mentally.

1. $4 + b = 12$
2. $7 + m = 18$
3. $p - 8 = 6$
4. $18 - 13 = y$
5. $9 - x = 2$
6. $q + 14 = 22$
7. $8 + d = 18$
8. $7 + 6 = f$

Write and solve an equation for each situation.

9. Twelve less than a number is sixteen. What is the number?
10. Eight subtracted from a number equals thirteen. What is the number?
11. The sum of nine and a number is twenty-eight. Find the number?
12. A number plus eleven equals twenty-five. What is the number?

Lesson 3-3

Pages 102–103

Identify any missing or extra information. Then solve if possible.

1. Monkeys at the zoo eat 9 bananas and 4 apples each day. How many pieces of fruit do the monkeys eat in one week?
2. Sandra has $21. She wants to buy cans of tennis balls for $4 each. There are 3 tennis balls in each can. How many cans can she buy?
3. Marco has soccer practice 3 days a week. He has 17 teammates. Practice lasts for 2 hours each day. How many hours does Marco practice soccer each week?
4. Kayla earns $5 per hour. She is saving to buy a new game that costs $36 dollars. How many weeks will Kayla have to work to earn enough money for the game?

Lesson 3-4

Pages 104–106

Write an equation that describes the pattern. Then use the equation to find the next three numbers in the pattern.

1.

Rule: ■						
Input (*b*)	4	6	10	14	20	24
Output (*x*)	13	15	19	■	■	■

2.

Rule: ■						
Input (*y*)	11	15	19	23	27	31
Output (*c*)	4	8	12	■	■	■

3.

Rule: ■						
Input (*f*)	$24	$32	$40	$48	$56	$64
Output (*q*)	$16	$24	$32	■	■	■

4.

Rule: ■						
Input (*m*)	$16	$19	$22	$25	$28	$31
Output (*p*)	$27	$30	$33	■	■	■

Lesson 3-5

Pages 108–109

Use any strategy to solve. Tell what strategy you used.

1. Ty wants to buy posters that cost $7 each. He has $50. How many posters can he buy?
2. Ian is eating pizza with 5 friends. They ordered 3 pizzas. If each pizza is cut into 6 slices, how many slices can each person have?
3. A vine in the park grows 2 inches every week. The vine is 13 inches tall now. How many inches tall will the vine be in 2 weeks? 4 weeks? 8 weeks?
4. Amy is putting photos in an album. Each page in the album can hold 4 photos. There are 32 pages in the album. How many photos can Amy put in the album?

Lesson 3-6

Pages 110–113

Show the equality is not changed.

1. $11 + 7 = 18$
   $11 + 7 + 8 = 18 + 8$
2. $28 = 12 + 16$
   $28 - 9 = 12 + 16 - 9$

Find the missing number in each equation.

3. $13 + 8 = 13 + \blacksquare$
4. $15 + 7 = 10 + 5 + \blacksquare$

Lesson 4-1

Pages 127–129

Organize each set of data in a tally chart and a frequency table.

1. George recorded the types of pets that his classmates have. His recordings are shown at the right.

Pets		
cat	cat	dog
cat	dog	lizard
dog	fish	bird
bird	dog	fish

2. Tina conducted a survey to find out the favorite sports of the children in the park. Her recordings are shown at the right.

Favorite Sports		
soccer	baseball	football
soccer	basketball	football
football	football	basketball
basketball	soccer	tennis

Lesson 4-2

Pages 130–133

Find the mode and median of the set of data. Identify any outliers.

1.

Students in Each Grade					
Grade	1	2	3	4	5
Number of students	26	22	27	24	22

2.

Roller Coaster Riders at an Amusement Park							
Roller coaster	1	2	3	4	5	6	7
Number of riders	46	38	41	17	45	39	36

Lesson 4-3

Pages 134–135

Solve. Use the *make a table* strategy.

1. Akira mailed invitations to his birthday party. The postage to mail each invitation was $0.39. Akira paid $2.34 in all for postage. How many invitations did he send?

2. During the soccer season, for every 3 penalty kicks he took, Jamil scored on 2 of them. If he scored on 12 penalty kicks, how many penalty kicks did he take?

3. Nick earns $7 an hour walking dogs. He works the same number of hours each week. Nick earns $252 in 1 month. How many hours does he work each week?

4. Maria bought some six-packs of soda. She bought 48 cans of soda in all. How many six-packs of soda did she buy?

Lesson 4-4

Pages 136–138

Organize each set of data in a line plot.

1. Number of seeds that sprouted

Seeds That Sprouted	
Week	Seeds
Week 1	6
Week 2	9
Week 3	11
Week 4	10
Week 5	9
Week 6	6
Week 7	9

2. Miles hiked by campers

Miles Hiked per Day	
Day	Miles Hiked
Monday	5
Tuesday	7
Wednesday	6
Thursday	4
Friday	5
Saturday	4
Sunday	3

Lesson 4-5

Pages 140–143

Use the graph to answer the exercises.

1. Which fruit did the farm produce the most of?

2. Which fruit did the farm produce the least of?

3. How many more pounds of strawberries were produced than pounds of plums?

4. Which two fruits added together equal the amount of the fruit that the farm produced the most of?

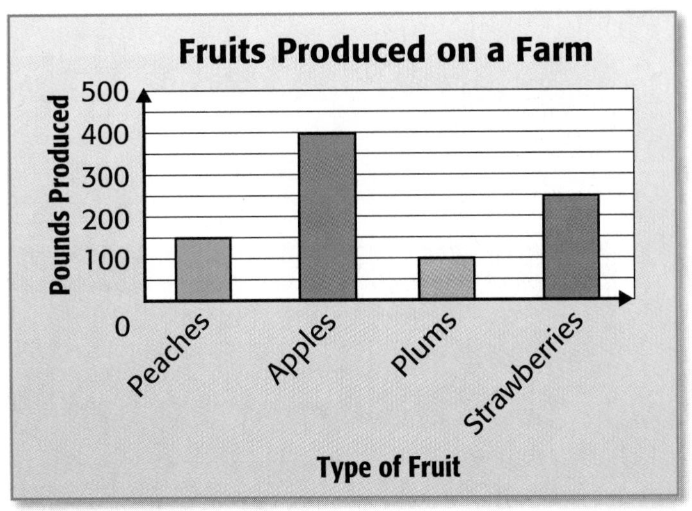

Lesson 4-6

Pages 148–149

Use any strategy to solve. Tell what strategy you used.

1. Luis has an aquarium with 47 fish. There are 12 orange fish, 13 blue fish, 9 white fish, and 8 yellow fish. The rest of the fish are red. How many are red?

2. There were 45 action, 60 comedy, 25 drama, and 50 mystery movies rented from a video store in one day. How many more comedies than dramas were rented?

Lesson 4-7

Pages 150–153

Use the line graph to answer the questions.

1. At what time were there the most skiers?

2. At which two times were there the same number of skiers?

3. How many skiers were there at 4 P.M.?

4. How many more skiers were there at 2 P.M. than at 12 P.M.?

5. Predict whether there will be more or less skiers at 5 P.M. than at 3 P.M. Explain.

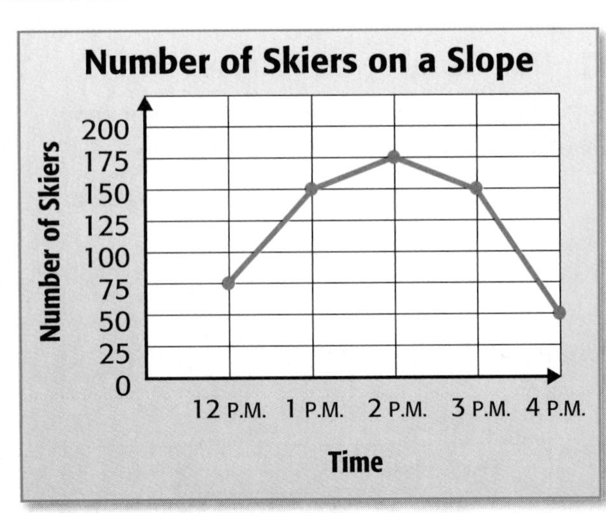

Lesson 4-8

Pages 156–159

Use the graph to answer the questions.

1. How many cups of lemonade were sold between 4:00 and 6:00?
2. How many more cups of lemonade were sold between 2:00 and 4:00 than between 10:00 and 12:00?
3. How many cups of lemonade were sold between 12:00 and 4:00?
4. Predict whether the number of cups of lemonade sold between 8:00 A.M. and 10:00 A.M. was greater or less than the number sold between 12:00 and 2:00. Explain.

Lesson 5-1

Pages 175–177

Copy and complete each fact family.

1. $3 \times 8 = ■$ $8 \times ■ = 24$ $24 \div ■ = 3$ $24 \div 3 = ■$
2. $9 \times ■ = 72$ $8 \times ■ = 72$ $72 \div 9 = ■$ $72 \div 8 = ■$

Divide. Use a related multiplication fact.

3. $27 \div 3 = ■$
4. $54 \div 9 = ■5$
5. $36 \div 6 = ■$
6. $88 \div 11 = ■$
7. $32 \div 8 = ■$
8. $50 \div 5 = ■$

Lesson 5-2

Pages 178–181

Identify the property shown by each number sentence.

1. $7 \times 4 = 4 \times 7$
2. $0 \div 15 = 0$
3. $3 \times (4 \times 5) = (3 \times 4) \times 5$
4. $24 \div 1 = 24$
5. $36 \div 36 = 1$
6. $(5 \times 8) \times 6 = 5 \times (8 \times 6)$

Copy and complete each number sentence. Identify the property used.

7. $6 \div ■ = 1$
8. $16 \times ■ = 0$
9. $14 \div ■ = 1$
10. $■ \times 8 = 8 \times 5$

Lesson 5-3

Pages 182–185

Multiply or divide.

1. 3×8 **2.** 5×5 **3.** 4×7 **4.** 2×9

5. $\begin{array}{r} 9 \\ \times 4 \\ \hline \end{array}$ **6.** $\begin{array}{r} 2 \\ \times 7 \\ \hline \end{array}$ **7.** $\begin{array}{r} 3 \\ \times 6 \\ \hline \end{array}$ **8.** $\begin{array}{r} 12 \\ \times 3 \\ \hline \end{array}$

9. $27 \div 3$ **10.** $32 \div 4$ **11.** $30 \div 5$ **12.** $15 \div 3$

13. $45 \div 5$ **14.** $28 \div 4$ **15.** $24 \div 4$ **16.** $45 \div 3$

Lesson 5-4

Pages 186–187

Tell which operation you would use to solve each problem. Then solve.

1. Sanjay and 3 of his teammates together scored 52 points in a basketball game. They each scored the same number of points. How many points did each boy score?

2. Sherri jogged 9 miles last week, which is 3 times as many miles as her sister and half as much as her brother. How many miles did her sister and brother jog?

3. There are 6 rows of desks in a classroom. There are 7 desks in each row. How many desks are in the classroom?

4. Roger earns $3,600 a year delivering papers. How much does he earn in one month?

Lesson 5-5

Pages 188–190

Multiply or divide.

1. 9×6 **2.** 6×8 **3.** 7×7 **4.** 8×10

5. 5×8 **6.** 9×5 **7.** 6×10 **8.** 7×9

9. $42 \div 6$ **10.** $48 \div 6$ **11.** $90 \div 10$ **12.** $56 \div 7$

13. $35 \div 5$ **14.** $81 \div 9$ **15.** $36 \div 6$ **16.** $72 \div 8$

Lesson 5-6

Pages 194–197

Multiply or divide.

1. $\begin{array}{r} 3 \\ \times\ 11 \\ \hline \end{array}$

2. $\begin{array}{r} 4 \\ \times\ 12 \\ \hline \end{array}$

3. $\begin{array}{r} 11 \\ \times\ 6 \\ \hline \end{array}$

4. 8×12

5. 7×11

6. 4×12

7. $11\overline{)88}$

8. $11\overline{)110}$

9. $12\overline{)48}$

10. $120 \div 12$

11. $99 \div 11$

12. $96 \div 12$

Lesson 5-7

Pages 198–199

Use any strategy to solve. Tell what strategy you used.

1. Manuel earns $4 for every 3 dozen cookies he sells. How much will Manuel earn if he sells 9 dozen cookies? 12 dozen cookies?

2. Laura has 24 jazz CDs and 7 country CDs. She has 2 times as many pop CDs as country CDs. How many CDs does she have in all?

3. Kim wants to buy a snowboard that costs $160. She has $88 in the bank. If she earns $6 an hour babysitting, how many hours will Kim have to work to earn enough money to buy the snowboard?

4. An art gallery has paintings on display in 7 rooms. There are 12 paintings in each room. How many paintings are on display in the art gallery?

Lesson 5-8

Pages 200–203

Multiply.

1. $6 \times 3 \times 4$

2. $5 \times 7 \times 3$

3. $8 \times 2 \times 5$

4. $9 \times 3 \times 2$

5. $6 \times 4 \times 5$

6. $9 \times 1 \times 4$

7. $8 \times 4 \times 3$

8. $3 \times 3 \times 12$

9. $10 \times 3 \times 5$

10. $6 \times 11 \times 1$

11. $9 \times 4 \times 2$

12. $12 \times 2 \times 4$

Lesson 5-9

Pages 204–207

Find all the factors of each number.

1. 36 **2.** 18 **3.** 16

4. 35 **5.** 11 **6.** 24

7. 48 **8.** 40 **9.** 23

Identify the first five multiples for each number.

10. 4 **11.** 7 **12.** 6

13. 12 **14.** 8 **15.** 9

16. 10 **17.** 1 **18.** 3

Lesson 5-10

Pages 208–211

Tell whether each number is *prime, composite,* or *neither.*

1. 1 **2.** 2 **3.** 14

4. 21 **5.** 33 **6.** 37

7. 41 **8.** 45 **9.** 57

10. What prime number is greater than 30 and less than 35?

11. What three prime numbers are greater than 40 and less than 50?

Lesson 6-1

Pages 225–227

Find the value of each expression if $v = 4$ and $x = 8$.

1. $x \div 4$ **2.** $6 \times v$ **3.** $x \div v$

4. $v \div v$ **5.** $x \times 7 =$ **6.** $5 \times v$

7. $(v \times 4) \div x$ **8.** $32 \div (x \div v)$ **9.** $(x \div 2) \times 9$

Write an expression for each situation.

10. a number divided by 5

11. The product of 3 and a number

12. a number divided by 10

13. 9 times a number

Lesson 6-2

Pages 228–229

Solve. Use the *work backward* strategy.

1. Tony has 14 baseball cards. His brother gave him 6 cards. He gave 3 cards to his friend. He bought 5 cards. How many cards did Tony have originally?

2. At a pet store, there are 3 times as many puppies as lizards and 4 more puppies than kittens. There are 5 lizards. How many puppies and kittens are there?

3. Gia works at a golf course 4 days a week. She found 12 golf balls on Monday, 7 balls on Tuesday, and twice as many on Wednesday as she found on Tuesday. She found 39 golf balls during her work week. How many balls did Gia find on Thursday?

4. Alberto rode on the Ferris wheel 7 times. He rode on the roller coaster 6 more times than the Ferris wheel. He took 28 rides altogether. How many rides did he take that were not on the Ferris wheel or the roller coaster?

Lesson 6-3

Pages 230–233

Find the value of each expression.

1. $(7 - 4) \times 6$

2. $5 \times 6 + 9$

3. $3 + 10 \div 5$

4. $6 + 12 \div 2$

5. $8 \times (3 + 7)$

6. $16 \div 2 + 3 + 6$

7. $x - (9 \div 9)$, if $x = 12$

8. $(9 - n) \times 7$, if $n = 4$

9. $(15 \div 3) + (r - 4)$, if $r = 7$

10. $(8 \times w) - 7$, if $w = 3$

Lesson 6-4

Pages 236–238

Solve each equation mentally.

1. $7 \times y = 63$

2. $36 \div m = 6$

3. $x \div 9 = 9$

4. $d \times 11 = 66$

5. $4 \times a = 28$

6. $100 \div c = 4$

7. $5 \times b = 35$

8. $n \div 9 = 8$

9. $25 \div p = 5$

10. $n \times 8 = 56$

11. $12 \times t = 48$

12. $40 \div g = 10$

Lesson 6-5

Pages 240–241

Use any strategy to solve. Tell what strategy you used.

1. Mike makes $4 an hour babysitting. Omar makes $6 an hour gardening. How many hours will Mike have to work to make the same amount that Omar makes in 8 hours?

2. Suna wants to make 5 bracelets and 3 necklaces. She plans to use 3 shells for every bracelet and 4 shells for every necklace. How many shells does she need?

3. Evan has twice as many pairs of mittens as boots. He has 6 times as many pairs of socks as boots. He has 18 pairs of socks. How many pairs of boots and mittens does he have?

4. Sam is replacing the wheels on 6 bicycles. He is also replacing the wheels on 4 tricycles and 3 wagons. How many wheels is Sam replacing in all?

Lesson 6-6

Pages 242–245

Write an equation that describes the pattern. Then use the equation to find the next three numbers.

1.

Input (a)	Output (q)
2	12
4	24
6	36
8	■
10	■
12	■

2.

Input (g)	Output (v)
21	3
28	4
35	5
42	■
49	■
56	■

Lesson 6-7

Pages 248–251

Show the equality is not changed.

1. $3w = 12$
$3w \div 6 = 12 \div 6$

2. $4y = 36$
$4y \div 6 = 36 \div 6$

3. $a \div 4 = 8$
$a \div 4 \times 7 = 8 \times 7$

4. $s \div 7 = 9$
$s \div 7 \times 9 = 9 \times 9$

Find the missing number in each equation.

5. $2 \times 5 \times 3 = 10 \times$ ■

6. $2 \times 8 \times 5 = 16 \times$ ■

7. $4 \times 6 \div 8 = 24 \div$ ■

8. $5 \times 9 \div 15 = 45 \div$ ■

Lesson 7-1

Pages 263–265

Multiply. Use basic facts and patterns.

1. 4 × 5
   4 × 50
   4 × 500
   4 × 5,000
2. 3 × 7
   3 × 70
   3 × 700
   3 × 7,000
3. 8 × 6
   8 × 60
   8 × 600
   8 × 6,000
4. 3 × 9
   3 × 90
   3 × 900
   3 × 9,000
5. 5 × 6
   5 × 60
   5 × 600
   5 × 6,000
6. 7 × 4
   7 × 40
   7 × 400
   7 × 4,000

Multiply. Use mental math.

7. 7 × 80
8. 60 × 6
9. 90 × 3
10. 500 × 7
11. 9 × 400
12. 8,000 × 5

Lesson 7-2

Pages 266–267

Decide whether each answer is reasonable. Explain your reasoning.

1. Ebony practices the guitar 30 minutes every day. Is it reasonable to say that she practices the guitar 3,000 minutes each month?
2. The soccer fields in a park are each 130 yards long. Is it reasonable to say that 4 soccer fields are a total of 1,560 feet long?
3. The chickens on a farm produce about 4,200 eggs per week. Is it reasonable to say that the chickens produce 600 eggs each day?
4. An album can hold 24 stamps on each page. There are 200 pages. Is it reasonable to say that the album can hold 48,000 stamps?

Lesson 7-3

Pages 268–271

Estimate each product.

1. 584 × 3
2. 484 × 5
3. 723 × 8
4. 3 × 692
5. 6 × $472
6. 9 × $460
7. 7 × 1,986
8. 8 × $5,420
9. 5 × 6,752
10. 3 × $478
11. 6 × $9,810
12. 8 × 3,755

Lesson 7-4

Pages 272–274

Multiply. Check for reasonableness.

1. 18×6

2. 28×5

3. $\$17 \times 9$

4. 2×99

5. 6×25

6. $7 \times \$43$

7. 5×73

8. $4 \times \$86$

9. 9×39

10. $3 \times \$92$

11. 8×78

12. $7 \times \$56$

Lesson 7-5

Pages 276–277

Use any strategy to solve. Tell what strategy you used.

1. Jesse bikes 224 miles each month. He bikes the same number of miles each week. How many miles does Jesse bike each week?

2. Movie tickets are \$7 for adults and \$3.50 for children. What is the total cost if three adults and five children go to the theater?

3. Rita is making muffins. There are 36 muffins in each batch. How many muffins will be in 3 batches? How many muffins will be in 7 batches?

4. At the zoo, the big cats are in a row. The lions are last. The jaguars are to the left of the tigers. The cheetahs are to the left of the jaguars. In what order are the big cats?

Lesson 7-6

Pages 278–281

Multiply. Check for reasonableness.

1. 538×3

2. 392×6

3. $\$256 \times 8$

4. 734×7

5. $\$493 \times 6$

6. $\$724 \times 4$

7. $6 \times 5,630$

8. $6 \times \$8,562$

9. $5 \times 2,845$

10. $4 \times 3,488$

11. $8 \times 2,376$

12. $9 \times 5,670$

Lesson 7-7

Pages 284–287

Multiply. Check for reasonableness.

1. $\begin{array}{r} 408 \\ \times\ 4 \\ \hline \end{array}$
2. $\begin{array}{r} 507 \\ \times\ 8 \\ \hline \end{array}$
3. $\begin{array}{r} 906 \\ \times\ 7 \\ \hline \end{array}$
4. 2 × 6,009
5. 7 × $3,408
6. 5 × 9,206
7. 3 × $8,702
8. 6 × 4,090
9. 9 × $6,205
10. 4 × 7,084
11. 8 × 9,502
12. 5 × 5,047

Lesson 8-1

Pages 299–301

Multiply.

1. $\begin{array}{r} 18 \\ \times 30 \\ \hline \end{array}$
2. $\begin{array}{r} 24 \\ \times 50 \\ \hline \end{array}$
3. $\begin{array}{r} 48 \\ \times 90 \\ \hline \end{array}$
4. $\begin{array}{r} 47 \\ \times 60 \\ \hline \end{array}$
5. $\begin{array}{r} 75 \\ \times 40 \\ \hline \end{array}$
6. $\begin{array}{r} 56 \\ \times 90 \\ \hline \end{array}$
7. $\begin{array}{r} 64 \\ \times 30 \\ \hline \end{array}$
8. $\begin{array}{r} \$49 \\ \times 60 \\ \hline \end{array}$
9. $\begin{array}{r} 85 \\ \times 70 \\ \hline \end{array}$
10. $\begin{array}{r} \$28 \\ \times 30 \\ \hline \end{array}$
11. $\begin{array}{r} 92 \\ \times 70 \\ \hline \end{array}$
12. $\begin{array}{r} 63 \\ \times 90 \\ \hline \end{array}$

Lesson 8-2

Pages 302–305

Estimate. Tell whether the estimate is greater or less than the actual product.

1. $\begin{array}{r} 38 \\ \times 26 \\ \hline \end{array}$
2. $\begin{array}{r} 63 \\ \times 44 \\ \hline \end{array}$
3. $\begin{array}{r} 59 \\ \times 37 \\ \hline \end{array}$
4. $\begin{array}{r} \$98 \\ \times 57 \\ \hline \end{array}$
5. $\begin{array}{r} 43 \\ \times 82 \\ \hline \end{array}$
6. $\begin{array}{r} \$67 \\ \times 38 \\ \hline \end{array}$
7. $322 \times 64 = n$
8. $668 \times 27 = n$
9. $982 \times 34 = n$
10. $441 \times 33 = n$
11. $877 \times 59 = n$
12. $799 \times 87 = n$

Lesson 8-3

Pages 306–307

Solve. Use the *act it out* strategy.

1. There are 4 tennis players at the court. Each one played one set of tennis against every other player. How many sets of tennis were played?
2. Keisha has $4.50 in her piggy bank. She has the same number of dimes and quarters. She has half as many nickels as dimes. What coins does she have?
3. Linda is 12 years old. Her mother is 2 years less than 3 times her age. How old is Linda's mother?
4. Jaime has 17 coins in his pocket. The coins have a value of $1.20. What coins does he have?

Lesson 8-4

Pages 310–312

Multiply.

1. 17 × 25
2. 56 × 33
3. $84 × 42
4. 62 × 55
5. 74 × 93
6. $65 × 48
7. 36 × 56
8. 49 × 77
9. $44 × 83
10. 64 × 95
11. $58 × 17
12. 75 × 73

Lesson 8-5

Pages 314–317

Multiply.

1. 104 × 18
2. 186 × 32
3. 207 × 49
4. 275 × 64
5. 377 × 53
6. 309 × 81
7. 452 × 37
8. 438 × 27
9. 588 × 39
10. 542 × 64
11. 663 × 46
12. 738 × 56

Lesson 8-6

Pages 320–321

Use any strategy to solve. Tell what strategy you used.

1. Natalie is thinking of two numbers with a sum of 13 and a product of 36. What are the two numbers?

2. The fish at the pet store eat 28 jars of food every week. How many jars of food will the fish eat in 4 weeks? in 6 weeks? in 8 weeks?

3. Ramón saves $15 every week to buy a skateboard. The skateboard costs $105. How many weeks will it take him to save half as much as he needs to buy the skateboard?

4. Every fourth grader washed 4 cars at the car wash. The fourth graders washed 283 cars in all. About how many fourth grade students are there?

Lesson 8-7

Pages 322–325

Multiply.

1. $1{,}877 \times 24$

2. $2{,}345 \times 62$

3. $3{,}906 \times 59$

4. $5{,}792 \times 48$

5. $6{,}504 \times 96$

6. $7{,}708 \times 85$

7. $8{,}544 \times 38$

8. $12{,}304 \times 65$

9. $17{,}455 \times 92$

Lesson 9-1

Pages 339–341

Divide. Check each answer.

1. $36 \div 3$

2. $60 \div 5$

3. $54 \div 3$

4. $70 \div 5$

5. $98 \div 7$

6. $91 \div 7$

7. $79 \div 3$

8. $66 \div 4$

9. $95 \div 7$

Extra Practice

Lesson 9-2

Pages 342–345

Copy and complete each set of patterns.

1. $48 \div 6 = \blacksquare$
   $480 \div 6 = \blacksquare$
   $4,800 \div 6 = \blacksquare$
2. $63 \div 9 = \blacksquare$
   $630 \div 9 = \blacksquare$
   $6,300 \div 9 = \blacksquare$
3. $\$40 \div 8 = \blacksquare$
   $\$400 \div 8 = \blacksquare$
   $\$4,000 \div 8 = \blacksquare$
4. $72 \div 9 = \blacksquare$
   $720 \div 9 = \blacksquare$
   $7,200 \div 9 = \blacksquare$
5. $\$27 \div 3 = \blacksquare$
   $\$270 \div 3 = \blacksquare$
   $\$2,700 \div 3 = \blacksquare$
6. $35 \div 7 = \blacksquare$
   $350 \div 7 = \blacksquare$
   $3,500 \div 7 = \blacksquare$

Divide. Use patterns.

7. $420 \div 6$
8. $300 \div 5$
9. $\$280 \div 7$
10. $\$210 \div 3$
11. $5,600 \div 7$
12. $7,200 \div 8$
13. $8,100 \div 9$
14. $1,600 \div 4$
15. $3,000 \div 6$
16. $\$2,700 \div 3$
17. $4,500 \div 9$
18. $5,400 \div 9$

Lesson 9-3

Pages 346–347

Solve. Use the *guess and check* strategy.

1. Ren bought 5 CDs for \$55. One of the CDs cost \$5 more than the others. How much did each CD cost?
2. Carmen has 49 more mystery novels than adventure novels. She has 223 novels in all. How many mystery novels and adventure novels does Carmen have?
3. The chickens on a farm eat 3 times as much grain as the turkeys do per week. The chickens and turkeys eat a total of 52 pounds of grain every week. How much grain do the chickens and turkeys each eat every week?
4. A toy store has at least 10 wagons and at least 10 tricycles on sale. There are a total of 89 wheels. How many tricycles and how many wagons are on sale?

Lesson 9-4

Pages 348–350

Estimate. Check your estimate.

1. $24 \div 4$
2. $510 \div 7$
3. $433 \div 5$
4. $476 \div 8$
5. $\$537 \div 6$
6. $298 \div 4$
7. $337 \div 8$
8. $\$259 \div 5$
9. $1,244 \div 6$
10. $2,240 \div 3$
11. $\$6,580 \div 9$
12. $8,256 \div 9$

Lesson 9-5

Pages 352–355

Divide. Use estimation to check.

1. $7\overline{)47}$
2. $8\overline{)39}$
3. $9\overline{)71}$
4. $6\overline{)33}$
5. $5\overline{)44}$
6. $8\overline{)62}$
7. $9\overline{)25}$
8. $6\overline{)45}$
9. $554 \div 8$
10. $462 \div 9$
11. $368 \div 6$
12. $659 \div 8$

Lesson 9-6

Pages 356–357

Use any strategy to solve. Tell what strategy you used.

1. What is the next number in the pattern 4, 14, 44, 134, ■?
2. Cristina has 7 coins with a value of $0.81. What are the coins?
3. There are 9 seals at a zoo. Altogether, the seals eat about 750 fish each day. About how many fish does each seal eat every day?
4. A plant produces about 45 new flowers every 2 weeks. After 8 weeks, how many flowers will the plant have produced?
5. At the drugstore, pencils are on sale for 8 for $1.25. Pens are on sale for 3 for $1.50. How much do 24 pencils and 12 pens cost?
6. Mei hiked for 20 minutes every morning from her campsite to the lake. She hiked back to the campsite every afternoon. Mei hiked for a total of 8 hours to and from the lake. How many days was Mei at camp?

Lesson 9-7

Pages 358–361

Divide. Use estimation to check.

1. $3\overline{)693}$
2. $2\overline{)764}$
3. $7\overline{)875}$
4. $4\overline{)936}$
5. $3\overline{)1,677}$
6. $6\overline{)2,558}$
7. $5\overline{)3,697}$
8. $9\overline{)2,938}$
9. $1,539 \div 2$
10. $7,564 \div 8$
11. $4,255 \div 7$
12. $2,687 \div 4$

Lesson 9-8

Pages 362–365

Divide. Use estimation to check.

1. $3\overline{)315}$ **2.** $4\overline{)837}$ **3.** $4\overline{)\$432}$ **4.** $9\overline{)976}$

5. $3\overline{)625}$ **6.** $4\overline{)438}$ **7.** $2\overline{)414}$ **8.** $7\overline{)756}$

9. $3\overline{)\$317}$ **10.** $5\overline{)1{,}039}$ **11.** $3\overline{)\$2{,}721}$ **12.** $9\overline{)9{,}459}$

13. $1{,}615 \div 2$ **14.** $4{,}363 \div 4$ **15.** $\$611 \div 3$ **16.** $1{,}236 \div 4$

Lesson 9-9

Pages 368–371

Divide. Use estimation to check.

1. $2\overline{)3{,}664}$ **2.** $3\overline{)4{,}671}$ **3.** $5\overline{)5{,}847}$ **4.** $6\overline{)7{,}248}$

5. $4\overline{)6{,}184}$ **6.** $8\overline{)9{,}872}$ **7.** $7\overline{)9{,}256}$ **8.** $6\overline{)57{,}888}$

9. $8\overline{)18{,}816}$ **10.** $9\overline{)33{,}786}$ **11.** $7\overline{)25{,}984}$ **12.** $6\overline{)23{,}678}$

13. $9{,}634 \div 8$ **14.** $59{,}510 \div 5$ **15.** $267{,}651 \div 9$ **16.** $165{,}785 \div 5$

Lesson 10-1

Pages 385–387

Identify each figure. Then tell the number of faces, edges, and vertices.

1. 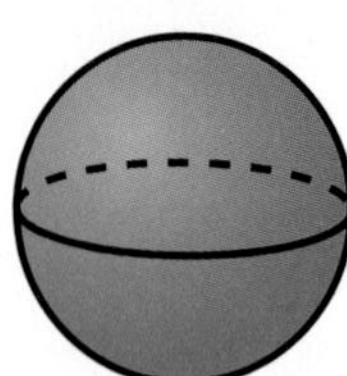

2. 

3. 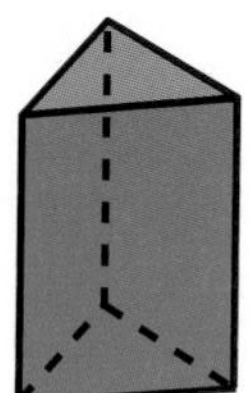

4. 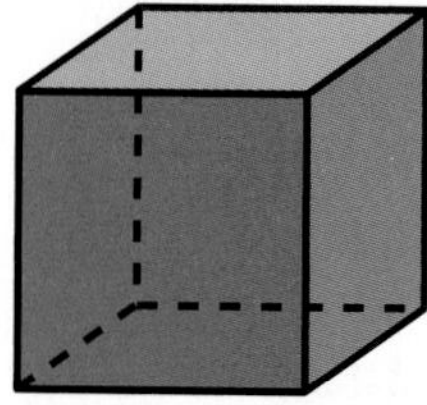

5. 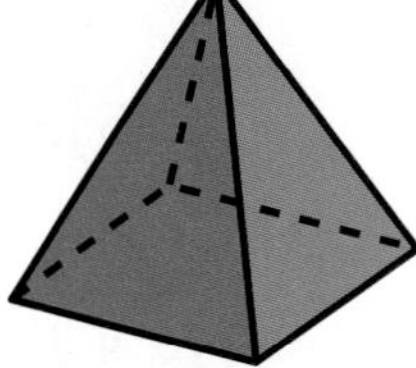

6. 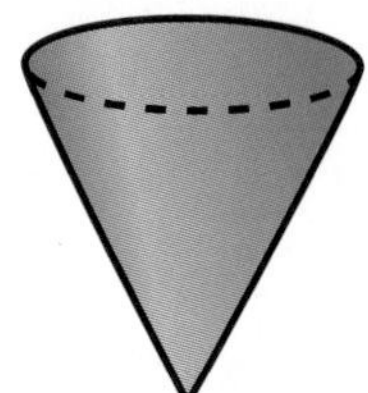

Lesson 10-2

Pages 388–391

Identify each polygon.

1. 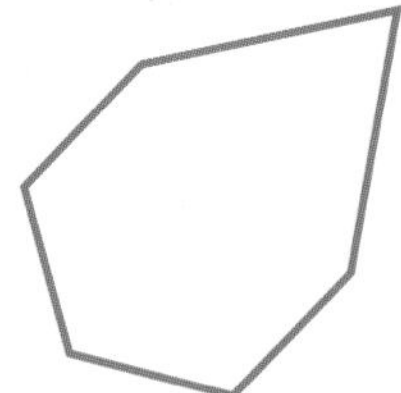

2. 

3. 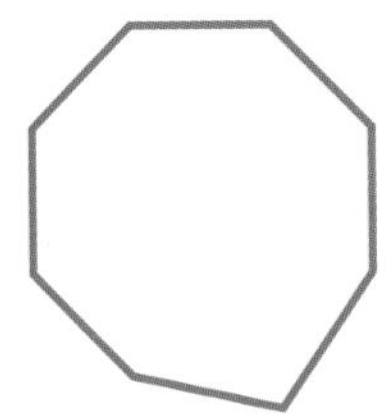

Tell whether each shape is a polygon.

4. 

5. 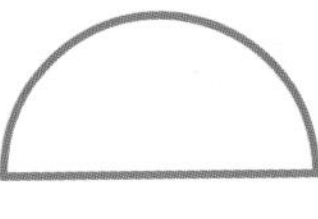

6. 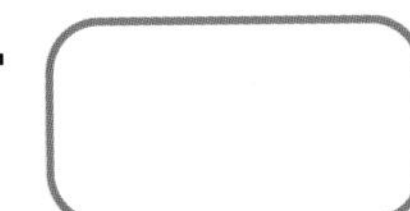

Lesson 10-3

Pages 392–393

Solve. Use the *look for a pattern* strategy.

1. A flowering plant produces 15 seeds on the first day of spring. On the second day, it produces 23 seeds. On the third day, it produces 31 seeds. Describe the pattern. How many seeds will the plant produce on the sixth day?

2. Copy and complete the table. What is the pattern?

Input	Output
3	21
5	35
7	■
■	54

Lesson 10-4

Pages 394–397

Identify each figure.

1. 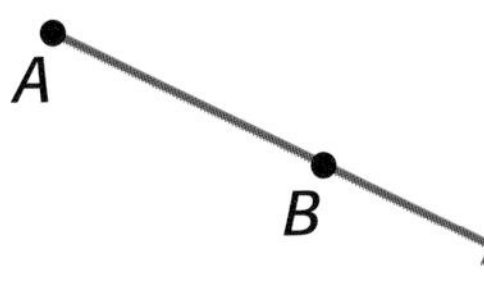

2. 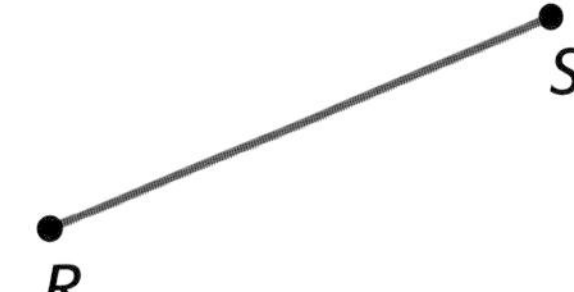

3. 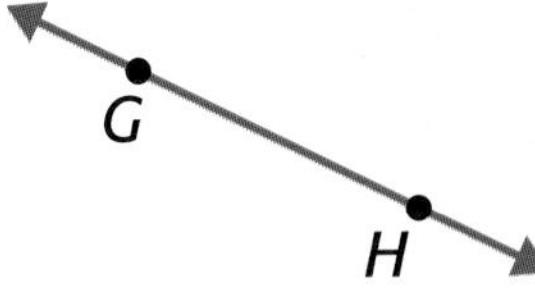

Describe the figure.

4. 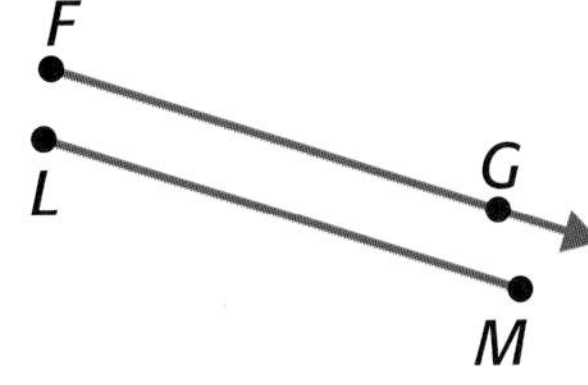

5. 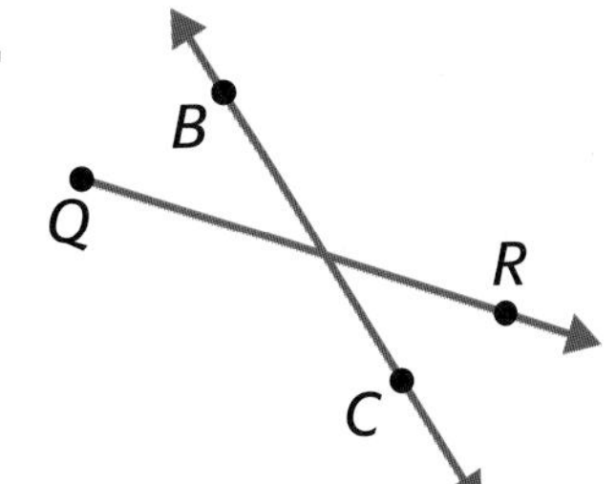

6. 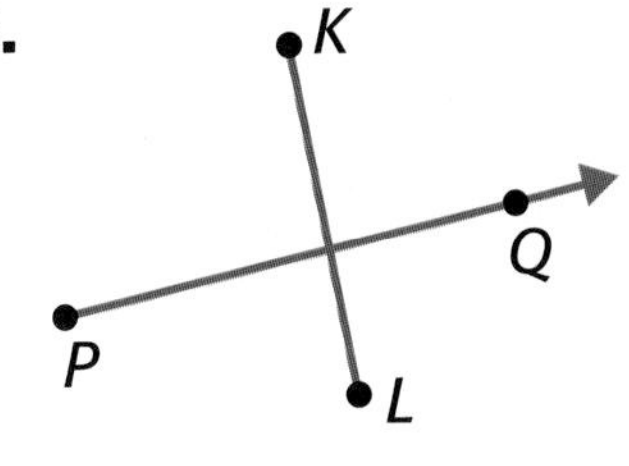

Extra Practice

Lesson 10-5

Pages 398–400

Write the measure of the angle in degrees and as a fraction of a full turn.

1. 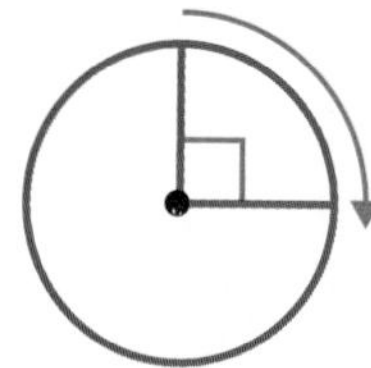

2. 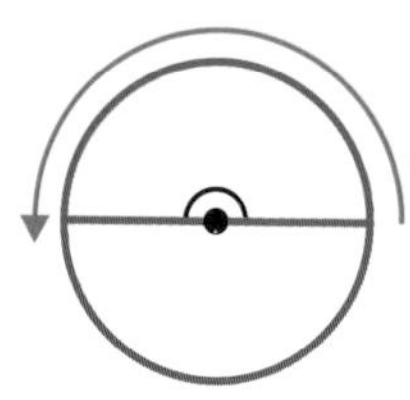

3. 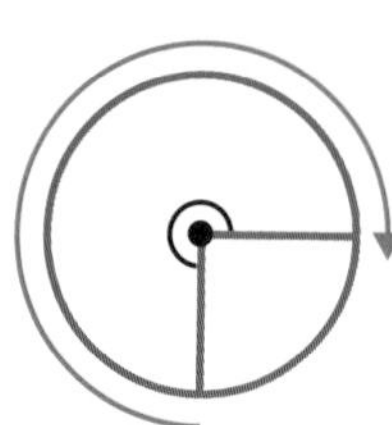

Classify each angle as *right, acute,* or *obtuse*.

4. 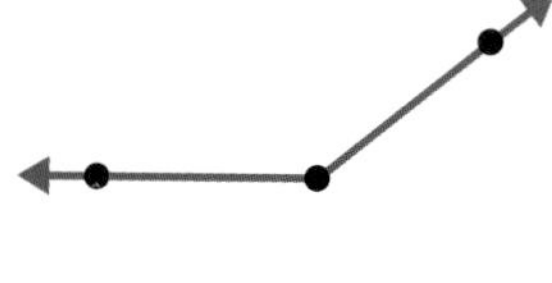

5. 

6. 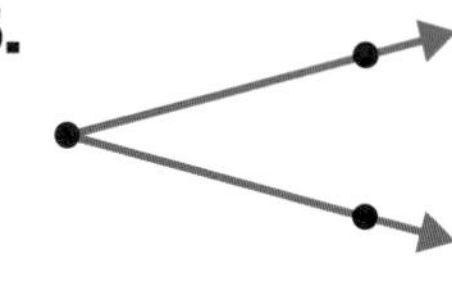

Lesson 10-6

Pages 402–403

Use any strategy to solve. Tell what strategy you used.

1. A number is multiplied by 4, then 9 is subtracted from the product. The result is 19. What was the original number?

2. For every 30 minutes that Julia swims, she rests for 15 minutes. In 3 hours of swimming, how many minutes will she rest?

Lesson 10-7

Pages 404–407

Classify each triangle. Use *isosceles, equilateral,* or *scalene* and *acute, right,* or *obtuse*.

1. 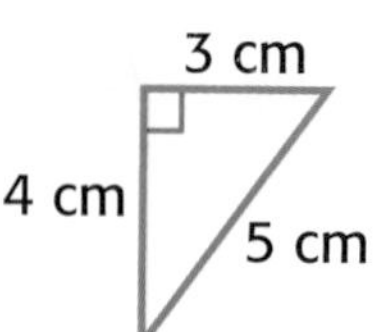

2. 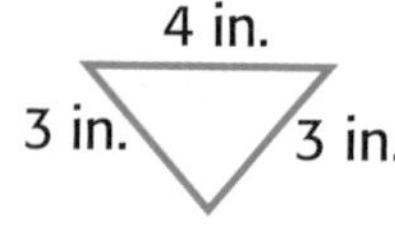

3. 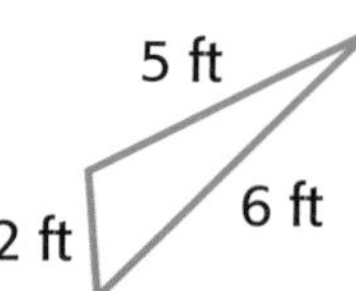

4. 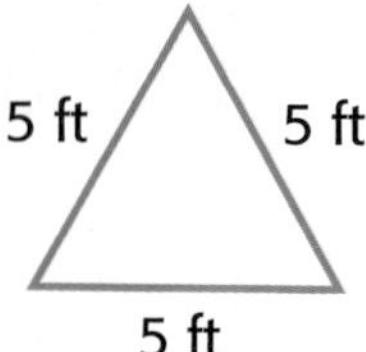

5. 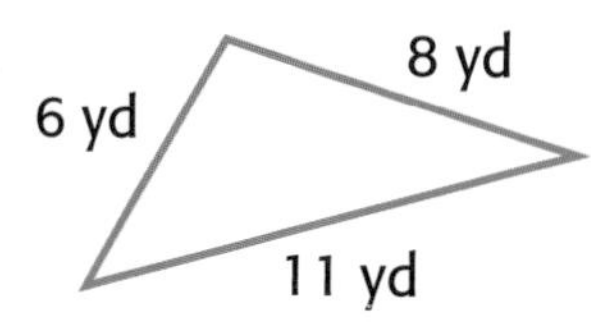

6. 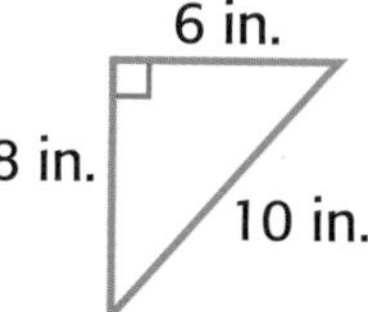

Lesson 10-8

Pages 410–413

Classify each quadrilateral in as many ways as possible.

1. 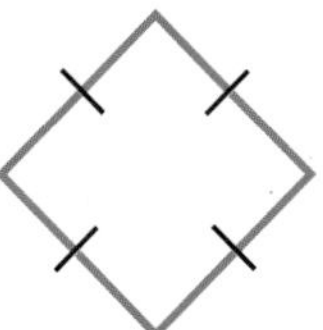

2. 

3. 

4. 

5. 

6. 

Lesson 10-9

Pages 414–417

Identify the part of the circle.

1. 

2. 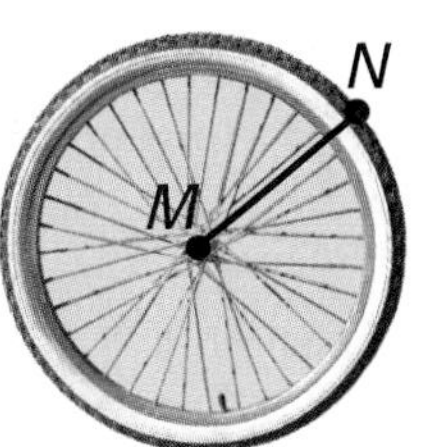

3. 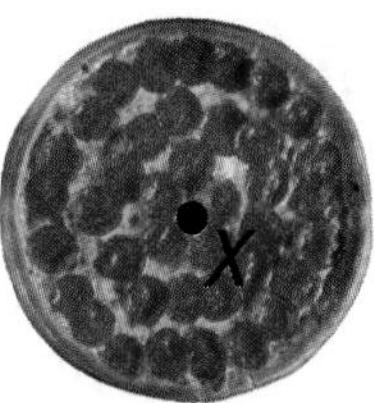

Identify the parts of the circle.

4. *GH*

5. *BA*

6. *H*

7. *DE*

8. *HI*

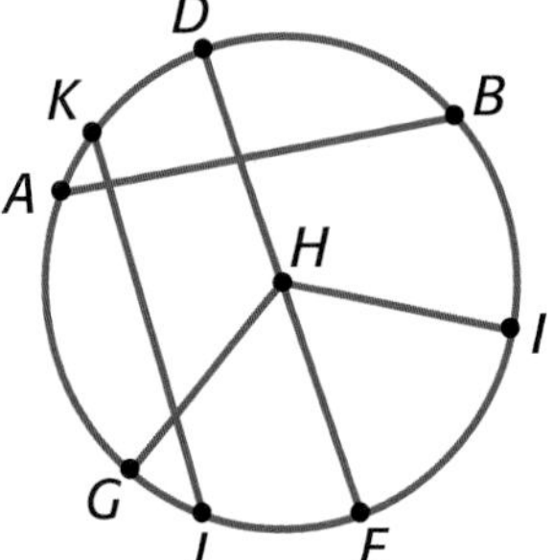

Lesson 11-1

Pages 431–433

Tell whether the figures appear to be congruent. Write *yes* or *no*.

1. 

2. 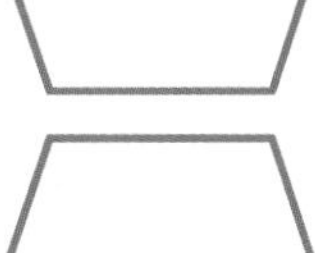

3. 

4. 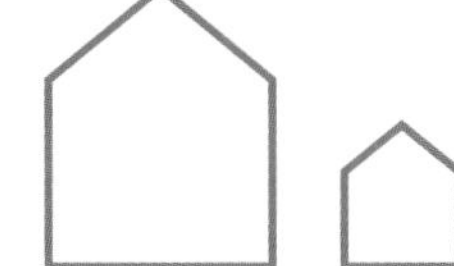

5. 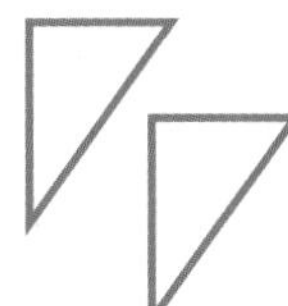

6. 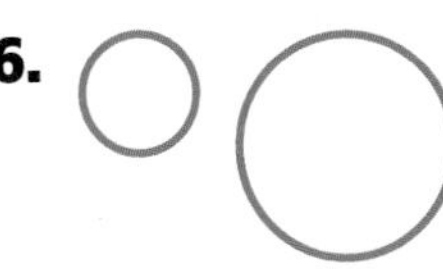

Extra Practice

Lesson 11-2

Pages 434–437

Tell whether each figure has line symmetry. Write *yes* or *no*. Then tell how many lines of symmetry the figure has.

1. 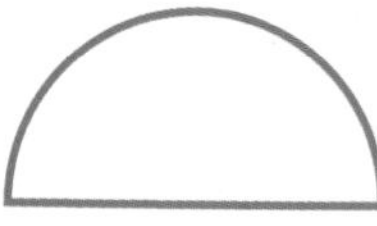

2. 

3. 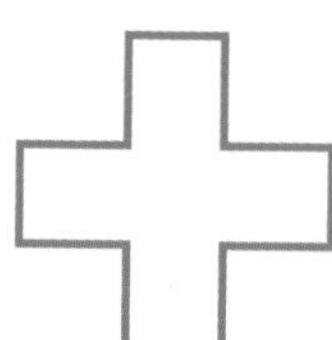

Tell whether each figure has rotational symmetry. Write *yes* or *no*.

4. 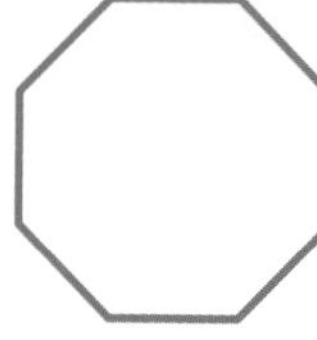

5. 

6. 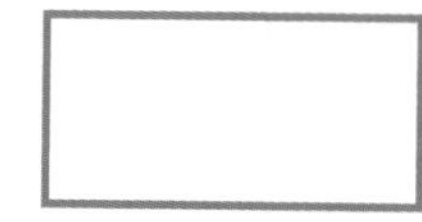

Lesson 11-3

Pages 438–440

Find the perimeter of each figure.

1. 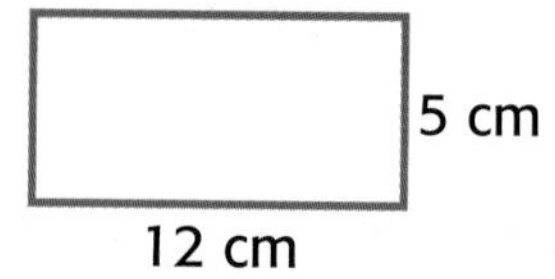

2. 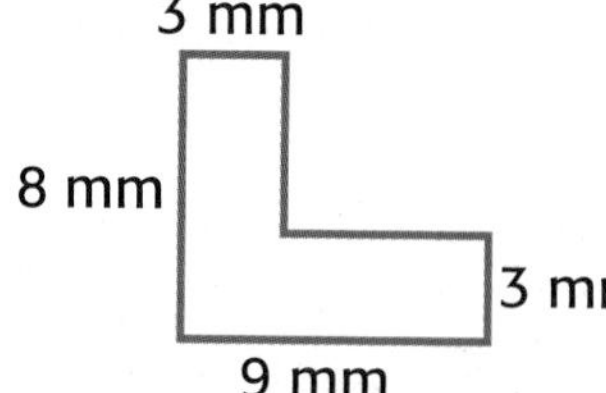

3. 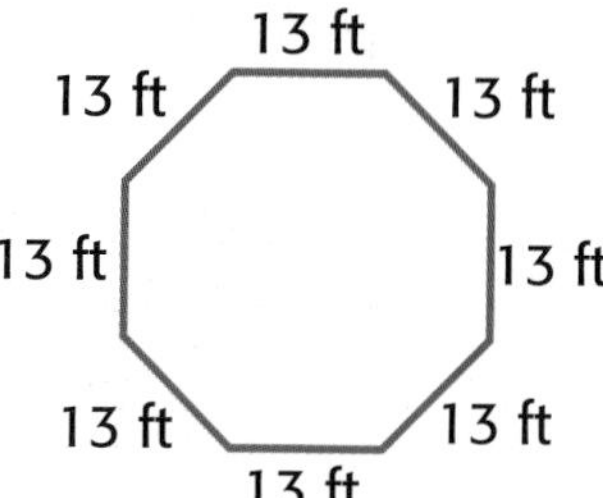

Find the perimeter of each rectangle in units.

4. 

5. 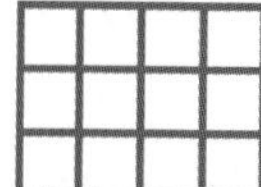

6. 

Lesson 11-4

Pages 442–443

Solve. Use the *solve a simpler problem* strategy.

1. Mark painted a mural on each of the 4 walls of his room. It took him 6 hours and 25 minutes for each wall. How long did it take him to finish?

2. Anita bought a sandwich for $3.35, a salad for $1.96, a glass of juice for $1.22, and a cookie for $0.85. How much did she spend for lunch?

Lesson 11-5

Pages 444–447

Find the area of each figure.

1. 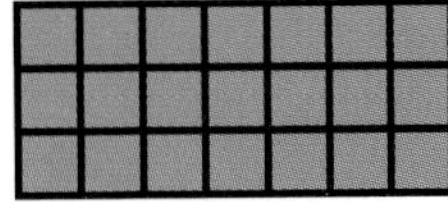

2. 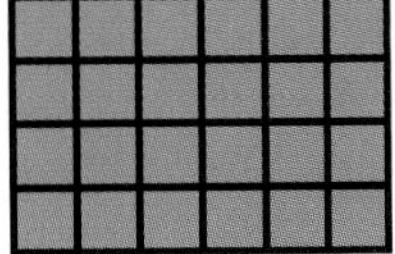

3. 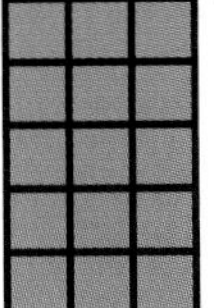

4. 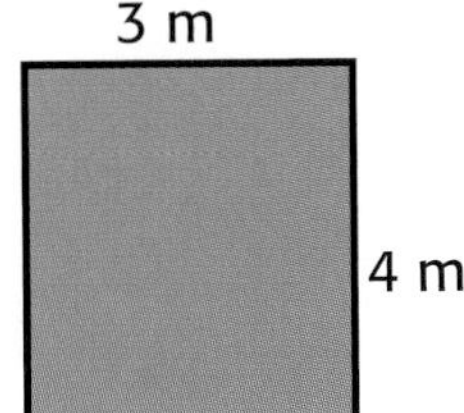

5. 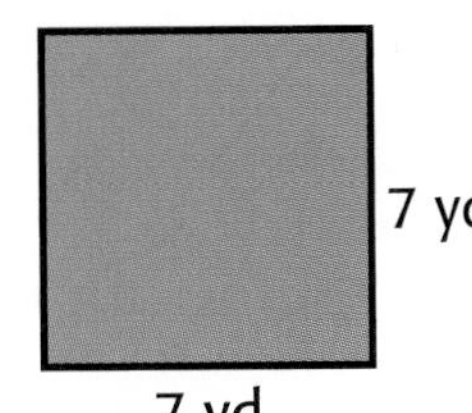

6. 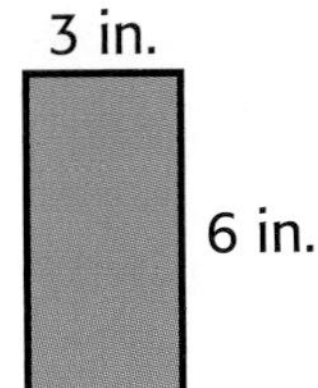

Lesson 11-6

Pages 452–453

Use any strategy to solve. Tell what strategy you used.

1. The perimeter of a rectangular yard is 20 meters. What are the possible lengths of the sides?
2. Stella bought 5 pencils for 75¢. How much would she pay for 12 pencils?
3. Each bunch of flowers has 12 tulips and 23 daisies. There are 6 bunches of flowers. How many flowers are there in all?
4. There are 324 apples at a market. There are 68 fewer apples than oranges and 127 more apples than limes. How many limes and oranges are there?

Lesson 11-7

Pages 454–457

Find the area of each figure.

1. 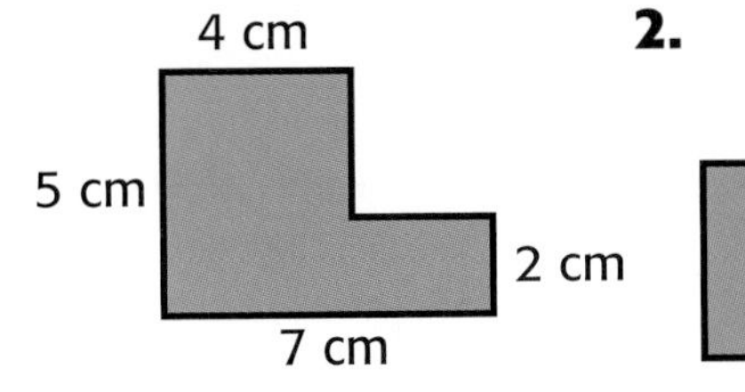

2. 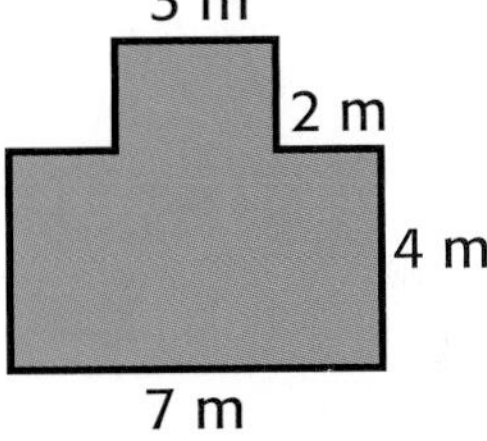

3. 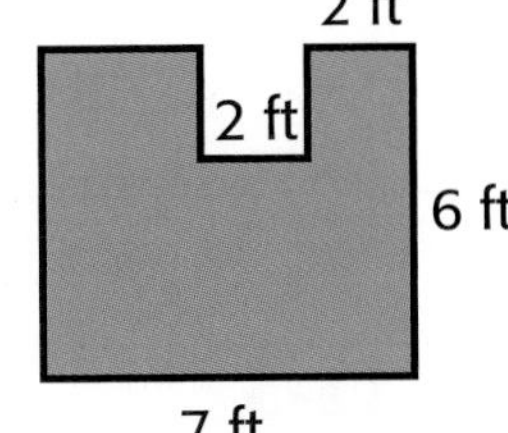

4. 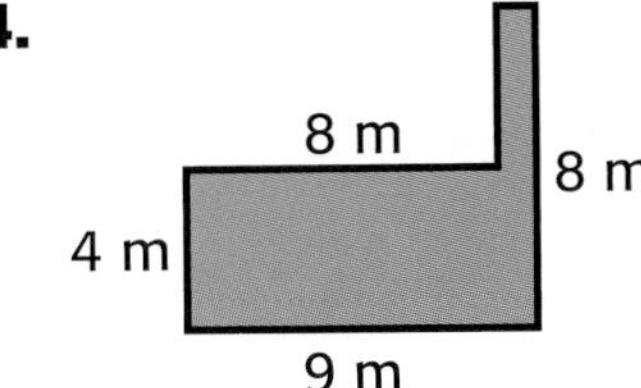

5. 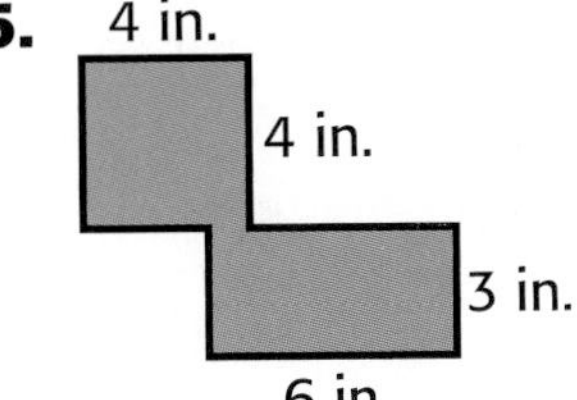

6. 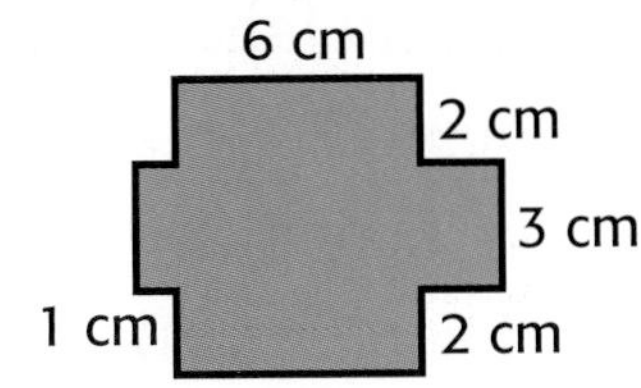

Lesson 12-1

Pages 469–471

Write the number that represents each situation. Then show the number on a number line.

1. Kaya spent $26 on a new pair of shoes.
2. Beth gave away 3 puppies.
3. Malcolm swam 8 laps in the pool.
4. A tree grew 12 feet in one year.
5. Steve ate 5 cookies for dessert.
6. Roberta does not have any pets.

7. Write the number of each letter on the number line.

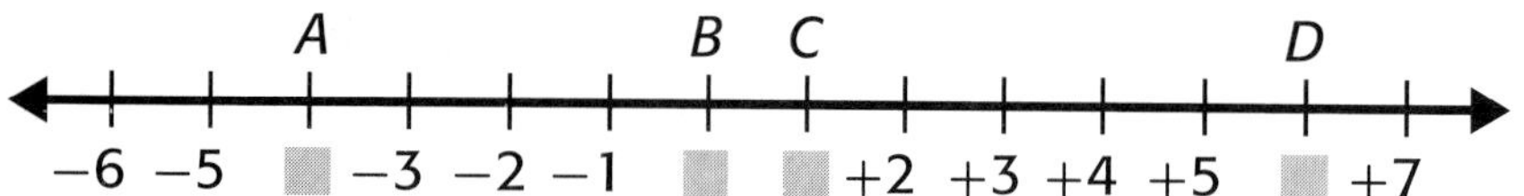

Lesson 12-2

Pages 472–475

Identify the letter that is located at each ordered pair.

1. (2, −4)
2. (−3, 4)
3. (7, 6)
4. (−4, −2)
5. (−2, 1)
6. (4, 0)
7. (−7, −6)
8. (7, −6)
9. (0, 0)

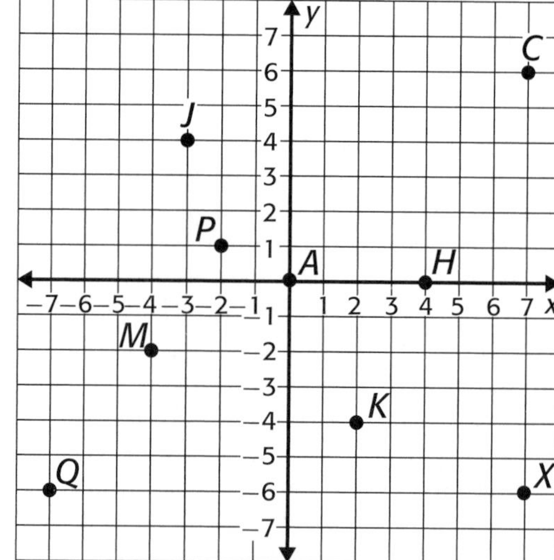

Lesson 12-3

Pages 476–478

Graph and label each point on a grid.

1. point *D:* (4, −3)
2. point *F:* (0, 6)
3. point *N:* (−3, 7)
4. point *O:* (−1, −6)
5. point *R:* (6, 5)
6. point *V:* (−4, 2)

Lesson 12-4

Pages 482–483

Solve. Use logical reasoning.

1. There are four buildings on a block. The bank is not next to the museum or the school. The library is next to the bank. The school is not first. What is the order of the buildings?

2. A group of 4 adults and 7 students rode a ferry. The cost for the entire group was $35.50. If the cost of a student to ride was $2.50, what was the cost for an adult?

3. The Bears won 18 games. The Lions won $\frac{1}{3}$ as many games as the Bears. The Sharks won 8 more games than the Lions. How many games did the Sharks win?

4. Mr. Myers is thinking of a number between 20 and 30. The number is not even, not prime, and not divisible by 3. What is the number?

Lesson 12-5

Pages 484–487

Copy and complete each function table.

1.

Rule: $y = x - 5$	
Input (x)	Output (y)
14	9
9	4
12	7
15	■
8	■
10	■

2.

Rule: $y = x \div 3 + 2$	
Input (x)	Output (y)
24	10
15	7
39	15
18	■
9	■
6	■

3.

Rule: $y = 6 \times x - 3$	
Input (x)	Output (y)
4	21
8	45
7	39
11	■
9	■
6	■

4.

Rule: $y = x \times x + 3$	
Input (x)	Output (y)
7	52
5	28
3	12
10	■
9	■
4	■

Lesson 12-6

Pages 490–493

Graph ten points on the graph of the function.

1. $y = x - 1$ **2.** $y = x + 2$ **3.** $y = 2x$

4. $y = x \div 3$ **3.** $y = 2x + 3$ **6.** $y = 3x - 2$

Extra Practice

Lesson 12-7

Pages 494–495

Use any strategy to solve. Tell what strategy you used.

1. A model home has 8 windows on the first floor and 7 windows on the second floor. There are 180 windows all together. How many model homes are there?

2. Radio station ABC plays songs that are $2\frac{1}{2}$ minutes long. How many songs can the station play in 50 minutes?

3. Emilio's sister is twice his age. In 6 years, his sister will be 3 times his age right now. How old are Emilio and his sister?

4. Leila bought a hat for $5, mittens for $7, and a scarf for $11. The cashier gave her $7 in change. How much did Leila give the cashier?

Lesson 13-1

Pages 507–509

Write the fraction that names part of the whole.

1. 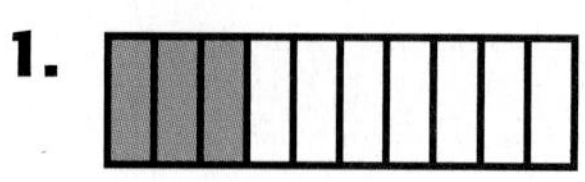

2. 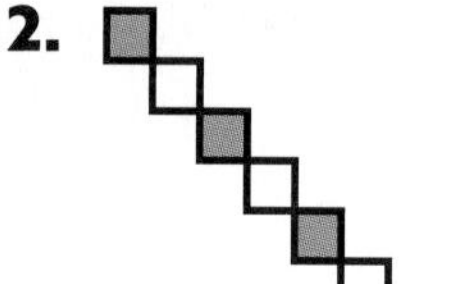

3. 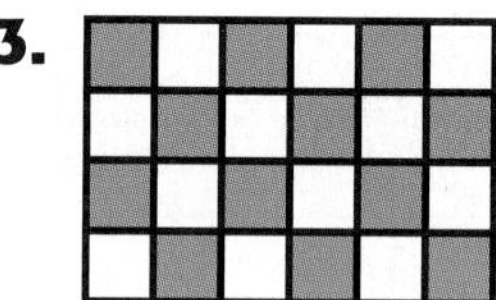

4. 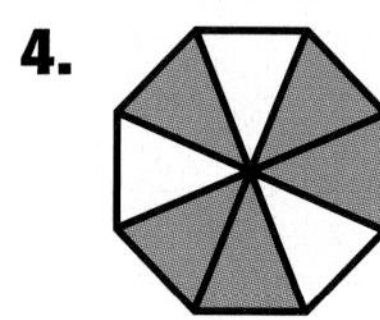

5. 

6. 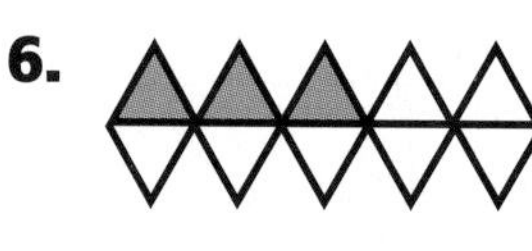

Draw a picture and shade part of it to show the fraction.

7. $\frac{3}{7}$ 8. $\frac{6}{7}$ 9. $\frac{2}{10}$ 10. $\frac{4}{5}$ 11. $\frac{7}{8}$

Lesson 13-2

Pages 510–513

Write the fraction for the part of the set that is blue. Then write the fraction for the part that is *not* blue.

1. 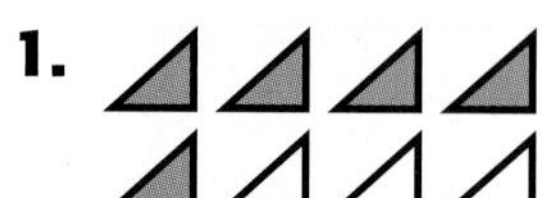

2. 

3. 

4. 

5. 

6. 

Lesson 13-3

Pages 514–515

Solve. Use the *draw a picture* strategy.

1. Four dogs are standing in a row. The great dane is ahead of the poodle. The terrier is not next to the poodle. The collie is next to the terrier and is not first. What is the order of the dogs?

2. There are 30 children at the park. $\frac{1}{2}$ are playing soccer. $\frac{1}{3}$ are playing football. The rest are on the swings. How many children are on the swings?

3. There are 16 CDs on a shelf. $\frac{1}{4}$ of the CDs are jazz. 5 are classical music, and 3 are blues. The rest are pop music. How many CDs are pop music?

4. There are 4 books on display. The cookbook is next to the history book but not next to the art book or the novel. The art book is third. What is the order of the books?

Lesson 13-4

Pages 518–520

Write the fraction for the part that is shaded. Then find an equivalent fraction.

1. 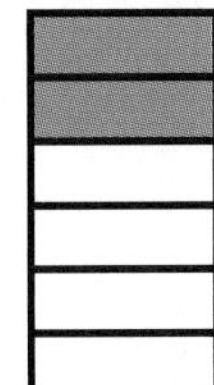

2. 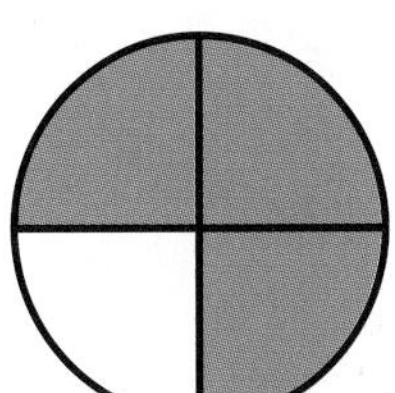

3. 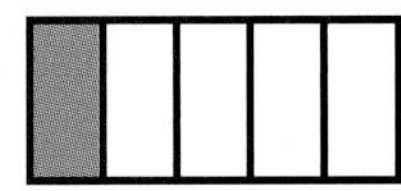

Find an equivalent fraction for each fraction.

4. $\frac{3}{12}$ **5.** $\frac{4}{10}$ **6.** $\frac{1}{4}$ **7.** $\frac{4}{6}$ **8.** $\frac{3}{7}$

9. $\frac{6}{18}$ **10.** $\frac{3}{8}$ **11.** $\frac{6}{9}$ **12.** $\frac{1}{2}$ **13.** $\frac{4}{20}$

Lesson 13-5

Pages 522–525

Write each fraction in simplest form. If it is in simplest form, write *simplest form*.

1. $\frac{3}{12}$ **2.** $\frac{4}{8}$ **3.** $\frac{2}{10}$ **4.** $\frac{8}{16}$ **5.** $\frac{3}{9}$

6. $\frac{16}{24}$ **7.** $\frac{20}{25}$ **8.** $\frac{30}{36}$ **9.** $\frac{9}{27}$ **10.** $\frac{12}{20}$

11. $\frac{21}{28}$ **12.** $\frac{18}{24}$ **13.** $\frac{11}{44}$ **14.** $\frac{20}{45}$ **15.** $\frac{6}{42}$

Extra Practice

Lesson 13-6

Pages 526–527

Use any strategy to solve. Tell what strategy you used.

1. There are 20 fish in an aquarium. $\frac{1}{5}$ of the fish are blue. $\frac{1}{4}$ of the fish are red. The rest are yellow. How many yellow fish are there?

2. Ramona started reading at 4:20. She stopped reading at 5:15. For how many minutes did she read?

3. Ten students are in the library. Three students leave the library as 5 students go in. How many students are in the library now?

4. Juan has 9 coins that equal 85¢. None of them are pennies. What are the coins?

Lesson 13-7

Pages 528–531

Compare. Write <, >, or =.

1. 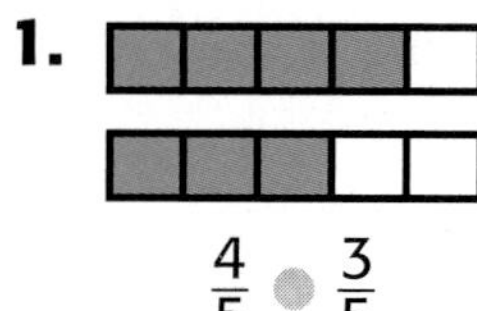

$\frac{4}{5} \bullet \frac{3}{5}$

2. 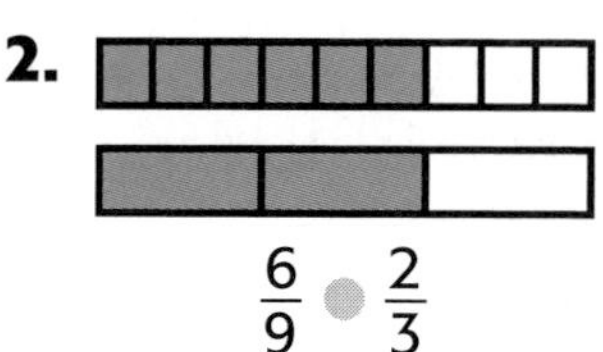

$\frac{6}{9} \bullet \frac{2}{3}$

3. 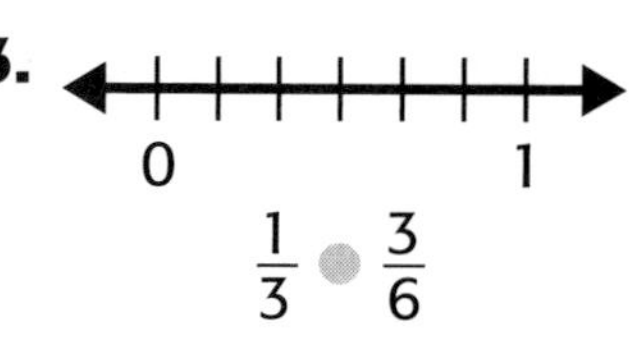

$\frac{1}{3} \bullet \frac{3}{6}$

4. $\frac{2}{5} \bullet \frac{1}{6}$

5. $\frac{6}{9} \bullet \frac{5}{10}$

6. $\frac{3}{8} \bullet \frac{1}{2}$

7. $\frac{7}{8} \bullet \frac{7}{12}$

8. $\frac{5}{5} \bullet \frac{4}{5}$

9. $\frac{3}{9} \bullet \frac{9}{12}$

Lesson 13-8

Pages 534–537

Find each sum or difference. Write in simplest form.

1. $\frac{2}{4} + \frac{1}{4}$

2. $\frac{3}{12} + \frac{3}{12}$

3. $\frac{3}{9} + \frac{2}{9}$

4. $\frac{4}{10} + \frac{2}{10}$

5. $\frac{2}{6} + \frac{2}{6}$

6. $\frac{3}{11} + \frac{5}{11}$

7. $\frac{6}{10} - \frac{2}{10}$

8. $\frac{9}{12} - \frac{4}{12}$

9. $\frac{8}{8} - \frac{5}{8}$

10. $\frac{5}{6} - \frac{2}{6}$

11. $\frac{13}{15} - \frac{8}{15}$

12. $\frac{4}{9} - \frac{2}{9}$

Extra Practice

Lesson 13-9

Pages 538–541

Write a mixed number and an improper fraction for each model.

1. 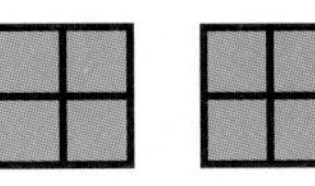
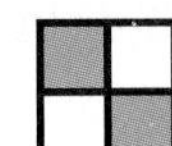

2.  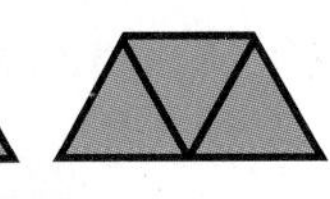
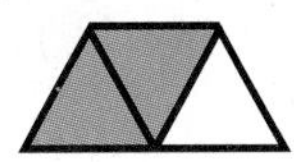

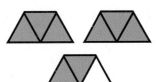

Write each as an improper fraction or a mixed number.

3. $3\frac{2}{3}$ **4.** $3\frac{1}{4}$ **5.** $3\frac{3}{10}$ **6.** $\frac{21}{4}$

Lesson 14-1

Pages 557–559

Write a fraction and a decimal for each shaded part.

1. 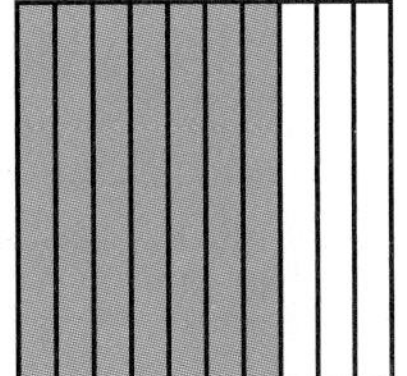

2. 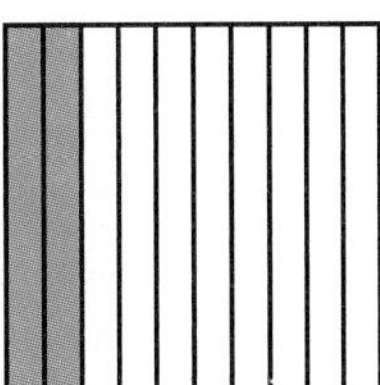

3. 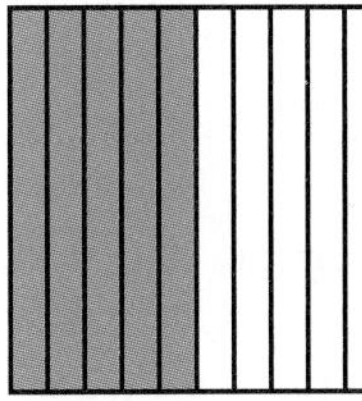

4. 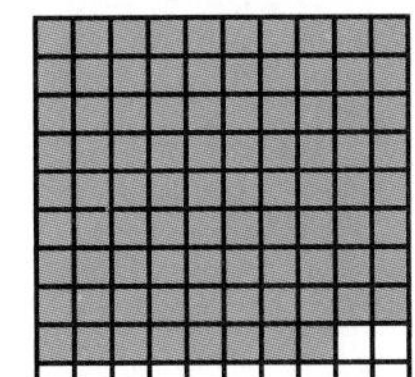

5. 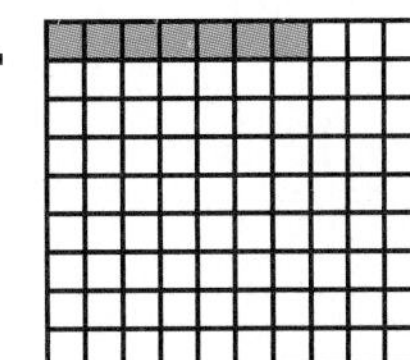

6. 

Lesson 14-2

Pages 560–563

Write each as a mixed number and decimal.

1. 

2.  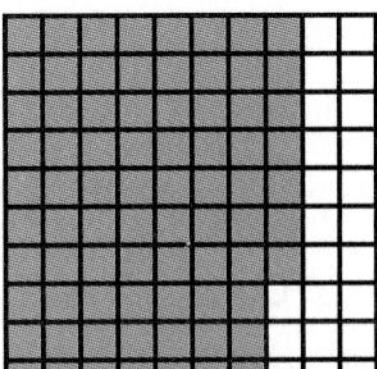

Write each as a decimal.

3. $4\frac{6}{10}$ **4.** $36\frac{33}{100}$ **5.** $83\frac{45}{100}$ **6.** $99\frac{8}{10}$

7. $15\frac{74}{100}$ **8.** $75\frac{3}{10}$ **9.** $62\frac{87}{100}$ **10.** $24\frac{5}{10}$

Lesson 14-3

Pages 564–565

Solve. Use the *make a model* strategy.

1. Marcus has 20 coins. One fourth are dimes. One fifth are nickels. The rest are quarters. How much are Marcus's coins worth?
2. There are 3 plants in a garden. The first plant is 3 times taller than the second and 2 times taller than the third. The plants are a total of 22 feet tall. How tall is each plant?
3. Emily walked halfway home from school. She walked back 3 blocks to find the book she had dropped. Then she walked home. She walked 20 blocks in all. How many blocks is it from Emily's house to school?
4. Simon is hanging wallpaper on 3 walls of his room. Each wall is 10 feet wide and 8 feet tall. Each roll of wallpaper covers 40 square feet. How many rolls of wallpaper does Simon need?

Lesson 14-4

Pages 566–568

Compare. Write $<$, $>$, or $=$.

1. 6.7 ● 0.67
2. 3.96 ● 3.09
3. 55.5 ● 55.50
4. 9.2 ● 9.22
5. 1.20 ● 1.19
6. 64.6 ● 68.4

Order from greatest to least.

7. 2.08, 2.98, 2.88
8. 53.03, 53.33, 53.13
9. 65.02, 6.86, 6.5
10. 0.78, 0.87, 0.08

Lesson 14-5

Pages 570–571

Use any strategy to solve. Tell what strategy you used.

1. A basement is rectangular in shape. One wall is 16 feet long. If the area is 304 square feet, what is the length of the other walls?
2. What is the next number in the pattern? What is the rule?

   8, 5, 12, 9, 16, 13, 20, 17
3. Bina began her chores at 3:30 P.M. She stopped at 4:20 to walk her dog. She started her chores again at 5:15 and stopped at 5:45. How long did Bina do her chores?
4. A pepperoni pizza is cut into 10 slices. A veggie pizza the same size is cut into 6 slices. Which is greater: 4 slices of pepperoni pizza or 3 slices of veggie pizza?

Lesson 14-6

Pages 572–575

Write a fraction and a decimal to describe the shaded part of each model.

1. 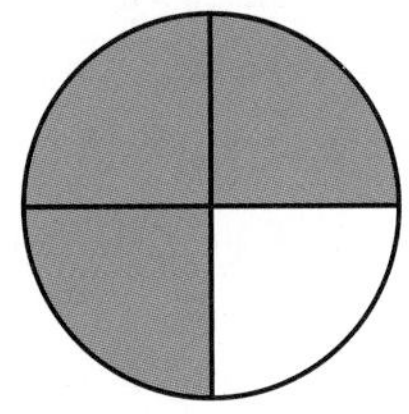

2. 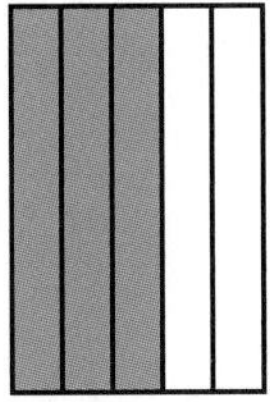

3. 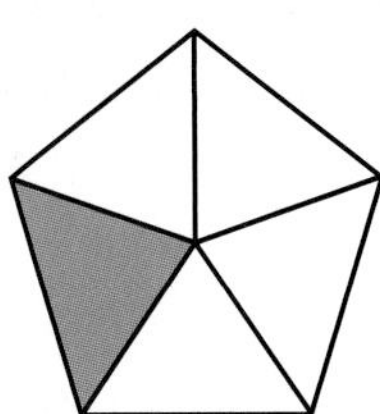

4. 

5. 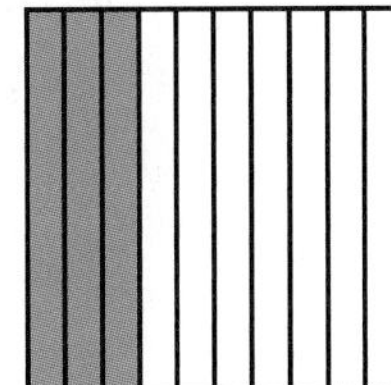

6. 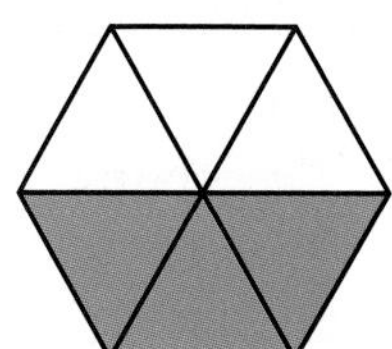

Lesson 14-7

Pages 578–581

Use a number line to compare. Write <, >, or =.

1. $\frac{25}{5}$ ● 4 **2.** 12.34 ● 12.3 **3.** $6\frac{1}{2}$ ● 6.89

4. $8\frac{1}{10}$ ● 8.75 **5.** 72.07 ● 72.70 **6.** 52 ● 5.02

Use a number line to order from greatest to least.

7. $67\frac{2}{100}$, 67.0, 67.70 **8.** 50.80, $\frac{4}{10}$, $\frac{4}{5}$

9. $\frac{25}{100}$, $\frac{2}{3}$, 33.3 **10.** $\frac{70}{100}$, 0.75, $\frac{4}{10}$

Lesson 15-1

Pages 593–597

Round to the nearest whole number.

1. 19.8 **2.** 46.21 **3.** 73.81 **4.** 32.41

5. 55.79 **6.** 38.11 **7.** 82.7 **8.** 25.5

Round to the nearest tenth.

9. 16.72 **10.** 93.39 **11.** 47.11 **12.** 33.76

13. 29.28 **14.** 73.64 **15.** 51.82 **16.** 85.83

Lesson 15-2

Pages 598–601

Estimate. Round to the nearest whole number.

1. 4.7 + 2.1

2. 5.3 + 4.2

3. $14.96 + $23.17

4. 17.67 + 23.78

5. 9.8 − 3.7

6. 13.3 − 7.2

7. 26.2 − 14.8

8. $25.8 − $16.2

9. 27.8 − 14.7

10. $38.91 − 26.78

11. 59.5 − 23.12

12. $83.32 − $54.86

Lesson 15-3

Pages 602–603

Solve. Use the *work backward* strategy.

1. Pedro has $3.75 left from lunch. He bought a taco for $1.60, a salad for $2.45, and milk for $0.95. How much money did he have before lunch?

2. Allison raked leaves for 45 minutes. She took a break for 15 minutes and then pulled weeds for half an hour. She finished her yard work at 8:30 P.M. What time did she start?

3. What is the least number of coins worth 25¢ or less that could be used to make $3.49? What are the coins?

4. A number is divided by 4. Next, 7 is subtracted from the quotient. Then, the difference is multiplied by 3. The result is 15. What is the number?

Lesson 15-4

Pages 606–608

Add. Use estimation to check for reasonableness.

1. 0.5 + 0.7

2. 0.8 + 0.7

3. 2.3 + 0.15

4. 6.4 + 9.34

5. 7.65 + 9.38

6. $7.25 + $6.49

7. 14.79 + 5.55

8. 11.46 + 4.93

9. 22.48 + 18.67

10. 17.99 + 12.99

11. 42.52 + 21.84

12. 6.4 + 3.6 + 2.8

13. 5.2 + 8.3 + 7.4

14. 6.6 + 4.7 + 9.9

Lesson 15-5

Pages 612–613

Use any strategy to solve. Tell what strategy you used.

1. There are two numbers whose product is 48 and difference is 8. What are the numbers?

2. A number is multiplied by 3. The product is subtracted from 50. The result is 11. What is the number?

3. A flower shop is selling 5 roses for $4. How much would 12 roses cost?

4. Dion surveyed 500 students to find out their favorite color. Blue was the favorite color of 7 out of 10 students. How many students' favorite color is blue?

Lesson 15-6

Pages 616–619

Subtract. Check your answer.

1. $4.8 - 2.3$

2. $6.9 - 3.3$

3. $8.3 - 2.7$

4. $5.2 - 2.8$

5. $3.78 - 1.44$

6. $7.56 - 4.43$

7. $9.45 − $2.06

8. $8.55 - 4.38$

9. $12.61 - 8.75$

10. $19.23 − $12.86

11. $26.74 − $16.95

12. $48.03 - 27.12$

13. 54.50 − 46.72

14. 38.04 − 23.60

15. 41.93 − 15.98

Lesson 16-1

Pages 631–635

Two 5–10 number cubes are rolled. Describe the probability of each outcome. Use *certain, likely, equally likely, unlikely,* or *impossible*.

1. What is the probability of rolling a number?

2. What is the probability of rolling a number that is less than 5?

3. What is the probability of rolling an even number?

4. What is the probability of rolling a number that is greater than 6?

Lesson 16-2

Pages 636–639

Use words and a fraction to describe the probability of each outcome.

1. an orange marble
2. a blue or green marble
3. a blue or yellow marble
4. a purple marble
5. an orange or blue marble
6. a marble
7. a blue or orange marble

Lesson 16-3

Pages 640–641

Solve. Use the *make an organized list* strategy.

1. Jim has 1 blue jacket, 1 green jacket, and 1 brown jacket. He has 1 tan hat and 1 black hat. How many different combinations of a jacket and hat can he wear?
2. Lee, Diego, Tara, and Irena will ride the Ferris wheel. Two people can sit in each car. What pairs are possible for the four friends to ride the Ferris wheel?

Lesson 16-4

Pages 644–646

Two spinners are divided into four equal parts. The grid shows the possible outcomes when each spinner is spun once.

Second Spinner

First Spinner	Red (R)	Blue (B)	Yellow (Y)	Green (G)
Red (R)	RR	RB	RY	RG
Blue (B)	BR	BB	BY	BG
Yellow (Y)	YR	YB	YY	YG
Green (G)	GR	GB	GY	GG

1. How many possible outcomes are there?
2. What is the probability of spinning two different colors?
3. What is the probability of spinning yellow on the first spin?
4. What is the probability of spinning blue on either the first or second spin?
5. What is the probability of spinning a primary color on either the first or second spin?

Lesson 16-5

Pages 650–651

Use any strategy to solve. Tell what strategy you used.

1. There are 12 students in a class. Eight are girls and 4 are boys. Their teacher will draw one of their names from a hat. What is the probability that a girl's name will be drawn?
2. There are 84 fish in a zoo aquarium. There are 4 colors of fish. Twelve are blue, 21 are black, 16 are red, and the rest are striped. How many striped fish are there?
3. Takara is taller than Ali. Ali is taller than Nicole. Megan is taller than Takara. List the girls in order from tallest to shortest.
4. Sara has 1 blue sweater, 1 pink sweater, and 1 purple sweater. She has 1 white skirt, 1 pink skirt, and 1 blue skirt. How many different outfits can she make?

Lesson 16-6

Pages 652–655

Draw a tree diagram to show all of the different breakfast/lunch/juice outcomes. Then find the probability for each situation.

Breakfast	Lunch	Juice
Bagel	Taco	Small
Cereal	Pizza	Medium
	Salad	Large

1. Find the probability of randomly choosing a bagel, a salad, and a medium juice.
2. What is the probability of randomly choosing cereal, a taco or pizza, and a large juice?

Find the probability for each situation.

3. roll a 3 on a 0–5 number cube and flip tails on a coin
4. roll an even number on a 0–5 number cube and flip a head on a coin

Glossary/Glosario

Math Online A mathematics multilingual glossary is available at www.ca.gr4math.com/multilingual_glossary. The glossary includes the following languages.

Arabic	Cantonese	Korean	Tagalog
Bengali	English	Russian	Urdu
Brazilian Portuguese	Haitian Creole	Spanish	Vietnamese
	Hmong		

Cómo usar el glosario en español:
1. Busca el término en inglés que desees encontrar.
2. El término en español, junto con la definición, se encuentran en la columna de la derecha.

English | Español

A

acute angle (p. 399) An *angle* with a measure greater than 0° and less than 90°.

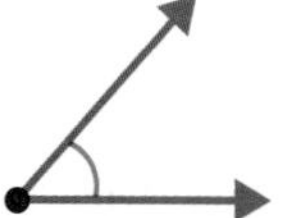

ángulo agudo Un *ángulo* que mide más de 0° y menos de 90°.

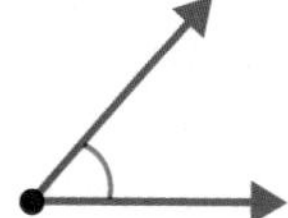

acute triangle (p. 405) A *triangle* with all three *angles* less than 90°.

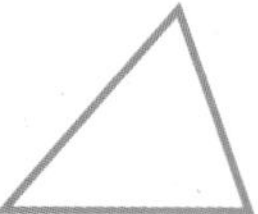

triángulo acutángulo Un *triángulo* cuyos tres *ángulos* miden menos de 90°.

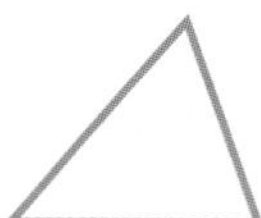

addend (p. 64) Any numbers being added together.

sumando Cualquier número que se suma a otro.

add (adding, addition) (p. 52) An operation on two or more *addends* that results in a *sum*.

$9 + 3 = 12$

suma (sumar, adición) Operación en dos o más *sumandos* que resulta en una *suma*.

$9 + 3 = 12$

algebra (p. 93) A branch of mathematics that uses symbols, usually letters, to explore relationships between quantities.

álgebra Rama de las matemáticas que usa símbolos, generalmente letras, para explorar relaciones entre cantidades.

angle (p. 398) A figure that is formed by two *rays* with the same *endpoint*.

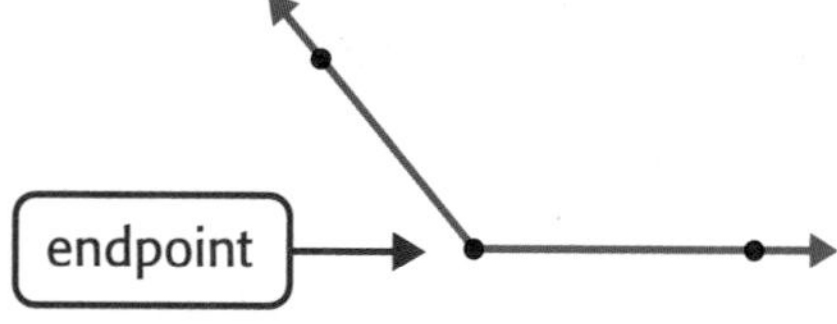

ángulo Figura formada por dos *rayos* con el mismo *extremo*.

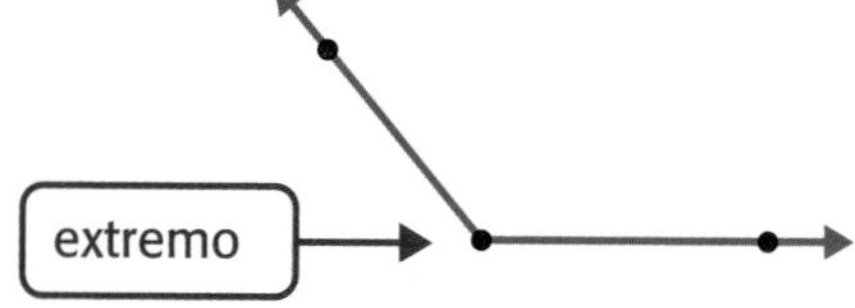

area (p. 444) The number of *square units* needed to cover the inside of a region or plane figure without any overlap.

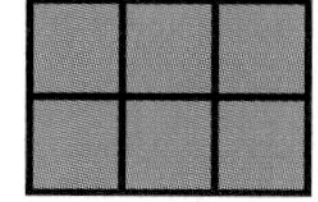

area = 6 square units

Associative Property of Addition (p. 55) The property states that the grouping of the *addends* does not change the *sum*.

$(4 + 5) + 2 = 4 + (5 + 2)$

Associative Property of Multiplication (p. 178) The property that states that the grouping of the *factors* does not change the *product*.

$3 \times (6 \times 2) = (3 \times 6) \times 2$

área El número de *unidades cuadradas* necesarias para cubrir el interior de una región o figura plana sin traslapes.

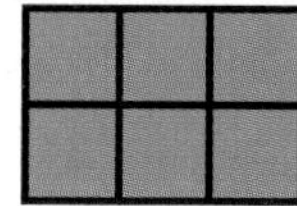

área = 6 unidades cuadradas

propiedad asociativa de la suma Propiedad que establece que la agrupación de los *sumandos* no altera la *suma*.

$(4 + 5) + 2 = 4 + (5 + 2)$

propiedad asociativa de la multiplicación Propiedad que establece que la agrupación de los *factores* no altera el *producto*.

$3 \times (6 \times 2) = (3 \times 6) \times 2$

B

balance (p. 110) An equation is balanced if both sides of the equals sign have the same value.

bar graph (p. 140) A graph that compares *data* by using bars of different lengths or heights to show the values.

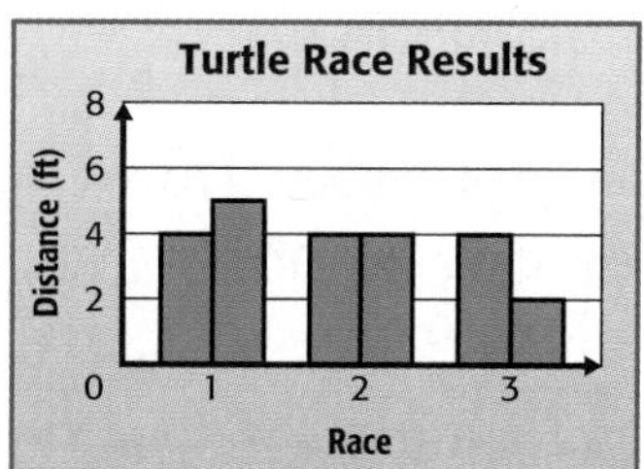

bilateral symmetry (p. 434) The property of a figure that allows it to be folded so the two halves match exactly.

equilibrar Una ecuación está equilibrada si ambos lados del signo de igualdad tienen el mismo valor.

gráfica de barras Gráfica que compara los *datos* usando barras de distintas longitudes o alturas para mostrar los valores.

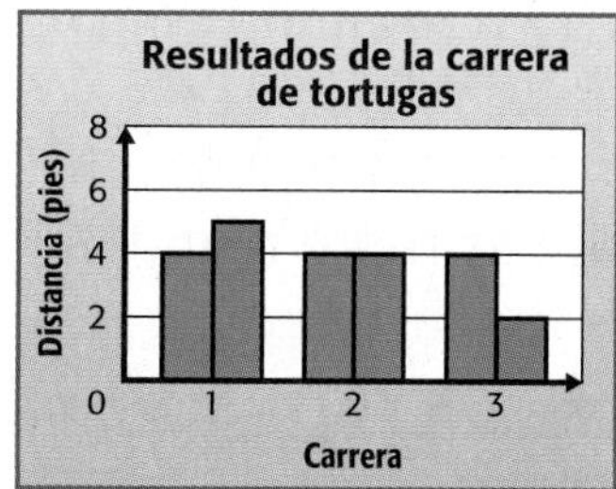

simetría bilateral Propiedad de una figura que le permite ser doblada de manera que las mitades se correspondan exactamente.

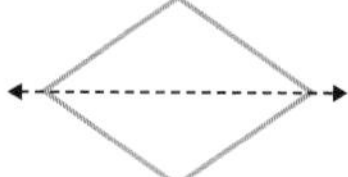

C

circle (p. 414) A closed figure in which all points are the same distance from a fixed point, called the center.

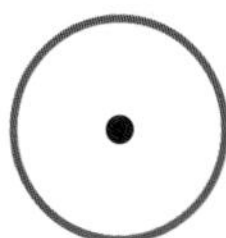

círculo Figura cerrada en la cual todos los puntos equidistan de un punto fijo llamado centro.

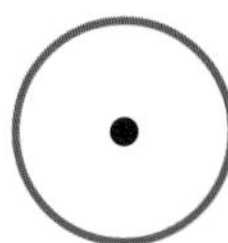

Commutative Property of Addition (p. 55) The property that states that the order in which two numbers are added does not change the *sum*.

$12 + 15 = 15 + 12$

propiedad conmutativa de la suma Propiedad que establece que el orden en el cual se suman dos o más números no altera la *suma*.

$12 + 15 = 15 + 12$

Commutative Property of Multiplication (p. 178) The property that states that the order in which two numbers are multiplied does not change the *product*.

$7 \times 2 = 2 \times 7$

propiedad conmutativa de la multiplicación Propiedad que establece que el orden en el cual se multiplican dos o más números no altera el *producto*.

$7 \times 2 = 2 \times 7$

compatible numbers (p. 348) Numbers in a problem or related numbers that are easy to work with mentally.

720 and 90 are compatible numbers for division because $72 \div 9 = 8$.

números compatibles Números en un problema o números relacionados con los cuales es fácil trabajar mentalmente.

720 y 90 son números compatibles en la división porque $72 \div 9 = 8$.

complex figure (p. 454) A shape that is made up of two or more shapes.

figura compleja Figura compuesta por dos o más formas.

composite number (p. 209) A whole number that has more than two factors.

12 has the factors 1, 2, 3, 4, 6, and 12.

número compuesto Número entero con más de dos factores.

12 tiene los factores 1, 2, 3, 4, 6 y 12.

cone (p. 385) A 3-dimensional figure with a curved surface, a circular base, and one *vertex*.

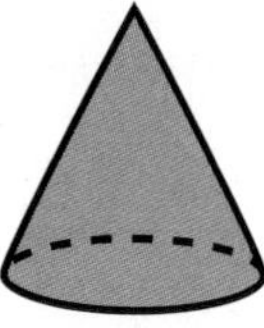

cono Figura tridimensional con una superficie curva, una base circular y un *vértice*.

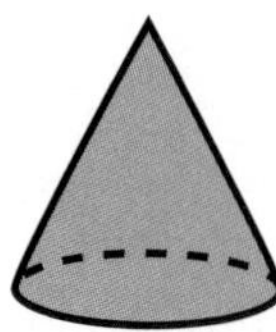

Glossary/Glosario

congruent figures (p. 431) Two figures having the same size and the same shape.

figuras congruentes Dos figuras con la misma forma y el mismo tamaño.

coordinate (p. 472) One of two numbers in an *ordered pair*.

In (1, 5), the 1 is the number on the *x*-axis. The 5 is on the *y*-axis.

coordenada Uno de los dos números de un *par ordenado*.

(1, 5) El 1 es el número en el eje *x* y el 5 está en el eje *y*.

coordinate graph or grid (p. 472) A graph that displays a set of points and gives the position of a point on a line.

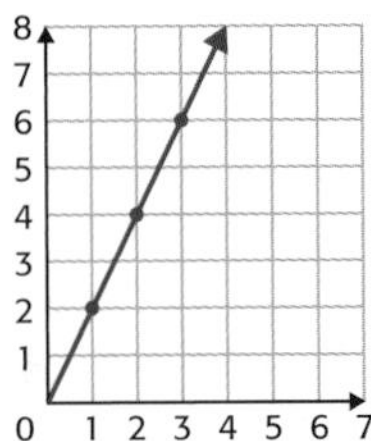

gráfica de coordenadas o cuadriculado Gráfica que representa un conjunto de puntos y da, en términos numéricos, la posición de un punto sobre una recta.

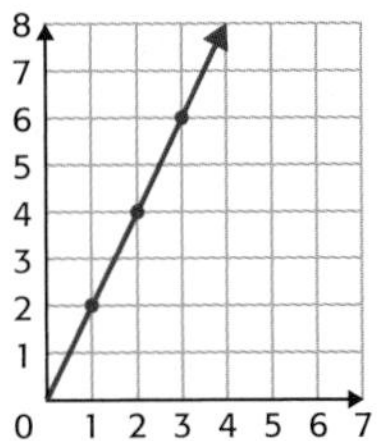

cube (p. 385) A 3-dimensional figure with six *congruent* square *faces*.

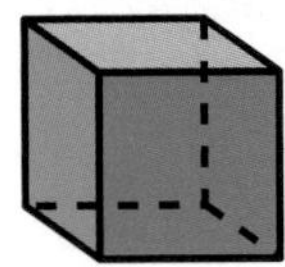

cubo Figura tridimensional con seis *caras* cuadradas *congruentes*.

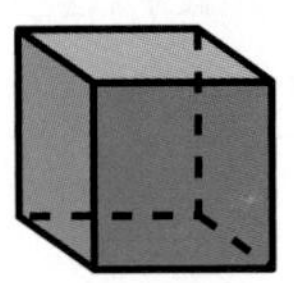

cylinder (p. 385) A 3-dimensional *figure* having two *parallel congruent* circular *bases* and a curved surface connecting the two *bases*.

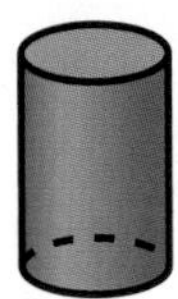

cilindro Figura tridimensional que tiene dos bases circulares *paralelas* y *congruentes* y una superficie curva que las une.

D

data (p. 127) Numbers or symbols, sometimes collected from a *survey* or experiment, to show information. Datum is singular; data is plural.

datos Números o símbolos que muestran información, algunas veces reunidos de una *encuesta* o un experimento.

decimal equivalents (p. 572) Decimals that represent the same number.

0.3 and 0.30

decimales equivalentes Decimales que representan el mismo número.

0.3 y 0.30

decimal/divisor

decimal (p. 555) A number that uses *place value,* numbers, and a *decimal point* to show part of a whole.

decimal Número con uno o más dígitos a la derecha del punto *decimal,* tales como 8.37 ó 0.05.

decimal point (p. 555) A period separating the ones and the *tenths* in a decimal number.

0.8 OR $3.77

punto decimal Punto que separa las unidades de las *décimas* en un número decimal.

0.8 ó $3.77

denominator (p. 507) The bottom number in a *fraction.*

In $\frac{5}{6}$, 6 is the denominator.

denominador El número inferior en una *fracción.*

$\frac{5}{6}$ 6 es el denominador.

diameter (p. 414) A *line segment* that connects two points on a circle and passes through the center of a *circle.*

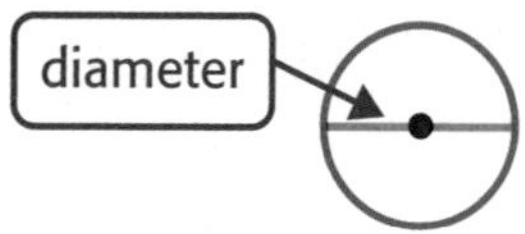

diámetro *Segmento de recta* que pasa por el centro de conecta dos puntos en un circulo y del un *círculo.*

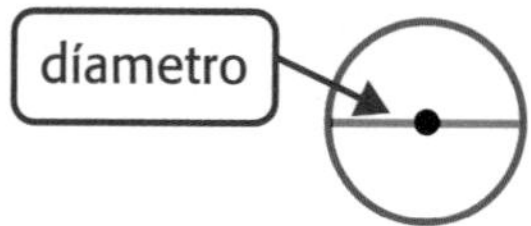

digit (p. 17) A symbol used to write numbers. The ten digits are 0, 1, 2, 3, 4, 5, 6, 7, 8, and 9.

dígito Símbolo que se usa para escribir números. Los diez dígitos son 0, 1, 2, 3, 4, 5, 6, 7, 8 y 9.

Distributive Property of Multiplication (p. 194) To multiply a *sum* by a number, multiply each *addend* by the number and add the *products.*

$4 \times (1 + 3) = (4 \times 1) + (4 \times 3)$

propiedad distributiva de la multiplicación Para multiplicar una *suma* por un número, puedes multiplica cada *sumando* por el número y suma los *productos.*

$4 \times (1 + 3) = (4 \times 1) + (4 \times 3)$

division (divide) (p. 170) An operation on two numbers in which the first number is split into the same number of equal groups as the second number.

división (dividir) Operación en dos números en que el primer número se separa en tantos grupos iguales como indica el segundo número.

dividend (p. 174) A number that is being divided.

$3\overline{)19}$ 19 is the dividend

dividendo El número que se divide.

$3\overline{)19}$ 19 es el dividendo

divisor (p. 174) The number by which the *dividend* is being divided.

$3\overline{)19}$ 3 is the divisor

divisor El número entre el cual se divide el *dividendo.*

$3\overline{)19}$ 3 es el divisor

double bar graph (p. 141) A *bar graph* that compares two related groups of *data*.

gráfica de barras dobles *Gráfica de barras* que compara dos grupos de *datos* relacionados.

E

edge (p. 385) The *line segment* where two *faces* of a *solid figure* meet.

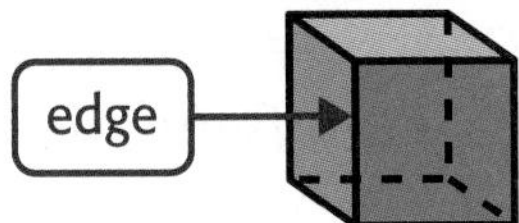

arista El *segmento de recta* donde concurren dos *caras* de una *figura sólida.*

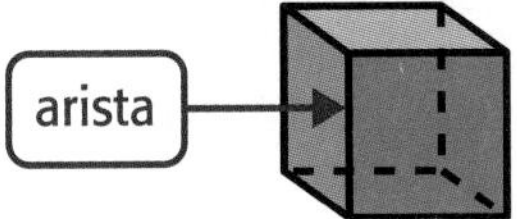

endpoint (p. 398) The point at either end of a *line segment* or the point at the beginning of a ray.

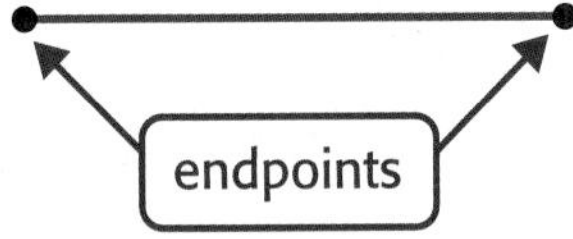

extremo El punto en cualquiera de los dos lados en que termina un *segmento de recta* o el punto al principio de un rayo.

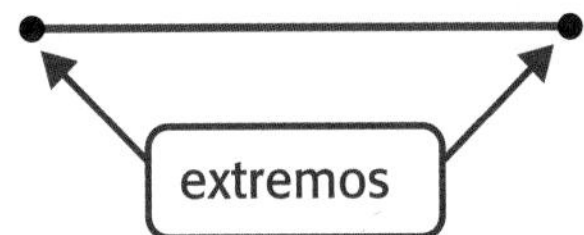

equally likely (p. 631) Having the same chance of occurring.

In a coin toss, you are equally likely to flip a head or a tail.

equiprobable Que tiene la misma posibilidad de ocurrir.

Al lanzar una moneda, es equiprobable que caiga cara o cruz.

equation (p. 96) A sentence that contains an equals sign (=), showing that two *expressions* are equal.

ecuación Oración matemátia que contiene el signo de igualdad, =, el que indica que las dos *expresiones* son iguales.

equilateral triangle (p. 404) A *triangle* with three *congruent* sides.

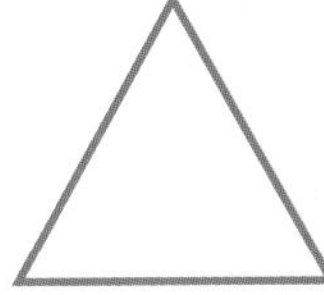

triángulo equilátero *Triángulo* con tres lados *congruentes*.

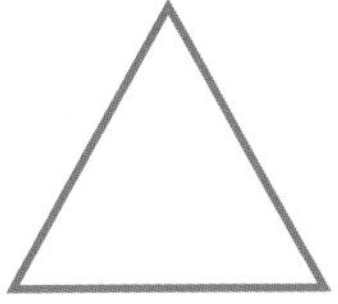

Glossary/Glosario

equivalent fractions (p. 516) *Fractions* that represent the same number.

$$\frac{3}{4} = \frac{6}{8}$$

estimate (p. 58) A number close to an exact value. An estimate indicates *about* how much.

47 + 22 is about 50 + 20 or 70.

expanded form/expanded notation (p. 18) The representation of a number as a sum that shows the value of each digit.

536 is written as 500 + 30 + 6.

expression (p. 93) A combination of numbers, variables, and at least one operation.

fracciones equivalentes *Fracciones* que representan el mismo número.

$$\frac{3}{4} = \frac{6}{8}$$

estimación Número cercano a un valor exacto. Una estimación indica *aproximadamente* cuánto.

47 + 22 es aproximadamente 50 + 20; ó 70.

forma desarrollada/notación desarrollada Representación de un número como una suma que muestra el valor de cada dígito.

536 se escribe como 500 + 30 + 6.

expresión Combinación de números, variables y por lo menos una operación.

F

face (p. 385) The flat part of a 3-dimensional figure.

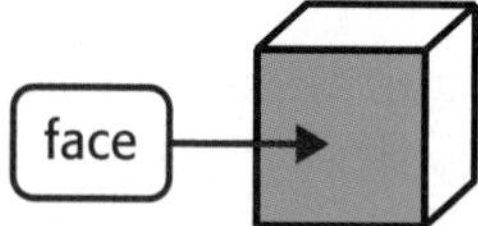

fact family (p. 175) A group of related facts using the same numbers.

5 + 3 = 8	5 × 3 = 15
3 + 5 = 8	3 × 5 = 15
8 − 3 = 5	15 ÷ 3 = 5
8 − 5 = 3	15 ÷ 5 = 3

factor (p. 204) A number that divides a whole number evenly. Also a number that is multiplied by another number.

fraction (p. 507) A number that represents part of a whole or part of a set.

$$\frac{1}{2}, \frac{1}{3}, \frac{1}{4}, \frac{3}{4}$$

frequency table (p. 127) A table for organizing a set of *data* that shows the number of times each result has occurred.

cara Parte llana de una figura tridimensional.

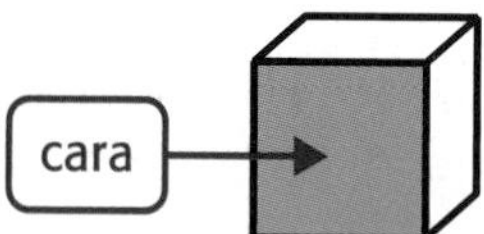

familia de operaciones Grupo de operaciones relacionadas que usan los mismos números.

5 + 3 = 8	5 × 3 = 15
3 + 5 = 8	3 × 5 = 15
8 − 3 = 5	15 ÷ 3 = 5
8 − 5 = 3	15 ÷ 5 = 3

factor Número que divide exactamente a otro número entero. También es un número multiplicado por otro número.

fracción Número que representa parte de un todo o parte de un conjunto.

$$\frac{1}{2}, \frac{1}{3}, \frac{1}{4}, \frac{3}{4}$$

tabla de frecuencias Tabla para organizar un conjunto de *datos* que muestra el número de veces que ha ocurrido cada resultado.

Glossary/Glosario

function (p. 484) A relationship in which one number depends on another number.

función Relación en que una cantidad depende de otra cantidad.

function table (p. 484) A table of ordered pairs that is based on a rule.

tabla de funciones Tabla de pares ordenados que se basa en una regla.

G

grid (p. 472) A group of horizontal and vertical lines, that intersects, forming squares.

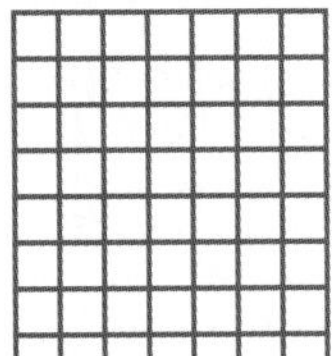

cuadriculdo Grupo de rectas horizontales y verticales que se intersecan formando cuadrados.

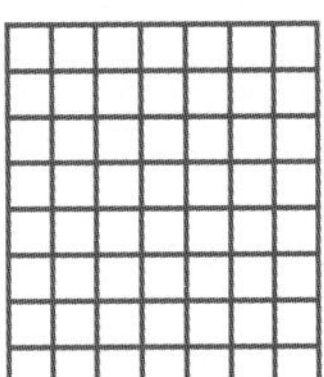

H

hexagon (p. 388) A *polygon* with six sides and six *angles*.

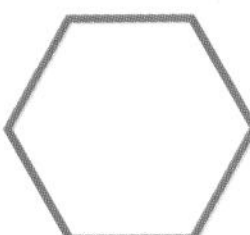

hexágono *Polígono* con seis lados y seis *ángulos*.

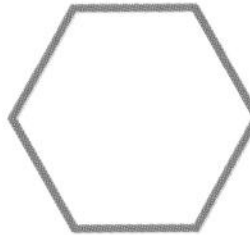

hundredth (p. 555) A place value position. One of one hundred equal parts.

In the number 0.5, 5 is in the hundredths place.

centésima Un valor de posición. Una parte de cien partes iguales.

En el número 4.57, 7 está en el lugar de las centésimas.

Identity Property of Addition (p. 55) For any number, zero plus that number is the number.

$3 + 0 = 3$ or $0 + 3 = 3$

propiedad de identidad de la adición Para todo numero, cero más el numero es el número.

$3 + 0 = 3$ ó $0 + 3 = 3$

Identity Property of Multiplication (p. 178) If you multiply a number by 1, the product is the same as the given number.

$8 \times 1 = 8 = 8 \times 1$

propiedad de identidad de la multiplicación Si multiplicas un número por 1, el producto es igual al número dado.

$8 \times 1 = 8 = 1 \times 8$

impossible (p. 628) An event that cannot happen. It has a probability of zero.

It is impossible to choose yellow.

imposible Un evento que no puede suceder, cuya probabilidad es cero.

improper fraction (p. 538) A fraction with a *numerator* that is greater than or equal to the *denominator*.

$\frac{17}{3}$ or $\frac{5}{5}$

fracción impropia Fracción con un *numerador* mayor que o igual al *denominador*.

$\frac{17}{3}$ ó $\frac{5}{5}$

intersecting lines (p. 395) *Lines* that meet or cross at a point.

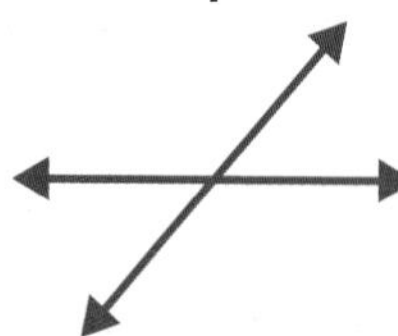

rectas secantes *Rectas* que se intersecan o cruzan entre sí.

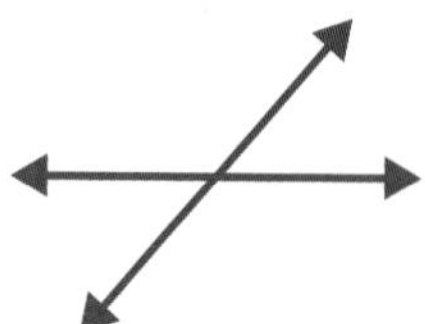

is greater than $>$ (p. 28) An inequality relationship showing that the number on the left of the symbol is greater than the number on the right.

$5 > 3$ 5 is greater than 3

es mayor que $>$ Relación de desigualdad que muestra que el número a la izquierda del símbolo es mayor que el número a la derecha.

$5 > 3$ 5 es mayor que 3

is less than $<$ (p. 28) The number on the left side of the symbol is smaller than the number on the right side.

$4 < 7$ 4 is less than 7

es menor que $<$ El número a la izquierda del símbolo es más pequeño que el número a la derecha.

$4 < 7$ 4 es menor que 7

isosceles triangle (p. 404) A *triangle* with at least 2 sides of the same length.

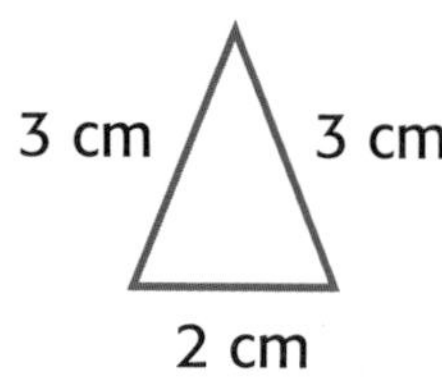

triángulo isósceles Un *triángulo* que tiene por lo menos 2 lados del mismo largo.

3 cm 3 cm
2 cm

L

like denominators (p. 534) When two or more fractions have the same *denominator* they have like *denominators*.

denominador común Cuando dos o más fracciones tienan el mismo *denominador*, entonces tienen *denominadores* comones.

like fractions (p. 534) Fractions that have the same denominator.

likely (p. 628) An event that will probably happen.

It is likely you will choose a red tile.

line (p. 394) A straight set of points that extend in opposite directions without ending.

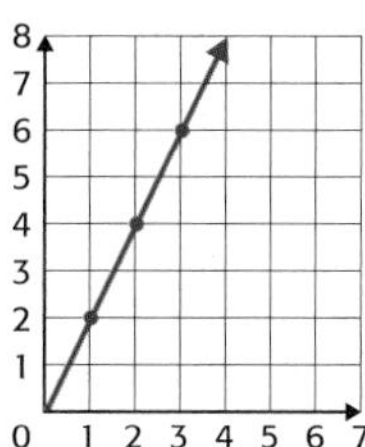

line graph (p. 150) A graph that uses points connected by *line segments* to represent data.

line of symmetry (p. 434) A *line* on which a figure can be folded so that its two halves match exactly.

line plot (p. 136) A graph that uses columns of Xs above a *number line* to show frequency of data.

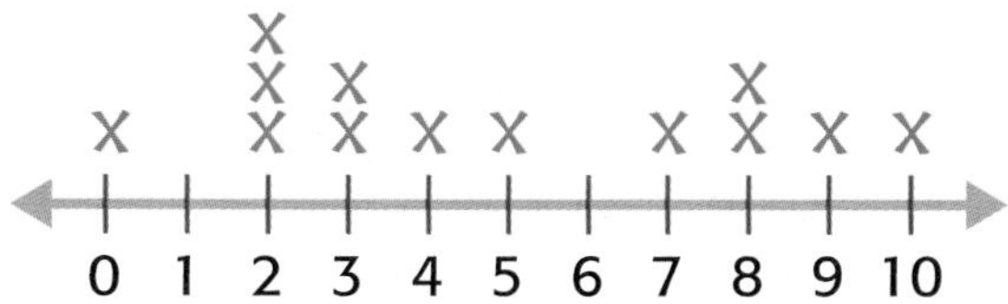

fracciones semejantes Fracciones que tienen el mismo denominador.

posible Un evento que probablemente sucederá

Es posible que elijas una baldosa rojo.

recta Conjunto de puntos dispuestos rectamente que se extienden en direcciones opuestas y sin fin.

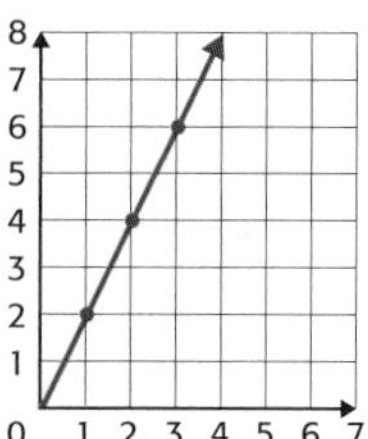

gráfica lineal Gráfica que usa puntos unidos por *segmentos de recta* para representar datos.

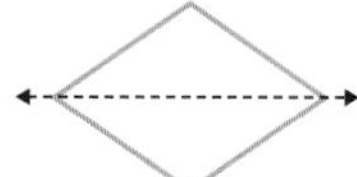

eje de simetría *Recta* sobre la cual se puede doblar una figura de manera que sus mitades se correspondan exactamente.

esquema lineal Gráfica que usa columnas de X sobre una *recta numérica* para representar frecuencias de datos.

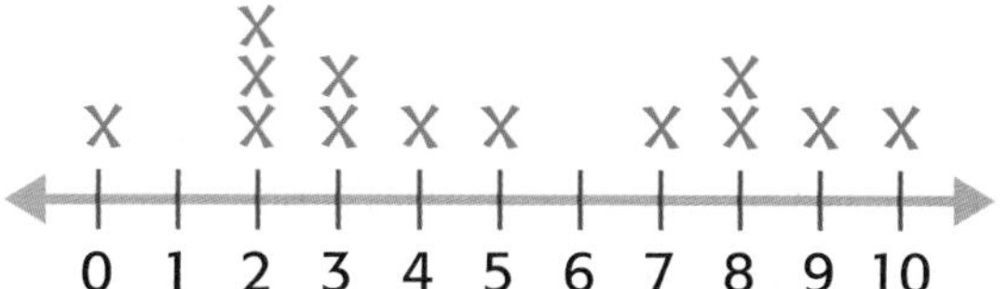

line segment (p. 394) A part of a *line* between two *endpoints*. The length of the line segment can be measured.

segmento de recta Parte de una *recta* entre dos *extremos*. La longitud de un segmento de recta se puede medir.

line symmetry (p. 434) A figure has *line symmetry* if it can be folded so that the two parts of the figure match, or are *congruent*.

simetría lineal Una figura tiene *simetria lineal* si puede doblarse de modo que las dos partes de la figura correspondan o sean *congruentes*.

M

median (p. 130) The middle number in a group of numbers arranged in numerical order.
The median of 3, 5, 6, 7, and 8 is 6.

mediana El número central de un grupo de números ordenados numéricamente.
La mediana de 3, 5, 6, 7 y 8 es 6.

minuend (p. 69) The first number in a subtraction sentence from which a second number is to be subtracted.

$8 - 3 = 5$

8 = minuend, 3 = subtrahend, 5 = difference

minuendo El primer número en un enunciado de sustracción del cual se restará un segundo número

$8 - 3 = 5$

8 = minuendo, 3 = sustraendo, 5 = diferencia

mixed number (p. 538) A number that has a *whole number* part and a *fraction* part.

$6\frac{3}{4}$

número mixto Número compuesto por un *número entero* y una parte *fraccionaria*.

$6\frac{3}{4}$

mode (p. 130) The number(s) that occurs most often in a set of numbers.

7, 4, 7, 10, 7, and 2
The mode is 7.

moda Número o números que ocurre(n) con mayor frecuencia en un conjunto de números.

7, 4, 7, 10, 7 y 2
La moda es 7.

multiple (p. 205) A multiple of a number is the *product* of that number and any whole number.
15 is a multiple of 5 because $3 \times 5 = 15$.

múltiplo Un múltiplo de un número es el *producto* de ese número y cualquier otro número entero.
15 es múltiplo de 5 porque $3 \times 5 = 15$.

multiply (multiplication) (p. 170) An operation on two numbers to find their *product*. It can be thought of as repeated *addition*.

multiplicar (multiplicación) Operación en dos números para calcular su *producto*. También se puede interpretar como una *adición* repetida.

Glossary/Glosario

N

negative number (p. 469) Numbers less than zero.

número negativo Números menores que cero.

net (p. 386) A flat pattern that can be folded to make a 3-dimensional figure.

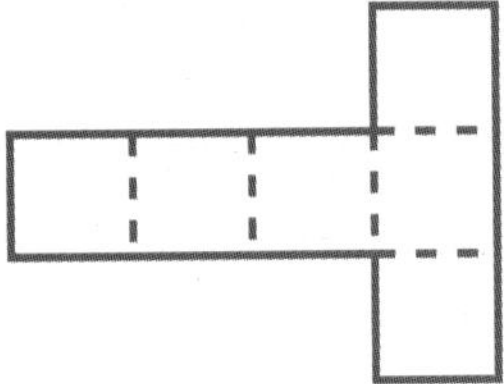

red Patrón llano que se puede doblar para formar una figura tridimensional.

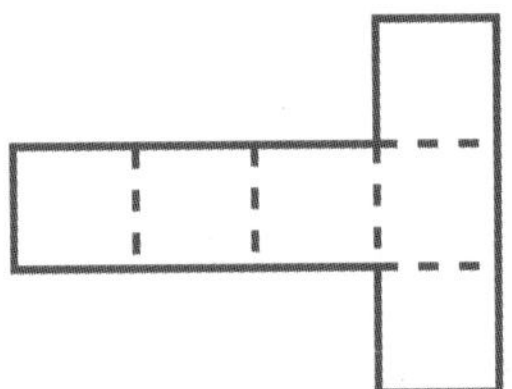

number line (p. 28) A line with numbers on it in order at regular intervals.

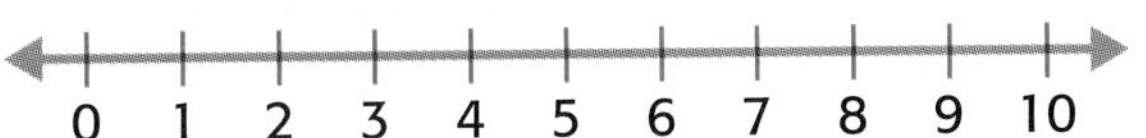

recta numérica Recta con números ordenadosa intervalos regulares.

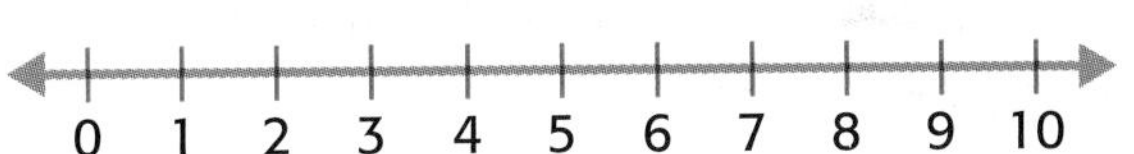

numerator (p. 507) The number above the bar in a *fraction*; the part of the fraction that tells how many of the equal parts are being used.

numerador El número que está encima de la barra de *fracción*; la parte de la fracción que te indica cuántas partes iguales están siendo usadas.

O

obtuse angle (p. 399) An *angle* that measures greater than 90° but less than 180°.

ángulo obtuso *Ángulo* que mide más de 90° pero menos de 180°.

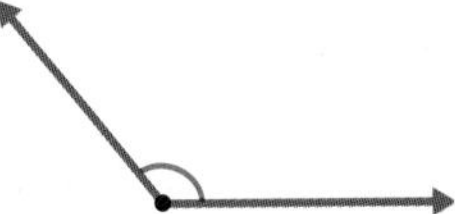

obtuse triangle (p. 405) A *triangle* with one *obtuse angle*.

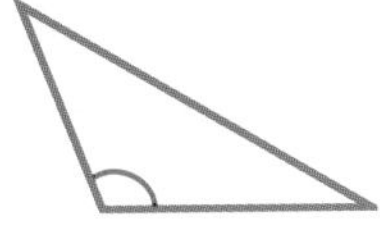

triángulo obtusángulo *Triángulo* con un *ángulo obtuso*.

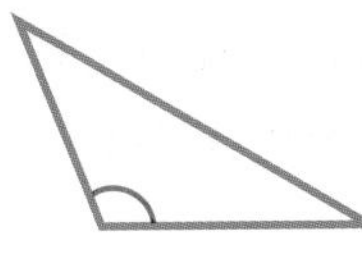

octagon (p. 388) A *polygon* with 8 sides.

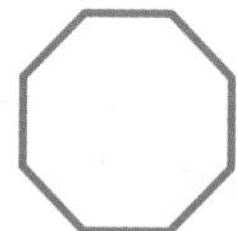

operation (p. 52) A mathematical process such as addition (+), subtraction (–), multiplication(×), or division (÷).

order of operations (p. 230) Rules that tell what order to follow use in evaluating an expression:
(1) Do the operations in parentheses first.

(2) Multiply and divide in order from left to right.
(3) Add and subtract in order from left to right.

ordered pair (p. 472) A pair of numbers that are the *coordinates* of a point in a coordinate plane or grid in this order (horizontal coordinate, vertical coordinate).

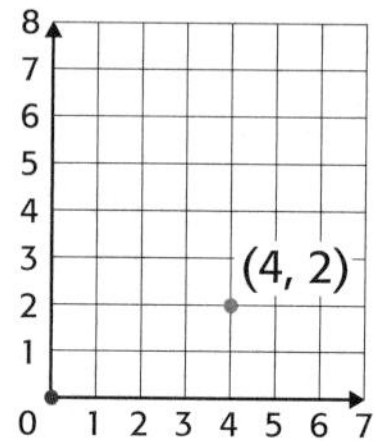

origin (p. 472) The point (0, 0) on a *coordinate graph* where the vertical axis meets the horizontal axis, (0, 0).

outcome (p. 631) A possible result of an experiment.

outlier (p. 131) A number in a set of data that is much larger or much smaller than most of the other numbers in the set.

octágono *Polígono* de 8 lados.

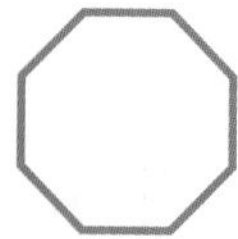

operación Proceso matemático como la suma (+), la resta (–), la multiplicación (×) o la división (÷).

orden de las operaciones Reglas que te indican qué orden seguir cuando evalúas una expresión:
(1) Evalúa primero las operaciones dentro de los paréntesis ( ).
(2) Multiplica o divide en orden de izquierda a derecha.
(3) Suma o resta en orden de izquierda a derecha.

par ordenado Par de números que son las *coordenadas* de un punto en un plano de coordenadas o cuadriculado, en este orden (coordenada horizontal, coordenada vertical).

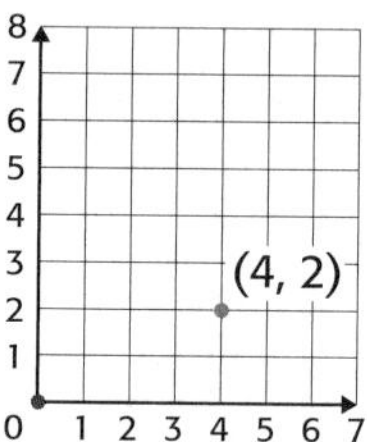

origen El punto (0, 0) en una *gráfica de* coordenadas donde el eje vertical interseca el eje horizontal, (0, 0).

resultado Resultado posible de un experimento.

valor atípico Número en un conjunto de datos que es mucho mayor o mucho menor que la mayoría de los otros números del conjunto.

P

parallel lines (p. 395) Lines that are the same distance apart. Parallel lines do not meet.

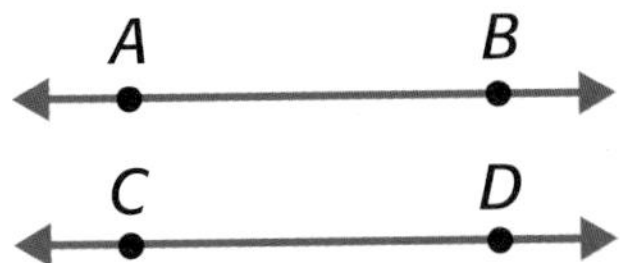

parallelogram (p. 410) A quadrilateral with four sides in which each pair of opposite sides are parallel and equal in length.

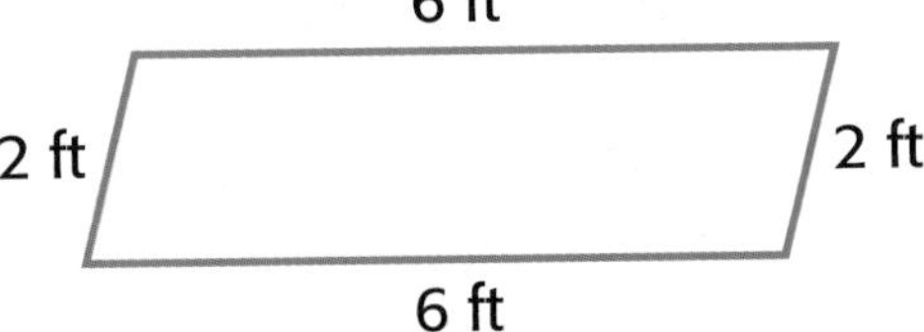

pentagon (p. 388) A *polygon* with five sides.

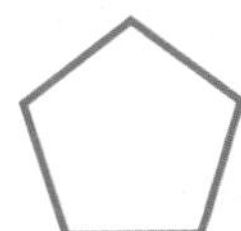

perimeter (p. 438) The distance around a shape or region.

period (p. 17) The name given to each group of three digits on a place-value chart.

perpendicular lines (p. 395) *Lines* that meet or cross each other to form *right angles*.

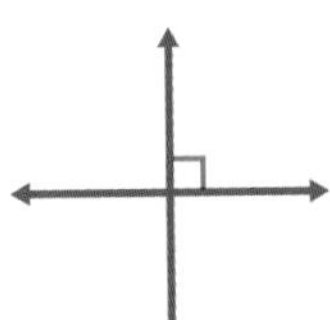

place value (p. 14) The value given to a *digit* by its position in a number.

plane figure (p. 388) A 2-dimensional figure that lies entirely within one plane such as a triangle or square.

rectas paralelas Rectas separadas por la misma distancia. Las rectas paralelas no se intersecan.

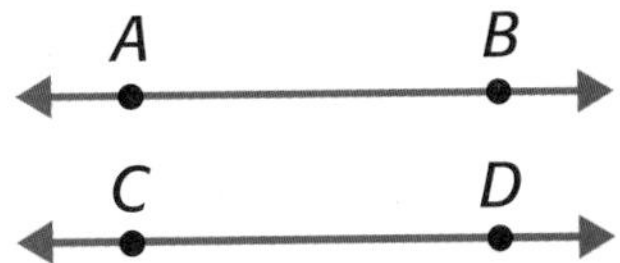

paralelogramo Cuadrilátero de cuatro lados en el cual cada par de lados opuestos son paralelos y de la misma longitud.

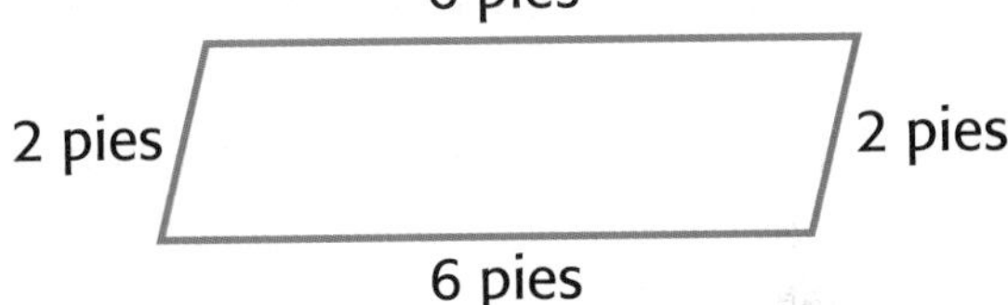

pentágono *Polígono* de cinco lados.

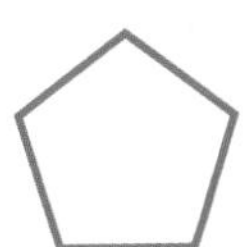

perímetro Distancia alrededor de una figura o región.

período Nombre dado a cada grupo de tres dígitos en una tabla de valores de posición.

rectas perpendiculares *Rectas* que se intersecan o cruzan formando *ángulos rectos*.

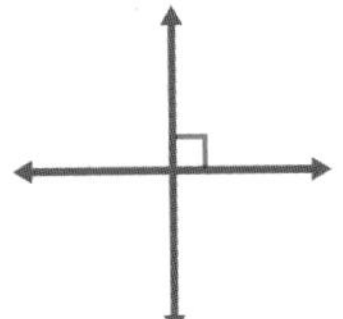

valor de posición El valor dado a un *dígito* según su posición en un número.

figura plana Figura bidimensional que yace completamente en un plano como un triángulo o un cuadrado.

Glossary/Glosario

polygon (p. 388) A closed *plane figure* formed using *line segments* that meet only at their *endpoints*.

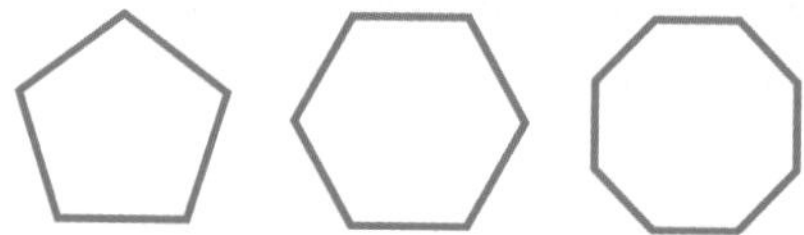

positive number (p. 469) Numbers that are greater than zero.

prime number (p. 209) A whole number with exactly two *factors,* 1 and itself.

7, 13, and 19

probability (p. 629) A number between 0 and 1 that measures the likelihood of an event happening.

product (p. 173) The answer or result of a multiplication problem. It also refers to expressing a number as the product of its factors.

pyramid (p. 385) A 3-dimensional figure with a polygon as a base and triangular shaped faces that share a common *vertex*.

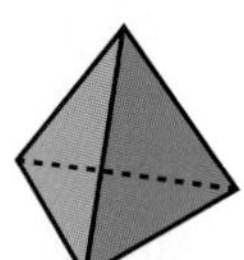

polígono *Figura plana* cerrada formada por *segmentos de recta* que sólo se unen en sus *extremos*.

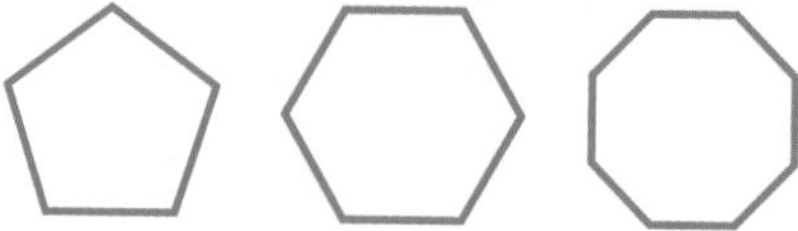

número positivo Números mayores que cero.

número primo Número entero que tiene exactamente dos *factores*, 1 y sí mismo.

7, 13 y 19

probabilidad Número entre 0 y 1 que mide la posibilidad de que ocurra un evento.

producto Repuesta o resultado de un problema de multiplicación. También se refiere a la expresión de un número como el producto de sus factores.

pirámide Figura sólida con un polígono como base y *caras* triangulares que comparten un *vértice* común.

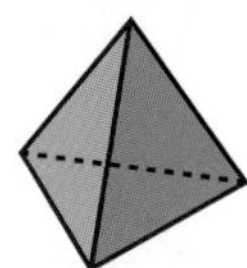

Q

quadrilateral (p. 410) A shape that has 4 sides and 4 *angles*.

square, rectangle, and parallelogram

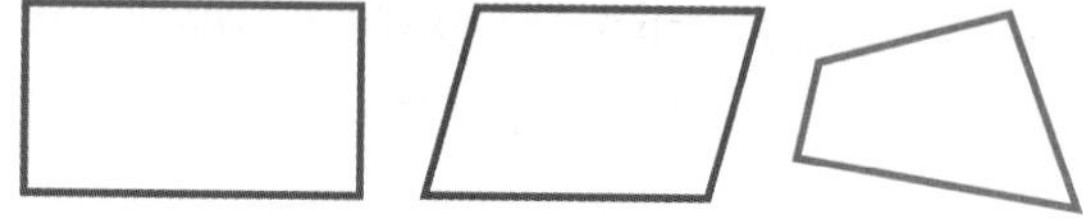

quotient (p. 337) The result of a *division* problem.

cuadrilátero Figura que tiene 4 lados y 4 *ángulos*.

cuadrado, rectángulo y paralelogramo

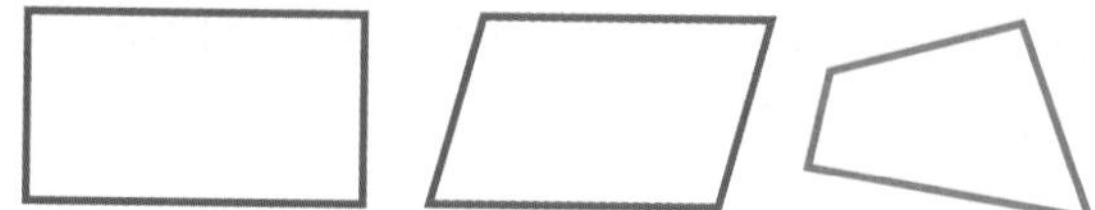

cociente Respuesta o resultado de un problema de *división*.

R

radius (p. 414) A *line segment* that connects the center of a circle to a point on the *circle*. The plural is radii.

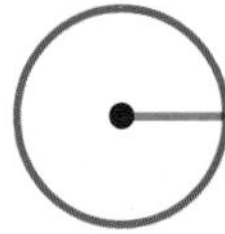

radio *Segmento de recta* que une el centro de un círculo con un punto del *círculo*.

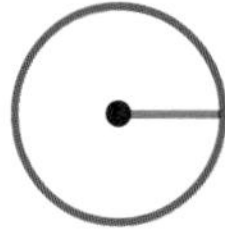

ray (p. 394) A part of a *line* that has one *endpoint* and extends in one direction without ending.

rayo Parte de una *recta* que tiene un *extremo* y que se extiende en una dirección sin fin.

rectangle (p. 410) A *quadrilateral* with four *right angles*; opposite sides are equal and *parallel*.

rectángulo *Cuadrilátero* con cuatro *ángulo rectos*; los lados opuestos son iguales y *paralelos*.

rectangular prism (p. 385) A 3-dimensional figure with six faces that are rectangles.

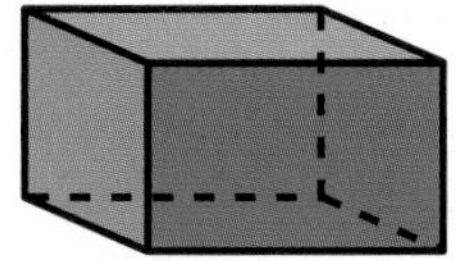

prisma rectangular Figura tridimensional de seis caras rectangulares.

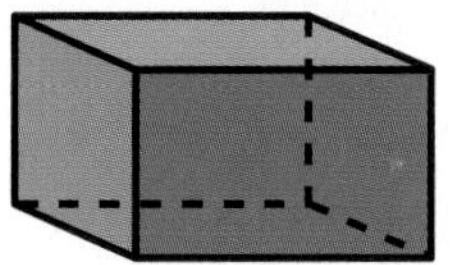

remainder (p. 338) The number that is left after one whole number is divided by another.

residuo Número que queda después de dividir un número entero entre otro número entero.

rhombus (p. 410) A *parallelogram* with four *congruent* sides.

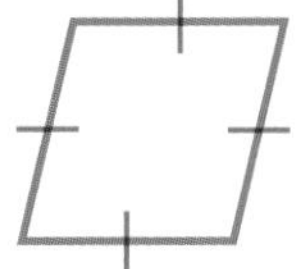

rombo *Paralelogramo* con cuatro lados *congruentes*.

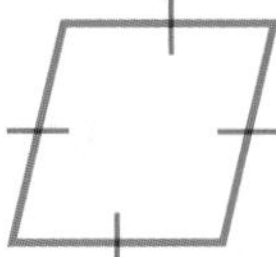

right angle (p. 399) An *angle* with a measure of 90°.

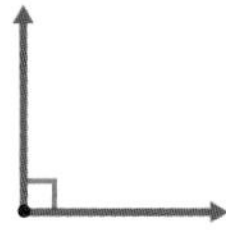

ángulo recto *Ángulo* que mide 90°.

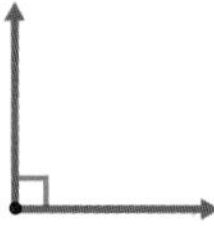

right triangle (p. 405) A *triangle* with one *right angle*.

triángulo rectángulo *Triángulo* con un *ángulo recto*.

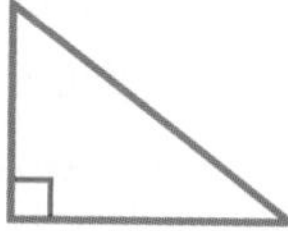

rotational symmetry (p. 435) A figure has rotational symmetry if, after a rotation of the figure about a point, the figure lies in its original position.

simetría de rotación Una figura posee simetría de rotación si después de rotarla sobre un punto la figura yace en su posición original.

round (p. 36) To change the value of a number to one that is easier to work with. To find the nearest value of a number based on a given *place value*.

redondear Cambiar el valor de un número a uno con el cual es más fácil trabajar. Calcular el valor más cercano a un número basado en un *valor de posición* dado.

S

scalene triangle (p. 404) A *triangle* with no *congruent* sides.

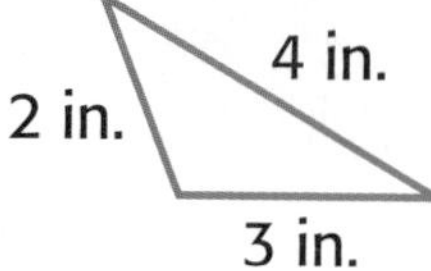

triángulo escaleno *Triángulo* sin lados *congruentes*.

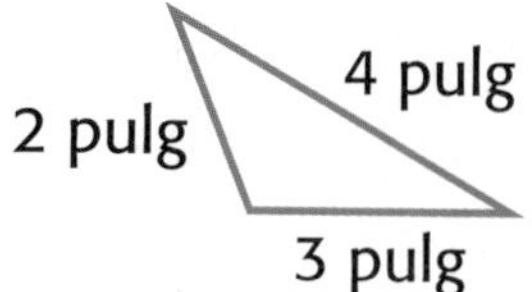

simplest form (p. 522) A *fraction* in which the *numerator* and the *denominator* have no common factor greater than 1.

forma reducida *Fracción* en la cual el *numerador* y el *denominador* no tienen un factor común mayor que 1.

solid figure (p. 385) A solid figure has three dimensions: length, width, and height.

figura sólida Una figura sólida tiene tres dimensiones: largo, ancho y alto.

sphere (p. 385) A solid or 3-dimensional figure that is set of all points that are the same distance from a given point, called the center.

esfera *Figura tridimensional* formada por el conjunto de todos los puntos equidistantes de un punto dado llamado *centro*.

square (p. 410) A rectangle with four *congruent sides*.

square unit (p. 444) A unit for measuring area.

standard form/standard notation (p. 18) The usual way of writing a number that shows only its *digits*, no words.

537 89 1642

subtract (subtraction) (p. 52) An operation on two numbers that tells the difference, when some or all are taken away. Subtraction is also used to compare two numbers.

$14 - 8 = 6$

subtrahend (p. 69) A number that is subtracted from another number.

$14 - 5 = 9$

↑ subtrahend

sum (p. 58) The answer to an addition problem.

survey (p. 127) A method of collecting *data*.

cuadrado Rectángulo de cuatro *lados congruentes*.

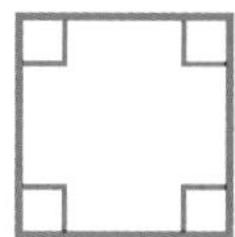

unidad cuadrada Unidad para medir el área.

forma estándar/notación estandard Manera habitual de escribir un número que sólo muestra sus *dígitos*, sin palabras.

537 89 1642

restar (resta) Operación en dos números que indica la diferencia, cuando algunos o todos son eliminados. La sustracción también se usa para comparar dos números.

$14 - 8 = 6$

sustraendo Un número que se sustrae de otro número.

$14 - 5 = 9$

↑ sustraendo

suma Respuesta o resultado de un problema de suma.

encuesta Método para reunir *datos*.

tally chart (p. 127) A way to keep track of *data* using tally marks to record the number of responses or occurrences.

What is Your Favorite Color?	
Color	**Tally**
Blue	𝍸 𝍷𝍷𝍷
Green	𝍷𝍷𝍷𝍷

tabla de conteo Manera de llevar la cuenta de los *datos* usando marcas de conteo para anotar el número de respuestas o sucesos.

¿Cuál es tu color favorito?	
Color	**Conteo**
Azul	𝍸 𝍷𝍷𝍷
Verde	𝍷𝍷𝍷𝍷

Glossary/Glosario

tally mark(s) (p. 127) A mark made to keep track and display *data* recorded from a survey.

tenth (p. 555) One of ten equal parts or $\frac{1}{10}$.

trapezoid (p. 410) A *quadrilateral* with exactly one pair of *parallel* sides.

tree diagram (p. 652) **a.** A diagram of all the possible *outcomes* of an event or series of events or experiments. **b.** A diagram of all the possible combinations of two or more objects or events being put together.

triangle (p. 388) A *polygon* with three sides and three angles.

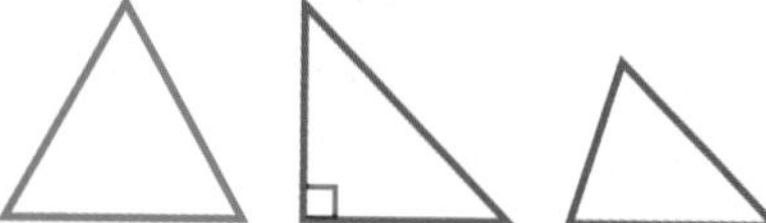

triangular prism (p. 385) A prism whose bases are triangular with *parallelograms* for sides.

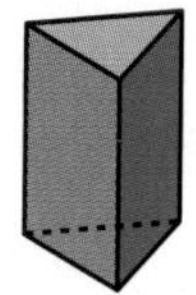

triangular pyramid (p. 385) A pyramid whose base is a *triangle*.

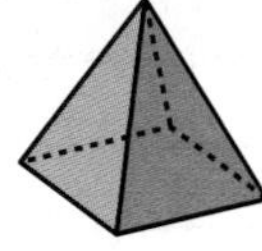

marcas(s) de conteo Marca que se hace para llevar un registro y representar *datos* reunidos de una encuesta.

décima Una de diez partes iguales ó $\frac{1}{10}$.

trapecio *Cuadrilátero* con exactamente un par de lados *paralelos*.

diagrama de árbol **a.** Diagrama de todos los *resultados* posibles de un evento o series de eventos o experimentos. **b.** Diagrama de todas las combinaciones posibles de dos o más objetos o eventos que se combinan.

triángulo *Polígono* con tres lados y tres ángulos.

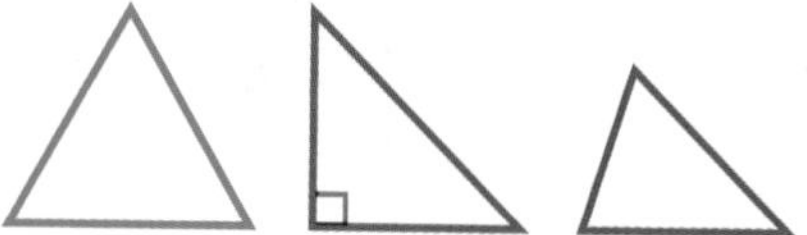

prisma triangular Prisma cuyas bases son triangulares con *paralelogramos* como lados.

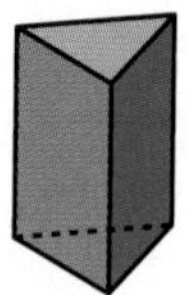

pirámide triangular Pirámide cuya base es un *triángulo*.

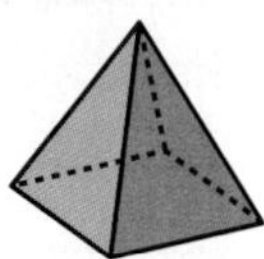

unlikely (p. 628) An event that is improbable or it will probably *not* happen.

It is unlikely you will choose a yellow tile.

improbable Evento que es improbable o que es probable que *no* suceda.

Es improbable que elijas una baldosa amarilla.

variable (p. 93) A letter or symbol used to represent an unknown quantity.

vertex (p. 385) The point where two rays meet in an *angle*.

variable Letra o símbolo que se usa para representar una cantidad desconocida.

vértice Punto donde concurren dos o más rayos.

X

***x*-axis** (p. 472) The horizontal axis (↔) in a coordinate graph.

***x*-coordinate** (p. 472) The first number in an *ordered pair* that indicates how far to the left or the right of the *y*-axis a point is. In (2, 3), 2 is the *x*-coordinate.

eje *x* El eje horizontal (↔) en una gráfica de coordenadas.

coordenada *x* El primer número en un *par ordenado* que indica la distancia a la izquierda o a laderecha del eje *y* a la cual se encuentra un punto. En (2, 3), 3 es la coordenada *x*.

***y*-axis** (p. 472) The vertical axis (↕) in a coordinate graph.

***y*-coordinate** (p. 472) The second number in an *ordered pair* that indicates how far above or below the *x*-axis a point is. In (2, 3), 3 is the *y*-coordinate.

eje *y* El eje vertical (↕) en una gráfica de coordenadas.

coordenada *y* El segundo número en un *par ordenado* que indica la distancia hacia arriba o hacia abajo del eje *x* a la cual se encuentra un punto. En (2, 3), 3 es la coordenada *y*.

Zero Property of Multiplication (p. 178) The property that states any number multiplied by zero is zero.

$0 \times 5 = 0$ $\quad$ $5 \times 0 = 0$

propiedad del producto nulo de la multiplicación Propiedad que establece que cualquier número multiplicado por cero es igual a cero.

$0 \times 5 = 0$ $\quad$ $5 \times 0 = 0$

Acknowledgements

Unless otherwise credited, all currency courtesy of the US Mint.

iv Doug Martin; **v** (bl br)File Photo, (others)Doug Martin; **vi** (l to r, t to b)courtesy Cheryl Avalos, courtesy William Bokesh, courtesy Patty Brown, courtesy David Chamberlain, courtesy Eppie Chung, courtesy Lisa Cirrincione, courtesy Carol Cronk, courtesy Ilene Foster, courtesy Grant A. Fraser, PH.D; **vii** (l to r, t to b)courtesy Suzanne Freire, courtesy Beth Holguin, courtesy Beth Holguin, courtesy Donna Kopenski, courtesy Kelly Mack, courtesy Kelly Mack, courtesy Juvenal Martinez, courtesy John McGuire, courtesy Donald Price, courtesy Kasey St. James, courtesy Art Wayman, courtesy Beverly Wells, courtesy Frances Whitney; **x–xi** Fred Felleman/Getty Images; **xii–xiii** Getty Images; **xiv–xv** Creatas/SuperStock; **xvi–xvii** Daniel A. Bedell/Animals Animals/Earth Scenes; **xviii–xix** Robert Lubeck/Animals Animals/Earth Scenes; **xx–xxi** Miles Ertman/Masterfile; **xxii–xxiii** George D. Lepp/CORBIS; **xxiv–xxv** David Muench/CORBIS; **xxvii** CORBIS; **1** Jeff Hunter/Getty Images; **2** Digital Vision, Ltd./Getty Images; **3** Joseph Sohm/Visions of America/Getty Images; **4** Stuart Westmoreland/CORBIS; **5** (t)Lonely Planet Images/Getty Images, (b)Fred Felleman/Getty Images; **6** Richard Cummins/CORBIS; **7** Alfred Saerchinger/zefa/CORBIS; **8** Jerry Alexander/Getty Images; **9** Michael Newton/Getty Images; **10** Robert Landau/CORBIS; **11** (l to r, t to b)Getty Images, CORBIS, S. Wanke/PhotoLink/Getty Images, Getty Images, Robert Landau/CORBIS; **12** Brad Mangin/CORBIS; **13** Greg Fiume/NewSport/CORBIS; **14–15** Isidor Stankov/iStockphoto; **19** Elizabeth DeLaney/Index Stock Imagery; **20** Ed-Imaging; **23** Claver Carroll/Jupiterimages; **24** (t)Brand X/SuperStock, (b)Pixtal/SuperStock; **26** Paul Seheult/Eye Ubiquitous/CORBIS; **28** Jeff Dunn/Index Stock Imagery; **32** (l)Ingram Publishing/Alamy Images, (r)G.K. & Vikki Hart/Getty Images; **35** Ed-Imaging; **36** (t)C. Borland/PhotoLink/Getty Images, (b)Matthias Kulka/CORBIS; **39** (l)Ed-Imaging, (r)Ryan McVay/Getty Images; **40** Ed-Imaging; **42** J.Berndes/A.B./Zefa/CORBIS; **42–43** (bkgd)Stuart Westmorland/Getty Images; **52–53** The McGraw-Hill Companies; **54** (l)CORBIS, (r) C Squared Studios/Getty Images; **57** Ed-Imaging; **58** (t)Image Source/Jupiterimages, (b)Index Stock Imagery; **60** Ralf-Finn Hestoft/CORBIS; **62** Gary Rhijnsburger/Masterfile; **65** (l)2006 Photos To Go, (r)Brand X Pictures/Alamy Images; **66** Getty Images; **68** Ed-Imaging; **71** 2006 Photos To Go; **72** Raymond Forbes/agefotostock; **73** Ed-Imaging; **74** Ed-Imaging; **75** Getty Images; **76** (t)Vladpans/eStock Photo; **76–77** Library of Congress; **79** George Doyle & Ciaran Griffin/Stockdisc/Getty Images; **80** (t)CORBIS, (bl br)Ed-Imaging; **81** CORBIS; **91–92** Digital Vision/PunchStock; **93** Don Smetzer/PhotoEdit; **95** Getty Images; **98** Stockdisc/Getty Images; **100** (l)Ed-Imaging, (r)William Howard/Getty Images; **101** Ed-Imaging; **102** Ed-Imaging; **108** Ed-Imaging; **113** (l)CORBIS, (r)Image Source/SuperStock; **114** (t)Joe McDonald/CORBIS; **114–115** (bkgd)Roine Magnusson/Getty Images; **115** Joe McDonald/CORBIS; **118** Getty Images; **124–125** Kwame Zikomo/SuperStock; **128** G.K. Vikki Hart/Getty Images; **130** (l)Creatas/SuperStock; **130** James Urbach/SuperStock; **133** Ed-Imaging; **134** Oliver Benn/Royal Philharmonic Orchestra; **135** (pencil)PhotoLink/Getty Images, (boat)C Squared Studios/Getty Images; **136** Darren Bennett/Animals Animals/Earth Scenes; **143–144** Ed-Imaging; **146** (c)Stockdisc/Getty Images; **146–147** (bkgd)Tony Craddock/Getty Images; **148** Ed-Imaging; **149** (tl cl bl)The McGraw-Hill Companies, (r)Ryan McVay/Getty Images; **150** (pansy)C Squared Studios/Getty Images, (ticket)D. Hurst/Alamy Images; **151** Daniele Pellegrini/Getty Images; **154** Ed-Imaging; **156** Chris Markes/agefotostock; **157** (l to r, t to b)Getty Images; **162** CORBIS; **170–171** Denis Scot/CORBIS; **175** The McGraw-Hill Companies; **177** John Blair/Alamy Images; **179** C Squared Studios/Getty Images; **180** BananaStock/Alamy Images; **182** Lon C. Diehl/PhotoEdit; **188** Getty Images; **190** Brian Hagiwara/PictureArts/CORBIS; **192** (soda fountain) Bettmann/CORBIS; (soda truck)Webster & Stevens Collection/Museum of History and Industry, Seattle/CORBIS; (drugstore owner)John Van Hasselt/CORBIS Sygma; **192–193** (bkgd)Tracy Hebden/Alamy Images; **192–193** (bubbles)Getty Images; **193** (l)SuperStock, (r)Rachel Epstein/PhotoEdit; **194** Tetra Images/Alamy Images; **195** D. Hurst/Alamy Images; **196** Kevin Schafer/zefa/CORBIS; **198** Thinkstock Images/Jupiterimages; **200** Ed-Imaging; **202–203** Ed-Imaging; **204** Dennis Macdonald/PhotoEdit; **205** Mark Richards/PhotoEdit; **206** StockTrek/Getty Images; **207** Ed-Imaging; **208** (l)StudiOhio, (r)The McGraw-Hill Companies; **210** Cathy Melloan Resources/Photoedit; **213** The McGraw-Hill Companies; **218** Jules Frazier/Getty Images; **222–223** Bill Brooks/Masterfile; **225** Jim Cummins/CORBIS; **226** Getty Images; **228** Elena Rooraid/PhotoEdit; **230** Pat Doyle/CORBIS; **234** Ed-Imaging; **240** Newstockimages/Punchstock; **242** Michael Newman/PhotoEdit; **245** Ed-Imaging; **246–247** (bkgd)Jeff Rotman/Getty Images; **247** (inset)Paul Springett/Alamy Images; **260** Denis Scott/CORBIS; **263** Jurgen Freund/JACANA/HOA-QUI/ImageState; **264** George Hall/CORBIS; **265** CORBIS; **266** (t)G.K. Vikki Hart/Getty Images, (b)C Squared Studios/Getty Images; **268** Ren Long/AP Images; **271** Ed-Imaging; **276** Ed-Imaging; **278** Richard Hutchings/PhotoEdit; **280** age fotostock/SuperStock; **281** Ed-Imaging; **282** (inset)Daniel A. Bedell/Animals Animals/Earth Scenes; **282–283** (bkgd)David Tipling/Lonely Planet Images; **284** Robin Lynne/Getty Images; **285** age fotostock/SuperStock; **287** (l)Jack Hollingsworth/Getty Images, (r)Ed-Imaging; **296–297** David Young-Wolff/PhotoEdit; **299** Cooperphoto/CORBIS; **301** Robert Lubeck/Animals Animals/Earth Scenes; **302** G.K. & Vikki Hart/Getty Images; **304** Colin Keates/Getty Images; **306** CORBIS; **310** Getty Images; **311** (l)Ryan McVay/Getty Images, (r)Michael Houghton/StudiOhio, (t)C Squared Studios/Getty Images; **312** C Squared Studios/Getty Images; **314** Getty Images; **316** (t)Getty Images, (bl)Ed-Imaging, (br)Ed-Imaging; **318–319** (bkgd)Steve Vidler/eStock Photo; **319** (inset)James Shaffer/PhotoEdit; **320** BananaStock/Jupiterimages; **322** Mark Newman/Photo Researchers; **323** Christian Petersen/Getty Images; **325** Ed-Imaging; **334–335** Paul Conklin/PhotoEdit; **337** Ed-Imaging; **339** Craig Lovell/CORBIS; **341** (l to r, t to b) Geoff Dann/Getty Images, Patti Murray/Animals Animals, GK & Vikki Hart/Getty Images, Ed-Imaging, Brand X/Jupiterimages; **347** Ryan McVay/Getty Images; **349** Stockbyte/Getty Images; **350** Adam Smith/Getty Images; **352** CORBIS; **353** Tony Freeman/PhotoEdit; **354** ThinkStock; **355–356** Ed-Imaging; **360** Brand X/SuperStock; **362** CORBIS; **365** Ed-Imaging; **366–367** (bkgd)Mauritius/SuperStock; **368** SuperStock, Inc./SuperStock; **369** Neal Mishler/Getty Images; **374** G.K. Vikki Hart/Getty Images; **378** C Squared Studios/Getty Images; **382–383** (bkgd)Masterfile; **384** Getty Images; **385** (t)GK Hart/Vikki Hart/Getty Images, (b)Thomas Northcut/Getty Images; **386** The McGraw-Hill Companies; **387** (tl)Jupiterimages; (tr)Stockdisc/PunchStock; **388** (t to b)S. Wanke/PhotoLink/Getty Images, Getty Images, CORBIS, Comstock Images/Alamy Images; **389** Getty Images; **390** (cl)C Squared Studios/Getty Images, (cr)Getty Images, (b)Bridgeman-Giraudon/Art Resource, NY; **391** Ed-Imaging; **394** CORBIS; **396** Brand X /ImageState; **400** The McGraw-Hill Companies; **401** photos.com; **402** Ed-Imaging; **403** CORBIS; **404** David Young-Wolff/PhotoEdit; **405** Miles Ertman/Masterfile; **408–409** Visions of America, LLC/Alamy Images; **409** (l)Mary Ann Sullivan/Bluffton University, (r)Visions of America, LCC/Alamy Images; **410** Werner H. Mueller/CORBIS; **411** (t)Alan King/Alamy Images, (c)courtesy George Hart, www.georgehart.com, (bl)Image Source/Alamy Images, (bc)Purestock/Jupiterimages, (br)Royalty-Free/CORBIS; **412** (tr)Burke/Triolo/Brand X Pictures/Jupiterimages; **412** (bl)Thomas Northcut, (bc)DK Limited/CORBIS, (br)Purestock/Alamy Images; **413** Ed-Imaging; **414** (tl)Peter Sebastian/Getty Images, (tr)CORBIS; **415** (c)The McGraw-Hill Companies, (r)Don Mason/CORBIS; **416** (l to r, t to b)Masterfile, CORBIS, The McGraw-Hill Companies, C Squared Studios/Getty Images, Getty Images, Brand X/SuperStock, CORBIS; **419** photos.com; **424** CORBIS; **428–429** Gary Gerovac/Masterfile; **432** photos.com/Jupiterimages; **433** (tl)Ralph A. Clevenger/CORBIS, (tr)Getty Images, (bl) rubberball/Jupiterimages, (br)Ed-Imaging; **434** Darrell Gulin/CORBIS; **435** Comstock/Alamy Images; **436** (tc)Getty Images, (cl)Colin Keates/Getty Images, (cr)Getty Images, (br)Gallo Images/Getty Images; **440** Michael Freeman/CORBIS; **442** (tl tr)CORBIS, (b)C Squared Studios/Getty Images; **443** Ryan McVay/Getty Images; **447–448** Ed-Imaging; **450** (l)Mark Cassino/SuperStock, (c)Iconotec/Alamy Images, (br)Jupiterimages; **450-451** Renee Morris/Alamy Images; **452** Ed-Imaging; **453** agefotostock/SuperStock; **454** Cardinale Stephane/CORBIS; **466–467** Lori Adamski Peek/Getty Images; **471** (t)CORBIS, (b)2006 Photos to Go; **473** Getty Images; **480–481** (bkgd)Getty Images; **481** Dennis di Cicco/CORBIS; **483** photos.com; **484** Brand X Pictures/Alamy Images; **487–488** Ed-Imaging; 492 Michael Houghton/StudiOhio; **494** Ed-Imaging; **495** 2006 Photos To Go; **504–505** (bkgd)Siede Preis/Getty Images, C Squared Studios/Getty Images; **510** The McGraw-Hill Companies; **511** (l)Don Farrall/Getty Images, (c r) Stockdisc/PunchStock; **512** George D. Lepp/CORBIS; **513** (l)Ed-Imaging, (r)Getty Images; **515** C Squared Studios/Getty Images; **520** (t)Getty Images, (bl br)Ed-Imaging; **523** Martin Harvey/CORBIS; **525–526** Ed-Imaging; **531** Getty Images; **532** (inset)Ed Taylor/Getty Images; **532–533** (bkgd)The McGraw-Hill Companies; **534** Myrleen Ferguson Cate/PhotoEdit; **541** (l)Punchstock, (r)Getty Images; **544** The McGraw-Hill Companies; **546** Getty Images; **552–553** CORBIS; **557** MedioImages/SuperStock; **560** David Muench/CORBIS; **561** Martin Harvey/CORBIS; **562** Kennan Ward/CORBIS; **563** (l)Ed-Imaging, (r)Getty Images; **564** Ed-Imaging; **570** Ed-Imaging; **571** (l)Michael Houghton/StudiOhio, (r)Michael Houghton/StudiOhio; **572** Greg Probst/CORBIS; **576–577** Digital Vision/Getty Images; **578** Stockdisc Classic/Alamy Images; **580** (l)Ed-Imaging, (r)Brad Wilson/Getty Images; **581** Ed-Imaging; **590–591** Robert Lubeck/Animals Animals/Earth Scenes; **593** Bob Krist/CORBIS; **594** Sam Greenwood/NewSport/CORBIS; **597** Ed-Imaging; **599** (tr)Michael Houghton/StudiOhio, (br)Michael Houghton/StudiOhio; **600** Mauritius/SuperStock; **602** CORBIS; **603** (bl)Getty Images, (bcl)Getty Images; **604** Ed-Imaging; **606** BigStockPhoto.com; **607** David Hosking/Alamy Images; **610–611** Donald Miralle/Getty Images; **611** (l)Empics/SportsChrome, (r)Rob Tringali/SportsChrome; **612** Getty Images; **613** The McGraw-Hill Companies; **614** Ed-Imaging; **616** Bettmann/CORBIS; **617** John Cancalosi/Peter Arnold, inc.; **619** (tl)Image Source/Getty Images, (br)CORBIS; **628–629** The McGraw-Hill Companies; **630** George D. Lepp/CORBIS; **634** (l)Getty Images, (r)Ed-Imaging; **635** Ed-Imaging; **637** The McGraw-Hill Companies; **640** Rob Gage/Getty Images; **646** (t)A&P/Alamy Images, (b)CORBIS; **647** (l to r)Stockdisc/PunchStock, Stockdisc/PunchStock, Stockdisc/PunchStock, photos.com/Jupiterimages; **648** (inset)James Hackett/eStock Photo; **648–649** (bkgd)CORBIS; **649** (inset)CORBIS, (eel)Peter Miller/eStock Photo; **650** Getty Images; **651** Getty Images; **653** (tl)Getty Images, (tr)Getty Images, (bl br)Getty Images; **654** Ed-Imaging; **658** Getty Images; **660** The McGraw-Hill Companies; **661** Getty Images; **664–665** Tim Fuller; **667** Comstock/Jupiterimages; **669** Ed-Imaging; **670** Jose Luis Pelaez, Inc./CORBIS; **671** The McGraw-Hill Companies; **675** (t)Comstock/Alamy Images, (b)D. Hurst/Alamy Images; **677** (bl)Ed-Imaging, (br)CORBIS; 678 NASA/CORBIS; **681** (bl)Getty Images, (br)Ed-Imaging; **CA09** photos.com; **CA1** Ed-Imaging; **R27** (tl)gds/zefa/CORBIS, (tc)Nancy R. Cohen/Getty Images, (tr)Burke/Triolo Productions/Getty Images, (bc)Tony Freeman/PhotoEdit, (br)2006 Photos To Go.

McGraw-Hill would like to acknowledge the artists and agencies who contributed to illustrating this program: **Cover** Mick McGinty represented by Mendola Artists; Argosy Publishing; Keith Batcheller, Gary Ciccarelli, Shawn McKelvey, Mark Snyder represented by AA Reps. Inc.

Index

Index

Index

O

Q

R

S

Measurement Conversions

	Metric	Customary
Length	1 kilometer (km) = 1,000 meters (m) 1 meter = 100 centimeters (cm)	1 mile (mi) = 1,760 yards (yd) 1 mile = 5,280 feet (ft) 1 yard = 3 feet 1 foot = 12 inches (in.)
Volume and Capacity	1 liter (L) = 1,000 milliliters (mL)	1 gallon (gal) = 4 quarts (qt) 1 gallon = 128 ounces (oz) 1 quart = 2 pints (pt) 1 pint = 2 cups (c) 1 cup = 8 ounces
Weight and Mass	1 kilogram (kg) = 1,000 grams (g)	1 pound (lb) = 16 ounces (oz)

Time	1 year (yr) = 365 days (d) 1 year = 12 months (mo) 1 year = 52 weeks (wk) 1 week = 7 days 1 day = 24 hours (h) 1 hour = 60 minutes (min) 1 minute = 60 seconds (s)

Multiplication Table

×	1	2	3	4	5	6	7	8	9	10	11	12
1	1	2	3	4	5	6	7	8	9	10	11	12
2	2	4	6	8	10	12	14	16	18	20	22	24
3	3	6	9	12	15	18	21	24	27	30	33	36
4	4	8	12	16	20	24	28	32	36	40	44	48
5	5	10	15	20	25	30	35	40	45	50	55	60
6	6	12	18	24	30	36	42	48	54	60	66	72
7	7	14	21	28	35	42	49	56	63	70	77	84
8	8	16	24	32	40	48	56	64	72	80	88	96
9	9	18	27	36	45	54	63	72	81	90	99	108
10	10	20	30	40	50	60	70	80	90	100	110	120
11	11	22	33	44	55	66	77	88	99	110	121	132
12	12	24	36	48	60	72	84	96	108	120	132	144

Formulas

	Perimeter	Area
Square	$P = 4s$	$A = s \times s$ $P = \ell + \ell + w + w$ or $P = 2\ell + 2w$
Rectangle	$P = \ell + \ell + w + w$ $P = 2\ell + 2w$	$A = \ell \times w$